IKE THE SOLDIER

★ ★ ★

IKE THE SOLDIER

★ ★ ★ ★ ★

AS THEY KNEW HIM

MERLE MILLER

A Perigee Book

★ ★ ★

DEDICATION

*For CAROL V. HANLEY, my collaborator in
the fullest sense. This book is as much hers as it
is mine.*

Perigee Books
are published by
The Putnam Publishing Group
200 Madison Avenue
New York, NY 10016
First Perigee Edition 1988
Copyright © 1987 by David W. Elliott

Copyright acknowledgments will be found on p. 827.

Library of Congress Cataloging-in-Publication Data

Miller, Merle, date.
Ike the soldier: as they knew him / Merle Miller.
p.   cm.
Reprint. Originally published: New York: G. P. Putnam's Sons, 1987.
Bibliography: p.
Includes index.
1. Eisenhower, Dwight D. (Dwight David), 1890–1969—Military
leadership.   2. Generals—United States—Biography.   3. United
States.   Army—Biography.   I. Title.
E836.M55   1988
355'.0092'4—dc19
[B]   88-9855 CIP
ISBN 0-399-51483-X

Book Design by The Sarabande Press
Printed in the United States of America
1 2 3 4 5 6 7 8 9 10

* * *

ACKNOWLEDGMENTS

Carol Hanley is one of many who assisted me in writing my previous book, *Lyndon*, and the only one I asked to stay on as my co-writer and researcher for *Ike*. She is also a close and dear friend. Carol worked with me from the book's inception in 1980 to its completion in 1986, and became as familiar with and as fond of Ike as I am. My debt to her is enormous and the dedication is a small token of appreciation.

I wish to thank David W. Elliott for his support and encouragement throughout the six years it took to write this book.

My thanks, too, to Alan Williams, my editor at G. P. Putnam's, who took over the first half of the manuscript in 1984, shaped and edited it and patiently saw the remainder of the manuscript through its lengthy gestation.

I am most grateful to Barbara Stroh, who typed and retyped the many drafts and revisions into beautiful manuscript pages; to Kathleen Hanley, who helped with the research and transcribed my early tapes of interviews; to John Reese, James Peterson, and Daniel Croswell, skilled historians and researchers in Kansas.

In Pennsylvania, Louise Arnold was particularly invaluable to me for her assistance in researching a wide range of material at the Eisenhower National Historic Site at Gettysburg, and later at the U.S. Military History Institute at Carlisle Barracks.

Once again the author owes a debt of gratitude to the staff of the Danbury Public Library for their generous assistance in finding needed facts and for their patience and understanding.

In addition to the Danbury Library, I used many other libraries for my research and they include the Butler Library Oral History Research Office at Columbia University; the National Archives and the Library of Congress in Washington, D.C.; the Dwight D. Eisenhower Library in Abilene, Kansas; the Herbert Hoover Library in West Branch, Iowa; the Franklin D. Roosevelt Library in Hyde Park, New York; and the Sam Rayburn Library at Bonham, Texas.

I am also thankful to the many friends I made at the U.S. Military Academy Library at West Point. Robert E. Schnare of Special Collections searched through old files and records for most valuable information; Elaine Eatroff, Rare Book Curator and Cataloguer, was particularly patient in finding facts I needed, even facts I had not requested; and Egon Weiss, Head Librarian, gave freely of his time and assistance.

Many offered information and assistance. John M. Manguso, Director, Fort Sam Museum, Fort Sam Houston, Texas; C. W. Munie, Historian/Curator,

State of Illinois Military & Naval Department, Camp Lincoln, Springfield, Illinois; Larry Adams, Curator, Mamie Doud Eisenhower Birthplace Foundation, Inc., Boone, Iowa; Gwen Goldsberry, owner and editor of the *Colorado Prospector* in Denver, Colorado; Ms. Bridget Janus, Librarian, *The Gazette*, Cedar Rapids, Iowa; Mr. Dan Fitzgerald, Manuscripts Department, Kansas State Historical Society, Topeka, Kansas; Mr. Larry L. Bland, George C. Marshall Research Foundation, Lexington, Virginia.

I am especially indebted to Eisenhower's many classmates, army and civilian associates, and relatives who granted me interviews and were generous with their memories. I am especially grateful to John Eisenhower who gave me many hours of his time and went out of his way to be particularly helpful.

Last, and surely not least, my thanks to the Hanley children, all eight of them, who so generously gave up their "Mom" for the duration of the writing of this book.

If we then ask what sort of mind is likeliest to display the qualities of military genius, experience and observation will both tell us that it is the inquiring rather than the creative mind, the comprehensive rather than the specialized approach, the calm rather than the excitable head to which in war we would choose to entrust the fate of our brothers and children, and the safety and honor of our country.
                                        —Karl von Clausewitz, On War

★ ★ ★
TABLE OF CONTENTS

* * *

INTRODUCTION

When I first started living with Dwight D. Eisenhower five years and six months ago, I was mainly interested in his presidency. He had, most people said with almost no effort, kept the United States at peace and prosperous for eight years. Despite a conspicuous number of friends who were members of what in his farewell address he called the "military-industrial complex," he had warned against the dangers of that lethal combination which has now brought this country close to economic collapse. He was not in awe of the Joint Chiefs of Staff. In fact, he worried about a time when there would be a president who did not understand "what those birds are up to." But the kind of man he was didn't interest me much—a dull, passive, lucky man who, as a soldier, had done nothing much remarkable. He had been a political general, a chairman of the board of directors, who had been told what to do by generals and civilians, Roosevelt and Churchill among them. I had spent some time looking into and writing about the lives of two other presidents of the United States. What had happened to *this* president before he was inaugurated was not of much interest to me. A chapter at most would handle it.

But as I worked, I discovered that Eisenhower—the man—before he became president was a story that has never been told. There have been over 100 full-length books about Dwight D. Eisenhower. He must surely be one of the most written about men of this century. But none of the books seemed to consider what kind of man he was and how he got that way, which is what this book attempts to do.

During the time of living with Eisenhower, I changed almost every preconceived idea I had about him. In the course of a year and a half of research, I uncovered a vast amount of material that had never been published; during interviews I learned of stories that had never been told. After another year, I thought: There is more to the man than the upstretched arms and the grin. Then I began to write.

It is very difficult to explain Dwight D. Eisenhower. He went so far, both farther and further than almost any American of this century, and yet he seemed not at all extraordinary. How then to explain his extraordinary journey from Abilene, Kansas, from the small, really quite shabby house on South East Fourth Street to all the places he went? Was it accident? Was it luck? Was he just a smiling country boy, an ordinary man, a run-of-the-mill graduate of West Point who happened to be in the right place at the right time?

No. It was none of these. He took the trouble to make it appear that way. He went to a lot of trouble to appear average, to seem ordinary, to appear guileless. And he fooled most people most of the time, including most of his biographers. A lot of people say they knew him; but I doubt they did. There was layer upon layer, and every time you thought that you really understood him, you realized that you didn't. He was generally considered to be a simple man, but he was not. He was most complex.

Dwight Eisenhower could and did outsmart, outthink, outmaneuver, outgovern, and outcommand almost anybody you'd care to name, including Winston Churchill, Charles de Gaulle, and yes, even Franklin Roosevelt. I don't know that he ever read Niccolò Machiavelli or La Rochefoucauld, but he practiced what they preached. Guileless? Don't be silly!

Eisenhower never let it all hang out. Usually he concealed his hand—he was, after all, a masterful poker player. He hung out what he wanted to let be known. He eluded everybody, largely, I imagine, because that's what he wanted to do. He took the trouble to be elusive. How else, to use the most obvious example, do you account for those bumbling nonsentences that emerged at presidential press conferences from a man who all his life wrote the most precise prose? The precision of his written prose and, often, his spoken prose, came not so much from what he had been taught in Dr. Holt's English classes at West Point, where he excelled, it came from reading aloud the King James version of the Bible. The cadence of those majestic sentences stayed with him all his life.

Eisenhower was far more familiar with himself than most people are, and while it would be too much to say that he was self-satisfied, he was certainly extraordinarily self-confident—to an almost unprecedented degree. When I asked John Eisenhower about his father's self-confidence, he said, "It was a combination of things. He was very popular at West Point; he was more mature; he had earned his living a little bit. He had gotten a Distinguished Service Medal. . . . Success sort of breeds success. In the old Army there in Washington in the thirties, Dad may have been a major, but he was still exposed to all the biggies—Pershing, MacArthur—he wasn't awestruck."

He had no time, ever, for contemplating what-might-have-been, brooding over what-might-have-been. He always felt the decision he had made was the best he could have made at the time he made it, based on what he knew at the time. Thus, he never indulged himself in regrets.

Also, he believed in the American system, and he believed in the people. He was a real American in that sense. Drew Middleton said Eisenhower had a sure grasp of the resources of the United States. He knew what he could do. Even at times when the army disappointed him, he was unshakeable. For example, after the Allied defeat at the Kasserine Pass, he said, "We'll get there, we'll get there." Once he told Winston Churchill, "I am probably the most optimistic person in the world."

Ike knew the value of making the right impression on the right people, whether it was Charlie Case, a lawyer friend in Abilene, Bernard Baruch, John J. Pershing, or the commander of every post at which he was stationed. Such an ability is deprecated by many people, but the alternative is making a wrong impression on people. It is not wise to point out the deficiencies of one's superiors—and Eisenhower never did.

He did not diminish, by word or deed, so far as I discovered, those who were competing with him for an appointment, promotion, whatever. He set out to demonstrate that he could do the job, whatever it was, better than his competitors, almost always with success, and when he failed, as in his early life in the army, he seldom brooded publicly. Privately, yes. He was not Job.

He often surrounded himself with sonsofbitches, not because he wanted to be popular but because he found it difficult to say no to his friends, or for that matter to people he didn't much care for. So he had hatchet men, Bedell Smith, his chief of staff when he was supreme commander in Europe, to name one, to do what had to be done.

He was a concerned man, happy when he was with his friends, but never really "at ease." One friend, Harry Anholt, said Ike was "a potentially destructive man. He was a man with a sword in his hand. . . . And he was expected to use it. Not by his own free will but by orders. And that's not a very pleasant thing to carry around." Another friend said he always got the impression that there was something inside Eisenhower that was always "crying to break out."

There were certain things he did not believe in, personal revenge, for example, personal vengeance. He did not believe in getting even; he did not hold grudges, but he did not forgive people either; if they had done something to offend him, they simply no longer existed.

With nations, Germany being the prime example, it was different. In July 1944, at his headquarters in Granville, France, he told Roosevelt's secretary of the treasury, Henry Morgenthau, "The ringleaders and the SS troops should be given the death penalty without question, but the punishment should not end there." He added that he felt the German people were guilty of supporting the Nazi regime and that made them a party to the evil that had been done. They were, he said, a paranoid people, and there was no reason to treat a paranoid people gently. "They have been taught to be paranoid in their actions and thoughts, and they have to be snapped out of it. The only way to do that is to be good and hard on them. I . . . see no point in bolstering their economy or taking any other steps to help them."

Eisenhower was a Christian; that is absolutely essential in understanding him. He was a Christian who for most of his life didn't believe you had to go to church to prove you were a Christian. He had been taught not to hate—the only thing to hate was evil. Hitler represented evil. Eisenhower had read the Old Testament back in Abilene, Kansas. The Old Testament God was stern. He punished transgressors.

John Eisenhower said his father was "imbued with a hatred of Nazism and all it entailed—he appeared . . . to approach his mission of defeating Hitler with the same attitude with which he attacked his opponents in bridge or poker— in both of which he was expert. He appeared to view any situation with the cold, calculating attitude of a professional, confident as he was throughout his life that the Almighty would provide him with a decent set of cards. He never wavered in his faith that he would win, but he appeared not to share the metaphysical feeling that God owed him anything specific, such as good weather on a given day."

The idea that Eisenhower was a pleasant, smiling, genial, friendly fellow who kept the British and Americans from fighting one another, and that's all, is not correct. Vernon Walters said, "When he landed in Europe, he had a mandate from the Combined Chiefs of Staff to, within two years, overthrow the Nazi Reich. Ten months to the day of the landing, he had accomplished that with losses far smaller than anybody in their wildest dreams had ever imagined."

His son, John, said, "Dad will be remembered much longer as a general than as a president. I'm quite sure of that. And the reasoning is quite simple. We've had by now—what is it?—thirty-seven presidents. We've only had one supreme commander, which is a little bit more of a distinction."

There was no one at the time who would have made a better supreme commander.

This book is different from my previous two books. It is not an oral biography, it is a biography. Also, it is not about a president, it is an impartial biography about the man. There have been various conceptions of him, and they have altered somewhat from book to book, but none of the principal conceptions has been wildly at variance with the others, and none has been discredited. Consciously or unconsciously most biographers would have us believe that Eisenhower was not like other men. Is the explanation that Eisenhower really was a paragon? Was he stainless, as so many writers would have us believe? Did Americans revere him because by circumstance he came to stand for everything they held dear?

Eisenhower has become not merely a mythical figure but a myth of suffocating dullness, the victim of civic elephantiasis. The myth-making process was at work during Eisenhower's lifetime; while he was still supreme commander, people paid to see him in waxwork effigy.

In trying to discern the actual man behind the huge, impersonal, ever-growing legend, one must understand that he was *not* a paragon. From the time he left West Point in 1915 until the end of his life, Eisenhower wasn't anything more than he was—a soldier.

What biographer Marcus Cunliffe said of Washington could also be said of Eisenhower:

Here was a man who did what he was asked to do, and whose very strength resided in a sobriety some took for fatal dullness; who on his own proved the soundness of America. A good man; not a saint; a competent soldier, not a great one; an honest administrator, not a statesman of genius; a prudent conserver, not a brilliant reformer. But in sum an exceptional figure.

What I hope emerges from these pages is a portrait of a fascinating man.

* * *

WHERE IT ALL BEGAN

At times the man who was to become supreme commander of the largest Allied army in history, a man who was to be known for his flawless memory had, or said he had, trouble remembering where he was born, but few things made him angrier than being called a *Texan;* he was, he inevitably said, a *Kansan.*

He was born in Denison, Texas, on October 14, 1890, too close to and on the wrong side of the railroad tracks. He grew up, also on the wrong side of the tracks, in an isolated town almost precisely in the geographical center of the United States, Abilene, Kansas. But the incredible journey he made really began on June 14, 1911, at that mighty, unarmed fortress on the west bank of the Hudson—West Point, New York. Eisenhower begins his best and most personal book, *At Ease: Stories I Tell to Friends*, published in 1967, only two years before his death, with an account of his trip to West Point in June 1911. "I traveled light," he said. "There was no need for more than a single suitcase."

It was a late start; he was almost twenty-one, but he got a late start at almost everything. In 1915 Eisenhower wrote of his West Point classmate Omar Nelson Bradley, "His most prominent characteristic is 'getting there.' " He could have been writing of himself.

Those who did not know him well thought of him as bland, relaxed, uncompetitive. He was none of those things. Whatever he undertook, whether it was personal or professional, he had to win. Late in life Eisenhower said, "I never give up a battle until I am licked, completely, utterly, and destroyed, and I don't believe in giving up any battle as long as I have a chance to win."

His son, John, said his father "couldn't do anything without making it work out. Trying to be best at it. He wasn't the kind of competitive person who would say, 'I have to put that guy down,' but he had to be better than everybody else. The things he chose doing, he was good at."

Eisenhower was not a patient man. He later said he was "a rather stern individual when I think I am being taken advantage of in any way or for any reason." He was the son of a Pennsylvania Dutchman with "all the temper of the Pennsylvania Dutch."

Eisenhower wasn't particularly fond of West Point much of the time he was there. He had not gone because he had dreams of military glory; that was for soldiers like his sometime friend, sometime enemy George S. Patton, Jr. He went to the Point because it offered a free education and opportunities to play baseball and football. The education turned out to be limited and uninteresting, and his athletic ambitions were frustrated. He often regretted that he had come and spoke of leaving. But late in life, as old men will, he remembered much of his time there with nostalgia.

When he was dying at Walter Reed hospital in 1969, his old friend Mark Wayne Clark, West Point class of 1917, visited him daily. Every afternoon around five, Clark would sit near his bed and talk with him for half an hour. Clark said, "He was really sick, all wired, emaciated, his head tilted, and weak as could be. But, you know, all he wanted to talk about was West Point, not about being president, not about being supreme commander, about D-Day, none of that. West Point was all, ever."

Ulysses S. Grant, class of 1843, the only other West Pointer who spent eight years in the White House, wrote in his *Personal Memoirs*, "I had rather a dread for reaching my destination at all . . . I would have been glad to have had a steamboat or railroad collision, or any other accident happen, by which I might have received a temporary injury sufficient to make me ineligible, for a time, to enter the Academy. Nothing of the kind occurred, and I had to face the music." It must be remembered, of course, that Grant lacked most of Ike's advantages as a plebe. According to his biographer, William S. McPhealy, "When Ulysses Grant reached West Point in 1839, he was still a boy. At 17 he weighed 117 lbs and was five feet one inch tall." Both Grant and Eisenhower were bored at West Point, and again as peacetime soldiers. Grant was so bored and depressed that in 1854, drinking heavily, he found it necessary to resign his commission. Eisenhower sometimes spoke of resigning, but he never really came close to doing it.

Eisenhower came to have a high regard for Grant. In 1946 when he was chief of staff of the army he wrote William Elizabeth Brooks, author of *Grant of Appomattox*, to say that not only had he read and enjoyed his book, but that many years ago he had read Grant's report to the secretary of war, submitted somewhere about the middle of July 1865. The first several paragraphs of that report

impressed me mightily—in them the Commander traced out his general idea or his general plan for the defeat of the Confederacy at the moment he was called upon to take charge of all the Northern armies. I think people frequently lose sight of the importance of this broad scheme which lies behind every move the Commander makes. As a consequence we see people—sometimes highly informed critics—attempting to separate one battle or one point of a campaign from the whole of the campaign and in doing so get it completely out of focus. Ever since I read that report my respect for Grant has been high, in spite of many bitter criticisms that I have read both of his military ability and of his personal habits.

With respect to this last item I am delighted that you have handled it so carefully and logically. It never seemed possible to me (and I have thought about it often during the months since December 1941) that a man who was so constantly under the influence of liquor could have pursued a single course so steadfastly, could have accepted frequent failures of subordinates without losing his own equilibrium, could have made numbers of close decisions which involved a nice balance between risk and advantage, and could have maintained the respect of such men as Sherman, Sheridan, Meade, and, above all, of President Lincoln.

Eisenhower was speaking not only of Grant's campaigns and battles; he was speaking of his own "single course" pursued steadfastly for winning the war in Europe, of the failures of his subordinates, of the many close decisions he had made involving "a nice balance between risk and advantage." And for the names of Sherman, Grant, Meade, one can substitute the names of almost any Allied generals, save Montgomery. And instead of Lincoln one would name Roosevelt, Churchill, de Gaulle, and, to be sure, Stalin.

No one ever accused Eisenhower of being "constantly under the influence of liquor," but he was accused of indecisiveness, indecision, dangerous affability, of knowing nothing at all about military strategy, and of never having heard a shot fired in anger. All that was said even before he got into politics.

Eisenhower was impressively broad of shoulder and, at five feet ten inches, taller than most of the incoming cadets. He was older; most of them were in their teens, but he was within a few months of being able to vote, although he did not vote until 1948, when he could have had the presidential nomination of either major party and even, many people thought, both parties.

His hands were large—"like elephant's feet," his brother Edgar said—and indicated a good deal about him. Harry Anholt, a friend who managed the Brown Palace Hotel in Denver before and during Eisenhower's presidency, said, "You could tell his hands had done a good deal of hard work when he was young. They were very large, and he told me he had frozen them a few times."

His wife, Mamie, remembered that when he began painting, many "experts" were surprised. They "didn't think he could pick up a paintbrush. . . . The knuckles of both Ike's hands had been broken because of football and baseball playing when he was young." Eisenhower himself often said his hands looked as if they were meant to hold an ax, not a pen.

In the summer of 1983, a statue of Eisenhower was dedicated at West Point; it overlooks the majestic plain. Almost everybody thought that the sculptor had done a good job, but there was one recurrent criticism. People who had never seen the man felt that the hands on the statue were too large.

As a new cadet, Eisenhower must have been conscious of his clothes that June day in 1911; they were poorly cut and had the look of the rube. In a photograph showing him in what he wore when he arrived at West Point, the sleeves of his jacket are too long and the jacket itself reaches almost to his knees. The trousers are also too long and baggy.

Many of the other entering cadets wore clothes that were for the most part well cut and seemed to fit perfectly. Many of them spoke of the class of 1915 plebe banquet they had attended on June 5 at the Hotel Drake in New York. The cost for the full-course dinner was $2.50, and room accommodations were made available to the incoming plebes for an additional dollar. But Eisenhower, for whatever reason, did not attend; nor did he stop in New York on his way to West Point. He later said the thought of stopping in that big city made him fearful. His only city experience had been a day and a night in St. Louis when he took the West Point entrance examinations, and then he had gotten lost.

If any of his fellow plebes were inclined to look down on him, they would soon learn that in West Point slang all plebes were "lower than whale shit," were "built wrong," "walked like turkeys"; their shoulders were "round as globes," and they were "so wooden that no one would believe that they wouldn't float if thrown in water."

When Eisenhower got off the train at the yellow-brick railroad station only a few steps away from the west shore of the Hudson, he was looking at one of the most spectacular views in America, the Hudson Highlands. George Washington called it "the Gibraltar of America," and it seems likely that in 1942 when Eisenhower spent a great many uneasy days on the real rock of Gibraltar he once or twice wished he had accepted an offer to become commandant at the Point. The academy itself, with its forbidding granite gothic buildings, was intimidating. "I was so scared, I almost turned back," he said.

But that feeling was temporary; as he was to discover, there was something comforting about the look of the place. It seemed settled, permanent, as if it had been there forever and would continue to be. The British had discovered at some cost during the Revolutionary War that it was impregnable. They had hoped to divide the rebellious colonists by taking it, but despite the treason of Benedict Arnold, they had failed. In the four years Eisenhower was there, he learned a great deal about what happened in that area during the Revolutionary War; those hills became more familiar than the flat plains of Kansas.

But on the morning of June 14, he was more aware of the intimidating climb up what was called "the long hill" to the adjutant's office, where he and the other entering cadets would abruptly cease to be civilians. They were to learn immediately that life at the academy was tough, at times brutal. They were the "scum of the earth." They were "entering purgatory for the first time." They were "Ducrot, too insignificant to be worthy of attention." They were "Mr. Dumgard, Dumbjohn, Dumflicket, Doojohn." "Drop those bags, mister. Pick them up, mister. That wasn't fast enough for me, mister. You hear me? That was not fast enough. Do not hesitate, mister. Drop those bags.

"There are only three answers to any question, mister. There are only three because you are so beastly you can only handle three. *If* you can handle three. You are subhuman, mister. You are beastly; that's why it's called Beast Barracks. The three answers to any question are, 'Yes, sir, No, sir, and No excuse, sir.' Now let's hear those three answers, mister. And brace yourself while you answer, mister."

Eisenhower said, "My impression of that first day was one of calculated chaos." As to the hazing that day and in the three weeks of "Beast Barracks" that followed, he said, "I had encountered difficult bosses before. . . . I suppose that if any time had been provided to sit down and think for a moment, most of . . . us would have taken the next train out. . . . But no one was given much time to think—and when I did it was always, 'Where else could you get a college education without cost?' "

The whole performance of "hazing" struck Eisenhower as funny, he said, "and in the semi-privacy of my room, I could laugh a little at myself and at the system. But whenever an upperclassman saw the sign of a smile, the shouting and nagging started again."

Eisenhower at West Point and later in life often said the system was ridiculous. But he did not rebel against it or try to change it much. It was that way throughout his life. He was not a man who tried to change things. Those who wanted him to improve things were inevitably disappointed. He was a man who went along with the status quo. That was true when he was a cadet; when he was a junior officer; a senior officer; when he was supreme commander. In French North Africa, for example, when as commander in chief of the Allied expedition there he hung on to the discredited Vichy officials rather than risk change. And as president he did not think it part of his job to educate the nation on the need for civil rights for Negroes. For that matter, he did not do much to interfere with the freewheeling reign of Joseph R. McCarthy. At the Point, there were never any courses on reforming the system. Instead, the cadets were taught to defend it when it was in trouble.

As for the brutality of Beast Barracks, Eisenhower later said, "There's a bunch of freewheeling boys and they have to be brought quickly into an attitude of obeying orders and they do this with methods that the new cadets sometimes think of as rather harsh. . . . Their purpose is not to make it easy."

By dusk that first day, not only had the plebes been hazed mercilessly, they had checked their civilian baggage and their civilian identities; they had been measured for uniforms and had been taught how to march, to salute, and to brace (stand at exaggerated attention). They had learned to do everything, *everything* on the double. They were not yet cadets, but by dusk they were no longer civilians either. By then they were wearing gray trousers and white shirts, and they were ready to be sworn in. They raised their right hands and repeated what was holy writ for West Pointers, the oath of allegiance. It was a moment Eisenhower never forgot:

I, Dwight D. Eisenhower, do solemnly swear that I will support the Constitution of the United States, and bear true allegiance to the National Government; that I will maintain and defend the sovereignty of the United States, paramount to any and all allegiance, sovereignty, or fealty that I may owe to any state or county whatsoever; and that I will at all times obey the legal orders of my superior officers, and the Uniform Code of Military Justice.

Eisenhower wrote of taking the oath:

Whatever had gone before, this was a supreme moment. . . . A feeling came over me that the expression "The United States of America" would now and henceforth mean something different than it ever had before. From here on in it would be the nation I would be serving, not myself. Suddenly the flag itself meant something. . . . Across half a century, I can look back and see a rawboned, gawky Kansas boy from the farm country, earnestly repeating the words that would make him a cadet.

The hazing bothered most of the other plebes much more. Not only were they young, most of them had had boyhoods that were privileged or sheltered. In Eisenhower's day there were no women, no blacks, no Hispanics, very few Catholics; and when he was a plebe there were three Jews, but not one of them graduated. Most of the cadets were solid middle-class WASPS. Eisenhower's roommate for the three weeks of Beast Barracks was quite typical. John Henry Dykes was from Lebanon, Kansas. His father and two uncles were doctors. According to John Henry's son, Delmar Spencer "Rooky" Dykes, "One of my dad's uncles was a friend of Charles Curtis." Curtis was a powerful Kansas Republican who became a U.S. senator and was Herbert Hoover's vice president. Dykes, like most cadets, had parents with power and what was just as useful to the politicians who appointed them: money.

According to Dykes, "I was probably the first cadet to meet Ike at West Point. When the class of '15 arrived, we were assigned two to a room in alphabetical order. Dykes was the last of the *D*s, Eisenhower was the first of the *E*s; so I drew Ike. For the next week . . . we went through the tough plebe indoctrination period called 'beast treatments.' The First Class officers made our lives miserable. They worked us over and chopped us down to size fast. We moved at a dead run all the time. We drilled, we shined brass buttons, we greased and cleaned rifles—and when taps blew at 10 P.M. we collapsed into bed.

"Ike took the hazing in his stride. When he was asked a question, he always began his answer with, 'Well, now . . .' I've noticed, watching his press conferences on TV, that even today he begins his reply to questions with, 'Well, now . . .'!"

When Eisenhower was president, John Mason Brown, in the *Saturday Review,* wrote, "Few men in public life could in a half hour have used 'well' and 'now' so frequently as traffic islands on which to pause before advancing an idea. Few could ever have said so often, after indicating that they were unprepared or reluctant to answer, 'But I will say,' 'But I must say,' or 'I can say,' or 'I do say,' and then plunged, out of a feeling of courtesy or obligation, into an answer. 'Well,' as he has used it, has been generally a filler-in while he collected his thoughts and a signal that he intended to reply. With him 'now' has marked the conclusion of one point in an argument and his transition to the next step in its development. Although both words in his use of them have Webster's blessing, his over-reliance on them has created, for readers of the transcripts, the impression that Eisenhower was inarticulate when he was not."

Another technique Eisenhower found useful at his presidential press conferences was also developed at the academy; there they called it "bugling," using many words to say nothing very much. According to Brigadier General Hume Peabody, West Point 1915, "One year, Ike and I were in math class together, and to appreciate my favorite memory of him, a knowledge of 'bugling' is necessary. Every cadet in the class usually recited on each day's assignment, first writing the problem on the blackboard. If he was not fully prepared he'd 'bugle'—stay at the board stalling and pray that before his turn came the bugle would sound recall from class.

"One day I was supposed to recite last. I hadn't the foggiest notion about my topic—as I had previously confided to Ike—and my only hope was to 'bugle.' I covered part of the board with meaningless figures and listened with a sinking heart to recitation after recitation. When the man before me finished reciting, there must have been at least five minutes left—but the axe never fell. Ike stood up and asked a question, then another and still another. The instructor was completely taken in and answered each question thoroughly. Then that blessed bugle blew and I was off the hook. No 'bugler' was ever more expertly rescued from his plight than I was by Ike that day so long ago."

Beast Barracks lasted three weeks. In addition to the hazing, there were endless hikes, close-order drill, field problems in strategy, calisthenics, and the cleaning of rifles, the shining of belt buckles—sometimes six times a day. Eisenhower's classmate Omar Bradley said they were "taught how to make a bed, clean and care for their room; when to shave; when to shine our shoes; and always, *always*, to say 'sir' to our superiors."

No plebe was ever complimented; none was ever treated as a human being. Eisenhower bore it all, though. He remembered the words his mother often repeated, "What man has done, man can do."

A 1980 guidebook for visitors to West Point indicates that the purpose of Beast Barracks—the guide calls it "the plebe system"—has not changed much in the over seventy years since Eisenhower was a plebe.

It says that the plebe "is subject to an intense, unremitting, and lengthy period of trial and training to test the steel of his soul. . . . Always under the surveillance of the upper classes—who outnumber plebes three to one—his every deficiency is detected, pointed out and corrected. . . . This system usually succeeds in weeding out individuals who do not have an intense desire to succeed at being a West Pointer. In those remaining, it roots out whatever bad habits of posture, self-expression, or attitude they may have brought to the Academy, and it incubates the precepts of the Corps, Duty, Honor, Country."

Dykes said that Eisenhower, during Beast Barracks, would say, "It won't always be like this." In his memoirs, Eisenhower says of Dykes, without naming him, that he "had come to West Point quite young. He . . . thought everybody was cutting him to pieces." Everybody in his hometown in Kansas who mattered had attended a farewell party in his honor. But West Point was clearly not for him—he once fainted on the drill field. But he did stick it out until after the first exams; then he failed math and returned to Lebanon.

Thirty-one years later when General Eisenhower was in Algiers, Dykes, then living in Enid, Oklahoma, wrote to him saying that the young men being commissioned as second lieutenants after three months' training in officer candidate schools were better trained than those commissioned in the First World War. "Of course," Dykes wrote, "the niches found for some twelve thousand officers commissioned directly from 'cits,' were apparently for considerations other than their value to the services, according to my observations. This of course can be expected, and I presume you have to make room for lots of them."

Ike liked to save unpleasant things for last; throughout his life, he liked to begin whatever it was on a cheerful note. When he was supreme commander reporting to Chief of Staff of the Army George C. Marshall, for instance, he always began with some pleasantries, then got down to the facts, which were often not cheerful. In reply to Dykes, he wrote:

It is a long time since June 1911, but I can still picture you exactly as you looked on the day we entered West Point.

Then to the serious business, the criticism:

> Please disabuse your mind from any thought that I have to "make room
> for officers commissioned for some reason other than their value to the
> service." I don't do any such thing. A man delivers or, if I can find out
> about it, he gets out. So far as I am concerned, the War Department has
> never in any way asked me to make room for anybody, and, knowing the
> type of leadership we have in the War Department, I know that no such
> request will ever be made of me . . . so far as I am concerned, no failure
> or error of mine can ever properly be attributed to inefficient subordinates
> foisted off on me for reasons other than efficiency.

When in December 1942 it was announced that Eisenhower was Allied supreme commander, Dykes wrote, "This will lead to the presidency in ten to
fifteen years." Eisenhower wrote back, "I don't think so, but I appreciate your
kindness."

According to Dykes's son, Delmar, "In 1952 Dad and three or four men
from Enid drove up to Abilene to see Eisenhower launch his campaign. Dad
hadn't seen Eisenhower since 1911, and naturally he was wondering if he'd be
recognized. Eisenhower spoke to several people in the crowd, then looked at
John Dykes, and without a second's hesitation he flashed the famous grin and
said, 'Hi, Johnnie.' Returning to Enid that night, Dad was a very happy man."

After the initial weeks of Beast Barracks came an interlude of summer camp
on the northeast corner of what was and still is known as The Plain. The day
Eisenhower moved into the tent that was to be his home for six weeks was
fearfully hot, and about a dozen boys, unable to take the heat and double-
timing, were taken to the hospital that day.

In summer camp Eisenhower learned close-order drill, stood guard duty,
hiked, and got in some target shooting. Sometimes he was part of a sham battle,
usually conducted in the surrounding mountains. The evenings were rather
dull, however, as there wasn't too much one could do in a tent barely eight feet
square. At the end of summer camp, he was assigned to F company, one of the
companies where the tallest cadets, most of them athletes, were assigned. The
reason cadets were assigned according to their height was so that when they
marched as a corps all hats, rifles and coats would be even.

Eisenhower's second roommate was still another Kansan, a plebe from Wichita he had met briefly when they both took the West Point examinations. He
was Paul A. "P.A." Hodgson. Hodgson, a sensitive, observant man, was Eisenhower's "wife" for four years and remained a close friend all his life. That
was true of most of Eisenhower's friends. The exceptions were rare and noteworthy. The two were assigned a small, efficient room with a cobblestone floor
and a fireplace for heat.

As a roommate, Eisenhower, according to P.A., "could be a sly one about
minor duties about the room; we were supposed to take turns opening the
windows at night and closing them first thing in the morning. But Ike dressed

so fast that he could linger in bed—and I, a slower dresser, always had to get out of my warm bed onto the cold floor and close the windows. I was always very careful about cleaning my part of the room whereas Ike was very nonchalant. But somehow I always got the demerits—he never did."

A West Point day began with reveille at 6:00; after roll call, the cadets marched to breakfast at 6:30. Then the cadets cleaned up their rooms, a task Eisenhower was happy to leave largely to P.A. Morning classes began at 8:00 and ended at noon, and after lunch they resumed at 1:00, continuing until 4:00. In a sense Eisenhower's day didn't really begin until after 4:00, which was time for sports. Then there was dinner and another brief free time. Most cadets used it for studying, but Eisenhower frequently found something better to do, like a quick game of poker.

Chapel was compulsory on Sunday, but otherwise, weekend schedules were about the same, just no classes. Inspections were endless. Cadets were not allowed to leave the grounds except for a special event like the Army-Navy game, and while you were a plebe, there were no furloughs and no summer vacation. P.A. said the whole thing was "rather grueling."

Academics began the first week in September. To Eisenhower, they were usually no problem, although he soon discovered that English was his best subject. James A. Van Fleet, the classmate who was to command a division and become a major general in France in 1944, said "Ike could express himself better than almost any member of the class. Consequently he was in the top section in English all the time. Some of the boys kidded him about it, claimed he was bookworming his way to the top. They kept it up until Ike pledged that he wouldn't open a book on English out of class for the rest of the term. He finally hit the bottom of the class. But he wouldn't crack a book until the class members released him from the pledge."

Clifford R. Jones, whose room was across the hall from Eisenhower's, said, "While all the rest of us were cramming like mad, I'd see Ike with his feet on the desk, reading a magazine."

In later years P.A. remembered that one two-hundred-word theme had to be turned in every Monday afternoon at 2:00. Hodgson worried all week over his. Not Eisenhower. After lunch on Monday, Eisenhower would say, "I need a nap. Call me at 1:30." After being wakened, P.A. said, Eisenhower would write until 1:55, and the theme would be only two or three words over two hundred and would inevitably earn a high grade.

Eisenhower had almost total recall. Then and later he had the infuriating habit of appearing not to listen to what was being said. He would often tap a pencil on a desk or doodle on a pad when someone was talking to him. But the speaker would almost always learn that Eisenhower could and would quote verbatim what had been said, not only minutes later but months and years afterward.

Robert B. Anderson, secretary of the treasury in Eisenhower's administration, said he had a very remarkable memory. "I used to be amazed, when I would go over to tell him about financing, and there might have been another financing [briefing] thirty days before, he would remember to the precise fraction of a point of interest what we had paid, and even after he was in the hospital, one of the last times I visited with him, we were talking about an event which happened, and he said to me, 'Oh, yes, I remember that.' He said, 'You remember, while we were talking, that Lucius Clay called me on the telephone and said thus and so.' Well, he remembered just precisely what Lucius Clay had said and exactly the context in which he said it."

Nancy Jansen McCarty, who worked with him as his personal secretary from 1967 to 1968, the year before his death, said that while he was working on what was to be a book about Churchill and Marshall (never finished), he could recall in detail not only what they had said to each other but very often what they had for lunch that day. His memory for what he had read was equally good whether it was the Bible, Shakespeare, an account of a battle, or a statistical report.

In 1943, when he was in England planning the Overlord invasion, his personal secretary was a WAC captain, Mattie Pinnette. She, too, was impressed with his memory and was grateful that he dictated in complete sentences.

At his first press conference after he became supreme commander of the Allied Expeditionary Forces, he was asked to make a statement for the newsreel photographers. He immediately dictated a three-hundred-word statement to Captain Pinnette. She typed it, gave it to him, and after he had glanced at it, he put it aside, and told the cameramen he was ready. Then, looking directly at the cameras, he made the statement without referring to the text; Captain Pinnette, who had a text, found that in speaking he made only two minor alterations and those were an improvement.

Eisenhower did write clear, precise English and he did write rapidly. He had what P.A. called in a letter home "a natural gift . . . a very direct and pleasing style." Those of us who remember the presidential press conferences may find that hard to believe. Eisenhower said of those conferences:

> I soon learned that ungrammatical sentences in the transcripts caused many to believe that I was incapable of using good English; indeed several people who have examined my private papers, many in my handwriting, have expressed outright astonishment that my writings and grammatical structure were at least adequate. By consistently focusing on ideas rather than on phrasing, I was able to avoid causing the nation a serious setback through anything I said in many hours, over eight years, of intensive questioning.

As a new cadet, Eisenhower was "reasonably popular," according to Alexander M. "Babe" Weyand, a fellow cadet and football player, "but for some reason he tried to project the image of a 'breezy westerner' as against what he called the 'effete easterner.' He pronounced *favorite* to rhyme with *kite*, *hostile* to rhyme with *file*, and he pronounced Rutgers with a soft *g*, as in German. He'd say, 'independent as a hog on ice,' 'underslung as a bull dog,' 'as sure as God made little green apples.' And if somebody didn't move quick enough he'd say, 'You hog-tied or paralyzed, mister?' "

He was also described as a "prankster." Weyand said, "As a plebe, he often pretended to be an upperclassman. He'd stand outside the door of another plebe and in a commanding voice boom out, 'Who lives in this house?' Whoever it was would drop everything and snap to attention until he saw that it was just another plebe.

"He would also shout 'at ease' at other plebes, but when he swaggered into another plebe's room, his smile was so warm and friendly that we all had to laugh."

William H. Britton, class of 1916, described Eisenhower as an "extrovert." He said when Eisenhower lived on the third floor and caught a cadet trying to sneak along the roof below his window to get to another division, he would dump a bucket of water on him. Whenever they heard a splash of water, they knew Eisenhower had caught another cadet. Britton said there were always snow fights during the wintertime, and "Ike was always in the thick of it."

One of Ike's extracurricular exploits that he often talked about as an old man had to do with the time he and another plebe, Layson Enslow Atkins, "Tommy," were found guilty of a minor infraction by an upperclassman named Adler and ordered to report to his room "in full-dress coats." They did exactly that, wearing the coats and nothing else. Eisenhower remembered that, "The sound that Corporal Adler let out was the cry of a cougar." Adler must have been surprised. As Eisenhower said, "The full-dress coat is a cutaway with long tails in back, and tailored straight across the waist in front." Such exposure at West Point in 1911 was unusual, and it is not surprising that Eisenhower never forgot it. Adler probably didn't either. He was so angry at the two cadets that he ordered them to report back to his room immediately after taps in complete uniform with rifles and crossbelts. They were braced against the wall of Adler's room so long that they both left their body outlines on it in perspiration. Eisenhower said, "afterward, we and the other Plebes had a lot of laughs—quiet ones—out of Adler's temporary discomfiture."

Major General Maxwell Taylor, class of 1922, said, "In later years I asked him how he had got along with the upperclassmen when he was a plebe at West Point. 'No difficulty,' he replied. 'One of them ordered me to report to his room after taps for inspection in my full-dress coat. I went in the full-dress coat—nothing else. After that I wasn't bothered.' "

Football practice also began in September. It was particularly rough in those days. The coach was Captain Ernest "Pot" Graves, and, according to Weyand, "Graves liked to see blood on your hands, and since at the time there were no face guards, drawing blood wasn't difficult. Graves said that everything that didn't draw blood was a love pat."

Marty Maher, the team trainer, remembered Eisenhower clearly. "He was always the first cadet on the field for practice and the very last to leave. I used to curse him because he would practice so late that I would be collecting the footballs that he had kicked away in the darkness. He never hit the rubbing table because he would always be out there practicing punts instead of getting a rubdown."

Marty, described as an athletic version of Mr. Chips, was beloved by generations of cadets during his more than fifty years at West Point. Eventually, with the help of Nardi Reeder Campion, Marty wrote an autobiography, *Bringing Up the Brass*, which was later adapted into a movie, *The Long Gray Line*.

Eisenhower never forgot Marty, who massaged his knee back to some use-fulness after he injured it in a football game. After the war, on one of his visits to West Point, while marching in an informal parade with other old grads and classmates, he spotted Marty sitting on a chair under a tree. He broke ranks, raced to the tree, and with a beaming smile of delight, hand outstretched, he exclaimed, "Marty!"

P.A. made the varsity team when he was still a plebe. Eisenhower did not. Weyand said, Eisenhower "talked such a good game we were all convinced he would make the squad but . . . he was too light, and as a result he was, to use one of his favorite expressions, 'fit to be tied.' "

"I weighed something on the order of 155 pounds," Ike said. "However, I was big-boned and was strong and had average speed." He was able to become a member of the Cullum Hall squad, which was comparable to a junior varsity at other schools. The squad played a short schedule, and Cullum Hall's equiv-alent of the Army-Navy game was against Riverview Military Academy in nearby Poughkeepsie. The coaches of the Cullum team and the Riverview team were great rivals. Weyand wrote, "Ike was conspicuous in Cullum's 11–6 victory."

"I showed up fairly well in the games we played," Eisenhower said, "and two or three times during the season was moved intermittently to the Varsity squad, but within two or three days, would be sent back as 'too light.' In high school I had played at end and tackle, but was converted by the picturesque Cullum Hall coach, Toby Zell, to a backfield position. At the season's end I was still a Cullum Hall player."

Since he had not made the varsity team, Eisenhower could not, as P.A. did, eat at the athletes' training table where the food was somewhat better and more plentiful. Moreover, at the training table a cadet just ate. At plebe tables, the plebes had to sit without lifting their eyes until they left the huge mess hall. They had to sit on the edge of their chairs, lifting food to their mouths at sharp right angles. After the food was in their mouths they had to put down their knives, forks, or spoons and keep their hands in their pockets until the food was completely chewed and swallowed.

In the spring of 1912 Eisenhower went out for baseball; the coach at the time was a hard-drinking, opinionated man, Sam Strang Nicklin, a former N.Y. Giants player. Colonel Russell P. "Red" Reeder, class of 1926, a longtime friend of Eisenhower's, said, "Ike was a place hitter, and Nicklin didn't like that. He wanted Ike to swing from the handle the way he, Nicklin, did it."

Eisenhower said, "I was good at bat, trained by my coach [in Abilene] as a 'chop hitter'—to poke the ball, in effect, at selected spots in the infield, rather than swinging away freely. The West Point coach took me aside to say that he thought highly of my fielding. But he could not use me unless I mastered his style of hitting. 'Practice hitting my way for a year and you'll be on my squad next spring,' he said.

"I practiced hitting the way the baseball coach had suggested, and during the summer months, whenever I had free time, I worked hard on the running track, practicing fast starts. By fall I had improved my speed considerably. I also set up a severe regimen of gymnastics to strengthen my leg and arm muscles. And I indulged my appetite at the table to the limit." But by the spring of

1913, when he might have tried out for the varsity baseball team and made it, Ike was unable to do so. By that time, due to a leg injury, he was incapable of participating in varsity sports of any kind.

President Eisenhower told Colonel Reeder in the Oval Office of the White House, "Red, not making the baseball team at West Point was one of the greatest disappointments of my life, maybe the greatest." Reeder said, "That was a great surprise to me." It must come as a great surprise to a great many people.

By the end of Eisenhower's plebe year, his class had been reduced from 265 to 212. He was 10th in the class of 212 in English. He was 39th in history; 30th in surveying (practical military engineering), and 39th in conduct.

Eisenhower became a "yearling" (third classman) and a corporal in June 1912. There were thirty-six corporals made and he ranked eleventh. P.A., who ranked seventh, wrote home, "It is almost like coming home to find yourself one of a big family of cadets instead of a pariah." The yearlings had no furlough. Instead they went to Camp Hasbrouck.

At summer camp as plebes, the main preoccupation had been staying out of sight; the second summer, between the year as a plebe and yearling status, it was all right to be seen, but the boodle had to be kept out of sight. Eisenhower understood boodle immediately; it was forbidden, and he had learned the joys of the forbidden back in Abilene.

Boodle had been defined by generations of cadets as "forbidden fruit, the contents of packages expeditiously secreted under a raincoat and smuggled into camp." Ike and his friends modified and improved on that unimaginative way of getting the boodle onto the academy grounds. They bought it from a friendly grocer in Highland Falls. It could not be delivered to the cadets by the grocer, an enterprising as well as trusting man; so he loaded it into a small boat and took it to an agreed-upon cove on the Hudson below the academy. Since the cadets were not allowed to have cash, the grocer would not be paid until after they graduated, and that was three years away.

The major problem for the cadets was getting out of the camp, getting the boodle from the cove, and bringing it up the steep cliff and back to the camp. The entire operation took ingenuity and considerable physical exertion. Eisenhower provided the ingenuity, leaving the physical exertion to others.

Fortunately, the camp was rather dark, individual tents being provided only with candles. As one cadet at the time said, "There were six companies, and each had its own tactical officer, who was supposed to keep his eye on things, but he just couldn't see much. At night the camp was a rather quiet, dimly lighted place."

According to Weyand, "To get out of camp on official business, you had to say 'all right' to the camp sentinel. That meant that you were leaving camp on an authorized mission; getting boodle was hardly that. But by crawling through an underground tunnel you could go to the latrine without passing the sentinel and saying 'all right,' which would have been a lie.

"From the latrine you could climb down to the river, get the food, and climb back up. And you had to do all that without being seen. It was, to put it simply, dangerous.

"Now Eisenhower avoided that danger, and I'll tell you how. It took considerable imagination; I guess he always had considerable imagination. There were screened windows on the latrine, and the frames were painted white. Now, the screens had to be removed when the cadets climbed out of the window and again when they climbed back in. There wasn't time enough to put the screws back in while the cadets were climbing down and back up the slope leading to the river.

"Eisenhower realized that if an upperclassman passed those screened windows while we were doing that the screw holes might be noticed; so he said we should put toothpaste over the screw holes, and we did, and it worked. It was a great idea."

It was indeed, and Eisenhower had a second great idea. He would guard the latrine while the cadets were climbing up and down to the river. He did that, a job requiring less risk and energy, and when the cadets were back in the latrine with the food, most of them understandably out of breath, he calmly wiped the toothpaste off the window frames, replaced the screws, and then shared the food with them. "And you know something," said Weyand, "nobody ever complained. To the contrary, we were grateful. After all, he thought of it."

There in three sentences is at least a partial summation of Eisenhower's phenomenal success. People didn't complain. They were grateful because most of the time "he thought of it."

Weyand said, "People are always talking about the fact that his grades at West Point were not exceptional. But you can see that in operations outside the classroom he was *outstanding*."

Eisenhower did sometimes sneak out the latrine windows. Colonel Charles C. Herrick, another classmate, said that, although being caught off the reservation was a serious offense, "It didn't worry Ike and some of the others. They'd sneak out the lavatory windows, and past the sentry post and off they'd go up the Hudson to Newburgh for coffee and sandwiches. Imagine! They'd travel thirty miles—fifteen there and fifteen back—just for chow. If any of those guys had been caught they'd have been thrown right out of the academy."

It must be assumed that the man who ran the restaurant in Newburgh was as generous and trusting as the merchant in Highland Falls, or that the cadets were breaking the rules and had money.

During Ike's plebe year, a number of cadets slipped out of camp for a beer. Despite the fact they had been cadets only a short time, they were caught, court-martialed, and dismissed. But authorities in Washington thought the punishment too severe and rescinded the dismissal and gave the offending cadets the privilege of "walking" the area for five hours a day Wednesday and Saturday afternoons until June. "I figure," said Weyand, "that beer cost them approximately 500 miles of walking per man."

Eisenhower never got caught leaving the post. "I was never in great scrapes at West Point," he said. "I never went off the post in civilian clothes, for example. I was given demerits for smaller offenses. I did not worry about demerits; however, some of my classmates worried over every one."

The list of Eisenhower's delinquencies at the academy is lengthy, but none of them is serious. These are typical:

Date	Offense	Demerits
27 Aug. 1911	Falling in without waistbelt when guard was turned out 1:15 p.m., 26 Aug.	1
30 Oct. 1912	Passing plates in a careless and improper manner at supper	2
11 Nov. 1912	Heat not properly adjusted at afternoon inspection	1
22 Nov. 1914	Tabletop dusty at morning inspection	1
20 May 1915	Not writing 200 words in Spanish composition for May 17 as required	2

Usually the reports were made by officers or other cadets. But in one instance Eisenhower turned himself in for "Not staying in area between tattoo and taps as directed." None of them was, as he often said of other matters, exactly "a federal offense."

At that time, cadets were allowed seven demerits a month; if a cadet got more than seven, he had to walk a one-hour tour for each additional demerit, no mean punishment, especially during a West Point winter. Wednesdays and Saturdays were set aside for that purpose.

None of Eisenhower's offenses, including the devious way of getting boodle, involved "lying, cheating or stealing"; therefore, he had not violated the cadet honor code of his day: "A cadet does not lie, cheat, or steal."

In 1946, when Eisenhower was chief of staff, he wrote his old friend and associate, Maxwell Taylor:

Since your visit to my office a few days back I have had West Point very much on my mind. . . . I think that everyone familiar with West Point would instantly agree that the one thing that has set it aside from every other school in the world is the fact that for a great number of years it has not only had an "honor" system, but that the system has actually worked. . . . We have succeeded early in a Cadet's career in instilling in him a respect amounting to veneration for the honor system. The honor system, as a feature of West Point, seems to grow in importance with the graduate as the years recede until it becomes something that he is almost reluctant to talk about—it occupies in his mind a position akin to the virtue of his mother or his sister.

Duty, Honor, Country. Everybody understood those. What a great many civilians have never understood is the fourth demand of a cadet, that he tell the truth in all official matters and that if he knows that a cadet, even himself, has lied, he must report that fact, knowing the guilty cadet will be immediately discharged from the academy. To many civilians, that meant being an informer; it meant ratting on a friend; it meant betraying a personal relationship to support an institution.

Eisenhower never questioned it.

The summer Eisenhower became a yearling, P.A. wrote home, "This being a yearling is some keen dope, believe me. I've been to three hops [dances] and a band concert but I haven't become well acquainted with any femmes."

Ike somehow met two young women that summer, possibly from one of the women's colleges near West Point, and convinced each one not only that she was the most important "femme" in his life but that she was the only one. He did not know that the two were close friends, but one week that fall he got letters from both saying that they would attend the same dance with him. According to P.A., on receipt of the two letters Eisenhower "looked wild and haunted for a day or two, but he thinks he has solved the difficulty now—and though still rather pale his appetite is returning."

All hops at West Point were chaperoned, and cadets had to be especially careful not to get demerits by what was called P.D.A., Public Display of Affection.

Eisenhower never got any demerits for P.D.A., but he did manage to get into trouble at the hops he went to "only now and then." His record shows a total of twelve demerits for "improper dancing."

In those days, "proper" young women wore dresses that swept the floor, and the sight of an ankle was considered offensive. Ike, a PS (parlor snake, in West Point slang—someone who liked to dance), and the daughter of a Spanish instructor were fond of quick turns and whirls. On one occasion, the young woman's ankles were both exposed. Eisenhower was warned not to let it happen again, but it did. His punishment tours for improper dancing were to be walked on specific dates, but because he was on crutches on those dates due to a football injury, he never walked his punishment tours. That led to the academy rule being changed. Instead of having to walk on certain dates, the punishment was changed to require walking for a certain number of hours. According to Weyand, "Eisenhower was very proud of the change he had effected."

Ike preferred poker to attending hops. He had learned how to play back in Abilene from a vagrant who could not read and had trouble writing his own name, but who, Eisenhower said, taught him "the rudiments of poker. . . . He dinned percentages into my head night after night around a campfire, using for the lessons a greasy pair of nicked cards that must have been a dozen years old. . . . Often, he would pick up part of the pack and snap it across my fingers to underscore the classic lesson that in a two-handed game one does not draw to a four-card straight or a four-card flush against the man who has openers." Naturally, very few "effete easterners" knew about percentages, so Eisenhower won most of the time. He recorded the results of the games in a book for payment after graduation.

Sometimes during a poker game, according to William Britton, "Ike and I would put on our raincoats with a can in each pocket and go to a dance in Cullum Hall and get in the ice-cream line, fill up the cans with ice cream and take it back [to the game]. . . . To this day I don't understand why we were allowed to go to the dance in improper uniform."

Or all the players would take a recess from a Saturday night game to stop in at a dance, known as a "Feed Hop," where they knew food was being served late in the evening. After consuming a number of sandwiches, they would rush back to continue playing.

Poker was not the only card game Eisenhower indulged in at the Point; he also learned how to play bridge, a game at which he became a master and one he liked so much that during the war he transported people hundreds of miles just so that he could have a decent partner. Britton remembers, "One day Ike said, 'Let's learn to play bridge. You get a partner, and I'll get a partner.' We started playing in Ike's room in November 1913. . . . We played every night, except Saturday, until April. . . . Ike and his partner beat us consistently. . . . One night there was a knock on the door. It was the sentinel making his inspection. Ike pushed the cards in the drawer of his desk as the sentinel opened the door. His quick thinking saved us a month of walking."

Mark Clark said that Eisenhower's bridge was like everything else about him. "He had to excel. He always had to excel."

In his second year at the Point, as a yearling, Eisenhower started out like most of his classmates, determined to make the incoming plebes as miserable as he had been the year before. He said, "I ran into a Plebe from my own state. . . . I demanded, with all the sarcasm and scorn I could muster in my voice, 'Mr. Dumgard, what is your P.C.S. [Previous Condition of Servitude]?' And added, 'You look like a barber.'

"He stood up, said, softly, 'I was a barber, Sir.'

"I didn't have enough sense to apologize to him on the spot and make a joke of the whole thing. I just turned my head and went to my tent where my roommate . . . was sitting. I looked at him and said, 'P.A. I'm never going to crawl [haze] another Plebe as long as I live. . . . I've just done something that was stupid and unforgivable. I managed to make a man ashamed of the work he did to earn a living.'

"And never again, during the remaining three years at the U.S.M.A., did I take it upon myself to crawl a Plebe."

Eisenhower's sensitivity to the feelings of others and his resolve never to humiliate anyone or allow anyone under his command to be humiliated lasted, with some few exceptions, for his entire career. When he was stationed at Fort Leavenworth in 1917–18, a classmate, John E. Harris, remembered that, "I was a major in an Engineering regiment, and Ike, a captain, commanded a big group of provisional officers—temporary second lieutenants who were getting six months of training to see if they qualified for permanent commissions.

I happened to be sitting in Ike's office one afternoon when we heard a commotion outside. A young first lieutenant was dressing down one of the temporary officers in a loud, abusive manner. The victim was obviously confused by the lieutenant's harshness and embarrassed by the crowd which had been attracted. Ike watched for a moment and then sent out an order to have the first lieutenant report to him "when he had finished."

When the lieutenant came in, Ike said sharply that he didn't care to know the circumstances of the incident—that no infraction could conceivably have justified the public humiliation to which the boy had been subjected. Then, his voice kinder but no less firm, he lectured the lieutenant on the responsibility that comes with authority. It was hardly a new idea, but Ike expressed it so eloquently yet so simply that I found myself listening as intently as the lieutenant. . . . At one point during his lecture I awoke to the fact that Ike's words applied as well to me as to the lieutenant. I learned an important lesson that afternoon, and I've never forgotten it.

★ ★ ★

WINNING AND LOSING

Eisenhower had spent the summer of 1912 improving his running speed, practicing fast starts, and further developing his leg and arm muscles. "As a consequence," he said, "I started the football season of 1912 weighing about 174 pounds and participated in West Point's first practice game, against a soldier team. In the latter half of the game, partly by good luck and partly by burning desire, I showed up quite well and for the first time attracted some attention from the varsity coaches, then headed by Captain Ernest Graves.

"After completing several post-game laps around the field, I trotted toward the gymnasium, overtaking and passing the coaching group. I was some 15 or 20 yards beyond it when Captain Graves called sharply, 'Eisenhower!' I stopped, ran back and saluted and, of course, said, 'Yes, Sir.' He looked at me and asked, 'Where did you get those pants?' They were hanging around my ankles. I replied, 'From the manager, Sir.' He said, 'Look at those shoes—can't you get anything better than that?' Again, I said, 'I am just wearing what I was issued.' It happened that the Cadet Manager, named Perkins, was in the group with Captain Graves and the latter turned to Perkins to say, 'Get this man completely outfitted with new and properly fitted equipment.' He went on to say a couple of other things, but actually I scarcely heard him; I was walking on air, because this was my first intimation that I would probably become a member of the Varsity Squad.

"Being dismissed by the Captain, I raced to the Club House at a ten-second gait and refused to leave until the manager came in and had me completely outfitted for the next day's practice. I think that that particular evening provided me the greatest personal thrill of my brief career at West Point."

He did not play in Army's first game that year, against Stevens Institute, but after that he played in every game until the Army team met Navy on November 16. Weyand said, "He started against Rutgers. Seemingly he did nothing noteworthy as Army won 19–0."

The *New York Times* did not agree; its sports reporter called Eisenhower "one of the most promising backs."

The next game was against those most effete of easterners, the Yalies. That year, however, the Yale team was considered by most observers to be the best in the country. Army lost, 6–0, but Weyand felt, "had he [Eisenhower] been started earlier . . . he might have saved the game."

The next week, in the game against Colgate, Graves sent Eisenhower into the game in the fourth quarter. Army won, 18–7, and the *New York Tribune* said, "The work of Eisenhower brought joy to the Army rooters." The West Point yearbook, *The Howitzer*, said, "Eisenhower could not be stopped."

Eisenhower said, "In one game an opposing player made a protest. He turned to the referee, who was standing close by my side, and said, 'Watch that man.' The referee with some astonishment said, 'Why? Has he slugged you or roughed you up in any way?' The man, who was probably green and overexcited, said, 'No! But he is going to.' I think this was the oddest thing that happened to me on the football field."

Eisenhower was a hero to his fellow cadets. Omar Bradley, a teammate, said, "In those days West Point was sports oriented to a feverish degree. . . . in organized team sports one learns the important art of group cooperation in goal achievements. No curricular endeavor I know of could better prepare a soldier for the battlefield."

That football was of great importance, there can be no question. "It has often been likened to war," Eisenhower wrote to General Maxwell Taylor in November 1945,

the razzle-dazzle passes to the Air Forces, the end sweeps to racing armored columns and the busting through the middle to the bone-shattering Infantry attacks. . . . The analogy is a good one in so far as each contest required guts, brains, physical power, skillful teamwork, and heart. But there is a vital difference. In war, victory is everything—and anything to gain it is fair! In football the game is the thing—the good clean fight with everything we've got, with victory the prize for excelling in the sum total of those qualities that, in the field of sport and good sportsmanship, make for perfection!

Eisenhower said that when he was supreme commander, "I noted with great satisfaction how well ex-football players seemed to fulfill leadership qualifications. . . . I cannot recall a single ex-footballer with whom I came in contact who failed to meet every requirement. Personally, I believe that this was more than coincidental. I believe that football, almost more than any other sport, tends to instill in men the feeling that victory comes through hard—almost slavish—work, team play, self-confidence, and an enthusiasm that amounts to dedication."

On November 9, 1912, Eisenhower was in the starting lineup of what was bound to be a tough game against the legendary Carlisle Indians. The star of that team was the immortal Jim Thorpe, a Sac Indian. Thorpe was arguably the best athlete of the first half of this century, and he had already been voted all-American. In the Olympics in the summer of 1912, he had won both the pentathlon and decathlon. He also played championship baseball and lacrosse and had won many track meets.

In 1913 he had to return all his gold medals because it was discovered he had played semipro baseball. He died in 1953, and it was not until January 1983 that the gold medals were returned to his family. The *New York Times* said that

Thorpe was "perhaps the best all-around athlete that America has ever produced."

Weyand wrote an account of the November 9 game for the West Point alumni magazine, *Assembly*, in 1968:

> Carlisle had a truly great team which scored 505 points during the season. It featured the exploits of the incomparable Jim Thorpe. Years later, [Carlisle Coach Glenn Scobey] Pop Warner assured me that he considered this to have been Thorpe's greatest game and, when I asked him, Jim verified that statement.
>
> With Ike plowing "up the middle," Army commenced moving. [Vernon] Prichard sent [Leland] Hobbs off tackle to a touchdown. Army had scored first, but then the redskins got mad and commenced taking the Army line apart. The backing chores fell to Ike and [Charles] Benedict, who had relieved Hobbs. Benedict was another "F" Company man. He and Ike were classmates and good friends. They worked in close harmony. When a runner came through the line the first to reach him tackled low, the other high.
>
> There is a story that never in his career, college or pro, did Jim Thorpe take time out for injuries. When he discussed the game with me, Ike chuckled and said, "When Bennie and I gave him the old one-two he proved as human as any of them." Carlisle took time out.

The *New York Times* reported that the time out lasted three minutes; no matter, nobody could stop Jim Thorpe. Weyand says, "Ike and Bennie tried another 'gang tackle,' but, that time, Jim saw them coming. He stopped short and they collided head-on. They were badly shaken up, and Graves relieved both of them, although Ike loudly protested that he was all right. . . . Eisenhower and Benedict were on the bench when Carlisle went on to win 27–6." According to the *New York Sun*, "Army has a rattling good back in Eisenhower, who was the best man to carry the ball in the Indian game." When Eisenhower was president, Weyand asked Thorpe if he remembered the 1912 encounter with Eisenhower. "With an economy of words, Jim nodded his head vigorously and grunted, 'Good linebacker.' "

Thorpe was perhaps not the only player in that 1912 football game who had played semiprofessional baseball.

On December 17, 1951, General Dwight Eisenhower, then supreme commander of NATO in France, received a letter from Bertram Jay Gumpert, a sports writer on the *New York Post*. Gumpert apologized for "writing trivia to one of the busiest men in the world, but I have a feeling he might welcome correspondence . . . from a newspaper man which for a change deals with neither politics nor military matters." Gumpert added that he had recently reviewed for the *Post* a book called *Great Sports Stories from* The New York Times:

> I ran into a story on Jim Thorpe's performance in the Carlisle-Army game of 1912. Starting at the right half for Army, but unmentioned anywhere but in the lineup, was a young cadet named "Eisenhower." . . .

Also, as you probably know, Thorpe is down on his luck (again!) and suffering from skin cancer. Perhaps a word or two from you might help his morale, and assist those trying to put him on his feet.

Gumpert saved the most important matter for a postscript. He wrote:

How many people know that if a young outfielder who played under the name of "Wilson" in the Kansas State League had remained in baseball he might have been a major leaguer, and, ultimately, a manager instead of a Five-Star general?

In his reply, Eisenhower thanked Gumpert for his letter and paid tribute to Thorpe as "one of the great athletes of our time." He was "sorry to learn that he is again in poor health and I am enclosing a check which is the necessarily modest contribution of a soldier. . . . The one thing I must ask is that you regard it as anonymous and as a confidential matter between the two of us."

But Eisenhower makes no mention at all of what was included in the postscript—a man "who played under the name of 'Wilson.' " That is an odd omission for a man always so careful to correct all errors about details of his life. But he did not take the trouble to say that he had never been "Wilson." If he hadn't been, wouldn't he have denied it?

After spending more than three years studying, thinking about, and trying to think like Eisenhower, I can with relative safety say that he would have. But the reader will have to decide.

The next question is when did "Wilson" play with the Kansas State League? Was it during the two years after Eisenhower graduated from high school and had nothing much to do except work in a creamery? That would be my guess.

According to the *Abilene Reflector-Chronicle Memorial Edition,* Eisenhower played center field in semipro baseball for a short time before entering West Point. There is no mention of the name Wilson.

Jim Thorpe was breaking the rules for Olympic athletes when he played semipro baseball, but Eisenhower, so far as is known, was breaking no rule at all by doing so. Why he might have chosen to call himself Wilson is not known.

In any case, whenever it was, and if it was, it would seem to demonstrate that even before he left Abilene, Eisenhower had more than enough guile to get along in the world outside.

The game after Carlisle was against Tufts on November 16. For a while Eisenhower played better than ever before. A classmate, Herman Beukema, said, "He carried the ball three times. He never held back. Nothing could stop him until he was carried off the field." Army won the game, 15–6, but Eisenhower did not celebrate the victory. The records of the West Point dispensary show that he was admitted for a sprained knee from a football injury "which occurred on November 16 at 4 P.M."

He was released from the hospital for the first time on November 21, and on November 26, four days before what everybody who had ever been at the Point considered the most important game of the year, Army against Navy, the *New York Sun* said, "Eisenhower is limping, but it is hardly likely that he will be kept out of practice. He is one of the Army's strongest offensive backs and a terrific line smasher."

The day the *Sun* article appeared, Eisenhower's football career ended forever, not in practice but in the new riding hall at West Point. The cadets were doing what they called "monkey drill," mounted gymnastics. Weyand said, "I was riding behind him when the accident happened. Suddenly my horse shied and there was Ike groveling in the tanbark, clutching his wounded knee.

"Of course if the football coach had been anybody except Pot Graves he probably would have quietly arranged for Ike to avoid that monkey drill."

Eisenhower said, "The doctors spent four days straightening my leg, a process so painful that I scarcely slept during the ordeal."

Joseph C. Haw, classmate, said before the class's fortieth reunion that when Eisenhower was in the hospital, another cadet there was very ill. "He began calling for the wardmaster, a surly so-and-so, who ignored him. Ike finally slid out of bed, balanced on his good leg and yelled at the wardmaster, 'Give him what he wants or I'll knock the living hell out of you.' Ike's buddy got attention. . . . Ike always championed the underdog."

Records at the infirmary show that Eisenhower was admitted ten different times for knee injuries. He did attend the Navy game, but on crutches; Army lost, 6–0, and Graves came up to Eisenhower after they had all returned to West Point and said, "You lost us the Navy game." Then the coach turned to the other cadets present and said, "Here I come up with the best line plunger and linebacker I've ever seen at West Point and he busts his knee in the riding hall."

Thirty-two years later, on November 29, 1945, Eisenhower, the five-star general who ten days before had become chief of staff of the U.S. Army, addressed the cadets and officers of West Point by telephone. He regretted that he would be unable to attend the forthcoming Army-Navy game. He added:

"From each of you on the squad I have a special favor to ask. . . . Due to an injury I never had the priceless privilege of playing against the Navy. So will you throw every block just a little harder—will you make every tackle a bit sharper—will you carry out every assignment on every play with just a little more precision? That will help make up, for me, for the tackles and the blocks that I always hoped to try against those crab-town pirates. . . . Good luck— and remember—It may be as tough as cracking the Siegfried [Line], but the Army did that—and it can do this! And do it good!"

Army did win, 32–13, but that may have been due to more than the exhortation from the chief of staff. West Point that year had one of the best, maybe *the* best team in its history, with considerable help from Glenn Davis and Doc Blanchard, the spectacular running backs, "Mister Outside and Mister Inside." Eisenhower and Benedict had been good—but never that good.

The Christmas of 1912 was surely one of the most dismal of Eisenhower's life. He was still in the infirmary, thus missing what would have been his first leave from the academy. He returned to his quarters on December 29, still limping.

While he was in the infirmary, the picture of the football team was taken for

The Howitzer, and the team captain, Leland Devore, did not postpone the taking of the picture so that Eisenhower could be included. "I don't think Ike ever forgave him for that," said Weyand. But on March 16, 1913, when he got his football A he "was very nearly tickled to death," according to his roommate, P.A. "He hasn't received his sweater yet, though, and so he can't wear it. He borrows mine occasionally so as to enjoy the sensation."

That month the cadet corps went to Washington to march in Woodrow Wilson's first inaugural parade. On March 3 they left on two trains of Pullmans and diners, and each cadet received a dollar for spending money. P.A. wrote, "Lord only knows when we'll find time to spend it. After the parade we are to be marched to the residence of a Mrs. Bradley to attend a reception and afterwards we are to be marched to the train."

It seems unlikely that any of the spectators on March 4, 1913, noticed a husky young corporal named Eisenhower in the front rank of F Company growling out of the corner of his mouth, "Dress up on the line. Dress up—watch that step!"

Eisenhower attended four other inaugurals in his lifetime, his own two and those of Harry S Truman and John F. Kennedy. He was in Washington as Pershing's chief of staff when Roosevelt was inaugurated in 1933, but there is no record he attended. His son, John, said, "My father disliked inaugurals. If he could have found a way of getting out of that one my guess is he would have."

Despite his many disappointments in 1912, Eisenhower continued to do reasonably well in his classes. He took a class in integral calculus. The professor one morning said that the next day the calculus problem would be "one of the most difficult of all." He then gave the lengthy and approved approach to the problem and the answer. As was often the case in West Point classrooms, Eisenhower was only half listening. He did hear and remember the answer to the problem, but the approach eluded him. That fact didn't worry him much. Since he was so good at figuring the odds in whatever it was, and since there were twelve cadets in the class, the chances were eleven to one that he would not be called on the next day.

But this time he figured wrong. The next day the instructor called him to the blackboard to solve the problem and explain the approach. First Ike wrote down what he knew, the answer. As for the approach, he had to make his own way through the woods; he had to and did use logic. And he arrived at the correct answer after some nervous minutes. But the instructor was furious. He said, "Mr. Eisenhower, it is obvious that you know nothing about this problem. You memorized the answer, put down a lot of figures and steps that have no meaning whatsoever, and then wrote out the answer in the hope of fooling the instructor."

As might have been expected, Eisenhower's face reddened; the veins in his forehead throbbed, and he was about to reply when a voice from the back of the classroom said, "Just a minute, Captain. . . . Please have Mr. Eisenhower go through that solution again." The voice was that of Major "Poopy" Bell— all the teaching staff at West Point had nicknames—an associate professor of mathematics, who had providentially come to the classroom on an inspection tour.

Eisenhower repeated his solution to the problem, and Poopy said, "Captain, Mr. Eisenhower's solution is more logical and easier than the one we've been using. I'm surprised that none of us, supposedly good mathematicians, has stumbled on it. It will be incorporated in our procedures from now on."

The calculus instructor never again gave Eisenhower a good grade. That year in mathematics he was 97th in a class of 177. In practical military engineering, however, he was 27th. And *The Howitzer* said, "His outstanding achievement as a yearling was a class standing of 16 in drill regulation—Infantry." This certainly was a portent of things to come in later years.

At the end of their second year at the Point, cadets got a furlough of about two and a half months. On the night before it began there was a hop, and, according to another member of Ike's class, John H. Cochran, "two-steps and waltzes were the only dances allowed. Well, maybe it was because of the furlough beginning the following day, or maybe because the girl was good-looking . . . this girl asked Ike to do the turkey trot—and Ike obliged. Well, sir, the Regular Army officer present took out his little book and down went Ike's name."

But before the officer could do anything about the charges, Eisenhower was gone. The following day at the graduation exercises Ike was named supply sergeant of F Company and off he went on furlough.

Eisenhower returned to Abilene in the summer of 1913. In his brother Earl's view, he was "the town hero, and he acted the part." He "lost no opportunity to impress us with what he knew and had done, and occasionally he would put on his uniform and parade through town, though I must admit he did this only a few times."

Ike had promised some of his friends in Abilene that on return there he would wear the cadet's full-dress uniform, and this was his first furlough. Earl remembered Ida spending an entire afternoon pressing Dwight's white trousers. "Dwight had told her, 'You know, mother, they have to be so well pressed that they will stand up by themselves.' Mother stuck at the job until they would do just that—literally." Milton and Earl helped him into his uniform, and by "help," Earl said, "I don't mean that we held his jacket for him while he slipped into it. Dwight lay on the bed while we eased his razor-sharp trousers on, one leg at a time. Then he stood up slowly, so as not to spoil the crease."

He never tired of bracing himself in a manner that would have pleased the most demanding of his hazers when he was a plebe. And the resplendent white dress uniform impressed everyone. The blond hair, the blue eyes, and the smile he forever wore impressed the young women on both sides of the tracks, including the one he most wanted to impress, Gladys Harding. She was considered the prettiest girl in town and probably the most talented; at the end of the summer, she was going off on a concert tour, doing "readings and playing the piano," often both at the same time. Eisenhower usually wore his dress uniform when he went to the Harding house on East Tenth Street.

One day when he got home, the white uniform unsoiled, he found his mother on a ladder trying to get the stovepipe down for cleaning. The large coal-burning stove along the east wall of the dining room had a five-gallon tank to heat the water for Saturday-night baths. The pipe Ida was wrestling with ran from the stove along the ceiling to the chimney.

Eisenhower did exactly what Ida planned he would; he said he would take care of it. So Ida got down from the ladder, and Ike "got up and tried to take the pipe apart, but it stuck. I gave it a big jerk," he said, "and the whole length crashed to the floor, including me. You never saw such a mess in your life. Mother and I started in to clean and it was a job."

That summer his next older brother, Edgar, was at Ann Arbor; Earl and Milton were too young to be considered serious rivals, and thus there was no family competition for the ubiquitous cadet. Because of his leg injury, Eisenhower could not, as he said more than fifty years later, even play "in the informal baseball league made up of such towns as Chapman, Herington, Junction City, and Salina." But he could and did act as umpire; the pay was $15 a game.

He umpired one out-of-town game, in Chapman, where there occurred what he called "a little incident," though he was never to forget it. In 1966, fifty-three years after it happened, he said that

> while waiting for game time, I had a bite of lunch downtown and, wandering around, saw a shooting gallery. I thought it would be fun to try a few shots at the moving targets. As a complete stranger in Chapman, and dressed in ordinary clothes, I could hardly believe my ears when I picked up a rifle and heard a man standing nearby say to another:
>
> "Okay, now, Mister, you've been bragging about your shooting. I just happened to see this soldier boy come in here and I'll bet you ten dollars that he can beat you on any target and in any kind of shooting you want."
>
> Although nothing had been addressed directly to me, when I heard this astonishing statement—nothing I was wearing identified me as a cadet or soldier—unaccountably, and for the first time in my life, a fit of trembling overcame me. My hands shook. Without a word, I laid down the rifle, having already paid for the shells, and left the place without a backward glance.
>
> Never before or since have I experienced the same kind of attack, even though today people somehow manage to call out, "Hey, Ike!" when I think I'm hidden incognito in an unmarked automobile. I think it was such a complete surprise to be revealed as a soldier, even without a uniform, that upset me. I wonder how the argument came out and how long it took my unsolicited sponsor to notice that the soldier boy was no longer present.

That summer, too, he was the hero of a boxing match in the basement of Sterl's department store. Eisenhower was not anxious for the fight. His opponent was taller and heavier than he, had boxed professionally in Kansas City, and had licked every amateur challenger in Abilene. Eisenhower had gained thirty pounds while at West Point, but his trick knee still bothered him and he was still wearing an elastic stocking.

Dirk Tyler was a black porter in a barber shop, who after his many claimed victories as a boxer, went around bragging, perhaps not a wise thing in a white Kansas town in 1913. Eisenhower's friend Bud Hoffman said that if Eisenhower didn't fight him, Tyler was "going to get himself into trouble."

Eisenhower reluctantly agreed to the fight; he later said that he was "scared stiff." But he saw at once that Tyler had no skill. He stood awkwardly with his arms crossed in front of him, then lunged at Ike with fearsome blows, but the West Point cadet simply danced around, looked for an opening, and saw it. He brought his left fist up against Tyler's chin, followed it with a right, and that ended the fight. Tyler had to be carried away.

Later in Normandy in 1944 he was to tell Kenneth S. Davis, his Kansas biographer, "Everybody had talked about Dirk so much I went out determined to use every bit of skill to protect myself. And then to find that boy didn't know the first thing about fighting . . . He telegraphed his punches from a mile away . . . Poor Dirk. Honestly, I've never been particularly proud of that scrap."

Happily, however, after the fight, Tyler stopped bragging. And, of course, Gladys heard about the victory. That summer Eisenhower, according to Davis, "dated her again and again, grasping greedily at a dreamed-of happiness which must necessarily be brief. . . . She listened with a genuine interest. She admired him tremendously, his sincerity, his rugged strength, his enormous vitality. With no other boy had she had so much fun."

Just how Davis found out what Gladys Harding was thinking is not known; she is not listed as among those he talked to in the early 1940s when he was working on *Soldier of Democracy*, but he does say that he had "long, fruitful interviews" with each of the brothers, including Earl.

Earl, Davis said, was "the exploited one" among the Eisenhower brothers, and, breaking Kansas liquor laws on orders from his older brother, he several times that summer with his own money bought six bottles of Muehlbach beer and raced with it to the Harding backyard. There he was met by Ike "who accepted the beer as his due and promptly dismissed his brother."

The summer had a happy ending as far as Gladys was concerned; she felt that her concert tour would bring her near New York City and that they might meet there during the Christmas holiday break. She also said that if she could, she might come to West Point during June Week the following year. As Davis wrote, "He hugged the promise to him as the miles roared under the wheels" of the train taking him back to the academy.

★ ★ ★

A GOOD GAMBLE

Eisenhower's last two years at the Point were not easy. The first bad news he got after he returned was that the charges of the officer who had caught him turkey trotting the previous June had gone through channels. His classmate John H. Cochran said, "When Ike got back, he was busted down to private, and he remained a private for a long time."

He did once more go out for football. He was no longer limping, and a new football coach, Charles Daly, a more amiable man than Coach Graves, allowed him to make the team. But he didn't last long. According to Babe Weyand, during practice, "the minute he was hit hard he was through."

Eisenhower said, "The football and medical authorities tried every experiment and exercise they could think of to get me back into condition. . . . They sent for all sorts of braces. I think they tried a dozen types during the year. None helped enough. . . . I learned to my dismay that rugged sports were denied to me from then on. . . . I found that I had to give up boxing. . . . I could not move laterally on my feet with any speed without renewed injury."

For the remainder of his life Eisenhower had to be careful in his movements. In 1966 he said, "Periodically in the past half century I have had to spend time in the hospital to recover from careless straining of that injured knee."

He said, "The end of my career as an active football player had a profound effect on me." Instead of giving more of his attention to studies, he gave less. "I was almost despondent and several times had to be prevented from resigning by the persuasive efforts of classmates. Life seemed to have little meaning; a need to excel was almost gone."

According to the author John Gunther, "The injured knee troubled him for years. He felt ashamed of it. He told me once, 'I was like a man with his nose cut off going out into society!' "

His roommate, P.A., said that he "was certainly a blue boy, for he loved football almost passionately." Eisenhower wrote Ruby Norman, a friend back in Abilene, "seems like I'm never cheerful any more. The fellows that used to call me 'Sunny Jim' call me 'Gloomy Face' now. The chief cause is this game pin of mine—I sure hate to be so helpless and worthless. . . . I'm getting to be such a confirmed grouch you'd hardly know me."

That fall he started to smoke, which was forbidden. He became rebellious, and one day "carelessly walked out of the barracks with the cigarette lighted. . . ." In another letter to Ruby, he wrote, "I feel right devlish tonight, you know—just like I could smoke a cigarette, and swear and do all the other mean things like drinking pop, and oh—I just know I'm feeling awfully tough."

Eisenhower continued smoking, and by the time of the Second World War he was smoking two, sometimes three packs of cigarettes a day. John Gunther in his brief, perceptive Eisenhower biography remembered lunching with him in Washington when he was chief of staff, "and between 12:45 and 3:00 P.M. he certainly smoked at least fifteen cigarettes." Gunther said, "He smoked like a furnace. . . . I asked him what brand of cigarettes he liked and he replied that it didn't matter in the slightest—he smoked anything."

He continued smoking "like a furnace" until March 1949, when he was president of Columbia University. His friend and physician, Major General Howard Snyder, remembered that moment in detail. "It was 3:00 P.M. March 21, 1949. He had an upset stomach. I had convinced him that he had to give up cigarettes for a while and then I added, 'As long as you have to give them up temporarily, why don't you make it permanent?' He had just reached for a cigarette. He stopped midway and put it back. That was his last smoke."

In the spring of 1950, when he was in Versailles as NATO commander, Diplomat Clare Boothe Luce came as one of many to persuade him to become the Republican presidential nominee in 1952. She saw that there were no cigarettes on his desk, unlike the time in 1944 when she had visited him in the European Theater of Operations and he had never stopped smoking. Mrs. Luce said, " 'Aren't you smoking?' He said, 'No, I quit. I had a little heart trouble, a little warning from my doctor, and so I quit.' " Mrs. Luce said, " 'Why, Ike, how did you ever do it?' He looked at me with disgust and said, 'How did I do it? I simply gave myself an order.' "

John Gunther asked Eisenhower if he minded when people smoked in his office. Gunther said, "He laughed, 'Oh, no. It gives me a sense of moral superiority. I had enough willpower to stop smoking, but they have not.' "

Coach Daly tried to cheer Ike up by giving him the first of what was later to seem an endless number of army coaching assignments. This one was with the Cullum Hall team. Eisenhower was assistant coach. He said, "My work was done under the supervision of an officer but he knew little of the game and when he did step in to coach, his actions were so resisted or misinterpreted by the squad that the head coach suggested that he give me considerable leeway."

Daly also saw to it that Eisenhower was in the varsity football team picture that year.

In coaching the Cullum Hall team, Eisenhower used the varsity formations and signals he knew so well. In spite of the fact that the squad only played secondary schools, they began doing so well that they started drawing large crowds of cadets.

At the end of his final season, the team members gave their assistant coach a pair of mother-of-pearl cuff links and studs. At the time Ike was given the gift, he was playing a Sunday afternoon game of poker. Later he said, "I stood up and expressed my surprise and gratitude but the ceremony having been completely informal, I was soon back at the poker game. Since then I have always regretted that I wasn't more deliberate . . . in expressing my appreciation because I was truly touched. It was probably more embarrassment than indifference that led me into such an exhibition of bad manners."

Football was not the only sport at West Point, and Eisenhower participated in as many others as possible. He did gymnastics in the new gym, learned to chin himself five times with his right hand alone and three times with his left and, according to his son, John, "learned to do the giant swing on the horizontal bar."

In 1925, when he was a major and coaching an army football team, the gymnastics he had perfected at the West Point gym greatly impressed the young man who was to become his naval aide during the Second World War. Harry C. Butcher and Eisenhower met in Chevy Chase, Maryland, and many years later, Butcher said, "One of the few things that stick in my mind about that evening was that all of us did various parlor tricks. Ike had one that none of us could do; he stood stiffly erect, slowly fell forward without moving a muscle, but at the last instant just before it seemed he would break his nose on the floor, his strong hands and muscular arms quickly broke the fall. He can still do the trick and does on appropriate occasions."

In *At Ease*, in which Eisenhower deals rather fully with his life and experiences at West Point, he says very little about what should have been his best and happiest year, the year he was a first classman.

He attended classes in Spanish, geometry, drill regulations, horsemanship, practical military engineering, civil and military engineering, and the science of gunnery. None of them worried him much nor interested him much. Most of the time he was not at all sure that he was going to become an officer. At West Point as for most of the rest of his life he had little doubt that if he decided to chuck the army he could do well at whatever else he chose. That year, in a letter to his friend Ruby, he even spoke of being an actor.

Dear Little Ruby

'Tis true I've not written for some time—I've never had such a protracted case of the blue devils in my life. Everything has gone wrong. . . . I lead the darndest, quietest, hum-drum existence you ever heard of. . . .

You know, I believe it would be great sport to play the leading man in one of those present-day five cent (selling for a dollar and a half) novels, don't you? . . .

Well, girlie, I'll write again pretty quick.

. . . As ever, good night, good luck.

Yours,
Ike

It was a rather melancholy period for Eisenhower, for although he still participated in the football games during his last year, it was not quite the same. He was a cheerleader, a cheerleader as he cabled Max Taylor on November 29, 1945, with a broken leg. "It is just thirty-one years since I last participated in a 'Beat the Navy' meeting! That year I was a 'Cheer Leader.' I'd like to ask this year's occupant of the same post whether he is any more successful than I was in impressing that gang with his eloquence in dodging the bombardment of catcalls and insults that was always my portion. Luckily I had a broken leg— The Corps was gentlemanly enough to abstain from physical violence against a cripple! Anyway, we licked the Navy!"

Ike, who had learned how to sew from his mother back in Abilene, designed capes that the cheerleaders slipped over their uniforms to spell out ARMY in black and gold. As a cheerleader, he also got his first practice at making speeches; the night before each game he would urge the cadets to support their team vocally the following day. According to one classmate, Major Robert L. Williams, "He was so eloquent that he made you absolutely certain that the team had to and would win. He was the best cheerleader we had during my four years at the academy. . . . I also remember one incident typical of his fair-mindedness. One Saturday afternoon the opposite team was penalized for some infraction or other and a spontaneous cheer went up from the plebes. Ike frowned, turned to the stands, and said, 'We don't cheer for a gain like that.' Suddenly everybody became quiet."

In May the graduating class of 1915 spent three days studying the battlefields of Gettysburg, where General George Gordon Meade, class of 1835, who had not been an extraordinary cadet, defeated the forces of General Robert E. Lee.

A short time after Ike returned from Gettysburg, Colonel Henry Alden Shaw, post surgeon at the academy, called Eisenhower to his office and told him that he had just finished reviewing his medical history as a cadet. Eisenhower later wrote, "This consisted almost exclusively of my torn-up knee and subsequent recurrences, which had me in the hospital from time to time."

Shaw also told him that while he would be graduated, because of his knee he might not be commissioned. The doctor had expected an outburst of anger at the news, but Eisenhower seemed not to be upset. He had come to the academy to get a free education; he had gotten it. He was quite prepared to resign from the army.

If Eisenhower learned anything at all at West Point, and he learned a great deal, it was that in the world outside of Abilene he could not only compete, he could, when he wished to, win. He had learned which fork to use and to enter and leave a room without stumbling over anything or anybody; he had learned that, until his injury, he could prevail against the best of them, whoever *they* were, on the football field. But he had acquired more than physical self-confidence; he had acquired mental self-confidence as well. He was still a hick, but he was a self-confident hick.

Shaw was surprised at Eisenhower's calm acceptance of the situation. The colonel said he would think the whole thing over. A few days later, Shaw, a coast artillery man, called Eisenhower back and told him that if he asked for a commission in the coast artillery, it would be granted.

Eisenhower said, "Colonel, I do not want a commission in the coast artillery." Shaw was apparently too astounded to ask why. Eisenhower on another occasion partially explained why. "Beyond keeping their equipment in readiness, oiling and greasing the ponderous machinery that elevated the guns for firing, and engaging in firing practice with dummy ammunition, a Coast Artillery Corps career . . . provided a numbing series of routine chores and a minimum of excitement. . . . Other arms of the service . . . referred to Coast Artillery posts as 'cottages by the sea.' "

In other words, a coast artillery assignment would be even more boring than the four boring years he was just completing. He couldn't tell Shaw that, of course. The colonel, Eisenhower said, "brought the interview to an end, and I thought, 'Well, that's that.' " He started "seriously" to consider a trip to South America. "I wrote for travel literature and costs."

But then Shaw called Eisenhower back yet again and told him that in going over his entire record he had learned that Eisenhower's most serious injury had been aggravated by a riding accident. "Mr. Eisenhower," Shaw said, "if you will not submit any requests for mounted service on your preference card, I will recommend to the Academic Board that you be commissioned." Eisenhower told Colonel Shaw "that my ambition was to go to the infantry," to which Shaw replied, "All right, I'll recommend you for a commission, but with the stipulation that you will ask for no other service in the Army."

It was not until thirty-one years later that Eisenhower learned from a classmate the full story of how he finally got his commission.

In April 1946 a classmate who had become head of the Department of Economics, Government and History at West Point, Colonel Herman Beukema, wrote to Eisenhower, then army chief of staff, "a medical board in 1915 had you slated for the axe until the chairman [Shaw] reversed a unanimous vote and carried the case to Washington. . . . I'll tell you the story some time if you are interested."

Ike immediately wrote back, "If you will send me now all the information you have in this matter I will appreciate it."

Beukema replied, "members of the board voted against commissioning you. He [Shaw] then called in the key people in the Tac [tical] Department, the Academic Board, etc., to comment on your cadet record. As a result he reversed the board and carried the split situation to Washington where it was agreed that you 'would be a good gamble.' "

Eisenhower did turn out to be a good gamble. But what is surprising is that he had made such a favorable impression on Shaw that the colonel three times went out of his way to help him. And he did so even after Ike had shown a markedly hostile attitude toward the colonel's own beloved coast artillery. Maybe it was just as Omar Bradley later said, "Ike liked people and it is awfully hard for them not to like him in return."

But there are many likable people in the world. Why was it that Colonel Shaw and later many others, including George C. Marshall and Franklin Roosevelt, felt compelled to help him? Mark Clark said it best. He said, "There was something about him that made you want to help him. I don't know *anybody* who didn't, certainly including me."

Graduating cadets were allowed to choose where they wished to serve, and Eisenhower picked the Philippines. Service there would be an adventure, a chance to play cowboys and Indians. The Indians in this case were the Moros in the southern islands. They were Muslims, who believed that killing Christians guaranteed them eternal life. They were still busy killing Christians, Americans, and Filipinos in 1935–39 when Ike finally got there.

Another factor in Eisenhower's asking for Philippines service was that a second lieutenant's pay of $141.67 a month would go farther there than it would state-side. The cost of uniforms also had to be considered. During the four years a cadet was at the Point, the treasurer of the academy took out of his pay each month the sum of $14 or $15 toward the purchase of his uniforms after he was commissioned.

"I went to the tailors and asked only for tropicals—khaki for field service and white for dress. I bought none of the other types of uniforms—olive drabs for garrison wear and the various types of blues for dress. These were expensive and I figured a number of years would pass before I needed them." Since his purchases were "far below average in cost," Eisenhower was given the balance on graduation, what he said was a "considerable sum of money—at least in my eyes."

Eisenhower and P.A. both worked on the yearbook, the 1915 *Howitzer*, and wrote many of the sketches that appeared under the graduates' pictures. P.A. wrote Eisenhower's, and it's a good, though sophomoric, evaluation of Eisenhower as he appeared in 1915. At the top of the page is a head-and-shoulders photograph of the cadet himself. To the right of the photograph are the words:

DWIGHT DAVID EISENHOWER
ABILENE, KANSAS
Senatorial Appointee, Kansas
"Ike"

Corporal, Sergeant, Color Sergeant, A.B. [Area Bird—one assigned to walk punishment tours in the area], B.A. [Busted Aristocrat—to a noncommissioned officer who has been reduced in rank to private], Sharpshooter; Football Squad (3, 2), 'A' in Football; Baseball Squad (4); Cheer Leader; Junior Meet (4, 3)

"Now fellers, it's just like this. I've been asked to say a few words this evening about this business. Now, me and Walter Camp, we think—"
—*Himself*

At the bottom of the page on the right is a photograph of "himself" in his dress gray uniform, his arms akimbo, and his stomach defiantly out, a rejection of the constant command when he was a plebe to "suck in your gut." The text reads:

This is Senor Dwight David Eisenhower, gentlemen, the terrible Swedish-Jew as big as life and twice as natural. He claims to have the best authority for the statement that he is the handsomest man in the Corps and is ready to back up his claim at any time. At any rate you'll have to give it to him that he's well-developed abdominally—and more graceful in pushing it around than Charles Calvert Benedict. In common with most fat men, he is an enthusiastic and sonorous devotee of the King of Indoor Sports, and roars homage to the shrine of Morpheus on every possible occasion.

However, the memory of man runneth back to the time when the little Dwight was but a slender lad of some "steen years," full of joy and energy and craving for life and movement and change. 'Twas then that the romantic appeal of West Point's glamour grabbed him by the scruff of the neck and dragged him to his doom. Three weeks of Beast gave him his fill of life and movement and as all the change was locked up at the Cadet Store out of reach, poor Dwight merely consents to exist until graduation shall set him free.

At one time he threatened to get interested in life and won his "A" by being the most promising back in Eastern football—but the Tufts game broke his knee and the promise. Now Ike must content himself with tea, tiddly-winks and talk, at all of which he excels. Said prodigy will now lead us in a long, loud yell for—Dare Devil Dwight, the Dauntless Don.

In later years the phrase "Swedish-Jew" puzzled a great many people, some of whom thought it somehow was an official West Point evaluation of him. And if so, what did it mean?

The Howitzer was not official; it was all written and edited by members of Ike's 1915 class and was filled with what undergraduates in whatever the institution consider humorous. During and after the war, several Americans sympathetic to the Nazis wrote letters to West Point asking to know whether or not Eisenhower was actually a Jew, as one of them said "in view of the role he played in the destruction of Gentile Germany." The matter also turned up in the 1952 presidential campaign when it was mentioned by the anti-Semitic Gerald L. K. Smith who wanted to demonstrate that Ike was a Jew, and what had been said in *The Howitzer* proved it.

P.A. referred to him as "Swedish" because he was blond and blue-eyed, and Swedes at the time were the subject of a good deal of folk humor, as were Norwegians. "My name is Yon Yohnson. I come from Visconsin; I work in the lumber mill there." At the time almost all Americans, including as we now know, such patricians as Eleanor and Franklin Roosevelt, indulged themselves in social anti-Semitism. Jews were sharp; they drove hard bargains; they outwitted Gentiles. Ike displayed all those qualities; therefore, P.A. was saying he was a Jew.

Like almost everyone else, Eisenhower treasured his class yearbook, and his son was not spared paying a good deal of attention to it. After all, if his father had his way, and he usually did, John would be in a *Howitzer* of his own some day. Brigadier General Frederic W. Boye said, "in the late twenties when he [Eisenhower] and Mamie were living in Washington, I stopped off to see them while passing through. After we had greeted each other, Ike turned to his son, John, who was then about five, and said gravely, 'John, this is a classmate of mine. Can you tell me his name?'

"John, who was seeing me for the first time, studied me closely for a few moments. 'Boye,' he said triumphantly. Ike laughed at my bewilderment, then said proudly, 'Fritz, this boy has gone over the yearbook with me so many times that he knows the names that go with the pictures as well as I do.' "

It was perhaps not so surprising that John should recognize Boye; as Eisenhower wrote on January 31, 1944, "One thing that has struck me very forcibly and through conversation I have learned that other old grads have been impressed in the same way, is the frequency with which one finds the older officer of today to be merely a more mature edition of the kid he knew as a Cadet. This is not always so and sometimes the exceptions are so glaring as to prove the rule. Nevertheless, General Bradley's present position, for example, could have been predicted accurately by anyone that knew him well thirty years ago. The same for George Patton, Everett Hughes, [Vernon] Prichard, and many, many officers of lesser rank. Frequently, I get a lot of fun checking up my present impressions of people with the impressions I had of them when they were very young and I am amazed to find how often these impressions are identical."

Eisenhower was one of the exceptions. One of his instructors gave the following impression of him as a cadet. "We saw in Eisenhower a not uncommon type, a man who would thoroughly enjoy his army life, giving both to duty and recreation their fair values, [but] we did not see in him a man who would throw himself into his job so completely that nothing else would matter."

There had been 265 plebes four years earlier; in front of the Battle Monument on June 12, 1915, there were 164 graduating cadets. Twenty-six of them became brigadier generals, twenty-three major generals, seven lieutenant generals, and two full generals. Bradley and Eisenhower got five stars each.

Ike graduated 61st in a class of 164, and his final standings of 28th in practical military engineering and 29th in drill regulations were considered very good. Only in one subject, math, was his final standing below the middle of the class.

As usual on graduation day, the West Point choir sang:

> The Corps! The Corps! The Corps!
> The Corps! Bareheaded, salute it,
>   With eyes up, thanking our God
> That we of the Corps are treading
>   Where they of the Corps have trod.
>
> Grip hands with us now, though we see thee not,
>   Grip hands with us, strengthen hearts.
> As the long line stiffens and straightens,
>   With the thrill that your pressure imparts.
>
> Grip hands though it be from the shadows
>   While we swear as you did of yore,
> Of living or dying to honor,
>   The Corps, and the Corps, and the Corps.

It was a stirring moment, as stirring as the time four years earlier when he and the other plebes took the oath of allegiance, but this time he was not exhausted; he was not a plebe; he was a graduate. He had taken the worst they had to offer, and he had prevailed.

The commencement address was by the secretary of war, Lindley M. Garrison. It was mercifully brief and—rare for graduation speakers—Garrison showed a real understanding of his audience.

> Whatever a man does under great stress, at a time of imminent crisis, can scarcely ever be the result of premeditation and deliberation at the instant of action; it is almost always the product of his instinct or second nature; that is to say, it is his answer in action of all that he has done and been up to that time. If he has been fortunate enough to receive in his plastic years those deep draughts of fine traditions, and they have permeated his system . . . he will come forth from whatever test he may be subjected to, worthily, and thus emphasize and justify the traditions which unconsciously guided his action.

More than fifty years later Eisenhower said, "West Point and all it means is so deep inside you that you are not so articulate about it. West Point did more for me than any other institution. . . . What they tried to teach the cadets was patriotism, honor, duty, and country. I say unashamedly it [the academy] tends to mold all who go there. And when anyone breaks the traits he has been taught, he always regrets it and is always ashamed. Maybe it is a characteristic of age to think this, but I think most graduates feel the same way."

Later that graduation day, Eisenhower and the other newly commissioned second lieutenants, many with girl friends and brides, went to New York City. The class dinner was held at the Astor Hotel, after which almost everybody went to see the successful Broadway musical *Chin-Chin*. Eisenhower's favorite number from the show, "It's a Long, Long Way to Tipperary," had been imported from England. The rest were American. It became one of his all-time favorites, along with such songs as "Abdul the Bulbul Amir," "Calamity Jane," "Clementine," "Beer Barrel Polka," "Oh, Bury Me Not on the Lone Prairie," and "I've Got Spurs That Jingle, Jangle, Jingle."

He was likely to sing such songs, usually off key, to audiences, willing and unwilling, for most of his life. Mark Clark said, "People tried to tell him that it was painful to listen to him, but I don't think he ever believed it. He was having too good a time."

The next morning Ike said a temporary good-bye to his fellow graduates, most of whom would serve with him at one time or another in the years ahead. In those days the army was small enough to be a kind of gentlemen's club for officers. They all knew each other; at least they all knew about each other. He checked out of the Astor and got on a train for the 1,400-mile trip to Abilene, where among the first to greet him was his mother, Ida. His journey, however, had just begun.

★ ★ ★

THE DOMINANT QUALITY

The three presidents I have written about had similar parents in that the mothers were strong and the fathers were not. Harry Truman's father, as his mother-in-law Madge Gates Wallace, often pointed out, was "a common dirt farmer," not a successful one, either. Lyndon Johnson's father was also an unsuccessful farmer, a failed "rancher," if you will. He served from time to time in the Texas legislature, never with much distinction, and he drank. Eisenhower's father refused to farm, but he failed at other things.

The three remarkable mothers had boundless ambition for their sons, and when their sons became famous, they were not surprised. When the war was won in Europe, Ida Eisenhower said, "Dwight always got what he went after."

Ida Elizabeth Stover was born on May 1, 1862, in Mount Sidney, Virginia, the second to last child of Simon Stover and his wife Elizabeth. At the time, Simon was forty-two and Elizabeth was forty, old to be parents of a baby. Ida had seven brothers, but they were all considerably older than she. "I suppose she was a little spoiled," her niece Nettie Stover Jackson said. "She was the only girl, and whatever she wanted, she got. At least that's what my dad said. Why, he just thought the world of Aunt Ida. So did all her sons."

The Shenandoah Valley around Mount Sidney is very beautiful; Woodrow Wilson, whose first inaugural Ida's third son would attend, was born in Staunton, a village nearby, in 1856. There are thousands of acres of rolling green farmland, orchards with peaches and cherry blossoms. The valley is usually peaceful, too, but not when Ida was an infant. The Yankees and the Confederates kept going north and south up that valley, and according to Mrs. Jackson, one thing her father remembered, "is the soldiers coming in wanting food and milk. There was a little spring house right there north of their house where they [Ida's family] kept the milk. They [the soldiers] just took what they wanted. Once, they tried to burn down the family's barn but failed." Mrs. Jackson went back to the family homestead in 1917, and "that barn that was built before the Civil War was still standing, but there were still parts where some soldier had fired into the barn. Aunt Ida always said that her mother told her she went out and yanked the gun out of his hand."

"My mother, back in Virginia, grieved herself to death when I was a little girl . . . because of the Civil War," Ida said. "I have hated war ever since." In 1946, when Ida was eighty-four years old and forgetful of many things, she still vividly remembered the stories her mother had told her of the Confederate soldiers coming to the house. Ida told her grandson John that what had happened had left her with strong pacifistic feelings for the rest of her life. According to John, she said, "Every time she saw a parade, when everyone else was out waving flags, she wanted to cry."

During the First World War, while her son Dwight was carrying out various frustrating army assignments in the States, anxious to get to Europe to confront the Hun firsthand, Ida, despite threats of arrest, distributed pacifist tracts on the streets of Abilene. Her son Milton said that everyone in town hated pacifists as well as everything German. "At one point," he said, "Mother was in real danger of being arrested because of her articulate pacifism and her German-sounding name. It was only the intervention of an influential friend that kept her out of jail."

During the Civil War, it might have been easier if the Stovers had been sympathetic with the Confederate cause, but they were not. Simon was drafted to fight for the Confederacy, but as often happened on both sides during that war, he hired a substitute for a thousand dollars. The substitute was killed, and Simon despite his age was again drafted. This time he decided to leave the Confederacy; he went North for a time, either to Ohio or Indiana, Nettie Jackson wasn't sure which. But before the war ended he returned to the Stover homestead, spending the days in a clump of woods back of the house, guarded by two fierce dogs.

So Ida's mother was left alone with her children, and there was always the frightening possibility that her absent husband might be arrested and charged with treason.

Ida was always upset by the way Virginians treated their slaves. Many years later in Abilene she said, "How they did abuse those Negroes. . . . It hurt me so that, little as I was, I wanted to do something about it! And I was going to if I ever had the chance. . . . It made my blood boil, the way they were treated.

"I wanted a home and a family, of course, but it took so long to achieve that, old age has overtaken me and I'm afraid I won't ever be able to do much about my second ambition. I always wanted to help to bring about racial equality. And I did do what little I could."

Ida's mother died when she was four and a half years old, and she and her brothers were shipped off to live with relatives. Ida went to the home of her maternal grandparents, who lived in another part of Augusta County. "Their farm was ten miles from any town, and the country school was backward." It was not usual in those days for fathers to care for their children. "It was just like being pulled up by the roots," Ida said.

The Links were in their sixties, and their daughter, Mary Ann Link, who had never married, was in her forties. She took care of her parents and was the housekeeper. She was a good cook, and she taught her niece to be a good cook, too. Ida was cooking and baking by the time she was seven, and she was always careful not to burn anything. "If I burned anything or took it out underdone, I was punished," she said. "I remember best the bare upstairs room where a quilt was always in progress," Ida said. "In winter my fingers got so cold I often botched the work and had to pull it out and do it over again—and not cry about it either."

"About the only good time we had was when I was permitted to go horseback riding with my brothers. I adored my brothers and imitated them. . . . I was a tomboy, but it didn't hurt me any. I was tough and wiry and could gallop, bareback, as heedlessly as any of my brothers over those wooded hills.

"We would make for the woods, get off our horses and sit around making plans. As soon as I was twenty-one and got my inheritance money [a small amount was left each of the children by their parents]—we were going to go off someplace together and I was going to college!"

Ida was a self-reliant child. She learned very early on not to let her feelings show. "Grin and bear it," she said, and did. But to grin and bear it had serious physical repercussions not only for her but for her son Dwight, who also most of the time kept his feelings to himself and suffered for it. During one crisis in France during the Second World War, one of the supreme commander's associates wrote, "General Ike had his standard assortment of minor headaches." But it was much more than headaches. Throughout his life the man known for his grin suffered from many ailments that doctors believed were caused by severe inner tensions—among them gastritis, shingles, high blood pressure, and colds. He seemed always to have colds. Kay Summersby, Eisenhower's driver and secretary when he was supreme commander, said, "he always had that grin at the ready," but underneath it all he was a man who "worried, worried, worried."

Ida often had painful headaches, and her sons would place cold cloths on her forehead or rub it to ease the pain. She later bought an ebony piano, and playing the piano relaxed her. But sometimes even that wasn't enough. Her grandson John remembered that once the mild-mannered, ever-agreeable Ida kicked a cat from a corner of the Eisenhower house all the way across South East Fourth

Street. Her son Dwight hated cats but so far as is known never kicked one. He did, however, according to his grandson David, keep a shotgun by the television set at his retirement farm at Gettysburg and gave orders "to shoot cats on sight."

She was fond of maxims and verses from the Bible. Her youngest son, Milton, refers to her as "a living Biblical concordance." As a girl in Sunday school she memorized 1,325 verses of the Bible, and until near the end of her life, she never forgot them. "She'd apply some passage in the Bible as nonchalantly as any common, everyday occurrence," Nettie said. Usually paraphrasing it. "He that conquereth his own soul is greater than he who taketh a city." She never hesitated to use them, either, along with endless folk sayings. "Sink or swim," she would say. Or "The Lord deals the cards. You play them." Or, "Perhaps you will be rewarded. If so, the reward will come by reason of your own efforts, not anybody else's."

Eisenhower didn't memorize verses of the Bible in Sunday school, but he had read the entire Bible twice when he left for West Point, the first time when he was twelve years old, and he could invariably summon up an appropriate Biblical quote. During the war one of his aides said that he could "quote Scripture by the yard," often to illustrate points made at staff meetings. When he was president of Columbia he gave a talk at the Riverside Church on Laymen's Sunday, October 16, 1949, and quoted from Romans 12:18, in which the simple virtues are emphasized, "If it be possible, as much as lieth in you, live peaceably with all men."

On another occasion, at a press conference, he told reporters to look up Song of Solomon 2:11–12, which reads: "For, lo, the winter is past, the rain is over and gone. The flowers appear on the earth; the time of singing has come. . . ."

Eisenhower also often used a well-worn maxim to make a point, "Never be more scared of the enemy than the enemy is scared of you." "A soldier's pack is not so heavy a burden as a prisoner's chains." "Weakness cannot compete with anything. Only strength can cooperate." "The plan may not be worth a damn, but planning is everything."

Yes, there was a great deal of Ida in her son Dwight.

When Ida's father died in 1883, her German grandfather Link became her legal guardian. He thought it was wrong for girls to know much, and Ida kept her ambition for a higher education to herself. But when she was eighteen, she went to Staunton to attend school. She earned her way by baking pies and cooking chickens in other people's kitchens and graduated from high school when she was twenty. The following school year, 1882–83, she taught at Limestone, near Mount Sidney, in a one-room schoolhouse.

On Ida's twenty-first birthday she received her small inheritance and, with her Aunt Mary Ann, went to Lecompton, Kansas. Several of Ida's brothers were already there. They had gone several years earlier to join a fundamentalist Dunkard colony.

That was the year when everything turned out happily. Ida bought an ebony piano, a Hallett and Cumston, manufactured in Boston in 1883, and whenever troubled or upset, she was always able, she said, to "play herself rested." The piano can still be seen in the Eisenhower home in Abilene. She also found to her delight that there was an institution of higher learning in Lecompton, Lane University, that offered courses in music. She enrolled immediately.

"But Ida loved Virginia," Nettie said, "and when the boys were growing up drove all the way back from Abilene one or two times. There were no paved roads, but she had a Dodge touring car, and she drove all the way back to where she'd been born and grew up. And she drove alone, back when a woman didn't travel alone. That took some doing. She was an unusual woman."

Aksel Nielsen, the Denver businessman who was perhaps Eisenhower's closest civilian friend from 1926 until his death, said, "He was always talking about his mother and how much she had done for him and the other brothers. He thought she was a great woman." In one of his frequent notes to himself in March 1942, Eisenhower wrote, "I think my mother is the finest person I've ever known."

He explained his feelings about his mother in terms that intellectuals deplored, that were dismissed as hopelessly corny. The thing that was often forgotten was that he meant them. During and after the war he often wrote for the *Reader's Digest*, and those articles sounded the way he talked all his life. He said in *At Ease* that his mother was "a worker, an administrator, a teacher and guide, a truly wonderful woman."

Eisenhower often mentioned Ida in personal letters, particularly those to his friends in Abilene and to his brothers. Shortly after the triumphant Allied landings in North Africa in November 1942, he wrote to his brother Edgar from his dank headquarters under the fortress of Gibraltar, "I would give a good deal if I could get out of this cave, in which my present office is located, and go see her for an hour or so."

On September 8, 1943, he answered a letter he received that day from his old friend and high school classmate, Frances Curry. She had written him a three-page letter reporting, among other things, that she had recently visited Ida and that his mother would like to fly around the world with her famous son.

It had been a busy day in Eisenhower's advanced command post near Carthage, and he had quite a few things on his mind, among them whether or not the Italian government would surrender that day and the equally urgent invasion of Italy at Salerno scheduled for the next morning. Yet he answered Miss Curry's letter that evening. He wrote, "It is quite true that mother would like to take a long plane ride—sort of a junketing trip. Nothing would give me more pleasure than to start on such a journey with her. Maybe I could get you to go along and keep the diary."

It would not have been Ida's first plane ride. Her son Arthur recalled a trip she made to Washington, "long before Dwight became a general." An army plane with an open cockpit was placed at their disposal. Ida climbed into it gaily, had a parachute strapped to her, and flew over the city of Washington. She said she found flying "a lot more sensible than crawling on the ground." But an air trip around the world would be something else again. In September 1943 she was eighty-one years old, but then she had driven a car until she was seventy-five.

On September 30 of that year, Eisenhower wrote Ida from his advance command post in Algiers, "I am looking forward to dashing out to see you the first time I get to the United States, even if only for a few days."

On May 10, 1945, he wrote to his brother Milton, "Please keep me informed . . . of mother's condition. It would be a source of never-ending regret to me to miss seeing her once again due to lack of information as to her condition." Despite the fact her memory was failing, Ida was fine. "I don't know what they are going to do with me," she told a neighbor. "They [the doctors] can't find anything wrong with me. It just looks like I am going to live forever!"

When Eisenhower returned to the States in June of 1945, he said, "The sight of my mother was one of the rewards of peace. Of course, she had paid the price of a lifetime of caring and working. As I first knew her, she was a tall woman, perhaps five feet six inches. She weighed about 135 pounds, with blue eyes and brown hair, untouched by gray. Now her hair was gray and, somehow, she was a little smaller."

On the last day of her life, an Indian summer day in September 1946, she took two rides in the familiar and loved countryside around Abilene, "coming home full of vivid memories of what she had seen," said Eisenhower.

Toward midnight, she asked her companion for a hot-water bottle. When the companion, Mrs. Robinson, gave her one, she said, "Please get right back to bed. You might catch cold." A few minutes later Mrs. Robinson "realized that she had died, quietly, with almost a smile on her face."

Lane University at Lecompton, Kansas, was founded in 1865. When Ida enrolled in September 1884 the eighteen-year-old institution, most of which was built on the foundation of what was once to have been the state capitol of Kansas, had ten faculty members. They offered classical, scientific, normal (teachers' training), commercial, shorthand, music and art courses. Bachelor of arts and master of arts degrees were awarded.

The university had been named after Jim Lane, who provided the founding gift of $2,000. Lane, a sometime abolitionist of dubious integrity, had served briefly as the first U.S. senator from Kansas.

There were about 200 students at the university when Ida enrolled there. The annual tuition was $30, and total expenses for a year were about $120, including books, room, and board.

David Jacob Eisenhower also enrolled at Lane, in 1884, against his father's wishes. Jacob Eisenhower, a successful farmer in Abilene, Kansas, wanted his son to be a farmer, too, but David, the rebel of the family, wanted to be an engineer, and he studied mechanics at Lane as a first step. He also studied rhetoric and Greek. He continued reading Greek, particularly a Greek Bible, until the end of his life. According to Dwight, "other translations made him nervous."

Ida was a year and three months older than David. She was one of the few women on the campus. "Because I was a girl," Ida said, "I was told I must listen, not talk, and not expect to go to school much." Most of her female peers were married at sixteen or seventeen.

David was on the debate team, and in 1885, his and Ida's last year at Lane, he upheld the negative of the topic, "Resolved, That Man Is Governed More by Circumstances than by Will." That same June Ida was in a "Concert for

Benefit of Lane University Library." And three days before David's debate she became valedictorian of her class.

Ida was popular with the male students as indeed all the outnumbered girls were. Going in and out of classes in her white shirtwaist and long dark skirt, she always appeared to be smiling.

She had large, strong hands, very much like those of her third son, Dwight. She was not conventionally pretty. She had broken her nose in a fall from a horse when she was a girl, and the nose was crooked; it gave her face a lopsided appearance. Her mouth was large and full, also like Dwight. Both of them smiled a good deal. "It doesn't take any more muscles to make you smile than it does to make you pout," she would say.

"Ike has the most engaging grin of anybody I've ever met," Mamie said, "though when he turns it off his face is as bleak as the plains of Kansas." His mouth was often described as lopsided, again like his mother's. Earl Endacott, the first director of the Eisenhower Library in Abilene and a lifetime friend of the family, said, "You take any picture of Ike, put a piece over half of it and then do the same on the other side. You will see two entirely different pictures. Physically, that is. One is smiling, the other is a serious college professor."

In 1944 an interviewer wrote of Ida, "Her famous son is very much like his mother; his features are like hers; his eyes are the same blue and he has the same friendly, easy smile, the same sociable manner, the same forthright honesty. And with it all the same dominant quality, sensed immediately."

Kenneth S. Davis, in his book *Soldier of Democracy*, said Eisenhower was "gentle . . . carefully regardful of other people. Somehow one did not expect such gentle kindliness from a man so deep of chest and voice, so tough-minded."

Nobody ever called David Eisenhower's manner dominant—except perhaps when he was punishing his sons, and he seldom smiled. He was notably taciturn, too, but then all her life Ida managed to talk enough for the two of them. Besides, as she often said in describing David, "Still water runs deep." David's voice was mellow, soft and guttural and Ida was attracted to him, she said, because he was "so much quieter than most, and fastidious in dress and in what he did and said. . . . Somehow books didn't seem so important after I met David at the University."

David must soon have decided—he did not decide things easily—that he would marry Ida. So he started calling on her at the house of her Uncle Will, who had come to Lecompton a few years before. Will's first wife had died; his second wife, Annie, was not a woman concerned with the feelings of others, especially a young man as sensitive and vulnerable as David. One night when David and Ida were sitting in the front parlor of the Stovers' house, Annie came in and said, "It is time all decent people was home in bed." David's swarthy face reddened as it was to do many times later in his life. No one was going to tell him when to leave a house, then or ever. David left the house, and Nettie Stover Jackson said he returned only once again, for his marriage, a ceremony Will Stover did not perform.

David and Ida were married at Will Stover's house on September 23, 1885, David's twenty-second birthday. According to the *Lecompton Monitor* and the *Hope Herald*, the ceremony took place "at the home of her uncle . . . the minister was the Rev. E. B. Slade. About 20 friends and relatives were present to witness the ceremony."

David and Ida did not return to Lane after the wedding.

Under the wedding announcement in the two newspapers was the following poem:

Double Bliss

Was just two years ago tonight
I saw a lady dressed in white
    And she was fair to see
Her curls hung round her lovely neck
Her soul looked out through . . .

The version I saw was incomplete; the reader will have to supply the last word or words. The ending is no doubt lost to posterity.

David, who was seldom carried away by anything, was so carried away by Ida, he wrote the poem and submitted it to the paper to commemorate the event. As far as I can determine, this was his first and last poem.

The marriage lasted fifty-seven years, until David's death in 1942. A year after he died, Ida said, "I never regretted marrying David."

★ ★ ★

A NICE LITTLE TOWN

David's father, Jacob, had put aside for each of his children the sum of $2,000, which they were to receive, along with 160 acres of land, when they were married. David, who hated the mere idea of farming, mortgaged the land and, using that money together with the $2,000 he had received as a wedding present, purchased a general store in the small village of Hope, Kansas, which was only twenty-eight miles south of Abilene.

It is not surprising that the young Eisenhowers were optimistic; they were going to start a business in a town called Hope, and David's partner was Milton Good, the son of Peter Good. David had worked on the farm of Milton's father during the summer of 1884; the farm was only eight miles from Jacob Eisenhower's homestead.

Like David's family, Milton D. Good was a member of a religious sect known as the River Brethren, an offshoot of the Mennonites. Milton had had several years of experience in "merchandising," clerking in a men's clothing store in Abilene. People said he was a born salesman; the *Hope Dispatch* was to describe him as "one of the best merchants that ever measured off a piece of bacon or weighed a yard of calico."

Some people found Milton a little too cheerful and hail-fellow, a teller of too many jokes. David, however, seemed to have no doubts at all about his partner. Milton had the experience, and David put up the cash for the firm known as Good and Eisenhower.

There were surely times later when Ida's perennial smile was forced, but not in September of 1885. She had married a seemingly ideal husband. He came from a substantial family. He was intelligent and learned. Who else did she know who read Greek for pleasure? And besides, all of Kansas was aflame with optimism that year. The population was increasing at an unbelievable rate; it had more than tripled in the fifteen years between 1865 and 1880 and continued to grow rapidly into the 1880s. Then, too, due to a wet cycle, crops had never been more bountiful, resulting in easy credit for farmers.

The building in which the new business was located had been built by David's father and was known as the Eisenhower building. It was divided by a partition. Abraham, David's brother, had his veterinary offices there, and on the second floor were two tiny apartments for the newlywed Goods and Eisenhowers. Their rooms were small, separated only by curtains and were hot and dusty from the unpaved streets. In the sub-zero winter, it was impossible to keep them warm, especially during the worst blizzard in Kansas history, in the winter of 1886.

In the benign autumn of 1885, Ida thought of none of those things. "Hope," she said, is "such a nice little town," and she scarcely minded that there was no water in the upstairs apartment and that the only staircase was outdoors. Of this humble first home Ida said to her niece Nettie Jackson, "I looked forward to fixing it up."

"She was smart, too," said Nettie. "It didn't take her long to learn how to handle David. I remember she told me that when they moved into that place in Hope she was working on the window shade and couldn't fix it, and she said, 'David, you'll *have* to help me get this shade up'; he said, 'I don't *have* to do anything.'

"So Ida told me, 'Thinks I, the next time I'll try a different tack,' and she did . . . when she was putting up the curtains. She said, 'David, I wonder if you *could* do this. I just *can't* seem to get it done.' Why, he was lickety-split at her side helping her. See the wisdom?"

The Goods and the Eisenhowers were young, happy, and prospering. At the time, most farmers everywhere in the United States bought their goods—food, clothes, feed for their livestock—at general stores, everywhere on credit. Farmers had money only at harvest time and thus paid up after their crops were sold. In rural America a man's word was his bond, and a handshake sealed all deals. Harry Truman, growing up in nearby Independence, Missouri, a few years earlier said, "You never had to sign a piece of paper when you made a bargain . . . you just lived up to what you'd agreed on. . . . That's what your word meant."

There were people in Hope who, while they liked the young Eisenhowers and Goods, found them too worldly. And some of the goods they sold were also too worldly; laces, for instance, velvet trimmings for women's dresses, cigars.

According to the Good-Eisenhower store's advertisements, the prices were so low that "they make your pocketbook laugh," and for almost two years a great many happy customers bought a great many things, worldly or not.

But in the harsh winter of 1886–87 tens of thousands of Kansas range cattle died of frost and starvation. And in the summer of 1887 there was not only an infestation of grasshoppers, the "wet cycle" ended.

Chris Musser, who was married to David's sister Amanda, kept a close eye on what went on in the store. After all, before there *was* a store David had asked Chris "to find out if I could get some money from Pennsylvania from your father to go into the mercantile and grocery business." Chris did write to his father, but the elder Musser had no money to lend; so Chris wrote to his uncle, Michael B. Musser, who lived in Mount Joy, Pennsylvania. He obligingly sent Chris a draft for $2,000, and after Ida and David had signed a mortgage on their land, this money was turned over to them, and they put it into the store.

By the fall of 1887, Musser remembered, "You could sell very well, but to collect was difficult." Corn was selling for nineteen cents a bushel, oats for nine cents a bushel, eggs were six cents a dozen. Four banks in Abilene closed, including the First National, in which Jacob owned stock.

"Everybody was broke," said Musser.

Milton Good and his wife left for Emporia, leaving behind a large number of unpaid bills, but he assured David and Ida, his other creditors and the Hope newspapers that he had "a little scheme" which promised to make him "a veritable Vanderbilt in wealth."

Things did not quite work out that way. Emporia was as depressed as Hope, and in a few months the *Hope Herald* ran a notice that the firm of Good and Eisenhower had been dissolved. Milton Good and his wife never returned to Hope.

For a while, David's brother, Abraham the veterinarian, drove the horse-drawn delivery truck and worked behind the counter with David; it became the Eisenhower Brothers' Store, but the drought continued, as did the losses.

If David had had enough capital to carry him another year, Chris Musser said, "he would probably have got through." He did not get through, however, and the whole experience was for him a humiliating failure; he failed several times again, but in those future failures there seemed to be no surprises for him. Withdrawn and angry, he seemed to expect what happened, even to invite it.

David's first forwarding address was Denison, Texas, which was prospering as Kansas had been in 1885. Before leaving Hope, David turned over the whole matter of the store's unpaid debts to a lawyer named Mahan. From David's meager assets, Mahan paid off many of the bills; he took what was left as his fee.

David also left behind a pregnant wife and a baby son, Arthur Eisenhower, who was born on November 11, 1886. Ida must have thought often of her mother, who had also been abandoned and left with young children when her father took off to avoid going to war. It had been difficult for her mother and it was just as difficult for her. Yet they both endured.

After Kenneth Davis's *Soldier of Democracy: A Biography of Dwight Eisenhower* was published in 1945, Eisenhower wrote an analysis of the book, sentence by sentence, pointing out its every error, its every wrong judgment. But he had no comment at all on what Davis said about his father's failure in Hope. Davis wrote, "It was his [David's] first, perhaps his greatest test, and he did not face it well. Actually, he did not face it at all. In self-violation, in violation of the frontier tradition of courage and self-reliance which he himself accepted, he sought only to escape from the scene of his humiliation. . . . The crisis at Hope caught him unprepared; his defenses were down. Thereafter he was almost always wholly defensive in his basic attitudes but his defenses were high and strong." Of Ida, Davis said, "She . . . fought back valiantly, and as instinctively as David had run away she had been strengthened rather than weakened by the experience."

Dwight's brother Earl said, "Maybe the tragedy, as far as Mother's part is concerned, is that she met Dad before she finished school, got married and started raising a family." Nettie Stover Jackson said, "That Hope deal humbled David. He just sort of gave up after that. He never seemed to try again. It was a sad thing to see. But Ida never gave up. She tried to figure out what had happened and why. She told me, 'I just studied everything I could study to find out if there was a way to get out of it.' "

Her son Dwight said, "My mother, for all her gentleness, was outraged by the injustice of my father's early business venture, particularly at the other partner's disappearance. She began to study law at home. For some years she read legal books, hoping that some day, somewhere they would meet up with the absconder—fully prepared to take legal action against him. Throughout the years that her sons continued to live under the same roof, this warm, pleasant, mild-mannered woman never ceased to warn them against thieves, embezzlers, chiselers, and all kinds of crooks."

David's failure made his sons eager to succeed, and while some were more successful than others, they were all demonstrably competitive, Dwight in particular. He not only succeeded; he spent as much time as possible with other successful men. He wanted to learn how they had done what his father had failed to do.

* * *

THE "RENEGADE TEXAN"

David was not by nature a happy man; even those who had known him in college, before the failure at Hope, remembered him as being gloomy, serious, much too serious, many thought. But the more than two years he spent in Denison were surely the most unhappy of his life.

Denison, in northeastern Texas near the Oklahoma border, was one of those cheerless towns that late in the nineteenth century were built around railroad tracks. It had been founded in 1872 when the tracks of the Missouri, Kansas & Texas (Katy) made it a center for cattle shipments north and east. The town itself was depressing enough for a man who had left everyone he knew back in Kansas and who was unable, then or later, to make new friends. But David's job must have made Denison even more unendurable. His job is seldom made clear in the biographies, but the 1890–91 edition of the city directory of Denison lists him as "an engine wiper at the Katy roundhouse." The job was one of the lowest forms of unskilled labor on the railroad. As a wiper, David had to scour the locomotives of grease and soot. The pay was $1.75 a day for a twelve-hour day, six days a week; his take-home pay was $10.50 a week.

It was by no means a happy period for Ida either. She was alone in the disheartening apartment above the failed store in Hope, and she was expecting. Edgar Newton Eisenhower was born on January 19, 1889. Ida had happened on the poetry of Edgar Allen Poe in college, and he quickly became her favorite poet:

> The happiest day—the happiest hour
> My seared and blighted heart hath known,
> The highest hope of pride and power,
> I feel hath flown.

Poe had spent a brief, unhappy time at West Point and was a drunkard as well as a poet and short-story writer. When her sons reminded Ida, as they took pleasure in doing, that Poe was a souse, she said, "I don't care. I still like his poems."

Edgar, in explaining who he was named after, added, "And Newton was the fellow who lay under the apple tree and had an apple fall down on him, and said, 'Well, that must be gravity.' So she named me after him. So I am a mixture. I am a poet and I am a scientist!"

Actually it was no surprise to Ida that her son Edgar became a lawyer. Hadn't she been reading all those law books during her pregnancy? "Mother always contended that my becoming a lawyer was prenatal influence. . . . 'I sort of concentrated on having an honest lawyer in the family,' she said."

David did not become reconciled to his son's being a lawyer until the end of his life. First, because of his own experience. And then, according to Edgar, "When he was an engineer at Belle Springs [an Abilene creamery], part of his job was to buy the oil that was used in the machines . . . [and] a young fellow came through Abilene selling oil. . . . Dad asked him what he had done before he got into the oil business, and he said, 'I was going to the University of Kansas and I was taking up law, but I made up my mind that I couldn't be a successful lawyer and be honest, so I gave it up and took up selling.' " Edgar said, "it made an impression on Dad in view of the fact that he had the other experience in his own business. It wasn't until many years afterwards that Dad finally confessed to me that he was wrong, that a lawyer could be successful and still be honest."

A month after Edgar was born, Ida and her two sons started for Denison, leaving behind the ebony piano she loved so much. Nettie Jackson said, "Aunt

Ida told me later that she'd never been so scared. Edgar was just a tiny baby. I'm sure she was scared. I'd have been scared to death. It was very unusual for women to travel alone those days, and sometimes in some places they wouldn't allow it. I just don't know how she did it."

David had found a trackside house in Denison, tiny and covered with soot from passing trains. To make matters worse, the house had a roomer, James Redmon, an engineer for Katy. Mrs. Jackson said, "I saw that house myself in 1948 or 1949. I'd heard about it and how close it was to the tracks, but it was closer, much closer, than I'd imagined. I'd have been scared for the boys, and I'll bet she was, too."

Denison itself was in many ways like Abilene in its wild period—cowboys, saloons, whores, and frequent murders. It was said that one man had been killed for every twenty-five feet of the business district. Still, there was an opera house in which the road shows of the day played briefly. The Eisenhowers, however, had no money for theater. There were nine hotels, each with a restaurant, but the Eisenhowers had no money to dine in a restaurant.

A peddler of hot tamales passed the house every day, six for a nickel. But a nickel was a nickel, and so to save money Ida learned how to make tamales herself. Later, back in Abilene, Eisenhower and his brothers peddled tamales—made from Ida's recipe—around town for extra cash.

When Ida told David that she was going to have another baby, he was not pleased; indeed, the news seemed to deepen his depression. It was difficult enough to take care of four on his salary; now there would be a fifth mouth to feed. To add to his sadness during that year, 1890, David's mother died back in Kansas, and he could not afford to return for her funeral.

That year he seemed to withdraw even farther from the real world. He took up pyramidology, drawing a huge plan of the Great Pyramid at Giza and the two adjacent pyramids. According to one biographer, the plan was almost sixteen feet square. Mrs. Jackson said, "I wondered how they had room for it. That house was so small—and with another baby on the way." David studied the chart avidly. He was convinced that those three pyramids, the Great Pyramid in particular, had the answers to all things past, present, and future.

Both David and Ida had wanted their third child to be a girl, but the birth of the healthy, blue-eyed baby boy on October 14, 1890, was a joyous event for Ida, and, as always, she showed it.

Many years later Eisenhower said of his birth, "My mother always said I was born in a violent thunderstorm and always 'feared' I'd lead a life of violence."

The roomer, James Redmon, was "the man who went for the doctor." Many years later he told the *Denison Press*, "I remember it quite well, the night I went for the doctor. . . . I was living in the house of the Eisenhower family. . . . I was in from the night run on the night that baby Dwight D. Eisenhower was born. Several women had gathered to do what they could, as they did in those days. I recall the room. It was downstairs where the mother was confined and the child was born. I was the only available man in the place with the exception of the husband, and so I hustled out of my apartment and went for the physician. . . . It was a cold night in October, the fourteenth, when the birth took place. He was the only baby in the locality for a while, and many of the neighbors came in and nursed the little fellow and kept 'company' for Mrs. Eisenhower."

Miss Jennie Jackson remembered being one of the neighbor women. She said she had bounced on her knee the baby the other Eisenhower brothers, who were all born in Kansas, called "the renegade Texan."

The name of the third son born to David and Ida Eisenhower is recorded in the family Bible in Ida's handwriting as D. Dwight Eisenhower. It does not say David Dwight Eisenhower, and when the name was early on changed to Dwight D., it was still only an initial. He was never called David; he was Dwight. And there is no doubt that after he was able to make his wishes known, and that was early in life, the last thing he would have wanted was to be named after his father.

The spring after Dwight was born, Jacob Eisenhower went to Denison and made his son David what he hoped would be a final and persuasive offer to get him to return to Abilene. Jacob had traded the Eisenhower building in Hope for three houses in Abilene, and he offered David and his family one of them. But David also had to have a job if he was to return, and Jacob persuaded his son-in-law, Chris Musser, to offer him one. The previous December, Musser had become foreman of the Belle Springs Creamery's new plant in Abilene.

Musser said of Jacob's plea to him after the latter's return from a short stay with David and his family in Denison, "He gave a very sad report of their condition. He asked me to give David a job. . . . I chose all my help, but there were no openings at that time. . . . One of the stockholder's sons was working at the plant, and we had to wait until he got another job before we had one for David."

On March 1, 1892, Jacob sent for his son. This time, no doubt gently prodded by Ida, who was pregnant again, David agreed to return. His total assets were $24, not enough to pay the family's fare from Denison to Abilene. Musser provided the necessary amount. He was a true Christian, a good member of the River Brethren, but what he did was surely for the sake of his wife, Amanda, and his father-in-law, Jacob.

On March 11 David signed a contract with the creamery, which was owned and operated by the River Brethren. He would work as a "refrigerating engineer," meaning he would see to it that the machinery kept running, hardly what he had in mind when he went to college dreaming of becoming a real engineer. He would receive a salary of $340 a year, $25 a month for six months, $30 a month for four months and $35 for two months.

So on his return, David was making less money in Abilene than he had made in Denison, and to complete the humiliation, the contract stated that he wouldn't get all the money when he had earned it. The contract stipulated, "At the end of each month 12% of the salary is retained until the end of the year when the full amount is paid." Musser wanted to make sure that David, scarcely a stable man in his eyes, stayed in one place and on one job for twelve months. David signed the contract with his usual Spencerian signature.

The time spent in Denison was seldom mentioned by the Eisenhowers during the somewhat better times in Abilene. There is only one mention of Denison in *At Ease*: "His [David's] first job was in Denison, Texas, where I was born." Clearly Eisenhower did not beguile his friends with stories about Denison.

On occasion, such as on the day he arrived at West Point, Eisenhower was even likely to forget the name of the town; on that day he wrote that his birthplace had been Tyler, Texas, 150 miles southeast of Denison. And when he was leaving the army forty-seven years later, in 1952, he again listed his birthplace as Tyler. Until Eisenhower became a candidate for the presidency, the whole idea of Texas and the fact that he was born there was a subject he preferred not to mention; and during the many times Eisenhower was stationed at army posts in Texas, he never once returned to Denison.

He finally returned to his birthplace in 1946, when he was fifty-five years old. On December 4, 1945, he had answered a letter from the president of the Dallas chamber of commerce asking him to visit Texas. He wrote that he had promised Speaker of the House Sam Rayburn "that at some time, convenient to us both" he would return to Denison, which was in Rayburn's congressional district.

Eisenhower became chief of staff of the army in November of 1945. He told Marshall that as chief of staff he wanted to accomplish two things: get universal military training in the United States and unify the armed forces. He also wanted to educate people on the need for international cooperation. Moreover, at a time when many Americans were talking about "cutting the army down to size," meaning the way it had been in the 1930s, Eisenhower had to worry about and work for good-sized appropriations, not only for the army but for the armed forces in general. Thus the friendship and support of Sam Rayburn was not only important; it was essential, and Eisenhower strove to accommodate him even when it involved a return to the Texas town where he was born.

So on April 20, 1946, Eisenhower and Mr. Sam went to Denison. They arrived by air at 11:30 A.M. They went to the birthplace at Lamar Avenue and Day Street and had strawberries and cream, scrambled eggs, homemade biscuits and coffee with Jennie Jackson. While Miss Jackson reminisced about bouncing the baby Eisenhower on her knee, photographers took an enormous number of pictures. Eisenhower grinned gamely through it all and continued grinning during a parade in an open car down Denison's Main Street and through a barbecue at the Denison football stadium.

Rayburn made a speech at the stadium: "Denison, I thank you for giving the nation General Eisenhower." Eisenhower, still grinning, also spoke: "I only wish that every man who served under me could have the same homecoming, because every one of them deserves it." In addition to the barbecued beef served at the stadium, Eisenhower and Rayburn ate baked beans, potato chips, pickles, and onions. Eisenhower drank water from a lister bag and then took a half hour's nap at the Denison Hotel. He declined with thanks an invitation from the hotel manager to stay overnight.

He returned to the birthplace at 3:00 and grinned while still more pictures were taken, most of them of him with Miss Jennie and Mr. Sam. As the flashbulbs popped, Eisenhower whispered to Rayburn, "I've had two meals in two hours, and I'm tired." Rayburn's reply is not known, but he knew that even in 1946 a great number of Democrats wanted to get rid of Harry Truman and have Eisenhower as the party's presidential candidate in 1948. Later, when he was asked what he thought about Ike as a Democratic presidential candidate, Rayburn said that the general had no political experience, no political interest, and no political philosophy. "Good man," he said, "but wrong business."

Eisenhower went directly from the birthplace to the airport where he took a plane south for Texas A & M. He spent the night there and the next morning received an honorary Doctor of Law degree. He also spoke at a sunrise service for the many men of the university who had been killed in the Second World War.

Except in years when he was running for the presidency, Eisenhower was emphatically *not* a Texan. He wrote his friend Charlie Case in July of 1942:

> A number of American newspaper clippings have come to my notice—all list me as a Texan. This comes about because of the locality of my birth, which was in that state. This fact is shown on the official records which is, of course, all that the newspaper men ever look at. I cannot even guess at the number of reporters I have told emphatically that I lived one year of my life in Texas and twenty in Kansas, together with the fact that Kansas is the home of my family. This makes no impression. In any event, I want you to remember that I am proud of my own home town—and that I've never claimed any place in the world as my home except Abilene.

Two years later the supreme commander of the Allied Expeditionary Forces in Europe was playing bridge in England with the genial George Allen, who wrote *Presidents Who Have Known Me*. Allen, who was to be influential in seeing to it that Eisenhower became a presidential candidate, asked him what state he had been born in. According to Harry Butcher, in July 1944 the supreme commander's naval aide, "Ike carefully explained that he was born in Denison, because his father had to move from Abilene to Denison to find employment in railroad work and subsequently had moved to Tyler, Texas, and then had returned to Abilene, Kansas, when Ike was two years of age. 'A chicken may hatch her eggs in the oven, but they're still not biscuits,' Ike said, and George roared."

★ ★ ★

AN ANGRY MAN

When David returned to Abilene, he was twenty-seven years old and a failure not once but twice, first in Hope, then in Denison. And everybody in town knew that he alone among Jacob's children had lost not only the $2,000 his father had given him but the 160 acres of land. And who had foreclosed the mortgage? Chris Musser, his brother-in-law, also twenty-seven and known around town as a comer, a young man with a good head on his shoulders, by Abilene standards a success.

Musser had even sent the money for the train fare to Abilene and he would be David's boss. Could any humiliation be more complete? David, understandably, retired deeper into himself and the mysteries of the Great Pyramid.

His son Arthur said, "he tried to prove prophecies for the future as well as prophecies in the Bible that had been fulfilled. By extending the lines of the pyramids, the passageways, the mechanical measurements, and all that sort of thing, he proved to his own satisfaction that the Bible was right in its prophecies. I want to point out, though, that when you reach a conclusion, you can always find evidence to prove your point, and I think that's what Dad did. He was very much satisfied with his chart."

Another of David's sons, Earl, said, "It was definitely the drawing of a draftsman. I think Dad loved draftsmanship." Edgar Eisenhower said, "Father was really a free thinker. . . . He read all the religious literature available. All his life he was searching for an answer. . . . He was looking for something. He wasn't satisfied with the formulas that were handed to him. . . . Not till the day of his death [did he find the answer]. He even left the last organization that he ever joined [Jehovah's Witnesses], because he couldn't go along with the sheer dogma that was so much a part of their thinking."

In *At Ease*, there is a seventeen-page chapter on Ida, but there is no similar chapter on David. Eisenhower almost never talked about his father, either. Aksel Nielsen, who was one of Eisenhower's oldest and closest civilian friends, said that in all the years they knew each other he couldn't remember a single conversation about Ike's father. "It just wasn't his favorite subject," said Nielsen.

David Eisenhower has been variously described as "severe," "stern," "glum," "just," "humorless," "serious," "brooding." His sons said he was a "thinker, not a talker, but when he talked he had something to say." "Mother was the talker in the family," Edgar said. "Probably one reason Dad never said much was because he couldn't when she had the floor. 'Mother,' he would say mildly, 'you state a good case,' or 'Well put, Mother, but slightly long.' Sometimes he'd start to tell a story and mother would break in and finish it for him."

David's grandson John said that he was stubborn. "For instance, we tried to get him to wear low shoes. He was wearing old-fashioned high shoes all the time, and so we went downtown and bought him a pair of low shoes, we thought for sure he would wear them. But he didn't. He was just too stubborn. He glowered, and I don't know whether he ever wore them. Probably not."

No one spoke of David as "cheerful." Nettie Stover Jackson, who often visited the Eisenhowers in Abilene, said she doubted if in his whole life David ever laughed aloud. She could not remember that in all the times she was with him he ever spoke to her at all "except maybe to say hello." His son Edgar said, "It was against his religion to hate anybody, but I do know he disapproved of some people. He was impervious toward those who annoyed or displeased him, often taking severe steps to teach them a lesson or two." Earl Endacott said of David, "He was very vindictive, not only to me but to everybody."

David's son Dwight was not vindictive, but he was not forgiving either. Once you were a friend, you were a friend for life. That is, as long as you didn't cross him or do something that he considered crossing him. John Eisenhower said,

"Dad could get over any disagreement very easily, as long as he won. [People] he doesn't have any confidence in . . . literally don't exist." His wartime aide, Harry Butcher, for example, in publishing *My Three Years with Eisenhower* in 1946, not only "crossed" the supreme commander, he embarrassed him and, in Eisenhower's mind, betrayed his confidences. John said, "Dad didn't win that one, so he may have carried a little bit more anger in Butcher's case than he would have in other people's cases."

Eisenhower did not, however, hate his old friend; he put him in what he called "the bottom drawer." Ike said he made it a practice to avoid hating anyone. "If someone's been guilty of despicable actions, especially toward me, I try to forget him. I used to follow a practice—somewhat contrived, I admit— to write the man's name on a piece of scrap paper, drop it into the lowest drawer of my desk, and say to myself, 'That finishes the incident, and so far as I'm concerned, that fellow.' " Butcher had not only ceased to exist, it was as if he never had existed. And how can you hate someone who isn't, who never was?

That "bottom drawer" was roomy and it was crowded. Eisenhower said, "The drawer became over the years a sort of private wastebasket for crumbled-up spite and discarded personalities. Besides, it seemed to be effective and helped me avoid harboring useless black feelings."

David's desk was always bare and clean, his accounts always balanced to the penny, and his dress was fastidious. Throughout most of his life he wore overalls, but they were spotlessly clean. One photograph of him "absolutely amazed" Mrs. Jackson. "It was taken outdoors, and he had his sleeves rolled and his collar unbuttoned. It just wasn't usual for him even to have his coat off, and especially to have a picture taken."

Until after he went to West Point, everyone in Abilene agreed that Dwight, almost defiantly, dressed sloppily, and his hair was frequently uncombed. His handwriting was also "sloppy," again almost defiantly so. When Eisenhower was a young boy, penmanship was taught in grammar school by the use of a copybook in Spencerian script. Yet "neither then nor since has my handwriting resembled Spencerian or the English language," he commented when he was in his seventies. "My handwriting remains angular and slurred."

In a letter to his mother in September of 1942 he said:

> I will have this letter written on the typewriter so that you can decipher it. As you well know my own handwriting is of a character that defies interpretation, even by myself.

Eisenhower's longtime friend and associate in the Army, General Alfred M. "Al" Gruenther said, "I don't think his handwriting was the worst in the world, but it is among the worst." Kevin McCann, who was Eisenhower's assistant from 1946 to August of 1951, and collaborated with him on several projects, including *At Ease*, had the job of interpreting what Eisenhower had written. He said his handwriting "looked as if it had been written on a lazy Susan. The words were upside down and every which way." Even though McCann became an expert, the words were sometimes undecipherable. When even McCann couldn't decipher them, he'd take them to Eisenhower who'd say, 'You figure it out. I don't know what it means.' "

According to Henry Jamieson, publisher and editor of the *Abilene Reflector-Chronicle*, Eisenhower, while visiting the Eisenhower Museum, studied the terse handwritten message that brought an end to the fighting in Europe and mumbled to himself, "I should have learned to write better than that."

After David's death, when Eisenhower was asked if he wanted anything from the house, the only thing he asked for was a sample of his father's Spencerian handwriting.

David was hungry for knowledge all his life, and he took courses in engineering from the International Correspondence School of Scranton, Pennsylvania. He told his son Edgar, "You must be inquisitive to learn. . . . You have to ask questions. For example, if two and two equals four, I want to know why the answer isn't five. I want proof. In this way my knowledge grows."

David worked as hard at the correspondence courses as he had in trying to solve the mysteries of the Great Pyramid. And on December 31, 1904, he received a certificate of completion for the following courses: "Arithmetic, Mechanics, Steam and Steam Engines, Dynamos and Motors, and Mensuration."

He liked to read. "Books . . . that's what he liked," said Ida. "At home, in what spare time he had, he opened a book and was lost." According to his son Edgar, his favorite author was a man named Stoddard, "whose lectures on travel and exploration were well loved in this period. . . . Through the pages of Stoddard, Dad, with his vivid imagination, visited all the corners of the world.

"Dad preferred to read about intellectuals, people who knew their own minds. He liked English history. It was American colonial times that he turned to, as though some ancestral self in him was retracing its steps."

According to Dwight's brother Milton, their father's mind resembled Dwight's "because it was completely logical—as logical as mathematics." Another brother, Earl, gave an example: "If he once got two points established in any proposition, then all other facts and ideas pertaining to that matter had to fall into place, else they were rejected." According to Earl, this logical method of reasoning enabled Eisenhower as president "to master a tremendous variety of subjects and problems, with a vast number of persons. He could do his work quickly, but thoroughly. He could keep constantly in touch with his principal advisers, including members of his cabinet."

David Eisenhower was opposed to cards, smoking, and alcohol. His son Dwight played cards, until late in life smoked excessively, and, though never to excess, drank. His son Arthur said that David was "always too serious." Another of his sons, Edgar, said, "Life to him was a very serious proposition, and that's the way he lived it, soberly, and with due reflection."

David never played with his sons; he never taught them games. He did not take them hunting or fishing; he did not swim with them; he showed no interest in who their friends were. It was perhaps for this reason that for a large part of his life Eisenhower sought out men who were older than he, surrogate fathers.

The first of them, a man he called "my hero," was named Bob Davis. Though most people at the time would no doubt have called him a tramp, Eisenhower saw him differently. "He had," he said, "long been a traveler, a fisherman, hunter, and guide. He was also a bachelor, a philosopher and, to me, a great teacher." Eisenhower probably chose to ignore the fact that Davis fished and trapped illegally and sold what he got in North Abilene.

Eisenhower often spent weekends with Davis on the Smokey Hill River to the south of Abilene. Ida gave him permission for such weekends; he had, he wrote, "my mother's blessing." Even so, the weekends must have been viewed with some disapproval by many people in town. Bob Davis was not the kind of man you invited to dinner, and there is no record that he ever shared a meal with the Eisenhowers.

Davis taught Eisenhower how to fish, "how to use a flat boat, with one paddle—to keep the paddle on one side and feather." Although it seems likely that Bob Davis had never heard of Socrates, he used the Socratic method of teaching, questions. "In the woods, it's raining. How do you find north? (The moss on the trees tends to be on the northern side. . . .) How do you catch a muskrat? . . . a mink?" And, most valued and profitable of all, Davis taught Eisenhower how to play poker. Eisenhower was well aware that his father violently opposed gambling of any kind, but that was all the more reason to gamble. "Bob was an illiterate and he had difficulty writing his own name. . . . But he knew poker percentages. . . . He dinned percentages into my head night after night around a campfire, using for the lessons a greasy pack of nicked cards that must have been a dozen years old." Poker was to remain Eisenhower's favorite and most profitable game until the late 1930s when he was to give it up abruptly. According to Raymond Daniell (in the *New York Times,* November 1, 1942), at one time, before the war, Eisenhower's winnings from playing poker amounted to $3,900, which was close to what his annual salary was.

John Eisenhower said of his grandfather David, "He was big on corporal punishment, and he tried to beat up his sons until they were big enough to beat him back." Earl said, "I never saw him show any signs of anger—like shaking his fist—or banging on a table, or anything like that in my life. Father was quiet, even when he was angry." Arthur attested that he never saw his father angry "except occasionally when he had to administer punishment."

Eisenhower described what happened when his father discovered that Edgar had dropped out of school to work for a local doctor. "I never before or after saw him so angry. At noontime that day, Edgar and I had come home for lunch and Father, in a surprise visit, from the creamery, found us in the barn. His face was black as thunder. With no pause for argument, he reached for a piece of harness, a tug it was called, at the same time grabbing Ed by the collar. He started in.

"A little over twelve years old at the time, I began to shout to my father to stop. Finally I began to cry as loudly as I could, possibly hoping that Mother would arrive on the scene.

"Father stopped his thrashing and then turned on me because I had come up behind him and tried to catch hold of his arms. 'Oh, do you want some of the same. What's the matter with you, anyway?'

" 'I don't think anyone ought to be whipped like that,' I said, 'not even a dog.' Whatever his reason, I suffered no punishment."

As happened so often when he made a harsh judgment, Eisenhower then softened it. "Now I know, and I am sure Ed does too, that only through instant and drastic action when he learned about the truancy could my father have persuaded him, a headstrong fellow, to change his attitude toward school."

Time tends to soften all our judgments, and in 1967 when Eisenhower wrote the above, Edgar's punishment did not seem as severe as it had in 1902. But he never physically punished his own son, John, who said, "Perhaps this stemmed from a fear that strong as he was, he might inflict serious bodily harm when his temper was aroused. Instead, he conducted discipline in a West Point manner. I was dressed down smartly on many occasions but never given a whack."

The work at the Belle Springs Creamery was neither very interesting nor very lucrative, but it was clean work, and David worked there uncomplainingly for twenty-four years. Then, in the summer of 1916, he went to a national convention of Jehovah's Witnesses in Washington, D.C. He sent a penny postcard back saying only one word, "Hot!" How he went and why he went and where he got the money to go we do not know. We do know that he was unceremoniously fired for going.

Earl Endacott said, "The River Brethren were very strict, and by that time he [David] had left them and joined the Jehovah's Witnesses. He wasn't as radical in that regard as the mother was, but the River Brethren didn't like it. Then he wanted to go to that convention, and they wouldn't give him any time off to go. He went anyway, and they fired him right after he got back. He resented that greatly. I remember one of the men who worked at the creamery had to go past the Eisenhower house to get to the creamery. But he didn't like to pass the house and did everything possible to avoid it. He knew if he started past the house David would stop him and talk to him about what a dirty deal he had got from that bunch at the creamery."

David, described by his son Edgar as a "plugger," was never out of work during the time the family lived in Abilene. When asked what his father's recreation was, Arthur said, "Work was his recreation. It was his passion."

The same year he was fired from the creamery, he started work as a mechanic at the Abilene Gas Company, which was part of the United Companies, at one time the employer of 25 percent of the work force of Abilene. It had been founded and at that time was still owned by yet another of the River Brethren, C. L. Brown, a progressive businessman who long before Social Security had initiated a plan that required those who worked for him to put 10 percent of their wages into a savings fund. United eventually had telephone and utility companies from the Rockies to the Alleghenies, as well as a number of lumberyards and a grocery chain.

David, according to the *Abilene Reflector-Chronicle*, "in 1916 became engineer for the gas plant of the United Companies and later local manager of the plant. He served as chairman for the employees' benefit and savings plan of the United Companies. . . . Each employee was required to save 10 per cent of his income and invest the same in bonds, a home, or sound stocks. . . .

"Mr. Eisenhower checked the 800 employees, saw to it that they made monthly reports of their savings and advised them on investments. He believed strongly in savings and preached it at stated meetings."

David's son Dwight was inclined to be careless about savings, but the woman he married more than made up for it.

Another example of David's being careful with money was the fact that after his return to Abilene from Texas he told the local merchants never to send him a bill; he would pay what he owed on the first day of every month, and he did. Twenty years after he initiated this system, he got a bill from one store. He went to the store, bill in hand, paid it, and never again traded there.

Dwight remembered his father's feeling about bills when he ripped his trousers, in an accident that nearly cost him a leg. He needed new trousers. He said, "I arranged with a storekeeper to let me have them until I could save the money to pay him back. I asked the man to say nothing to my father." But by another mistake the bill was sent to David. Eisenhower was still suffering from the effects of the accident when it arrived. He said, "He made no attempt to punish me but I could see that he was deeply disturbed by my violation of one of his basic principles. Never again did I take a chance that any indebtedness of mine would come to his notice."

After a working career which lasted forty-six years, David retired in 1931. He lived another eleven years. John said that during those years when he knew his grandfather, 1940–41, he had strokes where he was "having hallucinations and was seeing bugs." Once "I told him Dad couldn't come home for a certain thing because he was working so hard, and he sort of looked up and wept a bit."

When David died on March 10, 1942, Eisenhower was chief of the War Plans Division in Washington, working sixteen or more hours a day, seven days a week, and on constant call from Army Chief of Staff George C. Marshall. He was also on occasion giving advice to and writing messages for President Roosevelt. He was clearly too busy to attend the funeral in Abilene. Mrs. Jackson said, "Aunt Ida told me he just couldn't leave his desk. She said, 'He just eats right at his desk.' "

On March 10 Eisenhower wrote in his diary, "Dad died this morning. Nothing I can do but send a wire." The next day he wrote his further feelings, and they were largely concerned with his mother. A more direct man might have said what is clear, that Ida was a saint to have put up with David all those years. He said:

I have felt terribly. I should like so much to be with my mother these few days. But we're at war. And war is not soft—it has no time to indulge even in the deepest and most sacred emotions. I loved my Dad. I think my Mother the finest person I've ever known. She has been the inspiration for Dad's life and a true helpmate in every sense of the word. . . . I'm quitting work now—7:30 P.M. I haven't the heart to go on.

On March 12, the day of the funeral, he wrote:

My father was buried today. I've shut off all business and visitors for thirty minutes—to have that much time, by myself, to think of him. He had a full life. He left six boys, and, most fortunately for him, Mother survives him. . . .

His finest monument is his reputation in Abilene and Dickinson [Kansas]. . . . His word has been his bond and accepted as such, his sterling honesty, his insistence upon the immediate payment of all debts, his pride in his independence earned for him a reputation that has profited all of us boys. Because of it, all central Kansas helped me secure an appointment to West Point in 1911, and thirty years later it did the same for my son, John. I'm proud he was my father. My only regret is that it was always so difficult to let him know the great depth of my affection for him.

DAVID J. EISENHOWER 1863–1942

Eisenhower certainly never let his father know "the great depth of my affection for him." Whether he actually felt such affection is another matter.

David Eisenhower had very little money to leave to Ida or to his sons, and that had bothered him. Shortly before his death, Edgar saw him. "He was lying in bed and was not feeling well. . . . I said, 'Why, Dad, what is the matter?' And he said, 'Well, Edgar, I got something that has bothered me for a long time. I am not going to leave you boys anything.' He said, 'That breaks my heart.' And Dad cried, the first time I ever saw him cry in his life."

As Harry Truman said of his father, who was also not a success in the way we like to think of success, "You can't say a man who was the father of a president of the United States was a failure."

★ ★ ★

THE STEPPING STONE

The house on South East Second Street, where the Eisenhowers lived for seven years, was not much of an improvement over the one in Denison. They were once again near the railroad tracks, this time the tracks of the Union Pacific and the Santa Fe.

Those tracks split Abilene socially and economically; that was true of most small towns at the time. In Abilene on the north side of the tracks were the shops and the homes of the shopkeepers as well as the doctors, the lawyers, the schoolteachers, those who had the best jobs at United Companies. In general, those who wore shirts and ties and jackets to work lived on the north side of the tracks. The blue-collar workers, those who, like David, wore overalls to work, lived on the south side.

The Eisenhower house was tiny for a family of five, and by the time they moved out, they were seven. The lot was cramped. Eisenhower said of the backyard, "With wooden fences on each side and a coal and wood shed not far from the back of the house, [it] was large enough to swing a cat in, if it were a small one."

In 1898 David's brother, Abraham the veterinarian, who was also a preacher, and his wife, Anna, decided to move to California to convert the unconverted. He offered his house on South East Fourth Street to Ida and David for a modest sum, $1,000; he would charge no interest and they could pay when it was possible for them to pay.

It was a brotherly act of good faith, but David and Ida disagreed on whether to accept it. David saw no reason to move from the house on South East Second. Ida did, and as usual she won. In 1898 they did move, and the house on South East Fourth Street was theirs. It was originally in Ida's name, but on August 24, 1907, she sold it to her husband, David, for the sum of $1.00. After their death, the house was turned over to the Eisenhower Foundation in 1946.

Ida proved right. The wood-frame house was two stories high, and although it was only 23 feet square, it proved to be an ideal place to raise her boys. It was surrounded by nearly three acres of land and, since there were only six or seven other houses in the vicinity, there were many wide open fields to play in. They moved in on November 4, shortly after Eisenhower's eighth birthday. "I was getting along in years," Eisenhower said. "I heard for the first time mention made of my mother's age. In conversation with a neighbor, my mother said, as I recall: 'I've been married almost fourteen years and I am thirty-six years old.' And, she added, 'For the first time we have a home where my children will have room to play. I am most thankful.' "

Lincoln Elementary School was just across the street, and the C. W. Parker merry-go-round factory and winter carnival grounds were not far away. Mud Creek, where the boys swam and fished, was only three blocks away.

To Eisenhower, the house itself seemed like "a mansion . . . with its upstairs bedrooms. There were two fairly large bedrooms, with a miniature bedroom at the end of the hall. The first of the large ones was occupied by Father and Mother with the baby, Earl, in a cradle. Three boys slept in the adjoining room, Roy and I in one bed, Edgar in the other. Arthur . . . was awarded the little room. . . . Whether it was considered as an undeveloped bedroom or a generous closet, the rest of us envied his splendid isolation."

David had promised Abraham that when their father decided he wanted or needed to, he could live with David's family on South East Fourth Street for the rest of his life. Jacob decided he wanted to move in in 1900, and an addition, the first of several, was built onto the first floor. It provided two new downstairs bedrooms—one for Jacob and one for Ida and David. Jacob lived there until his death in 1906.

Eisenhower remembered him as "a patriarchal figure, dressed in black." He wore a beard with his lips shaved clean and talked with a Pennsylvania Dutch accent. "He kept a horse and buggy which, on occasion, he shared with us boys," said Eisenhower. "His importance, in my mind then, rested on the beard and the buggy and the horse; not on his success as a farmer, or as a leader of the family migration. Now I know otherwise."

"I remember Dad and my granddad always talked German to one another," said Edgar. He added, however, that David refused to speak German with Ida or with his sons. He didn't want them to be different from the other children in Abilene.

Abilene was perhaps a likely place for a president who came naturally to a middle-of-the-road position on most matters to grow up. It is only twenty miles east of the exact geographic center of the United States. The soil is excellent; most of the time the farmers were prosperous and brought prosperity to the Dickinson County town in which they shopped. Wheat and corn were the principal crops, and in Eisenhower's boyhood there were still native pastures with bluestem and buffalo grasses.

It is said that if you can live in Kansas you can live anywhere; the temperatures range from 20° below in the winter to more than 110° above in the summer. During July and August there are searing dry, hot winds.

When Abilene was founded in 1857, it was only a log-cabin hamlet and stagecoach stop with a population of 300. A few years later, in 1867, the town became the terminus of the cattle drives from Texas, at the point where the Chisholm Trail met the tracks of the Kansas-Pacific Railroad. Almost overnight the population grew to 3,000.

In the years between 1867 and 1871 the town was the wildest cow town in the United States. Most of the whorehouses the cowboys frequented were in what was called "Fisher's Addition." According to the *Abilene Chronicle*, that was "located east of Buckeye . . . about as far as where the Santa Fe railroad now comes into the city." The Eisenhower house on South East Fourth Street was in what had been Fisher's Addition; and the Belle Springs Creamery, where David Eisenhower and at one time or another all of his living sons were to be employed, is on the site of Drover's Cottage, what was at the time considered the best hotel in town.

In the winter of 1872, the citizens and the nearby farmers, whose unfenced wheat fields were frequently trampled by stampeding cattle, drew up a petition requesting all

> who have contemplated driving Texas cattle to Abilene the coming season to seek some other point for shipment, as the inhabitants of Dickinson County will no longer submit to the evils of the trade.

The petition was circulated all over Texas and was printed in all livestock journals and newspapers. The Texans got the message, and by the following spring, Abilene was free of cowboys; the whores moved west as did the gamblers; saloons closed and stores went broke. Abilene became what it is today, a painfully quiet, painfully dull town. It never regained the tough, colorful vigor of its four cowboy years. When the Eisenhower boys were growing up, Milton said the town "was quiet, perhaps smugly so."

In discussing his boyhood in Abilene, Eisenhower referred somewhat wistfully to "men I knew [who] were hardly candidates for the pulpit. Law-abiding though they were, they had their roots in that fascinating period of Abilene history when Wild Bill Hickok, the town marshal, made it famous—or less infamous."

Later, with seeming regret, he wrote, "I was nearly fifteen before I saw my first shooting scrape. . . . The shooter was standing on a walk, taking pot shots at a man who was setting a new sprint record from a point thirty yards away. The pistol looked very dangerous. Now I know that the little nickel-plated, snub-nosed weapon would have been harmful only in the case of a miraculous shot. . . .

"Across the street from our house lived a man named Dudley, who claimed he had served for a time as a young deputy under Wild Bill. His tales of the man's prowess with a revolver were entrancing. Other men well acquainted with revolvers and their use were the town marshal, Henry Engle, and the Wells Fargo agent, a Mr. Gish.

"Sometimes they went out to Mud Creek and would let me accompany them as they held a shooting contest. Occasionally, I was permitted to shoot several rounds. Each man carried his revolver differently. Gish wore his in a shoulder holster under his left arm. Henry Engle used a conventional holster on his right side. . . . I would watch intently as they would draw and shoot. While none of them had the skill I've seen in shooting exhibitions, they were all above average in marksmanship and at least two had personal experience in gunfights."

Also, there was his boyhood friend, Charlie Case's father, J. B. Case, who "[was] a first cousin of Mrs. George Custer . . . filled with tales and stories of the old west of the 1870s, and was a mine of information on the early days of Kansas."

No wonder Eisenhower read Westerns; they were about a way of life he had missed in Abilene, and he regretted it. There were six Zane Greys by his bedside when he died, and he was also fond of the work of Frederick Faust, who lived in Florence, Italy, and wrote Westerns under various pseudonyms, mainly that of Max Brand.

Sergeant Mickey McKeogh, General Eisenhower's orderly during World War II, wrote Mrs. Eisenhower every few weeks from Europe telling her "how the Boss was" and sometimes asking her to send things he knew the supreme commander wanted, most often "more Western stories, preferably with a lot of shooting in them."

McKeogh said, "It was sort of funny, considering the amount of shooting we were getting most nights, that he still wanted stories full of six-shooters and barroom brawls, but he did. Max Brand's stories were particular favorites of the General's."

One of the reasons Eisenhower enjoyed reading Westerns during the war and after was because they did not require any concentration. Mamie said he told her they were easy to put down and pick up despite any number of interruptions, including a night's sleep.

Eisenhower also liked Western movies, and one of his favorites was *High Noon*, with Gary Cooper. Cooper was the honest sheriff who was stalked through the deserted streets of a western town by four killers. In one scene Cooper escaped from a burning building by leaping onto a horse and riding out through a barrage of gunfire. Eisenhower, then president, watched the movie in the White House theater, and during that scene the president lost his usual aplomb. "Run," he shouted to Cooper, "run." After *High Noon* ended, with Gary Cooper and virtue triumphant, Ike turned to Mamie and said, "By golly, I never thought he'd make it."

Eisenhower was always fond of many of the people of Abilene, but after 1961, when he retired from the presidency, he and Mamie moved to Gettysburg, Pennsylvania, not Kansas.

"He never lost touch with Abilene at all and he maintained a love for Abilene," according to Henry Jamieson, editor of the *Reflector-Chronicle*. "This was his home. That was it. He told me at one time that one of his greatest desires would be to come back to Abilene and walk down the street alone, unrecognized, and be left alone. Which was impossible. You felt kind of sorry for him."

On the other hand, his son John said, "Abilene was a great symbol for him, a great place to be from. But what in hell would Abilene have to offer him? He was a gregarious man. He liked successful men. It was one of his characteristics. . . . Palm Desert, he spent a lot of time there, but Abilene, oh boy. There wasn't a chance he'd have retired there.

"I think, really, that this Abilene background was a very useful thing to Dad in dealing with Khrushchev, because when Dad said, 'You step across the line in Berlin and I'll shoot,' I think Khrushchev believed him, and I think he believed him more because of his background out here in Wild Bill Hickok country. They must have had a dossier at least three foot thick on Dad. And the background of what kind of people he came from, and he knew that Dad was an admirer of Tom Smith [town marshal martyred in a quarrel between two homesteaders] and less so of Hickok—but he was raised in that tradition, and when Dad said, 'I'll go so far, or you're going to get it,' I think Khrushchev believed him. I think the Abilene influence was more [important] than the West Point influence or Washington politics or the wartime."

In a letter dated January 14, 1952, to Maud Hurd, the wife of Arthur Hurd, who was a lawyer and an old friend of his from Abilene, Eisenhower said:

It would be difficult to tell you how much . . . I enjoyed your long and interesting letter. It told me more about Abilene than I have heard from anyone in years; it breathed a philosophy of life which is instinctively my own. Dickinson County is something deep within me. If I ever lose it, I shall be someone completely different from what I am or want to be. . . . It was refreshing to know that you still believe in self-independence; how well I remember an old Kansas saying, "Root, hog, or die"; another was "Sink or swim—survive or perish."

In a speech Eisenhower delivered in Washington on "Fair Dealing" on November 23, 1953, he said of his hometown:

I was raised in a little town of which many of you may never have heard. But out in the west it is a famous place. It is called Abilene. We had as our Marshal a man named Wild Bill Hickok. Now, that town had a code and I was raised as a boy to prize that code.

It was: Meet anyone face to face with whom you disagree. You could not sneak up on him from behind, or do any damage to him, without suffering the penalty of an enraged citizenry. If you met him face to face and took the same risks as he did, you could get away with almost anything, as long as the bullet was in front.

And today, although none of you has the great fortune, I think, of being from Abilene, you live after all by that same code, in your ideals, and in the respect you give to certain qualities. In this country, if someone dislikes you, he must come up in front. He cannot hide behind the shadow. He cannot assassinate you or your character from behind, without suffering the penalties an outraged citizenry will impose.

Carl Becker, in *The Heritage of Kansas*, wrote, "The passion for equality in Kansas is . . . the complement of the individualism and the idealism of its people. It has as the basis of it an altruistic motive, aiming not so much to level all men down as to level all men up. The Kansan's sense of individual worth enables him to believe that no one can be better than he is, while his confident idealism encourages him to hope that none can be worse."

It also teaches him to be self-sufficient. Henry Jamieson said, "It never occurred to him [Eisenhower] that the world owed him a living. He believed in getting ahead on his own." As an example, Jamieson quoted from Eisenhower's wartime diaries: " 'My God, how I hate to work by any method that forces me to depend on anyone else.' "

While visiting Abilene on October 13, 1959, Eisenhower said, "We are all met in the town that has for me a very deep, sentimental meaning. . . . It went through its heyday, let's say, of Wild West hilarity and even worse—and became a community of God-fearing, hard-working, simple people." Among those people were his grandparents, Jacob and Rebecca.

Jacob Eisenhower and his family arrived in Abilene for the first time from Elizabethville, Pennsylvania, in April 1878. Physically, it had not been a particularly arduous journey, three days by train. But emotionally there must have been a considerable strain on Jacob's father, Frederick, a weaver who was eighty-four and had never been out of Pennsylvania. There had been Eisenhowers there for 150 years; they had come from Switzerland, first having fled religious persecution in Germany.

Earl Eisenhower said, "I knew nothing about my ancestors until I was old enough to read myself; Dwight and Milton looked them up. Dad rarely talked about his relations." His son Dwight did. After his family's home was turned over to the Eisenhower Foundation in 1946, he enjoyed acting as a tour guide. One of his favorite heirlooms in the house was a solid walnut dresser that his grandfather Jacob had brought with him when he migrated to Kansas. Eisenhower would open the drawers and pull out an old nightgown and tell whoever it was its history. He would explain that it had been made by his great grandfather Frederick from flax raised on his own farm. On the couch in the living room, Eisenhower would point out a hand-loomed afghan Frederick had made from the wool of his own sheep. "Feel the texture," Ike would say. "It's over a hundred years old."

On one such visit to the house, Ike noticed that the coverlet Frederick had made was missing. He asked where it was and was told that Edgar had written asking that it be sent to him in Tacoma, Washington. Despite the fact that the contract for the foundation said that everything in the house should be left intact, an official of the foundation heeded Edgar's request and sent the coverlet.

When Ike was told what had happened, he blew his top. According to Earl Endacott, "Ike said 'Get the damn thing back . . . this is where it belongs.' " Just how the matter was worked out is not known by the foundation, but about two weeks later the afghan arrived from Tacoma. There was no covering letter from Edgar, but the coverlet was put back on the couch in the living room, and it is still there today.

The Eisenhowers were members of the religious sect known as the River Brethren, an offshoot of the Mennonites, which was formed around 1770 in Pennsylvania. They believed in trine immersion, the washing of feet, nonresistance and nonconformity with or to the world. They had a distinctive old-fashioned dress—the men in dark suits, the women with long plain dresses and bonnets. The heads of the men were uncovered since men, according to The Reverend A. L. Witter, Dwight Eisenhower's uncle, are "the glory of God." Women are not; thus they must not appear in public unless their heads were covered, usually with what was called a "prayer veiling," a kind of cap made of white material. Over that, the Brethren women usually wore a simple bonnet with no flowers, no ornaments. The women wore no cosmetics; the men did not wear neckties. The church was opposed to political activity, and the members did not vote until the presidential election of 1928, when they turned out to cast their ballots for Herbert Hoover over Al Smith, the great Catholic menace.

Frederick and Jacob had both married women older than they, and both wives had brought substantial dowries to the marriages. Frederick's wife, Barbara Miller of Millersburg, Pennsylvania, not far from Elizabethville, had enough money to pay for the building of a three-story house in Millersburg. Frederick did his weaving on the second floor; the other two floors were living quarters.

Jacob, a preacher-farmer, married Rebecca Matter, great-granddaughter of a Revolutionary War soldier. In 1854, he built a red-brick, two-story, nine-room house that is still standing. The first floor on which the family lived also served as a meeting place where the River Brethren held their religious services. The attic was kept open for strangers and travelers, and when that was filled they slept in the barn. Jacob never turned anyone away.

It was in this house that the last of Jacob and Rebecca's fourteen children were born, including Dwight's father. Of the eight boys and six girls, five boys and one girl died in infancy; one girl died when she was seventeen.

Before leaving Pennsylvania, Jacob had accumulated $13,000 in real estate, $8,500 for his house and land, and personal property worth $6,000. By the standard of his day, he could be considered wealthy. For the trip, the Eisenhowers had been joined by five other families including those of Jacob's sister Catherine and his brother Sam, a veteran of the Union Army.

Jacob's sixteen-year-old daughter, Amanda, wept when the family left Elizabethville. Many years later she said, "When we were on the train for the West, I wept as if my heart would break to leave all my old schoolmates and go I knew not where." To Abraham, thirteen, and Ira, eleven, the journey seemed a glorious adventure. David, who was fifteen, as usual did not reveal his feelings. The older three married daughters came to Kansas later.

The Abilene that greeted the River Brethren was small and quiet. All of

Dickinson County had been cleansed of visible sin. Kansas was about to go dry, which it still mostly is. Hard liquor is not sold in most bars, except those in motels, for guests only. However, there are bars in which beer only is sold, and there are also numerous retail liquor stores. William Allen White, the famous editor of the *Emporia Gazette,* once said that Kansans would continue to vote dry "as long as they can stagger to the polls."

According to Gladys Dodd's thesis, in certain parts of Dickinson County when the Eisenhowers arrived, playing marbles for *keeps* was forbidden every day of the week; during Ike's youth baseball was forbidden on Sundays. Ike's brother Arthur remembered the quiet that prevailed on the Lord's Day. "In our youth there were no movies, of course." Churches abounded, however; Eisenhower said, "From memory alone I can identify seven." In Earl Eisenhower's earliest boyhood recollections, "Abilene was a town of no paved streets. It had dusty roads. There were, of course, no automobiles. A boy could ride a bicycle, if he had one, along these dirt roads, but the horse-drawn buggy was the most usual means of transportation for the townfolk."

Eisenhower recalled: "Paving was unknown to me for a long time. Crossings of scattered stone were provided at each corner, but after heavy summer rain the streets became almost impassable because of mud. . . . In winter, snow could practically immobilize the community. I cannot recall when hard pavement was started in town, but it was not earlier than 1904 or 1905." According to Eisenhower's presidential appointments secretary, Thomas E. Stephens, he never got used to the idea. "In 1952, as we were walking down the street, Eisenhower commented, 'I still can't believe these streets are paved!' "

Milton Eisenhower referred to Abilene as "a safe little world." In Eisenhower's childhood, the town marshal was no longer a Wild Bill Hickok or a Tom Smith. There were no more outlaws. According to Eisenhower, he never saw the marshal do anything "except chase truant boys." He added that "the police force was one man, Henry Engle—who walked around making sure the stores in town were locked up and who spent the night watching trains go by or come in."

A short time before the Jacob Eisenhowers arrived in Abilene, there had been a debate by a nearby literary society on the proposition that "novel-reading is injurious to youthful minds." Miss Dodd wrote, "the affirmative won, of course."

But all these changes in and around the town were probably unknown to Jacob and other members of the River Brethren. They lived plainly, dressed plainly, and ate plainly, but they had nothing against making money. God favored capitalism. He wanted his Brethren to be prosperous. As they so often said to each other, "The Lord helps them that help themselves."

A year after arriving in Kansas, Jacob was farming 160 acres of land. He was delighted with the look and the feel of the soil; it was even darker and richer than he had expected, and the wheat was green and luxuriant that year. Jacob and the boys tilled the fields, and within a year, according to the 1880 census, half of the 160 acres was tilled—40 acres in corn; 40 acres in wheat. Eisenhower said that his grandfather, in addition to farming, had a dairy herd and poultry. In 1879, according to Eisenhower, his grandfather's butter production was a full thousand pounds, "more than six times the Dickinson County average. And grandmother that year had gathered 300 dozen eggs, twice the average of the county's farms."

When the Jacob Eisenhowers first arrived, the family spent the nights in a covered wagon. The following winter, however, Jacob and the boys built the house on the Eisenhower land, which was not far from the Smokey Hill River and the old Chisholm Trail. They also erected a barn and alongside it a Dutch windmill with wooden sails. This house was simpler than the red-brick Pennsylvania house, but here, too, there was a huge living room which could be and was used as a meeting room for the Brethren on Sundays and for "love feasts" once a year. Love feasts involved two entire days and evenings of praying, hymn singing, sermonizing, and yea-saying. There was also a lot of eating, and the drinking of wine—fermented until 1885, then unfermented—out of wooden cups.

There was also a third floor in the new house, to house passing strangers. On Sunday mornings, Brethren families from miles around would arrive at the Eisenhower farm, tie their horses, buggies, and wagons to a hitching post, and assemble in the living room. Jacob and the boys would hand out hymnals, and they all would sing praises of the Lord and pray. Jacob's sermons, spoken in a singsong Pennsylvania Dutch German, came from the New Testament but were seldom short and never cheerful. One mustn't expect much in the way of laughter on earth; the good times came in the hereafter.

David, despite his father's urging, never took to the Brethren; the other two boys, Abraham and Ira, delighted Jacob by becoming ministers. Both were total believers, with Abraham being particularly zealous. He succeeded in converting almost everybody he went after, but he failed with his elder brother and with David's son Dwight. David's other boys were not overly pious either.

★ ★ ★

IN THE TRUTH

David's sons all professed a firm belief in God, but they approached Him much less formally. Milton said, "after we reached the age of reason, they [the parents] did not insist that we go to church, they wanted us to do so as a result of our own convictions." Perhaps overexposed in childhood, none was a regular churchgoer as an adult, except Dwight, and that came only when he was persuaded that he had not only to be the political leader of the United States, but its moral leader as well. Arthur never joined any church, although, he said, "That doesn't mean I haven't got my mother's religion in my heart." Edgar said, "We boys are all religious, but we don't go around saying 'I'm a religious man' any more than we would say, 'I'm an honest man,' or 'I'm a clean man,' or 'I pay my bills.' "

It has often been stated flatly that Ida and David Eisenhower were River

Brethren. David's father Jacob and his brothers Ira and Abraham were indeed members of that sect, but Ike's cousin, The Reverend Roy L. Witter, son of A. L. Witter, said that, while Ida and David "worked along and came along for a number of years," neither was ever an actual member. Eisenhower, when president, explained that his parents "had been deeply religious people, though somewhat rebellious . . . not easily satisfied with any church."

When their eight-month-old son, Paul, died of diphtheria in 1895, both parents were shattered, and the River Brethren, though they tried, couldn't seem to help much. Three neighborhood women not only comforted them but offered them a new faith. They were Russellites; they and their successors, the Jehovah's Witnesses, were and are zealous in recruiting new members. The Russellite sect had, like the River Brethren, originated in Pennsylvania, not in the rural valley of the Susquehanna but in downtown Pittsburgh. The sect was founded in 1885 by Charles Taze Russell, who had a haberdashery there.

The women who were so helpful to the Eisenhowers in their grief were Mrs. Clare Witt, Mrs. Mary Thayer, and Mrs. Emma Holland. They said that if David and Ida Eisenhower read one of Russell's books, *Millennial Dawn*, and subscribed to and read his publication, *Zion's Watch Tower and Herald of Christ's Presence*, they would find the truth. There was, the three women said, no other way to understand the Bible. All other religions had either accidentally or deliberately, usually the latter, misled their followers. Could they come inside and explain?

It is part of the Eisenhower legend that it was not until Ida was in her dotage that she was somehow induced to become a Witness. In *Eisenhower: The Man and the Symbol*, published in 1952, six years after Ida's death, John Gunther, that usually reliable reporter, wrote, "Late in life she [Ida] became, of all things, a member of the sect known as Jehovah's Witnesses, which meant that she pledged not only to militant pacifism, but was an actual conscientious objector."

Eisenhower said, "A woman as individualistic as she was not able to accept the dogma of any specific sect or denomination." That is what Eisenhower wanted to believe and perhaps at times actually did, but Ida herself contradicted it.

In 1944 she placed the date of her conversion as a Witness as 1895; she wrote Richard Boeckel, who had become a Witness while in the U.S. Army, "as a witness of and for the Great Jehovah of Hosts (I have been such the past 49 years) I am pleased to write you and to urge you to faithfulness as a companion of and servant with those who keep the commandments of God and have the testimony of Jesus."

According to an account in a 1980 *Watchtower*, Boeckel was stationed at Fort Francis E. Warren in Wyoming when he first became a Witness, and in August 1944, while attending a United Announcers' Theocratic Assembly in Denver, he met Lotta Thayer from Abilene, a Witness and a neighbor of Ida's. Boeckel explained to Mrs. Thayer that it was difficult to serve God as a Witness in a military environment; she in turn said, "Do you know who my neighbor is? It's General Eisenhower's mother. She's one of Jehovah's Witnesses. Would you like her to write you?"

Ida's letter is dated August 20, 1944, and said that she generally refused to write to anyone on request, "because of my desire to avoid all publicity." She wrote:

I have been blessed with seven sons of which five are living, all being very good to their mother, and I am constrained to believe they are very fine in the eyes of those who have learned to know them.

It is always my desire and my effort to raise my boys in the knowledge of and to reverence their Creator. . . . I feel that Dwight my third son will always strive to do his duty with integrity as he sees such duty. I mention him in particular because of your expressed interest in him.

In the *Watchtower* account of the matter, it was said that one time when Boeckel refused, as a good Witness must, to salute his superior officers at Fort Warren, he said that he was a Witness and that his refusal to salute was "based on my understanding of the Bible." One officer reportedly said, "General Eisenhower ought to line you Jehovah's Witnesses up and shoot you all!"

Boeckel then, again according to *The Watchtower*, said, " 'Do you think he would shoot his own mother, sir?'

" 'What do you mean by that?'

"Reaching in my pocket and taking out Sister Eisenhower's letter, I handed it to him. . . . he read the letter . . . he handed it back to me. 'Get back to ranks,' he said. 'I don't want to get mixed up with the General's mother.' "

In any case we know that Ida did write the letter and we know from many sources that she did not, as some claim, including Milton, become a Witness "late in life." She was able to accept the dogma of the Witnesses from the time she was thirty-four and the mother of four small sons, all of them under the age of ten. She became a Witness because other Witness members had comforted her on the death of a fifth son. She remained one all her life.

Both Ida and David, but especially Ida, were avid readers of *The Watchtower*, and at the time of Ida's death there was a fifty-year collection in the house on South East Fourth Street. The publication had arrived by mail from 1896 to 1946. It was Milton who bundled up the fifty-year collection of the presumably embarrassing magazines and got them out of the Eisenhower house and away from the eyes of reporters. He gave them to a neighbor and Witness.

During the Second World War, a great many young men who were Witnesses, "ministers," asked to be and were excused from the draft; they did not believe that one human being was ever justified in killing another. About 3,500 other young men professing the same beliefs were not excused from the draft; they were sent to jail. Some young men like Boeckel became Witnesses while in the army and had very difficult times.

The fact that the mother of the Allied supreme commander in Europe was a Witness was considered big news, and there were many stories and pictures showing her recruiting other Witnesses, as active members are required to do. On May 18, 1943, Eisenhower wrote to Arthur:

Not long ago I saw a clipping in which some reporter made a point of the fact that our dear old Mother likes to go to conventions of her beloved Jehovah's Witnesses. As far as I am concerned, her happiness in her religion means more to me than any damn wisecrack that a newspaperman can get publicized—I know full well that the government is not going to measure my services as a soldier by the religious beliefs of my Mother. Moreover, at heart, the country has never had a more loyal citizen than she.

It was felt by some members of the family that Naomi Engle, Ida's nurse at the time, was putting undue pressure on her to have her picture taken signing up new members, for Naomi herself was a strong-willed Witness. She had arranged a Jehovah's Witness funeral for David even though he had made it clear before his death that he was no longer a believer. In the fall of 1944 Edgar wrote Naomi a stern letter saying that, while he believed in religious freedom, "I want Mother shielded and protected and not exposed or exhibited."

In October of that same year, Eisenhower's old friend J. Frances Curry wrote to him concerning the publicity about his mother. Eisenhower wrote back, "You are quite right in deploring the publicity that some of these people are trying to develop around her—I do not see, though, what I can do except to write to Milton, who is close by. It is a bit of a shock to me to learn that Naomi is rather pushing this kind of thing. I should think that her concern for Mother would lead her to discourage people flocking around for pictures, interviews, and so on. The answer is, of course, that she is perfectly innocent in the matter and is merely unsophisticated." The same day, he wrote to Milton asking him "to discourage Naomi from allowing reporters and photographers to harass Mother all the time."

A little later, innocent or not, unsophisticated or not, Naomi was discharged, it was believed, by Milton. According to Nettie Jackson, "The other woman they hired wasn't nearly as nice to her, and I think Aunt Ida missed Naomi."

Eisenhower's parents believed that, as Ida often said, "The fear of God is the beginning of all wisdom." He said of his parents in a speech in 1952, "Their Bibles were a live and lusty influence in their lives. . . . And they tried their best to instill it, its doctrines, its beliefs, its convictions, in their sons." There were prayers and blessings and Bible readings and amens before and after breakfast in the morning and, of course, before and after supper. Earl said, "Dad would read passages or he might pass the Bible around the circle and all of us got a chance to read." Even the Bible reading was competitive. A brother lost the privilege of reading if he made a mistake and another brother caught him, and the brother who detected the error took over.

As a boy, Eisenhower was understandably impatient with such tiresome solemnity. Mrs. Jackson said, "You know what a stool is, a chair without a back. Dwight would sit on a stool, and Ida said she didn't know how he did it, but he'd turn himself around on the stool and never make a sound, but the minute *amen* was said, he was facing the door and out the door. She was just puzzled about how he did it, and she worried about how he'd turn out."

At West Point, attendance at Sunday worship services was compulsory, and while there, Eisenhower was a member of the Young Men's Christian Association, which met on Sunday evenings for Bible study and also supplied teachers for the post Sunday School, in which capacity Eisenhower served during his First Class year.

After West Point, Eisenhower's attendance at church was sporadic, often nonexistent. But in 1951, when he was a likely presidential candidate, his not going to church and his refusal to profess any religious faith became an embarrassment, not only to Republican politicians but to his friends and staff. They urged him to join a church, any church, so long as it was white, Anglo-Saxon, and Protestant, and he must attend services on a regular basis, just as most voters did or pretended to or wished they did.

Such suggestions infuriated him. By God, he was not going to use religion in getting a nomination for the presidency. But in the spring of 1951, the intrepid Clare Boothe Luce went to Versailles to see him. One of his aides, Major General Wilton B. "Jerry" Persons, warned her not to ask the general about his religion. He would take off her head.

The first few minutes of Mrs. Luce's conversation went well. "He was always very relaxed and easy with me," she said. Mrs. Luce mentioned the unmentionable almost immediately. "I said to him, 'Ike, there seems to be one problem, and that's the question of your religion.' "

Jerry Persons had been right. Eisenhower was furious. His face reddened; he jumped out of his chair and, according to Mrs. Luce, said, "Now, I hope you're not going to bring *that* up. . . . Everybody on my staff has been after me to say what my religion is and what my church is. Now . . . I consider a man's faith is a matter between himself and God."

Unfazed, Mrs. Luce bore in on him: "Oh, but you do take it up with God, these questions?" Of course he did, Eisenhower told Mrs. Luce. How could he have gone through the war and ordered all that fighting, all those deaths, unless he asked God to support him and make him feel that what he was doing was right. But people kept asking him what his church was. "I would have nothing but contempt for myself if I were to join a church in order to be nominated president of the United States."

Well, said Mrs. Luce, wasn't the real question what kind of president he'd make if he didn't go to church on Sundays? "Think of all the little boys and girls all over the United States . . . pried out of bed in the morning by their parents and being told they should go to church . . . replying to their parents, 'Why do I have to go to church? The president of the United States has never gone to church and refuses to go to church.'

" 'Oh, boy,' he said, 'I never thought of that.' "

Mrs. Luce persuaded him he should go with Mamie to the Presbyterian church in Paris the following Sunday, and he did. He continued to attend the Presbyterian church wherever he was before and during the campaign of 1952. During the campaign—Mrs. Luce didn't remember where or how she, the candidate, and her husband, Henry, met, but they did—Eisenhower confessed that he'd never been baptized, but much as he wanted to be, he was damned if he was going to be baptized before the election.

There was much talk of God and religion and high moral principles during the 1952 crusade for the presidency, but Eisenhower did not get baptized. That happened on February 1, 1953; the service was performed by The Reverend Edward Elson, pastor of the National Presbyterian Church. Ida would have been pleased although she would probably have wished it hadn't taken her middle son sixty-three years to get around to it.

Robert Clark, a Washington correspondent, said, "Elson was very proud of the fact that Eisenhower had chosen to be baptized in his church and immediately prepared a press release that Eisenhower was unaware of. It said in essence that President Eisenhower throughout his military career was bouncing around from one military post to another and had never before had a chance to stake down his faith. Today he has been taken into membership at the National Presbyterian Church. The story was widely played in the press the next day, and James Hagerty, Eisenhower's press secretary, was summoned to Eisenhower's office. Eisenhower, who did not want any publicity about his religion, was livid. He told Hagerty to tell Elson, 'You tell that blankety-blank Elson if he ever again puts out a press release or does anything to inspire publicity about my going to church I will never go back to his blankety-blank church again!' "

Eisenhower continued to attend church with some regularity while he was president, thus setting a good example to the nation's youth, most of whom, like himself, would perhaps have preferred to sleep on Sunday morning. Eisenhower used to say that one of the best things about Sunday morning was that you could just roll over and go back to sleep.

John Bird, a campaign speech writer, remembered that one Sunday he went to the Doud house in Denver to work with the presidential candidate on a speech outline. "We were right in the middle of it when Mamie came down and said, 'Ike, it's time to go to church.' He said, 'Well, I think maybe I had better skip. We have this important speech.' She said, 'Well, if that's the way you feel about it . . . !' She flipped around and started up the stairs. And Ike gave us a kind of agonized look and he got up and said, 'Well, that's all, boys.' "

In a calmer moment, in an interview in her hometown newspaper, after Eisenhower's death, the former first lady said, "Ike was a religious man though he didn't feel it was necessary to go to church all the time. Sometimes, the last thing I'd hear him say in bed at night was, 'God, I did the best I could today.' And then he'd fall asleep."

His brother Roy's widow, Edna, said of Eisenhower, "There is something about him that enables him to lay down his troubles. . . . He can go to bed and sleep and let God take care of his troubles."

During his eight years in the White House, Eisenhower continued to talk about God a good deal; he even worked His name into presidential budget messages. Surely He did not want this blessed nation to go into debt. TRB in The New Republic analyzed one of Eisenhower's speeches, counting "eight mentions of Him, two 'Divines,' and two 'Crusades,' 'spirit' or 'spiritual' eight times and 'principle' (either singular or plural) sixteen times."

In his thesis on Eisenhower and the religious leadership of the president, James David Fairbanks wrote, "The best recent example of a president who well understood the essentially religious demands of his office and who was successful in carrying them out was Dwight Eisenhower. Eisenhower was not particularly sophisticated in either theology or sociology, but he seemed to possess an intuitive understanding of society's need for meaning and direction, a need that could only be fulfilled by appeals to transcendent values."

Arthur Krock probably spoke for most people in this country when he wrote in the New York Times, "The President effortlessly reveals the simple faith, the clean mind, the temperate and courageous parts of speech in controversy that especially appeal to the American people in their first magistrate." TRB also said that Eisenhower was "the wistful exponent of a simpler and lost America."

* ★ ★ *

MARCHING THROUGH GEORGIA

On May 22, 1944, two weeks before the largest invasion in history was launched on his order, Eisenhower wrote his brother Edgar, if they gave me some time and didn't check too closely on fact I could make you and me look like Tom Sawyer and Huckleberry Finn. Which one would you rather be?

Edgar was never Huck Finn, that happy outlaw; nor was he Tom Sawyer. Just as there was a good deal of Ida in Dwight, there was a good deal of David in Edgar. Dwight was not an outlaw either, but, like Tom, he was always aware "that it was not a hollow world." And he seemed to have been born with the knowledge of how to get people to do what he wanted them to do, what Twain called Tom's "great, magnificent inspiration . . . namely, that in order to make a man or a boy covet a thing, it is only necessary to make the thing difficult to attain." Eisenhower, like Tom, always knew how to make the Ben Rogerses of the world whitewash Aunt Polly's fence.

The Eisenhowers were poor when he was a boy, but Ike insisted that he was never aware of it. I once asked Wes Jackson, Nettie Stover Jackson's son, if he believed that, and he said, "Of course, I believe it." I said, "Surely it must have been difficult, even humiliating for him—wearing his mother's high-buttoned shoes to school." Jackson said he had experienced the same sort of thing. "You don't worry too much about what other people think. It was embarrassing, but it wasn't something that I felt I had a right to be embarrassed about. In fact, it made for me a sense of pride. I think the Eisenhower brothers, except perhaps for Edgar, had the same sort of thing. The standards of the family overrode the standards of the community. . . . The Eisenhower boys were healthy and they were not poor in spirit."

Eisenhower's feelings in the matter never changed. He never really understood what most people considered the necessity in the United States not only of feeling compassion for the poor but helping them. After the presidency he said, "We would have sneered at anybody who would have said we were underprivileged. We didn't know those words in those days, anyway. If either the town, or the county, or the government [the federal government] had tried to give us a dollar in those days, why everybody in town would have been out-raged . . . people were expected to work to take care of themselves."

Edgar never forgot the poverty of his youth. He said, "None of us ever had a new suit of his own until he was able to go out and earn it. Father's suits made over went right down the line." Even the boys' underwear was made out of David's, and "it was red," Edgar told his cousin Nettie. "Sometimes," he said, "[our] long stockings had holes in them and the long red underwear showed through." The other kids at school sometimes called the Eisenhower brothers the "red devils."

Edgar also had a vivid memory of shoes in his childhood. "I often wore my mother's old shoes, brogans, that buttoned clear up to the ankles. They weren't so bad. At least they didn't have high heels. You can imagine the reverence we had for new shoes. There was a special sort of importance about them, in our young eyes, and we had a real respect for them. I was wearing a pair of mother's old button-down shoes one day and met the son of one of the town's wealthy families. He was a pudgy youngster, spoiled, and he made fun of my shoes. I said nothing, so, to get my goat, the fat little kid tried another approach. It had been raining and there was a big mud puddle in the road. He was wearing a new pair of shoes. He walked up to the edge of the puddle, looked back at me to make sure I was watching, then he marched straight through the water. I was stunned. . . . Shoes were damned holy things to me. I resolved on the spot that some day I, too, would be in a financial position to buy new shoes, but even then I doubted if I would ever walk through mud puddles in them." Edgar said, "Being a little older than Dwight, I was perhaps more sensitive than he was . . . because I mentioned my feeling to him many years later and he said he never had any such feeling. I never outgrew it, however."

As far as it is known, Eisenhower did not, in his youth, resolve as his brother Edgar did, that some day he, too, would be in a position to buy new shoes, but in 1954 he was listed as "Among the most shoe-conscious folks ever to occupy the White House" by the publication of the leather and shoe industry. According to the article, Eisenhower had at least eighteen pairs of shoes, which included dress shoes, casuals, loafers, golf shoes, and lounging slippers, and, "No one can ever expect to find him with a hole in his shoe." (Unlike Adlai Stevenson.)

Edgar and Dwight were born a year and nine months apart. Edgar, the elder, was always the better athlete, and in adult life, the richer. In a letter dated April 10, 1944, Ike wrote to Edgar:

I am reminded that in everything in which we tried to excel as boys you were always vastly my superior. You could run faster, hit better, field better, tote the football better, and do everything except beat me at shotgun shooting. So it looks to me that if you have to tell many stories about our boyhood . . . you would always have to tell them that I was just the tail to your kite. . . . You and I were more closely associated than I was with any other individual, including any of the other brothers.

Both boys attended Lincoln Elementary School, across the street and about 100 yards from their house. Edgar, because he was older and stronger, was known as "Big Ike"; Eisenhower was "Little Ike." "The name was natural," Edgar said, "because the name Eisenhower was entirely too long for anybody to put up with." When Edgar left Abilene, he left the name "Ike" behind him, but when his younger brother went to West Point, his classmates referred to him as "Ike." The name stayed with him all his life and was likely the most famous nickname of this century. Sometimes in foreign countries it came out "Eek" or "Ik," but it was almost always said with affection. Ida called him Dwight, because she did not believe in nicknames. Edgar must have felt that there was room for only one Ike in the family, and that was he, Edgar. He was one of the few other people in the world who always referred to his brother as Dwight.

His fourth-grade teacher, Mrs. Van Ostrand, remembered, "Dwight was always full of fun—jolly and mischievous. Both he and Edgar were average students, although Dwight excelled in history." He loved ancient history, particularly Greek and Roman. That interest continued throughout his life, and when, for example, he was in North Africa as commander in chief of the Allied forces there, he took time off to visit the ancient city of Timgad in Algeria; the city had been founded in A.D. 100 by the Roman emperor Trajan. As a schoolboy in Abilene, however, he frequently neglected his other subjects to read ancient history, and sometimes he neglected chores as well. As a result, Ida sometimes locked the history books in a closet.

One day he discovered the key to the closet, and after that whenever his mother went shopping or was working in the garden he would unlock the closet and get out the books. He particularly was interested in ancient battles such as those of Marathon, Salamis, Zama, and Cannae. Remembering those days, after the presidency, he said, "I could never seem to get it into my head that all these things had happened two thousand years earlier—or that possibly I would be better advised to pay at least a little attention to current rather than ancient affairs."

The dates of the various battles were important to him, and in 1967 he said, "There are many unrelated bits of information about Greece and Rome that stick in my memory. Some are dates. I have a sort of fixation that causes me to interrupt a conversation when the speaker is one year off, or a hundred, in dating an event like Arabela." He also stopped reading certain books when the writer made a mistake in chronology. He said of his reading as a boy, "I read history for history's sake, for myself alone. . . . Except for my extracurricular reading of history, no school subjects set me afire until we took up the study of geometry [during high school].

"In grammar school spelling was probably my favorite subject. . . . I had learned that a single letter could make a vast difference in the meaning of a word. . . . I became almost a martinet about orthography, inclined to condemn as beyond redemption a man who confused principal with principle and the like. . . . Arithmetic came next because of the finality with which an answer was either right or wrong."

Later he was to describe himself in those days as either "a lackluster student or involved in a lackluster program." In a letter on October 30, 1947, to Pelagius Williams who had taught him history at Abilene, Eisenhower wrote:

I have often felt, as I look back, that you and your associates must have had a trying time with a group of healthy, vigorous Kansas boys who were far more interested in football and shooting rabbits than they were in the knowledge and sense that you tried to cram into our heads.

Eisenhower was more interested in baseball. He said, "Baseball players occupied a niche apart from all other human beings. For half the year their names were featured in the daily paper. They made immense sums of money—three, four, five thousand dollars, and all for doing what was fun."

In 1951 Milton and Ike were both offered large sums of money to participate in professional baseball; both were offered the prestigious and profitable position of baseball commissioner at a salary of $75,000 a year; both turned the job down. In a letter to Swede Hazlett, his friend from Abilene, Eisenhower wrote:

My refusals to consider the matter have been both prompt and emphatic. This has not meant that I was insensible to the compliment implicit in the suggestion, but it has meant that it is not the kind of work in which I felt it best for me to engage. . . .

I feel impelled to pause for a moment to make an observation concerning the topsy-turvey happenings that we accept, today, almost as commonplace. If, some forty-five years ago, anyone had suggested to two barefoot boys of the Dickinson County region that they would each one day casually— without even a second thought—dismiss an opportunity to take over an honorable and decent job paying $75,000 a year, the entire countryside would have, at that moment, broken into a very hearty laugh, not to mention a few snorts of derision. But that's the way it goes! I am not so terribly much richer in money than I was in those days (even though we had nothing then) but I guess that, in certain respects, my sense of values has changed considerably.

Later he applied terms of baseball to warfare. "We are playing in the big leagues," was one such comment. "You can't hit a home run by bunting. You have to step up there and take your cut at the ball." As president he confessed "to a boyhood hero worship for Honus Wagner, shortstop for the Pittsburgh Pirates, who led the National League in batting for eight years, and batted over .300 for seventeen consecutive years."

Most of the children at Lincoln Elementary School came from families rather like the Eisenhowers. Except for the carnival children. The Parker family moved to Abilene around the time David Eisenhower and his family returned there from Denison. The Parkers began with a merry-go-round factory. They imported skilled workmen from Germany to carve wooden horses and make organs. In 1900 the Parkers got into the carnival business; the Parker carnivals were known throughout the Middle West including, in my youth, Marshalltown, Iowa.

Carnival personnel spent the winter in Abilene in boxcars. The children of the carnival families went to Lincoln, which was only a block from where they lived. The town boys resented the carnival boys as too wild, rough, and dirty.

John Long, a grade-school classmate of Eisenhower's said that many fights took place on the school grounds during recess. "One of the largest of the carnival boys brought a long iron chain to school, and at recess he would take the chain and swing it around his head, walking toward us, daring anyone to try to take the chain away from him. He ruled the roost until one day Ike decided to tackle the boy.

"Dwight decided to use strategy," Long said. "Instead of walking in on the lad, as the boy walked toward him, he waited until the chain had swung away from him. Then Dwight dived for the carnival boy's legs and dumped him to the ground, grabbing the chain away from him. I tell you, Dwight became a hero to us boys from then on."

Remembering those boyhood fights, Eisenhower said, "The boy that was always ready to defend his rights, unconsciously assumed and was accorded a certain amount of superiority—he was 'let alone!'—almost the highest tribute that one could attain. Both the boy and his associates sensed that—though it was not talked about. Nobody paid any attention to it. Fighting and wrestling were standard games. They were pitting . . . strength and skill against each other in a competitive spirit."

According to Henry Jamieson, "Ida didn't approve of the boys fighting, but she didn't scold them too hard. Eisenhower came home one night with a swollen face. 'Was it a fair fight?' she asked. He said, 'Yes, it was a fair fight, and neither of us won.' She applied a cold pack to his face and that was all there was to it."

One time, according to Milton, "My brothers got into a lively fight in the house and a neighbor who was there tried to intervene. . . . Mother, without even looking at the two sons, said to the neighbor, 'Let them alone. Let them solve their own problems and things will be better.' "

Hungarian journalist Bela Kornitzer interviewed Eisenhower for a book he was writing, *The Great American Heritage: The Story of the Five Eisenhower Brothers.* "When I asked the President about his father's attitude toward his fighting, a faint smile appeared at the corners of his mouth, and he commented that his father never liked to see one of his sons licked by playmates. He preferred it the other way around. His father, he said, 'was a firm man who expected firmness to be a trait of his sons; . . . a man who much preferred his sons to be the winners.' "

The fraternal fights between Edgar and Dwight were more intense, and Edgar always won. Earl said, "There was no malice at all in those fights . . . but they sometimes fought until there were black eyes, and hair and everything else flying. But five minutes later they'd be out playing as calmly as you please. We were in close quarters practically all the time, and we were close together. . . . There's going to be arguments under those circumstances, and we had them. The older boys always won, because they were bigger. . . . The Eisenhowers learned how to defend themselves at all times, to never admit defeat and to never admit anyone was any better—no matter how good they were."

Edgar said, "When I look back on our youth, I don't remember that Dwight played with any other brother as much as he did me; but the occasion for a fight could be the simplest kind of thing. For instance, we might be walking with one another and he would try to trip me . . . he might take something away from me that I didn't think he was entitled to; then another fight was on. . . .

"We argued about everything. . . . If you look out the window and see that little patch of clouds over there, we would argue whether or not it would rain before the day was over. We would argue about why the world revolves in the way it does. We would argue about every conceivable subject that anybody brought up."

Whenever a reporter would say to President Eisenhower, "Your brother Edgar doesn't agree with you," he would reply, "We haven't agreed on anything since we were five years old." Even on trivial matters, they were still at odds. In 1949, when Eisenhower was president of Columbia, he made a speech to the American Bar Association in St. Louis. All the brothers were there. According to Milton, when reporters asked what had been the last time the brothers were together the following colloquy took place:

Edgar: "In June 1947 at Boulder Junction."
Eisenhower: "No, it was July."
Edgar: "I'll take that bet."
Reporter: "General, are you sure you're right?"
Eisenhower: "No, but I'm sure Ed is always wrong."

It happened that Ike was right. The last time was July 17, 1947.

In 1958 when Earl Eisenhower was asked whose side he took when brothers Edgar and Dwight disagreed he replied, "For sixty years now, no Eisenhower has agreed with any other Eisenhower." To agree, "I'm afraid we'd have to be in heaven."

Most of Ike and Edgar's fights ended up in a wrestling match, and Eisenhower later commented that he found Edgar's "arm twisting and toe holds not only painful but mortifying." He was determined to get even with him some day.

In the summer of 1913, when Eisenhower returned to Abilene from West Point for a two-month vacation, he felt confident he could lick Edgar and sent him a challenge: "anything he wanted, wrestling, boxing, barefisted or with gloves—or plain rough and tumble. Even then he got the best of me. In his reply from wherever his summer job had taken him, he wrote, 'I would be glad to meet you with boxing gloves at forty paces.' And he did not come home that season so I was robbed of sweet revenge."

Edgar didn't see Dwight from the time the latter went through Ann Arbor on his way to West Point until about fifteen years later at a family reunion in Abilene. "The first thing he said to me when he got off the train at night," Edgar said, was 'Fellow, I have been waiting for a long time to give you a whipping and this is it.' " Edgar said he finally talked him out of it.

The fights between Edgar and Dwight were never fought to establish any particular principle, "it was just another way of getting rid of excess energy," Edgar said. "The fights were not the kind you read so much about, like the one between Dwight and Wes Merrifield, the north-side champion." Lincoln

School went only up to the sixth grade. Seventh and eighth grades were at Garfield School. Everybody in town went there before entering high school, and Garfield was in enemy territory for the Eisenhower brothers, the north side of the railroad tracks.

According to John Asper, a boyhood friend, "There was antagonism between the north-side and south-side children—plenty of it. We wouldn't let the north-side kids south of the Union Pacific track if we could catch them and they wouldn't allow us north of the track. We could go up town, but if we got north of town, why it meant a fight."

The fight with Wes Merrifield, the north-side champ, took place soon after school started in 1903; Eisenhower was thirteen. Just who challenged whom is not now known. Merrifield wasn't any taller than Eisenhower, but he was a lot heavier, stronger, and very fast. Eisenhower was slight and possessed of ordinary strength and speed. There was no question among the spectators as to who would win, only how long Eisenhower would stay on his feet.

Kenneth Davis, in a 1945 article in the *New York Herald-Tribune*, called "Eisenhower's Toughest Fight," wrote: "Eisenhower kept boring in, hitting as hard and often as he could and taking all the punishment that Merrifield could give him. He took far more than he gave. Merrifield, with his superior strength and speed, landed innumerable solid blows on Dwight's face and body. Before long it seemed obvious that Dwight was beaten. His face was bruised and bleeding. Both eyes were blackened and swollen. His breath came in hoarse gasps through his swollen lips. . . . But it was here, where most fights end, that the amazing part of the fight began. Dwight wouldn't yield. Despite his weariness and the tremendous punishment he had taken, he kept coming in."

When Davis wrote of this same fight in *Soldier of Democracy*, it became longer, more dramatic and a lot less realistic. "The Eisenhower-Merrifield fight lasted two hours. After the first hour passed the crowd watched in hushed awe. . . . Both boys had long since fought beyond the limits of a purely physical courage and had entered the realm of moral stamina. . . . Behind the rim of the prairie far to the west the sun went down. Shadows blurred together to form an all-pervasive dusk. Neither boy had yielded. Neither had any intention of yielding. . . .

"At home Dwight barely managed to stagger up the stairs to his room. . . . Three days went by before he was able to return to school." No wonder after reading the Davis account in the biography Eisenhower commented, "Overdramatized—but it was tough." In response to questioning in 1954 concerning the fight, Eisenhower said he could not remember "exactly why the scrap took place," but with respect to the estimate of the time involved, his only response was "too long."

John H. "Six" McDonnell, a boyhood friend, said it was "the greatest fight I ever saw." G. M. "Bud" Hoffman, another boyhood friend said that he had "never seen anything like it since, and never expected to."

In his detailed account of errors and exaggerations in *Soldier of Democracy*, Eisenhower made no comment on what Davis said about what happened when he came home to Abilene from West Point in the summer of 1913, which would seem to indicate that it was accurate. Davis reported that Eisenhower said to Merrifield, "You remember that fight we had?" Merrifield said, "Do I? I'll never forget it." "Well, we called it a draw at the time," said Eisenhower. "At least I did. But I had far the worst of it. I'm willing to admit now that you really licked me then. . . . What I want to know is, do you have any ambitions now?"

According to Davis, Merrifield looked at the broad shoulders, thick chest, and muscular arms that Eisenhower had developed at the Point, and said, " 'Ike, I'm the most unambitious man in town!' "

Eisenhower also had no comment on what Davis said about his temper as a boy. "On one occasion . . . he flared up in sudden violent anger against Arthur over some trifling incident. A brick was lying at his feet, and before he had regained control of himself he had seized that brick and flung it with all his might at the head of his eldest brother. Fortunately, Arthur managed to duck in time. Dwight had fully intended to hit him."

Ida Eisenhower later commented to her grandson John that "Dwight, the third child, was the most difficult of all." From an early age he had exhibited a mind of his own and a terrible temper. More than once, she told John, he bloodied his head by beating it against a tree when things failed to go his way.

Eisenhower was more than mildly angry the Halloween when he was ten and not allowed to go trick or treating with Arthur and Edgar. His parents considered Dwight too young to go, and permission was denied. "I bellowed and did everything to get them to change their mind," Eisenhower said. "And off went my two brothers. Now, this is the last thing I remember about that incident until my dad had me by the collar and I was really getting a tanning. He had found me in the stump of an apple tree. For some reason I guess I thought the apple tree was to blame and I was there crying as hard as I could, beating the apple tree with my fists. After he got through with his punishment he says, 'Young man—to bed.' So, to bed I went."

About a half hour later his mother came into the room with salve for his hands and a few words paraphrased from the Bible. "He who conquereth his own spirit is greater than he who taketh a city." There was surely not much comfort in that, but Eisenhower, who liked telling the story, said that Ida added, "when you really got so angry at someone that you couldn't help yourself, that you weren't hurting them at all, they didn't even know it. So you are hurting yourself. In the meantime she began to wash my hands, put a little salve on them, and wrapped them up, and I think that was one of the most important moments of my life."

What did Eisenhower learn from these pious words of his mother? He told people they had taught him to curb his temper, but those who knew him well were skeptical. Bernard Shanley, special counsel to Eisenhower when he was president, remembered a time at Camp David when Eisenhower told with satisfaction how his mother had taught him to curb his temper. And Shanley, not always the most diplomatic of men, said, "Boy, what a lousy job she did."

Eisenhower was furious.

Shanley said, "It's amazing how few of the White House staff knew what a fearful temper he had. Tom Stephens, special counsel and appointments secretary, remembered that a stupid mistake by a staff member would infuriate him, and he would say, 'Well, I allow my staff members to make one mistake a year.' "

Discussing Eisenhower's temper in an article, "The President's Pet Peeves," Jack Anderson and Fred Blumenthal wrote, "He is seldom irked by the big problems he faces every day. But some minor irritation is apt to trigger his temper. . . . Then his face clouds, his eyes turn cold; his jaw stiffens. He explodes audibly, the words flying like shrapnel. Sometimes he flies out of his chair. But the outburst is short and quickly forgotten. . . .

"He expects his subordinates to be concise and accurate. If they ramble, he becomes irritated. He prefers oral briefings and insists on boiled-down reports. Said one aide, 'If you want to commit suicide bring him a lengthy report and call it a brief.'. . .

"When a presidential storm is brewing, Ike flashes danger signals that White House aides now recognize. If he wipes his hand slowly across his mouth or fidgets with the cap on his front tooth, it's a sign his patience is waning. Sometimes he jumps up and starts pacing the floor (although he does this too when in deep thought.)"

Kevin McCann, one of his oldest friends, said, "He used to get impatient at times because, after all, he always had too much to do and too little time. But essentially and enduringly with the people associated with him, he was a kind, considerate, thoughtful man, even a gentleman when their faults became most obvious." Another friend, General Al Gruenther, who was one of Ike's favorite bridge partners, said, "when he did blow it was never personal, it was blowing on a question of principle, that something should have been done . . . it was over in a matter of minutes."

John Gunther, in his book *Eisenhower: The Man and the Symbol*, said, "When he loses his temper he is apt to spell out words in an angry yell. He will say, 'Where is that memo? M-E-M-O!' "

The anger never lasted long, and Eisenhower would usually come out of it with a smile on his face. It also didn't take much, according to Anderson and Blumenthal, to dispel the cloud. "Once, after the President had endured a siege of bursting flashbulbs a photographer shouted, 'Hold it a minute!' Ike scowled, 'Why are you so slow?' he demanded. 'Mr. President,' the cameraman said, 'I'm a perfectionist.' The grim President changed to a smiling President."

Eisenhower knew about being a perfectionist; during his entire life he not only wanted to win at everything he did, everything he did had to be as nearly perfect as he could make it—business or pleasure, serious or frivolous. *Everything*. Mamie once said that "when he found he could not control his tennis strokes he used to beat his head literally against the wall."

When it was convenient, he could also pretend to be angry when he wasn't. In 1952, in setting up certain NATO negotiations, he took along as his translator General Vernon A. "Dick" Walters. Walters said, "On the way back to Paris we stopped in Italy to see Defense Minister Pacciardi. He had insisted that the Greek and Turkish forces be under an Italian commander. Both, however, had told Eisenhower that this was out of the question. Eisenhower suddenly appeared to misunderstand something that Pacciardi had just said and I had translated. His face flushed and he pounded the table indignantly. Pacciardi, after a few feeble attempts to explain that he had been misunderstood, gave in and accepted a U.S. commander for the Greek and Turkish sector of NATO. I was greatly crestfallen as it appeared to Pacciardi that I had mistranslated what he had said and that this had provoked Eisenhower's anger. I thought that my reputation as a linguist would be shot forever in Italy. The matter of the command settled, we returned to Naples airport and took off for Paris. I was sitting in the forward cabin feeling quite glum when General Eisenhower came forward, tapped me on the shoulder and said, 'Dick, if I sometimes appear to misunderstand what you say, it is just that I need a hook on which to hang my anger,' He added with a grin, 'It worked too!' "

As a boy, Eisenhower's day on most mornings began at 5:30. Ida said, "The boys took turns by weeks in getting up at 4:30 in the morning to build the kitchen fire and put on the mush." She would then get up and finish cooking breakfast. "Dad was the alarm clock," Edgar said. "Dad would come to the bottom of the stairs and call, 'Boys!' Then we would all get up. We didn't have any other alarm clock."

The boys all slept upstairs in what they called "the dormitory." For a while Arthur, being the oldest, had his own room which made him quite happy despite the size—6 × 7 feet. But when Ida hired a high-school girl, Florence Sexton, to help with the housework, Arthur moved into the dormitory.

During the cold winter months, when the temperature in Abilene drops to 17° below, there was an old-fashioned potbellied stove that furnished heat downstairs, but according to Edgar, "Before that little potbellied stove had cooked up a full head of steam in winter mornings, it was rugged getting out of bed. We avoided cold air as much as possible by putting on our clothes under the covers, so that when we got out we weren't hit by cold air. In our bedroom, we didn't have a fire. The only heat that came upstairs was from a small register in the ceiling."

None of the boys mention what it was like walking to the outhouse those cold winter mornings. There was no running water or indoor plumbing when the Eisenhowers first moved into the house. Edgar said, "A bathtub was something we had only heard about until we were in our teens. As kids we had to get used to taking our baths in a big galvanized washtub in the kitchen. There was always a scramble to see who got to go first. No seniority was involved— only fast footwork. The water had to be heated on the kitchen stove, and to save time all around, several of us often shared the same bathwater." In the summer the boys had to cart the water from outside where it had been heating in washtubs in the sun.

In the summer, when the temperature in Abilene was 100° or more, sleeping in the dormitory was equally uncomfortable. John Eisenhower, speaking of the summers he spent in Abilene, said: "I remember once Mother, Grandmother, and I were sitting there, and there was a wet sheet and a fan blowing off the wet sheet, cooling things off a little bit. But it must have been 110° or 113°, and there was no relief from that heat. . . . It was even hotter in the bedrooms, and when Dad was living there, there were no fans. The higher you went, the hotter it got. The way they stacked those kids in when they were small was really something."

Still, despite the heat and cold and the crowding, the boys were seldom sick, perhaps in part because of the knowledge of the remedies Ida always had in store for ills. If someone got an earache, Ida would get an herb from the garden, steam it in a tin can, and lay the patient down so that the vapor from the herb would filter into the ear and, presumably, cure the infection. The fumes were seldom pleasant smelling, and if the patient was not cured, the same treatment was repeated. According to Edgar, "Another of her pet medicines was sulphur and molasses. Mother doctored us with this gosh-awful tasting concoction each spring, just on general principles. And when she felt our systems weren't receiving all the iron they required, she made us take gunpowder. That's right, gunpowder! 'Tis hard to say whether or not it did any good, but we took it just the same."

Although drinking liquor was forbidden in the home, Ida had one bottle of spirits she kept for medicinal purposes "and it was seldom touched," according to Earl, who said, "It must have been in the house for twenty years."

David, who never even seemed to try to do anything about his temper, did not like to be kept waiting at any time, particularly in the early morning. The boys hurried downstairs, and David read a Bible lesson. The breakfast would be lengthily blessed and quickly consumed. Then David would leave for work, "usually carrying his lunch," Earl said. "If he wanted a hot lunch, it was one of the boys' duties to carry Dad his lunch. Dad never came home at noon." He worked twelve hours a day, six days a week, sometimes seven. So most of the boys' association was, of necessity, with their mother.

Soon after David left, Ida saw to it that the boys did the chores, the first of which was to accumulate kindling for the next morning's fire. And kindling was not easy to find in Abilene in those days. Edgar said, "We didn't have any trees that were being cut down, and we didn't have any boxes that were being broken up." Eisenhower said, "I was a great bawler . . . I was trying to get out of doing this, and I remember a neighbor lady coming in and saying, 'Ida, what are you doing to that child?' She said, 'He'll be all right as soon as he brings in the kindling.' "

Then there were the cows to be milked, the chickens to be fed, and the chicken houses and horse stalls to be cleaned. After school there were still more chores—doing the laundry, a task that was repellent both to Ike and Edgar, particularly when Milton and Earl were babies. Edgar said, "There was a part of the washing that wasn't too enjoyable," meaning the diapers. The white clothes had to be boiled, and whoever was not turning the washing machine had to bring the water for the five-gallon reservoir that was attached to the cook stove.

But Ike did not mind dealing with the baby buggy. Edgar said, "The way Dwight managed that job may illustrate something. The rest of us used to walk and shove the buggy along. But Dwight used to lie on his back with the buggy above him. He would grab the front axle and haul the buggy toward his head. As the rear axle came within reach, he grabbed it and sent the buggy in the opposite direction. And so on, over and over. The rest of us just pushed. He figured something out."

Roy Witter, Eisenhower's cousin, remembered that discipline in the Eisenhower household was strict but not, he said, "unreasonable. When 'yes' was said it was obeyed and when 'no' was said, it was obeyed, and the word was law. . . ." Ida's niece Nettie Jackson said, "Ida was really the power behind the throne, but she'd never let on. . . . Some of the time, though, she'd tell the boys she'd have to tell their father about something they'd done. . . . I tell you they did their best to avoid that.

"Most of the time she ironed out the problems as she went along. Whatever came up, right then and there she took care of it. She put first things first." Ida also told Nettie that she'd studied each of her boys; she knew that each one was different, and each one had to be treated differently.

The Eisenhower boys were taught not to hate. Earl once said, "The word 'hate' was never used in our family, except we hated evil. Outside of hating evil, we never hated anybody. We might have gotten angry with people. We might think they were wrong. We might pity them. But we never hated them. We liked everybody."

The boys never heard their parents raise their voices at each other or disagree. It was impossible to get Ida to disagree about anything. Why bother? She knew she'd get her way. Later her son Dwight seldom disagreed and almost always got his way. His parents must have disagreed many times over many things, but they did not do it in front of anybody else. They were possessed of what is today that rarest of virtues, reticence. So were their sons. Eisenhower's being reticent was ultimately balm not only to himself but to millions of others.

Politics did not interest David and Ida; that was a worldly matter, and their concern was with the Kingdom of God. Earl said, "I remember no political discussions in any way, shape, or form. I can't remember politicians or a single committeeman ever coming into our house. We probably discussed issues—but town issues more than those of the state or the country."

But in the fall of 1896 their sons became very interested in the presidential campaign. Eisenhower said, "Everybody in school had a button. McKinley buttons, bright yellow, predominated because there were few Democrats in the region.

"William McKinley was the Republican candidate, and he was to win the election. William Jennings Bryan was the Democratic candidate."

During the campaign, there was a torchlight parade of McKinley supporters on Buckeye Avenue in Abilene. Arthur, Edgar, and Dwight decided to join the parade, not because of any enthusiasm for the Republican candidate. It was simply something to do. Eisenhower said, "Each of us was handed a torch and mine was exactly my own height. We were told to shoulder torches, somewhat like shouldering arms. Off we went. . . . We got through the parade in our fashion, with no singed hair and without undoing McKinley. . . . but my parents missed not only my first appearance in parade formation but my first successful venture into politics. . . . That was one of my first brushes with political life until I found myself drawn into another campaign half a century later."

Milton said the fact that David and Ida weren't concerned with politics didn't mean that they were "aloof from life about them. They constantly helped others. . . . Evidently they felt that if a person were individually good, society could then take care of itself."

Edgar said, "They were neighbors in the true sense of the word. For instance, many a time I have gotten up in the middle of the night when it was snowing, when it was raining, and got a lantern to walk with my mother to the house of a neighbor who was sick and needed help. I know, for instance, that many of the neighbors used to come to us to borrow little things that were necessary to complete a meal; although we were poor, we always had enough to eat. . . . Whether they returned it or not didn't make any difference. It was part of Mother's and Father's way of living."

Since there were no girls in the family, the Eisenhower boys had to learn how to do a great many things that in those days were considered "woman's work," including cooking. On Sundays Edgar and Dwight had to cook Sunday dinner for the entire family. Happily, Eisenhower liked cooking then and for the rest of his life. Ida said, "Dwight could cook anything—stew, pancakes, vegetables—and I felt perfectly safe leaving him in the kitchen. He could make apple pie and many other kinds." She added that when his younger brothers were in the kitchen, "He was the boss. He was the commanding officer then."

"He constantly bragged about his Sunday-morning breakfasts and his Sunday-night suppers," said Edgar. "He had his own recipes for potato salad and vegetable soup. . . . He's enormously particular in making those dishes. But when he doesn't have time for more complicated things, he makes an old-fashioned beef and onion sandwich, using a healthy slice of extremely rare beef and about a three-quarter inch slice of Bermuda onion, putting them between two slices of whole wheat bread." Milton commented, "If you want to drive the neighbors away, try this some time."

As his grandson David said, "He got great satisfaction out of cooking because it was a project he could begin and see the fruition of within a matter of hours. This was so opposed to the tempo of his work as president and general."

John said, "He was quite a perfectionist in that [cooking] as well as other activities, and varied his recipes quite a bit. He would cook us a given size steak a certain number of minutes on either side, exactly. But then the big hazard of the whole exercise was that when his steaks were ready, he would give a yell for the family. We might be finishing a cocktail or something like that, but boy, forget it, you went to the table and you sat right down then because those steaks were *ready*. No delay; no fiddling around about it. . . . I think he personally preferred his steaks rarer than most people do. He used to say he liked them crippled and drug in, but actually he cooked them just to pink on the inside. Very, very artistically done. And it was a relaxation for him. . . . in Paris in 1960 when Khrushchev had broken up the summit meeting. People sort of wondered, well now what was he doing outside the embassy residence there cooking steaks? Well, he was enjoying himself, it was quite a relaxation for him. Before he could enjoy the big steaks, he used to love to make vegetable soup. I remember at Pearl Harbor, when he got the news of that and had done what he could, he just went down to the kitchen and started to make vegetable soup. Steaks were the same sort of therapy for him."

In *At Ease* Eisenhower included his recipe for vegetable soup, the most elaborate and time-consuming I have ever encountered, good enough, despite the fact that I have never been able to do what is suggested in the final paragraph of the recipe, "in the springtime when nasturtiums are green and tender, you can take a few nasturtium stems, cut them up in small pieces, boil them separately . . . and add about one tablespoonful . . . to your soup." When Eisenhower was president of Columbia University, a copy of the recipe appeared in a university cookbook. He got hundreds of letters from people asking him where they could buy nasturtiums.

When Eisenhower was a boy, his father got home around five and supper soon followed. According to Edgar, "Dad expected us to be on time at the table. If anyone was late, he would stand until the tardy one arrived. There he stood, stern and immovable, his clear eyes gazing across the room." Not until the last boy slipped into his chair would David sit down to say grace.

"You can imagine what an enormous amount of food six boys would eat," Ida said. "They especially liked fried mush with syrup—brown sugar, corn syrup or maple or other kind, or with puddin. . . . This was puddin—not pudding. . . . But first about the fried mush. It was cooked in this big iron kettle, using yellow cornmeal, salted to taste, stirring the meal into boiling water, and cooking it three hours. We let it cool, sliced it, then fried it slowly. Next we poured puddin over it. That was Dwight's favorite, and it made a little meat go a long way."

Here is how this favorite dish is made, according to Eisenhower's mother: "Use odd bits of pork, ham hocks, and such. Boil, together with bones, if any, for three hours. Let cool, then grind, very fine, two grindings. Salt and pepper to taste. Brown in a pan that is covered to prevent spattering, drain grease. Add water to make meat sauce, consistency of thick gravy. Heat again and work into smooth consistency. Spread on slices of fried mush, or on bread. After each use, cover or seal what remains with grease, to keep fresh."

Puddin remained a favorite of Eisenhower's. On February 18, 1943, he wrote Edgar from Algiers:

> your tale of puddin meat fairly made my mouth water. I think if I could have a good breakfast of mush and puddin some fine morning, I would not only think I was back in our Kansas boyhood days, but would fairly tear this place apart for the following week.

And on December 13, 1944, shortly before the Battle of the Bulge, Eisenhower had a strong craving for some puddin and wrote to Arthur:

> If you can find about five pounds of what we used to call "puddin" please wrap it up well and send it to Lt. Colonel James Stack, Operations Division, War Dept., Washington, D.C., with the request that he forward it to me. With it I would like one small box of cornmeal and one small box of whole hominy.
>
> It may sound to you as if I have a nerve asking you for all this but at least I can say in my favor that I have not asked anyone else for anything

during this war. Being my oldest brother you ought to do something to take care of me!

After supper the boys usually did the dishes and put them in the cupboard. According to Roy Witter, one boy would be at the dishpan, a second at the drying pan, and a third at the cupboard, and "they would toss the dishes over to each other like a ball, one to the other." Then the family would gather either in the front room or the dining room for more Bible reading, after which the boys did their homework. Until 1905 studying was done under kerosene lamps; after that the house had electricity. When David decided it was bedtime he wound the clock on the wall. All the boys remembered that threatening sound. Earl said, "When Dad started winding the clock, you might as well get ready for bed, for that was the bedtime signal." They had to go to bed on signal, and they had to avoid making too much noise. David was far more conscious of other people's noise than he was of his own.

Often after the boys went to bed, one or more of them would quietly climb out the upstairs bedroom window, which opened onto the roof of the front porch; the trellis on the side of the porch was easy to slide down and to climb. They all learned how to sneak out and back without making any noise. It was good fun and a dandy way to defy David, and the boys helped each other to accomplish it.

On Saturdays, even though there was no school, there were still chores. According to Earl, on a typical Saturday, "We would get up early, have breakfast, then start doing the chores at a breakneck pace. First we took all the rugs out of the house, beat them, put them back in place, dusted all the furniture, washed windows, and made the beds." Finally Ida would say, "All right, boys. You can go and play."

Ida said, "When all the boys were home, each was given a chore that would take from early morning until one or two o'clock. They worked hard because once they had finished they could play football or baseball or go to the river to play."

"If we had toys," Earl said, "we usually made them. We made our own sleds out of wood . . . we made slingshots and whistles."

"Our games at that time always seemed to involve running," Edgar said. "When you are running you are exhilarated. A moody lad doesn't get out and run and play Black Man, or Crack the Whip, or Shinny. It is only a happy boy that does those things. And those are the games we played, little simple things that we could make up ourselves; they were just a part of us."

The number of games was almost endless, according to Eisenhower's cousin, Roy Witter, "everything from pouring water on each other to snowballing. . . . Anything that was common to youth we engaged in."

Edgar and Dwight especially liked to play in the barn where they would hang from the rafters by their toes or play tag on the sloping roof, daring one another to lean precariously over the edge. They would sit side by side on Abraham's old veterinarian sign, legs dangling thirty feet above the ground. They snitched eggs and took them to the river and cooked them. They stole cherries from the cellar, and on happier Halloweens, when Dwight was able to join Edgar for trick or treat, they would, as Edgar remembered, "take somebody's farm wagon apart and put it together again on top of his barn. Or we might move his outdoor plumbing to a new spot; or take down a man's fence."

Surely the most hazardous undertaking was riding the rods under freight cars. Ike told Colonel Red Reeder how he and some of the other kids would ride the rods to the next town, wait, and then catch a train coming back. Reeder said, "It was against the law in every state of the Union, must have been, but if you have been to Abilene and don't drive, you will find it is still a difficult town to get in and out of. Perhaps he had discovered the only way!"

Eisenhower and Edgar often went fishing and hunting, two sports Ike enjoyed nearly all his life. He was not just a fisherman, he was a flycaster and a skilled angler. Ike particularly enjoyed trout fishing and cooking the catch over an open fire. He later said that next to golf and fishing, hunting was his favorite sport. He had a fine collection of pistols and shotguns, including at least three of the latter that were imported—a .410 gauge over and under, a 12 gauge and a 20 gauge, which was one of his favorites. On one side of the 20 gauge was his name and five stars, on the other a wild turkey. When he was returning from Korea on the cruiser *Helena* in the winter of 1952, he spent many hours shooting clay pigeons from the fantail of the ship. During the presidency his favorite hunting retreat was Milestone Plantation near Thomasville, Georgia. He would spend three to twelve days there every year hunting quail with his secretary of the treasury, George M. Humphrey. When ducks and quail were not in season, he used clay targets.

Hunting, as he reminded Edgar, was one of the few sports at which he was better than all his brothers. He was inarguably the best shot in the family. His favorite gun in his youth was a 16-gauge Model 1897 Winchester pump-action shotgun. Eisenhower brought home snipe, ducks, grouse, and quail, and he taught Milton and Earl how to shoot, but not without negotiating his usual shrewd bargain. To pay for the lessons, his younger brothers had to clean the birds he brought home.

One day when he was home alone, he accidentally killed a chicken. Chickens were valuable, and he was glad Ida wasn't around to see what had happened. According to John Eisenhower, "The problem was to put the bird where his mother would never see it. The simplest thing to do would have been to take the chicken's remains a long way off and throw it even farther away."

It didn't take young Dwight long to figure out that the simplest way to handle the problem of the dead chicken was to eat it. John said, "He plucked it, cleaned it, cooked it, ate the whole damn thing, and buried the bones."

Edgar had his own "chicken" story. He and Dwight found a "bottle of beer in the attic of a neighboring barn one day, and curious to know what effect it would have on chickens . . . caught a hen and poured the beer down its throat. Well, sir, you never saw anything like it in your life. From that moment on that crazy old hen was the funniest sight ever equipped with wings. She never walked; she always ran or flew. . . . She never hatched any chickens."

Eisenhower's only comment about the story was "Sounds wild, but it is fact!"

Sometimes on a weekend David would hitch the horses to the two-seated buggy and with Ida and all the boys drive to a farm four miles southeast of

Hope, owned by David's sister Catherine and her husband, Samuel B. Halde-man. "Those were great days in our lives," said Arthur. "We would leave Abilene in the morning and get to Hope just in time for supper. We all played, and what a time we had. And such food."

The Haldemans' son John remembered, "When Arthur, Milton, Dwight, and all the rest came to visit, they rode the calves, chased each other through the hayloft and with ball and bat in the cow pasture played rousing games of 'One-o'Cat.' " Another cousin, Harry Haldeman, who was a year and a half younger than Dwight, said of him later that "when they were growing up he saw no outstanding characteristics in him. Ike was just another one of us boys. . . . Oh, of course, when I look back on it now, I can see things I didn't know then. He could use his head when we were just kids—but at that time I didn't know how important his brains would be.

"One time I went up to Abilene to visit Aunt Ida and Uncle Dave for a couple of weeks and they sent me to school with Ike. I guess I was about eleven and Ike was ten. Ike got me out of a scrape I'll never forget. There was a great big Negro boy in the schoolyard, and he was the first colored person I'd ever seen in my life. I didn't have any better sense, I called that boy a name, and you know, he started to come for me, and I was sure he was going to just wipe the ground with me. But Ike spoke up and he talked him out of it. He told the boy I was just in town from the country and I didn't know any better. The boy waited to listen to what Ike said and there wasn't any trouble. I was sure grateful for that and I've never forgotten it!"

So far as food was concerned the Eisenhowers were almost self-sufficient. All the boys canned. Earl said, "Directed by our mother . . . we put up 400 to 500 quarts of fruit, 200 or 300 quarts of vegetables and as many as 150 jars of jellies and jams. We also made our own soup, and we butchered every fall." They even had a smokehouse, which David had improvised from the old windmill his father had built. Earl remembered David dismantling the twelve-foot-high windmill and turning the tank, which was four feet in diameter and eight feet high, upside down on the ground, cutting a small door in the side. "We used this as a smokehouse for a number of years," said Earl. They stored apples, cabbages, carrots, beets and other vegetables in what Earl said they called their own "deep freeze . . . a barrel that we kept buried in the ground with a thick cover, and straw underneath."

The vegetables and fruit they didn't can or eat, they sold. In addition to the family garden, David gave each of the boys a small plot of land on which he could grow whatever he chose. What they earned by sale of these vegetables they could use as they saw fit. They never made much money. (Earl remembered the summer that they "raised a whole five dollars.") In the first place, almost everybody in town had a garden. But Eisenhower made a point of planting his vegetables earlier than his brothers and, if he was lucky, he harvested them earlier. He also learned which vegetables were difficult to grow in small gardens and which were the most popular and profitable. Ida said Dwight was "very industrious about hoeing and tending the vegetables," although she said, "he disliked the job of shaking the bugs off the potato vines."

The boys loaded the produce into a wagon drawn by the old horse, Dick, and made their rounds. Their cousin Nettie said one day she was visiting them and "Dwight hitched up a buggy and took me out to show me where he went swimming, and where he went skating. When we were coming back, he said, 'Now, watch.' And pretty soon the horse pulled up to the gate of a house and stopped. It was the horse . . . they used when they sold vegetables, and that horse knew where everybody who bought vegetables lived. It stopped at every one of those houses."

Edgar didn't like the attitude of the customers; it was the old north-side arrogance again. He didn't like "the way they fingered our vegetables, taking only the nice ones and paying us only a slim price. Some of them even made nasty remarks about our produce, even though I knew our stuff was as good as could be found in town. I resented this. It admittedly made me feel a bit inferior." Eisenhower said he "never suffered this way. For one thing, I set the price fairly low to start with. . . . I would show the corn. If customers said the price was too high, I would pick up my pack and go on my way." He could not remember that there were many difficult customers, although "there were one or two homes to which we'd never go—unless we had something left after visiting all others."

Throughout his life, whenever there was land available, Ike would plant a garden. For example, at Fort Lewis, in Washington, where he was stationed in 1941, he planted corn, tomatoes, radishes, cucumbers, peas and beans.

Another venture with which the Eisenhower boys hoped to make money was launched during the week of the Dickinson County Fair. Edgar said it was his idea. He and Dwight and a friend named Walter Densler would sell hamburgers outside the main gate to the fairgrounds. Hamburger meat at the time was five cents a pound, and for another nickel you could buy a dozen buns. The boys bought the buns and meat on credit at a store owned by a brother of Walter Densler. Elsewhere they borrowed a gas stove and lumber. They built a stand which Edgar said "represented opulence." But once they were ready for business, they sampled their wares and found them so satisfying they ate almost all of them. It took weeks of selling vegetables to make enough money to pay back Walter Densler's brother.

One of Eisenhower's memories of his boyhood was less happy. In fact, it was lastingly painful and vivid. He was not quite ten years old and Earl was three. The two were playing in a small workshop attached to the barn. Eisenhower had placed a knife on a windowsill he thought was out of Earl's reach, but while he was looking the other way, Earl got on top of a box and grabbed the knife. When he jumped off the box, the blade of the knife flew up and punctured his eyeball. That accident did not blind the eye, but a second accident did. While neither accident had any appreciable effect on Earl's career, Eisenhower said, "It . . . always bothered me. I was with him when the first accident occurred and if I had been more alert, it would not have happened. My feeling of regret is heightened by a sense of guilt, even though my parents never charged me with any blame."

"I don't think Dwight ever got over that accident," Nettie Jackson said. "Aunt Ida was in Virginia when it happened. Dwight loved Earl, and he felt responsible." But this was a rare shadow cast over a boyhood Eisenhower later described as "far more fun and frolic than drudgery."

If Ike's and Edgar's boyhoods were not quite the stuff of Mark Twain nor of Norman Rockwell, still there were experiences that must have been cherished in their memories for the rest of their lives.

Abilene is situated on an angle between Mud Creek and the Smokey Hill River, both of which are usually lazy streams, but when there were heavy rains, Mud Creek would overflow, and the water would flood out over the town.

Once, when Dwight and Edgar were six and eight, Ida sent them out just before noon with their father's lunch to be taken to him at the creamery. But a flood, understandably, caused them to dawdle, and when they spotted what was left of a leaky old boat against a railroad embankment, the two boys could not resist climbing in and riding down through the flooded streets of town. Soon they were joined by several other boys, and the whole group started singing as loud as they could that rousing Civil War song, "Marching Through Georgia." Could there be any more exuberant and satisfying way to spend a beautiful spring afternoon?

Later, some older and larger boys climbed in the boat and sank it, and a neighbor told Dwight and Edgar that their mother was looking for them. They had completely forgotten to deliver David's lunch. When they got home, still dripping wet, they got a good licking, but it was one of Ida's lickings—nothing much—and even if it had been a David licking, surely it would have been worth it.

As Eisenhower said in later years, "As I remember, the life of all us boys together . . . We felt we had a pretty good thing going there."

★ ★ ★

NOT AT THE TOP, BUT CLIMBING

—*Motto of the Abilene High School Class of 1909*

Eisenhower entered Abilene High School, located on the north side of town, in the fall of 1904, when he was almost fourteen years old.

His cousin Nettie remembered him as "a big boy, very pleasant. You'd hear him coming two blocks away, whistling and singing." The division between the north and the south sides of town were less important in high school. Besides, Eisenhower had already made the transition when he crossed the tracks to go to seventh and eighth grades at Garfield School.

In Eisenhower's time and place, going to high school was by no means taken for granted. Money was scarce, and boys from working-class families dropped out of school as soon as they could find a job. Of the some 200 pupils who entered grade school in Abilene in 1897, only 67 went on to high school, and of that number only 22 girls and 9 boys were graduated, but it was still the largest class to date. Of the nine boys two were Eisenhowers, Dwight and Edgar.

Milton was later to write that, "He [David] and my mother were married after each had been in college little more than a year. Neither one, then, got the university education they both wanted, but they spent a good share of the rest of their lives making it possible for their sons to get the education they themselves were denied." Eisenhower wrote, "Mother and Father encouraged us to go to college. They said constantly, 'Anyone who really wants an education can get it.' "

Of the six surviving boys only Arthur, born at the time of David's business failure, the oldest and perhaps the most aware of the need for money, did not finish high school; his father never forgave him for that. Of the five other boys, four not only completed college, but went beyond. Milton became president of three colleges. Eisenhower's formal education did not end until 1929 when he was graduated from the Army War College.

All the boys did well in life. On his arrival in Kansas City, Arthur lived at a boarding house at the same time as Harry Truman. They became friends; as Truman was later to remember, "Arthur Eisenhower and I got along very well indeed. I'm sorry I can't say as much for his brother, the one you mention that went into the Army." Arthur started out as a messenger in a Kansas City bank and became its vice president. Edgar was graduated from law school at the University of Michigan and had a very successful corporate law practice in Tacoma, Washington. Earl attended the University of Washington, became an electrical engineer, was publisher and editor of a newspaper and manager of two radio stations (all owned by his father-in-law). Roy became a pharmacist and owned a popular and profitable drugstore in Junction City, Kansas.

Seven months after Eisenhower entered high school, he injured his left knee. He was to keep injuring that knee for much of his life. The first injury came when he was racing some friends on a wooden platform. He slipped and fell to the knee. As he much later wrote, "The damage seemed slight except for ruining a brand-new pair of trousers that I had bought and of which I was exceedingly proud. There was no bleeding; instead just a raw, red spot on my knee. The next morning there were no ill effects and I went to school." That evening, however, he didn't feel well and dropped off to sleep on the sofa, in what he described as a "kind of delirium."

His brother Earl, in a piece he wrote in 1954 for the *American Weekly*, said that while Ike was delirious it sometimes took two people to hold him down. "Somehow, in his feverish state, he imagined that the big clock at the foot of his bed was the town bully. So determined was Dwight to show that bully who was the better man that several times he jumped out of bed to swing punches at the clock."

His parents called Doctor Conklin, a thin, tall man who, as most doctors did in those days, wore a Vandyke. Conklin said the diagnosis was easy. Eisenhower had blood poisoning in his leg. If his condition did not improve, it might be necessary to amputate. Conklin came several times a day. Most of the time, Eisenhower was only semiconscious, sometimes not conscious at all. But one day Conklin said that the leg *had* to be amputated.

Edgar and Eisenhower remember what happened during the illness quite differently. In Edgar's autobiography, *Six Roads to Abilene*, he says that as he stood in front of the bedroom door, "I warned: 'Nobody's going to touch

Dwight. You're not going to operate on his leg, not even you, Doc Conklin.' I allowed Doc to enter the room only long enough to put medicine on Dwight's leg and change the bandages. We always believed in the power of prayer, and we prayed as we had never prayed before."

Eisenhower said, "This episode has often been told in biographies or magazine articles. One story said that my parents remained in prayer, day and night, for two weeks. This is ridiculous. My parents were devout Christians and there is no doubt that they prayed for my recovery, but they did it in their morning and evening prayers. They did not believe in 'faith healing.'

"My mother was the day nurse and a friend of hers the night nurse and they stayed constantly at my bedside. . . . When I heard Doctor Conklin talking about amputation, I became alarmed, and even furious. When Ed got home, I called him and made him promise to make sure that under no circumstances would they amputate my leg, 'I'd rather be dead than crippled, and not be able to play ball.' . . . After drastic measures, which included the painting of a belt of carbolic acid around my body, the progress of the disease was stopped."

He was not well enough to return to school that spring, however, and had to repeat his entire freshman year. That meant that he and Edgar would go through high school together. Edgar, who had been a year ahead of Eisenhower in grade school, dropped out of school in the eighth grade and got a job instead. He stayed out, he said, until "I suddenly realized my little brother Dwight had gone into high school and gotten ahead of me." The year Eisenhower was out with the knee injury, Edgar went back to school and completed the eighth grade. They both started high school as freshmen in the fall of 1905, and the two competitive brothers were even more competitive, though what went on in the classrooms was not important to either of them.

In 1947 a high school classmate, Mame McInerney (née Riordan), wrote him. "You won't remember me—I sat right behind you in study hall—Of course, everybody in Abilene sat right behind you. But I really did—I don't remember any great thrill—and I know I never, never saw anything on your paper I was safe in using." Eisenhower wrote back that he remembered her sitting in *front* (emphasis added) of him in study hall. "In fact, I had always attributed a certain amount of credit for my scholastic advancement to that arrangement."

Edgar and Dwight were interested in athletics, and Edgar was the better athlete. They both played on the football team. Edgar played fullback and was described in the yearbook as "the greatest football player of the class." Eisenhower played right end. He was not only slenderer, but Edgar was pleased to remember that his brother was not too fast. "His chest did not start expanding and his muscles didn't toughen until after he entered West Point."

When Eisenhower returned in triumph to Abilene in June 1945, the entire town turned out to cheer him. There was a parade with many floats, but the one that got the most cheers and applause was one carrying ten members of the former high school football team, including his brother Edgar, and Orin Snider, who coached the team when the Eisenhower brothers played.

Many of these same men also had been on the baseball team with Dwight and Edgar. One year, Edgar, who played first base, was captain. Dwight usually played center field. He and another teammate, Harry "Pat" Makins, were said to "stick around the left and center garden patches. They work together and keep the team in good spirits by their talking." Six McDonnell, a year younger than Eisenhower, was the pitcher. He was a first-rate ball player and after high school played for eight or nine years in the minor leagues. Eisenhower and Six became close friends, and through Six, Eisenhower met Joseph W. Howe, publisher and editor of the weekly newspaper, the *Abilene News*, who later proved helpful in getting Ike into West Point. Howe was a bachelor, a member of the school board, and a reader of books.

The school did not furnish athletic equipment and so, as Eisenhower remembered, "Each participant provided his own baseball shoes and gloves, but uniforms, balls, bats, and transportation required outside support." Early in the fall of 1908 the pupils formed the Abilene High School Athletic Association, charging each boy and girl twenty-five cents a month. Eisenhower won his first elective office that year, president of the association. In an article he wrote for the 1909 yearbook, *The Helianthus*, Eisenhower said:

> After electing Dwight Eisenhower president, Harry Makins vice-president and Herbert Sommers secretary and treasurer, we proceeded to do business.
>
> Deciding not to play any baseball in the fall, we started on football at once. . . . We were deprived of our coach, but nevertheless turned out a very creditable team. Unfortunately, however, only four games were played during the season, not giving the team a chance to prove its ability. But for the games that were played, the students supported the team loyally, and time and again the boys surmounted great difficulties, cheered on by the fierce enthusiasm displayed by our rooters.
>
> After the football season closed, we had to spend the winter dreaming of past victories and future glories, for A.H.S. boasts of no indoor gymnasium, and basketball was never played there. But we improved the condition of the Association itself, by drawing up a constitution, which makes the organization a permanent one, and each year it will simply be a question of electing new officers.
>
> Thanking the citizens of the town who have taken such an interest in the High School Athletics, and also our fellow classmates for their loyalty to us, we are yours for future victories on the gridiron by teams of dear old A.H.S.

Lelia Picking, a classmate, said "Dwight was really interested in this association, and worked hard to keep it going in order to compete with other schools. A small group of boys were the ones that really did the playing." Attendance at the games was never quite what the players expected, but, according to Miss Picking, "these [high school] days were days that were busy, busy days that were filled with work. We had very little time for recreation."

There weren't too many places for teenage boys in Abilene to get together. Sometimes they would congregate at the Beagle & Spader Billiard Hall where there were about ten pool tables and a couple of billiard tables, or a room in the back of Joe Howe's newspaper office that he fixed up so that boys who wanted to could meet there. Howe said Eisenhower and the boys used to box in the little room he provided for them. "He [Eisenhower] was a good boxer,"

Howe said. "He was not revengeful; he never went out looking for trouble, but at the same time, if he became unexpectedly involved, he never ran away from it."

Howe remembered him as "a real boy, who associated with real boys, did the usual boyish pranks." He couldn't recall Eisenhower ever being in any serious trouble. "I never knew him to miss a Halloween roundup or any other event wherein he could expend some of his surplus energy and have a good time. I never knew of his going out to hunt up the town bully just to lick him."

According to Howe, Eisenhower had two outstanding qualities: "He was especially observant. He could walk through a plant, or a building or manufacturing establishment, or watch someone who was adept at his work and be able to tell you everything he had seen. The other outstanding quality was his ability to listen to a conversation and then at the proper time to ask questions that would bring him the information he wanted."

Eisenhower seems always to have had a remarkable ability to observe, but he worked on it and improved it as he grew older. He always saw everything he wished to see and, if he wished, he remembered it accurately. He could all his life ask exactly the right questions to "bring him the information he wanted." And when he got the information, he put it to good use.

Eisenhower spent a lot of time in the Howe office, mostly in reading out-of-town newspapers. In those days, editors and publishers frequently exchanged newspapers. Eisenhower dropped in almost every afternoon to read the papers from New York, Cleveland, St. Louis, Omaha, and other faraway places. He told Howe, "I like to read what is going on outside of Kansas. Makes me realize that Kansas isn't all the world."

Howe also had a large library comprised not only of books he bought, but of complimentary copies from publishers for reviewers. "They wanted to 'get the small-town view of the publication,' " Howe said. "The boys would come to get a certain book to get information to write some essay, theme, or thesis. . . .

"I had a book, *The Life of Hannibal*. It started out with Hamilcar telling Hannibal what was expected of him. It told of some of his war strategy. Ike got to looking at it and then later began reading it. I do not know whether he ever finished it, but my reason for remembering it was that several other students looked at it and remarked it was too deep for them."

Eisenhower must not have found the book too deep, because Hannibal became his favorite general, and in later life he often referred admiringly to the Carthaginian, partly because for much of his life he, like Hannibal, "always seemed to be an underdog, neglected by his government."

During Eisenhower's first two years in high school, while a new high school was being built, classes were held in the old city hall on the corner of Fifth and Broadway. One of his teachers said, "In those days the students received their education midst the howling of dogs, the wailing of the prisoners, and the odor of the onions being cooked for the [Fire] Marshal's dinner." The marshal and his family lived underneath the school. There was also a large fire bell in the dome of the building, and sometimes it rang while the intricacies of algebra were being explained. That was a welcome signal to those boys who were members of the volunteer fire department. They dashed out of class to help bring out the ancient two-wheeled hose cart that was also housed in the building.

Eisenhower entered the new high school, located on Seventh Street, at the beginning of his junior year. The building was quieter, perhaps less exciting, but, according to him, it "invited pride and it attracted better teachers, teachers whose professional training was commensurate with the size and cost of the new facility."

Lelia Picking said that "With the change of location came many improvements in the general school system. The different branches of studies were divided into departments, and now only teachers who are efficient in a special line of work are employed. Each recitation room accommodates about thirty students. This is a great improvement over the old building, for there we often were compelled to recite in the study hall which was filled to overflowing. With an increase in the number of classes came a need for more teachers, so the faculty now consists of seven competent instructors."

The high school was a member of the North Central Association, a rigorous association that accredited schools "which possess organization, teaching force, standards of scholarship, equipment and character." Membership in this association secured admission, without examination, for graduates of Abilene High School to almost any college in the Midwest.

Eisenhower's grades improved, particularly in history and mathematics. He ranked one of the two highest in the school in the latter. The math teacher was Minnie Stewart, who thought that Eisenhower was brilliant, too brilliant to go to West Point and become a soldier. Miss Stewart later received an M.A. from Columbia Teachers College, and when it was announced in the summer of 1947 that Eisenhower would be the next president of Columbia, Miss Stewart, who was only a year older than he (it was common to certify teachers after a two-month summer course following high school graduation), wrote him that he was the third of her students to become a college president; the others were Milton, then president of Kansas State University, and Deane Malott, president of the University of Kansas. "With such men heading universities," she wrote, "I feel education can't go wrong."

As to the subjects taught at Abilene High School, Eisenhower did not like algebra; he said he "despised" it. "I could see no point in substituting complex expressions for routine terms, and the job of simplifying long, difficult equations bored me." But in his junior year in high school he realized that plane geometry was something else again. It was "an intellectual adventure, one that entranced me. After a few months, my teachers conducted an unusual experiment. The principal and my mathematics teacher called me to the office and told me that they were going to take away my textbook. Thereafter, I was to work out the geometric problems without the benefit of the book. In other words, the propositions, as well as the auxiliary problems, would be, for me, originals. This was a fascinating challenge and particularly delightful because it meant no advance study was required. They said that for the remaining months, unless the experiment was terminated by them, I would automatically receive an A-plus grade."

He performed the same kind of mental freewheeling in the integral calculus class at West Point when he worked out a problem in his own way and correctly—also without the benefit of a textbook and without any advance study.

The grading system for Abilene High School had changed that year from the percentage grading system to a I, II, III grading system. (I = 95 or better; II =· below 95 but better than 85; and III = between 85 and passing.) For the four marking periods that year he got four I-pluses in plane geometry as well as two in English history. His lowest grade was a III in language, one of the few things at which he never excelled.

Eisenhower had troubles from time to time in school, and when he did, he asked Joe Howe to help him out. Howe said that, like many schoolboys, Ike "was sometimes of the opinion that the teachers had it in for him."

High school students formed little after-hours clubs, most of them with pretentious and silly names, like The Bums of Lawsy Lou. "Ed and I never joined," Eisenhower said. "By the time I was old enough to be a member, I was gangly and awkward, with few of the social graces."

He certainly was gangly and awkward. In addition to incurring the injury to his own left knee, he fell off a ladder while painting the barn and nearly crushed his brother Earl's leg. And while digging a cistern for Ida, he swung his pick so carelessly that it went right through Edgar's shoe, severely cutting his foot.

Most of the time when Eisenhower wasn't in school, he had to work. Howe said, "He would take any job he could do and seldom complained about the work being too hard. . . . He never showed any bitterness about having to work."

Howe, who was chairman of the county Democratic Central Committee, said that he and Eisenhower sometimes talked politics; he was sure the boy was a Democrat. He was known as a good debater in high school, and he made a speech during his senior year at the Abilene Young Men's Democratic Club; the title was "The Student in Politics."

When in 1952 Howe, then an old man living in Emporia, Kansas, realized that Eisenhower was running for the presidency on the Republican ticket, he was greatly upset and wrote Six McDonnell who had introduced him to Eisenhower, protesting. McDonnell said, "He wrote me about four times, and I wrote him back. The last time I almost scolded him, telling him to quit worrying about such a thing. Even if Eisenhower had been a Democrat when he was a boy, there was nothing wrong with him changing his viewpoint. I said if he wants to be a Republican, that's his right, and don't you worry about it." It seems likely that Joe Howe continued to worry about it, however; in that part of Kansas once a Democrat, always a Democrat. And there were never many of them.

In Eisenhower's senior year, Commencement Week began on Sunday evening, May 23, 1909, at Seelye Theatre with the class sermon. The *Abilene Daily-Reflector* the next day said:

> The class sermon was by the Rev. Dr. F. S. Blayney, and while he did not announce his subject in specific words, his address was an exhortation upon self-reliance—a self-reliance which should be based upon carefully sought out truth and righteousness.

The theme was drawn from the first two and the last verse of the first chapter of Genesis and special attention was given to these words: "And the Spirit of God moved upon the face of the waters. And God saw everything that he had made, and behold, it was very good. . . ."

You are now commencing to organize and arrange in systematic form the foundation principles which you have learned in the class-room and the balance of your lives will be spent in perfecting your philosophy. . . .

In the class-room you have secured the foundation for your life's knowledge. Study to so build upon this foundation that when the great Saturday night comes God may look upon your life work and say, "Behold, it was very good. . . ."

The senior play was on Wednesday evening, May 26. It was a takeoff on *The Merchant of Venice*. Eisenhower was Launcelot Gobbo, the clown, while Edgar played the Duke of Venice. The only thing Miss Picking remembered about the production was that it took place during an epidemic of whooping cough and there was "no ban on attendance during illnesses" and while it was being performed, "we really whooped it up." The review in the *Abilene Daily-Reflector*, May 28, said of Eisenhower's performance, "Dwight Eisenhower as Gobbo won plenty of applause and deserved it. He was the best amateur humorous character seen on the Abilene stage in this generation and gave an impression that many professionals fail to reach." Eisenhower, fifty-eight years later, remembered not only the role he played but "for once in our school careers . . . I got more of the spotlight than Ed."

The commencement exercise was on Friday evening, May 27, also at the Seelye Theatre. It opened with the high school chorus singing "The Pilgrims' Chorus" from *Tannhauser*. The commencement address was given by Henry J. Allen, then editor of the *Wichita Beacon* and later governor of Kansas and a United States Senator. Following the presentation of diplomas, the girl's chorus sang "Summer Fancies," ending the program. Eisenhower's graduation from high school was, he said, "a great event." Surely two of the proudest parents at the graduation ceremonies that night were Ida and David. It had not been easy, but they had been firm about the necessity for an education.

In *The Helianthus*, Eisenhower once again finished second to Edgar. Agnes Curry wrote the class prophecy as if she were on a trip to New York City some time in the future. At her first stop, a hotel in Cleveland, she overhears a phone conversation and learns that another classmate, Bessie DeWolf, is president of a Cleveland college and decides to visit her there. Then,

the postman had brought the mail so I decided to look over the papers. I picked up one of the large dailies. . . . The politics always interested me a little so I thought I would run these over and all of a sudden I recognized the name Eisenhower. "If Eisenhower is elected president this year it will make his third term." Then I sat wondering if Edgar really would take the chair the third time.

"Say Bess, do you know what has become of Dwight?"

"Why yes! I hear about all the great men of the world. He is professor of history at Yale."

The caption under Eisenhower's picture in that same book read "Best Historian and Mathematician." But what should and did give an indication of the future of the two Eisenhower boys was the rest of the sentence, " 'Little Ike,' now a couple inches taller than 'Big Ike.' "

In the back of *The Helianthus*, the Central Kansas Business College of Abilene cribbed from Kipling for its advertisement, "The Half of Life Is 'If' "—

"If" you had invested only a small portion of your earnings in a business college course—you would be much further ahead today. Never too late to begin. See us today for terms, etc. We guarantee you a good-paying position when competent. . . . Hundreds of fine positions are open if you are prepared to possess one.

Eisenhower did not become familiar with Kipling's "If" until later. But it is not surprising "If" became Eisenhower's favorite poem and remained so for the rest of his life. John said, "That poem was one of his watchwords. He insisted that I memorize it, especially the last four lines. Those were his favorites. He really thought that was hot stuff."

> If you can walk with crowds and keep your virtue,
>   Or walk with kings—nor lose the common touch.
> If neither foes nor loving friends can hurt you,
>   If all men count with you, but none too much.
> If you can fill the unforgiving minute,
>   With sixty seconds' worth of distance run.
> Yours is the Earth and everything that's in it,
>   And—which is more—you'll be a man, my Son.

Eisenhower was not alone among Second World War leaders in admiring Rudyard Kipling's work, and "If" in particular. The writer and the poem were also favorites of Roosevelt, Churchill, and Patton.

★ ★ ★

A MATTER OF AGE

The summer after graduation, Eisenhower worked on the Bryan farm near Abilene. Mr. Bryan and his son worked every day, dawn to dusk, and Eisenhower learned how to handle horses with independent minds, much the way he later handled persons with independent, often wildly differing points of view. He also worked at the Rice-Johntz Lumber Company; "We carry the most complete stock of Lumber and Coal in Abilene; Bring us your estimates; We will treat you right," said the ads. Eisenhower, according to Earl Endacott, "became sort of a straw boss, an under-foreman. I found checks showing that he earned about fourteen dollars a week from the company, and J. T. Nicolay, Secretary and General Manager, was one of those who later wrote a letter of recommendation for him to go to West Point."

Edgar went to work that summer in the creamery; his salary is unknown, but according to Orin Snider, a boyhood friend of the Eisenhowers, Edgar almost immediately asked for a raise. When it was refused, he offered his resignation. His boss, part-owner Elmer Forney, not only accepted the resignation, but, Snider said, "kicked him out. Literally, too!" Edgar spent the rest of the summer working at various odd jobs, none of which pleased him, and he was never one to keep his complaints to himself or to hide his feelings, and these were very often feelings of hostility toward the world in general. In that, he was like his father, a resemblance that continued for the rest of his life. Edgar was a kind of talkative, financially successful David.

If Eisenhower had no firm plans for college, his brother Edgar did. He was determined to attend the University of Michigan at Ann Arbor and become a lawyer. So he and Eisenhower agreed that Edgar would go to the university and study law in the fall of 1909; Dwight would work and send his brother what money he could. Eisenhower said, "Ed and I had it all doped out. He was going to drop out [of the University] later, if necessary, to get me started. His choice of Michigan looked good to me and I was ready to join him two years later."

Eisenhower objected to Kenneth Davis, in *Soldier of Democracy*, describing the year 1909–10 as "aimless drifting, and the stream on which he drifted appeared to circle in a slow eddy, moving neither forward nor backward." Eisenhower's annotation says: "The mistake here is that I had the firm intention of going to Ann Arbor—two years after Ed entered. The arrangement was—I was to stay out a year—working at whatever would give me the most money. I was to help Ed who, by that time, we figured would have established some method in Ann Arbor by which the two of us, with Dad's help, could go on together from there."

David had not greeted the idea of Edgar's becoming a lawyer with enthusiasm. He had been cheated by a lawyer; therefore, all lawyers were crooks. He said, as Edgar remembered it, "If you'll change your mind and go to the University of Kansas and study medicine, I'll help you through. On the other hand, if you go to Michigan to study law, you'll be on your own." Edgar said, "There I was on my own, without a dime."

The money Edgar earned that summer was not enough, so he went to his patient, dependable uncle, Chris Musser, and told him his problem. He knew that Musser didn't much care for his brother-in-law David; Edgar describes Musser in *Six Roads to Abilene* as "a very understanding man." Musser was understanding enough to take Edgar to the Abilene bank of which he was a director, where he personally guaranteed a $200 loan for his nephew. The two of them decided not to mention the matter to David.

When the time came for Edgar to go to the university, Dwight left his job at the lumber company. He said, "I knew that I could earn more money at the creamery. . . . I said my good-byes and started off over there as an iceman." The job at the creamery—"Pure Ice Creams, Sherbets and Ices and Pure Creamery Butter"—involved handling large chunks of ice with a pair of tongs.

"The rest of the hours I spent helping load the wagons for delivery of the ice around town. . . . Though far from intriguing, the job did develop muscles. From iceman I was promoted to fireman. This exalted position was a tougher but better paying job."

He stoked fires under three large boilers. "We used slack (almost powdered) coal and clinkers formed periodically. With a slice bar, twelve feet or so in length, I would push the burning coal to one side, loosen the clinkers from the grates, then haul them out with a hoelike tool while another man turned a stream of water on the clinker. In this small inferno, life lost its charm."

All his life no matter what strains there were, including those when he was supreme commander of the Allied Expeditionary Forces in the Second World War and as president, Eisenhower had the enviable ability to take short naps. Many people thought that was something he had learned in the army; it wasn't. He learned that when he had to wake up every hour at the creamery to check the gauges of the boilers and, if they needed more heat, to stoke the fireboxes. His final job at the creamery, in the summer of 1910, was once more in the ice plant as assistant engineer, which meant helping inspect the machinery and keep it running—twelve hours a day, seven days a week. It paid what Eisenhower called the "impressive" sum of $90 a month.

When Edgar returned from Ann Arbor in June 1910, his stories about the campus, most of them exaggerated, made it sound like an earthly heaven, and Eisenhower was more than ever anxious to go in the fall of 1911. The university had a good football team, which made it even more desirable.

But that summer he became an even closer friend of Everett Edward Hazlett, Jr., a north-side boy, the son of a doctor and druggist, who was blond, mild-mannered, smart and shy. Everybody called him "Swede," and he became the first of those, outside Eisenhower's immediate family, who found him without flaw; Hazlett never changed his mind either.

He later said, "Ike was somewhat more than a year older than I, and lived in a different part of town, so we went to a different grammar school. . . . I never knew him intimately until we landed in the same high school. Here he was not only an excellent student but, what was more important in my eyes, the star halfback of the football team—what would be known as 'triple-threat' nowadays . . . he was calm, frank, laconic, and sensible, and not in the least affected by being the school hero." John called Swede his father's "closest confidant." Eisenhower wrote, "He was always a good person with whom to 'let go.' "

Their lives roughly paralleled each other for nearly thirty years, when Swede's changed for the worse. In 1939 a severe heart attack brought his promising career to an end. That was the year Eisenhower returned from the Philippines to begin the climb upward to supreme commander. Ike repeatedly reassured Swede that success did not change their relationship. In one letter he wrote to Swede that he would

admit for the sake of argument, (though without acknowledging any sense in the proposition) that so far as the headlines of the past few years are concerned, we are somewhat like Mutt and Jeff. I've been long; you've been short. You will remember that as between Mutt and Jeff themselves, comparative elongation made little difference, either in their recurring fights or in those instances when they were both on the same side of a question. What I am getting at is, so far as the Swede-Ike relationship is concerned, there is no "big" and certainly no "little" shot.

They remained friends until Hazlett's death in 1958, and Eisenhower wrote him often after the war. In a file at the Eisenhower Library in Abilene there are at least 150 letters Ike wrote to Swede. I spoke to "Ibby" Hazlett, Swede's wife, who was familiar with the relationship between her husband and Eisenhower in later years. She said that very often during the last years of her husband's life, because of the nature of his illness, it was necessary to have him hospitalized. When they arrived at a hospital, no matter where it was, there would always be flowers from Eisenhower waiting. A year before he died, Swede wrote Ike, thanking him for

your lovely chrysanthemums . . . and I appreciate deeply the thought behind them. . . . But then I have so many things to thank you for. First, of course, is for your continued friendship and confidence. You'll never know what that has meant to me, not only during these later years, but from the time I first knew you well, about fifty years ago.

When Hazlett was dying, according to Merriman Smith, "he was out here in Bethesda Naval Hospital. . . . Eisenhower at the end of the day would sit down and write him a two- or three-page letter by hand. Those went on every single day of the week for months and months. I don't know how many. I know it went on an awfully long time."

After Swede's death Ike wrote Ibby,

I can never quite tell you what Swede meant to me. While I am glad for his sake that he suffers no longer, his passing leaves a permanent void in my life.

Hazlett had attended Abilene High School for only one year, then transferred to a military school in Wisconsin. While there, he became interested in the U.S. Naval Academy at Annapolis, and in his senior year he applied for and got an appointment from his and Eisenhower's congressman, Rollin R. Rees. But despite the fact that he had taken a cram course in a school in Annapolis, he failed mathematics in his entrance exam.

The congressman reappointed him, and Swede returned to Abilene in the summer of 1910 to bone up on math. He found a job managing the office "of a very small manufacturing concern. . . . I spent many of my evenings at the creamery. . . . We played a bit of penny-ante poker, giving him the start that ended in his reputation as the best stud player in the Army. . . . We weren't above raiding the company's refrigerating room occasionally, for ice cream, and for cold-storage eggs and chickens, which were cooked on a well-scrubbed shovel in the boiler room.

"I talked a good deal about the Naval Academy, and gradually he [Eisenhower] became interested. At last it dawned on me that nothing could please me more than to have him go to the academy with me. So I proposed that he try for an appointment, too."

"It was not difficult to persuade me that this was a good move," Ike said, ". . . first, because of my long interest in military history, and second, because I realized that my own college education would not be achieved without considerable delay while I tried to accumulate money."

Two months before Pearl Harbor, on October 11, 1941, Eisenhower wrote Swede:

> To the fact that you were well acquainted with the methods of entering the Academies and my good fortune that you were my friend, I owe a lifetime of real enjoyment and interesting work.

Though Swede himself had Congressman Rees' appointment, there was also the possibility of getting an appointment from a U.S. senator from Kansas. One of those senators had no vacancies, but the other, Senator Joseph W. Bristow of nearby Salina, did. Bristow had been the first Kansan to be elected to the Senate by direct vote instead of by the state legislature. It turned out, although Eisenhower did not know it at the time, that Bristow was a close friend of Phil Heath, editor of the *Abilene Chronicle*.

During the campaign Bristow, a progressive Republican, a supporter of Teddy Roosevelt, and an enemy of railroads, monopolies, and big oil companies, had announced that if he was elected he would appoint young men to Annapolis and West Point as the result of competitive examinations rather than the wealth or political influence of their fathers.

On August 20, 1910, Eisenhower wrote the most important letter of his life up to then; he may have had some help from Swede, but Hazlett's prose style was ornate; the prose in the letter was sparse, direct, to the point, and, with one exception, accurate.

> Abilene, Kansas
> Aug. 20, 1910
>
> *Sen. Bristow*
> *Salina, Kans.*
>
> *Dear Sir*
>   I would very much like to enter either the school at Annapolis, or the one at West Point. In order to do this, I must have an appointment to one of these places and so I am writing you in order to secure the same.
>   I have graduated from high school and will be nineteen years of age this fall.
>   If you find it possible to appoint me to one of these schools, your kindness will certainly be appreciated by me.
>   Trusting to hear from you, concerning this matter, at your earliest convenience. I am respectfully yours,
>
>   *Dwight Eisenhower.*

Eisenhower had not taken the trouble to find out Bristow's first name, which was careless of him, but more important he was not about to become nineteen "this fall." Was that carelessness, too? Had he forgotten that he became nineteen on October 14, 1909; "this fall," on October 14, 1910, he would be twenty. Did the man with a perfect memory forget the year of his birth? Does anyone in control of his faculties ever forget that? Eisenhower very much wanted to go to Annapolis, and he knew perfectly well that the ages for entry to the Naval Academy were *between* the ages of sixteen and twenty. Later, as will be seen, he had many fancy explanations for the error, and so did Swede Hazlett, and so have those who have attempted to make Eisenhower into a man without flaws—and a bore.

After writing the slightly inaccurate letter to Bristow, Eisenhower began seeing everybody in town who might be helpful in obtaining the senator's appointment, and it is true that David's habit of paying his bills on time had helped the reputation of the Eisenhower family. Most of the leading businessmen wrote the requested letter, including the father of Ike's friend Charlie, J. B. Case ("For Nobby Clothing See the New Stein-Bloch Clothes at Case's"), J. A. Ward ("Wherever you go to do your jewelry shopping, you are bound to come to us before buying"), and C. S. Crooks, Agent for Wooltex Suits and "Graduating Dresses."

He also saw Charlie Harger, editor of the *Abilene Daily-Reflector*, who agreed to write a letter, although he told Eisenhower that he doubted if Bristow would pay much attention to it; he had supported the senator's opponent in the 1908 Republican primary. The person to see was Phil Heath, the senator's friend and political ally. Heath later remembered Eisenhower's coming to him. He asked if Eisenhower wasn't afraid he'd get seasick if he got to be a sailor. Eisenhower smiled and said, "I guess I can stand it if I do." Heath promised to and did write a letter to Bristow.

In a letter to Swede on February 12, 1952, Eisenhower said:

Actually,—if you will recall—the man who appointed me was one of the earliest so-called "Progressives," Senator Joseph Bristow. Mr. Harger was in the other branch of the Republican party, in those days called the "Stand Patters." As a consequence of this situation, Mr. P. W. Heath was the spearhead of my supporting phalanx. Others were Mr. Rogers, Mr. Ward (a jeweler), the Hurds, Mr. Litts, and dozens of others who wrote letters to the Senator in my behalf. Among these, of course, Mr. Harger was included. But I repeat that, so far as I am concerned, and *as of today*, he is the solely responsible individual (except for yourself) from whom I derived both confidence and inspiration.

In September Eisenhower read an announcement in the *Chronicle* from Bristow's office saying that on October 4 and 5 a competitive examination would be given for applicants to the service academies in the office of the state superintendent of public instruction in Topeka. Meantime, his letter of August 20 was not answered. He then wrote Bristow a second letter:

Some time ago, I wrote you applying for an appointment to West Point or Annapolis. As yet, I have heard nothing definite from you about the matter but I noticed in the daily papers that you would soon give a competitive examination for these appointments.

Now, if you find it impossible to give me an appointment outright to one of those places, would I have a right to enter this competitive examination?

This time Bristow replied immediately. Of course Eisenhower could take the exam in Topeka in early October. His instructions contained a proviso that the examination would apply to both academies if the applicant so chose. There wasn't much time, and Ike and Swede began immediately to study together. Hazlett had written to the Navy Department for copies of past examinations and Eisenhower remembered, "Day after day, during that summer, we asked each other questions and then graded the answers comparing them with those given in the naval documents." Soon, according to Hazlett, "Ike's God-given brain had sped him along until he was 'way ahead of his self-appointed teacher."

Eight candidates were in Topeka for the examination; it lasted two days, and Eisenhower scored 99 in grammar, 96 in arithmetic, and 94 in algebra, the subject he so disliked. He did much less well, 77, in geometry, which he did like, and in his favorite subject, history, he did poorly, 79 in general history, 73 in U.S. history. His overall score was 87 2/8, the second highest of all the Kansas candidates applying for West Point. Of the applicants for Annapolis, he came out first. But scoring the highest in the exam did not necessarily mean a candidate would receive the principal appointment. Eisenhower was wrong when he said in *At Ease*, "[I had come out] number two for West Point. I could expect a West Point appointment as an alternate only."

Bristow decided to give the principal appointment to West Point to Eisenhower and on the 24th wrote and told him so. The letters written to the populist senator by the merchants of Abilene and by Eisenhower's friends Phil Heath and Joe Howe must have convinced Bristow that despite Eisenhower's placing second in the exam—and it was only by a very slight margin second place—he would make the better all-around cadet. His character had been amply vouched for; he was a good athlete, and his father was a pillar of financial virtue. As the principal appointee, Eisenhower had only to pass the West Point entrance exam the following January (1911) to get the appointment.

On October 24, 1910, Bristow wrote a letter to George Pulsifer, Jr., of Fort Leavenworth, who had scored highest in the West Point exam, 89 4/8, telling him that he had decided to send Pulsifer's name in as an "alternate" for the West Point vacancy occurring next spring.

Under the rules of the War Department, as no doubt you understand, two alternate candidates take the entrance examination at the same time as the principal candidate, with the understanding that if the principal fails, the alternate who shows himself better qualified is to be admitted. The entrance examination will be held in Jefferson Barracks, Mo., on the second Tuesday in January.

The other alternate was Aaron A. Platner of Ellis, Kansas.

In his letter of the 24th to Eisenhower, Bristow also said that he needed more information for the secretary of war on Eisenhower's age and how long he had lived in Kansas. The very next day Ike answered the letter. In his unmistakable handwriting he wrote:

Your letter of the 24th instant has just been received. I wish to thank you sincerely for the favor you have shown me in appointing me to West Point.

In regard to the information desired; I am just nineteen years and eleven days of age, and I have been a resident of Abilene, Kans. for eighteen years.

Thanking you again, I am

Very truly yours,
Dwight Eisenhower

Jehovah's Witnesses do not celebrate birthdays; so it is quite likely that Ida did not bake a cake for Eisenhower on the day he became twenty. He himself referred to birthdays as "anniversaries," correctly claiming that a person is born only once. But whether it is called a birthday or an anniversary, a person is twenty only once in his life, and a man known all his life for his phenomenal memory cannot have forgotten how old he was only eleven days later.

But how could he possibly write Bristow and say he'd made a "mistake" as to how old he was? One of the reasons he received the principal appointment to West Point was because of his integrity and not, as Eisenhower claims in *At Ease,* because "The man who ranked above me in the West Point examinations failed to meet the physical requirements." George Pulsifer, Jr., had not failed to meet the requirements. According to U.S. Miltary Academy Library archival records, George Pulsifer passed the physical exam for admission in both January and May 1911. Pulsifer was not accepted for admission in January because he was the "alternate" appointee from Kansas. In order to attend West Point as a cadet in that year, the candidate had to fulfill three requirements: (1) pass the written (or academic) examination, (2) pass the physical fitness test, and (3) have an appointment from any of the following: congressman; president; regular army, or "at-large" appointment. (These occur when the academy has additional slots in a particular year.)

When one of the "at-large" appointments opened, it was granted to Pulsifer and he joined Eisenhower in the class of 1915. Pulsifer, a Kansan like Eisenhower, graduated 116th in the class of 164. This time Eisenhower outperformed him; he graduated 64th. In 1920, due to a disability, Pulsifer was retired from the army with the rank of major.

In the Kenneth Davis biography, the legend-making begins. We are reminded of Parson Weems and the cherry tree:

He [Swede] urged Dwight to write to the Senator, state his preference for the Navy, and ask for a reconsideration. Dwight muttered that it wouldn't do to "look a gift horse in the mouth." After all, he had stated his willingness at Topeka to enter either Annapolis or West Point. But he toyed with the idea until, a few days later, Swede happened to mention on *re-reading* [emphasis mine] an Annapolis pamphlet [he had] discovered that one must enter the Naval Academy *before* [emphasis Davis's] his twentieth birthday. Dwight and Swede had known, of course, that the age limits for entry were sixteen to twenty, but they had assumed that these limits included the twentieth year.

Assumed? Eisenhower, that most precise of men, *assumed* something so important? He didn't look it up? He didn't make sure? Come on now.
Davis continues:

"Well, that settles that," Dwight said. "They wouldn't need to know," Swede argued half-heartedly. "They haven't any way of proving when you were born. You could knock off a couple of years and nobody'd be the wiser."
Dwight shook his head. It would be risky. At such a juncture one would be a fool to tempt fate with a lie. And Swede could not but agree.

It should be noted that in the Davis version, Eisenhower at least considered telling a lie; and it should also be noted that in his meticulous corrections of the errors in *Soldier of Democracy*, Eisenhower makes no comment on the matter.
And there the matter rested until 1952. In its April 28 issue, *Life* magazine printed the wedding picture of Eisenhower and Mamie on its cover, and in ten pages of text and pictures, most of them dealing with Eisenhower's boyhood in Abilene, there was a reproduction of the first letter he wrote to Bristow on August 20, 1910. There it all was in Eisenhower's own handwriting: "I have graduated from high school and will be nineteen years of age this fall." By then, millions of people knew that Eisenhower, whom Henry Luce, publisher of *Life*, desperately wanted to be nominated for the presidency, had been born in October 1890. And some of the sharper-eyed among the more than five million who received the magazine deduced that he would not be nineteen "this fall," he would be twenty.
A representative of *Life* immediately got in touch with Eisenhower, and he said something he had not said before and did not say again, including in *At Ease*, written fifteen years later in 1967. "I was born 14 October 1890, as recorded in the family Bible. I remember clearly that some time late in 1910 or early 1911 I personally informed Senator Bristow that, having just learned of Naval Academy age regulations, I withdrew my application to that institution because of overage."
Henry Jamieson said in his book *They Still Call Him Ike*, "There is no correspondence in the Bristow collection to bear this out, but my information is that Ike informed him in person about his age on a visit to Salina." When I talked to Jamieson in 1982, he could not remember where he got the information about Eisenhower's trip to Salina. I told Mr. Jamieson that if he ever remembered or found any evidence to support his "information" to let me know. I

never heard from him. It is quite possible, of course, that Eisenhower did take the Union Pacific to Salina; it is only twenty-five miles from Abilene, but there is no mention anywhere that Bristow and Eisenhower ever met.

Again, it should be noted that there is no record anywhere, not in Abilene, not in Bristow's papers, of Eisenhower notifying Bristow of his ineligibility for entrance to Annapolis because of age. He received the principal appointment to West Point, and he was within the age requirements. A candidate could not be under seventeen or over twenty-two years of age at the time of admission to the academy. Best let sleeping dogs lie, as Ida would say.

Swede Hazlett was also questioned about the matter by *Life,* and in a letter to Ike written from his home in North Carolina, he said:

I have recently been involved in a tempest in a teapot concerning you, and I think you should know about it, especially as I gather you will be questioned on the matter.

Did you see the pictorial lay-out in *Life* on your boyhood? I thought it was splendid—but I also immediately caught the discrepancy in your age as between the family Bible and your letter to Senator Bristow. I thought that was because I was personally interested and that no one else would notice it. I was mistaken!

Monday I received a long-distance phone call from the *Life* representative in Raleigh who had traced me up here, saying that letters were pouring in questioning your veracity, and asking my interpretation of it. I told him I felt sure the Bible was right and that your saying you'd be 19 in October 1910 was purely *a slip of the pen,* based on the fact that you were *then* 19. On thinking it over, I backed this up that night with a "Letter to the Editor" pointing out that at the time you wrote the letter the only knowledge you had of entrance requirements was what I had told you, and that I was mistakenly of the belief that the 16–20 age limit to Annapolis was inclusive—that you were eligible until you were 21, and that there was absolutely no reason for you to dissemble in any way. Also that your innate honesty wouldn't have let you do it anyway. Hence, the "slip of the pen" theory seemed to me the only tenable one.

Today the "Letters Editor" of *Life* called me, and it seems they are quite steamed up about it, that more letters are coming in every day. I was questioned further and at some length. In particular, they wanted to know just when we found out that you weren't eligible for Annapolis. I told them that to the best of my recollection it was *after* you'd taken the compets in Topeka in November. All of this is as I recall it. My memory sometimes plays tricks on me, and perhaps your memory will dish up an entirely different story. But at any rate I thought best to let you know what I have told them. Especially as they indicated they might postpone the issue for a week in order to get in touch with you.

The whole incident seemed picayune to me, but it seems that your opposition is so jittery they'll snatch at trifles to defame you. If there is any way in which I can be made the goat of this affair, please know that I am entirely willing to serve.

One cannot dispute that Swede was "entirely willing to serve."

And there the "picayune" incident can end. The "jittery opposition" failed to prevent Eisenhower's election to the presidency in 1952 and his reelection in 1956.

When news of the West Point appointment reached the Eisenhower home, Dwight's brothers were, of course, delighted. His father showed no emotion at all when he found out. Eisenhower when he was president said that David was probably a little proud that a son had received the appointment. He couldn't be sure, though. Milton, the youngest son and thus the last to leave home, said that as David grew older "he was just as proud as punch of everything his sons did. . . . I saw father sometimes break down and actually brag about what he considered to be the achievements of his older boys."

David had more regard for college presidents, however, than soldiers or generals of the army. In 1948, before Eisenhower was installed as president of Columbia University, Milton and Edgar Eisenhower were standing beside their brother as he studied his inaugural attire in the mirror. Edgar told him, "Father would have liked this. He would have liked this even more than seeing you, Dwight, a general of the army. He had more regard for college presidents."

The day he found out he had got the West Point appointment had been, Eisenhower said, "a good day in my life. The only person truly disappointed was Mother. She believed in the philosophy of turn the other cheek. . . . It was difficult for her to consider approving the decision of one of her boys to embark upon military life, even though she had a measure of admiration for West Point because one of her instructors at Lane University, a favorite of hers, had been a West Point cadet."

Many years later in a television interview, Eisenhower said that Ida "didn't like it, but she never made the fuss about it that some people have tried [to make out]. . . . She just thought that for one of her boys to go into the army . . . was bad, rather wicked. And I know that she was sad."

Eisenhower said when the letter of appointment came he told his mother "she shouldn't worry because I hadn't yet passed the final examination." All she said was "It's your choice."

Neither parent attempted to dissuade him. After all, no one had kept Ida from coming to Kansas or going to Lane at a time when such things were rare for women. And no one had kept David from going to college when his parents would much have preferred that he become either a farmer or a preacher.

Between the tests in Topeka in October and the West Point examinations at Jefferson Barracks in January, Eisenhower returned to high school and took review courses in physics, mathematics, and chemistry. Joe Howe also remembered Eisenhower coming into his news office one evening after school to ask if he could borrow Howe's Century Book of Facts. "He said he guessed he would have to do some real studying now. He afterwards remarked that it certainly helped him."

He also played on the football team again. There were no rules in those days about postgraduates returning to the game, and Eisenhower weighed 160 pounds that fall and winter. He was twenty years old—there was no question of that in Abilene—and sixteen-year-olds on opposing teams must have been impressed at the mere sight of him. "In local towns I would be called Sweeney. It was Sweeney this, get out of there Sweeney. . . . I had to work rather hard. I always liked bodily contact, and the coaches, just because I loved to crash into someone, they put me in. I was fairly fast, I guess."

High school football was rough in those days. The players wore no helmets; they tied knots in women's stockings and wound them around their heads. For shoulder pads they used the sweat pads of horses. There were no colors to distinguish one team from the other, and sometimes in the heat of the game a player would discover that he was tackling a member of his own team.

But nobody made that mistake with Eisenhower. He played a number of positions, left tackle, halfback, and quarterback. Two days after he got back from Topeka, the Abilene team won a victory over Junction City, and they won decisive victories over St. John's, Enterprise, and Salina. Eisenhower was the star of every game, and it must have been a special pleasure to him that he was no longer competing with Edgar. Now *he* was "Big Ike," and he would remain that for the rest of his life—except in the mind of Edgar, who never surrendered the title.

In addition to going to school in the morning, playing football in the afternoon, and working in the creamery at night, Eisenhower dated Ruby Norman on occasion; she was bright and pretty and remained a cherished friend for the rest of her life. They usually went to a movie together.

He also on occasion made a little extra money playing poker at Callahan's Confectionery. Joner Callahan, who owned the store, was known and liked by practically everybody in town, and he provided a place in the basement for the young men of Abilene to meet, gossip, and play cards. After Eisenhower became famous, Joner created an "Ike's corner" in his store where he displayed pictures and news items about the local hero. And when Eisenhower came back to Abilene in 1945, Joner, then mayor, presented him with the key to the city.

On January 10, 1911, Eisenhower went to Jefferson Barracks just outside St. Louis to take the physical and academic examinations for West Point. It was a journey of about 400 miles, the farthest he had ever been away from Abilene. He said, "The farm boy was completely unprepared for the sights of the river metropolis."

One night he and another young man who was taking the tests went out on their own to see the wicked city. They rode in a streetcar to the end of the line, which was on the other side of the Mississippi and in another city, East St. Louis, Illinois. It was the streetcar's last run, and Eisenhower rightly said, "Now we had a problem." There was no other transportation, and Bob Davis's instructions about how to find his way out of a forest were of no use that night in East St. Louis. "A heavy fog lay over the city and we could not orient ourselves by the stars." The two young men were in something of a panic, and when they saw a light in a building, they knocked on the door. "The door, which was massive, began to open slowly, and the first thing we saw was the muzzle of a revolver." The man with the revolver proved to be an off-duty bartender, and he put down the gun and directed the young men to the bridge leading back to St. Louis. There they took the final 1:00 A.M. car back to the barracks. They had missed taps and had to get back to their bunks without being detected; so they did what Eisenhower did many times in the four years at West Point that followed: "We got over the wall undiscovered and sneaked into the building. So far as I know, no one ever learned of our silly escapade."

Back in Abilene, Eisenhower, knowing he had passed the physical examination, spent several uncomfortable weeks waiting to find out if he had passed the written test. "Then I was informed that I had passed. I was directed to report to the United States Military Academy on June 14, 1911."

On March 25, 1911, Eisenhower wrote to Bristow, advising him he had passed the entrance examinations:

Having learned from my parents that you are again in Salina, I take this opportunity of thanking you for my appointment to West Point.

Although I wrote to you immediately after receiving the appointment last November, it's [sic] value to me has been greatly increased, since I was notified that I had passed the entrance examinations. I took the examinations at Jefferson Barracks, Mo. in January.

One of my alternates, Mr. Platner, did not pass, but I understand the other one did. I have been ordered to report at West Point, June 14, of this year.

So trusting that you will accept my heartiest thanks for the great favor you have conferred upon me, I am,

Respectfully yours,
Dwight Eisenhower

That was Eisenhower's last communication with Bristow, but in April 1945 he once more expressed his gratitude, this time to Bristow's granddaughter, Mrs. Nevie Bristow Remling. She had written the Allied supreme commander that her grandfather had been proud that he appointed Eisenhower to West Point. Eisenhower replied:

I have always felt tremendously obligated to the late Senator Bristow and had I known his address, nothing could have prevented me from writing him to express my appreciation. I merely know that the last time I inquired about him during a visit to Kansas, he was no longer there and I gathered the impression in my little town, that he had died. I truly regret my failure to follow up more closely in the matter because I always looked upon him as one of the men who helped me as much as any other person of my acquaintance.

Eisenhower was to report to West Point on June 14. A minimum financial deposit was required from each new cadet to cover initial clothing costs, and he "had been able to save the necessary amount and had enough to pay my transportation costs. By the time I reached West Point, I would have a total of about five dollars cash in my pocket."

He reluctantly had to leave behind some "possessions to which I attached incalculable value"—including the 16-gauge Winchester repeater and his "smooth-haired wire [*sic*] terrier, Flip, who had been my outdoor companion for years. . . . After I left, she adopted Earl."

David said a brusque good-bye before going to work at the creamery. Milton, Earl, and Roy said a reluctant, envious good-bye. Earl and Milton were convinced they, too, ought to and could go to the Point. Ida walked to the front porch with her son, hugged him, and went back to her room, where Milton heard her cry "for the first time." In an interview in 1943 Ida said, "The hardest thing of all was when the last one left home. Then the house seemed so empty."

Eisenhower was going off to study war, but, as he later said, at the time "no one thought of war. I can hardly imagine a time when we were so free from talk of war or seemed so far from it."

Eisenhower made two stops on the trip from Abilene to West Point, first in Chicago where he saw Ruby Norman, who was studying violin at the Chicago Conservatory of Music, which was owned by the Ziegfelds, Flo's father and brother. He said, "She and I had been good friends during the final two years of my life in Abilene. I had been saddened when she went off to the city." He spent "a couple of evenings" with her; they went to the movies and visited the "sights." He also stopped in Ann Arbor and saw Edgar, who had lost twenty pounds as a result of an appendectomy and was disappointed at not being able to play football.

The two brothers rented a canoe, took a phonograph, and went paddling on the Huron with two coeds, singing songs, possibly Irving Berlin's two hits of that year, "Everybody's Doin' It Now" and "Alexander's Ragtime Band." It was, Eisenhower said, "up to that moment, the most romantic evening I have ever known."

He continued the journey reluctantly, and one senses that if there had been a way to stay behind, he would have done so. "I had a dismaying feeling that perhaps I had made a mistake in changing my mind about joining Ed at Michigan. It looked to me as if he were leading the right life."

U. S. Grant, on his way to West Point in 1839, had said, "I had rather a dread of reaching my destination." But there was no turning back for either of them.

★ ★ ★

THE SUMMER OF 1915

The journey from New York City back to Abilene the June following his graduation must have been one of the pleasantest of Eisenhower's life. He knew that he would be a hero back home and that he would do what he hadn't been able to do at the Point, strut around in dress uniforms, brag, exaggerate, and from time to time allude to his mysterious, romantic first assignment as a second lieutenant. True, he wasn't exactly a second lieutenant, not having been officially commissioned yet, and he didn't know where his first assignment would be, but that was a summer when nobody really cared about the literal truth. It was a joyous summer that, as so rarely happens in life, lived up to Ike's highest expectations.

He said, "Returning to my home, I set out to have a good time and did. . . . I was given upon graduation a considerable sum of money—at least in my eyes. This promised a fine vacation."

He was an umpire that summer for the informal Abilene baseball league, just as he had been during the summer of 1913. The pay was the same—$15 a game, and "was even more acceptable," Ike said, "because I received no income from the Army until the President could get around to signing my commission. . . . I probably wondered what kept President Wilson so busy that he couldn't sign and get it over with."

That summer, too, Eisenhower, at age twenty-four, fell in love with Gladys Harding, twenty-three, a blond, blue-eyed girl most people thought was the prettiest girl in Abilene. On returning home he had, as he wrote her, resolved "never to let you know that I care." But with Gladys, he found that impossible. He was at ease with her and that was unusual.

Eisenhower was almost never at ease with women. Three generals who knew him very well, Mark Clark, Al Gruenther, and J. Lawton "Lightning Joe" Collins all used the same words in describing him. They said he was "a man's man." On the other hand, it didn't bother him that many of the things he enjoyed doing, cooking and sewing, for example, were considered by many people at the time to be "feminine" pursuits. He seemed not to be aware of it.

Harry Anholt, an old friend and manager of the Brown Palace Hotel in Denver where Eisenhower spent so much time before, during, and after the presidency, said, "He was all man. He wouldn't even have his nails manicured, too unmanly. He was always courteous with women, but he didn't pay much attention to them. He had great rapport with men, especially intelligent men, but never with women. He was comfortable in a man's world. I think the only woman he was ever comfortable with was Mamie."

Maude Black, widow of Douglas Black, who had been chairman of the board of Doubleday & Company, Eisenhower's publisher, was also a close friend of the Eisenhowers. She said, "I knew him well enough to see that the furthest thing from his mind was women. You could just tell. At a social gathering he'd never sit next to a woman. He'd be off in a corner talking with the *men;* he enjoyed men. He did not enjoy women."

In high school, Eisenhower had had few dates. Henry Jamieson said, "I once asked Eisenhower why he saw so few girls when he was in high school. He laughed and said, 'I didn't have any money. I didn't have any clothes, and I didn't have any time.' " Once when he did have a date with a North Side girl, Myrna Hoffnell, she stood him up. When he arrived at the Hoffnell house, she was out riding with a young man who actually owned an automobile.

Eisenhower's friendship with Ruby Norman, the young woman he stopped off to see in Chicago on his way to West Point, was platonic. Ruby's daughter, Mary Jane Stineman, remembered "Mother used to say, 'I was his friend. Gladys Harding was his *girl.* She was the only girl he ever had in Abilene.' "

After two years at the Chicago Conservatory of Music, Ruby was awarded a teacher's certificate, but she chose to take a job with Chautauqua. A clipping provided by Ruby's daughter showed that her mother was a member of a six-girl orchestra, "The All-American Girls." According to one enthusiastic reviewer in Athens, Ohio, the young women were "idealistic and delightful." Nobody wanted them to leave town, and if they had to, they must return as quickly as possible, the reviewer said. Eisenhower was equally enthusiastic about Ruby's violin playing. He wrote her from West Point, "Sometimes I go darn near crazy to hear you play, and I've had my worst spell the last two days."

In 1913 he was going to have an eight-day Christmas leave in New York City, and it looked as if Ruby's Chautauqua group would allow her to be in the city at the same time. On November 20, clearly after considerable thought, he wrote "Dear little Ruby,"

Since you sort of asked my opinion on the matter I'll tell you this. Remember this is a "disinterested opinion"—as nearly as possible. Well, then, go home on Xmas vacation. I'd sure love to see you . . . but, well, I believe you'd enjoy yourself in the end by going home. Anyway, nothing can happen which will prevent us from being just as good friends as always . . . and if you'd spend your vacation in New York, we don't know *what* might happen. All very vague, I grant you, but meant well.

Not vague at all but undeniably well meant. So Ruby spent her Christmas vacation that year back in Abilene, and her daughter said, "To repeat, my mother and Eisenhower were just good, good friends, and they remained that all their lives."

In 1952, when Eisenhower's campaign train was going through Warsaw, Indiana, Ruby Norman Lucier asked if she could get on the train to see him. A functionary on the train said no, but she did get close enough for Eisenhower to see her, and, according to Mrs. Stineman, he shouted, "Ruby, my dearest old friend, you must hop on the train." Ruby did get on the train, and Eisenhower introduced her to Mamie. Later that same day Mamie wrote her a note:

What a delightful surprise to meet my husband's old girl friend! But I do think our meeting was ever so much more pleasant than what the movies lead us to expect from this classic situation. I am so glad you were able to board the train. And wasn't Ike funny when he said, "Does she admit it?" Seriously, though, it was wonderful meeting you, one of our strong supporters.

Ruby was active in Republican politics. Her husband was Ralph Lucier, who for a time was owner of the Tip-Top Café in Abilene, where Eisenhower spent a good deal of time in his youth; Ralph had also been a football teammate. Mr. and Mrs. Lucier attended Eisenhower's first inauguration on his invitation.

Eisenhower and Ruby exchanged letters until her death from leukemia in 1967. He was unable to visit her during her final illness because of his own poor health. He did, however, send her a copy of *At Ease*, which was published that year, and Mrs. Stineman remembers her mother laughing aloud at some passages and saying, "This is the first book that really sounds like Dwight."

In *Soldier of Democracy*, Kenneth Davis wrote, "His [Eisenhower's] real passion through all of his high school years was Gladys Harding. She had blue eyes and golden hair and a 'perfect complexion'; she was notably intelligent, and she had that North Side prestige which amounted to a psychological barrier between her and Dwight. . . . Under the circumstances she seemed to him as aloof, as unapproachable as a young goddess. He worshipped her silently, and from a distance." When Eisenhower corrected the inaccuracies in the Davis book, he made no comment on what was said about his feeling for Gladys.

Henry Jamieson said, "If he had a girl friend, I'd say it was Gladys. She was very good looking. Her father, Jay Harding, owned all the freight business in town. He had horses and wagons and a grazing business. They were a pretty well-to-do people and lived in a pretty big house, up on the hill, so to speak. Her father said, 'Get rid of that Eisenhower kid. He'll never amount to anything.' " Gladys did not do what her father told her to do, and Ike saw a good deal of her that summer at the Harding house, which was actually at 310 East Tenth Street, the first street south of the Union Pacific tracks and north of the Santa Fe tracks.

Eisenhower's only mention of Gladys in *At Ease* is casual: ". . . the South Side boasted more than our share of pretty girls—Gladys Harding, Ruby Norman, the four Curry sisters, and Winnie Williams."

If Davis is to be believed—and Eisenhower let the story pass without comment—"He [Eisenhower] was in New York during the brief Christmas holiday [in 1914], and he met Gladys there. They went dancing together and to the theater, and he was proud to introduce her to envious fellow cadets. But she was not able to come to June Week, either at the end of his third class year or for his graduation."

It is interesting, though, that there is no record of Eisenhower warning Gladys about what might happen if *she* came to New York on a Christmas holiday a year after he had given a "disinterested opinion" on that subject to Ruby Norman.

Gladys played the piano, and a short time after high school, like her friend Ruby, had taken a job with Chautauqua. In the wintertime, she toured with Lyceum. After a successful season with her "readings" and "pianologues" on the Lyceum circuit, Gladys was back in Abilene when Eisenhower returned from West Point the summer of 1915. She was to return to the circuit in the fall, but during the summer of 1915 she kept a hitherto unpublished diary, "1915—The Summer Dwight Came Back from West Point."

With the letters and her diary were a faded red rose and the remnants of a four-leaf clover; her son, Robert Brooks, said that they had survived because "mother took very good care of those things; they were perhaps her most prized possessions."

Had she ever mentioned that, had things gone differently, she might have been first lady? Brooks said, "No, she never mentioned it."

On June 22, Gladys wrote, "Stayed home in evening by my lonesome. *Dwight* came down. Rained all eve." Throughout the summer, every time Gladys mentions Eisenhower in her diary, and she mentioned him very often, she underlined his name, sometimes in red ink, sometimes in black. At the beginning of the summer, according to the diary, she and Eisenhower saw each other two or three times a week. By late August, just before she left to rejoin Lyceum, they often saw each other every night. They went to movies, to band concerts, to traveling road shows. They talked a good deal, and sometimes they just stayed at home. The Harding home.

It was not long before Eisenhower's "considerable" amount of money, several hundred dollars, "was completely exhausted." His father, he said, "was an understanding man and now that I was a grown fellow of twenty-five years, instead of his giving me an allowance, I made an arrangement to borrow sums from him to be repaid after my commission. This indebtedness didn't disturb me because I was sure I could soon pay it off."

A number of letters, hitherto unpublished, were written by Eisenhower to Gladys that summer and were delivered by him to the Harding house. Robert Brooks let me read and copy them as well as a covering note his mother had written saying, "Letters from Dwight Eisenhower when we were young and happy, 1914 and 1915. Not to be opened or published in any way whatsoever until after his death and Mamie's and also after my death."

Most of the letters are undated, but the first was dated August 17, though clearly written on the morning of the 18th. It said:

Dearest Girl:

It is 2:30 am. I've been to bed but couldn't sleep. Smoked a skag but that didn't help. I'm thinking rather fiercely and can't get settled. I'll write myself out to you and if I don't read this over in the morning I will send it to you.

I woke the folks when I sneaked downstairs to get this paper and pencil. I'm using a book for a desk and my bed for a chair. If I do send this please do me this favor. Tear it up. Please let it be just sort of a one-sided conversation with you the unwilling listener. So destroy all evidence of it. I think I appreciate you more this eve than ever before. I have a keener realization of your worth and sweetness and tell you how lucky I feel I am that you give me even a thought. Maybe it's only because I realize the date of your leaving is drawing so close, but I think the real reason is that I am awake to the fact that it was awfully hard to say the seven words Monday evening I wanted to hear so badly, and then too, I have not known before how much some of the ones of the past still mean to you. More than ever now I want to hear you say the three words more than I ever have. If ever you can say that to me and if you can you will because you promised. Then I'll know that I've won. From that time on, if it ever comes, I'll know you're mine, no matter where you go or what you do, whether you wear my ring would be of small consequence, such things as promises will be superfluous and I'll know that you'll wait. Nothing can change either you or me and that some day will mark the realization of my dreams. For, girl, I do love you and want you to *know* it. To be as certain of it as I am. To believe in me and trust in me as you do your dad. Please do not think that

I am assuming to be worthy of even the faintest spark of affection from
you. I know that I've made miserable mistakes, but, girl, I'm *trying*.

It seems so many thoughts crowd to my brain this eve, I'd like to talk
to you for hours. September 1 seems fiercely close, this parting is going to
be the hardest of my life. As I sat here smoking I tried to picture you as
you sat in front of your dresser the other night.

I know one thing you thought of is what you told me for the first time.
I don't know how much or how little you do love me but I do know that
you do not care now like I dare to hope that you will. As I look back to
my homecoming this summer and remember my resolution never to let
you know that I care, except in a friendly way, I wonder how I expected
to keep it. No matter what comes of it, it was inevitable that I should tell
you some time. If you find that nothing can ever come of it, well at least
sometime when the train is late, and you're sitting in a lonesome station,
[waiting] to jump to the next dreary town, remember that your soldier pal
loved you with the purest and strongest love he ever gave to a woman,
except his mother, and loved you as a man does the one woman whom in
his most cherished dream he hopes one day to call his wife.

I've been thinking too of how I told you this evening about jealousy.
Girl, I know I've no right to be jealous even if there were occasion to be
and also know that jealousy is one of the smallest and meanest traits a
fellow can let creep into his nature. But you see, dear, I need you so. When
I think of September 1, I begrudge every minute I can't see you until then.
I keep telling myself that you have other friends you will want to see and
that I am far luckier than I ever even dared hope. That makes the need
and hunger none the less.

And now good night. If you care you may put in your diary that on the
night of August 17 a boy wrote you a note. But as far as the note itself tear
it up and you will remember only bits of it and mayhap there be some
little part of it that will always remind you that your soldier boy really
loves you. Goodnight.

Dwight

On August 28 Eisenhower, wearing his white uniform, went with Gladys to
Union Station in Kansas City, and she left for New York and her Lyceum
engagements. Either before or after she left, Eisenhower checked into the Baltimore Hotel in downtown Kansas City, and he wrote her:

Sweet girl of mine,

I know you are not expecting this. You did not sleep last night so you
are probably safely in dreamland now. I did a lot of exercises trying to get
into a sleepy mood, but couldn't sleep very well so ate a piece of your
candy. It's in my suitcase you know. But this is what I want to say. You
said this eve that you thought I didn't love you as much since I knew you
cared. Girl, that knowledge made me adore you hundreds of times more
than before. It's hard to talk or express myself now. My heart seems to
choke me, and yet there is a certain happiness too. Even while seeing you

go, I know that you love me, and Oh, girl, that knowledge is the great and wondrous influx that will sustain me through this coming year and bring me to you again, to claim you forever and always. Now sweetheart, good night.

Your devoted Dwight

P.S. Well, It's honey, honey, bless your heart.

A week later, when he was back home in Abilene, he wrote her another lengthy letter:

I came upstairs and wrote you a note before going to bed. I wrote my heart out. I left it lying in my window. It rained a little so I wrote you another Wednesday morning, which I mailed. My brother called me up on the telephone. Roy, I mean, and said there was a girl here he wanted me to meet. Miss Shade is her name. She is a teacher in high school and I put it off as long as I could so I made arrangements to meet her Monday eve. I don't want to. Dearest, I feel you don't want Ruby to know you care for me. I'll try to keep it, but it means all to me, and I spect she'll guess it. I think you're mistaken in your idea of Ruby's attitude towards me. She's enthusiastic about Earl and never gives me a thought, except as a good friend. But at least she knows that I care for you, Gladys. . . .

Sweetheart, you made me feel so good when you told me how proud you were of my love. I didn't know I seemed such a man, a real man, and I don't care what anyone else thinks. It was a week ago tonight, I was down for the last time when we went to the station together. A week, just think. It seems months, and yet I can see you as plainly as you looked up at me and whispered the words I love you so well. I'd love to crush you in my arms tonight and cover your face with kisses, and I stand in front of your picture and love you and want you so badly.

After I came back from Kansas City, I met Charlie Case on the street. He stopped me and said some awfully nice things about you and then he said, "Ike, if you have any sense, you'll be a true sweetheart." He didn't know that you and I both know that I wouldn't be anything else. He didn't know that your love is my whole world. Nothing else counts at all. If he had known that he wouldn't have given me such advice, would he? And now Sweet, Goodnight. I hope you get lots of chances to write, and when you do please put everything in. I love you girl and shall never cease.

Your devoted
Dwight.

P.S. I wish you could know how my heart swells with pride and love as I read your letter. When I read it first I came up to my room and when you said "tears came to my eyes as I read your note," why honey all unconsciously my eyes filled with tears and I simply had to stop and whisper over and over I love you Gladys, I love you Gladys. And now my beautiful lady, I'm going to read your letter once more, then I'll meet you in dreamland if you will meet me there. And there, as sometime in reality, you shall be my dearest and closest friend, my own sweetheart and true blue *wife*.

There is no date on the following letter, but it seems to have been written after Eisenhower arrived at Fort Sam Houston and before he met Mamie:

Sweetheart, there's a hop at the——[illegible, probably the officers' club] which is just across the street from my house. The band played a medley just now "Farewell to thee," "Auld Lang Syne," and ended with "Home Sweet Home," although I was just crawling into my little bunk I am so sad and lonesome. Somehow when I get into a rather rebellious mood, I don't enjoy life at all. I was so happy last summer and now it seems as though you are sort of drifting as you said you would. Your life and work I think rather forces you to it. With me it's the same routine day after day and I have all my evenings to just think of you. I live in memory and in hope. You are so desirable and lovely, and how I miss you.

I heard from Mother today, she had just heard from Edgar . . . also Ruby wrote to me. I hate to confess it, but was terribly flat and uninteresting. Well, girl, write me a letter soon and make it big. Tell me all I want to hear and make it all first class. For girl you are concerned in everything I do. Why you are all to me. Goodnight girl and what's that about forgetting? Didn't we agree we were to ask that of each other sometime?

Always
Dwight.

I've done been true my gal to you.

Eisenhower first met Mamie on a Sunday in early October 1915, about three weeks after he first arrived at Fort Sam Houston near San Antonio, and he mentioned her for the first time to Ruby Norman on January 17, 1916:

Dearest Ruby:
'Tis a long time since I've written you, n'est-ce-pas? I've really started several times—but always something happens and I get side-tracked. It's 10 o'clock now—I'm on guard—and sitting in the guard house—

I scarcely ever write a letter any more. Yes—I reckon you'll say—"well, what's the trouble"—but there isn't so much. One reason is this—"you can't always hold what you have"—my life here is, in the main, uninteresting. Nothing much doing—and I get tired of the same old grind some times.

The girl I run around with is named Miss Doud, from Denver. Pretty nice—but awful strong for society—which often bores me. But we get along well together—and I'm at her house whenever I'm off duty—whether it's morning, noon, or night. Her mother and sisters are fun—and we have lots of fun together.

Eisenhower sounded a lot more interested in her mother and sisters than he did in Mamie, but he added that if Ruby wanted to know more about Miss Doud, he would be glad to tell her, "since [underlined twice by Eisenhower] I learned that G.H. cared so terribly for her work."

The contents of Gladys Harding's letter to Eisenhower are not known, but she must have said she had no intention of giving up touring, at least not immediately since ". . . she cared so terribly for her work."

Ruby Norman's daughter said, "Mother often said that Gladys was a very ambitious woman in those days." Besides, Gladys was being very successful on the Lyceum and Chautauqua circuits. The experience had to have been an exciting one for a young woman just out of a small midwestern town. No wonder she cared terribly. As for marrying a young second lieutenant, Gladys very likely agreed with her and Eisenhower's math teacher in Abilene, Minnie Stewart, who even before he went to West Point had told him, "There's just no *future* in the Army. You're just throwing yourself away." Most people not only in Abilene but in the entire country at the time agreed; there was no future in the army.

In Abilene, a great many people later claimed to have seen future greatness in Eisenhower, but if they did so when he was a boy and young man, they were silent. People in town generally agreed with Gladys's father, Jay Harding. Dwight Eisenhower would "never amount to anything."

It would appear that Gladys never said she would *not* marry Eisenhower. But she never agreed to, either, despite his desperate pleas.

On July 10, 1915, Gladys made a note in her diary to write to Eisenhower that same day in 1916, but on July 10, 1916, both she and Eisenhower were married. Eisenhower to Mamie Geneva Doud; Gladys to Cecil Brooks.

In *At Ease* Eisenhower does not mention Gladys's marriage, but he says of Brooks, a telegrapher, "because he was in touch with distant places, [he] enjoyed unique esteem. He was the radio and television of our day.

"Of Cecil Brooks, the telegrapher in the stock exchange office—we called it a bucket shop—rumor had it that he received a legendary salary—$125 a month. If that helped to set him apart from most men, he was even more notable because during a World Series he kept his wire open to the East until the games ended. . . . In the 1906 series of hitless wonders, I remember that truancy rose to unusual peaks. Few of us felt the classroom as important a center of learning as was Cecil Brooks's telegraph key."

Everybody in town knew Cecil Brooks, and most people had known his first wife, who had died in 1915 in childbirth. Some months after the death, Brooks asked Gladys for a date; she had refused. A proper mourning period had not yet passed, and besides, she was having dates with only one person, Lieutenant Eisenhower. But in June 1916 while still on tour, Gladys learned, possibly from Eisenhower himself, possibly from Ruby Norman, that in July Eisenhower was going to marry somebody named Mamie Geneva Doud. According to Mrs. Stineman, "She [Gladys] thought Dwight was going to marry her. And when she got the news that he was going to be married in Denver, she was furious. She went on the train to Kansas City, and on the train was Cecil Brooks. He asked her to marry him and she said yes. My mother told me this was to spite Dwight. So they were married in Kansas City on June 15th."

Eisenhower and Mamie were married in Denver on July 1. Mrs. Stineman said, "Gladys *had* to be married before Eisenhower, and she was, sixteen days before." The Brookses' marriage was not a happy one. Cecil Brooks, flattered to be the older man who married the prettiest young woman in town, indulged Gladys. Since by Abilene standards of the time he was well off, they had a housekeeper. After the housekeeper died, they never again ate at home; but only in restaurants. Mamie couldn't cook and didn't; Gladys could cook and wouldn't. Mrs. Stineman said, "Eating *every* meal in a restaurant was very unusual in Abilene." Not surprisingly, through the years Gladys put on a great deal of weight.

Mrs. Stineman said, "I always thought that Gladys didn't treat Cecil very well. When he died, she went into a total nervous breakdown. My mother, who was Gladys's best friend, said this was guilt, because she never really loved Cecil, and I thought, All these years I've known these people and I didn't know the story behind it. My mother was not one to gossip, and so when she told me that much, I knew it was the absolute truth."

Eisenhower never lost interest in Gladys and he continued to write her from time to time through the years. Most of the letters are quite impersonal, however, and not of much interest.

On June 9, 1943, when he was commander in chief of the Allied forces in North Africa and already a world-famous figure, Gladys wrote him a letter of congratulations, and he replied:

Dear Gladys:
   Since reading your letter of May 10, I am having great difficulty buttoning my blouse and getting my hat so it can touch the plates on my head. I think that when I get back to the old home town I will be in the state of mind merely to hop off the Union Pacific, stand in the middle of the street, and shout, "Here I am." And unless the whole town responds on an instant's notice, I will be sadly deflated.

                                                   Cordially,
                                                   Dwight

He never stopped asking other people in Abilene to say hello to her, to remember him to her, to inquire after her health. In a letter to his mother just before Pearl Harbor, on December 2, 1941, he wrote, "I should like for you to telephone Aunt Amanda . . . and Gladys Brooks, and give them my warmest regards."

In 1958, on one of his many triumphant returns to Abilene, Gladys was standing in front of the Catholic rectory across from the Eisenhower home. According to Earl Endacott, who was there, Eisenhower "had the caravan stop while he called her over to the car. They talked for a moment, and as the cars started to move on he reached over and gave her a big kiss."

Endacott repeated what everyone in Abilene believed, that "their affair became serious and lasted even after West Point. . . . It ended in a 'Dear John' letter."

Mamie reacted to the sight of the woman who, unlike Ruby Norman, had been a threat to her very much in a manner "the movies have led us to expect in this classic situation." According to Endacott, "She was furious and didn't bother to hide it."

Gladys liked the poems of Rudyard Kipling, and in October of 1915 gave Eisenhower a book of Kipling's poetry. It was inscribed in front, "Ike Eisenhower 21 October 1915 from GH." At the time of his death, it was among the books in his library at Gettysburg.

Gladys died in November 1959, and shortly before her death she gave her son a photograph of herself looking slim, extremely beautiful, and smiling. In a note to him, she said, "The picture of me hanging on the wall in the utility room is how I looked in days gone by. This is a picture I gave Dwight when we were dating back in 1914 and 1915. . . . When we broke up, we returned all mementos, etc., that we had of each other."

But Gladys had held onto his letters, a faded rose, the remnants of a four-leaf clover, and a diary of the summer of 1915, "when we were young and happy." And clearly very much in love.

★ ★ ★

FORT SAM

In September, with Gladys gone and his equipment fund spent, Ike received orders to go, not to the Philippines, the assignment he had requested, but to his least favorite state, Texas. The Philippines were quiescent, but relations with Mexico had steadily worsened since 1911, and increasingly members of the regular army were stationed along the common border. Service there was in general unpopular. Men were separated from their families; the climate was undesirable, and living conditions were poor.

Eisenhower not only did not want to go to Texas; he didn't welcome any domestic assignment, because it meant that he had to have all the required uniforms, not just those necessary for the tropics. And he was penniless. Fortunately he found a man in Leavenworth, Kansas, one Mr. Springe, who tailored very fine uniforms, said to be the best in the States—also very expensive, but he allowed Ike to buy his uniforms on credit, including, Eisenhower said, "a full dress coat (a big frock coat used only on the most ceremonial occasions) and evening or social full dress."

Mr. Springe's faith in Eisenhower was soon rewarded, because money started coming in to Ike from all those cadets who had lost to him in poker games at the Point. He also received the three months' pay that had been held back for the summer, more than $400.

Second Lieutenant Eisenhower had been assigned to the 19th Infantry, which had been billeted in Galveston, Texas, until an autumn cloudburst had flooded out the barracks there and it was transferred to Fort Sam Houston, near San Antonio, which everybody in the army called "Fort Sam." It was probably the best assignment in Texas that a young second lieutenant could have had, on a post where everyone of any importance either was stationed, had been stationed, or visited. Fort Sam was an army showplace in an area that, it was said, "produced strawberries in February and roses all year round." So many young officers got married while they were stationed at Fort Sam that everyone in the army called it "the mother-in-law of the army." Most important, it was peaceful. True, there was a war in Europe, but that had nothing to do with the army young Eisenhower was in. Woodrow Wilson would keep the U.S. out of it.

Eisenhower arrived on September 13, 1915. It was a good place to start an army career that was to last almost forty years. He served at Fort Sam until May 28, 1917, with the exception of short periods when he was on detached service with the Illinois National Guard at Camp Wilson, Texas, and with the Southern Department also at Camp Wilson.

Fort Sam looked like most army posts in the continental United States in those days. There were rows of long brick buildings trimmed in white and without individuality. The food was poor, both for officers and enlisted men. Eisenhower said it "lacked flavor, glamour, probably even nutrients. Tapioca pudding and mashed potatoes, often cold, seemed to be indistinguishable as well as permanent items on the menu." He volunteered for cooks and bakers school. "There I hoped to learn more about cooking for large groups of men." The purpose of the school was to train not only the enlisted cooks and bakers in their assigned duties, but also to train junior officers in mess management. Eisenhower was the most junior lieutenant in the regiment and the logical candidate for the job of mess officer.

He didn't learn enough, he said, "to qualify as a cook. But I did learn about the problems of trying to bring four-star cuisine out of recipes which use hundreds of pounds of ingredients and gallons of water. I knew enough so that I could discover what was wrong with the food that men in my command were getting. I have made things miserable on occasion for young captains or lieutenants, responsible for messes, who limited their inspection to questioning whether pots and pans were shined brightly enough. . . . I insisted that officers learn enough about their business, including the kitchen, to oversee it intelligently."

Marty Snyder, Ike's mess sergeant during World War II, said "From the beginning, I was aware of his interest in food. . . . At first, this may not appear to be a vital contribution to the war; for a while it didn't seem so to me. But one day when he had stopped in the kitchen of London headquarters, General Eisenhower observed, 'It's true that an army travels on its stomach, even if a soldier only travels from his typewriter to a file cabinet. Good food is more than sustenance. It's morale.' "

As chief of staff of the army, General Eisenhower sought to bring about improvement in the army's cooking. "Food is part of a soldier's pay," he said, "and it is my determination to see that none of his pay is going to be counterfeit."

High-ranking officers from all over the United States including many from Washington, D.C., made frequent visits to Fort Sam to inspect something or other and to rest, swim, or play golf in the sun. Thus, the senior officers on the post often were able to mention to the visitors the names of young officers who had impressed them. And in a very short time young Eisenhower had impressed everybody. He was soon to make an equally favorable impression on the many retired officers living in and around San Antonio.

Fifty years later, looking back on the days at Fort Sam, Eisenhower said, "It was impossible to become a general in peacetime. And I wasn't too concerned about promotion—I was more interested in doing my job well. Later when my son John wanted to go to West Point I told him never to think about promotion but to do his job well and make every boss sorry when he leaves."

There is something of an old-man-looking-too-rosily-on-his-youth in that. Eisenhower was never totally unconcerned with promotion; for one thing, he liked eating well, and each promotion brought an increase in salary, however slight. But with a single exception every boss *was* sorry when he left, and a great many bosses tried, very often successfully, to keep him from going anywhere, including to the Great War, thus, he was sure, ending forever his chance of attaining high rank.

Eisenhower was always able to do a job that would be admired by his superiors, but he tried never to be so outstanding that his peers were threatened by him. It didn't pay for a young officer to *appear* too competitive. One should not be known for one's sense of humor either; wit was looked on with suspicion on most army posts, just as it was during the 1952 and '56 presidential campaigns.

You were promoted when it was your turn to be promoted; your body had to be warm and you had to be sober most of the time to move up. A study of the peacetime army made somewhat later showed that it took, on the average, nine years of service to reach the rank of captain, eleven more to make major.

Afternoons were a trial since most of the time an army officer's work day ended at noon, and in the afternoons you were on your own. Some young officers succumbed to alcohol, and some to the women of the town—those who wouldn't have dreamed of sleeping with an enlisted man, but, when their husbands were at work, often found an attractive young officer welcome.

Life was lazy, and when he was president, Eisenhower was to remember a time at one of the early posts—they were all depressingly alike—when there had been an old army general, "Shooting Jim," who drooled when talking to Ike. According to Eisenhower's presidential secretary James Hagerty, "Ike and others used to bet quarters, on whether the drool would fall on the left or right side of Shooting Jim's jacket."

On his arrival at Fort Sam, Eisenhower reported first to George Willis Helms, who eighteen years after his graduation from West Point in 1897 was a captain and commander of F Company. In June 1943, Helms, then a retired colonel living in Virginia, wrote a letter to the Allied commander in Algiers, congratulating the one-time second lieutenant on his success.

In his reply of June 14, Eisenhower said

My dear Ginny:
    You told me not to answer your letter, but possibly you do not understand that my sole relaxation these days is the receipt of messages of good will from old friends. Your letter took me back twenty-eight years. I shall never forget the day I reported to you in Fort Sam Houston. Because I had some little reputation as a football player, you were apparently expecting a regular

Goliath, and expressed your immediate disappointment that I was a man of medium build and size. I even remember the names of many of the "F" Company non-commissioned officers and privates—that company was my first love in the military service.

I particularly cherish the good wishes of persons such as yourself who introduced me into the military service and took charge of my somewhat unruly and harum-scarum personality in time to keep me from getting too far off the proper track. I owe a lot to you personally; a fact which I never forget. . . .

P.S. I never addressed you as "Ginny" but neither Colonel nor Captain seems to be exactly appropriate. In any case, my purpose is only to make you understand how close I feel to you.

That first fall at Fort Sam, Ike had an orderly, his first. The orderly was Private Daniel S. Smiller, who remembered that "One day, a young second lieutenant came to the Fort and joined our company. His name was Eisenhower. . . . He was a strapping youth and seemed to know his way around. I reported at his bachelor headquarters . . . and looked after his trunks, etc., all being tagged 'Abilene, Kansas. . . .'

"One evening I had a date at San Antonio and needed a pair of civilian shoes, so I sneaked a pair of the lieutenant's without being caught. The next morning I arose early to replace them under his bed. As I was cleaning his room that morning, the lieutenant quietly remarked, 'If you want a pair of shoes, don't be bashful, ask me for them—don't sneak them out!' I was so embarrassed that I couldn't say anything. I was dumbfounded when he added, 'You can use those shoes any time—they are yours.'

"I thought I would be fired from my job. But he never again mentioned the incident."

Eisenhower was not always so understanding, however. His brother Arthur said, "In the early part of his military career, he was quite a disciplinarian. Once, for some infraction of the rules, he made a soldier dig a hole six feet long, two feet wide, and six feet deep. When the man reported to him that the job was done, Dwight ordered him to refill it."

The commander of Eisenhower's regiment, Colonel Millard Fillmore Waltz, West Point 1878, had been something of a hero in the Spanish-American War. He was short of stature, mustached, stocky, and ill-tempered. It was best for junior officers to keep out of sight when Colonel Waltz was around.

Ike's first meeting with the colonel had been short and formal. He had simply reported to his commanding officer. The second meeting was also short, but less formal. One evening Ike had made a bet with another second lieutenant that he could climb one of the cables holding the post flagpole in place, a distance of about fifty feet, hand over hand without touching the cable either with his feet or legs. Five dollars was bet, and the money was given to one of the spectators to hold. A time limit was set. Eisenhower took off his jacket and regulation blouse and began the climb. He had almost reached the top—that's the way he remembered it, anyway—when Colonel Waltz ordered him to the gound. Eisenhower said, "Sheepishly, I let myself down along the cable and as quickly as my feet touched the ground came to a stiff salute. First he ordered me to don my jacket, and then he offered a few suggestions for improvement. I was, it seems, foolhardy, undignified, untrustworthy, undependable, and ignorant. He wanted no more of this on his post. Once he had finished taking me over the coals, he stalked off, saying, 'There'll be no more of that on the part of anyone.' "

After the colonel left, the young lieutenants had a long argument about who won the bet. It was finally decided, as Eisenhower had maintained from the beginning, that the contest had ended in a draw; and the stakeholder returned the $5 to each contestant.

Later that year Eisenhower met the commander of the army's Southern Department, which covered the Mexican border from Brownsville to Yuma, Major General Frederick Funston. "Fighting Fred" Funston was the shortest general in the U.S. Army at the time, five feet four; his father, a Kansas congressman, had appointed him to West Point, but he had failed the entrance exam. Then, after a series of unbelievable adventures as a civilian, the governor of Kansas made him a colonel and put him in command of a regiment of Kansas volunteers. He had been a hero in the Spanish-American War, had served with Douglas MacArthur's father, Major General Arthur MacArthur, for two tours of duty in the Philippines during the insurrection there, and was commander of the Department of California at the time of the San Francisco earthquake in April 1906. It was generally agreed that, should the United States become involved in the war in Europe, Funston would command its armies.

It was Ike's reputation as a football player that brought him to the attention of the general. There were several military academies in and around San Antonio, and in the fall of 1915, shortly after Eisenhower's arrival at Fort Sam, the head of Peacock Military Academy offered Eisenhower the job of coaching the football team there. The pay for the season was "munificence itself," $150 for the season. But Eisenhower, though he needed the money, rather smugly turned down the offer, saying, "I was an Army officer, and therefore had no time for football."

A few days later, the famous General Funston walked into the officers' club where Eisenhower was having a few beers with other second lieutenants. The general "looked us over and said, 'Is Mr. Eisenhower in the room?' I stood up and said, 'Sir?' I couldn't imagine what he had on his mind." Funston bought Ike a drink, said that he understood Ike had been offered the coaching job. Eisenhower affirmed the fact, and Funston said, "It would please me and it would be good for the Army if you would accept this offer." Ike said, "Yes, sir," and the Peacock Military Academy had a new football coach, and the team had a winning season.

Once again it was football that brought him to public notice. The sports writer for the *San Antonio Express* spelled his name Eusenhauer but said, "Those who have seen this officer operate with a football squad believe him one of the best coaches in Texas—bar none. . . . He set about building Peacock up 'gradually' into a 'powerful' machine capable of holding its own with anything in the academy class in Texas. Peacock crowned its season with a defeat of Lutheran College in Sequin."

At the end of the season, Eisenhower wrote Ruby that he had attended a dance the team gave in one of the San Antonio hotels: "When I entered the ball room everybody stopped and started clapping and cheering. I blushed like a baby—Gee! Surely was embarrassed. . . ."

Most of Eisenhower's mornings at Fort Sam were spent drilling and training enlisted men who had little if any equipment to take part in a war President Woodrow Wilson said they would never have to take part in. But in May of 1915 a German submarine sank the *Lusitania*; one hundred and twenty-five American citizens were lost, and two years later America was in the war.

In the meantime, the main concern for most officers and enlisted men at Fort Sam and Fort Bliss, at El Paso, was what was happening on the Mexican border. An obstreperous Mexican outlaw who called himself Pancho Villa had to be captured and taught a lesson. But that would certainly not be a problem for men like Fighting Fred Funston or Brigadier General John J. Pershing, commander of Fort Bliss. Surely these warriors and a handful of other Americans could capture Villa and give him the hanging he deserved.

And so life at Fort Sam consisted largely in teaching men to hurry up and wait, to prepare for a war nobody thought would happen, to defend a country that would never be attacked. Later, *Fortune* magazine would reflect much public opinion of the peacetime professional army between wars: "To get into West Point you must have a mental age of over ten, but the enlisted man need only be able to read and write English. No one salutes him, and no one except the girl at the soda fountain thinks he is wonderful—and she not for long."

In a dance hall in San Antonio, a sign proclaimed that the dancing was for ladies and gentlemen. "Soldiers and dogs not allowed," it added.

★　★　★

MISS MAMIE

*Wanted—a wife. Modest young man of gentle disposition
and refined (?) nature desires to try matrimony with any coy
damsel willing to take the chance. Retiring but affectionate.
Prefer girl with money. Eisenhower.*
　　　　　　　　　　—Advertisement in the *want-ad*
　　　　　　　　　　section in the 1915 *Howitzer*

The dances at the Fort Sam officers' club were largely attended by young officers and their wives and by young women who were the daughters of well-to-do local families and the even better-to-do families from the north who had come to enjoy the winter sunshine of San Antonio.

In his letters to Gladys Harding, Eisenhower made a great point of how lonely he was, but that was something of a plea for sympathy. He wasn't lonely at all. He was surrounded by an exceptional crop of second lieutenants who were smart, ambitious, and on their way. Wade Haislip, a West Point classmate, during the Second World War was to command XV Corps in Normandy and in the campaign in the rest of France and the Rhineland. Carl A. Spaatz, class of 1914, was to become a lieutenant general and command the U.S. Strategic Air Forces in Europe. Jacob L. Devers, class of 1909, became a four-star general and commander of the 6th Army Group. Robert L. Eichelberger, also of the class of 1909, commanded the campaign to drive the Japanese from Luzon and the Southern Philippines. Walton H. Walker, class of 1912, became a lieutenant general and commanded the Eighth Army in the Korean War. Second Lieutenant Leonard T. "Gee" Gerow had graduated from Virginia Military Institute four years earlier. He was the commanding general of V Corps at Omaha Beach during the D-Day invasion and in 1945 was given command of the Fifteenth Army and promoted to lieutenant general.

Gerow was only two years older than Eisenhower, and they became friends at once and remained so for the rest of their lives. Gee liked parties and was a friend of a young woman who had had her coming-out party in San Antonio the previous spring. Her name was Mamie Geneva Doud. Everybody called her Mamie. She was eighteen and very popular with young, unmarried officers at Fort Sam. She was five feet three inches, had a good figure, fair skin, and bright blue eyes.

On Sunday afternoon, October 3, 1915, when Ike had been at the post about three weeks, Gee and Second Lieutenant James Byrom visited Major Hunter Harris and his wife, Lulu, at their home on the post, next to the bachelor officers' quarters. Among the other guests present were John and Elivera Doud from Denver, and their three daughters, Mamie, Mabel Frances, whom everybody called "Mike," and Eda Mae, "Buster."

Mike said, "We were all sitting on the Harrises' front lawn drinking grape juice. Gee Gerow and Jim Byrom were with us, and they started talking about this new second lieutenant, this big woman-hater named Eisenhower. They said he was good looking, and I don't know what all, and then the man himself appeared, and he was good looking." Eisenhower was officer of the day; he was wearing sidearms and a campaign hat at the rakish angle made popular by Theodore Roosevelt and his "Roughriders" in the Spanish-American War.

Mike said, "I think it is safe to say that Mamie noticed him right away, and so, for that matter, did I. He was always a person you noticed."

On his fiftieth wedding anniversary, Eisenhower said of that afternoon meeting, "I was going on guard duty when I was called across the street by a lady who lived on the post. I walked across and chatted a minute. There was this attractive-looking gal. She was wearing a great big flowered skirt that came up to here." (Ike pointed to a high waistline.)

Mamie on that same occasion said, "He was different from anyone else I knew. I think it probably was his vitality that appealed to me."

Eisenhower said, "I didn't know how long she was staying, but I invited her to take a walk with me. I found out later that she didn't like to walk, and that was a long walk we took."

Not only was the walk long, but she was wearing tightly-laced beige kid shoes that accumulated dust, pebbles, and sand. She also had to keep one hand on a large chipstraw sailor hat so that it wouldn't fall off, and the flowered cretonne skirt several times snagged on a bush, but Mamie, usually not a young woman to suffer in silence, did not complain. She already felt Ike was different; he was not, as she said, one of "those lounge lizards with patent-leather hair. He was a bruiser."

Mamie was born in Boone, Iowa, on November 14, 1896. She was a tiny baby, weighing less than four pounds. Her favorite uncle, Joel Carlson, described her as looking at birth "like a little plucked chicken." Although the Douds lived in Boone less than a year after Mamie was born, her ties were there rather than in Cedar Rapids, where she spent much of her childhood. She returned to Boone often, largely because she was so fond of Uncle Joel.

Joel was a most unusual midwestern male for the early twentieth century. In his youth, he had studied voice at the Chicago Conservatory of Music, where Ruby Norman was later to study. People in Boone said that he was stubborn and usually added that that was what you had to expect from a Swede. Even when Joel was a guest in the White House, he went to bed at his Boone bedtime, 9:00 P.M., no matter that he often had to leave in the middle of a movie being shown at the request of the president of the United States. Eisenhower must have respected Joel's independence of mind. In 1948, when he was president of Columbia University, he and Mamie gave him for Christmas a new Chrysler Winslow sedan, cost $2,424. When I mentioned that to Aksel Nielsen he said, "I never heard that, and you're right. It is extraordinary. They both were very careful with a dollar. . . . I knew they were fond of Uncle Joel, and he was a very nice man, but I didn't know they were *that* fond of him."

At the time of Mamie's birth, Boone had a population of 2,000 people, half of whom worked in the coal mines just outside town. It was surrounded by cornfields, and Mamie used to say, "Whenever they sing, 'Iowa, that's where the tall corn grows,' nobody's hand goes higher into the air than mine."

The house in which the future first lady was born is now a historical monument and has been restored to look the way it did in November 1896. It has five small rooms, and there is a sizable summer kitchen in the backyard. Mamie was born in the rear bedroom just off the dining room.

At the time, Mamie's maternal grandparents, Carl and Johanna Carlson, lived in a much larger and fancier house on Montana Street in Boone. Carl Carlson had been born Carl Jeremiahson on a farm in Sweden in 1841. Johanna was born nearby at about the same time. Following their marriage in 1867, Carl left for the United States, arriving at Boston in 1868. A short time later he changed his last name to the more pronounceable Carlson and went to Canada, but he stayed there only a short time. He then started west, arriving at Boone on Christmas Day 1871, where he decided to stay. A year later, he sent for his wife, who liked the Iowa village just as much as her husband did. Carl worked at odd jobs before settling down as a regular hand in a flour mill and soon had saved enough money to buy his own mill, which was one of the most successful in central Iowa.

Mamie's father, John Sheldon Doud—Sheldon was his mother's name—was of English ancestry. (Henry Doud came to the United States from Guilford in Surrey in 1639 and became one of the founders of Guilford, Connecticut.) John was tall, with gray eyes, strong features, and a ruddy complexion. He was born on November 18, 1870, in Rome, New York. His father, Royal H. Doud, was co-owner of a large wholesale grocery firm in Rome, but Rome was a tedious city for a man with a keen sense of adventure. So when John was six years old, Royal sold his share of Foote, Doud, and Company, and went to the growing, dynamic city of Chicago, where, with his brother Eli, he founded a meat-packing firm, the R. H. Doud Company, and made a fortune. He bought a handsome house in Oak Park and in 1895 retired.

John Doud was also an adventurous man. As a boy, he ran away from the home in Oak Park three times. Once, when he was fourteen, he served as a cook on a Mississippi steamboat, but he always returned. He studied both at the University of Chicago and Northwestern. He got a degree in mathematics from Chicago. Aksel Nielsen said, "He thought like a mathematician, like a certified public accountant where money was concerned. Here in Denver they used to say he had the first dollar he earned; that wasn't true, but he knew where every dollar *went*. He was very, very careful with money, and, putting it mildly, so was Mamie. She kept track of every dollar, of every nickel, too. They used to say, 'She held onto a dollar until the eagle screamed.'

"Maybe she learned that when she was a little girl. She had an allowance of three dollars a week, and when that was gone, her father saw to it that there was never any more, never."

Not long after he graduated from college, John went to Boone where he became a partner with his uncle, James Doud, in the meat-packing business. In the Boone newspaper at the time, Doud and Company said, "Our smoked meats and lards are the best the market affords."

The Carlsons were among the first people Doud met when he got to Boone, and on August 10, 1894, he married Elivera Carlson. (Much later in life she was nicknamed "Min," after a character in the "Andy Gump" comic strip.) She was tall, blond, blue-eyed, and only three months past her sixteenth birthday. Elivera, like her daughter Mamie, remained thin and trim all her life. When she and John Doud celebrated their golden wedding anniversary, she was able to wear her wedding gown. The couple spent their honeymoon in New Orleans, and in 1952, when Eisenhower was campaigning for the presidency, Min enjoyed pointing out the places where she and his father-in-law had been.

When Mamie was less than a year old, John Doud moved his family to Cedar Rapids, Iowa, the home at one time or another of the Wright brothers, Grant Wood, and Quaker Oats. John's job was as chief hog buyer for the Sinclair Company, the largest packing house west of Chicago.

John Doud had a passion for automobiles. When he moved to Colorado Springs in 1904 he had a green Rambler, the first car of any kind in town. He later had a Packard, a Pierce Arrow, a Winston Six, a Stanley Steamer, and an Oldsmobile.

The electric car he bought in Denver in 1912 cost $4,300. It had a two-and-a-half horsepower eight-volt electric motor and could travel 100 miles before the battery needed recharging. It was called "Creepy," its top speed being nineteen miles an hour. Mike (Mabel Frances) said, "Creepy was the only car Mamie ever drove that didn't frighten her. It had plum-colored upholstery, and there were vases that we kept filled with violets." The car is now on display at the Eisenhower Library in Abilene.

Mike said, "I don't remember much about Cedar Rapids. I was too young when we left, but I know Mamie loved it." "I remember attending family picnics," said Mamie, "and I remember riding on open streetcars and watching the circus pass our house on the way to the fairgrounds. And I'd see them again in the evening when they returned to the train yards. It was a beautiful way to grow up."

Isabel Ohler remembered many incidents from the days when she played with Mamie and her sisters. Several years older than the Doud girls, she often took Mamie to the matinee at Greene's Opera House. "If it happened to be something Mamie didn't like she would lay her head down in my lap and go to sleep." She remembered "shackin' a bob" with the girls, a term used for hitching a wagon to a sled. She also remembered the two-seated carriage the Douds had, pulled by a horse named Kate.

When Mamie was six years old, John Doud decided to retire. He had a million dollars, all soundly invested and enough to take care of himself and his wife for the rest of their lives and their four daughters until they were married. Eleanor was a year older than Mamie; Eda Mae had been born in 1900, Mabel Frances in 1902.

Elivera was uncomfortable in Iowa weather, 20° below in the winter and many days 100° and above in the summer. Cedar Rapids doctors said she was in what they called a "decline" that might develop into tuberculosis. So John Doud hired a boxcar and moved Kate (the horse) to Denver along with all their other belongings. He took his family to Colorado, first to Pueblo, then to Colorado Springs, finally to 750 Lafayette Street in Denver, where, Mamie said, "we lived forever!" It was, of course, to become the summer White House some years later.

Mike said that the house was "square, not very imposing, but beautifully comfortable. It was three stories tall; white columns rise three stories from the front steps; it's what they used to call plantation style—six bedrooms and two baths, a beautiful big dining room, a parlor, as Mama used to call it, and downstairs a big, beautiful billiard room. When I was a girl I thought we Douds were popular. It took me a long time to realize it was really the pool table that was popular. There was also a little kitchen downstairs where Mamie made fudge. She could make very good fudge."

Shortly after the family moved to Denver, John Doud discovered to no one's surprise that he could not stay retired. With the help of a Denver real estate tycoon, Aksel Nielsen, he began lending money, taking mortgages on the borrowers' property as collateral. When people could not repay, he foreclosed. His daughter Mike said, "Before you knew it, there was more income than outgo."

Mike said "It was a very comfortable life, a very happy life. We had a cook, a nurse—she came with us from Cedar Rapids—and a yardman. We had Landers, a houseman. He worked inside, but sometimes if the yardman didn't come, he worked outside, and he drove for us. We were a card-playing family. We played poker, hearts, and blackjack."

"I often think of what simple and good times we had in Denver," said Mamie.

"City Park was always fine for a picnic and the zoo—but mostly we went to Chessman Park because it was close. Later I was allowed to go on beefsteak frys in the mountains, but eleven o'clock was the curfew. I attended Miss Hayden's dancing school. She was quite a character with her long kid gloves and ball gowns that she wore at classes."

Mamie's education was haphazard, a fact that in later years caused her to feel inferior to the better-educated wives of other army officers, Bea Patton for example. And she never felt at ease with the wives of the professors at Columbia, the wives of the industrial giants her husband liked so much, or the wives of most politicians she met as first lady.

She was never much interested in books, though later in life she did read best-selling novels, particularly those by Taylor Caldwell, Daphne Du Maurier, and Victoria Lincoln. But education was not considered important for young women in Denver at the time; there was no profession open to them except teaching, and she would never have considered or been eligible for such a career. She was also in poor health much of the time, and the Douds traveled a great deal, to Panama, the Great Lakes, the Thousand Islands, and New York City. It would appear the Douds were more interested in fun and frolic than schooling for their children, another way they differed from the Eisenhowers, who were so tirelessly dedicated to education.

Mamie did attend and graduate from the Corona School, a grade school only a block and a half from the Doud house in Denver. Its most famous graduates were Douglas Fairbanks and Paul Whiteman (the orchestra leader). When Mamie graduated, she wore a white organdy dress and sang "Where the Four-Leaf Clover Grows" at the ceremonies. "Mamie had a good voice for singing, especially home singing," Mike said. "We used to sing a lot of Gilbert and Sullivan, and tunes like 'Meet Me in the Shadows,' and 'I Just Can't Make My Eyes Behave.' . . . Mamie could also play the piano by ear, and she was good."

In the winters, Mamie attended Mulholland School in San Antonio and in Denver she went briefly to East Denver High School. A friend, Miss Evelyn Griffin, who was in Mamie's ancient-history classes, said, "She was rather retiring though most friendly with classmates, rather more mature than the rest."

Her only complete year of high school was at Miss Wolcott's finishing school. Its physical facilities were impressive—a large auditorium with a stage and a huge organ, a studio where the young ladies were taught the fine arts, a bowling alley, a swimming pool, and a gymnasium. Miss Wolcott spoke much of the value of a sound mind in a sound body, but much more attention was paid to the latter. The motto of the school was, appropriately, Noblesse Oblige. Miss Wolcott used mottos the way Eisenhower's mother Ida used Biblical maxims. "The set of the soul determines the goal." Miss Wolcott also often said, "*Mens sana in corpore sano*."

Professor Robert F. Quarles, who taught geometry at Miss Wolcott's, did not comment on how well she did with Euclid, but he did say that she was "very demure. She chose to sit at the farthest seat from the teacher in the most remote corner of a large room. She was unassuming, modest, and a loyal member of the class."

One of Mamie's girlhood friends, Eileen Archibold (née Ewing), remembered her as a "gay, cheery girl who adored pretty clothes." The Ewings lived at 700 Lafayette Street, just a few houses away from the Douds, and the two girls spent their time playing with dolls and "dressing up." "She used to come down to my house all the time to get away from her younger sister." Mrs. Ewing would sometimes make the girls paper hats. "Mamie just loved to wear those hats." Her affection for hats was lifelong.

Mamie was a "belle and a leading spirit even as a little girl," recounted *Time* magazine in 1953. "When the rest of us were still getting kicked in the shins by boys," recalls Eileen Ewing Archibold, "one of them gave Mamie a snake skin. It was a real honor." Mamie made regular Saturday streetcar pilgrimages to the Orpheum Theater to drink in vaudeville performances by Blossom Seeley, DeWolf Hopper, Eva Tanguay, Harry Lauder, and other such glamorous figures. She dressed up in adult finery at every opportunity. Boys swarmed around the Doud house, and Mamie fed them cookies and Welch's grape juice, and allowed them to play at the pool table in the basement; as she grew older, they took her dancing.

According to Lester and Irene David in *Ike and Mamie*, "Mamie's first formal date was with Jimmy Cassell, whose grandfather, H. C. Brown, built the world-famous Brown Palace Hotel," where Eisenhower would launch his 1952 presidential campaign.

The Douds began spending their winters in San Antonio in 1910, when Mamie was fourteen. Elivera's health had greatly improved in Denver, but Eleanor had a bad heart, and the cold winters of Denver were thought to be too severe for her. Besides, the whole family enjoyed not only the climate of San Antonio, but the social life. Eleanor's death in 1912 was a serious blow to the entire family, but especially to Mamie.

The Doud house in San Antonio also had great charm. It was a large, white-shingled house with wide, curving verandas and tall Corinthian columns. Mike said it was "a lovely house, large and on a corner; it had a gallery all around it." It was here that Eisenhower went to pick up Mamie for their first real date. Mamie had kept him waiting four weeks for that date.

★ ★ ★

THE NATURE OF THE DUTY

The night after their first meeting, which in addition to the walk included a quick supper at the officers' club, Eisenhower phoned the Doud residence several times. When Mamie returned home from a date with somebody else, Landers would tell her that a "Mister I-something" had been calling her. Eventually he found her at home. "He asked me to go to the show on 'society night' at the Majestic. Well, all of us girls were always dated up for that night, so I told him it would be four weeks before I had an evening open."

There is no record of where Eisenhower and Mamie went on their first date. Soon, however, it became routine for him to call on her. Sometimes, though not often, he took Mamie out to dinner, usually to a Mexican restaurant called The Original on the San Antonio River. There they could have dinner for two for $1.00 or $1.25, tip included. The Orpheum Theater was also popular with Ike and Mamie. Not only could they see a movie, but six vaudeville acts as well.

After Eisenhower took Mamie home, he frequently walked the two miles to Fort Sam. The last jitney bus stopped running at midnight. It was a long walk, but he saved the nickel fare. "With debts to pay off, and a young woman to impress, I became, if possible, even more parsimonious."

Unlike most of Mamie's young men, Eisenhower was not intimidated by John Doud; he felt immediately at home with all the Douds, though Mike felt "he was too bossy; he threw his weight around a lot. He was very much a West Point man in manner, and at first I didn't care for that too much. But Papa liked him."

Sometimes Eisenhower would arrive at the Doud house when Mamie was out with somebody else; he would spend an enjoyable evening discussing the Mississippi or the Civil War with Mr. Doud. They both felt they knew every detail of every battle. Besides, John Doud was the first really successful man Ike had known. He appeared to be everything David never was, successful and secure.

Ike also worked out a strategy that was advantageous to him. "When Mamie had another date, I went to visit her mother. . . . I'd hang around until midnight and let the guys see me there when Mamie got back."

John Eisenhower said his father and Mrs. Doud "belied the standing joke regarding the relationship between a man and his mother-in-law. The two constituted a truly mutual admiration society and each took the other's part whenever a family disagreement would arise." Like Eisenhower, she enjoyed reading Westerns, and in later years they often exchanged paperback books. Elivera also liked to play the harmonica, and when her son-in-law and daughter were living in the White House, she often entertained them with a few harmonica favorites such as "School Days, School Days," and "There'll Be a Hot Time in the Old Town Tonight."

Aksel Nielsen said, "Mrs. Doud was a very proper person, stalwart, delightful." Elivera was also a cheerful woman, like Ida Eisenhower, but unlike Ida she had never known poverty. She insisted that her daughters not learn how to cook. "If you don't know how, you won't be asked to do it."

Ike's strategy worked. Less than two months after their first date he had eliminated all competition and was seeing Mamie every "morning, noon or evening" possible. That first Christmas he gave her a large silver jewelry box with her initials engraved on it. The gift was so expensive that both her parents insisted that it be returned at once. The gift was inappropriate, just too much for a couple not even engaged. Mamie said, "In those days, a young man didn't give a girl anything but gifts of candy or a book. My father's first impulse was to make me return the box." Mamie cried, and then she decided to convince her father that she should be allowed to keep the gift. She argued that "Ike and I are practically engaged." Then she sat down on the arm of his chair, rubbed his head affectionately and told him that he *really* wasn't bald, a demonstrable untruth. And then she appealed to an instinct even deeper than his vanity, his love of money. She told him that Hertzberg's, the store where Ike had bought the box, would not take it back because it was already engraved with her initials. Therefore, the store would not refund the purchase price. John Doud immediately saw the logic of that, and Mamie kept the box. It was in her bedroom at the White House and later in Gettysburg.

Mamie called her father "Pooh-Bah," after the character in *The Mikado* who liked to boss everyone around. John Doud had a prominent paunch of which he was very proud. It was proof that he never had to go without a meal. He was known to eat an entire pie at one sitting. Mike said, "I never saw Papa in my whole life without a coat." In the evenings he wore a silk smoking jacket, and in 1915 when Gladys Harding asked Eisenhower what he wanted for Christmas he told her a smoking jacket, and that is what she gave him.

John Doud also read Westerns, but when he died in 1951 the *Rocky Mountain News* noted that his library also included books by Dickens, Mark Twain, Somerset Maugham, Sinclair Lewis, and several Bibles.

Doud did not laugh much. At least not when John Eisenhower knew him. John remembered his grandfather as being "a very morose man"; but he taught his grandchild a great many Civil War songs, which he played on the piano and sang. "Then he would throw back his head and laugh and show his gold teeth all the way back. I can still remember every word of 'Rally 'Round the Flag, Boys.' "

John Doud, according to Aksel Nielsen, had not one mistress but two, neither of whom knew his real name. That was the reason he tried never to be photographed. Nielsen said, "He was a very secretive man. It was a secretive house."

John Eisenhower said, "There was always a closed feeling about that house." A biographer of Mamie wrote, "Mrs. Doud said that her husband had many acquaintances but was wary of forming close friendships. This exclusion of outsiders promoted overemphasis on family ties. 'We were always at the beck and call of each other,' she asserted. 'Now, looking back over the years, I think we were too self-contained, too clannish—but Mr. Doud wanted it that way. None of us ever stood up to him. We loved him too much.' "

Eisenhower and Mamie decided to become engaged, and on Valentine's Day 1916 he gave her a ring from Bailey, Banks, and Biddle. It was an exact duplicate of his West Point class ring, a large amethyst sunk in heavy carved gold, with their initials engraved inside. The wedding was to be in November, when Mamie turned twenty.

Soon after John Doud gave his approval to the marriage, Ike found that his application, made months before, to join the Aviation Section of the Signal Corps had been approved. In January he had written to Ruby Norman that he had tried, but couldn't "make it until next September. I'll get a lot more then— if I get in—and maybe I can make ends meet . . . ha ha you know me. I'll never have a sou." Not only would he make more money as a pilot, he told Ruby, the airplane some day was "going to have real value."

He was to report to the post hospital at Fort Sam to take a physical examination. "That night I went to the Douds' house walking on air," Ike said. "I liked the idea of flight training and of course the 50 per cent more pay held out great and glittering promise to a man on his way to marriage. To the assembled family I told my story. There was some chilliness in the atmosphere; indeed, the news of my good fortune was greeted with a large chunk of silence."

The silence did not last long. John Doud said that "if I were so irresponsible as to want to go into the flying business just when I was thinking of being married, he and Mrs. Doud would have to withdraw their consent." Flying seemed neither safe nor sane in 1916.

Eisenhower thought the matter over for two days, then capitulated. "As anxious as I was to try it, the Aviation Section was just another form of military service," he said. Since he was planning marriage, perhaps it was time to develop "a more serious attitude toward life, perhaps I should take a broader look at my future in the military. Possibly I had been too prone to lead a carefree, debt-ridden life. Now I would set my sights on becoming the finest Army officer I could, regardless of the branch in which I might serve." He announced to the Douds he would give up aviation.

As usual, he learned something from the experience, something he never forgot. It had, he said, "brought me face to face with myself and caused me to make a decision that I have never recanted nor regretted. The decision was to perform every duty given me by the Army to the best of my ability and to do the best I could to make a creditable record, no matter what the nature of the duty."

The son of Ida had spoken, and while it is easy to make fun of such a simplistic statement, and many of us did make fun of similar statements when he was president, Eisenhower meant what he said, and he did just what he said he would do for the next thirty-three years in the Army and, for that matter, in the White House. He performed every duty given him to the best of his ability— "no matter what the nature of the duty."

Mamie formally announced her engagement on March 17, St. Patrick's Day, at a party at the Garden of Allah, a restaurant, which had once been a theater, on Alamo Plaza in San Antonio. The date was one that Eisenhower always remembered, no matter how busy he might be. On that date in March 1944, a few weeks before the Allied invasion force would land in France, he wrote Mamie from London:

> No matter who might descend on me today, I'll let nothing interfere with writing you a note, because 28 years ago today you gave a party where you let it be known we were engaged.

Soon after the engagement, Mamie and her family went back to Denver. "As a symbol of my new seriousness and sacrifice, I stopped smoking ready-made cigarettes, which were then about $1.00 a carton," Eisenhower said, "and went back to rolling my own." Before the Douds arrived in Denver, President Wilson had called the National Guard into service. It was generally agreed that by the end of the year, perhaps much sooner, the United States would be at war.

Eisenhower remembered, "Throughout the winter of 1915–16 there had been a rising clamor for the United States to act more vigorously against both German submarine warfare, in which many of our ships had been sunk, and against Mexico, whose depredations across the border seemed to us unconscionable. Many people became impatient with President Wilson. He was well aware that America was not militarily capable of joining immediately in any major war abroad, and so he continued to apply reasonable arguments . . . to get the Kaiser and his subordinates to stop the inhuman submarine campaign."

On March 9, Pancho Villa had crossed the border from Mexico shortly before dawn with several hundred armed followers. They attacked the army post at Columbus, New Mexico, and before they were driven back across the border, fifteen Americans—eight civilians and seven soldiers—had been killed; in addition, stores and homes had been looted and burned. Eisenhower said, "This set off a reaction in the United States, and although Wilson seemed to be a most patient President he now decided that the time had come to punish the organized forces and irregular units that were causing us so much trouble. As a consequence, the so-called 'Punitive Expedition' was put together and given the mission of capturing Villa and totally dispersing his men. It was put under command of General Pershing." The National Guard was mobilized and Eisenhower left the post "to live in a camp [Wilson] where I became an Inspector Instructor of a Guard regiment. . . . My assignment was to the 7th Illinois Infantry under command of Colonel Daniel Moriarity. Fittingly, practically the entire regiment was Chicago Irish."

Moriarity had served with Teddy Roosevelt during the Spanish-American War, and they remained friends. Roosevelt said that it was easy to remember the names of the regiment's officers. "They're nearly all named Casey or Murphy," he said. Colonel Moriarity had held a National Guard commission since 1899; he was a stocky man with a mustache and a great storyteller whom everybody liked, including Eisenhower.

The new inspector instructor for the regiment got some idea of the kind of assignment it would be on the day he reported for duty. He was introduced to Father O'Hearn, the regimental chaplain, who suggested that they all have a drink before going to meet the colonel. Eisenhower declined, but the chaplain had a quick one. At Moriarity's headquarters, everybody except Eisenhower had a few drinks. Moriarity suffered from what he himself termed "the Irishman's disease"; he was seldom sober, and, Eisenhower said, "He was happy to have me, as an instructor, take over in effect the running of his regiment. I wrote all his orders, prepared reports and other official papers, and became the power behind the Irishman's throne."

An official history of the regiment said it was "engaged in field exercises, target practice, combat firing, maneuvers, and other activities incident to the highest type of intensive training." What the history does not say is that the young Irish soldiers had joined the National Guard as something of a lark; it gave them something to do during the summer, and they got paid for it. But at Camp Wilson they were far from home; they drilled in the hot desert sun, inadequately equipped, understrength, homesick, and afraid. Every unexpected noise made them think that Villa or some other Mexican was attacking. Most of them got drunk most nights, got in fights, got arrested, and had to be got out of jail the next morning. They also frequently contracted venereal diseases.

A photograph of Eisenhower taken at the time shows him in a garrison cap, standing on a parapet watching a maneuver with his hands stuffed in his pockets in an unsoldierly pose. Beneath him in the "model" trench, with its technically correct traverses, crouch slouch-hatted riflemen of the 7th, alert for the order, "Over the top and give 'em hell." Moving through the trenches, the men failed to keep their heads down, and Eisenhower told Moriarity, who was standing beside him, "If this were actual warfare, about half your men would be dead now, because they don't keep their heads down."

A private who heard the remark looked up from the trenches and said, "And you wouldn't be alive standing up there either, lieutenant."

Eisenhower made the soldiers work very hard, and they groused a lot, but in January 1944, after it was announced that he was going to command the Allied forces in Europe, some of the men remembered him well. One of them, Peter Rosin, told the *Chicago Tribune*, "Although his duties were of an advisory nature, he showed natural leadership. He was popular with officers and men alike."

Eisenhower, looking back on that assignment, said "It was one of the valuable years of preparation in my early career. Although I didn't have the primary responsibility of training, disciplining, and equipping such a large command, the arrangement made by the Colonel gave me the feeling of personal authority. I began to devote more hours of study and reading to my profession, although I did not neglect my courting, now carried on by correspondence."

Mamie, back in Denver, got more and more worried by what she read and heard. She was convinced that her fiancé would be sent to Mexico. "That seemed to Mamie like going around the world," said Eisenhower. He wrote her that his application to take part in the Punitive Expedition had been turned down, but that didn't help much. There was still the war in Europe to worry about. Relations with Germany were steadily getting worse.

Under the circumstances, Eisenhower and Mamie saw no reason to wait until November to get married. There was an exchange of telephone calls, and finally it was decided that the wedding would be in Denver at the Doud home in July—*if* Eisenhower could get a leave. The War Department had ruled that leaves and furloughs would be granted only in case of emergency. Eisenhower felt that "imminent marriage was just that." Colonel Moriarity did not agree; he refused Eisenhower's request but did send the request along to Fighting Fred Funston.

Football once again proved helpful, for Funston remembered the brief conversation of the previous fall, about Eisenhower's coaching the Peacock Academy team. He told Eisenhower that he remembered him very well. "I understand you want to get married," he said. "I confirmed that impression," said Eisenhower, and Funston granted him ten days leave, though he added that a marriage was possibly not what the War Department would consider an emergency, "but I'll take the responsibility," he said.

As usual, Eisenhower didn't have much money. Although it was Sunday, he got in touch with a friend at the Lockwood National Bank of San Antonio, and the friend told him that if there were any overdrafts during the wedding and honeymoon, the bank would honor them. Eisenhower said, "In those days the credit rating of an Army officer was of the highest order."

He had another friend at Hertzberg's Jewelry Store who not only opened the store but gave him on credit the $70 ring that had been picked out, with Mamie's help, earlier. "So with a new ring, new debts, ten days, and high hopes, I started on my journey," said Eisenhower.

His train was detained one day by floods in northern Texas, an experience that was to be repeated in June twenty-eight years later when a storm delayed the invasion of Europe by a day. The weather that followed in both cases was dazzlingly bright.

On the day of the wedding, July 1, 1916, Eisenhower found out that he had been promoted to first lieutenant.

The ceremony was scheduled to begin at noon in the "parlor" of the Doud house, and Eisenhower, understandably nervous, arrived early. Landers, the Negro chauffeur-butler, who when Eisenhower called had trouble remembering that the caller was a "lieutenant" and not a "mister," pressed the white uniform Eisenhower had bought to wear in the Philippines.

Eisenhower took his time getting dressed. Then he went and stood by the piano in the small but richly furnished front parlor. John Eisenhower later remembered that there always seemed to be too much furniture in the house, "lots of frills and bric-a-brac, lots of things to knock over." In addition to the piano, there were several rosewood chairs upholstered in petit point, each with its own small footstool. A large French clock stood on a table between two windows. The ceremony was performed by Dr. William Williamson of the Central Presbyterian Church in front of the white-tiled fireplace where four and a half years later the young couple would attend another ceremony, the saddest of their lives.

There were no outside guests; only the Douds and Eisenhower were there, plus a harpist on the stair landing. Some biographers of Mamie and Ike have suggested that the ceremony moved the four Doud women to tears. That is not the way Mike remembers it. She said, "The only thing I thought of was when I was going to get out of that frilly dress and back into pants. I think that was the first time I'd ever worn a dress—for that long anyway."

Mamie wore a floor-length cream-colored dress made of chantilly lace; she had on a tight-sleeved bolero jacket and a pink satin cummerbund. "She was very nervous, but nobody who didn't know her would have known it," said Mike. "Most people didn't realize it, but when she wanted to be, Mamie was very self-possessed. The steel in her didn't show, but she had it." Mamie later said the wedding was the only occasion on which she ever saw her husband nervous.

After the ceremony there was a champagne reception for a few of the Denver friends of the Douds, most of whom were astounded by Mamie's choice. Eileen Ewing Archibold said, "To begin with, everybody thought Mamie was too young to get married. Then, the Douds were well-off financially, and with all the other beaux she had, they felt Mamie could have done a good deal better. After all, he was only a soldier and a poor boy, and everybody felt he was marrying above his class."

Eisenhower cut the first slice of the wedding cake with his sword. It was customary for a West Pointer to cut his wedding cake with a sword, but in this instance the ceremony had special resonance. The groom was named Eisenhower, after all, and during the Middle Ages his ancestors had lived in Bavaria, and the name Eisenhauer meant "Iron worker or Striker of Iron." According to Earl Endacott, "The family must have engaged in farming and in making swords as well. The swords of this period all bear the mark *Eisenhauer,* and this meant that the blade had passed a severe test and was of superior quality."

Twenty-seven years later, in Sicily, Eisenhower came into possession of a saber "that was obviously made about the time of the Crusades." He told his son John, "It has our family name stamped on it in such a way as to lead me to believe that the maker rather than the owner of the sword was of our family. I am saving the thing and will show it to you some day."

After cutting and eating the cake, Mamie, who had changed into a silk dress, and Eisenhower, wearing a gray suit, took an interurban trolley to Eldorado Springs, a resort which was a short drive from the house, where they spent the night. They had been planning a quiet, private lunch at the hotel there before returning to Lafayette Street. But the Douds, who had never before had a daughter marry, decided that the newlyweds would welcome a surprise. So they all got in the car and drove to the hotel.

"We thought not only that they would be surprised but that they would like returning to Denver in the Packard instead of by trolley," said Mike, "and they were surprised, but I think not exactly in the way we had in mind. I think they would have welcomed a little more time alone. But Eisenhower didn't just marry Mamie; he married the entire Doud family."

Eisenhower, in *At Ease,* makes no mention of how he felt about the "surprise." He says only that they spent "one or two days" back at Lafayette Street, then took the Union Pacific to Abilene, where they spent only eight hours.

David met them at the station at four in the morning, and they went home for what Eisenhower called a "monumental fried chicken dinner." Ida, with the help of some neighbors, had, according to one account, in Dorothy Brandon's *Mamie Doud Eisenhower: Portrait of a First Lady,* prepared "fried chicken, potato salad, cakes, pies and jams and jellies . . . pickled pigs' feet, sauerkraut, baked beans, freezers of ice cream, and five-gallon cans of coffee." Another account, in *Red Carpet for Mamie,* by Alden Hatch, said that the menu included "Scrambled eggs and hams, grown and cured on the Eisenhower farm. Piles of golden griddle cakes. Steaks for those who wanted them. Thick yellow cream for the home-grown peaches, and country butter for the hot biscuits."

Both books were published in 1954, nearly forty years after the monumental meal. Whichever account is correct, Mamie's first meal in Abilene was more than ample.

Mamie, according to Mike, was especially fond of Ida. She was a very dear little lady, and they got on, she and Mamie, from the very first. Mamie said she noticed at once that Ike's mother had the same warm smile [as Ike]."

Eisenhower said, "After a full eight hours, we took the train again. For part of the time, we traveled the old Missouri-Kansas and Texas Railway, called the Katy Railroad, on which my father had gone to work in 1887."

In 1952 the Republican presidential candidate and his wife returned to Abilene. There was a parade in which there were many floats depicting various events of his life. According to Earl Endacott, "The float Ike seemed to enjoy the most was one showing the Ike and Mamie wedding. An engaged Abilene couple, dressed in costumes of the period, represented the pair. As the float went by, we saw Ike reach over and put his arm around Mamie and draw her close to him."

In 1966, the fiftieth anniversary of their marriage, Mamie and Ike talked to reporters about their long and largely happy marriage. What was the secret? Mamie said in essence what she had said twenty-three years earlier in another interview on the subject: "I've lived with him and listened to him for twenty-seven years—and he still fascinates me." In 1966 she said, "Even though Ike and I don't do the same things and have absolutely nothing in common, we always enjoy each other's company, and it is a joy to hear him talk. He is informed on almost everything. He's a brilliant conversationalist."

When asked the same question, inevitable on a fiftieth wedding anniversary, Ike said that in his opinion the best way to keep a marriage going was to have a sense of humor, to be understanding, and not insist on always being right. "Being right all the time is perhaps the most tiresome quality anyone can have," he said. In answer to the second inevitable question on such occasions—If he had it to do all over again, would he still marry the same person—he inevitably said, "That's the worst question I ever heard. There's only one possible answer."

Mamie then added a statement that would be widely criticized later. She said, "For any marriage to be successful you must work at it. Young women today want to prove something—all they have to prove is that they'd be a good wife, housekeeper, and mother. There should be only one head of the family—the man."

That was the way she was brought up, she said, and she had seen no reason to change what was, to her, sound practice. "Papa . . . was always the head of the household and all of us treated him that way. Every morning we would all come down to breakfast fully dressed. He never saw us at less than our best, and we grew up believing that was the way it should always be with a man. A man can toss his clothes on a chair or even on the floor. But let a woman do it, and the image of beauty and grace is shattered." She said that she and Ike had not long before gone for a walk and had seen a young couple, the woman's hair in rollers. "I think the General was appalled," she said. "I'm afraid that many young people today are so casual and modern that they leave nothing to a man's imagination. Where is the glamour if all the artifice is out in the open?"

Mamie managed to maintain an aura of femininity and youthfulness until the end of her life. She kept her figure trim and her skin smooth, and after the war she spent a spring vacation every year at Elizabeth Arden's Main Chance in Phoenix. "I have my own cottage," she said. "The full course is too strenuous for me. So I take a modified one. I diet on about 1,400 calories."

The secret of her youthfulness, she said, was "rest. Lots of rest . . . I try to spend one day a week in bed. A doctor once told me that if a woman would spend one day a week in bed it would do more for her face than all the face creams." The advice of Mamie's doctor did not receive wide medical acceptance, but in her case, it worked. Besides, she liked spending a lot of time in bed.

Mamie also felt wives should be interested but not involve themselves in their husband's work. "That's his business. . . . In all the years in the White House, I visited Ike's office only four times." Aksel Nielsen, who was present during one of Mamie's visits to the Oval Office, felt that Mamie's staying out was not wholly her idea. He said, "Ann Whitman [Eisenhower's personal secretary] was sitting in the office with a cup of coffee and Mamie took one look at her and said, 'Get rid of that.' Eisenhower was furious. He said, 'Mamie, you take care of your part of the White House and I'll take care of mine.' After that he did and she did."

"You have to feel you're a part of a man's life at the same time you know that he must run it himself," said Mamie. "Your job is to make it easier for him to do what he needs to do." She tried to do just that, and when the women's liberation movement was mentioned to her, she said, "I never felt the need to be liberated. I just wanted to be beside my husband, showing interest in his career, not mine." In the army you are a team, Mamie said. "His career is your career, his friends are your friends, and their wives make up your circle." She had no objections at all to that arrangement. "Whatever Ike did, I'd follow," she often said. "I'll always be an Army wife."

★ ★ ★

THE ARMY WIFE

In July 1916, shortly after Eisenhower and his bride returned to Fort Sam, a 1915 graduate of West Point was passing through San Antonio and decided to call on his classmate. Lieutenant John B. Wogan, later Major General Wogan, said, "The door of Ike's quarters was opened by a pretty girl wearing an apron and holding a broom. Now, our class had adopted an academy custom of giving a wedding present to every man who got married. The bridegroom had only to send an annoucement to the official academy jeweler, who then would ship the gift and bill each classmate for his share. But I hadn't received any such bill with Ike's name on it. Furthermore, we'd always considered Ike the true bachelor type—a good bet for the last man in the class to get married. Who was this girl?

"I stood at the open door, embarrassed, and inquired in my best stammer if she knew the whereabouts of Lieutenant Eisenhower. She replied that he was drilling with his company; would I like to come in and wait for him? I went in, still trying to figure it out. My confusion obviously amused her. Finally she rescued me.

" 'I'm Mrs. Eisenhower,' she said, smiling. 'Ike and I were married on the first of July.' "

The *Officer's Guide* describes an army wife as someone who "is equally at home in a cabin or a mansion, a fine hotel, a transport. She is a good mother and rears her family, generally under conditions which would seem impossible to her civilian sisters. . . . Her sense of Duty, Honor and Country are those of the Army itself."

Eisenhower had had four years to prepare himself for the realities of army life, but Mamie had had no preparation at all. True, she had often been on the post, having dinner at the officers' club or dancing with young officers. She had had meals at the homes of officers, but they were senior officers, and their homes, while seldom grand, had ample space.

In 1916 when Mamie first saw their quarters she very likely cried. They were to live in what had been Ike's bachelor's quarters, two tiny rooms and a minuscule bath. Forty-three years later, during a brief visit to San Antonio, Mamie was asked about her first home at Fort Sam. She was most explicit in describing the quarters. She said that she and the general had started their married life in "the building to the left-hand entrance of Infantry Post, the second stairway, the first floor, the apartment on the left." Officials of the army post were able to place a historical marker over the entrance to the quarters on the basis of the information provided by Mamie.

Everything about the place was shabby. Paint was peeling from the walls, and there was no money for paint. There was no electricity either, only two gas jets, one in the bedroom, another in the living room. There was no kitchen, but that didn't bother Mamie. "I'm not a cook," she would say. "I was never permitted in the kitchen when I was a girl." She did halfheartedly try to learn at the local YWCA but stopped going to classes after she learned how to mix mayonnaise.

Mamie's distaste for kitchens remained the rest of her life, although she did later learn to manage steak and potatoes, and, she said, "several other dishes Ike likes." Eisenhower said that he did "the only thing a fellow could do—I became the cook." During the war, Mamie often ate candy rather than cook a meal for herself. Sometimes she and other army wives in Washington would get together and take turns doing the cooking. Mamie, however, always preferred washing dishes.

At Fort Sam that first year, the Eisenhowers had to buy additional furniture, including an icebox. Mamie nevertheless insisted on renting a piano for five dollars a month. To make room for it, she stashed all the "inessentials," like Ike's field equipment, behind it.

When Mamie complained about their cramped quarters, and she sometimes did, adding that it didn't seem fair for captains and majors and colonels to live so much more comfortably, Eisenhower would say, "R.H.I.P." (Rank Has Its Privileges.) That answer never seemed very satisfactory to Mamie until very much later when she and Eisenhower lived in sumptuous headquarters like Quarters No. 1 at Fort Myer and in a château halfway between Paris and Versailles.

But the succession of rundown apartments and houses they lived in for so long cannot have been easy for the pampered daughter of John Doud, who when she asked for a diamond ring as a Christmas present when she was six was given one. The small gold band with a diamond chip can be seen at the Eisenhower Library in Abilene—along with the rest of Mamie's jewelry.

Mamie once said, "I call no place home. I have never allowed myself to get too attached to a place. . . . I guess you could say my hobby is fixing up homes for other people to live in. We'd be jogging along, like any young couple, then suddenly Ike would be tapped on the shoulder for some new and terrifying job. It would mean abandoning all our plans, plunging into the unknown—and usually setting up another household.

"Oriental rugs were ideal for service people," she said. "When you got orders to move, you would pack up all the family pictures and a few odds and ends and roll up the orientals. The Quartermaster Corps would move you, and somehow no matter where you were set down or what your quarters were like, the rugs and photographs would make the place seem homelike."

They also always took a plaque saying Bless This House, which hung in every house and apartment they occupied. The plaque or one with the same words still hangs to the left of the entrance of their last house, the only one they ever owned, in Gettysburg.

As to the various temporary homes they lived in—there were thirty-seven of them—Mamie always brought with her samples of wood painted pink and green, the colors in which her childhood bedroom had been painted. Whenever possible, she duplicated that color scheme.

From the time of her marriage until the end of her life, Mamie never really changed. Her interests, for the most part, were those of her girlhood in Iowa, Denver, and San Antonio, that of a well-off middle-class housewife of her generation. She continued to love pink and to wear pink ruffles; she wore her hair in bangs. She wore stockings tinted red, blue, purple, and green. Many people felt that a first lady should dress more conservatively, particularly one pushing sixty. No matter. Mamie paid no attention. She continued wearing them. After all, they came from Paris.

Mamie managed to keep occupied at Fort Sam, playing cards with other young army wives and going to dinner parties. She was popular and genuinely enjoyed being with other people. Wherever they were stationed, their quarters became a gathering place. She had no interest in outdoor life and did not care for sports, either as a participant or a spectator. She didn't even care for walking, but when First Lieutenant Eisenhower was involved, she decided she liked football.

The first year they were married, Eisenhower was coaching a football team at St. Louis College, a Catholic institution. Eisenhower's bride attended the games with all the Douds. Jim Sweeny, the team quarterback, told the *San Antonio Express*, "We thought more of him than we did any coach we ever had. We respected him from the time he showed up until he left and we fought as much for him and Mamie and the Douds as we did for the school. He was very frank and honest, and we learned more about honor and discipline from him than we did anywhere else."

Brother Laurence Duffy, who coached the younger boys on the field where Eisenhower was coaching the varsity, recalled that when Ike first arrived at the St. Louis practice field "We only had about eleven boys of any size. Ike looked the small-sized squad over and announced 'I could kill these boys off in a week.' . . . But he didn't." Ike's material was so slim that when he spotted husky fifteen-year-old Eugene Keller, a student from LaCoste, on the sidelines, he walked up to him and asked why he was not in uniform. Brother Duffy said Keller told Ike his parents wouldn't permit him to play football. "It was a very rough game in those days. With mock seriousness, Ike told Keller he had better be in uniform the next day or he'd take him behind the woodshed and whip him. Keller was out next day and saw service as guard."

The school had not won a game for five years. After Ike took over, its team tied the first game and won the next five. The team lost the last game, but its coach many years later said of the game, "With a combination of bad luck and nerves, we lost a close one." Brother Duffy said, "What Eisenhower did was amazing. We'd been beaten by lopsided scores—80–0, 50–0—the year before. Eisenhower handled the boys with precision and patience, and the boys held together the whole year."

The Fathers gave Eisenhower and his bride a victory dinner, "and thus started a friendship which has continued over the years. The college now has a different name. . . . but as late as 1962 I went out to see the faculty and the student body and we had a good time replaying the old games."

There were always a great many post activities, and an army wife was expected to take part in them. These included church, clubs, nurseries, Boy Scouts, Girl Scouts, and the thrift shop, where everything from old golf shoes to outgrown baby carriages were sold. As Maureen Clark, General Mark Clark's wife, said in her book *Captain's Wife, General's Lady*, "It is not always easy, and a wife plays a big part in her husband's career. In many cases she can make or break him by what she does."

At army parties, wives stood on one side of the room discussing things deemed suitable for women—cooking, knitting, taking care of babies, and, always, unendingly, prices at the post exchange. Prices at the post exchange, though they were usually only about half of what civilians had to pay, were always considered too high.

The men stood on the other side of the room discussing topics suitable for army officers—Pancho Villa, the war in Europe, and whether or not the United States would get in it.

Politics was little discussed by army officers in those days, but there was a presidential election in 1916, and most army officers at the time were for the Republican candidate, Supreme Court Justice Charles Evans Hughes, who was loudly supported by Theodore Roosevelt, who kept saying that the American people had had enough of Wilson's "milk and water" policies. However, Wilson won by a narrow margin, and continued to warn the Germans to stop the atrocities of submarine warfare. The Germans continued to pay no attention.

Ike hated to go to parties, according to his son John. "I can still see him out in the front room, dressed up and looking very uncomfortable, chewing nails while Mother sat in the back room fixing her hair. When she got him to the party, however, and he got to singing and talking with some friends, she had a very difficult time getting him to go home. He likes people and likes to exchange ideas with them, but he sure hates to doll up to do it."

It was expected of army wives that they be nice to the right people, and Mamie found being nice no problem, neither in the army nor in politics. "All my life I tried to do what Ike expected me to do," she said. That was not always easy. When Eisenhower was assigned to Camp Wilson, he was within commuting distance of San Antonio. But when he returned at night, it was almost always too late to go out anywhere—even if there had been some place to go. Army families in those days had little to do with civilians. In his book *Eagle Against the Sun*, Ronald H. Spector says of the American peacetime army, it "was sort of a 'gentleman's club' for its officers. Most of the 'club's members' were personally acquainted and they associated mainly with each other. . . . In the peacetime army, the main enemies were boredom and debt."

Mamie said of the Wilson period, "There wasn't much chance of Ike's being promoted . . . yet he used to read and study until two or three in the morning even though he had to be in the field at seven."

Sometimes Ike wasn't able to get back to Fort Sam. In her entire life, Mamie had never spent a night alone, and she was terrified, both for her own safety and for her husband's. When she complained, Ike said, "Mamie, I'm first an Army officer. I owe everything I am to the United States. You come second." What he said he did not have to repeat; it was demonstrably true for the rest of their life together. It was not what a young bride of nineteen, who all her life had been, in her words, "spoiled rotten," wanted to hear, but Mamie heard it; and it took several years, but she learned to live with it.

Eisenhower was never a demonstrative man. Julie Nixon Eisenhower said of the early days of the marriage, "When Mamie was married in 1916, it marked a wrenching break with her . . . sisters and her parents, to whom she had confided every emotion. She had to adjust to a husband who rarely verbalized affection and who had no use for small talk. A slap on the back or a pinch was Ike's way of saying 'I love you.' "

"There was a great deal of difference in our background," Ike said. "I was a boy in a family of six boys, and she was a girl in a family with three other daughters. She used to make a great deal about birthdays, anniversaries, and holidays." So Ike learned to keep a record of every birthday and anniversary.

Mamie was not a woman who worshipped material things. What she worshipped was the value of sentiment. Once when she was being photographed, she was asked to remove an old watch the photographer thought destroyed the graceful curve of her arm. She said she couldn't and wouldn't. Mamie's watch was the one Eisenhower had given her for their twenty-fifth wedding anniversary.

She did a good deal to teach Ike to be at ease—even with Winston Churchill and Franklin Roosevelt. John said, "She takes full credit for smoothing the edges off the rough-and-ready Kansan and for teaching him by example, and, on occasion, direct instruction, the manners of the higher born."

But she could be selfish and demanding. Ike said, "Mamie and I have had our difficulties. We were both strong willed." John agreed, "Both were strong personalities . . . [but] it seemed that the Old Man's views nearly always prevailed." Aksel Nielsen disagreed with John. "Mamie got her way more often than not. Most of the time Ike just shrugged his shoulders and gave in."

One incident early in their marriage turned out to be more than a spat. Eisenhower found out that Mamie had, without consulting him, sold the first two suits he'd bought after graduation. Both were double-breasted, and one was gray, the other navy blue. Dorothy Brandon, Mamie's biographer, said of the suits, "Both were made of striped material and far too 'natty and nifty' for her taste. . . . She formed an instant dislike for the garments when she first saw them during their courting days." At the time, however, Mamie kept her opinion to herself.

After the marriage and after the army ruled that soldiers could not wear civilian clothing when off duty, Mamie decided that the time had come to get rid of the inelegant suits; she would, she felt, be safe until after the war. She sold them to an old-clothes man, $10 for both suits. Eisenhower had paid $150 for each suit, a considerable sum for any suit in those days.

The quarrel that followed lasted a very long time, in part because Mamie, one of the more frugal first ladies of this century, was angry at herself: she had been bamboozled by an old-clothes man.

Nielsen said, "Mamie was frugal, frugal in the extreme, frugal sometimes to an embarrassing degree." In the White House it bothered her that the leftovers had a way of disappearing. "Leftovers make nice lunches . . . sandwiches for the staff. I don't want anything thrown out," she said. *She* never threw out anything, including dresses, hats, stockings, or shoes, and when she moved into the White House, it was necessary to turn what had been Bess Truman's bedroom into a closet.

After the presidency, when she was living at Gettysburg, Mamie had a dressing room with drawers filled with pocketbooks and purses still in their original glassine cases, cupboards filled with unopened bottles of some of the finest perfumes—all gifts she had received as first lady. A friend visiting her, on seeing them all, asked her why she didn't give them away. "You have got more than you will ever use," she said, "[and] they would make lovely Christmas presents to some of your friends." Mamie answered, "I couldn't do it. The people who gave them to me might find out!"

Mamie was always sensitive about electric bills, and after Ike's death, a house guest who couldn't sleep decided against reading on the dimly lighted front porch; instead, he read in the hall bathroom for several hours. When she got up the next morning, Mamie's first question was who had left the light on in the bathroom.

Mamie kept the family budget from the day they were married; Eisenhower just turned over the money he received to her and almost never complained or even asked what she had done with it. Mamie bought most of his clothes, underwear, shirts, neckties, and handkerchiefs; suits he had to buy himself, but after Mamie disposed of the $300' worth of "natty and nifty" suits for $10, Eisenhower's taste in that field dramatically improved. When in 1950 he was cited as a "best-dressed man," Swede Hazlett wrote him that he was "certainly the first Jayhawker ever to get such an accolade and will probably be the last." Ike replied that he had neither seen the story nor heard about it. He said: "My reaction to it is that some people must have a hell of a lot to do if they have time to devote themselves to such drivel." He said that his suits were made "by a Jewish friend of mine who has been in the mass-tailoring business all his life." He said the cloth and the cut of his suits were chosen by the tailor. "So far as my own intervention in such matters is concerned, one of Mamie's chief causes of complaint is that I will not even buy a pair of socks for myself."

Another quarrel early in the marriage occurred during a visit to Abilene. Eisenhower joined some old friends for a game of poker, and when he wasn't back by midnight, Mamie telephoned and demanded that he come home immediately. Eisenhower was losing a considerable sum of money, and he refused. "I wasn't going to come home until I made up my losses," he said, feeling, rightly, that Mamie would be much more upset over his losing a lot of money than being a few hours late in returning home. By 1:30, when he had made back the money he lost and more, he came home; the quarrel that followed was monumental.

On another occasion, however, he used the fact that he had to meet Mamie to get out of a crap game. He got into a game that had been going on for some time. He at first thought the two silver dollars he had were not enough for him to get in the game, but he was urged to get in anyway.

By the time he was supposed to meet Mamie, he had won $100. The other two officers were not happy at the prospect of his leaving with so much of their money; so he said, "I'll tell you what I'll do. Both of you seem to be losers in about the same amount. I'll take my two dollars, put them back in my pocket, and I'll divide my winnings in two equal piles. Each of you can take a roll. You can win or lose and it's okay with me. Lucky or not," Eisenhower said, "they couldn't see themselves taking a shot at fifty dollars each on one turn of the dice. So they politely refused, and the game was over." The following morning, Eisenhower sent a draft to Leavenworth completing his payments to the tailor. The only person left he owed money to was his father, and there is no record that he ever repaid him.

Ike was never a man who brought his troubles home. Mamie was fond of telling people that when he came home, "he came home to me." A short time after they were married, Ike was made provost marshal of the post. He did not discuss his new assignment with Mamie. One of his jobs as provost marshal was to patrol the red-light district of the Mexican section of San Antonio. One night, while patrolling Matamoros Street with two MPs, one walking with him, the other across the street, two bullets whizzed by, uncomfortably close. One of the MPs, a corporal, dragged the man who had fired the shots out of an alley, "not being unduly gentle about it," said Ike. "Hey, watch it," the man said, "I'm an officer." "I don't care what you are," said the corporal, "you shot at my lieutenant." The officer was turned in and fined five dollars by a National Guard court. Eisenhower said, "Penalties were stiffer later."

Ike was "frightened for Mamie. . . . there were many occasions when she had to be alone." So he bought her a .45 pistol and taught her how to use it. A little later he asked her to get the pistol for a rehearsal. It took quite some time to find it. The pistol was behind the piano with other what Mamie called "inessentials." It was also wrapped in Eisenhower's bedding roll, causing him to feel that in case of emergency the gun wouldn't be of much use to her. "I decided to keep on concentrating on trying to make the camp safer," he added.

On one occasion while at Fort Sam, Mamie was left alone for almost two weeks. Ike went on a march from Camp Wilson to Austin, Texas. More than 15,000 officers and men took part, and the 206-mile march and return lasted thirteen days. In addition to the soldiers, 5,000 horses and 200 trucks and wagons took part. It was said to be the greatest peacetime display by the U.S. Army since the Civil War, and when Austin was reached, the entire force was reviewed by the governor and General Funston and his staff, including Eisenhower. The parade lasted six hours. Nobody ever forgot that parade or the march. Sergeant Tom Blazina, who participated in both, recalled visiting Eisenhower in the White House. Ike said, "Sergeant, do you recall that hike to Austin?"

Blazina said, "Mr. President, could I ever forget it?"

"It was a long, hard, dirty hike," said the president.

"As I recall, you and all the staff officers made the hike on horseback," said Blazina.

"So we did, sergeant. But did you ever ride a horse over two hundred miles over hot, hilly, dirty roads?"

End of exchange, at least as Blazina remembered it.

Eisenhower surely remembered "Mugsy" on that march. Mugsy was his orderly when he was with the regiment, and during the march to and from Austin, everybody was hot and thirsty most of the time. One evening, without asking permission, Mugsy borrowed Lieutenant Eisenhower's horse, borrowed about thirty water cans, rode to the nearest town and filled them with thirst-quenching beer.

He returned the beer-filled cans to his thirsty friends and collected his profits. Eisenhower found out what had happened. According to Blazina, "Lieutenant Eisenhower was furious when he learned of the escapade. What he said to Mugsy can never be printed, but Mugsy did not lose his rank nor his job, but his conduct thereafter was exemplary."

At the end of the year, the 7th Infantry Regiment returned to Chicago. Eisenhower stayed behind at Wilson, but before the Chicago guardsmen left, a dinner was given to honor the first lieutenant. In a toast, one of the officers said, "This young officer has brought to us needed military information and many leadership abilities which as officers we did not have before. We honor him tonight for the modest but skillful way he has brought about these changes in our regiment. I believe that some day this young man will serve as military attaché to the Ambassador at [the Court of] St. James in London."

But when Major General Eisenhower went to London for the first time, in June 1942, it was not as a military attaché but as commander of the U.S. forces in the European Theater of Operations.

★ ★ ★

KEEPING THE COLONEL HAPPY

By early spring 1917 Eisenhower returned to Company F of the 19th Infantry. "The dangers and irritations along our southern border had been reduced and conditions between the United States and Germany had worsened. The War Department recalled many of the National Guard regiments and Camp Wilson, home of the 12th Provisional Division to which I had been attached, was now abandoned," he said.

Eisenhower was from the beginning certain that he would be part of the fighting of the First World War. Everybody said it was a "young man's war." He was young, not yet twenty-seven, and he was trained for combat. It was just a matter of being patient for a few weeks, a few months at most.

He later said:

As usual, our country was sadly—close to totally—unprepared. While we had mobilized a few more regular regiments in 1916, the strength of the Regular Army was awfully small. Intensive efforts had to start at once to bring our strength up to a position where it could participate in a conflict that had been raging in Europe for more than two years.

One of the methods for expanding the Army was to draw cadres of officers and men from each regular regiment to form either one or two more regiments around them with recruits. The 19th Infantry was directed to form the 57th and I was chosen to go with the new group. When Mamie and I got this news we were crushed. We had regimental spirit—in those days a man stayed with a regiment as long as possible.

His new assignment with the 57th Infantry, again at Camp Wilson, was the first of many in the years that followed that were unwelcome; he took them, though not without frequent bouts of grumbling and some little self-pity. He later told John that the transfer to the 57th was one of the greatest disappointments of his early career. "But he learned from it," said John. "He developed a certain philosophy very early that you never know what is good for you. It turned out he learned more than he would have if he'd stayed with the assignment he liked, with the 19th."

Colonel David Jewett Baker, West Point class of 1886, commander of the 57th, was, like Pershing, a problem for his staff. As a consequence of his initials, D.J.B., he was dubbed "Dumb John Baker" at the Point, a nickname which remained with him throughout his career. Arthur Nevins, a longtime friend of Eisenhower's who served as a second lieutenant under the colonel at the same time as Ike, said that the initials "gave him a label that he did not deserve in the least. He certainly was far from dumb, both mentally and in his speech." He was, however, "a most unusual character." Baker often would have to interrupt his talks to assembled officers because of an extended coughing spell; he suffered from asthma. "After recovering his breath he resumed his remarks exactly where he had left off," Nevins said, "and soon lit one of the hand-rolled cigarettes that were always arranged in a row on the desk in front of him. Then almost invariably he would proceed to make one of his characteristic caustic remarks regarding some officer in the group." One day it was directed at Nevins, who had previously put in a report for the loss of his pistol. Baker announced at midday officers' call: "There's too damn much ordnance being lost in this regiment. Why, a good soldier might just as well lose a testicle as a pistol."

Eisenhower was regimental supply officer. He joined the officers of his regiment on April 1, 1917. Camp Wilson was almost deserted when he arrived, but Colonel Baker told him that in two or three days three thousand recruits would reach there. They would arrive with nothing but the clothes they wore and whatever they carried in their barracks bags. The rest was up to Eisenhower, and altogether it was "enough to dismay a young man who had less than two years of commissioned service. . . . For the next five days, I was on the move almost around the clock."

With the help of an experienced supply sergeant named Alexander, who was clearly an expert "scrounger," trucks and tents were assembled—best not to question where they came from—and, Eisenhower said, "We somehow appropriated enough food to give them at least a meager sort of meal both the first evening and the next morning."

On June 1, the 57th, with its new supply officer, moved to Leon Springs, twenty-odd miles out of San Antonio. Ike said, "There was not a building or shelter on it of any kind. It did boast one well, from which we could draw fresh water."

Officers and men were in tents, which were hot, and the dusty, sandy field was hotter. "We were at full strength in numbers, at least, but the men were denied almost everything needed with which to prepare for war. The days were filled for all of us and we were working so hard that the Colonel determined that Sunday should definitely be a day of rest. Except for services by chaplains under the trees outdoors, we were free to do as we pleased."

There was no way to get back to San Antonio, and there seemed to be no way for Mamie to get to Leon Springs. She was pregnant; the baby was expected in late September. She was lonely in the apartment that had seemed too small for the two of them; now, although she was surrounded by her own furniture, some of it brought from Denver, it seemed too large. She occasionally gave parties for the other lonely wives. They played poker and whist, usually with matches as stakes. Mamie had learned from the Mexican cleaning woman how to make chili con carne and chicken la estancia. The table on which supper was served always looked elegant. Her sister Mike said, "There were never any paper plates or paper napkins. Wherever she was, Mamie always had her own silver and her own china."

One rainy day that summer, Eisenhower assembled a group of junior officers and enlisted men under a large tree just outside his tent to hear a lecture on supply in the field. It was a subject he'd learned only from textbooks and from his brief experience with Sergeant Alexander. He said, "While I was talking, the weather became more threatening. Then there was a terrific bolt of lightning, and all that I was conscious of was a sort of ball of fire in front of my eyes. . . . The next thing I knew I was lying on my back in the mud and an enlisted man was pushing down on my ribs, trying to bring me back from unconsciousness."

Being hit by lightning left Eisenhower with nothing worse than "a splitting headache." Captain Walton H. Walker was on the phone when the lightning hit the telephone line, knocking the receiver out of his hand and leaving him with a black-and-blue arm. Eisenhower said, "Colonel Baker often remarked that he was the only regimental commander in the Army whose entire staff had been struck by lightning and lived to tell about it."

Throughout his life Eisenhower kept in mind Ida's advice, "If you can't say something good about somebody, don't say anything at all." He kept that in mind even when he was president and tried and nearly succeeded in saying nothing publicly about such a thorn in his side as Senator Joseph McCarthy. He had it in mind near the end of his life when he was working on *At Ease*. There is not an unkind word anywhere about the man who during the Second World War gave him more trouble than all the other Allied officers put together, Field Marshal Sir Bernard Law Montgomery.

But in *At Ease* Eisenhower does say that being under Colonel Baker's command was something less than joyful. The colonel, he said, "was something of a dyspeptic and fussy about his meals. He complained constantly about the quality of the food and after having tried the mess officer's job on several other people, he gave me the position. This . . . was in addition to my other duties of trying to supply a regiment of 3500 men with mules, transportation, weapons, shelter, and all manner of hardware. . . . But supplying the colonel was its own war."

Ike found out that the colonel liked game, and "This gave me an idea." He and Walker liked to shoot and ride; so at four every morning they got on their horses and rode "to several fields in which we found doves in plentiful supply." The two hunted rather like the crowned heads of Europe; they shot without dismounting from their horses, and then an enlisted man came along and picked up the birds they had bagged.

Eisenhower said that he and Walker were anxious to "amuse the colonel," and when after a dove breakfast he would say, "Any of these for lunch?" they and "the best cook we had" experimented feverishly, concocting various dishes and "wasted a good many birds." They tried "broiling them with little pieces of bacon on their breasts." They made dove stew "adding a few mild vegetables—potatoes, carrots, and the like; finally we hit on making dove pies." One day a week the colonel got bacon and eggs for breakfast; another morning the cook prepared lamb chops, "dressing them up fancily." For the other five breakfasts, the colonel was served dove, and there were dove lunches and dove dinners as well.

Fifty years later Ike said, "The other officers got little attention because we were preoccupied with keeping the Colonel in a good mood. This was good for everybody; we all enjoyed life more when he was."

Everything worked out well for Eisenhower. In May he had become a captain, and Colonel Baker rated his work at Leon Springs as "superior."

John Doud was fond of quoting Mr. Micawber in *David Copperfield*, particularly when Micawber said, "Annual income twenty pounds, annual expenditure nineteen nineteen six, result happiness. Annual income twenty pounds, annual expenditure twenty pounds ought and six, result misery." Doud had said several times that once Eisenhower and Mamie were married they were on their own. "The well in Denver will have dried up," he said, also several times. Then, shortly after Eisenhower's twenty-sixth birthday, according to Mamie's biographer, Dorothy Brandon, Doud "took to disappearing for hours on end into San Antonio." When Min asked him what he was doing, he spoke of "odds and ends of business."

A little later, however, he told his wife that he had been looking for and found a runabout for the newlyweds, a secondhand black Pullman roadster with a jump seat. It was five years old, but the motor was in good shape. He gave the roadster to Ike and Mamie, perhaps adding, as he so often did, that financial self-restraint was the key to a happy marriage.

When Ike was not in San Antonio, which was most of the time in the summer of 1917, the Pullman roadster was under a lean-to back of his and Mamie's quarters. One Sunday morning, Mamie got up very early and climbed into the front seat of the car. She had decided to drive to Leon Springs. In 1953 she did not remember calling Eisenhower before starting out; in 1967 Eisenhower remembered that she had.

Mamie, again in 1953, said: "I'd never driven, so what! Papa let me steer the Packard plenty of times, and while Ike wouldn't allow any monkeying with the precious Pullman, I knew just what he did to get it into high gear. How he loved that car. . . .

"I said to myself, 'It's now or never,' and fumbled around with the ignition, which was fine as far as it went. But who was going to crank it up? I looked up and down the street. Sure enough, I was lucky; a sergeant was in sight. . . . I asked him to get the car started . . . he gave the handle a tug and *bang*! The motor caught. I backed out slowly, but must have had stage fright. The engine died, but the young man gave the crank another yank and the engine whanged away. I started forward, steering slowly until I was off the post, then went into high gear and kept going, ruts and all—it was as much fun as a roller coaster. Oh—until I reached Leon Springs."

Accounts differ about what happened next. Kenneth S. Davis said, "If Dwight had not been warned of her coming and had not been waiting for her at the gates she might have been forced to drive until the gasoline was gone. He leaped on the running board and showed her how to stop. She hadn't known."

Eisenhower went along with Davis and all the other biographers. In *At Ease*, he said, "I walked the mile or so to the entrance [of the camp] and waited. I was finally rewarded by seeing Mamie coming down the hill. . . . She got closer and closer and when I made out her words, she was saying, 'Ike! Get on, get on quickly—I don't know how to stop this thing.' " Eisenhower said he stopped the car, spent part of the rest of the day giving Mamie a few rudimentary driving lessons, after which "she became passably proficient. . . . I induced her to make an early start back. . . . Two hours later I got the welcome news that she was safely at home. . . . It was difficult to judge who was in more danger—the men on their way to war, or the women on their way to the men."

Again Mamie remembered it differently. She told Dorothy Brandon, "When I got there I just reached over and turned off the ignition, then yelled for Ike. He was surprised and very angry, but after he took me to lunch he got permission to drive me back to Fort Sam." We know for sure that as a driver Mamie was never more than "passably proficient" and that in the early 1930s she gave up driving entirely.

Eisenhower was seldom able to come back to Fort Sam that summer, but once when he did, he sat down and let out several of her dresses so that she could wear them until the baby was born. One was the white silk dress she had worn on their very brief honeymoon. Mamie herself made a layette, including a christening dress. They also had a serious quarrel; Mamie didn't remember what it was about, but she did remember that during the heated argument her ring struck Eisenhower's West Point ring and broke the amethyst. "He looked at it sadly for a moment," she said, "and then he quietly said, 'Young lady, for that fit of temper, you will buy me a new amethyst with your own money.' And I did—although parting with those dollars almost killed me."

At least once that summer Mamie's concern with money proved very useful. The regiment needed tools to cut trenches—in France, of course; they'd be in France any minute now—and shovel carriers to attach them to the packs of the troops. One day a huge box arrived containing the shovel carriers that had been urgently requisitioned. Almost the entire regiment, including the colonel, showed up to see the welcome box opened.

Eisenhower said, "The box, on the order of five feet by four by four, was bound up with strap iron and securely nailed. We got it opened up and looked in at our prize. Then our faces fell in dismay. They were shovel carriers, all right, but they were the old style and not the new ones with which the Army was then to be mass-equipped. . . . one look showed us that the equipment was not right and we sent it back."

A few months later, however, when Eisenhower was at another post, the army's ordnance department, then and now as vigilant as the IRS, sent him a bill for $22.04. He was the officer who had seen to the opening of the box; therefore, he was responsible for the nineteen items ordnance said were missing. Ike wrote a letter of explanation but had to send a check anyway. Fortunately, the ever-watchful Mamie pasted the canceled check on the back of her checkbook. Some months later he got still another bill for $22.04, and this time he simply made a copy of the canceled check and sent it to ordnance. That ended the matter in the eyes of the ordnance people, but Eisenhower said, "If this was my first encounter with bureaucratic blundering, it was far from the last before World War I was over. More humiliating than costly, in a way, I felt that in that nebulous region called the War Department, I had been found wanting."

By September Ike felt that the regiment was ready for active service in France. He would rather go as the commander of a company than as a regimental supply officer and mess officer; still, the main thing was to go. "We were sure that we were one of the best outfits in the whole Army and that we were destined for overseas duty."

But on September 20, four days before the birth of his first son, Captain Eisenhower was sent to Fort Oglethorpe, Geoorgia, to teach officer candidates. The colonel, perhaps more concerned with his own future without doves than without Eisenhower, asked that another captain be sent to Oglethorpe. The request was denied, the first of many such denials.

The 57th did not go overseas, perhaps giving Eisenhower some small, cold comfort. "For me this was a hard lesson that if the mills of the gods grind slowly and exceedingly small, the mills of the War Department seemed to grind to no purpose whatsoever."

Ike said, "My parting with Mamie was particularly difficult." It must have been much more than that, but there was some comfort in the fact that Mrs. Doud had arrived a few days earlier. Mamie said on another occasion, "I knew almost from the first day I married Ike that he would be a great soldier. . . . Nothing came before his duty. I was forced to match his spirit of personal sacrifice as best I could. Being his wife meant I must leave him free from personal worries to conduct his career as he saw fit."

At eleven o'clock on the night of September 23, Mamie got into the Pullman roadster, drove to the nearest mailbox and sent a letter she had written to her husband; he was on a field exercise at the time. When she got back to the post, Mamie complained of a stomachache, and as she many years later told Julie Nixon Eisenhower, "She thought it was due to the nervous tension of driving alone in the dark. So she ate an orange in the hope that would make her feel better. Mamie told me, 'Mama . . . took an awful long time to explain about the stomachache!' Mamie spent most of that endless night sitting up in a rocking chair."

The next morning she and Mrs. Doud went to the post hospital in an ambulance drawn by mules, Dorothy Brandon said; Julie said it was horse drawn. It was not comfortable; that much is certain, and there was considerable time lost while a nurse at the front desk asked Mamie what seemed to be an endless series of questions. Mamie shared a room with another patient, and the doctor took a long time getting there, but very early on the morning of September 24, 1917, Doud Dwight Eisenhower was born. Mr. Doud said that he needed a nickname; all the Douds had nicknames. She said that "Little Ike" would cause his father to be called "Big Ike," which she didn't like, and so she suggested that the baby be called "Icky," and he was. Oddly, when Eisenhower was in Europe during the Second World War, in his letters to Mamie he often referred to the child as "Ikky."

At the time his first son was born, Ike was in the field with the troops he was training. They "lived in trenches, constructed dugouts, and prepared for warfare on the Western Front. I came out of those trenches on the twenty-sixth of September and found a telegram dated the twenty-fourth, saying that my son had been born. His name was Doud Dwight."

★ ★ ★

FULL CIRCLE

The fall and winter of 1917 were cold, damp, and depressing, both at Fort Oglethorpe and in Europe where General Pershing and his troops were waiting to get into battle. The French at the time said, "The Yanks are over here now. But what are they doing over here? They are not fighting." Had Captain Eisenhower been overseas he would probably have been doing just what he was doing at Oglethorpe, overseeing the training and drilling of soldiers. Or he might have been coaching another football team.

Many of the officer candidates Ike was training at Oglethorpe were college men; the army seemed to feel that they would make better officers, but there were some National Guardsmen and enlisted men as well. Ike said, "The training was tough—designed as much for weeding out the weak and inept as to instruct. . . . Luckily, over the months I had been following the progress of the war and had read everything that I could find about minor tactics of infantry. We could put into practice what I had been reading as theory."

It was tiring, in many ways exasperating work, particularly for a man who wanted to be leading a platoon over the top on the Western Front. It must have occurred to Ike from time to time that if he had been a poor instructor he would very likely have been given a platoon and shipped overseas; by the spring of 1918 there were half a million American troops in Europe, and by July 300,000 more were arriving every month. But Eisenhower was not part of it; he was doing what he had been ordered to do; he did it because it was said to be "for the good of the country."

Some years later, when he was trying to decide whether he should run for reelection as president, he told his old friend Lucius Clay, who had been urging him to run, 'All that a person has to say to me is 'the good of the country.' . . . I probably yield far too easily to generalizations instead of demanding truth."

His work did not go entirely unnoticed, however; a young soldier named Edward C. Thayer wrote his mother at Worcester, Massachusetts:

> Our new captain, Eisenhower by name, is, I believe, one of the most efficient and best Army officers in the country. . . . He is a corker and has put more fight into us in three days than we got in all the previous time we were here. He is a giant for build and at West Point was a noted football player and physical culture fiend. He knows his job, is enthusiastic, can tell us what he wants us to do, and is pretty human, though wickedly harsh and abrupt. He has given us wonderful bayonet drills. He gets the fellows' imaginations worked up and hollers and yells and makes us shout and stomp until we go tearing into the air as if we meant business. . . . Eisenhower kept sending different ones of us up to the sentries with all kinds of answers to their challenges, to see if they know how to handle the situation. The rest of us stood around and laughed and smoked. Every now and then Eisenhower would jump on us and say we were having too good a time, call us to attention and put us through the manual for five minutes . . . but you could see that he enjoyed it all too.

On November 26 Ike was given still another unwanted assignment. He was ordered to Fort Leavenworth, Kansas, to instruct provisional second lieutenants. On the way, he stopped in San Antonio to see Mamie and his new son. The experience of seeing Icky for the first time must have been a deeply moving one, but nowhere does he say what he felt. Julie said, "Mamie had always expressed her emotions—every complaint, every thought, petty or important. Ike, to his dying day, found it difficult to express his feelings."

While in San Antonio, Eisenhower saw a friend, Lieutenant Colonel Gilbert Allen, who with him had been a member of the 19th Infantry. Allen was forming a machine-gun battalion for overseas service. Ike "instantly" applied for duty with the battalion, and Allen sent the application along to the adjutant general's office. It was instantly turned down with, Ike said, "a curt reply, adding only that I was considered to be a young officer with special qualities as an instructor. Disappointed, I trekked off to Leavenworth."

A few days after his arrival there, he was called into the office of the post commandant, where he was read a letter from the adjutant general saying that it had been noted that he had *several* times applied for overseas duty. The War Department "did not approve of young officers applying for special duty; they were to obey orders and, in effect, let the War Department run the war. . . . A man at a desk a thousand miles away knew better than I what my military capabilities and talents were; and he did not want to be bothered by any further exercises of initiative on my part."

After that the colonel added a few stern words of his own. Later in life Ike learned how to pretend to be angry if he thought that would be useful in getting what he wanted. But this time he was genuinely angry. "Sir," he said, "this offense—if it is an offense—was committed before I came under your juris-diction. If there is any punishment to be given out, I think it should be given by the War Department and not added to by yourself, with all due respect."

The colonel said that the captain was perfectly right and that he respected him for standing up for what he believed. Eisenhower left the office feeling friendly toward the colonel, "although my views of the War Department con-tinued to be beyond easy conversion to parlor language."

So he continued to train provisional second lieutenants, and he was in charge of bayonet drills, calisthenics, and exercises for the entire regiment. He hated the work, but as he later said, he managed to keep warm in a very cold winter. In early March 1918 he went to Camp Meade in Maryland to join the 65th Engineers, an assignment which delighted him because he had been told that his new unit was "the parent group which was organizing tank corps troops for *overseas* duty [emphasis his]. . . . Our first job was to complete the organizing and equipping of the 301st Tank Batallion Heavy. These men were to man the big tanks, a rarity on World War I battlefields where even the small 'whippets' were not common."

His men were equally delighted; they were volunteers and considered them-selves "*different*" (again, Eisenhower's emphasis). They "dreamed of over-whelming assault on enemy lines, rolling effortlessly over wire entanglements and trenches, demolishing gun nests with their fire, and terrorizing the foe into quick and abject surrender." Some of Captain Eisenhower's men may have had that dream; he certainly did.

Of course, there were no tanks available when he got to Meade, but he took the enthusiastic troops through the end of basic training, and in mid-March he was informed that the 301st was soon to go overseas and that "I was to go along in *command!*" (Again, emphasis his.) He hurried to New York and spent two days and most of two nights making sure that everything was ready for the troops to embark. "Too much depended on our walking up that gangplank for me to take a chance on a slip anywhere."

He went back to Meade and found that plans had once again been changed. Once again he was too good to be sent overseas, too successful at training troops; his "organizational ability" was too great. Most of those he had trained did go overseas, but some, presumably the less competent, did not and he was to take them to Camp Colt, "an old, abandoned campsite in Gettysburg, Pennsylvania, of all places. . . . My mood was black."

The title of the 65th Engineers was changed to the Tank Corps, under the command of Colonel Ira C. Welborn, West Point 1898. Ike's job was to train the corps, the only such unit in the U.S. Army. "I was required to take in volunteers, equip, organize, and instruct them and have them ready for overseas shipment when called upon." Tank crews were trained in the United States, England, and France. In France the training was for light tanks, in England for heavy tanks, and in the United States for both. Early in 1918 the War Department authorized a personnel strength of 14,827 officers and men in the Tank Corps of the AEF in England and France, and there were 16,660 in what was designated the Tank Corps in the United States. Colonel Samuel D. Rockenbach was the chief tank officer in the AEF; and Colonel Welborn was head of tank activities in the United States, including those at Colt. There would be no direct relationship between the two tank corps until after the war.

Ike was disappointed at the assignment and showed it. He was told it would only be a "temporary arrangement"; as soon as he had the training operation organized, Colonel Welborn "would consider his assignment overseas." Welborn's office was in Washington, and twice a week Ike had to report to him for instructions. Otherwise, Captain Eisenhower, less than three years out of West Point, was in command at Colt. "I was very much on my own. . . . I really began to learn about responsibility," he said.

In April, that unpredictable month, there was a heavy snowstorm, and the tents were unheated. Ike went into Gettysburg, which then had a population of 3,000, and bought every stove in town that would fit into a tent. Many of the tents still did not have stoves, however, and the captain felt that "the air should have been thick with complaints that Army negligence had exposed volunteers to premature death. Not so. They seemed to take the storm as a splendid way to demonstrate their robust health. To me, the spirit of the men proved the best disease preventive. . . . When the storm ended, we were ready to tackle anything in the way of work."

Ike liked the town of Gettysburg and the countryside around it. He had been there in 1915 with his West Point class, and he was familiar with the smallest detail of the three-day battle that took place there. Mamie didn't have much interest in the matter, but when she later came to Gettysburg, he nevertheless took her on long rides, telling her about the men who had fought there and what they had done. She said that he "knew every rock of that battlefield."

The tents of Eisenhower's troops were pitched on the scene of Confederate General George Pickett's famous and disastrous charge on July 3, 1863, which ended with what one Union soldier called "a vast mournful roar" and cost two-thirds of Pickett's men. In 1957 President Eisenhower and Field Marshal Viscount Montgomery toured the battlefield, and Montgomery said, "I would not have fought the battle that way myself." "If you had, I'd have sacked you," said Ike. A little later in front of the Lee monument Montgomery said, "A monstrous thing to have launched this charge." He shook his head sadly. "Monstrous thing. A monstrous thing."

Pickett had been last in his class at West Point in 1846; he perfumed his long hair and never appeared in public without carrying a riding crop. Ike identified much more with another officer who had taken part in that disastrous charge. Major General Isaac Trimble, who had been graduated from West Point in 1822; at the time of the battle he was almost sixty-two years old; he not only lost the battle, he lost a leg and was taken prisoner. Yet he took the trouble to draw a map of the battleground; he dictated to a young Union officer an account not only of the charge but of the three-day battle of Gettysburg, as he had observed it. The map and the "Remarks by Gen. Trimble" were given Ike when he was president by his ambassador to the Court of Saint James's, Jock Whitney, and Eisenhower said of Trimble, "As I walk in the back door of my office or leave by it, I pass a memento [the map and Trimble's remarks] of his stoicism in pain and in defeat and of his concern that the record of history be kept straight. . . . One must admire this aging man, in such desperate plight, who patiently went over the details of a battle lost so that the record might be correct. . . . Here, indeed, is a lesson against collapse into despair because all things seem lost." Ike many times during the bleak months at Colt was convinced that for him, all things were lost.

Later in April Mamie arrived with Icky. The four-day journey from San Antonio had been by day coach, and Mamie felt that only the kindness of the sleeping-car porter had made it possible. Icky was seven months old, and sometimes during brief stops in small towns, the porter would buy milk and put it in the refrigerator of the dining car.

Mamie was feeling considerable personal guilt. A woman she described as "an older Army wife" had persuaded her that it was foolish to bring her furniture all that way; it was simpler to sell it for cash and she could buy new and better furniture when she got to Colt. Mamie accepted the woman's advice and took the cash, $90. She said, "I know I was young, but not that young. Surely I could have applied simple arithmetic and figured out that ninety dollars would never furnish another apartment. What I exchanged for nine ten dollar bills cost originally nine hundred dollars. It's a wonder Ike didn't wring my neck." It was probably the last time she ever made such a costly error.

Part of the time at Colt they lived in a fraternity house with a gigantic ballroom but no kitchen. The cooking was done on an electric hot plate with two burners and the dishes washed in the bathtub. Ike spent as much time as he could with his family. "It was fun to have the chance to see my son growing up," he said.

On June 6 the first tank arrived—It was a seven-ton Renault which had been built in France by an American automobile company. It was ceremoniously unloaded from a railroad car and driven through the town to Colt. The *Gettysburg Times* reported that the tankers "were as happy as a playground full of children with a new toy . . . they knew about tanks only from hearsay and newspapers." Ike recalled in 1967, "We had not expected to see one until we reached Europe. Even at that, we couldn't be sure whether we would be operating them or facing them."

Two other Renaults arrived later in the summer, and they, like the first, were without weapons; in battles such as the famous British breakthrough at Amiens, tanks had either a machine gun or a small cannon mounted in a revolving turret. Again the men at Colt improvised.

Two British officers arrived at about the same time as the tanks; they acted as advisers to Eisenhower, who said, "Thus began my association with allies, a word that was to become vitally important as the years rolled on." They spoke "of a British political figure named Winston Churchill" who "had had a hand in producing the first tanks. They admired him extravagantly. I must say that from their descriptions, he sounded like a good chap."

In 1943 one of the British officers, F. Summers, a retired lieutenant colonel, wrote Eisenhower reminding him of the summer of 1918 at Colt. He asked Eisenhower to write the introduction for a book the corps was publishing. Eisenhower replied:

> No message that I have received in recent months has pleased me more than yours. I have often wondered where you were and what you were doing.
>
> I assure you that I could not have attempted to write a foreword for your book, except for my very great feeling of indebtedness for the advice and counsel you so kindly gave me years ago in the little town of Gettysburg— I hope I have profited somewhat by it.

In another letter written the same day, August 26, 1943, Eisenhower said that he had hurriedly written a foreword:

> More than a quarter of a century ago, the tank made its bow upon the battlefield as a clumsy, belly-crawling monster whose weakness in loco- motion and whose structural frailties were so glaring as to drive from the ranks of its adherents all except men of vision, of faith, and of fortitude. To those that were able to see in early failures only challenge to greater effort, we are indebted for the hastening of the German defeat in 1918.
>
> But more than this, imbued with a conviction that modern science stood ready to offer to armies speed of movement in battle with protection against the inevitable hail of small arms fire, they urged that there was thus pre- sented an opportunity through which the wise would prosper and the ignorant would meet disaster. Their number was all too few, but, fortu- nately, they persisted. Among them, none was more eloquent nor more farseeing than those distinguished soldiers that have contributed to this book. In a very marked sense, we owe to them the overwhelming nature of the Allied Tunisian victory—to say nothing of the triumphal odyssey of the British Eighth Army that began at El Alamein and has already reached Catania.

Ike realized that by the end of the summer there would be over 10,000 men at Colt, and once they were competent in basic drill, there would be little for them to do. To prevent them from becoming bored and to keep up morale, he set up a telegraphic school and a motor school. He went to Washington and managed to get a few swivel-type Navy guns, "we called them 'three-pounders,' " and although there was no ammunition, the troops drilled with them. There were some machine guns, and gunners were "trained . . . until they could take them apart blindfolded and put them together again." The guns were loaded on trucks, and the men were taught "to fire from mobile platforms at both moving and still targets."

Welborn approved of Eisenhower's imaginative training program. On April 19 and again on May 27, he had written to the adjutant general requesting Eisenhower be promoted to major.

Captain Eisenhower is attached to the Tank Corps and is in command at Camp Colt, which now has a strength of 4500 and will ultimately have a strength of 8000.

While Captain Eisenhower is a junior captain and is not eligible for promotion, according to the policy of the War Department, it is urgently requested that an exception be made in his case. He is doing important work, is deserving of promotion, and his duties can be better performed with the increased rank.

No action was taken; and on July 12 Welborn wrote another letter referring to his previous requests and the request of Colonel Clopton, director of the Tank Corps, Washington, that Eisenhower be promoted to major.

The adjutant general replied on July 16:

It is not stated that a vacancy exists for this officer in a higher grade. This information necessary before action can be taken.

On July 22 Eisenhower was promoted to the grade of major (temporary), with rank from July 18. "This appointment is to fill an existing vacancy."

The young major continued to win his superiors' approval, but not always without stepping on some toes. Ike met his first two congressmen while he was at Camp Colt, and he at once let them know what he thought of them. (As president, he dealt with congressmen indirectly and deftly; the *last* thing he allowed a congressman to find out was what he thought of him, particularly if he disliked the congressman.)

A junior officer at Camp Colt had been caught cheating at cards, and Ike gave him the choice of resigning his commission "for the good of the service," or being court-martialed. The young officer chose the former, and two days later his father and his congressman presented themselves in Eisenhower's headquarters. After a lively exchange between the congressman and the major, Eisenhower was asked to remove the words "for the good of the service" from the discharge. He refused, and the congressman "said he thought I was acting arbitrarily for a Major," Eisenhower recalled. "I'm acting as an Army officer protecting my command," he said, and that was the end of the matter—except that the congressman did get the young officer back in the army.

Most residents of Gettysburg welcomed the soldiers' presence, but there were some who "saw in them a source of quick and easy profit, catering to all their appetites." The second congressman showed up after Eisenhower had placed a guard around the hotel and bar of a man in Gettysburg who had violated orders by selling liquor to uniformed soldiers. When the angry hotel owner showed up to protest, he brought with him not only his congressman, but the congressman's secretary. After a short, lively discussion, the congressman said to Eisenhower, "I'll have to take up the question of replacing you"; to which Eisenhower replied, "You do just exactly that. . . . Nothing would please me better than to be taken out of this job. I want to go overseas. If they take me out of here, maybe I can get there." The congressman did complain to the War Department, and as a result Eisenhower got a letter from the assistant to the secretary of war commending him "for diligence in looking after the welfare and well-being of my soldiers."

That fall Major Eisenhower had to deal with "Spanish flu." The worst epidemic of this century, it was an outbreak that affected every country in the world, and in army camps in the United States it was estimated that influenza and pneumonia cost at least half as many American soldiers' lives as combat in Europe. The Spanish flu entered the United States through the port of Boston, and the first case was reported at Fort Devens, Massachusetts, on September 8. It was not diagnosed until September 13, and by that time there were 500 cases at Devens.

At the same time, orders were received at Devens to transfer 124 men to Colt for service as machine gunners in the Tank Corps. They left Devens on the 13th, and when one of them complained of being ill, he was returned to his quarters. The enlisted men were accompanied by an officer of the Medical Corps, Lieutenant T. J. Ferguson. While they were on the train, several of the men said they were ill; Lieutenant Ferguson decided they had "a touch of the grippe."

The train reached Gettysburg on the night of the 14th; Ferguson was not with them; he had gotten off the train and gone to the hospital in Lancaster, Pennsylvania, where he died a few days later. The medical officer at Colt who examined the men decided they were suffering from the effects of the typhoid shots they had had a few days before. They were assigned to a casual company which numbered more than a thousand men; a few days later several of the men from Devens were sent to the Colt hospital, where it was at last decided they had Spanish influenza.

The camp's chief surgeon, Lieutenant Colonel Thomas Scott, a National Guard officer from Oklahoma, showed rare ingenuity; he insisted that the patients be isolated and, according to Eisenhower, they were, "if only by putting canvas partitions between the beds. No more than four men were allowed in any tent; three whenever we had room. Each who had been directly exposed to the disease was, wherever possible, put into a tent by himself."

Ike said that Scott "used a number of strong sprays on patients," and, with the camp commander's permission, he experimented on the Eisenhower family and on the members of the headquarters staff.

"Each morning he would use two sprays on the throat and nostrils of each of us. One of them was intensely pungent and strong. On application, I felt as if the top of my head was going off. The other, I think, was a sort of soothing syrup to follow the first. The twice daily spray was anything but a tonic. Nevertheless, he insisted upon continuing this treatment on every member of my family and headquarters—though possibly he spared the baby. We were fortunate—or he was smart. Not a single person in my headquarters command or my family contracted the flu. Lieutenant Colonel Scott is another of those men to whom I will always feel obligated."

Mamie said, "It was a very sad time. Ike worked so hard and he was so upset about it. But there was nothing much he could do. . . . It was heartbreaking. You couldn't even get straw for the boys on the ground. There was just nothing."

Ike and Scott took other extraordinary precautions to prevent the spread of the disease. On clear days, tents were opened and all bedding aired in the sun. Wooden floors in the tents and elsewhere were scrubbed daily with a solution of Lysol and kerosene. On Ike's order, every man in the camp was given a medical examination daily, and anyone with a symptom of the disease was immediately put in one of the camp's five infirmaries. Men who were seriously infected were sent to hospital tents.

On September 30 Father W. F. Boyle made a parochial school in Gettysburg, St. Francis Xavier Hall, available to patients from Colt. Father Boyle said, "The lives of our soldiers are more important than a week or two of schooling for our children." Ike issued an order forbidding soldiers at Colt to attend church services in Gettysburg. MPs saw to it that there were never more than four tankers in a store at one time, and on October 1 Ike ordered the restaurants in town not to serve soldiers. MPs were posted on all roads leading into and out of the camp to make sure that soldiers without passes did not leave the camp, which was placed under quarantine by Eisenhower.

There were then 10,605 men under Ike's command at Colt, and between September 15 and October 5, 427 persons were admitted to the post hospitals; 106 were suffering from pneumonia, the rest from Spanish flu. But by the 24th Colt was, according to the *Gettysburg Times*, "practically free of influenza." Altogether, 150 men at Colt had died from the disease. Major Eisenhower issued a statement to the local newspaper thanking the people of Gettysburg for their "timely assistance during the recent regrettable epidemic." He spoke, he said, "on behalf of the officers and men of Camp Colt as well as their relatives and friends."

It had nothing to do with the fact that he had handled the epidemic very well, but on October 14, Ike became a temporary lieutenant colonel. He was twenty-eight years old that day. He knew that he would revert to his permanent rank of captain after the war, and he did, on June 30, 1920.

After the flu epidemic ended, the War Department decided to send the remaining troops at Colt to a camp in North Carolina, which meant little to Ike as Welborn had told him he would be in charge of the November shipment of troops overseas; that would be on November 18. They would sail from New Jersey, and Mamie would return to Denver with Icky.

"The move [to North Carolina] would not be made until after the November shipment of troops . . . was complete—and I would be in Europe and no longer responsible."

Welborn tried to get Lieutenant Colonel Eisenhower to change his mind about going overseas; he would recommend that he be made a full colonel, he said. Eisenhower refused. Rather than stay in the States, he would take a reduction in rank "to the average of my class—to major." Now nothing could interfere;

Eisenhower had planned everything. Except: "I had made no provision for imminent German defeat," he said.

On May 8, 1945, Brigadier General Norman Randolph, a classmate of Ike's at West Point who was also training men at Colt in 1918, wrote him:

As the bells and whistles announced the termination of hostilities in Europe today and as I listened to your broadcast I couldn't help thinking back to your office in Gettysburg on November 11, 1918, under similar circumstances. As we sat there stunned and disappointed by the fact that we had not gotten into the show I recall your saying "I suppose we'll spend the rest of our lives explaining why we didn't get into this" and "By God, from now on I am cutting myself a swath and will make up for this." Brother, you sure have made good on that last statement. . . . Knowing how bitter was your disappointment last time, I think I realize more than many others the happiness that is yours today—the crowning day of your life. . . . We are tremendously proud of you, old timer.

Philip K. McNair, another West Point classmate, also saw Ike shortly after the 1918 Armistice. "He was greatly upset," said McNair. He hadn't been sent overseas and now he never would be. He said that he had been educated to be a soldier, and when a war came along, he had to sit it out without even getting close to the battle. He was so keenly disappointed that when I left him I had the definite impression that he intended resigning his commission. I was sure that he and the Army were through."

With the end of hostilities, the War Department decided to close down Colt, and by early December Eisenhower had moved with his tankers to what was then called Camp Dix in New Jersey. As Ike was to learn again after the Second World War, the only thing men in uniform wanted when peace came was to take off their uniforms and go home. Ike said of November 1918, "Nothing at West Point or in the forty months since graduation had prepared me for helping to collapse an Army from millions to a peacetime core. The new problem kept us even busier than we had been in the middle of summer."

One of the men who wanted to and did get discharged at Camp Dix during that period in 1918 was Lieutenant George R. Goshaw. On March 7, 1946, he wrote to Ike from Alaska:

I have often wondered whether at times, your thoughts ever take the back trail to those days at Camp Meade, Camp Colt and at Dix during 1918. It was my privilege to serve under your command as sergeant when you were at Meade . . . later I was among the first troops that opened up Camp Colt before you arrived there and took over its command—later you approved the recommendation for a commission and then kept me at Colt—telling me when I requested an over-seas assignment, "that I would go over-seas when you went." Later at Dix, you kept me from needed sleep many nights by your continual winning at "seven-up" and "pitch." I now learn that you have continued to win at cards—no wonder, after getting such training at my expense. . . .

Apparently Ike decided not to let Goshaw go overseas as long as he himself couldn't, certainly not while Ike was winning at "pitch" and "seven-up." Goshaw continued:

> It was at Dix in December of '18 when I last saw you—You went to Georgia;
> I commenced my travels homeward to Alaska. . . . You made good, Ike. . . .

Ike had gone to Dix with between 5,000 and 6,000 men. However, what he called "a nucleus of a Tank Corps" was retained, and with the three Renaults and between 200 and 300 men Ike went on to Fort Benning, Georgia. He said, "The memory of that trip stays with me after more than forty-five years, etched deeply because of its discomfort. . . . The trip lasted for almost four days, each a year long."

Mamie and Icky were in Denver with the Douds. Buster, Mamie's favorite sister, had died of a kidney infection shortly before the Armistice. Mamie and Ike did not meet again until the following summer. The reunion was in Nebraska. Ike had no idea where he would be sent next, and he wasn't sure he cared. He had been offered a job by an Indiana businessman who had been one of his junior tank officers at Colt. He just might take the job.

As for his army career, "The prospects were none too bright. . . . I was still bothered on occasion by a bad knee, and saw myself in the years ahead, putting on weight in a meaningless chair-bound assignment, shuffling papers and filling out forms. If not depressed, I was mad, disappointed, and resented the fact that the war had passed me by. . . . Staying in the Army meant years of trying to stretch dollars and merge dimes. No one can be a more fearful worrywart than a young man trying to read his future in a bleak moment."

In March Ike was ordered back to Camp Meade. "For me this was full circle. Meade to Meade within one year." His commanding officer at Fort Benning, Colonel H. E. Eames, gave him an above-average rating for the period he served under him. "Although a young officer and ranking above his classmates, he was well-liked, had his command well in hand, disciplined and of high morale and efficiency."

Colonel Welborn recommended him for the Distinguished Service Medal for his work at Colt; it took him some time to get it, but Colonel Welborn said that he had "displayed unusual zeal, foresight, and marked administrative ability in the organization, training, and preparation for overseas service of the Tank Corps."

Ike sent a copy of Welborn's recommendation to his father, along with a note:

> *Dear Dad:*
> Just sending you above—as thought you'd be interested. There is no chance of getting one of the medals, but it shows Colonel Welborn's opinion of me.
>
> *Devotedly,*
> *Son*

In the long run, whether Ike admitted it or not, the experience at Colt in training and organizing troops was arguably far more valuable to him in the years to come than combat experience in France, where at best he would have been a company commander.

★ ★ ★

GENUINE ADVENTURE

At Meade life now seemed brighter. The Great War was over, and for a time, a very brief time, it did appear that the world had been made safe for democracy, though there had been a troubling revolution in Russia, and a great many people, including President Wilson, were worried about Communists in the United States. Allied troops were trying to defeat the Bolsheviks in Siberia, and in April, when asked where he would like to go when due for foreign service, Ike listed Siberia as his first choice. The others were France, the Philippines, and Hawaii.

Eisenhower was able to look on his own career with more satisfaction in that spring of 1919. He later said, "My education had not been neglected. . . . I had been singularly fortunate in . . . my first three-and-a-half years of duty. How to take a cross-section of Americans and convert them into first-rate fighting troops and officers had been learned by experience, not by textbook."

He became commander of a tank battalion and said that he would "prefer commission in Tank Corps. If same is made permanent branch, desire to stay with Tank Corps."

He came to regret that choice because there were not what he considered suitable quarters for Mamie and Icky, who were thus not with him. And he was still restless; there simply wasn't enough to do, as was usually the case in the peacetime army. Major General Floyd L. Parks, chief of staff of the First Allied Airborne Army during the Second World War, was at Meade living in the same bachelor quarters building as Ike that year. He remembered they "used to kill time on weekends by shooting pistol and rifle at the target range."

"There was every chance of going to seed," said Eisenhower. That was not about to happen to him. He and a few others started night school for junior officers who hoped to become members of the regular army after demobilization was completed. The classes met twice a week, and English, mathematics, and history were taught.

"We might have filled the time at the card table or the bar," said Ike, but when he and Major Sereno Brett heard about a truck convoy that was to travel coast to coast to publicize the army and to show that such a feat was possible, they immediately volunteered to join it.

Brett was a veteran of the war in France; he had served with the dashing

George Patton at St.-Mihiel; He had returned to the United States with Patton only a few weeks earlier. Ike said, "Sereno was of swarthy complexion, short, strong, and muscular. He had piercing brown eyes, the sort that seemed to look right through the person to whom he was talking."

Brett was filled with stories of what had happened in France, sometimes shading the truth in his and Patton's favor, and he no doubt mentioned the letter Patton had written to him, which said, "Not only did you work when we had nothing, not even hope, without a murmur . . . you fought on. . . . As far as I know no officer of the AEF has given more faithful, loyal, and gallant service." Brett was an extrovert; he was fond of practical jokes, and he was a good companion for Eisenhower that summer.

Eisenhower said of what was officially known as the First Transcontinental Motor Convoy of 1919, "In part prodded by the enthusiasts for a transcontinental highway and in part moved . . . to search out the military capabilities of automobile and truck, the War Department committed itself to the venture of a coast-to-coast convoy that was, under the circumstances of the time, a genuine adventure."

There were 81 vehicles as well as 37 officers and 258 enlisted men in the expedition. In *Overview*, the newsletter of the Eisenhower Foundation, in the fall of 1984, the expedition was described as one "which crossed the U.S. from east to west, much as the Olympic torch was carried across America this last summer—and at about the same speed! The convoy set a world-record pace for the time, however, traveling a total continuous distance of 3,251 miles from Washington, D.C., to San Francisco, in 62 days, only five days behind schedule. Average speed was 6 m.p.h. and average progress per day was a little over 58 miles. At every stop townspeople turned out to greet the soldiers, many of whom had recently returned from World War I, and to see the latest military equipment and listen to patriotic speeches."

In 1973 a magazine called *Constructor* had a lengthy account of the expedition that said, "The interstate highway system would probably have been built sooner or later, but the fact that it was built at all is due in large measure to the military. More important it happened because a military man who had some first-hand knowledge of the condition of the nation's roads was President when the Interstate Highway Act was passed in 1956. . . .

"Eisenhower gained his first knowledge of the condition of the nation's highways in 1919 when he accompanied an army convoy which left Washington on July 7, crossed the country and arrived in San Francisco Sept. 5, nearly two months later."

Ike and Brett missed the many speeches and ceremonies in Washington; they joined the convoy in Frederick, Maryland, the next morning as Tank Corps observers. The convoy was to proceed on the Lincoln Highway, which is now U.S. Highway 30. In 1919 it was a series of roads that Eisenhower said, "varied from average to non-existent. . . . We were not sure it [the trip] could be accomplished at all. Nothing of the sort had ever been attempted." He went on, he said, "Partly for a lark and partly to learn."

The convoy operated under what were said to be "wartime conditions"; according to the expeditionary adjutant officer it was assumed "that railroad facilities, bridges, tunnels, etc., had been damaged or destroyed by agents of an Asiatic enemy. The expedition was assumed to be marching through enemy country and therefore had to be self-sustaining throughout."

The convoy crossed Pennsylvania, Ohio, Indiana, and Illinois. It crossed the Mississippi at Clinton, Iowa, and then went to North Platte, Nebraska.

The article in the *Constructor* said, "On Aug. 1 the convoy reached the halfway mark at North Platte, Nebr. It had covered 1,660 miles, but the going was getting increasingly tougher. The roads were mostly sand, badly rutted, and narrow. The tires were wearing out and many had to be replaced. One truck skidded around a sharp turn and was so badly damaged it could not proceed. . . . The convoy was delayed for one day by heavy rains . . . which turned the road into a sea of gumbo."

In *At Ease* Ike calls North Platte *South* Platte and said of it only, "Mamie and all the Douds met the truck train at South Platte in Nebraska and went along with us for the next three or four days, as far, I think, as Laramie, Wyoming."

Mamie remembered things quite differently in 1952, just before she became first lady; she told Dorothy Brandon that not "all" the Douds went to North Platte. Two of them, Min and Mike, stayed behind in Denver to look after Icky.

Eisenhower had written her before the expedition began that the convoy would have an overnight halt in North Platte, 200 miles from Denver. He suggested that she might wish to join him there and said, as she remembered it, that if she came by train, she should leave Icky behind in Denver. According to Brandon, "Mamie finished her husband's letter and flew upstairs to find her father. Blotting a column of figures and laying aside his pen, Mr. Doud listened carefully while his daughter breathlessly read him Ike's letter." John Doud, the adventurer, had no intention of allowing his daughter to go to Nebraska by train; they would go together in the Packard. The trip, Brandon said, "would be rough, through the [Rocky Mountain] foothills, roads not much more than trails! The Nebraska prairie-land would be a bake-oven with not much in the way of roads. If Mamie was game, the trip was as good as made. She *was* game, and she kissed him extravagantly." Surely Mamie must have admired the prose in the Brandon book. It closely resembled the prose of one of her favorite writers, the romantic Fannie Hurst.

Brandon wrote: "The Army's endurance test with mechanized motor transport became front-page news as soon as the trucks roared out of Washington. Papa Doud and Mamie charted each day's run with pins on a map and did not need Ike's wire to tell them when to start for North Platte. At sunup next day, dressed in dusters, goggles, and pull-down hats, father and daughter made a final recheck of supplies, which included blankets, vital if they stalled overnight getting across the mountains. It was a risky journey, through the uninhabited foothills of the Rockies and sparsely settled Nebraska prairies. . . .

"With spirits as high as the snow-clad peaks that lay ahead, father and daughter sped out of town. All morning they snailed up the rocky grades. Often the Packard steamed like a kettle, forcing them to halt to cool off the radiator. . . . After noon, they dropped down to the sand and stubble of Nebraska, to mile after mile of emptiness. Only wagon tracks that had probably never been used by automobiles, guided them to North Platte."

They reached the town at dusk, and the next morning Mamie dressed at the hotel to meet her husband. She remembered wearing a "frothy cotton" dress "with black velvet at her wrists." Brandon wrote, with "her shining hair dipped and coiled to neat perfection. Mamie was without a doubt the prettiest girl in all Nebraska."

Mamie did not remember the mud; she remembered dust, and she remembered that John Doud had warned her against driving the Packard to the campsite where the convoy was to spend the night, but she did. "Finally, she heard a voice bellowing her name, and Ike, a grin on his dust-powdered face, leaned as far as he dared from a front seat, 'hollering like a kid on a roller-coaster.' . . . he had never looked happier or healthier." He may have been covered with dust, but there is no doubt that Ike was glad to see her. He said, "This was a fine interlude and I decided that it would be nice, being in the West already, to apply for a leave with my family at the end of the tour—if indeed we ever reached the end."

Mamie had come to North Platte not only to see her husband but to get what she wanted, which was to join her husband back at Meade. She "began to state her intentions expecting disagreement. Quarters or no quarters, she was going to Meade, if she had to live in a tent." To her great surprise, Eisenhower consented, provided only that she leave Icky back in Denver with the Douds. Mamie agreed to that. Later they must both have felt that it would have been better if Icky had never come to Meade.

The convoy went on, stopping in southern Wyoming at Laramie, Medicine Bow, Rawlins, Topton Station, and Fort Bridger. The public-relations officer reported that there the roads were "desolate and monotonous with clouds of dust. . . . The convoy rolled, tumbled, rocked, and tossed over an abandoned railroad single track grade with holes of varying depths and sizes." The convoy had its worst experience in Nevada when it ran into a huge sand drift; each of the eighty-one vehicles had to be pushed or pulled through the sand, and it took twenty hours to travel fifty miles.

The article in the *Constructor* reported that "Two tank trucks sank in the sand to a depth of 5 ft., requiring a major excavation to get them out. They hauled in railroad ties and built a section of a corduroy road. The drivers were subjected to extreme heat and water was rationed. . . . It was miserable, but the convoy moved doggedly on and finally reached Carson City where they were greeted by the governor and state officials. On top of all their other troubles, the men had to listen to another series of speeches."

Eisenhower loved to tell stories about that "genuine adventure," and he did so until the end of his life. "My son John has always been my most appreciative listener. He has heard them so often that he knows them by heart and often retells them himself. For all I know they may be passed on from generation to generation of Eisenhowers as family heirlooms."

There were "easterners" on the trip, and while Eisenhower does not say that they were "effete," he and Major Brett clearly considered them gullible. Word was circulated that the swarthy major was suffering from "shell shock," and to augment the talk Brett moved away from the others and placed his bedroll several hundred yards away. Eisenhower said, "While getting into his sleeping bag, he began to utter weird and strident cries. . . . In the morning when he woke, he'd give one or more of these whoops just on general principles."

As the convoy proceeded, Brett got stranger and stranger; his "fits" became more frequent, and the easterners got worried, particularly when a rumor was spread that an Indian attack was imminent. There was one easterner in particular whom they especially tried to hoodwink. "We had always intended to tell him long before we reached San Francisco. Instead we found that he had taken the whole thing seriously. Any attempt to explain it would humiliate him . . . so the half dozen of us involved pledged that we would never, as long as any of us was in active service, tell the facts to our friend. . . . I am sure that in the almost half-century since, he has had no inkling that what he and one or two others went through on that journey was as part of an audience for a troupe of traveling clowns." He and the others might have read *At Ease*, of course. After each hoax, the "traveling clowns . . . all went to bed, pleased with ourselves."

California had the best roads the convoy had encountered, but the official report said that "2 Rikers & Packard broke fan belts. Class B trucks had broken spark plug porcelain, broken fan belts & brakes required adjustment. Indian motorcycle broke control wire." Ike said, "But that was the last of our troubles except for final speeches." The governor of California spoke to them in Sacramento, "Their blood is the blood of the western country . . . strong—virile—self-reliant." "On the last day," Ike said, "the speeches ran on and on in a similar vein. The weather was fair and warm."

The convoy passed through 350 communities in eleven states as well as the District of Columbia. About 3,250,000 people had seen it, and it was estimated that 35,000,000 had read about it. Several hundred young men signed up for army service as a result, and the official report said that "all along the route, great interest in the Good Roads movement was aroused . . . [and] several states . . . voted favorably on large issues of road bonds."

The report added that the trip "forcibly demonstrated . . . the necessity for a comprehensive system of national highways, including transcontinental or through routes east and west, north and south, is real and urgent as a commercial asset to further colonize and develop the sparsely settled sections of the country, and finally as a defensive military necessity."

The recommendation may have been "real and urgent" and a "military necessity," but the *Constructor* article said "the report collected dust in the War Department's files for the next 35 years. It is significant that when the interstate system was finally approved in 1956 it came during the administration of one of the army officers who accompanied this pioneering journey."

Actually the journey proved very useful for that same officer in 1952 when he was running for the presidency on the Republican ticket. On the trip west in 1919, every time the convoy reached a town there was a welcoming committee. Ike said, "if only to demonstrate that I was not solely an Army propagandist, I tried to learn as much as I could about local interests. Much that I learned was quickly forgotten. But enough remained so that decades later it had its uses."

In 1952 in Fort Wayne, Indiana, he was as usual welcomed by a group of local Republicans; as usual they were in Ike's words "a little flustered . . . and, to put them at ease, I began to ask about certain local enterprises." Some of the businesses no longer existed, and the young people thought the presidential candidate had Fort Wayne mixed up with other Indiana cities, but an older man remembered that those companies had existed in 1919 and during the depression had moved away or merged. "This seemed to have a relaxing effect on the younger people in the group, they helped put me at my ease, and we had an animated conversation about the growth of cities like Fort Wayne."

In 1955, remembering the bumpy, often hazardous cross-country journey of 1919, Ike asked for a highway construction bill that would cost $101 billion over a ten-year period; that was a considerable amount for a budget-conscious president. Eisenhower said that his experience with the convoy "started me thinking about good, two-lane highways, but Germany made me see the wisdom of broader ribbons across the land. . . . After seeing the autobahns of modern Germany and knowing the asset those highways were to the Germans, I decided, as President, to put an emphasis on this kind of road building. When we finally secured the necessary congressional approval, we started the 41,000 miles of super highways. . . . This was one of the things I felt deeply about and I made it a personal and absolute decision to see that the nation would benefit by it."

In his presidential memoirs he wrote, "if peacetime prosperity kept on rising, the growing number of cars, used by the growing number of people, would slowly clog our road system and make the pace of today's traffic seem like a rushing river by comparison." That year (1955) the bill was passed by the Senate but failed in the House. In 1956 in his State of the Union message Ike again asked for "a grand plan for a properly articulated system that solves the problems of speedy, safe transcontinental travel; inter-city communications; access highways and farm-to-market movements; metropolitan congestion."

That year he was successful; the Federal Aid Highway Act passed both Houses of Congress, and on June 29 the President signed it into law. It was, he said, "the biggest peacetime construction project of any description ever undertaken by the United States or any other country." It would, he said, "change the face of America with straight-aways, cloverleaf turns, bridges, and elongated parkways. Its impact on the American economy" would be "beyond calculation."

At the end of the long transcontinental journey in 1919, Eisenhower got the leave he had requested, and he spent a happy month with his wife, his son, and the Douds. He had yet to make arrangements for Mamie and Icky to join him at Meade, and when the family started for their annual trip to San Antonio he went with them for part of the way. That trip, too, was hazardous. In Oklahoma the rain that had started shortly after they left Denver continued; again the roads were mud. "There were moments when I thought neither the automobile, the bus, nor the truck had any future whatever," he said.

They spent an entire week in a hotel in Lawton, Oklahoma, and while there they read every newspaper report about the 1919 World Series.

Of course, none of those reports prepared them for the ensuing Black Sox scandal that Eisenhower called "an all-time low for disloyalty and sellout of integrity. . . . The stories after each game, narrating the play, were strictly objective. But stark facts and objective reports could not give the whole story."

Ike, who as president was often criticized for taking too long to make up his mind on various issues, later said, "In the passage of years, whether because of the Black Sox scandal or not, I grew increasingly cautious about making judgments based solely on reports. Behind every human action, the truth may be hidden. But the truth may also lie behind some other action or arrangement, far off in time and place. Unless circumstances and responsibility demanded an instant judgment, I learned to reserve mine until the last proper moment. This was not always popular."

Eisenhower had thoroughly enjoyed the cross-country tour. Colonel Charles Miller, his commanding officer on the journey, said of him, "a good all-around officer, capable worker, willing and painstaking; intelligent; a good instructor; good military bearing; pleasing personality." His handling of his job, Colonel Miller said, had been "entirely satisfactory"; he had performed it "with energy and good judgment."

When Ike got back to Meade, most of his depression seemed to be gone. He found that Welborn was no longer his chief but was deputy to the new chief, Colonel Samuel D. Rockenbach, who had recently returned from France where he had been chief of the AEF Tank Corps. A solemn, hard-working man, unimaginative and narrow-minded, Rockenbach had been commanding officer overseas of a man Ike was to meet for the first time that fall of 1919, one who was both to delight and dismay him for the rest of his life, George S. Patton, Jr.

★ ★ ★

THE TORTOISE AND THE HARE

The difference between Eisenhower and Patton could be summed up in Aesop's verdict on the race between the tortoise and the hare: "Slow and steady wins the race." Colonel (temporary) George S. Patton, Jr., commanding officer, 304th Tank Brigade, was never slow and steady; Lieutenant Colonel (temporary) Eisenhower, second in command, 305th Tank Brigade, was seldom anything else.

Patton was born on November 11, 1885, five years before Eisenhower, on a 1,600 acre ranch near Pasadena, California. The remote ranch house was surrounded by eucalyptus trees and cedars. The Pattons had a housekeeper, half a dozen Mexican servants, a cook imported from England, and a governess. They stabled a dozen blooded horses, including Georgie's shetland pony, Peach Blossom.

Eisenhower's relationship with his father was distant; Patton's relationship with his father was abnormally close. After the older Patton's death, young George wrote in his diary, "I knelt and kissed the ground and saluted, not Papa, but the resting place of that beautiful body I loved."

At West Point, where in 1909 he graduated 46th out of 103, "Georgie," as he was called in *The Howitzer* and for the rest of his life, was on the football squad four years and broke school records in track and field.

In a West Point publication in which members of the class evaluated each other, Patton was called a "bootlick." During the Second World War "bootlick" became a "brown-noser," and Patton was frequently guilty of that when it suited his purpose. John Eisenhower said, "He would tell Dad 'I owe these stars to you and only to you,' and then he would cry a little."

Eisenhower was more subtle. When given a new assignment, he was always careful to find out what his superior officers wanted, and whenever he could, he did it. Patton was often described as flamboyant; he was "a character." He was unpredictable. Eisenhower was dependable, agreeable, predictable. Everybody thought from the beginning of Georgie's career that there were no limits to the heights he might achieve. For most of his life very few people thought that Eisenhower would achieve anything much.

Second Lieutenant George S. Patton, Jr., cavalry, the son of a wealthy lawyer, had married the even wealthier Beatrice Ayer, whose family had made millions— no one seemed to know how many—manufacturing textiles in New England. They had earned most of their fortune in the American Woolen Company.

It was known that Georgie's uniforms came from London's Savile Row; his boots came from Ugo Ferrini of Rome, and the pistols he wore at his hips were either pearl handled or ivory handled. He and Bea were often written up in the society pages of newspapers near the posts where they were stationed. It was known, too, that Patton did not need his army salary and often forgot to collect it.

Eisenhower's army salary was always essential to his and Mamie's survival, even when he was a four-star and five-star general. He was a poorly, though neatly dressed officer in or out of uniform. His taste in clothing was about the same, or perhaps slightly better, at the end of his life as when he left Abilene.

While Eisenhower was at Camp Colt training tank crews for overseas duty, Patton was already overseas in charge of the School for Light Tanks in France and of the First American Tank Center. Not only had he learned how tanks worked, how to keep them repaired and how the British-trained tankers used them in battle, he had himself tackled tactical problems and operated in tanks across trenches.

On September 26, 1918, while Eisenhower was concerning himself with Spanish flu among the troops, Patton "rallied a force of disorganized infantry and led it forward behind tanks under heavy machine gun and artillery fire" near Suippes, France. He had continued his derring-do until he was wounded in the leg. As the December 1918 citation for his Distinguished Service Cross went on to say, he had displayed "conspicuous courage, coolness, energy, and intelligence" as well as "extraordinary heroism in action."

In June of the following year he also received the Distinguished Service Medal, and later, when the AEF tankers returned home from overseas following the Armistice, Patton was immediately surrounded by reporters. The *New York Herald* had a story with the headline, COLONEL PATTON TELLS HOW BIG MACHINES BY HUNDRED ATTACKED THE GERMANS." The reporter described Patton's exploits on the battlefield, mentioned the D.S.C., said that he had "also been cited by the French for the Croix de Guerre," and there was a photograph of the young hero.

The only person who seemed to pay any attention to what Eisenhower was doing was Welborn, and the colonel's recommendation that Ike be awarded a Distinguished Service Medal was turned down. "It has been determined that the services performed by this officer, while efficient, are not exceptionally meritorous services to the government, performed in a duty of great responsibility within the meaning of the law authorizing the award of the Distinguished Service Medal."

When Eisenhower first met Patton in the fall of 1919 he was already a kind of legend, a fact Patton found unsurprising. He was convinced that he had been a hero and a legend in the past, that in fact there had been few battles in history in which he had not taken part. In North Africa in 1943, when General Sir Harold Alexander said to him, "You know, George, you would have made a great Marshal for Napoleon if you had lived in the 19th Century," Patton replied, "But I did."

Patton had been at Camp Meade briefly the previous spring but had not met Eisenhower. When he had arrived in late March, he was at the Benjamin Franklin Cantonment, which was the tank part of the post, the part where the troops were demobilized. The AEF Tank Corps, drastically reduced in size, merged with its U.S. counterpart, under the command of Colonel Welborn. In April Patton went to Washington on temporary duty in Welborn's office, formulating tank regulations and a course of instruction for the tankers. He was relieved from this temporary duty in September and returned to Meade on September 4, driving a spiffy new Pierce Arrow. He had written his father, "I can afford it and believe in enjoying myself between wars." Beatrice had a Franklin of her own. The Eisenhowers had a secondhand Model T.

It would have been quite natural for Eisenhower to have envied this living legend, only six years his senior (in rank), when he first met him, but if he did, he never said so. "Ike was not an envious man," said Mark Clark, who was very much one.

Eisenhower from the first admired and liked the fabulous, fortunate Georgie. He devoted most of a chapter in *At Ease* to their experiences at Meade. "When I returned to Camp Meade in the autumn, many changes had taken place. Senior Officers of the Tank Corps who had seen action in France, were back. Among these men the one who interested me most, and whom I learned to like best, was a fellow named Patton. Colonel George S. Patton was tall, straight, and soldierly looking. His most noticeable characteristic was a high, squeaking voice, quite out of keeping with his bearing. . . . Both of us were students of current military doctrine. Part of our passion was a belief in tanks—a belief derided at the time by others."

The many differences, personal and professional, between the two men seemed to disappear when they were discussing and working with what they both believed in, the tank. Eisenhower said, "George and I and a group of young officers . . . believed that they [tanks] should be speedy, that they should attack by surprise and in mass. By making good use of the terrain in advance, they could break into the enemy's defensive positions, cause confusion, and by taking the enemy front line in reverse, make possible not only an advance by infantry, but envelopments of, or actual breakthroughs in, whole defensive positions."

They experimented with the tanks they had at Meade, the light French Renaults and the American-made Mark VIIIs. At times even these two men had doubts about the future of the tank. It was clear that the Renaults were really too light for use in battle, that they were likely to balk when climbing even the lowest hill, and that they got stuck in the mud after the slightest rainfall. On the other hand, the Mark VIII was too slow, two awkward, and too difficult to maneuver.

"We devised a system of using Mark VIIIs to tow the smaller Renaults through depressions and up slopes where they, on their own power, could not make the grade," said Eisenhower. "On the side of each Mark VIII was an inch-thick steel cable, eighteen or twenty feet long. We used these as tow ropes to pull one, two, or three Renaults in tandem. This worked pretty well, increasing the small tanks' range."

One morning Eisenhower worked out an attack problem, and to carry it out, he and Patton attached three Renaults to a Mark VIII. It was to tow the smaller tanks through a deep, ruddy ravine. Eisenhower said, "Two of the Renaults became mired down, and the big tank had to give out maximum power.

"Patton and I were standing on the upslope as the big tank came through, crawling painfully to the top of the ravine. The noise was almost deafening; . . . in the midst of the racket we heard a ripping sound and we looked around just in time to see one of the cables part. As it broke, the front half whirled around like a striking black snake and the flying end, at machine-bullet speed, snapped past our faces, cutting off brush and saplings as if the ground had been shaved with a sharp razor."

That evening Patton said, "Ike, were you as scared as I was?"

"I was afraid to bring the subject up," said Eisenhower. "We were certainly not more than five or six inches from sudden death."

Perhaps as a result of that experience, Patton wrote a poem called "Fear:"

> I am that dreadful, fighting thing
> Like rat-holes in the flood
> Like the rust that gnaws the faultless blade
> Like microbes to the blood

They almost lost their lives again when testing a .30 caliber machine gun that became so hot with sustained firing that it continued to fire all by itself when they went to inspect the target. After that, Eisenhower said, "We decided that we had about used up our luck." They continued to experiment with the tanks, however. "In one respect, these circumstances were better than battle itself," said Eisenhower. "Trial and error and the testing of alternatives is experiment and research—but in action, you are offered few second chances."

One day at Meade Eisenhower and Patton completely took apart a Renault, as Eisenhower said, "item by item until there was no nut or bolt that had not been removed from the mechanism, including the engine. Now if a clock that has been disassembled can frighten the amateur, a tank, even a small one, is infinitely worse. I had doubts that we could ever restore the vehicle to running order.

"We started the reassembly during our afternoon hours and so carefully had we done the work, that no pieces were left over and the machine operated when we were finished." Their ingenuity was not applauded by their superior officers, however. They were told that they were wasting their time. The tank had no future, and if certain officers continued in their study and support of it, they wouldn't have much of a future either.

The American military was not alone in its indifference toward and opposition to tanks. Field Marshal Sir Douglas Haig, commander of the British Expeditionary Forces, and Marshal Joffre, commander of the French forces, both considered that the success of the tank the few times it was used in the First World War was accidental. It had no future, and when David Lloyd George, who became prime minister of Britain in 1916, suggested to them that horse cavalry might no longer be important or necessary, Haig and Joffre paid no attention except to say that civilians certainly did not understand military matters.

Eisenhower and Patton spent a good deal of time together. In addition to work, they played poker and spent a great many evenings, as Ike said, "studying and blowing off steam. . . . George . . . was getting prepared for Leavenworth [Command and General Staff School] and had sent for the back [tactical] problems. Then he said to me, 'Let's you and I solve these together.' He was . . . senior to me, and Leavenworth was still years ahead in my career; but I worked the problems with him. We began to solve them; and I found that as long as you didn't have any pressure on you, they seemed very easy. I liked them and got a lot of fun out of it. We'd go to his house or my house and the two of us would sit down, and while our wives talked for the evening, we would work the problems. Then I would open up another pamphlet, find the answer, and grade ourselves."

They even had themselves a most enjoyable game of "cops and robbers." While they were at Meade a number of robberies had occurred along the two-lane road leading from the center of camp to the main highway. One day the two adventurers put half a dozen pistols into a car—more likely the Pierce Arrow than the Ford—and, according to John Eisenhower, "started driving very slowly toward the main highway. Dad always said, 'We wanted to see what a fellow's face looked like when he's looking into the other end of a gun.' They were both going to pull guns in different directions and fix this guy. They thought they were going to be a two-man posse on the blacktop road there, but nobody stopped them. They were both disappointed."

The two men, so different in so many fundamental ways, as a result of the experiences they shared and the many mutual interests they had, became very close. Their wives never did.

Beatrice Ayer Patton was very different from Mamie Doud Eisenhower. Mamie was threatened by the outdoors and never took any exercise. Ike said, "She never has and never will consider outdoor sports a worthwhile way to spend her time." Beatrice loved being outdoors and riding and sailing. She had been educated largely in Europe and could speak French fluently; she wrote songs, pretty good songs; she wrote a book about Hawaii. She devoted a good deal of time and money to helping her husband achieve the glory and fame they both felt were his due. "He owed much of his success in the Army to his wife," Patton's biographer Martin Blumenson said. "In fact, it might be said that Patton was, as man and legend, to a large degree, the creation of his wife."

Mamie's biographer Dorothy Brandon put it delicately. "The close friendship between Ike and George Patton was never matched by their wives. . . . Mamie's only interest in sports was as a spectator at football games; her reading was confined largely to current events and an occasional novel. Although her family had better than average means, she had not traveled widely like Beatrice Patton, nor had she been associated with internationally prominent people. Mamie's orbit was domesticity. Her sparkle, wit and charm, her laughter, keen card sense and entertaining music, all made her the popular wife of a popular officer."

While Eisenhower was assigned to Meade, Mamie for some time was in a dismal furnished room in Laurel, Maryland, about "to throw in the sponge" and return to the Douds' home in San Antonio. Beatrice spent most of her time in a town house in Washington, which was just a little over thirty miles away.

Eisenhower and Patton were together at Meade for nearly a year. Eisenhower said, "One of the incalculable benefits I got from my friendship with George Patton was an invitation to meet a man who, as it turned out, was to have a tremendous influence on my life." Brigadier General Fox Conner, widely known as one of the real intellects of the army, was a close friend of General Pershing's. He had served as operations officer at general headquarters for Pershing in France, and after the war Pershing said no one, with the possible exception of himself, had been more important to American victory in Europe. Conner returned from France in September of 1919, and at the time Eisenhower met him was Pershing's chief of staff in Washington.

"When the Conners accepted an invitation from the Pattons to Sunday dinner, Mamie and I were included among the guests." What Eisenhower didn't know at the time was that the meeting had been prearranged. Patton had spoken so highly of Eisenhower that Conner went to Meade "to meet this promising young officer." Eisenhower was not aware of the purpose of the meeting, but he made a mighty impression on Fox Conner.

After dinner Conner asked to be shown around the tank schools, and Patton and Eisenhower took him down to the shops. Conner found a chair, sat down, and began asking questions, mostly about tanks, and most of them directed at Eisenhower. "Some could be answered briefly," Eisenhower said, "while others required long explanations."

During the session, which had lasted several hours, Conner had asked the temporary lieutenant colonel to express a great many opinions about the future of tanks, if any, and about the U.S. Army and its future, if any. Eisenhower's spontaneous answers were impressive.

On June 2, 1920, when Congress passed the National Defense Act, which abolished the Tank Corps and assigned tank units and personnel to the infantry, Patton asked to be relieved of his assignment with tanks and returned to duty with the cavalry. His request was granted and he was assigned to the 3d Cavalry. The Pattons moved into Quarters No. 5 at Fort Myer, Virginia, and the parties they gave were once again written up in the society pages of Washington's newspapers.

Eisenhower was still in the infantry, still commanding a brigade of heavy tanks when in November an article he had written about tanks appeared in *Infantry Journal.*

The article said:

A great many officers are prone to denounce the tank as a freak development of trench warfare which has already outlived its usefulness. Others, and this class seems to be in the majority, have come into contact with the tank so infrequently and have heard so little either decidedly for or against it that they simply ignore it in their calculations. . . .

[Some believe] that the man that follows this course of thinking is falling into a grievous error. . . . The tank is in its infancy, and the great strides already made in its mechanical improvement only point to the greater ones still to come. The clumsy, awkward and snail-like progress of the old tanks must be forgotten, and in their place we must picture a steady, reliable, and efficient engine of destruction.

Suppose we try to replace the Divisional Machine Gun Battalion by one company of . . . tanks. In making such a suggestion it should be understood that the idea is limited to the Motorized Battalion of the division. It is in no way meant to disparage the value of machine guns, and it is not in conflict with the idea supported by some officers of enlarging and unifying the machine-gun units in the division. Neither is it to be understood that it is proposed to limit the use and organization of tanks to one company per division. There must always be a large unit of tanks as army troops which can be used at the point or points most desired. Further, it is not contended that the replacing of the Divisional Machine Gun Battalion is absolutely necessary in order to include the company of tanks in the divisional organization. But by making such a proposition, it gives a ground for comparison with an organization and weapon with which officers in general are more or less familiar.

The article would seem to have been harmless, nothing inflammatory about it, simply a matter of carefully, diplomatically worded observations. Nevertheless, Eisenhower was summoned by a man very important to his career, Major General Frank L. Sheets, chief of infantry. General Sheets told Eisenhower that the ideas he had expressed in the article were wrong, that they were dangerous, and that in the future he was to keep them to himself. They were not solid infantry doctrine. And should the lieutenant colonel—he had just turned thirty— ignore what Sheets said, he would face a court-martial.

The Eisenhower-Patton career race was underway but by no means over. Anyone familiar with Aesop could have predicted the outcome. In the end,

Patton, as his biographer Martin Blumenson wrote, "missed the top rank of five stars. He was never a field marshal or a general of the armies like Marshall, MacArthur and Eisenhower during the war, [or] like Bradley, who was promoted in 1950 as U.S. Army Chief of Staff. . . . But he achieved something . . . far more important to him—enduring fame as a fighter. Like Horatio Nelson. He was a hero in the grand manner."

The two men remained friends until the 1940s, when "slow and steady" had clearly won the race. By then Patton found his old friend lacking in almost all the qualities a good general needed. Nowhere in his writing does Patton mention his first meeting with Ike, though he describes in details his first meeting with many other people. When he does mention Ike, either in his diaries or in his book, *War As I Knew It,* almost everything he says is critical.

Eisenhower many times during the war wished that he had never heard Patton's name, and while Patton's career was often in jeopardy, at least once Ike's was, too, because of what Georgie had done. If the tortoise and the hare ever developed a friendship Aesop does not mention it. He did, however, say, "I will have nought to do with a man who can blow hot and cold with the same breath," which is a perfect description of Patton.

★ ★ ★

THE DARK SHADOW

Mamie came to Meade for the first time in September 1919, shortly after Ike's return from his cross-country adventure. She left Icky behind in Denver. It was planned that a few weeks later Min Doud and Mike would take the baby by train to San Antonio for the winter. John Doud would come down to the house on McCullough Street in the Packard, and Mamie and Eisenhower could come for the Christmas holidays.

Many years later, after Eisenhower's death, Mamie looked back on their marriage and told Julie Nixon Eisenhower that "she blames herself for many of the strains on their marriage . . . and would like to go back and do some things differently. . . . More than anything else Mamie regrets that she gave in to the temptation to go 'home' to Denver so often. . . .

"It is easier to understand her frequent, prolonged absences when one considers some of the homes she and Ike shared," Julie observed. Mamie had not anticipated the room in Laurel; she had said that if Ike let her come to Meade, she would be willing to live in a tent, and indeed a tent might have been preferable. It was the only place Ike had been able to find, and Julie, relying on Mamie's memory, said it was "in a rooming house several miles from the post where the electricity was turned off at eight in the morning and did not go back on until after dark. Night after night Mamie sat in their gloomy room, waiting for Ike to come home—and the lights to go on. The only bathroom was down the hall. They ate at a boarding house around the corner."

Ike remembered, "Mamie had come alone . . . and had taken a room in . . . a small town a few miles from Meade. She stayed a month but because I could see her only a few evenings and because we both missed our little son, Icky, and worried about him while he was separated from us, she went back to San Antonio until we could all be together."

Dorothy Brandon said that the room was in Odenton, another depressing small town in Maryland not far from Meade, that the room was "clammy," that there was only one window, unwashed, that the landlady "was frugal with coal, and Mamie had to huddle in bed or bundle in blankets if she wanted to sit in a chair and stare out the streaked window at the intermittent traffic. Her breakfast came out of a paper bag."

After a stay of several weeks, said Brandon, "Mamie knew that she was doomed unless she found better accommodations . . . but . . . Ike was right; the war had brought too many new people into the area. No one showed any desire to move out. No one except Mamie Eisenhower. In dark defeat she packed up and caught a train for San Antonio."

Julie Eisenhower said, "Mamie's voice was anguished when she described the scene when she fled back home . . . half a century before. 'Ike begged me to stay . . . but I told him, "Ike, I can't live my life this way." '

"I threw in the sponge," said Mamie.

Ike came to San Antonio on Christmas leave, and he told Mamie that after the first of the year a duplex apartment would be available to them on the post at Meade, converted from a wartime barracks. A good deal of work still had to be done, however, and it seemed best not to bring Icky. He was to be left in Boone, Iowa, with Mrs. Doud's spinster sister, Eda.

By the time Mamie arrived on May 12, 1920, Eisenhower had found some odds and ends of furniture at the Meade dump and repainted and repaired them for the duplex. When Mamie got there, the meager furniture they had had at Colt had arrived, too, but the apartment still looked bare. Ike had made a dressing table for Mamie, decorating it with a remnant of flowered material. But they still had to sleep for a time on army cots.

The windows of their new quarters were large and clean; there was plenty of electricity, and Mamie would, Eisenhower said, "help me transform an ancient set of barracks into a home. . . . We scrubbed and waxed floors and brushed buckets of paint onto beaverboards nailed over the rough lumber partitions."

Actually, most of the work was done "with the help of soldiers who volunteered and whom I paid a nominal hourly sum. We had men who were skillful in revising plumbing. . . . The existing pipes were good for sanitizing thirty or forty men but were not much good for washing three people, one at a time. . . . All expenses of remodeling, renovating, and furnishing such barracks were to be borne by the officer himself."

The men even sowed grass in the sandy soil in front of the duplex and built a low picket fence around the front yard. "At the end, we were proud of the place which, counting labor and everything, had cost us about $700 or $800, not counting the labor Mamie and I had invested in the old barracks."

After the work was complete, Icky came east from Boone, probabaly accompanied by Mamie's Aunt Eda. Ike said, "For her trouble and his [Icky's] keep, we had paid her $100, somewhat under the going rates, I'm sure, but all we could afford out of our salary. When Icky arrived, we settled down."

It must have been the happiest time of his life up to then, that period beginning with Icky's arrival in August until just before Christmas 1920. Friend and postwar assistant Kevin McCann said, "That boy was everything to Ike. He would put on acts for him—lying on the floor and pretending to be a kitten, growling like a bull dog, playing the clown to make him laugh."

Icky was an engaging child. Like his father he was blond and blue eyed; he had an infectious grin, and, like his father, he loved the army, loved uniforms, loved parades, and loved football. His father said, "I was inclined to display Icky and his talents at the slightest excuse, or without one, for that matter. In his company, I'm sure I strutted a bit and Mamie was thoroughly happy that, once again, her two men were with her."

Ike was determined to be the kind of father David had never been, openly affectionate, and interested in whatever his son did. That was not difficult for him; as a parent there was a great deal of Ida in him and very little of David.

By this time Eisenhower was "entirely out of debt." He would be able to give Icky a good Christmas. He could also, with a salary of $320 a month, afford to hire someone to help Mamie with housework and child care. "We hired a girl in the neighborhood who was ready to work and who seemed both pleasant and efficient," Ike said. "When she accepted the job, a chain of circumstances began, linking us to a tragedy from which we never recovered."

On December 23 Mamie went to Baltimore with a number of other officers' wives to buy Christmas presents for the children of enlisted men. Icky's many presents were already piled under the tree in the living room. When Mamie got home, the maid told her that Icky seemed to have a fever. Mamie immediately consulted a doctor and described what she knew of the boy's symptoms; the doctor said just what most pediatricians would say today, particularly during the flu season. Keep him in bed a few days, and if he gets worse, call back.

Two days later, on Christmas day, Icky was so much worse that he couldn't get out of bed to open his presents. By that time, too, Mamie was in bed with a cold and a migraine headache. Ike played nurse for both his son and wife. Neither got better, and Icky got much worse. On the 27th the post doctor came to the house, examined the boy, and said that he had a severe case of scarlet fever. In those days, before sulfa drugs, the disease could be fatal, and, as Eisenhower remembered, when Milton was a boy, it almost had been.

Mamie was placed in quarantine, and Eisenhower took Icky to the post hospital in an ambulance. "We did everything possible to save him," he said. "The camp doctor brought in specialists from the nearby Johns Hopkins Medical School in Baltimore." Ike was not allowed in the boy's room, but he sat on a porch just outside. "I could look into the room and wave to him. Occasionally, they would let me come to the door just to speak to Icky. I haunted the halls of the hospital. Hour after hour, Mamie and I could only hope and pray. In those days, before modern medicine eliminated scarlet fever as a childhood scourge, hope and prayer were the only possibilities for parents. At the turn of the year, we lost our firstborn son."

Shortly after he had checked Icky into the hospital Eisenhower telephoned Min who, along with Mike and John Doud, was in Boone celebrating a Swedish Christmas with the Carlsons. Mike said, "Mother left almost immediately after Ike's call; I don't think she had much hope; in those days just saying the words 'scarlet fever' was enough to terrify most people. But she went. Mamie and Ike needed her."

Min arrived at Meade on the morning of the last day of 1920. Mamie was so depressed she seemed able only to speak in monosyllables, but Min, outwardly at least, was cheerful. Ike almost never left the hospital, and on January 2 he called home to say that Icky's crisis would be later that night. If he survived it, there was a good chance of complete recovery. If he did not, he would be dead by morning. That night Mamie and Min had the welcome company of a young lieutenant of whom Ike was fond. He was there to keep the two women company, stoke the fire, and, if they wished, play the piano. He was the favorite pianist at Meade at the time, and he did play. For most of the night no one spoke, and when Ike returned to the house early in the morning, accompanied by two other officers, he did not speak. A look at his face was enough; Icky had died.

Forty-six years later Eisenhower said: "I do not know how others have felt when facing the same situation, but I have never felt such a blow. Within a week he was gone. I didn't know what to do. I blamed myself because I had often taken his presence for granted, even though I was proud of him and of all the evidence that he was developing as a fine, normal boy. . . . For Mamie, the loss was heartbreaking, and her grief in turn would have broken the hardest heart.

"This was the greatest disappointment and disaster in my life, the one I have never been able to forget completely. Today, when I think of it, even now as I write of it, the keenness of our loss comes back to me as fresh and as terrible as it was in that long dark day soon after Christmas in 1920."

Mamie said, "For a long time, it was as if a shining light had gone out of Ike's life. Throughout all the years that followed, the memory of those bleak days was a deep inner pain that never seemed to diminish much."

In an interview in 1970, Mamie looked back to that January in 1921 and said it had been one of the most difficult periods in her life. "They had no serums, and . . . they [children] either got well or you lost them. Well, we lost him, and that was a very, very difficult time."

Icky's body was taken to the Baltimore railroad station by an honor guard, and from there the body, accompanied by Ike, Mamie, and Mrs. Doud, went to Denver where last services were held in front of the same fireplace where the young Eisenhowers' wedding had taken place three and a half years before. The burial was in Fairmont Cemetery, next to the graves of Mamie's two sisters, and the body remained there until 1966 when it was moved to the Eisenhower Meditation Chapel in Abilene, on the grounds where the library is and across from the house where Eisenhower was born.

Ike said in *At Ease*, "My wife and I have arranged that when it comes our time to be buried, to be laid away in our final resting place, we shall have him with us." In 1966, the year he partly dictated, partly wrote that book, he informed his old friend and supporter former Senator Harry Darby that he and Mamie wanted the boy's body brought to Abilene.

Earl Endacott, the first director of Eisenhower Library, said that no such provisions had been made in the original plans for the Eisenhower burial place. "It became necessary to tear out a portion of the concrete vault so that a place could be made for the boy at the foot of the adult graves." When reconstruction of the chapel was complete, Ike was notified, and on June 2, 1966, he flew secretly to Denver in an army plane to pick up Icky's body. Milton and Ike's longtime aide General Robert Schulz went with him on the trip.

Then the three men, still secretly, took the body back to Kansas, landing at the airport in Manhattan to avoid attention. A local undertaker met the plane, and the body, still accompanied by Eisenhower, Milton, and Schulz, was taken to the meditation chapel. The Reverend John Kellison of the Abilene Presbyterian Church and an army chaplain from Fort Riley conducted services. Then, Endacott said, "The casket in a wooden box was placed at the foot of the adult graves, and a short burial service was read by the two clergymen. As soon as the party left the chapel, the waiting workmen placed an already prepared concrete lid over the grave and the small headstone brought from Denver was placed in front. . . . Concrete was then poured over the hole and the terrazzo floor was refinished so that when the chapel was opened the next morning there was no evidence of the burial."

It was an extraordinary sentimental journey for a former president of the United States, and it was done in secret because Ike had no intention of letting the public know about the grief he still felt. He meant it when he said, "the keenness of our loss comes back to me as fresh and as terrible as it was in that long dark day soon after Christmas 1920."

Mamie missed the trip; she was in Walter Reed Hospital suffering from shingles, and when the doctors told her she couldn't go, she once again wept.

In late 1967, when he was on his way to Palm Springs by train, Ike stopped in Abilene and again visited Icky's grave. According to John, "He left upset. Mother called to say that the Boss was in bed with some sort of ailment, his spirits low." A few months later he had his third major heart attack, and that had a lot of emotional underpinnings. "Mother attributed it to the emotional impact of seeing the tiny plaque on the floor where the body of my older brother had been placed. She attributed a lot of things to it. . . .

"They were very good about not mentioning the death around me. Except every now and then Dad would say something—like how Icky, though he couldn't read the labels, could go through a stack of records and tell one from another. There were a lot of stories about Icky. . . . I really think his feelings were even more severe than he let on in *At Ease*. His feelings about Icky's death were very severe, very, all his life."

Privately, the death of Icky was often mentioned, particularly around the time of his birthday. On September 15, 1942, when Eisenhower was just getting used to his new job as commander of the European Theater of Operations in London, he wrote Mamie, "Some time ago you mentioned Aug. 24 as Ikky's [*sic*] birthday. I think you must have been thinking of September! Anyway, according to my feeble memory he would have been 25 on the 24th of this month." And on the 23rd he wrote her, "Tomorrow . . . Ikky would have been 25 years old. Seems rather unbelievable, doesn't it? We could well have been grandparents by this time."

On September 20, 1943, shortly after the first Allied bridgehead had, under Eisenhower's direction, been secured on the continent of Europe, he wrote her from his advanced headquarters at Amilcar, Tunisia, "This is the 20th of September and in four days more Ikky would have been twenty-six years old." On September 25, 1944, shortly after the triumphant Allied entry into Paris he wrote Mamie from Versailles, "I was going to write you today anyway because yesterday I thought so frequently of Ikky. He would have been 27 years old." And on September 25, 1945, he wrote Mamie from his now-peaceful headquarters in Frankfurt, again mentioning that they could have been grandparents. "It's difficult to realize that if Ikky had lived he would have been 28 today. We could easily have been grandparents—I'd have loved it. It would be especially nice to be with you today."

Eisenhower, for the rest of his life, sent Mamie flowers on Icky's birthday, usually yellow roses, the boy's favorite color, and he was particularly sympathetic when his friends suffered similar losses. His letters at such times showed remarkable empathy.

The noted writer of the *Inside* books, John Gunther, had covered the invasion of Sicily in 1943, and Ike and he had become warm friends, not usually the case with the general and newspapermen. After Gunther's son died of a brain tumor in 1947, a tragedy Gunther wrote about in his moving book *Death Be Not Proud*, he wrote Eisenhower that "Everything in my life was upset almost beyond arrangement by the death on June 30 of my 17-year-old son."

Ike wrote back on July 24.,

I am deeply shocked to learn of your son's sad passing and know well that neither success nor words of solace can much lighten the grave loss that is yours. A similar experience of my own, years ago, makes me particularly sensitive to the pain you will continue to bear.

In 1948, when his friend Louis Marx and his wife Barbara lost their twin girls at birth, Eisenhower wrote to him on January 27:

Inclosed [*sic*] is a note in which I have tried, though most inadequately, to tell Barbara something of the depth of my sympathy. . . . I want you to know that to you also I extend assurances of a deep and understanding sympathy. Our own first son died when he was quite a little boy and to this day I cannot think of it without experiencing again, at least in part, the very great grief that then seemed insurmountable. Nevertheless, receding time does bring at least a philosophical resignation.

The letter to Barbara, which was handwritten, said how shocked and distressed he was to learn she had lost her babies.

You have suffered a great tragedy and I do hope it will be of some consolation to you to know that all your friends, yours and Louis', will pray that you are given the strength to conquer your grief.

And in 1949, when Helen Hayes's daughter, Mary, died of polio, a handwritten letter arrived from Eisenhower, who was then president of Columbia University. "It was right after Mary died," Miss Hayes remembered, "and he told us about their loss, his and Mamie's loss of a son, and the terrible, horrible thing that it was for them. He used the analogy of a pit."

We were once in that same black pit, and if these words can help you out of that pit, I will consider writing this worthwhile.

Ike

P.S. If you attempt to answer this letter I'll be very upset.

Ann Whitman, Ike's personal secretary in the White Hoouse, said, "I came into the Oval Office one day and found him staring off into space. He turned to me and said very simply that he was thinking of the little boy. Upstairs, in the family living quarters, there would always be fresh flowers. Once he pointed to some—I can't remember what kind it was—and said: 'Icky always liked those flowers.' "

Malcolm Moos, the educator who was one of Eisenhower's speech writers, said that when he was working with the president on what was to be the most famous speech of his career, the farewell address dealing with the "industrial-military complex," "He was working furiously on one of the many drafts of that speech, and I was working with him. One day he stopped abruptly and asked if I had seen a particular phase of the Second World War; I forget which one. I told him that I had not, explaining that I had been in the ROTC but was rejected for active service because of physical infirmities resulting from scarlet fever. He nodded, then walked to the east door of the beautiful Oval Office and stood looking out at the White House lawn and beyond for several minutes. No further words were spóken. I felt it was time to leave."

Icky's death naturally affected the Doud family, as well, particularly John. Doud Dwight had not only been his first grandchild; he had been his namesake. His death meant that there were now three graves instead of two, and John Eisenhower remembered that, "Every Sunday the family would go to Fairmont Cemetery to change the flowers on the three graves and then sit silently for what seemed to a small boy an interminable length of time."

No wonder John felt a sense of exile when he was sent to Denver in the summer. The Doud house in Denver was not the happy-go-lucky place that Mike remembered, or that Eisenhower had found in 1915. To John Eisenhower, the Douds were "Very fearful people, especially at night. They didn't have just one line of defense in their home; they had several. You would lock the outside door and then you would have an inner key and you would lock the inside door. I couldn't figure out what made Pupah so morose. Shadow time he'd call it. Shadow time meant dusk."

When the Eisenhowers got back to Fort Meade from their sad journey to Denver in January 1921, friends on the post had taken away the Christmas tree and the unopened presents for their son. Ike and Mamie were forever grateful for that. Such thoughtful acts were the good part of life in the peacetime army. People not only knew about you, they cared about you. There was a clannish feeling that army people liked to think, probably rightly, civilians could neither share nor understand.

It turned out that the young girl Eisenhower and Mamie had hired to help with the housework and to help take care of Icky had been the carrier of the scarlet fever. Eisenhower said, "Although her cure was quick and she showed no evidence of the illness, the doctors finally concluded that she had brought the disease to the camp—and that our young son had contracted it from her."

Julie Eisenhower said, "Half a century later, Mamie was still unwilling to say much about how Icky's death changed her relationship with Ike. The pain is too deep. But there is no doubt that the loss of their beloved son closed a chapter in the marriage."

For a time, though probably neither ever said it aloud, Ike blamed himself for the maid being hired and for Icky's death, and for a time Mamie no doubt blamed herself. Then in their minds each blamed the other, and the dark shadow remained in each of their minds for the rest of their lives.

★   ★   ★

A GRAVE OFFENSE

Six months after Icky's death another blow fell, one that intensified Eisenhower's grief and pain. He was charged by the acting inspector general with "offenses of the gravest character for which he might not only be dismissed from the service but imprisoned." The whole episode, which lasted from mid-June until the end of 1921, was not something he would have brought home from the office to discuss with Mamie. The burden of it must have driven them even further apart. The trouble this time also concerned Icky. It had to do with the cost of supporting him in the two and a half months before the final, fatal trip to Meade.

The sum of $250.67 was involved. It was said that Eisenhower had knowingly violated army regulations by taking that amount for "commutation of quarters, heat and light for a dependent son, while during this same period his lawful wife was resident with him at Camp Meade, Md., and did with him, occupy public quarters, heated and lighted from public funds."

What he was said to have done was, according to the acting inspector general, Brigadier General Eli A. Helmick, West Point 1888, "illegal and unauthorized." He was charged with saying what was "false and untrue." It was recommended that he "be brought to trial upon charges."

There is no question but that Mamie during that period was living with Eisenhower in the converted barracks at Meade. As will be seen, in answering the charges against him Eisenhower does not deny that he and Mamie were living in the converted barracks; the money he took from the government for commutation was for the maintenance of his son, who was either in Boone or Denver from May 12, 1920, to September 1 of that year. Wherever Icky was, to charge the army for his separate abode was against regulations.

The army regulation Ike was accused of violating and, it would appear, did in fact violate was clear enough. It said, "Under the act of April 16, 1918, authorizing the paying of commutation of quarters, heat and light to Army officers who maintain an abode for a wife, child, or dependent parent only one abode is authorized for dependents in the order named, although such abode may be occupied by any or all such dependents within the officer's authorized allowance." Had he knowingly violated that regulation? Ike said no; his accusers said yes.

Neither in *At Ease* nor in any of his other writings does Eisenhower mention how close he came to trial and disgrace during the last six months of 1921. The chapter in *At Ease* called "The Tragic Road to Panama" discusses Icky's death in detail, but there is no mention of the grave offense with which Eisenhower was charged. His many biographers have been equally silent. But all the documents dealing with the case are available in his official army 201 file.

In *At Ease* Eisenhower says of the period from May 12 to September 1920, "Altogether, it was about two and a half months before we felt able to send for Icky, who was living with Mamie's aunt in Boone, Iowa."

But in a statement to the army, Eisenhower swore that during that period Icky was in Denver and that maintaining him there had cost $250.67, which he collected from the army. The army wanted the money back; but getting it back was just the first thing the army wanted. For a time, it looked as if the brilliant career of Dwight D. Eisenhower was over, which would have been a pity for him, for the army, and for the rest of us. It is an unexplained and unexamined part of his life, one of the few.

Eisenhower heard on June 14 that another officer on the post at Meade was in trouble for collecting commutation for more than one abode. He immediately went to the camp inspector to report the commutation he had received for Icky and was told it was unlawful; it was something that he, too, could get into trouble for. He then wrote a long letter to the adjutant general, never before published, in which he explained what he had done. It was probably the most difficult letter he ever wrote; and although in the end he was praised for writing it, and it proved useful in exonerating him, it was by no means his most effective.

The letter, which was dated June 17, 1921, said:

I have been informed by the Camp Inspector, that in his opinion I erroneously drew commutation of quarters for a dependent child from May 1, 1920, to September 1, 1920. The circumstances are as follows:

During the period I was on duty at this camp, which is classified as being in the field.

1. On May 12, 1920, my wife came to live with me in quarters which were converted barracks. A great deal of labor and personal expenditure was necessary before this building was rendered suitable for occupancy by an infant. Therefore for the period above mentioned I maintained an abode for Doud Dwight Eisenhower, who was my son. He was brought to live with me on Sept. 1, 1920, whereupon I immediately ceased drawing commutation for a dependent. The abode I maintained for my son, who was totally dependent on me for support, was at 750 Lafayette Street, Denver, Colorado.

2. The Camp Inspector states that inasmuch as my wife was occupying quarters with me at this camp, I was not entitled to commutation for the abode I maintained as above mentioned. I believe that this camp is classed as being in the field, that an officer is entitled to commutation for a dependent who is maintained elsewhere, without regard to the type of quarters occupied at this camp.

3. Copy of certificate signed by me in making claim for commutation described above, is enclosed. Attention is invited to the fact that this certificate does not call for a description of the type of headquarters occupied by an officer of the camp, but is simply a statement that an abode for a bona fide dependent was maintained elsewhere.

4. Request a decision as to whether I was entitled to commutation I drew under above conditions. In case it is decided that I was not entitled to same, request that this letter be referred to the auditor of the Army for a statement of the amount of commutation I drew between the dates mentioned, in order that I may refund the government.

Once the letter was written, Eisenhower probably put the matter out of his mind. He probably would have to repay the government for the commutation he had received, and while money was scarce, he could manage it. He had been careless, but the whole thing was nothing to brood about.

The letter's failure was apparent almost immediately. On June 21, only four days later, the adjutant general of the army replied (through channels):

Major Eisenhower's explanations and statements with reference to this matter are not thought to materially affect the issue. . . . The usual sources of definite information were open to Maj. Eisenhower, and he had only to make inquiry at Hq. Cp. Meade, Md., or Hq. Tank Center to be informed that the drawing of commutation under the circumstances he was then obtaining such allowance, was illegal and unauthorized. The Certificate[s] which this officer filed with his pay vouchers for the months of May to August 1920, inclusive, were on their face false and untrue. . . . and the result of this investigation leads me to the conclusion that . . . Major Dwight D. Eisenhower, Inf., be brought to trial upon charges based upon the facts as developed.

That same day it was recommended that Eisenhower's pay be stopped until the army got back its $250.67.

The adjutant general also wrote to the Law Division of the War Department for an opinion on the matter, at the same time requesting an investigation be conducted at Camp Meade.

On June 30 Colonel H. A. White, Judge Advocate, Chief, Administrative Law Division, wrote a long decision that concluded, "Major Eisenhower was not entitled to commutation of quarters for his dependent child during the above period—May 12 to September 1, 1920."

Colonel White, West Point 1895, did not give an opinion about what should be done. On July 6 General Helmick, acting inspector general of the army, rendered his report. He began it with the familiar charges and added excerpts of an interview with the accused.

Q: And you believed that in addition to the receipt of an abode for your family and heat and light in kind for them, you were also entitled to commutation of the same for your son who was living elsewhere?

A: My understanding of the law was that so long as I was actually maintaining an abode for a portion of my family and my station was in the field, in a cantonment, that I was entitled to commutaton without regard to any personal quarters occupied by me in the camp. I believed that the law was intended to give commutation to assist officers to maintain their families or parts of their families when not occupying public quarters and I know of no decision or opinion to the contrary.

General Helmick did not agree; he said that Eisenhower had taken the $250.67 "well knowing that he was already in receipt of quarters, heat, and light in kind for himself and wife, from the United States, for the same period."

Then Helmick proceded with the damning statement,

Major Dwight D. Eisenhower, Infantry, did for the period May 12, 1920, to August 31, 1920, sign certificates as follows: I certify that the foregoing account is correct that payment therefor has not been received; that I have not been absent on leave, either sick or ordinary, during the period covered by this voucher, except as stated above. AND NEITHER I, MY FAMILY, NOR ANYONE DEPENDENT ON ME HAS OCCUPIED PUBLIC HEADQUARTERS, NOR BEEN FURNISHED HEAT AND LIGHT BY THE UNITED STATES DURING THE PERIOD FOR WHICH COMMUTATION OF HEAT AND LIGHT IS CHARGED [Emphasis Helmick's], well knowing that his wife was occupying a public building as headquarters and that he and his wife were actually receiving an allowance of heat and light from the United States, in kind, during the entire period for which commutation was charged and received.

Helmick made two recommendations as a result of his findings:

a. That Major Dwight D. Eisenhower, Infantry, be brought to trial upon charges based upon the facts as developed.

b. That steps be taken at once to cause stoppage of pay to reimburse the United States for the amount erroneously received by Major Dwight D. Eisenhower, i.e., $250.67.

Eisenhower's pay was stopped on July 18, and the next day he paid the full amount to an officer of the Finance Department at Meade. That same day Colonel Rockenbach delivered an oral reprimand to Eisenhower; it seems unlikely that the chief of the Tank Corps was very harsh in his reprimand; he was, after all, an old friend of Georgie Patton's; they had fought together in France, and Rockenbach had recommended Patton for the Distiguished Service Medal. He was also a close friend of and fought in France with Sereno Brett, Eisenhower's companion in his cross-country adventure. They were all friends of Eisenhower's and, with their wives, had frequently dined together. Besides, Major Eisenhower was a passionate believer in the future of the tank, and there were not many of those in or out of the army in 1921. Nor were there many good football coaches, and since Eisenhower's arrival at Meade in 1919 he had, at Rockenbach's instructions, been coaching the Tank School's football team.

It might have seemed for a time after the reprimand that the nightmare was over, and on August 11 Eisenhower and Mamie went on a welcome forty-five-day leave in Denver. Helmick did not relax, however. On August 25 he turned the matter over to the III Corps Area at Fort Howard, which was not far from Meade, "for further investigation and appropriate disciplinary action." He also referred the case to the adjutant general, saying,

Attention is invited to the 8th Ind., and inclosure thereto in which it is stated no disciplinary action has been taken against this officer at Camp Meade. The reasons given for failing to bring Major Eisenhower to trial as recommended . . . are not concurred in.

Why was Helmick being such a stickler over what to most civilians would appear to be something inconsequential? Did he have a personal grudge against Eisenhower of which there is no record? I would guess not. Helmick was an old army man who went by the book. In the peacetime army, if you did not go by the book, if you failed to enforce every single rule, the whole shaky structure might collapse. The army in those days *was* the book. Any deviation was dangerous. It was better to be safe than sorry, and nobody ever got in trouble enforcing the rules.

Eisenhower's attempt to prevent an investigation had failed, and while he was acquainted with Major General C. J. Bailey, West Point 1880, commander at Fort Howard, and had been asked to and, thank God, agreed to coach the III Corps Area's football team (of which the general was a fervent fan), if the finding at Fort Howard was negative, he might be court-martialed and dismissed from the army.

While Eisenhower was on leave, he learned the nightmare wasn't over. In

September an officer at III Corps headquarters who was conducting the investigation wrote Eisenhower a letter offering what would appear to be another chance, "In order to afford him every opportunity to fully present his side of the case . . . describing in detail the present status of the matter, and asking that he make any further comment or explanation deemed desirable regarding his alleged illegal drawing of cash allowances for commutation of quarters."

There is no record in Eisenhower's 201 that he ever answered that letter. He may have felt, as he was later to tell the newspaperman Merriman Smith, "I can accept a fact for what it is, and I also can accept the fact that when you're hopelessly outgunned and outmanned, you have quite some thoughts about whether or not to make the fight. You'd rather let the fight come to you. You don't go out and pick quarrels when you know you're going to lose."

Or perhaps, as he much later told John Gunther, for months after Icky died he was "on the ragged edges of a breakdown." He was thirty-one years old. Neither his personal nor his professional life was going well. He had been turned down for the army's Infantry Training School at Leavenworth, which was a prerequisite for Command and General Staff School. Without the training offered by those two schools, no matter what else he did or how well he did it, his chances for advancement were limited, possibly nonexistent. Even a natural-born optimist, which he said he was, can get discouraged and depressed. There were times when he thought of the many disappointments of George Washington, and this may have been one of those times. Washington once said, "There is nothing that gives a man consequence and renders him fit for command like a support that renders him independent of everybody but the state he serves." He could still do his duty; he could still serve his state.

He would rest his case on his first letter.

Eisenhower returned to Meade on October 1, and on the 24th Brigadier General H. F. Hodges, West Point 1881 and at that time commander of the III Corps Area at Fort Howard, Maryland, wrote a soothing letter to the adjutant general.

It appears that the immediate commander of the accused administered to the latter . . . a verbal (probably oral) reprimand for the offenses covered in the inclosed charges. Just what was said by way of reprimand has not been shown, but whatever was said is believed possibly to have been sufficient to bar a trial on these charges, by reason of the provisions of the 104th Article of War. . . .

However, if it should be held that trial is not barred, it is recommended that duly-certified copies of the pay accounts, and certificates in connection therewith, upon which the accused drew his pay and commutation for the months mentioned in the charges, be procured and placed with these papers.

In other words, let the matter rest, but gather the relevant papers together *if* it should be ruled that a trial is *not* barred by the reprimand, "verbal (probably oral)." However, in Hodges' view, "whatever was said" was all that needed to be said.

But Helmick was not satisfied; on November 1 he again addressed the adjutant general. He repeated the charges, added that what Eisenhower had done was "false and fraudulent." Helmick felt ignorance of a regulation was no excuse at all, a fact that Eisenhower was, often portentously, to tell his son, John, and others as well. In the report, Helmick said:

Major Eisenhower is a graduate of the Military Academy, of six years' commissioned service. That he should have knowingly attempted to defraud the government in this matter or, as he contends, that he was ignorant of the provisions of the laws governing commutation for dependents are alike inexplicable. Before submitting a recommendation as to whether or not he should be brought to trial on these charges, it is desirable to have a full statement of his pay accounts as to commutation for dependents that may or may not have been drawn by him in the past.

Those were serious charges, the most serious so far. Helmick was not only saying that Eisenhower had lied about the period from May 12 to September 1, 1920, but that he had possibly lied in other instances as well, and only an examination of his total financial record could determine that.

For a time, Helmick was officially silent. Apparently no more financial irregularities were found, even by his anxious eyes.

By November 8, things began improving for Eisenhower. On that day "having been previously awarded the tank sweater and insignia," Ike was awarded (by Rockenbach) a "bar . . . for his untiring energy and devotion to the coaching of the Tank School Football Team during the season of 1921. The victory of the team can be largely attributed to his splendid efforts."

That was pleasing, but incidental. Much more important was that on December 7 orders were issued by the adjutant general of the army that would send Eisenhower to a new station, the Panama Canal Zone.

When Fox Conner learned that he was being sent to Panama as commander of the 80th Brigade, he immediately wrote Eisenhower asking him to come along as his executive officer. Eisenhower very much wanted the assignment, but the charges against him were still pending, and Rockenbach said no. Finally Rockenbach, knowing that the request for transfer would be refused, passed it along to the War Department. Disapproval was as instantaneous as anything in the War Department could be. Then General Pershing, Conner's boss and friend, took over as chief of staff of the army, replacing Helmick's friend and classmate, Peyton March. Conner immediately wrote a memo to Pershing:

Subject: Request of Fox Conner for Brigadier Adjutant.

He desires the detail of this particular officer (Maj. Dwight D. Eisenhower, Inf.) because he knows of his efficiency and because he is due for foreign service.

Eisenhower said, "The red tape was torn to pieces, orders were issued, and I was to arrive at the new station by January of 1922."

In this case the "red tape" was Acting Inspector General Eli Helmick. Helmick was not a stupid man. He had to realize that pursuing Eisenhower and forcing him to undergo a trial that might end his military career would not be looked upon with favor by the new army establishment, Pershing and Conner. Helmick still had another six years of active service, and he had no intention of being put on the shelf during those years. He wanted another star to take him into retirement. So Helmick retreated; he was no longer the Grand Inquisitor so far as Eisenhower was concerned. Still, he could not pretend there had been no charges; that would mean he had made a mistake. So on December 14 he sent a softened memorandum to the new chief of staff, reiterating all the charges about the separate commutation for Eisenhower's son. Was the oral reprimand given Eisenhower enough? As a stickler for rules and regulations, Helmick had to say he thought not.

The 104th Article of War does not confer jurisdiction on commanding officers to administer disciplinary punishment for grave offenses. . . . Therefore, since Major Eisenhower was charged with offenses of the gravest character for which he might not only be dismissed from the service but imprisoned, any action taken by his Commanding Officer under the 104th Article of War, in advance of the preferment of those charges, may not legally be made the basis of a plea in bar of trial for the same offenses stated in informal charges.

Then, having delivered his morality lecture, Helmick got to the "however," which cannot have been displeasing to Eisenhower, Conner, or Pershing. Helmick said:

The trial of Major Eisenhower is not recommended, however. While he was clearly not entitled to commutation for his son, there are no circumstances connected with his drawing same to indicate an intent to defraud the Government. Major Eisenhower's claims were made without ordinary prudence, but his frank avowal to the Inspector that he had drawn commutation for his son under the conditions stated must be weighed in his favor as showing a lack of knowledge on his part that his claims were false and fraudulent.

In other words, Helmick had done a complete about-face. In his earlier reports he had stated that Eisenhower's claim "that he was ignorant of the provision of the law governing commutations for dependents" was "inexplicable"; now he was saying lack of knowledge must be "weighed in his favor." No wonder in 1952 Eisenhower was able to tell Merriman Smith, "How do you get to be Army Chief of Staff . . . I have been in politics, the most active sort of politics in the military. . . . There's no more active political organization in the country or in the world than the armed services of the United States. . . . I think I am a better politician than most so-called professionals." Who could disagree?

Major Eisenhower still needed to be properly reprimanded, however, and it could only be done, according to Helmick, by "competent authority." In this case that was Assistant Chief of Staff, Brigadier General J. H. McRae, West Point 1886, whose office just happened to be next door to that of Fox Conner.

The reprimand from McRae read:

The Secretary of War directs:

1st. That a letter, substantially as follows be sent to Major Dwight D. Eisenhower, Infantry, through the Chief of Infantry.

With respect to the charges preferred against you for violation of the 94th and 98th Articles of War, in that you did draw commutation of quarters, heat and light for a dependent son while your lawful wife was resident with you at Camp Meade, Md. and did, with you, during the period for which commutation was drawn for your son, actually occupy public quarters, heated and lighted from public funds, the decision of the Secretary of War is that you not be brought to trial on those charges but be reprimanded instead. In arriving at this decision, due weight has been given to your disclaimer of any intent to defraud the Government and to the fact that you voluntarily subjected yourself to investigation nearly a year after the commutation was drawn by you. Your admitted ignorance of the law, however, is to your discredit, and your failure to take ordinary precautions to obtain from proper authority a decision as to the validity of your claims, is, in an officer of your grade, likewise to your discredit. Opinions of the Judge Advocate General and decisions of the Comptroller General are appropriately published for the guidance of all officers. A failure to conform to these opinions and decisions has, in the present case, led to these grave charges being properly preferred against you.

A copy of this letter will be filed with your record.

2nd. That all accompanying papers then be returned to the Office of the Inspector General for file.

As reprimands go, McRae's could be described as no more than a light tap on the wrist. While no officer would welcome having it as part of his 201, it would do him no actual harm, certainly not in Eisenhower's next assignment in Panama. His commanding officer there had almost certainly seen and approved the reprimand before it was sent. He may even have had a part in writing it.

The whole episode had lasted six months, and it turned out to be a total waste of time and money. The investigation must have cost the poverty-stricken peacetime army a good deal more than $250.67. It had, however, kept the acting inspector general occupied and no doubt feeling righteous.

In his final efficiency report at Meade, the friendly Colonel Rockenbach gave Eisenhower no "superior" ratings as he had in previous reports. He was listed as "average" in judgment and tact. And he was rated as "above average" only as a football coach and the commander of a heavy tank battalion. The lengthy statements on the charges against him were "inclosed." He was criticized, though mildly. "Having had independence of command for so long a time, his personal views influence his cooperation." But "He has an excellent command nevertheless and is an efficient officer. The morale in his battalion and among the athletes he has trained has been high." He was "an enthusiastic officer of greatest value to tank organizations."

Finally, there was the letter from Major General Bailey. He knew all about the trouble over the abode for Doud Dwight Eisenhower but, to him, football was clearly more important. He wrote:

Dear Major:
   It is with a feeling of gratification and pleasure that I take this opportunity of expressing my appreciation and thanks to you for coaching the Corps Area Football Team for its game against the Marines on December 3rd. You did an excellent job. Besides producing a good team for the championship game you developed for the Army a fine squad of football players, many of whom never had the good fortune of receiving such splendid coaching. The clean sportsmanship, endurance and fighting-to-the-finish spirit displayed on the field by your men was most commendable. Please convey to members of the team my most grateful thanks for their fine work.

Rockenbach also expressed his gratitude. He made his car and chauffeur available to Ike and Mamie during their final days at Meade. He gave them a farewell party and presented Mamie with a silver vase inscribed, TO THE MASCOT OF THE TANK CORPS FOOTBALL TEAM.

Later, Eisenhower said of his army experience in 1921, "If Meade was at times frustrating, it was also a school where I gained additional experience in handling men and in studying weapons."

On January 16, 1922, the Eisenhowers sailed for Panama—aboard the S.S. *St.-Mihiel*, according to Ike's 201 file, although in *At Ease* he calls the ship the *San Miguel*, which no doubt is close enough. But it seems odd that an army officer would forget about one of the most famous battles of the First World War. But then, before Panama, Ike was not only not much interested in battles; he seemed to resist such information.

It was Ike's first tour of duty outside the continental U.S. It was also to be one of the "most interesting and constructive" of his entire career. In Panama he would learn a great deal about the world and its history and, for that matter, about himself. He would become certain for the first time that he was going to be a soldier for life and, far more important, that he was a good one, possessed of a good mind.

No more was heard of the "grave offense"; Eisenhower never referred to it. Always able to forget people and events that he wanted to forget, the man with almost total recall would, no doubt, once the whole miserable episode was over, be totally unable to remember even the name of Eli A. Helmick. Surely in Eisenhower's mind, Helmick's name went into the bottom drawer; he had never existed, and the charges had never been made.

★ ★ ★

THE INVISIBLE FIGURE

Weather during the eight-day voyage was turbulent, and the Eisenhowers' Model T Ford hadn't been properly tied down. It arrived in Panama, as Eisenhower described it, "a rather sorry, although still mobile, vehicle."

Eisenhower said of the ship, "The accommodations were miserable. The Army Transport Corps evidently based their model loading pattern on advice given by sardine canners. . . . I was in charge of the enlisted detachment. Soldiers usually make poor sailors and my men were determined to prove the rule. We were busy day and night trying to make life easier for men who were convinced that neither they nor the ship would survive the voyage."

Mamie suffered as much or more than any of the soldiers. Though she didn't know it yet, she was pregnant. Julie Eisenhower many years later said that Mamie, because of her claustrophobia, "refused to sleep on the bunks one on top of another with only twelve inches between. Instead, she spent the nights on a short couch—so short she had to sleep in a jackknife position."

The Eisenhowers were met by one of Conner's aides who had made arrangements for getting them to Camp Gaillard aboard a train. Eisenhower said, "When we got to the point on the Canal nearest our station, we left the train to make our way to Gaillard. The first necessity was to walk hundreds of yards in the tropical heat across the Canal on one of the lock gates.

"For Mamie that walk was the worst possible avenue of entry to a foreign station. Crossing it, she probably thought that nothing in the United States was ever like this. . . . She thoroughly believed in the broadening influence of foreign travel—if she knew she could get back home soon."

In 1914 the Douds had taken a Caribbean cruise that stopped for one day in Panama; Mamie had fond memories of that brief stay, the grand tourist hotel, the colorful native shopkeepers, and the sun. She remembered the sun in particular; in Panama there would be no need to worry about whether coal stoves were properly stoked, no need to worry about interviewing a new maid once a week, either. There would be plenty of help available in Panama.

But from the beginning everything about Camp Gaillard was wrong for Mamie. When the French started work on the canal, the campsite was a beautiful residential district and was considered the healthiest part of the Zone. But it had been abandoned for many years, and it was very much on the wrong side of the railroad tracks; Mamie had never lived anywhere on the wrong side of the tracks.

At Gaillard all supplies had to be brought in, carried up a tortuous path that was forever crumbling. Very often the entire camp had to go without fresh supplies, eggs and milk, for example, for a week or more. Besides, the quality of the milk was always questionable.

Mamie, as she often said, had lived "in shacks with cracks," but the house at Gaillard was the worst. It was on stilts on a bluff above the canal; it was two stories, and the roof was made of sheet iron which invited rather than repelled the heat. The rooms in the house were large, though the smell and feel of mold was everywhere, and the rooms were dark and damp. Galleries ran all around the house to keep out the glare of the sun, and there was no glass on the windows, only screens and lattices. There was a steep, uncertain path leading to the house, and Mamie at first refused to go in. She was certain the steps would collapse if she did. Eisenhower cheerfully entered the house and returned a few minutes later even more cheerful, unbearably so. A little work was needed, he said, a little carpentry here and there, a little paint, and the lawn must be mowed. They would have a garden. It would be just like home in no time at all. In the meantime, they could stay at the Tivoli Hotel in downtown Panama City.

But the real heroine of that first depressing day was a small, white-haired woman who arrived shortly thereafter, Mrs. Fox Conner, who told the Eisenhowers that the Conner house had been in even worse shape when they arrived. She and her children had waited at the bottom of the hill, and Fox had gone to inspect the house they were to live in. When he returned he said that the house was "very beautiful" and added, according to his wife, "It is quite mountainous [here] and we will have riding. There is a swimming pool." But what was the house *really* like? asked his wife. "Well," Fox Conner said, "It's in bad condition, but if I can get some paint it will look better. It will cover the mold which now streams over everything. . . . I think that our house will be quite pretty."

Virginia Conner led Ike and Mamie through an opening in a hibiscus hedge to her home, and sure enough the repaired, partially rebuilt Conner house was comfortable, and the screens did seem to keep out the jungle, although, as Mamie was to discover, bats were a constant threat and could not be shut out.

There were also constant mud slides into the canal. One got used to them. They broke up the monotony of the day, but when Eisenhower returned to Panama after the war he was horrified to learn "that the entire post where we had once lived had slid into the canal and had to be laboriously dredged out of the main channel."

The Eisenhowers moved into their house after some fundamental repairs. The legs of their bed were in pans of kerosene to keep off the bedbugs, and there were various insects and hundreds of bats, which were not native to Panama. The French had imported them to eat the malarial mosquitoes. A law had been enacted that forbade the killing of bats, and, although the mosquitoes were gone, the bats remained, and the law was still on the books.

A bat got in the bedroom the first night they were in the house, and Mamie—totally wrapped up in sheets—shouted out for Eisenhower to kill it. Given a choice between obeying a civilian law and Mamie, he chose the latter. He grabbed a saber, and started slashing at the elusive creature. He jumped on chairs, on tables, and on the bed, missing the bat with every slash.

Mamie did dare to peer out from under the sheets, and she remembered, "Ike was so grim and earnest, I didn't dare laugh, but I felt like it. His long leaps and fancy sword play on the furniture was a riot. I kept thinking of Douglas Fairbanks, Sr., who was a great leaper and swordsman in the movies. Only, Fairbanks didn't fight bats."

The weather in Panama was almost unbearable. Fox Conner, Jr., said, "It rained around ten in the morning every day. Sometimes it rained all day and all night, every day and every night. Sometimes when you stepped out of the house it was more like swimming than walking. It was also hot as hell. There was no air conditioning, and there was nothing to do but suffer. It was very enervating, too. Sometimes just lifting food or a drink to your mouth wore you completely out."

Mamie did not like Gaillard with its moldy houses and uncomfortable climate. Mrs. Conner remembered, "She made no bones about how mad she was that they had been ordered to such a post." But the Eisenhowers had problems that went deeper than the discomfort of their surroundings. Their main problem had to do with each other. Mrs. Conner felt that their marriage had "reached a turning point. . . . It was evident that there was a serious difficulty at the time, largely, I think, because of the death of their child. They were two people drifting apart. . . . It was my feeling that their marriage was in danger. Ike was spending less and less time with Mamie, and there was no warmth between them. They seemed like two people moving in different directions."

Eisenhower spent most of his time with Fox Conner. Mrs. Conner said, "I never saw two men more congenial than Ike Eisenhower and my husband." Eisenhower looked back on the years 1922, '23, and '24 in Panama as among the "most interesting and constructive of my life. The main reason was the presence of one man, General Fox Conner." In 1933 he wrote in his diary of Conner, "A wonderful officer and leader with a splendid analytical mind. He is as loyal to subordinates as to superiors (and is quick to give credit to juniors). . . . I served as his brigadier exec for 3 years in Panama and never enjoyed any other 3 year period as much. Devoted to his family and to the service, he is a credit to both as well as to his country. He has held a place in my affections for many years that no other, not a relative could obtain."

Conner was a tall man who never lost his southern Mississippi accent. It was "hyed," not head; "nigra," not Negro. He liked Negroes but like most southerners of his time, he doubted if they were or ever would amount to much. He didn't think much of most foreigners either. His son, Fox, Jr., remembered that he "didn't like Armenians, and I remember one guy in his outfit, maybe an Armenian, he had a heavy accent, and he said he wasn't going to march. My father had him tied to a caisson, and he said, 'Now you march or you're going to be dragged.' The guy marched."

When Conner arrived at Gaillard, morale among the enlisted men had been poor and discipline worse. His predecessor had been careless, Virginia Conner thought he was insane. And the 20th Brigade wasn't really a brigade. Congress was not about to spend money for an army to fight a war that would never happen. So instead of the usual two or more regiments, the 20th Brigade consisted of a single regiment, the 42nd Infantry. The uniforms they wore had been bleached by the tropical sun and no two were the same color.

Conner's job was to reorganize and modernize the defense of the Canal Zone. To get the troops of his limited command into some kind of order was not easy, and Conner did it by the book. He was harsh; some people, junior officers especially, thought too harsh. A few considered him a martinet. Colonel Clarence Deems, Jr., who served with Conner, said he was "of the hard-boiled type—a Prussian in spirit. He was always right in his own estimation and did not seem to realize that others had their good points, too. He engendered antagonism, and in it the underlying feeling of that kind of loyalty that was enforced only, and not given in the outpouring of comradely affection."

The lieutenant colonel in charge of carrying out Conner's orders "decided to ignore any order my husband got out," Mrs. Conner said. "Ike had continually to follow up his orders to see that they were obeyed." That did not make him popular with fellow officers and the enlisted men. He was not popular; he didn't grin much, and he displayed none of the ease that made him so successful as Allied commander. Captain Rickard, who served in Plans and Training at Gaillard, and Captain James P. Murphy, who served as adjutant of the 42nd, both resented and disliked Eisenhower. Other accounts have it that he "handled his job categorically, without kid gloves; that he was impatient to the point of irritability with whatever seemed to him to be slipshod; that he aroused antagonism among the kinds of men who, in later years, would be stimulated by him to do their best work. Major Bradford Chynoweth, West Point 1912, had known Eisenhower at the academy and had been transferred to the canal by Conner on Eisenhower's recommendation. He remembered that the trainees in the Zone represented the "new army" and had to be built up to the standard of the old. "They needed lots of instruction. The Conner-Ike regime handled it more like the yearling corporal at West Point handling plebes. Breathe down their necks and bark at them. Be tough."

Conner and Eisenhower had somewhat similar backgrounds. The Conners, like the early Eisenhowers, had been farmers. Like Eisenhower, Conner as a boy was sometimes without shoes. Before the First World War, Conner went to Command and General Staff School, and he was determined that Eisenhower go there, too. To prepare him for it, Conner taught him to submit everything in the form of a five-paragraph field order, and he required Eisenhower to write one each day he served under him. Colonel Andrew Goodpaster, Eisenhower's staff secretary when he was in the White House, said that this was extraordinarily helpful. "This was training in logical thought to be sure to cover the issues comprehensively. . . . You have to talk about the mission, the terrain, and weather, detailed instruction, logistics and communication."

Conner had graduated in the top third of his class at West Point in 1898. He was too young to rise to a position like Pershing's in the First World War, although he was Pershing's G-3 (operations officer) at AEF headquarters, and during the Second World War he was too old to achieve combat command. He lived long enough to see his protégé become supreme commander of the invasion of Europe and achieve the greatest Allied victory in history. He died at the age of seventy-eight, the year before Eisenhower was elected president.

When Eisenhower joined Conner in helping devise new plans for the defense of Panama, the older man was convinced that there would be another war and that it would come in Eisenhower's lifetime. Virginia Conner reports that her husband many times said, "Anyone who will read the Versailles Treaty intelligently will see that there's another war in it. . . . [it is] the perfect breeder of a new war . . . in about twenty years." In an interview for the Hoover Library at West Branch, Iowa, Eisenhower, then near the end of his life, quoted Conner as saying, "You can't take the strongest, most virile people in Europe and put them in the kind of straitjacket that this treaty attempts to do." Eisenhower also said of Conner, "The whole business of the necessity of being prepared for war was a product of something that just seeped into me from the teaching of this man."

The teaching began one evening on the Conners' screened porch when Conner asked what Eisenhower called "a casual question" and found that "I had little or no interest left in military history. My aversion was the result of its treatment at West Point as an out-and-out memory course. In the case of the Battle of Gettysburg, for instance, each student was instructed to memorize the names of every brigadier in the opposing armies and to know exactly where his unit was stationed at every hour during the three days of the battle. Little attempt was made to explain the meaning of the battle, why it came about, what the commanders hoped to accomplish, and the real reason why Lee invaded the North the second time. If this was military history, I wanted no part of it."

Conner started his pupil off with three historical novels, *The Long Roll* by Mary Johnston; one about the Napoleonic Wars, *The Exploits of Brigadier Gerard;* and *The Crisis,* a novel about the American Civil War by the American Winston Churchill. After Eisenhower returned the novels, saying that he had liked them, Conner got him started reading the military history of the periods involved, especially the Civil War. Eisenhower said, "He had me read Fremantle's account of the Battle of Gettsyburg, as well as that of Haskell. The best outline or summarized history of the Civil War was, he thought, *Steele's Campaigns.* As I began to absorb the material of these books, I became even more interested in our Civil War, and we spent many hours in analyzing its campaigns." Eisenhower said Conner stimulated his interests in a period when some officers, to use his own words, were becoming "stultified."

Mrs. Conner remembered "They spent hours discussing wars, past and present." According to Fox Conner, Jr., "My father's method of teaching was very Socratic." He would ask Eisenhower "What was on Lee's mind? What did he know? What did he think he had to do? Why did he think that? What do you think the outcome would have been if his decision had been just the opposite? And at Gettysburg, why had Lee come into the North and exposed himself? And how can you explain Meade?"

Ike often went to Conner's copious library to borrow one book and returned to his own quarters with two. His reading included the works of Nietzsche, Tacitus, and Plato. "As I read each one, I tried to digest its main themes and important points—I could be sure that sooner or later the General would be asking me about them." He read Clausewitz's *On War* three times and later said that outside of the Bible that book had the greatest effect on him from a military point of view.

In Eisenhower's own workroom on the screened porch on the second floor of his quarters he had a drawing board on which he pinned large maps. In addition to books, he also studied various military technical journals. He was particularly fascinated by Napoleon's victories at Marengo and Austerlitz and the last campaigns in Italy. He also spent a lot of time studying the Battle of Leuthen and became so familiar with the details of Frederick the Great's victory that even after his retirement from the presidency he could remember them.

Eisenhower recognized that ancient battles were ancient battles. They would not and could not be repeated. It was Conner who pointed out to him that "in all military history only one thing never changes—human nature. Terrain may change; weather may change; weapons may change, etc., but never human nature." In his studies, Eisenhower concentrated on why certain commanders made the decisons they did, and later he would say, "War has always been a human drama. You can fill a battlefield with all the gol-darned machines that ever worked, and you'll still need some tough human beings to work them."

Eisenhower's evening conversations with Conner usually lasted until a late hour at night and continued the next morning, often on horseback. He said, "The best chance for such conversations was when we were out on reconnaissance. . . . We were constantly laying out routes and charting them on maps . . . so that we might be able to meet with considerable force any enemy landing on our sector of the Canal. . . ."

Eisenhower's horse during these rides was a large black gelding, Blackie, who was without beauty. Officially, he was fourteen years old when Eisenhower chose him from a group of about twenty horses available for officers. On the same day he chose a Puerto Rican orderly named Rafael "Lopez" Carattini. Lopez also chose a horse from among those allotted to enlisted men, and the party on horseback usually consisted of Eisenhower, Lopez, Conner, his aide, and his orderly.

In *At Ease*, Eisenhower spends six pages describing Blackie and how he trained him, far more space than he devotes to most people in the book, including Conner. But then Blackie proved to be notably educable and, like his master, he was not immune to applause. Blackie once won fourth prize at a horse show in Balboa in which most of the competing horses were thoroughbreds.

In June 1945, when Eisenhower was still at SHAEF headquarters in Germany, Rafael "Lopez" Carattini wrote him a letter reminding him of their days together in Panama, and on June 1, Eisenhower wrote back:

I remember you as well as if our days in Panama were only a few months rather than twenty years behind us. I wish I could have "Blackie" with me now. Moreover, all the things you mentioned in your letter almost made me homesick for the days we were riding the jungle trails together.

I am delighted that you have reached the grade of first sergeant.

P.S. On the chance that you would like to know what I look like now, I am enclosing the most recent picture I have had taken.

First Sergeant Carattini, then stationed at Warrenton, Virginia, cannot have been surprised at how one of the most photographed men in the world looked in 1945, but he was no doubt grateful for the photograph anyway.

As a result of his happy experience with the ill-favored Blackie, Eisenhower came to a conclusion that led, when he was president of Columbia, to the formation of the Conservation of Human Resources project, which he referred to as "one of my proudest memories of life at Columbia. . . . Far too often we write off a backward child as hopeless, a clumsy animal as worthless, a worn-out field as beyond restoration. This we do largely out of our own lack of willingness to take the time and the effort to prove ourselves wrong; to prove that a difficult boy can become a fine man, that an animal can respond to training, that the field can regain its fertility."

During the dry season, they were on horseback eight hours a day, "most of it at a walk. . . . We would make camp before dark," Eisenhower said. "Close to the equator, the sun sets early and during the long hours before bedtime, between 6:30 and 10:00, we sat around a small campfire and talked." Conner's questioning of Eisenhower continued, not only about the history of past wars and their leaders, but about more mundane matters, such as how far a mule could travel "before it ate all it carried?" And as his son said, Fox Conner "always waited for what he considered the right answer not just any answer."

Conner could quote Shakespeare at length and, according to Eisenhower was also somewhat of a philosopher. It was from Conner that Eisenhower first heard the maxims "Always take your job seriously, never yourself," and "All generalities are false, including this one," two quotations Eisenhower was fond of using for the rest of his life.

More than forty years later Eisenhower said, "Fox Conner was the ablest man I ever knew. . . . It is clear now that life with General Conner was a sort of graduate school in military affairs and the humanities, leavened by the comments and discourses of a man who was experienced in his knowledge of men and their conduct. . . . In a lifetime of association with great and good men, he is the one more or less invisible figure to whom I owe an incalculable debt."

Perhaps the most important belief Eisenhower absorbed from Conner was that another great war was inevitable. He urged Ike to be ready for it and, as part of his professional readiness, suggested he try for an assignment under Colonel George Catlett Marshall. "In the new war we will have to fight beside allies," Conner told Ike, "and George Marshall knows more about the techniques of arranging allied commands than any man I know. He is nothing short of a genius." Conner frequently said, "You and Marshall are a lot alike. I've noticed time and again that you attack problems the same way." Or, "Your mind has the same quality as Marshall's."

At the time Conner first talked about Marshall, Eisenhower had never met him, although everybody in the army in any position of power knew about the brilliant young officer who had graduated from V.M.I. in 1901. He had been first captain, clearly a man to keep in mind; he had distinguished himself in the First World War and in 1919 began five years as aide to General Pershing. When Pershing was Chief of Staff of the Army, Marshall did much if not most of his work for him, including the delivery of some speeches Pershing was to give.

It is rather interesting to note that while Eisenhower was still in Panama in 1924, Marshall and his beautiful but ailing wife, Lily, and her mother sailed there in the same ship in which the Eisenhowers had sailed from New York to Panama in 1921, the *St.-Mihiel.* The Marshalls and Mrs. Cole were on their way to Tientsin, China, where Lieutenant Colonel Marshall was to serve with the 15th Infantry. The Marshalls and Mrs. Cole stopped in Panama and were entertained by the Conners at a party with "lots of champagne." There is no record at the Eisenhower Library or anywhere else that Eisenhower and Mamie attended the party, and it is difficult to understand why they didn't. But even if the Eisenhowers were not present at that champagne party, it is quite certain that Fox Conner mentioned the brilliant young officer on his staff. It is also quite certain that Marshall made a mental note of the name Eisenhower. He always retained the names of young officers who were praised by their superiors. Yet despite this and Conner's suggestion that Eisenhower would benefit by serving under Marshall, the two men did not meet until 1929 in Washington.

Conner's experience in France in the first World War had convinced him that without strong leadership the Allies might again become what he called "their own worst enemies." His son said, "Father felt that the main difficulty would be the joint command, with armies composed of different nationals. In the last big breakthrough of World War I, remember, the French, English and Americans often wound up killing each other."

Conner felt that Eisenhower could provide the strong leadership required, and he proved abundantly right. During the Second World War the Allies did not kill each other. The British and the Americans and later the French and other Allied officers frequently cursed at each other, even threatened each other, often despised each other, but they largely kept their nationalistic antagonisms to themselves because their amiable supreme commander ordered them to do so or risk "being sent home in a slow boat, without escort." He took a hard line in part because he counted fostering Allied cooperation the second priority of his job. The first was defeating the Germans. Churchill once said to Ike, "What I like about you, Ike, is you ain't no glory hopper." A glory hopper would never have succeeded.

On July 4, 1942, nine days after he was designated Commanding General, European Theater, Eisenhower wrote to Conner from London:

> More and more in the last few days my mind has turned back to you and to the days when I was privileged to serve immediately under your wise counsel and leadership. I cannot tell you how much I would appreciate, at this moment, an opportunity for an hour's discussion with you on problems that constantly beset me. . . . Right now, aside from the old question of making firm agreements with allies, many . . . arguments involve internal organization—the same problems that you faced twenty-five years ago, and which have been the subject of bitter debate by some of our very able officers ever since. Such things as the . . . divisions of functions and responsibilities for the establishment of special schools, disciplinary barracks and like institutions. . . . I do not expect an answer to this letter, and certainly do not want to bother you with matters for which, you may be certain, I'll soon have answers. I hope they will be right. But, recently,

I've been so frequently struck by the similarity between this situation and the one you used to describe to me, that I thought you might like to hear something about it.

Fox Conner did answer Eisenhower's letter on July 20. In his reply he said:

Your present detail was, and is, widely approved. No better choice could have been made.

With all good wishes and great pride in you.

> As always yours,
> Fox Conner

When his memoir of the war, *Crusade in Europe,* was published Eisenhower wrote to the old man, saying

the thanks for *Crusade in Europe* should have been me to you, for I doubt very much that I should ever have been in a position to prepare such a memoir had it not been for the guidance and counsel I got from you.

And in *At Ease,* Eisenhower said, "I can never adequately express my gratitude to this one gentleman, for it took years before I fully realized the value of what he led me through."

★ ★ ★

SLIGHTLY TO THE REAR

In the years in Panama, while Eisenhower and Conner were working together, studying together, riding together, and talking endlessly together, Mamie became increasingly depressed and fretful. There was very little social activity on the post, bridge at the officers' club on Wednesday nights, a dance at the officers' club on Friday nights. That was all. Eisenhower went swimming in the Conners' pool next door; Mamie did not swim. The Conners had a tennis court; Eisenhower played there frequently; Mamie did not play tennis. Going across the locks to the city was a chore for her, so she seldom went to the city. She did all her shopping at the commissaries and the post exchanges. In those early days in Panama, Ike appeared not to need her.

The Conners, in addition to a son, had two daughters, Florence, eleven, and Betty, nineteen. Mamie was nearer Betty's age than Virginia Conner's, and in many ways Mrs. Conner treated her like a daughter in trouble. "I never knew how Ike felt," said Mrs. Conner, "as he knew Mamie was wearing down a path to my door. . . . She was letting herself go; she didn't seem to care how she looked, and I told her she ought to vamp her husband."

We know that Mamie took the advice about improving her appearance. She had her hair cut shorter, and the bangs that were to become so famous and controversial appeared for the first time. But the lethargy between the Eisenhowers, sometimes breaking out into open hostility, continued. Mrs. Conner said, "I never thought there would be a divorce—divorces were not nearly as frequent as they are now, or so easily obtained. But a cold, lifeless marriage could have resulted."

Then Mamie learned she was pregnant again. Eisenhower said, "The most important event during my Camp Gaillard assignment was the news that we were to have another child." The Douds were also happy with the news, but when they visited them and saw how they lived, they insisted that Mamie come to Denver for the birth of the baby. Mamie and Ike were easy to persuade and she started for Denver early in the summer, stopping off briefly in New Orleans. Eisenhower, who had missed the birth of Icky, had no intention of not being present when their second child was born. He applied for and was granted a leave.

John Sheldon Doud Eisenhower was born on August 3, 1922. Eisenhower said, "We had another boy, one who in appearance so resembled the one we had lost that, for my part, I was seldom able to see any difference between them when comparing their pictures at similar ages. . . . While his arrival did not, of course, eliminate the grief that we still felt—then and now—he was precious in his own right, and he did much to take our minds off the tragedy. Living in the present with a healthy, bouncing baby boy can take parents' minds off almost anything."

Several years after John's birth, in a letter to Mamie, Ike said:

The crowning thing you've given me is our son—he has been so wonderful, unquestionably because he's so much you—that I find I live in him so very often.

Eisenhower returned to Panama immediately, but Mamie stayed behind in Denver for several months. When she did come back, she brought a nurse with her, Kathryn Herrick, a large, cheerful woman who stayed with them until John was three and a half years old. Eisenhower said, "When she carried the baby under her arm, it looked as if she were carrying a corsage. John adored her and before he could talk, he was trying to sing songs to her." Some people on the post thought by having a nurse so long—her wages were paid by the Douds—the Eisenhowers were being indulgent, but foremost in their minds was the need of keeping their second son healthy.

The memory of Icky was also responsible for the fact that from the beginning Mamie was overprotective of John. "You know, John is doubly precious to us; we lost our first son when he was three, a year and a half before Johnny was born," Mamie said in an interview in 1965, her eyes filled with tears. Very much later she was to say, "It took me years, many years, to get over my 'smother love'—it wasn't until Johnnie had children of his own that I finally stopped all worrying."

Once, while the Eisenhowers were at a large ranch in Mexico along with Min, John wanted to qualify as a first-class Boy Scout. In a 1960 speech at a Boy Scout meeting in Washington, John's father, then president of the United States, referred to the family crisis John's wish caused. He wanted to march fourteen miles, a seven-mile walk to the front gate of the ranch at which they were staying and seven miles back. Mamie and what Eisenhower called John's "doting grandmother" insisted that the boy be accompanied by a car stocked with orange juice, Coke, water, and other supplies.

"Well, now, we had a storm," he said. "This got to be a hot argument. . . . And so, exercising what every man always thinks is his prerogative, I made the decision and said, 'Go right ahead, John; that will be all right.' " But, Eisenhower said, he got a good many "very tough looks" from Min and Mamie, and there was much talk between them "about a hard-hearted parent and an old soldier." The danger from coyotes was mentioned as well as the perils of rattlesnakes and wild cattle. "Finally, I had to surrender," said Eisenhower. He got in a station wagon and, staying a discreet distance from John, followed him, "always making sure that I could get back and report that nothing was wrong."

John returned without injury and, his father said, with "tremendous pride [and] self-confidence." From that, Eisenhower said he learned "a lasting lesson." John could do well on his own.

Mamie never really learned that lesson, and from time to time Eisenhower felt it necessary to tell her how he felt she should treat their son. In June 1944 when John, a newly commissioned second lieutenant, was visiting him in London and about to go to Fort Benning, Eisenhower wrote to Mamie, "He says you are going to visit him in Benning. I think that's fine, as it will be nice for you to know how he is living, etc., etc. But I think it would be unwise to stay too long. Undoubtedly he has some feeling (at least subconsciously) that he has always been carefully watched over. He is wondering how he will do 'on his own.' So he must be given a chance to be on his own before he comes up against really critical problems. . . . I think brief visits to him are more advisable than any long stay."

Their old family friend Mrs. Arthur Nevins said, "Mamie kept mothering John even after he was fifty years old. . . . She kept on worrying about him. He was always like a little boy to her. She would tell him to watch what he ate and to wear the proper clothes when it rained."

In 1964, at the Republican National Convention in San Francisco, John Bird, a writer who was working with Eisenhower on a magazine article, went to visit him in a suite at the St. Francis Hotel. "John was there, as was Mamie, in one of her beautiful robes. She was worrying about John because he had flown out in his own plane. I remember that she asked John, 'How are you going back?' He said, 'I'm going to fly back,' and she said, 'Well, promise me you won't fly over any mountains.' He said, 'Mother, how do you think I'm going to get out of here?' "

Eisenhower, who had been just as saddened by the death of Icky, reacted in a different way toward their second son. He did not allow himself to get as close to John as he perhaps should have. John's son, David, said, "My granddad and my father had a . . . correct relationship; by correct I mean formal." When I mentioned this to John he commented, "That's interesting. I would say formal. However, David was not around at some of the less formal moments. Dad and I were pretty close after the war—when we were sort of let down, both sort of stranded DPs there. He did more musing then than at any other time. I regret in a way you can't turn the clock back."

William B. Ewald, who assisted Eisenhower in writing the two volumes of his presidential memoirs, said, "Ike was exceptionally fond of his only child, John. I never heard John's name mentioned without seeing the President's face light up. The relationship of father and son is made exceedingly difficult when the father is as famous as Eisenhower. The offspring of important men have a tension-filled existence even as young children. No one treats them normally! There is always the added pressure of the son's trying to achieve as much as the father; and how can one measure up to a father who is a five-star general and a president?"

He also was expected to be what Icky might have been had he lived. Aksel Nielsen said, "John always had to live in the shadow of Icky and of his father. It wasn't easy."

Eisenhower always called his son Johnny; John called his father "the old man," or "the boss." Ike had extremely big bones, very large and powerful hands. Once in an interview with John, I said, "You are built differently than your father." John said, "I was never allowed to forget it. . . . Dad was never tough with me. He had me well frightened from the start and always boasted that he never had to lay a hand on me to make me mind. . . . Perhaps this stemmed from a fear that, strong as he was, he might inflict serious bodily harm when his temper was aroused. Instead, he conducted discipline largely in a West Point manner. I was dressed down smartly on many occasions but never given a whack.

"Dad himself was a terrifying figure to a small boy. He was powerfully built— in West Point he could chin himself five times with his right hand and three times with his left. . . . I could never measure up to these standards, try as I might. . . . Dad could never understand why I was not a star. The fact is that I was always painfully thin. Dad wrote from the Philippines when I was fourteen that I had to reach the weight of ninety-two pounds before I could play football. I stuffed myself on bananas and drank about a gallon of water one night before weighing in.

"He always swore he wouldn't force me to go to West Point," said John, "and he always pretended to try to talk me out of it. However, he gave himself away when he made me do foot exercises because my feet were too weak to pass the entrance examinations."

Eisenhower said he didn't push John to enter the academy. "I saw too many who were forced to go to West Point by parents who wanted them to get the free education. I counselled John. I told him that chances of promotion were not good, the promotion rate was low, and there was not much chance of getting to be a colonel. Under the old system of statutory retirement at age 64, I figured I would retire for age before I was promoted to colonel."

Edgar Eisenhower thought John would have been a good lawyer if he had decided to study law. "He had one of the most logical minds I had ever seen in a youngster. He would have been a great lawyer. Indeed, I think he had a good deal of difficulty determining whether to follow the law or to follow in his father's footsteps in the army. I used to talk to him about it, and I think his affection for his father overcame any desire he might have had to study law."

"At West Point," said John, "I was trying hard as hell all the time. . . . Dad, until his leg accident—when that riding master made him get on and off that horse doing monkey drill—was outstandingly good at riding. I was outstandingly bad. He was almost a demonstration man. He was very good—oh, yes. He was an expert horseman. And in his later years that was his favorite exercise. I was no good. I was absolutely non-simpatico with a horse. The same way with our disciplinary problems. Dad's were all intentional, his disciplinary difficulties. Mine were dumbness. It's true. I was a disaster."

Family friend and sometime-advisor Kevin McCann said that Eisenhower was "a good parent but a distant one over the years." John said, "There was a certain military wall between us. . . . I was not only his son, I was a young lieutenant who needed on occasion to be straightened out. I was always on the receiving end—I was like Beetle Bailey in the comic strip."

John himself found his father too army-conscious for comfort. "He thought I was too serious and criticized me for it," said John. "But I didn't graduate from the same academy he did. When he was there [at West Point] everybody got three months off between yearling and cow year, and the most important thing to happen was to have an undefeated football team in 1914. It was a completely different situation when I was there. We were second lieutenants, infantry. There was a war. . . . I thought Dad was a little bit out of his tree on that.

"I am certain that I was born standing at attention," said John. "Perhaps I was something like the top sergeant who was not born, but issued. With a few lapses of minor rebellion throughout my life, I am inclined to think that I remained in that posture, figuratively, for many years, until I was nearly forty. Certain factors contributed to this: 'a Spartan upbringing'; West Point training, and the circumstances of my father's meteoric rise to prominence during my early twenties. . . . I was always some sort of curiosity. And it affected the normal relations between a father and son, making it doubly difficult for me to establish my own identity."

In 1955 John, then a major, said, "I have found one thing, almost any trouble or frustration that I run through in the army, Dad has experienced at some time or another in his career, and he is able to be of great help to me sometimes when I run across something that really puzzles me as to why it exists."

When John was asked how being the son of the president of the United States affected him, he said: "Well, there's not too much to be bared on that score. I am used to it. . . . With each new change of station I am a curiosity for a while; however, in the course of time, things settle down to normal. Once you get settled down in a place, it doesn't make an awful lot of difference."

In his book, *Strictly Personal*, published in 1974, John said, "During the last decade—indeed, beginning with my father's departure from the White House in January 1961, I believe I have been successful in doing this, [establishing his own identity] and the natural mutual respect that existed between Dad and me during the last years of his life were rewarding indeed. But essentially this book is the story of a son living in the shadow of a great man, undergoing unusual experiences but at the same time trying to maintain a normal degree of independence."

Herb Mitgang, an editor of the *New York Times* who had been an editor of *Stars and Stripes* during the Second World War, went to the Normandy beach-head with Ike, John, and Mamie on the twentieth anniversary of D-Day. "I had an opportunity to observe the relationship between John and his father," said Mitgang. "In my view, and it is personal, not based on any documents or research, only my instincts and observations, I felt that Ike was a bit short with his grown son, a little inconsiderate of feelings. . . . I just felt that here was John seeking his father's approval and waiting for a kind word, not quite getting it from the old man. I almost said to myself, 'I wish Ike would give his son a pat on the back, a show of affection.' . . . I found John a very fine person, very considerate of everyone, very decent, and, I later discovered [on] reading his books, a very talented man.

"I felt that Ike didn't regard his son, his grown son, with enough respect as an individual among strangers, which we were."

When John was working on what became *Letters to Mamie*, by Dwight D. Eisenhower, published in 1978, he must have learned much more than he had known during his father's lifetime about the deep feeling his father had had for him.

In June 1942 Ike went to London for the first time, and in August he complained to Mamie:

> I've yet to hear from Johnny except for one short note (three lines) . . . Of course it's impossible for him to understand the loneliness of such a position as I had—it never occurs to him that his letters could be a *help* to me. I think if he knew that, he'd occasionally find time to write. Sometimes I think about the possibility that he may be just a bit spoiled. . . . Things have been easy for him . . . suppose he'd have had to start at 13 or 14 getting up at 4 or 5 in the morning working through a hot summer day to 9 at night—day after day—or doing his winter work with cold, chapped hands and not even gloves—maybe he'd think writing a letter wasn't so terribly difficult. . . .

He added, however:

> I've growled about J, send him my deepest affection. I'm so tied up in him it hurts.

In October 1944 he wrote from France, "I'm so wrapped up in that boy—but I keep reminding myself that he is a man, with a man's job to do and his own career to make. How I wish I dared go and stay with him." And on April 9, 1945, "God—how I hate to let him go whenever he comes to see me."

Ike had not wanted John to have the kind of boyhood he had had, and he went to great lengths to see that that didn't happen. As is so often the case in a father-son relationship, John saw the whole thing from an entirely different angle. He often said, "The only regret of my boyhood is that I was never put out on my own to earn my own living."

In 1956, when many people were giving Eisenhower many different kinds of advice as to whether or not he should run for reelection, John wrote him a long letter saying that the decision was his father's and no one else's, adding, "I shall try to analyze this as dispassionately as possible under the circumstances. I have the advantage in this matter that due to our close and affectionate relationship I have developed many reactions, outlooks, and prejudices similar to your own, to say nothing of our similar training in the matter of duty. I have the disadvantage that I am incapable of completely understanding the burdens of the presidency, not having experienced those burdens myself. . . ."

The judiciously worded letter ended, "You can still serve the nation well as a personal example (witness the case of General Lee) as a university president or as a writer and gentleman farmer. If you stay on, even a bridge expert can lose a hand if he gets no cards or inadequate cards to play with. At this point in the game the Eisenhower legend may be a more valuable national asset than Eisenhower the quarterback. . . . Recommendation: Don't run."

Shortly before his father's death on March 28, 1969, John was appointed by Richard Nixon to be the U.S. ambassador to Belgium. Eisenhower was "enthusiastic," his son remembered, but he was not surprised. John said, "As it turned out, he had known of this possibility for some time."

John's book about the Battle of the Bulge, *The Bitter Woods*, which was a best-seller, had been published two months earlier, and Eisenhower was proud of John's accomplishments as a writer. John is a better writer than his father; he has a rare ability to communicate the feeling of a time and a place.

John said of a visit to his father a few days before he died, "The boss lay with the oxygen tubes in his nose, suffering from a filling of the lungs and aware that this time he would not make it. . . . He had ordered a dozen copies of *The Bitter Woods* for me to sign for the doctors and nurses who had taken care of him."

Following Eisenhower's death, there was a week of public mourning that included what John called a "subdued but impressive rail trip to Dad's hometown of Abilene."

"Being so occupied [in preparation for Brussels] in the ensuing months, I had never had the chance to pause and endure the pain that accompanied the passing of a person who had been such an overwhelming factor in my life," he said. "As a result, the residue remained for an inordinate length of time—the doctors told me to expect the effects for as long as a year. I felt the pangs only periodically, when my feelings would well up—fortunately always in private. . . .

"One cartoon by Bill Mauldin, hardly a friend of the officer corps, got to me more than any other trigger. It depicted a World War II cemetery with a caption, 'Pass the word; it's Ike himself.' On seeing that cartoon in *National Geographic* one evening, I went to my bedroom and sobbed. Barbara [his wife] stuck her head in, took a look, and closed the door."

• • •

In October, in a solemn ceremony on the parade grounds at Gaillard, Fox Conner presented Eisenhower with a long-delayed Distinguished Service Medal. After having been twice denied, the award was finally approved by Conner's friend, John J. Pershing. The citation read:

> For exceptionally meritorious and distinguished services. While commanding officer of the Tank Corps Training Center from March 23, 1918, to November 18, 1918, at Camp Colt, Pa., he displayed unusual zeal, foresight, and marked administrative ability in the organization, training and preparation for overseas service of technical troops of the Tank Corps.

When Mamie returned to Panama with John and Kathryn Herrick, the relationship between the Eisenhowers changed. Eisenhower said, "The most absorbing interest in our lives was his [John's] growth into a walking, talking, running-the-whole-household young fellow."

Virginia Conner said, "After Johnny was born and Mamie felt better, she began to change, and I had the delight of seeing a rather callow young woman turn into the person to whom eveyone turned. She developed a sure and steady hand, and I have seen her, with her gay laugh and personality, smooth out Ike's occasional irritability."

Mamie was busy a good deal of the time with John, but she developed an outside interest as well. The enlisted men in the brigade were Puerto Ricans, and they were allowed to bring their families. Their wives proved to be notably fecund; it was said that there were more children at Gaillard than there were soldiers. There was no maternity hospital on the post for these women, and their babies were delivered hit-or-miss fashion in the enlisted area in Empire, just behind Gaillard. Mamie became the chairman of the money-raising committee to outfit a small post hospital—which the army agreed would be opened in a run-down building in Empire. She planned teas, picnics, bridge tournaments, and white-elephant sales. Lila Lee and Thomas Meighan, two of the most popular Hollywood stars of the time, were in Panama making a movie, and they were persuaded by Virginia Conner and Mamie to appear at a dance to raise money for the hospital.

The whole effort was a great success. Even the men were included in the project, organizing a clean-up squad to repair and paint the run-down building. Under the supervision of a Red Cross nurse, the ten-bed hospital was soon operating, largely as a result of Mamie's efforts.

In the winter of 1923, Mamie's sister Mike, then twenty, visited the Eisenhowers. Then Swede Hazlett arrived. The two friends from Abilene had not seen each other since Swede visited Ike at West Point at the time of his graduation in 1915. Hazlett was commander of a submarine and had been in fleet maneuvers in the area when his boat had to be brought to the submarine base at Coco Calo in the Canal Zone for repairs.

Hazlett was ashore for some time and spent every weekend with the Eisenhowers. He said, "Ike got me astride a horse again and we rode the bosque trails . . . in the evenings there was poker. This latter was bad news, for Ike and his army friends set a much higher standard for the five-card game than the navy.

"But what interested me most was his work, for the defense of the area. He explained the plans to me with the enthusiasm of genius. . . . In his study on the screened porch of his quarters . . . he puts in his spare time re-fighting the campaigns of the old masters. This was particularly unusual at a torrid, isolated post, where most officers spent their off hours trying to keep cool and amused."

Swede noticed another change in his old friend. "He takes his job seriously, and he loves his profession. Perhaps he had a touch of clairvoyance."

After Hazlett's sub was repaired, "I took him for a dip in Panama Bay. He enjoyed it thoroughly. I never had a passenger who was more avid for information. Whenever I was otherwise engaged he wandered through the ship, chatting informally with the crew—and they responded readily. I really believe that by the time he left the ship he knew almost as much about submarines as I did. That night we had a big party at the Union Club with Mrs. E., her sister, and some others. . . . I sailed the next morning, not to see him again for twelve years."

That summer, the summer of 1923, Ike felt the Panama heat even more than usual; he lost weight and complained of a pain in his right side. Doctors at the post hospital diagnosed the trouble as chronic appendicitis. For a while, Eisenhower ignored the pain, but as Fox Conner continued to remind him that he must be fit for high command at all times, he decided to do something about it. He went back to Denver on leave, where on October 3 he had an appendectomy at Fitzsimmons General Hospital. He was in Denver fifteen days before returning to Panama.

His rapport with Conner was unchanged, and while Eisenhower continued to work for Conner's approval, the general was anxious to appear at his best in the eyes of his protégé. One day while Conner was personally overseeing the shoeing of an old horse, afraid that if he left it to someone else proper attention might not be paid, the horse shied and jabbed its nose into the general's stomach. He fell backward out of a low window in the blacksmith's shop into a pail of water on the ground below. When a young aide rushed out to help him, Conner's first words were, "Don't tell Eisenhower."

In August of 1924 Eisenhower became a permanent major, and he received orders to return to the States. "Back into the rut I had started to dig for myself a decade earlier, I was ordered back to Meade—to help coach a football team," he said.

Mamie and John returned early in September. Before leaving, Mamie told Mrs. Conner, "You bawled me out and I thank you for it." Later that month Eisenhower followed in an army transport. He had been in the Canal Zone almost three years. There was one postscript to the Panama experience added more than thirty years later at the time of the Suez crisis. "In my telephonic and other communications with Prime Minister Eden," Eisenhower said, "I frequently expressed the opinion that the case as it stood did not warrant resort to force. I told Anthony that I doubted the validity of his argument that no one except the European technicians then operating the canal, were capable of doing so. Thirty years earlier I had been personally acquainted with the daily operation of the Panama Canal, a much more complex mechanism, and I could not wholly accept the contention that an exceedingly high level of technical competence was required throughout the operating organization at Suez."

The voyage back to the U.S. took six days; the transport was crowded, and Eisenhower shared a cabin with two junior officers from Gaillard who hated his guts. They had seen him as harsh and unrelenting, a kind of poor man's Fox Conner, a Fox Conner without the general's rank or authority.

But during the tedious voyage, they changed their minds. They played endless games of bridge, and Eisenhower not only consistently lost, he paid his losses cheerfully. Without Fox Conner looking over his shoulder, the man could be human.

★ ★ ★

THE WATERSHED

The return to Meade in September 1924 could not have been a pleasant experience for Eisenhower. It was the scene of the greatest tragedy of his life and the camp where his career had very nearly come to an end. Besides, he, John, and Mamie were back in the same converted barracks they had lived in three years before. This time the barracks were even shabbier; coal still had to be brought in for the stoves. If it rained, and it seemed to rain daily, the laundry had to be hung in the kitchen and the dining room. The fire escape was a knotted rope attached to a window in the upstairs bedroom.

Ike had been ordered back from Panama three months before his tour of duty there was officially to end. There was no national or international emergency. The main concern of the army once again appeared to be football. Eisenhower said of the transfer, "The War Department moves in mysterious ways its blunders to perform—this sentiment expresses my mood in the fall of 1924. Why . . . I was moved thousands of miles from Panama to the Chesapeake Bay to join three other officers in a football coaching assignment is still a cosmic top-secret wonder to me. Then and now, one guess would be as good as another."

The record made by the football team that autumn did nothing to improve Eisenhower's morale. It was a total disaster despite the fact that one of the four coaches was Vernon Pritchard, who had been the quarterback when Ike played on the West Point football team in 1912. Ike said of the 1924 season, "The players tried hard. We seldom won. . . . In the climax game against the Marines . . . we lost by 20–0 or something of that sort. For all of us . . . far from inspirational." After the season was over, Eisenhower was given another familiar and unwelcome assignment, commanding a tank battalion, "the same old tanks I had commanded several years earlier." He was to take over the command at Fort Benning after a sixty-day leave in Denver.

Major Eisenhower went to Washington to see Chief of Infantry Major General Frank L. Sheets, to ask if the orders could be changed and he be sent to one of the service schools. Sheets had twice before turned down similar requests from Eisenhower and now he did it a third time. "I should have known better," said Ike; this time "[Sheets] refused even to listen to my arguments, and said

I would have to go to Benning. . . ." Fortunately for Eisenhower, he now had a very good and very powerful friend in the army, General Fox Conner.

Conner had said that Eisenhower's work in Panama had been "superior." He had written on his protégé's efficiency report that he was "one of the most capable, efficient and loyal officers I have ever met. On account of his natural and professional abilities he is exceptionally fitted for General Staff Training." How well did Conner know him? "Intimately." Were there unfavorable entries against him during his service in Panama? "None made." What should be done with him when he got back to the States? "He should be sent to take the course at the Army Service School at Ft. Leavenworth."

By this time Conner, too, had returned from Panama; he was in Washington as deputy chief of staff to General John L. Hines, West Point 1891. Conner ran the office. Many times Hines did not show up at all, and when he did, according to Conner's son, "My father said he was far gone in drink." After his unsuccessful interview with Sheets, it seems likely that Eisenhower stopped by to see Conner. After all, his and Sheets's offices were both in the old State-War-Navy building just across the street from the Coolidge White House. The details of what Conner did, Eisenhower never knew, but a few days after he got back to Meade he received a telegram that said:

NO MATTER WHAT ORDERS YOU RECEIVE FROM THE WAR DEPARTMENT, MAKE NO PROTEST ACCEPT THEM WITHOUT QUESTION   SIGNED CONNER.

A few days later Eisenhower received a letter from Conner explaining what Eisenhower called a "novel arrangement"; temporarily he would no longer be an infantry officer; he would be under the jurisdiction of the adjutant general, who was in charge of recruiting. He would be the recruiting officer at Fort Logan, Colorado.

Certainly Eisenhower would have preferred to stay in the infantry; and on the face of it, the assignment was an insult. The Army Recruiting Service was for those who had not done anything bad enough to be dismissed for the good of the service or court-martialed but who nevertheless had to be got out of the way. At the time, it was almost as bad as being assigned to army G-2 (intelligence). "I got letters from some of my classmates," Eisenhower said later, "telling me I'd ruined myself, that the infantry would never have anything to do with me anymore. I think it sort of burned them up at the Chief of Infantry's Office, but it did turn out wonderful." In *At Ease*, he wrote: "Had anyone else suggested to me that I desert an arm for a service, I would have been outraged. . . . But with my solid belief in Fox Conner I kept my temper."

Conner's strategy was based on the knowledge that, if Ike went to Benning as ordered he would remain under Sheets's jurisdiction, and since Sheets seemed determined to hold Eisenhower back, he could have waited many, many years before going to Leavenworth. Therefore it seemed to Conner that the best thing to do was to get the major under some other jurisdiction, under the adjutant general, for instance. The adjutant general's office happened to be not far from Conner's; it also happened that there was a vacancy in the adjutant general's quota of officers at Leavenworth. As Eisenhower wrote in *At Ease*, General

Sheets had not been "converted by" what Conner had done; he had been "circumvented."

Finally, a new order arrived. The adjutant general had chosen Ike to go to the Command and General Staff School as one of his quota of officers; he would start the course in August 1925. "I was ready to fly—and needed no airplane," Eisenhower said, adding, "Certainly, had I been denied the good fortune of knowing Fox Conner, the course of my career might have been radically different. Because I *did* know him, I did go to Leavenworth."

Meanwhile, Eisenhower spent the months from the end of November 1924 to August 1925 in Denver as Fort Logan's recruiting officer. The job was not taxing, and during those months when he, Mamie, and John were living at the Doud house he became even more a part of what Min Doud called the "closed family corporation."

During most of that time, however, Ike readied himself for the treacherous days ahead at Leavenworth. Having missed Infantry School, which most of the students had attended, he felt "like [he was] being sent to college without a secondary education." Students who had spent the past year at one of the special service schools had a certain advantage from the start. An aide of Sheets's didn't give him much comfort by writing him, "You will probably fail." Ike confided his doubts in a letter to Conner and asked the general what he should do to get ready for the ordeal at Leavenworth. As usual, the general's reply was reassuring. He said:

> You may not know it, but because of your three years' work in Panama, you are far better trained and ready for Leavenworth than anybody I know.
>
> You will recall that during your entire service there [with me] I required that you write a field order for the operation of the post every day. . . . You became so well acquainted with the techniques and routine of preparing plans and orders for operations that included their logistics, that they will be second nature to you. You will feel no sense of inferiority.

Eisenhower nevertheless thought it necessary to prepare himself. He knew that Leavenworth was the toughest of all the army schools. In recent years there had been several nervous breakdowns and at least one suicide during the course. Ike knew that at Leavenworth there were no written tests; the principal technique was war gaming in which students decided how they would use their troops in various battle situations or maneuvers. "Problems are so drawn that you are required to bring to bear common sense and clear judgment in the application of the knowledge you have gained." The most helpful aid to study was the old problems used in former years. Eisenhower had had previous exposure to this type of gaming at Camp Meade when George Patton was preparing for Leavenworth and they had worked together to solve the "back problems." Ike said, "It was by no means a chore. I loved to do that kind of work . . . practical problems have always been my equivalent to crossword puzzles."

His friend Georgie had been an honor graduate in the 1923–24 class, 25th among 248 students, with an average overall grade of 88.948. Eisenhower borrowed the notes Patton had used, and according to Mamie, "He studied them to tatters." Ike knew that Patton had worked very hard at Leavenworth. On a weekend, when most students were playing hard, Patton wrote his wife, Bea, "I certainly busted all rules about studying today. I studied from 2:30 P.M. to 6 P.M. and from 7:15 to 11:45. . . . Still I hope to improve and I think some of the others will crack—I hope so." Ike never admitted he studied hard at Leavenworth, and he would never suggest that if some of the others in his class fell by the wayside, it wouldn't bother him too much.

By the time he arrived at the Command and General Staff School on August 25, 1925, he was quite confident that he would do well, and he did.

The Eisenhowers were at Leavenworth from August 1925 until late June 1926. It was and is a pleasant post on a plateau a hundred feet above the Missouri River, surrounded by rolling hills. The U.S. military prison was on the grounds and the federal penitentiary was adjacent. Occasionally a prisoner would break out of one of the institutions, and the sirens would sound until he was recaptured. The Eisenhower apartment was in Otis Hall, a red-brick building with white trim. It, too, was a converted barracks, but it was freshly painted and cheerful. There were twelve families in the three-story units. Four old friends, the Walton Walkers and Leonard T. "Gee" Gerow and his wife, Katherine, were already there.

Leavenworth is about thirty miles from Kansas City, and during the first part of September when classes began, the weather was described by one student as "sweltering." The commandant, Brigadier General Edward L. King, welcomed the class, and the instructors offered advice to the newcomers. One class member said of the advice received in the opening days, "We were assured that there were in the course no catch problems, no 'niggers in the wood pile'—that we would do well not to play hunches, or bone the personal equation [bootlick] individual instructors, not to follow previous problems blindly, but to tackle each problem with an open mind. . . . Above all, we were warned not to 'straddle' in solving a problem. . . . It was also emphasized that the purpose of the school is not simply to turn out staff officers, as some have supposed it to be, but equally to train every officer taking the course in high command."

Eisenhower's class of 245 was younger than any previous class, the average age being well under forty. The instructors found they were just as "serious," however, "but a bit more 'light-hearted.' " Morning classes began at 8:30 and lasted until noon. They consisted of either lectures or conferences on an assigned subject, and every lesson was accompanied by an illustrative problem. In the afternoon, from 1:00 to 5:00, sometimes later, problems were given. The first month the solutions did not count toward the student's standing.

Several courses were given. One, on military history, consisted of nineteen lectures on the campaigns of the World War and methods of historical research. Another was on Leadership. One of the two most important courses Ike took was in Tactical Principles and Decisions, which in addition to lectures, included marches, reconnaisance, attack and defense of a position, counterattacks, pursuits, river crossings, and tactical principles. The other was Command Staff and Logistics, in which he had to work out every detail of moving a division, both by truck and by rail, all over the map. Ike's success in this course had a great deal to do with where the problems were set. "Most of our problems were on the Gettysburg three-inch map. I had commanded a camp [Colt] here in 1918, and I became more familiar with the country . . . than you can imagine; so it never took me more than five minutes to stake out my problems where the others had to look up where the location of Seven Stars, Tawneytown, New Oxford and all the rest were. It would take the average fellow forty minutes and I'd take five."

Marking was impersonal. Papers did not bear the student's name, just identification numbers. In that way the instructors were ignorant as to whose paper they were grading.

Two years later, in the June 1927 issue of *Infantry Journal,* "A Young Graduate" attempted to give reassurance to officers about to go to Leavenworth. The "Young Graduate" was Eisenhower, who wrote that,

> Any student of average intelligence, possessed of an optimistic turn of mind and with enough self-confidence to trust his own common sense, will do well in the course, but have a most pleasant year while he was doing it.
>
> The first and most important thing for the student to do in the course is to *trust instructor.* Failure to follow this dictum, especially when the failure becomes chronic, is bound to result disastrously. The instructor, from the standpoint of Leavenworth requirements, must be considered as an expert on the subject he is teaching.
>
> Furthermore, don't be too critical concerning details with which you do not agree, it is possible to fail to see the forest because of the trees. Remember the philosophy of Molly Make-believe 'now abideth faith, hope & charity, these three'—*and greater than these is a sense of humor.*

One of the instructors, General Herbert Jay Brees, wrote Eisenhower on January 17, 1944, shortly after it was announced that he would command the forces invading Western Europe. Brees was then a retired major general and congratulated Ike on his appointment. The newly appointed supreme commander said in his reply of February 28:

> I know of no single year of my whole service that I go back to in my memories more than to my student year at Leavenworth, when you were in charge of instruction. Even today, if I could go back and rearrange the instructional course, based on the information that was then available to us, I think I would change only two details. The first of these would be to insist that all instructors treat war as the drama that it is rather than constantly reducing it to a science of marching tables and tonnage calculations. I do not decry the necessity for the scientific end of the education, I merely think that too many officers develop their thinking more and more along lines of mathematical calculations rather than realizing that calculations always go wrong. The second detail that I would change would be

a greater emphasis upon the Air Army, particularly in its role of supporting ground troops.

What I am trying to say is that I firmly believe that our school system, of which West Point, Fort Benning and Leavenworth are outstanding examples, is largely responsible for the very high average of professional training we have among our officers today. For this I feel that you can and should take a very considerable credit because I know that your many years of devoted service at Leavenworth were largely responsible for the excellent course of instruction developed there.

A welcome change from the indoor instruction was the "tactical ride." Another graduate of Ike's class wrote, "At 1:00 P.M. each student falls in with his section and mounts his assigned horse and the class of 250 rides off into the country to an unknown destination where each student receives a copy of the 'situation' and 'requirement,' the answer to which must be turned in at a designated hour. . . . Before writing a solution the student is allowed to 'reconnoiter,' on foot or horseback. The only map that can be used in these problems is a one-inch map showing the roads, the streams, but without contours—the ground forms, cover & so on must be determined by observation in the field." Eisenhower said, "Fox Conner had been correct. We had done this kind of 'war gaming' in Panama."

According to George C. Marshall's biographer, Forrest C. Pogue, when Marshall was at Leavenworth nearly twenty years before he never dallied after work. "A classmate recalls . . . When tactical problems might require a ride several miles out from the post, Marshall would always lead the way home. 'We never bothered to find the shortest way—all we did was to watch George Marshall and he would go off straight as a bee to a beehive and we would follow him.' " Ike hurried home immediately after the last class or maneuver, too.

Evenings were full. After a quick supper there was a great deal of reading and studying to do. "There are three generally recognized systems of study at Leavenworth," Eisenhower said. "These are called the single, the committee, and the pair or partner method. Each has its advantages and good points."

The committee system "is rather unwieldy, as there are too many men whose convenience and ideas must be suited. Too often when several men are working together some unfortunate characteristic of any one of them may vitiate the efforts of all." He added, "If you work entirely alone you are more apt to go stale, to go to one extreme or the other in the hours you devote to study, and consume too much time in working on details whose importance does not justify the effort made. . . .

"The partner system has most of the advantages of the other systems and none of the disadvantages, provided the partners suit each other. Each serves as a check on the other, study is less monotonous, and much time is saved in the staking out of illustrative problems, and in the assimilation of the broad principles of any subject. . . . The only caution to be observed is that the partner must not join up in haste and repent in haste."

Eisenhower chose as his study partner, Gee Gerow. They had been friends since they served together at Fort Sam, and Gee had an additional advantage.

He had just graduated first in his class in the Infantry School at Fort Benning, which Eisenhower had missed attending.

They converted a room on the third floor of Eisenhower's apartment into what Ike called "a model command post. The walls were covered with maps. The worktable was large and the bookshelves close at hand." Above all, he added, there was "no sound, household or military." While the two men were studying, no intrusions were allowed. John Eisenhower, who was three at the time, remembered "a new tricycle at Fort Leavenworth . . . an impressive pile of lumber stacked on the second floor of Otis Hall. . . . Mother singing to me in the car. But most vivid of all was the night I invaded Dad's attic study, normally off limits. He and his friend Gee . . . were poring intensely over a large table, eyeshades protecting them from the glare of a brilliant, low-hung lamp. I was too small to see what was on the table but stared in wonderment at the huge maps tacked on the wall. The two young officers were going over the next day's tactical problem. Dad and Gee welcomed me with a laugh and shoved me out the door in the course of perhaps half a minute."

Eisenhower, in the article he wrote for *Infantry Journal* after his graduation, said, "As in everything else, your daily habits at Leavenworth should be normal and reasonable. . . . If you study too much you will lose some of your ability to carry a fresh and active mind to the problem room. . . . Make yourself a schedule and stick to it. Make the limit of study 10:15 P.M. Get to bed at once and be sure you average a good solid eight hours sleep."

Forty years later he said, "As time went on, it was easy to identify those people who were studying too long and too hard at night and coming to daytime sessions . . . without fresh minds and an optimistic outlook. I established a routine that limited my night study to two hours and a half, from seven to nine-thirty. Mamie was charged with the duty of seeing that I got to bed by that time."

The advice he gave in 1927 is excellent advice indeed, but, as is so often the case with advice givers, he didn't follow it. The amount of time Eisenhower studied depends on the source. In *At Ease*, he said he studied only two and a half hours. Mamie remembered it differently. She told her biographer and friend, Dorothy Brandon, that Ike followed "a driving routine—a snatched early breakfast and a hurried dinner after day-long classes. Rarely did he wait for Major Gerow to arrive, so anxious was he to begin his evening grind. . . . Around midnight he would put in an appearance en route for a foray on the refrigerator."

Alden Hatch, also a friend of Mamie's and of Eisenhower's as well, wrote that, "Often Mamie woke at one or two in the morning to find her husband still fighting his theoretical battles, while the mounds of cigarette stubs littered every ashtray. Frequently he worked all night. All Mamie could do was to try to keep Johnny quiet and force her husband to take ten minutes to eat."

Saturdays were free and students were encouraged to "play hard," from Friday evening until Sunday afternoon. There were weekly hops on Friday night at the golf clubhouse, and for a moderate fee students enjoyed the privileges of tennis courts, the swimming pool, and an excellent eighteen-hole golf course. During the busy months at Leavenworth, Ike did find time to play golf for the first time. He liked it at once, and as in so many other endeavors, he was better at it than most. He played until very near the end of his life. And on February 6, 1968, when he was about seventy-seven he achieved what every golfer dreams about, a hole in one. He was playing at the Seven Lakes Country Club in Palm Desert on the thirteenth hole using a nine iron. Two weeks later, at the same hole, at the same country club, his brother Edgar did the same thing. Even at the ages of 77 and 79 the two brothers were still at it, but in this particular competition Edgar won: It was his fourth hole in one.

One of the great pleasures of golf after he got into politics was that the latter subject was not to be mentioned on the course; indeed no extraneous subject was to be mentioned while he was playing. He insisted on concentrating on each shot and talking about nothing but golf. Ed Dudley, the golf pro at Augusta National, said Eisenhower had "strong arms and wrists and was a perfectionist." Frequently when he had made mistakes in a game he would go back to the holes where he felt he had done badly and practice his shot over and over again until he was satisfied.

Classes were over the second week of June. The faculty board at the school met on the morning of June 16, 1926, and when the meeting ended, a little more than two hours later, it was announced that Eisenhower had been the top man with a mark of 93.08; Gerow's mark was two-tenths of a percent less. While Ike's final standing in the class was number 1, his standing for the course by months was as follows:

October	14
November	9
December	4
January	4
February	8
March	4
April	3
May	3

The board recommended Eisenhower for general staff duty as well as recommending him for the Army War College at what is now Fort McNair in Washington, D.C. George L. Byroads, the director of instruction at Leavenworth, described him as "an alert, forceful, resourceful officer, dependable and courteous." As the West Point alumni magazine, *Assembly,* noted in its spring 1968 issue, "If a point is reached in anyone's career when it turns upward, then possibly ranking first in his class at Leavenworth was this point in Eisenhower's career." He himself referred to the school there as "a watershed in my life."

Was Eisenhower surprised to find himself number one? The answer to that also depends on who is asked. John Leonard, a classmate, said, "Eisenhower said he was going to come out number one, and he did. Maybe just by the neck, but he did." Eisenhower, in his comments on the Kenneth Davis book, wrote that he "never dreamed I might be number one." Roscoe B. Woodruff, a less admiring classmate, said in an interview at the Eisenhower Library, "I kind of hate to say this, but they say one of the reasons he came out Number One was that he spent a lot of time in the faculty offices at the headquarters building. . . . It wasn't said maliciously, just casually, just casually. Ike was very well liked. They would just jokingly say, 'Well, he spends enough time with the faculty.' "

Eisenhower put it this way in his 1927 *Infantry Journal* article:

In addition to the instruction you receive in the conference room, during your study periods, and in the working of problems, you will gain a great deal by the absorbtion method. During recess between conferences you have splendid opportunities for dropping into the office of any instructor you'd like to see. The little talks you will have with these officers who have been through the mill and are now instructors intimately connected with the school will prove invaluable to you. Instructors are anxious to help, and you can ask specific questions or just sit around and listen to the general conversation. The insight into the school and the understanding of the whole course you will pick up in this manner is remarkable.

Many years later, Mamie summed it up best and most truthfully. She said, "I knew Ike would come out Number One. But when he made it I was so tumbled inside with gladness, it was days before I could eat properly."

Naturally, Eisenhower wrote his friend Georgie to tell him the good news and to thank him for the use of his notes. They had been a great help. Georgie wrote back on July 9:

Your letter delights me more than I can say. As soon as I saw the list I wrote you congratulating you on being honor but I had no idea that in addition you were no. ONE. That certainly is fine.

It shows that Leavenworth is a good school if a HE man can come out one.

You are very kind to think that my notes helped you though I feel sure that you would have done as well without them. If a man thinks war long enough it is bound to affect him in a good way.

I am convinced that as good as Leavenworth is it is still only a means not an end and that we must keep on [studying tactics].

Eisenhower understandably wanted to celebrate his success, and the next day after learning he had been top man he drove to Kansas City to see his oldest brother, Arthur, who at that time was vice president of the Commerce Trust Company. According to Earl Endacott, when Eisenhower went to his brother's office, "They talked for a few minutes about nothing much, and then Dwight approached his brother for a bank loan of $150. Arthur, with his banker's instinct, asked . . . what did Dwight have for security. Dwight said, Nothing. All he had was his future as an officer. Arthur told him that under those circumstances the bank could not make him a loan, but that he personally would do it.

"Dwight thanked him and took the money, promising to repay it as soon as possible. The money was to be used to throw a big party at the Muehlbach

Hotel for a few personal friends. Arthur said he was a softie to make the loan, but he agreed to go to the party, and through some influential friends—this was during prohibition time—he got some gin and whiskey."

The people at the party were Ike and Mamie, Arthur and his wife, and Gee Gerow and his wife. About midnight, Arthur called the president of the bank, George Dillon, to join the party, and he did.

Endacott said, "When Dillon arrived, he was greeted by all singing 'For he's a jolly good fellow.' Dwight was one of the loudest if not the best of the singers. The party lasted until after daybreak and Arthur said confidentially that he could never remember whether he was ever repaid for the loan, but he said it did not matter. He had had his money's worth."

After what was a day of recuperation, Arthur and Ike drove to Abilene for a rare family reunion. All the brothers were there, Dwight and Arthur from Kansas City, Earl from a small town in Pennsylvania where he was an electrical engineer, Milton from Washington, D.C., where he was assistant secretary of agriculture, Edgar from Tacoma, Washington, where he was already a very prosperous corporation lawyer, and Roy from Junction City, Kansas, where he had a drugstore.

The six brothers were in Abilene for three days, during which Ida served them fried mush and puddin, wore the knee-length white lace shawl Dwight had sent her from Panama, and smiled a good deal. David, unsmiling, said grace at each meal. At one point he announced that he'd be sixty-three in a few weeks but that he was as good a man as he ever was and that he would take on any one of them in a wrestling match. Dwight accepted the challenge and one afternoon they both took off their shirts and went to the backyard, along with the other brothers. Kenneth Davis does not say where Ida was. He does say, "Dwight was prepared to 'let the old man down easy.' He was almost thrown himself before he discovered, to his amazement, that he'd need all his strength and skill. For fifteen minutes the two grunted and strained before Dwight at last managed to pin his father to the ground. It was, certainly, a moral victory for David." Eisenhower, in his corrections of the Davis book, said of this odd wrestling match, "this is not true." His brother Milton, however, in an interview with Bela Kornitzer in 1955, remembered a wrestling match between Ike and their father at a different time and with a different outcome. The only thing that seems certain is that there was a wrestling match between father and son at one of the family reunions.

Later, Roy challenged his brothers to a golf game at the Abilene country club, and he won, shooting in the low seventies; the scores of Dwight, Arthur, and Edgar were in the low eighties. Another afternoon the six of them—possibly after a sampling of bootleg whiskey and gin—marched on Chestnut Street across the railroad tracks and through the business district. Ostensibly they were looking for Henry Engle, the chief of police, with whom they had had slight run-ins when they were boys. It is not surprising that the exhibition created a considerable stir in Abilene. Davis said, "The scene became part of the Abilene legend. Decades later, when curious visitors asked about the Eisenhower family, local citizens recalled the Big Parade of 1926 and smiled as they told about it."

On the last day of the reunion, Jeffcoat, Abilene's leading photographer, took a picture of the entire family on the front porch of the house. It is a remarkably solemn picture; five of the brothers and their father look as if they had just received some very bad news of a personal nature. Not even Ida is smiling. Dwight, seated on the second of two steps, is grinning broadly, wearing a dress uniform and high boots that some enlisted man at Leavenworth spent a good deal of time polishing. The Distinguished Service Medal is clearly visible on his uniform jacket; he was not yet the most successful member of that successful family, but he certainly looked to be the most confident.

The next morning Eisenhower and Mamie departed for a leave in Denver. He had been a major since July 2, 1920; he would remain one until July 1, 1936.

★ ★ ★

PRUDENS FUTURI

—*Motto of the U.S. Army War College*

Eisenhower had been in the army long enough to know that what he had done at Leavenworth would not have much effect on his immediate career. He was once more back in the infantry, and General Sheets was still head of that arm of the service. In May he had received orders that after his leave in Denver the War Department would send him to Fort Benning as executive officer of the 24th Infantry.

There had been two other possible assignments, one as the military instructor for an ROTC unit at "a northwestern university." The job offered a bonus of $3,500 a year to coach the university football team. The extra income would have been welcome, but he turned the offer down at once. "I don't think it's possible for a man to meet the requirements of two rather exacting jobs. If I have to coach football all the time, I might as well resign and . . . concentrate on the sport."

General King, commandant at Leavenworth, asked him to stay there another year as a teacher, but in the end, as before, Sheets prevailed. Eisenhower had hoped to go to the Army War College immediately after Leavenworth. It was considered that it was necessary to attend the college to achieve high rank. But that was not what the army had in mind for him.

In early August, Eisenhower and Mamie drove to Benning from Denver in a new 1927 Buick. On arrival he was asked to do what he had turned down $3,500 to do—coach the football team. He convinced the executive officer at Benning that he should not be head coach, but he was willing to take charge of the backfield. The season was not noteworthy, but by the time it ended Fox Conner, still deputy chief of staff, had once more arranged a better assignment for him. He was to come to Washington to write a guidebook on the battlefields in Europe on which American soldiers had fought. The book was to be published by the Government Printing Office, and it would be written under the watchful eye of General John J. Pershing, who was now chairman of the American Battle Monuments Commission. The book was to be, Eisenhower said, "a sort of Baedeker to the actions of Americans in war."

Before leaving Benning on January 15, Eisenhower got both good news and bad from superior officers. Colonel Walt C. Johnson said that he was "above average" as an executive officer with the 24th, but as a football coach, the colonel said, he was "superior." Eisenhower would have been happy to have the judgments reversed. Brigadier General Edgar T. "Windy" Collins had read Johnson's report and thought that certain ratings of Eisenhower were "low." Collins added, "Major Eisenhower . . . acted as Inspector and Assistant Executive for Training and Mobilization. In both capacities his duties were discharged in a superior manner. He is qualified to a very exceptional degree and is a very exceptionally efficient officer." It is not surprising that Windy Collins was someone Eisenhower later said he admired "tremendously," adding that the general was "keen, positive, impulsive, and mentally honest."

Although Mamie had traveled a good deal before, she had never been to Washington, and she found the streets puzzling, the taxis too expensive, and the prospect of keeping up a house too exhausting. She settled on a spacious three-bedroom apartment in the ornate Wyoming Apartments, a six-story building at 24th Street and Massachusetts Avenue, just behind Connecticut Avenue. The Wyoming had been recommended by friends, and Mamie liked it at once. Altogether, she lived there nine years. Eisenhower was beginning to collect oriental rugs, a hobby that persisted for the rest of his life and those brightened the floors of the apartment.

Ike started his new assignment in the old State-War-Navy building on January 21. The work was not easy. He had to take the mountain of material on America's participation in the Great War and organize and cut it so that it could fit into a single volume. The man who wrote the guidebook had to understand every battle in Europe, and he had to describe each battle in detail, as well as each monument commemorating the battle; moreover, as it would be critically read by the men who had fought and won and lost such battles the book had to be done in a prose style that would please not only these readers, including Pershing, but the most casual tourist who bought it from the Government Printing Office. Black Jack Pershing did not interfere with what Eisenhower did; nevertheless, his office was nearby, and his presence was always felt. Moreover, he frequently asked Eisenhower to act as his aide, an assignment the major did not greet with joy. He found the general "rather reserved and even remote in manner. . . . He had few visitors." Pershing was alway hours late for any appointment, and he usually did not get to the office until one in the afternoon and stayed until midnight. He expected those who worked with him, including his aide, to follow the same routine.

Ike felt that the job was one any qualified civilian could have handled. He was therefore elated when new orders arrived in March. Sometime between August 15 and 20, he was to report to the commandant at the Army War College, where he would be a student for the 1927–28 course. Pershing's executive officer, Xenophon Price, "thought I was passing up a shining future with the Battle

Monuments Commission. 'Every officer attached to the Commission is going to be known as a man of special merit,' he said. 'For once the [War] Department has given me a choice,' I said, 'and for once I'm going to say yes to something I'm anxious to do.' "

Price, as a member of the class of 1914, had known Eisenhower at West Point. He was to be one of the rare people to display dissatisfaction with, not to say dislike of, Eisenhower.

While waiting to attend the War College, Eisenhower completed *A Guide to the American Battle Fields in Europe*, which the *Encyclopaedia Britannica* was to say was "an excellent reference work on world War I." His name did not appear anywhere in the book, but almost everyone in the War Department knew that he had written it, and in less than seven months. Publication had been expedited "in order to have it available for the large number of ex-servicemen who intended to go to Europe in the fall of 1927." The whole thing was done in 282 pages, with lots of photographs—a masterful job!

Ike's assignment with the difficult general lasted only a little over half a year. Still, Pershing proved useful to him. On August 15, the general wrote a letter to the new and, it was hoped, friendlier chief of infantry, General Robert Allen. In it he said:

I wish to take this occasion to express my appreciation of the splendid service which he [Eisenhower] has rendered since being with us.

In the discharge of his duties, which were . . . difficult and which were rendered even more difficult by reason of the short time available for their completion, he has shown superior ability not only in visualizing his work as a whole but in executing its many details in an efficient and timely manner. What he has done was accomplished only by the exercise of unusual intelligence and constant devotion to duty.

Pershing was an old man, eighty-seven when these words were written, and yet the prose lacks the wooden quality of most of his letters and of his memoirs. It seems quite possible that in writing it he called for the help of his old friend Fox Conner. In any case, as intended, the letter impressed the new infantry chief.

Eisenhower pasted Pershing's letter in his battlefield guidebook and sent it home to Abilene inscribed, "To my mother and father . . . with love and devotion."

On August 16 Eisenhower entered the Army War College, a quiet post on the Potomac, just a streetcar ride from the Wyoming. The War College was, unlike Leavenworth, relaxed and was rightly called "the country club of the army." There were no tests and no grades. It was later named Fort McNair for Eisenhower's supporter and admirer, Lieutenant General Lesley J. McNair, known as the man who trained the U.S. Army for the Second World War. McNair was killed in Normandy when an American bomb fell short of its target. The post is one of the most beautiful the army has, with a broad, grassy parade ground, also used as a golf course, and handsome quarters for officers and noncoms; the houses were designed by Stanford White.

In a paper called "Dwight D. Eisenhower at the Army War college, 1927–28," Dr. Benjamin F. Cooling wrote, "The War College assignment proved to be merely an interlude for Eisenhower between assignments relating to the guidebook on the battlefields. But it was a valued interlude, for at the War College students learned to think about the big problems of the war—supply, movement of large bodies of troops, relations with allies, grand strategy. . . .

"The Army War College in the late 1920s was a pleasant, contemplative assignment for senior professionals of that generation. . . . One recent analyst said, 'To anyone subjected to the pressures at Leavenworth the War College seemed by contrast to be pleasantly contrived for a leisurely respite.' . . .

"Overall hung the 'lessons' and techniques of World War I. The curriculum was structured to reflect the staff organization of the American Expeditionary Force [AEF], as if every future war would be fought in the image of the one just past."

The commandant of the college in 1927 was Major General William D. Connor, West Point class of 1897, who said in his welcome to the incoming students:

"In a very large measure the period of your self-development begins right now for in this institution there are no marks applied to your daily work and there are no periodic tests or final examinations that you must undergo to show the faculty what progress you have made or what advantages you have accumulated during the year's work. From now on you become, more than ever before, subject only to the critical judgment of your fellow officers."

General Connor was describing what Major Eisenhower did most naturally and easily—earn the approval of his peers.

What Eisenhower learned at the War College was not totally without its uses in the Second World War. On March 22, 1943, American forces in North Africa, after the disaster of the Kasserine Pass, were beginning to do well. The Allied commander wrote Connor:

There is not any doubt about the extent of the influence that you are still exerting on operations in this war. Oddly enough, when the decision was made last November 11th to start rushing toward Tunisia in an effort to grab off the last foot that we could before the Germans could get in, I actually related to some members of my Staff your particular solution to a very "defensive-looking" problem we once had in the War College. When we were still wondering whether the French would fight us or help us, there were many people who counselled me to be more cautious, to develop my bases, perfect my build-up and bring in steadily the troops that we would need to wage a rather ritualistic campaign in that direction. Had we done this, we would probably now be fighting a rather heavy battle somewhere in the vicinity of Constantine, possibly even Tebessa and Souk Ahras, but anyone who has seen the terrain of North Africa can well appreciate that a very few troops, holding the coastline and the communications running eastward from Setif, could force upon any attacker the slowest and most costly of advances. Moreover, under those circumstances, we would have the airfields from which to help on our right and there would not exist any possibility of a junction with the Western Desert Forces.

When that argument was going on, I recalled the particular War College problem that made such an impression on me. We had been working on a problem of resisting invasion in Connecticut, and all the statistical technicians had worked out in detail the most advanced line that they could defend consistent with getting the logistics properly arranged and the necessary forces on the field. Your criticism of the problem was that it was one that obviously called for instant and continuous attack. I remember you said: "Attack with whatever you've got at any point where you get it up, and attack and keep on attacking until this invader realizes that he has got to stop and reorganize, and thus give to us a chance to deliver a finishing blow."

Each student at the college had to write what Dr. Cooling called "a research paper, then termed a 'Staff Memorandum,' and Ike chose the timely (if somewhat prosaic) topic, 'An Enlisted Reserve for the Regular Army.' . . . Eisenhower's paper, which he submitted on 15 March 1928, epitomized the principles emphasized in the War College Study at that time—brevity, lucidity, and practicality."

The report was seventeen pages long. According to Cooling, "Although the isolationist national mood of the twenties made overseas military involvement an almost taboo subject, Major Eisenhower approached the matter without hesitation. Connor's marginal comments cautioned him several times about the anathema attached to the term 'expeditionary force,' which Ike saw as one of the Army's primary missions."

The five months Eisenhower spent at War College were the most enjoyable of his career up to that time. Gee Gerow and Walton Walker were there, and another old friend, Wade Haislip, was there also. So was a man who was later to be very important to him, Everett Hughes, who had been one of Eisenhower's teachers at Leavenworth.

There were a great many parties in the Eisenhowers' apartment at the Wyoming, and Everett Hughes's wife, Kate, said of them, "Most of the time people were at their house. We'd gather there after the men had played their golf, or when they'd finished for the day at the War College. The men would stop at the Eisenhowers' for a drink and get to talking and then call their wives and we'd all go over. . . . Sometimes we'd go out to a Chinese or Italian restaurant, but mostly we'd stay at the Eisenhowers'. Mamie would have food for us, or sometimes each of us would bring something."

John Eisenhower remembered that when there was a social evening at the apartment, "Club Eisenhower," "I stayed in my room like all youngsters but would come out and join in for short periods of time. . . . Perhaps Dad's deepest admirer was Everett Hughes, who later became Inspector General in the European Theater and still later Chief of Ordnance. 'Uncle Everett' used to tell me at great length of my Dad's virtues. Your father is a man to watch! he admonished me one evening. I agreed, but in the light of the old man's disciplinary policies, I probably interpreted the statement a little differently from the way it was intended."

Milton was in Washington, too; he was on the information staff of the secretary of agriculture, Dr. William H. Jardine, a fellow Kansan. On Columbus Day that year, Milton married Helen Eakin, the daughter of still another Kansan, L. R. Eakin, who owned the largest department store in Manhattan, Kansas, where Milton and Helen had attended college. Eakin was also a director of a bank there, dabbled in real estate and oil, and before coming to Washington that year, was one of the richest men in town. While in Washington, he bought two thousand acres of farmland across the Potomac from the Lincoln Memorial. The land improved considerably in value a short time later when a new highway was built through it.

Eisenhower was best man at the wedding, which was in the Wyoming apartment. He wore his dress blues with the Distinguished Service Medal, and Milton and Helen cut the cake with his ceremonial sword.

Another frequent guest at the Wyoming was a close friend of Milton's, a personable—some people thought too personable—young man from Iowa, Harry C. Butcher. His job when he first knew the Eisenhowers was what some wags said was the most appropriate he ever had: he was editor of a farm magazine called the *Fertilizer Review*. Butcher later remembered that the parties in those early days in Washington were made considerably more lively by Major Eisenhower's own brand of bathtub gin.

At that time in Washington, Eisenhower was known as "Milton's brother." Most people who had met him were impressed with his friendly grin, but they couldn't help feeling that he was a little long in the tooth to be a major. At thirty-seven he ought to be at least a light (lieutenant) colonel. No, Milton was the one to watch.

Milton and his bride were frequently invited to the Coolidge White House. Milton said that they "became well acquainted with the Coolidge family, mostly on a social basis. My wife's parents, Secretary and Mrs. Jardine's closest friends, often joined the Jardines in White House affairs and my wife and I were included. . . . This experience gave me my first close-up look at a real, live President."

That same year Ike got as far as the front lawn of the White House when he took John to the Easter-egg hunt. The hunt was discontinued in 1942 because of the war and was not started again until Eisenhower's second year as president; he could well have thought back to the innocent spring of 1928 when there wasn't even a fence around the White House lawn.

Ike received a certificate of attendance from the War College on June 30, 1928. General Connor wrote a glowing comment:

Proficiency in theoretical training for High Command—Superior
For W.D.C.S. [War Department-General Staff]—Superior
Academic rating—Superior
Qualified for civilian contact and duty with civilian component.

For his next assignment, Eisenhower again had a choice. He could have joined the War Department general staff, which would have kept him in Washington and possibly given him a chance to avoid at least some of the blunders for which he felt the department was responsible. The other possibility was to return to the American Battle Monuments Commission to help revise the guidebook. He did not particularly want to work on the book again, but it meant a trip to Paris and a chance to see the battlefields he had written about.

This time he talked the matter over with Mamie. In 1965, looking back on that time, she said, "When Ike finished the War College in 1928 . . . General Pershing asked him to revise it [the guidebook to the American battlefields in Europe]. . . . Johnny was six and I thought it would be a grand experience for him to live in a foreign country. I asked Ike to take the foreign assignment and he did."

* * *

SOME AMERICANS IN PARIS

The whole thing started out well. John would go to the McJanet School for American children in Paris. Mamie, although she might at first have trouble in pronouncing the names of the shops and the streets in which they were located, would buy Parisian clothes on the Rue St.-Honoré, the Rue de la Paix, and the Place Vendôme. She did buy clothes, especially hats. Her husband said, "Mamie . . . was a specialist in the shops that ranged from the flea market and sidewalk stands to the *grands magasins.*" She still had most of these Paris clothes when she was first lady and when she retired to Gettysburg.

The plan also was that Eisenhower and Mamie would visit his battlefields, and John Doud and Min would join them and drive around France as they had the United States. If necessary, the Douds, who were looking forward to the trip as much as the Eisenhowers, would help take care of John. And they would all learn to speak and read French.

The Douds came to Washington from Denver in mid-July 1928, and on the 31st they all sailed from New York on a luxurious American liner. John said, "My sixth birthday occurred on board ship, and my recollection of the large birthday cake in the ornate dining room of the S.S. *America* remains strong. . . . The trip to Europe in 1928 seems to have stimulated my memory, for I remember many details."

The voyage across the Atlantic was smooth, but they were held up by a heavy fog at Southampton and did not cross the Channel to France until after dark on the 9th of August. The ship docked at Cherbourg, where fifteen years later Eisenhower was to dispatch airborne troops into the German-occupied Cotentin Peninsula.

By comparison, the problems Eisenhower faced at Cherbourg on August 9, 1928, were trivial, but he was at first annoyed, then furious to discover that his immediate superior in the American Battle Monuments Commission, Major Xenophon H. Price, Corps of Engineers, secretary of the commission, had not taken the trouble to send someone from the commission to meet them. Aksel Nielsen said of Eisenhower, "Nothing made him angrier than people not doing what they were supposed to do. He was impatient with incompetence."

Eisenhower then and there decided that when someone new to the commission, whether it be a clerk or a general, arrived, he would be met. He made sure that happened during his stay in France, sometimes himself going to meet whoever it was. That did not enhance his popularity with his superior officer.

It was after midnight when the Eisenhowers and the Douds finally were able to get on an overcrowded boat train for Paris. Ike's temper did not improve when at three-thirty in the morning they arrived in Paris at Gare St.-Lazare and were unmet. Although they knew that hotel reservations had been made for them, they did not know where.

No one at Gare St.-Lazare spoke English; it appeared that even the man from the Cook's had gone to bed. John Doud and Eisenhower had a lengthy discussion as to whether they should all spend the rest of the night in the station or take a chance and go by taxi to an unknown Paris hotel. Certainly, on that first trip to Paris in 1928, Eisenhower, like most Americans—and in many ways he was like most Americans—was convinced that the French overcharged you when they found out that you were from the U.S., that if you were not careful they stole you blind, and that they spoke an infuriating, largely incomprehensible language. He continued to be suspicious of Parisians during the time he served at the commission but changed his mind about the people of the French countryside.

John Doud and Eisenhower decided to risk the unknown. They all got into a taxi and trusted to the mercies of a wild, honest, even solicitous driver, who understood the word "hotel" after it was repeated several times in loud tones of voice. He took them to a satisfactory but modest hotel of which John Eisenhower remembered that "breakfast was limited to orange juice and croissants."

A few days later, Mamie, with the help of some resident army wives, found a ground-floor apartment at 110 Rue d'Auteuil on the Right Bank of the Seine. John said that the apartment was "about a mile and a half downstream from the Trocadero and the Eiffel Tower." It was "small but boasted a stone courtyard of perhaps eight by ten feet, adequate space for a six-year-old to play. I was able to find the apartment, near Pont Mirabeau on a visit nearly nineteen years later."

The apartment, owned by the Comtesse de Villefranche, had three bedrooms, a salon, a dining room, and a library. The kitchen was gloomy and had no icebox, and there never seemed to be enough heat. In one way it was rather like the Doud house in Denver. There was too much furniture, too many tables, too many figurines. Still, it was a considerable improvement over the military quarters they had lived in before. The apartment was also only a short walk from 20 Rue Molitor, where the commission had its offices, and Eisenhower walked home for lunch most days. The food, prepared by a succession of French cooks, was always too rich for Eisenhower's taste, always smothered in too many sauces. He frequently prepared sauceless meals himself.

They entertained a great deal, and the apartment soon became another "Club Eisenhower"—what Ike called "a sort of informal, junior-size American Express." The Pont Mirabeau became the "Pont Mamie." John said, "I don't ever remember any French people. The Americans stuck together; it was an American colony just as it later was in the Philippines. Americans abroad seem to want to stick together. French was not spoken; Dad's French was kitchen French at best."

Ike was rather defensive about his failure to master the language. Later, he said that, as president, "I am certain I could have been more effective in the many conferences I attended . . . if I had mastered at least one foreign language. . . . The deficiency was not totally my fault. A basic difficulty was my lack of talent for learning other languages, due largely to the fact that I was not exposed to them when young. Further, I am of the opinion that those people who cannot carry a tune or readily remember one have difficulty in languages; it is rare that I can distinguish or identify even the simplest words spoken in another language even though I have had fair familiarity with written texts in the same language. . . . In school I studied Latin, German, French, and Spanish, but I never wholly mastered them, and the resulting confusion in my mind made me incapable of using any one foreign language satisfactorily. In later years, when I was stationed in foreign areas, I had studied French and Spanish under professional teachers—with no appreciable results. I well remember how in 1929 under the tutelage of a Monsieur 'Freddy' for months in Paris, he expressed his opinion that I would never become much good in French. He said, 'Major, you are one of the best readers of French and translators of the written language that I have among my students, but you are the worst candidate as a French linguist I have ever tried to teach. You should stop wasting your money on me!' To this, out of native stubbornness, I replied, 'I'm inclined to agree, but I engaged you for one year of daily lessons, and I'm going through with it. I still hope for miraculous progress.' "

The miracle did not occur. Lieutenant General Vernon A. Walters, translator for many presidents, including Truman, Nixon, Eisenhower, and Reagan, was Ike's translator when he was head of SHAPE. He said, "I was fortunate during this period in being closely associated with General Eisenhower. This gave me an unusual opportunity to observe him under different circumstances and to watch how he dealt with different foreign leaders. Though he often expressed appreciation for my services, I could see how much more easily he could communicate with those who spoke English. I was conscious of this and did my best to make him as little aware as possible that what he was hearing was a translation. . . . The general did not have any facility in French or any other language and he frequently complained bitterly of it. I think it sort of puzzled him. He was a modest man, but he was not unaware of his gifts in many fields. And this genuinely puzzled him; how he could have lived in France for two years and not learned French. He used to say, 'I have a block where languages are concerned.' But as I once told him, 'General, the languages will get you a job as a head waiter or a courtier but . . . you've been amply compensated in other areas.' He grinned and laughed."

Ike once told John, "I think languages are a subject that only geniuses and crackpots can master." But John said, "Dad always figured out an equivalent English expression. For instance, the word *Reims*. Practically everybody in the army pronounced it *Reams*, to rhyme with *beams*. Not Dad, though, he said *Rants*, rhyming it with *aunts*, which is the proper way to pronounce it."

Mamie learned no French at all, despite daily lessons at the beginning of their stay. She used a pocket dictionary to communicate with merchants and the many cooks. The Douds didn't even try to master the language. Only John, at the McJanet School, learned to read and speak French.

In Paris that summer, the president of the American Olympic Committee, General Douglas MacArthur, over for the Amsterdam Olympics, gave an interview to a *Chicago Tribune* correspondent named William L. Shirer. MacArthur said, "We have one of the smallest armies in the world—nineteenth or twentieth among the nations. Even those little countries we created after the war, Rumania, Czechoslovakia, Yugoslavia, Poland, have a bigger army than the United States of America. At home there are practically no armed forces at all. Most of our soldiers are overseas or down on the Mexican border or sitting at desks. In case of an emergency we could count on a combat force of only two divisions—about twenty-five thousand men out of an army of a hundred and twenty-five thousand. . . . We have the worst-equipped army in the world. And the terrible thing is that our people don't give a damn. They're too busy making money. I'm truly concerned."

Eisenhower knew that what MacArthur said about the U.S. Army was true, but no one outside "Club Eisenhower" was interested in Eisenhower's opinions on anything. And he certainly could not have guessed that less than four years later, when he was assistant to MacArthur, then chief of staff, the general would ignore his advice and get into deep trouble in so doing. MacArthur would even fail to obey the orders of his commander in chief, Herbert Hoover, who had been elected president and inaugurated while Eisenhower was in Paris.

A few months after they arrived in Paris, the Eisenhowers were joined by another member of the commission, Captain George A. Horkan, his wife, Mary, and their son, George, Jr., "Bo," who, like John, was six years old. Bo Horkan said, "At the time, Major Eisenhower was writing a guide to the American battlefields in Europe and he traveled all over the battlefields of France. On occasion he would take John and me with him. I remember very vividly visiting Verdun, which had been fought over so violently, and we were shaken by the experience."

John's memory of Verdun was even more vivid. He said, "Most of the battlefields of France were flat, pleasant farming areas. On the other hand, Verdun was a forbidding place. A large portion of the town still lay in ruins from the war, only ten years before. Its most frightening place was a strong point named Fort Douaumont. As we approached the door of this grim, squat monster, a human skull—with one tooth—grinned at us from a recess. Without hesitation Bo and I decided that this was the time to leave and go to the bathroom. Dad, his mind on business, was annoyed. Somehow our natural needs were taken care of, and we stumbled our way through some of the eerie, dank passageways, with occasional dim lights to guide our way. Nearby we visited the 'Trench of Bayonets,' where perhaps a squad of Frenchmen, preparing to go over the top, had been buried alive by the impact of a nearby German shell. By some miracle the bayonets had remained sticking out of the ground, and the bodies of the victims had been left unmolested by the French as a national monument."

Ike saw the dank caves of Verdun not only in 1928 but in 1944. Both times he must have remembered that Fox Conner had told him that Verdun was the longest and bloodiest battle of the First World War; more than two million men took part in it, and more than one million were killed. Conner said it proved nothing to take such a stronghold, just to prove that you could do it; the French, using the slogan, "They shall not pass," had held on to it, and the Germans had tried to take it to show how strong they were. "It was all a shameful, shameful waste," said Conner. "It must never happen again. Trying to take something just to take it."

The supreme commander made no such mistake during the Second World War; he had a conference in Verdun on the morning of December 19, 1944, shortly after the beginning of the Battle of the Bulge. Eisenhower began the conference by saying, "The present situation is to be regarded as one of opportunity for us and not of disaster. There will be only cheerful faces at this conference table. True to his impulsive nature, General Patton broke out with, 'Hell, let's have the guts to let the —— — ——— go all the way to Paris. Then we'll really cut 'em off and chew 'em up.' Everyone, including Patton, smiled at this one, but I replied that the enemy would never be allowed to cross the Meuse."

In 1928 and '29, Eisenhower not only took the two boys, Bo and John, on trips to the battlefields, he often took Mamie. Once, they had a family picnic in the Argonne Forest, and John remembered that his father described in detail the battles fought there.

Ike also traveled with a driver-interpreter. "Whenever possible," he said, "I stopped along the road to join groups of road workers who were eating their noonday lunch. . . . When my chauffeur . . . and I would ask if we could join them, their custom was to offer something from their lunchboxes. I developed a habit of carrying a bottle of Evian and an extra bottle of *vin rouge*, something I did not drink myself, but which was always welcome."

His job "involved travel, all the way from the Vosges in northeast France to the English Channel, following the lines of trench warfare that had stabilized so rigidly between late 1914 and the weeks preceding the Armistice in 1918." Mamie remembered he would describe every battle site as if he had been there before. He would say, "Now, just over the next rise there should be a small stream. The land is swampy on this side and goes up in a V-shaped hill on the other. The 42nd Division lost 1,500 men taking that hill."

Bo Horkan said Eisenhower had a memory for topography. "There's no question about it. I think his experience in writing that guide gave him a grasp of the military terrain of northern Europe which was just absolutely invaluable, and there isn't any question that he had a better grasp of the weather and all the other factors that went into the movements across the great northern European plain than most people. . . . The general was a very determined man.

[If] he was going to do something, he did it, if it took all night and all day.

"In the Argonne Forest, Eisenhower was looking for the area in which Sergeant York had won the Congressional Medal of Honor [for his single-handed battling and capture of a German platoon]." That day in the Argonne, according to Horkan, "John walked ahead and said, 'Look at this funny thing,' and he kicked it. It was a hand grenade, and there was no way of knowing whether those things were live or not.

"The French farmers were suffering terribly, getting blown up; one a week was blown up when he went back to plow his land. These duds were everywhere, and in those days they didn't have the metal detectors we have now. It was really a very serious business."

Bo also remembered that Eisenhower took John and him "to Château-Thierry or St.-Mihiel, I don't remember which, to hear some remarks by General Pershing. Major Eisenhower took us up and introduced us to General Pershing, who was very, very friendly. On the way out there, we played a game called Stamp the White Horse. Every time you'd see a white horse, you'd lick your thumb and stamp it. This was 1928–29, of course, and to show you how times have changed, in a distance of twenty to thirty miles we were able to stamp over a hundred white horses. Stamp the White Horse was a game they used to play back in Kansas when Eisenhower was a boy."

In his spare time back in Paris, not that there was much, Ike found occasion to visit what George Horkan, Sr., referred to as "the old onion soup place on the Left Bank." Moreover, he often dropped in at a wax works, the Musée Grévin, a great favorite of his. In *At Ease* he recalled

Most of my friends had never seen anything of the sort before, and usually they were impressed. . . . This place—I suppose I was still an unsophisticated Kansan at heart—stayed in my memory as a unique Paris attraction.

"Twenty-five years later, after I had assumed Supreme Command of the NATO forces, I lunched in the Hotel Astoria with two members of the staff. They seemed tired and worn-out after the rush and pressure of getting headquarters ready for my arrival. . . . They insisted [that] . . . Paris was a dull town on a February afternoon. . . . Their last remark set me off and, completely wound up, I lectured on the wonders of the Musée Grévin. Either persuaded or wanting to escape my address, they agreed to go. After spending two hours or so wandering from one exhibit to another, they finally returned to the sidewalk outside. One of them asked disgustedly, 'Do you *really* suppose this was the most exciting spot he could find when he was still in his thirties?' "

Not long before they returned to the States in 1929, Ike and Mamie and another American officer, Major William R. Gruber, and his wife, Helen, made a seventeen-day tour through France, Germany, Switzerland, and Belgium. Ike kept a diary through most of the trip, and he found, as many American tourists did then and still do, that he liked the Germans, the German countryside, and

German food far better than the French people, countryside, and food. German food was served without sauces, for one thing.

When they were in the Black Forest, for example, he wrote,

We had lunch by the road and voted it the best one we've had. . . . The surroundings were perfect. Only a few of the roads are at all dusty, and the smell of pine, cedars, and the freshly cut hay in the valleys adds to a feeling of peace and contentment a visitor is almost compelled to experience in this region. . . . We have been enthusiastic about Germany, the people as well as the beautiful landscapes. It is hard to describe the little differences which one detects between the people of one country and those of another. However, one of the big points we have noted is the friendly way we have been treated everywhere. . . . In many cases, when we've made inquiries of one person, another with a knowledge of the country has stepped forward voluntarily with information, always tendered in the most courteous way possible. We like Germany!

Besides, as Eisenhower said, Germany was "the Fatherland. . . . Both Bill and I have our family roots in this country, as our names testify."

Eisenhower was also impressed with the Swiss countryside.

From the standpoint of scenery the trip was magnificent. Long deep pine covered valleys extending for miles, mountain streams trembling down the mountain sides of narrow gorges, their crests covered with snow and at their feet beautiful little mountain lakes all combined to make the trip . . . one which will never be forgotten by any of us.

Later, however, he was to forget the kindness of the German people, and was responsible for the ruination of their cities and countryside. They were the enemy. And although his doubts about the French, or "Frogs" as he called them, remained, they were his allies, and he treated them as such. One of them, General Charles de Gaulle, seemed to have every questionable and irritating quality of the nation he was to head, but Eisenhower overlooked all that as much as he could. He even concluded, difficult as it was, that de Gaulle was one of the greatest men he ever met.

While Major Eisenhower was serving in Paris, Xenophon Price made two reports on his fitness. In both he rated Ike as very few officers ever did in evaluating his perfomance; it was, Price said, "satisfactory." In one report he said what was true, that he had known Ike for eighteen years. He added in the second report that Eisenhower was "not especially versatile in adjusting to changed conditions." Price also said that "Family worries sometimes affect efficiency."

There is no record of any family difficulty during the Paris assignment, although John did have whooping cough in San Remo, interrupting their vacation there.

In his diary Eisenhower said of Price, and the Parisian assignment, "The year was very interesting to me, in spite of the old-maidish attitude of my immediate superior. . . . I was not so successful as I should have been in concealing my impatience with some of his impossible ideas and methods. However, we are good friends—in spite of the fact that from the standpoint of piling up a *perfect* record in the W.D. I was not sufficiently suave and flattering." He added, "Other officers serving in France on construction work for the Commisson were of very high caliber."

One of these officers was Major Wilhelm D. "Delph" Styer of the Corps of Engineers. After the Allies entered Paris in late 1944, George Horkan wrote Eisenhower saying that he had recently seen Styer, General Somervell's chief of staff. Horkan himself was then commanding general of the Quartermaster School at Camp Lee. He sent Eisenhower a number of Western magazines and asked if he had visited his old apartment in Paris, or 20 Rue Molitor, where the Battle Monuments Commission had its office.

Eisenhower wrote back,

To tell the truth, I have been in Paris only twice, each for a one-hour visit. I haven't even had a chance to run past my old apartment to see whether it is still there. I think it is, because the damage to Paris has been very slight.

In a 1966 *Parade* article, "Mamie and Ike Talk About 50 Years of Marriage," Ike was asked which assignment had brought them the greatest happiness. Eisenhower chose the years in Paris. He said, "We had a nice life and a nice group of friends. Our son, John, was going to a good school, and we had lots of fun and lots of company."

★ ★ ★

THE ASSISTANT TO THE ASSISTANT

The Eisenhowers sailed from Cherbourg to New York on September 17, 1929, on the S.S. *Leviathan* and went directly to Washington, to a three-bedroom apartment in the Wyoming. John started in the second grade at Kalorama Day School; a few months later he entered the newly completed John Quincy Adams School, just across the alley from the Wyoming. His father returned to the Battle Monuments Commission to make revisions on the guidebook.

Ike was not looking forward to duty with Pershing again. He said, "In his writing habits, the General was cautious and slow. Several times he asked me to draft speeches and in no case was I successful in producing anything he wanted. In drafting occasional letters, I was slightly more successful. In going over my work, he always edited carefully and with precise regard for the exact definition of words. If I had used the word 'exhaustively' I would find it changed to 'thoroughly,' if I used 'speedily' he would change it to 'rapidly.' "

Pershing was writing his memoirs, which were to be published in two volumes and dealt almost entirely with his experiences in the war. He used as the basis for the books a diary kept either by himself or by a member of his staff. Eisenhower said that "the entire format . . . was to be in diary fashion. This destroyed the continuity of any major episode, of course. A battle could not have a beginning and a body and an end for the very simple reason that it had to be told in the form of General Pershing's daily experiences, along with a score of other affairs coincident with it."

One day, despite his reservations about Eisenhower's writing ability, the general called him in and asked his help. "I'm unhappy about this description of Saint-Mihiel in the first part of September 1918—and also about the Argonne," he said. The latter battle lasted until the Armistice on November 11, 1918. "Read the parts of the book that cover these two periods and let me know what you think."

Two days later the major told the general what he thought, and it was surely not what Pershing wanted to hear, writers, whether they are civilians or soldiers, wanting only praise. Eisenhower said that the general should abandon the diary form for the battle of Saint-Mihiel and the Argonne campaign "and instead tell the story of each battle as seen from his position as the commander of the American Expeditionary Forces."

Pershing seemed to accept the suggestion and asked Eisenhower to rewrite the chapters, which the major did "with considerable effort." Pershing read the new chapters and said he liked them but would ask the man whose advice he asked as often as possible, Colonel George C. Marshall, then stationed at Benning.

A few days later Marshall came to Washington, and he and Pershing had a meeting that lasted all afternoon. Ike was not invited to sit in on the meeting. He said, "When his [Marshall's] conference with the General was done, he came out through my office. For the first time in my life, I met George Marshall. He did not sit down but remarked that he had read over my chapters. 'I think they're interesting. Nevertheless, I've advised General Pershing to stick with his original idea. I think to break up the format right at the climax of the war would be a mistake.' "

Ike's first exchange with Marshall was exactly the kind the colonel liked; he hated those who agreed with their superiors just to be agreeable. Eisenhower said "that there was some virtue in continuity. 'Although I still think,' I said, 'that each of the two battles ought to be treated as a single narrative with the proper annotations to give it authenticity.' "

Marshall, no doubt pleased at a show of independence, said that Eisenhower's idea was a good one, but that Pershing would be happier doing it the way he had done it. Marshall nowhere said what he thought of Eisenhower at that first meeting. Eisenhower does not say what he thought of Marshall either, but he certainly remembered that Fox Conner had said Marshall was a great man. Eisenhower no doubt also was impressed with the fact that Marshall did not sit down and did not smile; there was on that day and always a distance between them. Marshall once said, "I have no feelings except those I reserve for Mrs. Marshall." Harry Truman described Marshall as "the kind of man who always insisted that he be told exactly what was on your mind, and he never failed to tell you exactly what was on his."

In 1932 Pershing's *My Experiences in the World War* won the Pulitzer Prize for History; Eisenhower's work never won a Pulitzer. When he wrote *At Ease* in 1966, Eisenhower, sounding like all writers everywhere whose ideas have been rejected, said, "After General Pershing's books were published, a number of my friends—most of them in the Army and all of them interested in the story—remarked that it was difficult to get the entire account of the war clearly in mind. They objected to it as a chronological recitation, based so completely on dates and limited to the day-to-day movements of the General, that it was not as interesting as they had hoped. Given my own work, I am probably no man to pass judgments on memoir writing but I still have to agree."

On November 8, his revision of the guidebook completed, Ike got a new job, not with troops, but as assistant executive in the office of the assistant secretary of war—assistant to an assistant, as it were. Ten days before he took over in his new job came the great stock-market crash, on Black Tuesday, October 29, 1929.

The Great Depression frightened everybody, even those who did not seem directly affected by it. John said, "Dad's job required that his wardrobe include both civilian clothes and uniforms. My Grandfather Doud provided Mother with a full-time maid (for $50 a month) but that was a luxury item. Dad continued to pound into me that we were not wealthy people."

Mamie, John said, "managed the household single-handedly and efficiently. Every penny counted. My loss once of a $10 coat—which actually was not my fault—literally shattered her."

The Gerows were also living at the Wyoming, and Mamie and Katie Gerow shopped once a week at the commissary of the Army War College. They went by taxi; Mamie said that even with cab fare, she and Mrs. Gerow could still save money because food at the commissary was sold at cost. But on the return trip, the two women, to save a few cents on the fare, would get out of the taxi at Florida Avenue and carry their groceries up the hill to the Wyoming, a distance of more than a quarter of a mile.

Eisenhower's office was several miles away, yet he walked to save money. With his savings and his poker winnings, he bought Mamie a silver tea service, "Precious piece by precious piece," according to Julie Eisenhower.

Ike was working in the office, once again in the State-War-Navy building, of Assistant Secretary of War for Procurement Frederick H. Payne, an austere and ambitious New England businessman who was a friend of Hoover's and of the eccentric Oklahoma oil man who was secretary of war, Patrick J. Hurley. In his diary, Ike said that Payne was

a typical New Englander, about 56–8 years of age. . . . Little academic training, but lots of common sense and very shrewd. Tall and thin in appearance, he is straightforward and direct in action.

Very much intrigued with the social side of Washington official life and attends every dance-tea reception, etc., to which invited. Likes also to appear at conventions, dinners, etc., where he is invited to speak but cares very little *what* material appears in the speech. His thrill comes from the invitation itself—which he considers a recognition of his prominent position in the official world—and from meeting people. Devoted to his family. Friendly in all his contacts. An old-line Republican. Anti-prohibitionist. My principal contacts with him are through writing all his speeches.

Eisenhower's immediate superior was Major General George Van Horn Moseley, West Point 1899, who had been Pershing's G-4 (chief of supply) in Europe. Moseley was a cavalryman with extreme right-wing views and no hesitancy in expressing them. His recommendations to the general staff in dealing with malcontents in the United States were simple:

With all the troubles we have at the present moment in the United States why should we allow these aliens, who are now unlawfully within our gates, to work against us? It seems to me all such aliens should be gathered up and either returned to Russia or segregated and held segregated within the United States.

Moseley added that if the federal government found that the Communists could not be deported immediately, it should "gather up the worst of these offenders and ship them to a selected island in the Hawaiian group, where they could be held under federal control while awaiting deportation. . . . It might also have a very beneficial effect on the crime wave in America if the same procedure could be lawfully applied in clearing the country of the criminal class."

Eisenhower kept his feelings in the matter, as in almost all matters, to himself. It was quite some time later that he commented on Moseley in this period: "His outspoken reaction to public questions, often political, got him a bad press. Many who did not know the man himself may have thought him a reactionary or a militarist. The impression he created was a distortion, I am sure; he was a patriotic American unafraid to disagree with a consensus."

Anybody who did not think from what he said that Moseley was both a militarist, a reactionary, and worse, could not have understood the English language. As was so often the case, Eisenhower was defending an old friend not worthy of such defense. It is difficult to attack a man for being loyal to his friends. Besides, Moseley had written a letter about Eisenhower that was a most helpful addition to the major's 201 file. He said:

You possess one of those exceptional minds which enables you to assemble and to analyze a set of facts, always drawing sound conclusions and, equally important, you have the ability to express those conclusions in clear and convincing form. Many officers can take the first two steps of a problem, but few have your ability of expression. The subjects that you have worked upon have covered a very wide field. . . . My earnest hope is that you will guard your strength and talents carefully and that promotion may be given you in order that your government may use your talents in positions of great responsibility.

Under the revision of the National Defense Act of 1920, the assistant secretary of war was charged with the development of a plan for mobilizing matériel and industrial organizations in the event of another war. Ike, along with Colonel Gilbert Wilkes, West Point 1909, a member of the Corps of Engineers, was given the task of drawing up such a plan, and, as he wrote in his diary, he was happy to have the chance to learn "about the economic and industrial conditions that will prevail in this country in the event of a major war. . . . I now undertook work that was intriguing and frustrating."

The two men visited industrial plants, made studies of materials and their sources of supply and inquired "whether they could suggest improvements for retooling rapidly to produce matériel we might need in case of war." But the industrialists gave Ike and Wilkes little, if any, cooperation. Most of them were of the opinion that there would never be another war.

One industrialist who did cooperate was Bernard Baruch. "He was a man who was not only cooperative; he was anxious that the American public, as well as the armed services, understand the complexities of conversion to war." Ike visited Baruch to learn about the experience of the War Industries Board of World War I. "One of the questions was the organization of the government and the War Department itself for control of production." Baruch felt that in the event of another war prices, wages, and costs of matériel and services should be frozen. In so doing he hoped to avoid the inflation that accompanied previous wars. The two men had several meetings, and Baruch was able to convince Eisenhower of the soundness of his ideas, which the assistant to the assistant included in the industrial mobilization plan he was working on.

Baruch was probably the first in Ike's collection of rich friends. In 1926, through John Doud, Eisenhower had met Aksel Nielsen, who by Denver standards was very rich; but you might say Baruch was rich by international standards—he made a fortune in Wall Street, betting on the rise and fall of stocks, and was a millionaire before he was thirty-five. And Baruch was internationally known. He was adviser to presidents, had friends in the military—Pershing, who once during the depression borrowed $41,190 from him; and George C. Marshall, whom he met on a hunting trip in Louisiana in 1922. He was friends with all the right people, including Winston Churchill, who would stay with Baruch when he came to New York.

Baruch, like Eisenhower, represented all that was wholesome and right about the American way of life. Although the two had dissimilar backgrounds, one thing they had in common was their dedication to their country. A friend once said of Baruch that his love of country exceeded his love for any woman, which could also be said of Eisenhower.

In 1952 Baruch, a Democrat, endorsed Eisenhower's presidential candidacy; Ike was the first Republican nominee to earn his public support. When reporters asked Baruch if he would vote for Eisenhower he grinned all over. "When you see me look at him, you can tell I don't hate him. . . ." And when stopped by reporters once again on November 4, 1952, coming out of the polling booths twenty minutes before they opened, he said, "The damned thing won't work. You can't pull the lever." Later he admitted to the reporters, "I did vote for the General. . . . They wouldn't let me vote more than once." The night Ike won the election, one of the first telephone calls he made was to Baruch, thanking him "for his all-important support."

Baruch and Eisenhower remained friends until Baruch's death in 1965. Eisenhower said of Baruch, "Since the days of World War I, when I first learned of some of his accomplishments, he has been one of those leaders of thought and action who has commanded my respect and admiration. To this has been added in later years what has been to me a most satisfying and profitable personal acquaintanceship, so that I am continually conscious of a personal debt, which is all the greater because he has no consciousness of its existence."

In April 1930 Eisenhower and Wilkes began a series of field trips to find out what if anything could be done about the country's rubber supply in case the war nobody thought would happen, did happen.

Ike and Wilkes visited California, Texas, and Mexico, hoping to find out as much as they could about the guayule plant and the rubber it produced. The shrub grew like a weed in the deserts of Mexico. But where and how and when could it be grown in the United States on a large scale? What soil conditions were necessary?

It would seem that the two army officers were far from expert in such matters. But they were available, and the main problem of the army in those days was keeping its 118,000 officers and men occupied.

Eisenhower kept a diary on the trip, but it reveals nothing much except that the two men traveled in hot, uncomfortable trains, most of them crowded, that they saw a number of bad movies—"*Party Girl!!* Bah—!! *Terrible*"—that Ike was "developing a cold. Feel miserable," and that "Things in California are quite green—a real contrast to the long dusty miles in Kansas—Colo.—N.M. and Arizona." In Mexico they saw "many fields of guayule," and they concluded that "with the return of normal prices in crude rubber, the production of guayule rubber will be started in many parts of the U.S." That did not happen. Nothing at all happened as a result of their trip.

Eisenhower and Wilkes arrived back in Washington on May 8 and wrote a report that impressed General Moseley. He sent it to several businessmen, one of whom, C. H. Carnahan, president of International Rubber Company, wrote, "Having had to do work of this kind myself, I am in a position to appreciate the difficulties they had to overcome and the measure of conservatism which it was necessary for them to employ in reporting on a business with which neither of them was thoroughly familiar. I think they reflect great credit on the [War] Department."

The report was also sent to Baruch, who was also impressed. Years later, when he was called on by Roosevelt to plan for the mobilization of the United States and to find out what could be done about raw rubber, Baruch got out the report, as he wrote Eisenhower, "to see what we might do." Eisenhower commented, "He said my analysis of what would happen was quite valid and was very valuable to him."

One of Baruch's biographers, Jordan A. Schwartz, wrote: "The War Department showed an interest in the strategic value of rubber in 1930 when Baruch's most apt pupil in the military, Dwight Eisenhower, urged the growing of guayule rubber in the Western hemisphere." However, "interest in this highly adaptive strain of crude rubber continued to lag despite Baruch's best promotional efforts. As Nazi Germany embarked upon a course of self-sufficiency via production of synthetic rubber, both the Army and Baruch began to agitate for American purchase of stockpiles from an Anglo-Dutch cartel."

When Ike first took over as assistant to the assistant, most of the work he and Wilkes were doing was accomplished "on our own and in a rather isolated atmosphere. Indeed, the Chief of Staff of the Army, General [Charles] Summerall forbade any General Staff officer to go into the office of the Assistant Secretary of War." All this changed however, on November 21, 1930, when General Douglas MacArthur became, at fifty, the youngest chief of staff in the history of the army. Eisenhower said, "He was receptive of the ideas we had been advocating."

At the time MacArthur became chief of staff, the government was organizing a commission to study how to take the profits out of war. In June 1930 Congress passed a joint resolution creating a War Policies Commission "to study and consider amending the Constitution, so that, should there be a war, its burden would fall equally on everyone and it would be profitable for no one." The commission's chairman was the secretary of war, Patrick J. Hurley. The secretaries of agriculture, commerce, and labor as well as the attorney general were also members. So were four members of the House and four senators.

It was clear from the beginning that the commission would not accomplish much. In the hearings it held, many would be heard but few would be heeded. Profits during a war would continue to be enormous; wage earners would continue to ask for higher wages and threaten to and sometimes actually strike, if they wished; and soldiers would fight and die, while the nonfighting, profit-making patriots would be grateful to them—both those soldiers who survived the war and those who did not.

Even that New York City firebrand, Congressman Fiorello H. La Guardia, said to the commission, "The subject of equalizing the burdens of war and minimizing the profits of war is about the easiest of any to make a speech on, but probably the most difficult to work out in detail."

Eisenhower said, "These difficulties arise from a variety of causes. Pertinent statistics of past war experiences are by no means complete, nor are they easy to interpret intelligently. Every proposal made must rest to some degree upon abstract reasoning and even on pure conjecture. Class fears and prejudices are easily aroused—while a mass inertia engendered by the feeling that 'any war is a long way off' has likewise contributed to the defeat of efforts that would embody the considered opinions of those best qualified to speak."

Open hearings were held in March and May of 1931. During this time some fifty or more witnesses were heard. Before testifying they were given the opportunity of discussing their testimony with Eisenhower. Among the witnesses he saw and charmed were Walter S. Gifford of American Telephone and Telegraph, Daniel Willard of the Baltimore & Ohio railroad, Baruch, William L. Green of the American Federation of Labor, and Benedict Crowell, assistant secretary of war during the years 1917–20.

He studied those men carefully and concluded in his diary that among them there was "no great man . . . as we understood that expression when we were shavers. . . . We were taught the shibboleth of the 'super man'—possibly because it is easier to exaggerate than not. . . . Some men achieve goals for which numbers have been striving—and it is interesting to look over those qualified for 'Who's Who' or who have attracted special attention in some field, to try to make an estimate of their character, their abiliies and their weaknesses."

The hearings allowed a number of people to be heard whose views must have shocked and displeased Eisenhower, but when he discussed those people and their ideas in an article that appeared in *Infantry Journal*, November/December 1931, his tone was dispassionate. He said, "Among those who confined their attention almost exclusively to methods for preventing war were a retired admiral of the Navy, two ministers of the gospel, a leader of the Socialist party, an oculist, editors of so-called 'pacifist' leanings and officials of various peace associations."

Eisenhower could not really have ridiculed or villified pacifists, as MacArthur did with great regularity; he came from a family of pacifists, while MacArthur's father was, of course, a general.

The retired admiral, Samuel McGowan, testified in favor of a national referendum before war could be declared. He said, "The only good war is a war that doesn't take place; and it will never take place in this or any other country, if the people back home, the mothers . . . all through the country are allowed to have their way."

Newton D. Baker, the pacifist who had been secretary of war in Wilson's cabinet, said of the idea of a referendum, "Our people would be separated into opposite camps about war, and if a small majority decided in favor of the war, it would be a practical advantage to our adversary by our *going to war with a divided people whose feelings were split wide open;* it would put us in a very weak situation."

As for "conscription of property in case of war," which was widely approved by most pacifist organizations, Eisenhower quoted with approval Baruch, who was against any such proposal. Baruch said: "Nobody with any familiarity with industry could seriously urge a wholesale assumption by a Federal Bureau of the responsibility for management of any or all of the vast congeries of manufacturing establishments upon which we must rely for extraordinary effort in event of war. Even if such bureau management could prove adequate to the task (which it could never do) the mere process of change would destroy efficiency at the outset."

Eisenhower said that "most of" the pacifists who testified were for the League of Nations and the World Court; they wanted "withdrawal of the Marines from Nicaragua; independence of the Philippines; recognition of Soviet Russia, and revision of national policies with regard to Latin American countries. . . . Such expressions as 'peace-minded,' 'war-minded,' 'atmosphered in the psychology of war,' 'peace policies,' and 'preparation for peace' were used repeatedly, but no attempt was made to define them."

Obviously, although he does not say so, Ike considered such people soft-headed, but he did not appear to believe that they were all Communist subversives who ought to be rounded up and sequestered in the Hawaiian Islands. In fact, Ike added, "A listener gained the distinct impression that the members of this group, with possibly one or two exceptions, were earnestly and unselfishly laboring for the promotion of an idea in which they implicitly believed. One—Dr. Mercer Johnson—wore in his lapel the ribbon of the Distinguished Service Cross, won while serving with the A.E.F. in 1918."

Considering the fact that most of the readers of *Infantry Journal* were army officers who thought that people with such ideas ought to be dispensed with as quickly and painfully as possible, the assessment Eisenhower made is mild indeed.

True, he wrote that the Democratic national platforms of 1924 and 1928 declared, "In the event of war in which the manpower of the nation is drafted, all other resources should likewise be drafted. *This will tend to discourage war by depriving it of it profits.*" The emphasis was added either by Eisenhower or by an editor of *Infantry Journal*. Ike was wrong; the Democrats had that plank only in their 1924 platform; the Republicans, on the other hand, had a very similar plank in their platforms in both 1924 and 1928.

After hearing the testimony of all the witnesses, the War Plans Commission asked the War Department to propose a plan. Eisenhower spent ten days and ten nights completing the plan he and Wilkes had been drafting on industrial mobilization. "We finally prepared the paper," Ike said, "calling it a sort of basic plan for mobilization." The work paid off, too. General MacArthur said the paper was "masterly"—and he presented it before the commission on behalf of the entire War Department.

In *Infantry Journal*, Eisenhower devoted the last part of his article to his Plan for Industrial Mobilization.

The War Department Plan provides in detail for the orderly procurement of all supplies it will need so as to occasion the minimum of disturbance in the normal economic life of the nation. Beyond this it provides for a civilian organization to exercise, under the President, an efficient control over all resources. It makes provision for setting up promptly, in an emergency, all the administrative machinery that will be necessary.

The plan contained these conclusions:

Modern war demands the prompt utilization of all the national resources. Measures for transforming potential strength into actual strength must work in emergency with the utmost speed and effectiveness. . . .

The human burdens of war must be equalized in so far as possible. To this end liability for combat service must be determined under a selective service system developed along the general lines of that used in the World War.

The economic burdens must be equalized through:

a. Systematic registration of wealth and all accretions thereto during the period of the emergency; and tax legislation framed to place an equitable burden thereon.
b. Orderly and economic procurement by the government itself.
c. Strong and intelligent leadership . . . exercised through an organization adapted to the purpose.
d. Application of governmental controls . . . to prevent any profiteering at the national expense.
e. Prompt resumption of normal peace conditions upon the termination of war. During the progress of any war the President should appoint a committee to study and prepare plans for demobilization. . . .

All of the above demand an intensive and intelligent planning program carried out continuously in time of peace. . . .

Congress should satisfy itself at frequent intervals as to the progress of plans under development by requiring their presentation to appropriate committees of Congress.

Many of the witnesses gave their endorsement to the plan's general provisions. Howard Coffin, head of The Aircraft Production Board during the First World War, said that it was "splendidly conceived, and practicable in every respect." Coffin had said that the Eisenhower plan "would work with the maximum speed and effectiveness, with the least possible injustice to individual citizens."

Eisenhower said, "It seemed to make a general hit. We summarized it in a press release—and General MacArthur is to make a Movietone short of a synopsis."

"I received a letter of recommendation . . . Mamie had it framed," Eisenhower noted.

In the letter, which was dated November 4, 1931, MacArthur wrote:

I desire to place on official record this special commendation for excellent work of a highly important nature which you have just completed under my personal direction. You not only accepted this assignment willingly— an assignment which involved much hard work—performing it in addition to your regular duties in the office of the Assistant Secretary of War, but you gave me a most acceptable solution within a minimum of time.

This is not the first occasion when you have been called upon to perform a special task of this nature. In each case you have registered successful accomplishment in the highest degree.

I write you this special commendation so that you may fully realize that your outstanding talents and your ability to perform these highly important missions are fully appreciated.

It was a good letter to have added to one's 201. But by far the most important result of Eisenhower's work on the plan for industrial mobilization was that, as he said, "[It] gave me an early look at the military-industrial complex of whose pressures I would later warn. Except at that point, the pressures were exactly reversed."

During the years they lived in Washington, Mamie and Ike saw a lot of Milton and his wife; they played bridge with Harry and Ruth Butcher. On Saturdays during football season, their friends gathered at their apartment or at Milton's house to listen to army football games over the radio. Eisenhower, the most enthusiastic fan, had a large diagram of the entire football field on which he traced out the plays. Eisenhower played golf on occasional Sundays, usually with Colonel Jimmy Ulio, then Adjutant General of the Army. John said, "Though Dad had played the game little, he went after that game with the same intensity as in later years. . . . He seemed to wind up in the alfalfa an inordinate amount of the time, the air punctuated with certain expletives that I thought were not known to adults—only kids."

On less happy Sundays, Eisenhower put on a derby and striped pants and did what army officers did in those days; he and Mamie made formal calls to superior officers while John waited outside various apartment houses in the 1927 Buick. Occasionally they visited the Pattons. John remembered "silver horsemanship trophies covering a complete wall of the living room of their quarters." He was astonished that Patton "not only swore profusely around ladies but also encouraged all three of his children to do the same. . . . These visits, though rare, were always pleasant."

The most important social event for the Eisenhowers was the time they entertained Hurley and his wife; it was unusual for a mere major and his wife to take the secretary of war and his wife out to dinner, especially to the Willard, which in those days was considered the best hotel in Washington; it was also the most expensive, and it was said it was so near the U.S. Treasury building because you had to coin money to afford those prices.

The Eisenhowers got special rates because they were members of the Saturday Night Dinner Dance Club, a group of young civilians and military couples in Washington who gathered at the hotel every week. Despite the price reduction, the dinner was so costly that the Eisenhowers ate only stew and meat loaf for days afterward. Mamie said, "The party flowers cost almost as much as it took to feed us for a week. Added to the dinner check, they really upset our budget."

The Hurleys were suitably impressed, but Eisenhower was not impressed with Hurley. He said in his diary that the rich man from Oklahoma "is not big enough to go higher. . . . Affable but rather petulant. . . . Keen on favorable publicity and always solicitous of members of the press—no matter what the occasion. Meticulous as to details of dress and personal appearance—sometimes characterized by the unfriendly sections of the press as a 'dandy,' 'Fop,' etc. . . . He is jealous and unstable."

During this period, Eisenhower also attended the Industrial College of the Armed Forces, which had been set up in 1924 "in a little section of one room in the old Munitions Building" in Washington. It was "a forum . . . in which the questions arising in industrial mobilization could be discussed without regard to official solutions." Eisenhower said, "This was a school where officers, usually from the supply services, were trained in logistics, and especially in solving problems of converting a peacetime manufacturing plant to wartime schedules."

In the 1931–32 course Eisenhower was a part-time instructor and gave lectures at the school. In lecturing, he said:

I know that the present Assistant Secretary and his three predecessors and their executives have often stated most emphatically that the free opportunity offered here for the adjustment, coordination, and assimilation of divergent views is of the utmost importance to the student body, to the Army, as a whole, and to the development of logical thought on the problems involved in industrial mobilization.

In addition to all his other activities, the major was detailed to additional duty with the organized reserves of the III Corps Area as assistant unit instructor, 428th Infantry. Colonel W. W. McGannon, the senior instructor, said, "The talks indicated a deep knowledge of the subject and a thorough preparation. They were received by the audiences with the greatest interest. Major Eisenhower's platform presence and delivery make him a lecturer of unusual quality.

"His assistance as an instructor is greatly appreciated and has contributed in large measure to the success of the conference schools for Reserve officers of the Washington District."

As can be seen, Ike's time as assistant to an assistant, while not glamorous, was extraordinarily busy, and while outwardly, as always, he appeared cheerful, inwardly, as was to happen many times in the future, he was having trouble with his "insides." In his diary he wrote, "Lots of troubles with my insides lately. Have been bothered 5–6 years with something that seems to border on dysentery. Doctors have come to the conclusion that it is a result of nervousness, lack of exercise, etc. Am taking some medicine at the moment that for a day or so seemed to be exactly right—but now am apparently no different from usual." In another entry he noted, "Doctors report after long ex-ray [sic] exam, that they can find nothing wrong with my insides."

It was around this time he also began complaining of pain and stiffness in his back. John said his father had been "a real slave in Washington. He had arthritis. I guess he had an abcess, too—that was finally chiseled out. He was afraid he was going to be retired at an early age."

During this time in Washington, Eisenhower attracted the attention of some powerful men. Payne wrote yet another glowing report for the major's bulging 201. He said, "I know Major Eisenhower very well. In the preparation of studies and articles for my use, he has been superb." He added that he wanted to keep the major—but then who did not? No one, it seemed, wanted to lose him. "Here is a man I should always like to have with me," said one superior. And still another said, "I, too, have a feeling that I should like to keep him with me." Still another praised him for his "extraordinary literary ability." Another said that he had "greater skill in written expression of thoughts" than any officer he knew. Another said that the major "has no superior of his age and grade," adding that if there ever was another war, "he should be promoted to general rank."

Ike was grateful for all the letters, and they proved useful, but he still wanted troop duty. That was what being a soldier was all about. John remembered that his father worked very hard, and Mamie complained that he brought too much work home at night. John said, "Dad writhed in frustration in Washington during our seven-year stay. He . . . longed for line duty. Nevertheless, his time in Washington under Secretary of War Patrick J. Hurley, his successor George Dern, and Chief of Staff Douglas MacArthur gave him a feel for the Washington scene and the processes of government that he could be thankful for in later years."

★ ★ ★

THE INSUBORDINATE GENERAL

For a time in 1931, it looked as if Mamie might once again influence Eisenhower's career. She had done that in 1916 when he had given up going into the aviation branch of the army to marry her. In 1928, after he had finished his studies at the Army War College, he was offered two assignments, one to stay in Washington with the general staff, the other to go to Paris with the Battle Monuments Commission. He wanted to stay in Washington, but Mamie wanted to go to Paris. They went to Paris.

This time Mamie wanted to go back to San Antonio, "back home." The Douds were once again there for the winter. So Eisenhower reluctantly asked for a transfer back to Fort Sam, where he had started out sixteen years before; he had received three promotions since, and he had been a major for twelve years. Eisenhower said of going back to San Antonio, "[I] made up my mind only after a long struggle as I hate the heat, etc. Family was so insistent thought it best thing to do. Mamie is concerned chiefly with getting a place where servants are good—cheap—plentiful. I'd like a place that offers some interesting outdoor work. Dad, mother, and Mamie have talked about S.A. until it is apparent they're going to be all down in the mouth with any other selection. So I *asked* for it."

He was not disappointed when what he had *asked* for was refused.

At the end of January 1932, General William D. Connor, Eisenhower's mentor and friend at the War College, told him that he was going to West Point as superintendent and offered Ike a post as manager of athletics, to begin early the next year. He was also given the chance to return to Leavenworth to become commander of an infantry battalion stationed there. That would seem to have been the kind of troop duty he had for so many years insisted that he wanted, but he talked the matter over with Moseley and MacArthur, and both advised him against accepting either assignment. He took their advice without much of an argument.

In February MacArthur called Eisenhower into his office and advised him to stay in Washington until September 1933, thus completing a four-year tour of duty there. Eisenhower wrote in his diary, "Gen. MacA was very nice to me—and after all, I know of no greater compliment the bosses can give you than to want you hanging around." The next month he turned in his final recommendation to the War Plans Commission. He had a few documents to write, and when he said, "The long siege with the War Plan Commisson is completed."

Although for another eleven months he was still assigned to Frederick Payne's office, he worked for MacArthur full time. Once the assistant to the assistant attracted MacArthur's attention, the chief of staff called on him "to draft statements, reports and letters for his signature."

T. Harry Williams, the biographer and historian, once wrote that there have been two kinds of successful American military men, the seemingly easy-going, relaxed, smiling "Ike's" . . . and the "Mac's"—arrogant, distrustful of the democratic system, and dramatic. Seldom have the two been called upon to work together for a long period of time, but Eisenhower and MacArthur did for nearly a decade. It was not a halcyon decade for them or for the world.

In his book *The Soldier and the State: The Theory and Politics of Civil-Military Relations*, Samuel P. Huntington says:

> In contrast to MacArthur (who was a general), Eisenhower was still an unknown lieutenant colonel as the world moved toward involvement in World War II. While MacArthur . . . specialized in being different, Eisenhower specialized in adjusting to and reflecting his environment, absorbing the attitude and behavior patterns of those about him.

MacArthur, as chief of staff, worked in a grand office at a huge desk behind which was a large mirror framed in mahogany. At the time, he smoked cigarettes in a long holder. Like the man who was soon to be president, Franklin Roosevelt, the general frequently gestured with the cigarette and its holder in his right hand—perhaps the only thing he had in common with Roosevelt.

He had the only chauffeured limousine authorized by the War Department, and in his frequent trips to Capitol Hill to consult with congressmen, usually to ask for more money for the army, he went in the limousine. He never once offered Eisenhower a ride in or use of the car.

In an informal, off-the-record talk at the Overseas Press Club in New York after his years as president, Eisenhower spoke with considerable bitterness of those days in the early thirties with MacArthur. Stan Swinton, an Associated Press reporter who was present, said, "Eisenhower pointed out that the army was very small at the time, and he didn't have any money, didn't have an allowance for official business. He had to go to the disbursement officer and fill out vouchers to get money to go to the Hill to present a MacArthur report. Sometimes he went by taxi but most of the time by streetcar. After he went to the Hill and came back, if he had eighty-two cents in change he had to return it to the disbursement officer. He said, 'No matter what happens later you never forget something like that.' "

MacArthur, with whom Eisenhower was to work for so many years, seemed to have everything. His father, General Arthur MacArthur, had once been the army's senior ranking officer and had become a national hero for his daring deeds in the Philippines. Douglas had graduated first in his class at West Point in 1903. During the First World War, he had won the Distinguished Service Medal, Distinguished Service Cross, and seven Silver Stars. He had performed heroically at St.-Mihiel, Aisne-Marne, and the Meuse-Argonne. Everybody seemed to respect and admire him, and one admirer said, "If Caesar didn't look like MacArthur, he should have."

Pershing, however, was not among his admirers. MacArthur talked too much and too loudly for Pershing's taste. He was too visibly ambitious. Besides, in 1922, on Valentine's Day, MacArthur had married a very rich woman Pershing himself was said to favor, Louise Cromwell Brooks. A newspaper at the time called it the "Marriage of Mars and Millions." Even if he had not been a widower, Pershing would not have cared for that. The whole thing was vulgar. Pershing might have found comfort in the fact that of the 200 guests at the wedding in Palm Beach, only one was a friend of the groom. Louise had a number of well-publicized affairs during the marriage and showed up at many nightclubs with many different escorts, and in Reno on June 18, 1929, Louise was ironically granted a divorce on the ground that MacArthur had failed to provide support for her.

When he returned from the Philippines to become chief of staff, MacArthur also brought to Washington one Isabel Rosario Cooper, a beautiful Eurasian woman. He established her in a large suite in the fashionable Hotel Chastleton on 16th Street, N.W., and at his own expense, he had a second chauffeured limousine for Isabel.

Miss Cooper called MacArthur "Daddy." In *American Caesar,* the general's biographer William Manchester said that MacArthur also provided Isabel with an enormous wardrobe of tea gowns, kimonos, and black lace negligees. He did not buy her any street clothes because he didn't feel she ever needed to be on the streets. She was on the streets a great deal, however, and visited a large number of nightclubs in Washington and in Baltimore, all without "Daddy," who traveled a lot.

In September 1934 MacArthur, perhaps having heard of Isabel's nightclub visits and her affairs with various men in Baltimore, sent her a train ticket to California and passage on an oceanliner to the Philippines. She didn't go, however; she stayed on in Washington, and at one point when MacArthur was in a legal controversy with Robert S. Allen and Drew Pearson, authors of the column the "Washington Merry-Go-Round," he learned that Isabel might tell all on the witness stand. According to Manchester, "The General dispatched Major Eisenhower to find his jilted mistress; Ike couldn't do it; Pearson's brother, Leon, kept her out of sight in a Baltimore hideaway."

In 1960 Isabel committed suicide in Los Angeles; the death certificate said she was a "free-lance actress." After the war, when MacArthur was in Japan, his relations with the press were, as usual, bad. Manchester said, "Much of this was his own fault. His approach toward reporters was much like his attitude toward Isabel Cooper. . . . They were to be used as he saw fit and should remain mute and docile if he was busy elsewhere."

Eisenhower's observations on his being ordered to carry out a tacky search for the mistress of the chief of staff have not been recorded, but the incident cannot have improved his opinion of the general.

"In several respects," Eisenhower said, "he was a rewarding man to work for. . . . He never asked any questions; he never cared what kind of hours were kept; his only requirement was that the work be done. The difficulty was that I soon found myself engaged in a variety of reports, statements, estimates, and the like that kept me so busy I was in the office until 7:30 or 7:45 every night. . . . General MacArthur kept unusual hours, including luncheons or other absences from two to four hours and then stayed on in his office until 8:00. My hours became picturesque."

MacArthur seemed unaware of the fact that he caused inconvenience to others. Eisenhower said, "MacArthur could never see another sun, or even a moon for that matter, in the heavens as long as he was the sun. . . . He did have a hell of an intellect. . . . My God, he was smart. He had a brain. . . . He had one habit that never ceased to amaze me. In reminiscing or telling stories of the current scene, he talked of himself in the third person. 'So MacArthur went over to the Senator and said, 'Senator . . .' Although I had heard of this idiosyncrasy, the sensation was unusual. In time I got used to it and saw it not as objectionable, just odd."

Eisenhower was always upset at MacArthur's habit of mixing military and political matters. "My duties were beginning to verge on the political, even to the edge of partisan politics. . . . Most of the senior officers I had known always drew a clean-cut line between the military and the political. Off duty, among themselves and close civilian friends, they might explosively denounce everything they thought was wrong in Washington and the world and propose their own cure for its evils. On duty, nothing could induce them to cross the line they, and old Army tradition, had established. But if General MacArthur ever recognized the existence of that line, he usually chose to ignore it. At times, this could complicate life for himself and his staff."

MacArthur's handling of what became known as the Bonus Expeditionary Force was, at least until the 1950s, the most flagrant example of his contempt for civilian authority. It was a performance so theatrical that it is not surprising that many of his subordinates and some of his peers at the time called him "Sarah," for Sarah Bernhardt.

The Great Depression grew much worse in 1932. Nobody seemed to know how many unemployed there were that summer; some said 15 million; others said 17, maybe 20 million. Hundreds of thousands of young men were drifting around the country looking for work, many of them traveling in empty freight cars. Some hitchhiked, a few carrying signs that said, "Give me a lift or I'll vote for Hoover."

Early in the year a group of Communists demonstrated outside the White House singing "We'll Hang Herbie Hoover to a sour apple tree." Ike said in his diary, "The general economic situation has been such that 'pacifistic' organizations' propaganda and efforts have been more effective than ordinarily is the case."

Hoover frequently said that no one was starving, but it was generally agreed that millions of people were hungry. Secretary of War Hurley thought he had a solution. The country's best and most expensive restaurants, presumably including the one at the Willard, should wrap up their leftovers and distribute them to those in need. The eating clubs at Princeton almost immediately voted to give their scraps to those less fortunate.

Army officers were employed, but as Eisenhower wrote, "All salaries are to be reduced [in 1932], apparently by about 10%—the outlook for an Army officer on 'city' duty is none too cheering."

The outlook for most veterans of the First World War was even worse. In a bonus bill passed by Congress in 1924 over Coolidge's veto, the veterans were provided with an "endowment policy" that would pay them $1.25 for every day served overseas during the war and $1 for every day served in the United States. The money was to be paid in 1945 when, Ike said, "most of the Senators and Representatives would have left Washington and the earth. . . . This arrangement required them [veterans] to have one foot in the grave before they could enjoy the money. As times got hard, many veterans came to think of the deferred bonus as identical to a deposit in the bank. This oversimplification, without any legal base, became an intensely emotional idea at a time when millions of families were hard pressed to feed and clothe themselves or to meet the rent."

In December 1931 Congressman Wright Patman of Texas introduced a bill to pay the bonus immediately, but by the spring of 1932 the bill was still in committee, the subject of heated controversy. With the floor debates and crucial voting on the Patman bill expected in late spring, a force of about 15,000 unemployed veterans, led by one Walter W. Waters, descended on Washington to convince the federal officials of their plight.

Even before the arrival of the Bonus Army, Hoover had been convinced that most of its members were Communists, and it was felt that even if the bill passed both House and Senate, he would veto it. MacArthur said, "The American Communist Party . . . infiltrated the veterans groups and presently took command of their unwitting leaders." Ike, both then and later, took a calmer view of the veterans. Looking back on the matter in 1967, he said, "I would say there was no proof or evidence that . . . 'imperialistic Communism' had anything whatsoever to do with this . . . in those days we weren't ascribing everything that was disorderly to the Communists."

He said, "Except for 'Coxey's Army' in my boyhood, there was little or no precedent for the march itself. Thirty years before demonstrations would become an accepted mode of protest, the bonus veterans were pioneering direct action against Federal legislative authority. Both sides in the dispute were neophytes in conducting or facing such protests." A study by the Veterans Administration later showed that 90 percent of the bonus marchers had army or navy records, 67 percent had served overseas, and 20 percent had been disabled.

Ike said, "This bonus affair came up in a very unfortunate way. These people concentrated on Washington, and there were a number of old buildings along the Mall that had been marked by the government for destruction. They had been vacated, and the bonus marchers went into them just for shelter, rather then going out and making the little shelters that they did—the homemade ones with tin cans and cloth rags. . . . It was pitiful really. There were two or three thousand of these encampments. One was across the river in Anacostia, and then there were two or three right square in southwest Washington, on the Mall.

"To a number of citizens, they were a nuisance whose picketing and placards disturbed the quiet of Washington. To others, they were the menace of the Bolsheviks attacking the government at its very Capitol. In fact, most of them, after their arrival on Pennsylvania Avenue, however misled they may have been by a few agitators, were quiet and orderly. . . . But finally the government decided they had to go ahead with their contracts for demolishing these buildings and the work programs of reconstruction that would follow."

Waters from the beginning had with remarkable success insisted that the BEF be disciplined, "like the soldiers of the American Expeditionary force," he said. He had asked that he and several of his troops meet with Hoover to explain what they had in mind. But he was told that the president was much too busy. Instead, Hoover met some wrestling champions and a delegaton from Eta Epsilon Gamma sorority.

Some members of his staff thought that the president should explain his position to the American people on the radio, but Hoover refused. He hated the radio. When asked by an admirer if he got a thrill speaking on it, he said, "The same thrill I get when I rehearse an address to a door knob."

The Washington D.C. police chief was Brigadier General Pelham D. Glassford, who had been graduated from West Point a year after MacArthur. Glassford had resigned from the army the year before to take the job, and while they had known each other since they were both cadets, they did not agree on how to treat the Bonus Marchers. Glassford saw them not as a Communist menace but as fellow veterans down on their luck. He drove around Washington visiting them; he bought food for them out of his own pocket and persuaded the Salvation Army and other charitable institutions to provide additional food and clothing. He ordered his police to provide first aid when necessary.

On June 15 the Democratic House of Representatives passed the Patman bill, but it was defeated on June 17 by the Republican controlled Senate. Waters told the 8,000 estimated members of the BEF gathered on the Capitol steps that day, "Prepare yourselves for a disappointment, men. . . . The Bonus has been defeated. . . . This is only a temporary setback. We are going to get more and more men and are going to stay here until we change the minds of these guys. You're ten times better Americans than the Senators that voted against the bill."

After that, no one seemed to know what to do. Would these desperate Communists seize control of the Capitol, which they surely could have done? No. A newspaperwoman suggested to Waters that he and his troops sing "America," and they did. After that they quietly marched back to their shacks and the occupied buildings.

Early in July, Congress appropriated $100,000 to get the marchers home, and over 5,000 of the estimated 12,000 veterans accepted the offer and left the city. By the end of July there were an estimated 5,000 members of the BEF still in Washington. Since Congress had adjourned on July 16 without passing a bonus bill, there seemed no apparent reason why the BEF should remain in the capital. But many had no homes to return to.

As Eisenhower wrote in a report to Secretary Hurley:

In late July the evacuation of certain of the occupied areas in the vicinity of the Capitol became necessary in order that the government's . . . building program might proceed. On July 21st the Bonus leaders were formally notified by the police of this situation and requested to make prompt arrangements for the removal of occupants from the afflicted areas.

On the 28th, the buildings were still occupied, and the three commissioners who governed the District of Columbia ordered Glassford and his police "to clear those areas, using force if necessary."
Eisenhower's report said:

Accordingly, on the morning of July 28th a considerable body of police went to the encampment near Pennsylvania Avenue and 4½ [sic] Street and compelled the trespassers to evacuate. Within a short time large groups of men arrived from other camps, apparently under some prearranged plan, and a struggle for the possession of the disputed territory ensued. The police were overwhelmingly outnumbered and were quickly involved in a serious riot. The mob, composed of veterans and others who had intermingled with them, was incited by radicals and hot heads to a free use of bricks, clubs, and similar weapons. Several policemen were hurt, one most seriously, while another, in defending himself, was forced to shoot and kill one of the Bonus Marchers.

The district commissioners then went to Hoover and Hurley and told them that Chief Glassford had said he could no longer handle "the radicals and hot heads." It was necessary to call out the army. Glassford, who was among those hurt in the melee, later denied that he had asked the commissioners for federal troops. He did not mention that a brick thrown at his chest had knocked him down and that one of the "hot heads" had torn off his badge.

Most newspaper accounts at the time and many historians since have said that Hoover gleefully called out the army, but recent documents opened at the Hoover Library in West Branch, Iowa, show that he moved with great reluctance, that in fact he had some sympathy with the problems of the veterans.

Hoover never said or wrote exactly what he thought, but he did say some years later that in an oral order he had told Hurley to have troops clear the area in the business district and return the rioters to their Anacostia flats where they could be placed under guard. He denied that he ever ordered them driven out of the Capitol.

At 2:55 P.M. Hurley handed MacArthur the following:

To: *General Douglas MacArthur, Chief of Staff, United States Army*

The President has just informed me that the civil government of the District of Columbia has reported to him that it is unable to maintain law and order in the District.

You will have United States troops proceed immediately to the scene of disorder. Cooperate fully with the District of Columbia police force which is now in charge. Surround the affected area and clear it without delay.

Turn over all prisoners to the civil authorities.

In your orders insist that any women and children who may be in the affected area be accorded every consideration and kindness. Use all humanity consistent with the due execution of this order.

Patrick J. Hurley
Secretary of War

As late as the 1950s, some historians have said that when MacArthur received the orders from Hurley, he summoned his aide, Eisenhower, seized his riding crop, mounted his horse, and took personal command of the riot that was to follow. Eisenhower's personal account of what happened is considerably less inflamed. He said:

> As quickly as the order was announced to us, General MacArthur decided that he should go into active command in the field. By this time our relationship was fairly close, close enough that I felt free to object.
>
> I told him that the matter could easily become a riot and I thought it highly inappropriate for the Chief of Staff of the Army to be involved in anything like a local or street-corner embroilment. (Of course this was no "street corner" matter—but it still did not require the presence of the Chief of Staff in the streets.) General MacArthur disagreed, saying that it was a question of Federal authority in the District of Columbia, and because of his belief that there was "incipient revolution in the air" as he called it, he paid no attention to my dissent. He ordered me to get into uniform. (In that administration officers went to work in Washington in civilian clothes because a military appearance around the nation's capital was held to be undesirable.)

Ike, having lost in his first recorded disagreement with MacArthur, went to the Wyoming for his uniform; MacArthur sent an orderly to Fort Myer for his. In a famous photograph of the two that day, Eisenhower looks as if he wished he were anywhere else, while MacArthur looks delighted. In 1952 that photograph was widely circulated by the Democrats with the caption "General Ike Helps Rout Vets." It seems unlikely that it lost him any votes; it may even have gained him some.

When *The Eisenhower Diaries* were published in 1981, John P. Roche reviewed them in *The New York Times* and said of the famous photograph: "There is MacArthur in full regalia, complete with several decks of ribbons, looking sternly upon the 'battlefield' with the look of eagles in his eyes. Next to him is Ike, dressed in a regular unadorned uniform. If you take a close look at the expression on Eisenhower's face, you realize it is one of cold, caustic contempt. This is the closed Eisenhower, who later observed he had learned acting from MacArthur."

MacArthur brought to the battlefield about a thousand soldiers, including Third Cavalry troopers with sabers drawn; they were commanded by Georgie Patton, and he was supported by six midget tanks, a machine-gun unit, and tear gas. His men's rifles were at the sling.

Patton said, "The avenue was a sea of people. It took us half an hour to clear them out, and we—had to use force. As we passed the occupied building [where the scuffle had taken place] the Marchers cheered us and called, 'Here come our buddies.' The civilians in the crowd hissed us in a mild way. . . . It speaks volumes for the high character of the men that not a shot was fired. In justice to the Marchers it should be pointed out that had they really wanted to start something, they had a great chance here but refrained."

Eisenhower in the Hoover Library interview said, "The big thing was to move them [the veterans] out of those buildings, but there were others around in little hovels and huts no bigger than shelter tents. Finally the whole group got to moving back under the pressure of the soldiers toward the Anacostia Bridge. The orders were sent down by Colonel Wright, who was secretary to the General Staff, and finally by General Moseley, who was Deputy Chief of Staff, and Mr. Hoover, the President, saying, 'Don't allow any of our troops to go across the Anacostia Bridge.'

"I went up to the General [MacArthur] and said: 'There's a man here who has some orders about this.' He said, 'I don't want to hear them and I don't want to see them. Get him away.' He wouldn't listen to these instructions, and so far as I knew he never heard them, so the President's message to him just didn't get to him."

Eisenhower once again was softening the truth; the president's orders did get to MacArthur, and he ignored them. In his papers in the Library of Congress, General Moseley gives a far different account of what happened:

Sometime after the troops had completed their mission on Pennsylvania Avenue and before they had crossed the Anacostia Bridge with the view of cleaning out the camp on the other side, Mr. Hurley, the Secretary of War, directed me to inform General MacArthur that the President did not wish the troops to cross the bridge that night to force the evacuation of the Anacostia Camp. I left my office, contacted General MacArthur, and as we walked away, alone, from the others, I delivered that message to him and discussed it with him. He was very much annoyed in having his plans interfered with in any way until they were executed completely. As I told him, I was only instructed to deliver the message to him, and having done that, I returned to my office. Still later, I was asked from the White House if I had delivered the message and I stated that I had. Still later, I was instructed to repeat the message and to assure myself that General MacArthur received it before he crossed the Anacostia Bridge. I sent Colonel Clement H. Wright, then Secretary of the General Staff, to repeat the message to MacArthur and explain the situation as I had it from the White House. Colonel Wright contacted General MacArthur immediately and explained the situation to him fully.

As I now recall, Colonel Wright reported to me that the troops then had not crossed the Anacostia Bridge, but were advancing on the bridge. In any event, General MacArthur went on with his plan, carrying it through and compelling the complete evacuation of the large Anacostia Camp, which held most of the veterans. A mission of this kind was a very disagreeable one for the Army, but it was executed with precision and efficiency and entirely without bloodshed.

The point is not that the mission was disagreeable or that it was carried out without bloodshed, the point is that the chief of staff of the U.S. Army had disobeyed the orders of his commander in chief.

Eisenhower said that when MacArthur came to the Anacostia bridge, "he went with some of his troops across the bridge and, while no troops went more than two or three hundred yards over the bridge, that whole encampment started to blaze. Unquestionably the burning was started by the occupants themselves, but it was a very pitiful scene—those ragged, discouraged people burning their own little things."

This is yet another example of Eisenhower's convenient memory. The troops set the fires, no question of that. There were still photographs and newsreels showing MacArthur's soldiers lighting the fires. It was denied by the White House, but Journalist Howard Brubaker wrote in *The New Yorker* that the denials, including those of the War Department, made it clear that those around Hoover didn't waste time "looking at newsreels."

Roosevelt, then governor of New York, looking at photogrpahs of the rout, said that the whole thing looked like "scenes from a nightmare." He said of Hoover, there was nothing inside the man but jelly. He turned to his friend and adviser Felix Frankfurter, a man he was to put on the U.S. Supreme Court, and said, with grim satisfaction, "Well, Felix, this elects me."

After "the battle" had been won, MacArthur went back to the War Department, but before he left, Eisenhower said, "I remarked that there would probably be newspaper reporters trying to see him. I suggested it would be the better part of wisdom, if not of valor, to avoid meeting them. The troop movement had not been a military idea really, but a political order and I thought that the political officials only should talk to the press. He disagreed and saw the newspapermen that night."

MacArthur was most eloquent in his press conference. He said.

That mob down there was a bad looking mob. It was animated by the essence of revolution. . . . There were, in my opinion, few veteran soldiers in the group that we cleared out today; few indeed. I am not speaking figures because I don't know how many there were; but if there was one man in ten in that group today who is a veteran, it would surprise me. . . . I have released in my day more than one community which had been held in the grip of a foreign enemy. . . . At least a dozen people told me, especially in the Negro section, that a regular system of tribute was being levied on them by this insurrectionist group; a reign of terror was being started which may have led to a system of Caponeism, and I believe later to insurgency and insurrection. The President played it pretty fine in waiting to the last minute; but he didn't have much margin.

Some time later Hoover asked that Hurley and MacArthur publicly acknowledge their part in the rout. Both refused. Hurley said that MacArthur felt that such a public admission "would be bragging, that it would make him and Hurley heroes." They did not, he said, feel they should "hit the footlights."

The report that Eisenhower wrote for MacArthur's signature on the army's mission on July 28, 1932 said:

Its [the Army's] allotted tasks were performed rapidly and efficiently, but with the maximum consideration for members of the riotous groups consistent with their compulsory eviction. The results speak for themselves. Within a few hours a riot rapidly assuming alarming proportions was completely quelled, and from the time troops arrived at the scene of the disorder no soldier or civilian received a permanent or dangerous injury. Thus a most disagreeable task was performed in such a way as to leave behind it a minimum of unpleasant aftermath and legitimate resentment.

There was no doubt no time to report on at least one minor incident that happened at Anacostia. When the soldiers marched into one of the camps to burn what little the veterans and their families had left, one man came forward with a white flag. The soldiers chased him away, using sabers, bayonets, and tear gas. One man running from the tear gas had a baby in his arms; two days later the baby died, in part from the exposure to tear gas, in part from starvation.

The disillusioned Police Chief Glassford reported some time later that a veteran's wife said of the MacArthur troops, "These are the tin soldiers who dared to come only by night."

"No, these are the Regulars," replied Glassford.

On August 10 Eisenhower wrote in his diary, "As Gen. MacA's aide took part in Bonus Incident of July 28. A lot of furor has been stirred up mostly to make political capital. I wrote the General's report, which is as accurate as I could make it. I kept a copy. . . ."

I doubt that the report was as accurate as he could make it; it was no doubt as accurate as he knew he would be allowed to make it.

★ ★ ★

GOOD MAN FRIDAY

On February 20, 1933, shortly before Roosevelt was inaugurated, Eisenhower officially started working for MacArthur. He later said, "The second the Republicans lost control and I was no longer obligated to the Assistant Secretary of War, he [MacArthur] promptly took me over in his office.

"I wasn't really an aide. The job really didn't have a name. I called myself his good man Friday. My office was right next to his, and he could just call me at any time. He gave me chores—for example, I'd prepare the annual report of the Chief of Staff. He gave me a few ideas and I'd work them up." One of MacArthur's biographers, Frazier Hunt, said that Eisenhower "had the rare faculty of being able to put down on paper the exact shade of meaning that his superior desired. 'Ike got so he could write more like MacArthur than the General did himself,' was the way one officer who served on the General Staff at the time explained it. His mind was sharp and keen, and he had been perfectly trained in staff work."

In addition to the opportunity to do high-level staff work, "I was around men who were making decisions and listening to how they did it," Eisenhower said.

Their offices in the State-War-Navy building were separated only by a slatted door that did not come to the floor. Eisenhower's office was tiny, and behind his small, scuffed desk was a wall that needed a coat of paint. When Eisenhower had visitors on his side of the slatted door, "I always made sure that the door was closed because I didn't want to disturb the General." For his part, MacArthur scarcely had to raise his voice to summon his "amanuensis." "It was a dramatic voice," said the major. "He could have been a great actor."

On February 28, 1933, Ike wrote in his diary, "Right now everything is pessimism. For the past few days banks have been suspending payments in Michigan, Ohio, Maryland, Indiana—and finally this morning a large bank in D.C. followed suit. Today I've heard people advising all money in gold— eschewing bonds, bank deposits, stocks and all other types of money credit. Their feeling is that virtual panic is upon us—and their battle cry is 'Save himself who can.' " He added, "Right now I'm going to make one prediction. Things are not going to take an upturn until more power is centered in one man's hands. Only in that way will confidence be inspired. . . . For two years I have been called 'Dictator Ike' because I believe that virtual dictatorship must be exercised by our president. So now I will keep still—but I still believe it."

Eisenhower was not the only Kansan who believed that perhaps only a dictator could solve the problems of the United States. The governor of Kansas, Alfred M. Landon, who was to run against Roosevelt for the presidency in 1936, said, "Even the iron hand of a dictator is in preference to a paralytic stroke."

After FDR's inspiriting inaugural address on March 4, Ike noted in his diary, "While I have no definite leaning toward any political party, I believe it is a good thing the Democrats won—and particularly that one party will have such overwhelming superiority in Congress."

Later that month he wrote, "President has issued a proclamation suspending until next month *all* bank payments. . . . The moratorium itself is only a de-laying action [but] its announcement shows that the Pres. is going to step out and *take* authority in his own hands. More power to him!! . . . Congress has given the Pres. extraordinary powers over banks. . . . My own salary will be cut some more if these things come to pass. I cannot afford it—and will have to ask for relief from this city. Nevertheless he *should* do it—and if he doesn't I'll be disappointed in him."

Eisenhower never did have to ask the city for relief, and when he was president he took a poor view of people who had to ask the government, any government, for relief.

Once the banking crisis was over, Roosevelt went to work to set up a way to put unemployed young men to work in the forests of the United States. He had said, "The forests are the 'lungs' of our land, purifying our air and giving fresh strength to our people." A bill to set up the Civilian Conservation Corps was passed by Congress on March 31. The army and the Forest Service were designated to run the show.

By the end of July 1, three hundred CCC camps had been established all over the country, and 300,000 young men were at work digging ditches, raising bridges, protecting and improving parks, and building recreational areas. Most of the young men were from large cities, and what nobody really talked about was that 10 percent of them were black.

Much of the work of setting up the camps and the early training of the young men was done by the army, a task Eisenhower did not welcome. John said that his father felt that "the Army was trapped enough without having to take on the CCC chore." Eventually the officers' reserve corps did most of the work in supervising the camps.

Early in 1934 Edgar came to Washington as a representative of some West Coast lumber companies to set up a labor code under another of Roosevelt's "alphabet soup" agencies, the National Recovery Act, a measure that many businessmen, and certainly Edgar, thought meant socializing private enterprise.

The head of the National Recovery Administration was General Hugh S. Johnson, who had been a member of MacArthur's graduating class of 1903 at the Point. Johnson had frequent access to the president, which was still another reason the chief of staff hated the New Deal and New Dealers. Johnson got almost everything he asked for; MacArthur got almost nothing he asked for.

Roosevelt was worse than Hoover when it came to the army budget, which might have been expected from a man who had been assistant secretary of the navy during the Wilson administration. MacArthur several times went to the Oval Office and had several theatrical encounters with the president; after one of them he said that he vomited on the steps of the White House.

Since there were now three Eisenhower brothers in Washington at the same time, Ike asked Earl to join them. Earl had recently married the daughter of the owner and founder of a newspaper in a small town in Pennsylvania. Earl was about to become a member of the newspaper's staff. Except for Roy, the Eisenhower boys all married.

Earl and his bride drove to Washington, and a reunion was held at Milton's house in Falls Church, Virginia. The brothers cheered themselves up with a liberal sampling of Milton's homemade bourbon. It was said to be among the best in the area and was made in the basement of the house, near the furnace. It was aged for nearly a year, and was powerful.

Late in the evening, the four Eisenhowers got into a lively discussion of the New Deal. Earl said that arguing was one of the principal delights of their reunions. Edgar and Dwight argued against what was then sometimes called the Roosevelt revolution, Edgar being the more vehement of the two. Milton, who frequently went to the White House with his boss, Henry A. Wallace, the secretary of agriculture, and Earl defended Roosevelt and his policies. At one point Edgar got so angry at Earl that he said his brother's politics were the same color as his hair, red. The argument lasted until early the next morning, and it seems likely that by that time the Eisenhower brothers had consumed so much of Milton's bourbon that no matter what their politics were, their faces were red.

Eisenhower considered himself a failure at that time; Edgar was on a generous $50-a-day expense account and could keep whatever he didn't spend. Ike, meanwhile, had to account for sums as small as 82 cents to a warrant officer in the State-War-Navy building. And Milton was always walking into the Oval Office of the White House, closer to the president than his boss, Wallace, and like Hugh Johnson, getting almost all that he and his department asked for. After all, many more voters were farmers than soldiers.

When Ike's navy friend Swede Hazlett was ordered to Washington around this time, he found Eisenhower "still the same old Ike. . . . I had just been promoted to Commander, but he was still a major with no immediate prospects. I recall an occasional gripe about the Army promotion system, and how much better the Navy selection system was. I consoled him with the thought that in case of war the Army would expand so much more rapidly that it would eventually pull way ahead . . . of the Navy."

In his corrections of Kenneth Davis's *Soldier of Democracy*, Ike said, "The law governing Reg. Army promotion was passed in 1920. My situation in this respect was unfavorable, but if it had worried or 'dissatisfied' me, I'd have gone out. The plain truth was I'd long ago quit thinking about it and so far as Swede was concerned, I merely explained the circumstances that precluded any thought of promotion."

However, around that time, Eisenhower did almost resign from the army; a newspaper syndicate had either heard about or seen the reports that were regularly being sent to Congress over MacArthur's signature but, as many people knew, were written by Eisenhower. He was making $3,000 a year, and the syndicate offered him between $15,000 and $20,000 to write as an "expert" on military matters. He was tempted, but after talking the whole matter over with Milton, he decided against the offer. It is not known if he discussed the matter with Mamie. In any event, he remained in MacArthur's office as his "good man Friday" until his tour of duty as chief of staff ended in 1935, the same year the Tydings-McDuffie Act was passed into law, giving the Philippine Islands commonwealth status for ten years. After that they would be completely independent. To prepare for this, the Philippine government asked the U.S. government for a military mission to help set up a national defense system.

Manuel Quezon, the eloquent and handsome young president-elect of the commonwealth, insisted that MacArthur come to Manila as military adviser to the new government. MacArthur immediately accepted, and urged Eisenhower to come with him. By that time, the forty-five-year-old major was necessary to him. He told Ike he didn't want to bring in somebody new. "Nevertheless," Eisenhower said, "his emphatic insistence on my continuing with him was a distinction that I could not fully appreciate yet. . . . When General MacArthur lowered the boom on me, so to speak, I could not comfort myself with such perspective."

Ike had, of course, wanted to go to the Philippines in 1915 and 1919; by

1935 the islands had lost their appeal, and to go there with MacArthur was very nearly unthinkable. As he said, with customary understatement, "I was not ecstatic about the prospect. . . . I thought I deserved, after years of staff work, a chance to serve again with troops. [But] General MacArthur was still Chief of Staff and was very insistent that I go along with him for a year or so."

Ike's personal wishes were unimportant. "Whatever may have been going on inside me, I was in no position to argue with the Chief of Staff."

This time Mamie would not go with him. John was in his last year at John Quincy Adams School, and she thought he ought to be allowed to finish there, an idea that John, then thirteen, endorsed. If when John graduated Ike was still in the Philippines, they would join him.

Ike asked MacArthur how long he would have to stay in the Philippines. MacArthur said he didn't know, maybe a year, maybe more, a wholly unsatisfactory answer. The general did, however, say that Eisenhower could choose "one associate from the Regular Army to go along with us." He chose Major James Ord, who was a competent staff officer, a classmate and friend, who spoke fluent Spanish.

At worst, at the very worst, he would have a full tour of duty in the islands, four nightmarish years. He did not know and the general had no intention of telling him that on September 15 MacArthur had received a letter from the acting adjutant general. It said:

> You are hereby given the greatest latitude and general authorities in carrying out this all-important mission. . . . Your mission must be accomplished— ways and means are largely left to you. . . . The limitations of time on foreign service is waived in your case and that of the officers and enlisted men at your headquarters. [The law said that any officer who was on detached duty for more than four years either had to resign his commission or return to active duty.] It is expected that your term of service will be at least seven years, and probably much longer. Those under your immediate command will be relieved when you so request. . . . You stand relieved from duty on the General Staff and as Chief of Staff on December 15, 1935.

Seven years and probably much longer in the Philippines with MacArthur, with "Sarah," with General Impossible; had Eisenhower known of the letter and its threatening contents, it seems quite possible that he might have reconsidered that civilian job. At the very least he would have made a few phone calls, the first one to Fox Conner. He would not have gone to the Philippines. But he did not know, and it turned out that his years in the Philippines, four, not seven, were of incalculable value to him and to us.

MacArthur had assured Quezon that of course the Philippines could be defended, no problem, "if sufficient men, munitions, and money were available, and above all sufficient time to train the men, to provide the munitions, and to raise the money." None of those things were available in sufficient quantities then or ever.

Before leaving the United States, Eisenhower and Ord tried to draw up a plan outlining a territorial and administrative organization, a defense policy, and a citizens' military training program modeled on the Swiss system of compulsory military service. They tried to draw up plans that made sense financially and militarily. But before long, "Jimmy and I were muttering to ourselves that 'They also serve who only draft and draft.' . . . All Jimmy Ord and I could do was to assemble our proposals for a skeleton force that some day might have flesh put on its bones. We turned it in fingers crossed. . . . With the limited funds available, however, no matter how ingenious our schemes might be, we knew that we could not hope for any respectable force earlier than the date of complete independence—that is, the year 1946."

Thus Ike and Ord did not go to the Philippines with any great expectations. The only one with those was MacArthur. But then, as Harry Truman often said of him, "He thought he was God. He thought once he wanted something done, it was as good as done already." Ike said of their assignment, "Even though our Chief, Douglas MacArthur, spoke and wrote in purple splendor, his subordinates were restrained in the language we used about the future. We played it down as just another job."

Before leaving Washington, MacArthur wrote, in an effusive addition to Ike's 201:

Upon relinquishing the position of Chief of Staff, I want to leave a written record of my appreciation of certain important considerations connected with your work which have not been easy to describe in normal reports.

You were retained by the Secretary of War, and later by myself, on critically important duties in the Department long past the duration of ordinary staff tours, solely because of your success in performing difficult tasks whose accomplishment required a comprehensive grasp of the military profession in all its principal phases, as well as analytical thought and forceful expression. Through all these years I have been impressed by the cheerful and efficient devotion of your best efforts to confining, difficult, and often strenuous duties, in spite of the fact that your own personal desires involved a return to troop command and other physically active phases of Army life, for which your characteristics so well qualify you. In this connection I should like to point out to you that your unusual experience in the Department will be of no less future value to you as a commander than as a staff officer, since all problems presented to you were nevertheless solved from the viewpoint of the High Command. Then too, I have noted with satisfaction that you have never sought to employ staff authority in lieu of a proper application of leadership methods, but to the contrary, have invariably demonstrated an ability to organize complicated tasks quickly and efficiently, to secure cheerful cooperation from all concerned, and to carry group efforts to successful conclusion. The numbers of personal requests for your services brought to me by heads of many of the Army's principal activities during the past few years furnish convincing proof of the reputation you have established as an outstanding soldier. I can say no more than that this reputation coincides exactly with my own judgement.

* * *

THE MISSION

Eisenhower, Mamie, and John were in Denver with the Douds on October 1, when MacArthur and his party left Washington in a private railway car. Ike joined the party at the railroad station in Cheyenne, Wyoming, where he saw the curtain raiser of four years of temper tantrums, claims of betrayal, and what he described as "an explosive denunciation of politics, bad manners, bad judgment, broken promises, arrogance, unconstitutionality, insensitivity, and the way the world had gone to hell."

MacArthur had just been handed a telegram from Acting Secretary of War Harry H. Woodring, saying that President Roosevelt had appointed a new chief of staff, General Malin Craig, the appointment "effective this date." MacArthur had been promised by the president that he would remain chief of staff until December 15—at least that was what MacArthur thought he had been promised, though he realized that with Roosevelt you could never be sure—and that he would thus arrive in the Philippines with his resounding title intact and with four stars. The telegram meant that he no longer had the title and that he was also reduced to his permanent rank, major general. No wonder he felt "the world had gone to hell."

Nevertheless, he sent telegrams to Roosevelt and Woodring saying that Craig's appointment was "not only admirable but timely" and another to Craig saying "the entire Army will look forward with keen anticipation to what cannot fail to be a successful tenure of office."

So the trip did not start out well, and as time went on things only got worse. MacArthur was convinced that he had a great many enemies in Washington, and that feeling was not without foundation. Roosevelt said that the general was "the second most dangerous man in the country," the first being the fiery senator from Louisiana, Huey Long. He also said that MacArthur was "a potential Mussolini" with "a voice that might come from an oracle's cave." Harold Ickes, secretary of the interior, said, "MacArthur is the type of man who thinks that when he gets to heaven, God will step down from the great white throne and bow him into His vacated seat."

MacArthur was not a man who faced reality; Eisenhower, most of the time, did, and he realized even before getting on the ship for Manila that the mission would receive something less than enthusiastic backing from Washington.

The party that went aboard the S.S. *President Harding* on October 4 consisted of MacArthur, the general's aide, Captain Thomas Jefferson "T.J." Davis, the general's mother, Mary Pinckney Hardy "Pinky" MacArthur, who was eighty-four and ill, Major Howard J. Hutter, an army physician, and Ord and Ike. The journey lasted twenty-two days.

T.J. Davis, who throughout the war was Eisenhower's adjutant general, was a chubby, even-tempered South Carolinian whose relaxed personality enabled him without apparent effort to perform an adjutant's duties, i.e., to keep the records for headquarters, the roster of personnel, and to issue orders for and on the authority of the commander. There is no record of any friction between the two men. It might be said that Davis was the exact opposite of Bedell Smith.

Pinky was confined to her stateroom during the voyage, but MacArthur seemed to be having a very good time with a fellow passenger, Jean Marie Faircloth, of Murfreesboro, Tennessee, who was unmarried, had just inherited $200,000 from her stepfather, and adored soldiers, the general, it appeared, in particular.

Photographers were present when the party arrived in Manila, and in one picture MacArthur stands alone, a row of one at attention, lord of all he surveys, in a straw hat and white suit. He looked military, though; one could understand why a reporter in the First World War had said, "You could tell he was a soldier, even in a fur coat or a bathing suit." Eisenhower stood behind him, also wearing a straw hat and a white suit, but he did not look like a soldier. He looked like an unhappy civilian who wished he were almost anywhere else. Indeed, he would later write in his diary, "From the beginning of this venture I've personally announced myself as ready and willing to go back to an assignment in the United States Army at any moment. The general knows this if he knows anything."

Financially, the assignment was a good one. In addition to his regular army pay, Eisenhower received a salary from the Philippine government plus a liberal expense account, and he lived rent-free in a room at the Manila Hotel, which was owned by the Philippine government.

A short time after arriving, Pinky suffered a cerebral thrombosis and died. Newspapers in Manila said that she had been "the commonwealth's first soldier," and Ike said, "Her departure from his side, and from his counsels, affected the general's spirit for many months."

Manuel Quezon was inaugurated as the first president of the commonwealth on November 15, and in their first weeks in Manila, Eisenhower and Ord spent a good deal of time preparing for that ornate occasion. The inaugural was attended by Vice President John Nance Garner, seventeen senators, and twenty-six congressmen. There was in addition a crowd of a quarter of a million people. The festivities began at 8:15 on the morning of the 15th and lasted until early on the morning of the 16th and included a parade, endless speeches by a great number of Philippine and American officials, a state dinner, and an inaugural ball. A Japanese newspaper, *Yomituri*, congratulated the new commonwealth "especially because the Philippines can easily be reached by air from Japan and the [prospects for] Japan-Philippine trade are bright."

Once the inauguration was over, Eisenhower and Ord had to get down to completing work on what Eisenhower later was to call "a hopeless venture," a defense plan for the islands. Besides, MacArthur was making no sense; he was speaking of an army of thirty divisions, supported by 250 planes and sixty torpedo boats. Ike's longtime friend Kevin McCann said of that nonsense, "Repeatedly his staff told him that he could never achieve his goal on the sums allotted him. Yet he persisted, apparently in the hope that he could eventually get the necessary funds from the Philippine Government when the need arose. But he was wrong. For four trying years President Quezon held him to an $8,000,000 annual budget." In addition, the program to procure munitions for the small army was cut from a twenty-year period to ten years. But money was not forthcoming for that either, neither from Washington nor from Manila. The Filipinos were in at least one way like MacArthur; once they saw something on paper, many of them, including at times Quezon, thought it had been done. Besides, nothing must be allowed to interfere with corruption as usual. Corruption was a way of life with most of the Filipino establishment and with most of the 5,000 American colonists.

From the beginning, Ike was pessimistic. In January 1936 he wrote, "We must never forget that every question in Washington today is settled on the basis of getting votes next November. To decide this matter [allocating money for defense of the islands] completely in our favor would gain no votes, while to dissaprove [sic] the request and give the matter some publicity might be considered as a vote-getting proposition among the pacifists and other misguided elements of the American electorate."

Ike was never sure that the islands could build a defense against an invader. It might, he felt, "be necessary to content ourselves with an attempt to produce a military adequate to deal with domestic revolt," a constabulary. But even that was difficult, perhaps impossible. He dealt with the Filipinos better than most of the American colonists there. He did not speak of the "white man's burden" or of "white supremacy," which was heard so often at social gatherings; so far as is known he never said, "What can you expect? They're Filipinos."

On the other hand, he was aware that more than 2,000 native dialects were spoken and that very often those who spoke one could not understand any of the others. Almost nobody could write, though for years the American colonists had spoken of wiping out illiteracy.

Although the Philippines had been in American hands since 1898, there was still some fighting on islands to the south of Manila; the Moros on those islands, who were Muslims, believed that killing Christians improved their standing with Allah. MacArthur dismissed these outbreaks in the same cavalier fashion as he dismissed the possibility of a Japanese attack on the islands. He said to a magazine reporter in 1936, "Those Moro boys are all right. It's just that they don't understand. There aren't any newspapers down there, and you have to go around and explain things to them almost individually. Some of the Moros think the Filipinos are trying to enslave them; as soon as they learn that they're helping Uncle Sam, they're all right. There isn't going to be much trouble in that direction."

Ike wrote in his diary, "Among individuals [the Filipinos] there is no lack of intelligence, but to us they seem with few exceptions unaccustomed to the requirements of administrative and executive procedure. . . . We have . . . learned to expect from the Filipinos with whom we deal, a minimum of performance from a maximum of promise."

MacArthur never mentioned publicly the agrarian unease in the Philippines, although evidence of it was everywhere. An anonymous British manager of a sugar plantation said that there was in the islands "a general atmosphere of unrest . . . amongst the natives. There is a deep current of discontent which will sooner or later break out in open revolt." As for what Eisenhower was trying to do, training the natives to be soldiers, the Englishman said:

General MacArthur must have his tongue in his cheek when he sounds off about them or else he does not visit the training camps. I have visited a few here in the Provinces. The state of affairs is indescribable. They put a poor miserable third lieutenant, with at the most six months training, in charge of several hundred of these savages who have never known a moment's restraint nor discipline in their lives, and who are there at all much against their will, and expect him to keep order and discipline. They give him a few non-coms, who are rapidly promoted privates from the old constabulary, and who I rather suspect are the sweepings of the company that the Company Commander wanted to get rid of. These men speedily revert to type and become as dirty and sloppy as the recruits. No, mustn't call them recruits, might hurt their pride, "trainees" is the word. . . . There was no such thing as a salute, any one strolled up to the Lieutenant and spoke to him like a long lost buddie. Their clothing was dirty, the barracks were dirty, the equipment of the two sentries was such as to give a bitch wolf colic, it was so filthy. . . . You can imagine what will happen when they turn this herd of quarter-trained men back to their homes. They have learned foot drill and a few rudiments of military life. . . . [A man can] see fine houses . . . being built while he is still living in a shack that you could throw a cat through. He sees autos and hears of the parties in Manila, and all of that coupled with the well-known theory that he is taught in school, the one you know, about all men being equal, doesn't make him any more easy to handle.

In addition to all the difficulties in training men, there was never enough money. In February 1936 authority was finally received from Washington to purchase 100,000 Enfield rifles, and it was agreed that an additional 800,000 rifles would, unless something unexpected happened, be made available over an eight-year period.

There was a firm conviction both in Washington and in Manila that what some few alarmists called "the danger from the north"—Japan—was no danger at all. Paul V. McNutt, who was soon to become high commissioner in the islands, said that no defense at all was necessary, "not even a rifle"; so long as the American flag flew over the islands the Japanese wouldn't dare attack them.

It seems never to have occurred to Eisenhower or to the other American colonists that the Japanese were a serious threat. MacArthur called them "the Jap"; to many others they were "Charlie," and you couldn't take Charlie seriously as a soldier, sailor, or aviator. But in case of any attack, Eisenhower felt that the army he was trying to build could offer only "a passive type of defense" to an enemy invader. An enemy invader could be slowed by the Philippine troops, and then the United States would send reinforcements, probably from Hawaii.

Even after the attack on Pearl Harbor and the destruction of the U.S. Air Force in the Philippines, Clark Lee, the Associated Press correspondent in Manila, wrote, "The Japanese Army is an ill-uniformed, untrained mass of young boys between fifteen and eighteen years old equipped with small-caliber guns." Lee quoted an American army colonel as saying, "The Japanese troops invading the Philippines are distinctly fourth-raters. . . . These Charlies . . . can't shoot. Somebody gets hit about every 5,000 shots."

Back in the States after Pearl Harbor, a great many people were happily singing, "Good-bye, Mama, I'm off to Yokohama" and "You're a Sap, Mr. Jap." The liberal *PM* ran an editorial entitled "How to Beat the Japs in 30 Days." There were no air raid shelters in Manila nor were there ever any plans to build them. When the Americans there learned that shelters were being built in Japanese cities, they were delighted. They said, "Charlie's going to need them."

On July 1, 1936, his twentieth wedding anniversary, Ike became a lieutenant colonel, and in August, MacArthur was promoted; he became a field marshal in the almost nonexistent army of the Philippines.

Eisenhower was not pleased with the idea. He wrote in his diary:

A subject that has been much discussed among members of the Mission is the advisability of accepting higher rank [in the Philippine Army] for each of us under the provisions of the National Defense Act. To any such thought I have been unalterably opposed from the start, and have in fact gone so far as to inform the General that I personally would decline at this time to accept any such appointment from the Philippine Army in the event it were tendered to me. . . . In a locality where we are serving with so many American officers, most of whom believe that the attempt to create a Philippine Army is somewhat ridiculous, the acceptance by us of high rank in an Army which is not yet formed would serve to belittle our effort. . . .

Captain Davis and I have . . . strongly advised General MacArthur to decline, for the present, the acceptance of the title tendered him as Field Marshal.

He recalled telling MacArthur, " 'General, you have been a four-star general [in the U.S. Army]. . . . This is a *proud* thing. There's only been a few who had it. Why in the *hell* do you want a *banana* country giving you a field-marshalship? This . . . looks like you're trying for some kind of . . .' Oh, Jesus! He just gave me hell! . . . Probably no one has had more, tougher fights with a senior than I had with MacArthur. . . . I told him time and again, 'Why in the *hell* don't you *fire* me? . . . Goddamnit, you do things I don't agree with and you know damn well I don't.' "

Largely because of Eisenhower's loud disapproval, MacArthur for a time did hesitate to accept the title, but, eventually, Eisenhower said, "The general decided that he could not decline . . . without offense to the president [Quezon]. Anyway, he is tickled pink—and feels he's made a lot of 'face' locally."

In late August in an elaborate ceremony at the presidential palace, Quezon read a high-sounding manifesto making MacArthur a field marshal; Quezon's wife, Aurora, presented him with a gold baton, and the marshal wore a uniform he had designed himself. It was sharkskin, consisting of black trousers and white jacket, on which were his seven rows of medals.

MacArthur replied to Quezon in his usual flowery style, and Captain Bonner Fellers, liaison officer between the field marshal's office and the president, told him it was "a Sermon on the Mount clothed in grim, present-day reality. I shall never forget it." General Moseley wrote from Washington, "I was delighted that the commonwealth of the Philippine Islands . . . accorded you further promotion and new honors. There is little further that the Government can do for you now except to make you President of the United States."

MacArthur had insisted from the beginning that giving him the title of field marshal had been Quezon's idea, but Eisenhower saw the Philippine president in Washington in 1942 and later said, "When Quezon came to Washington during the war years, I had a chance to talk to him about it casually one day. I was surprised to learn from him that he had not initiated the idea at all; rather, Quezon said that MacArthur himself came up with the high-sounding title."

Criticism of the efforts of the mission grew both in the United States and in the islands, not because too little was being done but because any effort at all was considered to be unnecessary and dangerous. David H. Popper of the Foreign Policy Association said that MacArthur was a member of "a covert conspiracy to keep the United States in the islands." An article in *The Nation* said, "It is high time for this nation to reassert in unmistakable terms that the responsibility for policy-making on matters of national concern belongs, under our Constitution, to the civilian arm of the government. The recall of General MacArthur would serve that purpose."

In his April 1936 report, written by Eisenhower, MacArthur paid more attention to criticism in the islands; opposition to the defense plan came, he said, from those who were "secretly, if not openly subversive, or at least motivated by a selfish hope of personal gain through an attempt to make a political issue out of any effort to produce adequate security."

In a speech, also written by Eisenhower at MacArthur's direction, the field marshal said, "When the Philippine Defense Plan reaches fruition the people of these islands will be in a favorable posture of defensive security." Eisenhower may have written it, but he didn't necessarily believe it. He said, "General MacArthur's amazing determination and optimism made us forget [our] questions [about the effectiveness of the defense plan] at times, but they kept coming back in our minds."

MacArthur was not interested in air power. There were those in his command who felt he wasn't even aware of it. It was Eisenhower who organized a small "air force"; it was necessary, he said, if for no other purpose than to get to the training stations on the outer islands and in the mountains.

Much of the time Eisenhower wished Mamie and John were with him, but there were occasions in 1936 when he was glad they were back in Washington. He made a decision he saw no reason to consult or even tell his wife about. At forty-six he decided to do what she and her family had forbidden him to do twenty years earlier; he would learn how to fly.

"In the beginning of 1936," he said, "we fixed up a field outside the city limits, selected a few students, and started a miniature air force. The students learned rapidly and I decided to take flying lessons . . . from Captain Lewis and Lieutenant William Lee, the American instructors. Because I was learning to fly at the age of forty-six, my reflexes were slower than those of the younger men. Training me must have been a trial of patience for Lewis and Lee."

Lewis and Lee had, Ike said, been " 'borrowed' from the Army Air Corps. . . . We bought a few primary trainers." Lee remembered that Eisenhower started "coming out to the field even before we got our first aircraft together."

John Eisenhower, who himself became a pilot, said that his father "usually took the lessons before going to work in the mornings . . . and did snap rolls, loops and perhaps even Immelmann turns with the best of them. He never made solo cross-country flights to the best of my knowledge."

Lee said, "His flying was fair, but not as smooth as it could be. . . . On May 19, after flying with him for about twenty minutes, I got out and told him to get going. 'You mean you want me to fly it by myself?' asked Ike. 'Hell, yes,' I replied, 'you can fly it, so get along.' Off he went, alone, circled and landed several times. He was one happy fellow.

"You know the most amazing thing about him? It didn't matter where it was or what was going on, he could sleep anywhere; he could sit there in that plane, his arms across his chest, and he could fall asleep in about five seconds and stay asleep no matter what else was going on. A person who can do that is a person who's ready for anything, any kind of duty. It's just like a dog, it can sleep until you say 'Let's go,' and then he goes. I thought it was one of the greatest things about Ike."

Ike paid a good deal of attention to airplanes; he said of the training planes, "The engines were good, but the pilot who asked too much of one, in a steep climb, for example, learned that the roaring monster could retreat into silent surrender. . . . The seat of the pants was a surer guide to navigation than the few instruments and beacons we had. . . . To attract attention for a landing or a message, we buzzed a building until its occupants ran out. They never knew whether we were just visiting or in trouble. To communicate was a simple matter: you wrapped a message around a stone and dropped it as close as possible to them. We did have maps. One slight problem was that tropical landscapes, viewed from several thousand feet up, bore slight resemblance to the best map. . . . But it was fun."

Lee said that when a student was flying a BT-1, "We put a sandbag in the back seat and tied it to the seat for more balance. One day I remember Ike was flying solo in the ship. He came down once like he was going to land, but he went round once, maybe twice again. He finally got down and taxied up to the line. He was disturbed. He said he couldn't get the stick back.

"We looked back there and the damned sandbag had slipped forward. The stick wouldn't come all the way back. I don't blame him for being disturbed, because he wasn't an experienced pilot. I was an experienced pilot, but I'd have been disturbed over a thing like that."

Another of Ike's instructors, a young first lieutenant in the Philippine army,

Jesus A. Villamor, described another of Ike's flights. One morning Villamor arrived at the small airfield with a hangover and no breakfast. He said, "To top it all, I had already had to check out a number of other students, including many who were about to be washed out." Then he got Lieutenant Colonel Eisenhower. "I had to endure some twenty miserable moments flying with him. I grew more and more irritated as I watched him make mistakes time and again. In making turns, for instance, sometimes he would use the rudder first and other times the stick first. Naturally, skids and slips of the plane would result. And this despite my telling him [over the interphone] of his errors, and after my demonstrating the proper steps repeatedly.

"I should have taken into consideration the fact that it was a windy day and that smooth flying was difficult, if not impossible, especially for the type of plane we were flying. But I didn't. Instead, unable to stand it any longer, I grabbed the controls and landed the plane myself.

" 'Tell me, Colonel,' I continued impatiently as we stood beside the parked plane, 'surely you don't expect the plane to do things perfectly when you yourself don't follow the proper procedure, do you?'

"Ike didn't speak. 'Damn it, Colonel,' I said with all the vehemence I could muster, 'what the hell is your excuse anyway?' To that question Ike gave the only answer a West Point man can give. 'No excuse, Lieutenant.'

"The simplicity of his response stunned me. I suddenly realized how unfair I had been. And it finally dawned on me that I was just making a fool of myself. . . .

"His bearing, his manners, his attitude—all so aptly demonstrated in his simple reply—made me feel completely ashamed of myself. He could very easily have pulled his rank on me. Instead, he waited patiently, and, at the right moment, brought me down to reality in a simple, man-to-man fashion. It was clear to me then that this person I was shouting at was not just an ordinary army officer."

Many years later, in November 1945, Villamor met Ike again. Major Villamor had been a resistance leader on Mindanao and in the Visayan area before the islands were freed. Ike was Chief of Staff of the U.S. Army. Villamor brought with him a letter from an old friend of Eisenhower's, Major General Basilio J. Valdes, Chief of Staff of the Philippine Army. Valdes wrote, "Upon the rehabilitation of the Philippine Air Force, pilot ratings were reviewed and it was found that you had completed the prescribed course for Philippine Army pilots." Valdes had also sent a pair of wings, along with an extract of the special order awarding Eisenhower the rating of Airplane Pilot for having logged 350 hours of flying time during the period July 1936 to November 1939.

Eisenhower stopped flying after the Second World War, although on occasion he would, on a long trip, "move into the co-pilot's seat and take over the controls. But as the jet age arrived," he said, "I realized that I had come out of a horse-and-buggy background, recognized my limitations, and kept to a seat in the back."

The last plane he flew was reported to have been an open-cockpit biplane used for primary training in 1947. It had a top speed of 125 miles an hour.

Lee said he didn't think MacArthur ever knew about the flying lessons. "If

Ike wanted to learn to fly at forty-six years of age, we were more than glad to help him, and he was the kind of man we were happy to have aboard." He added, "MacArthur ignored the airplanes," a statement supported by the events of December 7, 1941.

Mamie found out that Ike had been flying the morning after she arrived in Manila, at breakfast; she was not happy with the news and said so on numerous occasions. She and John arrived in Manila shortly before the 1936 Presidential election, on the U.S.S. *Grant*. Mamie was pleased that Captain Arthur Nevins and his wife Anne had been on board the ship; he was assigned to Fort William McKinley, the headquarters of the Philippine Division, which was about nine miles south of Manila. He and Eisenhower had been in the same battalion at Leon Springs, Texas, in 1917. The two families were to remain friends for the rest of their lives.

The twenty-seven-day voyage had not been easy for Mamie, and her expectations were not great. "I had built myself up for a let down. I wasn't counting on finding anything delightful or delicious in such a hot place. I guess it was because the bad dream of the three years in Panama was my only comparison." She was also suffering from a stomach ailment that had almost kept her from making the journey at all.

Ike met her at the pier, and she was shocked to see that he was completely bald. He had shaved his head, he said, to keep cool. A second surprise was more pleasing. Ike was wearing his lieutenant colonel's leaves on his white uniform.

John had enjoyed the trip, and he said that the years that followed were "among the happiest" of his life.

Mamie found out almost immediately that the climate was just as bad as she had expected, maybe worse. Art Nevins was later to say that because of the climate, "everyone soon began counting the months, or boats, until he, too, would be leaving. . . . There was considerable joking as to whether the sun might not have addled the brains of an officer who had been in the islands a number of months. When an officer acted at all out of the ordinary, it was customary to say of him, 'Well, the old boy has missed too many boats.' "

The rainy season began about the first of June and lasted until about the middle of November. During that time it rained all day every day. Most of the time during the rainy season, Mamie didn't leave the Manila Hotel, although she was far from comfortable there. The six-story building was one of the handsomest in Manila, but the Eisenhower suite was not air-conditioned. A ceiling fan in the bedroom stirred up the air but didn't cool anything off. A large net over the bed had to be let down every night to protect her and Ike from things that crawled and things that flew. J. Lawton Collins, who was also in the Philippines in the 1930s and another lifelong friend, said, "There were armadas of mosquitoes; there were red ants that seemed to march in formations looking for human flesh. The cockroaches were as big as mice, or so it seemed." The net made the bed acutely uncomfortable for a woman who suffered from claustrophobia. Mike Doud Moore said her sister Mamie didn't like the Philippines. "She hated the heat. She didn't feel well in hot climates, and she was terrified of iguanas or spiders, or whatever they have out there."

Once, during an earthquake, a portable clothes closet fell across the bed. John remembered it was in the summer of 1937. "The quake had hit the island of Luzon in an intensity more severe than that of the 1906 earthquake in San Francisco. The folks had been out at a party at the time; but on their return they discovered that a giant *apparador* had fallen flat across the bed where Dad would have been sleeping. Had he been in bed, the crash might have killed him. That night, I was told, thousands of people slept in the Luneta, a large park between the Manila Hotel and the Army-Navy Club."

John didn't mind the hotel suite; in fact, after settling down there, he tried to stay as long as possible. "I was intensely interested in the 1936 political campaign and the effort to unseat President Roosevelt. The propaganda and the polls at the time showed Landon well ahead. Somehow I induced the folks to let me stay in Manila long enough to watch the returns at the Army-Navy Club. As they posted the sad news on the great bulletin board in the sweltering heat, I was aghast to witness the drubbing my candidate received."

John's father also had a lot of trouble over the 1936 election. MacArthur had been following the campaign in the weekly news magazine, *The Literary Digest*. In his diary Eisenhower said:

T.J. [Davis] and I came in for a terrible bawling out over a most ridiculous affair. The Gen. has been following the *Literary Digest* poll, and has convinced himself that Landon is to be elected, probably by a landslide. I showed him letters from Art Hurd, which predict that Landon cannot even carry Kansas, but he got perfectly furious when T.J. and I counseled caution in studying the *Digest* report.

I don't believe it reaches the great mass of people who will vote for the incumbent. We couldn't understand the reason for his almost hysterical condemnation of our stupidity until he suddenly let drop that he had gone out and urged Q. [Quezon] to shape his plans for going to the United States on the theory that Landon will be elected. Possibly he will, I don't know. But I hear the general is trying to bet several thousand pesos on it. . . . Why should he get sore just because we say "Don't be so d——— certain and go out on a limb unnecessarily." Both of us are "fearful and small-minded people who are afraid to express judgments that are obvious from the evidence at hand." Oh, hell.

The Art Hurd Ike referred to in his diary was an Abilene lawyer and an old friend. He was right. Landon did not carry Kansas that year; he carried only Maine and Vermont. Roosevelt received the greatest mandate since James Monroe, collecting 523 electoral votes to Landon's 8.

Ike also had been right; the *Literary Digest* poll did not reach the "great mass of people who will vote for the incumbent." The poll had been based on postcards sent to people who had their names in telephone books or on lists of registered automobiles. It had not occurred to the editors that in 1936 a great many Americans did not have telephones or cars.

On November 15 Ike wrote:

Boy, did the general backpedal rapidly. I hear he walked out to Q. on the first or second and "took back" what he had said at first. Accused *The Literary Digest* of "crookedness" when he heard Wall Street odds had gone up 4–1 on Roosevelt against Landon. . . . But he'd never expressed to T.J. or to me any regret for his awful bawling out of a couple of months ago.

After the elections, John's excuse for remaining in Manila had run out. "I was whisked off to Baguio, in the mountains of northwest-central Luzon. There, in Brent School, an Episcopalian mission, I was to remain for the next three and one half years."

MacArthur and Quezon, both with ample staffs, especially on Quezon's part, went to the United States late in January 1937, ostensibly to see Paul V. McNutt sworn in as the new high commissioner. McNutt, who had been governor of Indiana, was a handsome white-haired man who looked like a president and who planned to be the Democratic candidate for that office in 1940; it never occurred to anyone at the time that Roosevelt would even consider running for a third term—anyone except Roosevelt, anyway.

The MacArthur-Quezon trip was not a great success, partly because on his arrival in San Francisco Quezon told the press that the Philippine Islands could not wait until 1946; they must be free by the end of December 1938. Roosevelt did not take kindly to that announcement, and as a result, MacArthur said, "Quezon was practically ignored in the United States." Moreover, he said, "My request for supplies and equipment went unheeded by the War Department." As a result of their disappointment, the two men and their staffs went off to Mexico for a time, then Quezon went to Europe.

MacArthur returned briefly to Washington to rebury his mother's remains beside his father in Arlington National Cemetery. On April 20, in a civil ceremony at the New York Municipal Building, the general married Jean Faircloth, whom he had met aboard the *President Harding*. The groom and his bride returned to the Philippines almost immediately.

Even before he got off the ship in Manila, MacArthur said a number of things that were demonstrably untrue. He told a Philippine newspaperman that relations between the United States and the islands had seldom been better when in fact they had almost never been worse. He was asked if Japan posed any threat to the islands, and he said, "Never in word or deed, so far as I know, has Japan given any indication of a desire to absorb the Philippine Islands. Propaganda to that effect is generally traceable to those who have some ulterior motive to be served." He said finally that isolationists and pacifists in the United States "receive much more attention and space than they merit. They are very noisy but the noise they make is out of all proportion to their influence."

As a matter of fact, American antiwar groups had never been more powerful, as was reflected by the congressmen working on legislation and issuing statements that the United States was and would remain neutral.

In his shipboard interview, MacArthur also said that Roosevelt was planning to visit the islands in 1938, but Roosevelt had no such trip in mind and had never said he had. Ike made no comment; nobody asked him to, and even private comment at the Army-Navy Club was apt to get back to the general.

Although MacArthur and his bride seldom left their penthouse suite at the Manila Hotel, he seemed always to know what was said at the club. It was best to say nothing.

In a second interview, granted to newsmen soon after he got ashore, the general said a number of other foolish things: "The capacity of the Filipino officer and soldier, whether Regular, Reserve, or Trainee, to overcome difficulties, to absorb fundamentals of the military profession and to sustain a high morale and esprit while doing so, encourages a confidence in the successful outcome to the country's effort to prepare a respectable national defense."

This time Ike and Ord did feel they had to intervene. They took on the unpleasant task of telling the field marshal that most of the trainees were illiterate, that they had not even had toilet training, and that instead of absorbing "fundamentals of the military profession" the shoeless soldiers spent most of their time learning the fundamentals of public health. Not only did they not have shoes—they had almost no equipment, no tents, and no rifles. And they seemed singularly unable to "sustain a high morale and esprit." They wanted only to go back to their villages.

In his diary, Eisenhower noted that "with regard to the cadres the early inspections have been disappointing." He added, "In Southern Luzon conditions were found . . . to be very unsatisfactory. . . . The constant rains are, of course, partially responsible for this but many other defects were traceable to neglect on the part of the cadre officers and in some instances to distinct failure on the part of our Army Headquarters."

In July MacArthur sent Ord to Washington to try to do what he himself had failed to do, borrow or buy munitions from the War Department for the commonwealth.

One day while MacArthur and Quezon were in the States, Mamie decided to visit John at his school in Baguio. She had heard that the climate—at an altitude of 5,000 feet—was delightful, not unlike Denver. The city was only a two-hour plane ride from Manila, but Mamie was not flying after the narrow escape Ike had had in January. After John's New Year's vacation from Brent, on Sunday, January 3, 1937, his father and Lieutenant Lee flew him back to the school at Baguio. According to Lee, "We landed all right. . . . The field was built in a slope, but before taking off we had a—it says in my diary—fifty-minute debate. We could either take off downwind, downhill . . . or we could take off uphill and into the wind and have to clear a hump that was there. . . . We sat around in the airplane and talked and smoked. We were in a Bellanca, and those planes have big engines, 400 horsepower engines. I said, 'I think we can make it; there's just you and me but we've got over an hour of gasoline gone. I think we can make it.' He said, 'Well, you're the doctor, and if you think we can, let's go.'

"So we cranked it up and got it around and squared away and took off. Progress was slow going up that hill. . . . I wasn't picking up much speed to get over that hump, and to tell you frankly, I thought that was it.

"Ike was sitting there with his hands and arms across his chest, because he didn't have anyplace else to put them. I turned to him and I said, 'We ain't going to make it.' Just like that. And he just looked straight ahead.

"When I got up there I had nothing to do but try; so when I got up pretty close to the hill, I pulled back on the wheel, and we went over the hump.

"After we went over, I pushed that wheel forward as quick as I could, and I had picked up the speed. That's all I needed, flying speed, and as soon as I got it, I let the flaps up and we went on back.

"Ike said we didn't miss that hump more than a few inches. . . . I think we missed it a couple of feet. . . . But when we got back to the Army-Navy Club Ike bought a bottle of whiskey, and he handed it to me; he said, 'Here. You deserve this.' "

For her trip, Mamie hired a Filipino chauffeur to drive her on the 140-mile journey, most of it on a steep, one-way trail that seemed to go straight up at a ninety-degree angle. Carabaos pulling carts were everywhere on the road, as well as goats and pigs and children. In one mountain barrio, the car skidded and knocked over a young girl, who, while unharmed, was shaken by the accident. Mamie also appeared to be unharmed by the hazardous journey, but two days after she arrived in Baguio she was in the hospital, in a coma, her stomach hemorrhaging. The doctors said she was near death. Ike flew to her and stayed until the doctors assured him that she was out of danger.

The strain of working for MacArthur was beginning to take its toll on Ike. That year he had what doctors called a "partial stoppage" of the intestine. He continued to have such attacks for many years, and eventually an operation was necessary. By 1956, when surgery was performed, the partial stoppage was diagnosed as ileitis.

Mamie got back to Manila about the same time as MacArthur and Jean. Mamie was still weak, but she was able to go to a reception for the newlyweds. The two women liked each other at once, and they were very much alike— small, brunette women, devoted to their husbands and satisfied to be admiringly in the background. They often went shopping at the Philippine and Chinese markets in the morning. Mamie was by now used to the idea that rank has its privileges, but in visiting the ornate MacArthur penthouse suite she must surely have wondered from time to time if rank should be *that* privileged.

The MacArthurs didn't take much part in the social life of the city—too many movies; besides, Douglas was above all that. But according to Dorothy Brandon, "Of the approximately 5,000 Americans then living in Manila, not more than 500 persons—mostly married couples—had the requisite business, professional, and financial background to be acceptable as leaders of the dollar diplomacy."

The Eisenhowers were definitely near the top of those 500; at dinner parties, Mamie was usually seated next to Vice President Sergi Osmana of the commonwealth. But it was boring; always the same people, always the same discussions.

Journalist W. B. Courtney wrote of Manila social life, "Parties are wetter and held oftener; are bigger, showier, more lavish, and last longer, than in any other place in the world. Durability is required of guests."

When Jimmy Ord was in Washington in July 1937 doing what Eisenhower had wanted MacArthur to do, trying to raise money and obtain weapons for the almost invisible Philippine Army, Eisenhower wrote: "We have had recently a rush of social activity and I am exceedingly weary of it." And in another letter: "I have been swamped with work as you can well imagine. . . . To say nothing of the thousand and one details that come up in the office, I am pretty much on the run most of the time. On top of all this, we have had an unusual splurge of social activities, including formal dinners that it was impossible to duck."

A month before, MacArthur had had the pleasure of a visit from the agreeable Vice Admiral Mineichi Koga, commander of a Japanese naval squadron anchoring in Manila Bay, and the admiral gave a lavish party for the general on his flagship, *Iwate*. Such hospitality had, of course, to be returned, and Vice President Osmana and his charming wife gave a reception at the Manila Hotel for the admiral and officers of his staff. They were also entertained at the Army-Navy Club.

Eisenhower preferred to play bridge, and he played a lot of it in the Philippines. He was in fact known as "the bridge wizard of Manila." According to his son John, "He played a serious game. The bridge crowd played on the bottom floor of the hotel, and the stakes were a quarter of a cent a point. It was half a centavo. With his winnings, Dad gave me a beautiful camera which cost $34."

He often played both poker and bridge with Quezon, who was also considered an expert. Bridge and poker games, always stag affairs, often lasted all night in the presidential palace and on the presidential yacht. According to John, his father also played with Big Bill Tilden, reigning world tennis player, who was on a tennis tour. They played bridge in the Manila Hotel. As will be seen, Ike's winnings proved to be a significant financial crutch.

He continued playing bridge during the war, often with Al Gruenther, whom Alan Truscott, in his column "Bridge," described as "the bridge player among the generals and the 'general' among bridge players." After the war, Gruenther, in a letter to Charles Goren, a noted bridge expert and author of several books on bridge, said Ike was "a fine player. If he had the time to devote to it he would surely be classed as an expert. . . . His judgment is very sound, and he has real card sense."

When he was president of Columbia University, Eisenhower frequently played with friends on Monday evenings in his home at 60 Morningside Drive. Occasionally he played at the home of Douglas Black, president of Doubleday, publishers of *Crusade in Europe*, Ike's memoirs of the war. At the request of another Doubleday author, Somerset Maugham, Black arranged a game with Eisenhower. "They played right here in this apartment," Mrs. Douglas Black said. "I still have the score card. Willie [Maugham], when he was around here, he just wanted that. To play bridge with Ike. He was quite conceited and thought he played a fine bridge game, you know." However, after their first game, Ike commented to the Blacks, "He may be a great writer, but he sure as hell isn't much of a bridge player."

In 1950, when Ike was ordered to go to Paris as supreme commander of Allied forces in Europe, he took Al Gruenther as his deputy. "I'd like to take Beetle [Walter Bedell Smith]," he said, "but I think I'll take Al Gruenther. He's the best bridge player." In August of that year Gruenther had written to

Eisenhower describing a bridge hand in which he controlled his opponents' trump suit. In his reply, Ike said:

> On that particular occasion, you occupied the position that I constantly seek in a bridge game—that of ax-holder over an injudicious bidder. The only time I get a real feeling of frustration in bridge is when my partner, with such an opportunity, fails to take advantage of it.

When he returned from Europe to become president, Eisenhower found it necessary to find other partners, as Gruenther remained behind as head of NATO. In the frequent bridge games at the White House, particularly on Saturday nights, Chief Justice of the Supreme Court Fred Vinson was a regular, and occasionally world-class player Oswald Jacoby joined in.

As president, perhaps especially as president, he had the habit, according to James Hagerty, "of reviewing actions with people and expressing what he would have done in a similar situation, just like postmortem on a bridge hand." In early 1954, Lewis Strauss, chairman of the Atomic Energy Commission, held a press conference to discuss a new H-bomb which had enormous power but was miniaturized. According to James Hagerty, "In answer to questions, Strauss said H-bomb could 'knock out' any city, including New York City. On way down in elevator President said, 'Lewis, I wouldn't have answered that one that way, I would have said, "Wait for the move." But other than that I thought you handled it very well.' "

During the summer of 1937, Ike played a great deal of bridge, did a great many postmortems on his games, and surely reflected that for a man who would soon be forty-seven years old, things were not going well. There was almost daily trouble with MacArthur. For instance, as he wrote in his diary on July 9:

> Informed this morning by T.J. that the General called him in for a long talk. Subject was the General's readiness to dispense, at a moment's notice, with the services of any or all members of the mission. The occasion for the conversation was speculation on Ord's possible permanent [assignment] in U.S.—and the General's expressed irritation at what he termed the "conceit and self-centered" attitudes of various members of the mission. Said too many individuals were acting as if they were indispensable, and remarked that each was selfishly "looking out only for himself."
>
> It begins to look as if we were resented simply because we labor under the conviction . . . that someone ought to know what is going on in this army, and help them over the rough spots. However, from the beginning of this venture I've personally announced myself as ready and willing to go back to an assignment in U.S. Army at any moment. The General knows this if he knows anything, so I guess I don't have to make an issue of the matter by busting in and announcing it again.

That he was being considered by some Republicans as the party's presidential nominee in 1940 didn't seem to improve MacArthur's temper much that summer. Nor did it help his disposition when in August he received a shattering letter from the chief of staff, Malin Craig. It said, "Upon completion by you of two years of absence on foreign service you are to be brought home for duty in the United States. . . . There will be made available to you if practicable any command for which you express a preference."

The letter was polite enough, and MacArthur's reply was equally courteous. "I am naturally sorry to go. Particularly do I regret leaving unfinished a work which I regard as of transcendent importance. . . . I look forward with anticipation to whatever duty the War Department may have decided I should undertake in the service of my country."

Quezon was furious and sent Roosevelt a long cable but, as usual, where Quezon was concerned, nobody in Washington paid much attention.

On September 16, MacArthur, who had often thought of himself as the backbone of the U.S. Army, applied for retirement from that army. He gave a number of reasons, but the real one was that he could not possibly return to the States to take a lesser job than he had already had before coming to the Philippines. He was not about to serve as a corps commander under Craig; *he* had been chief of staff.

Roosevelt cannot have been surprised at MacArthur's retirement from active service, but when it took place, on December 31, the president said he had approved it "with great reluctance and deep regret." He thanked the general for his "outstanding service" to the country.

Meanwhile, in November MacArthur decided to continue as the Philippine military adviser. It was clear to everyone but him that the defense plan could not be carried out. Even he may have sensed it, however, because early in 1938 he decided that, since the Filipinos not only had no army but had very little bread, he would give them a circus—a big parade right through the main streets of Manila. The general was convinced, Ike said, that "the morale of the whole population would be enhanced if the people could see something of their emerging army in the capital city, Manila."

It meant bringing troops, if such a word could be used to describe such ill-trained and ill-equipped men, from ten districts to Manila. Just how they would be assembled and who would lead them in the triumphal march was uncertain. Although MacArthur had been retired from active service with the army, he was still head of the American advisory group. "I didn't like it," said Ike, "but it was an order, and Ord and I said, 'All right, we'll try to do it.' Jimmy and I estimated the cost. We told the General that it was impossible to do the thing within our budget. . . . But following the General's orders, we began to do the necessary staff work. . . .

"Among other details we had to arrange with island shipping firms to bring in the troops. It wasn't long until news of this reached the Philippine government. President Quezon called me in . . . [and] said he had heard about the planned troop movement, and asked me what it was all about.

"I was astonished. We had assumed that the project had first been agreed on between the President and General MacArthur." What happened when Quezon confronted MacArthur on what had been done behind his back and what had been planned involving his soldiers and his military budget is not known, but we do know that MacArthur defended himself by saying that he had never ordered the parade.

Ike said, "Here we were, we were flabbergasted, didn't know what to say. And finally, I said to him, I said, 'General, all you're saying is that I'm a liar, and I am *not* a liar, and so I'd like to go back to the United States right away.' Well, he came back . . . and he said, 'Ike, it's just fun to see that damn Dutch temper!'—he put his arm right over my shoulder—he said, 'It's just fun to see that Dutch temper take you over,' and he was just sweetness and light. He said, 'It's just a misunderstanding, and let's let it go at that.'

"Now, *that's* the time. From there on our relationships were never really close."

Lucius D. Clay, at the time a captain stationed at Fort McKinley, who later was to play so important a part in Eisenhower's military and political life, had another explanation for the coolness between Eisenhower and MacArthur. Clay said: "I was pretty cognizant of what happened. . . . A group of Filipino legislators felt that they could turn over the job of military adviser to Colonel Eisenhower and save a good deal of money. They were paying General MacArthur a much larger salary plus a very nice apartment on top of the hotel. . . . I know that General Eisenhower, then Colonel Eisenhower, had no part in this, and that he told those Filipino legislators that if they proceeded any further he would just have to ask to be sent home. However, this did come to General MacArthur's attention and I am sure that he just couldn't believe that this could have happened to him unless it had been instigated by Colonel Eisenhower. I think this is the real story of the rift."

There is no verification of Clay's surmise, but that there was a rift is certain. MacArthur's opinion of his subordinate never softened; he many years later called him "the apotheosis of mediocrity" and the "best clerk I ever had."

John Eisenhower said, "MacArthur was in very bad shape in those days [in the Philippines]. . . . He was living in a dream world. It sounded almost like the last days of Hitler, his impatience, his utter disregard of subordinates who had opinions different from his . . . the two younger officers [Eisenhower and Ord] believed that their chief had let them down and run for cover. It was important because it removed much of Dad's enthusiasm for his job. This zest was almost completely destroyed when shortly thereafter Jimmy Ord was killed in an airplane crash in the mountains of Baguio."

Eisenhower was in the hospital with another "partial stoppage" when Ord came to see him; that afternoon Ord was going to Baguio, and he mentioned that he was being flown by one of the Filipino student pilots. Ike, who flew only with American pilots, tried to dissuade him, but Ord "laughed and said, 'Our Filipino boys are doing very well. I'll use one of them. . . . See you late this afternoon.' "

His death was due not so much to the pilot's actions as to Ord's own rather childish attempt to drop a note from the air near the house of a friend. That did not make his death any less tragic, however; and Ike said, "Without my friend, all the zest was gone."

In September 1950, thirty-five years after their graduation from West Point, Eisenhower, in a message to their classmates, said, "Going back behind the days of World War II there was one classmate, Jimmy Ord, whose untimely death I shall always believe robbed our country of one of its most brilliant minds and potential leaders. He and I served intimately together for the two or more years just preceding his fatal accident. To his final day, he was the same vivid personality, the same keen thinker, the same witty entertainer that we knew so well in cadet days."

Ord was replaced by Lieutenant Colonel Richard Sutherland, who had been with the 15th Infantry in China. MacArthur was delighted with Sutherland; in the first place, his father was a U.S. senator from West Virginia. Frazier Hunt in his MacArthur biography said that Eisenhower and Sutherland "with their widely different military and family backgrounds developed certain cross-purposes. Sutherland gradually began to assume more and more power in the inner circle of the mission." Sutherland had graduated from Yale in 1916, been commissioned as a second lieutenant in the infantry, and served in the First World War. Shortly after he joined the mission, MacArthur wrote, "Sutherland has proven himself a real find. Concise, energetic and able, he has been invaluable in helping me clarify and crystalize the situation."

Sutherland's father was to become a Supreme Court justice; Clark Lee, the Associated Press correspondent in the islands, said the son was "brusque, short-tempered, autocratic, and of a generally antagonizing nature." Carlos P. Romulo, the Philippine leader, who was to become a close friend of Ike's both in the islands and later in the States, said that Sutherland was a "martinet."

In January 1942, when Ike was in the War Plans Division of the War Department in Washington, he received what he called a "most flamboyant radio[gram]" from MacArthur saying that in the event of the general's death, Sutherland should succeed him. That demonstrated, Ike said, that MacArthur "still likes his bootlickers."

Major General Charles Willoughby, whose opinions invariably reflected those of MacArthur, said of Sutherland, "Brittle in personality, aloof, a 'hard' man. Sutherland could not count on affection, but found associates who were willing to work with him on the basis of devotion to the 'old man.' " It is easy to understand why Eisenhower, not in Willoughby's sense a "hard" man, found the presence of Sutherland still another compelling reason to get out of the islands as quickly as possible. Sutherland stayed with MacArthur as his chief of staff during the Second World War, rising to major general.

Ike got away from the office as much as possible, often taking John with him. John said, "The Southern Islands were pretty much all the same—coconut trees, banana trees, and hard-working people on the sugar plantations. We saw the monument on Mactan Island where Ferdinand Magellan had been killed by the Philippine natives in 1521. We threw pennies to the divers in Zamboanga and saw the ramshackle tomb of the Sultan of Sulu."

There was one serious family problem that spring of 1938. On a trip to one of the outer islands with a friend, John was given a white cockatoo that he named Oswald.

"On docking in Manila, I took Dad aboard and introduced Oswald to him," John said. "Real outbursts of temper were rare with Dad—and he almost always recovered immediately—but when he did become angry it was spectacular. This time he outdid himself. 'There's nothing I hate worse than parrots and monkeys!' he roared. I thought this was a little illogical. . . .

"The incident created a temporary family crisis. Dad refused to sit in the same room with Oswald, but the door between our bedrooms was open. And every time Oswald said 'Agop,' I could see Dad wince, even from the rear." Agop was the only word in Oswald's vocabulary; John never found out what it meant. Eventually Mamie eased the crisis by finding a home for the bird with friends at Fort McKinley.

During this period, Ike, who had a private office in the Palace, spent a great deal of time with Quezon, and said, "President Quezon seemed to ask for my advice more and more. He invited me to his office frequently. This was partly because of the office hours General MacArthur liked to keep. He never reached his desk until eleven. After a late lunch hour, he went home again. This made it difficult for Quezon to get in touch with the General when he wanted him. Because I was the senior active duty officer, my friendship with the President became closer."

Quezon begged Ike to stay on. If he did not, the work already done would surely fail, and they would have wasted almost three years. Quezon, knowing Eisenhower very well, surely said that it was his duty to ask for a year's extension of his assignment. Ike, reluctantly, did. On March 3, 1938, the following radiogram was sent to the adjutant general in Washington:

UPON THE REQUEST OF THE PRESIDENT OF THE COMMONWEALTH LIEUT COL D D EISENHOWER HAS APPLIED FOR AN EXTENSION OF ONE YEAR OF HIS FOREIGN SERVICE TOUR . . . SPECIAL REQUEST FOR WAR DEPT APPROVAL IN THIS PARTICULAR CASE IN ORDER THAT COLONEL EISENHOWER MAY BE AVAILABLE TO CONTINUE THROUGH A CRITICAL STAGE IMPORTANT WORK IN CONNECTION WITH THE DEVELOPMENT OF EFFICIENT DEFENSE FORCES . . . MEDICAL EXAMINATION INDICATES OFFICER IS FIT FOR FURTHER TROPICAL SERVICE . . . IT HIGHLY DESIRABLE THAT COLONEL EISENHOWERS SERVICES BE CONTINUED AND SO RECOMMEND . . . REQUEST . . .

His tour of duty was extended from October 26, 1938, to October 26, 1939. That the extension had been a mistake was apparent almost from the beginning.

★ ★ ★

THE ELECTRIC TRAIN

In March 1938 Hitler annexed Austria, but the American colony in the Philippines took little notice. To Ike's dismay, when he and Mamie and John returned to the States that summer, they found that attitudes there were much the same. What was happening in Europe was deplorable but not the concern of Americans. Roosevelt did say that "our national defense is . . . inadequate for the purposes of national security and requires increase for that reason," and got the increase, too, $1.04 billion—the largest since the end of the First World War, but almost all the money went not to the army but to the navy; new battleships, aircraft carriers, and planes were to be built. The navy was, after all, the country's first line of defense.

The purpose of the trip to the U.S. was "to enable officer to familiarize himself with essential details in development of ordnance command aircraft and other technical materials needed by Philippine Army." The Philippine government was paying for the trip, and Ike himself hoped that he would be able to find someone somewhere in America who would be willing to help in the defense of the Philippines. Another purpose for the three-month home leave was that doctors in Manila had suggested that the stomach pains from which Mamie had been suffering almost since her arrival could be cured by a gallbladder operation. Naturally, she preferred to have it done in the States.

On June 26, the Eisenhowers boarded the S.S. *President Coolidge,* and Ike wrote in his diary, "Sailed from Manila on time, 5:00 P.M. Quarters 105–107. Sitting at Captain Ahim's table. Deposited with purser cash $360, traveler's checks, two packages, $3,000 and $1,010, also watch and chain."

They stopped first in Hong Kong. "Docked . . . at 8:00 A.M. Went to Repulse Bay Hotel. One large room for the three of us. Forty Mexican dollars per day. Exchange rate equals 3.20 Mexican dollars. Scheduled to leave here at 9:00 P.M. June 30."

In Shanghai, John said, "The economic situation was running wild . . . the exchange rate with the dollar in China had run out of all proportion. As a result, visitors such as our family could attend a luxurious movie, sitting in plush arm chairs for about four cents. A haircut cost between two and three cents."

Japanese officials in Yokohama were extremely arrogant toward most of the passengers, but, having been fully briefed on Ike's position in the Philippines, they were deferential with him, hoping no doubt to pick up a little information on what the mission was doing. Eisenhower was not helpful. He said, "I want nothing here; only to spend a few damned yen in your country."

At lunch that day most of the Americans on board the *Coolidge* were feeling very angry over the rude treatment the Japanese had given them, and when the band began playing "American Patrol" everybody in the ship's first-class dining room screamed and applauded. John said the passengers were "feeling superpatriotic."

On July 18 the ship arrived in San Francisco, and the Eisenhowers immediately went to Denver. Ike made several field trips, including one to Wichita, Kansas, to inspect what he called "airplane plants. . . . Arranged trip so as to cost government nothing except one-way trip from Abilene–Denver, making rest of trip by private plane.

"[Walter] Beech is confident his [Beechcraft] plane can be modified for military purposes. In fact he is now designing one for a South American government to use . . . somewhat bigger than present ship. Latest cost around fifty thousand dollars.

"Ample guns, etc. Speed 220, all other characteristics as to handling, etc., as good as present ship, of which eleven are in service. All reports good."

Ike went on several fishing trips, at least one with Aksel Nielsen, who said that Ike did not discuss his relations with MacArthur. "That was not his way. He did look awful, though; I'd seen him three years before, but I thought he looked ten years older in 1938, at least ten years older."

By August 22 Eisenhower was in Washington "to prevent adoption of policy that might limit our [the Philippine defense program] use of [United States] government property on loan basis." He went immediately to the War Department. "At first they were unsympathetic. As long as the Philippines insisted on being independent, the War Department's attitude was that they could jolly well look after their own defenses." So Eisenhower went to the top. In late August 1938 the top was the man MacArthur considered one of his worst enemies, Malin Craig, who in a year would be succeeded as chief of staff by a man MacArthur considered an even worse enemy, George C. Marshall.

Ike had no part in those quarrels; he told Craig that MacArthur was convinced, as was he, that "a friendly Philippines, with a government able to provide at least a delaying action in the event of an enemy invasion, was vital to U.S. interests." Craig agreed.

Eisenhower wrote MacArthur that he had "encountered nothing but the most sympathetic attitude toward your task and your plans, and have discovered that every official quickly sees eye to eye with us." He added that trips "such as this one are well worthwhile because personnel in the Department changes and indoctrination must therefore be intermittently continued." He added, "All the people I talked to in the War Department feel that you are making much more progress out there than they originally believed possible—they have become convinced that you're doing a worthwhile job, and in a fine way."

That was by no means true, but it would make MacArthur happy for a time, and Eisenhower had succeeded in doing what MacArthur and Ord had not done, persuaded not all but some men of power in Washington that the project in the Philippines, though difficult, maybe impossible, was at least worth a try.

He had succeeded in "begging or borrowing everything I could from the Signal, Quartermaster, Ordnance, and Medical Groups. I went to Wichita, bought several planes, then to Winchester Arms Company in Connecticut."

In his diary, he said, "Cost of New Haven trip. Receipts not available, except for Pullman seat. All tickets inter-urban type, collected and no receipt given. See certificate and statement of witness.

"We should carefully check net costs in ammunition from United States Ordnance and from Winchester, etc.

"Mr. Nelson says we paid more for .22 ammunition than his company would have charged us."

Mamie had by that time recovered from the gallbladder operation, and she went with Ike on the eastern trip, "but all expenses, of all kinds for her, were paid from personal funds, I habitually bought minimum accommodations for myself, no matter what I bought for her."

The stay in the United States included two trips to Abilene, the first in July when Ike stopped in Wichita, the second on September 8. On the second trip, his brother Earl was there. Earl said, "We were sitting with our parents in the patio trying to keep cool. Dad said he wished the floor had cement on it . . . he and mother liked to sit when the heat was bad in the house for here they could get some breeze.

"One of us spoke, I think it was Ike, and he said now was as good a time as any to get it done. We went up to town and purchased the necessary materials, mixing the concrete by hand in an old wheelbarrow. It was hard work, but we finally finished and stood back to admire our work. I turned to Ike and said that I supposed Edgar would now try to claim that he did this job. Without saying a word, Ike reached down and scratched . . . in [the] concrete:

1938

Sept. 8.

Dwight

Earl

Johnny

Boss—D. J. Eisenhower

"Ike said he didn't think Edgar could claim this job now."

After the hot job with the concrete, the Eisenhower men were tired and thirsty. As longtime observer of the Eisenhower family Earl Endacott said, "The mother made them a pitcher of iced tea. It seemed too weak to Earl, and he asked Ike if he didn't have something to liven it up. Ike said he just happened to have half a bottle of Philippine whiskey in his suitcase. They dumped it into the pitcher of tea and went to the front porch where the parents were.

"When they told the parents what they had done to the tea, the father jumped up mad and started for the front door, saying he was not going to stay out and have his neighbors see his sons drinking. The mother stayed with the boys, and they teased her into taking the drink. After taking a sip, she spit it out and said she couldn't see how they could drink such bad-tasting stuff.

"This shows the difference in the character of the parents. The mother, even though she didn't condone their drinking it, at least tasted it, while the father left the porch and remained sulking in the house."

John Eisenhower had still another memory of that short stay in Abilene in September 1938. "Earl was there, and we had a .22-caliber rifle and were target practicing with a target . . . up on the wall . . . of the chicken coop. Now, Earl had lived his whole life with one eye, and he didn't have to squint or anything like that.

"Dad was proud of being an expert rifleman, but Earl just shot circles around him, and Dad was furious. He was absolutely certain there was something wrong with his gun; so he went to the chicken coop . . . and put the damn gun in a vise and fired several rounds and all of them went right through the same hole.

"I've got pictures of that shooting episode in my album."

On October 10 Ike, Mamie, and John left Denver late in the afternoon, and in Tacoma they spent a day with Edgar. They probably had a lively discussion over what was happening in Europe; Edgar thought then, and he never changed his mind, that the United States should have nothing whatever to do with the squabbles over there. He thought that the army was a useless burden on tax-payers, and he thought that Roosevelt might be a Jew but certainly *was* a Communist.

In his diary Eisenhower said that he called on General Walter G. Sweeney at nearby Fort Lewis, adding that "Wayne [Mark] Clark is on the general staff there." Ike mentioned that he wanted to get away from the islands, and both Sweeney and his old friend from their days at West Point took note of that fact.

The Eisenhowers started their return voyage to the Philippines on October 13, sailing on the *Empress of Japan*. Eisenhower was disappointed that he could not get a stateroom with a private bath. It didn't matter to him, but he wanted Mamie to be comfortable. In a letter to T.J., he said, "This will be very severe on Mamie, as I imagine she will spend a considerable portion of her time in her stateroom."

They arrived back in Manila on November 5. Ike wrote, "Paid table steward $10.00 and Room Steward $10.00 as personal tips for voyage. . . . Both being Chinese made no attempt to secure receipts."

Ike thought their new suite in a recently completed annex to the Manila Hotel was too elegant, but Mamie loved it. It was air-conditioned, the French furniture was upholstered in brocade, the walls were paneled in damask, huge picture windows overlooked the bay, and the tiled bathroom had American plumbing. It was the kind of apartment in which the Eisenhowers could entertain, and they did. The guests at times included the new high commissioner, Paul V. McNutt, and his wife, Mary. McNutt told everybody that he planned to become president of the United States early in 1941, and there seemed no reason to doubt it. He looked more like a president than any candidate since Warren G. Harding. He talked like a president, too, saying very little in a baritone voice. He told Eisenhower and Mamie that as soon as possible after he moved into the White House, he would take care of Ike.

Of more immediate interest to Eisenhower was the fact that McNutt no longer thought that flying the American flag over the islands was all that was needed for their defense. He wanted a lot more money for the Philippine defenses, and he said so. What he said made headlines in the islands' newspapers, but most members of Congress were not much interested. Most of them felt that an army of 118,000 officers and men was large enough, perhaps too large. Maybe as president McNutt could do something about that.

In the meantime, it was apparent that Quezon had completely lost faith in MacArthur's ability to defend the islands. When Eisenhower was in the States, Quezon had made what was to have been a secret trip to Japan, secret even from MacArthur. But newspaper stories appeared saying that the president of the Philippines was trying to get a Japanese promise to respect the neutrality of the islands after they became independent. That, Quezon said, must be in 1940, not 1946.

Even in Manila Quezon said that what the mission was doing was useless. He told a large audience in Rigal Stadium: "The Philippines could not be defended even if the last Filipino were armed with modern weapons."

MacArthur paid little if any attention to such reality; he was spending even less time at the office these days. In February 1938 a son had been born, and the general, then sixty, spent a good deal of time with young Arthur MacArthur IV. From the day the boy was born, his father said that young Arthur would carry on the family tradition and go to West Point. Actually, Arthur did not;

after his father's death in 1964 he moved out of Waldorf Towers, changed his name, and moved into the East Village of Manhattan.

The Jewish Relief Committee of Manila had been organized after Hitler became chancellor of Germany. Ike said, "The Nazis were in the saddle and riding hard in central Europe. Among other things, they were persecuting unmercifully, and many of the Jewish faith were fleeing Germany, trying to find homes elsewhere in the world. In Manila, arguments started between those people who for some strange reason were supporters of Hitler, and the rest of us. It was difficult to keep arguments, even . . . at the Army-Navy Club, under control. The Philippines had undergone four hundred years of domination by Spain. The results were mixed. Almost without exception, though, the Spanish community was on Hitler's side, partly because they believed that Hitler supported the Franco government to which most of them gave their support. There was a considerable Jewish population in the city and I had good friends among them."

In her book, *Jews in Remote Corners of the World,* published in 1966, Ida Cowan said that in the 1930s the Philippine government "permitted European Jews having the required skills as teachers, professors, doctors, and lawyers to enter on a selective basis. In addition, temporary visas for two-year residence were granted others. Some of the immigrants on these visas started life anew in the Pacific as peddlers."

Many years after the war, Ike told Maxwell Abbell, president of the United Synagogue of America, "I grew up believing that the Jews were the chosen people, that they gave us the high ethical and moral principles of our civilization." He added that he and his brothers had been taught from the Old Testament.

When Ike was in London in 1942 as commander in chief, Milton, then president of Penn State, wrote him, "I was at a cocktail party . . . in Washington given by one of those real old dowagers. She said very nicely to me, 'You must come from a very nice family, young man. You have an important job here, and your brother is leading our troops abroad and I understand another brother is a banker. What a pity it is that you are Jewish.' I looked at her, sighed unhappily, and said, 'Ah, Madame, what a pity it is that we are not.' "

One thing is certain. Eisenhower did not repeat the anti-Semitic jokes that were so popular at the Army-Navy Club, and since everybody in the colony knew everything about everybody else that fact reached Manila's Jewish community.

In the late fall of 1938 the president of the Jewish Relief Committee of Manila, Alexander Frieder, along with others in the committee, came to Ike with a most unusual offer. He was asked to travel to Indonesia, Indochina, China, and anywhere else in Asia to find places where the refugees from Germany might find a home. He would be paid $60,000 a year with a liberal expense account. The salary for the first five years would be put in escrow and given to him if for any reason he had to give up the job.

Ike said, "The offer was, of course, appealing for several reasons. But this time, I had become so committed to my profession that I declined. . . . I became certain that the conflict General Conner had . . . predicted fifteen years earlier was likely to break out."

The fact that he had turned down such an appealing job offer did not mean that he was any happier in Manila; he was now almost fifty, an old man from his point of view, and it looked as if he might retire as a lieutenant colonel. But surely he did not have to spend his last days in the army working with men like MacArthur and Sutherland.

Many of the frustrations he felt were recorded in his diary, but it is significant that as this is written, more than forty-six years later, certain pages of the diary have not been released by John, his father's literary executor. It is impossible to believe that the pages have to do with security matters. He *never* recorded security information. Those pages almost certainly have to do with Eisenhower's frustrations, with his feelings about MacArthur. When asked about the missing pages, John said rather sharply, "I don't feel I owe opening those pages to the American public."

Ike continued in his campaign to get a transfer back to the States, and MacArthur continued to try to persuade him to stay on. The general said that as a mere lieutenant colonel in the army, Eisenhower would not be able to get an assignment even half as good as the one he had in Manila. When Eisenhower pointed out that to get a promotion to full colonel he had to have an assignment with troops, MacArthur appeared not to hear. And when, for example, in September 1936, Major General William D. Connor, Eisenhower's friend and supporter from the War College and now superintendent of West Point, asked that Eisenhower be transferred, presumably to the Point, MacArthur immediately replied:

SPECIAL CIRCUMSTANCES HERE MAKE IT IMPOSSIBLE TO CONSIDER OFFICER MENTIONED FOR ANY CHANGE OF DUTY . . . THANKS FOR CONSULTING ME.

In January 1937, when the adjutant general made the same request, Mac-Arthur's answer was:

COLONEL EISENHOWER DOES NOT DESIRE DETAIL OF COMMANDANT OF CA-DETS . . . I WOULD HAVE MOST SERIOUS OBJECTIONS TO HIS RELIEF FROM HIS PRESENT ASSIGNMENT . . . HE IS PERFORMING DUTY ANALOGOUS TO A CHIEF OF STAFF OF MY HEADQUARTERS . . . THE DUTY IS OF THE GRAVEST IMPOR-TANCE AND REQUIRES IN ADDITION TO GENERAL PROFESSIONAL QUALIFICA-TIONS SPECIALIZED KNOWLEDGE OF LOCAL DETAIL . . . HE COULD NOT ADEQUATELY BE REPLACED.

It seems unlikely that Eisenhower wanted ever to be commandant of West Point, a lackluster and thankless job hardly appropriate for an ambitious officer, and, indeed, later Eisenhower turned the job down; but MacArthur refused without consulting him. MacArthur was a firm believer in not burdening a subordinate officer with information that might make him reckless or dissatisfied with his service of MacArthur.

In the last eighteen years, Ike had had only six months of troop duty, and unless he could be assigned to troops he would spend the war that was coming behind a desk somewhere, a tired, forgotten, probably overweight lieutenant colonel, a regular army officer who had missed two wars. Of course, if he lived to be sixty and stayed in the army, he would automatically become a full colonel, a chicken colonel, no doubt a desk jockey.

However, he wanted at least to be a colonel who had served time with troops, and although it was not something he discussed with MacArthur, Ike had every intention of being transferred to Fort Lewis in the state of Washington. His visit there the previous year had convinced him it was the place to be. So, lest his old friend Mark Clark let the matter of transfer slip his mind, Eisenhower sent him a Christmas card. Clark replied, "It was certainly a pleasure to see you recently. I have kept track of the fine jobs you have had throughout your service and expect to see you reach the top."

Eisenhower cannot have been too surprised, therefore, when on May 24, 1939, he received orders from the War Department saying that he was "assigned to the 15th Infantry with station at Fort Lewis, Washington; upon completion of his present tour of foreign service, will join that station and report for duty, in accordance with orders to be issued by the commanding general, Philippine Department." That officer was not MacArthur. It was Major General W. S. Grant.

When he recorded his recollections of his last months in the Philippines, Eisenhower chose not to remember that he had been ordered in May to return to the States after his tour of duty ended on October 26, 1939. He said both in *Crusade in Europe,* written in 1947, and *At Ease,* published in 1967, that he asked for permission to return to the States *after* the war began. It is more dramatic that way, but it is not true. From May 24 on, there was no question that Eisenhower would return to the States and to Fort Lewis.

The next day, Eisenhower wrote Clark that his new assignment made him feel "like a boy who has been promised an electric train for Christmas." He asked about living quarters on the post and about a school for John. Clark, who had helped arrange the assignment, replied that both he and Sweeney were delighted. He sent pictures of the post and added, "When you arrive, please know that Mrs. Clark and I want to take care of you and the family until you get settled."

In subsequent letters, Clark told Eisenhower the best way to ship a car from San Francisco to Fort Lewis and, no doubt with Maurine Clark's help, he sent on the number of windows in the house the Eisenhowers would occupy and the sizes of those windows. That was so that Mamie could buy material for the curtains in the Philippines, where everything was cheaper.

Originally, the Eisenhowers were to have returned to the States by army transport but, with the comfort of Mamie once more in his mind, Eisenhower asked that his tour of duty be extended a few weeks so that they could travel by commercial liner. That request was granted on August 1.

The war that Fox Conner had predicted began at daybreak on September 1. Eisenhower later said, "That summer the Germans were massing against the Polish frontiers 60 infantry divisions, 14 mechanized and motorized divisions and armored cars. To oppose them the Poles could mobilize less than a third that strength in all categories. Their force was doomed to quick destruction under the fury and weight of the German assault. But the Polish Army, easy victim though it was to Hitler's war machine, far surpassed the United States Army in numbers of men and pieces of equipment. . . .

"The American people still believed that distance provided adequate insulation between us and any conflict in Europe or Asia. Comparatively few understood the direct relationship between American prosperity and physical safety on the one hand, and on the other the existence of a free world beyond our shores. Consequently, the only Americans who thought about preparation for war were a few professionals in the armed services and those far-seeing statesmen who understood that American isolation from any major conflict was now completely impossible."

Eisenhower did not then or for some time in the future know the awful dimensions of what was happening in Germany, but from the beginning, the war against the Nazis was a crusade; it was a battle of good against evil, white against black. It was an Old Testament war led by an Old Testament man.

He agreed completely with the man who was to be a close friend and who was often to keep him up late, Winston Spencer Churchill, who after he became prime minister said, "Victory at all costs, victory in spite of terror, victory, however long and hard the road may be, for without victory there is no survival."

On September 3 Prime Minister Neville Chamberlain told Britain and radio listeners all over the world, "This morning the British ambassador in Berlin handed the German government a final note stating that, unless we heard from them by 11 o'clock that they were prepared at once to withdraw their troops from Poland, a state of war would exist between us. I have to tell you now that no such undertaking has been received, and that consequently this country is at war with Germany."

Ike heard the announcement "over an antiquated radio that, under favorable conditions, pulled in transoceanic messages." The radio was in the home of a friend, Colonel Howard Smith, a member of the Public Health Service in Manila. Australia, New Zealand, and France also declared war against Germany that day, and Chamberlain formed a War Cabinet, making Churchill First Lord of the Admiralty.

The night he learned Europe had gone to war, Eisenhower summed up his thoughts on the matter in a letter he wrote to Milton:

This evening we have been listening to broadcasts of Chamberlain's speech stating that Great Britain was at war with Germany. After months and months of feverish effort to appease and placate the man that is governing Germany, the British and French seem to be driven into a corner out of which they can work their way only by fighting. It's a sad day for Europe and for the whole civilized world—though for a long time it has seemed ridiculous to refer to the world as civilized.

If the war that now seems to be upon us, is as long and disastrous, as bloody and as costly as was the so-called World War, then I believe that the remnants of nations emerging from it will be scarcely recognizable as the ones that entered it. Communism and anarchy are apt to spread rapidly, while crime and disorder, loss of personal liberties, and abject poverty will curse the areas that witness any amount of fighting. It doesn't seem possible that people that proudly refer to themselves as intelligent could let the situation come about. Hundreds of millions will suffer privations and starvation, millions will be killed and wounded, because one man so wills it . . . the absolute ruler of eighty-nine million people. And by his personal magnetism, which he must have, he has converted a large proportion of those millions to his insane schemes and blind acceptance of his leadership. Unless he is successful in overcoming the whole world by brute force, the final result will be that Germany will have to be dismembered.

For a long time after the war began, it didn't look like much of a war. It was, people said, "a phoney war," a "sitzkrieg." Ike found that it "completely bewildered" him. In an October letter to his friend Gee Gerow he said:

For the moment it appears that the struggle is economic in nature. The Allies apparently believe that with control of the seas they will finally force Germany, in spite of her access to all southeast Europe and Russia, to break down. Certainly it seems obvious that neither side desires to undertake attacks against heavily fortified lines. If fortification, with modern weapons, has given to the defensive form of combat such a terrific advantage over the offensive, we've swung back to the late middle ages, when any army in a fortified camp was perfectly safe from molestation. If we assume that no violations of the flanking neutrals will occur, and further that in the air, as on the ground, virtual stagnation is to occur, what, will you tell me, is the answer.

On November 30 what appeared to be a real enough war broke out. Russian troops invaded Finland, and Russian planes bombed Helsinki. The gallant little democracy that had been created by the Allies after the Great War and had regularly paid its war debt, immediately earned everybody's sympathy. Roosevelt compared the Russian attack to the "dreadful rape of Poland" and deplored "this new resort to military force."

Meanwhile, the Eisenhowers were planning to leave the Philippines on December 13. MacArthur continued to urge Ike to remain under his command, and Quezon was even more anxious that he stay. By that time, the Philippine president had almost no relationship with MacArthur. Most of the time, if MacArthur wanted to see him, Quezon said he was too busy. One time the angry MacArthur told one of Quezon's assistants, "Jorge, some day your boss is going to want to see me more than I want to see him."

If Eisenhower left the islands, that would mean Quezon had no American he felt he knew and could trust in Manila. Ike said that, during this period before he left, the Philippine president told him, "We'll tear up the old contract. I've already signed this one and it is filled in—except what you want as your emoluments for remaining. You will write that in."

That offer was so alluring that Ike felt he had to discuss it with Mamie and John. John said, "For practically the only time in my recollection we held a family council, called without a doubt, to enable Dad to clarify his own thoughts. I could tell from our conversation that Dad's mind was already made up. 'The only reason left for me to stay in this place,' he said as he paced the floor of our living room, 'is the extra money the Philippine government is giving me. Other than that, there's not much to keep me here.' " Mamie, of course, wanted to go; she hated the tropical islands; John did not. "I wanted to finish school at Brent. . . . It took little time for Dad to decide to ask for relief from duty with MacArthur and return to the States."

He told Quezon that no amount of money would cause him to change his mind. "My entire life has been given to this one thing, my country and my profession," he said. "I want to be there if what I fear is going to come about actually happens."

Ike said that Quezon "finally accepted my decision and before long we had a beautiful farewell luncheon in the Malacañan Palace overlooking the river that flowed past." There were about 150 army, navy, and civilian friends of the Eisenhowers at the luncheon. Quezon presented Ike with the Distinguished Service Star of the Philippine government "for services of extraordinary value to the Commonwealth." In his presentation, Quezon said, "Among Ike's outstanding qualities the quality I regard most highly is this: whenever I asked Ike for an opinion I got an answer. It may not have been what I wanted to hear, it may have displeased me, but it was always a straightforward and honest answer."

MacArthur's farewell letter said that he regretted the end of Eisenhower's four-year tour of "distinguished and invaluable services in assisting in the initial development of the defense plan." His contributions to building the nonexistent army had been "stamped indelibly at all times with superior professional ability, unswerving loyalty and unselfish devotion to duty . . . sound judgment and unflagging enthusiasm have contributed greatly to the monumental progress thus far attained."

It was a typical MacArthur letter, flowery and not very accurate. Eisenhower's enthusiasm had been far from unflagging a good deal of the time, and it is certain that he did not feel that progress on the Philippine defense army had been "monumental."

He may have felt that the whole thing didn't matter much. He later said that at the time he was leaving the Philippines, "I was certain that the United States had been drawn into the whirlpool of the war, but I was mistaken as to the manner of our entry. I assumed that Japan would make no move against us until after we were committed to the European war. Moreover, I was wrong as to the time. It seemed to me that we would be compelled to defend ourselves against the Axis within a year of the war's outbreak."

On the morning of December 13, the general and Jean MacArthur came to the Eisenhowers' stateroom to see them off, bringing with them a going-away bottle of whiskey, which John felt was Mrs. MacArthur's idea. Nevertheless, John said, the fact that the general was there at all "was uncommon for this normally thoughtless and egocentric man." John said that his father and MacArthur "still held a sort of peculiar mutual admiration, despite their differences."

In their last meeting for more than six years, the two men did not talk of Japan's increasing threat to the Pacific. Eisenhower said that they spoke of "the gloominess of world prospects, but our foreboding turned toward Europe—not Asia."

A year later Eisenhower wrote MacArthur from Fort Lewis where he was commander of the 3d Infantry Division, "So far as the U.S. is concerned, the guns . . . are not yet roaring. But how long they can keep silent remains more of a guess, it seems to me, with every day that passes. Once they really open up, I'll expect to see you in the middle of it."

Much of what Eisenhower had done in the Philippines had been boring, much of it maddening, depressing, and useless, but a good part of what he had learned proved valuable to the Allied cause and to himself. It was what he knew about the Philippines that caused him to be asked to come to Washington a little less than two years later.

Major General W. S. Grant, Commanding Officer, Philippine Department, said of Eisenhower: "An admirable officer in every respect; possesses extraordinary literary ability; performing duties which in scope and responsibility are comparable to those of an Assistant Chief of Staff of the War Department General Staff; recommended for General rank in time of war."

Eisenhower said about leaving the islands, "For me, the next six years would be thronged with challenges and chances, work and decisions, for which all my life I had been preparing."

★ ★ ★

WAR GAMES

When the Eisenhowers returned to the States in 1939 they stopped in Tokyo and found the Japanese to be a pleasant and agreeable people. That had been true in the Philippines, where Japanese immigrants were arriving in ever-increasing numbers, many of them with cameras. They seemed to take pictures of everything, especially on beaches and around military installations. They worked hard; they smiled incessantly, and they were forever asking questions. They often made notes on what they saw and were told.

On the trip the Eisenhowers made across the Pacific in 1938, the Japanese they met were equally obliging and inquisitive. For example, in Yokohama a number of natives volunteered their services in helping the Eisenhowers find bargains in the shops and serving as guides. One such volunteer made a mistake; according to John, he "indicated a knowledge of Dad's background. So we knew we were being followed." In Kobe a taxi driver, without extra charge, took the lieutenant colonel, his wife, and son through a rainstorm that was accompanied by landslides, "to reach the places we wanted to go. Dad had no objection to these services on the part of the Japanese Government. They were convenient and he in truth had no espionage in mind."

Immediately after they had gone through customs in Tokyo, "apparently by pure chance," said Eisenhower, a young Japanese who had recently graduated from an American university appeared and introduced himself. He was, he said, an assistant postmaster, and he added that friends had told him about Eisenhower's work in the Philippines. He was most interested in Eisenhower's "impressions of the Filipino people." The young assistant postmaster served as a guide for the Eisenhowers, helped them find bargains in the shops in Tokyo, "and in a dozen ways made himself agreeable and helpful." He spoke of his hope for lasting friendship between Japan and the United States, "for which," Eisenhower said, "he professed great admiration and affection. . . .

"He seemed to have unlimited time to devote to us, and I assumed that he made it a practice to meet and talk with visiting Americans, possibly in nostalgic memory of his student days. Some weeks later, however, when I mentioned him to others who had passed through Japan shortly before or after that period, I found no one who had met him or any other government official." Eisenhower had felt, he said, that "there was nothing unusual about a transitory visit from another lieutenant colonel." However, the Japanese had a highly sophisticated intelligence system. The United States had almost none.

Eisenhower learned first hand how inadequate American intelligence was a little more than two years after his return to the States from the Philippines, when he was called to Washington by Marshall and shortly thereafter became chief of the newly reorganized War Department Operations Division, the OPD. In that position he discovered what he called "a shocking deficiency that impeded all constructive planning existed in the field of Intelligence. . . . Our one feeble gesture in this direction was the maintenance of military attachés in most foreign capitals, and since public funds were not available to meet the unusual expenses of this type of duty, only officers with independent means could normally be detailed to these posts. Usually they were estimable, socially acceptable gentlemen; few knew the essentials of Intelligence work. . . .

"In the first winter of the war these accumulated and glaring deficiencies were serious handicaps. . . . The chief of the division could do little more than come to the planning and operating sections of the staff and in a rather pitiful way ask if there was anything he could do for us."

One intelligence officer—Eisenhower called him "one of our better attachés"—came to Washington to report in essence that continuing the war was useless. The Allies could not possibly win. The Germans had 40,000 combat planes in reserve, all with trained crews, waiting to go into action. There were also enough reserve army divisions to sustain a completely successful invasion of the British Isles. Eisenhower and his staff in the OPD did not believe the report; the German army had just been stopped before Moscow, and none of the reserve of "40,000 combat planes" had been used, although, Eisenhower said, their "employment would have insured the destruction and capture of such an important objective as Moscow."

It was clear that something had to be done and done fast about American intelligence, and it was, but it took time. The British, unlike the Americans, had not looked upon spying activity "with repugnance," and "in the early days of the war the British were able to supply us, out of their prior war experience, much vital information concerning the enemy," Ike said.

On his trip back to the United States from the Philippines in 1939, Eisenhower tried to relax, but he was not successful. John said, "In the mornings he would sit and watch the sea, but in the afternoons he was up on the bridge learning from the captain how to navigate a ship. . . . He was slightly impatient with me because I was willing to watch the sea all day long. Dad's general interest in everything was remarkable to me, who am inclined to be easygoing." Eisenhower also wrote a lengthy report for Quezon on how to defend the Philippines in the unlikely event that the islands were invaded by anybody. As his friend Aksel Nielsen said, "He called his autobiography *At Ease,* but he was never really at ease; he tried to relax, but I don't think he ever succeeded."

In 1954, when Eisenhower was president, Joseph A. Loftus, then White House correspondent for the *New York Times,* said that "Eisenhower is most at ease when his physical being is on the move—at least his hands. This he acknowledged to newsmen when they asked him how Mrs. Eisenhower liked his televised speech to the nation. 'Mrs. Ike gave me a good report,' he allowed, 'but she said I moved around too much. She said, "Can't you ever keep still?"' 'You know,' he added thoughtfully, 'Mamie is right. I never am still, physically. I always have to move around. I've always been that way.' "

Eisenhower arrived back in San Francisco with Mamie and John on January 16, 1940. He was glad to be back in the States after so many years in what he must have felt was exile. He was no longer under the uncomfortable, at times almost unbearable command of a general who had ignored his every request for a transfer, who had berated, denigrated, and humiliated him, both publicly and privately. It would also be good to be away from the bigoted minds of most of the members of the Army-Navy Club. It would be good to be out of the tropics; he would welcome the changing seasons of Fort Lewis.

The first order Eisenhower got when he reached San Francisco was not encouraging. There had been an emergency change in his orders, and instead of going to Fort Lewis for troop duty, he was placed on detached service. He was to stay behind and make plans to bring all the troops of the IX Corps Area, under the command of Lieutenant General John L. DeWitt, to California for special training. Eisenhower explained to DeWitt his anxiety to be with troops; the general said he understood and, unlike MacArthur, he lived up to his word.

Eisenhower and Mamie took an apartment, and John went to stay with Edgar in Tacoma until his mother and father got settled at Fort Lewis. While he was in San Francisco, a city he liked, Eisenhower ran into an old friend, Colonel James Byrom, West Point 1914, who had been at Fort Sam the day in 1915 when Ike first met Mamie. Byrom, who was to go to the Philippines shortly, thought Eisenhower looked thin and tired, and said so.

Eisenhower immediately registered that bringing all the IX Corps troops to California would take so long that some of them, the members of the National Guard from Minnesota, for example, would arrive in time only to get back on the train to go home. Eisenhower suggested to the colonel in charge of the operation that there ought to be two mobilization points for the troops, one nearer the outskirts of the corps area. The colonel was, Eisenhower said, "a stickler for orders." He said, "There will be no shift from the specifications given us."

The colonel also forbade Eisenhower to discuss the matter with DeWitt, but a few days later Eisenhower saw the general.

DeWitt was inspecting an army field exercise on a beach in southern California, and the new army chief of staff was with him. George C. Marshall, who had been stationed in the Philippines in 1902 and 1903, remembering the abundance of servants available to army officers in the islands, said to Ike, "Have you learned to tie your own shoes again since coming back, Eisenhower?" Ike grinned and said, "Yes, sir, I am capable of that chore anyhow."

That was the second time the two men had met, the first having been ten years earlier in the offices of the Battlefield Monuments Commission in Washington, but Marshall asked no questions about Eisenhower's experiences in the Philippines; he gave no indication that the lieutenant colonel's name was in his little black book as one of the officers he considered promising.

DeWitt took Eisenhower aside and said, "How're you getting along with the planning?" Ike ignored the colonel's orders and deftly explained the problems. "I told him about the difficulty in transportation but said we were carrying out the plans as ordered.

"He said, in mixed surprise and annoyance, 'If this is true, why haven't you been in to see me?'

" 'Because the colonel said I shouldn't bother you. He said he would straighten it out.' "

DeWitt straightened the colonel out, and Eisenhower drew up his plan for two concentrations of troops. "I completed the work in a few days.

"Then I was free to go up to Fort Lewis."

On February 2 Eisenhower went to Camp Ord, California, where he joined the 15th Infantry as its executive officer and, better yet from his point of view, as commander of its First Battalion. The 15th was considered one of the best if not *the* best regiment in the U.S. Army. Many of its members were veterans of a long stay in Tientsin, China; it had once been commanded there by Marshall, and the Chief of Staff of the Army would certainly be interested in the officers of his old regiment, including Ike. Besides, the 15th was part of the 3d Division, "The Fighting 3d," which in the First World War had been known as the "Rock of the Marne." There were many who thought that the 3d had outfought and outsoldiered MacArthur's gaudier Rainbow Division, an idea that could not have displeased Eisenhower.

The regiment was on maneuvers, appropriately called "war games," and when the games were over, the 15th and Eisenhower went north to Fort Lewis. "After eight years of desk and staff duty in the rarefied atmosphere of military planning and pleading, I was again in daily contact with the two fundamental elements of military effort—men and weapons," Eisenhower said. "In case of war such outfits would be the bulwark of American defense and the spearhead of our retaliation, should there be a sudden attack on us. . . . There was unlimited opportunity for men and officers to prove their professional worth."

One of the first things Eisenhower discovered after his arrival at Fort Lewis was that his battalion was undermanned, underequipped, and there was a shortage in housing. Congress was not about to pass legislation making up those shortages. Early in 1940 the army had asked for 166 planes; it got 57, and there were no four-engine bombers among them. Congress decided that such planes would be considered "aggressive weapons." The total strength of the U.S. Army at the time was 241,612 officers and men. Later in the spring, however, the army moved up a notch. It became the 19th largest in the world.

Despite the shortage in housing, the Eisenhower quarters at Fort Lewis were in every way the best they had had since their marriage. The house had a long front hall with a dining room on one side and a living room on the other. Beyond the living room was a glassed-in front porch. The kitchen was large, and had the Eisenhowers had a butler, there was a pantry for his use, plus a servants' room and a servants' bath. Upstairs were a master bedroom, two other bedrooms, a sleeping porch, and two baths. The Eisenhowers had sent for their furniture, which had been stored in Pennsylvania and Washington, D.C., and it arrived before they did.

Almost all the officers on the post were against the New Deal, but many of them, including the Eisenhowers, lived in houses built by the Public Works Administration, created by FDR. Eisenhower was never a New Dealer, but he was, as his son, John, said, "charitable toward much of what Roosevelt was trying to do." His brother Edgar, as John said, considered President Roosevelt "a work of the devil."

Ike and Edgar were still competitive, even in the matter of John's future. When John was staying with his uncle in Tacoma, Edgar discovered that his younger brother's son had a "legal" mind. He told John that he should not become "a professional killer," meaning a soldier, like his father.

Instead, Edgar said, John should become a lawyer, and if he did so decide, Uncle Ed would pay his way through a college of his choice for four years, plus an additional three years of law school. Then, if John joined Edgar's law firm, he would pay him twice what he would have earned as a "professional killer" at any comparable stage of John's career"—until you're earning more. Then, you're on your own."

Eisenhower wanted his son to go to West Point and be a soldier, but he at least went through the motions of letting the young man decide for himself. He pointed out what John already knew, that his father had been a commissioned officer for twenty-five years and was only a lieutenant colonel; that he had attended all the schools the army had to offer and had done well in all of them, graduating at the top of his class in the most important, the Command and General Staff School; that his ratings had all been what Eisenhower called "satisfactory," but which John was surely aware were almost all superior—and none of that had mattered at all so far as advancing his career was concerned. Until you became a full colonel in the army in those days, all promotions were only on the basis of seniority.

Eisenhower said, "John must have wondered why I stayed in the Army at all. To give him the less gloomy side of the picture, I said that my Army experience had been wonderfully interesting, and it had brought me into contact with men of ability, honor, and a sense of high dedication to their country. . . . My ambition in the Army was to make everybody I worked for regretful when I was ordered to other duty.

"John listened seriously and promised to think it over."

In the end, John decided to go to West Point. When he broke the news to his uncle, he said, "I can argue with you, Ed, and love it. But I could never work for you." John said in his book *Strictly Personal*, "Despite the fact that I sometimes wondered about this decision in later years, I believe it was right, as Ed and I always remained warm friends."

Shortly after his arrival at Fort Lewis, Eisenhower and the rest of the "short" 3d Division went down to Monterey, California, for "extended maneuvers."

"Through the day, like everyone else on maneuvers, I sweated and accumulated a grime of caked dust," Eisenhower said. "At night we froze. Never in any one stretch did I have more than two hours' sleep." He wrote his old friend Courtney Hodges, who had just become a brigadier general, that he had been "having a grand time."

John, who joined his father in the field, said Eisenhower loved everything about being assigned to troops and was "ecstatic." John said he used the extra cot in his father's wall tent, and that the two of them "witnessed the beginnings of a growing army—new tanks, the new 81-mm mortar, and night firing by machine guns, using tracer ammunition." At mess one night, John said that he "sat down at the end of the table next to a couple of lieutenants who were on the receiving end of Dad's relaxed but peremptory orders.

"One day a demonstration of the 81-mm mortar had been conducted by a Lieutenant White. White had spent hours adjusting his weapons with great results. After the appropriate accolades, the Old Man had said, 'Now Lieutenant White will move the mortars three hundred yards to the rear and fire again.' The result had been a disaster. Lieutenant White groused all through the evening meal about the affair, seeming, apparently, to hold me somehow partially responsible. I viewed his problems with a certain detachment."

The three-day exercise went off well enough, but it proved very little. The officers and men were neither trained nor equipped in any way for the Second World War; they really were not ready to have done battle in the First. If what he was doing was, compared to what was happening in Europe, unrealistic, that fact did not bother Eisenhower; it seems not even to have occurred to him.

At least Eisenhower was satisfied with his poker games while in the field. Mark Clark said that Major General Sweeney, the commander of the 3d Division, was "a lovable, crap-shooting, wild Irishman who liked to play poker and have parties. He didn't much bother with military matters. I was the plans and operations officer and had done most of the work in planning the details of the maneuvers.

"Another of my duties was to line up players for Sweeney's poker games; he played every night, and he always insisted that there be at least six people. The stakes were rather modest; you could lose at most maybe forty or fifty bucks a night. The game would start immediately after mess, about seven o'clock, and Sweeney had an alarm clock he set for midnight. He didn't want any strangers in the game, but one night a couple of officers had gone into Monterey, officers who usually played, and there simply weren't enough players. Now Sweeney had met Eisenhower the year before and had met him and watched him since he arrived at Fort Lewis, but he didn't know anything about Ike's poker playing. So I told Sweeney that Eisenhower had got back from the Philippines with a pocket full of money, and I suggested that he join the game. Sweeney agreed. He said, 'Have him here by seven o'clock.' ''

That was a statement Sweeney was to regret, because when the game ended at midnight Eisenhower not only had all the money he had brought, he had $50 more, much of it Sweeney's. Clark said, "The general was furious, but he still said, 'Have Eisenhower here by seven o'clock tomorrow night. I'm going to get back what I lost.' ''

Several games were played after that, both during the California maneuvers and back at Fort Lewis; Eisenhower continued to win, and he put aside enough money to buy Mamie an expensive gift for their twenty-fifth wedding anniversary and, while still at Lewis, bought a new car, a Chrysler Royal. "We thought it was a terrific car," said John. "It cost a thousand dollars, and we kept it until 1944."

Sweeney may have been unhappy with Eisenhower's success at poker, but after the war games he wrote a firm letter of commendation:

I wish to commend and compliment you upon the success you attained as Chief Umpire during the recent field exercises and maneuvers participated in by the 3d Division and attached units at Camp Ord, California, from April 12th to May 8th, 1940.

It was due to your initiative that the Umpire System was organized and molded into a working team which enabled me to control and direct the exercises. The smooth functioning of the Umpire System contributed greatly to the success of our training period.

Your ability, tact, untiring energy and devotion to your work reflected great credit upon yourself and upon the Umpire group as a whole.

Eisenhower returned to Fort Lewis after the maneuvers. He and Wayne (Mark) and Maurine Clark and Mamie spent a good deal of time together that spring and summer. Mrs. Clark said, "We went to their home often for cracked-crab dinners and they came to our house for the same thing. That is, it was cracked crab during the first three weeks or so of each month. The last week of the month was different. By that time nobody had any money left for crab. The gaiety subsided before each pay check as we were brought face to face with the high cost of living.

"Any parties held were quiet affairs. Usually it would be necessary to serve only a dessert and coffee and then go to the post movie. The show would end early, we would say good night in the theater lobby, and everybody would be home by 10:30. . . . Ike and Wayne worked together very closely. Ike was full of ideas about how to fight a war, and used his battalion to test theories. Wayne told me, 'That Ike is always trying something new. He wants to experiment. I think he is using that battalion to test every rule he ever read in the book.' ''

Eisenhower said of early 1940 at Fort Lewis, "The officers and men lacked any sense of urgency. Athletics, recreation, and entertainment took precedence in most units over serious training. Some of the officers, in the long years of peace, had worn for themselves deep ruts of professional routine within which they are sheltered from vexing new ideas and troublesome problems. . . .

"The Army concentrated on spit and polish, retreat formations, and parades because the American people, in their abhorrence of war, denied themselves a reasonable military posture."

Burton S. Barr, who was to become a leading Republican politician in Arizona after the war, was a second lieutenant and platoon leader in Eisenhower's First Battalion when its commanding officer arrived. "He made an immediate impression on everybody," said Barr. "He seemed to know what he was all about and what the Army was all about, and there was no room for nonsense.

"One of the first things he did was to call all the battalion officers together, and he said, 'If any of you think we are not going to war, I don't want you in my battalion. We're going to war. This country is going to war, and I want people who are prepared to fight that war.'

"I tell you, nobody, *nobody* was talking like that at the time. People were going around saying, 'War? What war? I don't see any war.'

"What Eisenhower said was scary, but nobody quit the battalion. He was pretty popular among the men, but he was no easy task master."

Barr said:

I'll never forget one lesson I learned from Eisenhower that summer. One day my platoon was on the range, and up comes Ike. He comes down the line, and I made myself busy doing something—I was always busy when I saw him—as far from him as possible.

He went over to a kid who had a brain it would have taken a search team to find, and Ike said to him, "Show me your score book." That's the first thing everybody had to do when he went to the range, put down his name. But there was no name in this kid's book. In fact there was nothing at all, zero.

Now who is to blame? The kid? Oh no. His platoon leader is to blame, and I heard Eisenhower's voice say, "Barr, come here!"—He walked away so that the other men couldn't hear, and I got to where he was very quickly. Now, I've heard about being eaten out, and I've seen it, but this was unique. This wasn't being eaten out. This was Eisenhower having a buffet supper, and I was the complete meal. To this day, and I'll be sixty-five my next birthday, I remember every word of it.

I knew that my company commander—I was in A company—had invited Eisenhower to have lunch with us that day, and I decided I'd have lunch with B company. I wasn't going to take a second bawling out.

But the minute I started toward B I heard that voice, "Barr, come here." I went up to him a second time, and he said, "I'm going to tell you something, lieutenant, and you'd better listen carefully. This morning you did something wrong, and I bawled you out for it. *That was the end*. We don't carry grudges around here, not for an hour, not for half an hour, not at all. Now, you eat lunch with your own company." Suffice it to say, I did, and I never forgot that. I've practiced it, too. Whatever people think of me politically, I don't think you'll find anybody who'll say that I carry grudges.

So I learned something fundamental from Eisenhower.

Eisenhower found the attitudes of most officers and their wives at Fort Lewis pretty much the same as those in the Army-Navy Club back in Manila. The war was a bore; it had nothing to do with us, and maybe Hitler was right. After all, our ambassador to the Court of Saint James, Joseph P. Kennedy, was saying that the British would be defeated.

"Even the fall of France in May 1940 failed to awaken us," Eisenhower said, "and by 'us' I mean many professional soldiers as well as others—to a full realization of danger. The commanding general of one United States division . . . offered to bet, on the day of the French armistice, that England would not last six weeks longer—and he proposed the wager much as he would have bet on rain or shine for the morrow."

Eisenhower on the other hand was convinced that the United States must do everything possible to prevent a British defeat; that Britain was "the sole remaining belligerent standing between us and starkest danger."

That summer Eisenhower, or "Alarmist Ike" as he was known around Fort Lewis, led his troops in taking part in another "war game." The battalion had to march twenty-five miles in five days and do battle with the troops of the Washington National Guard. Things did not work out quite that way. Eisenhower said that the terrain was cut-over land, "some of the most difficult terrain in the country . . . stumps, slashings, fallen logs, tangled brush, pitfalls, hummocks, and hills made the land a stage setting for a play in Hades. . . . At times, I was really fagged out. But all of us learned lessons that would pay off in combat. The experience fortified my conviction that I belonged with troops; with them I was always happy."

When he was at work on *At Ease*, Eisenhower may have forgotten or, more likely, put aside in his memory the fact that the 15th Regiment did not really do battle with the troops of the Washington National Guard. Instead, the 15th met up with soldiers of the 30th Infantry Regiment, commanded by Colonel Robert Lawrence Eichelberger, who as a lieutenant general was to make a considerable reputation in the Pacific war under MacArthur's command.

As Burton Barr remembered the 1940 maneuvers in Washington State, Eichelberger's regiment and Eisenhower's battalion confronted each other at a road junction, and the two commanding officers, "while they weren't fighting each other physically, were fighting with words. They were both very, very angry. I remember Eisenhower shouting, 'How in hell did your 30th get in with my 15th? We're both supposed to be fighting the Washington National Guard, and we're supposed to be getting them to surrender.'

"It was a real mess, but troops were surrendering, all kinds of troops, some of them no doubt troops of the Washington National Guard. Everywhere you looked soldiers were surrendering. But they were surrendering because if you surrendered you got out of the heat and the dust and got on a truck. Who wouldn't surrender?

"Ike was saying, 'We're doing great. We're winning. We're capturing troops.' I don't know how I got the guts, a second lieutenant to a lieutenant colonel, but I said, 'Colonel, all these guys want is to get on a truck. If you've got enough trucks to haul all of them, you'll get all of them to surrender.' I have to say this to his credit, he laughed, and he said, 'I guess you're right.' I didn't know much about war, but I knew enough to realize that what was going on wasn't very realistic. It was good exercise, and a lot of people got suntans."

In July 1943 Eisenhower once again met up with Burton S. Barr, this time at a North African port from which a part of the invasion of Sicily was soon to be launched. Eisenhower was then Allied supreme commander in the Mediterranean and was an international hero fresh from great victories in Tunisia. Barr said, "He was wearing four stars on each shoulder, and he took one look at me and recognized me immediately. I was a major and had been a second lieutenant the last time he'd seen me back at Fort Lewis. He put out his hand and asked how I was. We shook, and he looked at my major's leaf. You know what he said? He said, 'Barr, how did you get promoted so rapidly?' "

In his diary in late September Eisenhower wrote, "During the war of 1917–1918, many interesting things happened to me that later slipped from my memory. That experience suggested that when a new emergency arose—if ever—I'd try to keep a brief diary, so as to have a day-by-day account of outstanding events. This is the beginning of such an effort. . . . Right now the so-called 'Battle of London' is progressing. It is a German bombardment of England by air, apparently conducted with two main objects:

(1) To cut off British imports.
(2) To cause enough damage to England's morale, material resources, industries, and military forces, that an invasion by sea will be feasible.

"England seems to be standing up better than had been anticipated."

In early September Eisenhower's old friend George Patton wrote him a letter that gave Ike "reason for outright elation . . . almost a guarantee that in case of war I would not be left at home." Colonel Patton was stationed at Fort Benning, Georgia, as commanding officer of the Second Armored Brigade; he suggested to Eisenhower that he ask for a transfer to the division of which Patton's brigade was a part, the 2d Armored Division. He and Ike were, after all, veterans in the use of tanks.

Eisenhower answered the letter immediately. "I am flattered by your suggestion that I come to your outfit. It would be great to be in the tanks once more, and even better to be associated with you again.

"Since you did not specify the capacity in which I might serve in the armored division, maybe I should tell you that by requirement of law and preference, I'm at long last doing 'command duty.' It's not only that, like yourself, I like to work with soldiers, but I'm weary of doing desk duty. I suppose it's too much to hope that I could have a regiment in your division, because I'm still almost three years away from my colonelcy, but I *think* I could do a damn good job."

On October 1 Patton replied, "In view of my present make it seems likely that I will get one of the next two armored Divs which we firmly believe will be created in January or February depending on production. If I do I shall ask for you either as Chief of Staff which I should prefer or as a regimental commander. You can tell me which you want for no matter how we get together we will go PLACES. . . .

"Again thanking you and hoping we are together in a long and BLOODY War."

T.J. Davis, who had served with Ike in the Philippines, was then in the adjutant general's office in Washington and presumably had some influence with the brass in Washington. Naturally, Eisenhower wrote him about Patton's offer. He said, "My ambition is to go, eventually, to an armored outfit. George Patton has told me that at least two new armored divisions are to be formed early next year, and if he is assigned in command of one of them he intends to ask for me, possibly as one of his regimental commanders. That would be a swell job and I only hope that the War Department won't consider me too junior in rank to get a regiment. I realize that I am quite conceited to entertain the idea, but I have noticed that in certain instances regimental commands have been given to Lieutenant Colonels. It is always possible, therefore, that the War Department might be charitably inclined in my case."

In Patton's next letter, written on November 1, he said, "If I were you I would apply for a transfer to the Armored Corps NOW. There will be at least one vacant regiment shortly and no other Lt. Col. in the div. except possibly Jones ranks you and I don't bother with rank anyhow. . . . If you have any pull, use it for there will be 10 new generals in this Corps pretty damned soon.

"Give my best to Mamie and here's LUCK."

It is perhaps not coincidental that during this time Eisenhower jotted down in his diary, *Fox Conner, 1316 New Hampshire Ave. N.W. Washington.*

By that time Mark Clark was in Washington in General Headquarters of the Army (GHQ) directly under George Marshall, and Eisenhower wrote him asking that he "try to make sure that I would be let alone for awhile so that I would be available for the Armored Force when the time came. By no means did I want the reputation of an eager beaver—but having a temporary success as a fugitive from the staff, I hoped to remain so.

"For a few weeks I continued to dream about an armored command under George Patton. But the roof fell in shortly after the middle of November. . . ." At that time, Eisenhower was handed a telegram from his classmate and old friend Gee Gerow. Fifteen years had passed since they had studied so hard at the Command and General Staff School, and Gee now was a brigadier general and head of the War Plans Division (WPD) in the War Department. The telegram said:

I NEED YOU IN WAR PLANS DIVISION DO YOU SERIOUSLY OBJECT TO BEING DETAILED ON THE WAR DEPARTMENT GENERAL STAFF AND ASSIGNED HERE PLEASE REPLY IMMEDIATELY

"Shock waves of consternation hit me," said Eisenhower. In the opening line of the letter he wrote in reply, he said, "Your telegram, arriving this morning, sent me into a tailspin." He almost immediately suffered an attack of shingles, "the first and last of my life." The doctors advised him to go to the hospital for treatment, but he refused. He added, however, that "straight thinking, in the midst of physical pain and a disturbing query, was a little difficult."

In his diary, he said, "I'd like to stay with my regiment—but it looks like I were sunk. [*sic*]" He later said, "In the few hours between the arrival of Gerow's telegram and my reply, I reviewed in my mind and tried to evaluate the ramifications of this new development. There was the possibility that once again— should we go to war—I'd be shut out of combat duty. I did not want to be considered as a slacker or a cry baby but I honestly felt that after all my years of almost constant staff assignments, I really deserved troop duty."

The letter, presenting "as factually as I could my record and my wishes" was, he felt, "one of the most important I have ever written." In it he carefully said what he had said so many times before, that he would go where he was ordered to go. But he added:

> I have consistently indicated my desire to stay with troops, either with the 15th, or, if possible, in command of one of the mechanized units to be organized in the spring.
>
> At various times I have had informal reports from Washington, to the effect that I had been requested for positions on certain Corps and Division staffs. My informants have told me that in each such instance the War Department (Chief of Infantry) has declined to give favorable consideration, on the ground that I needed duty with troops. . . .
>
> All the above seems to be a lot of beating the devil around the bush. However, it is almost necessary to recite these things to you so that you can understand the reason for the somewhat confused state of mind in which I now find myself. Oh yes! Another thing I should probably tell you is that General Thompson is merely waiting favorable action on a recommendation of his, regarding a new assignment for his Division Chief of Staff, before putting my name before the War Department to fill that position.

He added that if it was decided that he had to take the Washington assignment, he and Mamie looked forward to renewing their close relationship with the Gerows. It turned out later that Mamie wanted desperately to go to Washington. But, considerately, she did not say so then.

He ended the letter saying what was to turn out to be painfully true. "Actually, Gee, the job of staying with a regiment is a damn near hopeless one." He added, however, that Lieutenant Colonel Wayne (Mark) Clark was "one of the finest officers in our Army." He asked Gee to have a talk with him; "at least I could recommend others."

Eisenhower's immediate fate had already been decided; he would stay behind a desk, working with a major general who was nearly sixty and who was the kind Lesley J. McNair, head of Army Ground Forces, had in mind when he described a "metallic general, one who has silver in his hair, gold in his teeth, and lead in his pants." Major General C. F. Thompson, Eisenhower's immediate superior, had been a member of the West Point class of 1904. In August Thompson had called Eisenhower into his office and said that if he became, as he hoped and planned, commander of IX Corps, which included the entire northwest of the United States, he wanted Eisenhower to be his chief of staff. Eisenhower had said yes. What else does a lieutenant colonel say to a major general?

In the meantime Eisenhower was "temporarily" serving as executive officer of Fort Lewis. McNair and "an inspecting group from GHQ" were not impressed with Thompson, and he did not get command of IX Corps. That job went to General Kenyon A. Joyce, the kind of man McNair described as a "sparkplug leader." McNair was almost deaf and was fifty-seven years old, but he was the kind of man who went up steps two at a time. He was later to be head of a phantom army under Eisenhower's command in England, but before that he was more responsible than anybody else for training millions of young American civilians to be soldiers. Joyce's name was later to be put on a very small list of the best generals Eisenhower had ever worked with.

A great many people have said that Eisenhower was "lucky," that he fell into plum assignments that he had not earned, that his career was blessed, that for him it was easy all the way. The period just before America entered the war firmly refutes this.

What Eisenhower had prayed would not happen in the fall of 1940, did happen. Joyce arrived on the post on October 24, and Eisenhower wrote in his diary two days later, "I'm still on same job. In fact he [Joyce] has asked for me for his corps staff, G-3 [mobilization and training] I think. I'm sure the A.G. [adjutant general] will turn it down. I devoutly hope so—because I have only two alternative ambitions—one is to be in the 15th—the other to command a new armored regiment." It was a gloomy time.

Whatever the low state of Eisenhower's own morale that fall and winter, he strove to do something to improve the morale of the troops under his command. "Dad was . . . very aware of their hardships," said John. "He was particularly conscious of them as compared to the members of his own staff who, he felt, had it soft. He never treated his own staff with the respect he treated anyone in the field."

Eisenhower devoted one of the five Notes in *At Ease* to the subject of morale. He said:

> There is at least one striking difference between the American soldier and numerous other soldiers in history. The Army, however, as far back as the days of Von Steuben, learned that Americans either will not or cannot fight at maximum efficiency unless they understand the why and wherefore of their orders. To Von Steuben, after his professional career in Europe, where troops were only pawns to be moved about the board of war without consideration of them as individual human beings, this was a wonder. To meet it, changing his own practice and attitude completely, he worked to develop in Washington's army an understanding by the individual—down to the last private—of his place in the scheme of battle and of the training drudgery necessary for him to maintain that place honorably.

On October 21 Ike had written to his friend T.J. on a matter of morale.

> I don't know whether you are acquainted with the winter climate of the great Northwest, but one of its characteristics is long and dark afternoons

and evenings that must necessarily be spent indoors. This feature of our winter makes us particularly sensitive to all suggestions that seem to have a definite value in producing and maintaining a morale and contentment, particularly among enlisted men.

This afternoon there came to my desk (I am temporarily acting as Post Executive for General Thompson) a request for some musical instruments. It is a new unit and therefore without funds of its own with which to buy the instruments desired. The Commanding Officer reports that there are some very good musicians in the outfit, who are voluntarily devoting their time to practice, and that the men, particularly the recruits, take a tremendous interest in the effort. . . . While pondering the matter I happened to remember that you are in the Morale Division of the Adjutant General's office, and the hope was born that you might be in a position to do something about the matter. . . . There is no desire to build up a big military band. Rather, the effort is to produce a small orchestra that could provide entertainment for the men during the evenings and, when the organization can arrange a dance of its own, to furnish the music. A couple of saxophones, a trumpet or two, drums, something called a sousaphone, and possibly a clarinet would certainly be all that would be needed. At least such an assembly of instruments would furnish the backbone of the equipment required and the rest could be secured by contribution, and so on.

Would you nose around in your inimitable way to find out whether or not such a thing could be put over? . . . I must confess that I write this letter with only a modicum of hope that anything can be done about it— but it struck me as such a worthy project that I didn't want to deny you a chance to work on it a bit.

Ike's pessimism was well founded. In a reply to T.J.'s letter telling of his failure to get any musical instruments, Eisenhower said, "An official letter went forward the other day on the subject of recreational facilities, in which it was recommended that a set of instruments be provided at the rate of one set per each Service Club established at Posts. So I imagine that sooner or later the matter will get to the War Department on an official basis." In that letter to T.J., Eisenhower repeated once again that he wanted to remain with the 15th Infantry.

Eisenhower had somewhat more success with a morale matter that involved the entire regiment. John said, "The 15th Infantry—I believe it was Dad's doing—was enamored of the 'Beer Barrel Polka.' The regiment, it was claimed, would march only to that piece of music. Thus, when the 3d Division would pass in review, the band would stop when the first elements of the 15th reached the line and burst into the 'Polka.' Trivial as this matter may seem, it was the stuff of which morale was made."

Burton Barr said, "I imagine there were some officers and men in the 15th who had never heard of the 'Beer Barrel Polka,' but everybody soon learned that Eisenhower liked it very much indeed, and pretty soon we were all humming it or singing it or marching to it. It was a great tune. On the night Eisenhower celebrated his birthday at the officers' club he sang it. I was celebrating my own birthday. He was born in 1890, I was born in 1917. So he bought me a drink. But I stood at attention while drinking it. I didn't find him an officer you could relax with."

November 14 was a "hectic day." It was Mamie's birthday and it began with good news; at 9 A.M. a telegram arrived saying that John had won Senator Arthur Capper's principal appointment to West Point. John's father noted, "That's a great load off our minds, with nothing to worry about now except his phys. condition." But the letter he received from T.J. was not an encouraging one. Early that month Major General Walter Krueger had put in a request to the War Department for Ike to become chief of staff of VII Corps; Krueger had only recently become corps commander, and one of the first officers he asked for was Eisenhower.

Krueger was nine years older than Ike and had been born in East Prussia. He had come to the United States as a child and been educated in the Middle West, but until the end of his life he spoke with a heavy German accent. He had fought in the Spanish-American War and reenlisted after that war as a private. His entire army career, including wartime service in the Pacific under MacArthur, lasted forty-four years.

T.J. said in his letter that Krueger's request for Eisenhower had been turned down, as Eisenhower said, "on the ground that I was *too junior* in rank. God knows I've told everyone I want to stay with troops—but it never occurred to me the W.D. [War Department] would give such a reason."

In a letter to T.J., Ike said:

In view of the fact that the War Department thinks I am too junior to be a Chief of Staff of the Corps, it seems evident that they will consider me too junior for commanding a regiment. Therefore, I want to stay right in the 15th Infantry.

It strikes me that this business of being so particular about the details of rank is, to say the least, somewhat amusing under existing circumstances. When a man has reached the age of fifty . . . and is some two and one-half years away from his eagles, it seems that the matter of rank could be so adjusted that the War Department could put a man wherever they want to.

On November 30, despite his junior rank, as Eisenhower said, "My active service with troops came to an end. Orders arriving that day detailed me to the General Staff Corps, assigned to duty as Chief of Staff, 3d Division, Fort Lewis, effective immediately. I was back on the staff—but at least with the designation 'General Staff *with* Troops.' I had escaped Washington and, to that extent, felt lucky."

Eisenhower's morale must have improved somewhat late in 1940 when he learned that the "metallic general" (Thompson), about whom he and McNair had had grave doubts, had no doubts at all about Ike. In his efficiency report on Eisenhower, Thompson said, "He has the highest potentiality for command or staff duty. . . . He is highly suitable for all civilian contacts. . . . He is affable, energetic, dynamic, zealous, original, loyal, capable, dependable, and outstanding."

The general added that Eisenhower was "superior in handling of officers and men, in performance of field duties, in administrative and executive duties, in training troops, in tactical handling of troops (units appropriate to officer's grade)."

On December 11, 1940, Ike wrote to MacArthur, telling him of his year in the States, after his return from the Philippines.

> A very merry Christmas to you and yours, and may 1941 be the finest year you've yet lived. . . .
>
> It did not take me long to find out, after I came home, that it is well nigh impossible for a field officer who has been through the schools to remain quietly with troops these days. When I hit the dock at San Francisco I caught a month D.S. [detached service] on secret work in 4th Army Headquarters. Then after serving two months with the 15th Infantry, I had to make a personal appeal to the Army Commander to get out of a long training cruise with the Navy, and having been excused from that I served as Chief Umpire of the Division during a month of maneuvers. . . .
>
> After we came back here, a number of suggestions, some of them official in character, were made that I go on Staff duty, but I declined on the plea that I'd been with troops only four months. However, in September I received a local order to serve as Post Executive during our great building and expansion boom. While on that job, General Krueger asked the War Department to detail me as his Corps C/S [chief of staff]—just after the War Department had sent me a wire saying it was contemplating assigning me to Washington in War Plans Division. Again, I repeated my sob story, and, when both those projects were dropped, thought I was in the clear. But then along came another request—and this one was approved; so now I'm Chief of Staff, 3d Division, with station at Fort Lewis.
>
> My case is not particularly unusual . . . I'm luckier than most in that I don't have to pack up and move.

Pearl Harbor was a year away.

* * *

A COLONEL NAMED EISENHOWER

For much of the world 1941 was a year of trauma, but for Eisenhower it was a very good year indeed, when all that he had ever hoped and worked for happened. Then there were the surprises, pleasant and extraordinary.

On March 1, under Special Orders No. 49, he was relieved from assignment and duty as chief of staff, 3d Division, and assigned to duty as chief of staff of the IX Army Corps, commanded by Kenyon Joyce. "Although my post was still Fort Lewis, my duties were considerably enlarged," he said. "The Corps was made up of all posts, camps, and stations, in the northwestern part of the country." That same month he was appointed colonel (temporary), with rank from March 6.

Eisenhower was delighted with his most recent promotion. He had achieved a lifelong ambition, something very few men ever manage. He was a full chicken colonel. And he was annoyed, at least he pretended to be, when fellow officers at the post predicted that he would soon be a brigadier general. "Damn it," he told John, "as soon as you get a promotion, they start talking about another one. Why can't they let a guy be happy with what he has? They take all the joy out of it."

On May 16 Walter Krueger was given command of the Third Army, and when shortly thereafter the Third's chief of staff decided to retire, Krueger knew that he wanted Eisenhower for that position. This time Krueger knew better than to go through channels. He wrote to a man he had known since they served in the Philippines together early in the century, George Marshall. Krueger told Marshall that he wanted a man "possessing broad vision, progressive ideas, a thorough grasp of the magnitude of the problems involved in handling an army, and lots of initiative and resourcefulness." Did such a paragon exist? He did. Krueger supplied the name, Dwight D. Eisenhower.

On June 24 Eisenhower was ordered to go to San Antonio "and report to the commanding general, Third Army, for duty with the General Staff Corps. The travel directed is necessary in the military service."

Eisenhower and Mamie arrived in San Antonio on July 1, their twenty-fifth wedding anniversary. It was also John's first day at West Point, an institution he viewed from the beginning with little awe. He recalled that MacArthur had called entering West Point as a cadet his "highest honor."

"Forty-two years after MacArthur, I was entering West Point under similar circumstances, as an Army brat," said John. "But my emotions, as the hour approached, were somewhat more mixed than the way MacArthur in his old age described the hour. My feeling, so well remembered, was one of controlled, determined trepidation."

When the son of a classmate of his father's braced him, John reacted very much the same way his father had. He found the whole thing ridiculous. "I nearly burst out laughing with relief. After all the anticipation, I was finally there. The ball game had begun."

At Fort Sam, Ike and Mamie were driven in a staff car to a handsome house at 177 Artillery Post Road. Eisenhower was not satisfied with it, however; he found it "small" and wrote Gee Gerow that "we are rather avoiding settling too firmly, believing something a bit more desirable will become available." Two months later something better did turn up next door, a fourteen-room red brick house at 179 Artillery Post Road; it had five bedrooms and a huge lawn. Eisenhower described it to Everett Hughes as "a house as big as a stock barn."

Shortly after his arrival at Fort Sam, Eisenhower began to get together what was to become his "family," two members of which stayed with him until the end of the war. The first was Lieutenant Ernest R. "Tex" Lee, a native of San

Antonio. As a mere colonel Eisenhower was not entitled to an aide; so Tex became his executive officer, largely performing the duties normally assigned to an aide. Tex was an excellent gofer. He had the gregarious, unflappable personality of a happy salesman. He had been an assistant manager of a Metropolitan Life Insurance agency in Chicago and more recently the sales manager of a Chevrolet agency in his hometown. He had begun his military career in a San Antonio high school, had been in the army reserve corps and by studying nights had become a second lieutenant in the reserve.

When Eisenhower arrived at Fort Sam, Lee was already there as administrative officer and he expected to be replaced with an officer of Eisenhower's choice, but after looking him over for ten days, Ike asked him to stay on.

Tex was in his early forties and wore glasses. According to Kenneth S. Davis, he was "built much like Eisenhower's brother Edgar, with receding black hair above a high forehead that was markedly narrower than the cheeks below it." His hearty manner put off some people, but Eisenhower seemed not to mind, though they were never close. (Lee is not mentioned at all in *At Ease* and only once in *Crusade*.) He was a humble man, not a Uriah Heep to be sure, but inarguably Tex got along with most people.

A few days after he became Eisenhower's offical executive officer, Lee interviewed for orderly a young private from Corona, New York, who before he was drafted had been a bellman at the Plaza Hotel in Manhattan, Michael James McKeogh, Mickey.

Lee's questions seemed to be casual. Mickey said that he was "asked if I drank. I figured he meant did I drink twenty-four hours a day, and I said no."

So he got the job. Mickey also served as a striker, being paid an extra $10 a month by Eisenhower to help Mamie in the fourteen-room house on Artillery Road. In a book he wrote after the war, with the help of mystery novelist Richard Lockridge, Mickey said of Mamie, "She is a very lovely and gracious person, and she can put anyone at ease, no matter where he comes from. She also has very exact ideas about how she wants pictures hung."

Life at Fort Sam had not changed much since the Eisenhowers had been there twenty-five years earlier. The officers and men had Wednesday and Saturday afternoons free and all day Sunday. Six days a week officers wore civilian clothes, and, Mickey said, Eisenhower dressed like "a conservative professional man." He had three suits, one single-breasted gray, a double-breasted blue suit, a brown tweed suit, and a tuxedo. He always wore white shirts and conservative red and blue ties. He bought his clothes and uniforms ready-made—except for his riding breeches, which were hand tailored.

"He was the best-dressed soldier in the world in his riding outfit," said Mickey. "When he was in his pink breeches, high boots, and pink wool shirt, everybody would just stand and look at him. He wore that uniform a good deal later, on inspection trips. He was a Clark Gable in that, and in his summer uniforms."

Except in Mickey's eyes, however, Ike was never known as one of the army's fashion plates. There MacArthur outshone him, and so did Patton. Eisenhower was never much for spit and polish, either at West Point of afterward. John said, "Before he had orderlies to take care of such things for him, [he] had always managed to avoid them [spit and polish] whenever possible. He used to shake his head at the loving care with which his friend George Patton would polish brass. When Chief of Staff of IX Corps at Fort Lewis, for example, the then Colonel Eisenhower, slaving hard at organizing and training, habitually wore a wool shirt rather than the more formal blouse and pinks that the commanding general preferred. The general had once mentioned the deplorable condition of Dad's belt buckle. Dad forthwith had given a sergeant a dollar and told him to buy eight brand new belts. It was then the duty of the sergeant, whenever a belt buckle became tarnished, to produce a replacement from his drawer."

While serving as Krueger's chief of staff, Eisenhower said he "was brought closer to the problems of the Army of the United States as a whole. . . . The situation contrasted favorably to that of a year earlier. The Army of the United States now totaled approximately 1,500,000 officers and men. However, grave deficiencies still existed. Vehicles, modern tanks, and anti-aircraft equipment were critically short. Supporting air formations were almost non-existent. Moreover, the approaching expiration of a year's service for National Guard units and Selective Service soldiers was a constant worry. . . . In June we feared the exodus of men, beginning in September, would not be matched by a comparable inflow."

What Eisenhower did not say was that inside and outside training camps all over the United States, hastily written scrawls appeared everywhere saying OHIO. That meant "Over the Hill in October." The Selective Service "trainees"—in those days they were almost never called "soldiers"—had been drafted for one year, and after that one year, the draftees would leave even if they had to go AWOL—or so the defiant letters on barracks and latrine walls would have the world believe. Did much of anybody really intend to go AWOL in October? Probably not. But it was difficult to take seriously training in which broomsticks were substituted for guns and trucks were labeled "tanks." Besides, those drafted had simply held unlucky numbers. The lucky guys were still wearing civilian clothes and making fortunes at their jobs.

In July Roosevelt asked Congress to extend National Guard service and the draft from one year to thirty months, which the Senate acceded to on August 7. The August 12 vote in the House was close; the extension was granted by a vote of 203 to 202. After that nobody in the army said much about going over the hill in October. Most of us in training stopped kidding ourselves; we were soon going to be in a real war.

In August American and British leaders met on board H.M.S. *Prince of Wales*, at Placentia Bay in Newfoundland. There, for the first time, a discussion of a cross-Channel invasion of Europe was discussed, and it was agreed that "there would not be needed vast armies on the continent such as were required in World War I. Small forces, chiefly armored, with their power of hard-hitting, would be able quickly to win a decisive victory." (By late March 1942 a specific plan, code-named ROUNDUP, was prepared, to be implemented in the spring of 1943; when the cross-Channel invasion took place in June 1944, it was code-named OVERLORD.)

. . .

That summer and fall of 1941, relations between the United States and Japan continued to deteriorate. On July 26 Japanese assets both in the United States and Britain were frozen, and that same day Roosevelt ordered that the Philippine Army be incorporated into the U.S. Army. In addition, MacArthur was brought back into the Army of the United States as a temporary lieutenant general. He would command both the Philippine troops and the American troops in the area. MacArthur received a great many cables congratulating him, but there is no record that Colonel Eisenhower was among the well-wishers. Ike did, however, write a letter to General Joyce, referring at least indirectly to MacArthur's reinstatement. He said, "The Philippine situation is a curious one. That may be the place where the shooting starts, but even so, I don't see how it can ever be anything but a secondary theater."

Meanwhile, the Third Army, under the command of General Krueger, was about to take part in the largest peacetime maneuver before the Second World War. The Third was to try to "invade" the United States, and Lieutenant General Ben Lear's Second Army was to "defend" the country against the invasion. The maneuvers were to take place in Louisiana during the month of September.

In a letter to Joyce, dated July 25, 1941, Ike said:

The opening date of maneuvers is rushing toward us, and with each passing day it seems we discover new problems that must be solved before the shooting starts. This army of eleven divisions stretches from Arizona to Florida, and concentration plans are not easy to perfect. But I'm hopeful that we'll get the job done, possibly well. . . . You must know how deeply I appreciate the generosity of your final report on me. I sincerely hope that others besides the clerks and Adjutant General in the War Department see it, not only because of what you said, but more particularly because *you* said it.

Eisenhower had known for a long time that his performance in the maneuvers would be closely watched. The dusty roads of Louisiana would not be like the dusty (and ignored) roads in the state of Washington; here the top men in the War Department would be paying close attention. "We didn't know how soon war would come, but we knew it was coming," Lesley McNair, director of the war games, told a reporter much later. "We didn't know when we'd have to fight, but we knew it might come at any time, and we had to get together something of an army pretty darn fast. We didn't dare stop for the progressive and logical building of a war machine. As a result, the machine was a little wobbly when it first got going. The men knew it. The officers knew it. Everybody knew it."

Mark Clark, deputy director, said, "The . . . maneuvers were typical. . . ." Under orders from McNair to "keep the directive as simple as possible," Clark "got an automobile map of Louisiana and drew a big goose egg in the Shreveport area, where Lear would assemble his army. I drew another for Krueger's forces, and in front of each I put a broad line which no troops would be permitted to cross before a given signal. I gave each army a mission that would bring them into contact; McNair said that was fine and go to it, limiting the maneuvers to the state of Louisiana."

In addition to the 342,000 men in the two opposing armies, a company of paratroopers as well as an experimental armored corps were to be used for the first time. The latter included the 1st and 2d Armored Divisions, the 2d commanded by Major General George S. Patton.

Months earlier Lieutenant Colonel LeRoy Lutes, who was assistant chief of staff of the supply section of the Third Army, had been ordered to arrange logistics for the areas the men of that army would "occupy." Lutes, who was to become a close friend of Eisenhower's, had graduated from a military academy in 1908, had enlisted in the National Guard and become an officer of the regular army right after the First World War. Eisenhower said, "His brilliance . . . was to bring him, long before the end of this war, the three stars of a lieutenant general."

Before the OVERLORD landings in Normandy, Lutes worked with Eisenhower's headquarters in London planning ways to supply troops once they had landed in France. His experience three years before in Louisiana had been extremely helpful. There the Third Army troops had had 11,500,000 pounds of bread and 8,500,000 pounds of meat, part of it dried beef. Any veteran of the peacetime army can testify that very few days passed when "shit on a shingle," creamed chipped beef on toast, was not served. KPs on the maneuvers had to peel 9,000,000 pounds of potatoes. Altogether more than 18,000,000 meals were served, and the forces under Lutes's command were able to provide one roll of toilet paper each day for every forty-five enlisted men.

Mickey McKeogh got sick from the food during the maneuvers. "The doctor said it was the diet I was getting and ordered me on a diet of poached eggs and milk. . . . The cooks were using about a pound of lard to fry one potato. The Boss went over to the kitchen and raised hell. The food got better, and I got pretty unpopular around the mess hall."

On August 11 Eisenhower left Fort Sam for Camp Polk, which was not far from the gulf coast and the Texas border. In a letter to Gee, he had said, "All the old-timers here say that we are going into a God-awful spot, to live with mud, malaria, mosquitoes, and misery." The area more than lived up to that description. Ike's friend James Stack said it was an area "where I don't think any human beings have been for fifty years. We found snakes all over the place, rattlers. We killed fifteen, twenty rattlers a day, and we were just torn apart by the ticks. A lot of men had poison oak. . . . It was a hundred degrees in the day time and forty or thirty at night. You would go down and take a shower, and by the time you got back you were just as dirty and sweaty as you were when you left. Because of dysentery, all the mess equipment had to be scalded before and after we ate."

Eisenhower's quarters were in a barracks at Camp Polk. Mickey said, "I'd go to his room the first thing in the morning and take care of things for him, straightening up his room, finding clean laundry for him, and things like that. It was one of my jobs to see that his uniforms were pressed and his clothes sent to the laundry. And I did odd jobs around the office and drove him sometimes and generally made myself useful. That's an orderly's job—to make himself useful and take care of the boss. . . . He never let any of the men be imposed upon, and he wouldn't let any of the other officers do it. I remember once down there when we were going into a car park at night and a major was directing the cars in, using a flashlight in the blackout. He directed our car very carefully, and right into a ditch. Then he started to bawl out the man who was driving, a corporal named Wood.

"The Boss really got sore at that. He got out of the car and I wouldn't want to have been that major. The Boss pointed out . . . that if we were in a ditch . . . the major had put us there, not Wood. The major had to stand there and take it, and it was the sort of thing that made us all proud of the Boss, and glad to be working for him."

In a paper presented to the Kansas History Teachers Association in 1971 F. Patrick Murray said, "From September 15–28, 1941, nineteen divisions took part in the maneuvers . . . the biggest war games undertaken by the Army prior to World War II and . . . the culmination of the Army's large unit training exercises before the war.

"The outcome . . . was not prearranged. Though the Army's general headquarters gave Lear and Krueger a wide strategic direction, the tactics and results were up to their own initiative and daring, plus the ability and resourcefulness of their men. Krueger's forces were part of a hypothetical invasion bridgehead on the Texas and Louisiana Gulf Coast and were acting as a screening force for other invasion troops, supposedly by pushing north behind them. Lear's job, as vanguard of the defending forces, was to stop Krueger and push him back into the Gulf."

There were to be no "winners" or "losers"; it was simply an enormous game. Marshall had said, "I want the mistakes made down in Louisiana, not over in Europe, and the only way to do this thing is to try it out, and if it doesn't work, find out what we need to make it work."

The official viewpoint notwithstanding, for the many young reporters covering the event there would certainly be "winners," and there would be "losers." Eisenhower did not like losing, and he seldom did—whether he was playing golf or bridge or poker or waging war.

On the day the maneuvers began, Eisenhower wrote a letter to Joyce:

Our big war started this morning. The customary lull in the flow of early reports has set in, and I should have a few minutes in which to answer your deeply appreciated letter. We have three Corps in line; all attacking to the northward from the Lake Charles area, while the Cavalry Division (56th Cavalry Brigade Attached, and with an Anti-Tank Group on Call) is covering our left on the left bank of the Sabine.

Eisenhower told Joyce that Lear's Red Army had five infantry divisions, one cavalry, and two armored divisions—and George Patton, whom many thought worth a division by himself. Krueger's Blue Army had no armor. Each force had about 350 combat planes. He went on to say,

The weather has closed in so much that air operations are almost out of the question. . . . But operations early this morning were quite productive of results, both as to information and tactical effect. We've located at least a large part of the hostile mechanization, and if we can stymie it in the swamps and batter it to pieces with our A-T Groups, those Reds are going to be on the run by the day after tomorrow. If the hostile tanks can preserve their freedom of action, the battle will probably become a confused dog fight. Maybe we're just overconfident, but we *think* we can take care of ourselves. Anyway, we're attacking all along the lines.

In addition, Eisenhower told Joyce, the maneuvers would help the army get rid of the inept among its officer corps. He said:

We've started *real* reclassification. So far, one Major General and one Brigadier are, along with a flock of lesser fry, awaiting results! A lot more must go, in my humble opinion. . . . We hear that General Marshall is due here tomorrow. It may be that he will take the trouble to tell General Krueger the whys of the promotion difficulty in my case. Certainly, the implication of the present imbroglio is that I, along with a generally acknowledged incompetent, cannot be promoted. Though I always make allowances for my own egotism, I still hope that my friends will differentiate as to reason, even where circumstances *appear* identical.

The letter turned out to be a two-page, single-spaced typewritten essay, and it may seem strange that on such a morning Eisenhower found the time. It must, however, be remembered that that morning, the man who had planned the maneuvers for his Blue Army was useless. All he had to do was wait for the "lull in the flow of early reports" to end so he could find out if things had happened the way he had planned for them to happen. And that day writing letters was a way of relieving tension.

Eisenhower said, "During maneuvers, my tent turned into something of a cracker-barrel corner where everyone in our army seemed to come for a serious discussion, a laugh, or a gripe. These visitors prolonged my hours and considerably reduced sleeping time. But I never discouraged those who came to complain, for I was often astonished to see how much better they worked after they unburdened their woes; and, of course, the harder they worked the smoother things went for us at army headquarters."

Robert Sherrod, one of a number of newspapermen who dropped into Eisenhower's tent, recalled, "In 1941 I became a military reporter, an embryo war correspondent, and one of my first assignments was to the swamps of Louisiana in the summer of 1941. Down there, I heard that the brightest young fellow around was a colonel named Eisenhower. . . .

"I've forgotten who directed me to him, but I did go down and had quite a long and enlightening talk with Colonel Eisenhower, who was very articulate . . . so much more articulate than any other officer I encountered during the Louisiana Maneuvers that I was deeply impressed by him. . . . He was a deeply impressive man. He looked like a soldier. He talked like an educated man. He was very forceful, altogether, as I've said, the most impressive man I'd seen.

"An odd thing happened there. Eric Sevareid and I had gone down to Louisiana on the train together. Eric had just come from the Blitz in London and he knew something about wars and being under fire, but he didn't know anything about the U.S. Army. So we traveled around a bit during the maneuvers. We'd get separated and I'd see him again. He'd say, 'Well, what do you make of this whole thing? Who should I talk to down here?' I'd say, 'Well, there's a colonel named Eisenhower who makes more sense than any of the others, as far as I can tell.'

"Afterwards, about 1946–47, Eric wrote an autobiographical book called *Not So Wild a Dream,* and in that he gives me credit for discovering General Eisenhower, which was rather amusing to me."

In his book, Sevareid wrote that he observed both Clark and Eisenhower during the maneuvers. "Two of the maneuver directors walked in. One I knew— General Mark Clark. The other, who answered my questions with quiet precision and looked at me with remarkably steady eyes in a relaxed face, was introduced as Eisenhower. . . . Two men with the same training and beliefs. As the succeeding years passed, my own daily life and the life and death of countless others were to become mixed up with the thought processes and instincts of these two personalities. I was to see one of them become the victim of the natural pressures of his position and fame, while the other became their master, his heart expanding rather than contracting under duress until he was more than a mere leader of men."

In his widely syndicated column, Drew Pearson paid Eisenhower a great compliment. He said, "Colonel Eisenhower . . . conceived the strategy that routed the Second Army. . . . Krueger's chief of staff has a steel-trap mind plus unusual vigor. . . . To him the military profession is a science and he began watching and studying the German Army five years ago."

Eisenhower wrote that in what the column said, the "author attributed credit to me that should have gone to General Krueger. I still have no idea why I became the target for his praise."

The reason Eisenhower became "the target" was no doubt because one of the column's leg men had stopped by at "crackel-barrel corner." Eisenhower treated the press the way he treated enlisted men, with respect, though he preferred reporters remain at a distance. He knew, too, that reporters, like enlisted men, could instantly spot a pretentious phony, and he took the trouble not to be one.

As Eisenhower wrote a friend, "In the fall of 1941 . . . flash bulbs were a fairly novel element in my daily life, and I was only an unknown face to those who used them. During the critique at Camp Polk a group shot was made of General Krueger, Major E. M. Holden, a British military observer, and me; in the picture my two companions were correctly identified, but I appeared as 'Lt. Col. D. D. Ersenbeing'—at least the initials were right."

The first phase of the maneuvers ended on September 19, and Ben Lear's

Red Army had clearly been outmaneuvered or, as the newspapers said, defeated. Twice, Lear had had to evacuate his command post. To make matters worse, propaganda pamphlets had been dropped on the Red Army saying:

Your commanders are withholding from you the terrible fact of your defeat. Your gasoline stores have been captured. From now on, if you move, you do it on the soles of your shoes. Your food stores have been captured. Your dinner tonight is going to be what was left over from yesterday. No one is going to bring up any of the steaks that the men of the Third Army will have tonight. Rout, disaster, hunger, sleepless nights in the forests and swamps are ahead of you—unless you surrender.

At the halfway mark of the maneuvers, on September 19, the umpires ruled that Lear's Second Army had been almost completely destroyed.

During the lull between the two phases of the maneuvers, Krueger and his staff, including Eisenhower, went to the state capital, Baton Rouge, to have dinner with the governor, Samuel H. Jones. More than three and a half years later, on March 7, 1945, a day when Eisenhower learned that First Army troops commanded by his friend Courtney Hodges had made the first Allied crossing of the Rhine, over the bridge at Remagen, Jones wrote Eisenhower:

Dear General:

I thought you would be interested in the following true story.

It happened back in 1941 when General Krueger was commanding the Third Army and General Lear the Second Army in the big Louisiana Maneuvers.

In a lull during the maneuvers, General Krueger flew over to Baton Rouge and paid a visit to the Governor. He brought with him his entire staff and as the then Governor I gave a luncheon at the Executive Mansion for the General and his staff.

During the course of the meal the General said to me: "Governor, I want you to know my Chief of Staff. He's the Colonel down the table. He has one of the brightest minds in the American Army. In my opinion he's 'going places.' "

To which I replied:

"General, I missed the Colonel's name. What did you say his name is?" Whereupon the General replied: "Eisenhower."

Some time after that I have had occasion to remind General Krueger of his role as a prophet.

Those who think that Eisenhower was "always lucky" cannot have considered the weather; the weather never seemed to favor him. That bad luck began in Louisiana; when the second phase of the exercises began on September 24 a hurricane swept over the entire area. Once again, however, the Third Army was victorious. By September 28, when the maneuvers ended, Krueger's armor was just outside Shreveport; by late afternoon, when McNair ordered a cease-fire, the city was surrounded, and its waterworks had been seized by the Third.

Hanson Baldwin said in the *New York Times*, "Had it been a real war, Lear's forces would have been annihilated."

McNair later had a great many unpleasant things to say about the exercises, the lack of discipline for one thing, but he took the time personally to congratulate Eisenhower on what he had done; so did Marshall, who had briefly visited Louisiana during the final days.

Eisenhower's efficiency report for the period covering the maneuvers was signed by Krueger. In it, Krueger said Ike's duties performed during the period and the manner of their performance were superior; physical activity: superior; physical endurance: excellent; knowledge of his profession: superior. In answer to the question, For what command of duty would you specifically recommend him in the event of war?, Krueger replied, "Command of Division." And to the question, Of all general officers of his grade personally known to you, what number would you give him on this list and how many comprise your list?, Krueger answered, "No. 2 on a list of 170."

No doubt Eisenhower knew he had done a superior job. After all, he perfectly matched the qualities necessary for a senior commander, set out in a letter to Gee:

There is a tremendous job facing every senior commander in this Army. The nervous energy and drive that are required in bringing a large unit along toward high training standards is tremendous; only people who are highly trained professionally and who have an inexhaustible supply of determination can get away with it. It is only rarely that the necessary qualifications are combined in one person. Some of them have plenty of drive but are totally unacquainted with training standards and methods in the smaller units, while others are technically proficient but have not the iron in their souls to perform the job.

One of the things that is causing the greatest trouble is that of eliminating unfit officers of all grades. But it is a job that has got to be done.

The last year has made a tremendous difference in the physical stamina of the men and in their ability to take care of themselves. Just before we started the problem in which we are now engaged, the tail end of a hurricane visited this section of the country and the Army got a good drenching. Yet when the problem started at noon yesterday, everybody was full of vim and ready to go. I do not know how long this problem will last but I can assure you that in Armies of about a quarter of a million you don't do things in a hurry. You have to take time to unwind things, even for minor changes in plans and orders.

Eisenhower surely counted on a promotion after the maneuvers, but his old friend Clark, knowing that, decided to keep him in suspense for a while. Every officer who took part in the maneuvers was present for the final critique, and Eisenhower was in the front row. Clark, after going over what had happened in the maneuvers on a large map, was handed a list of officers who had been promoted, ten to be major generals, and ten to be brigadiers. Clark said, "I glanced at it quickly; Ike was number three on the list to be brigadier generals, but I read out the whole list—with one exception. I deliberately left out Ike's name. I tell you, you could hear a pin drop, and I didn't dare look at his face. I knew what must be going through his mind, and I knew his face had to be red, and that vein . . . had to be throbbing, but I left out his name, and I said, 'That's all, gentlemen. Congratulations.' People started getting up, and then I banged the gavel, and I said, 'Please be seated. I have an apology to make. I have made a grievous error. I neglected to mention the name of another officer to be brigadier general; he is number three on the list.' I could hear Ike say, 'You sonofabitch. I'll get you.' He came up on the platform. 'I could kill you,' he said. I said, 'Ike, I couldn't resist the temptation.' "

Some days it was as if they were still at West Point.

A number of officers did not get promotions, among them Major General Ralph E. Truman, whose National Guard division, the 35th, had been held in reserve most of the time. After the maneuvers, Truman, who was Harry Truman's first cousin, was assigned to an administrative post. His place was taken by Major General William Hood Simpson, West Point 1909, a bald, quiet, and effective man, effective in or out of combat. Eisenhower was later to say that Simpson was one of the best if not the best of all his generals. "If Simpson ever made a mistake as an army commander, it never came to my attention. . . . Alert, intelligent and professionally capable, he was the type of leader that American soldiers deserve."

Almost all of the newspaper and magazine accounts of the maneuvers mentioned how well the Third Army's supply services had done, and LeRoy Lutes, too, became a temporary brigadier general.

Eisenhower's sister-in-law Mike was at Fort Sam at the time; her second husband, George Gordon Moore, had recently been commissioned as a captain. "Mrs. Krueger told me that the general was *very, very* impressed with Ike," said Mike, "and I guess that was the first time anyone in our family realized that he was going places."

When Eisenhower returned to Fort Sam, a parade was held in his honor; he refused a proposed gun salute, saying he thought it would be a waste of gunpowder. He told Clark, "I'm completely overcome. . . ."

Despite a new star, Brigadier General Eisenhower was none too happy. He said, "The maneuvers ended. I got, instead of a command, the star of a brigadier general." He said to Gee, "Things are moving so rapidly these days that I get almost dizzy trying to keep up with the parade. One thing is certain—when they get clear down to my name on the list, they are passing out stars with considerable abandon."

T.J. Davis, who was still in the adjutant general's office and had become a lieutenant colonel, wrote him a letter of congratulations, and Eisenhower replied, "You know how much I appreciated your note. But what do you mean, 'How does it feel to be a B.G.' I'm working harder than ever; I used to be a deck hand, now I'm a stevedore. . . . I might get east for a few days in a month or so. I'll wire you in advance if I can come."

Another man to receive recognition after the maneuvers was Major Gruenther, who was to be a lifelong friend of Eisenhower's as well as his favorite bridge partner. Gruenther was only forty-two, another midwesterner, from Platte Center, Nebraska. He had been graduated from West Point twice. The first time, 4th in a class of 277, in 1917. Members of that class were graduated but not given their commissions. The army at that time had too many second lieutenants; so the 1917 graduates were sent back to the Point for another term. On November 1, 1918, at the age of nineteen, Gruenther became a second lieutenant. Like General McNair, he was an artilleryman, and he was quickly and widely recognized as an "army brain." It was a reputation he was never to lose.

That other army brain, General McNair, said of Gruenther after the maneuvers that the young major was capable of a much higher command, and in October Gruenther became a temporary lieutenant colonel on Krueger's staff, and as deputy chief of staff, served under Eisenhower. He served with Eisenhower during much of the war, and he succeeded him as Supreme Allied Commander in Europe (SACEUR).

Eisenhower had brains, too, and what was more, he had another quality that helped him greatly and which he took great pains to cultivate. People liked him and trusted him. His presence was not threatening. Mark Clark once said, "I suppose not *everybody* liked him, but I never heard anybody say he hated Ike's guts."

From Marshall's point of view, the maneuvers were a success in three important areas: it was demonstrated that the equipment of the United States Army was inadequate; the morale of the troops had improved; and he had found those colonels who would be good general officers.

General Krueger in his memoirs said, "Toward the end of the Louisiana Maneuvers when General Marshall asked me whom I regarded as best fitted to head the War Plans Division, which I had headed several years before, I named Eisenhower, though I was loath to lose him."

★ ★ ★

THE FIRST ANSWER

Ike said of the Louisiana Maneuvers that they "provided me with lessons and experiences that I appreciated more and more as subsequent months rolled by. . . . October and November were as busy as the months preceding the maneuvers. Measures to correct defects [uncovered] in Louisiana were begun at unit level; in many cases the return movement offered an immediate opportunity."

If there was one thing he did not want at the time it was an order sending him to Washington, D.C., where he seldom went happily, not even to the White House in January 1953. He wanted to continue as a field officer. He had demonstrated that he was a good one, had been complimented by Krueger, McNair, and Marshall, but still Krueger had recommended him for yet another behind-a-desk, paper-shuffling office job, in the War Plans Division.

He would be ordered to Washington while others of his age and rank would go off to Europe or the Pacific and make reputations for themselves and earn additional stars for their shoulders. For him, the Second World War would be much like the First, a war he would sit out. In the days just before Pearl Harbor, the most exciting prospect for Eisenhower's immediate future appeared to be a two-week leave around Christmas, and he and Mamie planned to visit John at West Point.

Eisenhower said, "Although the Washington negotiations with the Japanese ambassadors were nearing their dramatic climax at the beginning of December, a relaxation of tenseness among the civilian population was reflected within the Army. It seemed that the Japanese bluff had been called and war, at least temporarily, averted in the Pacific. . . . My daily paper, on December 4, editorialized that it was now evident that the Japanese had no desire for war with the United States."

On December 7, George C. Marshall went horseback riding in the morning. When he returned to Quarters No. 1 at Fort Myer, the offical residence of the Chief of Staff of the Army, which in due time Ike and Mamie would occupy, he got a telephone call asking him to come to his office in the Munitions Building. It was not until after lunch that day that he heard the message: "Air Raid on Pearl Harbor. This is not a drill."

When news of Pearl Harbor reached Fort Sam Houston, Eisenhower was taking a nap; he had left word at his office to be called if anything important happened, and after Tex Lee called him, he went immediately to work. He said, "Within an hour . . . attack orders began pouring into Third Army headquarters from the War Department." Antiaircraft units were dispatched to the West Coast, where many people were sure an attack would come at any moment. Antisabotage measures were ordered everywhere. In addition, Eisenhower said, "General Krueger's headquarters had to send out instructions to a hundred stations as rapidly as they could be prepared and checked. It was a period of intense activity."

On December 8 Congress declared war on Japan; on the 11th, Germany and Italy, faithful to the pact they had signed with Japan affirming the unity of the three nations, declared war on the United States. In his message to Congress following that act, Roosevelt said, "Never before has there been a greater challenge to life, liberty, and civilization."

Early on the morning of the 12th Eisenhower got the call from Washington that he had been expecting and dreading. A sharp, abrupt voice, that of Walter Bedell Smith, then a colonel and secretary of the general staff, said, "Is that you, Ike?"

"Yes."

"The Chief [Marshall] says for you to hop a plane and get up here right away. Tell your boss that formal orders will come through later."

Eisenhower said that Mamie "hurriedly packed a bag for me." The day was rainy with high winds, and commercial planes were grounded. Tex Lee, faced with his first big assignment, that of getting his boss to Washington as quickly as possible, persuaded a young army pilot to fly his C-45 through the storm, and Mickey McKeogh drove Mamie to the airport to see Ike off. She said that he was "hurried and unhappy. . . . I knew he was hoping the Washington duty would be temporary."

The pilot of the plane got as far as Dallas and gave up. Eisenhower made the rest of the journey by train.

Before he went to a new post, Eisenhower always took the trouble to find out as much as possible about the man who was to be his new commanding officer. This time his new CO had the most important job in the army and one of the half dozen most important in the Allied war effort. Eisenhower had seen him, always briefly, three times before. Marshall had not been extravagant in his praise, he never was. A man was expected to do his job well.

Marshall had been chief of staff since September 1939, and his likes and dislikes, his strengths, his foibles, and his impressive achievements had become well known. For one thing, Eisenhower knew that it would not be necessary for him to speak warmly of Douglas MacArthur in Marshall's presence. The two men, both born in 1880, had never been close. Marshall's official biographer, Forrest C. Pogue, said: "The difference between Marshall and MacArthur lay more in their temperaments and styles than in ancient quarrels and fancied injuries. . . . Marshall . . . lacked the florid touch and the flair for self-dramatization that helped make the Pacific commander a striking and effective figure. These were not qualities that the Chief of Staff held against his brother officer—Marshall recognized that showmanship could be a valuable asset to a field commander—but they were not to his taste."

Eisenhower knew, moreover, that he and Marshall would never exchange their personal views of MacArthur. Marshall's personal views on most things were not shared with anyone. For example, Mrs. Marshall said, of the night of December 7, "George said nothing except that he was tired and was going to bed. I sat there trying to think of something I could say or do that might help him, but words are futile at a time like that, so I passed his door and went into my room. I knew he would rather be alone."

We can be sure that by the time Eisenhower's train reached Union Station in Washington, everything he knew about the chief of staff was neatly catalogued in his mind, ready for use when he needed it. General Andrew J. Goodpaster, Eisenhower's staff secretary in the White House, said, "He was always a tremendous man for analyzing what was in the other fellow's mind, what options were open to the other fellow, and then what line he could take best to capitalize on or exploit the possibilities, always having a great regard for the options open to the other man."

In answer to a telegram, Milton met Eisenhower's train; he had driven in from his home in Falls Church, where Eisenhower was to stay until Mamie arrived in mid-January. During that time he never saw Milton's house in daylight.

On the morning of December 14, Milton drove Eisenhower directly to the old Munitions Building on Constitution Avenue where Marshall had his office. The Pentagon was being built on the other side of the Potomac.

Eisenhower reported at once to the chief of staff. Marshall made no effort to put him at ease. Eisenhower said, "Without preamble or waste of time the Chief of Staff outlined the general situation, naval and military, in the western Pacific. The Navy informed him that the Pacific fleet would be unable for some months to participate in major operations. . . . At that moment there was no assurance that the Japanese would not quickly launch a major amphibious assault upon Hawaii or possibly even upon the mainland. . . . The Navy Yard at Cavite, just outside Manila, had been damaged very severely by Japanese bombers on December 10. That portion of the modest task force comprising the Pacific fleet which was disposed at or near Manila consisted largely of small divisions of submarines. The largest warship in the Asiatic fleet was the heavy cruiser *Houston* at Iloilo.

"Against a strong and sustained attack, forces such as these could not hold out indefinitely. All the evidence indicated that the Japanese intended to overrun the Philippines as rapidly as possible, and the problem was to determine what could now be done.

"Marshall took perhaps twenty minutes to describe all this and then abruptly asked, 'What should be our general line of action?' "

Eisenhower, "hoping I was showing a poker face," asked for a few hours, and Marshall said, "All right," dismissing him.

The desk in the War Plans Division (WPD) to which Eisenhower had been assigned was not far from that of Gee Gerow, then head of the division. Gee was about to get a job Eisenhower would then have preferred, command of the 29th Division. It seems unlikely, however, that on the tense Sunday morning of December 14 they did more than exchange pleasantries.

Eisenhower put a sheet of yellow paper in the typewriter on the desk assigned him and with two fingers started typing.

Marshall had not thought it necessary to mention what Eisenhower called "the psychological effects of the Philippine battle upon people in the United States and throughout the Pacific. Clearly he felt that anyone stupid enough to overlook this consideration had no business wearing the star of a brigadier general. . . . Obviously, if I were to be of any service to General Marshall in the War Department, I would have to earn his confidence; the logic of this, my *first answer*, would have to be unimpeachable, and the answer would have to be prompt. A curious echo from long ago came to my aid."

The memory was of Fox Conner and those long days and nights in Panama, when the general told Eisenhower that a second world war was inevitable, that it would be fought with allies, and that George Catlett Marshall, who would certainly have a good deal to do with that war, was "close to being a genius."

Eisenhower immediately decided that such a man would have to have an answer that was "short, emphatic, and based on reasoning in which I honestly believed. No oratory, plausible argument, or glittering generality would impress anyone entitled to be labeled genius by Fox Conner."

Eisenhower's double-spaced written answer to the Marshall assignment began, "Assistance to the Far East." Under the heading "Steps to be Taken," he listed:

> Build up in Australia a base of operations from which supplies and personnel (air and ground types) can be moved into the Philippines. Speed is essential.
> Influence Russia to enter the war.

The brief text largely had to do with getting planes—pursuit, heavy bombers, and transport planes—to Australia. It ended with "Bombs and Ammunition."

Initially, utilize the bombs and ammunition now in Australia and to be carried on carriers and fast merchant vessels with planes. Establish fast merchant ship supply service from U.S. to Australia for maintenance. Ferry from Australia to Philippines.

The entire report was only about 300 words, "short," "emphatic," and based on Eisenhower's reasoning. He used it as the basis for what he said to Marshall when he returned to his office for a second interview later that same Sunday.

" 'General,' I said, 'it will be a long time before major reinforcements can go to the Philippines, longer than any garrison can hold out without any direct assistance, if the enemy commits major forces to their reduction, but we must do everything for them that is humanly possible. The people of China, of the Philippines, of the Dutch East Indies will be watching us. They may excuse failure but they will not excuse abandonment. Their trust and friendship are important to us.' "

He went on to tell Marshall, "Our base must be Australia, and we must start at once to expand it and to secure our communications to it. In this last we dare not fail. We must take great risks and spend any amount of money required." Eisenhower had, as Goodpaster said, "analyzed what was in the other fellow's mind," and had shown "a great regard for the options open to the other man."

Marshall did not seem overjoyed or overwhelmed at the brilliance of the junior officer; he acted like a confident man who was chief of staff of an army that was ill-equipped, short of men, and already humiliatingly defeated in many areas of the world—but an army that would continue to fight and would prevail. He said, "I agree with you." Eisenhower noted, "His tone implied that I had been given the problem as a check to an answer he had already reached. He added, 'Do your best to save them.' "

On December 19, Eisenhower was permanently assigned to Washington. His first WPD job title was Deputy Chief for the Pacific and Far East. Early the next day he wrote to Krueger:

This is literally the first minute I have had to make even the briefest kind of report to you. I arrived here Sunday morning and have been working incessantly ever since with never more than a few brief hours for sleep.

My immediate assignment is as an assistant to Gerow to lighten the burden of this office. The rapid, minute-by-minute activities of the Army seem to be centered through this place, because no one else is familiar with everything else that has been planned in the past. As quickly as this work can be centralized properly the pressure should ease up some, but there is no prospect of it becoming "normal."

Up to yesterday I was determinedly clinging to the hope that I could return to your headquarters at a reasonably early date. That hope went glimmering when I found out last night that my transfer has been made a permanent one.

I was not consulted and naturally I have never been asked as to my personal preference. This of course is exactly as it should be, but it does not prevent my telling you how bitterly disappointed I am to have to leave you, particularly at this time.

In his reply Krueger said:

As you know, I had little hope of keeping you with the Third Army for long, but scarcely expected that you would be taken away this early in the game. However, I am sure that your new position offers a wider field for your abilities, and is in the best interests of the service. . . . I am deeply appreciative of the fine work you did here as my Chief of Staff, and sincerely hope that the experience you gained on the catching end will not be obliterated entirely by the press of your work on the pitching end.

My very best wishes to you in the new and wider field of usefulness that lies before you. I know that you will make an outstanding success in whatever position you may be called upon to fill. But I regret that, for the time at least, it is to be staff rather than command.

On December 12, the day Eisenhower left San Antonio for Washington, Winston Churchill boarded the battleship *Duke of York* for the same destination. The ship sailed from Greenock in Scotland on a wet and windy day.

The stormy weather continued all across the Atlantic, and Churchill remained below deck most of the time. He said, "Many serious reasons required my presence in London. . . . [But] I never had any doubt that a complete understanding between Britain and the United States outweighed all else, and that I must go to Washington at once with the strongest team of expert advisers who could be spared."

He did bring along an impressive list of advisers, and Brigadier General Eisenhower, although he mostly sat on the sidelines during the forthcoming conferences, worked closely with all of them later in the war. Perhaps his favorite was Sir Charles A. Portal, Marshal of the Royal Air Force, Chief of the Air Staff, of whom he said, "His distinguishing characteristic was balance, with perfect control of his temper; even in the most intense argument I never saw him show anger or unusual excitement." Admiral of the Fleet Sir Dudley Pound, Chief of Naval Staff and First Sea Lord, was sixty-four years old, but in the years ahead he was to be largely responsible for the successful outcome of the Allied war in the Atlantic. Lieutenant General Sir Hastings L. Ismay, nicknamed "Pug" for his bulldog visage, more than anyone else ran the British war machine. General Sir John Dill also came along; he had been thought by Churchill to be too cautious to continue as chief of the Imperial General Staff and had recently been replaced by Sir Alan Brooke, whose relations with Eisenhower were never wholly harmonious. Brooke remained in London.

After the British and American meetings in Washington, Dill stayed behind as the personal representative of Churchill, working with the combined chiefs of staff. He was a most fortunate choice for this position, and was able to do the nearly impossible in interpreting the British to the Americans and vice versa. After his death in 1944, Roosevelt said that he had been "the most important figure in the remarkable record which had been developed in the combined operations of our two countries." Sir John was buried in Arlington National Cemetery, the only foreigner to be so honored.

Next to Churchill, the most important man in the British delegation was Max Aitken, Lord Beaverbrook, who was Churchill's Minister of Supply and the publisher of three vastly popular London newspapers, the *Daily Express, Sunday Express,* and *Evening Standard,* which were soon to make Eisenhower's name a household word.

This first series of meetings between Churchill and Roosevelt and their advisers to take place after Pearl Harbor had been given the code name ARCADIA, but there was nothing pastoral about it. The differences between the Allies were deep and complex, and the careful staff work done by the British on the way to Washington turned out to be largely a waste of time, as did what had been done by Roosevelt's staff. The two leaders made most of the decisions in the evenings at the White House. Churchill was a guest there from the evening of his arrival on December 22 until his departure on January 14. Roosevelt's adviser Harry Hopkins insisted that one night Roosevelt wheeled himself into Churchill's room and found the prime minister naked, just out of the bath. Roosevelt apologized, but, according to Hopkins, Churchill said, "It's quite all right. The Prime Minister of Great Britain has nothing to conceal from the president of the United States."

Churchill claimed that he had never greeted Roosevelt without wearing at least a towel.

During the three weeks of the ARCADIA discussions, Eisenhower attended meetings largely as a spectator, on Christmas Day and on December 29, 30, 31, as well as January 9 and 10; he never met Churchill. Frequently Marshall read reports at ARCADIA meetings that Eisenhower had written. Ike several times listened to lengthy, often acrimonious debates over whether or not there should be an Allied landing in North Africa. (The operation was first code-named GYMNAST, then SUPER-GYMNAST. Eventually it would be carried out under the code name TORCH.) Churchill hoped that the operation would take place in a few weeks; Marshall and Eisenhower did not want it to happen at all. Both were opposed to what they called "peripheral strategy." If Germany was to be defeated, it could in their opinion only be done by a direct cross-Channel invasion of the continent. Roosevelt at one time or another was on both sides of the question. When he was with Churchill, he supported him; when he was with his chief of staff, he appeared to support his view.

There was always complete agreement on one matter, the importance of keeping Russia in the war. If the Soviet Union collapsed, the Germans could use all their strength against the Western powers. It was feared, too, that if the Soviet Union was desperately weakened and Stalin felt that Britain and the United States were doing very little to help, he might once again sign a non-aggression pact with Hitler.

There was apparent agreement on a "massive landing" in Europe in 1943, but the timing was not actually agreed on, and the invasion could be across the Mediterranean, from Turkey into the Balkans, or by landings in Western Europe. The British favored the former, the Americans the latter. It was agreed, however, that wherever the landings took place, they would be "the prelude to the final assault on Germany itself, and the scope of the victory program should be such as to provide means by which they can be carried out."

Eisenhower worked right through the holiday season that year, as did most of the officers in the War Department. On Christmas Day, in addition to an ARCADIA meeting, he attended a joint conference of the chiefs of staff and took notes. Later that evening he went to his brother Milton's house alone. Mamie, who had remained in Texas, was visiting their son John at West Point. She stopped off in Washington on her way back to San Antonio and stayed at Milton's, but she scarcely saw her husband. Milton remembered that during that period Eisenhower usually got to the house in Falls Church late at night and "would go at once to our children's bedroom, wake them, and have a relaxing chat. . . . While these nightly visits were underway, my wife would go to the kitchen and prepare a light but nutritious meal, nearly always including a pot of cocoa, which helped Ike get to sleep. . . . He would leave our home early in the morning. Our cook and houseman would get up at six-thirty in order to serve his breakfast by seven. He was in his office by seven-thirty each day . . . " where he remained at his desk for a "skimpy" lunch and dinner. "Every day the same—7:45 A.M. to 11:45 P.M.," Eisenhower wrote in his diary.

New Year's Eve was different, however. On that day he did manage to get out of the office for lunch. Later that evening, back in the office and still hard at work, he took a short break to write and unburden himself to his friend LeRoy Lutes. Lutes was about to come to Washington to join the Services of Supply. Eisenhower wrote, "Just to give you an inkling as to the kind of madhouse you are getting into—it is now eight o'clock New Year's Eve. I have a couple hours' work ahead of me, and tomorrow will be no different from today. I have been here about three weeks and this noon I had my first luncheon outside of the office. Usually it is a hot-dog sandwich and a glass of milk. I have had one evening meal in the whole period. . . . I can tell you frankly that you will never have time to find a place to live, even if any places were available." At the bottom of the letter Eisenhower wrote, "Happy New Year!"

During the first week of January, Eisenhower noted in his diary, "Tempers are short. There are lots of amateur strategists on the job, and prima donnas everywhere. I'd give anything to be back in the field. . . . The conversations with the British grow wearisome. They're difficult to talk to, apparently afraid someone is trying to tell them what to do and how to do it. Their practice of war is dilatory.

"Chief of Staff out of town one day. Would be a relief except we've so much work we can't catch up anyway so we'll go home at 10 P.M. as usual."

As was to be the case during most of the war when Eisenhower was working under great stress, his health suffered. In his diary, he noted, "Two days of feeling bum. Hope it's only flu. Afraid it may be shingles coming back. . . . "

The last ARCADIA meeting was held on January 12. Churchill said, "The most valuable and lasting result of our first Washington Conference . . . was the setting up of the now famous 'Combined Chiefs of Staff Committee.' " Marshall had been convinced since America's entry into the war that only a totally combined chiefs of staff would work; the British tried, without success, largely due to Marshall, to keep some tactical matters separate and in London. By the end of ARCADIA, however, Marshall's victory was complete. The Combined Chiefs were firmly established in Washington.

After the conference, the "Atlantic First" strategy remained intact. Just how the invasion of Europe would be carried out was still unsettled, though both sides tended to think they had won.

Despite apparent agreement between the Allies, only one matter was not subject to argument during the ARCADIA meetings or later; that was that "only a minimum of forces necessary for safeguarding vital interests [in the Pacific] should be diverted from operations against Germany."

Eisenhower said, "Our planning and organizational work sometimes involved differences in national conceptions that struck at the very foundation of our basic plan. These points were discussed in an atmosphere of cordiality and objectivity, but they were nonetheless serious. Whenever I found myself opposed to the views of the Prime Minister, he was, of course, supported by his War Cabinet and technical advisers. That differences should occur was inescapable and natural. Varying situations in national geography bring with them differences in military doctrine, and special war experiences bring with them strong differences in projected strategy."

In most major arguments, Americans, their interests often articulated by Eisenhower, won, in large part because the United States had become stronger and more important in the war than Britain. Almost nobody noticed at the time, but one empire was ending and another was beginning. When Eisenhower became president in 1953 he recognized that fact; he recognized that the war he had played so large a part in winning had not only defeated Germany, which was what he had intended; it had also defeated Great Britain, which he had not had in mind.

★ ★ ★

A MAN OF RESPONSIBILITY

The first months of 1942 were not a happy time for Eisenhower. He soon realized that while George Marshall had none of the wild irrationality of Douglas MacArthur, he was not an easy superior officer. No one ever described his rare, reluctant, and brief smile as a grin. He was often described as "reserved," and one cannot help wondering how Marshall would have fared with the reserved English had he become supreme commander. Eisenhower made everybody feel at ease in his presence. Almost nobody felt at ease in Marshall's presence. In many respects he was a lot like Eisenhower's father, David. No one, not even Mrs. Marshall, suffered the delusion that they were close to Marshall. General Walter Krueger, commenting on Marshall's detachment, said, "If you really tried to find out what he was like, he clammed up, and you never discovered what he was really thinking."

Marshall had a quick temper but was far more successful than Ike in concealing it. In his last speech to the cadets at VMI, he said, "Don't be a deep feeler and a poor thinker." He was on a first-name basis with no one, including, it was said, his wife Katherine. He often called her "Lily," the nickname of his first wife. Mark Clark said, "He never called Ike 'Ike,' he never called me Mark. He was never familiar with people. He was all business." When once, in 1945, he called Eisenhower "Ike," he promptly used Eisenhower five times to make up for it. It bothered him when President Roosevelt called him George, and later, when FDR told him, "Everyone calls me Franklin; why don't you call me Franklin?" Marshall said, "I'll try, Mr. President." He couldn't remember names. He almost always called his longtime aide Frank McCarthy, Frank McCart*ney*; his secretary Miss Nason, to Marshall, was "Miss *M*ason." Sometimes he could not remember a name at all. He would say, "You know who I mean, red eyes." From that, whoever it was would have to figure out who best fitted that description, not always an easy task. Eisenhower never forgot a name. Apart from his inability to remember names, however, Marshall possessed "a wicked memory," according to his wife. "He never forgets a brilliant performance and he never forgives a dullard. Mediocrity seems to make little impression on him, except by way of irritation."

Although they never became close friends, the chief of staff and Eisenhower had a great many things in common. Marshall was born on December 31, 1880, in a small town not far from Pittsburgh—Uniontown, Pennsylvania—and his boyhood had many similarities to Eisenhower's. Both fathers had awesome tempers. The elder Marshall used a willow stick for punishment; David Eisenhower used a hickory stick. Like Ida Eisenhower, Marshall's mother, Laura, had a lasting influence on his life.

Marshall, like Ike, wanted a field command. Both were good with troops, although neither man spent very much time with them. It was the regret of both their lives. Harry Truman once said of Marshall, "Of course, he wanted a field command and he'd have been wonderful at it, but Roosevelt convinced him his job was in Washington as Chief of Staff, and that's what he did, and he did it without a single complaint." Clark said, "When we needed Eisenhower, we had him; when we needed Marshall, we had him."

Both Marshall and Eisenhower were dedicated professional soldiers. But they were very different men. For example, Eisenhower, as we know, was a prolific writer; Marshall was not. He did help Pershing organize his memoirs, but the only book Marshall himself wrote, between 1919 and 1923, was brief, totally impersonal despite its being called *George C. Marshall, Memoirs of My Services in the World War 1917–1918*, and without penetrating or even interesting insights. It had been turned down by Houghton Mifflin in 1924; it "needed more work," a phrase familiar to all authors. Marshall never found the time for that work nor, it would seem, did he have much interest. Shortly before his death, he asked his wife to see to it that the manuscript be burned, but a copy turned up in the attic of the Marshall house in Leesburg, Virginia. It was published by Houghton Mifflin in 1976, still needing more work.

Eisenhower's *Crusade in Europe* was long, lucid, and enormously profitable; for reasons that infuriated most professional writers, including this one, he was allowed to take advantage of the "capital gains" tax. He also profited handsomely from *Mandate for Change, Waging Peace, At Ease,* and *In Review*—a compilation of material, mostly personal, from his previous four books.

Marshall's approach to such matters was quite different. In a speech at the U.S. Air Force Academy in Colorado, his offical biographer, Forrest C. Pogue, said that Marshall was determined not to write a memoir after the Second World War, "saying that he had not served his country to sell his story to a popular magazine." Even when he agreed to cooperate with a biographer, he stipulated that the writer must be selected by a responsible committee in whose deliberations he would have no part, and that any payment received from the book or articles based on his statements or his papers could not go to him or any member of his family but must be given to a nonprofit foundation to aid further research.

Eisenhower was never described as imperturbable, but Marshall often was, and he did appear to be "not easily excited, calm." On the morning of June 6, 1944, Frank McCarthy called the Marshall home and, according to Mrs. Marshall, said, "Is the general there? It's supremely important." Mrs. Marshall called the general, who came to the phone and said, "Yes, Frank, I see." Then, Mrs. Marshall said, "he hung up. I said, 'Frank told me it was supremely important and that's all you said. What did he tell you?' " General Marshall said, "He told me that the troops landed during the night." Mrs. Marshall said, "You didn't ask how things were going." Marshall said, "At this distance don't you think that's Eisenhower's problem?"

Ike said of his early association with Marshall, "During the frantic, tumultuous months I spent in the War Department in the Planning Section and later as Chief of Operations, I was with General Marshall every day. I knew about his reputation, of course, but before long I had conceived for him unlimited admiration and respect for my own reasons. He inspired affection in me because I realized the burden he was uncomplainingly carrying. He never seemed to doubt that we could win, even when the Philippines had fallen."

Later Ike said, "Of Americans I have known personally, I think that George Marshall possessed more of the qualities of greatness than has any other."

Eisenhower's job in the War Department was in large part to do what could not be done, and he knew it could not be done. It was to furnish enough reinforcements to the Philippines so that the islands could hold out against the Japanese onslaught. It had been decided at the ARCADIA conference, though not clearly stated, that what Eisenhower had said in his first report to Marshall was true—the Philippines could not be saved, but it was necessary to go through the motions. Enough help could not be sent in time. Everyone agreed on that, and everyone avoided saying so. Ike knew that the officers and men fighting there, many of them friends, could not hold out for long.

Soon after Ike's arrival in Washington, it was decided that the best, possibly the only way to get supplies to the islands was to hire men and ships to run the

Japanese blockade. Eisenhower and Marshall agreed that the man for this mission was Patrick J. Hurley, who had been Herbert Hoover's secretary of war. Roosevelt had just appointed him ambassador to New Zealand, but Hurley, a feisty Oklahoman, wanted more active service. So Roosevelt sent him over to the Munitions Building to see Marshall. Hurley, it will be remembered, had lavishly praised MacArthur's heroism in dispersing the Bonus Marchers and was a certified MacArthur enthusiast, eager to help. He was given a huge sum of money and told to proceed at once to Australia and spend whatever was necessary to run the Japanese blockade of the Philippines. According to Marshall, he first made Hurley a temporary brigadier general. Then, to keep the loose-lipped Hurley from sharing the good news with the press, he sent him to the War Plans Division. There, according to Marshall, Eisenhower and Gerow were "to keep him . . . and take him to a plane shortly after midnight."

Eisenhower and Gerow each gave Hurley a star for his uniform and got him on the plane. But the assignment proved more difficult than dispersing Bonus Marchers. Only three of seven ships that sailed from Australia got as far as Cebu; none of the ships reached Bataan, and only a thousand tons of supplies reached the garrison in Luzon. A few submarines got through, but that was all. By the middle of January, the defenders of Bataan were on half rations, Filipino rations.

MacArthur's forces were pinned down in the island of Corregidor and in the Bataan peninsula. A Filipino friend of Eisenhower's, Carlos P. Romulo, who was to become one of the early leaders of the United Nations, said of the main tunnel on Corregidor where as many as 5,000 soldiers and Philippine civilians, including Quezon, were quartered, "The smell of the place hit me like a blow in the face. There was the stench of sweat and dirty clothes, the coppery smell of blood and disinfectant, coming from the lateral where the hospital was situated, and over all, the heavy stink of creosote, hanging like a blanket in the air that moved sluggishly when it moved at all."

Under the circumstances, the impatience of MacArthur and, later, Quezon was understandable, but Eisenhower was impatient, too. On January 29 he wrote in his diary, "MacArthur has started a flood of communications that seem to indicate a refusal on his part to look facts in the face, an old trait of his. He has talked about big naval concentrations . . . he complains about lack of unity of command, about lack of information. He's jittery!" And on February 3, "Looks like MacArthur is losing his nerve. I'm hoping that his yelps are just his way of spurring us on, but he is always an uncertain factor."

If in the past Ike's assignment to Washington had been irritating, by February it had come close to being unbearable. Brigadier generals, some of them not as bright as he, were preparing their troops for battle. And what was he doing? He was acting as a messenger boy for MacArthur and Quezon. MacArthur's dissatisfaction seemed to grow every day, and he passed each complaint along to Washington, phrased in the familiar MacArthur hyperbole. But the American public needed a hero at that time, and MacArthur's forces at least were fighting back, and his communiqués were optimistic. On February 8, however, Eisenhower may very well have decided, as Harry Truman did in 1951, that MacArthur had "missed too many boats" to the mainland of the U.S. Quezon was ill with tuberculosis and certain that in his lifetime the islands would never be free again, and since he thought that Washington was to blame for most of his troubles, he suggested that if the United States would remove its troops from the Philippines and grant independence to the islands, he would do his best to persuade the Japanese to remove their troops. The high commissioner to the Philippines, Francis B. Sayre, approved of the proposal, and MacArthur's accompanying message said, "So far as the military angle is concerned, the problem presents itself as to whether the plan of President Quezon might offer the best possible solution as to what is about to be a disastrous debacle. . . . Please instruct me."

It was a ticklish business to reply to Quezon's outlandish suggestion. Secretary of War Henry L. Stimson tried, as did Admirals Harold Stark and Ernest King. Sumner Welles, under secretary of state, worked on the message, and so did Marshall. But in the end, the man who drafted almost all of it was Dwight Eisenhower. It was not only an important assignment; it was one that must have given him grim pleasure. For FDR's signature, he wrote a firm reminder to MacArthur to do what he was in Manila to do—his duty. The message said, "American forces will continue to keep our flag flying in the Philippines so long as there remains any possibility of resistance. I have made these decisions in complete understanding of your military estimate that accompanied President Quezon's message to me. The duty and necessity of resisting Japanese aggression to the last transcends in importance any other obligation now facing us in the Philippines."

The message also said, "I authorize you to arrange for the capitulation of the Filipino elements of the defending forces when and if in your opinion that course appears necessary and always having in mind that the Filipino troops are in the service of the United States."

On February 9 Eisenhower wrote in his diary, "Spent the entire day preparing drafts of president's message to MacArthur and Quezon. Long, difficult, and irritating. Both are babies. But now we'll see what happens. Tonight at 6:45 I saw the president and got his approval to sending the messages."

MacArthur's reply was equally stern but seemed to indicate that he had never supported the Quezon suggestion. "My plans have already been outlined in previous radios; they consist of fighting [only] present battle position in Bataan to destruction and then holding Corregidor in a similar manner. I have not the slightest intention in the world of surrendering or capitulating the Filipino elements of my command. . . . There has never been the slightest wavering among the troops. I count on them equally with the Americans to hold steadfast to the end."

Mamie and Mickey McKeogh arrived in Washington around this time. Mickey drove the Chrysler east from San Antonio, and Mamie came by train. Again she had supervised the packing of their belongings. She once said, "I could have made quite a career out of running a transfer company. Or maybe I overestimate my ability; our belongings just about pack themselves. I might have less luck with other people's 'untrained' possessions." She spent a week at Milton's house in Falls Church, then found a three-room apartment at the

Wardman Park Hotel. John remembered the apartment as being on the same floor as that of Secretary of Agriculture Henry A. Wallace, and directly above that of Secretary of State Cordell Hull.

Eisenhower did not have many evenings at home, but it was pleasant to have Mamie there when he did. She fussed over him, coddled him, and amused him with inconsequential conversation. She seldom asked how things had gone at the office, and he seldom told her.

When Mickey arrived on February 7, he found a room not far away, "and then for a while I spent most of my time driving Mrs. Eisenhower around Washington. It was about ten days after I got to Washington that I first saw the Boss, who was working eighteen to twenty hours a day."

He had driven Mamie to the Munitions Building to pick up "the Boss." Mickey said, "He came out and I was standing by the car, holding the door open. The first thing I thought was that he was more tired than I'd ever seen him; all of his face was tired. But he smiled when he saw me, and that did what it always did to his face; even when he was tired. I saluted, but he didn't return the salute. Instead he held out his hand and said, 'Mickey, I'm glad to see you.' . . . His voice was tired, like his face. He got in the car without saying much of anything and all the way back to the hotel he said almost nothing. He was never talkative, but that day he was very silent."

It was just the day before that Eisenhower had become assistant chief of staff, head of the War Plans Division (WPD). His friend Gee Gerow, whom he had replaced, was quite brilliant but did not possess Eisenhower's self-confidence and decisiveness. John Eisenhower said it was too bad "the way Dad replaced Gerow there. Gerow had sort of run himself out. Dad and Gee had been very close through the years, but during the war, when Gerow was commander of the Fifteenth Army, they were no longer close." Gee's watch had not been a happy period for the Allies, and when he left for his assignment as commander of the 29th Division he said to Eisenhower, "Well, I got Pearl Harbor on the book; lost the Philippine Islands, Singapore, Sumatra, and all the NEI [Netherlands East Indies] north of the barrier. Let's see what you can do."

Even though he was being replaced, Gerow's final report on Eisenhower was most generous. He said that the performance of his classmate at Command and General Staff School had been, since he arrived in Washington, superior; he rated him excellent in physical endurance, superior in the knowledge of his profession; he recommended that in wartime Eisenhower should have "the highest command in the Army." On a list of 111 officers known personally to him, Gee said he considered Eisenhower the "best officer of his rank in the entire army."

John J. McCloy, who at the time was assistant secretary of war, said Marshall had told him when General Gerow was relieved, "We're going to put a new man in charge of War Plans who may at some stage be destined for pretty high command."

Eisenhower's old friend Art Hurd in Abilene wrote him a letter congratulating him on his impressive new appointment:

The *Kansas City Times* this morning had the story of your added responsibilities and for the third time in a year, I wish to extend congratulations.

My prophecy is that within twelve months, I will write another letter about the addition of another star. There are not so many rungs left in that ladder extending above your head.

I have just talked to your Mother, thinking that she might have some message for you. She said to tell you that your father's condition is not any worse nor has it improved. [He was ill with arteriosclerosis.] He lies down most of the time. Your mother had not heard the latest news about you and I am taking a copy of this morning's *Times* down to her in a few moments. . . . I am tempted to write a letter to John and tell him what a smart boy he is in picking out his dad.

Ike's secretary during those hectic days was a handsome young woman from Buffalo, New York, named Helen Dunbar, and she, too, kept a diary. She said that every day began with "a planning conference, a blitz." Such sessions sometimes lasted from twelve to fourteen hours, and one of her jobs was to keep Eisenhower supplied with Philip Morris cigarettes and vitamin pills. She said that he was "always in a rush."

Being highly circumspect, she recorded next to nothing about war reports or the work in Eisenhower's office. But she wrote a good deal about her boss:

There is never anything discourteous, questioning or sloppily said in any of his letters or inter-office memoranda. Everything is suitable and polished. He can draw words out of his mind like MacArthur and his memory is meticulous.

She wrote of a report on the Philippines that Eisenhower dictated to her:

It was six pages long, detailed, specific . . . all of it from memory and it was accurate.

He uses every opportunity and chance and every person who comes along, not to the other's disadvantage, as others do, but justly and equally. His time is planned for, and he makes the most of it.

Once shortly after she started working in the War Plans Division she put through a call to another general, and Eisenhower had to wait while she did it. After he hung up, he said, "Miss Dunbar, you get the guy on the phone first or I'll wring your neck. I can't lose a minute around here." She said, "His eyes twinkled, but I got the message."

Among the visitors that crowded in the Munitions Building every day was Lucian K. Truscott, Jr., who was to go to London to work with Mountbatten on plans for commanding amphibious operations. Colonel Truscott, who had worked with Eisenhower at Fort Lewis, said, "There was everywhere the sense of urgency, of hurry, as though time were pressing, and everywhere an air of mystery as though all could tell of deep, dark secrets. . . .

"His methods had not changed from those I had been familiar with the year before at Fort Lewis. Every problem was carefully analyzed. There was the same extraordinary ability to place his finger at once on the crucial fact in any problem or the weak point in any proposition. There was the same ability to arrive at quick and confident decisions. And the same charming manner and unfailing good temper."

If others treated winning the war casually, Ike did not. He was working seven days a week from eight in the morning until ten o'clock at night, and at times he would even come back to the office in the middle of the night to tie up loose ends. Marshall had learned early on that Eisenhower did what he was asked to do—and always more. He also learned that Eisenhower was able, unlike his predecessor, to act on his own: Eisenhower did not burden Marshall with unnecessary decisions. Years later, on his seventy-fifth birthday, in October 1965, Ike told Merriman Smith that he once had what he called "a Dutch-uncle talk" with President Lyndon Johnson.

> I told him what I thought, although you can't be as blunt as you'd like to be when talking to the President. I told him that when I was operations officer in the War Department that I moved whole divisions in and out of the country and that I reported to General Marshall about it only when I saw him on Saturday mornings for our review of the week. . . .
>
> A man with the responsibilities of the President should not allow himself to be bogged down in detail. For one thing, in a war or combat zone, this can be upsetting emotionally and throw off judgment.
>
> The President's job is to know exactly what the problem is that he should solve and then decide how to solve it. Then he's got to find his lieutenants, his preconsuls and then trust the man he himself picks and say, "Now you do this within the limits I give you."
>
> Do you send troops to Lebanon or don't you? Now, it's up to somebody to find where the troops are, exactly what kind, what's the date they're going in and so forth. The President of the United States should not burden himself with all of those things.

One decision Eisenhower made without consulting Marshall, and perhaps the one that caused him the most prolonged worry, involved the *Queen Mary*.

The British had given the Americans permission to use their fastest, largest, and most luxurious liners, the *Queen Mary* and the newly commissioned *Queen Elizabeth*, to transport troops. When Eisenhower found that the *Queen Mary* was in New York harbor, he "moved a whole division out of the country" aboard her, bound for Australia, without telling Marshall.

The journey was a long one, with the first stop at Rio de Janeiro to refuel. There the *QM* was seen by an Italian agent who cabled Rome that the ship, "with about 15,000 soldiers aboard, left this port today steaming southeast across the Atlantic." The ship then sailed for the Cape of Good Hope and was to proceed across the South Pacific to Melbourne. Eisenhower slept fitfully those nights, convinced that the *Queen* either had been or was about to be sunk by a submarine. It arrived safely, however, with its precious cargo intact. Indeed, in five years the great British passenger liners transported 200,000 troops and never once sighted a U-boat.

In *Crusade in Europe*, Eisenhower wrote, "I do not remember whether General

Marshall knew of this incident at the time, but it was the kind of thing that we kept from him when possible. There was no use burdening his mind with the worries that we were forced to carry to bed with us. He had enough of his own."

On the other hand, biographers of Eisenhower have noted that when Ike told Marshall that the ship was safe, the chief of staff said, "I received that intercept at the same time as you did. I was merely hoping that you might not see it and so I said nothing to you until I knew the outcome."

Ike hadn't liked most of his army assignments, and he didn't like this one. In a letter to retired Major General Daniel Van Voorhis, he said, "Gee and I have really played tag with each other all along the line; but this is the first time I really envy him. My heart is in the field and it is hard to sit at a desk on days such as these. The powers that be have put me in this backbreaking job—so all I can do is hope."

Georgie Patton, as usual, had the assignment Ike wanted: commanding general of I Corps. He had written that, with Ike in the War Department, "we will eventually beat hell out of those bastards—You name them; I'll shoot them." Ike wrote back:

> I don't have the slightest trouble naming the hellions I'd like to have you shoot; my problem is to figure out some way of getting you to a place to do it. . . . It was a personal disappointment to me to come to Washington. . . . This thing is too serious to worry about anyone's personal preferences, so I have wrapped up in cotton batting all my ideas about troop training and laid them away in mothballs. You'll have to do that end of the job.

In a letter to his friend General Krueger, dated February 19, he complained that his job was "a slave seat. . . . I have been here ten weeks next Sunday and in that time I have never left the office in daylight and Sundays and all holidays are exactly the same as all the others."

On Sunday, February 22, Roosevelt decided that because MacArthur had become such a symbol of Allied strength in the Pacific, he must not be taken prisoner. Therefore, he must abandon his troops, a humiliation for any commander, and proceed first to Mindanao and then to Australia. "You are directed to make this change as quickly as possible." It was made clear that the order, signed by Marshall, was that of the president. "Instruction will be given from here at your request for the movement by submarine or plane or both to enable you to carry out the foregoing instructions. You are authorized to take with you your chief of staff, General Sutherland."

After he sent the order, Ike wrote in his diary, "Message to MacArthur was approved by the Pres and dispatched. . . . In a war such as this, when high command invariably involves a president, a prime minister, six chiefs of staff, and a horde of lesser 'planners,' there has got to be a lot of patience—no one person can be a Napoleon or a Caesar. And certainly there's no room for a Pope [Civil War general John Pope] or a Gates [Revolutionary War general Horatio

Gates]. It's a backbreaking job to get a simple battle order out, and then it can't be executed for from three to four months."

In commenting on Kenneth Davis's book *Soldier of Democracy*, in which Davis used a quote by Jules Romain to the effect that simple ideas are sometimes hard to apply to masses of armed men in a highly emotional atmosphere, Eisenhower, perhaps thinking of himself, said, "A shrewd observation—one writer said the 'military genius is the man that can do the average when everyone else is going insane.' "

There was considerable doubt in everybody's mind, including MacArthur's, as to whether he would carry out the order of a man he despised, his commander in chief. And Eisenhower had his own doubts about the wisdom of the move. He wrote in his diary, "I cannot help believing that we are disturbed by editorials and reacting to 'public opinion' rather than to military logic. 'Pa' Watson [General Edwin M. Watson, FDR's military aide] is certain we must get MacArthur out, as being worth 'five army corps.' He is doing a good job where he is, but I'm doubtful that he'd do so well in more complicated situations. Bataan is made to order for him. It is in the public eye; it has made him a public hero; it has all the essentials of drama, and he is the acknowledged king on the spot. If brought out, public opinion will force him into a position where his love of the limelight may ruin him." On the 24th he added, "MacArthur says, in effect, 'Not now.' I think he is right." It should be noted that nowhere during these months did Ike express any sympathy or understanding for MacArthur's real difficulties.

At sunset on March 11, after several more sharp prods from Washington, MacArthur left the islands for Australia by PT boat.

Almost two and a half years later, on September 25, 1944, remembering the trouble he had taken and the time he had expended in 1942 to help MacArthur, Eisenhower closed a personal report to Marshall by saying, "To end up this long letter, you might not mind a personal note. It is that you take for your 'bedtime reading' a little book written by Frazier Hunt called *MacArthur and the War Against Japan*. You will be quite astonished to learn that back in the Winter of 41/42, you and your assistants in the War Department had no real concern for the Philippines and the forces fighting there—indeed, you will be astonished to learn a lot of things the book publishes as fact. I admit that the book practically gave me indigestion. Something you should know before considering this suggestion further."

The day MacArthur left the Philippines, Eisenhower learned that his father had died. David was seventy-nine, the same age his son Dwight would be at the time of his death in 1969. Eisenhower's duties were so pressing that he was unable to do more than send a telegram.

In addition to the troubles he was having with MacArthur, there were also joint army-navy problems, and that day his anger exploded into his diary, particularly against Admiral Ernest J. King, who as commander in chief of the U.S. fleet and chief of naval operations was to have a good deal to do with the Allied naval victory and who would become a close associate and admirer of Eisenhower's. Not that day, however. Eisenhower wrote, "One thing that might help win this war is to get someone to shoot King. He's the antithesis of cooperation, a deliberately rude person, which means he's a mental bully. . . . This fellow is going to cause a blow-up sooner or later, I'll bet a cookie. . . . Gradually some of the people with whom I have to deal are coming to agree with me that there are just three 'musts' for the Allies this year—hold open the line to England and support her as necessary; keep Russia in the war as an active participant; hold the India–Middle East buttress between Japs and Germans. All this assumes the safety from major attack of North America, Hawaii and Caribbean area. . . . We lost 8 cargo ships yesterday. That must stop, because any effort we make depends upon sea communication."

On March 14, he felt a further need to justify in his diary his anger over King. "Lest I look at this book sometime and find that I've expressed a distaste for some person, and have put down no reason for my aversion, I record this one story of Admiral King.

"One day this week General [Henry H. "Hap"] Arnold sent a very important note to King. Through inadvertence, the stenographer in Arnold's office addressed it, on the outside, to 'Rear Admiral King.' Twenty-four hours later the letter came back unopened, with an arrow pointing to the "Rear," thus: [Here a long, heavy arrow has been drawn in a diagonal line underneath and pointing to the word "Rear."] And that's the size of man the navy has at its head. He ought to be a big help winning this war."

Sometime later Eisenhower replaced this last sentence with "Must have been someone of the admiral's staff, as he's too big to let a little thing like that bother him." After the war and upon his return to Washington, Eisenhower discovered the diary notes of 1942, which he had left behind, and was chagrined to observe his treatment of King. "In glancing back over old notes I see that Admiral King annoyed me. In justice I should say that all through the war, whenever I called on him for assistance, he supported me fully and instantly."

Although many of the troops MacArthur left behind in the Philippines were understandably bitter, his escape to Australia was greeted as a great triumph by the press; on March 18 the banner headline on the front page of the *New York Times* said, MACARTHUR IN AUSTRALIA AS ALLIED COMMANDER. MOVE HAILED AS FORESHADOWING TURN OF THE TIDE.

Eisenhower did not agree; on March 19 he wrote in his diary, "MacArthur is out of Philippine Islands. Now supreme commander of 'Southwest Pacific Area.' The newspapers proclaim the move—the public has built itself a hero out of its own imagination. I hope he can perform the miracles expected and predicted; we could use a few now. Strange that no one sees the dangers. Some apply to MacArthur, who could be ruined by it. But this I minimize. I know him too well. The other danger is that we will move too heavily in the Southwest. Urging us to that direction now will be: Australians, New Zealanders, our public (wanting support for the hero), and MacArthur. If we tie up our shipping for the SW Pacific, we'll lose the war."

He later wrote, "Professional military ability and strength of character, always required in high military position, are often marred by unfortunate characteristics, the two most frequently encountered and hurtful ones being a too obvious avidity for public acclaim and the delusion that strength of purpose demands arrogant and even insufferable deportment. A soldier once remarked that a man sure of his footing need not mount a horse."

By March 20 Eisenhower had been in Washington a little more than three months; he had carried out every assignment without hesitation; he had demonstrated an ability to make decisions without bothering the chief of staff; he had successfully dealt with a great number of important people, including the president of the United States; he had worked to the point of total exhaustion without audible complaint. Since March 9 he had been serving as the first chief of the War Department's Operations Division (OPD), as the reorganized, expanded WPD was now known.

It had been clear to Marshall even before Pearl Harbor that the War Department had to be reorganized; there was indeed too much clutter; there were too many people doing too little, too many meaningless titles, too many departments. In January he had chosen Eisenhower's brilliant West Point classmate, Major General Joseph T. McNarney, to do the job. Eisenhower said that McNarney was "possessed of an analytic mind and a certain ruthlessness in execution which was absolutely necessary to uproot entrenched bureaucracy and streamline and simplify procedures . . . a selfless soldier. Any views he may ever present to you will be his honest convictions and without any thought of the effect upon himself. I regard him as one of our finest. . . . He is tough but most sensible."

Now that the United States was in the war, Marshall also needed an agency which in Eisenhower's words "could assemble and concentrate the sum total of strategic information for General Marshall's attention and through which, after he had reached a decision, his commands could be implemented. This agency, in other words, would be the Chief of Staff's personal command post. The creation of the Operations Division . . . was the answer to this need."

Marshall had observed Eisenhower very carefully during this period; he knew how desperately Eisenhower wanted a field command. How would Eisenhower react if he was told that he would not get what he wanted, that he would spend the rest of the war behind a desk in Washington? On March 20 Marshall decided to find out. The two men were discussing the promotion of another officer, and Eisenhower said, Marshall "stopped to give me a bit of his philosophy on the subject. 'The men who are going to get the promotions in this war are the commanders in the field [Marshall said], not the staff officers who clutter up all the administrative machinery in the War Department and in higher tactical headquarters. The field commanders carry the responsibility and I'm going to see to it that they're properly rewarded so far as promotion can provide a reward.'

"To illustrate his point, General Marshall cited a number of cases in World War I where outstanding leadership of combat troops seemed to him to have been ignored. His opinion was that the staff had been constantly favored and pushed ahead of field commanders. This time, he said, he would reverse the practice. Finally, possibly because he realized that I had been brought from the field into the War Department on his personal order, he turned back to me and said:

" 'Take your case. I know that you were recommended by one general for division command and by another for corps command. That's all very well. I'm glad they have that opinion of you, but you are going to stay right here and fill your position, and that's that!'

"Then, to underscore the point, he said, 'While this may seem a sacrifice to you, that's the way it must be.' "

Eisenhower "impulsively broke out," saying, "General, I'm interested in what you say, but I want you to know that I don't give a damn about your promotion plans as far as I'm concerned. I came into this office from the field and I am trying to do my duty. I expect to do so as long as you want me here. If that locks me to a desk for the rest of the war, so be it!"

Eisenhower rose; the distance between Marshall's desk and the door must never have seemed longer, but he walked that last mile; he turned at the door and thought he saw a slight smile on that usually unrelenting face. Eisenhower returned to his own office and set down his opinion of the chief of staff. It is a pity that the document is lost to history, but the next day Eisenhower was calm as he wrote, "Yesterday I got very angry and filled a page with language that this morning I've 'expurgated.' Anger cannot win, it cannot even think clearly. In this respect, Marshall puzzles me a bit. I've never seen a man who apparently develops a higher pressure of anger when he encounters some piece of stupidity than does he. Yet the outburst is so fleeting, he returns so quickly to complete 'normalcy,' that I'm certain he does it for effect. At least he doesn't get angry in the sense I do—I blaze for an hour! So, for many years I've made it a religion never to indulge myself, but yesterday I failed."

Many years later Eisenhower said, "A question arose in my mind that I have never been able to answer satisfactorily. Had the years of indoctrinating myself on the inconsequential value of promotion as a measure of an Army man's worth influenced my reply to him? Certainly, in the years past, knowing that I was locked in because of age and grade, I had known a wonderful sense of freedom from awe when in the presence of superior officers. But without my outburst I often wonder whether General Marshall would have had any greater interest in me than he would have had in any other relatively competent staff officer."

That same day, still smarting, he went to West Point with Mamie. It was the first time he had left the office for any length of time since taking up his post; it was also the first time he had been back at the Point since his graduation, but nostalgia was not his primary emotion. Twenty-seven years had passed; one war had ended, and he had missed it; another had begun, and he was to miss this one, too. John said, "During the visit, Dad told me a little bit about his work with General George C. Marshall. He had been informed by Marshall a few days earlier that he would be retained as Chief of War Plans for the duration of the war and remain a brigadier general. Dad seemed to expect me to be unhappy at this turn of events, but I was not; to me as a plebe the grade of brigadier general seemed tantamount to a god. But Dad, disappointed himself, took it philosophically and at the end of the pleasant visit went back to his duties."

Back on the job in Washington, on March 25 Ike gave Marshall an historic thousand-word memorandum he had drafted, a succinct blueprint for conduct of the global war, headed *Critical Points in the Development of a Coordinated Viewpoint as to Major Tasks of the War*. He wrote:

The first question that must be definitely decided is the region or theater in which the first major offensive effort of the United Powers must take place. . . . We are principally concerned in preventing the rise of any situation that will automatically give the Axis an overwhelming tactical superiority; or one under which its productive potential becomes greater than our own.

The loss of either England or Russia would probably give the Axis an immediate ability to nullify any of our future efforts. The loss of the Near East or of England would probably give the Axis a greater productive potential than our own.

Consequently the immediately important tasks, aside from protection of the American continent, are the security of England, the retention of Russia in the war as an active asylum, and the defense of the Middle East. . . .

All other operations must be considered in the highly desirable rather than in the mandatory class. . . . Foremost among these is probably the support of Australia and New Zealand and the lines of communication thereto. . . . The principal target for our first major offensive should be Germany, to be attacked through western Europe. . . .

Eisenhower ended by emphasizing "the tremendous importance of agreeing upon some major objective toward which we can all begin turning our coordinated and intensive effort."

The memorandum really said nothing that he had not been saying to anyone who would listen since shortly after he first arrived at the War Plans Division, but this time the words had an immediate and enormous effect. Marshall had lunch at the White House that very day, and he presented the proposal to Roosevelt; Stimson; Frank Knox, secretary of the navy; Lieutenant General H. H. Arnold, chief of the U.S. Army Air Forces; and Harry Hopkins, presidential aide and unofficial assistant president of the United States and friend of Marshall's. Roosevelt's was the final and most important voice, and he approved the plan and asked Marshall to work out the details; it was given the code name BOLERO and involved a buildup of American forces in England in preparation for a cross-Channel invasion of France.

Roosevelt directed Marshall and Harry Hopkins to go to London at once to get Churchill and his military advisers to approve the plan. That approval was not easily or immediately forthcoming, but in only fourteen weeks, the work and the words of Dwight D. Eisenhower had come to the favorable attention of everybody in Washington planning an Allied victory. That was about to happen in England as well.

Two days after Marshall had lunch with Roosevelt, Eisenhower found out he was promoted to major general (temporary). He said, "Still a permanent lieutenant colonel, but the promotion is just as satisfactory as if a permanent one. I suppose one could call it the official 'stamp of approval' of the War Department."

To persuade Roosevelt that Eisenhower should have a second star, Marshall had told the president, as Eisenhower put it, "that, as his operations officer, I was not really a staff officer in the accepted sense of the word. Under his [Marshall's] direction, he said, all dispositions of the Army forces on a global scale—and this included the Air Corps—were my responsibility. I was *subordinate commander*."

In a letter to John on March 29 he said, "Ever since I left West Point, which was a week ago today, I have been looking for an opportunity to write you. . . . Following Dad's funeral, all the boys decided they wanted to give his watch to you. . . . I now have it in my possession. As a matter of interest, I took the number from the watch and wrote to the Elgin Company where it was made to find out the year in which it was sold. It left the Elgin factory about 1886, so it is now about 56 years old. It is apparently in very good condition, but I am having it cleaned and oiled and also having the fact of its presentation to you engraved on the back. . . . The watch is a very thick and heavy one and not a comfortable one to carry; nevertheless, I am sure you will appreciate the deep affection of your five uncles in desiring you to have it."

Only a man with a precise mind and a need to know the smallest detail about everything that touched his life would have taken the trouble to write to the Elgin Company to find out the year a watch was made.

Then, in a P.S., Eisenhower said, "I was appointed a Major General day before yesterday, so apparently the Chief of Staff did not mean what he said about making me serve in the War Department in the grade of Brigadier."

In the letter Eisenhower gave the addresses of the five uncles so that John could write thank-you notes, and the next day he himself took the time to write to Edgar, who before Pearl Harbor had repeatedly said that the United States should stay out of the war. Now Edgar wanted that war over with as quickly as possible.

Eisenhower said, "You are no more anxious than I to get this war over with. The difficulty is that there are so many things that we didn't do in the last twenty years that their accomplishment now is a matter of weeks and months. It cannot be done in a minute. There is no use going back over past history either to regret or to condemn; although I was one of those that for the past two years has preached preparedness and tried to point out the deadly peril into which the United States was drifting. I don't see any point in telling anyone else that he was wrong." (In other words, he was saying: Edgar, what has been true all our lives is true once again. You were wrong, and I was right.)

"We have got a fearful job to perform and everybody has got to unify to do it," he continued. "No other consideration can now be compared to that of defeating the powers that are trying to dominate. . . . We have got to win and any individual in this country, so far as I am concerned, that doesn't do his very best to fulfill his part of the job is an enemy. This applies whether he's a doctor, soldier, laborer, professional man, or just another taxpayer. . . . As always, With Affectionate regards."

That Eisenhower still hoped, in spite of everything, that he would have field duty is borne out by a March 30 entry in his diary: "Paragraph 1, Special Orders 79, War Department, announced me as major general (temporary) Army of the United States, dating from March 28, ranking from March 27. This should assure that when I finally get back with troops, I'll get a division."

Meanwhile, he felt that the situation in the Philippines was growing critical, and on the last day of March wrote, "For many weeks—it seems years—I've been searching everywhere to find any feasible way of giving real help to the P.I. We have literally squandered money; we wrestled with the Navy; we've tried to think of anything that might promise even a modicum of help. I'll go on trying, but daily the situation grows more desperate."

On April 1, 1942, Eisenhower and Mamie moved into one of the desirable brick houses at Fort Myer reserved for senior staff, and although he was probably not then aware of it, he had passed all the tests, including one of his own: he had proved that he need not mount a horse.

* * *

A KANSAN GOES TO LONDON

The day Ike and Mamie moved to Fort Myer was the day Marshall presented BOLERO, the plan for the rapid buildup of American manpower and equipment in the British Isles, at the White House. It was immediately approved. ROUNDUP, the cross-Channel invasion plan, was also agreed on without much argument. It called for thirty American divisions (a million men) and eighteen British divisions, supported by aircraft from both countries, to take part in a landing in the Pas-de-Calais region of northern France in the spring of 1943.

The first consideration of the U.S. and Britain in the spring of 1942 was to keep the Russian army of eight million men in the war. Neither ROUNDUP nor BOLERO promised any immediate help to the Russians, so a third, contingency plan, SLEDGEHAMMER, was approved during the lunch. It provided that if the Russian army appeared near collapse, British and American forces would make an emergency landing on the coast of France somewhere between Le Havre and Calais in 1942, possibly as early as September 15. Roosevelt felt certain that Churchill would not greet all these suggestions with delight, and he asked Hopkins and Marshall to go to London to explain and argue for the decisions that had been made in Washington. On April 4 Hopkins, Marshall, and their party left Baltimore for London in a Pan American clipper. Because of an engine failure on their plane, they had to stay two days in Bermuda. The engine was repaired, and Hopkins and Marshall left Bermuda on the morning of April 7. The next morning they were greeted in London by a smiling Churchill. He asked them to meet with him that afternoon at 10 Downing Street.

The Americans spent the weekend at Chequers, Churchill's country home, after which Hopkins cabled Roosevelt, "All well. Harry." Marshall sent an equally enthusiastic cable to Stimson, and the two Americans returned home convinced that their mission had been a total success. Churchill himself sent a message to the president: "Former Naval Person to President Roosevelt, I have read with earnest attention your masterly document about the future of the war and the great operations proposed. I am in entire agreement in principle with all you propose, and so are the Chiefs of Staff."

John Eisenhower wrote in *Allies*, "Two nations marching together, shoulder to shoulder, was heady wine. But hardly had Marshall and Hopkins set foot in the United States than the hangover set in on both sides of the Atlantic."

Eisenhower wrote in his diary, "BOLERO is supposed to have the approval of the Pres. and Prime Minister. But the struggle to get everyone behind it, and to keep the highest authority from wrecking it by making additional commitments of air-ship-troops elsewhere is never ending.

"The actual fact is that not 1 man in 20 in the Govt. (including the W. and M. Depts) realizes what a grisly, dirty, tough business we are in! They think we can buy victory."

After the war Ike said, "History has proved that nothing is more difficult in war than to adhere to a single strategic plan. . . . This one was no exception— realization of the plan was far removed from its making, and countless occasions were to arise when argument, blandishment, and exhortation would seek its abandonment. . . ."

Also after the war, he wrote, "The general belief in England then was that the operation was possible only 'after German morale had cracked,' but years later W.C. said he had always believed in it when 'we'd manufactured the gear.' "

Churchill's obstinate opinions on the subject were not easy to take at the time.

When Marshall returned from London on April 19, Eisenhower noted in his diary, "He looks fine. I hope that, at long last, and after months of struggle by this division, we are all definitely committed to one concept of fighting. If we can agree on major purposes and objectives, our efforts will begin to fall in line and we won't just be thrashing around in the dark." Alas, the thrashing around in the dark was to continue, and what Eisenhower was to call "the blackest day in history" was still three months away.

May did not begin well anywhere in the world for the Allies. On the first day more Japanese troops landed on Mindanao, and Corregidor was shelled and bombed. All of central Burma had been overrun. That same day Mandalay fell to the Japanese; the road to Mandalay was closed, never to reopen. Kipling's Far East was dead; Burma became independent in 1948.

Just before midnight on May 5 the Japanese landed on Corregidor, and on the 6th Eisenhower wrote in his diary, "Corregidor surrendered last night. Poor Wainwright; he did the fighting in the Philippine Islands, another got such glory as the public could find in the operation. Resistance in the P.I. will quickly close, so it lasted five months.

"General Mac's tirades, to which T.J. and I so often listened in Manila, would now sound as silly to the public as they then did to us. But he's a real hero! Yah."

Eisenhower had heard often enough from that assiduous student of Ecclesiasticus, Ida, that "envy and wrath shorten life," and he tried, on occasion with success, to stifle both, but at times he found himself not so much envious as angry at life's injustices. In the spring of 1942 MacArthur was a hero, all right. He had been awarded the Medal of Honor by the president. The citation had praised "his gallantry and intrepidity above and beyond the call of duty in action," his "heroic conduct," his "calm judgment in each crisis," his "utter disregard of personal danger under heavy fire and aerial bombardment." According to the *New York Times,* thirteen babies born in the city between March 1 and April 8 had been named Douglas MacArthur Jones, Douglas MacArthur Smith, etc. MacArthur Roads were springing up everywhere; there were several MacArthur Streets and MacArthur Parks. There was a MacArthur Narcissus, and a number of young men and women were dancing the "MacArthur Glide." Newspaper reporters referred to the general as the "Incredible Warrior," "Destiny's Child," and the "Lion of Luzon."

On the 8th the U.S.S. *Lexington,* the "Lady Lex," was sunk in the Battle of the Coral Sea; that day, too, the Germans began an attack in the Crimea.

But on the morning of May 6 the emphasis was on landing craft, when Eisenhower attended a meeting with a subcommittee of BOLERO called the Special Committee on Landing Craft for the Continent. The questions discussed were, Eisenhower wrote, the ones "on which I begged the answers last February." Nobody seemed to know or even want to find out anything about such craft, yet the questions would seem basic for a nation that was planning to take part in a cross-Channel invasion later that year. As listed by Eisenhower they were:

Who is responsible for building landing craft?

What types are they building?

Are they suitable for cross-Channel work?

Will the number of each type be sufficient?

Obviously, after the meeting his questions were still unanswered. He wrote, "How in hell can we win this war unless we can crack some heads?"

At times that spring it was necessary to take the commander in chief to task. On April 29 Roosevelt's naval aide at the Pacific War Council had said that the president wanted "to have in Australia 100,000 troops in addition to the personnel of Air Force required to maintain 1,000 planes." On May 4 Ike wrote a memorandum, to be signed by Marshall, saying that what Roosevelt proposed was impossible. Eisenhower once again advocated "an early offensive on the continent of Europe. . . . I believe that the most important consideration is the gathering of the largest force of ground troops possible in the British Isles at the present time. . . . If instead the number is to be decreased by more than 50%, then our recent proposal to the British Government for 1942 has, in effect, largely been cancelled."

Marshall made a few minor changes in what Ike had written and sent the memo to the president. Roosevelt did what presidents had done before and have since. He said that he had never called for an increase of American strength in Australia; he had simply wanted to know if "this properly could be done." He now understood that it was "inadvisable" and added, "I do not want BOLERO slowed down." The president also sent a memo to the secretaries of war and navy, the chiefs of staff, and Harry Hopkins saying that there was to continue to be a holding pattern in the Pacific. The major offensive was to be in Europe."

The memorandum clearly had been a success, and a few days later Eisenhower wrote a memo to Marshall that was to have a great deal to do with his own future.

Subject: Establishment of Western European Theater of Operations.

1. Discussion.
1. The decision of the President relative to the putting into execution of the BOLERO plan makes it advisable to set up a theater of operations for the operations envisioned in this plan and to designate a United States commander of the theater of operations and of all U.S. Army forces to be employed therein.

In early May 1942 Eisenhower had little reason to think he would ever have an Allied command in London; he had never been to England or had a close English friend, yet he showed a real sensitivity to British feelings when his friend from Fort Lewis, Colonel Lucian K. Truscott, Jr., came to see him in the Munitions Building before going to London to organize American soldiers into units like the British Commandos. Eisenhower told him, "If you do . . . organize such units, I hope that you will find some other name than 'Commandos' for the glamor of that name will always remain—and properly so—British." When the time came, Truscott called his American troops Rangers because "few words have a more glamorous connotation in American military history."

It was generally agreed around the Munitions Building that, since most of the troops involved in the ROUNDUP invasion of France in the spring of 1943 would be American, the commander of the operation should also be an American. The consensus was that that man would be Marshall, possibly with Eisenhower as his chief of staff. Perhaps with this in mind, Marshall decided to send Ike to England. The chief of staff also wanted Eisenhower's opinion of a man who, although Marshall hadn't said so, had made a poor impression on him when he was in London, Major General James E. Chaney. Chaney had gone to England a year earlier as Special Army Observer, London; now Marshall felt that Chaney, Commander of United States Forces in England, and his staff were failing to play an effective role in the war.

On May 21 Eisenhower wrote in his diary, "I'm taking off on the twenty-third with General Arnold and others for a trip to England. We want to see how things are going there on our offensive plan. . . .

"My own particular reason for going is an uneasy feeling that either we do not understand our own commanding general and staff in England or they don't understand us. Our planning for BOLERO is not progressing. We'll be gone about a week."

The fact that Eisenhower was going to London was announced to the press, but nobody much cared about an obscure major general going on an overseas errand, the purpose of which wasn't even mentioned. One wire-service reporter decided to do what was then called "an over-nighter," a story written at night that might, if nothing much else happened, be a space filler the next morning. There is no record that his story was ever printed anywhere, but an exchange between the reporter and a public information colonel in the War Department was preserved in Eisenhower's 201 file. The colonel, Gordon Ordway, was told by the reporter that he needed some background material on Eisenhower.

ORDWAY: "I don't know what we can give you. What sort of thing do you want?"

REPORTER: "What are some of the things that have happened to him in his past life?"

ORDWAY: "Nobody here can tell you that. You are in need of a personal friend."

REPORTER: "That is what I am looking for. Do you know anybody?"

ORDWAY: "I can't think of anyone off hand. . . . If I only knew somebody who knew him intimately I would tell you."

REPORTER: "Has General Eisenhower written any books or articles for magazines?"

ORDWAY: "Not that I know of."

REPORTER: "Will you give me some idea of what he did in the Philippines?"

ORDWAY: *No response.*

REPORTER: "Can you give me any idea of his military philosophy?"

ORDWAY: "No. I am sorry. I know so little. I hope I have not confused you too much."

At that time very few people in Washington or anywhere else outside of Abilene and the army inner circle knew much about Eisenhower; to those who considered themselves "in" in Washington, he was simply "Milton's brother." Milton was the one who went to the White House all the time, who was in charge of what most people, including Roosevelt, felt was essential to the winning of the war—getting Japanese and Japanese-Americans out of their homes on the West Coast and elsewhere and herding them into what were called "relocation centers" but were really, as Roosevelt himself later said, "concentration camps."

By the time of the landings in North Africa in November 1942 that had changed forever. Milton, much to his annoyance, became known as "Ike's brother." Stephen E. Ambrose wrote in his biography of Milton that when somebody said to him, " 'I'd like to shake your hand. I admire your brother so much,' . . . Milton handled such scenes with his usual grace, but inwardly he seethed."

Eisenhower and his party started for London in the early morning of Saturday, May 23. With him were Mark Clark and Lieutenant General H. H. Arnold, who most of the time displayed an amiable disposition and thus was known as "Hap." He was four years older than Eisenhower and had been graduated from West Point in 1907. According to Eisenhower, Hap wanted to "make a deal with the British to effect some kind of reallocation in airplanes. Under present arrangements, we cannot build an air force; all our planes are taken up so rapidly that we cannot train."

They landed first in Montreal, then flew to Goose Bay, Labrador. The weather was bad, and three hours later the pilot turned back, and the party spent the night at Gander, Newfoundland. The weather was still bad the next morning, and the three generals spent the day skeet shooting. It was Eisenhower's first full day of leisure since he had arrived in Washington the previous December.

They got to Prestwick, Scotland, on May 25, and, as Eisenhower wrote, they "visited activities in connection with an amphibious exercise that had just been called off. . . . The British . . . assault-landing craft and tank-landing craft could cross the channel only in very calm weather. . . .

"During the day we passed the birthplace of Robert Burns and saw one of the spots where Robert Bruce was supposed to have spent considerable time."

On the night of May 25 Eisenhower made what might be called his first British conquest. He shared a railroad compartment from Glasgow to London with Lieutenant General Sir Humphrey Gale of the British General Staff. They may or may not have discussed the fact that they had been born in the same month of the same year, but whatever they discussed, Gale later said that he had never met a man he liked so much at first meeting, adding that the American had a sense of humor.

Eisenhower would soon charm and delight a great many other Englishmen, most of them soldiers, but the most important civilian as well—Winston Churchill. He failed completely with two military men, however, Bernard Law Montgomery and Alan Francis Brooke. Neither was ever charmed by the man from Kansas.

When Clark and Eisenhower arrived at Victoria Station in London, a smart-looking young woman from County Cork was waiting for them. When the war began in September 1939, Kay Summersby had joined Britain's Motor Transport Corps. Before that she had been a model for Worth of Paris, which she described as "the cream of the couturiers." By the time she met Eisenhower, she was divorced from her husband, a young British publisher, and engaged to a young army captain, Dick Arnold, West Point 1932. In all his writings Eisenhower mentions Mrs. Summersby only once, in *Crusade in Europe*. He lists her as a member of his staff: "Kay Summersby was corresponding secretary and doubled as a driver." That May morning, however, she must have been a welcome sight; she was pretty, and she was wearing a well-cut uniform in a city where most women had not been able to buy any new clothes for almost three years. She was cheerful, too, most of the time, although that morning she was angry. The train was late; she had been assigned to two officers who were only major generals, and instead of getting into the Packard, which they apparently didn't see, they got into the car of Ambassador John G. Winant and went to the American embassy. Kay returned to American theater headquarters at 20 Grosvenor Square. Then she went to lunch, and when she came back to Grosvenor Square she found that her two officers were "walking toward my khaki-colored Packard. They were nondescript, although one was shorter than the other." She drove the two men to Claridge's, and "General Eisenhower remarked, 'Thank you. Tomorrow morning at nine, please.' I had driven them exactly two blocks."

As he had expected, Eisenhower was not impressed with the Americans at 20 Grosvenor Square. They still wore civilian clothes, worked eight-hour days, and took weekends off. Lucian Truscott had found that they "repeatedly expressed their views that no American officers should be working members of any British staff" and that if Americans *had* to have contact with the British, it "should be done by liaison officers from the theater headquarters." They resented American military visitors and spoke disdainfully of "freewheeling missions," of people who were "running the war from Washington," and of those interlopers who were "infringing on the rights of the theater commander." Truscott was such an interloper, and even more so was Eisenhower, who said in *Crusade*, "Upon our arrival in England we met the United States commander, Major General James E. Chaney. . . . He and his small staff had been given no opportunity to familiarize themselves with the revolutionary changes that had since taken place in the United States and were completely at a loss in their earnest attempts to further the war effort. They were definitely in a back eddy, from which they could scarcely emerge except through a return to the United States."

As Eisenhower later said to other officers, Chaney and his staff clearly were about to go home, "on a slow boat, without escort."

That evening he attended a dinner given by Air Chief Marshall Portal. Eisenhower, in *Crusade*, expressed his admiration for Portal in terms used to describe no other British officer. "He was a profound military student—but with it all a man of action—and quiet, courteous, of strong convictions. It was a pleasure to discuss with him any problem of war, whether or not it pertained exclusively to his own field of the air. He enjoyed great prestige in British military and civil circles, as well as among the Americans of the Allied command."

Eisenhower was from the beginning less enthusiastic about the English officer he met the next day. He and Clark attended a field exercise commanded by Montgomery, in the Kent-Sussex area. Clark remembered that Monty "was late, very, very late, and he shook hands stiffly, making it very clear that we were mere major generals while he was a lieutenant general. He told us, 'I'm sorry I'm late, but I really shouldn't have come at all. I'll make it brief.' He turned to a big map on the wall and, with a pointer, started showing us where the troops were, the German troops and his. Ike took out a pack of cigarettes, lit one and in a minute or so, Montgomery, not turning around, said, 'Who's smoking?' 'I am, sir,' said Eisenhower, and Montgomery said, 'Stop it. I don't permit it here.' Ike dropped the cigarette on the floor, stepped on it, and looked at me, very red faced. Monty took a few minutes more, then said, 'That concludes my presentation. Sorry to be so abrupt.' He shook hands, and out we went."

Eisenhower wrote of the encounter that Montgomery "explained the exercises to us. General Montgomery is a decisive type who appears to be extremely energetic and professionally able. I would guess his age at 58 years." (Montgomery was fifty-five, three years older than Eisenhower.)

Kay Summersby remembered that on the way back to London Eisenhower said something "about that sonofabitch, meaning Montgomery. . . . He was furious . . . really steaming mad." She looked into the rear-view mirror and saw that "Eisenhower's face was flaming red and the veins in his forehead looked like worms."

The next day, May 28, Eisenhower and Generals Chaney and Somervell (Lieutenant General Brehon Burke Somervell, commanding general of the Services of Supply—Army Service Forces) met with the British Chiefs of Staff to discuss ROUNDUP, which Ike described as "an assault to be launched early in 1943, conducted during its initial stages by British troops supported by possibly ten or twelve American divisions. This general idea presupposed the existence in England of an air force capable with some reinforcement of carrying out the preliminary and supporting action that we believed to be necessary. It presupposed, also, British capacity for assisting materially in the quick delivery of all the amphibious equipment we would need, and, of course, contemplated the regular arrival of new divisions from the United States in sufficient strength to support the attack constantly and to enlarge the operations against the enemy."

Eisenhower told the assembled British and American officers, "The first thing to do is to name a commander for the operation." That suggestion cannot have come as too great a surprise for anyone there. Nor can Eisenhower have found the next question startling. Whom, he was asked, would you name as commander of this expedition?

Ike pretended that the question was unexpected, and then he tried out what might be called his Kansas small-town act on the assembled Englishmen and Americans. As he related it:

> Still thinking of an operation in early 1943, when the British would necessarily provide the major portion of the forces during initial stages, I replied, "In America I have heard much of a man who has been intensively studying amphibious operations for many months. I understand that his position is Chief of Combined Operations, and I think his name is Admiral Mountbatten. I have heard that Admiral Mountbatten is vigorous, intelligent, and courageous, and if the operation is to be staged initially with British forces predominating I presume he could do the job."
>
> My remarks were greeted with an amazed silence. Then General Brooke said, "General, possibly you have not met Admiral Mountbatten. This is he sitting directly across the table from you." My failure to recognize him when I entered the meeting and my later personal remarks about him naturally caused a moment of embarrassment. Nevertheless, I stuck to my guns and retorted, "I still say that the key to success is to appoint a commander and give him the necessary authority and responsibility to carry out the planning and preparatory work that otherwise will never be done."

The meeting was merely for an exchange of ideas and nothing was done. Almost needless to add, however, from then on Admiral Louis Mountbatten was my warm and firm friend.

Of course. The handsome, colorful Lord Louis would appear to be a man who had everything, but as La Rochefoucauld pointed out, the one thing a person can never get enough of is flattery.

Is it possible that Eisenhower did not know that he was sitting across the table from one of the most photographed, most written about men in England? Hardly. Eisenhower never attended a formal meeting of any kind without being briefed in advance on who was to be there. He certainly did not attend this most important meeting without knowing as much as could be known about everybody involved, particularly a close friend of Churchill's, recently named chief of Combined Operations by him. Since Mountbatten was only forty-one, younger than most of his peers in the services, Churchill gave him a lot of seemingly unnecessary but nevertheless pleasing titles; he was an air marshal, a lieutenant general, and a vice admiral. He also sat on the Chiefs of Staff Committee.

Marshall had spent a good deal of time with Mountbatten, a fact that he seems likely to have mentioned to Eisenhower. The chief of staff had been impressed with the fact that the vice admiral had got all the branches of the services to cooperate with him, something Marshall had not always been able to do. He asked Mountbatten, "How did you do it?"

"Well, after all, we all speak the same language," said Lord Louis. "And come to think of it, you speak English, too, of a sort. Why don't you send me a few American officers?"

Lucian Truscott was one of those officers, and he wrote to his wife of his first meeting with Mountbatten, which was eleven days before Eisenhower appeared not to recognize him, "I was prepared to some degree by the accounts I had of Admiral Mountbatten from General Marshall, Eisenhower, and Al Wedemeyer [of the WPD]."

Before he left for London, Truscott, a polo player, had been told by Eisenhower not only that Mountbatten played polo but that he had written a book about it. Since the polo book had been published under the pseudonym *Marco*, this shows the degree of Eisenhower's prior interest in Lord Louis.

Finally, Eisenhower had left Washington with "notes to take to Great Britain." The third item on his list was

Discuss with Lord Mountbatten:
a. Possibility of his coming to the United States for a visit.
b. Selection of picked men from 34th Division to participate in Commando Operations.
c. The extent to which more American officers should be included in Lord Mountbatten's staff.

If Lord Louis became a "warm and firm friend," Eisenhower did not do so well with General Sir Alan Brooke, also a member of the British Chiefs of Staff. Brooke, commander in chief of the Home Forces, and the hero of Dieppe, was not on that day or any other impressed with Eisenhower as a soldier. He, like Eisenhower, kept his frustrations and anger to himself, but carefully recorded them in a diary. At the time of the battles in Tunisia, he wrote, "As Supreme

Commander what he [Eisenhower] may have lacked in military ability he greatly made up for by the charm of his personality."

Eisenhower and Clark did a good deal of traveling in England, in part, according to Clark, "so that we could see where their troops were and their defenses against a possible German invasion." On Saturday, May 30, after a visit to the Dover defenses and consultations with several high-ranking British officers, Clark and Eisenhower were driven by Mrs. Summersby around London, to the sites of the worst bomb damage during the Blitz, which had lasted from September 1940 to May 1941. The bombing had killed 44,000 civilians, wounded another 50,000, and in London alone had left 375,000 people homeless. Kay was able to describe vividly what had happened. She had been on duty twenty-four hours at a time during that period.

Eisenhower was very moved by her account. At one point he said, "Poor people, poor London." He was also curious about "women at war." According to Kay, he asked "how we got along with our male colleagues; how we managed in the rough spots." What he learned, she said, "grew into a near-obsession, that women could safely and efficiently replace . . . men [in the rear echelons]— a conviction which he helped translate into actual practice long before Normandy and still supported vigorously after the war."

That evening Eisenhower, Clark, and Arnold had drinks at Claridge's and discussed who ought to replace Chaney. Arnold remembered that they agreed it had to be someone who had the "experience and knowledge of our way of doing things"; in addition, he had to be "fully acquainted with our War Department plans" and must have the confidence of General Marshall and the secretary of war. According to Clark, "He [Ike] never said so, but it was clear to me that he very much wanted the job, very much."

Before Clark and Arnold got into a serious discussion of who had all the qualities necessary for the job, Eisenhower excused himself. It is not surprising that the two men agreed that the commander simply had to be Ike. Clark said, "It was obvious, and I asked Arnold to tell Marshall about the discussion and pass our recommendation along to Marshall when he got back to Washington. He did it, too. I don't think Ike was too surprised."

Ike must have felt some satisfaction in knowing that Arnold and Mountbatten were flying to Washington on June 1, Mountbatten to see both Roosevelt and Marshall, Arnold to see the chief of staff. It was not unreasonable to expect that on the way they would mention Eisenhower and that his name would come up in their conferences. Moreover, Mountbatten was to have dinner both with the president and Hopkins.

On the 31st Eisenhower and Clark wanted to see Buckingham Palace. The palace was closed on Sundays, but when the custodian told King George about two high-ranking American officers wishing to visit, the king agreed and said that he and the queen would stay in their quarters to avoid embarrassing the Americans. But that Sunday turned out to be such a beautiful spring day that the king and queen seated themselves in a small garden on the grounds. When they heard the custodian's voice and realized that he and the two visitors were coming toward the garden, their majesties ducked behind a hedge and got out by crawling through a low opening in the garden wall.

Eisenhower returned to England in June as commanding general, replacing Chaney, and paid an official visit to the king and queen. At that time, according to Harry Butcher, the king told Eisenhower about the two American officers who had visited the palace when he and the queen were in the garden. "He described the visitors as one very tall and the other simply tall," Butcher said. "Ike completed the king's story by identifying the generals."

When Eisenhower and Clark left London, Kay Summersby drove them to Northolt airfield. By then the three had learned a good deal about each other. The Americans had learned that Kay was not only attractive and a good driver; but she was possessed of high good humor, knew a great many people, and was helpful in suggesting ways that could help Americans win British approval.

At the airfield, Eisenhower gave her something rare in London in the spring of 1942, a box of chocolates.

He said, "If I'm ever back this way, I hope you'll drive me again."

"I'd like that, sir," said Mrs. Summersby.

★ ★ ★

A PRECIOUS FRIENDSHIP

The day before Eisenhower got back from London, Mountbatten told both the president and Marshall that Ike had made a most favorable impression on him and on the other Britishers he had met. Clark and Arnold also told the chief of staff that if Chaney were replaced, they felt that Ike was best qualified to succeed him.

Eisenhower reached Washington on June 3, and he at once wrote a memorandum to Marshall. "It is immediately necessary to dispatch to England the man who will be the Commander of the 1st Corps to take part in the assault. I have thought this matter over at great length, and, as a result, I recommend that General Clark be sent for this job. . . ." No wonder Marshall later told Clark, "It looks to me as if you boys got together."

In that same memo, Eisenhower said, "During my visit in England, I also gave a great deal of study to the identity of the individual who should now be commanding our Forces in England. I was very hopeful that my conclusions would favor the present incumbent. For a variety of reasons, some of which I intimated to you this morning, I believe that a change should be made. I recommend General McNarney as the best-fitted individual to fulfill the various requirements enumerated in a previous memorandum to you on this subject. . . . I believe that General McNarney has the strength of character, the independence of thought, and the ability to fulfill satisfactorily the requirements of this difficult task."

McNarney was an excellent suggestion, but Eisenhower cannot have been much surprised that Marshall rejected his suggestion. McNarney had only recently, at Marshall's direction, reorganized the War Department and only three months earlier been made deputy chief of staff. Marshall was not about to shift him to London almost immediately.

Besides, by then Marshall had had three recommendations that Ike himself go to London. He had also been in daily, sometimes hourly association with Eisenhower for six months, and although he hadn't told Ike so, he liked what he had seen.

The man was confident; he was quick. He was able to make decisions on his own. He easily saw what had to be done to solve a problem, and he did it without bothering his superior. He was never boring and never stupid, and he was neither awed nor terrified, as so many people were, of the aloof chief of staff. That had impressed Marshall that first Sunday in December, and it still did. Finally and perhaps most important, the man had great charm, a charm that Marshall must secretly have envied, and it was transportable. It worked on both sides of the Atlantic. Eisenhower was ready to move on, and as a good father figure should, Marshall was going to make it possible for him to do so.

On June 6 Eisenhower gave Marshall still another memo: "No matter whether you decide to retain General Chaney or to designate another officer for command in Europe, I believe it highly desirable to promote the individual concerned. There will soon be at least 4 Major Generals in the Command, and the promotion is logical for that reason."

The directive Eisenhower gave the chief of staff on the 8th was not new; it was a revision of the basic outline Ike had written on May 12, describing in detail the Allied strategy for the war. It said of the man who ought to be sent to London, "As a first condition, he must enjoy the fullest confidence of the Chief of Staff. . . ." Ike certainly had that and knew he had that—no harm, however, in reminding Marshall of it. He added that the man sent "*will exercise unity of Command over both United States Army and Navy Forces in that region* [emphasis mine—M.M.]. . . . It must be clearly understood, particularly by the British, that he is, for the U.S. troops, a Theater Commander in every sense of the word."

There was much more in the document that Eisenhower was later to refer to as "the Bible." "I remarked to General Marshall that this was one paper he should read in detail before it went out because it was likely to be an important document in the further waging of the war. His reply still lives in my memory: 'I certainly do want to read it. You may be the man who executes it. If that's the case, when can you leave?' Three days later General Marshall told me definitely that I would command the European theater. . . .

"Of course command now does not necessarily mean command in the operation—but the job before the battle begins will still be the biggest outside that of the C/S himself."

That night Ike jubilantly wrote in his diary, "The chief of staff told me this morning that it's possible I may to go England in command. It's a big job; if the U.S.-U.K. stay squarely behind BOLERO and go after it tooth and nail, it will be the biggest American job in the war."

Three days later, on June 11, 1942, Eisenhower was named commander of U.S. forces, European Theater of Operations (ETO), with headquarters in London, effective June 25, 1942. He wrote in his diary, "The C/S says I'm the guy. He also approves Clark for Corps CG [commanding general], in England, and gives us the II Corps. Now we really go to work. Hope to leave here by plane on the 22nd."

It has often been said and written that Ike was "flabbergasted" and "thunderstruck" when he found out that he had got the job. Al Gruenther, who was later to join him in London and who frequently played bridge with him, said, "Anybody who says that never sat down at a bridge table with him."

Before returning to England, Eisenhower had a number of people to see, memos to write, and matters to be cleared up. One of those matters had to do with being sure that the navy understood that there was to be complete unity of command in London. That meant clearing the matter with Admiral King. Brigadier General Thomas T. Handy, who succeeded Ike as head of the Operations Division, said, "Old Ernie King was meaner than hell, but he was a strong man, and he was a hell of a big asset to the war effort. . . . He was a cool one, but, boy, he was hard-boiled, and when you got him on your side, he was on your side all the way."

The whole thing turned out to be easy. King readily agreed that the navy was part of the unified command under Eisenhower, an army major general. That was a revolutionary idea for a man who a few weeks before had refused even to read Ike's memos. Now he was agreeing that an army officer was for an indefinite period able to give orders to navy officers. It had never happened before, and there would no doubt be considerable resistance on the part of some navy officers. But should Eisenhower encounter any naval resistance to his authority, he was to get in touch with King at once. And when Eisenhower told King that he knew it was unusual, but he would like to have his friend Commander Harry Butcher as his aide, King said, "Let's do it, just because it is unusual."

Ike did want to see John before going overseas on his awesome new assignment, and he wrote him, saying:

Confidentially, I am soon to leave the United States for an indefinite stay. Naturally I am anxious to have a few hours with you just to say goodbye and have a good talk. . . .

Mamie intends to return to the Wardman Park Hotel where she will take a small apartment. She will have a room for you when you come down next fall with your pal.

P.S. The bosses are certainly giving me a tough job this time. I will tell you about it when I see you.

When he got his father's letter, John asked for a leave for the following weekend. "This would constitute a precedent," he said, "but the authorities at the Academy were generous enough to grant my request." At the time the American public was very sensitive to precedent-breaking for the sons of famous men, particularly if they were Roosevelts, but Eisenhower was not yet a famous man; he was a colorless officer going to Britain to command an inactive though growing theater, geographically closer to war but still by no means part of it.

When Mountbatten heard the news of Eisenhower's appointment he wrote, "My very sincerest congratulations. . . . It is we in England who really ought to be congratulated at our great good fortune that you should be selected for this vital job."

Eisenhower had to have been pleased with the letter, but would have been much less so if he had known that Churchill, with Mountbatten's enthusiastic support, had already persuaded his cabinet that there would be no landings in Europe that year unless the Germans "were suddenly and unexpectedly demoralized." At the moment, that did not seem likely since Rommel's troops were rapidly approaching Tobruk.

Despite the crisis in North Africa, shortly before midnight on June 17, Churchill, Brooke, Ismay, and the prime minister's private physician, Lord Moran, started an air journey for Washington. Churchill came with one main idea—to persuade the Americans that a cross-Channel landing was impossible and that a landing in French North Africa was necessary. Many years later Marshall said that he was not surprised at what Churchill wanted or that he was successful in getting it. "We failed to see that the leader in a democracy has to keep the people entertained. (That may sound like the wrong word, but it conveys the thought.) The people demand action. We couldn't wait to be completely ready. Churchill was always getting into sideshows. If we had gone as far as he did we never would have gotten out. But I could see why he had to have something." Moran said that Churchill had set for himself what "was not an easy task. . . . Those whom the president trusted, Hopkins, Marshall, and the rest, were of one mind. There was only one way to shorten the war, and that was to set up a Second Front in France. No one but Winston could have hoped for a hearing in such circumstances." No wonder the prime minister kept humming an inane little song to himself, "We're here because we're here because."

Churchill said, "I had to work by influence and diplomacy in order to secure agreed and harmonious action with our cherished ally, without whose aid nothing but ruin faced the world." That meant, in simpler language, that he, Ismay, and Brooke had during their short stay in Washington to practice witchcraft, magic, and chicanery, which they did. When they left Washington, they had succeeded in confusing everybody, but they had for all practical purposes ended any American hope for a landing on the continent of Europe in 1942 and possibly 1943 as well.

The Churchill party arrived in Washington on the evening of the 18th. Churchill stayed at the British embassy that night, and the next morning, after meeting with Marshall, left for Hyde Park where he was to be a guest of the president. While the prime minister was en route, Marshall sent Roosevelt a telegram warning:

YOUR GUEST . . . IS PESSIMISTIC REGARDING BOLERO AND INTERESTED IN AUGUST GYMNAST AND ANOTHER SIMILAR MOVEMENT IN NORWAY

When Churchill landed at the small airport near Poughkeepsie, New York, Roosevelt was waiting to greet him and witnessed what Churchill called "the roughest bump landing I have experienced."

Roosevelt did not want any substantive discussions the first day; he was, he said, "expecting more information from Washington." The information consisted of a letter from Stimson urging that the president continue his support of a cross-Channel invasion. Stimson's letter was accompanied by a letter from Marshall saying that his entire staff, Eisenhower, McNarney, and Arnold approved of what it said.

That afternoon, in Washington, at a meeting in the Munitions Building at which Eisenhower took notes, Marshall and Brooke as well as John Dill and Ismay agreed that the buildup of American troops in Britain and Ireland, BOL-ERO, would continue, that plans for a possible cross-Channel invasion that year "should be studied further" but only be undertaken "in case of necessity."

The next morning at Hyde Park Roosevelt and Churchill and Hopkins got down to business; it was as well that Brooke and Marshall were not there. Churchill gave Roosevelt a memorandum on "the immediate strategic decision before us." It said, "No responsible British military authority has so far been able to make a plan for September, 1942, which has any chance of success unless the Germans become utterly demoralized, of which there is no likelihood. Have the American staffs a plan . . . ?" The prime minister frequently asked questions to which he knew the answers. He knew that the Americans had no such plan. Therefore, it followed that "in case no plan can be made in which any responsible authority has good confidence, and consequently no engagement on a substantial scale in France is possible in September 1942, what else can we do? Can we afford to stand idle in the Atlantic theater during the whole of 1942? Ought we not to be preparing within the general structure of 'Bolero' some other operation by which we may gain positions of advantage, and also directly or indirectly to take some of the weight off Russia? It is within this setting and on this background that the French Northwest Africa operation should be studied."

It was all over, really. It was just a matter of waiting for the inevitable agreement of the Americans and of Ismay and Brooke. There would be no landing in Europe in 1942, and one would take place in French Northwest Africa. From the beginning it was recognized that the latter, code-named TORCH, would be difficult. As it turned out, TORCH would be as difficult as any Allied undertaking of the Second World War, and a man who, as they say, had never heard a shot fired in anger, Dwight D. Eisenhower, would be its supreme commander.

Roosevelt, Hopkins, and the prime minister started from Hyde Park late on Saturday night and got back to Washington at eight the next morning, Sunday the 21st.

Brooke and Dill had planned to spend a quiet Sunday visiting Mount Vernon, but that morning Brooke was told that he was to have lunch with the president. During a meeting between the British and Americans in the Oval Office, news arrived that was to bring the importance of North Africa vividly into everybody's mind. Brooke said, "I can remember this incident as if it had occurred yesterday. Churchill and I were standing beside the President's desk talking to him, when Marshall walked in with a pink piece of paper containing a message of the fall of Tobruk. Neither Winston nor I had contemplated such an eventuality and it was a staggering blow." Churchill called it "one of the heaviest blows I can recall during the war. Not only were its military effects grievous, but it had affected the reputation of the British armies. . . . I did not attempt to hide from the President the shock I had received. Defeat is one thing; disgrace is another."

Roosevelt immediately said what a good ally should say: "What can we do to help?" Churchill didn't hesitate. He said, "Give us as many Sherman tanks as you can spare and ship them to the Middle East as quickly as possible." The Americans agreed, and shortly thereafter 300 tanks and a hundred self-propelled 105-mm guns were sent to the Suez Canal. Brooke said of that Sunday afternoon, it "did a great deal towards laying the foundations of friendship and understanding built up during the war between the president and Marshall on the one hand and Churchill and myself on the other." On his way home, Brooke wrote in his diary, "It has been a very interesting trip and real good value."

John, who had arrived at Fort Myer for a weekend leave, was sitting with his father on the front porch "when word came in that . . . Tobruk . . . had fallen during the latest Nazi offensive in North Africa." He said, "It made the Old Man pensive for quite a while." Father and son talked about the depressing way the war was going. "News from around the globe had consisted of one disaster after another ever since Pearl Harbor on December 7, 1941, but this setback [Tobruk] for the Allies had come as a particular surprise."

When John had arrived on Saturday, the first question he asked his father was what his job was going to be overseas. "Oh, I'm going to be the commanding general," Eisenhower said. John said, "This came as somewhat of a surprise, as the jump from a colonel who was Chief of Staff of the Third Army at Fort Sam Houston the previous October to commanding general of an entire theater of war in the course of six months seemed astronomical. It was."

John probably did not realize it at the time, but his father's sudden, worldwide prominence was to have an effect on his own life as well. He later said that as a result "of Dad's new-found prominence . . . I found that . . . I was treated a little differently, even by my classmates. I was suddenly thrust into a sort of reflected prominence, even though I was only a yearling. It was a heady feeling in a way and caused little inconvenience—so long as I remained within the cloistered walls of Hell-on-the-Hudson." That "reflected prominence" has bothered John Eisenhower ever since.

The father and son talked, too, about West Point. John was "surprised to find that we had not so much in common on the subject as I thought. The structure of the place had changed little—this was still June 1942—but our views of it differed. In the twenty-seven years since his graduation, Dad had perhaps developed an overly rosy picture of the place. He thought of it mostly in terms of athletics, pranks and fun."

John parted with his father shortly after noon on Sunday. "His leave was too short to let him see his father off," said Mamie. "So they shook hands at the front door. Ike stood and watched John walk down the steps. John turned. He saluted his father, and his father returned the salute. They made me cry."

After John left, Mamie continued packing. She had decided against going to Denver to stay with the Douds. By remaining in Washington she would be able to see John often, either in Washington or at West Point, and she would get her husband's airmail special-delivery letters sooner. She also hoped that there would be frequent firsthand news from officers in the War Department who would be going to and returning from London. Besides, in Washington there were many "war widows" like herself who were also old friends.

The next morning, the 22nd, Eisenhower took the time to write his son a long letter.

Dear John:

If nothing interferes, I will be leaving here tomorrow between 8:30 and 9. I cannot tell you how delighted I was to have the opportunity for a nice long visit with you. It was much more satisfactory than any call I could have made on you at West Point itself.

I want to tell you once more how proud I am of you and your record to date. I hope, too, that as you go through West Point you will have as much fun as is possible during war time, when, of course, everything takes on a very serious aspect.

Knowing how busy you are, I hesitate to ask you to write me, but I would like you to know that an occasional letter from you would be the finest present I could get in England. If you could use about ten minutes after chapel each Sunday to drop me just a note, I will be most apprecia-tive. . . .

Good luck to you and just keep going like you have started. *Goodbye and good luck*—

P.S. Please don't write me at the expense of your letter to Mamie. After all, she will always forward your letters to me and she looks forward to your weekly notes.

That same day Eisenhower went to the White House to meet the president. Harry Hopkins was there, and, Ike said, "Matters discussed were of a general nature pertaining to BOLERO and the exact nature of the assignments for General Clark and myself in London. The president had been informed of an appoint-ment General Clark and I had with the prime minister for 5:30 that same afternoon, so after a brief visit the meeting broke up."

The meeting was very brief indeed. According to White House records at the Roosevelt Library it lasted only eight minutes, from 1:02 to 1:10 in the after-noon.

Churchill in *The Hinge of Fate*, volume IV of his history of World War II, has the day wrong; he says that his meeting with the two generals was on June 21.

On June 21, when we were alone together after lunch, Harry [Hopkins] said to me, "There are a couple of American officers the president would like you to meet, as they are very highly thought of in the Army, by Marshall, and by him." At five o'clock . . . Major-Generals Eisenhower and Clark were brought to my air-cooled room. I was immediately impressed by these remarkable but hitherto unknown men. They had both come from the President, whom they had just seen for the first time. We talked almost entirely about the major cross-Channel invasion in 1943, "Round-up" as it was then called, on which their thoughts had evidently been concentrated. We had a most agreeable discussion, lasting for over an hour. In order to convince them of my personal interest in the project I gave them a copy of the paper I had written for the Chiefs of Staff on June 15, two days before I started, in which I had set forth my first thoughts of the method and scale of such an operation. At any rate, they seemed much pleased with the spirit of the document. . . . I felt sure that these officers were intended to play a great part in it [Round-up], and that was the reason why they had been sent to make my acquaintance. Thus began a friendship which across all the ups and downs of the war I have preserved with deep satisfaction to this day.

When he was writing *Crusade,* Eisenhower remembered that he had met with Roosevelt and Churchill, who was "a guest at the White House." He added that their meeting had resulted in "no more than an informal chat. It had no military significance, but it was the first time I ever had a personal talk with either of these two men. Tobruk, in the African desert, had just fallen to the Germans and the whole Allied world was thrown into gloom. These two leaders, however, showed no signs of pessimism. It was gratifying to note that they were thinking of attack and victory, not of defense and defeat."

Exactly what was said at the first meeting between the two men is not of great significance. It clearly wasn't very important. What was important was that they did meet, sized each other up, and liked each other. In 1965, at the time of Churchill's funeral, which Eisenhower attended, the former general and ex-president said, "Out of the war came an association, and abiding and to me a precious friendship was forged; it withstood the trials and frictions inescapable among men of strong convictions, living in an atmosphere of war."

When the British party left for England on the 25th, its members were convinced that they had succeeded in doing what they had set out to do. Churchill's triumph was far from complete, however. Even in New York newspapers the headlines told of trouble back home: ANGER IN ENGLAND, TOBRUK FALL MAY BRING CHANGE OF GOVERNMENT, CHURCHILL TO BE CENSURED. Roosevelt was fortunate; in the United States a national leader was elected for a four-year term, and he served out that term, no matter what happened. It was, the prime minister said, "a bad time. I went to bed, browsed about in the files for a while, and then slept for four or five hours until we reached London. What a blessing is the gift of sleep."

For Eisenhower, in addition to dealing with the British in those final days before leaving for London, there were other distractions as well. On the 20th he was visited by his old friend from the Philippines, Manuel Quezon. Quezon offered Eisenhower an annuity of $100,000 or more, what the general called "an honorarium for services rendered during the period I was acting as military adviser to the Philippine government." Eisenhower diplomatically turned down the offer, explaining that it was "unquestionably legal and that the president's motives were of the highest" but someone might misunderstand and that "any gossip on such a matter might reflect upon the Army and the War Department."

Eisenhower was wrong. Accepting the money was not "unquestionably legal." To the contrary, a very clear army regulation said that "every member of the military establishment . . . is bound to refrain from . . . acceptance by an officer of gift or any emolument from a person or firm with whom it is the officer's duty as an agent of the government to carry on negotiations."

When MacArthur was leaving the Philippines for Australia in March, Quezon gave him a cash award of $500,000. Major General Richard Sutherland got $75,000, and various other high-ranking officers on MacArthur's staff got large amounts. Both Roosevelt and Stimson knew about the matter, but nothing was known of it publicly until 1979, when an article on the subject was published in the *Pacific Historical Review*.

Eisenhower did accept an official citation from Quezon, and he said, "The president accepted my explanation [about the money] and stated that the matter was ended once and for all." He told Marshall what had happened, but he very likely did not mention it to Mamie. The Eisenhowers could have used the money.

Before Eisenhower left his office in the Munitions Building for the last time, his secretary, Helen Dunbar, presented him with a photograph of himself that she said she had "hijacked" and would he autograph it? "You bet," he told her. "Matter of fact I'm flattered you want one." Miss Dunbar said that when all the staff of OPD had been assembled, "It was all light banter . . . some scene from a book or a movie." Ike shook hands with everyone, told each that he would miss him or her, and hoped to see everybody in London.

Eisenhower, Clark, Mickey, and Tex Lee left from Bolling Field just outside Washington on June 23 at a little after nine in the morning. Clark's family, his wife, Renie, his daughter Ann, and his son Bill, a cadet at West Point with John, had come to the airport to see him off. But public displays of affection were not for the Eisenhowers. Ike had called Ida the night before to say good-bye and had said good-bye to Mamie in the house at Fort Myer. "I didn't go to the airport," said Mamie. "He wanted it that way. But he asked me to stand under the flagpole at Fort Myer so that he could see me when the plane crossed." Mamie did. "I stood under the flagstaff in the front yard where I knew Ike would be sure to look. The plane roared in very low. I waved and tried to tell myself I saw Ike at a window waving—but I didn't. I was crying too hard."

Eisenhower saw her, though, and wrote her from London, "In spite of our turn, when we took off at Bolling, I could see small figures and movement in the open space around the flagpole at Myer.

"I think I did not tell you before that when I came over here our plane flew directly up the river in front of West Point. We had a grand view of the place and I wondered whether J. may have happened to notice us."

After a stop at Gander and another at Prestwick, the party arrived at Northolt outside London on the evening of the 24th. Mountbatten was there to greet the Americans, and so was Colonel John Clifford Hughes Lee, "Jesus Christ Himself" Lee, who was to be commanding general of the Service of Supply in the ETO for the rest of the war. Lee sometimes thought that he, not Eisenhower, was supreme commander, and he caused Eisenhower a lot of trouble. But that was all ahead. At the moment, Eisenhower was looking forward to the challenging new assignment, one of the first in his career when he was not assistant to anybody, was nobody's chief of staff or deputy. He was on his own, but that didn't concern him much. He was not a man normally troubled with self-doubt.

The theater commander's first worry was not the Germans but the Americans, those thousands already there, the tens of thousands more on their way, and the ones he would have to send home. The latter were on their own; the others were given a pamphlet, most of which was written by a Yorkshireman who had spent a great deal of time in the United States, Eric Knight. Knight was the author of a very popular wartime novel that later became an even more popular movie, *This Above All*. The pamphlet said, "You are coming to Britain from a country where your home is still safe, food is still plentiful, and lights are still burning. . . . So stop and think before you sound off about lukewarm beer, or cold boiled potatoes, or the way English cigarettes taste. . . . Be FRIENDLY— but don't intrude anywhere it seems you are not wanted. . . . Don't . . . make wisecracks about the war debts or about British defeats in this war.

"NEVER criticize the king or queen. . . . If you want someone's friendship, don't snatch it; wait for it. . . . Get acquainted."

A great many people on both sides of the Atlantic said that trouble between the British and the Americans would impede the war effort by months, perhaps years, but there was very little trouble, even after the Negro troops arrived. That was very largely due to the example set by and the guidelines established by the theater commander. Don Cook, a man who observed the general for many years, wrote of him, "Remarkable from the day he set foot in London was his deep, visceral dedication and determination to make Anglo-American cooperation a living and working reality. He brought with him a simple conviction about this which was as basic and unshakable as his own patriotism. Moreover, he made it work. . . . Eisenhower was probably the least chauvinistic American and the least chauvinistic military commander in history. He never lost his American patriotism or pride; he simply added another patriotism to it."

★ ★ ★

20 GROSVENOR SQUARE

Things began going badly the very first night. He was driven from the airport to Claridge's, then as now considered one of the most fashionable hotels in London, and he hated it. The sitting room of his suite, 408, had gold walls, and the bedroom was pink. He felt, he said, as if he were living in sin, and in a week he moved to a less elegant hotel, the nearby Dorchester, which he thought was more American. It was noisier, anyway.

Brigadier General Charles G. Bolte, who had been Chaney's chief of staff before Chaney had returned to the States a few days earlier, and the other high-ranking members of the American delegation were already in residence at the Dorchester and liked it. According to Bolte, "Eisenhower asked me to move into Claridge's, which was a very blue-stocking thing, and I said, 'I can if you want me to,' but I told him, 'You ought to move into the Dorchester because Claridge's is a pile of sugar. A bomb and it'll dissolve. The Dorchester is steel and concrete.' He didn't like it, but he moved into the Dorchester."

The Dorchester was located across Park Lane from Hyde Park, and Eisenhower's suite there was more conventional and had the added advantage of a fireplace. When wood could be found, Ike liked an occasional fire, even in late June. Mickey said, "The General loves an open fire, not so much for the warmth as to look at. He loves to sit in front of a fire and just look into it, and it is handy to throw his cigarette butts into. He always throws them into a fireplace if there's one around. . . . The General hasn't much use for ash trays at any time. He knocks the ashes off his cigarettes by tapping his hand against something—the arm of a chair, the edge of his desk—and he believes that cigarette ashes are good for carpets. Mrs. Eisenhower doesn't share that belief."

The suite at the Dorchester had three rooms, two bedrooms, one of which was soon to be occupied by Harry Butcher, and a living room.

In his first report to Marshall, Ike promised to do what proved to be almost impossible to do. He said, "I shall try to apply your dictum—'Persuade by accomplishment rather than by eloquence.'" He did try, but in the early days the British much of the time seemed determined to keep him from doing anything at all.

He had thought he was there to prepare for an Allied invasion of the continent in 1942. But the year was nearly half over, and no preparations appeared to have been made; and except for his friend Mountbatten, whom he saw almost immediately after his arrival, the British seemed to be avoiding him. Brooke was simply not available to him, and Churchill was busy fighting off a censure motion in the House of Commons.

On June 30 Ike wrote Marshall, "I can discover little if any progress in the formulation of broad decisions affecting the operation as a whole. . . . General Brooke . . . has been practically incommunicado since his return from Washington. . . . There seems to be some confusion of thought as to the extent of the British commitment toward a 1942 operation."

A week later, he wrote, "Am somewhat uncertain as to existing agreements, if any, concerning 1942 operation, but request information as to whether you believe that British and U.S. forces in Great Britain should now begin concrete preparations, including assembly of shipping and landing craft, so as to make possible an operation no later than September 15 in the hope that it will prove feasible." Those were not easy messages to write. He was a theater commander, but he was unable to find out what was going on in his own theater and was asking for help from Washington.

In the beginning Eisenhower did alienate a few of the British by pretending to be too tough. He used phrases such as "Kill the Hun," and would often remark, "I can be hard-boiled too—if I have a man by the throat." Others of the British thought that they could take him in. Few ever did. The one Britisher who seemed frank and open to him, although he often was not, was Mountbatten. On June 26 Ike had made arrangements to go with Lord Louis on an exercise in Scotland in which tanks would be landed in darkness. On July 1 Eisenhower said in his diary, "Went as a member of Lord Louis' party to witness some secret exercises in Scotland, north of Prestwick. The exercises were over about 5 P.M. Went to bed on Lord Louis' yacht and got up at eight. Visited a combined signal school run by Lord Louis' group and then went on to Prestwick."

In the meantime Eisenhower built up his staff for the European Theater of Operations U.S. Army (ETOUSA), which, although it would grow rapidly, on his arrival included only 55,390 officers and men. He had Clark as his deputy commander and chief of all ground forces in ETOUSA. U.S. troops in northern Ireland were under the command of Major General Russell P. "Scrappy" Hartle. Hartle was an agreeable fifty-three-year-old career officer, a graduate of the University of Maryland. The U.S. Army Air Forces were under the command of Major General Carl "Tooey" Spaatz, West Point 1914, with whom Eisenhower was to have a long, generally agreeable, and admiring association. Major General Charles H. Bonesteel was in command in Iceland, and J. C. H. Lee was in charge of supplies.

At 20 Grosvenor Square, on the morning after he arrived, Eisenhower had the first of an almost unending series of staff meetings. He was dismayed by the mood of defeatism on the part of both U.S. and British forces, resulting from the recent fall of Tobruk, and what he said that morning set the tone for what was to be the spirit of the Eisenhower command until the war ended: "Pessimism and defeatism will not be tolerated. Any officer or soldier who cannot rise above the obstacles and bitter prospects that lie in store for us has no recourse but to ask for instant release from this theater. And if he shows such attitude and doesn't ask for release, he will go home anyway. . . . We're here to fight and not to be wined and dined."

Many people secretly scoffed at what he said; it was too much, too corny, too Rotarian. Most of the scoffers were soon, in a phrase Ike used often in those days, on their way home "on a slow boat, without escort." Those who stayed soon discovered they were on a tight-run ship.

The change in attitude around 20 Grosvenor Square was soon apparent. Kay Summersby, who was shortly to become a member of the Eisenhower wartime family, said that the motor pool for headquarters "had once been rather a social center; we went to work around 10 in the morning, took an hour and a half for lunch, knocked off about teatime in the afternoon. Now it was run strictly on military lines. Headquarters had been reorganized. Instead of the easy-going group of 'observers' whose schedules included long liquid lunches and early cocktail hours, 20 Grosvenor Square was peopled by army men . . . on a seven-day week. General Eisenhower had come over to do a job; he was wasting no time."

When Lieutenant Colonel John Dawson Laurie, Lord Mayor of London, asked Eisenhower to have dinner with him and the Lady Mayoress, Ike did what he had asked others to do socially. He declined. He wrote Laurie, "The amount of work falling upon me as Commander of the U.S. Army in Europe absorbs my time to the extent that I must rigidly limit my participation in social activity. Consequently I have found it necessary to decline all invitations to social-official functions except where a connection with the combat effort of our two countries is indicated."

From the beginning of Eisenhower's stay in London, one of his most important jobs, one he had anticipated back in Washington, was getting thousands of American soldiers arriving every week to accommodate themselves to the British and British ways and vice versa. One of the first Britishers Eisenhower consulted in the matter was Pug Ismay. Brooke would have been no help at all. He hated Americans. Pug did not; he was from the beginning, as Eisenhower said, "devoted to the principle of Allied unity." In his memoirs Ismay said of Eisenhower, "Frankness, sincerity, and friendliness were written all over him. But, with it all, he was master in his own house. . . .

"One of his first questions was a revelation. Whom should he see about making arrangements to ensure that good relations were established between his troops and the civil population in England? His soldiers were apt to regard themselves as crusaders who had come over to Europe to help us out of a mess, and to think that they should be treated with the utmost generosity and consideration. The British people, on the other hand, who had been fighting alone for more than two years, would tend to resent the discomforts and deprivations which the arrival of these self-styled crusaders would inevitably involve. Unless something were done to enable both sides to understand each other, there was bound to be irritation and bad feelings."

Ismay told Eisenhower he should see Brendan Bracken, minister of information, the colorful young man who had succeeded in publishing, in politics, and in becoming a very close friend of Churchill's. Bracken lived at 10 Downing and was, some people said, the prime minister's natural son. It was clear that he was what Churchill wanted a son to be, a success; Randolph failed at things. Bracken and Eisenhower got along immediately. Bracken said, "He says 'Yes' or 'No' right away and has got a reason for it."

Most Americans did not feel any great rush of affection for the British. They said that British soldiers were "underpaid, undersexed, and under Eisenhower." The British said that the Americans were "overpaid, oversexed, overfed, and over here." They also felt that the Americans were overdecorated. The reason for the Good Conduct Medal eluded them. You got a medal just for staying out of trouble? Preposterous. One story that everybody heard who was stationed in England at the time went, "Heard of the three Yanks who went to a war movie? One immediately fainted, and the other two got a medal for carrying him out."

On July 19 in a memorandum to Hartle, Clark, Lee, Spaatz, and Bonesteel on British-American relations, Eisenhower said:

> Among the matters that are causing me constant concern are the great difference between the pay scale of our men and the British; considerations involving the quality and quantity of rations; methods for promoting proper

relationships between our men and the British Army and the British public; standards of discipline, including military courtesy, and training programs. . . .

There is no need to recite again the risks we run, collectively and individually, of creating ill-feeling through, what the British will consider, lavish expenditure of money. . . . Because of strictness of food rationing in the United Kingdom, I believe that each man should carry with him a day's ration in kind, which ration should be as large as possible in components difficult to obtain here. An excess in meats, fats, and sweets would seem to be indicated. Company commanders and mess sergeants could so arrange that the man going on pass got somewhat more than his proportion of these items and the whole matter would present little difficulty if handled skillfully.

The program was not a complete success. Some GIs themselves ate the extra ration when they went on leave; others used it to get personal favors of one kind or another, but most did not. Some British shopkeepers and restaurant owners overcharged the many Americans who never understood British money, but there were also few of those. One GI who worked in intelligence headquarters near Grosvenor Square said of Eisenhower, "It was generally known that he wanted all red tape cut for better relationships between the British and the Americans." He was a man "who could blend these forces into one happy and united team, where national rivalry was not so much ignored as unthinkable."

On September 4 a letter was sent from the Home Office in London to chief constables, saying, "It appears that . . . difficulties may be caused by the presence among the population of coloured troops."

When Eisenhower was asked about "the coloured troop problem" at his press conference, he said, "Prior to my arrival in England, censorship had been established by American headquarters on stories involving minor difficulties between Negro troops and other soldiers, or civilians. These incidents frequently involved social contacts between our Negro soldiers and British girls. The British population, except in large cities and among wealthy classes, lacks the racial consciousness which is so strong in the United States. The small-town British girl would go to a movie or dance with a Negro quite as readily as she would with anyone else, a practice our soldiers could not understand. Brawls often resulted, and our white soldiers were further bewildered when they found that the British press took a firm stand on the side of the Negro."

Eisenhower announced at that press conference that censorship of incidents involving Negro troops had been lifted. Some correspondents thought he had gone too far, that, in Eisenhower's words, "troublemakers would exaggerate the importance of the incidents and that the reports, taken up at home, would cause domestic dissension. I thanked them but stuck to my point, with the result that little excitement was ever caused by ensuing stories. It was a lesson I tried always to remember."

The one time in North Africa when the general briefly forgot that lesson the results were disastrous.

According to Butcher at that same press conference, "As background he [Ike] told them his policy for handling colored troops would be absolute equality of treatment, but there would be segregation where facilities afforded. The colored troops are to have everything as good as the white."

Norman Longmate, the Englishman who wrote *The G.I.s: The Americans in Britain 1942–1945,* commented, " 'Ike' himself, born in Texas, was no liberal reformer, but his attitude to colour as a military problem was within its limits, sensible and honourable."

When the war began the navy accepted Negroes only as mess attendants. The Marines would not accept them at all, and in the army for most of the war, total segregation existed. That was official government policy, approved by Franklin Roosevelt in 1940. Intermingling of the races "would produce situations destructive to morale and detrimental to the preparation for national defense." The Red Cross dutifully segregated blood plasma donated by Negroes and whites. Stimson until the end of his life believed that Negroes were intellectually inferior, and so did most American soldiers. But, while there were many brawls and even occasional gunfire, caused usually by Negro men associating with white British women, most of the time an uneasy peace prevailed.

In July 1942 *Stars and Stripes* said what was true then and largely remained true while American troops were in England: "The Negroes have found the people ready and willing to make them feel at home."

Discipline was much on Eisenhower's mind during this period. It was something civilians and most new soldiers did not understand. Without discipline there could not be morale, and, as he was to say at the end of the war and believed for the rest of his life, "Morale is the greatest single factor in a successful war."

Saluting was absolutely essential to good discipline, but to most of the citizen soldiers in London in those days, the author included, it was silly and it was stupid. What did saluting have to do with winning the war? It need hardly be said that the general did not agree.

One day not long after his arrival he was driven the distance between the officers' club and an enlisted men's mess and was saluted only once, by a British soldier, although the car was proceeding at the slow speed of ten miles an hour and the stars of his rank were clearly visible on his license plate.

He returned immediately to his headquarters and dictated a memo to be distributed to all officers and enlisted men in the theater. It said that if he ever again observed any laxity in saluting he would personally get the name of the offender and would hold his commanding officer responsible. Saluting improved, particularly when cars and officers wearing two stars were seen.

Kay Summersby had been driving for Tooey Spaatz, and about a month after Eisenhower's arrival in London, she went with Spaatz to Hendon airfield where to her surprise she met Ike returning from one of his many inspection trips. He was delighted to see her, and two days later she was again driving for him. Once again, rank had its privileges.

His driver had been Albert Gilbey, and in his first letter to Mamie, written on June 26, Eisenhower told her that he had been assigned a driver, "an old-time Britisher," who was "safe and sane, and seems to know every crook and cranny of the country. I think we'll get along fine."

That driver, "Lord Gilbey," as he was called, was a veteran of the First World War and was, according to Kay, "a little slow." It was certainly safe to tell Mamie about Gilbey, but Ike did not mention that Kay had become a member of his staff until the following March when Kay's picture appeared in *Life* magazine, showing her on her way to join his headquarters in North Africa.

When Kay once more reported for duty as Eisenhower's driver in London she said that, although he was "in the midst of a new staff conference, the General took time out to chat and to hand me a veritable treasure; oranges, lemons, and grapefruit. They were part of a load he had brought back for British commanders. I was humbly appreciative for a share. The General apologized because some of the fruit was bruised."

Gilbey stayed on as a driver, too. "I got most of the few day trips," said Kay. "He made the night runs."

Kay was nicknamed "Skib" by Eisenhower's London family because she came from Skibereen, Ireland. She came from a good but by no means wealthy family. Her father had been a colonel in the army, and she was very useful to Eisenhower not only as a driver and later as a secretary answering letters written to him by admirers, but she knew how to deal with British aristocracy, and who was to sit where at the rare parties he could not avoid. In fact she did very much what Mamie had done for him when they were first married; she helped smooth some of the rough edges.

Anthea Saxe, also a driver during the war and a close friend of Kay's both during and after it, said, "She was very beautiful in those days. She was charming and gracious, and she was gay and witty. She had a lot of energy and drive, and she took his mind off the war.

"She was also extremely capable and perhaps more important was very close mouthed. She never blabbered about anything, and he trusted her. She once told me that he felt he couldn't trust all his aides but that he knew he could trust her, and that she was the only one."

Other people were infuriated simply because she was a woman. In those days women in uniform were generally regarded as second-class citizen soldiers. They were either all whores or all lesbians, or both. One general was certain they could not be trusted with military secrets. They got PWOP, pregnant without permission, and they were without exception ugly. A soldier wrote his sister, who was thinking of becoming a WAAC, "Why can't these gals stay home and be their own sweet self, instead of being patriotic." A Marine officer welcomed Marine women in uniform by saying, "Goddamn it all. First they send us dogs. Now it's women."

Harry Butcher and Eisenhower's old friend from MacArthur's staff during the years in the Philippines, T.J. Davis, arrived in London on July 2. Davis, now a full colonel, told amusing stories, and many of them were about MacArthur. Butcher and Davis had more or less the same opinion of the national hero, then issuing frequent and flamboyant communiqués from Australia. Butcher was absolutely essential to Ike at that time. He would say, "There are days when I just want to curl up in the corner like a sick dog, but Butch won't let me. That's why I need him. To keep me from going crazy."

Kay said, "I always thought of Butch as playing the role of a favorite younger brother—full of admiration, but with enough brash confidence to speak up when he disagreed with the General."

Butcher on Eisenhower's order began keeping a diary, beginning on July 8, 1942, ending on July 10, 1945. On the latter day, the buoyant and victorious general had returned to Washington from a vacation in White Sulphur Springs. Butcher said, "I talked with Ike last night about writing a book. I said I could do the human-interest and personality story from the diary. He agreed and immediately began outlining to me the problem of writing a book.

"In saying good-bye, General Ike's last words to me as he boarded the plane were:

" 'Don't make any mistakes in a hurry.' "

Butcher did not do what he told Eisenhower he was going to do; he did not write a book at all; he simply cut down the original 640,000 words in the diary he had been ordered to keep as part of his official duties and had it published by Simon and Schuster under the title *My Three Years with Eisenhower: The Personal Diary of Captain Harry C. Butcher, USNR, Naval Aide to General Eisenhower, 1942 to 1945*. In the introduction to the book, "Operation Doorstop," Butcher said, "As this book took shape, I debated with myself the advisability of asking General Ike to read it. We corresponded on the subject and we came to the conclusion that it would be inadvisable for him to treat my effort differently from that of other reporters. Consequently, he has not seen the manuscript and I wish to make clear to the reader that this book is my responsibility and not General Eisenhower's. . . . I will send him an autographed copy but have written him that when the material is published, I should not only go to Tahiti, but will dig myself a deep foxhole and crawl in. Nevertheless, I would like to be a mouse hiding behind a stack of the Westerns on his night table when and if he ever finds time to read this stuff."

Eisenhower found time to read the book all right, and he felt that Butcher had totally betrayed him, and he continued to feel that way for the rest of his life. Just to begin, a diary written on the order of one's superior officer is hardly personal; the material did not even belong to Butcher, and he had no right to publish it, nor did Eisenhower ever understand when Butcher in July 1945 spoke of "writing a book" that publishing great parts of the diary was what he had in mind. Moreover, the book did a great disservice in publishing Eisenhower's supposedly private comments, often when he was annoyed and tired, on other world leaders and Allied officers, Churchill, de Gaulle, and Montgomery, to name only three.

On publication of the book, Butcher's name immediately went in Ike's "bottom drawer," and in Eisenhower's own account of the war years, *Crusade in Europe*, Butcher is mentioned only four times. On page 60 he is identified as "my naval aide, Commander Harry C. Butcher." On page 77 Ike speaks of "a diary of the time" when the landing in North Africa, by then called TORCH, was being planned in the early days in London. On page 133 Ike noted that "Commander Harry Butcher and Captain Ernest Lee were personal aides" on his staff during the war. Butcher is mentioned one final time, on page 133, as "Commander Butcher, my personal aide." In his massive book *The President Is Calling*, Milton Eisenhower does not mention his old friend Butcher at all.

John Eisenhower said, "I find it more difficult to be angry than the rest of them. I know he did wrong, but what the hell. Milton has never forgiven him. Butcher is an affable, salesman-type, shallow-type fellow. A huckster. I can see why they [his father and Milton] didn't want to have any more to do with him. He was good to me as a kid. He was damned good for my father for a long time, except he couldn't be trusted, and with that finally came the reluctant conclusion. It was criminal. He could have been sued, I think. That was one of his main duties during the war to keep that diary. Dad didn't want to be bothered with any law suits. I don't know whether he ever considered that or not. But I think that since Butcher came off smelling like a rose by Butcher's standards, it was worth it to Butcher to lose Dad's friendship. So my guess is that Dad would have said, 'why that sonofabitch' every time he would have mentioned Butcher's name.

"But when Dad was finding his way around, going through what I call the apprenticeship period, it was a damned good thing to have Butcher around."

On December 15, 1945, the first installment of Butcher's book appeared in *The Saturday Evening Post,* and it included a most embarrassing paragraph in the August 26, 1942, entry. "We lunched alone at the flat. We had soup, and Ike undertook to demonstrate how the Prime Minister eats his soup—if 'eats' is the word. Being short and stockily built, the P.M.'s chin isn't very much above the soup plate. He crouches over the plate, almost has his nose in the soup, wields the spoon rapidly. The soup disappears to the accompaniment of loud and raucous gurglings. While showing me how it was done, Ike almost choked."

On December 22, a week after the article appeared, Eisenhower spent a good part of the afternoon with Butcher, who agreed to rewrite that paragraph, to which, Eisenhower said, "I took such earnest exception." He did rewrite it— but not much. In the book the paragraph says, "Since the P.M. is short and stockily built, his chin isn't very much above the soup plate. He crouched over the plate, almost had his nose in the soup, wielded the spoon rapidly. The soup disappeared to the accompaniment of loud gurglings."

Butcher also made reference in the book to Eisenhower's "suppressed yawn" while attending a dinner party at Churchill's home.

Eisenhower, in a letter he wrote to Butcher on December 26, said what he felt deeply about and never forgave.

My feeling is that you were admitted into a circle where every individual had a right to believe that the matters discussed were to remain secret. Your admission into that circle was by the fact that as my aide I was responsible for bringing you into the secret. In the over-all story there is no objection that I can see to your telling about these things except in those instances where, because of the mention of personalities or other equally delicate subjects, I or any other participant in the discussion had every right to believe that the matter died at the instant it was born. There is no possibility of my giving you any line of demarcation, but you know how repugnant it would be to me ever to appear in the position of having violated good faith.

Butcher had done just that—violated good faith; and while it was not re-pugnant to him, it was to his former friend and commanding officer.

Churchill made what was perhaps the best summation of the whole Butcher affair in a letter to Ike dated January 26:

I have skimmed over the Butcher article and I must say I think you have been ill-used by your confidential aide. The articles are, in my opinion, altogether below the level upon which such matters should be treated. Great events and personalities are all made small when passed through the medium of this small mind. . . . I am not vexed myself at anything he has said, though I really do feel very sorry to have kept you up so late on various occasions. It is a fault I have. . . . It is rather late at my age to reform, but I will try my best.

To which Ike replied (January 30, 1946):

Your comments on the "Diary" echo my sentiments. Incidentally, I assure you that I never complained about staying up late. I didn't do it often and certainly I always came away from one of those conferences with a feeling that all of us had gotten some measure of rededication to our common task.

When Butcher and T.J. first arrived in England they were met at the airport by a man who was to be a lifelong friend of Eisenhower's, George E. Allen. Allen was a cheerful man who had made a good deal of money without, as he often said, ever doing much work; he knew a great many people, including several presidents, and was later to be the author of a kind of autobiography, *Presidents Who Have Known Me*. He had come to England and Ireland on a kind of vague goodwill mission. He was an old friend of Butcher's. "If war could be made happy, George could do it. He was a good tonic for Ike," Butcher said of him in the diary. Allen in his own book added, "As a matter of fact, I wasn't feeling happy about the war at the time and I probably needed a tonic more than the General did. And I got it. He was and still remains one of the most confidence-inspiring men it has been my good fortune to know. If he ever entertained the slightest doubt about the outcome of the war, he never betrayed it by so much as a crease in the forehead. He never underestimated the diffi-culties, but neither did he question the ability of the United States and its Allies to meet and overcome them. I was so impressed with his determination that I told him about Knute Rockne's contempt for the 'good losers.' Good losers get into the habit of losing. Rockne boys would tear their hearts out by the handfuls on the rare occasions when Notre Dame lost."

Eisenhower had not played against Rockne's Notre Dame team when he was at West Point, but in 1944 an imaginative radio sports announcer, Bill Stern, told a story about Eisenhower and the famous football coach that was later reprinted in a magazine called *Coronet*. According to the story, a professional boxer known as Frankie Brown had challenged young Eisenhower to a match. The two men fought, and the bout was declared a draw. It turned out, according to the story, that Brown's real name was Rockne, and he went on, as Stern so often said, to become the famous Knute Rockne, and Eisenhower went on to become General Eisenhower. When the general was asked about the story by Charles Harger of Abilene, he said that he had done some boxing as a boy "on a strictly amateur basis."

"In later years I got to know Rockne and he and I had several interesting conversations. I admired him a lot but there is no basis whatsoever to the story to which you refer. I have no idea how it ever got started . . . a number of other stories have been circulated about me that are fully as mythical."

On July 4, the day of Butcher's arrival, Sevastopol fell to the Germans, who took 90,000 prisoners. The British continued to suffer great losses at El Alamein, and the Germans continued to sink a great number of Allied ships. But that night six American planes for the first time joined the RAF to bomb airfields in Holland.

Eisenhower had to make a speech that day at the opening of the Washington, a club for servicemen, an engagement Bolte had accepted for him before he arrived. He was furious that, according to Bolte, "he had been sucked into a thing that was insignificant compared to what he felt he had been brought over to do. . . . When he got up, the red blood was rising in his neck."

Allen and Butcher had written a speech for him. "The General was properly grateful," said Allen. "With such a writing team, he said, he'd soon establish a reputation as an orator. . . . He made a speech all right, and it was a masterpiece. But there wasn't a word of the Butcher-Allen script in it. It was a ten-minute off-the-cuff talk about the Allied cause. It was an inspiration to England particularly and to the whole free world. It was simple, from the heart, and eloquent. I recognized then a fact that my experience with General Eisenhower has since confirmed; that he needs a ghost writer about as much as I need more starch in my diet."

On the evening of July 4 Eisenhower attended a reception given by the American ambassador. He shook the hands of most of 2,650 people, and the next morning, according to Kay, "his right hand was terribly swollen. At the dinner that evening he also smoked a great many cigarettes, and Ambassador Winant later had to tell him that in England it was the custom not to smoke a cigarette until after the toast to the king. Eisenhower was furious and told Winant that that dinner was the last one he would ever attend in England."

He did not quite live up to that pledge, however; a little later he attended a dinner party given by Mountbatten, who had heard what had happened at the American embassy. Immediately after the soup course, the accommodating Louis rose, toasted the king, then said to Eisenhower, "Now, General, smoke all you want."

Everybody in England heard and talked about that, and it further endeared the folksy general to the English public.

On July 5 Eisenhower had received an invitation that he could not turn down. Churchill had invited him and Clark to Chequers. John Eisenhower said, "With Dad's background, coming from Abilene, being an unknown Army officer when Churchill was the Colossus of the world, he couldn't help being flattered." From the beginning, however, Ike was wary. He was aware, as he was to say, that "when the prime minister turned the sun lamp on you, you were in trouble.

He almost never turned it off until he got his way. Or thought he got his way. He was the most persuasive man I have ever known, and the most persistent."

That first day when Churchill greeted the two Americans, he wore carpet slippers and what Clark called "a baggy smock." He continued wearing them until 2:30 the next morning, when he allowed his visitors to go to bed.

Churchill often spent a good deal of the morning in bed, and almost every afternoon he took a nap so he could stay up late, and his guests of necessity did, too. Kay said, "The only thing Ike really deplored about the P.M. was his habit of staying up until all hours. By nature Ike was an early-to-bed, early-to-rise man. The P.M. was the opposite."

On that first visit Eisenhower and Clark made to Chequers, Churchill got to the point immediately. "He led us down a winding path through the woods until we came to a secluded beach where we sat down and talked about coming events. . . . It was typical of the Prime Minister that he lost no time in stating his views. He stressed to us that he was in favor of postponing the cross-Channel operation and undertaking an invasion of northwest Africa at the earliest possible date." The argument was not settled that day or that night.

There is no record of what was served at dinner at Chequers that night. Churchill later said, "Irish stew turned out to be very popular with my guests, and especially with General Eisenhower. My wife was nearly always able to get this."

But Clementine Churchill did not always get Irish stew, and at No. 10 Downing Street, where Eisenhower also dined frequently, onion soup and game pie were often on the menu. Walter Bedell Smith, who was shortly to become Eisenhower's ill-tempered chief of staff, said in a letter to Marshall:

> I am feeling completely fit again but I must confess that I was miserable for about ten days, and an evening with the Prime Minister together with his onion soup and game pie finished off the business. I spent five days in the hospital with the best care and emerged very much myself again. The memory is still strong and I can pass up the exotic dishes without a tremor. . . .
>
> Our relations with the prime minister are on a most informal basis. Unfortunately, this happy state of affairs carries with it the obligation for a weekly dinner at No. 10 Downing Street which is usually terminated about 2:00. Since I retain my sense of humor I must confess that I derive some comfort from the look of patient resignation on the face of Isme [*sic*] and the C.I.G.S. [Chief, Imperial General Staff—Sir Alan Brooke] as they brace themselves for hours in a straight-backed dining room chair and listen to Mr. Churchill's flights into the stratosphere, which they have heard over and over again.

In that same letter Smith said, "General Eisenhower continues to enjoy the complete confidence and support of the Prime Minister and of the British Chiefs of Staff."

That was not quite true, and Smith knew it wasn't quite true. Marshall, being a realist, knew it, too.

Food wasn't the only hazard at Chequers: there was no central heating and it was impossible to get warm there. Ike said that the house, which dated back to about 1480, was "a damned icebox." After the first visit he never went there without wearing two suits of underwear.

Chequers, the general said, was "rather unpretentious but a very good type of English brick architecture of that time. The principal feature of the house is an enormous living room with the ceiling running completely to the roof, around which are built various offices, dining rooms, and dens. On the second floor is a nice movie theater at which the prime minister entertains not only his guests, but all of the retainers of the household."

On that first visit to Chequers, the movie shown was *The Tuttles of Tahiti,* an American movie starring the English-born actor Charles Laughton. "Fortunately it was in the lighter vein and was hilariously funny," Ike said. "All of us, including the prime minister, had a thoroughly good time."

The bedrooms were all small, and in Eisenhower's that first night was a book on the history of the house. "I could not go to sleep without reading that part applying to my own room," he said. "I slept in an enormous oak bed, four-poster, with enormous bulges on the posts at intervals, each elaborately carved, the whole surrounded by a canopy [of] solid oak, apparently about six inches thick. . . . This room was supposed to have been frequently used by Cromwell, whose daughter had married the then owner of the house. Cromwell's picture hung in the room where I slept."

Eisenhower and Clark were up early the next morning, but their host was not, and after they had inspected a guard of honor made up of Coldstream Guards, Churchill leaned out his bedroom window and shouted, "Ain't they a fine body of men?" Eisenhower agreed; the shortest, he said, was "at least six feet tall."

On their way back to London the two Americans discussed their differences with Churchill. Clark later accurately wrote, "Once he had decided that a certain course of action was proper and would produce the best results for the allied cause—and particularly for Great Britain—he relentlessly pursued that course, ruthlessly eliminating obstacles in his path." The Americans did not win a single argument with Churchill in 1942, but later Eisenhower frequently won over "the prime," and to his credit, when Churchill was convinced of the rightness of a certain action, he became its most enthusiastic backer.

John Eisenhower said that in the beginning of his father's relationship with Churchill, "Dad was in the driver's seat. He was representing the United States, which was the senior partner. He was also in a position where he could say 'no' to Churchill. . . . Churchill's overtures and his courting of the Americans was calculated."

Within a very short time Churchill became quite fond of Eisenhower and at dinner parties disregarded strict British protocol by almost always placing him to his immediate right, which was considered the chair of highest honor. As the lowest-ranking general present, this honor should not have been given him. Almost all the men he associated with and gave orders to outranked him.

But Churchill described Eisenhower as "a great, creative, constructive, and combining genius." In an address to the English Speaking Union in London in 1951, after Eisenhower became Supreme Allied Commander Europe (SA-

CEUR), Churchill said in a dramatic low voice, almost a whisper: "What shall I call this man? How shall I refer to him? By what title shall I address him— this—this soldier, this great soldier? This educator and historian? This great educator and great historian? This statesman, for truly he is one of the great statesmen of all time. Why, I shall call him what I have ever called him, and what I shall always call him, Ike."

Eisenhower had an equally high opinion of Churchill. On December 8, 1954, the president wrote his old friend Swede Hazlett, "Not long ago my old friend Winston reached the venerable age of four score. . . . The occasion was made one of celebration throughout the Empire, and our own papers were filled with reminiscent accounts of his experience and accomplishments. Some of them were, I thought, reasonable and accurate; others extravagant.

"Unquestionably he is a great politician and a great war leader. In addition, he has displayed many of the qualities of a great man. For my part, I think I would say that he comes nearest to fulfilling the requirements of greatness in any individual that I have met in my lifetime. I have known finer and greater characters, wiser philosophers, more understanding personalities. But they did not achieve prominence either through carrying on duties of great responsibility or through giving to the world new thoughts and ideas of such character as to bring to them by popular acclaim the title of great."

Kay Summersby said that while Eisenhower was in London that summer and fall he was "impatient, tired and nervous. . . . He was losing weight and the wrinkles on his face were suddenly too deep for a man of fifty-two. He was drinking more coffee, smoking cigarettes, and getting less sleep than ever." She said that he almost never sat still, and on those rare occasions when he did "his fingers would be tapping on the table." Internally, Eisenhower was filled with discontent. In his first letter to Mamie, he said, "I cannot tell you how much I miss you. An assignment like this is not the same as an absence from home on maneuvers. In a tent, surrounded by soldiers, it seems natural to have to get along alone. But when living in an apartment, under city conditions, I constantly find myself wondering, 'Why isn't Mamie here?' You've certainly become necessary to me."

He later wrote Milton, "It is a rather lonely life I lead; every move I make is under someone's observation. And as a result, a sense of strain develops that is entirely aside from the job itself. At home a man has a family to go to."

"I live in a gold fish bowl," he told Mamie. "This job would be far easier, and far more efficiently done if you could only be here."

As usually happened when he was under stress, his body reacted. Butcher went with him to the London Clinic "where he received a new type of injection for the neuritis in his shoulder. The treatment proved more rigorous than either of us had anticipated, and I certainly hope it works. . . . The doctor seemed quite hopeful of success for the treatment, which required insertion of the needle in several places in a small area and forcing a flow of novocain through the joint where the fourth rib joins the backbone."

On July 10 Eisenhower had added a third star to his shoulders and car, but the additional rank did not improve his chance of promoting a cross-Channel invasion.

On July 8 the "Former Naval Person," Churchill, in London, cabled Roosevelt in Washington, "No responsible British general, admiral, or air marshal is prepared to recommend 'SLEDGEHAMMER' as a practicable operation in 1942. The Chiefs of Staff have reported, 'The conditions which would make 'SLEDGEHAMMER' a sound, sensible enterprise are very unlikely to occur.' "

Eisenhower got the message; no one seems to know just how, but on that same day he saw Brooke, Portal, and Ismay in his office; on the 10th he reviewed the disappointing decision with the British Chiefs, and on the 11th he told Marshall, "The British Staff and Prime Minister have decided that SLEDGEHAMMER can not repeat not be successfully executed this year under the proposition that the invading forces must be able to remain permanently on the continent. They have reached that conclusion primarily because of the lack of suitable craft to land and maintain a force of sufficient size to do this job. They believe that failure would bring almost disastrous results and that even a partial success would cost more in its adverse effect on next year's operation than would be gained by holding a tiny foothold expensive to maintain."

"They" had decided that. He had not been asked what he thought. But he told Marshall, "My own position has been that if ordered to conduct an offensive this year an attempt at SLEDGEHAMMER in spite of its obvious risks and costs would be preferable to GYMNAST or other major expedition intended to open up an entirely new front in this theater."

But SLEDGEHAMMER was not about to happen, a circumstance Ike later decided was for the best. In *Crusade*, he said, "Later developments have convinced me that those who held the SLEDGEHAMMER operation to be unwise at the moment were correct in their evaluation of the problem. Our limited-range fighter craft of 1942 could not have provided sufficiently effective air cover over the Cotentin or Brittany peninsulas, against the German air strength as it then existed. At least, the operation would have been very costly. Another reason is that out of the northwest African operation flowed benefits to the Allied nations that were felt all through the war and materially helped to achieve the great victory when the invasion actually took place in 1944." Lacking the advantage of hindsight, however, he did not feel that way in the summer of 1942.

On July 14 Eisenhower had what he called a "conference" with the press. Ray Daniell, head of the London bureau of the *New York Times*, presented a list of complaints of the correspondents stationed there. It said that they and their work were looked on with "disdain." Ike replied that he worked with the correspondents on what Butcher called "a basis of complete frankness and trust." He said that the correspondents were "quasi members of my staff," and he charmed everybody. Edward R. Murrow, an old friend of Butcher's from the Columbia Broadcasting System, called after the conference to say, according to Butcher, "that Ike had made a grand impression." Daniell in the *Times* said that the general had given "an excellent demonstration of the art of being outspoken without saying much of anything."

Eisenhower himself claimed to be "quite astonished at the outburst of publicity that followed the announcement of my appointment over here. I think that all this comes about mostly because newspaper strategy is forever trying to open up a second front next week. . . . Recently here I went through an ordeal of one hour's picture-taking in my office. Some of the photographers were from American newspapers, so I suppose that sooner or later there will be some more of this."

On July 15 Roosevelt decided to send a party headed by Marshall, King, and Hopkins to London to get a commitment for some kind of action in the European Theater that would involve American forces in 1942, preferably before the elections on November 3. Hopkins had dinner with the president that night, and he took notes on what Roosevelt said. "I am not content with the British cabinet position. I want to know what our men on the ground—Eisenhower, Clark, and Stark—think. Do they agree with the British cabinet? Can you get a confidential report to them?

"Even though we must reluctantly agree to no SLEDGEHAMMER in 1942, I still think we should press forward vigorously for the 1943 enterprise. . . .Will they also give up 1943? . . . My main point is that I do not believe that we can wait until 1943 to strike at Germany."

Churchill wisely sent his private train to Prestwick to meet the visiting Americans on the 17th; he wanted the train to come first to Chequers so that he could get to them before they saw their fellow Americans. But Marshall and King decided to go directly to London.

When Butcher found out that his old friend Steve Early was in the party, he asked for and got Eisenhower's approval to meet the party, and he, Hopkins, and Early stayed up very late. The latter two played gin rummy, and, Butcher wrote, "I bet on Steve, unfortunately."

On the 19th, according to Butcher, "Ike worked hard all day. Kept two stenographers busy, writing a proposal to be used by General Marshall and Admiral King with the British."

The next day, July 20, the Eisenhower arguments as well as those of Marshall and King themselves were presented to the British. The Americans were not successful. Alan Brooke wrote, "After lunch at 3 P.M. we met Marshall and King and had long arguments with them. Found both of them still hankering after an attack across the Channel this year to take the pressure off the Russians. They failed to realize that such action could only lead to the loss of six divisions without achieving any results."

There were more meetings on the 21st, and Brooke observed, "Marshall admitted that he saw no opportunity of staging an offensive to help the Russians by September. He missed the point that after September the Russians might be past requiring assistance." Moreover, said the man from Ulster, the weather would be such that a cross-Channel invasion was "practically impossible."

The next day, a day that Eisenhower was to say might be "the blackest day in history," the Americans admitted their failure. When Roosevelt heard the news, he was not particularly surprised or dismayed. Plans had to be made at once to join the British in a landing in North Africa, and it must not be later than October 20, a date comfortably before the chancy congressional elections. "Full speed ahead," said Roosevelt.

Eisenhower's reaction was quite different. He said that what had been decided "rejects the thought that the allies can do anything to help the Russians remain in the war as an effective fighting force. . . . It is quite clear now that ROUNDUP may never come off."

On the evening of their victory, according to Brooke, the "Chiefs of Staff gave dinner to the Americans at Claridge's. On the whole, went well."

The next day he wrote, "My birthday—59! I don't feel like that."

That, too, was an unhappy day for Ike. Butcher said, "Saw Ike and General Clark at breakfast. The proposal for a second front has definitely been turned down by the British as too risky and too unlikely really to help the Russians.

" 'Well, I hardly know how to start the day,' Ike said. 'I'm right back to December fifteenth.' "

Not only did it appear that Eisenhower was back to square one, the day after he first came to Washington, almost eight months before, all he had said and written and advocated, appeared to have been wasted effort. Furthermore, he did not yet know the worst. The diversionary expedition into North Africa would be led by the man who—possibly except for Marshall—had fought hardest against it: himself.

Three days later, on July 25, in Marshall's suite at Claridge's, the American chief of staff told Eisenhower that if all went the way he hoped, Eisenhower would be "deputy Allied commander" of what had been GYMNAST and was now TORCH. On the other hand, Marshall said that Eisenhower might be supreme commander of the expedition, and he told him that King had said, "The best man you can possibly get is right here and available—General Eisenhower."

Later that summer, still not in a happy mood, Ike wrote his old friend Fox Conner, then retired. Conner had told Eisenhower that he was for a cross-Channel attack, and Eisenhower wrote back, "I quite agree with you as to the immediate task to be performed by the Allies. I have preached that doctrine earnestly for the last six months—to everyone who would listen to me. . . . I believe in direct methods, possibly because I am too simpleminded to be an intriguer or to attempt to be clever. However, I am no longer in the places where these great questions have to be settled. My only job is to carry out my directives as well as I can. I sincerely trust that I will be able to do my duty in accordance with your own high standards."

On August 2 Colonel Al Gruenther, Eisenhower's old friend from the Louisiana maneuvers, arrived in London. Many years later Gruenther remembered that when he reported to Eisenhower in his and Butcher's suite at the Dorchester, "He [Eisenhower] was not the cheerful man I remembered, and he had aged ten years."

The next day Eisenhower told the British that he was making Gruenther his deputy chief of staff for the planning of TORCH. During that meeting Eisenhower asked Captain Charles E. Lamb of the Royal Navy, "With TORCH to be our immediate assault, when do you figure ROUNDUP can be done, if ever?" Lamb was Director of Plans, Admiralty.

His reply was a masterpiece of circumlocution. According to Butcher, the captain "answered to the effect that if Russia holds out, if the Middle East stays safe, and if Turkey is still neutral, or at least not actively with the Axis, then the Germans will be locked in Russia for another winter. (A lot of 'ifs'!) This will give time to decide on ROUNDUP. It may be accomplished late in 1943, but probably not until 1944.

" 'In other words,' Ike said, 'ROUNDUP may be described in aviator's language as 'ticking without load.' ' "

"Ticking without load" is an Air Force expression used to describe an idling propeller.

Butcher added that "Ike . . . at no time expressed an unwillingness to go forward with the assault [on North Africa] and is somewhat fearful that his honest appraisal of the dangers may be misconstrued as fear rather than deliberation."

Another man who was not enthusiastic about TORCH was Joseph Stalin. The job of telling him that the operation in Africa would take place instead of a second front in Europe fell to the old warrior, Churchill. Roosevelt's advice about what Sir Winston should say to Stalin was less than forthright. He suggested that Churchill tell Stalin that there was to be action against the Nazis in 1942 but not tell him of its exact nature. He did add, however, that "we should attempt to put ourselves in his place, for no one whose country has been invaded can be expected to approach the war from a world point of view."

After Churchill's two-day and two-night visit to Russia—Stalin was as fond of drinking and late hours as the prime minister—he cabled Roosevelt, "I am definitely encouraged by my visit to Moscow."

On August 25 Clark and Eisenhower had dinner with the prime minister; he told the Americans that he had been so persuasive with Stalin that he had said of TORCH, "May God prosper that operation." He also said that the operation should go forward as soon as possible and with as much strength as possible.

That would be Eisenhower's job.

★ ★ ★

MAELSTROM

By the end of August Eisenhower's shoulder was bothering him again; he was overworking, and he was finding it difficult to sleep.

He had what were really two full-time jobs, one as commander of ETOUSA, the other as the man planning and very likely to command a precarious invasion—or was it a liberation?—about which almost everybody had doubts. TORCH was to be the first attempt at a major amphibious landing since the Allied disaster at Gallipoli in 1915, the year Ike graduated from West Point. Most people blamed Churchill for that, and his wife Clementine said, "The Dardanelles haunted him for the rest of his life." The memory did not, however, cause the prime minister to question the necessity for TORCH. He said in his memoirs that he fully supported the operation from the beginning and never changed his mind.

All amphibious landings are risky, but during the entire war none involved more intangibles than TORCH. According to Butcher, Eisenhower felt the Allies were "undertaking an operation of a quite desperate nature which depends only in minor degree upon professional preparation or on the wisdom of military decisions. He is reminded of the return of Napoleon from Elba."

In a letter to Mamie on August 28, Eisenhower said, "Since July 18 one's life here has been one hectic day after another with most of the nights the same. Important messages arrive at all hours of the night and frequently must be delivered to me without delay. One night they came so thick and fast that I just couldn't get any sleep." And a few days later he wrote Patton, who was about to become part of the confusion as commander of the Western Task Force in the TORCH landings, "You are undoubtedly keeping well abreast of the changes in conceptions—I feel like the lady in the circus that has to ride three horses with no very good idea of exactly where one of the three is going to go. However, there is one mighty fine feature of this whole business and that is that you are on that end of it. . . . I think Wayne [Mark Clark] and I are standing up pretty well under the load, although this morning I am in somewhat of an irritable mood because last night when I hit the bed, I started thinking about some of these things all over again and at two-thirty was still thinking. I suspect that I am just a bit on the weak-minded side when I allow myself to do that, but anyway it doesn't happen often. We are keeping our tails over the dash board and look forward to meeting you one of these bright fall days."

He missed John, and in a letter to Art Hurd back in Abilene Ike said, "I would certainly pay one devil of a lot if I could have him here by my side right now. He would get more good as a prospective army officer out of this maelstrom than he will in six months where he is."

If Gallipoli haunted Churchill for the rest of his life, Dieppe dogged Mountbatten for the remainder of his. His biographer Philip Ziegler says, "With the possible exception of the partition of India, no episode in Mountbatten's career has earned him as much criticism as the raid on Dieppe. It is the only point on which he showed himself invariably on the defensive."

On the morning of August 19 a thousand British commandos and American Rangers plus more than 5,000 Canadian troops made an amphibious assault on the town of Dieppe on the French coast. Allied intelligence was poor, and the plans made both for the landing and for the evacuation that was to follow were careless and incomplete. The Germans were expecting the invading force, and naval and air support were almost nonexistent. More than 3,400 of the Canadians were casualties. Of these, almost 2,000, many of them wounded, became prisoners of war.

Not long after the OVERLORD landings in Normandy, Eisenhower wrote to Mountbatten, "I often think of you and the early work you did in promoting efficiency in Combined Operations. I remember telling a Canadian general only two or three weeks ago that except for Dieppe and the work of your organization and the Canadians at that time we would have been lacking much of the special equipment and much of the knowledge that went into this particular operation."

That was true, but whether the lessons learned were worth the great cost has never been satisfactorily settled. The Germans were delighted with the Allied failure, and there was considerable embarrassment over the fact that although only a dozen American officers and fifty American enlisted men took part in the raid, American newspapers carried headlines like, U.S. AND BRITISH INVADE FRANCE and U.S. TROOPS LAND WITH COMMANDOS IN BIGGEST RAID.

The result was a mild reprimand to Eisenhower from Marshall, asking him to be conservative in his estimate of American participation in the raid. As a result, Eisenhower decided against giving medals to any Americans until after the Canadians, the British, and the Fighting French had been decorated. "The tail shouldn't wag the dog," he said.

Eisenhower never forgot that he was a man who only fifteen months before had been a lieutenant colonel, that he had never been in battle and that he was surrounded by men who not only outranked him but who, many of them, had been in battle in two wars. John said that he took the trouble to, and succeeded in, appearing "simple, self-confident and stable" but that the pictures taken of him during this period and later "gave no indication of the tremendous battle he was fighting with himself to combat exhaustion, frustration, and the normal doubts."

It was therefore a great relief when in late August Butcher found a "hideout," a place where Ike could relax. It cost about $32 a week, and the owner agreed to maintain the garden, including the vegetables. All Eisenhower and his family had to provide were bed linens and food.

Telegraph Cottage, as it was called, was in Kingston, a quiet suburb less than forty miles from 20 Grosvenor Square. It was surrounded by twenty acres of woods, lawns, and a vegetable and rose garden. Beyond the woods was a nine-hole golf course, and the cottage had five bedrooms and a single bath. It was without central heating, but there was a fireplace in the living room and a large stove in the kitchen that made most of the house comfortable most of the time. The single telephone was a direct line to Eisenhower's headquarters on Grosvenor Square.

Ike was able to relax there, and he frequently wore a pair of straw slippers that he had bought while still stationed in the Philippines, GI slacks, an old shirt, and a half suede, half smooth leather jacket.

Mickey was in charge of housekeeping details and in addition helped the general dress and undress, changed the blades in his razor, squeezed the toothpaste, and even ironed his shoestrings.

Two sergeants took care of the house and of what Eisenhower called "a simple mess." One of them, Sergeant John Alton Moaney, became Eisenhower's valet after the war. Moaney, a black from Maryland's Eastern Shore, was never called by his first name. John Hunt, Johnny, another black, from Petersburg, Virginia, was Eisenhower's cook from the pre-TORCH days in England through the OVERLORD operation.

By the end of the summer, the family, usually including Kay, was spending most of its time at the cottage. The general wrote to Mamie, "Our cottage is a godsend. Butch says I'm human again." He was never able to forget the war completely, however. At Churchill's insistence, an underground bomb shelter was installed, much to Eisenhower's dislike. Another reminder, half a mile away, was a decoy that flared into flame when German bombers came within six miles, in order to divert attacks from important industrial and military installations. To those in Telegraph Cottage, it was very disconcerting.

The general was not alone in finding the fall of 1942 a difficult time. In 1953 Churchill's doctor, Lord Moran, asked him which had been the two most anxious months of the war, and the prime minister said they had been September and October of 1942. He told Eisenhower many times that his people needed a military victory, and so did he. Unless he had one before the end of the year, he might be forced out of office. At one time, the hostility of the French to the British notwithstanding, Churchill and the British Chiefs had thought of putting a division of British troops ashore in North Africa but abandoned the idea on the grounds that it might lead to charges of bad faith.

On September 5 Roosevelt sent Churchill a one-word telegram: "Hurrah!" The details on TORCH had been agreed on. Churchill replied, "O.K. full blast."

On September 8 Eisenhower and Clark had their usual Tuesday dinner with the prime minister. He read large parts of a speech he had made that day in the House of Commons. When he asked Eisenhower how soon the North African attack would take place, Ike said, "November 8—sixty days from today." The prime minister had wanted the attack earlier but went along with Eisenhower's decision. As he wrote Roosevelt, "In the whole of TORCH, military and political, I consider myself your lieutenant, asking only to put my point of view before you. . . . This is an American enterprise, in which we are your helpmates."

Early in August Patton had been in London for preliminary planning for TORCH and then had returned to Washington. On September 5 Eisenhower wrote Georgie that the British and Americans "were very close to final agreement" on TORCH. He said, "In spite of difficulties, you can well imagine that my feelings are merely those of great relief that final decision and definite plans now seem assured. The past six weeks have been the most trying of my life and had it not been for the fact that I had in this thing, as my principal mainstays, you and Clark, I cannot imagine what I could have done."

"The plan has finally been settled," said Patton, "and I feel very calm and contented. It still can be a very desperate venture if the enemy does everything he should, and we make a few mistakes. I have a sure feeling we will win." He told his friend Ike that while the picture was still "gloomy," when he and his troops started for the beaches "we shall stay there either dead or alive, and if alive, we will not surrender."

Everything seemed brighter, especially at 20 Grosvenor Square, after September 7. On that day Brigadier General Walter Bedell "Beetle" Smith arrived to become Eisenhower's chief of staff, though Marshall had tried to keep him in his own office in Washington as long as possible. Ike once said that no man was indispensable but that Smith came as close to it as any man could. And that very night at Telegraph Cottage Beetle cheered everyone up by telling what had gone on in Washington so far as TORCH was concerned; he told his listeners that the operation "will be a pushover."

Beetle had been born in Indianapolis, Indiana, five years before Eisenhower. He had enlisted in the army in the First World War, gone to an officers' training camp and been commissioned as a second lieutenant. He fought in France and after the war stayed in the army. His rise, like Eisenhower's, had been steady though unspectacular. Marshall had met him many years before at the Infantry School at Fort Benning; Smith had been secretary of the school, and his name had immediately gone into Marshall's little black book.

Pogue in his biography of Marshall says of Smith, "Those who worked under him dreaded both his tongue and his exactions. . . . On reaching a newly established headquarters, he liked to pull out his watch and give the staff two minutes to produce a given paper or put through an important telephone call. . . . Smith was the lean and hungry type Marshall needed for a ruthlessly efficient office, and he leaned heavily on him as Secretary General Staff and Secretary of the Combined Chiefs of Staff in 1941–42. In an army where Marshall depended on officers like Eisenhower and Bradley to do their jobs quietly, to conciliate, to persuade, he required others, like Smith, who could hack a path through red tape and perform hatchet jobs when time and tradition and the dead hand of the past threatened to block progress." Smith, like Butcher, was a friend of Roosevelt's press secretary, Steve Early, and, like Eisenhower, he was fond of men of wealth and power and, sure enough, among his friends was Bernard Baruch. Both Eisenhower and Smith had short tempers, and Smith made full and successful professional use of his. The two men occasionally shouted at each other, but their anger seldom lasted long. They were never close socially. Smith played chess; Eisenhower never did. Ike read Westerns. Smith, in addition to a taste for military history and biography, liked the novels of Joseph Conrad and Ford Madox Ford. Eisenhower saw a lot of Bradley and enjoyed his company. Smith thought Bradley was dull. Eisenhower enjoyed relaxing with friends and exchanging stories and gossip. Smith never indulged himself in small talk. For Eisenhower one of the minor joys of 1942 was singing, off key, the newly published song "One Dozen Roses." Nobody ever heard Smith sing. Very few people who served under him had ever seen him smile. He suffered from an ulcer, which some people thought was responsible for his rudeness. Eisenhower's old friend Allen Nevins, however, said that Smith's ulcer had nothing to do with it. "Smith was just naturally mean," said Nevins.

Chester B. Hansen, one of Bradley's aides, said, "If you got the A treatment from Smith, you took the afternoon off. If you got the B treatment you took the rest of the week off. If you got the C treatment you started cleaning out your desk." Ruth Briggs, Smith's secretary and good friend in London and thereafter, said, "He was terrifying. He would rattle off questions and orders with the speed of a machine gun, and the air would be blue with profanity."

Many people not under his harsh command saw an entirely different man, among them Major General Sir Francis de Guingand, Montgomery's chief of staff in the 21st Army Group, who said, "Bedell Smith and I became great friends. I so enjoyed those evenings spent together at his house either near Versailles or Rheims. We did a lot of business and thrashed out a lot of troubles. He was a most delightful host and is the most generous man I have ever met. He had a wonderful way of creating a pleasant atmosphere around him and rightly or wrongly, I believe this close association between us was responsible for the avoidance of any friction between our two Headquarters."

Drew Middleton of the *New York Times* said, "As our ancestors used to say Smith had a mind like a steel trap, and he was Ike's sonofabitch. You had to have one, especially in an Allied command. You don't want the senior American firing a Briton or a Frenchman. You want somebody else to do it so that Ike remained inviolate at the top of the pyramid. Besides, Smith knew the Army backwards and forwards, and he had come up through the ranks. He wasn't a West Pointer. Therefore he had none of the commitments of the West Point Protective Association."

It is no wonder that Eisenhower called Smith the "general manager of the war." He did a good deal of the time-consuming staff work, thus freeing Ike to make the critical decisions. Smith also did the traveling that Eisenhower had neither the time nor the energy to do. He frequently went to Washington to confer with Roosevelt, with Marshall, with Hap Arnold, and numerous others. When Eisenhower was in North Africa he sent Smith to London to talk matters over with Churchill and Brooke. It was Smith who carried on secret peace negotiations with the Italians and later with the Germans in the Netherlands, and it was Smith who received the Italian surrender and presided over the German surrender in May 1945.

Because of his ulcer, Beetle went to the hospital frequently and for long stays. After the Germans surrendered, his health broke down for a long period, and he was not present when SHAEF was dismantled. He said that it was just as well. He might have displayed more emotion than he wished. In a letter written to Air Chief Marshal Tedder in July 1945 he said, "I am not too articulate where my feelings are concerned."

His services with Eisenhower continued for the rest of his life. Ike said, "Remember, Beetle is a Prussian and one must make allowances for it," and another time he said that Beetle was like a crutch to a one-legged man. It was certainly good to have him around in the weeks before the TORCH landings.

Robert Murphy's presence at Eisenhower's London headquarters proved to be less fortunate, even though he was welcomed and trusted and came with very high recommendations from everybody, including the president of the United States.

Ike had never heard Harry Truman's definition of an expert as "a person who can't learn anything new because if he did he might find out he wasn't an expert any more." That was a perfect description of Murphy.

He was a tall, slightly stooped man, and what was left of his hair was sandy. He had the carefully cultivated manner of a man who had done very well in the best prep and Ivy League schools. He had adopted that manner twenty-five years before when he first started to work for the State Department. Actually he was the son of a frequently unemployed, heavy-drinking railroad laborer in Milwaukee, and he had gone to Marquette University on a scholarship. He had been a member of the State Department since 1917, a large part of the time with the American embassy in Paris and more recently as consul general in Algiers. He was also Roosevelt's personal envoy to French Africa, and it was known that the president thought highly of Murphy's advice on French matters.

After the German victory in the summer of 1940, the French government in the southern, unoccupied part of France had been headed by the friend and ally of Black Jack Pershing from the First World War, Marshal Henri Philippe Pétain who in 1942 was eighty-six. The motto of his state was "Work, Family, and Fatherland," of which the Nazis heartily approved. Pétain had surrounded himself with an unsavory group of Frenchmen, including Pierre Laval, a fervent admirer of Hitler and probably the most hated man in France. Another man close to the marshal was Admiral Jean-Louis-Xavier-François Darlan, commander of the air, sea, and land forces under Pétain. He was almost as hated in France as Laval. Just before Pearl Harbor, the American ambassador to Vichy France, Admiral William D. Leahy, had written to Roosevelt that Pétain was a "feeble, frightened old man, surrounded by self-seeking conspirators." He had urged Roosevelt to reconsider his attitude toward the Vichy government, but Murphy, then in Algiers, advised against any change in policy. The United States, he said, "should not slam the door in the French face now." He said his "contacts" had told him that. And they probably had. Darlan said of Murphy that he was "skillful and determined, long familiar with the smart world and apparently rather inclined to believe that France consisted of the people he dined with in town."

By the time Murphy came to London in 1942 neither his opinions nor his dinner companions had changed much. He distrusted Charles de Gaulle. Murphy said that he had never heard of de Gaulle until the general had flown to England to become head of the Free French after the armistice in 1940. He added, "It was understandable why many politicians distrusted him." He advised Roosevelt to have nothing to do with him, and the president happily accepted that advice. He didn't like de Gaulle either. Stimson said, "To the President, de Gaulle was a narrow-minded zealot with too much ambition for his own good and some rather dubious views on democracy."

Murphy was traveling under the name of Lieutenant Colonel McGowan—Marshall had said, "Nobody pays any attention to a lieutenant colonel"—and before his arrival Butcher said that he was "the hotshot on relationships with the French in Morocco. . . . He might be described as the head of the American fifth column set up there." His title was Head of the Civil Affairs Section for TORCH.

Marshall had met Murphy-McGowan in Washington and cabled Ike, "He [Murphy] impressed me very favorably and can be of great assistance in developing the situation from both the political and civil administrative angles."

Murphy, in a lieutenant colonel's uniform, arrived in London on September 16, and he, Eisenhower, Butcher, and at one time or another a great many advisers spent most of the night at Telegraph Cottage discussing what Murphy thought would happen when the Allies landed in North Africa. They would not be met with cheers at the beach. All the officers in the French armed services had taken an oath of allegiance to Marshal Pétain, and it was expected that most of them would live up to it and oppose any violation of French North Africa's loyalty to the Pétain government in Vichy. True, McGowan-Murphy had set up an underground of sorts, people of many political opinions who were united in only one, that the Nazis must be defeated. But just how its members would react to an Allied landing that included the British no one could say for sure. The situation was unique. Was the landing an invasion or was it a liberation? No one including Roosevelt seemed quite sure of that, and the confusion continued long after the landing. Eisenhower couldn't even pronounce the names of most of those who either would applaud or oppose the landing of the troops under his command.

Murphy said of Eisenhower's feelings:

> In 1942, American soldiers and diplomats had to contend with large areas of ignorance. That African venture probably was more unpalatable to Eisenhower than any other assignment in his distinguished career. The General disliked almost everything about the expedition; its diversion from the central campaign in Europe; its obvious military risks in a vast untried territory; its dependence upon local forces who were doubtful at best and perhaps treacherous; its bewildering complexities involving deadly quarrels among French factions, and Spanish, Italian, Arab, Berber, German, and Russian politics. Eisenhower listened with a kind of horrified intentness to my description of the possible complications.

During what he called his "marathon conversation" with Eisenhower, Murphy spent a good deal of time touting the virtues of General Henri Giraud, who had been wounded in the First World War and was considered something of a hero. In April 1942, at age sixty-three, he had made a dramatic escape from his German captors and made his way to Vichy. He had been described by a fellow Frenchman, diplomat and economist Jean Monnet, as "tall, with a clear blank gaze, conscious of his own prestige, inflexible on military matters, hesitant on anything else." The old man probably could be smuggled out of France, and Murphy was sure a great many Frenchmen in North Africa would rally to his support.

Murphy told Eisenhower that he knew nothing at all about military matters and almost immediately proved it by saying that of course Giraud would insist on supreme command of all the troops taking part in the landings. Eisenhower, not losing his temper, explained that since only American and British troops would be involved it seemed unlikely that a French general could or would be placed in charge.

Murphy said, "We covered all the points about Africa which had been bothering me. . . . I explained how . . . French officers . . . feared that Americans would underestimate the strength needed to establish themselves in Africa." Eisenhower insisted that the date of the landings, November 8, be kept from even the most trusted among the French until four days before they took place. Murphy reluctantly agreed but later said, "With the miserable communications existing in the two thousand-odd miles of territory from Tunis to Casablanca, four days' notice was fantastically inadequate for any coordination with our French friends. In fact we lost the friendship of some of them who were indignant over the method used." Indeed, the poor communications in the area and from the area were to cause Eisenhower a good deal of trouble; they almost got him dismissed.

• • •

After the long meeting with Murphy, Eisenhower cabled Marshall, "I was very much impressed by Mr. Murphy. . . . I believe much good was accomplished." He couldn't help adding, "Smith has taken a great burden from my shoulders—I truly appreciate the sacrifice you made in his case."

The morning after the conference at Telegraph Cottage, Murphy flew back to Washington. Butcher said, "If all that he anticipates in the way of French cooperation comes to pass, many of our worries will have been needless. However, he couldn't answer the two big questions: 1. Would the Spaniards fight, especially in Spanish Morocco, and would they attempt to close the Strait of Gibraltar or attack Gib airdrome and harbor? 2. What would happen in France itself?"

Eisenhower was not at all sure that all or even most of the 120,000 troops and officers that the French kept in North Africa would immediately rally to Giraud's support, as Murphy had said, and he proceeded on the assumption that they would not. He had to have enough strength to land and to push forward no matter what. He told Marshall on October 12, "Material preparations consume so much time and progress seems often to be so slow that occasionally impatience is almost certain to turn into irritation and irascibility. On the whole, however, I think we have every reason to be satisfied with the way things are moving along. . . . If nothing untoward happens, I believe the plan, as finally approved, will develop almost perfectly up to the point of departure."

After that, what would happen so far as the weather and enemy resistance were concerned "only the future can tell. . . . My own conviction is that, with a decent break in the weather, we should get on shore firmly and quickly and, at the very least, should find divided councils among the French, which should prevent them offering really effective resistance. . . . I am anxious that no document, which might be captured, will contain anything tending to nullify the effects of the Presidential promises of completely fair and friendly treatment for the French population. . . . *We must take no chance that a document captured or found ashore can be used either to stir up the Spaniards or to convince the French that we are double-crossing them.*"

Actually Eisenhower's trouble with documents that might or might not fall into enemy hands began in England long before the landings.

De Gaulle's headquarters knew something was afoot; a great many people in England at the time suspected that, but the Gaullists in England were told nothing of plans for TORCH. That was largely Roosevelt's doing. He told his son Elliot, "De Gaulle is out to achieve one-man government in France. I can't imagine a man I would distrust more. His whole Free French movement is honeycombed with police spies, he has agents spying on his own people. To him, freedom of speech means freedom from criticism. Why should anybody trust completely the forces backing de Gaulle?" Besides, he added, after the war de Gaulle wanted all the French colonies returned to France, and Roosevelt was not about to allow that to happen if he could help it.

Churchill had great difficulties with de Gaulle, but in a secret speech to the House of Commons on December 10, 1942, he said, "I continue to maintain friendly personal relations with General de Gaulle and I help him as much as I can. I feel bound to do this because he stood up against the men of Bordeaux and their base surrender at a time when all resisting will-power had quitted France. All the same, I could not recommend to you to base all your hopes and confidence upon him."

If Eisenhower's commander in chief had been more tolerant of de Gaulle and recognized that even before TORCH it was said by many of its leaders that at least 90 percent of all those in the resistance supported de Gaulle, Ike's task in North Africa would have been considerably easier, and he would not have had to deal with Giraud, whom most members of the resistance considered a "pure fascist," or make a deal with Darlan, who was even more heartily hated.

Churchill had warned that so far as intelligence was concerned, de Gaulle's headquarters in England were "leaky," and on September 18 an officer from there came to Eisenhower's office to say, "Sir, I am directed by General de Gaulle to inform General Eisenhower that General de Gaulle understands that the British and Americans are planning to invade French North Africa. General de Gaulle wishes to say that in such case he expects to be designated as Commander in Chief. Any invasion of French territory that is not under French command is bound to fail."

Eisenhower's expression did not change. He said, "Thank you," and the French officer saluted and left.

That was one of Eisenhower's better answers, but the incident did not help him sleep at night. Did de Gaulle headquarters really know about the Allied plans or was what happened a simple attempt to find out?

Actually, as early as August 27 de Gaulle had sent telegrams to two of his supporters saying, "I am convinced by many indications that the United States have taken a decision to land troops in North Africa. . . . The operation will be launched in conjunction with an impending British offensive in Egypt." De Gaulle hadn't been told, but he had made a very good guess.

Throughout the war Eisenhower was always acutely aware of the importance of security, in the months before TORCH, especially so, but at that time a dismaying series of events took place. The first occurred the day after the final strategic plans for TORCH were agreed on by Ike and Mark Clark. Simultaneous landings were to be made in the areas of Casablanca, Oran, and Algiers. The beachheads were to be quickly expanded so that complete control of western Algiers could soon be achieved. Eventually, the Allies were to have possession of the whole North Africa area from Rio de Oro to Tunisia, thus making possible air operations against the enemy in the whole Mediterranean area.

On September 7 the page of Butcher's diary outlining those plans was found to be missing. Butcher said, "If some enemy spy has managed to get that sheet, all our hope of attaining surprise is already in vain. . . . Had to tell Ike today, though I hated like poison having to add to his worries. He was considerably upset but was so considerate I could have wept. . . . I'm responsible and probably should be sent home on a slow boat, unescorted, to use one of Ike's favorite expressions."

Butcher stayed, but the page was never found. A few days later Beetle wrote a letter to Lieutenant General Sir Frank Noel Mason-MacFarlane, governor and commander in chief of Gibraltar. The letter contained not only the date and the places of the landings but the strength of the Allied forces. The letter was in the possession of a British naval officer who was a passenger in a plane shot down by the Germans off the coast of Spain.

The man's body had been washed ashore and found by the Spanish, then returned to the British. The letter was found still sealed in the tunic pocket of the body. It could, however, have been opened, read, and possibly copied by the Germans. True, sand in the buttonholes of the tunic would seem to indicate that the body had not been searched. But who could be sure?

The next unsettling incident concerned a letter Churchill had written to the Combined Chiefs suggesting BONE as an additional landing force for TORCH. A secretary had for some reason taken the letter out of his office and had lost it when he was getting on a London bus not far from the office. The letter was picked up on the street by a charwoman who took it home and gave it to a roomer in her house, a British airman. The airman immediately took the letter to the chief of air security.

The whole thing had an unreal quality, one of Graham Greene's "entertainments," perhaps, with a perfect cast: a careless, possibly suspicious secretary, a concerned char, her airman lodger, and, finally, the safe chief of air security. But was it all that simple? The paper on which the letter had been written was dry, and it had begun to rain almost at the same time the secretary got on the bus. Thus, it must have been found by the char seconds after it was lost. But had someone else in that brief interval seen the letter, copied it, memorized it? The commander of TORCH lost a good deal of sleep wondering about that sort of thing.

An invasion needs maps, and a large number of maps of the area had been printed in a small country town and were being brought to London by truck when a number of the maps fell off. They were found by the police of a nearby village, who saw that the area involved was French North Africa and called de Gaulle's headquarters to find out if the maps belonged to them. General Sir Hastings Ismay, the man so close to Churchill, said in his memoirs, "It would have been very awkward if the officer to whom the inquiry was addressed had asked to see a copy of the map. Fortunately he suspected nothing, and answered in the negative. Once again we breathed a sigh of relief. Our guardian angel had been looking after us—perhaps better than we deserved."

On October 12 Ike wrote his old friend from OPD days Charlie Gailey back in Washington, "Dear Charlie: Thanks for your swell letter—but, what the hell do you mean by 'people returning from England say your health is fine.' Why shouldn't it be? Never felt better in my life, and as the big day approaches, feel that I could lick Tarzan."

The letter may have cheered Gailey, and when he saw Mamie, as he did frequently, he probably passed the happy news on to her, but the letter Eisenhower wrote to John a few days later was considerably more realistic. He said, "When you get to high places in the Army, this business of warfare is no longer just a question of getting out and teaching the soldiers how to shoot or how to crawl up a ravine or to dig a fox-hole—it is partly politics, partly public-speaking, partly essay-writing, partly social contact, on to all of which is tacked the business of training and disciplining an Army. All in all, there's never a dull moment—but there are many in which a fellow wishes he could just get into a hammock under a nice shade tree and read a few wild west magazines!"

His birthday celebration at Telegraph Cottage on October 14 came just at the right time. Mickey had gotten a small cake with three candles, and a Scotch terrier, then six weeks old, was introduced and named Telek. Many have said that the name was a contraction of Telegraph Cottage, though that would seem to be spelled *Telec*. Kay Summersby says that the name was a combination of Telegraph and the first letter of her given name, which seems more logical. Telek was actually owned by Mrs. Summersby, who took care of him most of the time. Summersby was at the party, but her name is not included in Butcher's guest list. "Clark, Beetle, T.J., Major Lee, Mickey, and I had a so-called 'surprise' at Da-de-da. [At the time, the code name for Telegraph Cottage.] The birthday cake had three stars and three candles."

A great many songs were sung, many of them written especially for the occasion by members of the family. Lyrics had been copied and handed around. One, sung to the tune of "Yankee Doodle," went

> When clouds of war in 'forty-one,
> Came thundering down upon us,
> We had to pick a Man of Steel,
> To fight the foe Ger-Manus.

> Send 'em "IKE" arose the cry,
> From the hills and valleys,
> He's the man to crack them down,
> and stow them in the galleys. . . .

The song had nine choruses, all of which were sung, with Ike singing the loudest. The cable from Marshall was both welcome and reassuring. It said,

MY PRAYERS, BEST WISHES AND COMPLETE CONFIDENCE TO YOU ON YOUR BIRTHDAY.

MARSHALL

By October 16 Murphy had returned to Algiers from Washington, and at a meeting with French officials there discovered that Admiral Darlan had found out that the Allies were planning to invade either Casablanca or Dakar. The admiral also believed that the Germans were going to move into French North Africa, using bases on the Spanish mainland and in Spanish Morocco to do so. The admiral added that if the Allies promised him full support and aid, he would take charge, releasing the French fleet to the Allies.

Marshall was understandably suspicious of the admiral's sudden change of heart. Darlan had bitterly hated the British during most of his career, and he despised de Gaulle, whom the British were supporting. In 1940 he had been convinced the Germans would win the war and had welcomed them with considerable enthusiasm. By the fall of 1942, however, he had decided that the

Allies would win and was willing to shift his support. That opportunistic decision did not make him a hero in the eyes of most people. After Darlan's death Eisenhower said of the admiral, "His reputation was that of a notorious collaborator with Hitler [and] his mannerisms and personality did not inspire confidence and in view of his reputation we were always uneasy in dealing with him." But in London in 1942 Eisenhower's interest was in landing his troops with as little resistance as possible, and maybe the colonial French would rally to Darlan. Better yet, why not a team? Why not use both Giraud and Darlan? Giraud would be governor of all French North Africa, being responsible both for its civilian and military affairs. Darlan would be commander of all the military forces there and commander of the French navy. Thus when the Allies landed there would be immediate and total cooperation. After the landings had been made and after North Africa had become a base for future Allied operations, Darlan would take over Clark's job as deputy Allied commander, and Clark would take command of the Fifth Army.

It all sounded good, and when Ike met with Churchill and the British Chiefs of Staff he cannot have been too surprised to discover that they accepted the plan with enthusiasm. Churchill, as usual, got to the point immediately. The point was the French fleet at Toulon, and the prime minister said, "Kiss Darlan's stern if you have to, but get the French navy." In *Crusade* Eisenhower, as was usually the case, phrased the remark more delicately: "Just before I left England Churchill had earnestly remarked, 'If I could meet Darlan, much as I hate him, I would cheerfully crawl on my hands and knees for a mile if by so doing I could get him to bring that fleet of his into the circle of Allied forces.' "

Eisenhower had asked Murphy to set up a secret meeting on the Mediterranean coast to which high-ranking American officers would come to talk over matters with high-ranking French officers. On October 17, a Sunday, word came from Marshall that the meeting was to take place on the following Thursday, October 21. Clark said when he saw that cable, he thought, "This was it—this was a job I wanted to do.

" 'When do I go?' I said to Ike.

" 'Probably right away,' he answered."

The meeting with, among others, General Charles Emmanuel Mast, Giraud's representative in Algiers, was to take place in an isolated villa on the Algerian coast.

When Clark and his party got to the Eighth Air Force bomber base at Polbrook, the weather was too bad to fly for the two Flying Fortresses that were to take them to Gibraltar. The party included very valuable, very high-ranking personnel, including Brigadier General Lyman L. Lemnitzer, the G-3 [operations] of Eisenhower's headquarters; Colonel Archeleus L. Hamblen, G-4 [supply]; Captain Jerauld Wright, U.S. Navy liaison officer with TORCH; and Colonel Julius C. Holmes, a one-time State Department career officer who spoke French. They took off the next morning at six, Lemnitzer in one plane, Clark in the other. If Clark's plane was forced back or shot down, Lemnitzer was to take over. They got to Gibraltar a few hours later and conferred with several British officers, including Lieutenant N. L. A. Jewell, commander of the submarine that would take them to the agreed-on point below the villa.

The Americans boarded the submarine, the *Seraph*, that night, traveling all night and most of the next day on the surface of a calm sea. The submarine reached the African coast on the morning of the 21st, but there was too much light to make a safe and secret landing. So Clark and the party spent an uncomfortable day on the submerged *Seraph*. On the night of the 22nd the prearranged signal light appeared, and the Americans made a hazardous though exciting scramble ashore. They climbed up the steep slope to the villa, hid their equipment, and waited for Mast and the others to arrive. Murphy had met them on the beach.

The Mast party arrived at the villa on the morning of the 22nd, and while the meeting was necessary so far as the French were concerned, not much was settled and very little of any real importance was learned. Clark lost his pants when a rubber boat capsized as he attempted to board it in preparation to return to the *Seraph*, but he had a great story to tell about hiding in a wine cellar—"an empty repeat *empty* wine cellar"—when local police, alerted by suspicious Arab servants at the villa, arrived. The police departed, and after darkness that night the Americans left the villa with their boats, and Clark lost his pants in the disturbingly high surf. It was the kind of boyish adventure that Clark loved—he was the hero—and after it was over he told the story again and again, to Churchill, to the king, and to war correspondents attached to Eisenhower's temporary headquarters at Gibraltar, each time embellishing it a little. Clark thus became one of America's first war heroes and received a good deal of publicity plus several proposals of marriage from women who admired his left-side profile in newspaper photographs. For his efforts he got a Distinguished Service Medal (DSM), and later Murphy got one, too, perhaps supporting the English contention of the time that the Americans were overdecorated.

While Clark was having his adventure, Eisenhower made an inspection trip in western Scotland. The landing in North Africa was just three weeks away, and he wanted to see what he called "the final and most ambitious training in landing operations."

Butcher, Mickey, and Kay went with him. The party left London early in the morning, and Butcher, whose diary did not reveal that Kay was along, recorded only the bleakness of the trip. Kay remembered that the general's private railroad car, the *Bayonet*, was really quite comfortable. It was paneled in teak and had a private office for the general, sleeping quarters, and a sitting room. She and Ike did some work, then played bridge and napped.

The general and his party got off the train at Kentallen, about fifty miles north of Inveraray, and in deep mud and heavy rain, Kay drove at the head of a ten-car caravan. She said, "The driving was sheer hell. Not only were blackout conditions rigidly observed, but on these rural Scottish roads there were no white lines painted in the center. . . . I could see nothing. I pushed ahead, daring to go only ten or twelve miles an hour, not even that. Ike was impatient at my snail's pace."

The 1st Division, which was to become the famous "Big Red One," was to take part in amphibious landings in the darkness that were supposed to resemble

those the division soon would be making in North Africa. At each point where
the simulated landings were made, Ike got out of the car and sloshed through
the mud to the beach to talk to the officers and men. Everything he saw and
heard depressed him. The men were simply not ready for actual combat. He
kept saying, "They'll be sitting ducks if they don't sharpen up."

One young officer told Eisenhower that the troops had just received a con-
signment of bazookas, which Ike knew was "the infantryman's best weapon of
defense against tanks." The officer and his men were leaving for North Africa
the very next day, and he "was at a complete loss as to how to teach his men
the use of this vitally needed weapon. He said, 'I don't know anything about
it myself except from hearsay.' " Butcher said, "The whole demonstration was
disappointing, and Ike felt pretty low on the return trip."

In a letter to Mamie written after the disheartening journey, Ike said that he
was "dizzy in the head and weak in the stomach." He told her of the trip,
adding that "during the whole time I was either in an automobile or on a train
and one night was up the whole time." He did not mention the teak paneling
in the *Bayonet;* he did not mention playing bridge; he did not mention Kay.
He did say, "Please remember that I love you—that you're precious to me and
that I'd do a lot better work anywhere, any time, if I had you with me."

In his report to Marshall, he said, "I have just returned from a rather difficult
inspection trip in Scotland. . . . The exercises that I witnessed had, as usual,
both encouraging and discouraging prospects. The men looked fine and without
exception were earnestly trying to do the right thing. I spoke to scores of them,
in the pitch dark, and found that their greatest weakness was uncertainty! Most
of them did not know exactly what was expected of them. This extended all
the way from challenging to actions in tactical moves. All this, of course, is the
business of the officer—the Major, the Captain, and the Lieutenant. It is at
this level of command that we have our most glaring weaknesses and it is one
that only time and eternal effort can cure. We are short on experience and
trained leadership below battalion commander, and it is beyond the capacity of
any Division Commander or any Colonel to cure these difficulties hurriedly.
Time is essential."

In nineteen days, most of which would be spent aboard troop ships, the
officers and men taking part in TORCH would make an amphibious landing on
a scale unprecedented in history, and the natives might or might not be friendly.
Murphy, who at first seemed to know all about them, now seemed to know
nothing about them or changed his mind about what he knew almost daily. It
is not surprising that Eisenhower was neither cheerful nor confident when he
returned to London. To make matters worse, Beetle's ulcer flared up, and
Eisenhower ordered him to bed.

"The pressures were getting to Ike," said Kay. "He was impatient, tired and
nervous, his temper at the ready. . . . The General was worried about himself.
'I've got to get in shape,' he kept saying, 'before North Africa.' "

"The unsatisfactory showing of the maneuvers, added to the more important
worries of Ike, contributed to what he described as 'a state of jitters,' " said
Butcher. "He called me into his office, said he couldn't concentrate. . . ."

Eisenhower wrote Marshall, "The real strain comes from trying to decide
things for which there is no decision—such as, for example, what is to be done

if the weather throughout that whole region simply becomes impossible along about the time we need calm seas. If a man permitted himself to do so, he could get absolutely frantic about questions of weather, politics, personalities in France and Morocco, and so on. To a certain extent, a man must merely believe in his luck and figure that a certain amount of good fortune will bless us when the critical day arrives."

On October 24, still not having heard what happened to Clark, Eisenhower decided he wanted to be completely alone, and he set out to drive to Telegraph Cottage; he had no driver's license, wasn't sure of the way, and was unaccustomed to driving on the left side of the road. Still, he made it and had a few hours to himself, being joined for dinner by Beetle. As Kay Summersby later said, "I've since wondered what some conscientious M.P. would have done in stopping that big Packard and finding a three-star general driving alone."

Eisenhower was planning to leave London for Gibraltar on November 2. "To account for my absence from London an elaborate story was circulated that I was making a visit to Washington." On October 30 Butcher had, he said, "my first experience with 'cover.' " A story had come from the States saying that Eisenhower was being brought back to Washington for "consultation." Colonel Morrow Krum, a public relations officer, "came running, wanting to know what to tell newspapermen." Butcher, a one-time reporter and editor, wanted "to retain some aspect of integrity" and took Krum in to see Beetle so that he "could give the official answer. He said that it was supposed to be a secret, and so far as headquarters is concerned, the answer to inquiring newsmen is 'no comment.' " Naturally, Eisenhower's "return" made headlines in every American newspaper.

Eisenhower was very worried about what Mamie would think when the stories appeared and considered sending a cable to Marshall asking him to tell her in strict confidence what was going on but didn't send it. He didn't even want the code clerks to be in on the secret.

That same day he wrote Mamie a letter "not to be opened until November 14." It said, "On the day you open this letter you'll be 46. I'd like to be there to help you celebrate and to kiss you 46 times (multiplied by any number you care to pick). . . . The crowning thing you've given me is our son. He has been so wonderful, unquestionably because he's so much you—that I find I live in him so very often. Your love and our son have been my greatest gifts from life. . . . I've never wanted any other wife—you're mine, and for that reason I've been luckier than any other man."

Whatever his doubts about the success of TORCH Eisenhower never expressed them or showed them in public. General Thomas Handy said, "He *always* put on a cheerful face, always. But we had been told *definitely* that landing on the west coast of Africa at that time of year was impossible. *Impossible.* And always the things we didn't know were much more numerous than the things we did know.

"But if you're the head of something, you can't take a defeatist attitude toward it. Ike couldn't go around saying 'I'm opposed to it.' If he felt that strongly about it the only thing for him to do was to tell them to get somebody else to do the job. But a hell of a lot of jobs have been done that a lot of people thought were *impossible*. You *win* wars by doing the impossible thing. The Germans had been doing it for *years*. All through the first part of the war the Germans did things that *everybody* said were impossible."

In his last days in England in 1942, Eisenhower said farewell to the king and was pleased that he hadn't had to worry about backing away without falling. "He came right to the door with me," Eisenhower said.

On October 31 he had a small dinner at the cottage with Clark, Butcher, Beetle, T.J., and Kay. Mrs. Summersby wrote, "The festivities could scarcely be described as gay."

Eisenhower had asked Kay if she would like to go to North Africa. In *Eisenhower Was My Boss*, she said that she was excited about the trip because her American fiancé would be taking part in the invasion. She wrote that she told Eisenhower she "would do *anything* to be somewhere near him. Ike knew about Dick."

The day before Eisenhower was scheduled to leave he received an urgent message from Murphy reporting that Giraud could not leave France for North Africa until November 20. He asked that the invasion be put off for two weeks.

Eisenhower immediately forwarded the message to Marshall, saying, "It is inconceivable that McGowan [Murphy] can recommend such a delay with his intimate knowledge of the operation. . . . It is likewise inconceivable to me that our mere failure to concede to such demands as have been made would result in having the French North African Army meet us with serious opposition. Recommend the President advise McGowan immediately that his suggested action is utterly impossible in the present advanced state of operation, and that we will proceed to execute this operation with more determination than ever." (Actually, Murphy did not have a detailed knowledge of what was planned for TORCH. As he wrote in his evasive autobiography, *Diplomat Among Warriors*, "Everybody assumed that somebody else had briefed me thoroughly, but nobody had.")

Marshall forwarded Eisenhower's message to the president, along with Murphy's. On the 2nd Roosevelt responded to Marshall, "I fully concur in General Eisenhower's recommendation. Please inform him to that effect at once." Marshall did, adding that the U.S. Chiefs of Staff and Dill, acting for the British Chiefs, "are in complete accord with your views on this matter."

It is no wonder Eisenhower said, "Nothing more could now be done in London. It was a relief to lock up the desk."

On the evening of November 2, Kay drove Eisenhower to the Cannon Street Station and bid him good-bye. But the next morning he was back again. According to Kay, "They had arrived safely in Bournemouth only to find their B-17s grounded by nasty weather. Flight to Gibraltar was out of the question; authorities refused to let the rank-packed train stay in Bournemouth as a juicy target for Nazi air raiders. So they all came back to London."

Since Eisenhower was presumed to be in Washington, he had to spend the day in what Kay called, "the old reliable security hideaway, Telegraph Cottage. Every man there was as nervous as an expectant father, and as one irreverent companion put it, 'I was as nervous as a pregnant nun.' "

On Thursday, November 5, the Eisenhower party was once more back at

Bournemouth, but the pilot, Major Paul Tibbets, who was later to fly the plane that dropped the atomic bomb on Hiroshima, felt that the weather was such that it was too dangerous to attempt a takeoff. Eisenhower did what he seldom did. He pulled rank. He wrote Beetle on the 6th, "We had an anxious moment or two getting off the field at Bournemouth, but I think that most of the passengers didn't know exactly what the hazards were. The final decision as to whether or not to take off was put squarely up to me as a command matter and, since the pilots clearly indicated that it was a hazardous undertaking, I had a bad moment until all planes were in the air and straightened out to sea."

As John Eisenhower wrote many years later, "The six Flying Fortresses [actually only five—the sixth had mechanical trouble], supposedly destined for Washington, took off through the rain and fog and headed south toward Gibraltar. Whatever lay ahead, the 'most anxious months' were over."

★   ★   ★

THE ROCK OF GIBRALTAR

The weeks to come would be both politically hazardous and physically uncomfortable. When Eisenhower and his party arrived on the Rock in the afternoon of November 5, three Allied task forces were on the high seas headed for North Africa. The landings at Casablanca, Oran, and Algiers were scheduled for 1:00 A.M. on Sunday, November 8. Air support would be from Gibraltar, and 350 cargo ships and transports were involved, as well as 500 warships. Mussolini had said that the gigantic convoy was headed for North Africa, but nobody paid any attention. British intelligence had spread the myth that the ships were headed for Malta, which had been under almost constant attack from the air since the war began.

It was almost unbelievable that the convoy had not been attacked. The ships could be seen by enemy agents on both sides of the strait, in Tangier and Algeciras; surely they had been observed. But there was no attack. Was the reason the air cover provided for the convoy? Was it that Allied cover operations had been so effective? Was it stupidity on the part of Axis intelligence? Peter Tomkins, a member of the Allied Psychological Warfare Branch who landed in North Africa with the American troops, said, "It was, as we later learned, a mixture of the three."

On arrival at Gibraltar Eisenhower was met by Lieutenant General Sir F. N. Mason-MacFarlane, who had reported to Eisenhower's headquarters in August that any unusual activity on the Rock would be known in Berlin within twenty-four hours and that if as a result of TORCH comings and goings Spain should get into the war on the side of the Axis, both the air station and the naval base at Gibraltar would at once go out of commission. That, of course, had not happened at the time of Ike's arrival, and the governor offered him comfortable sleeping quarters in his mansion. Eisenhower had very little time for sleeping during the next eighteen days, and his headquarters, where he spent almost all his time, were, he said, "the most dismal setting we occupied during the war."

Eisenhower's office, shared with Clark, was deep inside the Rock, a damp, eight-square-foot room lighted by a single, naked bulb. "Through the arched ceilings came a constant drip, drip, drip of surface water that faithfully but drearily ticked off the seconds of the interminable, almost unendurable, wait which occurs between completion of a military plan and the moment action begins."

Colonel Benjamin A. Dickson, West Point 1918, who at the time of the landings was G-2 [intelligence] of Patton's II Corps, said of the quarters, "Inside the Rock the tunnels and galleries had been continually enlarged and extended since the start of World War II by two companies of Canadian engineers, hard-rock miners with the latest tools. The result was an underground with water mains, sewers, heating, ventilation, power and light. The office portions were sheathed and paneled and the batteries, magazines, troop quarters, storerooms and reservoirs were all finished appropriately, according to their usage. On the face of the Rock, where the Prudential Life Insurance Company's sign should have been, there was a criss-cross of water catchment ditches running into underground cisterns. As a Command Post it offered the greatest security ever known." It also had facilities for communicating with all three of the landing forces.

At ten o'clock on the night of the 5th Eisenhower informed London that Allied Force Headquarters, Gibraltar was officially open. He had more than forty-eight hours to wait for reports on the landings, and during that time he studied weather reports, rechecked every detail of the plans he had worked on in London, conferred with Admiral Sir Andrew B. Cunningham, commander of the TORCH naval forces, sent messages to Marshall and the Combined Chiefs, and wrote letters.

The atmosphere in Ike's office was understandably tense. He said, "One could feel it in every little cave makeshifting for an office. It was natural. Within a matter of hours the Allies would know the initial fate of their first combined offensive gesture of the war."

Of the three landings, Casablanca was the one that worried him most. John Eisenhower, who some years later visited the landing area himself, said, "Pessimists estimated that out of the year only twelve days enjoyed seas fit for landings of assault craft; the surf often rose as high as fifteen feet." The surf could determine whether the landings succeeded or failed, and First Lieutenant Beardwood, a young Signal Corps meteorologist, was attached to G-2 section at Gibraltar, and every day he flew to the Azores to make observations. According to Dickson, "When he returned he consulted a notebook full of cabalistic symbols and then produced his predictions. . . . The long range weather forecast on the landing for the Western Task Force was forbidding. The Atlantic surf was booming on the Moroccan coast with combers eighteen feet high. A gale south of Iceland was sending these seas across the broad ocean. Surf over five feet is lethal in an amphibious landing."

Another problem at Casablanca that was difficult to predict was the attitude of the resident general of Morocco and commander of all French forces in North Africa, Auguste Noguès, a man who couldn't make up his mind whether he was for or against the Axis, earning him the nickname of "General No-Yes." Unfortunately, at the time of the TORCH landings he decided he was the faithful servant of Marshal Pétain and thus would resist the invasion.

The reaction of the French colonists was unpredictable. Back in London, Ike wrote, "The Allied governments had hoped that the people would, upon our entry . . . blaze into spontaneous revolt against control by Nazi-dominated Vichy."

That was one of the most naive hopes of the war. As Eisenhower was soon to discover, most of the colonists did not want to throw off the Vichy yoke. They didn't even consider it a yoke. They were grateful to the Germans for helping to keep the natives quiet. As for the Nazis' attitude toward the Jews, the colonists found no fault with that. They had always been anti-Semitic. And they had no objection to the fact that Jewish businessmen were being forced to sell everything they owned at very low prices. The colonists were grateful for the bargains. As for the concentration camps, the French colonists, like the Germans back home, managed to make themselves unaware of such matters.

In general, the French colonists in North Africa were very much like the American colonists Eisenhower had known in the Philippines, clannish, bigoted, and politically reactionary. Harold Macmillan, who was to be a lifelong friend and admirer of Eisenhower, said, "These people were by no means penitent about their past. . . . Nor were their hearts always changed when they changed their coats."

After the war ended, Eisenhower wrote Cunningham, "The other day someone asked me what particular period I would probably remember longest in this war. The subject was intriguing enough to demand an hour's conversation and out of it I came to the conclusion that the hours you and I spent together in the dripping tunnels of Gibraltar will probably remain as long in my memory as will any other. It was there I first understood the indescribable and inescapable strain that comes over one when his part is done—when the issue rests with fate and the fighting men he had committed to action."

Later Eisenhower often relieved tension by painting, but before and during the war he wrote long personal letters. They were often on matters far from cosmic. On the 6th he wrote Beetle to say that he had discovered "that there is a channel of communication between yourself and me, to which system the British have no access." Therefore, if Beetle wanted to send a message he didn't for whatever reason care to share with the British, he could do so, and that included personal messages to Eisenhower and the principal members of his staff. He added, "Please find out from Kay how Telek is and include a short statement in any message to me—such as Telek OK, or Telek very sick, or whatever is applicable. I am quite anxious about the black imp."

Telek had been ill when Eisenhower left London, but in answer to his letter, someone in London, probably Beetle, sent him a cable, "Telek is fine."

Ike also wrote Mamie on the 6th:

By the time this can reach you the newspapers will have told you that I'm in the Mediterranean area . . . so now you will understand why, for the past few weeks I've been sounding a bit mysterious. . . . I have a new title "Allied C-in-C" in this region. It's high sounding, but won't amount to much unless all this goes with a swing. Before you get this note, you'll know all about it. . . . With a lot of luck, maybe I can do something here that will hurt the Axis—and that's what I live to do.

Good luck, dear—and please get all the happiness you can. I love you— heaps—and I do not want you to make yourself miserable in worry over me. Have a good time, but don't forget your

Ike

On the evening of the 6th he and Clark went to their room but understandably found that they were not sleepy. Clark said, "We got into our pajamas, sat down, and had a drink. Ike was complaining about having to stay cooped up in Gibraltar while I went off to Algiers to get things ready for the arrival of the command staff. I said, 'Ike, that's your penalty for being the supreme commander.' We had a few drinks, and then we got started talking about codes. I remember Ike said, 'Let's think up a code that's just between ourselves. . . .'

"So we got out two pads and two pencils, and we wrote down a lot of names— matching each with a code name—like Churchill—Jim; Roosevelt—Bill, and so on.

"Finally we had another drink, and one of us—we've argued since about which one it was—said, 'There ought to be a code word that just means a son-of-a-bitch.' We laughed, and I said, 'If we just use S.O.B., the Germans will decode it; they know what it means.' We thought about it, and finally I said, 'How about YBSOB—yellow-bellied sonofabitch?'

"We agreed, and when I got to Algiers, I started sending messages to Eisenhower using the code YBSOB because there were a lot of them around at the time.

"A few nights later in the middle of the night I got a cable from the president, Roosevelt, by way of Eisenhower. The message said, 'I'm readying Clark's dispatches from . . . Algiers with great interest. And he has my sympathy. . . . But there occurs a word that appears so frequently I'm led to believe it's a typographical error. It is YBSOB.'

"Eisenhower, in sending Roosevelt's message along to me, said, 'I transmit to you the president's message for you to reply direct.'

"So I sent a message to the president, saying, 'The word YBSOB is not a typographical error. It means yellow-bellied-son-of-a-bitch.'

"Three days later I got a message from the White House. It said, 'I appreciate your frank message. And I agree with you on the necessity for having a word like that available. I only wish I had invented it when I first came to Washington, for there are a lot of them around here, too.' "

So far as I can discover Eisenhower kept his and Clark's addition to the language to himself. Clark used it frequently at press conferences in Algiers and he used it when I visited him more than forty years later at his home in Charleston, South Carolina, and each time he said it, it was as if it were for the first time.

After a few hours' sleep Eisenhower was back at his command post. He wrote a lengthy message to Marshall:

Dear General,
   It is now 9:30 Saturday morning. Tonight we start ashore. . . .
   Recent messages from McGowan [Murphy] clearly indicate that he has a case of jitters. I assume that you have seen copies of all his communications, including the one demanding as diversions for Torch, a landing in southern France of more than 50,000 soldiers, coupled with simultaneous attacks in Norway and Western France. . . .

He did not have to say that what the jittery Murphy suggested was ridiculous; Marshall would know that.
   He added:

We are standing, of course, on the brink and must take the jump—whether the bottom contains a nice feather bed or a pile of brickbats! Nevertheless, we have worked our best to assure a successful landing, no matter what we encounter. As I look back over the high-pressure weeks since July 24th, I cannot think of any major item on which I would now, if I had the power, change the decision that was made at the time. . . . If, of course, some unexpected development should make this operation appear as a failure, much of the work that has been done will be discredited by unthinking people, and the methods that have been followed will be cited as erroneous. I do not believe that a final success or failure, which is going to be determined by a number of factors beyond anyone's control, should blind us to the fact that before this war is won the type of thing that we have been doing for the past many weeks will have to become common practice between the British and American services.

On the eve of D-Day, November 7, the young meteorologist told Eisenhower that at Casablanca the next morning the surf would be down, generally to about three or four feet, five at most. "My greatest fear had been dissipated," Eisenhower said. And he made the crucial decision that the landings would proceed as planned. (Colonel Dickson later recommended that Beardwood be given a Legion of Merit, which was done. Some Americans did earn their decorations.)
   That afternoon Eisenhower and Butcher drove up a winding road toward the summit of the rock to find the Barbary apes that are supposed to bring good luck. Eisenhower found one and patted it on the head. Then he returned to his command post and, later in the afternoon, briefed the four correspondents accredited to his headquarters. They were, he said, part of the family, and the public needed to know all the facts.
   Admiral Cunningham, a notably cheerful man, had good news, which was that the Axis expected to drive back the Allies from an attempted landing in Sicily. And there was further good news that afternoon. Beetle, authorized by Churchill, cabled that in the second battle of El Alamein 30,000 prisoners had been taken, 350 tanks and thousands of vehicles destroyed or captured. Rom-

mel's forces were in full retreat, despite Hitler's order to fight to the last round, the last man. As General Sir Harold Alexander said in his report to the prime minister, "Ring out the bells!"

H. Freeman Matthews, who was to be Ike's acting chief of civil affairs in Algiers and was later a member of the U.S. delegation to Potsdam, wrote Eisenhower in the summer of 1945, "I was interested to see you quoted in today's press as saying the night you were most worried in the last three years was that of November 7/8, 1942. I have a vivid recollection of that night myself. If you felt any nervousness as you sat in your tunnel office at Gib and listened to your own voice coming in on the radio [announcing the invasion], you certainly did not show it."

Eisenhower wrote back, "November 7–8 1942—are days that will live in my memory for all time." In an unpublished section of *Crusade,* a section more emotional and more revealing than a good deal of what was published, he wrote, "Without confidence, enthusiasm and optimism in the command, victory is scarcely attainable.

"During those anxious hours, I first realized, I think, how inexorably and inescapably strain and tension wear away at the leader's endurance, his judgment and his confidence. The pressure becomes more acute because of the duty of a staff constantly to present to the commander the worst side of an eventuality. The seriousness of the possibilities are reflected in the demeanor of the staff members and the commander inherits an additional load in preserving optimism in himself and in his command."

The biggest worry for everyone was a worry, it turned out, that need not have concerned anyone. When would Giraud—his code name was KINGPIN—show up? Or would he show up at all? Murphy, his main advocate, who had arranged for the five-star general to take part in the operation, didn't know his whereabouts. In his autobiography, Murphy described his first meeting with the man who was to cause the Allies, Eisenhower in particular, so much trouble. Shortly after the war began, Murphy said, he was at a Paris railroad station, Gare du Nord, watching some French conscripts on their way to the front. "By coincidence I found myself standing next to a tall, very erect French officer in uniform whom I recognized as General Henri Giraud, a celebrated hero of World War I." Giraud was also there to see the conscripts, many of them drunk, all of them unkempt and untrained. But the general seemed not aware of such matters. According to Murphy, he said, "This time things will go better for us. *On les aura!*" Murphy thought that remark proved the general was "a man exceptionally buoyant." Others might have concluded that the old man was not so much buoyant as stupid, particularly since the French army in the Second World War did considerably worse than it had done in the First. Eisenhower found KINGPIN to be stupid, arrogant, intransigent, and unpopular. Giraud had been a general when Ike was still a major so it is perhaps not surprising that he treated him throughout as if he were at most an impertinent captain.

Giraud had been picked up near Lyon, where he lived, by the *Seraph,* a British submarine commanded by an American. (In order to have the submarine technically under American command, Ike placed Captain Jerauld Wright, a staff member, aboard.) It was the same submarine that had taken Clark on his African adventure, but Giraud did not know that the *Seraph* was British; he hated everything British and, had he known, he might not have gone; thus the American commander, the first of the many accommodations to the French general's sensibilities.

But where was he? In midafternoon Eisenhower's headquarters received a disquieting message from the *Seraph*, "Task gone. Radio failing." Clark said, "Nobody could figure it out at first, but then somebody, probably Cunningham, figured out that it should have said, 'Task done,' and that was exactly what happened. A flying boat with the general aboard arrived at the Rock about an hour later."

Clark said, "He looked awful, like a man suffering from a very, very bad hangover. He needed a shave, and he had a handlebar mustache that drooped. Altogether there was nothing impressive about him. I couldn't imagine anybody getting enthusiastic about him."

Colonel Holmes acted as interpreter. Ike said he could understand Giraud's French fairly well, but "I insisted on using an interpreter, to avoid any chance."

The meeting began with Eisenhower explaining that a statement had been written to be signed by Giraud to the effect that the United States had learned that Axis soldiers were preparing to invade French North Africa; to prevent that, American troops were intervening. French officers and soldiers of the French army in North Africa were to do their duty. The line written for Giraud was, "I resume my place of combat among you."

But the idea of being a spear carrier did not appeal to Giraud, a fact that he made clear immediately. He said, "As I understand it, when I land in North Africa I am to assume command of all Allied forces and become the Supreme Allied Commander."

Clark said, "I didn't dare look at Ike. I just didn't dare. I might have started laughing. I don't know what I might have done. I just didn't look at him. He said exactly the right thing under the circumstances. He said, 'There must be some misunderstanding.'

"One thing was sure about Giraud. He wasn't bluffing. He had been led to believe, I was never sure how, that he was to be the supreme commander. You couldn't help feeling a little sorry for the old man, but you couldn't let on how you felt, either."

At the end of three hours Giraud went off to have dinner at Government House with General Mason-MacFarlane. The only good news was from Casablanca, where the surf was going down.

The argument continued after dinner, and after a time Eisenhower, who most of the time had held his temper in check, turned matters over to Clark. In dealing with Giraud, Clark acted as Beetle Smith did so many times; he was the bad cop. He lost his temper and cursed and threatened and demanded.

In a message to Marshall, Eisenhower added in longhand, "10 P.M. I've had a 4 hour struggle with KINGPIN. He—so far—says, 'Either I'm Allied C-in-C or I won't play!' He threatens to withdraw his blessing and wash his hands of the affair. I'm weary! But I'll send you a radio later tonight, after this thing is finished."

Clark's more aggressive approach to Giraud made no dent either, and finally Giraud said, "I shall return to France."

"Oh, no, you don't," said Clark. "That was a one-way submarine. You are not going back to France."

The debate continued, getting nowhere, and eventually Eisenhower suggested that since they were all tired they should go to bed. Giraud agreed, and before he left said what turned out to be his only totally accurate statement of the long encounter: "Giraud will be a spectator in this affair."

That was all he could ever have been. If only Murphy had not gone to the Gare du Nord in the summer of 1939, Giraud might have returned peacefully, and the Allies might have been spared one of the more ludicrous misjudgments of the war.

After Giraud left, Ike radioed the Combined Chiefs, "Six hour conference between AMERICAN EAGLE [Clark], KINGPIN [Giraud] and the Allied Commander in Chief has just terminated." It was then after midnight. He went on, "My impression, shared by the EAGLE and Cunningham, is that KINGPIN is playing for time and that he is determined, knowing that there will be some French resistance, not to lay himself open to the charge of being in any way responsible for the shedding of French blood. . . . He is choosing to wait to see what happens. His method of gaining time is to insist upon a point which as a soldier he is well aware the Allies cannot accept. If we are generally successful tonight, we will not be surprised to find him more conciliatory tomorrow morning. . . .

"Latest news that we have been able to get from North Africa indicates that we may expect considerable resistance which, if true, shows that Mast, operating in the name of KINGPIN, has not been effective."

In other words, Murphy's advice might prove to be totally wrong, and indeed it was. But not only was he not discredited; he got a medal, and Eisenhower continued to trust him and count on him for the rest of Murphy's career. In fact in 1959, as president, Eisenhower took Murphy along on an eleven-nation tour "to give me invaluable assistance on the intricacies of this journey."

At 2:40 A.M. on November 8, Commodore Royer Dick, Cunningham's chief of staff, came into Eisenhower's office to report "Landing successful, A, B, and C Beaches, Eastern Task Force." Mark Clark said, "After that, the messages came in rapidly and most of them looked good."

The Eastern Task Force of the invasion, 23,000 British troops and about 10,000 Americans, was under the command of Major General Charles W. Ryder, regular commander of the 34th Infantry Division; he had been a classmate of Eisenhower's at the Point, and after the landing he was to return to the 34th. The temporary command had been given to Ryder to emphasize the American character of the landings. Afterwards the command was to be given to the unsmiling Scot then waiting at Gibraltar, Lieutenant General Kenneth Anderson, commander of the British First Army.

The troops under Ryder's command were landed on a desolate beach four miles from the agreed-upon spot where members of the French underground were waiting to guide them to their destinations in Algiers. As a result there was an uneasy thirteen-hour delay in their arrival in the city. Still, resistance was slight.

The commander of the Center Task Force was Major General Lloyd R. Fredendall, who found it unnecessary to leave his ship while his troops, about 40,000 of them, landed and seized Oran. French resistance was bitter and sustained, but the First Division, the Big Red One, under Major General Terry de la Mes Allen, had by the 10th achieved the first of its great victories. Apparently on the voyage from western Scotland to Oran the officers and men had learned how to use their bazookas and how to do better in real battle than in simulated landings.

The Western Task Force was commanded by Patton, but there were those who doubted that even the unsinkable Georgie could bring his troops into such a physically inhospitable port as Casablanca.

Under the direction of No-Yes Noguès, the French troops, whom Major General Ernest Harmon, commander of the 2d Armored Division, found "belligerent, surprisingly ill-informed, and quite willing to fight," did fight. It was not until November 10th that Noguès reluctantly ordered a cease-fire.

Harmon said, "Except for the stubbornness and lack of vision on the part of a few men in French high Army and Navy command, there would have been no battle. It needn't have happened."

One division commander in Casablanca at the time of the landings, General Émile Béthouart, head of the French Expeditionary Corps to Norway in 1940, tried, unsuccessfully, to aid the Allies. For his trouble he was imprisoned by Noguès and faced possible execution until Eisenhower secured his release.

By 4:30 A.M., although there was no word from Patton, it was apparent that at least on two fronts things were going more or less as expected, and Eisenhower and Clark put their cots in their office and took short naps. While Ike and Butcher were shaving in cold water in the lavatory that morning, they agreed that the strategic success achieved by the two landings indicated that the missing page of Butcher's diary had not been stolen, but burned.

Ike found time to write Mamie:

I hope you won't mind my writing at least part of this letter by dictation. Frankly, I am so weary that I just haven't the courage to pick up a pen. We got no sleep at all last night. . . .

As you must have heard over the radio, I am in command of an expedition moving in North Africa. . . .

P.S. I've had an hour's sleep and feel pretty well. It seems to me that life is one long conference—I start another right away!

Mamie was playing cards at Milton's when the landings started, and, Milton later wrote, "Knowing that the announcement of the invasion . . . would be broadcast at nine o'clock that evening, I kept a radio on so that we would not miss the initial part of the broadcast. . . .

"When the invasion announcement was made, and a personal statement by General Eisenhower rang through the room, Mamie was silent. Tears came to her eyes. . . . When the program ended and the excitement had diminished, Mamie turned to me and said, 'Milton, I am proud of you for not telling me.' "

Katherine Marshall was at a night football game in Washington; the general had begged off; he said he had to stay in the office. Mrs. Marshall said, "There came in the middle of a play, a voice from the loud-speaker, 'Stop the game! Important announcement! . . . The President of the United States has announced the successful landing on the African coast of an American Expeditionary Force. This is our second front.' "

Roosevelt had been at Shangri-la (Camp David) when the landings started. Grace Tully answered the phone; the message was from the War Department. After Roosevelt was given the message he said, "We have landed in North Africa. . . . We are striking back."

It had taken a long time and a great many humiliating defeats, but eleven months after Pearl Harbor, after Tobruk, Hong Kong, and Singapore, we were, as Roosevelt said, striking back. TORCH had succeeded. As Robert E. Sherwood said in *Roosevelt and Hopkins*, "At a White House conference some time later, General . . . Handy . . . expressed the opinion that, 'TORCH was unquestionably the most complex operation in military history, and perhaps it still retains that distinction, even after OVERLORD.' General Marshall had firmly opposed it, and so had General Eisenhower, who is quoted as having described the day when the decision was made by Roosevelt as possibly the 'blackest day in history.' Yet the decision having been made, it was carried out with extraordinary skill. Counting every mistake that was made in the military operations, it was a brilliant performance. The same could not be said for the concurrent and subsequent political conduct of affairs."

Before meeting with Giraud for the second time, on the 8th, Eisenhower summoned his naval aide, Butcher. "Here's what he handed me, in his own hand," Butcher said.

Worries of a Commander

1. Spain is so ominously quiet that Gov. of Gib. reports himself uneasy.
2. No news from Task Forces. Reports few and unsatisfactory.
3. Defensive fighting, which seemed halfhearted and spiritless this morning, has blazed up, and in many places resistance is stubborn.
4. No Frenchman immediately available, no matter how friendly toward us, seems able to stop the fighting. (Mast et al.)
5. Giraud is in Gibraltar, manifestly unwilling to enter the theater so long as fighting is going on.
6. Giraud is difficult to deal with—wants much power, equipment, etc., but seems little disposed to do his part to stop fighting.
7. Giraud wants planes, radios.
8. We are slowed up in eastern sector when we should be getting toward Bone-Bizerte at once.
9. We don't know whereabouts or conditions of airborne force.
10. We cannot find out anything.

After finishing the list and giving it to Butcher, Eisenhower and Clark had another two-hour conference with Giraud. Ike said later, "A good night's sleep did something to change General Giraud's mind at the next morning's meeting [and] he decided to participate on the basis we desired. I promised that if he were successful in winning French support I would deal with him as the administrator of that region, pending eventual opportunities for the civilian authorities to determine the will of the population."

Eisenhower cabled the Combined Chiefs that agreement had been reached and that "I recognize him as the leader of the effort to prevent Axis aggression in North Africa, the Commander in Chief of all French forces in the region and the Governor of the area."

That night, much to Eisenhower's great satisfaction, "I slept long and solidly, better than I have at any time in the last fourteen weeks."

Sometime around 11:00 A.M. the next morning, November 9, Clark and Giraud took off for Algiers in separate planes, Clark to set up advanced headquarters; Giraud "to do his utmost to stop all resistance to us and to begin organizing the French forces for employment against the Axis."

In a letter to Beetle later that day, Ike said of Giraud:

He wants to be a big shot, a bright and shining light, and the acclaimed saviour of France. . . . It isn't the operation that's wearing me down—it's the petty intrigue and the necessity of dealing with little, selfish, conceited worms that call themselves men. Oh well—by the time this thing is over I'll probably be as crooked as any of them. Giraud, in his first conference with me, even made a point of his rank. Can you beat it? Yet he's supposed to be the high-minded man that is to rally all North Africa behind him and to save France. . . .

To turn to more pleasant things! The operation—in spite of my resentment that we have to waste time and resources fighting people that are supposed to become our allies—is proceeding as well as we had any right to expect.

With Giraud and Clark on their way to Algiers, and the operation going well, Eisenhower found time to consider his own position at the moment. It was a surprisingly optimistic document, jotted down in longhand in the early afternoon. He called it "Inconsequential thoughts of a commander during one of the interminable 'waiting periods.' "

War brings about strange, sometimes ridiculous situations. In my service I've often thought or dreamed of commands of various types that I might one day hold—war commands, peace commands, battle commands, etc. One I now have could never, under any conditions, *have entered my mind even fleetingly*. I have operational command of Gibraltar. The symbol of the solidity of the British Empire—the hallmark of safety and security at home—the jealously guarded rock that has played a tremendous part in the trade development of the English race! An American is in charge and I am he. Hundreds of feet within the bowels of the rock itself I have my

CP. I simply *must* have a grandchild or I'll never have the fun of telling this when I'm fishing, gray-bearded, on the banks of a quiet bayou in the deep South.

Again, what soldier ever took the trouble to contemplate the possibility of holding an allied command of ground, air, and naval forces? Usually we pity the soldiers of history that had to work with allies. But we don't now, and through the months of work we've rather successfully integrated the forces and the commands and staffs of British and American contingents. . . . I am proud of this British-United States command. The final results I don't know, but I do know that every element of my command—all United States and British services—are working together beautifully and harmoniously. That's something. . . .

It was something all right. At fifty-two he had achieved all he ever dreamed of doing and more. He had it made and knew he had it made. Those things are rare in anybody's life.

★ ★ ★

FRIDAY THE THIRTEENTH

On November 9 Eisenhower sent a generally cheerful report to Marshall, but he did have to say that time was going slowly. "We are in the afternoon of the second day and I don't mind confessing to you that it seems like it's been at least a month since 1:00 A.M. yesterday morning." He also complained about his trouble with the French:

If we had come in here merely to whip this French Army, I would be registering nothing but complete satisfaction at this moment. I am irritated though to think that every bullet we have to expend against the French is that much less in the pot with which to operate against the Axis. Worse than that, every minute that we lose will mean a week of reorganization and straightening out later, and I am so impatient to get eastward and seize ground in the Tunisian area that I find myself getting absolutely furious with these stupid Frogs.

He then expressed his dissatisfaction with Giraud who was, he said, "doing everything possible to kill time until the French have quit of their own accord. After that he wants to step in and become the knight in shining armor that rallies all North Africa and becomes finally the Saviour of France."

His real trouble with the Frogs had not yet begun; it was trouble that was to spread over the entire Allied world, and he was to be the center of it and the villain.

In his message to Marshall on the 9th, he added:

Since yesterday afternoon we have had Darlan in protective custody at Algiers. Clark left for that area today, where he will establish my Advanced CP. He has been empowered to treat with Darlan and to do his best to get real advantages out of Darlan's influence with the French fleet. But to show you what I have on my hands in the way of temperamental Frenchmen— Darlan states that he will not talk to any Frenchmen; Giraud hates and distrusts Darlan. It's a mess! I get weary of people that have no other thought but "ME."

The plan had been for the planes carrying Clark and Giraud to leave the Rock for Algiers at about the same time, but shortly after Giraud's plane left, bad weather closed in, and Clark's departure was delayed for five hours. When Giraud arrived at an airport about forty miles from the city, there were no cheering crowds to greet him, and Murphy almost immediately told him that "it had become necessary to bring Darlan into the picture." The old general was surprisingly philosophical about the matter, however. According to Murphy, "Giraud had no desire to engage in any political controversy. His only interest was to preserve French sovereignty and to make sure that French commanders had an appropriately important share in military operations conducted on French soil."

Clark was less patient and less polite. When Murphy told him that he had been negotiating with Darlan and that the admiral, not Giraud, had popular backing among the colonists and the generals, Murphy said, "Clark astonished me by the sharpness of his reaction. 'This really messes things up!' he exclaimed." And Clark added in his diary that night, "What a mess! Why do soldiers have to get mixed up in things like this when there is a war to be fought?"

By that time it was apparent even to Murphy that the French leaders in North Africa would not rally to Giraud, but would give support to and obey the orders of Darlan.

As soon as Murphy found out that the Allied troops had landed on the morning of the 8th, he went to the opulent villa of General Alphonse Juin, commander in chief of ground forces and the ranking army officer in North Africa. Before going, Murphy found that the resistance groups he had helped set up were operating as planned and had soon taken over the city's police and power stations as well as communication and transport centers and the military headquarters. He told Juin that American expeditionary forces either had or were about to land all along the coast of North Africa. He did not mention that the British were also involved and, as he had been told, he exaggerated the size of the landing force, saying that half a million men were involved. Juin was at first furious, but after a time, he said, "If the matter were entirely in my hands, I would be with you. But, as you know, Darlan is in Algiers. He outranks me, and no matter what decision I might make, Darlan could immediately overrule it."

Though he was later to pretend he had not known, Murphy was well aware that the controversial admiral was in Algiers, and he said, "Very well, let us talk with Darlan."

In his autobiography, published in 1964, Murphy said, "The melodramatic role played in the African campaign by Admiral Darlan provoked one of the bitterest controversies of the war. For more than two years Darlan had been broadcasting anti-British and anti–de Gaulle statements from Vichy, and apparently collaborating closely with the Nazis. British and de Gaulle propagandists naturally did everything possible to discredit him. So when an arrangement was made with Darlan in Algiers, protests in the United States and Great Britain became so intense that they distracted from the brilliant military achievements of the campaign, and threatened to affect seriously the reputations of those responsible for making the agreement with Darlan, including Eisenhower."

Murphy might more accurately have said, "especially Eisenhower."

Darlan purportedly was in Algiers because his son Alain was in a hospital there, suffering from polio. Nobody really believed that, however, especially Murphy; he said, "That night at Juin's residence I entertained no doubts whatsoever about bringing Darlan into our enterprise, because my authorization in this matter had come from Roosevelt himself."

In October Darlan had sent a representative to Murphy to say that the wily admiral just might stop supporting the Nazis and come over to the Allies. The representative also said that Darlan had heard that the United States was planning an assault on Dakar or Casablanca and that it would be soon.

Darlan had often used his son as a political agent, and in September Alain had left Vichy for Tunisia disguised as a traveling salesman. Alain said, "I know that before my departure for Tunisia . . . my father said to me: 'I hope soon, thanks to a direct line of communication, at last to be able to have more precise and surer information, from those interested, on the plans of the Americans.' "

Alain had gone from Tunisia to Algiers, where he had been stricken with polio. He was sent to the Maillot Hospital there. Darlan arrived in Algiers on November 6 and saw his son the next day. Alain said, "Despite the optimistic affirmations of the doctors, my father decided, after I got better on November 6, to stay on a few days and not leave until the morning of November 10."

By that time the Allied forces would have arrived, and Darlan would be available. As he later said, he had already decided that the Allies, not the Germans, would win the war, and he wanted to be on the side of the winners. The winners, not yet sure they were winners, wanted him, too, but a good deal of hocus-pocus went on at the time and continued when the participants wrote their memoirs. Darlan did not find time to write a memoir.

Was Darlan's presence in Algiers a surprise? Did the Allies not know that he was prepared to cooperate with them? In Eisenhower's *Crusade in Europe*, published in 1948, he said, "There was no question that Darlan's presence [in Algiers] was entirely accidental, occasioned by the critical illness of his son, to whom he was extremely devoted."

Yet back in London on October 17 Butcher had written, "Today a succession of messages from 'Colonel McGowan' [Murphy], relayed via general Marshall, came tumbling in, the news both good and bad. Good, in that Darlan wants to play ball, which means the French Navy as well as the Army may be self-neutralized. . . .

"Representatives of Darlan have informed Murphy most secretly that the

French government at Vichy has learned . . . that the U.S. plans military operations soon against Dakar or Casablanca or both. . . .

"Murphy recommends that Darlan be encouraged on the basis of securing his co-operation with Giraud. Darlan expected in Algiers within a week. . . ."

In 1946 when Eisenhower was Chief of Staff of the Army, John Wallace Carroll, a respected journalist and author, who had been director of the London office of the Office of War Information at the time of the Allied landings in North Africa, wrote him:

> I am now writing a book about psychological warfare in Europe in which I pay considerable attention to that operation [TORCH]. I am taking the line which I took with the British propaganda agencies the time—that the agreement with Darlan was not a matter of choice but of sheer military necessity. I am citing all available evidence to show that Darlan's presence in Algiers on November 8 was an accident and not brought about by us.
>
> This latter contention has now been brought into question by an entry in Harry Butcher's diary for October 17, 1942. As you may know, Butcher says that Darlan informed Murphy of his willingness to join the Allies and that you thereupon worked out a "formula" to obtain his cooperation by making Giraud governor of North Africa and Darlan commander of the armed forces.
>
> This suggestion of collusion with Darlan is so contrary to everything else that I have gathered that I hesitate to accept it as fact.

Eisenhower's headquarters took some time to draft a reply to Carroll's letter. The first draft was written by Air Force Major General Lauris Norstad, director of plans and operations, for Eisenhower's signature, and said, "I have your letter concerning the Allied negotiations with Admiral Darlan. The view which you propose to express on this subject in our forthcoming book is substantially correct. . . . American authorities received advance indication that Admiral Darlan was going to Algiers and a later notice that he was actually there at the end of October. It was also reported that the Admiral was interested in making contact with American representatives with a view toward cooperating with Allied forces— or getting on the bandwagon, as emissaries of General Giraud described it. . . . The records concerning the invasion of North Africa are still retained in classified files and therefore unfortunately are not available for public research at this time. . . ."

In a note accompanying his draft of the proposed letter to Carroll, Norstad said, "No records on this subject are as complete as the personal knowledge of the C/S. Suggest he read this carefully."

Ike did read it carefully, and his simplified reply was an almost total lie. The only thing he says that can go without challenge are the words, "The whole Darlan affair was an extremely complicated one. . . ." The letter, dated September 17, 1946 said:

Dear Mr. Carroll:

The proposition you advance in the second paragraph of your letter to me dated September 11 is correct. The whole Darlan affair was an extremely complicated one but the action taken arose from military necessity and his presence in Algiers on November 6 was purely accident, brought about by the grave illness of his son.

I have not read the Butcher diary and therefore do not know exactly what he had to say about this matter but I can tell you that there was absolutely no contact with Darlan prior to the arrival of General Clark in Algiers and no attempt was ever made by anyone connected with the expedition to contact Darlan prior to that time. From what I am told regarding Butcher's statement I assume that there was some casual remark around headquarters from which Butcher made a wrong deduction. There was no question that he tried to keep an honest diary but there is equally no question that many things went on of which he knew nothing and equally true that at other times he got only one little part of the story.

I repeat that you are absolutely correct in the line you are taking as explained in paragraph two of your letter.

Sincerely,
Dwight D. Eisenhower

In December Carroll asked for permission to quote parts of the Eisenhower letter; such permission was understandably refused. An aide talked to Carroll and explained, in the words of the aide, that "the Chief of Staff felt that he was giving information in his letter and not writing for publication—a quote would be undesirable but there was no objection to a footnote mentioning verification by General Eisenhower." And when John Wallace Carroll's *Persuade or Perish* was published in 1948, he said exactly what Eisenhower wanted him to say.

As for Harry Butcher's diary, Eisenhower by September 1946 *had* read what he had written, both in the book and in the large excerpts that appeared in *The Saturday Evening Post;* Butcher's problem was not that he knew too little; he knew and had told too much. Darlan had indeed been expected in Algiers; he got there not "within a week" after October 17. He arrived on November 6, ready and eager for any offers, and offers were almost immediately forthcoming, almost resulting in Ike returning to the States a permanent lieutenant colonel.

Part of the trouble in those early days in North Africa was that many people expected Eisenhower to be what he was not. He was never a reformer, and he never had any desire to be one. In North Africa reform was not part of his mission. He had not been ordered to change the government there, to institute civil liberties, to rescind anti-Semitic laws and customs, to improve the lot of the natives, or to institute democracy in a society that could at best be described as feudal. His orders were to drive Rommel out of Africa as quickly and at as little cost as possible. But for most of November 1942 he spent relatively little time on that. He found himself immersed in French politics about which he knew nothing and cared nothing, and in so doing he found himself for the first time in his life being publicly criticized and humiliated.

He did learn something about French politics and, for that matter, about American politics as well. He learned that his esteemed commander in chief, Franklin Roosevelt, could not always be counted on to tell the truth or live up to his promises. The president told quite a few lies in the late fall and early winter of 1942, and while it was far from the first time in his life that he had lied, he had never before told so many lies that were circulated to so many people.

Clark flew to Algiers early in the afternoon of November 9 accompanied by General Anderson, who was to take over Ryder's command. Clark was not surprised by the fact that Darlan was in the city. He said that the day before, when he and Ike had been involved with those interminable negotiations with Giraud, "I was busy until a late hour. . . . I asked General Mason-MacFarlane to sound out Giraud on a question that had been worrying me—the presence of Admiral Darlan in Algiers. The governor later reported back that Giraud had been asked about his attitude toward Darlan, who seemed likely to be the key man in any effort to get the French fleet to come over to our side, and that Giraud had been asked about Darlan if in exchange we could get such a prize as the fleet. He didn't, however, have much regard for or faith in Darlan."

Clark also said that "General Ryder had advised Ike as early as November 8 . . . that he was acting to take Darlan into protective custody. The surprise in regard to Darlan, therefore, was chiefly the fact that the French official with whom we have had to deal looked to him as the man with the greatest authority in North Africa. I took a great deal of blame later for dealing with a collaborator at Algiers. Ike backed me up, but I suppose he must have had many moments of doubt when the heat was really on from Washington and London."

Clark did not meet with Darlan until the morning of November 10th, and his immediate dissatisfaction with the man had to do not with his slippery politics but his appearance. He was "stubby," he was "ingratiating," and he was "little." Clark, who was six feet two, put a great reliance on height, and to him Darlan was always "the little fellow."

That first morning at the Hotel St. Georges Clark "looked coldly" at the little admiral "and asked Murphy to explain to him the necessity for getting to the point of the conference at once.

"We have work to do to meet the common enemy," said Clark. "Is he ready to sign the terms of the armistice? It will cover all French North Africa. It is essential that we stop this waste of time and blood."

The admiral said that he agreed that the fighting should be stopped, but there were complications. Pierre Laval, the trusted adviser of Marshal Pétain, was on his way to Berlin, and until his return it would be impossible for Admiral Darlan to conclude any lasting agreement.

"Then there's no reason to continue these talks," said Clark, rising. He would put Giraud in charge of everything, and he would place Darlan and his entire party under what he called "protective custody."

Clark's earlier adventures in North Africa were shortly to be front-page news in almost every newspaper in America, and everything he did during those early hours in Algiers had the air of melodrama, perhaps because he had with him Colonel Darryl Zanuck, already a famous Hollywood figure, and Zanuck was taking pictures, moving and still, of everything Clark did, possibly for use in something to be called *The Mark Clark Story*.

When Eisenhower learned of Zanuck's presence in Algiers he informed Clark:

"Someone tells me that this man Zanuck has gotten into Algiers. . . . I sent word to him that he was not to go down there. If he is there, you tell him that he will obey my orders as long as he is in this theater, or I will have him out of here so fast he won't know what's happening to him. I am not going to have a bunch of free-lancers dashing around here flouting established authority. Please tell him this in no uncertain terms."

When Darlan returned from a short private session with his staff, he began writing a cease-fire order. All French military forces, the air, army, and navy, were at once to stop hostilities against the Allies. As for the French fleet at Toulon, Darlan said he would try to get it but doubted that he could. When Murphy escorted him to his car, Darlan said, "Would you do me a favor? Please remind Clark that I am a five-star admiral. He should cease shouting at me and treating me like a junior lieutenant." Murphy did relay that message, but it did little good. Clark did not like foreigners and was rude to them, even the British. It is not surprising that he was not seriously considered for Eisenhower's job.

When word arrived that Pétain had rejected the armistice, fired Darlan, and ordered that he be replaced by General Noguès, the admiral told Clark that he would have to revoke the cease-fire order. To prevent this, Clark had Darlan placed under house arrest in the villa of Admiral Raymond Fenard, who had the title of Delegate General of French North Africa. Most of the French with whom the Americans worked had high-sounding titles, and very few Americans took the trouble to try to understand the humiliation they felt for their defeat by the Germans. Eisenhower was like most of his fellow countrymen in the beginning, but he was capable of learning, and he did. After a while they were no longer "Frogs"; they were Frenchmen; they had suffered defeat, and their country and colony were poverty-stricken.

On the day Darlan was arrested, November 10, Oran fell, and at a press conference Eisenhower said that everybody, including General Fredendall, commander of the Center Task Force, "did a fine job. He [Fredendall] started in and made a job of it. . . . I'm sure proud of my boys. . . . After their long sea voyage there was no longer any question of the hardihood of our soldiers. . . . The Air, Navy, and ground forces cooperated beautifully."

Details of what was going on in Casablanca were meager, Eisenhower said, "but Patton is progessing steadily, and I am quite sure that because we didn't hear anything it doesn't indicate things are going bad for us." He did not add that he had sent Georgie a somewhat impatient telegram, "Algiers has been ours for two days. Oran defenses crumbling rapidly. . . . The only tough nut left is in your hands. Crack it open quickly and ask for what you want."

In a message to Beetle, he said, "Reports from Patton still meager. . . . If he captures Casablanca by noon tomorrow, I will recommend both him and Fredendall for third stars."

Casablanca did fall to Patton on the 11th, just before noon, and when the French commander, Noguès and Admiral Michelier, appeared at his headquarters, Patton congratulated them on their gallantry. "The Navy did fight to the end," said Georgie. "The army really quit. . . . I closed the conference with champagne and many toasts."

The French officers drank $40 worth of champagne, but Patton felt it was worth it.

That same day Hitler's troops began taking over unoccupied France, which shocked the French commanders loyal to Pétain and was to make it easier for many of them to obey Darlan's cease-fire order. It seemed generally to have worked, and on the 11th the admiral was released from house arrest. Clark began a long series of angry meetings with Darlan and Giraud and, after his arrival from Casablanca, Noguès. Noguès was no easier to handle than the other two Frenchmen, and Clark continued to issue threats, slam doors, and indulge in temper tantrums. He sent frequent cables about his troubles to Eisenhower, "The measure of my anger at some of the men with whom we had to deal was indicated by the occasional appearance in my messages to Ike of YBSOB."

Eisenhower had planned to go to Algiers on the morning of the 12th, but the weather made the trip impossible. He cabled Clark, "Naturally, I approve of everything you have done. My only purpose in coming down was to bring up the last piece of ammunition we had and simply lay down the law with a bit of table pounding. Unfortunately, since I don't speak French any such attempt would have lost much of its force, but I had actually prepared my little speech in my own mind and was determined to refuse to listen to any more argument. It was my idea simply to say that you had explained the whole situation . . . and that they would now get together and come with us and be the future Marshals of a greater France, or they would go into oblivion."

Later that day he decided to radio to Clark the speech he would have made if in Algiers instead of Gibraltar. "Is each [French officer] so afraid one of the other that he recoils from thinking of himself as a Ney?"—Napoleon said that Marshal Michel Ney was "the bravest of the brave" and his most trusted and loyal soldier—"Are they ready to admit that you and I love our country more than they do theirs? . . . If they engage in petifogging struggles for personal power, they will destroy themselves and will be deserting France in her hour of need." He told Clark that he could read the telegram to the French officers if he wished. There is no record that Clark did read the message to them.

The French were not the source of all Eisenhower's troubles. The Combined Chiefs had decided that Eisenhower had had almost total success and that the difficulties of TORCH were behind him. They thought that the planned buildup of forces to the size that had been planned back in London was now unnecessary and that Eisenhower should return to London for a conference on future strategy. Perhaps, it was suggested, an attack on Sardinia should be launched. Ike cabled Beetle:

I am unalterably opposed to any suggestion at this time for reducing contemplated TORCH strength. . . . Rather than . . . talking at this time of possible reduction we should be seeking ways and means of speeding up the buildup with a view of cleaning out North Africa. . . .

I am disturbed by the apparently bland assumption that this job is finished. It would take only five minutes on the ground to convince anyone that nothing could be (actually) further from the truth. We are just started on a great venture and I must insist that there be nothing now but the firmest and most intense support, in order that a good beginning may not be destroyed by any unwarranted assumptions.

On the morning of the 13th Eisenhower cabled Marshall, "I am leaving at once for Algiers in the effort to crystalize the confused political situation. The quarrels among the principal French personalities are exasperating and Clark needs help. I expect to return here this evening."

Eisenhower, Cunningham, and several aides including Butcher left the Rock in a Flying Fortress accompanied by three P-38 fighters late in the morning, and early in the afternoon Murphy told the other Americans that the French had finally reached an agreement. Darlan, Giraud, and Noguès, joined by Juin, granted to the Allies the use of French ports and railways. Darlan would see to it that the French civilians cooperated militarily with the Allies, and the Allies in turn would leave untouched the French administrative control of North Africa, including, although the "Darlan deal" did not say so, suppression of free speech, and, when deemed necessary, executions and imprisonment of those who dissented. Giraud's control of the armed forces in the area was to be kept quiet for the time being. Noguès was to retain control of Morocco, and, finally, the French were to be provided with supplies, civilian and military. The status of the fleet at Toulon was still not settled.

Murphy was no longer taking part in the proceedings. He told Eisenhower, "The whole matter has now become a military one. You will have to give the answer." Eisenhower added, "It was squarely up to me to decide whether or not the procurement of an armistice, the saving of time and lives and the early development of the workable arrangements with the French were worth more to the Allied forces then the arbitrary arrest of Darlan, an action certain to be accompanied by continued fighting and cumulative bitterness. Local French officials were still officially members of a neutral country, and unless our governments were ready formally to declare war against France we had no legal or other right arbitrarily to establish, in the Nazi style, a puppet government of our own choosing."

Actually, Eisenhower had made up his mind what to do before leaving Gibraltar. He called in his staff and said:

The military advantages of a cease-fire are so overwhelming that I will go promptly to Algiers and if the proposals of the French are as definite as I understand, I shall immediately recognize Darlan as the highest French authority in the region. None of you should be under any misapprehension as to what the consequences of this action may be. In both our nations, Darlan is a deep-dyed villain. When public opinion raises the outcry, our two governments will be embarrassed. Because of this, we'll act so quickly that reports to our governments will be on the basis of *action taken*. I'll do my best to convince our governments that the decision was right. If they find it necessary to take action against this headquarters, I'll make it clear that I alone am responsible.

Eisenhower, Cunningham, and the others in their party started back to Gibraltar on what should have been a routine flight, but the weather was very bad, and the plane ran short of fuel. Gruenther, back at headquarters in the Rock, said, "We worried with that plane every second of the trip, and most of the time we were sure it would never make it. They never got the message on the plane, but since there was no visibility here because of the fog, *no* visibility, we tried to get them to fly to another destination. It turned out (a) They probably didn't have enough fuel to go anywhere else and (b) They didn't get the order. Ike later said, 'My staff was mad as hell at me. They accused me of disobeying orders, but the fact is we never received them.'

"The visibility was less than forty feet when the pilot brought the plane down on that tiny, tiny field. I don't know how he did it. It was a kind of miracle."

Late that Friday the 13th—it was after dark when the plane landed—Eisenhower sent Beetle a cable telling him of the agreement, adding that it was "important that the first publicity come from the group itself. I have faithfully promised this so please make sure that no repeat no mistake occurs. Still some faint hope of securing fleet but not repeat not too promising."

According to the *New York Times,* that same night Darlan announced that he had "assumed full responsibility for French interests in North Africa." He added that Pétain had given his blessing to the whole undertaking and said that de Gaulle was not repeat not included in the arrangement.

The reaction was not long in coming. Butcher said, "By Saturday morning Ike had a cable from Beetle in London, saying the deal was being coolly received. There are no objections from the U.S.A., so far. Ike had to explain the deal, primarily because of the nonannouncement of Giraud's participation—he being the guy Ike had previously blessed. Six pages of his crisp prose were required to tell the British his American point of view re [the] French, shared by the British as well as Americans on our staff, and most certainly regarded as an achievement by Murphy, who had been living with the French for many, many years."

Not only was there no criticism from the United States, but that day Ike received a congratulatory message from Roosevelt which so pleased him that he sent it to all the elements under his command. It said, "Both personally and on behalf of the American people I send sincere congratulations to you and every member of your command on the highly successful accomplishment of a most difficult task. Our occupation of North Africa has caused a wave of reassurance throughout the nation not only because of the skill and dash with which the first phase of an extremely difficult operation has been executed, but even more because of the evident perfection of the cooperation between the British and American forces."

Even Stalin joined in the praise, saying, according to the *New York Times,* that "the American and British campaign in Africa has turned the military and political position in Europe radically in favor of the Allies, opening the way for the early collapse of the German and Italian Axis."

In his long reply to the Combined Chiefs, Eisenhower got to the main point immediately, saying, "Can well understand some bewilderment in London and

Washington with the turn that negotiations with North Africa have taken. The actual state of existing sentiment here does not repeat not agree even remotely with some of prior calculations." This was a polite way of saying that most of what Murphy had told him before the landings was dead wrong.

He went on:

The following salient facts are pertinent and it is extremely important that no repeat no precipitate action at home upset such equilibrium as we have been able to establish:

Foremost is the fact that the name of Marshal Pétain is something to conjure with here. Everyone from the highest to lowest attempts to create the impression that he lives and acts under the shadow of the Marshal's figure. The civil governors, military leaders and naval commanders will agree on only one man as having an obvious right to assume the Marshal's mantle in North Africa. That man is Darlan. . . . The gist of the current agreement is that the French group will do what it can immediately to assist us in taking Tunisia. The group will organize French North Africa for effective cooperation and will begin reorganization, under KINGPIN [Giraud], of selected military forces for active participation in the war. It will exhaust every expedient in an effort in controlling and pacifying the country. . . . Without a strong French government of some kind here we would be forced to undertake complete military occupation. The cost in time and resources would be tremendous. In Morocco alone General Patton calculates that it would require 60,000 Allied troops to hold the tribes quiet and in view of the effect that any tribal disturbance would have on Spain, you can see what a problem we are up against.

The KINGPIN is now so fully aware of his inability to do anything by himself, even with Allied moral and military support, that he has cheerfully accepted the post of military chief in the Darlan group. He fully agrees also that his own name should not repeat not be mentioned in connection with this movement for a period of several days. . . .

I realize there may be a feeling at home that we have been sold a bill of goods, but I assure you that these agreements have been arrived at only after incessant examination of the important factors and with the determination to get on with military objectives against the Axis and to advance the interests of the Allies in winning this war. . . .

Finally, it must be clearly appreciated that if Darlan is repudiated and we attempt to dictate the personnel of the coalition to run this section of the world, the following will be the consequences: (a) Our hope of securing organized cooperation in this region will be gone at great cost to us in additional troops and in stagnation of operations. (b) All French Armed Forces in this region will resist us passively and in some cases actively. (c) Our hope of getting Tunis quickly will not repeat not be attainable because Esteva will not repeat not cooperate. (d) The opportunity for gaining some assistance from remaining French naval, air and military units will disappear. (e) The last glimmer of hope with respect to the Toulon fleet will be gone.

He saved the best, the most provocative as well as, he surely hoped, the most convincing for last. "I suggest that if the two governments after analysis of this radio are still dissatisfied with nature of agreement made that a mission of selected British and United States representatives, and including Free French if deemed advisable, be immediately dispatched to his headquarters." American and British governments and de Gaulle decided against such a mission, immediately or ever.

When Eisenhower reread his "long telegram" while writing *Crusade* he was able to say, "Even after long retrospective study of the situation I can think of little to add to the telegraphic explanation."

Roosevelt was delighted with the message, so much so that he read it aloud to Hopkins. In his book about the two men, Robert Sherwood, who heard the reading, said, "It was a remarkable statement of Eisenhower's reasons for the Darlan deal. Roosevelt . . . read it with the same superb distribution of emphasis that he used in his public speeches . . . sounded as if he were making an eloquent plea for Eisenhower before the bar of history. . . .

"Roosevelt attached great importance to Eisenhower's confession of astonishment at the situation as he found it in North Africa; it did 'not even remotely resemble prior calculations.' When the supreme commander of a major military operation like that . . . indicates that there must have been something wrong with his Intelligence Service. . . . The headquarters of Robert Murphy in Algiers and all the American consulates in that area . . . were centers of Intelligence with large staffs which included observers of unquestioned competence as well as courage. Yet Eisenhower was astonished when the local French failed to hail Giraud as a conquering hero. This led to a display of political crudity which made the U.S. government look amateurish."

The whole thing made Eisenhower seem to many people in the United States and Britain not only amateurish but a man either too stupid to understand what Fascism and Nazism were all about or, worse, sympathetic to either or both. Most editors of American newspapers, however, felt that it was Eisenhower's business to make decisions that would "save lives and shorten the war." It was up to the country involved to choose its own government, the majority of the editors said, a statement with which Eisenhower agreed, but just how a new government was to be set up in a country not yet "liberated" or "freed"—both words were used at one time or another to describe what we were doing in French North Africa—had to be set aside for the moment.

On November 13, the day before Eisenhower composed the long "telegraphic explanation" Roosevelt had liked so much, Darlan had announced that he had established a provisional government with himself as head. The next day he rescinded his pledge of loyalty to Pétain, saying that the marshal was under the control of the Nazis. That same day he appointed Giraud president of all French forces, land, sea, and air. Giraud almost immediately ordered the French military forces in the North African area to begin resistance to Axis troops. Both the Germans and the Italians began pouring troops into the area, and it would no doubt have shortened the war and made it less costly had the supreme commander of TORCH been able to order his men into battle immediately; but in November and December 1942 Eisenhower was largely concerned with other matters. He was too busy defending himself from people he had assumed were his friends to have much time for attacking the Axis enemy.

At a press conference on the 15th, Eisenhower said of Darlan's plan, "The working arrangement is very satisfactory." He said he had gone to Algiers to meet with "a whole flock of admirals." They, too, had approved of Darlan's plan.

But it appeared for a time as if almost nobody else did. First of all came the outraged voice of a man Ike had known and liked in London, Edward R. Murrow. Murrow's nightly broadcasts from London made his voice, next to Roosevelt's, the most listened to and influential of any American's. He attacked the "Darlan deal" from the beginning. Why, he wanted to know, were we cooperating with a man like Darlan instead of with the Free French? They had, after all, shed blood fighting the Nazis. It was men like Darlan who had praised and cooperated with the Axis. He said, "There is nothing in the strategic situation of the Allies to indicate that we are either so strong or so weak that we can afford to ignore the principles for which this war is being fought."

Even the amiable Ernie Pyle, the columnist who by the war's end would be loved by millions of GIs who felt he spoke for them, said, "We have left in office most of the small-fry officials put there by the Germans before we came. We are permitting fascist societies to continue to exist. . . . The loyal French see this and wonder what manner of people we are."

All true, but there were not too many "loyal" French in North Africa in November 1942; they became "loyal" only after a few Allied victories.

The criticism grew, from London, from Washington, and from supporters of de Gaulle in England and in North Africa. Sir Percy Harris, a Labour Member of Parliament, said that the "Darlan deal" was "the one sinister side of the African campaign and was one of the most mysterious chapters of the war."

Eisenhower was not generally a man called upon to defend his actions, and he was amazed and disheartened at the furor. To him the whole thing was simple. "Our basic orders required us to go into Africa in the attempt to win an ally—not to kill Frenchmen.

"I well knew that any dealing with a Vichyite would create great revulsion among those in England and America who did not know the harsh realities of war; therefore I determined to confine my judgment in the matter to the local military aspects."

That satisfied no one, however; the furor continued and grew, and the only immediate comfort, and it wasn't much, came in a cable from Churchill: "Anything for the battle, but the politics will have to be sorted out later on."

Ike wrote Mamie, "Since I cannot even guess at how much the home newspapers print of this affair, I don't know what your particular mental picture of it may be. But so far as I'm concerned it's primarily more work, more anxious moments, and more nervous expenditure. I work all day—12–14 hours in a dungeon—get a late dinner and go to bed; up and start all over again. Get around this great area very infrequently. . . .

"Yesterday I received a letter from Edgar. . . . he told me mainly about my mother, who cannot understand why I'm in Europe."

He told Beetle, "I am not committing ourselves to anything that is not essential to immediate operations, and God knows I'm not . . . trying to be a king-maker. . . . I do not understand why anyone should think that I am trying to set up a permanent political regime, or why it should be thought I fail to recognize the crookedness or intense unpopularity of Darlan. But I do know that the so-and-so, on his own hook, is trying to get Dakar into our camp. I am keeping out of any conversations concerning it, because Dakar is not repeat not in my area. But I do feel that the Allies should not repeat not hesitate to take advantage of any favorable situation in that line that this fellow can bring about." Up to that time, the governor general of French West Africa had refused to allow either Allied or Axis ships to use Dakar, but he was at least listening to what Darlan was proposing.

Ike even found he was defending himself to John:

From what I hear of what has been appearing in the newspapers, you are learning that it is easy enough for a man to be a newspaper hero one day and a bum the next. The answer is that just as one must not let his head get swelled too much by a bit of acclaim, he must not be too upset and irritated when the pack turns on him. Apparently, the people who have been creating the storm do not like Darlan. The answer to that one is "Who does?" The only thing that a soldier can use for a guide is to try to do what appears right and just at the moment of the crisis. If it turns out wrong—or if it even appears to turn out wrong—the reaction may be serious, but there is no other course to follow. . . . This is not meant as a defense or any real explanation. It is really just a bit of philosophy.

By the 16th, according to Sherwood, "The storm of criticism of the Darlan deal had reached such proportions that Hopkins, [Roosevelt's speechwriter Samuel] Rosenman, and I strongly urged the President to issue a statement to the press. . . . When Roosevelt read it, he made substantial revisions, all of them calculated to make the language tougher and more uncompromising."

The statement came to the point immediately. It said, "I have accepted General Eisenhower's political arrangements made for the time being in Northern and Western Africa.

"I thoroughly understand and approve the feeling in the United States and Great Britain and among all the other United Nations that in view of the history of the past two years no permanent arrangement should be made with Admiral Darlan. People in the United Nations likewise would never understand the recognition of a reconstituting of the Vichy Government in France or in any French territory. . . . The present temporary arrangement in North and West Africa is only a temporary expedient justified solely by the stress of battle."

The president referred again "to the present temporary arrangement in Algiers and Morocco" and repeated that "Temporary arrangements made with Admiral Darlan apply, without exception, in the current local situation only."

That particular statement was perhaps the most repetitious of the tens of thousands of statements released during Roosevelt's many years in the White House. Darlan, not surprisingly, resented the repetitions and in a letter to Clark said, "I am only a lemon which the Americans will drop after they have squeezed it dry."

Later Roosevelt said to the press that he was quoting "an old Bulgarian proverb of the Orthodox Church: 'My children, you are permitted in time of great danger to walk with the Devil until you have crossed the bridge.' Mind you," he added to the reporters, "this is okayed by the church."

Roosevelt frequently found old "proverbs" and "sayings" that were not discovered by anybody else, but no one ever questioned their authenticity. In those far off and innocent days that would have been considered rude.

On the same day Roosevelt made the statement, Harry Hopkins drafted a letter for the president to send to Eisenhower. It read in part, "I want you to know that I appreciate fully the difficulties of your military situation. I am therefore not disposed to in any way question the action you have taken. Indeed you may be sure of my complete support of this and any other action you are required to take in carrying out your duties. You are on the ground and we here intend to support you fully in your difficult problems." The note continued, "(1) . . . we do not trust Darlan, (2) . . . it is impossible to keep a collaborator of Hitler and one whom we believe to be a Fascist in civil power any longer than is absolutely necessary. (3) His movements should be watched carefully and his communications supervised." A copy of the letter was sent to Churchill.

There was no objection to the deal in the Soviet Union. In a letter to Churchill, Stalin said, "It seems to me that the Americans used Darlan not badly in order to facilitate the occupation of Northern and Western Africa. The military diplomacy must be able to use for military purposes not only Darlan but, 'Even the devil himself and his grandma.' "

The Russian ambassador to the United States, I. M. Maisky, said that the reference to the devil was from "an old and strong Russian proverb." Stalin liked convenient proverbs and sayings, too.

Despite Roosevelt's public statement defending the deal, the criticism continued. The uproar was too passionate; too many people, including many in the Allied services, felt personally betrayed. I was very much among them. In various bars on various islands in the Pacific that fall and winter, I remember asking people who never had an answer and seldom wanted to hear the question, "What the hell is this goddamn war all about, anyway?"

It has always been easy to criticize the agreement with Darlan, and it was suggested then and has been since that de Gaulle supporters should have been placed in the top civilian and military positions.

Drew Middleton, who was then a correspondent for the *New York Times* and has been its military correspondent since 1970, said in his book *Our Share of the Night:*

I did not think then nor do I think now, that this could have been accomplished without further bloodshed. Even had the Allies been able to force their will upon the North African French at that time, there were not enough DeGaullists in North Africa to fill all the jobs held by Vichy men.

In the end the Allies would have had to supply the administrators from our already slender resources of manpower while at the same time maintaining the DeGaullists in office with our troops.

Eisenhower, "as the man who had made the decision, might have been made a scapegoat," his son John said. "His career was more in the balance than he realized, though the fact that he had taken the personal risk of the deal on himself eventually increased his stature with his political bosses." But on November 23, when Ike left the Rock for Algiers, he was eager to get down to the business of being a soldier again. He had told Beetle, "My whole interest now is Tunisia. When I can make the Allies a present of that place the AGENT [code name for Churchill] can kick me in the pants and put a politician here who is as big a crook as the chief local skunk."

★ ★ ★

A BITTER DECISION

On his way to Algiers Eisenhower stopped in Oran to have lunch with Major General Lloyd R. Fredendall, commander of II Corps.

Fredendall, a man who talked like a vulgar first sergeant, though presumably not in the presence of his commanding officer, was to cause Eisenhower a good deal of trouble before the battle for Tunisia was over.

At the Oran airport Ike and his party first encountered what was to delay and defeat the Allied forces for the rest of that fall and winter—mud. "We landed on a hard-surfaced strip but then could not taxi a foot off the runway because of the bottomless mud," he said. "A huge tractor appeared and, with men placing great planks under the keels of our Fortress, pulled us off a few yards so that incoming aircraft would still be able to land. Tactical operations were at a standstill so I spent the morning inquiring into problems of supply, housing, and food. It was on that occasion that I first met Air Force Lieutenant Colonel Lauris Norstad, a young officer who so impressed me by his alertness, grasp of problems, and personality that I never lost sight of him. He was and is one of those men whose capacity knows no limits." Norstad, thirty-five, West Point 1930, was to become General Norstad and to serve as Supreme Allied Commander, Europe.

"The general [Eisenhower] was tired, and he looked much older than in his pictures," Norstad remembered. "But he was cheerful, and the thing that always impressed me about him was that he *looked* in charge of things. When he was around, you didn't have to ask who was boss. You knew.

"As for the mud, I was used to mud. I grew up in mud country in the Dakotas, but the mud in Tunisia was different. There seemed to be nothing but mud, oceans of it, and it was impossible to get anything clean, including yourself."

The Eisenhower plane had burst a tire when landing. When it had been repaired, the general and his party flew to Maison Blanche airport near Algiers. The official headquarters, a modest suite at the Hotel St. George, consisted of three bedrooms and a parlor. There was a small fireplace in the room Eisenhower used as an office. "It was very nice and seemed fairly modern," he said.

"This harbor, lying just outside my window, is crowded with ships. It is situated within easy bombing distance of Sardinia, Bône, Philippeville, and this place must all be adequately protected by day and by night. It seems to me certain that sooner or later we are going to get some very heavy bombing raids, particularly by night, on these ports."

Indeed several air raids took place that first night, and the general was furious over what he considered inadequate defenses against them. He was particularly upset about the effect the raids would have psychologically on the Arabs and the French.

The general's headquarters in Algiers started out small but quickly grew to be the largest headquarters anywhere. Eisenhower wrote Marshall that his principal objective was "the capture of Tunisia in an effort to throw the enemy back into the Bizerte stronghold, where we will try to confine him closely while bringing up additional means for the final kill."

Tunisia had to be taken. It was the key to the Central Mediterranean. The Corsican port of Ajaccio was 300 miles to the north. Toulon and Marseilles were only 400 miles away; the British base at Malta, 230; Palermo in Sicily, 190; and Cagliari in Sardinia, 170 miles.

The Germans were equally determined to stay. Dr. Goebbels said, "The Fuehrer has decided that Tunis must be held as long as possible and has opposed every compromise proposal."

Getting reinforcements for the Allied troops was not easy. Railroad facilities were almost nonexistent. The port of Bône was small, damaged, and under heavy and constant air attack. Motor transportation and labor supplies were minimal, and the distances to be traveled were always great.

Some things in war never change, and the desert war in Tunisia in 1942 was not very different than it had been for Hannibal's troops when they fought against those of Scipio Africanus Major in 202 B.C. The sand was the same. The lack of water was the same, and transport moved slowly, often not at all, and human errors abounded. Rommel said of his own time, "The mismanagements, the operational blunders, the prejudices, the ever-lasting search for scapegoats, these were now to reach the acute stage. And the man who paid the price was the ordinary . . . soldier."

Almost every soldier and officer of any nationality agreed. And in addition to the human errors and the enemy there was the always menacing desert itself. Major General Matthew Bunker Ridgway, commander of the 82nd Airborne, said, "A fine dust clogged the nostrils, burned the eyes and cut into the throat like an abrasive. . . . The ground was hard, and covered with loose boulders, from the size of a man's fist to the size of his head."

Eisenhower shortly after his arrival in Algiers wrote Ismay, "Upon reaching here, I sensed that every individual was suspicious of everyone else—every man was sure all others were crooks and liars. This atmosphere tended to make difficult any progress in obtaining the concessions and cooperation desired by the U.S. and U.K. I immediately started a personal campaign to establish for myself a reputation for the most straightforward, brutal talk that could be imagined. I refused to put anything in diplomatic or suave terminology, and carefully cultivated the manner and reputation of a complete bluntness and honesty—just a man too simpleminded to indulge in circumlocution."

It was neither the first time nor the last that Eisenhower did that—got tough and pretended he was too simpleminded "to indulge in circumlocution." As he added in a handwritten afterthought to Ismay, "After all, I couldn't adopt any other attitude and act naturally."

The general also felt it necessary to put on a little "dog." "We will necessarily have to preserve a position of the dominating influence in the region," he said, "and even such a matter of appearances will have its effect not only on the native population but apparently on these Frenchmen." Even before coming to Algiers he had asked Butcher to get a villa, "a place where I can entertain at will for almost any size of party, and will have my private office in my quarters. . . . I am going to have a very fine layout."

The day after the general arrived in Algiers, headquarters personnel moved into two rented villas. His own Villa dar el Ouard (villa of the family, in Arabic) was large, but there were only two bedrooms and baths as well as four servants' bedrooms and baths. There was plenty of floor space for visitors with bedrolls, and there were often a number of those. The gas and water mains had been destroyed by enemy bombs, thus neither heat nor water were available. When Kay Summersby arrived in late December, she found the whole thing "ugly, filled with uncomfortable French furniture, and a general appearance of dreariness."

The general did not keep his hardships from Mamie. She was, after all, in a cozy, warm apartment in the Wardman Park in Washington, and he wrote her, "Sometime when I can have an hour to write I'll try to tell you how I live. For the moment all I can say is that 4 of us stay in a big-looking but most uncomfortable place on a hillside overlooking the city. It's sort of a combination of Moorish-Spanish architecture with French habits controlling the inside. Awful."

In another letter he wrote of the inadequate food. "We have an army cook who does as well as he can out of the type of rations we get. I haven't had fresh fowl or beef since coming to this country. All of us live mostly on mutton and canned 'willie' so far as the meat ration is concerned. . . . None of us is starving, but we do get occasional yens for a good turkey dinner with all the trimmings."

His meager diet did not last long, however. Mickey wrote that during the first two weeks in Algiers, "Probably the most important thing I did was to find food for the house. . . . I made a deal with one of the troop transports and got eggs and meat and coffee and butter from it, and I found and rented a freezing compartment in a cold-storage warehouse and gradually, by keeping my eyes open and keeping at it, I kept the boss and the rest of us pretty well fed." Eisenhower did not mention to Mamie that his diet had improved.

The weather never stopped being a problem, an unexpected one for the general and for most of his troops. Africa was sunny, wasn't it; and the skies were blue? Wasn't the temperature forever mild? Eisenhower told Mamie he had "expected to find . . . people bathing on the beaches." Instead, the skies were incessantly gray. The days were sunless, and the temperatures were bone-chilling. "I haven't been really warm since arriving here except in bed," he said.

As always, minor irritations were numerous. Butcher had managed to procure a phonograph and had asked London for some records. The general asked for two in particular, those all-American favorites, Dvořák's "Humoresque" and "The Anvil Chorus" from Verdi's *Il Trovatore*. He had also wanted "The Last Roundup," but he told Mamie that that was unavailable in London. "All in all I feel well," he said to her, "and I think I am going as strong as ever. We work all day long, go to our house where four of us sleep surrounded by guards at every door (there is even one just outside my bedroom, which makes me feel like—) and then get up and start all over again."

In a P.S. to one letter, he said, "We are engaged in a battle in Tunisia, which you can find on your map. So far it goes pretty well, but this business of war is chancy, so I just keep on trying to drive ahead and don't become too hopeful and hysterical on the one hand nor too depressed by disappointment on the other."

The continuous November rains made Allied aerial activity impossible; the B-17s had to be propped up under the wings or they would have disappeared in mud. The Germans, on the other hand, had two all-weather airfields, one at Tunis, the other at Bizerte. Moreover, the rain did not stop German troops from pouring into Tunisia. By the beginning of December, Allied intelligence estimated that enemy strength was about 31,000, 20,000 of whom were Germans.

On December 29 there were 50,000 enemy troops in Bizerte-Tunis-Sousse area; and by late January Axis strength in Tunisia was up to 112,000, including 81,000 Germans. Of the number of Germans in Tunisia, Eisenhower commented in a cable to Marshall, "It is noticeable that it is the Hun and not the Wop that is defending this particular spot."

The best news for the Allies that fall came from Russia. On November 19 the Red Army had counterattacked from points north and south of the German salient in Stalingrad. In five days' time it was certain that the German forces were trapped in the city. On that day, November 24, Eisenhower wrote Mamie, "The Russian fight continues to stir me to the depths of my soul. They're hitting so hard that no one can fail to admire them. I hope they kill a million Huns— even more! And I wish we could be hammering at the d—— Germans this instant, just as hard and on as big a scale as the Russians."

In his own life, however, there were no heroic actions. There was no action at all, not even any exercise. He told John, "I must begin to get a little bit of exercise daily, or I'm going to suffer for it. Long and confining hours, seven days a week, all the time wrestling with difficult decisions based on conflicting reports and the doubts and fears of subordinates, finally produce a load that can be carried only if a man keeps in fine physical shape."

On Saturday, November 28, Eisenhower, accompanied by Clark, made his first trip to the front to visit Lieutenant General Kenneth Anderson, commander of the British First Army. It was, not unexpectedly, cold and rainy the morning the two generals left on what Clark, a man impatient of protocol unless it was *his* protocol, called a "Boy Scout" trip. With Eisenhower, as many trips as possible to the front were a necessity, not only to visit his subordinate commanders but, whenever possible, to be seen by the troops. He also wanted to find out firsthand what was happening outside his headquarters. He neither liked nor entirely trusted most written reports.

The two generals made the journey in a semiarmored Cadillac, led by a jeep and a scout car. Another scout car was in the rear. Mickey and Clark's orderly were in a quarter-ton truck. Butcher said, "Plenty of .50-caliber guns, but elevation for antiaircraft guns for defense against enemy aircraft, from which principal danger might be expected, was disquietingly low."

Before leaving, Eisenhower heard the disconcerting news that Hitler had announced he was taking Toulon, by force if necessary, and that "a large part" of the French fleet had been scuttled.

The 500-mile trip to Anderson's headquarters in a village beyond Constantine was both hazardous and tedious, and it was not a success. Eisenhower's relationship with Anderson was never warm. The Britisher was not deliberately rude like Montgomery: he was simply cold and uncommunicative. Eisenhower was not at his best during this period, either. He was learning that planning and carrying out combat action was more difficult and unpredictable than planning maneuvers in the state of Washington or in Louisiana. Much of the drive ahead in Tunisia had been easy; holding the points seized was more difficult, particularly with the enemy pouring in troops and equipment. Besides, for almost the first time in his career Eisenhower seemed uncertain. His troops were uncertain, too; most of them had been hastily and carelessly trained, and they had never been under fire. It was impossible to tell how a man would react in battle until he had been in battle; that was to prove almost disastrously true in the case of Fredendall.

Of course Eisenhower mentioned none of these things in the letter he wrote to Beetle and the "gang" in London after his return to Algiers late on the evening of November 29. The letter had the happy sound of a boy's report from summer camp. True there had been some irritations and inconveniences, but they had been easily overcome.

"We went . . . into town where we expected to find a large headquarters," he said. "The headquarters had been moved and we were stranded. . . . At this juncture, through the aid of a French policeman on a bicycle, we found an American Vice Consul and he, in turn, led us to a delightful French family who took us in for the night. . . . We got started out from there again the following morning about seven o'clock. By this time we decided that the scout cars, although imposing looking and contributing largely to our feeling of importance, were in the way when it came to making time over winding mountainous roads. So we left them behind. From that place on, we had the feeling that a . . . plane might come sweeping out of the air at any time to take our rear window as his target, but no such incident occurred and so had a very uneventful journey."

Anderson's troops consisted of three inadequately armed and incompletely manned brigades of infantry and one obsolescent tank. The troops had been repeatedly bombed by Germans flying out of the hard-surfaced airfields, and it was generally known that more enemy ground troops were arriving every day.

"Yet on the whole morale was good," Eisenhower said. "The exaggerations [of hardships the troops had suffered] were nothing more than the desire of the individual to convey the thought that he had been through the ultimate in terror and destruction—he had no thought of clearing out himself."

The trip back to Algiers was even more disheartening than the trip to the front had been. "The driver," Eisenhower wrote, "was far from being like Kay, and he constantly had us in a state of nervous tension. . . . He tried to pass a bicyclist without sounding his horn . . . the bicyclist decided to make one of the unaccountable turns we have come to expect from them. The result was that we took the front wheel of the bicycle. . . . An hour or so later the driver suddenly announced that we were without gasoline. . . . He apparently decided it was too much trouble to put the filled cans in our car and thought he could get the trucks and jeeps to carry it for him. We finally got to a British airfield and got the few gallons that they could spare." Eventually the battery of the car ran down, and it was without lights and had to be towed back to Eisenhower's villa, arriving, Eisenhower wrote, "just at midnight behind a half-ton truck. . . . All of this may have contributed to the sourness of my outlook and to the acuteness of my stomach pains." The fact that the bicyclist was a twelve-year-old Arab boy and he had been killed can't have helped, although, according to Butcher's diary, "The French lieutenant who happened to see the accident held the poor boy entirely at fault."

Ike said that if any of the London gang had "any romantic anticipations involving an Arab Rudolph Valentino type, I advise you to come prepared with a half-dozen scrubbing brushes and at least a barrel of strong washing powder. With this equipment to work long and earnestly on some likely looking individual and then with a number of yards of clean muslin with which to drape him to your satisfaction, I think you might get a plausible imitation of what the movies have shown us. As the desert hero stands at the moment, he typifies filth, squalor, rags, and laziness. I must admit, however, that the dirt-stained imitation of a circus tent that he wears as a robe lends to his carriage, particularly at a distance, a certain dignity. Moreover, as he stalks along in his stately filthiness, he seems to be perfectly content with his lot—and obvious contentment always creates in others a desire to learn its cause."

The fighting in Tunisia was always uppermost in his mind, but Ike did on occasion find time to make more general observations on North Africa than the fact that most Arabs did not bathe regularly.

He told John, "Of course, I have seen only the coastlines, but the cities are rather nice looking, being built largely of a light-colored stone, and are usually situated so as to give a very pleasing effect, especially from the air. . . . On the north coast there is a large European population and some of the hotels are very modern."

"The poverty of the country, brought about by two years of virtual blockade, is evident everywhere," he wrote Mamie. "Money is little good because there is nothing to buy. No cloth, no coal, no wood, and scarcely any other item except meat (chiefly a poor grade of mutton) which seems to be reasonably plentiful. People, even poor people, don't want to work for money, because there is nothing to buy with the money. . . . The country is a very divided one in sentiment. Millions of Arabs are a very uncertain quantity, explosive and full of prejudices."

The morning after his return from the trip to the front, Eisenhower was sick with a cold. The doctor in charge of the headquarters dispensary prescribed "rest, paregoric, and customary treatment for colds." He found the time and energy to write a lengthy report to Marshall on the trip. He dictated it from his bed. He said of Anderson that he "is apparently imbued with the will to win, but blows hot and cold, by turns, in his estimates and resulting demands. . . .

"Even by using transport airplanes for supply of critical items, the logistics situation is one to make a ritualist in warfare go just a bit hysterical. From Algiers to the eastward, we can run a total of 9 small trains a day. 2 of these have to haul coal to operate the railroad; 1 is the barest minimum to keep the population from starving. This leaves 6 for military purposes, and since we have been trying both to crowd troops forward, particularly armor, and to supply what we have already there, you can see that reserves of munitions and rations are almost at the vanishing point . . . motor transport is something we just don't have and, in spite of impressing every kind of scrawny vehicle that we can run, we have not been able to do much by road, except in pushing forward parts of Armored Units. . . . So far as we can, we ship by sea to Bône, but the job of providing air cover is one that is just a bit beyond our means. However, [Admiral] Cunningham is bold and in spite of some losses we have gotten a lot of stuff forward that way."

As he often did he saved the good news for the last: "Upon my return from the East this morning, I was handed a most commendatory message sent me by the Secretary of War." (Stimson had said, "This is to convey my admiration and appreciation of your masterly conduct of the campaign thus far as well as my best wishes for your success in Tunisia. I know it will be a tough pull but I am confident that you will thoroughly succeed.")

Although the general's cold hung on for months, the next morning, December 1, he was feeling much better. At 10:30 he pinned a DSM on Clark's chest and cabled Marshall that Clark was to command the U.S. Fifth Army, a decision that a great many people, soldiers, and civilians, felt was not his best. Most soldiers in the Fifth Army itself felt it was his worst.

In the afternoon Eisenhower went with Ryder to visit several hospitals in which were officers and men who had been wounded in battle. Eisenhower insisted that Ryder be the one to pin Purple Hearts on the eighty-seven officers and men. They were Ryder's troops, and the Allied commander in chief had no intention of stealing his glory. Many of the men were from the 39th and 34th Infantry divisions, a large number from Iowa and Minnesota, and the general shook their hands and asked where they were from, where they were hit, and if they expected to get out soon. The questions were routine, but the soldiers Eisenhower asked the questions of almost always felt that he wanted to know, that he actually cared. For one thing Eisenhower *looked* at them, and he listened. Most generals, Bradley excepted, just asked the questions and, unhearing, moved on to the next man.

When Eisenhower returned to his headquarters he found that Patton had arrived from Western Task Force headquarters in Morocco. Eisenhower didn't know it, but behind his back Georgie's attitude to him had changed, in fact Eisenhower was not fully aware of the depth of the change until after the war when Patton's posthumous book, *War as I Knew It*, was published in 1947. Eisenhower read an early excerpt that was published in the November 1, 1947, edition of *The Saturday Evening Post*. In it Patton alleged vehemently that SHAEF prolonged the war and lost thousands of additional lives when it "prevented George Patton from winning the war in September, 1944." After reading the excerpt, Eisenhower commented, "I am beginning to think that crackpot history is going to guide the future student in his study of the late conflict."

In his diary Patton noted that he had been in Algiers on December 1 and found that "Ike is sick, has a cold, but is low too—lacks decision." Patton had dinner with what he called "the sacred family—Ike, Clark, and Davis, the Adjutant General." Georgie was not of the family; he was an outsider, invited to share a meal at the table of the those who had, he felt, surpassed him. The tortoise had outdistanced the hare.

Patton found out that night, too, that Clark was to command the Fifth Army. "I had expected this but it was a shock," he said. "It means that I simply have a corps. 'The best laid plans of mice and men.' I felt so awful that I could not sleep for a while, but I shall pass them yet."

Eisenhower's opinion of Patton had not altered in the slightly more than a month that had passed since the TORCH invasion. On December 10, in evaluating the events since the landing, he also evaluated the officers who had taken part in it. Two British officers, Admiral Cunningham and Air Marshal Tedder, had measured up. The general said, "I regard them both as top-flight leaders. I am sorry that Tedder is not an actual member of this organization. Among the American commanders, Patton I think comes close to meeting every requirement made on a commander. Just after him I would, at present, rate Fredendall, although I do not believe the latter has the imagination in foreseeing and preparing for possible jobs of the future that Patton possesses. Clark is an unusual individual and is particularly strong in his organizational ability and orderliness of his mind. Unfortunately, I have not yet seen him in a position where he has had to carry the responsibility directly on his own shoulders, but there seems to be no reason why he should not measure up in this respect.

"I think, however, that for the next several months he will deliver for several reasons. First, he is getting command of the Fifth Army, for which he has begged and pleaded for a long time. Second, the job, for the moment, is one largely of organization and training, and in these fields I think Clark had no superior."

Eisenhower was right about Patton as a commander; the mistakes Georgie made were in other areas. But Eisenhower overestimated the capabilities of both Fredendall and Clark. Both made errors that were costly in lives, time, and money. Eventually he dealt with Fredendall, but he never dealt with the deficiencies of Clark, never even seemed to realize that he had deficiencies. Perhaps they had been too close too long, a friendship going back to their days together at West Point, though it was not renewed until Clark played a central role in rescuing Eisenhower from the Philippines and MacArthur. Ike was grateful for that, many felt too grateful and at much too high a price. Eisenhower repeatedly wrote good letters and made good notes in his diary about weeding out the inefficient and incompetent, but when it came time to do it himself, he nearly always faltered. That happened when he was president, too. He lacked the ruthlessness that he so often saw as a virtue in others, his classmate McNarney, for one. It was part of the fundamental decency of the man. It was also a serious flaw.

The Combined Chiefs had decided on a major attack against the enemy on December 9, but during the first week in December the Axis were pushing back the Allied lines, and the Germans were strafing Allied troops day and night. "Courage, resourcefulness, and endurance, though daily displayed, could not completely overcome the combination of enemy, weather, and terrain. In early December the enemy was strong enough in mechanized units to begin local but sharp counterattacks," said Eisenhower.

Anderson concluded that the December 9 attack was impossible, indeed that "any major attack for several weeks afterwards" was "out of the question. I am very sorry, but there it is. . . . It would do nothing but harm to push in recklessly when I am unready," he said.

Eisenhower delayed making up his mind for a day or so. In a letter to Tom Handy back at OPD, he said:

I think the best way to describe our operations to date is that they have violated every recognized principle of war, are in conflict with all operational and logistic methods laid down in textbooks and will be condemned, in their entirety, by all Leavenworth and War College classes for the next twenty-five years. . . .

As you know, the sketchy forces we were able to get inside the Tunisian border were not in sufficient strength to sweep the Germans out of the way; and the French in the critical corner of the region would not take a definite and prompt stand in our favor. . . . As quickly as I saw opposition building up in Tunisia, I realized that Anderson, with his own forces, was not going to be strong enough to seize Tunis; and so I immediately began combing the area to find everything that could move and could be gotten up to him. . . .

During all this period we found it increasingly difficult to give any air cover to our infantry, since each rain would put our fields out of operation. In any event, the closest field we had to the front line was a hundred miles away, and the enemy's—two of which were all-weather—were within fifteen miles. We used our bombers against both the airfields and the port facilities, but we did not have enough strength of this kind to render the fields usable or to stop his reinforcement.

From a logistics viewpoint, the situation became worse from the day we started.

On December 9, the day the Allied attack was to have been launched, Eisenhower postponed it. That same night Patton, as ordered, returned to Algiers. He was very excited and pleased. His plane had been fired on three times by Allied antiaircraft gunners during the journey. Eisenhower sent him to the Tunisian front to find out why the Allies were losing so many tanks, and he found and reported to the Allied commander that our M3 Grant tanks were too light, their turret-mounted 37-mm guns could not penetrate the German Panzer IV's armor, and their 75-mm guns, because they were mounted on the hull, were restricted in their arc of fire. Moreover, the ammunition available appeared to have been made for training exercises, not combat.

The future looked brighter, however. M4 Sherman medium tanks, faster, more heavily armored and with 75-mm guns mounted in power-driven turrets, were about to arrive in Tunisia.

Patton said, only in his diary, not to the two officers involved, "Ike and Clark were in conference as to what to do. Neither had been to the front, so showed great lack of decision. They are on their way out, I think. . . . Too damned slick, especially Clark."

Publicly at least, Eisenhower was not too upset by the news Patton brought back. He wrote Butcher on the 10th, "All in all, I would rate our prospects for the present as good. We are having our troubles; so is the enemy. If we can make up our minds to endure more and go further and work harder than he does and provided only that the comparative logistics of the situation do not favor him too, we can certainly win!"

He was equally optimistic in his report to the Combined Chiefs. "I am still absolutely unwilling to give up the thought of an all-out attempt to win the critical area. It is my conviction that we must strive to avoid settling down to a logistic marathon. While the difficulties, as presented to me by the air, the ground, and the supply organizations, are tremendous and undoubtedly definite risks are assumed, I still insist that if we can only be fortunate to get a spell of good weather, we can do the job."

Privately, however, he had doubts about the operation, and there was really no one in Algiers he felt close enough to, to share his private misgivings. He often wished he had someone like his West Point roommate, P. A. Hodgson around to help him clarify his thoughts and feelings. But P.A. was at good old Fort Sam in San Antonio, serving as executive officer. He had just returned to active service after having received a disability retirement in 1941.

In a long and revealing letter written on December 4, the general told P.A.:

For some reason, during these past hectic weeks, I have found myself more and more frequently wishing that you could be here for a day or a week, just to go over with me a thousand things that range all the way from major problems to inconsequential details. The pressure of work on a job like this seems to result in making personal activity resemble a whirlpool, with the individual constantly getting closer to the center and, therefore, with his contacts limited progressively to fewer and fewer people. I find myself resenting this and frequently try to break out of its clutches, at least mentally, by wondering what someone else would say or think about particular questions.

Possibly one of the reasons that I think of you so often is because you were always so stubborn you would never believe anything or anybody— even me—and I have no doubt that attempting again the perfectly hopeless job of convincing you might, at least, serve to clarifiy my own weaker mind.

Anyway, this afternoon when I found that for some unaccountable reason my office was free of staff officers, commanders, visitors, politicians, and all other types of humanity, I jumped upon the chance to send you word of greeting and an inquiry as to how you are getting along. . . .

I should like to tell you, in some detail, something about the nature, objectives and developments of this campaign. However, I established stringent censorship rules that I require everybody else to observe, so I have made it an invariable practice to say nothing about such things except in official telegrams to London and Washington. I can say, however, that high command in war carries with it a lot of things that were never included in our textbooks, in the Leavenworth course, or even in the War College investigations. I think sometimes that I am a cross between a one-time soldier, a pseudo-statesman, a jack-legged politician and a crooked diplomat. I walk a soapy tightrope in a rainstorm with a blazing furnace on one side and a pack of ravenous tigers on the other. . . .

In spite of all this, I must admit that the whole thing is intriguing and interesting, and is forever presenting new challenges that still have the power to make me come up charging.

On December 7 Eisenhower had received an encouraging cable from Churchill. The prime minister was, he said, "filled with admiration" at the way Eisenhower was conducting the campaign. He had been "absolutely right" to run all the risks in the race for Tunis. Churchill was sorry the general was being bothered "by all this Darlan business," and he added, "Please think of me as a fairly solid fortification covering your rear and go for the swine in front with a blithe heart."

The PM's letter helped Ike's morale considerably, and it improved even more when on the the 11th Beetle and Milton arrived. It was always a pleasure to have Smith at his side, and Milton, the diplomat, had been sent by the president to try to straighten out the uproar over the "Darlan deal." Other objectionable French leaders were also involved, Milton told Murphy, Noguès in particular. He said that his brother was even being called a "fascist." "Heads must roll, Murphy!" he said. "Heads must roll."

Milton was then associate director of the Office of War Information (OWI), and he had personally suggested to Roosevelt that somebody, possible Harry Hopkins, be sent to North Africa to straighten out the mess. His brother was the center of most of the criticism, and the whole thing might, he said, end Ike's career. Roosevelt liked the idea of sending someone but said that Milton himself, not the ever-ailing Hopkins, should go to Algiers.

Once there, Milton got in touch with Drew Middleton, who told him that the only press communications cable connecting Africa and the United States and Europe had been severed by a sunken ship. Thus, correspondents in North Africa were unable to send out their stories by wire, and the only news of what was going on was coming from broadcasts made by the powerful Radio Maroc in Rabat. The staff members were all ardent Gaullists and thus vociferously opposed anything that was favorable to men like Darlan. On Milton's orders, the Gaullists were soon replaced by an eager young graduate of Princeton,

C. D. Jackson, who was later to play a large part in Dwight Eisenhower's political career. Cable service to London was soon restored, and that, too, helped to make available differing points of view from North Africa.

Marshall also tried to aid the general. In a letter to Elmer Davis, head of the OWI, the chief of staff said that he hoped Davis could help Eisenhower with his press relations. He said, "I am very much worried about the terrific pressure being put on him more or less to do the impossible. . . . I want to give him the chance to do what he was sent to Africa to do and I hope you can find some way to take off the pressure and bring the press to a practical realization of his difficulties, without advertising them to the enemy." In his reply Davis promised that his organization would "do what it can to help."

Milton stayed in Algiers ten days. He did not see much of his brother, but Ike felt that the visit was very helpful. He wrote to an army public relations officer in the War Department, "Unquestionably my brother's visit to this sector has accomplished a lot of good. Not only did I learn for the first time of some of the intricacies of the press relations problem at home, but he was able to uncover for us many weaknesses here that had been heretofore overlooked, either because of the press of overwork and lack of personnel or because we simply could not find out what was happening."

December 24 had been chosen as the day for what the general called "our final and most ambitious attack. Our chief hope for success lay in our temporary advantage in artillery, which was relatively great. But reports from the Tunisian front were discouraging; the weather, instead of improving, continued to deteriorate. Prospects for another attack grew darker."

Early in the morning of the 23rd, Eisenhower once more started for the front, this time accompanied by Butcher and Brigadier John F. M. Whiteley, his British deputy chief of staff. In his book Butcher headed his recollections of the journey "General Mud—and the Assassination of Darlan." They encountered what Eisenhower called "miserable road conditions from the moment we left Algiers. I met General Anderson at his headquarters on the morning of December 24 and with him proceeded at once to Souk el Khemis." V Corps, which was to make the attack, had its headquarters there, in a farmhouse; and in the muddy yard were various farm implements that must have been familiar to Butcher, the Iowa farm boy who had once edited the *Fertilizer Review*. Hayracks were used to hide slit trenches, and tunnels in haystacks were used to quarter some soldiers. No vehicles were allowed since their tracks might be seen from the air.

What Eisenhower saw caused him to make what he termed "a bitter decision." He called off the attack.

The general had "observed an incident, which, as much as anything else, convinced me of the hopelessness of an attack. A motorcycle was stuck in the mud just off the road, and four soldiers were trying to get it out. With every attempt the motorcycle sank deeper . . . and the soldiers finally gave up, leaving the machine sunk in the mud.

"We went back to headquarters," said Eisenhower, "and I directed that the attack be indefinitely postponed. . . . In such circumstances it is always necessary for the commander to avoid an attitude of defeatism; discouragement on the part of the high commander inevitably spreads rapidly throughout the command and always with unfortunate results. On that occasion, it was exceedingly difficult to display any particular optimism."

Anderson told Eisenhower that the attack could not possibly take place for at least six weeks, and a short while after that, according to Butcher, a "message came via telephone from General Clark, and it was put in terms so guarded that Ike suspected, but wasn't sure, that Darlan had been shot."

Just why Eisenhower would have "suspected, but wasn't sure, that Darlan had been shot" is never explained, never even discussed. Curious.

Clark in his book *Calculated Risk* does establish one fact. The Americans had finished with Darlan, "the Little Fellow." On the 23rd at a luncheon given by Darlan for Allied officials, the admiral turned to Clark and said, "Tomorrow the Axis press will say I gave this luncheon because a gun was pointed at my head." Clark replied, "If the rest of the luncheons were as good as this I would get my gun out every week." Darlan chuckled.

"A few minutes later, while I was talking to Mme. Darlan about the possibility of taking their stricken son to Warm Springs for treatment, I said (with the ulterior hope of getting a reaction from Darlan on his removal from the North African political scene), 'I think it could be arranged for Admiral Darlan to go, too, if he chooses.'

"I watched Darlan narrowly for a reaction. He nodded and said, 'I would like to turn this thing over to General Giraud; he likes it here, and I don't.' "

Late the next afternoon Murphy rushed into Clark's office. " 'They've shot the Little Fellow,' were his first words.

" 'You mean Darlan?' I asked. 'Where is he?'

" 'He's on his way to the hospital,' said Murphy.

" 'Let's go,' I said, heading immediately for the car."

Later Clark said what could not be denied, and indeed nobody tried to deny it. "Admiral Darlan's death was, to me, an act of Providence. It is too bad that he went that way, but, strategically speaking, his removal from the scene was like the lancing of a troublesome boil. He had served his purpose, and his death solved what could have been the very difficult problem of what to do with him in the future."

In those days before Harry Truman set up the CIA, political assassination on a government level was something that foreigners were familiar with, Americans never. Assassination was even more un-American than spying.

What had happened? About 2:30 in the afternoon of December 24, a twenty-year-old Frenchman named Bonnier de la Chapelle entered the summer palace in which Darlan had his headquarters. Some said the young man was a Gaullist, others that he was a royalist; Murphy later observed that the assassin came from a good family.

He signed the register and filled in a request to see a French employee, then waited in the corridor leading to Darlan's office. After a long lunch, Darlan returned to the summer palace and started for his office. Chapelle shot him twice, and the admiral died about an hour later in the same hospital in which his son was a patient. The young assassin tried to escape but was captured and taken to police headquarters. On Christmas morning he made a confession in writing and signed it. The police commissioner burned it immediately, and on the morning of December 26 Chapelle was shot by a firing squad. The court-martial records are still sealed.

A year after he was executed, according to the Associated Press, "A group of about 50 persons, the majority of whom fill official positions under the orders of General de Gaulle, celebrated the anniversary of the death of Fernard Eugène Bonnier de la Chapelle, who assassinated Admiral Darlan, by placing a wreath on his tomb and observing a minute of silence."

Later an Algerian court of appeals annulled the sentence, saying that Darlan had been an enemy of France and that what Bonnier had done was in the interest of the liberation of France.

In his biography of de Gaulle, Bernard Ledwidge says, "De Gaulle . . . in his Memoirs points the finger of suspicion at the Americans without actually naming them. He suggests that the exponents of the 'Temporary expedient' had come to feel that Darlan was now counterproductive and had therefore arranged for his elimination. As evidence in support of his theory he advances the indecent haste and the secrecy with which the assassin was put to death. Not even his name was revealed to the press before his execution, and there had been no time to interrogate him adequately. It was as if those in authority were anxious to conceal what might lie behind his deed—and those in authority were Giraud and the Americans."

After examining all the theories and the plots and subplots and rumors surrounding Darlan's death, Anthony Cave Brown, a biographer of William J. "Wild Bill" Donovan, founder of and leader of the Office of Strategic Services (OSS), said, "The fact seems to be that there was no official American involvement in the Darlan affair and it was solely the work of a group of hotheads . . . with, perhaps, French connections."

According to one de Gaulle biographer, Don Cook, a young American war correspondent, Virginia Cowles, was in London before the assassination, and at a dinner party she heard a number of Frenchmen denouncing Darlan and the stupid Americans. Miss Cowles said, "Darlan is a Frenchman and the French ought to be able to deal with him themselves." A few days later an anonymous Frenchman called her and said that if she watched the newspapers she would see that her advice had been taken. Two days later Darlan was shot.

It seems unlikely that the mystery surrounding Darlan's death will ever be solved completely, and it is equally unlikely that the Allied high command in Algiers had anything to do with it, beyond applauding it, that is. The day before he was murdered, Darlan told Murphy, "You know there are four plots in existence to assassinate me. Suppose one of these plots is successful. What will you Americans do?"

Murphy said that the admiral spoke of his own possible death as if he were discussing somebody else's.

At 10:00 P.M. on Christmas Eve Eisenhower and Butcher started back to Algiers. They had breakfast in Constantine, where the news of Darlan's death was confirmed. They were back at the St. Georges by 6:00 P.M. on the 25th. Butcher said, "Ike's comment while en route home from the east was that Darlan's death ended one problem, but no doubt created many more."

Eisenhower sent his regrets to Darlan's widow, attended his funeral, and said good things about him at a press conference, making it clear, however, that his praise applied only to the six weeks he had known the admiral.

On the 26th Eisenhower told the Combined Chiefs, "The continued rains have made impossible any decisive attack in the near future. By actual test, we have discovered that we cannot maneuver any type of vehicle off the roads and, since our real hope for victory lay in the skillful maneuver and use of our artillery to provide the punch necessary to blast the enemy's armor, the original plan has met an impasse. . . . The abandonment for the time being of our plan for a full-out effort has been the severest disappointment I have suffered to date."

★ ★ ★

POWER PLAYS

January 1943 was not a good month for Eisenhower; he nearly lost his life when a plane in which he was a passenger came close to crashing in the Atlas Mountains; he faced the possibility that he might have to return to the States in disgrace, return to his permanent rank of lieutenant colonel, and retire; not only that, he would have a reputation as a Nazi or a fascist or both. Moreover, near the end of the month he was given a grandiose title with no real power. It appeared that he would be reduced to arbitrating quarrels between querulous French generals, shaking hands, issuing pompous statements, presiding at banquets, and entertaining visiting dignitaries.

New Year's Eve, at least, went well. As one of his guests at the dinner party he gave, Brigadier Ian Jacob, said, "He finished the evening at 1:30 A.M. by calling and making a grand slam vulnerable, which put the seal on his happiness." The guests at the dinner party were nine men and five women, among them Kay Summersby.

The next day in writing Mamie about his victory at bridge he did not mention Mrs. Summersby; in fact it was some time before Mamie knew that she was there. In his January 1 letter to Mamie, Ike said:

Darling girl:
    Last eve I wrote you my *final* letter for 1942. This morning I've been fighting for the time to send you my *first* of 1943. . . .
    For the first time here (and the second since leaving Washington) the household had a party last eve. 14 for dinner, nine men and five ladies. The biggest incident so far as I was concerned was a bridge hand I held. We'd played about four rubbers and were finally on the last one; both

vulnerable. I picked up—Hearts A, K, Q, J, XXXX—Spades, A, K, Q, XX. After picking myself off the floor, where I promptly fell—I studied the matter over, I wanted to bid 7 hearts, finally, but wanted to get there so as to get doubled and give me a chance for redouble. If I said 2 hearts, my partner might say 2 N T or 3 Ds or Cs. Then I'd bid spades. Since my 8 hearts made it almost certain that my partner held more spades than hearts, it seemed clear that finally I'd end up in 7 spades, where I did not want to be. I'd almost surely have to trump the first trick and that would leave me only 4 trumps if spades were called. So my first bid was 7 hearts. I still figured that my opponents might have at least 1 Ace and would double. It happened that one opponent held 2 Aces, but would not double. The hand was a lay down. . . . I promptly started for bed, where I went as soon as I got rid of all the guests. . . . Well, Sweetie—maybe this description is not as marvellous as I thought the hand was—but it had been so long since I touched a bridge card that I felt very proud of myself.

Kay arrived in Algiers on December 23 when Ike and Butcher were on their way to the front. She had sailed from Greenock, Scotland, in early December on a troopship that was sunk near Oran. Kay and her companions, among them the famous photographer-writer Margaret Bourke-White, had spent a miserable night, most of them in lifeboats, before being picked up by a British destroyer. She had seen her fiancé, Lieutenant Colonel Dick Arnold, briefly in Oran, then was flown to Eisenhower's headquarters in his B-17.

During her first week in Algiers, Ike invited her to his villa for dinner. She said, "Life in Algiers was not too much different from life in London. It was only the landscape that was different, and at that we still had those familiar barrage balloons dotting the sky." There were a great many air raids, and they played a good deal of bridge. "Ike had the place of honor, in front of the fire," said Kay, "and although he complained that his backside was getting roasted, he was obviously glad of the warmth. He was developing another of his colds. Sometimes it seemed as if his colds had colds."

When she first arrived, Kay stayed in a maternity hospital, the Clinique Clycine, which was only five minutes away from Eisenhower's headquarters in the St. Georges. But within a few days, at Eisenhower's suggestion, she moved to a small house shared by five WAAC officers she had known in London, including Ruth Briggs, Beetle Smith's secretary and a superb bridge player.

The others she shared quarters with were Mattie Pinnette, Ike's secretary-steno; Martha Rogers, Louise Anderson and Arline Drexel. Kay was to share living quarters with these five women throughout the war—in London, in France, and in Germany.

Mamie found out that Kay was in North Africa from the February 22 issue of *Life*. If Mamie didn't buy it herself, no doubt a large number of army wives in Washington made sure that she saw it. The magazine contained Margaret Bourke-White's detailed account of the bombing of the *Strathallen*, although, of course, the ship was not named. The headline read *Women in Lifeboats, Torpedoed on an African-Bound Troopship, Photographer Finds Them as Brave in War as Men*. Bourke-White wrote about boarding Lifeboat No. 12, saying that among the passengers was "the irrepressible Kay Summersby, Eisenhower's pretty Irish driver." She said that Kay was one of the first who "began joking." Kay "announced her breakfast order. She wanted eggs sunny-side up and no yolks broken. One soldier said he'd take his brandy with a dash of hot milk in it."

Nothing in the story was likely to have comforted Mamie back at the Wardman Park. "A splendid big Scottish girl, Elspeth Duncan, one of General Eisenhower's clerical staff, made the best rower of all. . . . Lieutenant Ethel Westerman of Englewood, N.J., on her way to be chief nurse of the General Dispensary Headquarters, still had her rosary, and blonde, petite Jeanne Dixon of Washington, D.C., secretary to General Eisenhower, had saved her prayer book." There were several pictures of the women in the lifeboats, and many of them were very attractive, but Mamie rightly decided that "the irrepressible Kay Summersby" was the one she had to worry about. And she wrote Eisenhower immediately. On March 2 he replied:

You are all that any man could ask as a *partner* and a *sweetheart*.

So *Life* says my old London driver came down! So she did—but the big reason she wanted to serve in this theater is that she is terribly in love with a young American Colonel and is to be married to him come June—assuming both are alive. I doubt that *Life* told that. But I tell you only so that if anyone is banal and foolish enough to lift an eyebrow at an old duffer such as I am in connection with Waacs—Red Cross workers—nurses and drivers—you will know that I've no emotional involvements and will have none. Ordinarily I don't try to think of all the details surrounding my existence when I write to you—they are all unimportant compared to the real things I like to talk to you about. And, by the way, my own driver is a Sergeant Drye [*sic*].

While those years as commander of the U.S. forces in the European Theater of Operations were triumphant and satisfying for Eisenhower, they were the hardest of her life for Mamie, particularly after rumors started that he was having an affair with Kay, who almost everyone agreed was his mistress.

On January 2 a most elegant English gentleman, the Honorable Harold Macmillan, arrived at Eisenhower's headquarters. Eisenhower did not know that Macmillan was a close friend of Churchill's, that he had been a Tory member of Parliament since the 1920s, and that he was head of his family's distinguished publishing firm. The general had not officially been told that Macmillan was coming or for what; all he knew was what he had heard on the radio.

Eisenhower did not grin when he saw Macmillan. He said, "Pleased to see you, but what have you come for?"

Macmillan tried to explain that he was to be Minister Resident at Eisenhower's headquarters. But, he said, "The conversation began to languish. Happily, I thought of my own background and I began to ask whether he knew my mother's state. 'What do you mean, your mother? Why should I know that?' 'My mother was born in Indiana,' I said, 'at a little town called Spencer. So I'm a Hoosier.' This disclosure gave him pleasure, and after that we got on better."

Macmillan said of his first meeting with Eisenhower, "Although it was an inauspicious start, our relations were destined to ripen into a close comradeship and friendship, and to last over many years of war and peace."

Eisenhower later wrote of his "old friend," Harold Macmillan, "I had first become acquainted with Macmillan in Algiers in 1943, where he was assigned as my political adviser. From the start I found him more than competent; my high opinion of him had been frequently expressed in later years, publicly and privately."

In January 1957, when Macmillan succeeded Anthony Eden as prime minister of Britain, President Eisenhower wrote to congratulate him, adding:

"Welcome . . . to your new headaches. Of course you have had your share in the past, but I assure you that the new ones will be to the old [as] a broken leg is to a scratched finger. . . . Knowing you so long and well I predict that your journey will be a great one. But you must remember the old adage, 'Now abideth faith, hope and charity . . . and greater than these is a sense of humor.' "

In his first interview with Macmillan, Eisenhower complained at the names he was being called. "I'm no reactionary," he said. "Christ on the Mountain! I'm as idealistic as hell. Now that poor Darlan has been killed we've got this Giraud and no one can attack his record. We're going to get a new governor for Algeria. It's a guy called Pie-row-ton. They tell me he's a fine guy." The "they" was undoubtedly Murphy, who was once again wrong. Murphy later said that he had not done enough investigating into the affairs of Marcel Peyrouton, but the fact that Peyrouton had been minister of the interior of the Vichy government had been widely publicized both in the American and the British press. It was also well known that he had been responsible for tens of thousands of enemies of the Vichy government being jailed and tortured. He had been in Interior when the first decrees against French Jews were issued. Besides, as Murphy later said, the idea of using Peyrouton had been Darlan's.

Whose idea it was didn't matter. Peyrouton, under Eisenhower's order, came from Argentina, where he had been the Vichy ambassador, to serve in Algeria. The protests, almost all of them directed at Eisenhower alone, were in many cases even greater than the protests over Darlan.

Eisenhower's health continued to suffer. He had had what was later diagnosed as "walking pneumonia" since he first arrived in Algiers on November 23, and on January 7 after what Butcher described as "a solid month of colds, sniffles, and general below-par physical condition, Ike laid in bed until lunch, then got up and sat by the fire. . . . Carpetbags under his eyes."

That same day Arthur Krock, the Washington columnist of the *New York Times*, came to Eisenhower's defense saying that "an authoritative person," had told him that Ike was being "required to fight two wars when one is enough for any man to handle. . . . the President at a Cabinet meeting told all present that in North Africa General Eisenhower is the boss and he did not want him interfered with or undermined by anyone. The President added that Robert Murphy, the State Department's representative, was in charge of civilian affairs, but he wished to make it clear that when he said under, he meant under.

"Despite the plaguing to which the authoritative person quoted above referred, General Eisenhower had been assured by the responsible American authorities and told he need not worry too much about defending his course of action." It seems unlikely that Ike saw that column; he seldom saw an American newspaper in those days, and at the time, far from getting support from Washington and from the president in particular, he was only getting additional headaches.

Actually the bad news began in December; on the 23rd Eisenhower had been told by Marshall that the Combined Chiefs of Staff and the president of the United States and the prime minister of Great Britain were considering plans to meet in North Africa "in the near future." Were there facilities for such a meeting in Morocco? "Some of the party, including myself, could visit your headquarters. Please give me your opinion on feasibility and practicability of holding meeting as indicated."

Unofficially, Eisenhower was not overjoyed at the idea. However, it was decided that the best place to hold the conference was in Casablanca, and as the local commander, Patton was in charge of security for the awesome visitors; still, Eisenhower was Patton's commander, and it was his theater, a place where security was difficult, perhaps impossible. It was said that fifty American dollars and probably a great many fewer could buy the assassination of anybody in the medina of Casablanca.

Security was not the only problem, either, probably not even the most important. There was the grave danger that the prime minister and the president would arrive with ideas, quite likely dangerous and unwelcome ideas, about the conduct of the war. Churchill thought that he had inherited the military genius of his ancestor, the 1st Duke of Marlborough, and Roosevelt felt that a stint as assistant secretary of the navy had qualified him to be a military strategist.

Eisenhower liked and honored both men, but he couldn't help thinking how much better off everybody and everything would be if they stayed out of his theater. War was his business and politics was theirs, and at the moment his troubles about Darlan and those involving Peyrouton made it seem quite likely that he could never be elected to anything, and that was the way he wanted it. Roosevelt, on the other hand, was thinking of the trip as a lark, a welcome vacation in the sunshine after the gray fall and early winter of Washington.

The main purpose of the meeting was to discuss Allied strategy following the capture of Tunisia. Stalin had also been invited but said he was too busy with military matters to attend. Besides, he was unhappy with the continued absence of a second front.

On New Year's Eve, while Eisenhower was winning at bridge, Roosevelt and his friends and family at the White House saw Humphrey Bogart and Ingrid Bergman in *Casablanca*. Robert Sherwood said, "Very few of those present . . . had any idea as to the significance of its selection."

From January 7 until the 13th Eisenhower spent most of his time in bed. On the 11th and 12th doctors took his blood pressure; it was high both days, 168, but according to Butcher, the doctors said that it wasn't "at all unusual for any man who has been and is going through what he is." He did make one hurried trip to Constantine to confer with Anderson and Fredendall at the advance command post. Then he returned to his office for work on the 13th, and there he got what was really the first good news since he arrived in Algiers. It was a letter from McNarney, saying that he knew from daily conferences with Marshall that "You have his complete confidence." McNarney added, "You amaze me with your ability to keep your composure and your sense of humor."

In his reply, Ike said, "I quite agree with you that the gaining of the Chief's confidence is the biggest compliment that can be paid to any officer in this or any other army."

About his composure and his sense of humor he added:

There is no use denying that at times discouragement has piled on top of discouragement with such rapidity as to threaten my sense of humor. Except for the knowledge that you and people in the department understood the matter and were backing me up in meeting a military crisis, I shudder to think what might have happened. There have been many times when I could have taken action that would have been far more popular, at least for public consumption, than what I did. Entirely aside from all other considerations, I don't see how a fellow could follow that path and last long in any army.

The biggest disappointment we have is the delay in launching a final all-out offensive for Tunisia. Sometimes I get so impatient I want to run up to Medhez-el-Bab, grab a rifle myself and start fighting Germans. It is a real exercise in self-control to keep yourself doing your own job and pounding away at it day after day. . . .

Out of current negotiations will unquestionably come very important decisions, but until we get Tunisia these are not I feel going to affect this force greatly. However, I am delighted to be looking forward beyond that phase of the thing, because—as I told the Chief—some day we have got to go across that Channel if we are going to whip Germany. You and I have always agreed on this point, and I am counting on you to stick with me in this conviction.

Eisenhower did not then know that when he got to Casablanca on the 15th a divided American delegation would meet with a united British delegation that had in mind preventing a crossing of "that Channel" in 1943. Once again the British won. As Eisenhower's successor at OPD, Handy, said, "We were snowed under at Casablanca on the planning level. There wasn't any question about that."

For a man opposed to imperialism, Roosevelt often acted in a most imperial manner, and that happened before he arrived in Casablanca for the troublesome conference.

The president did not seem to understand the circumstances under which the Allied forces under Eisenhower were in North Africa, and he did not seem to want to take the trouble to understand. On January 3 he sent a secret telegram to Churchill saying, "I feel very strongly that in view of the fact that in North Africa we have a military occupation, our commanding general [Eisenhower] has complete control of all affairs, both civil and military. Our French friends must not be permitted to forget this for a moment. . . . If these local officials will not cooperate, they will have to be replaced. . . . I am not quite sure whether Eisenhower can hold Giraud in line, but I shall soon find out."

Eisenhower saw the cable through the British Foreign Office, and he was both furious and frightened by what it said. In the first place, the Allies were not occupying the area, and Eisenhower could not order Giraud to do anything. Suppose that proud Frenchman refused. Suppose he resigned. Suppose he simply said no as he had several times at Gibraltar.

If Giraud refused to do what Eisenhower demanded and said, in essence, "Okay. You take over the job," Ike would have to take over the job, "in addition to his other duties," in army parlance. Patton had said that if the Allies were on their own in Morocco, it would take 60,000 soldiers to keep the peace, or even try to keep the peace. In addition, the French guarding the Allied lines of communication to the front would be withdrawn, and so would the French combat troops, which would be brought back to Algiers, Oran, and Casablanca. As Butcher said, "Instead of active help from our re-created ally, we would have little help, probably passive resistance à la Gandhi, or possible resumption of French fighting Americans *pour l'honneur*."

If any of those things happened, it would, Butcher added, be necessary to "kiss Tunisia good-bye until we can build up with troops and equipment, not only to pursue the Tunisian objective, but to police the great expanse of French North Africa."

If what the president ordered were to bring on French resistance, Butcher added, "Ike said he would of course carry out the order, but would then ask to be relieved, which would no doubt mean reversion to the rank of lieutenant colonel and retirement."

But did one tell his commander in chief that his ideas were dangerous nonsense? One did not. One told the Combined Chiefs of Staff that, "A review of the military situation, as it now stands, quickly demonstrates that only intensity of effort, full and effective military cooperation from the French, and freedom from diversions and dispersions can give us any promise of victory in the approximate future. The latest intelligence reports indicate that the enemy has in Tunisia some 50,000 troops with at least 250 tanks."

On the 5th in a "for your eyes only" personal message to Marshall, Ike guardedly said, "We have learned that in some quarters at home there is an apparent conviction that we are in North Africa fully capable of carrying out our military mission and, if need be, of controlling the population by force. . . .

"I am writing this message for your exclusive and confidential information with the request that when opportunity arises you do what you can to correct or soften this view at least to the extent that during the ensuing critical weeks we do not receive any arbitrary instructions which might precipitate a military crisis.

"We did not take the easy, safe course, and I know you have always agreed that the decision to rush ahead although risky was fully justified. . . . I will be prompt in reporting to you personally when the time arrives that we are strong enough to disregard, if so ordered, French and other viewpoints. The immediate effect of non-cooperation now would be catastrophic. . . . This matter is purely military."

It seemed unnecessary to mention that the "some quarters" he referred to were in the White House.

Fortunately, by the time Roosevelt arrived for the Casablanca conference the whole thing appeared to be forgotten. Roosevelt's principal interest appeared to be to do what Churchill wanted him to do and to arrange a "shotgun marriage" between de Gaulle and Giraud. None of the Americans were very serious at Casablanca.

Eisenhower made plenty of mistakes of his own during this nervous period. In late November and for part of December he had imposed censorship on political reporting from his theater, and it was not until the end of January that the censorship was ended. He had not wished to resort to this measure, "even though from a good motive. . . . Because of general dislike of censorship, I had to be convinced that the reason for such action was important. In this case it was."

He had undertaken the move largely on the advice of Murphy and Macmillan, who had hoped to bring about some kind of rapprochement between Giraud and de Gaulle. The followers of the two men for weeks had been calling each other names in broadcasts and in print. The application of censorship made the name-calling a private matter. Eisenhower said, "I think the censorship had some of the desired effect, and it was lifted the second I learned that Giraud and de Gaulle had agreed to meet at Casablanca."

Ike was a man seldom troubled by regret, and he did not often admit to error. However, according to Robert Sherwood in *Roosevelt and Hopkins*, "Years later . . . Eisenhower said to me that he believed this action had been a mistake—that 'Censorship is never the answer.' "

In any case, censorship was less than totally effective. When Lincoln Barnett, a *Life* correspondent who had been ordered out of North Africa for a censorship violation, wrote on February 23, thanking the general for not making the punishment more severe, Eisenhower replied:

Dear Barnett:
Perhaps you will not object to my giving you one little item from my own habits of life—or—to put it in language a bit more flowery—from my philosophy. An offense once committed and punished is, so far as I am concerned, forgotten. Neither the offender nor those who are compelled to take action in the case should allow it to assume such an importance, thereafter, that it precludes the possibility of washing clean the slate. You committed a grave offense and it was quite true that the action I took in the case was less severe than my staff advocated; but I have no doubt about your basic abilities and, moreover, about your integrity of purpose in this desperate war. I feel that your zeal as a reporter and your recognition of the elements of drama in a particular story, led you into an error which I feel quite sure you will not repeat. So you must not let any such thing ruin your future usefulness; on the contrary, you should now go ahead as if the thing had never happened and re-establish yourself, not only in the good opinion of your employers but in the confidence of all those with whom you have to deal. I rather recoil from appearing in the role of lecturer and am just a bit hesitant about sending to you what I have dictated. However, I do feel, honestly, what I have just said and I hope you will take it in that spirit.

Eisenhower flew to Casablanca on the morning of January 15. Roosevelt and Churchill were already there. Churchill had arrived at Anfa, the suburb just outside Casablanca where the conference was held, early in the morning of the 13th; the villa that was to be his while there was part of a beautiful hotel compound overlooking the sea. Churchill immediately met with his advisers, telling them to be patient with the one-time British colonists, the Americans. The British arguments, he said, should be as "the dripping of water on a stone." Portal said it more directly. "We are in the position of a testor who wishes to leave the bulk of his fortune to his mistress," he said. "He must, however, leave something for his wife, and his problem is to decide how little he can with decency leave apart for her."

Handy did not attend the conference, but he heard tales of the British successes from many colleagues who did, particularly Brigadier General Albert C. Wedemeyer. Handy said of the British, "One thing they understood, the Prime Minister above all, was the principle of the objective. You headed them off one way and they'd come at you in another way. Their Army, their Navy, their Air Force had got together and agreed on a *British* view. Our people, our Army and Air Force and Navy people, they all had their own point of view, and they were all behind the eight ball."

Arthur Bryant, Brooke's biographer, said of Casablanca, "The British were quite clear about what they wanted, and, under Brooke's chairmanship, presented to their political chiefs and allies an unshakeable front. Behind them and the Defense Minister was a streamlined professional organization, the result of years of evolution and experience. For every argument they advanced they were able to produce chapter and verse, with plans and statistics worked out to the last detail."

The chapters and verses, the plans and statistics, were all in a converted 6,000-ton British liner that had arrived in the port at Casablanca, along with a staff of clerks. Whenever a difference of opinion arose between the British and the Americans, the clerks immediately found the answer to whatever it was, and it always turned out that the British answer was not only the right one; it was the only one.

Thus, the British had come to the conference convinced that a cross-Channel invasion of the continent was out of the question for 1943. The Americans reluctantly—Marshall was particularly reluctant—agreed. The chief of staff had come to the conference on the 13th, the same day Churchill arrived. The British wanted what the Americans did not want, more activity in the Mediterranean. One British observer said that his American cousins looked on the Mediterranean "as a kind of dark hole, into which one entered at one's peril" and that if large forces were employed there "the door would be suddenly and firmly shut behind them." The British won that one, too. It was decided at Casablanca that the Allies would drive northeast through Sicily to Italy. Churchill called it "the soft underbelly" of Europe, which proved to be one of the least accurate statements made during the war.

Sir Ian Jacob, who was secretary to Brooke during the conference, said, "When the British chiefs saw how the land lay and the size of our party, they suddenly woke up to the fact that they had left most of their clubs behind."

Roosevelt had arrived in Anfa on the 14th, taking over a second great villa not far from Churchill's. Their respective staffs had to make do with the hotel itself. Macmillan said that Churchill's villa—"The Emperor of the East's villa"—was loosely guarded while that of Roosevelt—Macmillan called him "Emperor of the West"—"was difficult to assess. If you approached it by night searchlights were thrown upon you, and a horde of what I believe are called G-men, mostly retired Chicago gangsters, drew revolvers and covered you." The whole thing, Macmillan said, was a "mixture between a cruise, a summer school and a conference . . . when they got out of school at five o'clock or so, you would see Field-Marshals and Admirals going down to the beach for an hour to play with the pebbles and make sand castles."

Eisenhower had taken Butcher with him to Casablanca. Butcher had one great political asset; he talked a good deal through perfect teeth and a perpetual smile; and he never managed to say anything much. Besides he knew Harry Hopkins, who had come with Roosevelt to North Africa. Ike's naval aide was very much at home with the people then in power in Washington. Butcher had an agreeable personality, and had he chosen to go into politics, he might well have been successful.

The plane on which the two men traveled was a creaky B-17, retired from combat duty, and they stopped at Oujda, where Eisenhower conferred briefly with Clark. There is no record of what Clark and Ike said to each other, but later that day at Casablanca Patton, after meeting with Eisenhower, said, "He and Clark are at outs." That may or may not have been true, but Patton said of Eisenhower, "He thinks his thread is about to be cut."

When Butcher and Ike continued their flight over the Atlas Mountains, Eisenhower said that "The journey became somewhat hazardous owing to the loss of two engines. Under order of the pilot, Captain Jack Reedy, we flew the last fifty miles of the journey with all the passengers standing by the nearest exits, equipped in parachutes and ready to jump on an instant's notice. With an anxious thought for an old football knee, I was delighted that I did not have to adopt this method of disembarkation."

Butcher said that during the flight "The propeller shaft had broken, preventing feathering, and causing danger of disintegration."

When Ike took off his parachute, he dislodged one of his stars and asked Butcher to help him get it back in place. Butcher had great difficulty in doing it, and Ike said, "Haven't you ever fastened a star before?"

Butcher said, "Yes, sir, but never with a parachute on, sir."

Over the Casablanca landing field, Eisenhower said, the pilot "got one more engine working briefly and with increased power made a fine landing."

Eisenhower, who wanted to return to Algiers as quickly as possible, ordered the plane to be repaired immediately, and about an hour and a half later, when he was in a meeting with the Combined Chiefs of Staff, he got a message from the commander of the airfield saying, "It is impossible to repair your plane. It's being scrapped immediately and will never fly again."

Eisenhower said, "When I saw that report, the realization of how lucky we had been to make the landing struck me with full force."

An old friend, Major General Ira C. Eaker, commander of the Eighth Air

Force, was in Casablanca for the conference, and he loaned Ike his own plane to return to Algiers the next morning.

Patton met Eisenhower and Butcher when they arrived at the Casablanca airport. Patton said, "I took them to Anpha [*sic*] and met Admiral King, who, when off duty, is most affable." The British encouraged King to talk a good deal. As Brooke said, they felt that " 'Uncle Ernie' would take a less jaundiced view of the rest of the world if he had been able to shoot his line and really get it off his chest."

Eisenhower was not at Casablanca to make decisions. He was there to be looked over by his bosses, the president and the prime minister and the Joint Chiefs, and it was apparent from the beginning that he had better impress them. Butcher said, "Eisenhower's neck is in a noose, and he knows it." Sherwood said, "For a time there was some doubt whether Eisenhower would remain in command for HUSKY [the invasion of Sicily that was being planned]. General Alexander, who outranked him, was now moving into Tunisia from the south with the victorious British forces under the field command of General Montgomery. Here was tough professional competition for Eisenhower at a moment when his own position was most insecure, and I believe he would not have been greatly surprised if he had been put under Alexander or transferred elsewhere."

Eisenhower, unlike the British, had come to the conference with no notes at all. He had told Marshall before the conference, "I shall be ready to render a complete accounting for prior decisions and actions. . . . I plan to do it from my own memory and do not intend, unless you otherwise direct, to bring with me a group of staff officers and records to fill in technical details. I feel so confident of my complete familiarity with all major factors that I think technicians would be a mere hindrance."

Immediately after his arrival Ike had lunch with Marshall and King. Butcher said, "This was the first of a series of unending conferences for Ike. He kept on with them until well after midnight."

Sherwood said that there was "quite a family gathering" in Roosevelt's villa. Hopkins' son Robert was there. He was an army sergeant, and Eisenhower had ordered him to come from Tunisia to meet his father. Two of Roosevelt's sons, Colonel Elliott Roosevelt and Lieutenant Franklin, Jr., were there, and so was Churchill's son Randolph, a captain in the British Commandos, the British Special Service Brigade. The presence of Roosevelt's two sons was widely criticized in the American press, and a great many soldiers in and near the theater complained that since their fathers were not president they never got to go anywhere. (I felt that way and said so, many times.)

In meeting with the president and the prime minister, Eisenhower spoke at length, and he spoke, as he said he would, without notes. Said Sherwood:

He stated his case to the president and prime minister with courage and conviction. . . . He made no attempt to disguise his ignorance of European politics, having spent most of the prewar years in the Philippines. He said that when the name of Peyrouton was mentioned to him by Darlan and Murphy he had no idea who the man was and no knowledge of his background except that he had once been a successful official in Algiers, Tunisia, and Morocco. Eisenhower felt that this appointment should be checked with the State Department, which first said, "Yes" to it and then "No" and finally "Yes." (Eisenhower of course did not know that the "No" was from [Under Secretary of State Sumner] Welles and the final "Yes" from [Secretary of State Cordell] Hull.) He defended his much-criticized action in imposing political censorship on North Africa on the ground that the de Gaullists were pouring hostile propaganda from their station in Brazzaville and he did not want to advertise the conflict to the world by permitting the radio stations in Morocco or Algiers to talk back in this verbal war.

Roosevelt thought Eisenhower looked "jittery." Sherwood in his account of the conference added that, "Eisenhower had ample reason to seem jittery." He mentions the "bad cold" that had turned into what he calls "severe grippe. . . . Although the initial operation under his [Eisenhower's] command had been an inspiring success, he had subsequently seen the high hopes for quick victory in Tunisia frustrated; far worse than this for a good soldier was the bewildering political mess in which he found himself involved and for which he was so ill-prepared."

Ike did get some good news that day. Alexander said that the British were about to take Tripoli and that, if the port had not been destroyed, the Eighth Army would be at the southern border of Tunisia by the first week in March.

Early that evening Ike got word that Roosevelt wanted to see him alone. He said, "This was one of several intimate and private conversations I had with Mr. Roosevelt during the war. His optimism and buoyancy, amounting almost to lightheartedness, I attributed to the atmosphere of adventure attached to the Casablanca expedition. . . . While he recognized the seriousness of the war problems still facing the Allies, much of his comment dealt with the distant future, the post-hostilities tasks, including disposition of colonies and territories. . . .

"We went over in detail the military and political developments of the preceding ten weeks; he was obviously and outspokenly delighted with the progress we had made. . . . While both of us were aware that the Axis forces in Africa could not withstand the pincers effect that . . . Alexander's forces and our own were developing, President Roosevelt's estimate of the final collapse was, in my opinion, too sanguine by many weeks. Under his insistence that I name a date, I finally blurted out my most miraculous guess of the war. 'May 15,' I said. Shortly thereafter I told Alexander of this and he, with a smile, said that in answer to the same question at the conference he had replied 'May 30.' "

Roosevelt "constantly" referred to French North Africa and its inhabitants "in terms of orders, instructions, and compulsion. . . . He . . . continued, perhaps subconsciously, to discuss local problems from the viewpoint of a conqueror. It would have been so much easier for us if we could have done the same!" Ike said.

What looked in Casablanca like good news turned out to be very bad news. Eisenhower was told that it had been decided that "the British Eighth Army and the Desert Air Force, coming up through Tripoli and lower Tunisia, would be assigned to the Allied forces under my command when once they had entered the latter province. During the day I spent at Casablanca I was informed of this general plan, but not until General Marshall later came to Algiers did I learn that it had been definitely approved."

Macmillan visited the president while both Eisenhower and Churchill were in Casablanca. He said:

> I found the president in a great bed. . . . At the head of the bed was sitting Churchill and, standing to attention like a Roman centurion on the other side, our Commander-in-Chief, General Eisenhower. As I came in through the door, the President threw up his hand in friendly greeting. "Hello, Harold," he called. "It is fine to see you—fine." Murphy soon joined us and a short discussion followed about conditions in North Africa. When I left, General Eisenhower came out with me. He seemed somewhat surprised. "You never told me," he said, "you were a friend of the President." "Well," I replied, "I don't think I am a particular friend but I have seen him several times in the United States and we have some friends in common." "How strange you English are," reflected the General. "If you had been an American, you would have told me that you were on Christian-name terms with the President of the United States." I replied, "Well, I am not sure that I am—not mutual; but that's just his way of being friendly." The General seemed still more perplexed. But, curiously enough, this little incident served me well with him.

Eisenhower, who always had a sharp eye for where the power was, naturally would have been more impressed with the fact that Macmillan knew the president than that his mother had been born in Indiana.

Eventually, while Eisenhower was with the president and the prime minister, Hopkins and the Combined Chiefs joined them. Ike stayed up until 1:30 talking with Georgie, and the next morning, as had been planned before leaving Algiers, he gave Patton another DSM.

Then he and Butcher flew back to Algiers in Eaker's B-17. What he learned in Casablanca had in general been disappointing to Eisenhower. His future was still in doubt because he had done what his bosses, particularly the president and the prime minister, had wanted done, but when it had proved to be unpopular, according to Butcher, "the President and the Prime Minister . . . had their noses to the political winds and weren't going to get caught holding the bag for a general who had made an unpopular decision and hadn't yet got Tunisia." Roosevelt had made it clear to Marshall at Casablanca that there was simply no good reason for giving Ike another star.

Butcher said that while Ike was at the conference "his work and leadership had been taken rather for granted. His bosses hadn't been at all effusive in praise. . . . But such is the life of generals. . . . They have tossed out awards and promotions to Ike's subordinates (or rather Ike has). . . . Ike remains a lieutenant general, with his three stars dimmed by the four- and five-star subordinates."

One thing Eisenhower had said to Roosevelt impressed the president, so much so that he repeated it to Hopkins. Ike had said, "I believe in a theater commander doing these things [choosing Darlan and Peyrouton] without referring them back to his home government for approval. If a mere general makes a mistake, he can be reprimanded and kicked out and disgraced. But a government cannot kick out and disgrace itself, not at any rate, in wartime."

But the president had not mentioned how he felt to Eisenhower.

Eisenhower must have had a few unkind thoughts about British behavior at Casablanca, but he kept them, as he often said, "in the family," and when he heard that friends like Handy and Gailey felt that the Americans had been betrayed at the conference, he wrote Handy a soothing letter:

Dear Tom:

The great meeting has passed into history and I hope that history will declare the decisions to be wise ones. Frankly, I do not see how the "big bosses" could have deviated very far from the general course of action they adopted. ROUNDUP, in its original conception, could not possibly be staged before August of 1944, because our original conceptions of the strength required were too low. Inaction in 1943 could not be tolerated and, unfortunately, distances are so great that we could not devote 1943 to one enemy and 1944 to another. One may question, if so minded, the specific objectives chosen, but in all such cases the pros and cons are usually rather evenly balanced and I am happy that a firm decision was reached.

There is one thing concerning which I have probably written you before, in which you and your division can always be of help. It is the matter of refusing to deal with military problems on an American vs British basis. I am not so incredibly naive that I do not realize that Britishers instinctively approach every military problem from the viewpoint of the Empire, just as we approach them from the viewpoint of American interests. But one of the constant sources of danger to us in this war is to regard as our first enemy the partner that must work with us in defeating the real enemy. . . .

He then explained how he had tried to achieve a partnership in his dealing with the British. He said:

The second anyone brings up an idea that sounds to me as if it represents a purely national rather than a United Nations attitude or viewpoint, I challenge him openly on the spot. I *think* that the results have been good. . . . I am not British and I am not ambidextrous in attitude. But I have got a very wholesome regard for the terrific tasks facing the United Nations in this war, and I am not going to let national prejudice or any of its evils prevent me from getting the best out of the means that you fellows labored so hard to make available to us. I do not wish to belabor the point, but it is a very important one and I commend it to your quiet reflection—it is never out of my mind for a second.

Two days after Eisenhower returned to Algiers, the Combined Chiefs agreed that the next operation would indeed be an invasion of Sicily.

The last day of the conference, Sunday, January 24, was probably the most important, in part because Giraud and de Gaulle had their pictures taken together, physically together anyway, and at a press conference in the afternoon Roosevelt said what a great many among the Allies, including Churchill, Marshall, and Eisenhower, wished he had not said. He said that the Axis powers must surrender unconditionally; no alternative was possible. And in a very large sense Eisenhower's recent troubles were responsible for that statement. Sherwood said, "His timing of the statement at Casablanca was attributable to the uproar over Darlan and Peyrouton and the liberal fears that this might indicate a willingness to make similar deals with a Goering in Germany or a Matsuoka in Japan."

On the 21st most of the American leaders, including Roosevelt and Hopkins, had had lunch with Clark's Fifth Army troops—boiled ham, sweet potatoes, and fruit salad, eaten al fresco while an artillery band played the "Missouri Waltz" and "Deep in the Heart of Texas."

That same day word was received at the conference that de Gaulle, thanks largely to the efforts of Anthony Eden and Churchill, had agreed to come to the conference. Giraud was already there, and he had been agreeable throughout. De Gaulle was not; Hopkins said he was "cold and austere," and in his first meeting with Roosevelt he had not been a success; on the other hand, de Gaulle had not returned to England.

On Sunday morning de Gaulle was a little less austere, and Churchill appeared in Roosevelt's suite while the president was being his most charming; the prime minister played the bad cop and shouted at the general, *"Mon general, il ne faut pas obstacler [sic] la guerre."* ("General, you must not obstacle the war.")

Then, according to Hopkins, "de Gaulle . . . agreed to a short statement, and before they [de Gaulle and Giraud] could catch their breath, the president suggested a photograph."

Then the four men went into the garden of the hotel compound. It was crowded with reporters and photographers, most of whom had flown in from Algiers. The two French generals did not smile, but they did shake hands; one observer said, "They did it as if they were touching sabers."

Churchill said, "The picture of this event cannot be viewed in the setting of these tragic times without a laugh."

The statement issued said, "We have met, we have talked. We have registered our agreement on the end to be achieved, which is the liberation of France and the triumph of human liberties by the total defeat of the enemy. This end will be attained by the union of all Frenchmen, fighting side by side with their allies."

Later at that same press conference, Roosevelt announced his policy of unconditional surrender; it was as if the idea had just occurred to him. "Some of you Britishers know the old story—we had a general, U.S. Grant. His name was Ulysses Simpson Grant, but in my early days, and the Prime Minister's early days, he was called 'Unconditional Surrender' Grant. The elimination of German, Japanese, and Italian war power means the unconditional surrender by Germany, Italy, and Japan. That seems a reasonable assurance of future world peace. It does not mean the destruction of the population of

Germany, Italy, or Japan, but it does mean the destruction of the philosophies in those countries, which are based on conquest and the subjugation of other people."

The idea had not been spontaneous; it had been discussed before Roosevelt left Washington and discussed with Churchill earlier in the conference. Roosevelt had not, however, told the prime minister that he intended to announce it in public, and Churchill was at first annoyed. Later he said that he had "frequently defended the decision. . . . It is false to suggest that it prolonged the war. Negotiation with Hitler was impossible. He was a maniac with supreme power to play his hand, which he did, and so did we."

Marshall said, "I think there was quite a possibility that the Germans and Japanese might have conceded the war a little earlier if it had not been for the unconditional surrender formula. However, I think it had a great psychological effect on our people, on the British people, and on the Allied people generally, as well as on the Germans when it was made . . . because we had been going through a period of defeats and now this came out as a declaration that we were going into this thing to the finish."

On the day before the press conference, Roosevelt, Churchill, and Hopkins had met with the Combined Chiefs and agreed on the conduct of the war for the rest of 1943. The battle of the Atlantic was considered most important; "security of sea communications" had to be achieved. In the second place came "assistance to Russia in relation to other commitments."

In the third place came something called "Operations in the Mediterranean." Sicily was to be captured, with the target date "the favorable July moon." Eisenhower was to be supreme commander.

Fourth, the American buildup in Britain was to continue and be intensified. The Americans were to begin daylight precision bombing, and nighttime bombing by the RAF was to continue. That was a small American triumph. The British didn't really think daylight bombing was feasible.

And although it wasn't to be that year, the British did commit themselves to a cross-Channel invasion. A British general, Frederick W. Morgan, was to be Chief of Staff to Supreme Allied Command. The work done by Morgan and his staff—soon to be known as COSSAC—in outlining the plans for an invasion proved to be invaluable for the man who did the job.

Finally, operations in the Pacific were to be continued "with the object of maintaining pressure on Japan." Burma was to be reconquered and the Burma Road was to be reopened.

The British were very pleased with what had happened. They had got what they came for; the liner, the documents, and the clerks had been a success, but then so had the prime minister and his staff, Brooke in particular. Churchill, apparently without irony, said, "I love these Americans. They have behaved so generously."

Eisenhower did not yet know what had been decided, but on January 19, three days after his return to Algiers, he wrote in his diary,

The past week has been a succession of disappointments. I'm just writing some down, so as to forget them.

a. The French began showing signs of complete collapse along the front as early as the 17th. Each day the tactical situation has gotten worse. We will be pushed to make a decent front covering Tunisia.

b. The aggressive action and local attack I had planned for the 24th and following days had to be abandoned.

c. The newspapers want my scalp for "political censorship"—but there is *none*. Has not been for two weeks. Why the yell?

d. Peyrouton's appt. to succeed the worthless Chatel has been received with howls of anguish at home. Who *do* they want? He is an experienced administrator and God knows it's hard to find many of them among the French in North Africa.

e. We've had our r.r. temporarily interrupted, twice. I'm getting weary of it but can't move the troops (even if I had enough) to protect the lines.

On the morning of the day Roosevelt was announcing his policy of unconditional surrender, Marshall, and his assistant, General Brehon, Somervell, Wedemeyer, Arnold, King, and Sir John Dill flew to Algiers. Marshall was very pleased with Eisenhower's quarters. He said he found them "homelike." Mickey had spent the previous day giving the house what he called "extra licks . . . getting everything polished up." Marshall was to have Eisenhower's room, and a red satin cover had been put on the bed. When Ike was showing the chief of staff the room, Telek got on the bed and, according to Eisenhower, "did what all little puppies do when they can contain themselves, or their bladders, no longer.

"General Marshall apparently detected a look of acute embarrassment on my face because he took it all with a grin and said, 'Apparently the dog doesn't realize who's to sleep here—or'—and he paused a second and then added—'or maybe he does!' "

There were no alerts that night, and the next morning before leaving, King said that he had had his first good night's sleep in a long time, then, aware that Ike's mood was less than joyous, he took the trouble to tell him that the navy and the whole country were behind him. He said that the three-star general had done a great job, which was the only compliment Eisenhower had had from anybody for some time. Butcher said that it helped Ike's morale. "It has seemed to me that so far as recognition is concerned, Ike has always been the bridesmaid, never the bride, but time will correct this."

During the visit, Marshall seemed more concerned with Ike's health than with strategy or French politics. Butcher felt that "his whole attitude toward Ike was that of father to son."

At breakfast on the morning of the 25th—Ike was already at work—the chief of staff "ordered" Butcher to see to it that Eisenhower didn't spend too much time at the office, that he take a nap and have a rubdown from a masseur every evening before dinner, and to try to get him to take some exercise, preferably horseback riding, which Marshall and Eisenhower both loved. Butcher was told, he said, to be sure that Ike did "things that relax his mind and body, so he can have a fresh point of view while meeting ever-pressing decisions.

"He may think he has troubles so far, including Darlan," said Marshall, "but he will have so many before this work is over that Darlan will be nothing. . . . He is too valuable an officer to overwork himself."

It was not until Marshall got to Algiers that it became definite that the British Eighth Army and the Desert Air Force would be under Eisenhower's command once they had entered Tunisia. As he had expected, Alexander would be his deputy, with Tedder commanding the air forces, and Cunningham continuing as naval commander. In other words, he would have three British assistants, all of whom outranked him, all of whom had more experience than he, and none of them burdened with military or political failure. At first glance the whole thing looked very good to him. "This development was extraordinarily pleasing to me," he said, "because it meant, first and foremost, complete unity of action in the central Mediterranean, and it provided needed machinery for effective planning and strategical co-ordination."

For once the expert bridge player and the master at poker was napping. He had been outthought and outmaneuvered by a man who was an ally but was not a friend, not then or ever, General Alan Brooke. On January 20, a few days after Casablanca, Brooke in his diary said, "The back of the work here has been broken and thank God for it! . . . At one time I began to despair of our arriving at any sort of agreement. Now we have got practically all we hoped to get when we came here.

"They [the Americans] are difficult, though charming people to work with." Then he deprecated three Americans. Of Marshall, he said, "[his] thoughts revolve round the creation of forces and not on their employment . . ."; of King, "[his] vision is mainly limited to the Pacific . . . although he pays lip service to the fundamental policy that we must first defeat Germany and then turn on Japan, he fails to apply it in any problems connected with the war." And Arnold "limits his outlook to the air and seldom mixes himself with other matters."

Getting to Eisenhower took a little longer. Brooke said, "On this date we had achieved another marked success. We had got agreement on the organization of Higher Command in North Africa. . . . It was clear that centralised command was essential to command the First and Eighth Armies and the American and French forces, but who was to be placed in this responsible position? From many points of view it was desirable to hand this command over to the Americans, but unfortunately up to now Eisenhower . . . had neither the tactical nor strategical experience required for such a task. By bringing Alexander over from the Middle East and appointing him as Deputy of Eisenhower, we were carrying out a move which could not help flattering and pleasing the Americans in so far as we were placing our senior and experienced commander to function under their commander who had no war experience. . . . We were pushing Eisenhower up into the stratosphere and rarified atmosphere of a Supreme Commander, where he would be free to devote his time to the political and inter-allied problems, whilst we inserted under him . . . our own commanders to deal with the military situations and to restore the necessary drive and co-ordination which had been so seriously lacking."

Eisenhower had not seen Brooke's diary—it was not published until 1957— but a man who had taken a good deal of trouble to understand the British point of view in these matters should, one would think, have wondered if the British general was not up to something. Yet it took Eisenhower some time to realize that he had been boxed in, that Brooke had him exactly where he wanted him, back in Algiers making small talk, shaking hands, reaching political decisions that were bound to be unpopular with some group or other, shelved with a high-sounding title. The title was commanding general of the North African theater, and he was to continue as commander in chief of the Allied forces there.

If Marshall warned him that something strange and suspicious was afoot, there is no record of it. Shortly after Marshall returned to Washington, Eisenhower wrote Handy, "The short visits that I had with him were more than stimulating, and I feel better able than ever to carry my own little burden when I realize how cheerfully and effectively he is marching under the heavy load he is carrying."

Marshall's advice notwithstanding, Ike had only one rubdown; then he dispensed with the masseur. On the 28th he was up at 7:00 and at the office at 8:15. He was furious; the charwomen ought to get their work done early so a man could breathe some fresh air.

The Russians continued to win the only Allied victories, in the Caucasus, in Tikhoretsk, and in Stalingrad. In Tunisia the American and French troops were withdrawing into the Faid Pass. Ike wrote Mamie on February 2, "Yesterday . . . all the news was bad! It takes a lot at times to keep the old grin going; but I'm always firmly of the belief that if one keeps on working and driving things will be better soon. So while my head may get bloody, it's never bowed." He advised her to pay their 1942 income tax "*early!* . . . I believe in taxes. I like to pay what the government expects of me. . . .

"At times I get so homesick for you that I want to jump up and down all over the floor of this office."

On the 3rd he had lunch with Patton and Clark. Clark was in command of the Fifth Army and was to build up what he called a "huge and intensive" training program that included, in Clark's words, "training for amphibious landings that put the men through countless tough experiences and prepared the teams that later made possible our thrusts against the European Continent. . . . There also were centers for airborne troops, tank destroyers, engineers and battle training." Patton was to command the American forces in the assault on Sicily, and at lunch Eisenhower said, according to Patton's diary, " 'George, you are my oldest friend, but if you or anyone else criticize the British, by God, I will reduce him to his permanent grade, and send him home. . . .'

"Later I asked Clark if I had been accused. Clark said no, and that Ike talked to him the same way. Clark thinks General Marshall told Ike to do it to all of us. 'Cromwell, beware ambition, by it the angels fell.' "

The next day, feeling that he had perhaps spoken too harshly to his "oldest friend," Eisenhower wrote Patton a few more words of advice, saying that "it occurred to me that part of my conversation with you may have sounded as if I were irritated. I feel sure you understand that I had nothing in mind but the friendliest of intentions." He advised him, however, to " 'count ten before you speak.' This applies not only to criticism of Allies, a subject on which I am adamant, but to many others. A man once gave to me an old proverb. It was this: 'Keep silent and appear stupid; open your mouth and remove all doubt.' I do not mean this applies to you, as you damn well know, but I do mean that a certain sphinx-like quality upon occasion will do one hell of a lot toward enhancing one's reputation.''

The letter didn't comfort George much; such well-meant letters seldom do. Patton wrote a reply, saying that maybe his trouble was that he didn't act "sufficiently over-awed in the presence of high personages and therefore speak too freely.'' He never sent the letter, and his troubles in Sicily resulted from what he said and did in the presence of people who were not "high personages.'' He outranked everybody, and his attacks were not on Allies but on two young soldiers in his command.

Churchill and his party arrived in Algiers on February 5. Eisenhower had not been happy before they arrived, and he was not happy while they were there. Eisenhower had not mentioned security to his distinguished guest, but, as he later wrote Marshall, "I have had a crowded two weeks, starting with the visit of the prime minister on the 5th and 6th. Providing for his protection was quite a mental burden upon us, since we had received a message from London indicating that a definite attempt would be made to knock him off.''

Churchill arrived at Maison Blanche airport on February 5; he was brought to the headquarters in Algiers in an armored car that had its windows smeared with oil and mud for purposes of camouflage. It proceeded to Algiers by a circuitous route. Brooke, who was driven to Ike's headquarters in his own car flanked by a man with a tommy gun and with Eisenhower himself armed with a pistol, said, "I could see Eisenhower was somewhat worried with the responsibility of having him [Churchill] on his hands.''

The prime minister stayed in Cunningham's villa; Churchill wrote Roosevelt that it was "next door to General Eisenhower's. Both are surrounded by barbed wire and heavily guarded and patrolled. . . . I do not propose leaving precincts. No one considers in these circumstances any danger, provided precautions are taken.''

Churchill had insisted on a luncheon for twelve, and the guests included both Giraud and de Gaulle as well as three Vichy Frenchmen many people considered unsavory, Noguès, Pierre Boisson, and Peyrouton. Churchill said simply, "I told them that if they marched with us we would not concern ourselves with past differences. They were dignified, but anxious.''

It was to have been a short stay, and Churchill and his party left for the airport at midnight, but a magneto on the prime minister's plane was not functioning, and he happily returned to Cunningham's villa where a soft bed, hot water, and a plentiful supply of booze were available. One of Cunningham's aides said that the prime minister had secretly sent someone to Maison Blanche to remove the magneto. Churchill himself said, "It was obliging of the magneto to cut out before we started rather than later on.''

Finally, on Sunday night, the 7th, Churchill and his party took off for England. "This was my last flight in 'Commando,' which later perished with all hands, though with a different pilot and crew,'' Churchill said.

Just what was accomplished by the dangerous trip was not clear. Brooke, a bird-watcher, was pleased with the fact that he "discovered the same African blue-tit that I saw in Marrakesh." But during the visit Eisenhower began to realize that his high-sounding title didn't mean much unless he had the authority to go with it. But did he?

He was now commanding general of a new theater, the North African Theater of Operations (NATOUSA), and Lieutenant General Frank M. Andrews had become commanding general of the American forces in Europe.

Eisenhower expressed his concern to Marshall on February 8. Churchill had said that shortly after he got back to London he was going to announce the new command arrangement concerning Eisenhower, Tedder, Alexander, and Cunningham. Eisenhower said:

There will probably be innocently created through these announcements, a popular impression of overriding British control of this great area and operation. . . . We must rigidly avoid the creation of a popular or official belief that we are going back to command by council rather than by individual.

In a second telegram to Marshall that same day he said:

I am thinking of the inevitable trend of the British mind toward "committee" rather than "single" command. . . . For example, in the Air paper the statement is made that after following out the general organization prescribed, further details will naturally be left to the *Air Commander-in-Chief*. So far as I am concerned no attention will be paid to such observations. It is my responsibility to organize and win battles. . . .

I do not consider that there is anything vicious or even deliberate in the British actions; they simply reflect their own doctrine and training just as we do ours. But when the two governments accept the principle of unified command—which means a Task Force Commander—in a particular theater, I not only believe that they must leave him a considerable freedom in organizing his own forces as he sees fit, but that when it becomes necessary to organize subordinate task forces, he should be free to do it under unified command, if he so chooses.

Marshall immediately took Eisenhower's two angry messages to Roosevelt, and the president cabled Churchill, "I agree to your announcing on February 11 the placing of your Eighth Army under the command of General Eisenhower and the appointment of Alexander as Deputy under Eisenhower, and also the appointment of Tedder. It is my opinion that cooperation by French forces will be best if the American Supreme Command in North Africa is stressed, and I consider it inadvisable to release to the enemy any information whatever as to the details of the duties of Alexander or Tedder. I am glad you are safely back. You have accomplished marvels."

Churchill's reply said, "I will act in the way you wish, but I cannot guarantee that there will be no criticism." He quoted from a note he had received from

Minister of Information Bracken saying that he was "having quite a bit of trouble in persuading some of the newspapers not to criticize American handling of the North African campaign. If General Eisenhower's appointment as Supreme Commander is stressed and General Alexander's and Air Marshal Tedder's respective functions are left vaguely undefined, I think we must expect a spate of criticism from the British press."

Churchill added, "I shall utter the most solemn warning against controversy in these matters and every effort will be made by Bracken behind the scenes. Please do the like on your side to help your faithful partner."

So the Britishers, with all that rank, had won a battle, but an American lieutenant general who wasn't doing too well either politically or militarily had won a war, and on February 11 he became a full general. John said of the experience, "He was now alert to a title's being one thing and authority another. He would never forget that lesson."

Eisenhower was made a four-star general on February 11, the twelfth officer in the history of the United States Army to be so honored; the first had been U. S. Grant. When he was in Algiers, Marshall had said that he would try to get Ike a fourth star, and on January 27 Eisenhower cabled him, "There is a personal favor I should like to ask of you. Immediately before any public announcement is made of the possible nomination of which you spoke to me, would you please have someone call Mamie and tell her over the phone. As a matter of sentiment, I should like her to be the first, outside of official circles, to hear of it. I will be very grateful."

On February 9 Marshall cabled Eisenhower that he would personally call Mamie about the promotion, and a cable on the 11th said that he had "telephoned your friend at ten this morning," adding that the nomination had gone forward at noon. Later that day Ike received a telegram from Mamie, "Congratulations on your fourth star."

That was not the first word he had about the promotion, however. On February 9, the news was broadcast on the BBC. That night Captain Barney Fawkes, of the *Maidstone* submarine mother ship, had telephoned Tex Lee with the news. Lee informed Butcher, and, Butcher said, "Ike walked into the room as I was replacing the receiver. . . . I offered him my hand and said, 'Congratulations.'

" 'What for?' he asked, not putting out his hand.

" 'On being a full general.'

" 'How do you know?'

"As I declared the source, he stuck out his hand, but almost simultaneously burst out: 'I'm made a full general, the tops of my profession, and I'm not told officially. Well, maybe it isn't true. How did you say you heard it?'

"I told him again. . . .

"Then he believed it but was still grousing because he hadn't been informed officially."

He was in fact nervous and he was angry. As he later wrote Mamie, he knew that Marshall wanted to get him that fourth star, but he also knew that the bad personal publicity might make it politically hazardous to promote him, and he knew that his commander in chief was not a man who took chances politically on so minor a matter as promoting an unpopular career man in the army. So he was understandably unsettled when the news came to him from an unofficial source. Besides, the fact that the BBC was the first to report the news didn't please him. He didn't quite trust the British Broadcasting Corporation, which was forever reporting "British victories," but when the Americans won a battle it was always an "Allied victory."

The significance of the fourth star was, as John said, "far greater than a mere promotion. For one thing, the rank itself, since World War I, had been reserved for only one man, the Army chief-of-staff, and that only on a temporary basis. Attainment of the rank put General Eisenhower, for the moment at least, in the position of being the 'Pershing' of the war in Europe. He had taken twenty-eight years to achieve that honor."

That night he called in Mickey, Hunt, Moaney, and two waiters, Henry Clay Williams and Foster, and promoted each of them one grade. He told Butcher, "You can get yourself an aide of your own." Everett Hughes, Kay, and the five WACs came for dinner and drinks, and Ike sang all the words to "One Dozen Roses" several times. Butcher noted that he "let out all stops when he came to 'Give me one dozen roses, put my heart in beside them, and send them to the girl I love.'

"Mamie's ears must have burned."

The presence at the dinner of Kay and the WACs was not mentioned.

That was, as Kay said, "the general's last carefree evening for many a week." Early the next morning he left for Constantine and an extended inspection of II Corps. "It was my first trip as a four-star general," he said. The victory was not complete, however. He added, "I was still a lieutenant colonel in the Regular Army."

* * *

TURN OF THE TIDE

The trip to Constantine was long, muddy, and often dangerous. It was Kay's first combat drive, and she immediately found out that it was nothing like driving the general over the quiet country roads of England. A scout car was in the lead, followed by the general's sedan, a weapons carrier, a backup sedan in case something happened to the general's, and in the rear a second scout car. Air attacks were possible in many places along the road, and snipers, Arabs and French sympathizers with the Axis, were believed to be everywhere in the area. German paratroopers were dropped frequently to blow up bridges and interrupt Allied communications. If they saw an enemy motor convoy, it was felt certain they would try to destroy it. "Chilly, rainy weather added a final hazard," said Kay. "Driving a general in wartime is far from glamorous."

As soon as the men along the way saw Kay at the wheel of the sedan they whistled, hooted, and made various vulgar remarks that caused Eisenhower to mutter about the lack of discipline. Kay said, "I attempted not to smile, pretending that I neither heard nor saw the wholly natural reactions of these men to a woman, *any* woman."

The soldiers also gossiped, and at the time Eisenhower was severely criticized for what many said was "flaunting" his intimate relationship with Mrs. Summersby. No one doubted that they were sleeping together, and most people felt he shouldn't have brought a woman into a combat zone anyway.

A story repeated everywhere at the time and later in Europe had the sedan breaking down on an isolated road. Kay got out, lifted the hood, and started tinkering with the motor. According to the story, Eisenhower remained in the back seat of the car for a time, then got out, took a tool out of the trunk, walked to the front, and asked, "Screw driver?"

Kay was said to have replied, "We might as well. I can't get the goddamn motor fixed."

Just what was passed along to Mamie is not known, but she must have heard all the gossip and all the criticism, most of it more than once.

Major General Ernest N. Harmon, who traveled in Eisenhower's sedan many times, didn't agree with the criticism. He said that Kay was "pretty, she was English, she was fearless, and she handled an automobile better over a bad highway than any man in my whole division. . . . I remember passing a truck train stopped by the side of the road. The men were all out urinating against the tires of the trucks. I speculated briefly on Miss Summersby's reaction, but then she volunteered that she wasn't bothered in the slightest. She was used to seeing that sort of thing, she said."

The first stop was at the beautiful walled city of Constantine, late in the afternoon of the 12th. The city had been fought over since the time of Julius Caesar, and in mid-January Eisenhower had established an advance command post there. He said he wanted it "so that I may maintain close touch with commanders and insure coordinated action by all ground and air forces available." His own headquarters in Algiers were becoming embarrassingly large; it would soon include a thousand officers and five thousand enlisted men. Lucian Truscott said that the size of his Algiers headquarters caused Eisenhower "much concern. Differences in organization, equipment, procedures and national characteristics between British and American forces resulted in much duplication of effort. Had all forces been British or American, the size of the headquarters could have been reduced by half. Most staff officers like to be close to the throne, and many of them are empire builders at heart. There is more prestige in belonging to a top headquarters than to a lower one even though the duties may be identical."

Truscott was deputy chief of staff, and the purpose of his command post at Constantine was, he said, "to furnish General Eisenhower with an office closer to the front than AFHQ [Allied Force Headquarters] so that all information concerning the situation . . . would be available to him in either place."

Anderson as head of the First Army was to control all operations in Tunisia, but the French, whose troops occupied a considerable sector of the front and whose cooperation was necessary, would still not serve under the British. According to Eisenhower, French leaders insisted "that there would be a rebellion in their Army if I insisted upon this arrangement, because of ill feeling still enduring from the British-French clashes in Syria, Oran, and Dakar. The British First Army was on the left, the French forces in the center, and the American forces on the right, but all occupying parts of a single, closely interrelated battlefront, and all dependent upon a single, inadequate line of communications. It was an exasperating situation, full of potential danger."

When Ike's fears were realized, Truscott's headquarters didn't prove to be of much help. Communications between Algiers and Constantine were difficult, and Truscott, though he was a competent officer, was outranked by almost everybody he dealt with. He was only a brigadier general. Besides, it was understood that he was a coordinator, not a commander, a kind of housekeeper for the boss, Eisenhower. Moreover, the distance between Algiers and Constantine was so great, nearly 700 miles, that Eisenhower didn't get there very often.

It turned out intelligence generally was quite poor. For instance, no one paid much attention when on January 30 the Germans moved forward and defeated a French garrison at a mountain trail called Faid Pass. It was the beginning of the battle for the Kasserine Pass.

During the disheartening early months of 1943, Eisenhower must often have thought of his boyhood hero, Hannibal, who here in this same difficult North African terrain, at the end of the Second Punic War (202 B.C.), had suffered his final, humiliating defeat at the hands of the Roman general, Scipio Africanus Major. During the winter and early spring of 1943, Eisenhower and his troops suffered a series of humiliating defeats, sometimes at the hands of German Colonel General Jürgen von Arnim, a true Prussian from a military family, a sullen man for whom Eisenhower felt only contempt.

Ike's appreciation of Field Marshal Erwin Rommel, who had arrived in Tunisia in January, was different; he was an enemy general, of course, a Hun, but he was also a brilliant general, and Eisenhower recognized that fact. Eisenhower must also have realized that he and the field marshal had a good deal in common. They were less than a year apart in age; Rommel had been born in 1891. Both had spent most of their lives in obscurity; both had chosen the infantry as their branch of service; both had had many unwelcome military assignments and performed them creditably and usually with notable success; and for both, perhaps the most unwelcome assignment of all was the one in North Africa. Rommel was convinced that the battle was lost before it began; Eisenhower thought the expedition was a sorry substitute for what should have been a cross-Channel invasion of Europe.

When Eisenhower got to Truscott's headquarters on February 12, he was told by the brigadier general that the Allies must, in his opinion, destroy Rommel's army before it escaped into the Tunisian bridgehead. In a memorandum Truscott gave Ike, he added, "In one respect only have Axis forces demonstrated superiority; the ability to concentrate superior means in local areas and to retain the initiative. This fact may be attributed to shorter lines of communications and perhaps to more experienced leadership."

He later said, "Little did we realize how soon the Boche was to underscore my remark as a masterpiece of understatement."

Before leaving Algiers, Eisenhower had been told by his G-2 (intelligence) officer, British Brigadier Eric Mockler-Ferryman, that General Arnim was adding his Fifth Panzer Army to Rommel's forces so that the Germans could make a major thrust through the pass at Fondouk, a soft point in the Allied line where the British and French troops were divided.

On the morning of the 13th, Eisenhower, Truscott, and their party left for II Corps headquarters near Tebessa. The sedan stopped first at a British air base at Canrobert, then at an American base at Youks les Bains. Ike was delighted with what he saw among the American airmen. They were living under primitive conditions, eating K and C rations almost exclusively, were under constant air attack from the Germans, and yet their morale was demonstrably good.

Eisenhower's pleasure did not last long. He arrived at the II Corps command post shortly after noon, and while he had been warned that Major General Lloyd Fredendall's headquarters, which he seldom left, were unusual, he cannot quite have been prepared for their grotesque quality. Earlier that month (February 4) he had written Fredendall that he must stop criticizing the British, adding "I expect you . . . to enhance the reputation of the American Army with the British and the French and create in them a confidence in our armed forces that will have a beneficial effect throughout the remainder of the war." He went on:

> One of the things that gives me the most concern is the habit of some of our generals in staying too close to their command posts. Please watch this very, very carefully among all your subordinates. Speed in execution, particularly when we are reacting to any move of the enemy's, is of transcendent importance. Ability to move rapidly is largely dependent upon an intimate knowledge of the ground and conditions along the front. As you well know, this can be gained only through personal reconnaissance and impressions. Generals are expendable just as any other item in an army, and, moreover, the importance of having the general constantly present in his command post is frequently overemphasized. The same thing applies to commanders of all grades, and I sincerely hope that you will make this a matter of primary interest in the handling of your forces.

Although Fredendall cannot have known it, Rommel had said almost the same thing. He said, "There are always moments when the commander's place is not with his staff but up with the troops. . . . The higher the rank, the greater the effect of the example."

No matter what anybody said, Fredendall had no intention of leaving his headquarters; after all, in Oran he had stayed aboard the troopship while the officers and men under his command took the city. Eisenhower apparently did not find this behavior unusual. To the contrary, shortly thereafter he gave

Fredendall a Distinguished Service Medal. The citation said that he had "demonstrated the highest quality of leadership," and Ike commended the fifty-eight-year-old general for "exceptionally meritorious service . . . brilliant leadership and resolute force."

Fredendall was a stocky man, coarse, often incomprehensible in his speech, but able to make it clear that he despised not only the British and the French but most of his American subordinates and superiors as well. His command post was seventy miles from the front, in underground shelters blasted in the rock of a deep canyon, and most American officers were embarrassed when they saw it, many covering their chagrin with a wisecrack; they called it "Shangri-la, a million miles from nowhere," or "Lloyd's very last resort." Truscott said, "Although I had warned General Eisenhower what to expect, his reaction to the location and to the tunneling which was still in progress was that of nearly everyone who saw it for the first time. There were some acid comments."

Eisenhower himself said in *Crusade*, "Second Corps Headquarters had established itself in a deep and almost inaccessible ravine a few miles east of Tebessa. It was a long way from the battlefront, but, considering the length of the lines and the paucity of roads, it was probably as good a site for the main headquarters as was available." But in 1947 he was softening his opinion to avoid hurting Fredendall, who had received a disability retirement from the army in 1946. Besides, Ike hesitated to attack anyone who had taken part in the crusade, no matter how inept or short-lived his contribution had been. Al Gruenther once said, "You will notice Ike almost never criticized anybody who was in the Army to anybody who wasn't, and he had a very special feeling for those who'd been with him in Europe."

Eisenhower certainly did not think that the command post was "probably" in "as good a site . . . as was available" when he saw it in February 1943. And he had to know that he should sack the man who had selected it on the spot. On February 24 he wrote Gee, who was back in Scotland as commander of the 29th Division:

> The only thing on which I would venture to give you the slightest advice is that you must be tough. You may not be able to discover among your men those that will be the best battle leaders, but you can find those who are this minute endangering the battle success of your whole command. They are the lazy, the slothful, the indifferent or the complacent. Get rid of them if you have to write letters the rest of your life. . . .
>
> For God's sake don't keep anyone around that you say to yourself "He may get by"—he won't. Throw him out and I am sure your theater commander knowing the deadly seriousness of all this, will back you up to the hilt.

Yet on February 13th, faced with a man about whom he should have had no doubts at all, a man who couldn't possibly "get by," Eisenhower, according to Truscott, "discussed the situation and plans." He also had discussions with Anderson.

Just before dusk, Ike, Truscott, a member of Truscott's staff, and another from Fredendall's set off for the front. Kay stayed behind at the extraordinarily safe corps headquarters. The convoy was smaller now, one Bantam (jeep) armed with a machine gun, Eisenhower's sedan driven by Truscott's driver, Sergeant Barna, another sedan with Major General Lowell Rooks, who was G-3 (operations) at the Algiers headquarters, and a second Bantam in the rear.

Eisenhower saw "a number of things that were disturbing" that night. He said, "The first of these was a certain complacency, illustrated by an unconscionable delay in perfecting defensive positions in the passes. Lack of training on the part of commanders was responsible."

The 1st Armored Division of Major General Orlando P. "Pinky" (for his red hair) Ward was almost totally dispersed. Fredendall and Ward detested each other, which was the main reason for the dispersal. The division had been divided into two combat teams, A and B. Combat Command B was headed by an old friend of Eisenhower's, Brigadier General Paul M. D. Robinett, a man with a considerable ego who did not mind that Fredendall had told him to bypass Ward if he had any problems and come directly to corps headquarters. He disliked obeying anybody. And that night he was right about one very important matter. Eisenhower's G-2, Mockler-Ferryman, had predicted that the German attack, if and when it came, would be almost exactly where Robinett and his combat team were, Fondouk. Robinett didn't think so; his reconnaissance teams had found absolutely no evidence to support such a claim, and he had passed that finding along both to Fredendall and to Anderson, both of whom discounted it. In *Crusade* Eisenhower said, "I was convinced of the accuracy of his report and told him I would take the matter up the next day with the corps and the army commanders."

The next day was too late; the next day it didn't matter.

From Fondouk, Eisenhower and his party went to Sidi Bou Zid opposite Faid to inspect Combat Command A, headed by Brigadier General R. A. McQuillin, who was an old friend of Truscott's; in the army in those days, everybody still knew almost everybody. All was very quiet on McQuillin's front; men more experienced in combat might have found it suspiciously quiet, but that night the Americans did not. Eisenhower went for a brief walk in the moonlight. In the distance to the east he could see the mountains surrounding the Faid Pass.

Some nervous sentries fired near the convoy on its way back to Fredendall's headquarters. And a little later the driver of Ike's sedan, Sergeant Barna, did something Kay did not do during the entire war. He fell asleep at the wheel, and the right wheel of the sedan went into the ditch. Nobody was hurt, and the convoy got back to Fredendall's headquarters at 5:30 in the morning. At 4:00 that morning the Germans had launched an attack through the Faid Pass in the direction of Sidi Bou Zid, almost exactly where Ike had taken his moonlight walk in the desert. The news was disconcerting, but Eisenhower was assured the attack was small, nothing to worry about.

So he decided to do what he must have been dreaming about since he was a boy in Abilene and Ida locked up his Greek and Roman history books. With Kay once more at the wheel of his sedan he went to Timgad, and he, Truscott, Tex Lee, and Kay spent more than an hour wandering through the streets of the city that had been founded by the Roman emperor Trajan in A.D. 100.

Timgad had been abandoned by the Berbers in the seventh century and not rediscovered until 1881. A triumphal arch, a forum, a library, and a great many Roman houses were still intact, and the Americans spent more than an hour wandering through the city. Truscott said that they "stood on the walls where Roman soldiers had once stood guard. We were not unmindful of the fact that not so many miles away, American soldiers were fighting on ground where Roman legions had once borne their victorious eagles."

They got back to Truscott's advance command post in the middle of the afternoon, and none of the news was good. McQuillin's reserve tank battalion had been destroyed and a battalion of corps artillery had been overrun. It was clear at once that the early reports had been too optimistic. A great many infantry troops had also been lost; no one knew how many. Eisenhower told Marshall on the 21st, "The night before the attack I visited the exact spot from which it was launched and thereafter remained in the east until it became evident that the new line would have to be established west of Sbeitla–Feriana and that considerable rehabilitation and rebuilding of formations would be required. This was my job."

Arnim, who disliked Rommel to about the same degree Fredendall hated Ward, had headed the attacking forces. On the night of the 14th, Rommel was in command of the troops that forced the Allies to abandon Gafsa, another small village that was important largely because it was near the airfields at Thelepete. The airfields also fell to the German troops, and in his report to Marshall, Ike called their loss "a real tragedy. . . . It was on my responsibility alone that we attempted to operate along a forward line, which it was obvious could not be held passively against any concentrated, determined attack. . . . To me it seemed, as always before in this campaign, that the risks involved, assuming tactical efficiency on our part, were fully justified. Now we have the picture of the enemy, on our side of the valley, doing as much, and trying more, than we did on the other side. . . . I am provoked that there was such reliance upon particular types of intelligence that general instructions were considered inapplicable. In this connection and for your eyes only, I have asked for the relief of my G-2. He is British and the head of that section must be a British officer because of the network of special signal establishments he operates."

Mockler-Ferryman's replacement was General Kenneth Strong, who was to remain Eisenhower's G-2 for the rest of the war.

In an unpublished section of his diary written on February 20, Butcher told what had happened:

> An explanation of the defeat, as seen by Ike, lies in a misinterpretation of radio messages we regularly intercept from the enemy. This source is known as ULTRA. It happens that our G-2, Brigadier Mockler-Ferryman, relies heavily on this source. It has frequently disclosed excellent information as to the intentions of the Axis. However, the interpretation placed by G-2 on the messages dealing with the attack—an attack we have been expecting for several days—led Mockler-Ferryman to believe that a feint would be made where the attack actually occurred through Sidi Bou Zid, and that the real and heavy attack would come farther north. . . . Basing his judgment on the reliability of ULTRA, Mockler-Ferryman was confident the main attack would come in the north. . . . General Paget left this morn-

ing *en route* to the U.K. and is to handle with Sir Alan Brooke . . . the replacement of Mock in such a way that he will not be discredited. . . . However, Ike insists we need a G-2 who is never satisfied with his information, who procures it with spies, reconnaissance, and any means available.

Actually, in spite of his charge that Mockler-Ferryman was "too wedded to one type of information," ULTRA was to remain Eisenhower's most used and most trusted intelligence source for the rest of the war.

Whatever unease Eisenhower may have felt after he reached Constantine on the 14th he, as usual, kept it to himself. In a message sent from there to the Combined Chiefs he said that, yes, there had been "a hostile attack that developed against our Faid position on the morning of the 14th. . . . During the course of the day confused fighting took place in the region west of Faid and east of Sbeitla. . . . Provided that the operations planned for today are reasonably successful, I consider our position will be satisfactory but will not, repeat not, be so favorable from the standpoint of launching eventual offensive operations."

His report to Marshall on the 15th was equally relaxed. It was also less than truthful when discussing the American troops. He did not mention "a number of things that were disturbing." He said, "I know you would have been impressed could you have seen the magnificent spirit displayed everywhere by the American enlisted men. . . . Not a man had a complaint and while all spoke with delight of the prospect of white bread and some other items which are beginning to become available, they seemed to realize the difficulties of transportation which made ammunition and fuel take precedence over bulky rations. . . . I assure you that the troops that come out of this campaign are going to be battle wise and tactically efficient."

His account of what he found at II Corps' command post was, to put it kindly, fanciful. He said, referring to his letter of February 4, "In a recent letter to you I enclosed a copy of one I had sent to Fredendall. The effect was most noticeable. He is quick to take a hint and I was impressed by his thorough knowledge of his battlefront and of all his troop dispositions. He is working incessantly, and for the past several days has had little rest. Yet he seems fit, and I am placing a lot of confidence in him."

Ike also apologized for not having had time "to express to you adequately my appreciation with respect to my recent promotion. I hope you understand."

That same day, while he was still at Constantine, he wrote Mamie. John said the letter "was one of his most revealing." Periods of great combat activity, when headlines were being made, were times of relative inactivity for him as he waited for reports from the front. And away from the harassments of Algiers—with momentous events pounding around him—Eisenhower the letter writer was at his best. He told Mamie that 15th day of February, the day after they had become engaged in 1916,

How I'd like to be back, with you, to February 14 of 27 years ago!!!
I'm not in my regular quarters and have been moving rapidly for the past few days. Now I'm waiting at the only place where I can quickly get

a piece of news for which I have need. When I arrive I'll have to decide whether or not I'm to go back to my normal spot, or hike off again in the other direction. Most of my days are like that; many of my minor problems involve making the best guess as to *where* I myself *should* be the next day— sometimes the next hour.

Your telegram of congratulations on my latest and final promotion came just before I left my headquarters. Strangely enough, my first news of the incident came through the British Broadcasting Co. I wouldn't believe it, although I knew the matter was under consideration at home. I knew also that General G.C.M. [Marshall] wanted to do it—but I was in no position to know whether or not the newspaper argument developed out of some of the moves here might have made my promotion politically inexpedient. Actually, I didn't have much feeling about it. I am human enough to want the official approval of my past actions that such an unusual advancement implies—but anyone worthy is so concerned with the enormity of the tasks . . . that what the world calls success or promotion does not loom up as particularly important. It is true I do not often write to you of my responsibilities, although you, better than anyone else, would understand the feelings I'd try to express. . . . My technical boss is a combined body of men (8) [the Combined Chiefs] that is divided into two parts by the Atlantic Ocean. Moreover, an active theater of war must be commanded on the spot. So the boss in that one has only one real confidant—his pillow, and only the underneath side of that! Loneliness is the inescapable lot of a man holding such a job. Subordinates can advise, urge, help, and pray— but only one man in his own mind and heart can decide, "Do we, or do we not?" The stakes are always high, and the penalties are expressed in terms of loss of life or major or minor disasters to the nation. No man can always be right. So the struggle is to do one's best, to keep the brain and the conscience clear; never to be swayed by unworthy motives or incon-sequential reasons, but to strive to unearth the basic factors involved and then do one's duty.

It is not always easy—in fact the strain comes from not being sure that the analysis has been carefully and accurately made. And when it is clear that the only logical answer is certain to bring criticism; even possibly official misunderstanding by superiors, then is when such things as pop-ularity, favorable press, possible promotion, etc., etc., must be disregarded as the ant crawling across the floor.

He then discussed his acceptance of Darlan and said that he had realized before he did it that his decision would be "bitterly assailed by many, particularly those who think that all human beings think in terms of self only. The same ones are now probably giving me the devil for not having captured Tunisia— but I wonder where those people think my front lines would be now if I had not accepted poor Darlan at that moment. . . .

I'm simply trying to say that in a job like this so many things are so big that even a fourth star fails to cause any great internal excitement. I appreciate the confidence of my superiors—and I feel damned humble in the fact of it, but I do not feel that I've "arrived"—or that my major job is finished. I've just begun and though the prospect is, in some phases appalling, I can do my duty only if I steer myself to the requirements and meet them to the best of my ability. When you remember me in your prayers, that's the special thing I want—always to do my duty to the extreme limit of my ability.

It certainly was the best letter he ever wrote to Mamie; it was among the best he ever wrote to anybody, and it was certainly the most personally revealing. Of course he had wanted "official approval of my past actions," and by that he meant much more than just the so-called deals he had made with Darlan and Peyrouton; he meant the "past actions" of the twenty-eight years since he had been commissioned a second lieutenant. He had gotten that approval, and it was both satisfying and somewhat frightening. Those eight shadowy men on both sides of the Atlantic were indeed his bosses, and they could fire him if they did not like what he had done or disapproved of what he had not done, but they were not where decisions had to be made. They were at home in Washington or London; he was there; he was johnny-on-the-spot, and he alone had to decide what his duty was, and he had better decide right.

For most of his life since graduating from the Point he had been a subordinate, one who could and did "advise, urge, help, and pray." Now there was no one to turn to. He had a combat assignment, his first, and a good many people, some with great pleasure, were taking the trouble to point out that he had never heard a shot fired in anger.

He had three Britishers in his command who all had had considerable experience in combat. He respected them, and they in turn respected him, but it is impossible to imagine him sitting down to discuss anything but an Allied strategic plan with Tedder or Alexander, for that matter, even with Cunningham, that jolly, red-faced sailor, who had been a destroyer captain in the First World War and had had flag rank since 1932. Eisenhower had been a major in 1932.

No, the best thing was to confide only in your pillow, "and only the underneath side of that!" Of course he was lonely.

He also told Mamie on the 15th:

I hope this letter does not sound morbid. I don't mean it so and I love you so much that I always like you to realize exactly how I feel about things; and for some reason I felt like attempting to explain today. I try to keep fit, optimistic and calm—both my temper and my disposition are sometimes sorely tried, but I think I do a pretty good job of controlling both, even if poor Ernest [Tex Lee] and Mickey sometimes suffer a bit. They know I don't mean to hurt their feelings, so occasionally they have to let me blow off. Secretly, I think an outburst on my part amuses rather than alarms them.

He did not always like Mamie to know how he felt. To the contrary, he almost never shared his feelings with her, but that day in Constantine he must have felt somehow exposed, and that though he had won a victory, he might lose his personal war. He might still be sent home in disgrace; he might be dismissed from the crusade after a single, unsuccessful battle. He had been forgiven his so-called deals, but now had almost 50,000 square miles of territory to conquer, and he had called the whole thing off once; he had said it was hopeless. That was the first strike; the second was when he "dealt" with two unsavory Frenchmen; now was his third time to step up to the plate, and he knew as only an old baseball player could know, that if he struck out this time, he was finished.

Moreover, and this must have been the most terrifying thought of all, the whole thing was really out of his hands. What happened depended largely on what Axis officers and troops did. As for his own troops, the most crucial segment of them at the moment were commanded by a man who was either a coward or a madman and quite likely both. He could have discharged him and hadn't, but if he had, what instant replacement was there? And what would bringing in a replacement in the midst of a battle do to the morale of the other officers and the enlisted men in II Corps?

Help was on the way; Alexander would soon arrive. Rommel would soon give up on a battle he had had no heart for, and Eisenhower would soon, in his son's words, write letters "dealing with matters such as an injured right thumb . . . the income tax for 1942, and the peccadillo of a gift for Mrs. George Marshall."

Meanwhile, February 16 started out with more bad news. At 1:00 A.M. Truscott told Eisenhower that Fredendall had told him that more than a hundred American tanks had been destroyed in two days; two battalions of artillery had been overrun; two battalions of infantry had been lost, and, as Truscott put it, "no one knew how much more!"

Fredendall had said that the first day's losses would "include sixty-two officers and 1536 enlisted men, about half killed or missing."

Eisenhower decided to return at once to Algiers, and he got there at 7:00 that evening. He learned that not only were the Allies in trouble with the Germans, Giraud had just passed on the disheartening news that the Arabs, having learned of the Allied defeats, might decide openly to side with the Axis.

Kay Summersby said, "Headquarters had all the cheer of an empty funeral parlor. News from the front . . . was increasingly bitter to swallow. . . . General Eisenhower was . . . glum and weary with these worries, plus the first home-front criticism of his combat direction."

Beetle was in Tripoli, and Eisenhower immediately conferred with his deputy chief of staff, Brigadier John F. M. Whiteley, and it was decided to send troops to the front immediately. He told Butcher that he did not want to talk about what he had learned at the front, "business," as he put it. He said "he had a bellyfull of such talk, having done nothing else for five days."

He was awakened during the night to be told that Anderson felt that troops had to be withdrawn to a line he and Eisenhower had agreed on earlier that month when they met at Tulergama. Eisenhower did not disagree, and the next morning, Butcher said, he was "pounding the table with staff members, insisting that everything possible be done to rush help to the front."

Alexander arrived that afternoon, and he said all the things he should have said, that he was delighted to be working under Eisenhower, that he realized that the sector was American, and that while his present assignment was necessary, it was also a privilege and a pleasure. Ike said all the right things back.

Alexander was an affable man, and although he and Eisenhower had some difficulties later, Ike always respected him. He said, "Alexander seems to have a genius for getting people to work for him just because they want to get a pat on the back from their Commander." On the 18th Alexander went to the front in the rain, and although he was cheerful by nature, what he saw did not impress him. His comments on Fredendall's headquarters are not recorded, but he did a few days later inform Churchill, "Have just returned from three days on the American and French front lines. . . . Broadly speaking, Americans require experience and the French require arms. . . . I am frankly shocked at the whole situation as I found it. . . . Hate to disappoint you, but find victory in North Africa is not just around the corner."

He was not much impressed with Eisenhower either. He told Brooke, "There is no policy and no plan. This is the result of no firm direction or centralised control from above."

Alexander was already a veteran both of the First World War and the Second. In the First he had become a lieutenant colonel, been wounded twice, and decorated three times. In the Second he had seen action at Dunkirk and in Burma and Egypt. In the last assignment, he had been Montgomery's commanding officer. "Monty" got most of the acclaim, but Alexander seemed not to mind. Brooke found him much like Eisenhower; he said they were both "men with a genial gift for accommodating and reconciling divergent views."

In a speech to the House of Commons on February 11, Churchill had said, announcing the new command arrangements in Africa, "In General Eisenhower, as in General Alexander, you have two men remarkable for selflessness of character and disdain of purely personal advancement. Let them alone; give them a chance; and it is quite possible that one of these fine days the bells will have to be rung again. If not, we will address ourselves to the problem, and in all loyalty and comradeship, and in the light of circumstances, I appeal to all patriotic men on both sides of the Atlantic Ocean to stamp their feet on mischief-makers and sowers of tares wherever they may be found and let the great roll into battle under the best possible conditions for our success."

Alexander's first order was to Anderson, commander of the First Army, an unsmiling man who never suffered from overconfidence. The order got immediately to the point:

Your immediate task is:
(a) To stabilize the front in the southern sector.
(b) To reorganize and regroup your forces in order to allot separate sectors
    to:—
        British
        American
        French
We must regain the initiative at the first available opportunity and keep it.

Truscott said of the order that it seemed to him "most untimely—rather like telling a man who had a bear by the tail to 'hold on.'"

On the 25th, when he was "to keep my memory straight . . . setting down my recollection of events leading up to the current situation on the battlefront," Eisenhower agreed with Alexander "on the essentials of this situation. . . . We agree that the first thing is the concentration of all troops into nationalistic components and the immediate rehabilitation of the divisions, particularly those that have been partially used up." Eisenhower didn't say so, not even in the privacy of his diary, but the dispersal of the divisions under his command had been yet another error of Fredendall's, and it had proved a disaster in every way.

On the 18th, the day after Alexander arrived and was on his way to the front, Eisenhower wrote a somewhat boastful letter to his competitive brother Edgar:

This morning I received a congratulatory message from you. . . . I rather doubt that any civilian would fully understand what a unique thing it is in our Army to have a "Four-star" gentleman hanging around. So I don't suppose there's any use to try to tell you how astonished I was when they finally put the finger on me. In this case, unfortunately, I am forced to admit that the force of circumstances—rather than any peculiar individual merit—was largely responsible. The Allied command has given me a command so wide in scope and so large in numbers that I suppose it would have been embarrassing for our government to have failed to promote me. . . .

Your tale of puddin' meat fairly made my mouth water. I think if I could have a good breakfast of mush and puddin' some fine morning, I would not only think I was back in our Kansas boyhood days, but would fairly tear this place apart for the following week. . . .

With respect to your offer of service, I can tell you flatly that there are several places here I could use you beautifully, but being my brother I wouldn't have you unless you were forced on me by the War Department.

Eisenhower had not received congratulations from his son, and he did not take the matter philosophically. He was furious. On February 27, John had written him that a friend was having trouble with West Point discipline; the latest promotion was not even mentioned. So Eisenhower began his reply, on March 20, with a stern lecture, the type of lecture with which John had long been familiar. "I know that, as they always have in the past, cadets jeer at the disciplinary standards the Technical Corps is always trying to instill in them. But I tell you this—if I could have in this entire force, today, the discipline of the United States Corps of Cadets, I could shorten this campaign immeasurably. Discipline wins battles. . . . Discipline makes a man salute—it also makes him hang on to his machine gun, firing it to the last round in the face of what appears to be an overwhelming attack."

Then he got to the real point of the letter, his disappointment and anger not at what his son had said but at what he had not said. As always, he approached the matter sideways. He said he had "chuckled over the fact that you did not even mention my promotion." You can be sure that whatever he had done he had not chuckled. He went on, "When I was made a B.G., you wrote a full page about it. When I was made a Major General, you asked me to defer all future promotions until you had gotten to be a Yearling. You congratulated me, at least feebly, on being a Lieutenant General; but you paid not the slightest attention to the fact that I finally got my 4th star."

After that, trying ineptly to hide his hurt, he said, "I do not mind confessing that I really got a laugh out of it because I have had so many messages of congratulations that I suppose I just naturally expected you to fall in line with the rest. As a matter of fact, you are the only one that had the sense to see it doesn't amount to a tinker's damn in the winning of this war—and that is all that concerns me."

John saw through the camouflage, of course. He said, "Regrettably, I never realized how much the promotion meant to my father. News of the Battle of Kasserine Pass reached the United States simultaneously, and my concern about it tended to overshadow the news of the promotion."

On February 19 Rommel and Arnim launched a joint attack on Kasserine and Sbiba, but the American forces there held fast.

On the 20th despite the resistance of the British 26th Armored Brigade the Germans got to within ten miles of Thala, and detachments of the 10th and 15th Panzers drove through the now-famous Kasserine Pass. That morning Eisenhower held an off-the-record press conference. He said that he assumed full responsibility for the defeat, adding, without naming Fredendall, that as Butcher said, "American armor was in small packets, which permitted the concentration of German armor to overwhelm them. However, the Americans showed great fighting spirit."

At dawn on the 21st the enemy renewed his attacks, and drove Robinett's Combat Command B to a point only eight miles from Tebessa. But a counterattack from a battalion of the 6th Armored Division, with the help of a company of tanks, regained the lost ground. In the north the Germans were stopped short of Thala by massed artillery and the pounding of Allied planes.

Truscott said, "This was not the end of the Kasserine battle, but it was to be the high water mark in the tide of the German storm."

Two days earlier, on the 19th, Fredendall had called Truscott and told him that Ward had to be fired, and Truscott sent the message along to Eisenhower. The two men had talked over the possibility of bringing Major General Harmon, commander of the 2d Armored Division in Morocco, to II Corps, and Ike decided to do it. On the 20th he sent a message to Fredendall telling him that Harmon would arrive at the Tebessa headquarters "as quickly as flying weather will permit," and he added, "From all I can learn . . . General Ward did a rather excellent job tactically during the operation. I believe that his present discouragement is due possibly to physical exhaustion and to the great strain under which he has been operating for many days and which culminated in the attack all along his front. I believe that he has qualities which must not be lost to the service."

If Ward was replaced, the message said, he should be directed to report to Eisenhower, and Fredendall should be "particularly careful to avoid any criticism that might prove detrimental to his future utilization."

Harmon arrived at the Algiers headquarters on the afternoon of the 21st, and Ike told him that American forces had been overrun at Kasserine, and he described the hostility that had developed between Fredendall and Ward. He said he did not want to relieve Fredendall in the midst of battle, that Harmon should go to the Tebessa headquarters as deputy commander of the corps, and that his "first job is to do the best you can to help Fredendall restore the situation."

He said that he would explain more of what was going on and what he thought ought to be done when he and Harmon went to Constantine that night. He didn't really do that, however, and Harmon went to Tebessa not quite sure how he was to proceed and convinced that Ike was equally uncertain about what should be done.

The party started to Constantine at 3:00 in the morning of the 22nd. Kay was again the driver, and Butcher and Whiteley also went along. They arrived late in the afternoon, and Truscott said, "I briefed General Harmon on the situation and conditions as I knew them, and he then departed for II Corps."

Eisenhower stayed in Constantine and in the evening talked by telephone with Fredendall, who said that the day had been quiet, with only minor skirmishes. He thought that the Germans were regrouping for another attack. Eisenhower disagreed. He thought that Fredendall should counterattack immediately and said so. Fredendall said that both he and Anderson thought that he should wait a day. According to Eisenhower, he said that the enemy had " 'one more shot in his locker' and believed that he should spend the next twenty-four hours in perfecting and strengthening his defenses, rather than in the attempt to concentrate enough strength for a counterattack in the direction of Kasserine. No one could quarrel violently with this decision; my own convictions and desires were based upon an anxiety to take instant advantage of the fleeting opportunity for trouncing the enemy before he could recover from his embarrassing position."

Despite the fact that he was commander in chief, Eisenhower did not insist that his "convictions and desires" prevail. He let Fredendall and Anderson have their way, and that capitulation was a costly one. Martin Blumenson in *Kasserine Pass* suggests that an immediate Allied counterattack would have destroyed many, perhaps most of the German troops.

It was later said that the green American troops learned a great deal from the Kasserine experience, but so did their commander in chief. He was never again so indecisive, so cautious, so hesitant to use his authority.

Harmon arrived at Tebessa at 2:00 in the morning on the 23rd. He said, "As I walked into the headquarters, Fredendall and his staff were sitting around looking very glum, and they handed me an envelope saying, "Here it is. The party is yours.' " Harmon opened the envelope and found a typewritten order placing him in charge of "the battle in progress."

Then Fredendall, having had quite a few drinks, went to bed for twenty-four hours, and Harmon took over. With a driver and two young officers from the sleeping major general's staff, he started on a trip to the front. He stopped first at Ward's headquarters and told him that he was now his commanding officer, not easy since Ward had been at the Point in 1914 and Harmon had graduated three years later. Ward seemed not to mind, though; indeed he appeared to be grateful. Harmon said, "We are going to hold today and counterattack tomorrow. Nobody goes back from here." Ward did not disagree.

Next, Harmon visited Brigadier Cameron C. G. Nicholson, deputy commander of the effective 6th Armored Division. Nicholson delighted Harmon when he said of the enemy troops, "We gave them a fucking bloody nose yesterday, and we are going to give them another fucking bloody nose tomorrow."

A few minutes later Brigadier General S. LeRoy Irwin, an Eisenhower classmate, came to Nicholson's division headquarters to say that Anderson had ordered him to move his artillery brigade from Thala to a town called Le Kef, about fifty miles to the rear. Harmon, who had already decided that he was on "a real no-glory assignment," immediately countermanded Anderson's orders. He told Irwin to stay where he was.

Harmon said, "I figured if I won the battle, I would be forgiven. If I lost, the hell with it anyway." When he got back to Tebessa he announced that he planned to counterattack the next morning. No one had much of anything to say to that.

On the afternoon of the 23rd, Eisenhower, Truscott, and Whiteley went to Tebessa. Eisenhower asked Truscott to have his sedan brought to the Fredendall headquarters so that he could ride back to Constantine in that instead of a Bantam. Truscott did what was asked but decided that Kay ought to stay in Constantine. "I doubted that General Eisenhower would want her in the forward area under the circumstances," said Truscott. "I made a mistake. It was the only time in all our associations that General Eisenhower showed irritation with me. Miss Summersby was the only driver in whom General Eisenhower had complete confidence for black-out driving at night." Obviously he wasn't "flaunting" Kay; he was simply using the person best qualified for the job.

Kay made her position clear to the other drivers. When another WAAC driver, Inez Scott, arrived in the North African theater during this period, she said, "I soon learned that Kay Summersby considered herself as being the top dog as far as drivers were concerned. She let me know in no uncertain terms the very first day that . . . she was General Eisenhower's personal chauffeur and that the only time I *might* drive the General would be if she was assigned to some other duty."

Eisenhower conferred with Fredendall and the commander of the 1st Infantry Division, Major General Terry Allen. Everything was quiet along the front, and this time Eisenhower did what he should have done the day before. He insisted that the Germans should, as Truscott put it, be destroyed "before they could escape."

But in what II Corps' G-2 Benjamin "Monk" Dickson, described "as one of the greatest tent-folding acts of all time," the Germans did escape. "Dawn found the Kasserine Valley empty of German troops except for a rearguard at the entrance to the pass; Rommel had vanished in the night. He left II Corps feeling like the Union Army after Gettysburg."

That evening, the 24th, Eisenhower returned to Algiers to find his friend and classmate, Omar N. Bradley, but Ike felt no sense of jubilation. Butcher said, "The proud and cocky Americans today stand humiliated by one of the greatest defeats in our history. This is particularly embarrassing to us with the British, who are courteous and understanding. But there is a definite hangheadedness."

Mickey said, "He [Eisenhower] sat down at the piano in the house in Algiers the night we got back from that inspection trip. He had a habit, when there was a piano, of sitting down at it now and then and playing 'Chopsticks' with two fingers. He looked worried and tired and the smile wasn't there—not in his eyes anyway. I thought it was strange that he should sit down to play 'Chopsticks,' which he usually did when he was feeling satisfied with the way things were going. He started to pick out notes, very slowly. It wasn't 'Chopsticks.' He picked out taps very slowly on the piano and then he got up, without saying anything, and went off to bed. I don't think I ever saw him lower than he was that night."

Eisenhower said, "Although with regard to the strength of the forces engaged on both sides the Kasserine affair was a mere skirmish in proportion to the Ardennes battle, yet there were points of similarity between the two. Each was an act of desperation; each took advantage of extraordinary strength in a defensive barrier to concentrate forces for a blow at Allied communications and in the hope of inducing the Allied high command to give up overall plans for relentless offensives."

A few days later the German troops were back where they had started on Valentine's Day. They had gained no territory, but they had humiliated the Americans, and most of the British, including Anderson and Alexander and certainly Brooke, were far from courteous and understanding; they were contemptuous.

The operation had by their own estimate cost the Germans 736 men killed and wounded, and 252 more were missing. Fourteen guns were lost, sixty-one motor vehicles, six half-tracks, and twenty tanks. Italian losses seem never to have been tabulated, but II Corps took 73 German prisoners and 535 Italian.

The cost to the Americans was 300 killed, 3,000 wounded, and almost 3,000 missing in action out of 30,000 who took part. More than 7,000 replacements were needed in II Corps after Kasserine.

Rommel was soon relieved of his command, and about 300,000 men were left behind to battle hopelessly under the command of Arnim.

In a memorandum to Marshall written immediately after the battle on February 24, Eisenhower said, "After our troops recovered from the initial shock of open battle they began giving a steadily improving account of themselves throughout the fighting and the last phases of the enemy advance encountered stout defensive action and some sharp counterattacks on our part. . . .

"In spite of very heavy losses, the troops are in good heart and a change in temper is particularly noticeable. They are now mad and ready to fight. A certain softness of complacent attitude that was characteristic of all units only a few days ago has disappeared."

Later he said, "The turn of the tide at Kasserine proved actually to be the turn of the tide in all of Tunisia."

Harmon stopped off at the Algiers headquarters on the 28th, and when Eisenhower asked him what he thought of Fredendall, Harmon said, "You ought to get rid of him." Eisenhower then asked if Harmon wanted the job. "I hesitated a moment, for it was a temptation," said Harmon, "but then I said, 'No, ethically, I can't do that. I have reported to you that my superior is no good. It would look like I had sold him down the river . . . to better my own assignment.' " So Harmon returned to his 2d Armored Division in Morocco. And Fredendall stayed right where he was.

On March 2 Eisenhower sent Fredendall a very strange message. It said, "This morning I sent identical telegrams to you and the three Division commanders." The division commanders under Fredendall's II Corps command were, Allen of the 1st, Ward of the 1st Armored, and Ryder of the 34th. The telegram said, "As an American I am proud of the way in which American troops, in the recent battling, recovered from initial shocks and speedily demonstrated a readiness to slug it out with the enemy. Our troops are rapidly becoming battlewise and their future operations are certain to bring discouragement to the ranks of our enemies. Front line units now have the urgent task of replacement, rehabilitation, and training, and I assure you that I am straining every nerve to bring your magnificent organization up to strength as quickly as it is humanly possible. . . .

"I hope that every man in your command realizes that I have complete confidence in his readiness and ability to do his full part alongside our gallant allies in driving our enemies out of Africa. Please accept my personal thanks and congratulations on your fine record of leadership."

To Fredendall, he said, "In the case of these three Division Commanders, I believe that we have good sound men and, therefore, the job is to make the very best use of each."

That meant he was not going to fire Ward as he had been asked. He went on:

> There is no question at all in my mind of you having proved your right to command a separate and fairly large American force on the battlefield. . . .
>
> I would not leave you in command of that Corps one second if you did not have my confidence. . . .
>
> Among the things that please me most is the fact that after several days of rough handling and constant retreat, you were able—through your efforts and your personality—not only to hold the position that had to be held but were able to stage at least minor counterattacks that showed that the subordinates under you had not lost their fighting spirit.

After reading that message Fredendall might well have decided that he was in for a third star as well as a second DSM. Although he had gone to bed for twenty-four hours during the battle he had "through your efforts and your personality" done what had to be done, and he had the confidence of his commander in chief. If he had not, he would not have held his job "one second."

Still, although Fredendall was doing such a wonderful job, and his three division commanders were doing terrific jobs, Eisenhower did add, "With the establishment of an American sector, it may be that you will need some additional assistance in the way of staff officers. If you do, give me a list of the best men you know. Don't trifle with mediocrity or with people that just get by. Let me know your needs in this line as early as possible, if any."

Yet the very next day, in a cable to Marshall, Eisenhower seemed to be having some doubts about the man who had been in the chief of staff's little black book. He said:

Please do not look upon any communication I send you as a defensive explanation. Not only do I refuse to indulge in alibis but, frankly, I feel that you have given such evidence of confidence in me, that I never experience the feeling of having to defend my actions. . . .

Today, I am writing about personnel. The problem plagues me all the time. As you know, I have had my moments of doubt about Fredendall and I have spent much time in travelling just to assure myself that he was doing his job successfully. . . . By every yardstick that can be produced for measuring an officer he is tops—except for one thing. He has difficulty in picking good men and, even worse, in handling personnel. He is too good to lose. . . . his assignment is critical at this moment because Alexander is depending on the II Corps, as an *independent* American organization to conduct a speedy attack. I have discovered that a man must take the tools he has and do the best he can with them, but in this case I must either find a good substitute for Fredendall or must place in his command a number of assistants who are so stable and sound that they will not be disturbed by his idiosyncrasies. . . . Fredendall's staff I consider weak, and I am searching the theater to pick him up a good man or two to reinforce him. I want him to have every single thing that it is possible for him to have.

Those last murky sentences are surprising given the fact that they were written by a man known for his incisive prose. The real answer was hiding; it was to "find a good substitute for Fredendall."

Back in Washington the chief of staff seemed to have guessed that Eisenhower was in trouble and that he needed help but was reluctant, perhaps too proud to ask for it. In any case, even before Eisenhower had finished his message to Marshall, he received a cable from him. "What about Fredendall? Has recent fighting confirmed your opinion or given you another impression?"

The reply to that was easy, and Eisenhower's prose was once again precise and to the point, though he did leave room for both him and Marshall to backtrack. He said, "Just as your #3238 arrived I was preparing a message to you on the same subject. In the past two days I have developed grave doubts about Fredendall in his future role. I am having a final conference with Alexander this evening and tomorrow. Fredendall is a good fighter, energetic, and self-confident and I have encouraged him to the limit by the fullest expressions of confidence in his work."

The first part of that last sentence is complete fiction. The second part is true, though greatly understated.

Eisenhower went on, "His difficulty is in handling personnel in which field he is in constant trouble while I am not sure that he is big enough to command an independent sector under Alexander. A most vital job is facing the II Corps which will operate as a purely American unit in a somewhat independent role. I am making still another visit to see him tomorrow morning and it is possible that I will relieve him if this is necessary. His good qualities and experience should still not repeat not be lost to the Army."

The next morning Eisenhower went to Tebessa again, and he relieved Fredendall of his command. Just what was said is not known, but he was certainly not harsh with the man. In *Crusade,* he said, "I had no intention of recommending Fredendall for reduction or of placing the blame for the initial defeats in the Kasserine battle on his shoulders, and so informed him. Several others, including myself, shared responsibility for our week of reverses. But morale in the II Corps was shaken and the troops had to be picked up quickly. For such a job Patton had no superior in the Army, whereas I believed that Fredendall was better suited for a training job in the States than he was for battle leadership."

Eisenhower was never a man who enjoyed someone else's defeat—unless the someone else was a Nazi or, in his later years, a Communist.

When Fredendall got back to the States, a great many people considered him a hero. After all the *New York Times* on February 25 had said that he and Alexander "were in active command of the operation that halted the enemy threat to Allied communications." Fredendall was given a training command in the Second Army and that year became a lieutenant general.

John Eisenhower said of his father's reluctance to relieve Fredendall, "Had Eisenhower, at that time, possessed the confidence he would develop during the next year, he might not have been so lenient."

Handy put it another way. He said, "In France Eisenhower would go out in the field, and if he saw an officer hesitate unduly or saw him do something absolutely wrong, he relieved him on the spot."

On the afternoon of March 5, Eisenhower met Patton at the Maison Blanche airport, and Ike told him, Patton said, that he was to replace Fredendall because the fighting in Tunisia "was primarily a tank show and I know more about tanks."

The next day, back at headquarters in Algiers, Eisenhower wrote some advice for Patton. He said Georgie did not have to prove that he was courageous. "I want you as corps commander—not as a casualty." He then proceeded to tell him exactly the opposite of what he had recently told Fredendall. "In actual battle under present conditions a Commander can really handle his outfit only from his Command Post, where he can be in touch both with his Commander and with his subordinates."

He then told Patton to do what he had not done in the preceding days. He said:

> You need have no doubts whatsoever about enjoying my fullest confidence. I mention this again because it affects your handling of personnel under you. You must not retain for one instant any man in a responsible position where you have become doubtful of his ability to do his job. We cannot afford to throw away soldiers and equipment and, what is even

more important, effectiveness in defeating our enemies, because we are reluctant to damage the feelings of old friends. This matter calls for more courage than any other thing you will have to do, but I expect you to be perfectly cold-blooded about it. . . . If a man fails you, send him back to me and let me worry about it. I will give you the best available replacement or stand by any arrangement you want to make.

While firing a subordinate is difficult, giving advice to his successor is not.

★ ★ ★

AN AUSPICIOUS OMEN

During Marshall's visit to North Africa for the Casablanca conference, he suggested to Eisenhower that Ike needed someone to act as his "eyes and ears." Someone to observe and listen to what was being said and was happening in the field and report back to the commanding general. It was a job that, it turned out, would be misunderstood by some, but in a cable to Marshall, Eisenhower said, "The nature of the work involved here requires brains, tact, and imagination more than it does thorough acquaintanceship with the theater, so that any man of ability might be able to operate efficiently after a week of indoctrination." He attached a list of twelve active major generals he thought could do the job and the name of one retired general. The third name on the list was that of O. N. Bradley, his 1915 classmate at the Point. In the twenty-eight years since their graduation they had never served together and had seen each other less than half a dozen times.

Marshall chose Bradley for the assignment because he thought he was the best qualified. He had had his name in his little black book for a very long time.

Bradley was then stationed at Camp Gordon Johnson on the desolate gulf coast of Florida, training the division he commanded, the 28th, for an amphibious landing. On February 16 he received a telephone call from Lesley McNair's office in Washington telling him that he was being sent overseas. He was not told where, but the caller did say, "You're going to join your classmate. I can't say anything more over the phone."

Bradley knew then that he would be joining Eisenhower in North Africa. He and Ike had very similar backgrounds. His father had at times been a farmer, but more often he was an underpaid teacher in one-room schools in Missouri. Bradley had been born in 1893 in Clark, Missouri. Neither Bradley nor Eisenhower was considered an outstanding cadet; both were more interested in sports than in scholarship, but, as Bradley was to point out later, every member of the 1914 baseball team who stayed in the army became a general.

Both Bradley and Eisenhower were members of F Company while cadets, but they were not especially close. Like Eisenhower, Bradley did not get an overseas assignment during the First World War, and in the years ahead neither had a spectacular career. In the years between the wars, Bradley was stationed at twenty-eight different posts. He did, however, have one advantage over Ike. He attracted the attention of George C. Marshall in 1929; Eisenhower had to wait more than a decade to do that. In 1929 Bradley reported to Lieutenant Colonel Marshall, assistant commander of the Infantry School at Fort Benning, Georgia. Bradley was an instructor in tactics at the school, and the following year, Marshall, assistant commandant of the school, made Bradley chief of the weapons section. In 1940 Marshall, then chief of staff, made Bradley assistant secretary of the general staff. In February 1941 Marshall made him commander of the infantry school. That same month Bradley became the first member of the class of 1915 to get a star.

On February 24 Bradley reported to Eisenhower's office in the Hotel St. Georges. Bradley said, "Slumped in a chair before his situation map, a long stick in his hand, Eisenhower outlined my mission." He was, Eisenhower said, to go to the front "and look for the things I would want to see myself if I only had the time. Bedell will give you a letter telling Fredendall and the others that you are to act as my eyes and ears."

It did not take Eisenhower long to realize that in "Brad" he had someone special. As early as March 20, in a letter to Handy, Ike said of the man who was to serve with him for the rest of the war, "Bradley is . . . on the job. What a godsend it was to me to get that man!"

In February 1948 when Bradley was to take over from Eisenhower as chief of staff Ike wrote to his old West Point roommate, P. A. Hodgson:

Tomorrow, the 7th, I quit the job of Chief of Staff. Bradley is taking over, a circumstance which is of great gratification to me. Throughout the war he was not only an outstanding commander, but he was my warm friend and close adviser. I think I may claim some right to at least a casual recognition in the field of strategy, organization, and in developing Allied teamwork. Bradley was the master tactician of our forces and in my opinion will eventually come to be recognized as America's foremost battle leader.

But Ike's warmest tribute to Brad was recalled in a memorial tribute to Eisenhower after his death. Congressman W. G. Daniel of Virginia reported that Eisenhower had once said to him, "When Stonewall Jackson was killed at Chancellorsville, General Lee is reported to have said, 'With the death of General Jackson, I have lost my right arm.' Had I lost Bradley in Europe, I would have lost both arms."

When Bradley went to the Tunisian front early in 1943 he took with him a letter addressed to all U.S. commanders. It said:

Major General O. N. Bradley is visiting your headquarters as a personal representative of the Commanding General, North African Theater of Operations, to discuss questions of interest to you concerning American troops under your command. Please give him every possible cooperation and assistance.

Bradley's mission was not popular. Fredendall treated him with contempt and ignored him as much as possible, but Bradley did not tell Eisenhower his opinion of the man until Ike arrived at the Tebessa headquarters on March 5. According to Bradley, "Eisenhower asked me to join him . . . on the porch of the small European stucco house in which we were meeting.

" 'What do you think of the command here?' he asked.

" 'It's pretty bad,' I replied. " 'I've talked to all the division commanders. To a man they've lost confidence in Fredendall as the corps commander.' "

Eisenhower said that he had already ordered Patton to come from Morocco. "He'll report in tomorrow to take command of II Corps," he said.

On March 8 Ike told Marshall, "The plan I tentatively adopted was to have Patton because of his local prestige, experience, and qualities of leadership take charge of the immediate work of rehabilitating the II Corps and to remain in command until after completion of the next offensive phase which will terminate when the Eighth Army has gotten into the open north of the Gabès Gap, I hope by the end of this month. Bradley is now associated closely with Patton and it was my first intention that upon completion of the next phase I would send Patton back to his job of preparing the Western Task Force [for the invasion of Sicily] and place Bradley in command of the II Corps."

Patton made certain immediately that no one could have any doubt about the fact that changes had been made at II Corps. Bradley said that when Patton arrived late in the morning of March 7, "Even the Arabs plodding through the muddy streets picked up their robes and scurried into the nearest doorways. The armored vehicles bristled with machine guns and their tall fishpole antennas whipped crazily overhead. In the lead car Patton stood like a charioteer. He was scowling into the wind and his jaw strained against the web strap of a two-starred steel helmet. . . .

"In the words of Eisenhower, Patton was to rejuvenate the jaded II Corps and bring it to a 'fighting pitch.' By the third day after his arrival the II Corps staff was fighting mad—but at Patton, not at the Germans."

Patton made clear immediately on his arrival that helmets were always to be worn, and so were leggings, correctly threaded; neckties were also required, and that meant everyone, officers, noncommissioned officers, and privates. Nurses working in hospital tents had to wear helmets, and so did auto mechanics. Patton himself seemed to be everywhere at once seeing that his harsh rules were enforced.

G-2 Dickson said, "He was as quick as a hair trigger to enforce this penalty. . . . One cold afternoon I watched while a Signal Corps lieutenant took off his helmet to scratch his head. He was spotted by Georgie and immediately fined $50." Enlisted men were fined $25 for infractions of the rules about uniforms.

Everybody hated the new orders, but, as Bradley said, "Each time a soldier knotted his necktie, threaded his leggings, and buckled on his heavy steel helmet, he was forcibly reminded that Patton had come to command the II Corps; that the pre-Kasserine days had ended, and that a tough new era had begun."

Patton immediately made it clear to Eisenhower that he did not want Bradley around as a spy; Bradley had to be under his command or get the hell out. He shouted over the phone to Beetle, "We're awfully hard up for a good Number Two man as deputy corps commander. . . . If it's all right with Ike, I'm going to make Bradley my deputy commander." Eisenhower gave his approval, and Bradley became deputy commander of the corps.

Alexander observed the two men together, and he said that they were:

Two completely contrasted military characters; the one impatient of inaction, the other unwilling to commit himself to active operations unless he could clearly see their purpose. On one of my visits to the American headquarters, I was fascinated to hear this characteristic exchange:

PATTON: "Why are we sitting doing nothing? We must do something."
BRADLEY: "Wait a minute, George! What do you propose we do?"
PATTON: "Anything rather than just sit on our backsides."

Both were good soldiers. Patton was a thruster, prepared to take any risks; Bradley, as I have indicated, was more cautious. Patton should have lived during the Napoleonic Wars—he would have been a splendid Marshal under Napoleon.

At first Patton was impressed with Alexander. "I was very much taken with Alexander. He is a snob in the best sense of the word—very alert and interested in all sorts of things including genealogy. . . . He seemed to agree with most of my [military] ideas. I really think he is a good soldier and much more talkative than he is supposed to be."

This amiability was not destined to last, however, and Ike knew Georgie well enough to prepare for a quick change of mind. He wrote Patton on March 6, "I expect you to respond to General Alexander's orders exactly as if they were issued by me. I want no mistake about my thorough belief in unity of command."

On the 8th Eisenhower wrote George on another matter, one that, with Patton, it was seldom necessary to touch on. Was it possible that the II Corps was not being aggressive enough? He said:

Dear George:
    In the operational report for March 7 I saw the following remark with respect to II Corps.
    "No patrolling but no contact with enemy."
    This raises a question in my mind of why we don't patrol aggressively enough by day and by night to make contact? Would it not be good for our own troops? Would not such action be in conformity with the old dictum, "Contact once gained must never be lost"?

Patton's handwritten reply of March 13 reported that since March 8 his patrols had taken "eighty-nine prisoners. . . . Anytime you have any suggestion tactical or otherwise I shall be delighted to get them as you know that so far as I am concerned your ideas are tops."

Patton now had four divisions under his command, the 1st was led by the boisterous Terry Allen and Brigadier General Theodore Roosevelt, Jr., Teddy's son, who was a frequent drinking companion of Allen's. From the beginning, Patton had doubts about Pinky Ward as leader of the 1st Armored, and he proved to be right. The remaining two divisions, the 9th and the 34th, were held in reserve in case of an attack from Rommel's forces. It was some time before the Allies learned that Rommel had left North Africa on March 9; the field marshal stopped in Rome to convince Mussolini that the fight in Tunisia was hopeless, but he failed, and he failed to convince Hitler and was forbidden to return to North Africa. Rommel's command was taken over by Arnim, a great admirer of der Fuehrer, who even wore a mustache very much like his master's.

Eisenhower's first task when he replaced Fredendall was to help Montgomery get through the Mareth Line, an old French fortification which ran twenty-three miles from the Atlantic to the Matmata Hills. The line was heavily fortified, part of it underground. From the beginning it was clear that Alexander was keeping American troops in a subsidiary position because he did not trust the Americans to mount a major offensive. It was necessary to establish a forward supply center for Montgomery's troops, and Patton's troops were to help set up that supply center, to take over the forward airfields, to assist Montgomery, and to draw off enemy forces fighting him. Those were not welcome assignments for a man who disliked the British in general and Montgomery in particular. While he waited for the battle to begin, Patton continued to emphasize discipline. On the 14th he said in his diary, "Think the soldiers are improving a little. Am sure it does good [for me] to be seen. Yesterday I took a walk and collected 8 soldiers and 2 lieutenants for improper uniforms. Had them fall in and follow me—quite a procession."

The Montgomery attack was scheduled to begin on March 20, and Patton was to take Gafsa a few days before that and make a series of feints toward Maknassy. His troops took Gafsa on the 16th, and Patton immediately became a national hero back in the States. Actually, what Patton called "the great and famous battle of Gafsa" was no battle at all. As troops of the 1st Division approached the village, it fell with almost no opposition and the American division moved on toward El Guettar and Maknassy.

On the 15th Eisenhower had told Marshall that he planned to visit Patton for several days, and he left shortly after breakfast on the 16th and returned in the evening on the 19th. He reported to Marshall that both the 1st Infantry and the 1st Armored divisions had done a good job, but that "bad weather and execrable conditions of roads" made the advance of the latter "exceedingly difficult. . . . The prolonged rains in this part of Tunisia at this season of the year have been most unexpected, yet I believe that this condition will soon pass and more activity ensue. The officers and men of both divisions are in fine shape and eager to fight. Patton, assisted by Bradley, has done a splendid job in a very short time, and I have no fears of the outcome if we can produce any fight along the line of Gafsa–Maknassy–Faid."

In that same message Eisenhower told Marshall that he had received a copy of an exchange of messages between Churchill and Stalin. Churchill had told

Stalin that he hoped the Axis troops would be cleared out of North Africa by the end of April, and Stalin's gruff reply said, "It is evident that the Anglo-American operations [in Europe] will not only not have been expedited but on the contrary they have been postponed till the end of April." As for HUSKY, the planned invasion of Sicily, Stalin said, "Fully realizing the importance of Sicily. I must however point out that it cannot replace the second front in France."

Eisenhower was upset by the fact that Churchill "has apparently commited himself definitely to the June HUSKY date. All planning constantly reveals new complications and increased demands, whereas it is reported to me this evening that shipping in sight fails to meet minimum requirements by forty-two vessels. While I will immediately go into these matters, it appears that possibly the seriousness of the problem facing us has not been appreciated by AGENT [Churchill]. I have been given until April 10 by CCS [Combined Chiefs of Staff] to make a final report on possibilities. I notice that AGENT has been basing his calculations on a completion of the Tunisian campaign in April, whereas Alexander refuses to make an estimate earlier than May 30. Personally, I believe that the current operation should be completed in five to six weeks after the Eighth Army breaks through the Gabès bottleneck."

So Churchill was causing concern on the part of Eisenhower, and two of the commander in chief's deputies, Bradley and Patton, were having trouble with another Britisher, Alexander, who on March 19 sent a directive to their command post setting forth the plans for the final conquest of Tunisia. The 9th Infantry Division was to be transferred to Anderson for an attack on Bizerte to be led by the British First and Eighth Armies. Bradley said, "The directive alarmed me when I saw it . . . for it . . . meant that II Corps would be pinched out of its fair share in the final victory campaign."

Patton's reaction was predictably more explosive. He wrote in his diary, "I kept my temper and agreed. There is nothing else to do, but—I can't see how Ike can let them [the British] pull his leg so. It is awful. . . . The more I think about the plan of pinching us out, the madder I get, but no one knows that, except me."

With Patton's permission, Bradley went to Haidra, where the British were all accommodation. The last thing anybody had in mind was to "pinch out" the Americans. The whole thing had to do with roads and was a matter of logistics. Alexander would, as Bradley said, "find it impossible to support II Corps over existing roads on that Northern Tunisian front."

Bradley was not taken in, however. He thought the plan was bad in every way. Alexander would be denying himself the use of an entire corps, albeit American, three full divisions, and "I did not believe he could afford to waste them." Furthermore, taking the 9th division away would once more break up II Corps "into separate American bits for indiscriminate assignment to any Allied command," and it violated the principle that "American troops would fight under American command." Finally, Bradley felt that the American troops had won the right to an American victory under the American flag. The Alexander plan would "irritate friendly relations between our forces."

He was sure Eisenhower did not know about Alexander's plan and flew to

Algiers to explain his and Patton's feelings in the matter. Bradley, unlike Patton, did not think that Ike had "sold out" to the British, but he did think that "As Allied commander in the Mediterranean Eisenhower walked a chalk line to avoid being branded pro-American by the British command. For his command had become a test of Allied unity in the field, and any such label would surely have destroyed Eisenhower's effectiveness as an Allied commander. As a result of these precautions . . . some Americans tended to look on Eisenhower as too pro-British."

Bradley saw Eisenhower in the afternoon of March 22 and the morning of the 23rd. Indeed Ike did not know of Alexander's plan. "He listened apprehensively to my explanation," said Bradley, who went on to tell him what he already knew, that the people of the United States wanted a victory and that American troops ought to be able to fight under an American command, an idea that also cannot have escaped Ike's attention.

So what did Brad have in mind?

According to the account of the war written by one of his aides, Lieutenant Colonel (then Major) Chester B. Hansen, Bradley "gestured toward the map on his wall.

" 'Move the entire II Corps up north,' he said. '—not just the Ninth Division and then let us go after Bizerte on our own.' "

Eisenhower agreed, and later on the 23rd he sent a message to Alexander that began:

> As we have agreed, I continue to communicate to you freely on matters that seem to me important, in the confidence that nothing I say will be taken by you as unjustified interference in your special province. I think that only the closest of understanding between you and myself can ever produce the results that we seek, not only at this moment, but in any further tasks our two governments may assign to this whole team.

So much for diplomacy, tact, the smoothing of possibly ruffled feathers. Then he got down to the business at hand.

> I desire . . . that you make a real effort to use the II Corps right up to the bitter end of the campaign. . . . I would consider it unfortunate if the developments of the campaign were such that participation by American troops, in an American sector, was deliberately eliminated as the crisis of the campaign approaches. I believe that our units are learning fast. Their morale, technique and physical condition improve daily, and the idea of U.S.-British partnership that is so essential to the final winning of this war, constantly grows in strength. . . . I am convinced that when the time arrives for the final attacks, the II Corps will be a real asset and one capable of delivering sturdy and effective blows, unless, of course, it should become badly depleted in the meantime. It will be just as bold and aggressive as you tell it to be.

The words were not totally what Bradley had hoped for, but they were strong enough; Alexander would get the message; American forces were to fight together under American leadership. Besides, Alex—they were by now Alex and Ike to each other—was not Anderson, and he was not Montgomery. John Gunther said about this time, "When you mention Monty to people, they may curse or grin. Every time I asked somebody about Alexander, I got a reaction of pleasure, genuine warmth, and admiration."

On the 29th Ike sent Marshall a copy of the letter and said, "I am enclosing copy of a letter I recently wrote General Alexander. In the main it is self-explanatory. It was brought about by the fact that his outline plan for a continuation of the Battle of Tunisia seemed to me to be a bit on the slow, methodical side and, in addition, appeared to contemplate the eventual pinching out of the U.S. II Corps. I have taken up both these matters verbally, and Alexander sees eye to eye with me in principle; however, I felt that a letter, which could be circulated among members of his staff might have a wholesome effect."

On the 30th and 31st Eisenhower visited Montgomery's command post south of Gabès. It was only their second meeting; the first had been at Montgomery's headquarters in England the previous summer. This time Eisenhower did not smoke in Monty's presence, and, knowing that Montgomery liked to go to bed early, he excused himself and as Montgomery's biographer Nigel Hamilton put it, "hit the sack" shortly after dinner.

In an April 5 letter to Marshall, now in the Eisenhower papers, Eisenhower reported his visit.

In the early part of the week I made a trip to Montgomery's headquarters and had a most interesting time. I was particularly fortunate in getting to traverse critical portions of the Mareth position (by jeep airplane) before the debris of battle had been cleared away. Many lessons were plain right on the ground. Montgomery is of different caliber from some of the outstanding British leaders you have met.

According to Hamilton, the letter also said, "He [Montgomery] is unquestionably able, but very conceited. For your most secret and confidential information, I will give you my opinion which is that he is so proud of his successes to date that he will never willingly make a single move until he is absolutely certain of success—in other words, until he has concentrated enough resources so that anybody could practically guarantee the outcome. This may be somewhat unfair to him, but that is the definite impression I received."

He did add, however, "Unquestionably he is an able tactician and organizer and, provided only that Alexander will never let him forget for one second who is the boss, he should deliver in good style. The . . . esprit and efficiency of the Eighth Army and Desert Air Force are obvious to anyone."

Monty, for his part, wrote in his diary on the night of the 30th: "General Eisenhower stayed the night with me. He knows practically nothing about how to make war, and definitely nothing about how to fight battles. He is probably quite good at the political stuff." And to Brooke the next day he said, "He knows nothing whatever about how to make war or to fight battles; he should be kept right away from all that business if we want to win this war."

Monty complained to Alexander that "Eisenhower . . . brought no bedding! I suppose they think we live in hotels.

"I liked Eisenhower. But I could not stand him about the place for long; his high-pitched accent, and loud talking, would drive me mad."

Shortly after Ike's return to Algiers, another inter-Allied dispute broke out, this one between Patton and a hard-nosed New Zealander, Air Vice-Marshal Sir Arthur Coningham, commander of the First Allied (North African) Tactical Air Force.

At the time in that theater what was called a sitrep, a situation report, was issued every twenty-four hours to tell higher and adjacent headquarters what had gone on during the previous twenty-four hours. On April 1 Patton's II Corps sitrep said that front-line troops in the corps area had been "continuously bombed all morning" by German planes. The reason, the report said, was that "Total lack of air cover for our [ground] units has allowed German air force to operate at will."

That seemed to mean that Coningham's tactical air force was not doing what it was supposed to do, provide air cover for Allied ground troops. When Coningham read the report he was furious, and he sent a report to all headquarters in the theater and to Eisenhower's headquarters saying that II Corps was making a good deal over very little. Four men had been killed in the raids, the New Zealander said, and there had been "a very small number wounded." It was to be hoped, the air marshal said, that II Corps was not using the air force "as an alibi for lack of success on the ground . . . such inaccurate and false reports should cease."

Coningham's boss, Tedder, saw the inflammatory message and immediately recognized that it "could have led to a major crisis in Anglo-American relations." He telephoned Eisenhower, and, although they had a bad connection he said that he sensed that Ike was "deeply concerned." Tedder apologized for Coningham's message and said that it would immediately be withdrawn and that Coningham would apologize.

Eisenhower saw the whole thing as a personal failure. He was not doing his job; he was not achieving a peaceful cooperation between the Allies. If he had been, a thing like this would never have happened. He was so upset that he drafted a cable to Marshall saying that he should be relieved of duty. He did not send it, however, and no copy of the message has been preserved. It was the second time in less than four months he had thought of becoming a lieutenant colonel stateside. That was the last time—on the record anyway—that he considered it.

Coningham's apology was only twenty-seven words long. It said that his complaint had been "withdrawn and cancelled," and he added that he had not said that "II Corps personnel are not battleworthy." That had been an error in transmission. What he had actually said was *"few* corps personnel are not battleworthy."

The apology by no means satisfied Patton. He remained "quite mad and very disgusted," and in a letter to Eisenhower said that he considered Coningham's words an "altogether inadequate apology to the United States troops, many of whom have marched and fought over hostile country since the 17th [of March]."

On April 5 Eisenhower explained the whole matter to Patton; at least he thought he did. He said:

I had already taken up, prior to receipt of your message, the matter of unjustified distribution of adverse criticism made against your Corps. . . . However, I realize also that the great purpose of complete Allied teamwork must be achieved in this theater and it is my conviction that this purpose will not be furthered by demanding the last pound of flesh for every error, when other measures should suffice. Moreover, I am certain that the officer concerned quickly appreciated the gravity of the incident and has already taken steps to alleviate the effect. . . . In connection with this matter I am since informed that there was a certain amount of unwise distribution of your sitrep. Who was to blame for this is immaterial and I do not intend to pursue the matter further. . . . General Alexander would be extremely hurt if he felt that at any time you had failed to make to him proper representations about personnel or any other matter affecting efficiency, morale and esprit in your unit, merely because of the mistaken belief that since he is a British officer, you must not presume to offer any advice or counsel prior to his making of a final decision. . . . Please do not look on this as a lecture, I am simply trying to present for your consideration, views that I deem to be of the highest importance in the further prosecution of this campaign. . . .

P.S.   General Alexander has told me that your Corps is not to be pinched out of the coming campaign. . . .

Patton was by no means satisfied. He said after reading the message, "It is noteworthy that had I done what Conygham [sic] did, I would have been relieved. Ike told me later that he could not punish Conygham because he was a New Zealander and political reasons forbad. Unfortunately I am neither a Democrat or a Republican—just a soldier."

Also on April 5 Eisenhower wrote a far from cheerful message to Marshall; he said that Butcher had returned from almost a month's stay in the States where he had found that "many people are considering the war already won and are concerning themselves with considerations of 'after the war' jockeying for position. It seems amazing to me that people do not understand that right here in Tunisia we are still facing a great battle with extensive losses and before we get much further along these will be multiplied."

He also said that:

The past week has been a most trying one and was notable for one incident that disturbed me very much. This involved a very unwise and unjust criticism of the II Corps by a senior member of the British Air Force. . . . The man's superiors moved rapidly to correct the error and to minimize the damage. There were, of course, as usual, two sides to the story but there was really no excuse for the thing happening. However, I never get really discouraged because I realize that the seeds for discord between ourselves and our British allies were sown, on our side, as far back as when we read our little red school history books. My method is to drag all these matters squarely into the open, discuss them frankly, and insist upon positive rather than negative action in furthering the purpose of Allied unity.

In the same message he told Marshall he was sending Pinky Ward home. Not only was Ward not Fredendall's type of tank commander; he was not Patton's either. Every morning Ward's 1st Armored Division, which was holding a crucial pass, was attacked by the Germans, and every morning it withdrew a few thousand feet. In the afternoon it simply retook what it had given up. Patton replaced Ward with Harmon. Eisenhower had earlier told Marshall "I completely agree with General Patton as to the necessity for this action," and recommended that Ward be incorporated "immediately into the training system at home. He has been personally gallant, was slightly wounded, and has been decorated for bravery. . . . He has not been fully able to recover from initial shocks and exhibit the necessary sturdiness of purpose to rehabilitate the morale and fighting spirit of his organization."

Harmon took over command of the 1st Armored Division and Ward returned to the United States to take command of the Tank Destroyer Center; eventually he commanded the 20th Armored Division, which had a distinguished record later in Europe.

On April 7 a happy and historic event occurred for the Allies. A reconnaissance party from Montgomery's Eighth Army met with one from Patton's II Corps on a desert highway between Gabès and Gafsa. The three British scout cars and five American armored cars advanced somewhat uncertainly at first. Then they rushed toward each other. Sergeant Joseph Randall from State Center, Iowa, said, "Hello, you bloody Limey." And a red-haired soldier from London who was wearing a blue beret said, with proper British restraint, "Very glad to see you." The British had with difficulty pushed the German forces back almost 1,500 miles, and the Americans had, also with difficulty, driven the Germans back 140 miles from the Kasserine Pass.

Things moved swiftly for the Allies after that. Sfax fell on the 10th, the vital port city of Sousse was evacuated by Axis troops taken by the British on the 12th. At midnight on April 15 Patton, as had been planned, turned over command of II Corps to Bradley and returned to the planning of HUSKY. The next day Eisenhower wrote a message to Bradley saying that while the 1st and 9th divisions of II Corps had "established for themselves reputations as sound fighting units . . . the 1st Armored and the 34th Infantry Divisions have been subjected to quite severe criticism. . . . We must remember that in both cases there were many extenuating circumstances, which we have not attempted either to publicize or to discuss at any length. Beyond all this, the experience of the British Army in its early days in the desert was, in some instances, far more unfortunate than has been our own."

He said that in a telegram he had received from Marshall he learned that "faulty censorship" at his Algiers headquarters had caused to be attributed to American units "the blame for not securing a more decisive victory over Rommel in the south and cutting him off during his retreat. This has had a most disheartening effect at home and apparently morale is suffering badly. . . . The sector you have been given is not well suited for sustained and heavy attacks; the character of the country and the paucity of communications make your task a difficult one. But we must overcome these difficulties."

Finally, he said:

Let me offer one item of advice. It is that you must be tough with your immediate subordinates and they must be equally tough with their respective subordinates. We have passed the time when we cannot demand from troops reasonable results after you have made careful plans and preparations and estimated that the task can be accomplished. A General Officer reported to me this morning that a battalion of infantry working under him requested permission to withdraw and reorganize because it had a total of *ten killed* during an attack. We have reached the point where troops *must* secure objectives assigned by Commanders and, where necessary, we must direct leaders to get out and *lead and to secure the necessary results.*

In Bradley's case that advice was unnecessary; he was tough on himself and on his subordinates, but he never raised his voice to do it, and he often went to the front in a battered jeep, looking more like a GI than a general, and he always asked the right questions.

By the time the change in command took place an Allied victory in North Africa was certain, yet it would be almost a month before the fighting stopped. The Allies had encircled the enemy, and the circle was made smaller almost daily—but always at a cost. Hitler, as had happened many times before and would happen many times again, refused to recognize the inevitable. In his mind the Axis forces could stay put as long as they wished. Mussolini felt that the Allies could be held back until winter.

At the northern end of the circle were 30,000 Americans, the respected, experienced 1st and 9th divisions; on the other side were 20,000 Germans. The hilly, rocky red earth was ideal for defense, but they had no air force, no artillery, not many supplies, and very little chance to get reinforcements.

The final big drive of the Tunisian campaign began on April 19. Alexander's plan was for Anderson's First Army to make the first thrust, along with one of Montgomery's armored divisions. The Eighth Army and II Corps would make the secondary attack.

Montgomery began the operation with a night attack on the 19th, but it was not a success, and he stopped the attack for four days to regroup. He was still regrouping when the main attack began on the 22nd and 23rd. In the beginning the Germans, duly forewarned, held firm against the First Army. Anderson was assigned more of Montgomery's troops by Alexander, but no breakthrough was achieved.

On April 23rd the 1st and the 9th divisions moved forward, and three days later the 1st stopped short of Longstop Hill, which was to become the famous Hill 609. Bradley sent the 34th Division forward on the 26th, and four days later it had captured the hill.

"With this successful attack against Hill 609," said Bradley, "the 34th rid itself of the poor reputation with which it had emerged from Fondouk."

On April 22, the day before the 1st and the 9th began their attack, Eisenhower and Butcher flew to Alexander's headquarters for a conference with the British general and with Giraud. After that they went by jeep to Bradley's headquarters. Bradley took them to Terry Allen's 1st Division headquarters, where Allen was laying out plans for the dawn attack. That was encouraging, and so was the news that a number of German six-engine Me 323 transport planes, each of which could carry 120 troops, had been shot down over the bay of Tunis. Ike and his naval aide returned to Algiers that evening where they learned for the first time that Arnim had taken over Rommel's command and that the British Eighth Army had taken Enfidaville.

On Easter Sunday Butcher said that Eisenhower was "waiting as patiently as possible for news of a breakthrough. . . . He is shooting the wad. If they [the Allied forces under his command] can't break through, then he may be on his way home, defeated.

The advance went well from the beginning. Bradley sent Ryder's unfortunate 34th Division to take the famous Hill 609. He told Ryder, " 'Get me that hill, and you'll break up the enemy's defenses clear across our front. Take it and no one will ever again doubt the toughness of your division.' . . . Seldom has an enemy contested a position more bitterly than did the German high on Hill 609. For he knew once that rampart fell, he had no choice but to withdraw to the east, and thus open a path to Mateur on the flank of his Tunis line."

By April 30, the 34th, assisted by tanks, had secured the hill, and the bravery of the officers and men of that division was no longer in question. Drew Middleton wrote, "When they build the monuments for the men who won this war, remember 609 with its poppies as red as any that bloom in Flanders, and the Americans who died there as grandly as any who died in the Argonne or at Gettysburg or Bunker Hill." The 34th went on to fight in Italy, and in two years in the mountains there it spent 605 days in the line and suffered 20,000 casualties, about one and a half times its full strength.

On Easter Sunday Butcher had said, "Ike's position just now is something like that of a hen setting on a batch of eggs. He is waiting for the eggs to hatch, and is in the mental state of wondering if they will ever break the shell."

During the first week in May it became apparent that Eisenhower would *not* soon be on his way home. True, as he told Marshall on the 5th, "Even the Italian, defending mountainous country, is very difficult to drive out, and the German is a real problem." On the other hand, he said, "We outnumber, out-tank, and out-gun him." The battle ahead would still be difficult, because "the mountainous terrain in itself imposes very slow and laborious cross-country movement; while the enemy with his use of innumerable land mines and skillful utilization of the ground for emplacing machine guns and mortars, has made our task a tough one."

The Allies had learned some things, however, and the lessons "have *not* been developed by planners; they are the result of earnest consideration by the ground force commanders."

As for the invasion of Sicily, Ike said, "Anticipating similar conditions in the mountainous coastlines of HUSKY, all of us have come to believe it best to attack in the strongest possible forces on the vital southeastern coastline and avoid dispersed landings, which might leave us in a series of small pockets all around the coastline and with no real possibility of operating rapidly toward a common junction." Eisenhower continued to learn from his mistakes. As Gruenther once said, "He was the most educable man I have ever known."

In his May 5 letter to Marshall, Eisenhower said, "As to the current battle: Yesterday the II Corps took Mateur, continuing the good work and great improvement that began with the assumption of command of the II Corps by Patton in March. Bradley is bringing the whole corps along in fine style . . . [it] must soon be classed as an outstanding tactical organization. . . . I would like to use the First, Third, and Forty-Fifth Divisions as the assault units for HUSKY. . . . Tomorrow morning we start the big drive which we hope and believe will see us in Tunis in a day or so."

It must not be thought, however, that Ike was concerned only with the current battle; he was thinking beyond that, beyond Sicily even. Among other things, he was thinking about the uniforms American soldiers would be wearing the next winter. He told Marshall in that same May 5 letter that it was "almost impossible to look neat and snappy in our field uniform. Given a uniform which tends to look a bit tough . . . the natural proclivities of the American soldier quickly create a general impression of a disorderly mob. . . . I suggest that the Quartermaster begin now serious work to design a better woolen uniform for next winter's wear. In my opinion, the material should be very rough wool, because such material does not show dirt and is easily kept in presentable condition. Something on the order of the British battle-dress would be indicated, although I think our people should be able to design a better woolen uniform for next winter's wear."

Nothing in Eisenhower's life was wasted. The sewing he had had to do back in Abilene and chosen to do for Mamie plus his experience in designing uniforms for the cheerleaders at West Point was to lead to a welcome change in appearance and, for that matter, the morale of several million American soldiers. The Eisenhower jacket, which further improved the appearance of American GIs, as well as, in slightly modified style, that of American women, came somewhat later.

On May 7 Eisenhower and Butcher once again flew to Bradley's headquarters and visited the command posts of the 34th and 1st divisions. Not all the news was good. Allen, although he had been ordered to hold a defensive position, had attacked, met serious opposition, suffered many casualties, and had withdrawn. Allen, despite the brilliant successes of his division, was on the way out, to be succeeded by the less flamboyant, more sober Major General Clarence R. Huebner, who had risen from the ranks.

Back in Algiers that evening it was learned that the 9th Division had taken Bizerte, and Anderson's First Army had taken Tunis. Both had happened since Eisenhower had had lunch with Bradley, but he refused to celebrate. Time enough for that when all the Axis forces had been driven out of North Africa.

He did not have long to wait. It was learned on the night of the 7th through what Butcher called an "intercept," probably ULTRA, that the Axis leaders had a plan to evacuate 30,000 Italians and 25,000 Germans to the Italian mainland. On the 8th Cunningham radioed his ships, "Sink, burn, and destroy; let nothing pass."

At noon on May 9 a surrender was signed on the II Corps front. It was 182 days after the TORCH invasion and was the first unconditional surrender of the Germans to American forces. Bradley's message to Ike said, "Mission accomplished." Ike's reply the next day, May 10th, said, "Your message is a model of brevity, clarity, and emphasis. I am bursting with pride over the magnificent fight . . . and the magnificent fighting team you are commanding."

On the 11th Churchill added his congratulations to Eisenhower from the king and the War Cabinet. He said, "The simultaneous advance of British and the United States armies side by side into Tunis and Bizerte is an augury full of hope for the future of the world. Long may they march togeher, striking down the tyrants and oppressors of mankind."

Eisenhower's message to Churchill said, "With the Hun in Tunisia surrendering by the thousand, with the remainder of his forces here disorganized and short of supplies, I feel that we can safely assume a successful completion of this particular phase of the TORCH operation. It seems to me a very appropriate time in which to tell you once again of the profound gratification that I have invariably felt for the unwavering support you have given me. My feelings in this regard are all the deeper because of the circumstances that from the standpoint of your Government, I am a foreign soldier."

By this time Eisenhower's name had become a household word all over the world, and he began hearing from a large number of old friends and from people who suddenly remembered being old friends.

On May 10, the day of the last organized Axis resistance in Tunisia and wholesale surrenders began, Gladys Harding Brooks, the woman Ike at one time had wanted to marry, wrote him from Abilene—seven handwritten pages. "Dear (General) Dwight," the letter began. It had been a long time since anybody had called him Dwight.

> The fall of Tunisia! With kings and Queens—a Prime Minister, the President of our United States—here and there—all sending you "Congratulations" as well as hundreds of others all over the world—May we too send ours and just repeat again and again how wonderful we all think you are & oh! how proud we are of you!!!

She told him that a portrait of him had been unveiled in Abilene. "Mr. Helms painted the picture, y'know & while it's lovely & all that—yet I'll have to confess—that it doesn't do you justice. You're better looking I'd say & have more sparkle—animation—'what have you' etc; etc; etc!"
She underlined each "etc" five times.

> The soldiers who visit us here—week after week—admire it; want to know all about you. They go up and down to see where you lived: & I know some stop and see your Mother. . . .

In the newsreel at the show the other eve: it showed the battle going on "over there" & there were five or six spots showing you ["you" underlined three times]. One was of you & Gen. Patton in the rain. You said something out of the corner of your mouth & I'd say from that look [underlined twice] in your eye, too—that you were plenty mad [underlined twice] right at that moment. . . .

Have you heard the song, "You Ought to be Born in Texas"?

It rhymes all the famous & notables who were born there & you're in that, too.

Soooooooooo—you see song, poetry, news shows, conversation, papers—everywhere—your name is on everyone's lips! . . . How proud your wife and son must be of you—as well as your mother & all your family & all of us, too!!!!!! ["All" is underlined four times; "us"—five.]

Our most sincere Good Wishes and Congratulations.

Gladys and Cecil

It seems unlikely that Cecil Brooks had much to do with the writing of the letter.

Eisenhower replied on June 10:

Dear Gladys:

Since reading your letter of May 10 I am having great difficulty buttoning my blouse and getting my hat down to its accustomed place on my head. I think that when I get back to the old hometown I will be in a state of mind merely to hop off the Union Pacific, stand in the middle of the street and shout "Here I am." Unless the whole town responds on an instant's notice, I will be sadly deflated. I cannot tell you how nice it is, however, to have a whole town that is completely prejudiced in one's favor. . . .

Please give my mother a ring and tell her that I am as well as ever and still looking forward to the day when I come home. Special good wishes to you and Cecil.

In June 1815, while the Battle of Waterloo was still being fought, the Duke of Wellington said, "Nothing except a battle lost can be half so melancholy as a battle won." Eisenhower did not feel that way, and while he still did not take time out to celebrate, he did write Mamie on May 12:

Today I write you with a lighter heart than I have carried in many a moon. As the papers tell you . . . we have just about completed the current job, and though my confidence has been so complete that I predicted this victory, long ago, to take place in middle of May . . . the fact that it is all but done lifts a big load from my mind. I only wish that it were the *final* battle of this war and that I could be catching the next plane for home and *you!!* But I'm afraid that happy day is still a long way off.

Loads of love, sweetheart, and don't forget your

Ike

That day, too, Colonel General Jürgen von Arnim surrendered the remaining Axis forces in North Africa. When Arnim, who so much admired Hitler, was brought through Algiers on his way to captivity, some members of Eisenhower's staff thought that the victorious Allied general should see the defeated colonel general. Eisenhower disagreed. True, to allow Arnim to pay a call on him was "a custom of bygone days," but Eisenhower said, "The custom had its origin in the fact that mercenary soldiers of old had no real enmity toward their opponents. Both side fought for the love of the fight, out of a sense of duty or, more probably, for money. . . . The tradition that all professional soldiers are really comrades at arms had, in tattered form, lasted to this day.

"For me World War II was far too personal a thing to entertain such feelings. . . . Because only by the destruction of the Axis was a decent world possible, the war became for me a crusade in the traditional sense of that often misused word. . . . I told my Intelligence officer, Brigadier Kenneth Strong, to get any information he possibly could out of the captured generals but that, as far as I was concerned, I was interested only in those who were not yet captured." Eisenhower did not deviate from that stern rule until the final surrender on May 7, 1945.

The German general was far from the most important problem presented by the prisoners taken. None of the army schools Eisenhower had attended had had courses on what an American general should do when he was faced with the care and feeding and, as soon as possible, the evacuation of what some said might be a quarter of a million of them.

B. H. Liddell Hart, in *History of the Second World War*, said that, "As to the size of the final bag [of Axis prisoners] in North Africa, there is a lack of certainty. On May 12 Alexander's headquarters reported to Eisenhower that the number of prisoners since May 5 had risen to 100,000 and it was reckoned as likely to reach 130,000 when the count was complete. A later report 'gave the total bag at about 150,000.' But in his postwar dispatch Alexander said that the total was 'a quarter of a million men.' Churchill in his Memoirs gives the same round figure but qualifies it with the word 'nearly.' Eisenhower gives it as '240,000,' of which approximately 125,000 were Germans. But Army Group Africa had reported to Rome on May 2 that its rationing strength during the month of April had varied between 170,000 and 180,000—and that was before the heavy fighting of the last week of the campaign. So it is hard to see how the number of prisoners taken could have exceeded this strength by nearly 50 per cent. Administrative staffs who are responsible for feeding troops do not tend to underestimate their numbers."

As for plans to evacuate the POWs, transportation had been meager and unsatisfactory before their influx; now it was impossible even to move the 1st Armored Division to Morocco to protect the Allied rear, much less transport prisoners.

By May 13 the Cape Bon peninsula was in Allied hands, and all Axis resistance in Africa came to an end. On May 19, during a visit to Washington for the TRIDENT conference, Churchill made a triumphant speech to Congress:

The African excursions of the two Dictators have cost their countries in killed and captured 950,000 soldiers. In addition nearly 2,400,000 gross tons of shipping have been sunk and nearly 9000 aircraft destroyed, both of these figures being exclusive of large numbers of ships and aircraft damaged. There have also been lost to the enemy 6200 guns, 2550 tanks, and 70,000 trucks. . . . Arrived at this milestone in the war, we can say, "One continent redeemed."

Harold Macmillan said, "At no time, perhaps, in the whole of the Second World War did the prestige and power of British stand so high. . . . Owing to the modesty and charm of General Alexander and of the other British officers— Tedder and Cunningham—the Americans felt no jealousy, but rather shared with brotherly affection by which each nation saluted the other's prowess. No less credit was due to General Eisenhower, the Supreme Allied Commander; for it was under his authority and through his guidance that the whole Allied forces were welded together."

On May 20 a victory parade was held in Tunis, an idea that, according to Butcher, Eisenhower "abhorred. . . . He has asked that it be laid on as a combination of victory and commemoration of those who sacrificed their lives, but it turned out to be just a Victory Parade."

The parade lasted more than an hour longer than had been planned, and Eisenhower had to stand at attention most of the time. Macmillan said, "Eisenhower, with true courtesy, had placed Giraud at his side and immediately behind them stood Cunningham, Alexander, and Tedder. Each side of the platform was guarded by a Churchill tank."

After the parade a lunch was given at the palace of the French president-general, at which Giraud said, according to Macmillan, "that when he had seen the Eighth Army at Sfax, he thought they must be unique. Now that he had seen the First Army, he realized that it was as good. He said that in his whole life he had never seen such a body of men. All that old Ike could do was say ecstatically to me and others (and repeat it the next day) that he had never believed it possible to dream of having such an honour as to command an army like this. Really, it has been a grand day."

Patton did not agree. He thought the parade "was a goddamn waste of time." Eisenhower had not invited him or Bradley to be with him on the reviewing stand. Moreover, according to Patton's biographer Ladislas Farago, Eisenhower had added "insult to injury" by having on the platform "Allied commanders, many of whom had watched the campaign from Algiers, and even from London or Washington. Patton was disgusted."

Eisenhower asked Macmillan to fly back to Algiers with him in his B-17. "As we passed Bizerte we saw approaching the first convoy to attempt the Mediterranean passage since 1941," Macmillan said. "It had left Gibraltar a few days before and was to reach Alexandria without loss. To look down upon this great armada was indeed to see a striking proof of what had been at last accomplished. I turned to Eisenhower and said, 'There, General, are the fruits of your victory.' He turned to me and smiled, smiling through his tears, for he was deeply moved, 'Ours, you mean, ours—that we have all won together.' "

Life magazine said that what had happened in North Africa "was more than a military victory. It was a victory for United Nations friendship. On the shoulders of General Eisenhower, commander in chief of all Allied land, sea, and air forces in North Africa, fell a task without precedent in military history. He was the first American ever to hold supreme command over thousands of British fighting men. Upon him as master strategist and coordinator rested the future of joint Anglo-American command. He did not fail. Thanks to his skill and tact, an interlocking staff of brilliant men—Alexander, Montgomery, Tedder, Spaatz, Anderson—functioned with superb efficiency. It was an auspicious omen for the tasks ahead."

The general did not relax, however. On the 13th, he wrote Marshall:

> Sometimes I think it would be most comforting to have a disposition that would permit relaxation—even possibly a feeling of self-satisfaction— as definite steps of a difficult job are completed. . . .
>
> Unfortunately, I always anticipate and discount, in my own mind, accomplishment of the several steps and am, therefore, mentally racing ahead into the next one. The consequence is that all the shouting about the Tunisian Campaign leaves me cold. I am so impatient and irritated because of the slowness with which the next phase can unfold, that I make myself quite unhappy. I am convinced that if I could undertake HUSKY today with only two divisions, I could gain a bridgehead and an advantage that would make the further conquest a very simple affair. Just as I suffered, almost physically, all during January, February and March while the enemy was fortifying his positions in Tunisia, so now I resent every day we have got to give him to perfect and strengthen HUSKY defenses. I have gotten so that my chief ambition in this war is finally to get to a place where the next operation does not have to be amphibious, with all the inflexibility and delay that are characteristic of such operations.
>
> I hope that out of your present conversations in Washington will come some final agreement as to the specific line the Allies are to take in winning this war.

In a letter to John the next day, he said, "This phase of the job is all done except for the shouting and the cleaning up. We have been through the plebe course and now have to catch our breath while we think of starting the yearling grind."

★ ★ ★

THE FIRST STEP

Many times during the war when there was not much news reporters would return to the fact that while Eisenhower's mother was a pacifist and a Jehovah's Witness, her son was leading the Allied troops in the bloodiest and most destructive war in history. Moreover, he was to tell newspapermen in the spring of 1943, "I'm not one who apologizes for hating his enemies."

Such stories about his mother always annoyed him, and on May 18 he wrote his brother Arthur that he had seen a clipping

in which some reporter made a point of the fact that our dear old mother likes to go to conventions of her beloved Jehovah's Witnesses . . . As far as I am concerned her happiness in her religion means more to me than any damn wisecrack that a newspaperman can get publicized. . . . I know full well that the government is not going to measure my services as a soldier by the religious beliefs of my Mother. Moreover, at heart, the country has never had a more loyal citizen than she. Actually, the newspaper account indicated that the whole convention made a devil of a fuss over her; showing that even people who proclaim themselves pacifists at heart are not above getting on the publicity bandwagon, even though that publicity is generated out of a circumstance which they publicly deplore. Moreover, I doubt whether any of these people, with their academic or dogmatic hatred of war, detest it as much as I do. They probably have not seen bodies rotting on the ground and smelled raw stench of decaying human flesh. They have not visited a field hospital crowded with the desperately wounded. But far above my hatred of war is the determination to smash every enemy of my country, especially Hitler and the Japs—or to put it more simply, my hatred of war will never equal my conviction that it is the duty of every one of us, civilian and soldier alike, to carry out the orders of our government when a war emergency arises. As far as I am concerned, Stephen Decatur told the whole story when he said, "Right or wrong, my country."

On May 12, the day Arnim surrendered, the TRIDENT conference began in Washington. It was the largest Allied gathering of the war up to then, and, as Robert Sherwood said, "a confident atmosphere prevailed. . . . It was the first of all the conferences that was held with tabulations of actual victories over Germany on the books—and hopes were high for the achievement of a better world in the future."

Things had now changed for Germany. Eisenhower said, "The Germans . . . were compelled after Tunisia to think only of the protection of conquests rather than of their enlargement." And his friend Tom Handy said, "After Tunisia we were pushing the Boche. They were scared of what *we* were going to do, where we were coming next."

Churchill had come across the Atlantic on the *Queen Mary*, largely to persuade Roosevelt that after the great victory the Allies under Eisenhower would achieve in Sicily, Italy must be got out of the war, and Turkey must be got into the war. As for the first, the prime minister said that "the collapse of Italy would cause a chill of loneliness [to settle] over the German people, and might be the beginning of their doom." The defeat of the Italians would also be helpful to the Russians, he said. It would take troops from the eastern front and send them to the Balkans to replace the Italian forces there. He repeated that he wanted as much as the Americans a full-scale invasion of Europe from the

United Kingdom but added that the plan must offer "reasonable prospects of success."

That last upset Marshall and Stimson, because they didn't know what it meant. In fact, Marshall found himself consistently puzzled by the prime minister. He later told Sir Charles Wilson, Churchill's personal physician, who was to become Lord Moran, "I did not think the moment had come for a decision. It would be better . . . to decide what to do when the attack on Sicily was well underway. I wanted to know whether Germany meant to put up a stiff resistance in southern Italy. . . . I wanted more facts. I wanted to ask Winston a dozen questions, but he gave me no chance. He kept telling me what was going to happen. All wishing and guessing."

This time the Americans did not act like dutiful colonials. While Churchill had done a great deal of homework on shipboard, the Americans had prepared themselves, too. And at one point when Marshall, who was usually at Roosevelt's side during meetings of the conference, told Brooke that the Americans regretted having so easily committed themselves to TORCH and HUSKY, Brooke rather peevishly asked, "What strategy would you have preferred?"

"The cross-channel attack," said Marshall. "We should finish the war more quickly."

"Probably so," said Brooke, "but not in the way we hope to finish it."

But this time neither Marshall nor Roosevelt nor the other Americans present were put off or persuaded by Brooke or his prime minister. The British disagreed among themselves, and Churchill seemed to be caving in to Roosevelt and Marshall. Brooke said of the prime minister at the conference, "There are times when he drives me to desperation. . . . Winston's attitude at the White House Conference was tragic."

They did agree on one thing, that the cross-Channel invasion should take place on May 1, 1944, and that the initial assault should be by nine divisions, two airborne. They agreed that constant bombing, by day and night, should be continued and intensified, the climax coming in April 1944.

The Allies agreed, too:

That the Allied Commander-in-Chief North Africa [Eisenhower] will be instructed, as a matter of urgency, to plan such operations in exploitation of HUSKY as are best calculated to eliminate Italy from the war and to contain the maximum number of German forces. Which of the various specific operations should be adopted, and thereafter mounted is a decision which will be reserved to the Combined Chiefs of Staff.

That was not what Churchill had come to Washington for, and he was furious. It was a victory for the Americans, for Eisenhower in particular, and he hadn't even been at the conference. Nevertheless, as Churchill said, "Post-HUSKY is in Eisenhower's hands." So he decided to go at once to Algiers to consult with the man in charge, and he persuaded Roosevelt to allow him to take Marshall with him. Without Marshall, he said, it would look as if he were trying to put something over on the Americans, and that would never do.

Churchill concluded that Roosevelt "is a tired man." He told Sir Charles,

"His mind seems closed. He lost his wonderful elasticity. . . . He is not willing to put pressure on Marshall. He is not in favor of landing in Italy. . . . I only crossed the Atlantic for this purpose. I cannot let the matter rest where it is."

Marshall had been planning a trip to the southwest Pacific, but on orders from his commander in chief he agreed to the African safari. He told Stimson that he "seemed to be merely a piece of luggage useful as a trading point."

The party, which included Brooke, arrived at Maison Blanche in the afternoon of May 28. Brooke said, "Lovely clear day and a very good view of all the country. . . . Eisenhower, Cunningham, Alexander, and Coningham were all on Maison Blanche aerodrome. Drove up to Eisenhower's house where I am in same room I had last time."

The prime minister was to have gone to Cunningham's villa, where he was staying with the admiral, but he did not. Cunningham did not have to be persuaded to do anything; he would do as he was told. Eisenhower needed a good deal of persuading. So Churchill got into the car with Ike. Unhappily, no record exists of what was said on the drive to Cunningham's villa, but Churchill had more to tell Eisenhower, much more. Butcher said, "Although Ike had the Prime Minister driven to the Admiral's house, the PM didn't even stop there to rest. He immediately trundled with Ike down the driveway to our house. There, with General Marshall and the Admiral, they gathered on the front porch, the PM finding a confortable chair and seeming settled for the duration. An informal conference, pleasant to kibitz on, continued until time to get ready for dinner."

Churchill almost never stopped talking while he was in Algiers, at least not when he was awake, and he seemed never to go to bed. One morning for breakfast he had nothing but a bottle of white wine, with soda water and ice. When the prime minister got back to London, Sir Charles Wilson (Lord Moran) said, "Winston is so taken up with his own ideas that he is not interested in what other people think. It is as if he had lived for years in a foreign country without picking up the language."

Eisenhower did not expect that the Churchill visit would go easily. Beetle had been Ike's representative at the meetings of TRIDENT, and he had returned on the 25th to report that while Marshall wanted to invade the continent through France, the English had not been convinced. Moreover, at the conference Churchill had been critical of Eisenhower because, the prime minister said, he had not made plans to invade Sicily immediately after the victory in Tunisia. Butcher said, "Beetle said he [Churchill] seemed completely to overlook our continued shortage of landing craft." The Tunisian victory had been very popular, but, Beetle felt, Eisenhower's contribution to that victory had been generally ignored. The real hero in the United States as elsewhere was Montgomery. The documentary film about the British victory at El Alamein, *Desert Victory*, had been widely released and widely praised. Roosevelt said that it was "the best thing that has been done about the war," and Stalin had announced that it would be shown not only to Russian soldiers but "among the widest masses of our population." Montgomery said, "I did not know I was becomng a celebrity"; but when he was in London in May, he went to the theater, where the Broadway success *Arsenic and Old Lace* was playing to a packed house, and when it was over the audience stood to cheer Monty, who was sitting in a box. Outside the theater, people stood ten deep to see and try to touch him. According to Montgomery's biographer Nigel Hamilton, he "now began to enjoy himself so much that Brooke was obliged to send him a preemptory summons to return to the field of war and attend the great council of war which Churchill, on his way back from London, had convened in Algiers."

During the TRIDENT talks another unfortunate thing happened to Eisenhower, and Beetle could not have helped noting with some satisfaction that it would not have happened if he had been in Algiers instead of Washington. On May 17 AFHQ's G-3 sent a cable signed with Eisenhower's name asking for a change in the Psychological Warfare Plan for HUSKY; the cable said in essence that asking for unconditional surrender was a mistake, that it was "an intimidation of the Italians by threat" and that the policy would strengthen resistance in Sicily. The cable said, "I therefore strongly recommend that the statement of policy be amended." It should state the Italians themselves should choose between continuing the war and ceasing hostilities. If the Italians on Sicily did stop fighting, the act would be "accepted by the Allies as evidence of good judgment, entitling them eventually to a 'Peace with Honor.' " Finally, the Allied governments would pledge "full nationhood" for Italy as soon as the Axis were defeated. Thus, the only obstacle to an honorable peace in Italy was the policy of the Fascist government.

Eisenhower had not seen the cable before it was sent, but that did not save him from Roosevelt's idée fixe, and Churchill agreed with the president, as did the Combined Chiefs, who transmitted the president's irate message, "Most certainly we cannot tell the Italians that if they cease hostilities they will have a peace with honor. We cannot get away from unconditional surrender. All we can tell them is that they will be treated by US and the British with humanity and with the intention that the Italian people be reconstituted into a nation in accordance with the principles of self-determination."

Churchill approved the statement, and it was sent along to Ike not so much as a reprimand as a reminder to him and his G-3 and anyone else in his command that when the president of the United States spoke of "unconditional surrender," he meant just that.

On May 30 Eisenhower sent Beetle a sharp message telling him what he already knew. "Please see to it that the Psychological Warfare Section does not send to Washington or London any more messages suggesting broad policy or changes in existing directions from Combined Chiefs of Staff without referring them, in each case, to you.

"I am exceedingly irritated by the recent incident in which the expression 'Peace with Honor' was used."

Altogether, late May 1943 was from Eisenhower's point of view not the best time for Churchill to come to Algiers. The general wanted to spend all his time planning what the troops under his command were going to do in HUSKY, and the prime minister was interested only in talking about what those troops should do after HUSKY. That first afternoon and early evening, seated on the front porch of Ike's villa, Churchill began his argument, and he continued it that night at dinner, when he, Eisenhower, Marshall, and Beetle were guests of Admiral

Cunningham. Butcher said, "The PM recited his story three different times in three different ways. . . . He talks persistently until he has worn down the last shred of opposition. Ike is glad to have General Marshall on hand."

The first formal meeting of what became known as the Algiers conference took place in the afternoon of the 29th, and the first item on the agenda was the bombing and proposed land attack on Pantelleria, a small, rocky island between Tunisia and Sicily that had been under naval and aerial bombardment since the 13th. It was said to have a garrison of 10,000 soldiers and was called the "Gibraltar of the Central Mediterranean." After the Italians on the island had surrendered, Eisenhower told Hap Arnold, "The Air Corps demanded Pantelleria as a starting point for air operations in HUSKY and I agreed with them that it was necessary." He said later, "I directed the assault to be made somewhere in early June and to be preceded by a most intensive air bombardment. I told the commanders and staffs that I believed the Italian morale would be so shaken by the bombardment we could put on the island that an Infantry assault would probably never have to be made." Most of the British, including the officer in charge of the landings, Major General W. E. Clutterbuck, were convinced from the beginning that it could not be taken without costly, crippling casualties. That was a point of view from which Alexander never wavered. Even the usually friendly and dependable Cunningham was at first skepical about the project. So was Tedder, but he, after some argument became convinced that the airfield on the twenty-three-square-mile island was essential to the successful invasion of Sicily.

Eventually, Cunningham came around to Eisenhower's point of view. And Strong reported in his book *Intelligence at the Top* that, "When the conversation had gone on for some time, Eisenhower turned wearily to Cunningham and said, 'Andrew, why don't you and I get in a boat together and row ashore on our own. I think we can capture the island without any of these soldiers.' "

Eisenhower had already told Marshall that while "some of the people carrying responsibility toward it [taking the island] are shaking their heads, . . . I believe it will work. If it won't, when everything except the character of the beaches is in our favor, we had better find out—once and for all—just what is involved in operations of this kind."

Churchill, who was seldom inclined to argue over what he considered inconsequential matters when he had something big in mind, voiced no objection to the invasion of Pantelleria, which was code named CORKSCREW. He suggested at that first formal meeting that Eisenhower explain his plans for HUSKY.

Eisenhower said that if HUSKY was a quick success, in order to avoid a period of inactivity for the troops, the Allies should invade mainland Italy. That was just what Churchill wanted. Marshall's position was also unchanged since the TRIDENT meetings in Washington; he did not want any commitments in the Mediterranean that would take troops or matériel that would be necessary for the cross-Channel invasion. He also wanted to avoid making a decision until the Allies found out what happened after the HUSKY landings, and he was in favor of landings in Corsica and Sardinia. Fewer troops would be required. Naturally, Eisenhower agreed with his chief, and Marshall suggested that Ike set up two entirely separate headquarters, one to plan for an invasion of Sardinia and Corsica, the other to be concerned with the possible landing in southern Italy.

In *Hinge of Fate,* Churchill said, "Although much lay in the balance, I was well satisfied with the opening discussion. . . . I now prepared what I called 'Background Notes,' setting forth the whole case for the attack on Italy. . . . I circulated this document to the principals before we met again on Monday, May 31."

He was not willing to wait for Monday to pursue his argument with Eisenhower, however. On Sunday, before dinner, Churchill's aide called the Eisenhower villa to see if the prime minister could come to see the general at 10:45 P.M. As Butcher noted, "The date jolted the free and easy lounging he needed so badly. . . . Ike and I sat reminiscing while waiting for the Prime Minister. Ike was growling because of the necessity of spending another night, probably until 1:30, going over the same ground, i.e., 'Keep on until you get Italy,' which the P.M. has already covered, re-covered and uncovered—and there were really no serious questions of difference between the two."

The whole thing was not without its humorous aspects. Butcher said to Eisenhower, "Would you ever have thought a year ago, certainly two years ago, that you would be in Algiers, in far-off Africa, the Allied Commander of a great and victorious army, sitting in a villa, awaiting a late night call from the Prime Minister of His Majesty's government and growling because the PM was fifteen minutes late? . . . Ike enjoyed the picture, upon which he elaborated, going back to his boyhood days when he had been variously a cowboy, a boiler stoker in a creamery, and a semipro ballplayer." (Eisenhower had, of course, never been a cowboy and was no doubt indulging himself in wishful thinking.)

When Churchill did arrive to continue his case for an invasion of Italy, he added a new gimmick. He said that the British people would be proud to cut in half their already short rations for a month if the shipping space saved would help to provide additional space for supplies needed in the invasion of Sicily.

There was no point in arguing. Even his wife, Clementine had said, "I don't argue with Winston. He shouts me down. So when I have anything important to say I write a note to him."

Eisenhower that Sunday night repeated that it was too early to make a commitment. A good deal would have to do with what happened in Sicily. The prime minister left at 1:10 in the morning. He said he hoped that he and Eisenhower would have Christmas dinner in Rome.

The less than cordial relationship between Eisenhower and Brooke did not improve during the late May and early June meetings in Algiers. In *Crusade* Ike remembered that Brooke told him in a private conversation that he was quite willing to consider postponing the May 1, 1944, date agreed on in Washington for OVERLORD. He might even be willing to do away with the project completely. Eisenhower remembered that Brooke said he "favored a policy of applying our naval and air strength toward the blockading of Germany and the destruction of its industry but avoiding great land battles on the main fronts.

He held the belief that in ground conflict in a large theater we would be at a great disadvantage and would suffer tremendous and useless losses."

Eisenhower added, "Any suggestion or intimation of abandoning OVERLORD could always be guaranteed to bring Marshall and me charging into the breach with an uncompromising, emphatic refusal to consider such an idea for an instant."

Brooke later said that he had never expressed doubts about a sustainable cross-Channel invasion. John Eisenhower diplomatically said, "This divergence was undoubtedly only a misunderstanding; and whether Brooke really said what Eisenhower later recalled is unimportant. The fact was that Eisenhower at the time understood Brooke to be having second thoughts on OVERLORD, and this belief colored his attitude toward the CIGS [Chief, Imperial General Staff] from that time on."

The conference in Algiers had begun well for Eisenhower, and a week later, on June 3 when it ended, he was in an even stronger position. He had impressed everyone except Brooke and Montgomery, who had come to Algiers directly from his triumphant personal appearances in London. According to an extract from that meeting sent to Patton, "Montgomery . . . said that all his commanders had complete confidence in the present plan and that troops would be filled with enthusiasm when they stepped ashore. . . . His officers were completely happy about the whole thing."

According to Nigel Hamilton, things were far from perfect, however. "Jealousy was rife. But refreshed and invigorated by his trip home, Monty was determined at least that the Allied invasion of Sicily be a resounding success."

Butcher said, "The film *Desert Victory* had contributed greatly to his [Montgomery's] popularity. I learned that Beetle, fortunately, also was aware of the lack of coordinated American moving-picture coverage of our operations, of the diverse groups now fumbling in this field, and is prepared promptly to get it co-ordinated."

The final meeting of the conference took place late in the afternoon of June 3, in Eisenhower's villa. It was largely concerned with bombing the railroad marshaling yards in Rome, and it was decided that, as Churchill put it, "there was no valid reason for refraining from bombing this target, provided the attacks were made by day and due care was taken to prevent damage elsewhere. General Marshall and I undertook to seek authority from our respective Governments authorizing such action."

Then Montgomery spoke, and after that a great number of high-sounding compliments were exchanged. Churchill said that he "paid . . . tribute to General Eisenhower. I said I would take home the feeling of confidence and comradeship which characterized action in this theater. I had never received so strong an impression of cooperation and control as during my visit. It would be impossible to embark on an undertaking under better augury. I said that I should not like to go away without reaffirming my full confidence in General Eisenhower and without expressing my admiration of the manner in which he had handled his many great problems." The man from Abilene who had come so far in so short a time said that any praise belonged to the officers around the table. He added that while there were times when there might be differences of opinion in the headquarters, those differences were never on national lines. The last was not quite true, but under the circumstances it was the right thing to have said.

The prime minister added that Marshall and Brooke "warmly concurred" and that "we all parted on the best of terms. . . . Soon the German nation was to be alone in Europe, surrounded by an infuriated world in arms. The leaders of Japan were already conscious that their onslaught had passed its zenith. Together, soon Great Britain and the United States would have the mastery of the Oceans and the Air. The hinge had turned."

So the real victor in Algiers had been Eisenhower. He had proceeded cautiously, patiently, seeming to insist on nothing, and gaining almost everything. Churchill's "Background Notes" and his endless, repetitive arguments had been a waste of time for both him and his patient listeners. Brooke reported that on the way back to London, "P.M. in depth of gloom." Memory is kind. When Churchill was writing his account of the Algiers meetings in 1950 he said, "I have no more pleasant memories of the war than the ten days in Algiers and Tunis."

When Lord Moran read the typescript pages of those days, he said to Churchill, "You old dear, I'd not like you half as much if you had antennae." Fortunately Churchill did not know what he meant. He said, "Some of you doctors get queer ideas about what is in people's heads."

Eisenhower's antennae were in excellent condition. His friend and associate Lauris Norstad said, "Eisenhower was the most intense listener I have ever known. He not only heard and remembered what you said; he seemed to know what you were thinking when you said it and why you said it."

On June 7, four days after the prime minister and his party left Algiers and after Marshall had returned to Washington, Eisenhower, accompanied by Cunningham and a party including Butcher, went aboard the British destroyer H.M.S. *Aurora* at Bône, and started for Pantelleria. Because of the doubts of almost all his associates about CORKSCREW, Eisenhower said, "I engaged to make a personal reconnaissance of the place."

Cunningham told Eisenhower that the area had been mined except for the narrow channel they were in, which had been swept.

Eisenhower asked if there were floating mines, and Cunningham said, "Oh, yes, but at this speed the bow will throw them away from the ship. It would be just bad luck if we should strike one."

The next morning, June 8, Eisenhower was up at six after a restless night, and at breakfast that morning Cunningham decided that the *Aurora* would not be a witness to the aerial and naval bombardment of the island, as had been planned. It would be a participant. Moreover, it led the naval bombardment and fired 150 rounds from nine six-inch guns and got to within 7,000 yards of the shore.

Eisenhower wrote the commander of *Aurora*, "I was impressed by the efficiency displayed by your officers and crew. I hope the presence on the bridge of the Commander-in-Chief of Naval Forces and myself did not disturb you too much. The performance was exhilarating. I understand other ships engaged on our mission were attacked by the enemy. Apparently the *Aurora* carries a charmed life."

He was encouraged by what he had seen. The experience, he said, "convinced me that the landing would be an easy affair and resistance would be light. . . . I directed definitely that the plans go ahead as ordered."

As Eisenhower had predicted, the operation on June 11 was a success. More than 6,000 tons of bombs had been dropped on the island, and even before the first troops had reached the tiny harbor, where the landing was to have taken place, the senior Italian naval officer on the island, which had been blockaded since May 14, surrendered his forces "through lack of water."

Lampedusa, a neighboring island, even smaller than Pantelleria, had a radar station, and its garrison surrendered to a British pilot who landed when his plane ran out of gas. A third tiny island in the area, Linosa, surrendered because its citizens decided they'd be better off under the Allies than under Mussolini. The fact that the three small islands were then occupied by the Allies meant that there was no enemy outpost south of Sicily.

The relatively small victory of CORKSCREW must have meant more to Eisenhower than the giant victory in Tunisia, perhaps because he had in a sense *not* acted as an Allied commander. Indeed, the British had to a man been opposed to the operation and except for Cunningham had remained in opposition. As a result, Ike had really acted like an American commander in the field, trusting his own judgment and his own instincts, and he had been right. He was pleased with himself, and he deserved to be.

The next day, June 12, he wrote Mamie, "Just a note as I want to spend a few minutes for the assembly of a bunch of newsmen at a press conference. They want to know about the operation we completed yesterday.

"I graduated [from West Point] 28 years ago today and met you about four months later. Also, yesterday, the 11th, marked my four months of wearing four stars; so it was a nice day to capture 15,000 prisoners."

The letters he received from Mamie had not been cheerful. In a reply he had written her on the day of CORKSCREW's success, he said, "Your letters often give me some hint of your loneliness, your bewilderment, and your worries in carrying on your own part in this emergency. . . . You never seem quite to comprehend how deeply I depend on you and need you. So when you're lonely, try to remember that I'd rather be by your side than anywhere in the world." It is also obvious from Eisenhower's reply to one of the letters that Mamie had been doing some private investigating among her friends in Washington concerning Kay's fiancé. He said, "You mentioned my driver, and a story you'd heard about the former marital difficulties of her fiancé. You said it was a 'not pretty' story. Your letter gave me my first intimation that there was any story whatsoever—I didn't know anything about it. In any event, whatever guilt attached to him has been paid in full. At the same moment that your letter arrived I received a report that he was killed—by a mine! . . . Here we considered him a valuable officer and a fine person. I'm saddened by his death. . . . War is often sad."

The news of Dick Arnold's death was devastating to Kay, who wrote, "He and a friend, a captain, both engineers and intimately familiar with mines, had been walking across an area well-marked with the usual white mine tapes.

Suddenly the captain stumbled on a trip-wire. He was seriously wounded by the explosion. Dick was killed instantly."

Arnold had been commander of the 20th Engineers in Lucian Truscott's 3d Infantry Division. According to Truscott, Arnold had been killed "about 1100 hours, June 6 in Sedjewane Valley while on inspection of mine clearing work, being carried out by elements of his command." The message from Truscott had not reached Eisenhower until the day the Pantelleria garrison was surrendered. Eisenhower himself took charge. He cabled Truscott asking for as complete an account of Arnold's death "as is practicable. If you will direct that special care be taken in marking and caring for his grave I will be very grateful to you. Please give me exact details of grave's location." Eisenhower added that Kay was anxious to have certain personal items in Arnold's possession, "a blue dressing gown, a silver cigarette lighter and a brown leather pocket purse with his initials on it. . . . The bond between them [Kay and Arnold] was common knowledge to everyone that knew them both. I feel that sending these articles to her without listing them on the personal effects will not constitute any violation of the spirit of the regulations."

Ike himself told Kay what had happened, and she said the general "was kindness personified." He suggested that she take some time off. " 'We can spare you,' he said. 'There's no one at the farm [a secluded villa outside Algiers acquired by Butcher]—go out there for a while. You can ride and get away from everyone; I know that's what I'd want.' He paused. 'I guess there's not much I can say, Kay.' "

Kay did not take Arnold's death well. Her old friend Anthea Saxe remembered that she "went into a complete nervous breakdown. . . . Eisenhower was marvelous. He helped her tremendously through this difficult time. He gave her a lot of things to do to keep her busy."

During this period Kay took on a second job. The General complained that his personal mail was getting so heavy "it's almost a full-time job in itself," Kay said. Then "as though struck by an afterthought, he added, 'How would you like to take it over, Kay?' I jumped at the opportunity." The letters, according to Kay, "reached the proportions of a paper tidal wave by the time he was on the Continent." In North Africa there were at least fifty a week. Kay said, "Peculiarly no writer ever blamed the general personally for a particular grievance, whether it be the Darlan fiasco . . . a wounded husband or a sadistic C.O. . . . Very few wrote him with awe; they were respectful but informal, in a style of correspondence with a favored uncle or a city councilman." Taking on the new job meant that Kay was in the headquarters all the time, and, she said, "I soon became part of the real official family. Before, I had been among the outside, after-hours intimates; now I was in the 'paper world,' the official inner circle." In any case, Kay's second job brought her closer to Eisenhower. Arnold's death and Kay's extreme sorrow meant that she was more than ever dependent on him. But no need to mention any of that to Mamie.

There was little time to celebrate his victory at Pantelleria. The next morning, Saturday the 12th, GENERAL LYON, King George VI, arrived. According to Kay, who drove Eisenhower to meet the king, his "visit was so hush-hush that we drove to Maison Blanche airport just as usual, with only the motorbike escort to clear our way. No special guards were provided. At the field, we moved down to a distant corner and joined the British High Brass, including Admiral Cunningham and Air Chief Marshal Tedder. . . .

"On the trip through Algiers Butcher and I pretended to be earless machines. But we couldn't help eavesdropping on the King of England. He was buoyant and friendly with General Ike, the first to admit his downright excitement at getting out of embattled England for the first time since the war started. . . . [He] sat back stiffly and drove himself into a tizzy trying to decide whether he should return the salutes of British troops who recognized their King in our car. After twitching hesitantly several times, he gave in and returned the salutes steadily." Eisenhower thus faced a problem that has troubled very few Americans ever. The road was lined with troops who recognized their king and saluted him. Should Eisenhower return a salute meant for the king? At first he decided that since he was Allied commander, he should follow the British custom and let the superior officer, in this case the king, return the salutes, but then Ike found himself being an American and, as he had done all his life, he began returning all salutes. Butcher said, "After we had dropped the King, we agreed we had done our bit without a hitch, with the possible exception of having intruded on the King's right to return his own salutes, Ike being only mildly concerned but fearing the King had never been told the difference between the American and British customs."

The king seemed not to have noticed or minded. The next morning he presented Eisenhower with the Grand Cross of the Most Honourable Order of the Bath. The *Chicago Tribune* made no comment on the matter, but it had been annoyed when Eisenhower's old boss, MacArthur, was given the G.C.B. The *Tribune* said the whole thing was an invidious British attempt to embarrass MacArthur when he ran for president.

The king was taken to the villa of Lieutenant General Sir Humphrey Gale, the chief administrative officer at Eisenhower's headquarters. That evening the king gave a dinner party. Macmillan later said, "The king was in excellent form. . . . He was very good with Eisenhower, who was himself in excellent shape—interesting, amusing, not too shy or too much at ease—in fact, the real natural simple gentleman which he is.

"After dinner, in the chief sitting room of the villa, the little ceremony took place to which Eisenhower had looked forward with great and genuine pleasure. The king took the General a little apart . . . and presented him with the G.C.B. with a few very well chosen phrases." The honor brought Eisenhower, as Kay observed, "as close as a foreigner could come to an outright title. His pride . . . was such that he never appeared in public without the thick maroon ribbon among his growing collection."

On the afternoon of June 12th, between the time Ike left the king at General Gale's villa and the dinner with him, Eisenhower held a unique press conference, unique for a general anyway, and unusual for a man who not long before had imposed censorship on all news from North Africa. He called all the correspondents in the North African theater together and announced that the next Allied operation in the theater would be an invasion of Sicily and that it would be "sometime next month." He confided in the correspondents, he later said, "paradoxically, to maintain secrecy. . . . I felt I had to stop speculation by war reporters as to the future intentions of the Allied Forces. I knew the Germans were watching us intently, and it is astonishing how expert a trained intelligence staff becomes in piecing together odd scraps of seemingly unimportant information to construct a picture of enemy plans. . . . It seemed certain that if reporters seeking items of interest for their papers and radio networks should continue to report on activities throughout the theater, the enemy would soon be able to make rather accurate deductions as to the strength and timing of our attack, even if we should be successful in concealing its location." So, he later wrote of the correspondents in Algiers, "I decided to take them into my confidence. . . . I immediately placed upon every reporter in the theater a feeling of the same responsibility that I and my associates knew."

He explained that Patton's Seventh Army would attack the southern beaches of Sicily and that Montgomery's Eighth Army would attack the eastern beaches south of Syracuse. He said that Alexander would be in command of the ground operation, and he described the air campaign that would, the Allies hoped, "destroy the German air forces and . . . cut his sea and land communications as well as soften his defenses."

The air offensive would, he said, be conducted so that the enemy would decide that the western end of Sicily was to be attacked. "I informed them [the newspaper and radio correspondents] that we would use airborne troops in the operation on a much larger scale than had yet been attempted in warfare. The attack was carried out exactly in this fashion on the night of July 9."

As will be seen, the airborne operation had difficulties that had not been anticipated, but the operation in general went off pretty much as planned in its early stages. It got into difficulties later, and so did both Montgomery and Patton, the former because he moved too slowly, the latter because he could not control his temper.

The press conference was, however, a great success. The flattered correspondents, none of whom betrayed Ike's trust, thought that he had done what he did because of a suddenly developed fondness for reporters. That was not the case. Eisenhower understood that reporters were necessary, and he knew how to charm them, as he did everybody else, but most of the time even when he was a presidential candidate and president he treated reporters like raw recruits who hadn't yet learned to salute properly and were certainly out of uniform most of the time.

On July 1 Eisenhower gained another press supporter. He spent an hour and a half briefing Raymond Clapper, one of the most famous Washington correspondents of the time, on plans for HUSKY. Butcher said, "When he finished, Clapper . . . said he had never before been excited in an interview. Ended his conversation by practically nominating Ike for President. Ike and I have picked up this theme and are already forming our cabinet. Beetle will be head of the Gestapo, as he likes to cut throats. T.J. will be Postmater General, and I am tentatively slated, subject to good behavior, for Secretary of the Navy."

It was all a great lark in those days, a joke, the idea of an army officer not yet a permanent full colonel being president of the United States.

Planning for HUSKY continued, and Eisenhower, as had been the case before

TORCH, was nervous and irritable. He was also suffering from the disease that was suffered by almost everyone in the theater at one time or another, including the king, the African "pip," or as some called it, "the GIs." Eisenhower also said that he felt "as if my stomach were a clenched fist."

On the 3rd he wrote Churchill, "An atmosphere of tension pervades every headquarters in this theater. Nevertheless I am happy to report that there is likewise a degree of confidence and that everything that foresight and careful planning can do has been or is being done."

Eisenhower left Algiers for Tunis on the afternoon of July 6 and spent the next day at his two new advance posts, one near Carthage (code name FAIRFIELD REAR), the other on the bay of Tunis (code name FAIRFIELD ADVANCE). In the afternoon of the 8th, two days before the invasion, he and his party arrived in Malta. His headquarters were in Verdala Palace, the summer residence of the governor, the 6th Viscount Gort.

Eisenhower's office was not grand, however. The room was ten by fourteen feet, and a table covered with a gray blanket served as his desk. The room had a clay floor and an oil burner; like the pre-TORCH headquarters at Gibraltar, the room in the Verdala Palace was damp, so damp, in fact, that he couldn't light a cigarette. Two correspondents were covering the invasion, E. J. Gilling for the British and John Gunther for the Americans. Eisenhower asked them for a cigarette. "All cigarettes, wet or dry, are very scarce," said Gunther.

The general's bedroom was also small and damp and had a stairway leading to a dungeon where prisoners had once been chained. The British had white-washed the staircase, but the atmosphere was still not cheerful. In the afternoon he briefed the two reporters, and Gunther was immediately impressed. Eisenhower, he wrote, had "tact, candor, freshness . . . [was] indisputably genuine . . . [had] modesty. . . . He will not allow correspondents to dateline anything as from 'General Eisenhower's headquarters.' He insists on the term 'Allied headquarters.' One more item: I never saw him wear more than two decorations, although many of his men are bedecked like awnings."

During the afternoon before the invasion, which was to be on Saturday morning, July 10 at 2:45, Eisenhower called in Butcher to, as Butcher noted in his diary, "outline his idea for a book he would like to do after the war; has jotted down twenty-four names of important persons he had worked for or with, not political, and including every big name I ever heard of. Said he was of a mind to write his experiences with and impressions of each. Said he would paint each one's character, and around each tell some stories which would make his book useful as a history. Told him that truth wouldn't prevent him from being sued for libel and he might have a merry time defending himself in court after the war if he pursued his fancy. . . . Tore up his notes? But not a bad idea."

A little later, as he had done on Gibraltar before TORCH, the general wrote Mamie a letter:

I'm again in a tunnel, as I was at the beginning of last November, waiting, as I was then, for news! Long before you receive this you'll know whether or not our present venture is a success and you will have been spared the agony of waiting . . . anything can happen. It is 10:00 P.M. I should have some reports tomorrow.

In circumstances such as these men do almost anything to keep them from going slightly mad. Walk, talk, try to work, smoke (all the time)—anything to push the minutes along to find out a result that one's own action can no longer affect in the slightest degree. I stand it better than most, but there is no denying that I feel the strain. . . .

It would be fun to have you and Johnny here with me in this little dungeon. There would be lots of things to talk about. . . . After looking around a bit we could settle down and talk about the family, and what we're going to do when I can come home again, and where we'll live and so on, and so on. We could easily keep going through the night.

HUSKY should have been easier for Eisenhower than TORCH; in North Africa he had been in charge of all operations, ground, sea, and air. Here he had his deputy Allied commander, Alexander, in direct charge of ground operations, Cunningham for the navy, and Tedder for Air. At that point Ike had done all that he could do except call the whole thing off, if that became necessary. For a time it looked as if he might have to do just that.

That evening, on the way from Cunningham's headquarters to his own, Eisenhower saw that most of the windmills on the island were rotating alarmingly. The wind quickly increased to a forty-mile-an-hour gale, and at dinner, where Mountbatten was a guest, Ike said, "To be perfectly honest it doesn't look too good." The wind was from the west and was blowing gigantic waves onto the shore where the Americans were to land. Several staff members had suggested that the landings be postponed, which would have meant a delay of two or three weeks before another invasion could have been mounted. Eisenhower decided to go ahead, and after dinner he and a party, including Cunningham, Mountbatten, and Butcher, visited a lighthouse on the southeast tip of Malta to see the towplanes and troop-carrying gliders fly over. It still did not look good, particularly when he saw the transport planes bucking the high winds, but he returned to the office, and four hours before H-hour sent a message to Marshall:

Everything has proceeded as planned and with known losses at sea confined to three MT vessels. The operation will proceed as scheduled in spite of an unfortunate westerly wind that may interfere some what with the landings of US troops. All of us hope to have good news for you tomorrow.

After sending the message Eisenhower returned to Cunningham's headquarters, where the first news of the success or failure of HUSKY would be received. He went to his bedroom in the cavern, rubbed the lucky coins he habitually carried in his pocket, and fell into a deep sleep. The next morning he learned that the landings had begun as scheduled.

HUSKY was the largest amphibious operation in history; more than 3,000 ships were involved and almost 500,000 Allied soldiers were to take part. There were units of the RAF, the American air forces and navy, the Royal Navy, as well as British and American armies. In the first stages of HUSKY, nine divisions were afloat, two more than in the first stages of Overlord the following year.

Eisenhower was in charge of it all, and he looked, according to John Gunther, "like a perfectly confident and unworried father awaiting the birth of a healthy baby." You can be sure he did not feel that way.

One important element in the early success of HUSKY was that the enemy was surprised by it, and Operation MINCEMEAT was in large part responsible. The Germans had believed that the Allied invasion was headed toward Sicily, mostly because at 4:30 in the morning of April 30 a British submarine, *Seraph*, had surfaced briefly in the middle of a fleet of Spanish fishing boats not far from the port of Huelva on the Gulf of Cádiz. The sub released the body of a man wearing a lifejacket and carrying a great many papers; more suspicious minds might have thought there were too many papers. The man was a Major William Martin, and his papers said that he was a Royal Marine. The letters and documents were artfully designed to foster the idea that the Allies were not preparing to attack Sicily—that was simply a "cover"—but were headed for Sardinia, Corsica, and Greece. All had been written by members of British naval intelligence in London, chief among them Lieutenant Commander Ewen Montagu, who later wrote an engaging book, *The Man Who Never Was*, telling how Operation MINCEMEAT was conceived and executed.

The letter achieved exactly what the British naval intelligence planners had in mind. The body drifted ashore and was picked up by Spaniards, who opened the briefcase, found that the next Allied operation would be against Sardinia and Greece, and gave the documents to the Germans, who photographed them, sent the film to Berlin, and then returned the documents to the briefcase and gave the body to the British vice consul in Huelva.

The Germans were completely taken in, and a Panzer division was moved from France to Greece, followed by 180 aircraft.

The Allies were also lucky. The night before the invasion the German radar operators were seeing what they considered too many "blips" on their screens, so many in fact that they were sure the screens were malfunctioning. So, much as the American radar operators at Pearl Harbor in 1941 had done, the Germans did not report what they had seen until the next morning. By that time Allied forces were ashore, Patton's Seventh Army on the Gulf of Gela between Licata and Scoglitti. Shortly thereafter Gela, Licata, and Vittoria had been taken. The British had landed near Syracuse and taken it by the end of the day.

When Eisenhower saw Gunther and Gilling he said, "By golly. By golly, we've done it again. I don't understand it." He cabled the Combined Chiefs of Staff and the British Chiefs, "Reports as of 11:00 A.M. state that leading waves of both Seventh and Eighth Armies are successfully ashore. Seventh Army . . . in communication with their paratroops. Small vessels carrying supporting weapons somewhat delayed due to rough weather yesterday and last night, no intensive enemy reaction yet reported. Weather has improved. Today is the critical period, but air forces will provide assistance against mobile reserves until supporting weapons are landed."

Shortly after midnight Sunday the 11th General Alfredo Guzzoni, who had come out of retirement to take command of the Axis forces on Sicily, issued an order for the soldiers under his command to counterattack Patton's forces at Gela. His troops were poorly equipped, poorly trained, and without enthusiasm for battle. Sporadic fighting took place most of the morning, but the Axis forces never reached the beaches. Before noon, with sixteen of their tanks burning on the battlefield, the enemy pulled back. By that time Patton had arrived on the beach, and General Hobart Gay, Patton's chief of staff, wrote that Patton's "presence in the front lines had a great deal to do with the enemy attacks failing."

On the night of the 10th Eisenhower went to bed immediately after dinner with Lord Gort and slept until 5:30 the next morning. Sporadic reports that came in through the day indicated that all was going well, and Eisenhower sent a message to the Combined Chiefs and the British Chiefs, "Reports on today's operations indicate satisfactory progress with slight opposition. Seventh and Eighth Armies by 2359 hours 11 July expect each to have landed approximately 80,000 men, 7,000 vehicles, 300 tanks and 900 guns. Port of Syracuse reported in good working order."

That afternoon Ike and a few others from headquarters spent an hour on one of the beaches in Malta. He was nervous, and after reclining on the sand for a while, he dug holes with a stick. Then he returned to headquarters and made plans to visit Patton and Montgomery on Sicily. The party, including several British and American high-ranking officers, Butcher, and the two newspapermen, Gilling and Gunther, went aboard the British destroyer *Petard* late that night, and Eisenhower slept in the captain's cabin until five on the morning of the 12th. Eisenhower visited Patton on board Vice Admiral H. Kent Hewitt's flagship, *Monrovia*, and he reprimanded the Seventh Army commander because of the sketchy reports that had been sent to headquarters. Patton, who had expected praise for what he and his troops had accomplished, was furious. He said, "When I took him in my room to show him the situation [on the map] he was not much interested but began to compare the sparsity of my reports with the almost hourly news bulletins of the Eighth Army. . . . I think he means well, but it is most upsetting to get only piddling criticism when one knows one has done a good job. He is now wearing suede shoes a la British."

Eisenhower had hoped to visit the battlefield at Gela, but after Patton told him that it would take an hour and a half in a landing craft just to get there, he changed his mind. He and his party returned to *Petard*, which was fired on from a battery hidden in a woods beyond the beach. The ship's commander, nervous at having Eisenhower aboard, provided cotton for his ears and a helmet. The latter was much too small, and Ike said, "If I use this, I'll need two men to hold it on." Then he turned to Gunther and said, "They treat me like a bird in a gilded cage." Then, perhaps imitating the dialect of the characters in his favorite radio program, *Amos 'n' Andy* he said, "I'se a valuable fellow, that's what I is."

As the ship steamed along the coast, Ike continued talking to Gunther, who wrote that "his informality, his use of homely language is disarming; but he never loses a nice healthy dignity; and don't think he lacks force. You get a sense that he's very sure of himself, very shrewd, very tough, and conscious of his own worth."

Eisenhower wanted to meet an officer of the 1st Canadian Division, the first soldiers from Canada to be under his command. He told Marshall, "I must say that the sight of hundreds of vessels, with landing craft everywhere, operating along the shoreline from Licata was unforgettable. I went ashore in the Canadian sector merely to welcome the Canadian Command in this Allied Force. Everybody I saw was in good heart and anxious to get ahead."

Gunther had in his own mind already written the lead for his dispatch, "The American commander-in-chief of the allied forces of liberation set foot for the first time on the soil of occupied Europe today." But that was not quite the lead he wrote. In *D-Day*, his story of the Sicilian invasion, Gunther said, "It gave me an odd feeling to be the third American to set foot on this part of Axis Europe. The first was General Eisenhower, the second his naval aide, Commander Harry Butcher. It happened I was right behind them. . . . The place was a beach near the southeastern tip of Sicily off Cape Passaro. The time was 10:24 A.M. Monday, July 12. . . . I had hoped Eisenhower would say something in the Stanley-Livingston tradition, for instance, 'My name is Eisenhower.' What the commander-in-chief did say was good enough. There was no warning whatever that he was arriving. He walked up to the first British officer we saw, a colonel with a long dusty mustache and said, 'Good morning, I'm General Eisenhower.' The British colonel almost passed out with surprise."

The general and his party, including Gunther, had come ashore in a DUKW, an amphibious truck, and then were driven inland for about a mile, where they found a very junior Canadian officer, Captain J. E. Moore of Vancouver, but that was good enough, and, making a stop for a conference on H.M.S. *Hilary*, Eisenhower returned to *Petard* and was back in Malta at 2:30 in the afternoon of the 12th.

On Tuesday the 13th Gunther had an interview with Air Marshal Keith Park, the Air Officer Commanding, Malta, and he asked what the Britisher thought of Eisenhower. "By Jove, what a man," said Park. "A magnificent coordinator, don't-you-know? And so *simpatico*. You know what that word means, don't you? *Simpatico*. He's a good mixer, but not too much so. And by Jove, what a person to rely on."

* * *

HOLDING PATTON'S HORSE

For a while the Sicilian campaign looked easy. Many Italian soldiers simply became part of the civilians who were cheering the progress of the Allies. Tens of thousands of other Italian soldiers were delighted to become prisoners of war. By the end of the campaign 135,000 Axis soldiers had been captured, most of them Italian. Brigadier General Maxwell D. Taylor, West Point 1920, commander of artillery and second in command of the 82nd Airborne Division, said, "Most of the way it was as pleasant a campaign as one is likely to find in war. No one was very angry at anyone. The Italians had no desire to die for the King or Badoglio [Mussolini's successor], much less for Hitler. In the towns we passed through, the villagers greeted us as liberators and many rushed up to ask in broken English about relatives in America." The 82nd marched 150 miles in six days.

Eisenhower told Marshall on July 17, "Morale in the Italian Army is low and we have some evidence on which to base a belief that the population, generally, is very friendly to us. However, we have had some cases of sniping in the rear areas. One night three soldiers had their throats cut almost on the beaches. I hope that the Rome bombing (day after tomorrow) does not work in reverse, so far as morale is concerned."

On July 15 Eisenhower had told the Combined Chiefs and the British Chiefs:

The air operation against the marshaling yards at Rome has tentatively been set up by Tedder and myself for Monday, July 19. Exact details as to timing will be communicated to you when we can make reasonable predictions on weather and you will be kept constantly informed of any modifications of plan. The operation will involve practically the entire strategic force in the Mediterranean, employing approximately 400 bombers and dropping more than 1,000 tons of bombs. Targets for the heavies will be the marshaling yards and for the mediums will be the important airfields a short distance to the south thereof.

No one was anxious to bomb the Eternal City, but the Germans, knowing of that reluctance, were using Rome as the center of their communications system.

The raid went off as scheduled, and it was one of the largest of the war. As planned about 1,000 tons of bombs were dropped, and more than 500 bombers took part. The Lorenzo and Littorio railroad yards were hit in the morning, the Ciampino airfields in the afternoon. Of Rome's 400 churches only the Basilica of San Lorenzo was damaged. Many hundreds of civilians were wounded and killed, however. No air raid shelters had been built by Mussolini.

At the time of the raid, Hitler was in Italy conferring with Mussolini about the situation in Sicily, and, as usual, the Fuehrer was telling Il Duce what he had to do. Hitler said that the new secret weapon he was building for use against England would be ready by winter and that Italy must be defended, "so that Sicily may become for the enemy what Stalingrad was for us." Mussolini promised to do everything that Hitler asked, but he must have known that he was making an idle promise. He had never really believed most of what he said anyway.

When he got back to Rome, black clouds of smoke were rising from the bombed city, and the next day when he saw the king, Victor Emmanuel said, "We cannot go on much longer. Sicily has gone west now. The Germans will double-cross us. The discipline of the troops has broken down."

In a message to Marshall on July 17 Eisenhower had said that recent evidence showed that "the German is pushing forces into the toe of Italy with the intention of pushing them over into Sicily. My own guess is that he will largely abandon the western part of the island and attempt to take up a line running north westward from Mount Etna. This line would be one that, with German troops alone, he might believe he could hold for a considerable time. I rather think he has given up hope of making the Italians fight effectively."

Eisenhower was right about what the Germans had in mind. The Allies had to prevent that from happening. Their troops had to go around Mount Etna and get into Messina before the Germans built up their strength there. The job of driving up the inland road to Messina was to have been Patton's, and the road was in the American sector, but after Montgomery found that the coastal road leading to Messina was too strongly defended for his taste, he decided, without consulting either Patton or Alexander, to send one of the two corps under his command up that road as well.

Alexander, who still had doubts about American competence in combat, backed up Monty, leaving Patton's Seventh Army with the humiliating job of protecting the Eighth Army's rear and flank. In his diary Patton said, "Went to lunch at 1250. General Alexander . . . and members of his staff arrived at 1310, so I had to quit eating and see them. They gave us the future plan of operations, which cuts us off from any possibility of taking Messina. It is noteworthy that Alexander, the Allied commander of a British and American Army, had no Americans with him. What fools we are."

He was furious, but remembering Ike's warning about losing his temper, Patton practiced instead some Ike-like cunning. He decided that since it appeared impossible for his troops to take Messina, he would settle for Palermo. He did not tell Alexander that, however; he asked and got permission to take Agrigento and Porto Empedocle, which would give him a port to bring in supplies for his troops.

Patton was not surprised when Alexander warned him that the operation must be limited in scope. Georgie had already decided that one of Alexander's problems was that his head was too small. No wonder he had trouble making decisions.

"Monty is trying to steal the show," Patton wrote his wife, Beatrice, "and with the assistance of Divine Destiny [Eisenhower] may do so but to date we have captured three times as many men as our cousins."

On the 20th Alexander, realizing that Montgomery could not take Messina without help, ordered that both Patton's Seventh Army and Monty's Eighth should, together, drive the Germans across the strait, Patton attacking to the north, Monty from the south.

As yet Patton had done very little that was noteworthy in Sicily, but back in the States a great many people were convinced that he was winning the war without much help. Bea was very busy building up that idea. In a radio interview she said of her husband, "He has always felt that wars are won not by the best tanks or the fastest airplanes, or the most powerful guns, but by the fightingest men. . . . He's not only a great student of tactics and history, but he brings the past right into the present and applies it to the situation at hand. When he was in Africa, he used to write me about Hannibal."

In that same radio broadcast Beatrice said of Patton, "Invariably he writes of visiting the wounded in field hospitals." Soon, without any help at all from

Beatrice, millions of people all over the world were to know about two of Patton's visits to field hospitals.

On July 21 Patton said in his diary, "I really feel like a great general today— all my plans so far have worked. I hope God stays with me."

On the 18th Patton had put his Seventh Army deputy commander, Major General Geoffrey Keyes, West Point 1913, in command of a provisional corps, and on the 22nd it entered Palermo, having advanced almost 100 miles in four days, most of it by foot. The achievement added greatly to Patton's reputation in the States, but the Germans were still in Messina.

Eisenhower told the Combined Chiefs and the British Chiefs of Staff on August 5:

> My present estimate is that a feeling of restrained optimism with regard to Sicily is justified and that the clean-up may come sooner than the thirty days estimated by some of our commanders last week. It seems possible, according to Allied G-2, that an opportunity for a quick victory existed during the early days of the invasion. If this was so I did not sufficiently appreciate the situation. In any event the present enemy position does not seem to have much depth and once we are through his main defensive line, it is likely that progress will be rapid. On the other hand, the Germans have used the time to build a strong fortress area, thick with anti-aircraft, on the Reggio side of the narrows and this will have its effect on our efforts to interfere with his evacuation when the break comes.

On July 25 Mussolini was arrested, and Marshal Badoglio was asked to form a new government. Badoglio was seventy-one, and while he had been a supporter of Mussolini's for a very long time, he had from the beginning opposed the Italian military liaison with Germany. Eisenhower received the news the next morning before breakfast, but he was not elated. Perhaps because of the Darlan experience he was wary. He told Butcher that he "regretted existence of rapid communications." Butcher wrote, "If we were still in the day of sailing ships, he thought he could deal more quickly and advantageously with the Italians than is possible when he has to communicate to both Washington and London and wait for the two capitals to concur or direct."

Eisenhower did not know then that the leaders in those two capitals would almost never concur on what should be done about Italy. Hitler, however, knew exactly what to do. Rommel had just been posted to Greece, but Hitler at once ordered him to gather a force in the Alps for probable entry into Italy. Rommel did that and more. He crossed the Italian frontier and took over the Alpine passes. The Italians protested meekly, but by September Rommel had eight divisions in northern Italy. They acted as a reserve for General "Smiling Albert" Kesselring's ten divisions in the south. The disaster had begun.

Ike had been in Tunis conferring with his senior commanders when he heard that Mussolini had been fired. That afternoon he flew back to Algiers, and in the evening he had dinner with Secretary of War Henry L. Stimson, who had just been in England consulting with Churchill about what the Allies should do next. While Stimson was there, Churchill had received the news that Montgomery had met heavy German resistance at Catania. The prime minister had been alarmed by the news and as a result he had told Stimson what from his experience in two wars the American already knew, that the Germans were great fighters. He also once again expressed his doubts about the feasibility of a cross-Channel invasion. According to Stimson, "He repeated assertions he had made to me in previous occasions as to the disastrous effect of having the Channel full of the corpses of defeated Allies. This stirred me up and for a few minutes we had at it hammer and tongs. I directly charged him that he was not in favor of the ROUNDHAMMER operation [modified ROUNDUP for late 1943]. . . . On this he said that, while he admitted that if he was C-in-C he would not set up the . . . operation, yet having made his pledge he would go through with it loyally."

Stimson did not mention the argument in Algiers, but he did find that Eisenhower agreed with Marshall and other American officers in Washington and London, that the attack on Italy should be limited in scope and that its main objective should be the capture of air bases in the Foggia area. Those bases were essential for the mounting air offensive against Germany.

When Stimson returned to Washington in August he sent a memorandum to Roosevelt emphasizing that and adding that the Italian operation the Americans, including Eisenhower, had in mind must not in any way interfere with the cross-Channel invasion. He added that in this area the British, Churchill in particular, did not agree.

After meeting with Stimson a few days later Roosevelt said that the secretary of war and he agreed completely on everything. The president's later actions left some doubt about that, but then none of the Americans, including Roosevelt, Stimson, and Eisenhower, got what he wanted in Italy, and neither did any of the English, including Churchill.

On July 26 Eisenhower's first interest was in what the Italians were going to do immediately. He wanted to offer them "peace with honor." But that is not what either Roosevelt or Churchill had in mind. Actually, they both changed their minds several times, and "rapid communications" between London, Washington, and Algiers were in the days and weeks ahead almost incessant and often infuriating in their inconsistency. At the same time Eisenhower had to deal with two difficult French generals, several Italian officers of high rank, some of them disguised and with psudonyms, and above all an American general, his old friend George Patton, who had to be saved from a general court-martial. And in this affair, Ike found it necessary to withhold the truth from the man to whom he owed so much, General Marshall. No wonder Eisenhower would be forced to take briefly to his bed.

On July 27 he informed the Combined Chiefs and the British Chiefs of Staff:

Yesterday I met all commanders in Tunis. Plans for operations against the mainland of Italy were reviewed and I ordered the preparation of the following alternative plans: (a) BUTTRESS, as previously conceived. (b) AVALANCHE, employing Fifth Army with a United States and British Corps and contemplating French followup formations.

The military significance of recent political changes in Italy ought to be revealed during the next few days, and it will then be possible to decide which of the two plans to put into effect. My one concern is speed of action and all our efforts are bent on launching the next operation as soon after the completion of HUSKY as it is humanly possible to do so.

In addition, a plan is being prepared for a small force of a division, together with an airborne division, to rush into Naples at short notice in the event of a complete Italian collapse or a rapid German withdrawal from southern Italy.

BUTTRESS meant that the Allies would land on the toe of the boot of Italy; AVALANCHE provided for a landing on the west coast, farther north but below Naples. Another alternative considered was a landing on the islands of Corsica and Sardinia.

On the day Ike met with his senior commanders the CCS held an emergency meeting and decided to launch AVALANCHE as soon as possible. That news delighted Churchill, who was opposed to a landing in Sardinia or on the toe and, as he put it, crawling up the leg of Italy "like a harvest bug from the ankle upwards." For once, Marshall agreed with him. They also both agreed that the main Allied purpose in the immediate future was to "knock Italy out of the war." But exactly what that meant and what would happen after the knockout nobody seemed to know.

In the meantime the HUSKY operation had to be completed, and on August 16, the day before Patton's and Montgomery's troops both entered Messina, Ike sent an encouraging report to the Combined Chiefs and the British Chiefs:

> The Sicilian phase of the campaign is now drawing rapidly to a close. In spite of every effort by all three services, the enemy is succeeding in evacuating considerable numbers of personnel and light equipment. At the Commanders in Chief meeting today it was concluded that crossing of the straits should be attempted as quickly as necessary supporting guns and supplies could be accumulated. Present indications are this date will be between September 1 and September 4. Assuming no great change in general situation, AVALANCHE will be launched target date of September 9. Since a ten-day interval between the two assaults would greatly alleviate our difficulties in landing craft, we are straining to make the first assault at the earliest possible date.

On June 11 when Eisenhower had told Marshall about his satisfying success at Pantelleria he also said, "I am particularly pleased that the operation turned out as it did because I had to take the decision for its capture in the face of much contrary advice. . . . Moreover, today marks the completion of my twenty-eighth year of commissioned service and I believe that I am now legally eligible for promotion to colonel."

He was indeed legally eligible, and he received an order to report for an examination to see if he was physically fit to become a full colonel. He did that on the morning of August 10. The doctors found that he was subject to "hypertension" and that his blood pressure was much too high. He was ordered to go to bed for a rest, preferably for a week—but two or three days at least.

He stayed out of the office that afternoon and the next, but that evening he had to entertain at dinner four senators who were in his theater to study postwar problems. The senators were Richard Russell (Georgia), R. Owen Brewster (Maine), James M. Mead (New York), and Albert B. Chandler (Kentucky). Russell was on the Senate Military Affairs Committee and was to prove extremely useful to Eisenhower when he was president. Ike found that the Georgia Democrat was much more understanding of his foreign affairs policy than most members of his own party.

Although there is no record of what was said at that dinner in the Eisenhower villa it seems unlikely that the general looked upon the senators' mission with any great enthusiasm. What happened when the war was over was not his business; when that happened he would be sitting under a cool shade tree someplace, fishing. His job was winning the war, and the enemy in Sicily seemed stronger with each passing day, retreating more slowly than before, destroying bridges and roads, and leaving deadly mines everywhere. Why couldn't the senators concern themselves with the business at hand? When he was president, he had that same trouble with a great many senators. They were forever concerning themselves with the future. Dealing with the present was, as always, politically precarious.

Ike spent the afternoon of the 12th away from the office, but he cannot have been enjoying much peace of mind. That morning he had received a cable from Marshall saying that he was to use in the Mediterranean only those resources already available there and that, beginning November 1, seven U.S. divisions already under his command would be sent to England to take part in the cross-Channel invasion now planned for the following spring, an invasion that almost everyone agreed would be commanded by Marshall. A great many people were also convinced that a subordinate of Marshall's would be sent to Washington to handle domestic matters that the army concerned itself with and to "oversee" what was going on in all theaters of war in which the United States was involved. That subordinate, most people felt, would be Eisenhower. Butcher said, "If he has to return to Washington to take this backbreaking job, his heart will be practically broken. But he's a soldier."

The general managed to stay out of the office on the 13th, 14th, and 15th, but, as Butcher said, "He has only one speed and that is superspeed." On the 13th, while he and his naval aide were having coffee, he jumped out of bed several times to lecture Butcher on the "mistakes" he had made in his recent army career. He said that the approach to Italy had been too cautious, which was true, and that in Sicily the Allies should have landed on both sides of the Strait of Messina, cutting off the island from mainland Italy and preventing the escape of Axis troops and equipment. That also was true. Butcher added that "Patton's great progress gives Ike a warm glow, as there are many Army officers who could not see through Patton's showmanship and boisterousness to discern his fine qualities of leadership, on which Ike banked so strongly."

On the 16th Eisenhower flew to Tedder's headquarters at La Marsala for another meeting with his senior commanders, returning to Algiers that night.

There he learned that Lucian Truscott's 3d Division was nearing Messina. The following morning the Americans would enter the city.

In his diary Patton said, "I feel that the Lord has been most generous. If I had to fight the campaign over, I could make no change in anything I did. Few generals in history have ever been able to say as much." The next day he added, "Few people, especially generals, have no regrets, but in this case, I have none."

Ida Eisenhower was fond of repeating the proverb, "Pride goeth before destruction, and a haughty spirit before a fall." One of the many differences between George Patton and Ike is that the latter never indulged himself in hubris.

On the morning of the 17th Eisenhower had returned to the dispensary and found out that even so brief a rest had done him good. His blood pressure was down. That morning, too, T.J. had called Butcher on the interoffice phone to say that Brigadier Frederic A. Blessé, chief surgeon at Allied headquarters, had news from Sicily that, Butcher said, "was most alarming and implicated General Patton. T.J. thought General Ike should see Blessé as soon as possible, to get the full report."

Blessé and Eisenhower met around noon, and the doctor told him what thousands of soldiers in the Seventh Army knew at least in part. Patton had made himself liable to a general court-martial by striking and verbally abusing two soldiers in his army. The first incident had taken place on August 4.

On that day, after a visit to the front, Patton had asked his driver to take him to an evacuation hospital, the 15th, which, like most such hospitals close to the front, was under canvas. There he had seen Charles H. Kuhl, an infantryman from the 1st Division, who was, according to doctors in the hospital, suffering from "psychoneurotic anxiety state, moderately severe." To Patton, those words were meaningless jargon. Such a thing as a "psychoneurotic anxiety state" did not exist.

He asked Kuhl what was the matter with him, and the soldier said, "I guess I can't take it, sir."

Patton was furious. He called the soldier a coward, slapped his face with his gloved hand, grabbed him by the scruff of the neck and shouted to a nearby doctor, "Don't admit this sonofabitch." Then he looked down at Kuhl and screamed, "You hear me, you gutless bastard? You're going back to the front at once."

He then kicked the soldier out of the tent. A few minutes later several medical corpsmen picked Kuhl up and carried him to another tent. He was found to have a temperature of 102.2°, had been suffering from diarrhea for a month, and had malaria.

It is perhaps true, as Patton's admiring biographer, Ladislas Farago, wrote, "Had General Patton been able to control his nervous temper after the first incident in the admission tent of the 15th Evacuation Hospital, his slapping of an apparently sick soldier would never have become public knowledge. The slapping created no hysterics in the tent. It was discussed only in passing at the hospital and the story never got beyond it. It was not reported to higher echelons by the medical staff, and Kuhl had been willing to overlook the unhappy incident. In describing what had happened to his family, he said, 'Forget it.' "

But what happened on August 10 could not be forgotten. Patton said in his diary, "At another evacuation hospital . . . saw another alleged nervous patient—really a coward. I told the doctor to return him to his company and he began to cry, so I cursed him well and he shut up. I may have saved his soul if he had one."

The soldier was Private Paul G. Bennett, a twenty-one-year-old farmer from South Carolina who had enlisted in the army before Pearl Harbor. He had recently become a father for the first time and had been afraid that he would be killed before he saw the baby. On August 6 his best friend in his field artillery battery had been wounded, and Bennett kept saying that the German shells were "going to land on me." A medical officer of his unit ordered that he be evacuated although Bennett had begged to be allowed to stay with his outfit. Patton arrived at the evacuation hospital a few minutes after the South Carolinian was brought in.

The official army history tells what happened without flourishes:

[He] dropped in unexpectedly at the 93rd Evacuation Hospital (Colonel D. E. Currier, medical commander) where he was met by Major Charles B. Etter, the hospital's receiving officer, and taken to the receiving tent, where fifteen patients had just arrived from the front. Patton started down the line of cots, asking each man where he had been hurt and how, and commending each. The fourth man Patton reached was a soldier of Battery C, 17th Field Artillery Regiment, who had been previously diagnosed at a clearing station as suffering from a severe case of shell shock. He was huddled on his bunk and shivering. Patton stopped in front of the bed and as was his way, asked the soldier what the trouble was. The man replied: "It's my nerves," and began to sob. Patton instantly furious, roared, "What did you say?" The man replied: "I can hear the shells come over but I can't hear them burst."

Patton turned impatiently to Major Etter and asked, "What's this man talking about? What's wrong with him, if anything?" Etter reached for the soldier's chart but before the doctor could answer Patton's questions, Patton began to rave and rant: "Your nerves, hell; you are just a goddamned coward, you yellow son of a bitch." At this point, Colonel Currier and two other medical officers entered the receiving tent, in time to hear Patton yell at the man: "You're a disgrace to the Army and you're going back to the front to fight, although that's too good for you. You ought to be lined up against a wall and shot. In fact, I ought to shoot you myself right now, goddam you." With this Patton reached for his pistol, pulled it from its holster and waved it in the soldier's face. Then as the man sat quivering on his cot, Patton struck him sharply across the face with his free hand and continued to shout imprecations. Spotting Colonel Currier, Patton shouted: "I want you to get this man out of here right away. I won't have these other brave boys seeing such a bastard babied."

Reholstering his pistol, Patton started to leave the tent, but turned suddenly and saw that the soldier was openly crying. Rushing back to him, Patton again hit the man, this time with such force that the helmet liner he had been wearing was knocked off and rolled outside the tent. This was enough for Colonel Currier, who placed himself between Patton and the soldier. Patton turned and strode out of the tent. As he left the hospital, Patton said to Colonel Currier: "I meant what I said about getting that coward out of here. I won't have these cowardly bastards hanging around our hospitals. We'll probably have to shoot them sometime anyway, or we'll raise a breed of morons."

This time what happened could not possibly be hushed up. It had been witnessed by a large number of shocked hospital staff members and was soon known all over the Seventh Army. At midday on the 17th, Blessé brought Eisenhower an official report on both incidents.

At first Ike pretended, or maybe even believed, that the whole matter was of small importance. He said that whatever the cause of Patton's actions, he would have to be given a "jacking up." Butcher did what he so often did; he said what Eisenhower wanted to hear and what he himself believed. "I added my nickel's worth, that regardless of method Patton had done a swell job," Butcher wrote in the diary. Butcher never upset his boss or anyone else with disturbing original thoughts.

The false feeling of security did not last long, however. Eisenhower knew that something had to be done and done fast, and it would be far more than a "jacking up." At the end of the day he saw Blessé for a second time. He asked the doctor to make an investigation of the matter, warning him that total secrecy must be maintained. He said, "If this thing ever gets out they'll be howling for Patton's scalp and that'll be the end of Georgie's service in this war. I simply cannot let that happen. Patton is *indispensable* to the war effort—one of the guarantors of our victory."

The same afternoon Ike sent Lieutenant Colonel Hamilton Long from Massachusetts, who was theater medical consultant, on a desperate and also confidential mission to look into the matter. He asked Long to send him a frank report "for my eyes only."

Then Ike began the painful task of writing his old friend George in longhand. He did not mention Long, but he said:

Dear General Patton:
This personal and secret letter will be delivered to you by General Blessé, Chief Surgeon, Allied Headquarters, who is coming to Sicily in connection with matters involving health of the command. . . .
I am attaching a report which is shocking in its allegations against your personal conduct. I hope you can assure me that none of them is true, but the detailed circumstances communicated to me lead me to the belief that some ground for the charges must exist. I am well aware of the necessity for hardness and toughness on the battlefield. I clearly understand that firm and drastic measures are at times necessary in order to secure desired

objectives. But this does not excuse brutality, abuse of the sick, nor exhibition of uncontrollable temper in front of subordinates.

In the two cases cited in the attached report, it is *not* my present intention to institute any formal investigation. Moreover, it is acutely distressing to me to have such charges as those made against you at the very moment when an American Army under your leadership has attained a success of which I am extremely proud. I feel that the personal services you have rendered the United States and the Allied cause during the past weeks are of incalculable value; but nevertheless if there is a very considerable element of truth in the allegations accompanying this letter, I must so seriously question your good judgment and your self-discipline as to raise serious doubt in my mind as to your future usefulness. I am assuming, for the moment, that the facts in the case are far less serious than appears in this report, and that whatever truth is contained in these allegations represents an act of yours when, under the stress and strain of winning a victory, you were thoughtless rather than harsh. Your leaderhip of the past few weeks has, in my opinion, fully vindicated to the War Department and to all your associates in arms my own persistance in upholding your preeminent qualifications for the difficult task to which you were assigned. Nevertheless, you must give to this matter of personal deportment your instant and serious consideration to the end that no incident of this character can be reported to me in the future, and I may continue to count upon your assistance in military tasks.

In Allied Headquarters there is no record of the attached report or my letter to you, except in my own secret files. I will expect your answer to be sent to me personally and secretly. Moreover, I strongly advise that, provided there is any semblance of truth in the allegations in the accompanying report, you make, in the form of apology or otherwise, such personal amends to the individuals concerned as may be within your power, and that you do this before submitting your letter to me.

No letter that I have been called upon to write in my military career has caused me the mental anguish of this one, not only because of my deep personal friendship for you but because of admiration for your military qualities; but I assure you that conduct such as described in the accompanying report will *not* be tolerated in this theater no matter who the offender may be.

Sincerely. . . .

The next day, in a message to Marshall, Eisenhower did not mention the Patton matter, though he did mention his name. He said, "For your personal information on the American side of the ground organization, Generals Patton, Bradley, and Keyes, and each of the division commanders have been outstanding. Leadership throughout the command has greatly improved. Our soldiers literally kept marching when no skin was left on the bottom of their feet and fought magnificently and successfully in one of the most unrelenting offensives in which American troops have ever participated."

Eisenhower no doubt felt that, although what would be done about Italy had to be decided in Washington and London, what was to be done about Patton had to be handled in the theater. Maybe it would go away. Maybe George could explain what happened; possibly the whole thing was exaggerated.

The matter did not go away. On the 19th Demaree Bess of *The Saturday Evening Post* gave Butcher a statement of complaint about what had happened in the 93rd Evacuation Hospital. Included in the report was a simple, frightening declaration, "If I am correctly informed, General Patton has subjected himself to a general court-martial by striking an enlisted man under his command." He said that he and the other correspondents who had investigated the case had not written about it but that what had happened could not be kept secret indefinitely. Quentin Reynolds of *Collier's*, who always had an opinion on everything, often only slightly exaggerated, said that at least 50,000 American soldiers would shoot Patton if they could.

"Ike is in the position of having to deal severely with a general who has commanded an army in one of our country's most successful operations and who is the best ground soldier developed so far by the Allies," said Butcher. "Just one of the many worries which plague the Allied commander-in-chief."

Long's preliminary report was the first to reach Eisenhower, and it verified everything Major Etter had said about what happened in the 93rd Evac. Long also added the hardly comforting words, "The deleterious effects of such incidents upon the well-being of patients, upon the professional morale of hospital staffs, and upon the relationship of patient and physician are incalculable."

As president, Eisenhower did what is not uncommon with presidents, he appointed a great many committees to look into matters that he did not wish to confront. He did somewhat the same thing with what newspapers were later to refer to as "the slapping incident." He had already dispatched two investigators, Blessé and Long, and now he sent a third, Major General John Porter Lucas, West Point 1911, a friend of both his and Patton's, to look into what had happened. Lucas, who was soon to face troubles of his own at Anzio, dutifully took off for Sicily.

Butcher said, "All the press, while not printing the story, are incensed." Eisenhower called a group of reporters into his office and told them he was doing everything in his power to keep Patton in command. He said that Patton's "emotional tenseness and his personal impulsiveness are the very qualities that make him, in open situations, such a remarkable leader of an army. . . . I feel . . . that Patton should be saved for the great battles facing us in Europe." Once more the reporters agreed not to write the story, but Eisenhower knew that it could not be kept quiet much longer, and that night, Butcher said, the general "sat in my room for half an hour, debating the question [what to do about Patton], not so much with me as with himself. He's sweating it out."

Patton knew he was in serious trouble when on the 20th a cable arrived "From the Commander in Chief, personal to General Patton":

General Lucas will arrive at Palermo airfield between five and five-thirty this afternoon. It is highly important that you personally meet General Lucas and give your full attention to the message that he will bring you. In the event that it is impossible for you to meet him personally, be certain to have transportation awaiting him and leave word as to the place where he can reach you quickest.

That same day, before Lucas arrived, Blessé delivered Eisenhower's letter to Patton. After reading it, he was far from contrite. He said in his diary that night:

General Blessé . . . brought me a very nasty letter from Ike with reference to the two soldiers I cussed out for what I considered cowardice. Evidently I acted precipitately and on insufficient knowledge. My motive was correct because one cannot permit skulking to exist. It is just like any communicable disease. I admit freely that my method was wrong but I shall make what amends I can. I regret the incident as I hate to make Ike mad when it is my earnest study to please him.
General Lucas arrived at 1800 to further explain Ike's attitude. I feel very low.

Patton does not mention striking the two soldiers, which was the court-martial offense. No, he "cussed them out for what I considered cowardice. . . . My motive was correct because one cannot permit skulking."

The day after receiving Eisenhower's letter Patton did call in Private Bennett and, according to his diary, "explained to him that I had cussed him out in the hope of restoring his manhood, that I was sorry, and that if he cared, I would like to shake hands with him. We shook." It will be noticed that once again Patton had only "cussed out" Bennett, no mention of slapping him and later hitting him so hard that his helmet liner fell off or of the general's reaching for his pistol and saying that he ought to shoot the soldier as well as threatening him with death in front of a firing squad. Patton added in his diary that, "General John A. Crane, to whose brigade he [Bennett] belongs, stated to me afterwards that the man was absent without leave and had gone to the rear by falsely representing his condition to the battery surgeon. It is rather a commentary on justice when an Army commander has to soft-soap a skulker to placate the timidity of those above."

What General Crane is said to have said to Patton is simply not true. It surely can be said that as of the night of August 21 Patton had learned nothing at all from the experience. The fault was all in the "timidity of those above," meaning Eisenhower.

But Georgie had an enjoyable evening. Bob Hope and his "troupe called on me at the office. . . . They sang and carried on until after midnight. I put myself out to be amusing and human as I think it may help, if this business about the shirkers comes up."

On the 22nd Patton called into his office "all the doctors and nurses and enlisted men who witnessed the affair with the skulkers. I told them about my friend in the last war who shirked, was let get by with it, and eventually killed himself. I told them that I had taken the action I had to correct such a future tragedy."

That is the first time but by no means the last that Patton's dead friend was mentioned. The general also said that he regretted "my impulsive action." But at least one member of his audience was not impressed. Dr. D. E. Currier was not impressed. He felt that what Patton said was "no apology at all" but "an attempt to justify what he had done."

The next day, Patton said in his diary, "Private Charles H. Kuhl . . . came in. He was one of the two men I cussed out for skulking. I told him why I did it, namely, that I tried to make him mad with me so he would regain his manhood. I then asked him to shake hands, which he did."

Later when the whole matter of the slappings became a cause célèbre, a letter Kuhl had written to his family in Mishawaka, Indiana, became public. In it he said, "General Patton slapped my face yesterday [the letter was written on August 5] and kicked me in the pants and cursed me. This probably won't go through, but I don't know. Just forget about it in your letter."

In the meantime Eisenhower was concerned not only with Patton's misconduct but with what the Italians wanted or did not want as well as what Washington and London wanted. Then, too, he had a war to fight, although a great many people seemed to think that war was already won or at least that it would be over before Christmas.

In a letter he wrote to Edgar on August 21, he said, "I should like very much to know what basis the prophets are using who say that the war will be over before Christmas. Naturally, since there are 130 million people in the United States, each one could pick a day from now on and some one individual would surely be right. . . . In the letters I receive from the United States nothing disturbs me more than the complacent attitude 'that the war is won.' . . . At any rate, I can tell them all this: When you give a German division a good position to hold, it takes a lot of fighting and a lot of grim work and big casualties to break him out of it. The German is a determined and resourceful fighter and there are still a lot of them in the German Army."

In the message on the 24th, Eisenhower told Marshall, "Foreseeing a future need of yours for senior U.S. commanders who had been tested in battle, I have been watching very closely and earnestly the performance of American commanders here and I have been trying to arrange affairs so as to give a number of them opportunity to demonstrate their capabilities. . . .

"First Patton. He has conducted a campaign where the brilliant successes scored must be attributed directly to his energy, determination and unflagging aggressiveness. The operations of the Seventh Army in Sicily are going to be classed as a model of swift conquest by future classes in the War College in Leavenworth. The prodigious marches, the incessant attacks, the refusal to be halted by appalling difficulties in communications and terrain, are really something to enthuse about. . . . He never once chose a line on which he said 'we will here rest and recuperate and bring up more strength.' On the contrary, when he received an order from Alexander that made it look as if he was to remain rather quiescent in the Etna region he immediately jumped into a plane, went to Alexander, got the matter cleared up, and kept on driving."

So much for Georgie's many virtues and successes. He was not, however, a perfect commander. "In spite of all this George Patton continues to exhibit some of those unfortunate personal characteristics of which you and I have always known, and which during this campaign caused me some most uncomfortable days. His habit of impulsive bawling out of subordinates, even to personal abuse of individuals was noted in at least two specific cases."

If Patton was reluctant to face what he had done, his commander in chief was in that letter even more so. Marshall could not possibly have guessed from what Eisenhower said, what actually had occurred. "I have had to take the most drastic steps, and if he is not cured now, there is no hope for him. Personally, I believe he is cured—not only because of his personal loyalty to you and to me but because fundamentally he is so avid for recognition as a great military commander that he will ruthlessly suppress any habit of his own that will jeopardize it."

That last was pure wishful thinking. Eisenhower had no evidence that Patton was suppressing any habit at all. From Patton's point of view he had done no wrong. To the contrary, he had persuaded two soldiers to stop skulking, and they had been grateful for it. They couldn't wait to shake his hand and tell him so.

"Aside from this one thing," Eisenhower told Marshall, "he has qualities that we cannot afford to lose unless he ruins himself. So he can be classed as an army commander that you can use with certainty that the troops will not be stopped by ordinary obstacles."

In other words, from Eisenhower's point of view, the matter was over and done with. George was sorry; he would never do it again, whatever it was, and the chief of staff need not concern himself with the messy details.

What a pleasure it must have been for Eisenhower to get to the next man, Bradley. He said, "There is very little I need to tell you about him, because he is running absolutely true to form all the time. He has brains, a fine capacity for leadership and a thorough understanding of the requirements of modern battle. . . . He has the respect of all his associates, including the British officers that have met him. I am very anxious to keep him in this theater as long as we have any major operations to carry out."

At the time Bradley kept his opinions about what should be done about Patton confined to his staff, but after the war he said, "I would have relieved him instantly and would have had no more to do with him. . . . He was colorful but he was impetuous, full of temper, bluster, inclined to treat the troops and subordinates as morons. His whole concept of command was opposite to mine. He was primarily a showman. The show always seemed to come first."

On the 29th Eisenhower flew to Catania and had lunch with both Patton and Bradley, as well as, among others, Montgomery. It was the first time he had seen Patton since the trouble began, and Georgie found him "most effusive. We had lunch with Monty. . . . Ike decorated him with the big cross of the Legion of Merit.

"Then I handed Ike my letter [of remorse] about the incidents of the two soldiers. He just put it in his pocket."

After lunch Eisenhower and Montgomery went to Messina. A great many photographs were taken. According to Butcher, "Monty's photographers were on the job." At Messina one picture was taken of the two generals looking across the strait. It was a picture Ike was to remember with some bitterness later. The Italian mainland was only two miles away.

The next day Eisenhower met with his commanders in chief, including Alexander, in an olive grove near Catania. Then he flew back to Maison Blanche airport, and when he returned to his office, Butcher said, "he cleaned up accumulated messages."

Just when and where Eisenhower read Patton's remorseful letter is not known. It was the kind of letter he would surely want to read privately and perhaps more than once. And after reading it he must have taken some time to think over its rather startling contents. It was written on the official stationery of the Headquarters Seventh Army.

My dear General Eisenhower:

Replying to your letter of August 17, 1943, I want to commence by thanking you for this additional illustration of your fairness and general consideration in making the communication personal.

I am at a loss to find words with which to express my chagrin and grief at having given you, a man to whom I owe everything and for whom I would gladly lay down my life, cause for displeasure with me.

I assure you that I had no intention of being harsh or cruel in my treatment of the two soldiers in question. My sole purpose was to try and restore in them a just appreciation of their obligation as men and soldiers.

In World War I, I had a dear friend and former schoolmate who lost his nerve in an exactly analagous manner, and who, after years of mental anguish, committed suicide.

Both my friend and the medical men with whom I discussed his case assured me that had he been roundly checked at the time of his first misbehavior, he would have been restored to a normal state.

Naturally, this memory actuated me when I inaptly tried to apply the remedies suggested. After each incident I stated to officers with me that I felt I had probably saved an immortal soul.

Very respectfully yours,
G. E. Patton, Jr.

Eisenhower apparently saw no need to answer the letter; at least there is no record that he did. He must have wondered, however, about Patton's curious friend and schoolmate "who, after years of mental anguish, committed suicide." Clearly what Patton was saying was that he had done Kuhl and Bennett a big favor. He had saved them from anguish and suicide.

In the meantime Patton was making various speeches that he considered apologies, although those who heard them frequently did not. When he spoke before the famous 1st Division, he used such vulgar language and spoke in such a vainglorious way, one man said "almost as if in mistreating those guys he had won a battle," that the men were shocked into silence. Major General Clarence R. Huebner, who had recently taken over command of the 1st, said, "I assembled 18,000 men, and Patton made a speech, a very good speech, in which he explained that he was sorry. But when he was finished, not one man clapped or said anything. There was no applause. They knew Patton was wrong, but they also knew it was something to get over with and forget as soon as possible."

Huebner does not explain that one of the men slapped, Private Kuhl, had been a member of the 1st Division.

Major Charles Burta Etter who had been at the 93rd Evacuation Hospital on August 10 when Private Bennett was assaulted, said, "The apology went like this. We were ordered to the General's office. . . . We stood at attention while he told us that a good friend of his, in a fit of depression, had committed suicide during World War I. He felt that if someone had been 'rough with him' and 'slapped some sense into him,' his life might have been saved. He explained he considered his action for the soldiers' own good. He felt that we should understand his, the General's motives, that we must realize our responsibilities as officers, and watch over personnel who were in trouble. "With that as an explanation of his conduct, we were advised to forget the incident and dismissed."

For a time it looked as if that was just what had happened; everybody had either forgotten what had happened or was ready to overlook or forgive it. In a message to Marshall on September 6, Eisenhower said, "With respect to Patton, I do not see how you could possibly submit a list for permanent Major Generals, on combat performance to date, and omit his name. His job of rehabilitating the Second Corps in Tunisia was quickly and magnificently done. Beyond this, his leadership of the Seventh Army was close to the best of our classic examples."

That was all true, but one might question the accuracy of what followed:

It is possible that in the future some ill-advised action of his, might cause you to regret his promotion. You know his weaknesses as well as his strengths, but I am confident that I have eliminated some of the former. His intense loyalty to you and to me makes it possible for me to treat him much more roughly than I could any other senior commander, unless my action were followed immediately by the individual's relief. In the last campaign he, under stress, it is true, indulged his temper in certain instances toward individual subordinates who, in General Patton's opinion of the moment were guilty of malingering. I took immediate and drastic measures, and I am quite certain this sort of thing will never happen again.

You have in him a truly aggressive commander and, moreover, one with sufficient brains to do his work in splendid fashion. . . . Incidentally, I think he will show up even better in an exclusively American theater than an allied one.

The last two observations are accurate, the final one in particular; Patton was not meant to work with allies. But the rest of what Ike said was not true, and thousands of people under Eisenhower's command would have known that it wasn't true. Moreover, eventually, the facts were certain to reach the chief of staff.

That happened, and when it did, the whole thing surely demonstrated to

Eisenhower that if he had been frank with Marshall from the beginning, he, Marshall, and the entire U.S. Army would have been better served. As it was, even Stimson had to get into the act, and that proper Bostonian proved as able to say what was not true as anyone else. As Arthur Krock said, what "would probably have been only a sensation shows signs of becoming a *cause célèbre*, producing public suspicion concerning what really goes on among our troops abroad and widespread distrust of the attitude of commanding generals toward matters of legitimate public information."

A great many people back in the States now knew what had happened at the two evac hospitals, possibly including the president, Marshall, and Stimson. But the public at large did not find out until Sunday, November 21, when Drew Pearson said on his weekly network program that Patton had slapped "a battle-weary soldier," that he had been reprimanded by Eisenhower, and that Ike had made him apologize before his own soldiers. Pearson predicted that Patton would never have another important wartime assignment.

The story was picked up by a great many other columnists and reporters, including John O'Donnell, a columnist of the *New York Daily News* who said that the soldier Patton had slapped was indeed a malingerer and a Jew and that Jews with power in Roosevelt's New Deal had covered up the story.

The whole thing could not have come at a worse time. Eisenhower had just been host to Roosevelt, Marshall, Harry Hopkins, and, among others, Admiral King. They were on their way to conferences, and both the president and the admiral had told Ike that he was about to be returned to Washington to become acting chief of staff. The coveted job of commanding Operation OVERLORD [the Normandy invasion] would go to Marshall.

The last thing Ike needed on the 22nd was to hear that the slapping or slappings—the first stories referred to only one slapping—had become a national scandal. Only two days later, on the 24th, he was to fly to Cairo where he would again have to confront all those who had in one way or another been embarrassed by the story, including the president, Hopkins, and Marshall. He would also have to confront Brooke, who wouldn't at all mind Ike's embarrassment; he might even enjoy it. Admiral King was friendly enough, and he would be there, too. But an admiral never much minded when army generals got into trouble, and here were two of them in trouble at the same time. On the 26th Ike was again to go to Cairo, accompanied by Marshall. This time Roosevelt was to present him with a Legion of Merit, assuming that the Patton incident and his handling of it hadn't caused the president to change his mind.

What Marshall and Eisenhower said to each other about the matter is unknown, and we do not know when the chief of staff first learned of it. Forrest C. Pogue said, "There is no evidence of a report on Patton's soldier slapping until November, when Drew Pearson broke the story that correspondents in Sicily had agreed to keep secret." Rumors of what happened must have reached Marshall's Pentagon office, however, and he may have been as anxious not to know officially as Eisenhower was to keep him from knowing. As president, Ike often was delighted not to know about a great many things, and he pretended not to know about a good many others. In that sense his experience with the Patton matter may have proved very useful.

But the whole country was immediately aroused by what Patton had done or was said to have done. Several congressmen issued pontifical statements denouncing Patton. An American Legion post in Iowa asked for an immediate investigation saying, "These are American soldiers and not Germans. If our boys are to be mistreated, let's import Hitler and do it right."

The first statement issued by Eisenhower's headquarters, on November 22, was a disaster. It said that Patton was still in command of the Seventh Army and that he had not, repeat not, been reprimanded by Eisenhower. According to a reporter for the *New York Times* the statement "disgusted everybody who heard it. The feeling was that the Army should either have ignored Mr. Pearson's broadcast or answered it with the whole truth." The next morning, on the 23rd, Beetle told reporters the previous statement had been "the truth but not the complete truth." He said that he had been "a little ashamed" of having told reporters something "with my tongue in my cheek." For once Beetle had succeeded in charming his audience, and then he turned the whole matter of explaining what had happened to Merrill "Red" Mueller, of NBC, who had been in on the "Patton incident" from the beginning.

By that time the correspondents in Algiers were satisfied, but Marshall still was not. That same day he cabled Eisenhower, saying that a great deal of publicity had been given to the matter. He asked for the facts about what had happened and what Eisenhower had done about it. Eisenhower's reply of the 24th was about 1,200 words long, and it repeated some of what he had said before, that the "mainspring" of the drive from Gela to Messina had been Patton. Ike said that Patton "drove himself as hard as he did members of his army and, as a result, he became almost ruthless in his demands on individual men." When he "encountered two unwounded repeat unwounded patients who had been evacuated for nerve difficulty or what is commonly known as 'battle anxiety' . . . he momentarily lost his temper and upbraided the individuals in an unseemly and indefensible manner, and in one of the cases he cuffed the individual involved so that the man's helmet rolled off his head." One of the men did "have a temperature."

Eisenhower did not mention the other ailments suffered by both "unwounded, repeat unwounded" men. He failed to mention Patton's threat of a firing squad or that Georgie had reached for his own pistol to do the job. But then he did not mention Patton's friend who had committed suicide after all those anguished years either.

Eisenhower then told Marshall about the letter he had written to Patton and about the investigators he had sent to Sicily. He did not, however, quote from their findings. He said that he made "a short visit there myself to determine whether or not there was any resentment existing in the Army against General Patton." Neither he nor the other investigators had found anything to make him doubt that "the corrective action described above was adequate and suitable in the circumstances. . . . As a final word, it has been reported many times to me that in every recent public appearance of Patton before a crowd of his own soldiers, he is greeted by thunderous applause."

Quite likely Eisenhower did not know about the 1st Division's stunned silence. He probably did not know that the doctors and nurses throughout the theater had been outraged by Georgie's posturing pretense of apology. And that was probably just as well. The bliss of ignorance is at times absolutely necessary.

Ike sent a personal message to Patton on November 24 "for his eyes only (Code clerk, when you have decoded this message take it personally to General Patton and to no repeat no one else): The flood of newspaper accounts in Washington concerning incidents in which you were involved in the latter part of the Sicilian campaign has continued today. It is my judgment that this storm will blow over because our reporters here have generally sent forward very accurate stories including an account of my action with respect to you and of your corrective measures. I must stress again to you the necessity for acting deliberately at all times and avoiding the giving way to impulse. In this particular instance if any inquiry is made from you by the press, I insist that you stick to the facts and give a frank exposition of what occurred. In addition, you could, I think, invite any such press men to visit units still under your command to determine for themselves the state of morale.

"I do not, repeat not, desire that you make a formal statement for quotation at this time but I repeat that you are authorized to give representatives of the press a frank account of the whole matter."

By that time Ike knew that any "frank account" from Patton would largely have to do with the classmate and friend who could and should have been saved from suicide. Maybe Patton actually once had such a friend. It was certainly helpful to have him dead.

By now, fortunately, Eisenhower was not alone in defending and trying to keep his old friend in action. After Pearson, in the words of the secretary of war, "spilled the beans" about what Patton had done in Sicily, Stimson came to the rescue both of him and of Eisenhower. The old man sent a letter to Senator Robert R. Reynolds, chairman of the Military Affairs Committee, hinting that serious military matters had been involved in Patton's being retained in high military command. "The military reasons referred to above are still important to Allied operations in the Mediterranean theater," Stimson said, "and consequently must remain secret for the present . . . but I assure you that they will eventually be disclosed. At the time it will be made evident why a general discussion of details of this affair prior to the completion of certain strategic plans was directly contrary to the military interests of the United States and of our allies. General Eisenhower was obliged to consider this matter from a military viewpoint rather than that of what is termed 'public relations.' "

Stimson went on, "General Eisenhower in his last report has again reported that these instances [of violence] have not affected General Patton's standing as a tactical leader, one who successfully concluded, in record time, a complicated and important military campaign, and one whom his officers and men would again be willing to follow into battle. He reports that the serious aspect of this case is the danger that the Army will lose the services of a battle-tested Army commander, and also afford aid and comfort to the enemy."

Patton again got in trouble in the spring of 1944, and again he was protected by Eisenhower and Stimson. In his biography of Stimson McGeorge Bundy said, "Once more he [Stimson] supported Eisenhower's courageous acceptance of such annoyances and his refusal to relieve Patton. Perhaps no decision of the war was more triumphantly vindicated by events than this one; in the summer of 1944 Patton became almost overnight the idol of many of the same newspapers and politicians who had most loudly demanded his removal in 1943."

The important thing is to have a happy ending. In this case the ending was very happy indeed, and in this case, there were heroes everywhere you looked, which has seldom happened since.

By the end of the war Eisenhower had changed his opinion of Patton as a general and as a man, but there is no evidence that he ever regretted saving Patton's neck during the summer and autumn of 1943. Long after the war and after Ike had been president he was asked by Bruce Catton, the historian, if he remembered "that occasion in the fall of 1861 when President Lincoln came to General McClellan's house to see him and McClellan simply went upstairs and went to bed and left him cooling his heels? Do you think that is rather significant in its revelation of McClellan's frame of mind at that time?"

Ike said, "It was, indeed. And he saw himself as the great, new Napoleon. But, on top of that, I think . . . it reveals something about Lincoln. Mr. Lincoln . . . is supposed to have said when an associate said to him: 'Why did not you resent this and correct this man?'—and Mr. Lincoln replied: 'All I want General McClellan to do is to win a victory. If he will do that, I will hold his horse.' Here was a man that was dedicated to one thing . . . winning for his nation an end to the great war. So, I think this is as revealing about Mr. Lincoln as it was about General McClellan."

What Eisenhower was doing in 1943 was holding Patton's horse so that he could win a victory. That Ike should have said what he said about Lincoln and McClellan is very revealing about Eisenhower.

★ ★ ★

THE SOFT UNDERBELLY

Patton was not the only general Ike had trouble with that summer and fall. He had to deal with several Italian generals who couldn't decide whether Italy should continue on the side of Hitler or join the Allies. He had to mollify the two French generals, who disliked each other intensely, and bring them into some kind of agreement that would be beneficial to the Allies and, presumably, to themselves and their country.

Monty was, as always, a troubling British general. In Sicily he seemed either to move too slowly or not to move at all. He and Patton were not friendly. Montgomery at times pretended not to be unfriendly, but he really, as a subordinate said, "never . . . gave real credit to anyone else." Patton didn't even pretend to be friendly. He considered the advance toward Messina a race. "This is a horse race, in which the prestige of the U.S. Army is at stake," he said. "We must take Messina before the British."

Montgomery's staff, after the war at least, denied that the British had looked on the advance as a race. Eisenhower's friend and admirer, Montgomery's chief of staff, Major General Francis "Freddie" de Guingand, said, "It was all balls, that, about who was going to get to Messina first. We were *delighted* when we heard that Patton had got to Messina first." As for the scene in the movie in which Patton marches into Messina, de Guingand said, "Absolute cock, in the film, Monty marching at the head of the highlanders—all balls!"

De Gaulle observed Eisenhower closely during this period, and while the relations between them were not easy, the Frenchman made a shrewd appraisal of the American:

He was a soldier. To him, by nature and profession, action seemed natural, immediate, and simple. To put into play, according to time-honored rules, specific means of a familiar nature—this was how he envisaged warfare and consequently his task. Eisenhower approached the test trained for thirty-five years by a philosophy beyond which he was in no way inclined to go. Yet now he found himself invested with an extraordinarily complex role. Removed from the hitherto rigid framework of the American Army, he had become commander in chief of a colossal coalition. Because he had to lead the forces of several peoples in battles on which the fate of their states depended, he was to see national susceptibilities erupt into the tried and tested system of the units under his orders.

It was a piece of luck for the Allies that Dwight Eisenhower discovered in himself not only the necessary prudence to deal with these thorny problems, but also an attraction toward the wider horizons that history opened before his career. He knew how to be adroit and flexible. But if he used skill, he was also capable of audacity.

In the first week of August, as the Allied troops continued the drive to Messina, the crowds of cheering Sicilians disappeared, and the German and Italian troops were increasingly dug into the rock terrain on the northwestern slope of Mount Etna as well as the mountains to the south and west. The battle for Troina lasted six days, and the 1st Division fought back more than twenty German counterattacks. The Seventh Army continued its advance, however, and on August 6 Patton moved his camp to a new command post in an olive grove. He wrote Beatrice that it was a place "where Hannibal may also have wandered if he ever came this way." The "incidents" in the evac hospitals did not seem to trouble him. On the 15th he wrote Bea, "It was funny to see our men sitting down among German corpses eating lunch. . . . Our men are pretty hard."

At dawn on the 17th Lucian Truscott, commander of the 3d Infantry Division, was on the heights above Messina. He had been ordered to wait for Patton, and when Georgie got there he shouted, "What the hell are you all standing around for?" Then he and an American party, including Truscott, entered the city. A British armored patrol arrived a few minutes later. Truscott said, "General Montgomery had no doubt been anxious to beat General Patton into Messina for he had landed a patrol a few miles down the coast for the purpose of being there before us. The race to Messina had been won."

After that, for some time nobody except Ike seemed in a hurry to go anywhere.

In a press conference on August 18 Eisenhower said that the outcome of the campaign in Sicily represented "a real victory," which cannot be denied, though it was a costly one. According to the *New York Times*, Ike also said, "The cooperation between the American Seventh Army and the British Eighth Army was a 'one-two punch' that Alexander 'could bring into action whenever he desired.' " That could have been denied but wasn't, and there was no discussion of the fact that the Germans escaped from Sicily with 40,000 men and 10,000 vehicles, and the Italians with over 70,000 men, which should have dimmed the sense of triumph.

The victory in Sicily did, however, supply good news for the opening of the QUADRANT conference in Québec, which took place from August 14 to 24. Roosevelt, Churchill, their chief advisers, and the Combined Chiefs took part. A target date of May 1, 1944, was affirmed for OVERLORD, and the controversial landing in Southern France, then called ANVIL, was decided on, despite the opposition of Churchill. The prime minister went back to Washington with Roosevelt and was there when British and Canadian troops under Montgomery's command crossed the narrow Strait of Messina on September 3.

It was decided at Québec that Eisenhower should send representatives to Lisbon to meet with General Giuseppe Castellano, who said he had been sent by the Badoglio government to negotiate an unconditional surrender with the Allies if at the same time the Allies would allow the Italians to switch from the German side in the war to the Allied side, an idea both Roosevelt and Churchill looked upon with suspicion.

What followed looked and sounded like a very bad Italian comic opera. Eisenhower called in Macmillan to help him. He had decided that very day, August 18, to send Strong and Beetle to Lisbon to meet with Castellano, who was traveling under a false passport saying that his name was Raimand Imas. According to Macmillan, "The rest of a hot morning was spent in an atmosphere of amateur charades." Beetle and Strong could not go to Lisbon in uniform without arousing the suspicion of the German secret service and the international press. So civilian clothes were provided. These included for Beetle what Macmillan called "an appalling Norfolk jacket . . . some grey flannel trousers which fitted him very ill [and] some kind of dubious hat with a feather in it."

Strong, who looked like the caricature of an American's idea of an Englishman, wore horn-rimmed glasses, had a receding chin, and was dressed for the expedition in what Macmillan described as "a very improbable costume." Their appearances, however, turned out to be the least of the worries of Strong and Beetle and Eisenhower. A good deal of rhetoric was exchanged at the time about how Italy was to be "knocked out of the war" but exactly how that was to be done and what would happen after it had happened was never very clear in anybody's mind.

Eisenhower had been more than unusually impatient with Montgomery that summer. Kay said, "I often heard him grumble, 'Why doesn't Monty get going? What's the matter with him. Why doesn't he get going?' . . . Such statements were made in careful privacy. They never tarnished Monty's press."

It seemed to Eisenhower to take Monty forever to get across the Strait of Messina and begin the long, difficult drive—though at times drive scarcely seemed the word—up the toe of Italy. And in a postwar interview Eisenhower was less careful of tarnishing Monty's press. He said that he had been "pressing for speed all along." He added:

I believe there is a picture of Montgomery and me looking across the Strait from Messina. I believed that the Germans would withdraw, that we could make a landing practically unopposed. General Montgomery wished to have everything fully prepared and thought there would be considerable German opposition. Meanwhile there was General Patton moaning—asking that he be allowed to make the crossing. I told General Alexander I believed we could do it in a rowboat. We sat there in Messina from 17 August until 3 September.

Ike flew to Sicily to visit Montgomery in Catania on August 29. The two of them drove for two hours along the tortuous and hazardous road to the headland where they looked at the Italian mainland, just two miles away. After spending the night at Monty's headquarters, Ike returned to Algiers, stopping first at Alexander's camp near Cassibile for a meeting of his commanders. That was the day he got promoted twice (from lieutenant colonel to brigadier general on the permanent list) and added an Oak Leaf Cluster to his DSM. He told Marshall that this recognition was "most heartwarming and encouraging," especially "in these intense days."

Strong's and Beetle's trip to Lisbon to meet Castellano had not been a success. The two Allied representatives were not authorized to tell Castellano anything of importance about what their countries had in mind for the future militarily, and the Italian general was not authorized to sign any kind of surrender, conditional or unconditional. So both sides returned to their home stations, Castellano taking back to Rome what were called the "short terms" for surrender, drawn up by Ike. They provided, without frills or weighty explanations, what Strong called "terms for a military armistice" that had to be accepted unconditionally.

AVALANCHE, the Allied landing at Salerno, was to be on September 9, and Eisenhower learned that there were more enemy troops there than had been anticipated. On August 28 Beetle, under Ike's direction, sent a cable to the Combined Chiefs, saying, "The risks attendant on AVALANCHE, which have been pointedly put to you and which we are perfectly prepared to accept will be minimized to a large extent if we are able to secure Italian assistance just prior to and during the critical period of the actual landing. Even passive assistance will greatly increase our chances of success and there is even some possibility of the Italians being willing to immobilize certain German divisions. It is these factors which make me so very anxious to get something done now."

But what should that something be? Everybody had an idea, but everybody's idea was different. Churchill, for instance, was totally dedicated to retaining the king, the seventy-three-year-old, antidemocratic Victor Emmanuel III. The Americans, Roosevelt in particular, were supporters of Count Carlo Sforza, a genuine anti-Fascist who had spent the years when Mussolini was in power in exile. Both the president and the prime minister were reluctant to let Eisenhower handle matters by himself. After all, he had handled North Africa with a minimum of interference, and the result had been the "Darlan deal."

Churchill and Roosevelt were not even willing to accept Eisenhower's "short terms" for the Italian surrender. While they were in Québec they had accepted what were called "long terms" for that surrender, drawn up by anonymous men in the British Foreign Office and the American State Department. They were, Macmillan said, "a planner's dream and a general's nightmare" and were "remote from realities."

As for "rapid communications," Macmillan observed that Eisenhower was "getting pretty harassed. Telegrams (private, personal, and most immediate) pour in on him from the following sources: (i) Combined Chiefs of Staff (Washington), his official masters; (ii) General Marshall, Chief of U.S. Army, his immediate superior; (iii) The President; (iv) The Secretary of State; (v) Our Prime Minister (direct); (vi) Our Prime Minister (through me); (vii) The Foreign Secretary (through me)."

Finally, on August 31 Roosevelt gave Eisenhower his approval for the general to negotiate an immediate surrender on his own "short terms." The "long terms" could for the time being be postponed. Castellano said he could not accept the terms unless guarantees were given that sufficient Allied troops would be landing in Italy to protect the Italians from German reprisals. On September 2 Castellano got permission to sign. Smith, who was in Cassibile, Sicily, was authorized to sign, and Eisenhower flew there from Algiers to witness the ceremony. The secret signing was done by both sides by 4:30 P.M. on September 3, and then Castellano was given the longer, harsher "long terms." Eisenhower had no great enthusiasm for the matter. He felt that Castellano had been tricked, which was true. Smith said, "There was a certain amount of bluff. We had only limited means for the invasion of Italy, and we led Castellano to believe that our invasion would be in greater strength than was actually intended."

A bottle of whiskey was produced, and, according to Strong, "We drank out of rather dirty glasses and Bedell Smith, Castellano, Montanari, and I had our photographs taken together. We were under no illusions about the difficulties that would face our troops in the near future and there were no celebrations. . . . We picked branches from the [olive] trees to keep as mementos of the occasion."

At dawn on that same day Montgomery's troops had landed at Reggio di Calabria on the toe of Italy. Eisenhower said, "The allied invasion of the continent of Europe was an accomplished fact . . . ten days later than I had hoped it could be done."

The Italians continued to be concerned about what the Germans would do when the capitulation was announced on September 8. The Allies had no troops near Rome, and Castellano was sure that if the Germans got into the city without a fight they would loot and rape and take over the government, in which case the Italians would be worse off than they were before Mussolini was fired.

The Germans did have four divisions near the city, but they were without much fuel or ammunition. The original plan for AVALANCHE had called for the 82d Airborne to be dropped near Naples on the night of the 8th. The paratroopers were to blow up the bridges over the Volturno River, thus preventing the Germans from arriving to block mountain passages through which Clark's Fifth Army had to move on its way from Salerno to Naples. Clark had said that the troops of the 82d were to be his "left arm."

But Clark was to lose that "left arm." Eisenhower decided—and it was among the most daring and precipitous decisions he made during the war—to shift the drop of the 82d from Naples to Rome, where it was to capture airfields and railroad yards and join the Italian troops available there in holding Rome against the Germans until reinforcements arrived.

Then-Brigadier General Maxwell Taylor said of the plan, GIANT II, "I was struck both by the attraction of the mission—the opportunity which it afforded the division to take part in a truly history-making operation—and by the many difficulties to be overcome in a short period of time. . . . Also I was impressed . . . with the loose undertakings into which Castellano was entering, often with considerable pressure from General Bedell Smith . . . who was conducting the discussions. Little as I knew of the situation in and around Rome, I could not believe that the Italians could do all the things to which Castellano was agreeing."

The plan was elaborate in the extreme, calling for combined parachute and air landings over a period of several days at five airfields near Rome, plus a small seaborne force that was to come up the Tiber with artillery and antitank weapons to reinforce the landings. Taylor was not pleased with the unconcerned way Castellano said everything would be taken care of—lighting the airfields in a prearranged way, for example, providing hundreds of trucks for the airborne troops, the fact that the airfields were so far from Rome, two of them twenty-five miles away, and the large number of antiaircraft batteries in and around Rome. "Finally," Taylor said, "the American commanders [of the expedition] would have to be furnished with the latest intelligence regarding both the German and Italian forces. Castellano accepted all these requirements without much hesitation."

Taylor and the 82d's commanding officer, Matthew Ridgway, had their doubts, however, and they persuaded Alexander and Smith that someone should go to Rome to find out what Taylor called "the state of things and to determine the feasibility of the operation." It was decided that Taylor himself and an air force colonel, William Tudor Gardiner, a fifty-three-year-old former governor of Maine, would make the trip.

The two officers, pretending they had been rescued at sea by the Italians, got to Rome by dusk after a series of adventures. Taylor said they were "the advance guard of the Allied invasion which was not to reach the city until nine months later." They first saw General Giacomo Carboni, who was in command of the defense of Rome. Everything the Americans said alarmed Carboni, particularly the fact that the Italian surrender was to be announced by Eisenhower at 6:30 P.M. on September 8. The Italian general said that there were 12,000 German troops near Rome and that 36,000 more could quickly be summoned, which was exactly what would happen when the surrender was announced.

Carboni said that his own troops were not only outnumbered but were very ill-equipped. Some of the units had no more than twenty rounds a gun. He said that both the air drop and the announcement of the armistice must be postponed.

The two Americans were noncommital but asked to see Badoglio. After a time they went in Carboni's car through numerous checkpoints in the blacked out city to Badoglio's villa. If caught they could have been shot by a firing squad at once. Badoglio, in pajamas, greeted them around midnight. He was tired and, when he was told about the plans for GIANT II, he was horrified. He said that the whole thing would end in disaster, not only for the Allies and the city of Rome but for all of Italy; he was terrified of the Germans. Taylor and Gardiner, asked him to send a message to Eisenhower saying what he believed.

The old man then drafted his message in longhand:

Due to change in the situation brought about by the disposition and strength of the German forces in the Rome area, it is no longer possible to accept an immediate armistice as this could provoke the occupation of the capital and the violent assumption of the government by the Germans. Operation GIANT II is no longer possible because of lack of forces to guarantee the airfields. General Taylor is available to return to Sicily to present the views of the government and await orders.

A little later Taylor sent his own message to Ike:

In view of the statement of Marshal Badoglio as to inability to declare armistice and to guarantee fields, GIANT II is impossible. Reasons given for change are irreplaceable lack of gasoline and munitions and new German dispositions. Badoglio requests Taylor return to present governmental views. Taylor and Gardiner awaiting instructions.

After a most anxious wait that didn't end until three o'clock the next afternoon, Taylor and Gardiner were told that Eisenhower had ordered them returned to his advance headquarters at once. They later learned that some of the planes and troops that were to have taken part in GIANT II had been already in the air when that calm, careful American officer, General Lyman Lemnitzer, deputy chief of staff to Alexander, had personally carried the message of the cancelation to the fields of departure. The planes in the air were recalled without mishap.

It is impossible to say what would have happened if GIANT II had not been canceled. After the war, however, it was learned that the Germans did not, as General Carboni had said, have 12,000 troops to take over the airfields from the Italians. Field Marshal Albert Kesselring, the German commander, had only two battalions available to attack. Only a few German antiaircraft units were near the Eternal City; a panzer division was about sixty-six miles northwest of Rome, and a parachute division was to the south. Kesselring greatly feared just such an attack as proposed for GIANT II, and on September 9 he "kept his binoculars trained on the sky all . . . day, watching for enemy planes that never came." After the landings at Salerno he decided to occupy Rome, but the Italian resistance was such that it took two days of fighting before the city was taken.

Kenneth S. Davis was less than admiring of the general's decision when he wrote *Experience of War: the United States in World War II*, published in 1965. In that book he said, "It appears that Eisenhower would almost certainly have won the great prize he sought if he had boldly gambled with the 82nd, permitting the Rome drop to be executed despite the forebodings of Carboni and Badoglio and against the advice of Taylor. There are some who claim that the arrival of American paratroopers would have triggered a rising of the Rome civilian population which, of itself alone, could have overwhelmed the relatively few Nazis who then oppressed them. In the event . . . Rome was condemned to eight long months of torture by Hitler's brutes. . . . Clark's loss of the airborne support on which he had heavily counted . . . brought the Salerno operation very close to failure."

We know that Eisenhower did not lose his enthusiasm for GIANT II. After the war, in an interview with an Army historian, he said, "I wanted very much to make the air drop in Rome, and we were all ready to execute that plan. . . . I was anxious to get in there."

Kenneth Strong shared that view. In a similar interview with an army historian in 1947, he said, "My opinion is that the cancelation of GIANT II was a great mistake. If the airborne division had been sent . . . the Italians would have welcomed us, and they would have held the airfields for us."

In his autobiography, *Intelligence at the Top*, Strong is sparing in his approval of Taylor. He said that the paratroop officer had learned nothing in Rome that he had not been told before undertaking the risky mission; nevertheless, he advised against it. Strong's final comment is short and to the point. He said, "We briefed Taylor thoroughly on the situation before he left and placed a large sum of money in lire at his disposal. On his return he gave it all back to me except for twenty lire; I have ever since regarded Maxwell Taylor as a very careful and scrupulous man."

As was so often the case, Eisenhower was much more generous in his summing up. In *Crusade* he said of GIANT II, "At the last moment either the fright of the Italian government or the movement of German reserves as alleged by the Italians—I have never known which—forced the cancellation of the project. But in the meantime Brigadier General Maxwell D. Taylor, later the gallant commander of the 101st Airborne Division, had been hurried secretly to Rome, where his personal adventures and those of his companion added another thrilling adventure to the whole thrilling story [of the secret negotiations at the time]. The risks he ran were greater than I asked any other agent or emissary to undertake during the war—he carried weighty responsibilities and discharged them with unerring judgment, and every minute was in imminent danger of discovery and death."

Taylor, who was to become a less than cautious military adviser to Kennedy and a great favorite of the clan, never doubted, at least publicly, that he had been right. He said of his and Colonel Gardiner's journey, "Our trip to Rome was not wasted, although a mistake avoided brings none of the satisfaction of a feat achieved."

Wednesday, September 8, was not a good day for Eisenhower. He got up early and shortly after breakfast was handed the infuriating message from Badoglio saying that an immediate armistice was impossible. The general was even angrier when he found that the usually reliable Beetle had, without consulting him, sent the message on to the Combined Chiefs of Staff. Smith said that

Eisenhower was in conference with his commanders, adding that they probably would call off GIANT II, and asked the Combined Chiefs to pass on its "thoughts on whether or not, repeat not, we should proceed with the armistice announcement for the tactical and deception value." That last especially angered Ike. That was his business, deciding whether or not to proceed with the armistice announcement.

Beetle did not make many mistakes, but when he did, it was a beaut, and there must have been a few times when Eisenhower thought of replacing a man who was very nearly irreplaceable.

Ike immediately dictated a message to Badoglio that demonstrated just how angry he was:

> From Allied Commander in Chief to Marshal Badoglio: I intend to broadcast the existence of the Armistice at the hour originally planned. If you or any part of your armed forces fail to co-operate as previously agreed I will publish to the world full record of this affair. Today is X Day and I expect you to do your part.
>
> I do not accept your message of this morning postponing the armistice. . . .
>
> Plans have been made on the assumption that you were acting in good faith and we have been prepared to carry out future operations on that basis. Failure now on your part to carry out the full obligations of the signed agreement will have most serious consequences for your country. No future action of yours could then restore any confidence whatever in your good faith and consequently the dissolution of your government and nation would ensue.

Ike had a late lunch with Bradley at his villa in Amilcar, and his classmate said, "He looked drawn and worried. 'Badoglio has gummed up the works! . . . We've just had to call off Ridgway's air drop on Rome.' Eisenhower was referring to arrangements for the Italian surrender and his plan to land an airborne division on the edge of Rome. The joint announcement of Italian surrender was to be made at 6:30 that evening. And at 8:30 the next morning Clark was to land at Salerno. Now, with only a few hours left before going on the air, Eisenhower had no assurance that Badoglio would honor his surrender agreement with a simultaneous broadcast from Rome. Unless that broadcast went on the air with Eisenhower's from Carthage, the Germans would seize the Italian transmitters and brand our statement a hoax."

Later in the day Eisenhower had Castellano brought to Amilcar, and he kept him waiting in the courtyard for half an hour. Castellano had had no part in what Badoglio did, but he was Italian and had been less than dependable when talking about what the Italians could do when the Americans landed in Rome, which they now would not do. Eisenhower had Castellano stand at attention before him while Ike, seated, read the entire message he had sent to Badoglio. Other Allied commanders were seated at the same table, among them Cunningham and Tedder.

If the whole charade gave Ike a great deal of understandable pleasure, he had still by 6:30 that evening received no word from Badoglio. Nevertheless, the message he had recorded earlier was broadcast over Radio Algiers:

This is General Dwight D. Eisenhower, commander in chief of the Allied forces. The Italian government has surrendered its armed forces unconditionally. As Allied Commander-in-Chief I have granted a military armistice, the terms of which have been approved by the governments of the United States, Great Britain, and the Union of Soviet Socialist Republics. . . . Hostilities between the armed forces of the United Nations and those of Italy terminate at once. All Italians who now act to help reject the German aggressor from Italian soil will have the assistance and the support of the United Nations.

An anxious hour and a half passed, and then Badoglio went on the air and ordered all Italians to stop fighting Allied forces and to resist "attacks from any other quarter." Shortly thereafter, as agreed in the surrender terms, the Italian fleet started for Malta. The Allies were delighted that Italy was out of the war. Eisenhower said to Kay, "One down—and two to go." It was by no means that simple, however. In his report on what was in polite language called the "Italian tragedy" or the "Italian foul-up" Ike said, "For three years we strained to break their spirit. We . . . succeeded only too well."

The first disappointment was that of the troops on the ships headed for Salerno. They heard the Eisenhower announcement over the ships' loudsheaker systems, and many, probably most of them, thought that there would be no opposition when they went ashore. One soldier said, "I never again expect to see such scenes of sheer joy. We would dock in Naples harbor unopposed, with an olive branch in one hand and an opera ticket in the other." It was not to be.

As had happened when he waited for the first news of TORCH and HUSKY, Eisenhower busied himself by writing letters. One was to John:

By the time you get this letter you will know that today was a very full one for me and crowded with anxiety. However, being made as I am, it is also crowded with hopefulness. I am probably the most optimistic person in this whole world. Everybody else sees all the risks and dangers and I guess I am just a wishful thinker, because I just shut my eyes to such things and say, "We will go ahead and try to win." One of these days I will probably get a bloody nose—but I hope it isn't this time.

And he wrote Mamie:

Don't be shocked to get a typewritten note, but at the moment I am just too worn down to go over to the office and start writing.

Please don't think I am sick or in any danger of being so, but this is September 8 and long before you get this note you will have read in the papers enough that will show you why I happen to be rather stretched out at the moment????

In a second letter to Mamie that same day, he said:

Here I am once more—waiting in a forward post for news of the development of plans. This is the thing that is making an old man of me. . . .

I thought it rather curious that you didn't send me a teletype when the President announced making me a permanent Major General and awarding me such a generous citation. Maybe, to you the incident did not constitute a significant personal honor—I thought it most unusual and was deeply appreciative.

I have to make a two-hour auto trip in a few minutes—I could do the same journey in one hour by plane (including rides to airfields) but sometimes I just get tired crawling in and out of planes. So I take one of my staff officers occasionally and go off by car. The roads are not too good and we meet much traffic, but at least I am out of reach of a phone for awhile, and the method of travel is a bit of change. (Last winter I hoped I'd never have to take a car trip again.) Lots of love, my darling—you're always in my thoughts.

AVALANCHE was precarious from the beginning, and after the war Eisenhower said that of all the operations he commanded, it came closest to strategic disaster. Churchill, after it was over, said it had been "a close-run thing."

Before the operation was launched, Eisenhower said that a great many people in his headquarters "frequently expressed doubts about going on with AVALANCHE. I felt that the possible results were so great that even with the meager allotments in landing craft . . . and air force, we should go ahead. I so informed the Combined Chiefs of Staff." The decision to proceed "was solely my own, and if things go wrong, there is no one to blame except myself."

Ike had wanted the first landings in Italy to be farther north, near Rome, but Salerno was the last area for which aerial support was possible. The invasion force included 700 ships and landing craft and 55,000 troops. During the first month, about 115,000 men, as well as 100,000 tons of supplies and 30,000 motor vehicles, were landed on a thirty-six-mile stretch of beach. Montgomery's forces were 150 miles to the south, and to Ike's impatient eyes they seemed to be making very little if any progress.

The main assault was at 3:30 A.M., and no cheering natives greeted the American soldiers. The beaches were lit by flares, and there was heavy artillery fire from the German installations on the high ground just beyond. "Men squirmed through barbed wire, ground mines, and behind enemy machine guns and the tanks that soon made their appearance, working their way inland and knocking out German strongpoints wherever possible," said Clark.

By dawn the awkward, ugly but extremely useful DUKW's began bringing in tanks and big guns. Each DUKW carried a 105-mm howitzer, twenty-one rounds of ammunition, and a seven-man crew. The crews and their guns went to work as soon as they were unloaded, on the open beaches, without cover. One howitzer knocked out five tanks and caused eight others to withdraw from the scene of action.

By 6:45 that morning Eisenhower learned that the first landings had been made. Subsequent reports stated that while there was never enough air power, B-17s and B-25s were continuing to bomb the roads that led to Salerno Bay. At 6:00 that evening Eisenhower was able to dictate a long, quite optimistic report to the Combined Chiefs of Staff and the British Chiefs. He was not too modest to point out:

> Due to my refusal to accept evasive and dilatory action on the part of the Italian government, Badoglio went through with his part of the armistice program last evening.

Part of the Italian fleet was already on its way to place itself in Allied hands, as promised. Eisenhower had been told, he said, to expect little help from the Italian army, and that was proving to be the case. There were also no reports on any movements of the Italian air force.

> I feel that AVALANCHE will be a matter of touch and go for the next few days. If we had a lift to put in one more infantry division immediately the matter would be almost a foregone conclusion, but if the enemy really appreciates correctly the speed of our buildup, we are in for some very rough fighting. All of us are aware of this and everything possible is being done. . . .
> We are using every possible expedient to speed up Clark's buildup. . . . The purpose of these moves is to keep the enemy upset and worried in the southern end of the boot so that he will be discouraged from making too heavy a counterattack on Clark. . . .
> While I do not discount the possibility of a very bad time in the AVA-LANCHE area, my belief is that the enemy is sufficiently confused by the events of the past twenty-four hours that it will be difficult for him to make up a definite plan and that by exploiting to the full our sea and air power, we will control the southern end of the boot to include the line Naples–Foggia within a reasonable time. Our greatest asset now is confusion and uncertainty which we must take advantage of in every possible way.

Serious trouble started on September 11, and the German attack on the British forces was so strong that Clark sent an American regiment north to close the gap between the two beachheads. German aerial attacks on the Allied ships were heavy, and a hospital ship, eight landing craft, a Liberty ship, and four transports were sunk. On the 12th additional German troops arrived from the toe of Italy, and Clark had no troops to send to close the continuing gap. The Germans began an attack on the American forces in the afternoon of the 13th. Two American infantry battalions drew back almost immediately and the enemy took more than 500 prisoners. By evening only two American artillery battalions and Clark's headquarters were holding the almost nonexistent line between the Germans and the sea. As was to happen in the Battle of the Bulge in December 1944, anybody who could hold a gun and fire it was drafted into a loose defense line behind the artillery, and for a time Clark thought the operation might have to be abandoned. In *The West Point Atlas of American Wars* the authors say:

At nightfall the German attacks ceased, but the exhausted Allies had to struggle to reestablish their lines along the best available defensive position. Losses had been heavy; many units had been completely scattered. During the night, two battalions of the 82nd Airborne Division were dropped into the beachhead. . . . During 14 September, the Germans pushed constant probing attacks all along the Allied front, seeking a weak spot. Thanks to splendid naval and air force support . . . all the German assaults were broken up. More Allied reinforcements, including elements of the British 7th Armored Division, poured in. By the 15th the beachhead was safe.

On the 13th Eisenhower cabled Marshall:

We are very much in the "touch and go" stage of this operation. Internally the Italians were so weak and supine that we have got little if any practical help out of them. However, almost on pure bluff, we did get the Italian fleet into Malta and because of the Italian surrender [the British] were able to rush into Taranto and Brindisi where no Germans were present. Our hold on both places is precarious but we are striving mightily to reinforce. . . .

I went out the other day with Admiral Cunningham to watch the Italian fleet sail by.

Considering for a moment the worst that could possibly develop . . . I would merely announce that one of our landings had been repulsed—due to my error in misjudging the strength of the enemy at that place. But I have great faith that even in spite of currently grim reports, we'll pull out all right. Our Air Force, the fighting value of our troops, and strenuous efforts by us all, should do the trick. Besides, the German must still be worrying some about sabotage and unrest in his rear. I wanted to visit Clark tonight, but when Alexander also felt that he should go, I had to stay back because of Alexander's immediate command responsibility and the fact that we should not both go at once.

Once again Eisenhower's optimism and faith were justified.

A large part of the victory was due to the fact that Lieutenant General Carl "Tooey" Spaatz, deputy commanding general of the Mediterranean Allied Air Forces, had, with Tedder's approval, agreed that for the first time heavy bombers would be used in a tactical role close to the beachheads. The effectiveness of the bombing so impressed Eisenhower that by the time he started planning OVERLORD he insisted that the Allied heavy bombers be under his command to be used as he saw fit in support of the troops on the beaches of France.

At breakfast on the morning of the 16th, Eisenhower discussed with Butcher what he had learned about the QUADRANT conference in Québec. According to Butcher, "So far, we have little fact to go on, except that a grand-scale cross-Channel invasion of France has been decided on for the spring of 1944, and a new code name assigned—OVERLORD replacing the old ROUNDUP. Ike's view was punctuated by a comment that if the Salerno battle ended in disaster he would probably be out."

But the battle did not end in disaster, and as Eisenhower later wrote in his diary, "by the evening of the sixteenth (on which day I visited the Fifth Army) the immediate danger was over and we could reorganize preparatory to taking up the advance. . . . From that time on, the Germans began to use the terrain most effectively to delay our advance. Demolitions and mines were their chief weapons, coupled with rearguard actions in all the passes through the very mountainous country."

On October 1 what was left of Naples fell to the Fifth Army; the city was without lights and a water supply, both destroyed by the Germans; factories and public buildings had been burned; land mines were everywhere; the port was a wreck; the railroads Mussolini had been said to make run on time were no more. All criminals had been released from jail, the sewers had been blown up, and, giving Eisenhower and millions of others in the Allied nations still another proof that the war against the Nazis was a crusade, there was the outrage committed at the University of Naples, which had been founded in 1224 by Emperor Frederick II. In a dispatch to the *New York Times* Herbert L. Matthews described it:

The Germans broke into the university after having carefully organized their procedure, with dozens and dozens of five-gallon gasoline tins and supplies of hand grenades. They went from room to room, thoroughly soaking floors, walls, and furniture, including archives that went back for centuries. Then they threw in hand grenades. There was something apt about it, something symbolic about the whole German attitude. It did not matter to the Germans that they were destroying the accumulated wealth of centuries of scientific and philosophical thinking.

That same day, on the other side of Italy, Foggia, along with its complex of modern, well-equipped airfields, fell to Montgomery's Eighth Army. The airfields were of great value to the Allies because until their capture the fighter cover for AVALANCHE had had to come from Sicily. Now both fighters and bombers could and did use those fields.

It was a time of great, though temporary, optimism for most Allied leaders, including Eisenhower. On October 1 he sent a message to Marshall saying that he hoped to be north of Rome "in six or eight weeks." Three days later he added that he and Alexander were in agreement that "we will have Rome by the end of October. I had originally intended to move the main Allied Force Headquarters to Naples, but because Rome is a better prospect from the long-term viewpoint and because of our belief that we will capture it at a reasonably early date, I think I shall not move until I can make the jump straight into Rome. . . . We are pushing hard to get the necessary force into Italy to bring about the major engagement as early in the winter as possible."

Such optimism became at least questionable when Hitler ordered Kesselring to hold out indefinitely in the hills and mountains south of Rome. He also ordered Rommel, who was in command in the north, to give Kesselring more artillery and two additional infantry divisions.

Eisenhower did not know of these orders for some time, and apparently neither he nor any of the other Allied leaders gave much if any thought to what would happen if the Germans decided to stay in Italy and fight for every foot of the forbidding ground. That was surely one of the most costly and bloodiest oversights of the war.

On October 13 Italy declared war on her recent ally, but the Allied soldiers, many of them still in summer uniforms despite the frigid temperatures, continued their costly way up the boot toward Rome. Once again, as had happened a year earlier in Tunisia, General Mud was in command. Lucian Truscott, commander of the 3d Division, said, "Incessant rains did more to delay our advance than either German demolitions, which were bad enough, or German delaying action. Along the main highways there were piles of fine big trees which the Germans felled to interlock across a road, in places where there was no way round. Booby-trapped and mined, these were formidable obstacles. . . . Bypasses were rarely possible." And by the end of 1943 the Allied advance was stalled along the Gustav Line, which was anchored by Cassino.

Trench foot was another enemy; so were the swollen rivers, and to the Italians, so was hunger. In one of the cartoons Bill Mauldin drew for *Stars and Stripes*, and eventually the world, there was his bearded, dirty, weary soldier with a mess kit looking at a tiny, thin, little Italian girl holding out an empty pail. The caption was, "The Prince and the Pauper."

In October in addition to his other duties, Eisenhower had to entertain a great many visitors, including the U.S. Ambassador to Moscow, Averell Harriman, and his daughter Kathleen; Secretary of the Treasury Henry Morgenthau, Jr.; and Secretary of State Cordell Hull. It sometimes seemed, as Butcher said, that visiting firemen took most of the general's time. On October 15, however, he was able to celebrate his own fifty-third birthday, what he called in good Jehovah's Witness fashion, his "fifty-third anniversary." Mamie, on hearing of the celebration at which Kay was present, reacted unfavorably. We do not know what she said in her letter about the matter, but on November 10 Eisenhower wrote:

I'm sorry if I failed to tell you anything about my birthday party. [Tex] Lee worked it up and having heard my desire to taste lobster again, he procured some on the black market at the highest prices I ever heard of. Luckily I did not learn the cost until after the dinner or I would have choked.

He had Air Chief Marshal and Lady Tedder, Capt. Brigg (a AC in office of C/S), Mrs. Kay Summersby, my driver and secretary, Colonel [James] Gault, a British officer I like a lot, Lee himself and one or two junior staff officers. We had a really fine dinner, everybody cleared out at 10:00 and that's all there was to it. . . .

The people that work for me intimately (my own official FAMILY) are:

Butch—diary, visitors, house.

Lee—office, trips, transportation, adv C.P.

Marshall—in charge of clerks. No. 1 stenog. In charge of office when rest are gone. He is a W.O.

Kay Summersby—1st driver—in charge of unofficial mail from unknown people.

Mickey—Personal, orderly and chief factotum.

Sgt. Farr—Steward.

Miss Chik—

Miss??—

Miss Ray—stenographers and clerks (Enlisted WACS).

Miss Scott & Hargreaves (drivers) WACS.

Several cooks—houseboys—etc.

That is the whole group. All are nice—and I think are all personally devoted to me. So far it's been quite a happy family. Most of them seem to feel they know you and John—you're often talked about.

On his birthday, too, the *Washington Post* carried a press-service report predicting a political future for him:

Eisenhower Urged
for President

New York, Oct. 4 (INS): Tank Corps Post No. 715 of the American Legion in New York City is on record last night as determined to boost the candidacy of Gen. Dwight D. Eisenhower for President of the United States.

A resolution to that effect was adopted by the post September 21, but not made public until now. The resolution said the members of the post had "no knowledge or concern as to the political affiliations or beliefs of General Eisenhower but considered him presidential material by reason of his outstanding "leadership qualities."

Eisenhower's old friend George Allen sent him the clipping from the *Post*, asking, "How does it feel to be a Presidential candidate?"

Eisenhower wrote in pencil on Allen's note, "Baloney! Why can't a simple soldier be left alone to carry out his orders? And I furiously object to the word 'candidate'—I ain't and won't." He gave Allen's note and his reply to Butcher, telling him to mail it back to Allen.

Eisenhower was once again being attacked in the British and American press, particularly the more liberal newspapers, for appearing to agree to another "Darlan deal." After all, Badoglio had not opposed Fascism; he had supported it, indeed had been a member of the party since 1936. He had, moreover, led Mussolini's forces against Ethiopia and in Spain, and he had opposed Mussolini joining Hitler's war against France not for moral reasons but because he knew that Italy was not prepared for war. We were in the war to defeat Fascism and Naziism. Was it necessary to recognize and give power to Fascists and Nazis, even those on a secondary level, simply because they were available? If we did that, what was the war all about, anyway?

Harry Hopkins in a memorandum to Roosevelt said that he did not believe Italy should be recognized as a "cobelligerent" in the war:

> I hope you will not encourage Eisenhower to recognize Italy as a co-belligerent. This will put them in exactly the same position as our other allies. Nor do I think there is enough evidence that Badoglio and the King can be trusted for us to arm any of their divisions. I should think that Eisenhower could quietly look the other way if some of the armistice terms are being violated, such as Italian naval ships being used to transport our troops, or Italian bombers from Sardinia fighting the Germans. . . .
>
> I cannot see that a declaration of war by Badoglio gets us anywhere except a precipitate recognition of two men who have worked very closely with the Fascists in the past. I think we should get every possible advantage out of them, but I don't think we are under any obligation to them. . . .
>
> I would not throw out Badoglio, but recognition would be an inevitable step? Could you not tell Eisenhower to keep on as he is for the present and make the decision in another week?

Macmillan said of the criticism, "The so-called leaders of public opinion, especially in the press, were only too prone to blame us for another infamous deal. . . . Generosity to a defeated enemy and the Christian desire to help and sustain a suffering population are often stronger the nearer one approaches the scene of war."

On November 9 Roosevelt did what Hopkins advised. He cabled Eisenhower, "At this distance it is my opinion that the top man in Italy is very old and I have been informed that he does not click well except in the morning before lunch. Furthermore, the world over here places little reliance on him and clearly remembers his appeasement policy in regard to Mussolini for twenty years." The American public wanted a democratic form of government in Italy, the president said, and it did not seem that either the king or Badoglio could encourage this. But what did Eisenhower, as the man on the scene, think?

Eisenhower in his reply on the 10th said that his opinion of Victor Emmanuel

> is the same as yours and reports which I have received from Italy lead me to believe that he does not repeat not count for much although his house remains a rallying point for the military and naval factions.
>
> Our own position, of course, is much stronger than it was when we entered North Africa and confronted a somewhat similar political situation because we are prepared, if necessary, to continue military government in fact if not repeat not in name, to include the Rome area. We will not repeat not turn over areas to the control of the Italian government until the

government has assumed a complexion appropriate to the principles for which the United Nations are fighting this war.

In other words, Italy would be ruled not by the king or by Badoglio or anyone else until there was, in Eisenhower's words, "a broad-based, anti-Fascist coalition government." That, although Eisenhower did not say so to the president, was undoubtedly the first lesson he had learned from the bitter times in North Africa. A second was implicit in his further words: "We do not repeat not propose to exercise political censorship and will refrain from expressing opinions of [on?] internal political matters."

Also on November 10, Eisenhower answered a letter from Arthur Capper, the Republican senator from Kansas who had been responsible for John's appointment to West Point and who was to play a major role in helping John's father get the Republican presidential nomination in 1952. Capper said that he had recently been in Kansas where "a great many of our best people told me they would like to see you become the Republican Candidate for President." Among the clippings the senator sent the Allied commander in the Mediterranean was one with the headline SENATOR CAPPER ENDORSES GENERAL EISENHOWER FOR PRESIDENT IN 1944.

Ike did not dismiss Capper's suggestion as easily as he had that of George Allen; he said that it was "most gratifying to hear that one's efforts are favorably regarded in his own home State." He added, however, that he had a job to do, "a gigantic job, and for any soldier to turn his attention elsewhere would constitute a neglect of duty to his country."

On November 15 Eisenhower flew to Malta to meet Churchill; the prime minister was traveling on the battle cruiser *Renown* and did not arrive there until the 17th. He was ill with what he described "as a heavy cold and sore throat." He spent most of his time in bed in the San Anton Palace, but felt strong enough to pin medals on Alexander and Eisenhower. The decorations were the only two of their kind in the world; each had on it the numbers 1 and 8, for the victorious 1st and 8th British armies in North Africa. Churchill said the two generals were "taken by surprise and seemed highly gratified when I pinned the ribbons on their coats."

That day, too, the prime minister told Eisenhower that it was by no means certain that Marshall would command OVERLORD. The appointment might, Churchill said, go to Eisenhower. He was sorry, he added, that what was surely the most coveted assignment of the war could not go to Brooke, but it had to go to an American. "It is the President's decision," he said. "We British will be glad to accept either you or Marshall."

As for OVERLORD, Eisenhower said that when he met with the prime minister in Malta, "He told me that originally it was intended that General Brooke should command in England and the Mediterranean command should remain undisturbed. However, when the Americans, at Québec, insisted upon American command in England, it became politically necessary (and the truth of this statement is obvious) that the British should have command in the Mediterranean. He said that later proposals of the president's were, however, to the effect that General Marshall should take over strategic direction of the whole

European campaign, while General Brooke should actually command in England, and I should remain in command here. This, the prime minister said, he could not accept. There were many sidelights that the prime minister gave to me on the whole proposition. However, these were not particularly important, and at the time of my meeting him, he felt that the original proposal would go through as first approved; namely, that General Marshall would take command of OVERLORD in England and I would possibly go to Washington."

Faced with such maddening contradictions, with the fact that one's fate and future were being treated so offhandedly many people would have been angered. Only a man who put duty above everything else, would have done without protest what Eisenhower was ordered to do. Eisenhower simply observed privately that he and Marshall seemed to be no more than "a couple of pawns in a chess game, each compelled to await the pleasure of the players."

The war in Italy continued to go badly. The authors of *The West Point Atlas of American Wars* say, "The whole mountainous countryside had been organized into a series of defensive positions—the exact names and locations of which are still not well-defined. Demolitions and mine fields blocked every avenue of approach; machine gun and mortar positions were well dug in—many blasted out of solid rock—and camouflaged to disappear into the rugged scenery; German artillery had registered on all roads, trails, and possible sites for bivouac and assembly areas. It was to be another Battle of the Wilderness, with craggy Italian mountains in place of Virginia thickets, fought in bitter winter weather." Eisenhower rather mildly observed later, "The Italian avenue of approach did not in itself offer a favorable route from which to attack decisively the German homeland."

One thing had proved certain. "Knocking Italy out of the war," which had seemed so simple, so painless in Washington and London and at times in Algiers, was going to take a long while, cause a great many casualties, and accomplish not very much. At times that war was like the trench fighting of the First World War. One military historian, James L. Stokesbury, has said, "Few soldiers of World War II experienced the kind of deadening, soul-destroying fighting that characterized the earlier war, but most of those who did experience it fought in Italy."

Another of Eisenhower's tasks in November was to arrange for quarters for the leaders who were about to meet in Cairo, from the 22nd through the 26th. Not only was Ike to see to it that suitable quarters were found, he was, he said, responsible for "insuring safe passage through our area." News of the meeting had somehow got to the Germans, and it was suggested by Admiral King, who was with Roosevelt on the way to Egypt, that the meeting place be changed to Khartoum, almost 1400 miles to the south. Eisenhower decided against the change, and he also decided that, against the advice of the Secret Service, it was safe for him to meet the president of the United States at a quay west of Oran, thence to go with him to LaSenia airdrome and ride in the presidential plane to Tunis. According to Butcher at the time of the Casablanca conference, "The Secret Service mingled with our troops and even patted them on the hips while they were at parade for the President's inspection when he was en route from Casablanca to Rabat. The Secret Service seemed overzealous when it suspected that American soldiers, who had taken the oath to support the president of the United States—their Commander-in-Chief—might attempt to assassinate him. Just the fact that the Secret Service failed to take into account the Army's loyalty made Ike furious at that time. Now . . . they even intimate that it would be unwise for a four-star general, the Theater Commander, to meet the president and accompany him to the airdrome."

As was to happen often in the eight years between 1953 and 1961, Eisenhower prevailed over the Secret Service.

Eisenhower met the president, who with his party was aboard the new battleship, the U.S.S. *Iowa*, at the quay near Oran on the morning of November 20. According to Admiral King, who was with the president, Ike was "smiling and pleased to see his commander-in-chief." The general "showed no signs of worry about the success of the Italian operation, for which he had full responsibility and for which many of us did not think he had sufficient forces."

As had been planned, Ike flew with the president to the El Anouina air strip near Tunis. He had arranged with Kay to drive him and the president to what was to be Roosevelt's villa. Eisenhower's villa was nearby. When Kay parked Ike's Cadillac alongside the presidential plane, the *Sacred Cow*, Mike Reilly, chief of the Secret Service, shouted, "You're not expecting to drive the president, are you, lady?" Kay said that driving the president and her boss was exactly what she had in mind. Reilly was, she said, "on the verge of apoplexy, and he started thumping on the door of the Cadillac, shouting, "No woman ever drives the president! No woman ever has—or ever will as long as I'm boss here. Certainly no Limey woman!"

After several other sharp exchanges, Reilly won, and Kay had to show an American sergeant, male, how to operate the Cadillac she considered her own. She drove Butcher, Harry Hopkins, and Admiral King back to Tunis in another car, and a few minutes after her three passengers got out, Reilly walked over to where she was standing and said, "It's okay for you to get back in your own car now. They've gone in the house." A few minutes later she had her revenge. She was told by an officer of the Roosevelt party, "The President has asked to meet you."

Kay said that when she walked into the library of the villa, "General Eisenhower, who nodded encouragingly, stood by the fireplace. President Roosevelt sat by the window, half hidden by his two sons, Elliott and Franklin, acquaintances from my African days. Admiral Leahy stopped talking as the general moved over and said, 'Mr. President, this is Miss Kay Summersby, the British girl you asked about.' " Roosevelt told Kay that he had heard "quite a bit" about her and asked, "Why didn't you drive me from the plane? I'd been looking forward to it."

"From some deep storehouse of the past I produced a maidenly but maddening blush. 'Mr. President, your Secret Service wouldn't let me drive!' " Everybody laughed, and Roosevelt asked, "Would you like to drive me from now on?" Kay said that it would be a privilege, and Roosevelt said, "Very well. You shall drive me then. I'm going on an inspection trip soon."

Later Kay drove the president to Elliott's photo reconnaissance wing, not far away. After dinner young Franklin, who was serving on a destroyer, invited her to have dinner with his father and brothers and their associates. Ike was also a guest, and just before he left for the dinner, King told him that he hated "to lose General Marshall as Chief of Staff, but my loss is consoled by the knowledge that I will have you to work with in his job."

The president had been having such a good time that he decided to stay over another day to visit the Tunisian battlefields. Originally Ike had planned to include Bizerte on the tour, but he decided that since going to that seaport city would involve crossing the harbor channel in a landing barge, the danger that the barge might be bumped and overturned was too great. So he changed the route to go to Medjez el Bab on the south side of the Medjerda River and return on the north side of the river. Kay drove, and the president, who considered himself on vacation, just as he had during the Casablanca conference in January, talked of many things. He told Eisenhower that he had been deeply disappointed that the TORCH invasion had taken place after rather than before the 1942 congressional elections; he spoke of the fall of Mussolini, and he said that he often had differences with Churchill, but added, "No one could have a better or sturdier ally than that old Tory."

They also discussed the recent battles in the area as compared to those between the Romans and Carthaginians. They both were familiar with the battle of Zama in 202 B.C. in which the Romans had won a great victory over the Carthaginians. The exact location of the battle was not known, but the president and the general agreed that since the Carthaginian general, Eisenhower's boyhood hero, Hannibal, had used elephants it must have been fought in the plains rather than the mountains.

Roosevelt also mentioned the command of OVERLORD, but not in any way that can have been any too pleasing to Eisenhower. He said, "Ike, you and I know who was the Chief of Staff during the last years of the Civil War but practically no one else knows, although the names of the field generals—Grant, of course, and Lee and Jackson, Sherman, Sheridan, and the others—every schoolboy knows them. I hate to think that 50 years from now practically nobody will know who George Marshall was. That is one of the reasons why I want George to have the Big Command—he is entitled to establish his place in history as a great General."

Eisenhower remembered that Roosevelt added, "as if thinking aloud, 'But it is dangerous to monkey with a winning team.' I answered nothing except to state that I would do my best wherever the government might find use for me." According to John Eisenhower, "This encounter was the only time that Roosevelt mentioned the OVERLORD command to Eisenhower before the decision was made."

During the ride, Telek had been in the front seat of the Cadillac next to Kay, and she remembered that while the general and the president were talking, the dog "decided to take one of his flying leaps. The General gasped and caught him in midair, just before the bundle of Scottie landed on the President's legs. 'I'm sorry, Mr. President,' the General apologized."

After that, the three of them discussed the breed of dogs they all loved,

Scotties. Roosevelt was, after all, the owner of the most famous Scottie in the world. Kay said, "The President continued to play with Telek. Suddenly he pointed to a rare grove of trees and remarked, 'That's an awfully nice place. Could you pull up there, Child, for our little picnic?' "

On Roosevelt's invitation, according to Kay, she sat in the back seat of the car with the president, and "General Eisenhower remained outside to hand in delicious chicken sandwiches. . . . Coffee was the only other item on the sparse menu, as the General was afraid to offer lettuce or other green vegetables to the President in this disease-ridden climate."

Eisenhower's account of the presidential picnic as recorded in *Crusade* is shorter and different. He wrote that after his and the president's talk about Hannibal and the elephants, "I wandered off to inspect some burnt-out tanks while the President and his driver had their lunch."

The president and his party flew to Cairo to meet with Chiang Kai-shek on Sunday evening, November 21, the night Pearson made the Patton broadcast. Butcher said, "Late yesterday [This was written on November 23], when we returned to AFHQ, I found to my dismay but not surprise that Drew Pearson had broken the story about General Patton's eccentric activities during the Sicilian campaign."

Three nights later, Eisenhower, on instructions from Roosevelt, flew to Cairo. He took with him several members of his family, including Kay, two WAC officers, Ruth Briggs and Louise Anderson, and Tex Lee. They flew in a C-54. Eisenhower told Kay, "There's no use wasting all the space on this big plane. Besides, it may be the only chance you'll ever get to visit the Middle East." The flight was smooth, and Kay said, "After a few rubbers of the usual Eisenhower bridge, the plane turned into a snoring dormitory."

The next day Eisenhower met with the Combined Chiefs. Marshall gave a dinner that Ike attended along with Hap Arnold, Brooke, Portal and Tedder, and Admirals Cunningham and King. As he was leaving the dinner, one of the guests thanked Marshall for a fine Thanksgiving dinner. Eisenhower said, "I turned around in complete astonishment and said, 'Well, that shows what a war does to a man. I had no idea this was Thanksgiving Day.' "

On the 26th Roosevelt gave Ike the Legion of Merit, and the general again met with the Combined Chiefs. The president told Ike something he was not for some time to tell the American people. According to Ike, Roosevelt said that, "much as he'd like to go back to private life, it looked as if he'd have to stand again for the Presidency."

It was not until the following July that the president wrote a letter to Harry Truman's Missouri friend, Robert E. Hannegan, chairman of the Democratic National Committee, saying that after twelve years in the White House he did not wish to serve again but if he were nominated and if "the commander-in-chief of us all" ordered him to serve again, as a "good soldier" he would do so. His running mate was to be a man with whom Eisenhower later had a good deal of trouble, Senator Harry S Truman of Missouri.

Eisenhower did not vote in the 1944 presidential election, but his son John felt that, if he had, he would have voted for Roosevelt. He would have agreed with millions of other Americans who, as was said at the time, did not believe in "changing horses in the middle of the stream." Besides, Eisenhower knew firsthand what a confident and successful commander in chief of the American armed forces Roosevelt had been.

When Marshall had seen Eisenhower earlier that week, he had, as at Casablanca, been alarmed at Ike's appearance and ordered him to take a two-day vacation. Ike was not overjoyed with the idea, feeling that it might be a way of giving him a small reward before telling him that what everybody by now assumed, was true: The chief of staff was to command OVERLORD, and Eisenhower would be sent back to Washington for a desk job. Still, an order was an order, and he admitted to Kay—she said it was the first time ever—that he was in fact tired. "He usually blew his top if anyone so much as intimated that he looked tired," she said.

Tedder had a welcome suggestion about the short vacation. Ike should go up the Nile to Luxor, site of some of the most beautiful ancient Egyptian tombs and temples. Tedder also lent Ike his C-47 and a British archeologist friend, a Major Emery. The party included Kay, Tex Lee, Ruth Briggs, Louise Anderson, and Colonel Elliott Roosevelt.

They flew to Luxor on the 27th, and that night and the next day they visited the tombs and temples on both sides of the river. "It was like walking right into those musty times," said Kay. Emery "explained the human side of old Egypt, too. Slaves may have carried out the heavy labor on the big pyramids . . . but they were workers with certain inalienable rights. There is evidence that they often resorted to a supposedly modern union device: strikes. . . . The major told us of one obelisk . . . quarried out of pure granite, in one piece, without seam or joining."

According to Kay, Emery and Ike "frequently wandered off alone in pursuit of some dim fact; other times we looked around to find them far in a distant chamber, discussing a point of ancient life as compared to one of today. General Ike was happy as a kid, making no attempt to hide his natural enjoyment, protesting frequently that we moved along too quickly. . . . When we emerged from the last tomb in the late afternoon, we shook our heads as if we had jumped across hundreds of centuries."

That night Eisenhower slept fourteen hours. "The next morning he looked like a different man," said Kay. They returned to Cairo early on the 29th, and Marshall was so pleased with the change in Ike that he insisted on another trip immediately. This time they went to Jerusalem, the party including Kay, Anderson, and Briggs. They had lunch at the King David Hotel, but after that the journey, which included visits both to Jerusalem and Palestine, was a disappointment. They found everything too noisy and commercial. At one point a group of American monks eagerly ran out of their monastery to greet the famous general. One of them, who was from Kansas, was particularly annoying. According to Kay the monk "hung on to the general's arm as though they were fraternity brothers at a class reunion."

A number of postcards and other souvenirs had been pushed on the general and his party during the tour, and that night Ike gave Kay a postcard that was a souvenir from the one quiet place they had seen that day, the Garden of Gethsemane. On the card the general wrote, "Good Night—There are lots of things I wish to say—You know them—good night."

Eisenhower himself said of his brief holidays, "This was my first glimpse of these areas, and the intense interest that I felt in viewing the remains of ancient civilizations came closer than had anything else during the war to lifting briefly from my mind the constant preoccupation with military problems."

Back in Algiers, the atmosphere was not restful for Eisenhower. Everybody said that he might as well start packing, because right after the first of the year he would be going back to Washington. Nobody said it to him directly, but a great many people thought about and talked about the fact that the Patton "slapping incident" and Ike's handling of it could not have improved his chances for the supreme commander's job. The whole thing had created a nasty political unroar back in the States, and Roosevelt, that ultimate politician, wouldn't promote a man responsible for two brouhahas—first Darlan, then Patton—in less than a year. There was also the fact that he had appeared to be too eager to hold hands with still another politically unsavory European, Badoglio. On December 6 Butcher said, "Oddly, though we have no information and don't expect any until the General sees the President, now expected at Tunis tomorrow evening, we seem to have taken for granted that we are to go back to Washington. While we still put an 'if' in our plans, Ike is considering the 'round-the-world' route, including a visit to MacArthur and possibly to Lord Louis."

Eisenhower did not attend the meetings of EUREKA, the conference at Teheran that took place between November 28 and December 1. It was the first meeting of the "Big Three," Churchill, Roosevelt, and Stalin, and what happened there pushed Roosevelt into making a decision he wasn't ready to make. The man who really did it was Stalin. As was so often the case, Churchill summed the whole thing up at the beginning of EUREKA. He said, "We have in our hands the future of mankind."

In the second session, on the 29th, Stalin looked directly at the prime minister and asked what he had asked many times before, never to his mind receiving a satisfactory answer. "I wish to pose a very direct question to the Prime Minister about OVERLORD," he said. "Do the Prime Minister and the British staff really believe in OVERLORD?" The Russian leader wanted a simple, affirmative answer. "Yes" would have done nicely, but Churchill did not give him such an answer. Perhaps he was incapable of it. The prime minister said, "Provided the conditions previously stated for OVERLORD are established, when the time comes, it will be our stern duty to hurl across the Channel against the Germans every sinew of our strength."

Stalin, with reason, found that a less than satisfactory answer, and a little later he asked another question, this one of Roosevelt, and got an answer he didn't like. "Who will command OVERLORD?" he asked. Roosevelt said that that had not been decided, and he whispered to Admiral Leahy, who was sitting next to him, "That old Bolshevik is trying to force me to give him the name of our Supreme Commander. I just can't tell him because I haven't made up my mind."

In *Roosevelt and Hopkins*, Sherwood said, "Roosevelt must have been sorely tempted at that moment to name General Marshall as supreme commander and have done with it, but he did not do so, for reasons known only to himself. He said that the decisions taken at this Conference would affect the choice of the particular officer, and this probably meant that he would appoint Marshall only if the command involved *all* of Western and Southern Europe instead of OVERLORD alone."

Stalin angrily replied that until such a commander was named, the OVERLORD operation was not to his mind "real." According to Leahy, "It was evident that Stalin wanted to have that appointment announced while he was in Teheran." That didn't happen, but it was decided that when OVERLORD was launched, then planned for May 1944, the Russians would at the same time start an offensive in the east and there would be an additional Allied landing in southern France. The latter was deliberately left hazy, largely because the British, Churchill in particular, didn't want it to happen.

From Teheran Roosevelt returned to Cairo, and while there he had three days of meetings with Churchill and the Combined Chiefs. On December 5, a Sunday, Roosevelt, in Sherwood's words, "made the momentous decision concerning the supreme command for OVERLORD. He made it against the known preference of both Stalin and Churchill, against his own proclaimed inclination to give to George Marshall the historic opportunity which he so greatly desired and so amply deserved." Harry Hopkins had come to see Marshall the night before, saying that the president was, as Marshall described it, "in some concern of mind over my appointment as Supreme Commander. . . . In my reply I merely endeavored to make clear that whatever the decision, I would go along wholeheartedly with any decision the president made. . . . I declined to state my opinion."

On Sunday Marshall called on Roosevelt at his villa, and the president said more or less what Hopkins had said the night before. Marshall repeated that he would go along with whatever the president decided, that, in his words, "the issue was too great for any personal feeling to be considered. I did not discuss the pros and cons of the matter. If I recall, the president stated in completing our conversation, 'I feel I could not sleep at night with you out of the country.' "

It was a considerable tribute at what otherwise must have been a heartbreaking moment for Marshall. According to Pogue, Roosevelt "presumably said, 'Then it will be Eisenhower.' If he did not say it at once, he said it shortly afterward." Messages to Chiang Kai-shek and Stalin were sent, saying that OVERLORD and the landing in southern France, ANVIL, would be the first priorities. Then Marshall drafted the following message to Stalin for the president's signature. "The immediate appointment of General Eisenhower to command of OVERLORD operation has been decided on."

After the message was sent, Marshall in a characteristically kind act got the draft he had written and wrote at the bottom: "Dear Eisenhower. I thought you might like this as a memento. It was written very hurriedly by me as the final meeting broke up yesterday, the president signed it immediately. G.C.M."

"This thoughtful gesture constituted the real passing of the torch to Eisenhower," said Pogue, "and with it Marshall reassured the Mediterranean commander of his backing. Renouncing his great ambition, Marshall delivered the charge he had most coveted into the safekeeping of the officer he had been grooming for a key role since the beginning of the war. The Army that the Chief of Staff had prepared would go to victory under the command of an officer of Marshall's own choosing."

Before breakfast on Tuesday, December 7, Eisenhower received a cable from Marshall that seemed to assume that Ike already knew he was to be supreme commander. It said, "In view of the impending appointment of a British officer as your successor . . . please submit to me . . . your recommendations in brief as to the best arrangement for handling the administration, discipline, training, and supply of American troops assigned to Allied Force under the new command." Not having seen the president's announcement as yet, Eisenhower said, "I was unable to deduce his meaning with certainty."

Later that morning, however, Eisenhower flew from Maison Blanche to Tunis. He said, "The President arrived in midafternoon and was scarcely seated in the automobile when he cleared up the matter with one short sentence. He said, 'Well, Ike, you are to command OVERLORD.' " Just two years had passed since Colonel Eisenhower had settled in for one of his rare daytime naps at Fort Sam, only to be awakened by the news from Pearl Harbor.

* * *

THE SULTAN

On December 8 Ike flew with the president and his party, including Hopkins, to Malta, where Roosevelt gave Lord Gort an inscribed testimonial from the people of the United States to the people of Malta praising their bravery. Then the general and the president flew to Sicily, where Roosevelt reviewed some troops and gave a Distinguished Service Cross to Clark and a Legion of Merit to Beetle.

While Eisenhower was with him on the president's *Sacred Cow* Roosevelt told Ike a number of things that he already knew, one, that the assignment in London would involve more than mere military matters. According to Sherwood in *Roosevelt and Hopkins,* the president said that the general would be "surrounded by the majesty of the British government and the powerful personality of Winston Churchill." Churchill still believed, Roosevelt said, that really the only way the Allies could lose the war was to fail in a cross-Channel attack.

That cannot have been encouraging news for the man just appointed to command that attack. Eisenhower knew that the prime minister was eloquent, persuasive, annoying, and nearly indefatigable. He also knew that just before the Teheran conference Churchill had for a short time lost his voice entirely. Ike cannot have helped thinking, as other people did from time to time, that if Churchill were voiceless more often, many things would be easier. Ike did not know on December 8 that three days later the prime minister would descend on his Carthaginian headquarters, somewhat diminished by illness, but not much and not for long.

Roosevelt was somewhat concerned with a matter that did not seem of any real importance to Eisenhower—what the general's new title should be. "He toyed with the word 'Supreme' in his conversation but made no decision at the moment," said Ike. "He merely said that he must devise some designation that would imply the importance the Allies attached to the new venture."

In *At Ease* Eisenhower said that the last time he saw Roosevelt, a month later, in Washington, "He asked me whether I liked the new title 'Supreme Commander,' and I acknowledged that it had the ring of importance, something like 'Sultan.' "

At Malta the *Sacred Cow* had been delayed with some mechanical troubles just long enough for it to be impossible for Roosevelt to start his trip home on the 8th. Eisenhower said, "The Secret Service men were irritated and fearful, but the president confided in me that he had made up his mind to stay at Carthage an extra night and if a legitimate reason had not been forthcoming, he would have invented one. I remarked that I assumed the president of the United States would not be questioned in dictating the details of his own travels. He replied with considerable emphasis, 'You haven't had to argue with the Secret Service.' "

On December 9, Roosevelt and his party boarded the *Iowa* again and started back to the States. Back home, when the president first saw Stimson, he said, "I have . . . brought OVERLORD back to you safe and sound on the ways for accomplishment." The statement may have been more optimistic than the facts warranted, but it sounded good. OVERLORD did now have a commander, and the Christmas season was beginning. However, it was already apparent that many costly and bloody battles were ahead in Italy. By going to London Eisenhower was spared the long agony and the bitter recriminations of the Allied failure in Italy. Had he stayed, the Italian failure would have been his.

Rumors of Eisenhower's appointment started almost immediately. On the 16th Hanson W. Baldwin said in the *New York Times*, "Gen. Dwight D. Eisenhower, who at one time was slated to succeed General Marshall as Chief of Staff, is more likely under the recent change of plans, to become Supreme Anglo-Saxon Commander in the European Theater. An invasion of Western Europe will probably be commanded by an American." The next day the *Times* reported that the "usually authoritative Army and Navy Register" would in its issue of December 18 say that Eisenhower would go to London as supreme commander and Marshall would remain in London as chief of staff.

Morale in Ike's headquarters in Algiers had improved greatly. "We now feel that we have a definite and concrete mission," said Butcher. "This adds zest to living and interest in pursuing the objective. It has . . . made a remarkable difference in Ike. Now he is back to his old system of incessant planning and thinking out loud of qualifications for this or that man for certain jobs."

The "powerful personality" Roosevelt had warned Eisenhower about arrived in Amilcar on the morning of December 11. His plane had first landed at the wrong airport and then flown to one near Eisenhower's villa. Churchill said, "Ike, always the soul of hospitality, had waited two hours with imperturbable good-humour. I got into his car, and after we had driven for a little while, I said, 'I am afraid I shall have to stay with you longer than I had planned. I am completely at the end of my tether. . . .' "All that day I slept, and the next day came fever and symptoms at the base of my lungs which were judged to portend pneumonia. So here I was at this pregnant moment on the broad of my back amidst the ruins of ancient Carthage."

The fact that he was ill did not prevent the prime minister from making demands on Eisenhower. He insisted that Beetle remain in the Mediterranean to assist Ike's successor. Ike said that his being separated from Beetle was something that was not even discussable, but Smith could remain behind long enough to indoctrinate the new theater commander.

In general, the prime minister treated his illness as a kind of internal war that had to be waged on enemies who had no business being where they were and had to be routed. He said, "After a week's fever the intruders were repulsed. I hope all our battles will be equally well conducted." Lord Moran and his associates had been good generals.

Winston's daughter Sarah came to visit him during his illness. She was reading *Pride and Prejudice,* and her father said of the characters in the Jane Austen novel, "What calm lives they had, those people! No worry about the French revolution, the crashing struggle of the Napoleonic Wars. Only matters of controlling natural passions, so far as they could, together with cultured explanations of any mischances."

Even on a sickbed Churchill was not content with a calm life, and he arranged it so that no one around him could be very calm either, including Eisenhower. Butcher wrote in his diary, "Last evening, Ike, after a preluncheon conference with the CIGS [Brooke], lunch with the PM, and talk for an hour after lunch, then dinner at 8:30 and further talks, was completely whipped down—even his voice was hoarse. He got in eight hours sleep and today is ready for more."

On the 15th Churchill had a mild heart attack, and the next day Brooke wrote in his diary, "Lord Moran tells me that he thought the P.M. was going to die last night. He thinks him a little better as regards the pneumonia, but is worried about his heart." By the 19th Moran was able to say, "The Prime Minister's temperature is normal, and the signs of pneumonia are disappearing."

Brooke, who had arrived with the prime minister, was in a more mellow mood than usual. On the 11th, the day he arrived, he told Eisenhower that he was having trouble with Churchill "mainly on the question of his [Ike's] successor. . . . I . . . asked him to assist me in making it quite clear to the P.M. what the organization should be. . . . Ike's suggested solution was to put Wilson in Supreme Command, replace Alex [ander] by Monty, and take Alex home to command the land forces for OVERLORD. This almost fits in with my idea except that I would invert Alex and Monty."

General Sir Henry Maitland "Jumbo" Wilson, who had been head of the British Tenth Army in the Middle East, did succeed Eisenhower in the supreme allied command. Wilson was a colorless man of sixty-four who was not a threat to younger, more ambitious men.

Brooke said, "I discovered that, as I had expected, he [Eisenhower] would sooner have Alex with him for OVERLORD than Monty. He also knew that he could handle Alex, but was not fond of Monty, and certainly could not handle him."

Churchill, as usual, prevailed, and when Wilson's appointment was made public, at the same time it was announced that Alexander would remain in operational command of the armies in the Mediterranean and that Montgomery would become commander in chief of the 21st Army Group under Eisenhower. Churchill for a time had been unable to decide between Alexander and Montgomery for the OVERLORD assignment, but Brooke did the final persuading, and Monty greeted the new assignment with delight. Alexander could remain with the fiasco in Italy; the OVERLORD assignment, he said in his diary, could be "a very fine job, and it will be about the biggest thing I have ever had to handle."

Eisenhower in *Crusade* said that he had "expressed a preference for Alexander. . . . I regarded Alexander as Britain's outstanding soldier in the field of strategy. He was, moreover, a friendly and agreeable type; Americans instinctively liked him." However, "General Montgomery was assigned to command the British forces in the new operation, a choice acceptable to me." He added that Montgomery was very popular with British enlisted men and that was "the greatest personal asset a commander can possess." He added, too, that Monty had very great ability in "what might be called the 'prepared' battle. In the study of enemy positions and situations and in the combining of his own armor, artillery, air, and infantry to secure tactical successes against the enemy, he is careful, meticulous, and certain."

At the end of the war, however, without mentioning Montgomery by name Ike indicated that he did not think highly of the things Monty was best at. He said, "Although a minimum of tactical risk should be taken when the general situation is adverse, the opposite prevails when a commander has present in the theater the moral and physical assets for general victory. In the general offensive the cautious attempt to provide for certainty in every tactical operation is the enemy of great strategical gain. Risks must be taken, and they must be shouldered by the highest commander."

On the 18th Eisenhower and Beetle flew to Caserta, a few miles north of Naples, to establish an advance command post there. "By such a move I could be closer to the scene of operations," Ike said. "It is always a good thing to move a headquarters when its personnel begin to get so well 'dug in' as they were in Algiers—when directing staffs become too much concerned with the convenience of living they grow away from troops and from the real problems of war."

On Sunday, December 19, Eisenhower, Beetle, and Clark visited the American part of the Fifth Army front. There is no record of what the men said to each other. But earlier that month, before he learned that he was to command OVERLORD, Ike had visited the front and said that he had been right earlier in feeling "that winter operations in Italy would be accompanied by the utmost hardship and difficulty, especially as they would be undertaken without the constant support of our great asset, an overwhelming air force. I felt that maintenance of morale would require careful control of operations and the best efforts of all commanders. Certainly I intended to be close by to help." Now he knew he would not be close by to help, and he must have felt a mixture of relief and of guilt.

On the 20th, when Eisenhower arrived at the new headquarters Butcher had requisitioned, he was tired and depressed by what he had seen on the front lines the previous day, and, according to Kay, he "protested vehemently when he saw his office: a sumptuous room big enough for a railroad station or an airplane hangar, carefully conceived to impress the ego of the brassiest of visitors. It was adjoined by a mirrored, dwarfing, intimidating reception chamber. In short, nothing could have been further from the Eisenhower idea of a small, modest office accessible to any member of his staff. He was especially irate over the gigantic, potted palms, which added an extra, Tsarist touch of power."

Butcher had also requisitioned a hunting lodge on a mountainside nearby where, he felt, Eisenhower "could sit and contemplate before the fireplace or even warm his backside by an Italian-type high earthen stove in the living room." The lodge had previously been occupied by Prince Umberto, son of Victor Emmanuel III, who after the war was for thirty-five days to be King Umberto I until the people of Italy in their wisdom voted to abolish the monarchy.

The lodge was ornate, dusty and damp, and when he first arrived, Eisenhower sat down in the living room, which had a stove and was warm. A few minutes later Mickey came down the stairs shouting that there was a rat in the general's bedroom and that he was afraid of rats. The commander of OVERLORD rose from his warm seat, announced that if he couldn't shoot a German he could at least shoot a rat, and put on his spectacles. Then, armed with a .32 automatic pistol he went up to the bathroom. He complained that the light was bad, but he shot anyway. The rat had been sitting on the toilet seat, and Eisenhower's first shot nicked the seat, but the rat, unharmed, jumped to a pipe above. With his second shot, Eisenhower nicked the tail of the rat, which leaped a foot higher, still clinging to the pipe. The man about to become supreme commander of the Allied Expeditionary Forces then shot a third time, and the rat fell quivering to the floor. Henry Clay Williams, a staff waiter, finished it off with a large stick of firewood. As Kay later put it, "After three or four near hits by General Dwight D. Eisenhower, head of the straightest shooting Army in the world, things were so bad that someone else had to come in and club the poor animal to death."

The next morning Eisenhower, Beetle, and Lee visited Montgomery's headquarters. He did not yet know that he had the 21st Army Group command, and his chief of staff, de Guingand, said, "We all thought we would hear the answer—but we didn't." Montgomery didn't hear officially that he was about to return to England until Christmas Eve. His lyrical biographer, Nigel Hamilton, said, "There was low cloud and heavy rain making flying impossible. But Monty was over the moon."

The island of Capri had on Eisenhower's order been set aside as a rest area for combat troops, but General Tooey Spaatz, a moody, bad-tempered man with a fondness for luxury, decided that the huge villas on that opulent island ought to be taken over by high-ranking air force officers, himself foremost among them. His temper cannot have been improved by the secret cable he received from his commanding officer two days before Christmas. This time Eisenhower got to the point immediately:

I have just learned that air force administration of recreational activities at Capri is so organized as to reserve facilities exclusively for air force officers. This is directly contrary to my policies and must cease at once. In permitting the air force to take administrative charge of these matters on the Isle of Capri I did so on the assumption that the place would be run in exact accordance with policies I have so often expressed to you. Please have the officer in charge call at Fifth Army headquarters with the least possible delay and confer with G-1 so that a program may be worked out whereby all British and American personnel in this area, particularly from combat units, may be assured of proportionate opportunity in taking advantage of these facilities. Naturally I assume you are unaware of the methods that have been pursued to date, but I expect your orders in the circumstances to be so positive that there can be no possible misunderstanding or future error in this regard.

Under present plans I will land at El Aouina some time Saturday morning. I will send you my ETA [Estimated Time of Arrival] so that you may meet me there to assure me that this matter has been completely straightened out.

What happened the day before Christmas did not improve Ike's temper. He and his family went to Capri for what was to have been partly a pleasure trip and partly a chance for him to look into matters himself. The pleasure was short-lived, despite the fact that the weather was beautiful. Kay called it "a gorgeous afternoon filled with bright sunshine and a soft breeze, the one clear day we saw during our entire visit in Italy. . . . We toured the famed resort in jeeps, captivated by the indescribable color, the luxurious air of semi-tropical leisure, and the attractive, gay little villas.

"General Eisenhower, however, spotted a villa which wasn't exactly miniature. 'Whose is that?' he asked, pointing. 'Yours, Sir,' was the reply. The General reddened, then nodded at another house, so fabulous it appeared on loan from Hollywood. 'That one belongs to General Spaatz,' our guide answered. Ike asked about several others, before erupting. 'Damn it, that's *not* my villa! And that's not General Spaatz' villa! None of those will belong to any general as long as I'm boss around here. This is supposed to be a rest center—for combat men—not a playground for the brass!' (The villas were decommissioned within hours after we left, reserved for the men who really need them.)"

That day, Christmas Eve, Roosevelt in a broadcast from his home at Hyde Park announced that Eisenhower would command the invasion of Europe, that Montgomery would head the British troops under Eisenhower, and that Spaatz would be commander of "the entire American strategic bombing force operating against Germany." The president also paid special tribute to Marshall and to Admiral King, and he said that during Churchill's sickness, "The heartfelt prayers of all of us have been with this great citizen of the world." He paid tribute to Stalin, too, saying "I believe we are going to get along very well with him and the Russian people—very well indeed."

Francis Trevelyan Miller in *Eisenhower: Man and Soldier* wrote, "When Mother Eisenhower heard that her Dwight had been made Commander in Chief of the Mighty Allied Forces in World War II, she sat silently and is said to have remarked, 'I feel sad when I realize that the responsibility was delegated to Dwight on the Eve of the Coming of Christ.' "

Ida may have thought something like that, but there is no reliable record that she ever said it. Her son's title was Supreme Commander, Allied Expeditionary Force, (SCAEF), and he said, "This sounded very imposing and inspired Commander Butcher, my naval aide, to say that his major problem for the next week or so would be to design special stationery to carry my exalted title."

Despite the new job and the exalted title, Christmas was not a happy day for Eisenhower. He went to Churchill's villa in Carthage where the discussion, led by the rapidly recovering prime minister, was concerned with an operation about which Eisenhower always had his doubts, a proposed amphibious landing at Anzio. "I . . . pointed out that the landing of two partially skeletonized divisions at Anzio, a hundred miles behind the front lines as then situated, would not only be a risky affair but that the attack would not by itself compel the withdrawal of the German front. Military strategy may bear some similarity to the chessboard, but it is dangerous to carry the analogy too far. A threatened king in chess must be protected; in war he may instead choose to fight! The Nazis had not instantly withdrawn from Africa or Sicily simply because of threats to their rear. On the contrary, they had reinforced and fought the battle out to the end. In this case, of course, one of the principal objects was to induce the enemy to reinforce his Italian armies, but it was equally important that this be done in such a way that our own costs would be minimized. It was from the standpoint of costs that I urged careful consideration of the whole plan. I argued that a force of several strong divisions would have to be established at Anzio before significant results could be achieved. . . .

"The Prime Minister was nevertheless determined to carry out the proposed operation." And of course Churchill prevailed. He asked for and got what Eisenhower considered an insufficient force, two divisions. "If I had asked for a three-division lift, I should not have got anything," he said in *Closing the Ring*. "How often in life one must be content with what one can get! Still, it would be better to do it right."

The day after Christmas Eisenhower wrote Mamie a far from cheerful letter:

I came down to the office bright and early this morning to write you a special letter. It is now 11:20 and I've got my first chance to pick up a pen. . . .

During the past few weeks I've led the existence of a traveling man. Been to Cairo—(Jerusalem for a two-hour visit—Tunis—Italy—Sicily—Oran—etc. Some places I stayed two hours—some a whole week. You can see that I've had little time for routine existence! My latest trip to Italy was completed last night—it lasted a week! . . .

I think I've had a good case of homesickness lately. Nothing has been exactly right and everybody about me is having a rough time. I try to hang on to some shreds of a good disposition, but it does get tough at times. Now, with a move staring me in the face I don't know what I'm going to do with some of the people I've depended upon. If I have to live in a

London hotel a while these boys will be out of a job—yet I'll need them later! Oh well—Lee will do something about it.

Well sweet—I love you for trying so hard to make my Xmas a nice one, and you sent me the one thing I really wanted—a good picture of yourself. But Xmas as such falls pretty flat here—all days seem to be the same. I truly hope next year we'll be together, and I hope further that when we get this war won our long partings will be at an end. All my love—always. Happy New Year!!!

Your
Ike.

On the 28th Eisenhower had a meeting in Algiers with Monty, and the English general said in a message to Brooke that Ike "has told me that he wants me to be his head soldier and to take complete charge of the land battle."

Among the last messages Ike received before leaving the Mediterranean theater was one from de Gaulle; it could not have been more conciliatory:

I want to tell you that the French Committee of National Liberation has full confidence in you in the employment of the French forces that it is placing under your command for the next Allied operation.

On the 29th Eisenhower replied, saying that "[my] chief of staff . . . tells me that many of the misunderstandings that seemed to be impeding complete coordination between us have been largely eliminated." Moreover, he added, Smith said "that a large part of the credit is due to your very understanding attitude toward these matters."

The next day Eisenhower paid a farewell call on the French general, and their meeting was, according to Butcher, "a love feast." So the troubles with the difficult Frenchman seemed, thanks largely to Eisenhower's efforts, to be over. Trouble with de Gaulle started again, however, when Eisenhower was in London; this time the problems were largely caused by the American State Department and the British Foreign Office.

Among those Eisenhower was taking to London, and they were the best men in the Mediterranean theater, were Tedder, who was to be his deputy, and Admiral Sir Bertram Ramsay, who was to become naval commander in chief of the Allied Expeditionary Force for OVERLORD. (Cunningham had replaced Sir Dudley Pound as first sea lord in October.) Both were brilliant choices, and, Ike said, Tedder had proved in the Mediterranean that he was "not only a brilliant airman but . . . a staunch supporter of the 'allied' principle as practiced in that command." Ramsay "was a most competent commander of courage, resourcefulness, and tremendous energy. . . . We sometimes laughed among ourselves at the care with which he guarded, in British tradition and practice, the 'senior service' position of the British navy."

As for the Americans Eisenhower would take with him, Spaatz of course would go to London; so would General Courtney Hicks Hodges, a nongraduate of the class of 1908, who was to command the U.S. First Army. Hodges was so self-effacing that at one point Eisenhower thought maybe a publicity man should be assigned to try to make him a little more colorful. It was a pity that Patton, who had much more color than was necessary or desirable, could not share some with Hodges. Eisenhower wanted Hodges to "live by Bradley's side during the later stages of planning and preparation and . . . actually accompany him into the operation. In no repeat no event will I ever advance Patton beyond army command, but the above arrangement will give us time to determine whether it should be Bradley or Hodges that moves back to the army group once it is necessary to insert this formation into the line."

In that same message to Marshall, Ike said, "Frankly, I am very disappointed to leave here before we could attempt at least one ambitious shot at Rome, but the time element allows of no indulgence of personal desire. Consequently, I will stick to my schedule of going to the U.K. about January 10."

As things turned out it was a pity that Eisenhower did not go directly from Algiers to London, but Marshall, always conscious of the well-being of the officers directly under his command, ordered Eisenhower home. The cable on the 29th said:

> Now come on home and see your wife and trust somebody else for twenty minutes in England. . . . Things have been going ahead in the UK for a long time [since the previous April] . . . under a wise and aggressive man [COSSAC chief General Sir Frederick Morgan] and [Bedell] Smith has already been there. You will be under terrific strain from now on. I am interested . . . that you are fully prepared to bear the strain and I am not interested in the usual rejoinder that you can take it. It is of vast importance that you be fresh mentally and you certainly will not be if you go straight from one great problem to another.

That was one of the few messages from Marshall that Ike did not welcome, and he was right. He had, in fact, resisted taking the furlough until Marshall made it an order. He considered that going to the States for so brief a visit was a waste of valuable time. After all, OVERLORD was to be in May, and very little had been done, and much of what had been done, Eisenhower considered wrong. What he did not know was that the trip home would do more than waste his time. It would be painful for him and for Mamie.

In *Crusade* Eisenhower said of the unwelcome journey, "I could accomplish little by a visit to Washington until I had been in London at least long enough to familiarize myself with the essentials of the problems there. General Marshall did not agree. . . . Strictly speaking my commanders were the Combined Chiefs of Staff, but realizing General Marshall's earnestness in the matter, I quickly cleared the point with the British side of the house and made ready to leave for the United States. After a week I planned to return briefly to Africa to complete the details of turning over the American command to General [Jacob] Devers, who had not yet arrived from London. All this could consume time, the most precious element of all."

In studying Morgan's COSSAC plan Eisenhower found that he approved of the general strategy, but he was alarmed at the proposal that three divisions were enough to make the first assault with only two to make a follow-up landing. He told Beetle, "I'd like to assault with twelve divisions." That would have been impossible. Even if a troop buildup of that proportion could have been made, not nearly enough landing craft would be available. There were never enough landing craft for Eisenhower's amphibious landings. In the case of OVERLORD, Ike made a compromise proposal, "I must have at least five divisions in the first assault and two to follow." Montgomery and Smith were to go to London immediately to start carrying out his plans.

Eisenhower, Butcher, and Mickey left Maison Blanche airport for Marrakesh and the States early in the afternoon of December 31. Three convalescent soldiers and two others shared the C-54 with them, and Ike asked two of the convalescents to make up a foursome to play bridge.

The party arrived at Marrakesh around 6:00 in the evening. Churchill was staying in the same villa he had been in after the Casablanca conference. The prime minister was still not fully recovered but, Lord Moran said in his diary, "As the P.M. grows in strength, his old appetite for the war comes back. . . . He is organizing an operation all on his own. He has decided that it should be a landing behind the lines at Anzio. If the Chiefs of Staff are not available, there are plenty of lesser fry to work out the details." It was clear, Butcher said, that Churchill "had practically taken tactical command in the Mediterranean. This feeling, plus the knowledge that General 'Jumbo' Wilson was desirous of keeping Allied Force Headquarters at Algiers, so far behind the lines, left Ike with a rather unsatisfactory impression as he departed from the theater."

The three Americans left at 4:45 on the first day of what was to be a crucial year in Eisenhower's life. The plane was fired on by a Portuguese shore battery near the island of São Miguel in the Azores. They spent three hours having the plane refueled in Terceira. Then the plane left the Azores, and eleven hours later arrived in Bermuda, where they spent another two hours. They reached Washington at 1:30 A.M. on Sunday, January 2. Nothing good happened after that.

The first disaster occurred when Butcher and Eisenhower brought two recently born puppies fathered by Telek to the Wardman Park; both were wearing Scotch-plaid leashes and collars, and both immediately made messes, first on Mamie's oriental rug and then on Ruth Butcher's rug in the apartment across the hall. Mamie had heard all about Telek, and she had read about Telek, and she had disliked everything she knew even before the accident of Telek's offspring on her oriental rug. The dogs had to be got rid of at once. Eisenhower gave one puppy to Milton's son Buddy, and the other went to a friend of and adviser to Franklin Roosevelt, Paul Porter.

Eisenhower was in Washington until the afternoon of January 13, and none of the time spent together was easy either for him or for Mamie. It had been eighteen months since they had seen each other, and Eisenhower had changed greatly. John said that his father "had gained a little weight and was noticeably older. His demeanor was increasingly self-assured. (The General's habit of announcing the termination of a visit created a reaction from his independent wife; he had been living too long in an atmosphere where every minute counted.)" He was unable or unwilling to relax, and his temper, so controlled in the presence of Churchill, was much less so when confronted with Mamie's chatter and complaints. In addition, there was the annoying problem of secrecy; John called it "a triumph of security." The Germans had said in a broadcast before Eisenhower's arrival in the States that they expected a midwinter assault across the Channel. Therefore it certainly would not do for it to be known that the commander of that operation had gone home.

Marshall's aide, Colonel Frank McCarthy, was in charge of Ike's security, and very early on the morning of the general's arrival, McCarthy saw to it that Ike, the stars removed from his overseas cap and those on his shoulder hidden by his overcoat, went down a servant's stairway at the Wardman Park and joined McCarthy in a black sedan parked at the back entrance of the hotel. Eisenhower was then driven to the Pentagon where he had a long meeting with Marshall. That evening there was a party at Butcher's apartment. Among the guests was Steve Early, Roosevelt's press secretary and Butcher's friend. Early had got fifty oysters and steaks from the famous Harvey's restaurant on Pennsylvania Avenue. There were also two chickens, fresh eggs, and butter. It should have been a gala evening, but there was unease in the air.

The next morning Eisenhower saw Roosevelt at the White House; he saw the president twice again, on the 5th, and on the morning of the 12th. What was discussed is not known; Roosevelt did not allow records kept of what was said in such meetings. But Eisenhower said, "Mr. Roosevelt was temporarily ill with influenza but seemed quite cheerful and kept me at his bedside for more than an hour as we discussed a hundred details of past and future operations. As always he amazed me with his intimate knowledge of world geography. The most obscure places in faraway countries were always accurately placed on his mental map. He took occasion to brief me on his post-hostilities occupational plans for Germany. He definitely wanted the northwest section as the United States area but listened attentively as I voiced my objections to dividing Germany into 'national sectors.' I admitted all the difficulties of true joint occupation but said we should insist upon that plan as the only practicable one—and one, moreover, which would quickly test the possibilities of real 'quadripartite action.' I urged, again, that occupied territories be turned over, as quickly as possible, to civil authority. He seemed impressed but did not commit himself." Roosevelt did not live to put his ideas on postwar Germany into effect, but his ideas prevailed; Eisenhower's did not.

So within a week Ike had disagreed with two Allied leaders, Churchill and Roosevelt. In both cases what happened was disastrous, but Ike's ideas, if they had been carried out, might have had equally unfortunate results. About Anzio, however, one thing was certain; Eisenhower had been right that war was not a chess game. The Germans, according to the *New York Times*, "did not divert troops from the Cassino front to counterattack at the beachhead, but, taking a long chance that the beachhead was no more than a threat against their communications, have waited until divisions could be brought in from the north to mount a counteroffensive."

We do know of one specific exchange between Roosevelt and Eisenhower while the general was in Washington. Eisenhower told the president that while he was with Churchill in Marrakesh, Lord Moran complained that whenever he got near the prime minister to read the thermometer, Churchill removed it from his mouth and announced his own temperature. Eisenhower quoted Churchill as saying, "I always do that. I believe these doctors are trying to keep me in bed." According to Eisenhower, Roosevelt said, "Oh, that's nothing new. I've been doing that for years. I don't trust those fellows, either."

On the evening of January 3 Marshall gave a party for Eisenhower and several other commanders at 1806 I Street in Washington, an old house bought several years earlier by a small group of men who wanted a place where "they [could] cook oysters, lobsters, and ducks to suit themselves, and put away a lethal sort of drink based on Medford Rum." Eventually the club had fifty members, and Marshall was invited to entertain there. That night a large number of congressional leaders were present, including several ranking members of the House and Senate Military Affairs Committees.

Eisenhower was the last speaker; he described the Mediterranean operation and added that the question he found most difficult to answer was when a soldier in the field asked, "What about the strikes?" He said that both he and the soldiers under his command needed an answer to that. Marshall a few days before at an off-the-record press conference had said that the railroad strike then going on and a threatened steel strike had made an early end to the war impossible. Eisenhower's speech was never reported, but what Marshall had said was eventually published, and various labor leaders issued a great many bitter statements on the matter.

Later on the night of January 3, Eisenhower and Mamie started to West Point to see John. They traveled in Marshall's private railroad car, and McCarthy went with them. John said, "Shortly after the turn of the year, in early 1944, I was sent for by the officer of the day. Dad, I learned for the first time, had secretly returned to Washington directly from North Africa. Colonel Frank McCarthy . . . was in the O.D.'s office, having come to West Point to pull me out for the remainder of the day. To my astonishment—and to that of the O.D.—Frank told us that Dad and Mother were on a railroad car pulling into a siding near the East Shore Station down on the river at that very moment. Within moments I was whisked into a staff car for the short ride down to the tracks. During the afternoon a handful of friends from the post also came down for a visit; and as a special treat that evening I was allowed to invite three cadets down for dinner."

The three Eisenhowers were alone together only for a few minutes, and those were not comfortable. John said that he wished his father good luck, "but he was obviously rather preoccupied, impatient to get on with the new job of planning the invasion. (His no-nonsense life of the past eighteen months had sharpened his manner somewhat; Mother at one time chastised him for his abruptness. He growled amicably, 'Hell, I'm going back to my theater where I can do what I want.')"

Eisenhower, Mamie, and Colonel McCarthy returned to Washington that night, and the next day, the 5th, Ike had more conferences with General Marshall and met again at the White House with Roosevelt. The president showed Eisenhower a cable from Churchill in which the prime minister asked that Wilson take over Eisenhower's command at AFHQ on the 8th. Eisenhower happily agreed and decided that under the circumstances he would not have to waste more time by returning to Algiers. It would be better to go directly to London from Washington. He cabled that decision to Smith, adding that Devers should take over the American command (NATOUSA) on a date he and Smith agreed on. Eisenhower would, he said, like to return to North Africa "purely as a visitor within a week or ten days after I reach my new station merely to say good-bye to the main officers to whom I am indebted for fine service. I would count on staying there one day only."

The chance for that day never happened, but before leaving Algiers, Eisenhower had expressed his gratitude to troops in his command and all that they had accomplished in the little more than a year since TORCH. In the beginning, he said, "Our fortunes appeared to be at a low ebb. All this was changed by your skill, your determination, and your devotion to duty. . . . You have established yourselves on the mainland of Europe. You are still advancing. Until we meet again in the heart of the enemy's continental stronghold, I send Godspeed and good luck to each of you along with the assurance of my lasting gratitude and admiration."

On the night of the 5th, again using Marshall's private car, Ike and Mamie started for White Sulphur Springs, West Virginia; there the army had recently taken over the famous Greenbrier Hotel, and at Marshall's request, the cottages on the grounds were being used for army officers home from overseas assignments and their wives. The Eisenhowers were there on the 6th and 7th.

On the morning of January 8 Ike flew alone to Fort Riley, Kansas, where he was picked up by an army car and driven to nearby Manhattan; Milton in September had become president of what was then Kansas State College. The Douds were there, along with Arthur and his wife. Naomi Engle had driven Ida over from Abilene. Eisenhower had been told that she might not recognize him, but she did. Nothing was the same, however. Ida was almost eighty-two, and her mind was largely concerned with things in the past, when her sons were boys and when she and David were young. His brothers, too, noticed that Eisenhower was less at ease than he had been. The reunion, spent in Milton's large house on the campus, was strained.

Eisenhower returned to White Sulphur Springs on the 9th, and on the 11th he and Mamie returned to Washington. The next morning he again saw Roosevelt at the White House. The president was still ill in bed with influenza. Eisenhower said, "At times, it must appear, the entire high command, civilian and military, shared the same illness. Perhaps this is not too far from the truth; perhaps fatigue and concern and responsibility were taking their toll."

Eisenhower said, "In none of the various talks I had with the President were domestic politics ever mentioned except casually. His son Elliott, whom I sometimes saw both in Africa and in England, likewise avoided politics as a subject of conversation except to refer to himself, occasionally, in a jocular tone, as the 'black sheep and reactionary of the family.'

"As I left the President, I said, 'I sincerely trust that you will quickly recover from your indisposition.' He quickly replied, 'Oh, I have not felt better in years. I'm in bed only because the doctors are afraid I might have a relapse if I get up too soon.' I never saw him again."

That afternoon and again the next morning Eisenhower had further meetings at the Pentagon; he made a recording urging people to buy war bonds and met with, among others, Milton's old boss Elmer Davis, director of the Office of War Information. He returned to the Wardman Park and said good-bye to Mamie. According to Kenneth Davis her final words to her husband were, "Don't come back until it's over, Ike. I couldn't bear to lose you again."

That evening at seven o'clock he, Butcher, and Mickey took off for London and, after stopovers in Bermuda and the Azores, arrived at Prestwick airport at 1:20 A.M. on the 15th. They went by rail to London, to be met by Kay who had been flown from the Mediterranean. As Eisenhower later wrote, "It is well for man to avoid superstitions, gossip, rumors, and, perhaps, portents. If I had taken what greeted me on arrival in London on January 16, 1944 as a portent, I should have turned back. The fog in the streets was the heaviest it had ever been my misfortune to encounter. . . . Our automobile lights could not penetrate the heavy, yellowish curtain more than a few inches." Kay remembered that driving through that pea soup "was something like trying to swim underwater at night, with one's eyes open. . . . I coaxed the Packard down to Cannon Street Station, the same place from which General Eisenhower left for North Africa."

Seeing the fog, Ike said, "Now I know I'm back in London. . . . Think you can make it, Kay?" Kay said that she could, and, after a hazardous journey through the foggy streets arrived "in the general vicinity of what appeared to be Grosvenor Square, I decided to get out and determine exactly where we were. . . . I had to bend over and feel my way along the street's surface, groping for the sidewalk. A dim light glowed several feet away at some sort of doorway. . . . " 'Here it is!' I shouted, holding fast to the blast-wall headquarters entrance. 'This is 20 Grosvenor!' " According to Kay, Eisenhower went inside, and after "a quick check on incoming cables . . . reappeared within a few minutes."

From there, she said, they went a short distance away to Hayes Lodge, "which was to serve as the General's home and headquarters in the city. It was pleasant, after the fog, to step inside and collapse into the plush chairs." The general liked it very much. " 'But I'd still rather live in Telegraph Cottage, out of town,' he said wistfully."

That day Rommel had been given tactical command of the German troops that would face the invading Allies. The next six months would be a busy time for both generals.

★ ★ ★

THE FINAL PLAN

In one polite paragraph in a letter to Marshall, Eisenhower summed up his stay in the States that January. He said:

I must thank you again for the great trouble you took in making my visit home a pleasant one. I really got a definite rest, and although my wife complained that a brief visit, after almost two years, was almost worse than waiting until my return could be a permanent one, I am absolutely certain that she loved the White Sulphur Springs layout.

In *Past Forgetting* Kay is quoted as saying that when Ike returned to London, "he told me a bit about his stay in the States.

" 'After two days I started getting itchy,' he said. 'I wanted to get back here and get to work. But Marshall insisted that I needed the whole twelve days as vacation. Some vacation. I spent as much of it as I could in the Pentagon.' He stopped and then said, 'Oh my God, I almost forgot. I saw the President while I was in Washington, and he asked after you. . . . He sent you his very best wishes and he gave me something for you.' " The gift for Kay from the president was an inscribed photograph. Much of *Past Forgetting* is undependable, but the above has the ring of truth, and Kay's friend, Anthea Saxe, verified the fact that Kay did have an autographed picture of Roosevelt.

Kay also quoted Eisenhower as saying, "There was the very devil to pay from the moment we walked in with those two pups until I left." That was true. What seems less credible is quoting Eisenhower as saying, "It wasn't only the dogs. The big trouble was . . . I kept calling her Kay. That tore it. . . . I kept calling her Kay. Every time I opened my mouth to say something to Mamie, I'd call her Kay. She was furious." That sounds much less likely. Once maybe, even twice but if he did it "every time," he needed a rest even more than Marshall realized. However, there is little doubt that Kay was much on his mind at the time—and on Mamie's mind. Kay had become an important part of his life, and in London their relationship, although nobody was quite sure what it was, was even more discussed than it had been in North Africa. There the natives did not speak English.

On the 16th, the day after he arrived in London Eisenhower sent a message "for immediate delivery to Mrs. Eisenhower at the Wardman Park Hotel, Washington, D.C."

Trip finally completed with only one unfortunate incident, the theft of my bag of pecans and chocolate. I am truly disappointed because I wanted to try the vitamin chocolate. We brought the package as far as this city but then it disappeared. While our visit together was often interrupted and the pain of parting was as bad as ever, I am still glad I made the trip. I feel much better after having those ten days with you. Please take care of yourself and don't become worn out by Washington life. I am writing thank you notes to all that were so kind to us. Much love.

After Eisenhower left Washington, Mamie once again fled to San Antonio and stayed there for the rest of the winter. In a letter to her written on the 20th Ike said:

My darling:
I left Washington a week ago tonight and this is the first letter I've written, although we did send messages along the route and I sent a special teletype as soon as I got to my office. As I suspected, I've found a heaped up stack of work waiting for me—and I've just started. I get too tired to write—eat—or do anything else.
I've just called upon his Majesty. That is—I suppose you call them "calls." Anyway, when you receive word—you go. Stayed only 40 minutes this time. Mickey decked me out in my best!
I find myself very glad I came home—even though things did seem to be a bit upsetting! I guess it was just because we'd been separated so long, and before we could get really acquainted again, I was on my way.

On the 24th he wrote:

Last evening there was delivered at my house a sweet letter from you, just as you'd finished packing and were waiting for the car that Stack was sending to take you to the train. It was the third letter I'd received since coming here and all of them have been wonderful—quite the nicest you've written since I left home in June '42. My trip home has paid dividends!

He was still worried about her, however, and at times not even sure of her whereabouts. He wrote John on the 31st:

I have had a terrible time trying to keep up with Mamie's whereabouts. When I was in the States she said that she was going to Hot Springs, Arkansas, for two to three weeks and then to Texas. Just as I arrived here I had a message from her saying that her address would be the Majestic Hotel, Little Rock, Arkansas. The next day I received a message from Washington saying that Mamie was in Hot Springs. It all defeats me but I think I am perfectly safe in sending my letters to Texas because they will scarcely arrive there before she does. On the other hand I feel rather helpless in trying to send a teletype because I would not know where to direct it. She is, of course, leading a hectic life and probably it does not occur to her that she has given me two or three different pieces of information on the same subject. But it will all straighten out soon.

On the twenty-eighth anniversary of their engagement he wrote:

> What a day—I've had at least six visitors since starting on what I intended to be a real Valentine letter. Each interruption makes it just that much more difficult to say what I really wanted to tell you, which is that I'm lucky to have had you to see or send a message to every Valentine's Day for 28 times. Quite a record in itself—even if you were only an ordinary woman. But considering that everyone loves you—most deservedly—I wonder how my luck has held so long. Take care of yourself, my sweet— maybe on next Valentine's Day, I can crack your ribs instead of hurting your eyes with a scrawl like this—I love you—always.

This time Eisenhower had come to London, he said, "to undertake the organization of the greatest fighting force that the two Western Allies could muster. . . . Now began again the task of preparing for an invasion, but by comparison with the similar job of a year and a half earlier, order had replaced disorder and certainty and confidence had replaced fear and doubt." His staff this time, in addition to Beetle, included Ramsay, Tedder, Montgomery, Spaatz, and Bradley. The previous August, back in Algiers, Eisenhower in a message to Marshall had assessed the value of Clark, Patton, and Bradley. He knew them all well, and he respected them and felt comfortable with them, his old classmate Bradley in particular. At that time Marshall had said that he wanted Bradley to go to England to command the army that was getting ready for the cross-Channel invasion. In a message to Marshall on August 27, 1943, he said of Bradley, comparing him to Patton and Clark:

> Of the three, Bradley is the best rounded in all respects, counting experience, and he has the greatest characteristic of never giving his commander one moment of worry. . . . He has had some little experience in planning amphibious operations, but his function in preparing for the Sicilian show was a subordinate one, especially with all the intricate co-operations with navy and ground forces. However, his ability is such that he could solve this part of the problem very satisfactorily.

But Eisenhower must have felt that he had been less than enthusiastic in his assessment of Bradley, because in a later message, he said:

> I have been thinking over what I told you in my telegram of the other day reference Bradley. . . . The truth of the matter is that you should take Bradley and, moreover, I will make him available on any date you say. I will get along. . . .

On September 2 the chief of staff cabled Eisenhower that he should have Bradley ready to go to England where he would "head an army headquarters and will also probably have to develop an army group headquarters in order to keep pace with the British planning and requisitions." On September 9 Bradley and his staff flew to London, and in the months ahead, Bradley, as always, did what he had been sent to do, but in his mind one large question remained unanswered. Who was to be the ground forces commander in chief for the invasion? He said, "If there was to be a ground force commander-in-chief it was desirable that he be an American, for the Americans would eventually outnumber the British more than three to one on the ground. But who . . . was he to be? At that time not an American field commander rivaled the stature of either Alexander or Montgomery. If the ground force commander in chief were to be named, the odds were heavily in favor of one of these British soldiers. Consequently, the issue was tactfully dropped and hidden away in the files."

On January 17, 1944, at his first press conference in London, Eisenhower announced that Brad, the man called "the doughboy's general," would lead the U.S. forces in the invasion of Europe. According to Bradley, who had not yet talked to Eisenhower and who got the news in the London *Daily Express*, "For the moment that statement [Eisenhower's] was not clear, for it did not indicate whether Eisenhower meant First Army on the assault or the Army Group as an opposite number to Monty. It was not until later that Eisenhower said he meant the Army Group."

One of the most important meetings of the war took place at Norfolk House on the morning of January 21. The house had once belonged to the family of the Duke of York, and George III had been born there. That day the imperialists and the colonists sat side by side, and a colonist named Eisenhower was in charge. The parking places were assigned according to rank, but when Kay arrived with the supreme allied commander she was not pleased to find that the No. 1 spot which had been designated for Eisenhower's Packard was occupied by "the flashy, shiny, black Rolls-Royce which could belong to only one man in all of England: General Montgomery. I was furious, as only a rank-conscious army driver can be."

Eisenhower told her it didn't matter and went into the meeting, which, according to Beetle, "brought together for the first time in their new assignments the men who would direct the over-all strategy and tactics responsible for Germany's defeat in the West. It secured agreement on the only major revisions which were to be made in plans for the cross-Channel assault." This time, as Smith points out with satisfaction, it was not necessary to introduce Eisenhower to anybody: "Almost every man present was an old friend, tried and tested in previous Allied undertaking." Tedder, Ramsay, Bradley, Montgomery, and Leigh-Mallory were there. Air Chief Marshal Sir Trafford Leigh-Mallory was the least familiar among them, and he was to prove the most difficult from the first meeting to the last. He said at the January 21 meeting and many times in the future that Eisenhower's plan for using two American airborne divisions to help secure the landings at Utah Beach on the Cotentin Peninsula would involve too great a risk; there would be an alarming number of casualties, as many, he said, as 75 percent or more.

It seemed during the anxious months preceding the invasion that no one liked or quite trusted Leigh-Mallory; no one wanted to serve under him, including the British. Eisenhower had to have heard the bitter criticism, still he did nothing.

When Brigadier General James Gavin of the 82d Airborne came to England from Sicily, he met with Leigh-Mallory. He remembered the British officer saying, "Now I want you chaps to tell me how you do this airborne business." Gavin tried, but Leigh-Mallory after a while said, "I don't think anybody can do that." "We just got through doing it in Sicily," said Gavin, but Leigh-Mallory remained unconvinced, and late in May when he came to Portsmouth he again protested against the "futile slaughter of the two American airborne divisions."

That was not what Eisenhower wanted to hear from the air chief marshal, and he later remembered, "I went to my tent, alone and sat down to think. Over and over I reviewed each step [of the invasion]. . . . I realized . . . that if I deliberately disregarded the advice of my technical expert on the subject and his predictions should prove accurate, then I would carry to my grave the umbearable burden of a conscience justly accusing me of the stupid, blind sacrifice of thousands of the flower of our youth."

Moreover, if the air chief marshal was right, "the effect of the disaster would be far more than local; it would likely spread to the entire force." On the other hand, as Eisenhower had already explained to the Combined Chiefs and the British Chiefs, "To assist the assault on the Cotentin an airborne division would be landed on D-Day to seize the exits from the beaches; followed, probably by a second airborne division in approximately twenty-four hours."

As Beetle had said at the time and later, "The reasons [for the airborne landings] were compelling. Behind the landing area stretched the low ground the Germans had flooded. A few roads crossed the marshy, mile-wide strip, but unless airborne troops were put down on the firm ground behind to seize the roadheads and engage the defenders, the narrow causeways across the marshes could be raked by enemy fire. Our troops would take heavy casualties, forcing their way inland from the beaches."

There were other considerations, but finally, in Eisenhower's mind, "Leigh-Mallory's estimate was just an estimate, nothing more, and our experience in Sicily and Italy did not, by any means, support his theory of pessimism. Bradley, with Ridgway and other airborne commanders, had always supported me and the staff in the matter, and I was encouraged to persist in the belief that Leigh-Mallory was wrong! I telephoned him that the attack would go as planned." Eisenhower preferred optimists to pessimists.

Happily, Leigh-Mallory was indeed proved wrong. Despite great difficulties, most objectives were eventually reached, and casualties were not as high as had been feared. Beetle said later, "It is a matter of record that losses to the airborne elements in the first drop were less than 2 percent. Total losses for the entire operation were less than 10 percent." And when the attack was successful, Eisenhower said that Leigh-Mallory "was the first to call me to voice his delight and to express his regret that he had found it necessary to add to my personal burdens during the final . . . days before D-Day."

Another major problem discussed at the Norfolk House meeting on January 21 was the shortage of landing craft. That problem, too, was to persist during that winter and spring in London. As Churchill once said, "The destinies of two great empires . . . seem to be tied up in some goddamned things called LSTs." The shortages meant, it was decided, that the OVERLORD landings had to be postponed for a month. More warships and convoy vessels were also necessary, in Smith's words, "to load, land, and supply the increased landing force. Five initial infantry divisions and two in the follow-up meant that a total of seven divisions must be landed in assault boats on D-day. A threatening shortage of landing craft and supporting warships continued to hang over the operation till late in March, when we were finally assured of the number we should need."

Montgomery and Beetle had been busy since their arrival in England earlier that month, and Montgomery not only had his car parked in the No. 1 position outside; he took command inside Norfolk House as well. Eisenhower presided, but Monty prevailed. If many of his audience hadn't known better, they would have thought that the whole idea for a cross-Channel invasion had been Monty's. The work done by Morgan and his staff in drawing up plans for the invasion was largely ignored. Morgan, chief of staff to the Supreme Allied Commander, COSSAC, was unpopular with many of his British colleagues for tending to side with the Americans; in Monty's mind he was "a deserter"; he had sold out to the Yanks.

Now Monty strode up and down and explained that the Americans would land in Normandy on the right and push toward the ports of the Loire, Cherbourg, and Brest. The Canadians and the British would land on the left and "would deal with the enemy main strength. In the initial stages, we should concentrate on gaining control of the main centers of road communications. We should then push out our armored formations between and beyond these centers and deploy them on suitable ground. In this way it would be difficult for the enemy to bring up his reserves and get them past these armored formations." Montgomery said that success had to be quick. The battle, indeed the war had to be won on the beaches, an idea with which, it would be found, Rommel agreed. He always thought that what happened on the first day would be crucial.

Ike was not happy with what happened on January 21. There were consolations! The postponement of the invasion meant that there would be an extra month for bombing the Germans, and by June spring thaws would have dried up enough so that the Russians, not impeded by mud, could continue their offensive, but Eisenhower in the main was forced to accept less than he wanted, less than he thought was necessary.

As the British writer Max Hastings was to say forty years later in his book about OVERLORD, "Eisenhower understood that in some respects his authority was that of a constitutional monarch. The power that he held was less important than the fact that his possession of it denied it to others. Eisenhower lacked greatness as a soldier and tolerated a remarkable number of knaves and mischief-makers in his court at SHAEF. But his behaviour at moments of Anglo-American tension, his extraordinary generosity of spirit to his difficult subordinates, proved his greatness as Supreme Commander. His failures were of omission, seldom of commission. It remains impossible to conceive of any other Allied soldier matching his achievement."

The atmosphere of strained relations was not a new experience. On April 4 Eisenhower wrote Marshall's assistant, William Somervell:

Dear Bill:
The current stage of preparation is a replica of the others I have been

through. As the big day approaches tension grows and everybody gets more and more on edge. This time, because of the stakes involved, the atmosphere is probably more electric than ever before. In this particular venture we are not merely risking a tactical defeat; we are putting the whole works on one number. A sense of humor and a great faith, or else a complete lack of imagination, are essential to the project.

When Eisenhower emerged from the January 21 meeting, his car was in its proper space; Kay had remarked to Monty's driver, "There must be some mistake." The mistake was corrected, and when Eisenhower got in the car, Kay was, she said, "beaming a purely feline smile. The General," she added, "wasn't interested in such trifles. He was quiet on the ride to Grosvenor Square."

Among the many disappointments at the meeting had been Churchill's opposition to ANVIL, the landing in southern France that Eisenhower had hoped would be at the same time as OVERLORD. In a message he sent to the Combined Chiefs, he said, "OVERLORD and ANVIL must be viewed as one whole. . . . I regard ANVIL as an important contribution to OVERLORD as I feel an assault will contain more enemy forces in southern France than a threat. The forces both U.S. and French are in any case available; and the actual landing of these forces will increase the cooperation from resistance elements in France."

That battle was won, but not easily, and even after the invasion in Normandy had succeeded, the argument over ANVIL continued. Moreover, even after the war, Churchill continued to believe and to say that the operation had been a costly mistake.

On February 12 Eisenhower officially assumed command of OVERLORD. The assignment was awesome, involving in part

Task. You will enter the continent of Europe and, in conjunction with the other United Nations, undertake operations aimed at the heart of Germany and the destruction of her armed forces. The date for entering the Continent is the month of May 1944. After adequate Channel ports have been secured, exploitation will be directed towards securing an arena that will facilitate both ground and air operations against the enemy. . . .

Command. You are responsible to the Combined Chiefs of Staff and will exercise command generally in accordance with the diagram at Appendix. . . . [This is a diagram indicating the chain of command.]

Logistics. You will be responsible for the coordination of logistical arrangements on the continent. You will also be responsible for coordinating the requirements of British and United States forces under your command. . . . In preparation for your assault on enemy occupied Europe, Sea and Air Forces, agencies of sabotage, subversion and propaganda, acting under a variety of authorities, are now in action. You may recommend any variation in these activities which may seem to you desirable. . . .

Responsibility will rest with the Combined Chiefs of Staff for supplying information relating to operations of the Forces of the U.S.S.R. for your guidance in timing your operations. It is understood that the Soviet Forces will launch an offensive at about the same time as OVERLORD with the object of preventing the German forces from transferring from the Eastern to the Western front. The Allied Commander in Chief, Mediterranean Theater [Wilson] will conduct operations designed to assist your operation including the launching of an attack against the south of France at about the same time as OVERLORD. The scope and timing of his operations will be decided by the Combined Chiefs of Staff. You will establish contact with him and submit to the Combined Chiefs of Staff your views and recommendations regarding operations from the Mediterranean in support of your attack from the United Kingdom. The Combined Chiefs of Staff will place under your command the forces operating in Southern France as soon as you are in a position to assume such command. You will submit timely recommendations compatible with this regard.

As Beetle later said, "In the military system the chain of command is absolute. Each commander in that chain is responsible as an individual for his own decisions. In turn, he is responsible to the next higher commander. General Eisenhower, as Supreme Commander of the Allied Expeditionary Force, was responsible for each decision his subordinates made. This, in turn, indicates how carefully the high commander must weigh the choice of his division, corps, and army commanders, since, if a subordinate commander fails, it is the Supreme Commander who is at fault for having placed him in a position of command."

All true, and Eisenhower made mistakes in choosing his subordinates, but they were few in number. There is very little to be said for America's peacetime army. It was small; it was badly trained, poorly equipped, and, as we have seen, turned dangerously inward. It was an island surrounded by a sea of uncaring, more often contemptuous civilians. Many if not most of its members were incompetent, lazy, drunken, uncaring. But there were a few good men, and in general they were very good men indeed. If you were ambitious, and Eisenhower was, you kept an eye on them, and Eisenhower did. Marshall had his little black book for the officers he considered promising. Eisenhower didn't need a book. He just kept them in mind, and when the time came, that paid off, for him, for the Allied armies, for all of us.

What happened in those months was, according to Max Hastings, "the greatest organizational achievement of the Second World War, a feat of staff work that has dazzled history, a monument to the imagination and brilliance of thousands of British and American planners and logisticians which may never be surpassed in war."

Besides his military duties, according to the *New York Times*, Eisenhower had to "Coordinate and execute dozens of subsidiary policies emanating from all the capitals of the major Allied nations. He is concerned not only with waging war but with diplomacy . . . and a thousand other problems associated with smashing the German army."

And as if that weren't enough, during the period from his arrival in London until the invasion was launched, he inspected a great number of Allied units, often wearing what he called his "goop suit." It consisted of long, overall-type trousers that came up to his armpits. The bottoms were buttoned around his shoes. His coat was usually a heavy battle jacket, and instead of a military cap, he wore a knitted helmet. On such occasions he almost never wore any ribbons or decorations. His presence, however, never went unnoticed. He would have been pleased had he known that one American corporal watching him climb over a tank said, "He looks sort of like the guys you know at home, not like you'd expect." He *did* travel in some style, though, in a special train that had an office, room for staff cars and a radio-equipped jeep which followed him through the countryside so that he could constantly be in touch with his headquarters.

As usual when he was overworked and depressed, Eisenhower's health suffered. As he wrote to Mamie on the 24th, "I'm having a flare-up with my insides, accompanied by shooting pains! I think it's just the old trouble, but at times it's worrisome." And early in February he wrote, "What a time I've had recovering fully from the cold I first caught about November 15! Personally I think my trouble is as much cigarettes as germs—but it simply seems impossible for me to be truly moderate in the matter of smoking. I'm just a weak sinner."

On January 22, the day after the meeting at Norfolk House, the landing at Anzio, code name SHINGLE, took place. For a time it looked as if Churchill had been right about his much-favored project. There would be an easy victory, and while he and Eisenhower had missed having Christmas dinner in Rome, perhaps the Allies could celebrate the Easter holiday there. That year Easter was on April 9.

Eisenhower had been dubious about SHINGLE from the beginning, and even before leaving the Mediterranean he had made that fact clear. "It was from the standpoint of costs that I urged careful consideration of the whole plan. I argued that a force of several strong divisions would have to be established in Anzio before significant results could be achieved. I pointed out also that, because of distance, rapid building up of the attacking forces at Anzio would be difficult and landing craft would be needed long after the agreed-upon date for their release."

So far as SHINGLE was concerned, Eisenhower was more of a realist than Churchill, and that was to prove increasingly true as time went on. The landing was made at the prewar luxury beach resort under the command of Major General John P. Lucas, West Point 1911. Lucas, who was only a few months older than Eisenhower, was well thought of by his fellow officers, including Ike. According to Lucas's friend James Gavin, Lucas was "a widely read man of unusual intelligence and sensitivity." In December, knowing that he would be commanding OVERLORD and leaving the Mediterranean, Eisenhower had recommended that Lucas be given the Fifth Army while Clark became theater commander. That did not happen, but at the time of the landing, Lucas commanded the invading VI Corps, which consisted of one British and one American division.

There was almost no opposition on the beach, and by nightfall of the first day, 36,000 troops and more than 3,000 vehicles had been disembarked. The Allied plan was for the troops of the Fifth Army to cross the Rapido River and link up with VI Corps, which was to drive inland to cut the highways that were the major supply and escape routes for the German forces to the south. Then the triumphant Allies would march to Rome, leaving the unhappy Germans behind them. But on the night of the 20th the crossing of the swollen Rapido had not gone as planned. A few troops of the 36th Division, the Texas National Guard, did get across the river—but at great expense. Not a single one of the 700 men of one battalion managed to get to the other side. The few Texans who had succeeded were slaughtered by the Germans. Altogether the 36th suffered 1,681 fatalities at the Rapido, and the bitterness in Texas, particularly against Clark, still remains.

Even before he knew about the disaster at the Rapido, Lucas had had grave doubts about SHINGLE. He wrote in his diary, "They will end up by putting me ashore with inadequate forces and get me in a serious jam. Then who will take the blame?" He later told Gavin that he did not have enough troops in VI Corps to make the landing and go on to Rome. Clark, he said, ordered him to carry out his orders or be relieved of his command. Clark did not tell Lucas that he, too, thought the whole operation was hazardous, even foolhardy.

So Lucas carried out his orders, but he was still to be relieved of his command. Only Churchill, whose idea SHINGLE had been, whose support for it had never wavered, and on whose shoulders blame should have fallen, escaped censure. And he blamed others for the failure. "I had hoped we were hurling a wildcat on the shore," he said, "but all we got was a stranded whale."

The day after the Anzio landing, Butcher said in his diary, "SHINGLE has started out well"; a few days later, on the 29th, he said, "The battle at Anzio is going slowly. At lunch Ike wondered what was causing the slowness." The slowness continued, and on February 8 when Eisenhower's old friend, Wes Gallagher, then Associated Press correspondent, arrived in London he said, "The reason for failure to exploit the beachhead was fear of the various generals to take responsibility. . . . If Ike had been there, he would have said, 'Go ahead, the responsibility is mine.' "

The Germans called Anzio "a prison camp where the prisoners feed themselves." There were 70,000 such prisoners, along with 18,000 vehicles. Axis Sally, the German propaganda broadcaster, had a special song for the men, "Between the Devil and the Deep Blue Sea." It was generally felt that Lucas should have moved out at once, but he did not. Some people said he suffered from a "Salerno complex." On one short visit to Anzio, Clark allegedly said to Lucas, "Don't stick your neck out, Johnny. I did at Salerno and got into trouble." Whether Clark said it or not, Lucas certainly did not stick out his neck. Instead of moving out after the landing he built up a defense for a German attack he was sure would come. There was no such attack. And while the Germans built up their strength, 88s were fired into the vulnerable "prison camp," and one division lost more than a third of its strength, almost 5,000 men. The Germans by the end of February had three divisions on the heights overlooking the beach, and it wasn't until May that the Allied forces were able to break out.

Eisenhower tried to take an optimistic view of the operation. He later said, "In the final outcome the Anzio operation paid off handsomely. . . . The move undoubtedly convinced Hitler that we intended to push the Italian campaign as a major operation." Forty years later historians have uncovered no evidence that that was true. But it must be assumed that the idea of failure of another Allied amphibious operation upset the man who was planning the largest amphibious operation ever. Perhaps the best estimate of the meaning of Anzio came from Nazi General Albert Kesselring, who said, "Anzio was the enemy's 'epic of bravery.' We felt we were opposed by equals. Our enemy was of the highest quality."

The arrival of Patton on the morning of January 26 cannot have contributed to Eisenhower's peace of mind. Georgie flew into the Cheddington airport, thirty-five miles north of London, but his presence in England was kept secret from the British and American people for some days.

Butcher and General J. C. H. Lee met Patton at the airport, but from the moment he stepped off the plane the arriving general was unhappy. Patton and Lee were both members of the class of 1909, but the deputy supreme commander was a pious man who never cursed; the two men had little in common. Had Ike sent Lee there as a deliberate insult to Patton? Georgie wasn't sure. The day was cold and foggy, and Patton realized that he was, as he said, making "my twenty-seventh start from zero since entering the U.S. Army. Each time I have made a success of it, and this one must be the biggest."

The news Georgie got in London was not encouraging. He was to be commander of the Third Army, most of which was still in the States, but the advance party would arrive in England on the *Queen Mary* in a day or two. It was a good assignment, but he would no longer be, as he had been in Morocco, Tunisia, and Sicily, the top American field commander. He would be part of a team. He said, "All [the personnel in the Army] are novices, and [we are] in support of Bradley's First Army—not such a good job, but better than nothing."

According to Butcher, when Patton visited Eisenhower at his office, the supreme commander, in addition to telling him of his new command, gave him "a severe bawling out for failing to follow Ike's instructions of counting ten before issuing an order or by taking any abrupt action. Patton . . . most contrite. . . . He is a master of flattery and succeeds in turning any difference of views with Ike into a deferential acquiesence to the view of the Supreme Commander. For instance, he told Ike during a lively discussion of history that anyone would be foolish to contest the rightness of the Supreme Commander's views, particularly as he is now—in Patton's words—'the most powerful man in the world.' Ike glumly and noncommittally passes off such flattery."

Patton in his diary did not mention the reprimand, but he did say, "Ike asked me to dinner; Kay, Butcher, a British Aide-de-Camp, and a WAC captain were present. Ike very nasty and show-offish—he always is when Kay is present—and criticized [J. C. H.] Lee for his flamboyance which he—Ike—would give a million to possess." Patton was not very good at analyzing what went on in other people's minds, and much of the time he must have been puzzled and surprised by what was happening in his own. One thing is certain. Eisenhower would not have given a million to possess Lee's flamboyance; it was the flamboyant people who caused trouble.

Patton's word, given on his arrival in England cannot have reassured Eisenhower much. Butcher reported that after the dressing-down, "Patton said . . . that hereafter he certainly would be more careful as to the place he has a tantrum and certainly will not choose a hospital."

In the weeks that followed, Patton by his lights did his best to stay out of trouble. He made inspection tours, and in one speech before the invasion he said:

I am not supposed to be commanding this army—I am not even supposed to be in England. Let the first bastards to find out be the Germans. Some day I want them to rise on their hind legs and howl: "Jesus Christ. It's that goddamn Third Army and that son of a bitch Patton again." . . . There's one great thing you can say when it's all over and you're home once more. You can thank God that twenty years from now when you're sitting by the fireside with your grandson on your knee and he asks you what you did in the war, you won't have to shift him to the other knee and say, I shoveled shit in Louisiana.

That speech was not reported in the press, but what he said on April 25 before the Welcome Club of Knutsford, England, *was* reported and was widely commented on both in England and the United States. The Welcome Club had been started by the charitable women of Knutsford for the supposedly homesick soldiers under Patton's command. Patton had said that he would not make a speech at the club; he would be "too prominent." He arrived fifteen minutes late, but he still created quite a stir among the fifty or sixty people present, most of them women. He was asked to say a few words, being assured that they would be off the record. He did say a few words, and they nearly ended his career. As he remembered it, he said:

Until today, my only experience in welcoming has been to welcome Germans and Italians to the "Infernal Regions." In this I have been quite successful. . . .

I feel that such clubs as this are a very real value, because I believe with Mr. Bernard Shaw, I think it was he, that the British and Americans, are two people separated by a common language, and since it is the evident destiny of the British and Americans, and, of course, the Russians to rule the world, the better we know each other, the better job we will do.

A club like this is an ideal place for making such acquaintances and for promoting mutual understanding. Also, as soon as our soldiers meet and know the English ladies and write home and tell our women how truly lovely you are, the sooner the American ladies will get jealous and force this war to a quick termination, and I will get a chance to go and kill Japanese.

Looked at casually the speech might seem trouble free; it was courteous; it quoted George Bernard Shaw, who had in fact said that, and it flattered the middle-aged women who heard it outrageously. As Butcher said, Patton was "a master of flattery." Besides, the speech was off the record, wasn't it?

It wasn't. And the first reports did not mention the fact that Patton had at least included the Russians among the rulers of the world. The British press did not pay much attention, but in the United States the speech made the front pages of most newspapers. The kindest critic said that it was "unfortunate." Marshall, on the morning of April 29, cabled Eisenhower, "Newspapers today carried reports of General Patton's statements reference Britain and America's rule of the world. We were just about to get a confirmation of the permanent makes [permanent Army promotions; Patton's was among those on the list before the Senate]. This I fear has killed them all."

Eisenhower had been away on an inspection trip, which included an amphibious landing exercise by the 4th Infantry Division followed by a discussion on his train of what they had seen with Bradley and Gee Gerow, who was to be commander of the V Corps at Omaha Beach on D day. Ike had returned to London on the 28th, and he replied to Marshall's cable of the next morning, saying that the chief of staff's message was

> my first intimation that Patton had broken out again. . . . Apparently he is unable to use reasonably good sense in all those matters where senior commanders must appreciate the effect of their actions . . . and this raises doubts as to the wisdom of retaining him in high command despite his demonstrated capacity in battle leadership. In this case the only excuse he gave to Smith, who has talked with him, is that he spoke to about sixty people at a private gathering and did not repeat not know that any representative of the press was present. . . .

> While his exact remarks on this occasion were incorrectly reported and somewhat misinterpreted in the press, I have grown so weary of the trouble he constantly causes you and the War Department that I am seriously contemplating the most drastic action. I am deferring final action until I hear further from you. Specifically I should like to know whether you still feel, after the lapse of several days, that his latest statements have caused such serious reaction at home as to prevent the War Department securing congressional approval of any of its recommendations. Regardless of the answer to the above question do you consider that his retention in high command will tend to destroy or diminish public and governmental confidence in the War Department? If the answer to either of the above is in the affirmative then I am convinced that stern disciplinary action must be taken so as to restore the situation. I request that you give me a reply as soon as convenient and I will then make final recommendation.

This time it looked as if Eisenhower would have to do what he liked least— fire somebody, in this case, an old friend.

In a later message on the 29th, Marshall quoted a critical editorial in the *Washington Post* and added, "Like you, I have been considering the matter on a purely business basis." He added that if Eisenhower felt that Hodges could do as good a job fighting the Germans as Patton, "all well and good. If you doubt it then between us we can bear the burden of all the present unfortunate reaction. I fear the harm has already been fatal to the confirmation of the permanent list."

In a second message Ike sent to Marshall on the 29th, his attitude had softened. He said that he was "weary of his [Patton's] habit of getting everybody into hot water through the immature character of his public actions and statements." On the other hand, "In this particular case investigation shows that his offense was not as serious as the newspapers would lead one to believe, and one that under the circumstances could have occurred to almost anybody." That is true— almost anybody—except of course Marshall and, it hardly need be added, Ike.

Eisenhower sent Patton a message, also on the 29th, saying that after examining all the evidence about what happened, he understood Patton thought he was talking privately and "upon the spur of the moment" but that Patton should "understand thoroughly that it [the incident] is still filled with drastic potentialities regarding yourself." Furthermore, if in the future Georgie was "guilty of any indiscretion in speech or action that leads to embarrassment for the War Department, any other part of our Government, or for this Headquarters, I will relieve you instantly of command."

On the 30th Eisenhower cabled Marshall that he had sent for Patton "to allow him opportunity to present his case personally to me." But he added that from everything he knew at the moment, "I will relieve him from command and send him home unless some new and unforeseen information should be developed in the case." He thought Hodges could command the Third Army, but "Patton has proved his ability to conduct a ruthless drive whereas Hodges has not."

The next morning, May 1, Marshall sent Eisenhower what had to have been a comforting message. He said:

> The decision is exclusively yours. . . . Send him home if you see fit, and in grade, or hold him there as surplus if you so desire, or . . . continue him in command if that promises best for OVERLORD. . . . Do not consider War Department position in the matter. Consider only OVERLORD and your own heavy burden of responsibility for its success. Everything else is of minor importance.

When Patton appeared at 11:00 in the morning of May 1, Ike had not yet made up his mind what to do. He said, "George, you have gotten yourself into a very serious fix." Patton was again contrite and flattering. He said, "Before you go any farther, I want to say that your job is more important than mine, so if in trying to save me you are hurting yourself, throw me out." There were further fawning words, and then Eisenhower said that Patton's mistakes had caused trouble not only with the War Department but with the entire country, that he had told Marshall that, as Patton put it, he was "washing his hands of me," and that "his hand was being forced in the United States."

By the end of the interview Patton's future was still uncertain, but Patton said, "When I came out [of Eisenhower's office] I don't think anybody could tell I had just been killed. . . . I feel like death, but I am not out yet. If they will let me fight, I will; but if not, I will resign [from the army] so as to be able to talk, and then I will talk and possibly do my country more good. . . . All the way home, 5 hours, I recited poetry to myself."

On the 3rd Eisenhower told Marshall that he had decided to keep Patton. Relieving him "would lose to us his experience as commander of an Army in battle and his demonstrated ability of getting the utmost out of soldiers in an offensive operation." That day he told Patton the same thing. He said, "I do this solely because of my faith in you as a battle leader and from no other motives. . . . I expect you to plunge into your task of preparing your army with undiminished vigor."

Eisenhower later remarked that Patton's "emotional range was very great and he lived at either one end or the other of it. I laughingly told him, 'You owe us some victories; pay off and the world will deem me a wise man.' "

★ ★ ★

O.K. WE'LL GO

"It seems no exaggeration to say that General Eisenhower, with his historic role, faced problems of such heroic range that they required the judgment of a Solomon, the military mind of a Napoleon, the diplomacy of a Prime Minister," said Kay Summersby.

Walter Bagehot, the nineteenth-century English economist and journalist, defined the kind of supreme commander Eisenhower was in another way. He said, "The soldier—that is, the great soldier—of today is not a romantic animal, dashing at forlorn hopes, animated by frantic sentiment, full of fancies as a love-lady or a sovereign; but a quiet, grave man, busied in charts, exact in sums, master of the art of tactics, occupied in trivial detail; thinking, as the Duke of Wellington was said to do, *most* of the shoes of his soldiers; despising all manner of éclat and elegance."

Ike sometimes worked twenty hours a day during the late winter and spring of 1944, and he had little time for exercise. He was tense, nervous, and irritable, and he was sometimes annoyed by things that normally did not bother him at all—his treatment by the British press, for example. He usually paid little attention to cricitism, but early in February he wrote in his diary, "Much discussion has taken place concerning our command setup, including newspaper evaluations of personalities and abilities. Generally speaking, the British columnists (not the chief of staff or the prime minister) try to show that my contributions in the Mediterranean were administrative accomplishments and 'friendliness in welding an allied team.' They dislike to believe that I had anything particularly to do with campaigns. They don't use the words 'initiative' and 'boldness' in talking of me, but often do in speaking of Alex and Monty."

He went on to say that Cunningham and Tedder had been the "bold" commanders in the Mediterranean; and it was he, Eisenhower said, who "peremptorily had to order the holding of the forward airfields in the bitter days of January 1943. I had to order the integration of an American corps and its use on the battle lines (if I had not done that Tunisia would have evaded us a much longer time). I had to order the attack on Pantelleria. And, finally, the British ground commanders (but not Sir Andrew and Tedder) wanted to put all our ground forces into the toe of Italy. They didn't like Salerno, but after days of work I got them to accept." True, "no British commander ever held back when once an operation was ordered. We had a happy family. . . . But it wearies me to be thought of as timid, when I've done things that were so risky as to be almost crazy. Oh hum."

And in a letter to Mamie on March 29, he wrote:

All my conferences this morning have been of the irritating type. People had misquoted me, others have enlarged on my instructions, still others have failed to obey orders. So I had a big field day, and ended up by tanning a few hides. I feel positively sadistic—but I undoubtedly got a certain amount of satisfaction out of the process. One secretary, one aide, one staff officer, and one other are all a bit tanned, I hope!

Early in March he had been able to move his headquarters, which then included 4,000 people, to Spaatz's Eighth Air Force cantonment in Bushy Park, not far from Wimbledon and a short drive from London. The headquarters' code name was WIDEWING, and the buildings were rickety and seemed to disintegrate a little every day. It was said that one reason the war had to be won quickly was to avoid the total collapse of WIDEWING. The floors were concrete and damp, and it was often so cold that Butcher wore his heaviest GI underwear, and his teeth sometimes chattered.

Ike's own office was, as usual, unpretentious. Kay said that it shocked "visitors who expected grandeur in the Supreme Commander's Inner Sanctum." It was about twenty feet square, and his desk was square with three flags on top, those of Britain and the United States and his own flag with four white stars. Photographs of Mamie, John, and Ida were also on the desk, and there were signed photographs of Roosevelt, Marshall, and Cunningham on the walls, as well as maps that were covered with a locked silver screen when anyone under the rank of lieutenant general came into the room. A safe in one corner had mosaic photographs of places where operations were taking place and would take place in the future. There was a swivel chair behind the desk, and in other parts of the room were two overstuffed chairs, a couch, and a radio.

One of the buzzers on the supreme commander's desk summoned Kay, another, Captain Mattie Pinnette.

Several telephones were on a table within easy reach of Eisenhower when he was at his desk, one of them a sea-green "scrambler" for secret conversations with people like the prime minister.

At ten every morning and four every afternoon Eisenhower did what people like Patton deplored; he had tea, usually with Kay. Occasionally he would inspect the kitchen, and Marty Snyder, who was headquarters mess sergeant, said, "Other officers often did the same thing, but somehow their presence in the kitchen always made the enlisted men uncomfortable. Eisenhower was different. There was a casualness about him that immediately put everyone at ease. Sometimes he'd glance at the stoves to see what was cooking, but he seemed to make a point of trying not to be in the way. The men sensed this and liked him for it. . . . Nor was he patronizing; the men would have hated that. He was himself."

Around the time he moved his office to WIDEWING, Eisenhower settled in Telegraph Cottage again. It, too, was unpretentious, badly heated, damp. But he was happier there than anyplace else during the entire war. Snyder was a masterful scrounger, and there were almost always fresh eggs, cream, fresh fruit, and white flour for the bread. Obtaining such delicacies was not easy, but, Snyder said, "I managed—or else I wouldn't be telling about it now." There were endless games of bridge at the cottage, and it was difficult to find enough Westerns to keep the supreme allied commander occupied.

More than a million and a half Americans arrived in England from the end of June 1943 to the launching of OVERLORD. Between February 1 and June 1 Eisenhower inspected twenty-six divisions that were training for or merely waiting for the invasion. He visited twenty-four airfields, warships, depots, shops, and other military installations. He talked with the men, according to Kay, "never, to my continual astonishment, . . . repeating himself. Waiting for the next inspection, we played bridge." During his inspections, Eisenhower usually asked about the food; the subject always interested him, as befits a good cook. He asked about equipment. He asked where you were from. And, always, he asked if anybody was from Abilene. From Kansas. Were there any farmers? What are you planning to do after the war?

Eisenhower was not at his best when handling humor; his was Rotary Club stuff, material suitable for mixed company—he hated dirty jokes—at the officer's club on a Friday night. One story that served Eisenhower well on inspection trips, both with British and American soldiers, concerned two privates who had just seen a general go by in a big car. The first private said, "Boy, that's one job I'd like in the Army." The second said, "There're disadvantages. For one thing, you'd never be able to look forward to a promotion."

He was never unaware that many of these young men would be killed or wounded. As he wrote Mamie in April, "It is a terribly sad business to total up the casualties each day—even in an air war—and to realize how many youngsters are gone forever. A man must develop a veneer of callousness that lets him consider such things dispassionately; but he can never escape a recognition of the fact that back home the news brings anguish and suffering to families all over the country. . . . War demands real toughness of fiber—not only in the soldiers that don the uniforms but in the homes that must sacrifice their best."

It was by no means necessary for Eisenhower personally to inspect the troops under his command, but he said, "Soldiers like to see the men who are directing operations; they . . . invariably interpret a visit, even a brief one, as evidence of the commander's concern for them. . . . It pays a big dividend in terms of morale, and morale, given rough equality in other things, is supreme on the battlefield."

As had been true during his previous stay in England, Eisenhower concerned himself greatly with relations between the British and his American soldiers. British soldiers were still underpaid, undersexed and under Eisenhower; the Americans still overpaid, oversexed, and over here. On January 23 a Mr. Maxwell Taylor of Hertfordshire wrote the supreme commander saying that he understood "the matter of Anglo-American understanding" was important to the general and he wished to report something he had seen that morning. An American officer got on a bus and seated himself. He was smoking a cigar, and when "a rather fussy and perhaps ridiculous Englishman" told him that he should go to the top of the bus, that smoking inside was prohibited, the American said, "Don't be so typically English; you ought to be in an institution." Taylor said that an argument followed, and he added, "I do feel that your compatriots, especially senior officers, are doing their country an ill-service by such tactlessness."

Eisenhower replied immediately:

Dear Mr. Taylor:

I truly thank you for the trouble you took in reporting to me the incident related in your letter. My only regret is that I do not have the name of the offending American officer; if I did, I assure you that he would never again be guilty, in this Theater, of such a breach of good manners and of such direct assault upon the good relations that must obtain between our two countries.

You are completely right in assuming that the matter of maintaining a firm Anglo-American partnership for the purpose of winning this war is close to my heart. There is no single thing that I believe more important to both of our countries, and I request merely that if ever again you are witness to such an incident you will make such effort as you can to identify the offending individual.

The day he replied to Taylor, Ike sent a memorandum to his deputy theater commander, J. C. H. Lee, "I am particularly anxious that all communications and projects dealing with injuries by American forces to British civilians, and all related subjects be communicated promptly to the American ambassador. . . . I know that this is probably your custom already, but I assured the Ambassador that I would personally tell you of my deep interest in the subject."

Actually, relations between the Americans and the British were better than ever in early 1944, perhaps because of the cross-Channel journey the soldiers of both nations were so soon to make. An artillery captain in Bradley's army group said, "I've never seen a people gripped by such a sense of euphoria as the English that year. . . . Life had been simplified by the common knowledge that in this fateful hour only two possibilities remained—life or death."

Nothing was left to chance. Officers would send their trunks to storage; every soldier would have both a D and a K ration; every truck would have a full gas tank and enough extra gas for a 150-mile trip. The principal American landings would be made on two beaches, one near St.-Laurent-sur-Mer on the northern coast of Calvados, another near St.-Martin-de-Varreville on the southern part of the east coast of the Cotentin Peninsula; the British and Canadians would invade north of Caen. The night before, two U.S. airborne divisions would drop around Ste. Mère-Eglise and a division of British airborne would land east of the Caen Canal.

Beetle said, "Except for the single worry of the weather, we were never concerned about our ability to penetrate the Atlantic Wall. . . . The hazardous expedition would depend on four factors of weather." First, there had to be a low tide so that beach obstacles could be seen and destroyed. Second, the low tide had to be late enough in the morning so that there could be an hour of saturation bombing of the German beach defenses before the Allied landings were made. On the other hand, the landings had to be early enough for there to be a second low tide before it got dark. That was so the second wave of landings could be made.

For the airborne landings that were to take place at 0200 on D-Day, a full moon that rose late was necessary so that pilots of the planes carrying the troops could get to the drop zones in darkness but have enough light to see them. Finally, the often choppy English Channel had to be calm enough so that the more than 5,000 ships and hundreds of smaller craft could be controlled and not run into each other, and to prevent the assaulting forces from being too seasick to get off the ships.

"Finally," said Beetle, "we hoped for a fair wind blowing inshore to drive the smoke and dust of battle toward the enemy." Realistically, he added, "It was foolhardy to imagine that all the conditions would be perfect."

Eisenhower's meteorologists told him that the best day for the landings would be June 5. Of course they could not make any real predictions about the wind, the sea, and the storms on that day. "Those were in the hands of fate," said Beetle. Nevertheless, on May 17 Eisenhower decided, at least tentatively, that D-Day would be June 5.

The final meeting of the Allied planners was on May 15, at St. Paul's School. It was a chilly day in London, the distinguished participants wore their overcoats the entire day. The lecture room was dark, and while the king, Churchill, Field Marshal Smuts, and the British Chiefs of Staff sat in their chairs, the other brass sat on wooden benches behind them. No one seems to know why Montgomery chose to make St. Paul's his headquarters, but we do know that he attended school there from 1902 to 1906, that he had an undistinguished record, that he had never been summoned to the headmaster's office—he was an obedient boy—and that he took some pleasure in the fact that that office was now his office.

Immediately after the meeting Leigh-Mallory dictated an account of the meeting: "The audience looked down from their crescent-shaped auditorium upon a vast coloured map, on a scale of about six inches to a mile of . . . that portion of the north coast of France in which the Allied invasion is shortly to be launched.

It was a curious experience to see so great and vital a secret, written so large and revealed to so large a company. With the help of this great map and with charts and maps hung upon the walls the exposition of OVERLORD plans went forward."

The meeting began at 9:00, and at that hour Montgomery posted two American MPs at the locked doors of the room. They were large men, wearing white helmets and white holsters for their guns. One observer thought they looked "absolutely terrifying." Shortly before the meeting began, there was a great pounding at the doors; Montgomery looked angry, but the pounding continued, and finally Monty ordered the doors opened. Patton walked in, predictably late, an entrance appropriate for a star. Then Eisenhower rose and undramatically opened the meeting. He said, as Leigh-Mallory remembered it, "Here we are . . . on the eve of a great battle to deliver to you the various plans made by the different Force Commanders. I would emphasize but one thing, that I consider it to be the duty to anyone who sees a flaw in the plan not to hesitate to say so. I have no sympathy with anyone, whatever his station, who will not brook criticism. We are here to get the best possible results and you must make a really cooperative effort."

Montgomery spoke next. He was, as Leigh-Mallory recalled, wearing "a very well-cut battle dress with a knife-like edge to the trouser-creases. He looked trim and business-like. He spoke in a tone of quiet emphasis making use of what is evidently a verbal trick of his, to repeat the most important word or phrase in a sentence more than once." General Ismay, who was present, thought Monty must have been reading the speech Shakespeare has Henry V deliver before the battle of Agincourt,

He that hath no stomach for this fight,
Let him depart.

"Montgomery was quite first-class," said Ismay. "His general line was: 'We have a sufficiency of troops; we have all the necessary tackle; we have an excellent plan. This is a perfectly normal operation, which is certain of success. If anyone has any doubts in his mind, let him stay behind.' " He also said, among other things, that he would take Caen on the very first day of the invasion, but that is not what happened, and long after the invasion, every GI in Europe was asking, "When is old Monty going to get off his can and start fighting?" Monty ended his speech by saying that the success of OVERLORD would depend on the people at St. Paul's that day. He said: "We shall have to send soldiers to this party 'seeing red.' We must get them completely on their toes; having absolute faith in the plan; and imbued with infectious optimism and offensive eagerness. Nothing must stop them. If we send them into battle this way—then we shall succeed."

Field Marshal Jan Christian Smuts also spoke. The old prime minister of South Africa—he was seventy-four at the time—seemed to be everywhere Churchill was that spring. Kay called him "the inevitable Smuts."

Churchill was his usual eloquent self, gripping the lapels of what Leigh-Mallory called "a black, short overcoat, looking something like a frockcoat."

The prime minister said, "I am hardening on this enterprise. I repeat I am now hardening on this enterprise."

Eisenhower took those words to mean that the prime minister had in the past had doubts about OVERLORD and said as much in *Crusade*. In *Closing the Ring*, Churchill said that Eisenhower had "taken this to mean that in the past I had been against the cross-Channel operation, but this is not correct. If the reader will look back . . . he will see that I wrote . . . to General Marshall on March 11 . . . 'I am satisfied that everything is going on well. Ike and Bedell will probably tell you they are well pleased. I am hardening very much on this operation as the time approaches, *in the sense of wishing to strike if humanly possible, even if the limiting conditions we laid down at Moscow are not exactly fulfilled.'* "

Brooke never hardened on OVERLORD, and for that reason alone it is perhaps just as well that he did not get the command he so much wanted. The man who did get it expressed no grave doubts about the operation, publicly or privately. Ike later said that he was as close to being a one hundred percent optimist as a man could be, and he was right. He told a reporter, speaking of Anzio, "I was not there then, but the Allies do not attack to be thrown back. I never considered failure because I do not ever let my mind think upon it that way."

At the May 15 meeting, Eisenhower assured the king that victory was certain. He said that OVERLOARD would have "the greatest armada of transports, landing craft, and warships the world has ever seen." In addition there would be 11,000 Allied planes in the sky. Later he remembered that even Churchill "got caught up in the atmosphere of confidence and conviction. The smell of victory was in the air." The supreme allied commander closed the meeting at 4:30. He said, "In half an hour Hitler will have missed his one and only chance of destroying with a single well-aimed bomb the entire high command of the Allied Forces."

Eisenhower was always security-conscious, some people thought too much so. There were signs everywhere in England, "Careless Talk Costs Lives" and "Like Dad, Keep Mum." In a February memorandum on the subject of security Eisenhower had said, "Although it will be impossible to prevent the enemy from becoming aware of the preparations which are being made for the liberation of the Continent, the success or failure of coming operations depends upon whether the enemy can obtain advance information of an accurate nature. It is only by the most stringent observance on the part of each individual that the enemy may be prevented from obtaining this vital information."

Yet the breaches in security were terrifying. On May 18, three days after the meeting at St. Paul's, a German radio broadcast said that the Allied invasion would be "any day now." That was neither surprising nor frightening. The Germans had to be aware of the buildup of troops in southern England. And they had to know that the landing would be as early in the summer as possible.

There were twelve copies of the basic OVERLORD order in the British War Office. No information of the war was more secret or more important. The twelve copies appear not to have been secured in a guarded safe or even by a paperweight, because a sudden gust of wind blew all twelve copies out the open window. They fell among a crowd of pedestrians in the street below. Within minutes everybody in the War Office was on the street searching for the twelve precious sheets of paper. Eleven were found, but the twelfth was not. One copy was all the Germans needed to know everything about the Allied plan for the invasion. Two tense hours passed, in an incident Alfred Hitchcock would have appreciated, before a stranger handed the twelfth copy of the order to a British sentry outside the War Office. The sentry did not ask the man's name. He was never identified.

The month before, a West Point classmate of Eisenhower's, Major General Henry J. Miller, who was chief supply officer of the Ninth Air Force, raised yet another glass at a cocktail party at Claridge's Hotel and said that he would swear the invasion would take place before the middle of June. When challenged, he offered to take bets on the date. Eisenhower heard about the matter, and despite their close and old friendship, he reduced the general to his permanent rank, and Colonel Miller was returned to the States. So was a naval officer, who was also drunk and dangerously indiscreet at a cocktail party. Eisenhower wrote Marshall, "I could cheerfully shoot the offender myself."

In a letter to Miller, Eisenhower said, "I know of nothing that causes me more real distress than to be faced with the necessity of sitting as a judge in cases involving military offenses by officers of character and good record, particularly when they are old and warm friends."

Another incident involved an American soldier—he happened to be of German descent—who mistakenly sent a package with important secret papers to his sister in Chicago instead of to the proper address in the War Department. The whole matter on investigation appeared to be no more than an honest mistake, but it still worried Eisenhower.

An episode that could have proved fatal to OVERLORD occurred on June 4. On that day, after many of the ships taking part in the invasion were in the Channel, a woman working in the Associated Press office in London "practiced" on a tape with the sentence, "Eisenhower's forces are landing in France." The "practice" sentence was soon transmitted all over the world, including Moscow and Berlin. The message was canceled in twenty-three minutes, but the episode did not improve Eisenhower's temper. Butcher said, "Ike looks tired and worn. The strain is telling on him. He looks older now than at any time since I have been with him." It is not surprising that Eisenhower was smoking six packs of cigarettes a day, lighting one with the butt of another.

One of the lesser but nevertheless troublesome problems he had worrying him was Mamie, her dissatisfactions, her complaints, the rumors that circulated about him and about her, magnifying the strains of separation.

Throughout the war, rumors about Mamie's "drinking problem" were almost as widespread as those about Eisenhower and Kay Summersby. Henry Jamieson said, "It was an old, old story, one that happened many times during the war. It was tied to a whirl in which the wives of many officers who were overseas started to drink too much. For a year or even two, Mamie was part of that whirl, worrying too much, drinking a little too much. . . .

"It reached a point where members of the family became concerned about her, afraid that she might be approaching an alcohol problem. I must emphasize that it had not reached that point. Still, one close family member talked seriously to her and Mamie quickly understood what was happening and where she would be drifting. She stopped at once. And after that, she took only a single drink at any gathering."

The rumors continued, however, and it was known that she had a formidable drinking companion in Ruth Butcher, but then war "widows" did drink heavily, and not only in Washington. One particular vicious rumor had it that Mamie had been so drunk that for a long period she had to crawl around the Wardman Park apartment on her hands and knees. Merriman Smith, the White House correspondent for UPI, said that this rumor came about due to Mamie's inner-ear problem. He said, "She sometimes found it necessary to touch somebody to get a point of reference or cross a room."

She suffered from labyrinthitis, an inner-ear infection that causes dizziness, nausea, and visual disturbances. Many people preferred to think, however, that she was drunk when she held on to someone when climbing stairs or in a crowd.

Mamie was very much aware of her position and did her best to keep her decorum in public. After her husband's death she told Julie Nixon Eisenhower, "I respected him [Ike] so much I didn't want to do anything to disappoint him. Julie added, "Her face was uncharacteristically sad, as if she were looking back on the times when she had disappointed him."

During the war, when driving for pleasure was frowned upon and gasoline rationed, Mamie tried not to take taxis. According to a mutual friend in Washington, she was afraid that if she did "she may be used as a horrible example and thereby 'bring disgrace upon Ike'—so she walks most places."

She made little attempt, however, to understand the pressures on him, and her letters to him were seldom cheerful or encouraging. She complained, and she announced her suspicions, and repeated the gossip she had heard. Ike, on the other hand, tried to understand the problems she was facing, sometimes with success. For example, in March 1943, at a time when it looked as if he might be sent home in disgrace from North Africa, he sent his old roommate from West Point, P.A., a most perceptive and sympathetic letter concerning Mamie, in which he said:

> Mamie has undergone a real strain in the last two years. Not only did she move all her household effects with annoying frequency, but she also had both John and me leave her in quick succession and, on top of that, came all this rush of publicity that has worried her a lot. I must say that one of the nicest things about her, is her own natural dignity and good taste— many a woman would have either through ignorance or lack of tact made a holy show of herself in the same circumstances. From all sides I hear that Mamie's handling of herself has not only been admirable but has won the universal approval of everyone in the Army who knows anything about such things. I can not tell you how proud I am of her.

The press was far less sympathetic, and the fact that she had returned to San Antonio had not gone unnoticed. An article in the *Washington Daily News* that was picked up by the United Press on March 1 said that she had left Washington because "people pursued her as the wife of the invasion commanding general."

The story mentioned that she had been living in Washington "at a hotel with her friend, Mrs. Harry Butcher, wife of General Eisenhower's naval aide." The publicity cannot have pleased Eisenhower, and he had even more to unsettle him when she returned. She had heard more gossip about him and Kay, and she wrote him about it. In his reply on May 12, he said:

> This morning I received the first letter you wrote to me after returning to Washington. It was most welcome and interesting, although you finished with a dark "such tales as I've heard since returning to Washington." I know that people at home always think of an army in the field as living a life of night clubs, gaiety and loose morals. So far as I can see (and admittedly my chances of seeing such things is limited) the American forces here are living cleaner and more nearly normal lives than they did in Louisiana—California—etc. when we were in large encampments. 99% of officers and men are too busy to have any time for anything else. In the larger cities such as London, there are undoubtedly numbers of officers and men that are living loosely, but it is also true the picture painted by gossips are grossly exaggerated. So far as the group around me is concerned, I know that the principal concern is work—and their habits are above reproach.

On May 21 he wrote his wife still another unhappy letter. Mother's Day had been on the 14th, and he had forgotten it. On May 14 he had returned to London from an extensive and tiring inspection of Canadian and British troops and had no doubt given some thought to the meeting the next day at St. Paul's. No matter that in less than three weeks he would undertake, as the *New York Times* later said, "to deliver 300,000,000 people in western Europe from Nazi bondage." No matter that the British do not celebrate Mother's Day and thus Eisenhower was not reminded of it by ads and editorials in the newspapers. Mamie was annoyed. He had forgotten a sacred day, and she expressed her displeasure to her husband. In replying, he said:

> I am truly sorry that Mother's Day came along without my ever knowing it. My impression was that it was a June Sunday, and since I never hear the day mentioned over here, I was just stupid about it. . . . But anyway you shouldn't hold me guilty of negligence merely because I may be forgetful. God knows I am busy; and I do try to write you often.
> Please don't get annoyed with me. I depend on you and your letters so much, and I'm living only to come back when this terrible thing is over. So if any omission of mine gets you irritated, please remember that after all, you're mine, and all I have—and I'm yours, always.
>
> *Loads of love,*
> *Ike*

During this difficult period of planning and writing, an unidentified officer in Eisenhower's command told a reporter for the *New York Times*, "His job makes a Roman proconsul look like a Mayor of Sandusky by comparison." Butcher did his best to dream up new ways to get the supreme commander to relax. He set up a badminton court on the lawn at Telegraph Cottage, but Eisenhower seldom used it; he did occasionally go horseback riding, often with Kay.

That spring he seemed to be particularly observant of the beauties of nature. John said that it was "as if his senses were sharpened by what was soon to come. Rarely in his writings did he go into such detailed description" as in his letters to Mamie on the 24th and 30th of May. On the 24th he wrote:

> Last eve at 5:30 I seized a chance to ride a friend's horse in one of the big parks (something like Rock Creek Park). I should like to be able to describe to you the flowers, birds, deer and shrubbery. Even more I should like to give you some idea of the antics of the hordes of rabbits—little bunnies ranging in size from that of a mouse, on up to full grown mammas. I was all alone—(my friend sometimes rides with me. He is Sir Louis Greig, in charge of the Park)—so I could go exactly where I pleased. Pheasants, partridge, wild duck, crows—in one instance being pursued by two king birds—brilliant red trees that I'm told are hawthornes [*sic*] sometimes the flowers are white whole massed banks of rhododendrons?? and lovely blue fields that look like blue bonnets to me. I kept wishing you could be with me to see it. I know you'd have loved it.

On May 29 Leigh-Mallory once again said that if the parachute operation was carried out, disaster would result. He told the supreme commander that "at the most 30 per cent of the glider loads will become effective for use against the enemy" and said the operation probably would "yield results so far short of what the Army C.-in-C. expects that, if the success of the seaborne assault in this area depends on the airborne, it will be seriously prejudiced."

That was certainly nothing Eisenhower wanted to hear, but he replied on the 30th; he was later to say that the decision to drop the airborne troops against such opposition was the most difficult of his life. He said:

> Thank you very much for your letter of the 29th on the subject of airborne operations. You are quite right in communicating to me your convictions as to the hazards involved and I must say I agree with you as to the character of these risks. However, a strong airborne attack in the region indicated is essential to the whole operation. Consequently, there is nothing for it but for you, the Army Commander and Troop Carrier Commander to work out to the last detail every single thing that may diminish these hazards.
>
> It is particularly important that air and ground troops involved in the operation be not needlessly depressed. Like all the rest of the soldiers, they must understand that they have a tough job to do but be fired with determination to get it done.
>
> I am, of course, hopeful that our percentage losses will not approximate your estimates because it is quite true that I expect to need these forces very badly later in the campaign.

That was the kind of encouragement, the sort of Dutch-uncle talk that a company commander might have to give to a nervous second lieutenant about to embark on his first combat mission, not a message from a supreme commander to the man who commanded the Allied Expeditionary Air Force. Still, if he didn't do it, who would? Mark Clark said, "He [Ike] once told me, 'You can delegate a lot of small authority but big authority, never. The most important things, which are usually things you'd just as soon not handle, you have to handle.' "

In the letter he wrote her that day, he did not share his misgivings with Mamie. He said:

Whenever I have a chance to write you these days I find myself wondering what you'd like to hear that I can talk about. Naturally, I don't keep accurately informed as to the details of censorship regulations, so I have the uneasy feeling that there is almost nothing I can say.

I've been so busy I don't even play a rubber of bridge any more—in fact, I seem to live on a network of high tension wires. . . .

This country, at this time, is a mass of rhododendrons(?). I'm sure I've never seen them so common elsewhere. Another flower that is everywhere is one they call Azalia [sic]. Lilacs, too, are prolific.

I've travelled over much of the country, but my trips are so hurried that I have no real idea of the geography. When this d—— war is over we'll have to come here and hire a little Austin to tour the place. I think we'd like it.

Eisenhower also tried sketching during that period. His first attempt was a large pine tree that could be seen from the window of his office at WIDEWING. He received materials for the sketch and a few rudimentary instructions from a Red Cross woman, but the attempt was a failure. He wrote "baloney" on the unfinished drawing and discarded it. Butcher wrote, "Ike's desire to sketch is, to me, just another example of his boredom and impatience with the planning period."

Minor health problems plagued him. He had a sore left eye from too much strain and had had a ringing in his ear for a month. There were compensations, however. On the 26th of May he had lunch at Buckingham Palace. He was the only guest, and he told Butcher that the king and queen were "nice people to be with. Even if they weren't King and Queen you would enjoy being with them. The Queen . . . is more talkative than the King. . . . Ike . . . might have been embarrassed when the King mentioned to him that he had dropped his napkin to the floor, but he wasn't. . . . Service was somewhat cafeteria style— each getting up and delving in the modest array of food on a side table. So far as Ike was concerned, the friendliness and companionship of the threesome was reminiscent of any . . . friends in Tacoma, San Antonio, Washington, or Abilene."

Brigadier Kenneth Strong, Ike's unpretentious and reliable G-2 officer, arrived in late May from Algiers, and his presence at Eisenhower's side always made him feel more confident. Strong was another British officer Monty considered a "deserter" for openly confessing to liking Americans.

Eisenhower insisted that written intelligence reports be short, preferably no more than a single page in length. That was also true when he was president, causing a great many people to conclude that his powers of concentration were limited. But both as supreme commander and as president he preferred oral reports. Strong said, "Eisenhower had an immense talent for listening to oral explanations and distilling their contents. . . . this gave him an opportunity to question uncertainties and to probe below the surface of the apparent points at issue. I found that a visit to him was worth a pile of memoranda, especially as he was so often looking far ahead of current events. He never insisted on seeing the raw Intelligence on which judgments were based, as I am told that Churchill always did."

There was no way of keeping from the Germans the fact that a great military buildup was going on in England and that it would lead to an invasion of France. But when? And where? On the latter, the German high command was in disagreement. Field Marshal von Rundstedt, the top commander in the West, thought that the invasion would be at the narrowest, most obvious place, the Strait of Dover. Rommel, in command of Army Group B in northern France, did not presume to know where the invasion would be; so he began fortifying all the beaches. He had concluded that the crucial period for the Germans would be the first forty-eight hours of the invasion. Hitler, like von Rundstedt, was sure that the main invasion would be across the Dover straits, but that a small feint would be made in Normandy. All three Germans were sure that at some point major attack would be made in the Pas-de-Calais area, at least north of the Somme. They kept the entire 15th Army there even after the invasion.

Eisenhower said in *Crusade*, "The defenses [in the Calais area] were so strong that none of us believed that a successful assault from the sea could be made except at such terrific cost that the whole expedition might find itself helpless to accomplish anything of a positive character, after it got ashore. But we counted upon the enemy believing that we would be tempted into this operation, and the wide variety of measures we took for convincing him were given extraordinary credence by his Intelligence division."

Eisenhower learned about the elaborate plans to deceive the Germans shortly after his arrival in England. He was told by Brigadier Stewart Menzies, head of MI-6 of the British intelligence service, that while his presence in London would not be known to the British and American press for some days, the Germans had known almost immediately that he was there. Menzies personally had given this information to a German spy whose code name was TATE.

Menzies said that TATE had landed in England by parachute in September 1940, been picked up by the English, had broken under intense interrogation, and had agreed to become a double agent. There were twenty such double agents in England, Menzies said, their activities carefully supervised by the British, and the Germans on the continent trusted all of them. They were thus very valuable to the Allied cause.

Naturally, most of the information these double agents sent back was false, but for the Germans to continue to trust people like TATE it was necessary from time to time to allow them to send true and verifiable information, usually things that the Germans would sooner or later learn anyway. Ike's arrival in England was such a matter, and the same was true of Patton. The Germans knew all about him and had great respect for his fighting ability. Thus, it was he who was to head the fictitious First U.S. Army Group (FUSAG); the Germans were led to believe that Patton's FUSAG would make the Pas-de-Calais landing. The whole plan of deception had the code name FORTITUDE. A bogus oil dock was built at Dover, directly across the Channel from Calais. It looked fairly authentic when viewed from a distance; it had, after all, been built under the direction and with the work of some of the best technicians in the British film industry. Patton's FUSAG command was made up of the real U.S. Third Army and Canadian First Army, which were scheduled to land in Normandy in the second week of June, but the Germans were led to believe that it would take part in the main invasion across the Pas-de-Calais that would follow a feint in Cherbourg. Eisenhower said, "Both deceptions succeeded admirably."

There was also a totally nonexistent British Fourth Army supposedly being built up in Scotland. Its headquarters were in the basement of Edinburgh Castle, and it consisted of twenty-eight overage officers and 334 enlisted men, most of them radio operators, who were real enough. They sent fictitious messages between units that were also fictional, simulating the radio traffic that might attend a massive buildup; imaginary football games were played by these imaginary units and duly reported in the real Scottish press. Some Allied troops did not keep mum; they talked and talked in various Scottish pubs and revealed "secrets" to any German agents who happened to be in the same pubs at the same time. Norwegian-English dictionaries started turning up in unexpected places, and so did topographical maps of Norway. The object was to pin down the twenty-seven German divisions in Scandinavia by threatening an Allied invasion. Through ULTRA interceptions, the supreme commander learned that the Scottish operation had also succeeded. The twenty-seven divisions would not be transferred south, where they would later be desperately needed. Altogether the Americans learned a lot since late 1942 when Eisenhower first arrived in Washington, and "the chief of the [intelligence] division could do little more than come to the planning and operating sections of the staff and in a rather painful way ask if there was anything he could do for us." The supreme commander had learned a lot, too.

The deceptions were a great success, and the supreme commander, generally considered a plodding, unimaginative man, was responsible. It was he who had taken the chance.

Major General J. Lawton "Lightning Joe" Collins, who commanded VII Corps, many years later said of that spring in the south of England, "It took an act of faith to believe that the Germans didn't know exactly what was going on in the south of England in the weeks just before the invasion. There wasn't a port from Portsmouth to Plymouth that wasn't overflowing with landing craft of one kind or another; every road was jammed with equipment and troops, and some roads were widened to take care of the heavier vehicles. A few bombs could have wiped out most of the invasion army. I guess it was a combination of God, the success of the Allied air forces in wiping out most of the German air forces, and luck. Luck definitely played a part in it." A quarter of a million Allied troops were assembled in the rural areas of southern England for more than a week, and, Collins said, "there was not a leak, intentional or accidental, in the newspaper press or through private channels of operations in England. In addition, the people living in the vicinity . . . were not permitted to enter or leave the area. But . . . the people of Devon accepted the restrictions on freedom of movement and communications and kept their mouths shut, while the British press cooperated fully. I wonder if it could happen again—certainly not in America."

On June 1 Ike sent two messages to Marshall, the first said:

Personal from General Eisenhower to General Marshall eyes only. BIGOT [This was the code name for documents containing information about the assault phase of OVERLORD.]: Weather forecasts while still indefinite are generally favorable. I will keep you informed on this point. Everyone is in good heart and barring unsuitable conditions we will do the trick as scheduled.

The second message to the chief of staff had to do with Marshall's stepson, of whom he was very fond, Lieutenant Allen Tupper Brown, who had been fighting in Anzio. It said:

Personal for General Marshall signed Eisenhower SHSAC [Supreme Headquarters Supreme Allied Command]: I have just learned that your stepson has been lost in battle. To you and Mrs. Marshall I send sincere and understanding sympathy. May the merciful God help you to bear this added burden.

By the morning of June 2 Ike had moved his headquarters from WIDEWING to the advance command post from which he was to launch the invasion. His new headquarters were about a mile from the British Naval War College, at Southwick House near Portsmouth. Southwick House was comfortable, but Eisenhower's headquarters office was not. It was in an army 2½ ton truck. He called it "my circus wagon." There was a tiny study, in one corner of which Kay had a desk, an even smaller living room, a galley, an observation deck enclosed in glass, a chemical toilet, a shower behind a screen, and a washbasin with hot running water. In the bedroom there was a bunk covered with a blue and white tablecloth. Beside the bed were the Westerns, and in the bedroom were pictures of Mamie and of John in his cadet's uniform. Visitors usually sat on the bed to talk. The three telephones were for "scrambled" calls to Washington, to No. 10 Downing Street, and to Beetle and other Allied leaders back at WIDEWING.

The atmosphere outside was not cheerful. Kay found the woods surrounding the trailer a place where "sunshine was exiled, where rain soaked our entire canvas headquarters days on end, giving everything a damp, musty odor; it was a long jump from London or Algiers. The Prime Minister and Field Marshal Smuts were headquartered on a special train parked at Southampton."

While he was at Portsmouth, Eisenhower, always an early riser, would be the first to arrive at the officers' mess in Southwick House. When Marty Snyder got there at 6:30 in the morning, Ike would be alone in the kitchen, "frying eggs or mixing pancake batter. This was relaxation for him, but I knew he was the kind of man who was busy concentrating on his own problems even when he appeared idle, so after exchanging greetings, I would let him alone."

On June 2 Eisenhower had a meeting at Southwick House with his invasion staff. He had dinner with Montgomery at Monty's headquarters, "after which," according to Monty, "we went up to Southwick House for a conference with the Meteorological experts on the weather. The weather looked reasonable, but the experts were worried about a depression over Iceland. It was decided to lay on the operation for the 5th June, without any change, with another Meteorological conference at 9:30 P.M. on the 3rd June."

On the morning of the 3rd, Eisenhower returned to WIDEWING for both morning and afternoon appointments with, among others, J. C. H. Lee, Spaatz, and Tedder. He returned to his advance command post that afternoon and had dinner with Smuts, Ernest Bevin, then minister of labor and national service, and Churchill.

Eisenhower's disagreements with the prime minister had been frequent during the months of preparation for OVERLORD. The climax, however, came that evening. According to Kay, the prime minister had arrived "in a stew because the King, Ike, and all the military-political advisers absolutely refused to let him ride on an invasion ship. He played grumpily with a cat at mess, feeding it milk from a saucer on the table."

"Churchill told me he was coming along with the invasion, and I told him he couldn't do it," said Eisenhower. "I was commander in chief of this operation and I wasn't going to risk him because he was worth too much to the Allied cause. He thought a moment, and then he said, 'General, do you have operational command of all of these forces?' I said, 'Yes. That's right.' He said, 'But you are not responsible administratively for the make-up of the crews.' I said, 'No, that's right.' He said, 'Well, then, I can sign on as a member of the crew of one of His Majesty's ships and there's nothing you can do.' I said, 'That's correct, but, Winston you will make my burden a lot heavier by doing it.' We left it at that. . . . Luckily the king learned of his intention and sent word that as long as the prime minister felt it desirable to go along on the operation, the king thought it would be his duty to go along, too. . . . The prime minister didn't want the responsibility for the king going, so he didn't go either. That's the way it was done.

"Churchill was a staunch little fighter; that's all."

The prime minister did not forget the matter, however; in *Closing the Ring* he took the trouble to point out that the cruiser squadron with which he had proposed to journey across the Channel "was, as I had justly estimated, not exposed to any undue danger. In fact, it did not sustain a single casualty."

The weather report on the evening of June 3 did little to cheer Eisenhower. The depression over Iceland was moving south, and the high-pressure system approaching the Channel from the Azores was being pushed back. According to Monty, "This meant that the prospect of a good belt of high pressure over the Channel area on the night 5th June and on the 6th June, was receding. . . . This was awkward."

At 4:00 the next morning the weather was pleasant. There was little wind, and the stars were visible, but the weather report, Eisenhower later remembered, "was the worst ever. They talked about gales hitting the Normandy beaches and winds up to 45 miles an hour. It meant landing would be impossible."

Still, Eisenhower went around the room to find out what his associates thought; Admiral Ramsay would not commit himself. Tedder was for postponement, and, although he chose to forget it in his memoirs, Montgomery was for going without delay. Eisenhower decided on a delay of at least twenty-four hours. It was that decision, the decision to postpone, that Eisenhower later remembered as his most difficult. On June 4, 1952, when he was in Abilene for the laying of the foundation of the Eisenhower Museum he said, "This day, eight years ago, I made the most agonizing decision of my life.

"I had to decide to postpone by at least twenty-four hours the most formidable array of fighting ships, and of fighting men, that was ever launched across the sea against a hostile shore. The consequences of that decision at that moment could not have been foreseen by anyone. If there were nothing else in my life to prove the existence of an almighty and merciful God, the events of the next twenty-four hours did it. I believe that that decision at the moment could possibly have cost us additional thousands in lives. The greatest break in a terrible outlay of weather occurred the next day and allowed that great invasion to proceed, with losses far below those we had anticipated. And one of the great factors in the low loss of life was the fact that the weather was so bad the surprise was practically complete."

The day that followed that early morning decision was not an easy one. Ike had a series of meetings at Southwick House, with Churchill, Smuts, with the Commanders in Chief, and with de Gaulle. Foreign Minister Anthony Eden brought the French general to Churchill's train in Southampton where the two men had a short, unhappy exchange, largely having to do with Roosevelt and his inhospitable attitude toward de Gaulle. A short time later the prime minister escorted the Frenchman to Ike's "circus wagon." He was, the prime minister said, "most ceremoniously received. Ike and Bedell Smith vied with one another in their courtesy. Presently Ike took him to the map tent and in twenty minutes imparted to him the whole story of what was about to happen."

Also, before de Gaulle left, Eisenhower showed him a copy of a proclamation he proposed to make to the people of occupied Europe, the French in particular. Eisenhower's words had already been recorded, and he wanted the general to record a message to be broadcast following his own. De Gaulle refused. Eisenhower's message, he said, made no mention of him or of his provisional government. In fact, he said, it appeared to him that the British and Americans were planning to run France all by themselves, and if he spoke to his people after Eisenhower, it might seem that he was endorsing those plans, and that he had no intention of doing. Then he stalked out of the command post into the rain, which got more intense every minute.

De Gaulle went back to the Connaught Hotel in London and drew up his suggestions for Eisenhower's message. He sent it to the supreme allied commander on the morning of the 5th. But, he later wrote, "As I expected, I was told it was too late, for the proclamation had already been printed."

Eisenhower, whose day had begun at 4:00 that morning, had yet another meeting at night. At ten o'clock, his senior commanders, and their chiefs of staff gathered in the library at Southwick House. Beetle was there; so were Tedder, Leigh-Mallory, and Montgomery. Eisenhower was wearing olive drab battle dress.

The head of the SHAEF Meteorologic Committee, RAF Group-Captain J. M. Stagg, spoke first. There had, he said, been a welcome change in the weather. The rain front would clear out about midnight; winds would be more moderate; cloud conditions would be favorable for heavy bombing on the 5th and the 6th, and the cloud base at H-hour on the night of the 6th, just might be high enough to allow spotting for naval gunfire.

That was good news, but it was not *very* good news; in his account of the meeting on cross-Channel invasion, official army historian Gordon A. Harrison, said, "After listening to the forecast, Admiral Ramsay reminded the commanders that there was only half an hour to make the decision, and that if Admiral [Alan G.] Kirk's forces were ordered to sail for a D-day on Tuesday, June 6, and were later recalled they would not be able to sail again for a Wednesday rendezvous, the last day for two weeks on which light and tidal conditions would be suitable for the assault."

Beetle yet again took a realistic point of view; it was possible, he said, that the naval gunfire would not be spotted on Tuesday the 6th, but if the invasion were to be postponed now, it could not be tried again until the 19th. That meant troops would have to be unloaded from their ships with God alone knew what security risks, not to mention what would happen to troop morale during the long, tedious and terrifying wait to reembark. In addition, postponement from the 6th to the 19th meant the loss of thirteen days of fighting weather on the other side of the Channel.

Leigh-Mallory, as usual, worried about what the cloudy weather might do to the air forces; Tedder, the amiable, anxious-to-please deputy commander, thought the bombing would be "chancey." Eisenhower the optimist said, "We have a great force of fighter-bombers." So much for the pessimists. Eisenhower was right; more than 10,000 Allied planes supported the landings. Then he turned to Montgomery, "Do you see any reason why we should not go on Tuesday?" The usually cautious Monty once again said, "I would say—Go!"

"The question is," said Eisenhower, "just how long you can hang this operation on the end of a limb and let it hang there." According to John, his father "then sat by himself, head bowed, hands folded." A little later, at 9:45, Eisenhower said, "I don't like it, but there it is. . . . I don't see how we can do anything else. I am quite positive we must give the order."

There was, of course, still the possibility that the weather would get so much worse that his decision would have to be reversed. The rain seemed more insistent than ever when Eisenhower returned to the trailer.

He undressed almost immediately and got in bed, said a silent prayer, and closed his eyes. It seems unlikely that he went to sleep or missed the sound of a single raindrop on the roof. At 3:30 A.M. he rose, dressed, and had a cup of coffee. The rain had not let up. Indeed, it seemed even more ominous now. Years later, remembering that rain, he said, "Our little camp was shaking and shuddering under a wind of almost hurricane proportions and the accompanying rain seemed to be traveling in horizontal streaks."

When he got to Southwick House, his commanders were already gathered in what had been the library. There were still a few books on the shelves. Coffee was served, and shortly after 4:00, Stagg and his associates arrived. This morning the Scot seemed if not cheerful at least less worried. Strong said that the meteorologist was "a man of 'sharp mind and soft speech,' and his judgment was thoroughly trusted by Eisenhower. To everyone's surprise the Group-Captain reported that a totally unexpected change in the meteorological situation had occurred. A fresh weather front had been located which gave some hope of improvement in conditions during the daylight of June 5 and throughout Tuesday, June 6. It was thought that this improvement would be followed by variable conditions lasting until Thursday, the 8th. . . . Eisenhower, looking considerably more cheerful, proceeded to ask each of his commanders in turn his opinion of the effect of this forecast on his operation."

Leigh-Mallory was still dubious. Tedder advised caution. Montgomery again said to go. Ramsay said that under the circumstances the landing was in fact feasible but, because of the anticipated weather, the troops would not have the full support of naval gunfire. There was silence then; some people later remembered it as being lengthy, as long as four minutes, but that could not have been. The meeting was to disperse at 4:15, and it had not begun until 4:00. Eisenhower thought maybe forty-five seconds elapsed.

Then the man from Kansas said, "O.K., we'll go."

★ ★ ★

PIERCING THE HEART

All that spring the BBC had been broadcasting strange messages before, during, and after its newscasts. They were sent in the clear, and there must have been people on both sides of the Channel who thought that the solemn men who read the news had taken leave of their senses. They would say, "The children are bored on Sundays" or "The crocodile is thirsty" or "The tomatoes should be picked" or "Napoleon's hat, is it still at Perros Guire?" The words were in French, of course, or in French dialects. Those *messages personnels* were for the French underground, alerting its members to attack German troops at various places or to blow up railways or communications facilities. One message was unique, however. It involved two lines from Verlaine's poem, *Chanson d'automne* ["Autumn Song"]. The first was to tell the underground that the long-awaited invasion was not far off. It was broadcast on the night of June 1: "*Les sanglots longs / Des violons / De l'automne*

[The long sobs of the violins of autumn]." The second line was broadcast on the night of June 5, and it meant that the invaders were on their way, *"Blessent mon coeur / D'une langueur / Monotone.* [Pierce my heart with monotonous languor]." The identity of the person in Allied intelligence who chose those lines to announce to the French underground that the greatest invasion in history was imminent is not known, but he had a waggish sense of humor.

On the night of June 5, Oberstleutnant Helmuth Meyer, the intelligence officer of the German Fifteenth Army guarding the Calais sector, heard the line, knew what it meant, and rushed to his commanding officer, Generaloberst Hans von Salmuth. The general was playing bridge and was not much impressed with what Meyer told him. He did, however, put his army on alert. Then he returned to his bridge game.

Field Marshal Rommel could have alerted the entire German Seventh Army, but he was on his way to his home near Ulm on the Danube. Before leaving he had written Admiral Friedrich Oskar Ruge, his naval adviser, "It eases my mind to know that while I'm away the tides will not be suitable for landings. Besides, air reconnaissance gives no reason for thinking they are imminent."

Hitler was in a heavily drugged sleep back in Berlin, and no one dared to wake him. Albert Speer said, "In recent days Hitler had kept saying that the enemy would probably begin with a feigned attack in order to draw our troops away from the ultimate invasion site. So no one wanted to awaken Hitler and be ranted at for having judged the situation wrongly."

Rundstedt, who was having dinner at the time the line from Verlaine was broadcast over the BBC, decided that the message was a false alarm. The Channel was far too choppy for an invasion. Besides, as one of his officers said, "Does anyone think the enemy is stupid enough to announce his arrival over the radio?" No one did.

There were two things concerning OVERLORD about which Ike could do nothing after his early-morning decision of June 5. One was the weather, which turned out to be his greatest asset: It was the kind of weather the Germans almost to a man decided made an invasion landing impossible. The other was German activity, but it turned out there was almost no German activity. He didn't know that on the long day of June 5, of course, and felt helpless. He had given the orders, and others would have to carry them out. What happened next was up to the officers and men on the 4,000 ships headed for Normandy and on the crews and the troops getting aboard the thousands of aircraft that would soon fly across the Channel. Eisenhower read at a Western; he drank a good deal of coffee. He smoked innumerable cigarettes, and he looked at the sky, which was dark and threatening.

Later that morning Kay drove him to the South Parade Pier in Portsmouth, where British troops were being loaded into three LCI(L)'s. He smiled, and some of them smiled back. It was said in England that Eisenhower's smile was worth twenty divisions, but he never said that, and he didn't think it. On his return he played a game of checkers with Butcher. It ended in a draw. At lunch he and Butcher talked about Washington politics, including a story about the spectacularly unpleasant racist senator from Mississippi, Theodore G. Bilbo. After lunch he had a press conference lasting more than an hour. He spoke of what he called "the greatest operation we have ever attempted," and, according to Butcher, "he held them on the edge of their chairs. The nonchalance with which he announced that we were attacking in the morning and the feigned nonchalance with which the reporters absorbed it was a study in suppressed emotion which would interest any psychologist."

The *New York Times* correspondent said that Eisenhower "had had little sleep in the preceding twenty-four hours, but it could never be guessed, watching his stride, fresh and alert, between his office on wheels and his wardroom lined with maps." In his visits with the airborne troops he had displayed "calm confidence." At the press conference the "only sign of the weighty decision on his mind was an occasional tap of his finger for emphasis and the lighting of one cigarette after another."

Beetle called from WIDEWING. De Gaulle was not going to make the broadcast. All right then, said Eisenhower; if de Gaulle didn't come through, he would deal with someone else. It was simply another of what Butcher called "those last-minute things that worry the devil out of the SC." No wonder a member of his staff had said the day before that "no one in the world could carry the political and military problems as well as Ike."

Sometime during the day Eisenhower wrote a note that he later put in his wallet. Eventually, he gave it to Butcher, explaining that he had written such notes before each amphibious operation. He had secretly torn up the others. This one, he thought, might be of some interest. It said:

> Our landings in the Cherbourg-Havre area have failed to gain a satis-
> factory foothold and I have withdrawn the troops. My decision to attack
> at this time and place was based upon the best information available. The
> troops, the air, and the Navy did all that Bravery and devotion to duty
> could do. If any blame or fault attaches to the attempt it is mine alone—
> July 5.

In *Six Armies in Normandy,* John Keegan, senior lecturer in war studies at the Royal Military Academy at Sandhurst, wrote, "These were the words of a great man and a great soldier. The greatness of Eisenhower as a soldier has yet to be portrayed fully." It should perhaps be added that Eisenhower's state of mind can be judged by the fact that this most precise of men dated the note *July 5*.

Several years later, on the twentieth anniversary of D-Day, Ike spoke with Walter Cronkite about the note. "I don't know exactly who found out about it," he said, "but it was published. What I did was this. From the beginning I had been partly responsible for this plan. I had been on the staff, head of the staff that originally outlined this operation way back two years ago. From all those two years I believed in this thing, I believed it would defeat Germany, and consequently I felt not only as a commander but as sort of a fellow who'd been trying to convert everybody to the need of this thing, I felt a particular responsibility. So I wrote a little thing that soundly assumed that we were going to be defeated, but I told no one else about it; and it must have been an aide who got this thing out and told people about it. I just said the landing had been a failure and it's no one's fault but mine. I was the one who picked out—I knew

I couldn't fail except on weather—I was the one that was responsible for the decision to go and all the fault belongs to me, and that's that.

"If it did fail you know this—I was going into oblivion anyway so I might as well take full responsibility."

At 6:00 that evening Eisenhower, Kay, and a small party, including several reporters and two army photographers, took off for Newbury to see the paratroopers of Maxwell Taylor's "Screaming Eagles," the 101st Airborne Division. It was surely on the supreme allied commander's mind that Leigh-Mallory had said that three-quarters of these men would be casualties within hours.

The supreme allied commander arrived unannounced, but, according to Keegan, "His appearance among the waiting sticks [of men], sitting tensed under the wings of their planes in the gathering dusk, created a muted sensation. Corporal Kermit Latta was struck by the 'terrific burden of decision and responsibility' which showed on his face and by the sincerity of his effort to communicate with his young soldiers. He paused to speak to their group, and we can detect in his exchanges something of the deft personal appeal which was to make him the United States' most popular postwar President:

" 'What is your job, soldier?'

" 'Ammunition bearer, sir.'

" 'Where is your home?'

" 'Pennsylvania, sir.'

" 'Did you get those shoulders working in a coal mine?'

" 'Yes, sir.'

" 'Good luck to you tonight, soldier.' "

This exchange demonstrates that Eisenhower not only spoke to soldiers, he saw them as well. That was and is rare for generals. Montgomery, for example, spoke to soldiers with great success, but he did not see them. He allowed them to see him.

The photographs taken by the two army photographers that showed Eisenhower with groups of the Screaming Eagles with their blackened faces were among the most famous of the war, and many years later when discussing them, Eisenhower was asked if it was true that there were tears in his eyes when he turned away from these troops. He said:

I don't know about that. It's possible because it's an operation you started, and you know there are going to be losses. You know there are going to be German troops in the area where they are dropping. You know there will be all sorts of flak, and you would think if a man didn't show a little emotion it would show that he was probably a little inhuman. . . . You just had to make decisions . . . and I wanted to do something that would be to my country's advantage for the least cost. You can't say *without* cost; you know there's going to be a cost.

After all, Leigh-Mallory had said that three-quarters of these men would be casualties; Ike had sent them anyway, hopeful that the Englishman was wrong.

The most famous of the photographs shows Eisenhower with a clenched fist raised. Just before the fortieth anniversary of D-Day, a reporter for the *Wash-*

ington Post tried to identify and find the men of the 101st in that photograph. It was a difficult job. In the story printed in the *Post* on June 6, 1984, the reporter, Daniel St. Albin Greene, wrote, "The only clue Army information office could provide was an old photograph. A caption on the back, in fading purple ink, says the picture shows Eisenhower issuing the order of the day: 'Full victory—Nothing else.' It also lists 11 names of men 'presumed to be in the scene.' . . . It took a lot of digging but four of them were finally found. . . . Each vividly remembers the evening the Allied commander dropped in to see them off. He walked among the troopers and tents at the 101st Airborne camp near Newbury, England, chatting here and there with individuals and groups. Although Eisenhower's clenched fist and expression suggest a more urgent topic, Strobel [one of the four] is sure they were talking about Michigan fishing when the picture was taken. Strobel also remembers Eisenhower's comely British chauffeur, Kay Summersby. 'Many of the soldiers assumed she was Eisenhower's lover.' "

Kay said in her diary that night, "General Taylor was about the last person to get aboard his ship. E. walked with him to the door of the C-47. By this time it was getting quite dark. We returned to the 101st headquarters with several members of his staff, had some coffee, and then proceeded to climb to the roof of the building to watch the aircraft circling over the field, getting into formation. It was one of the most impressive sights that anyone could wish to see, visibility was perfect, all the stars were gleaming. E. stayed for about half an hour."

In *Eisenhower Was My Boss*, she remembered that after the planes had taken off—he had saluted each plane as it passed—"General Eisenhower turned, shoulders sagging, the loneliest man in the world."

"Without a word, he walked slowly toward the car. . . .

" 'Well,' Ike said quietly. 'It's on.'

"He looked up at the sky and added, 'No one can stop it now!' "

They got back to the supreme commander's headquarters at 1:15 A.M. Butcher said, "We sat around in the nickel-plated office caravan in courteous silence, each with his own thoughts and trying to borrow by psychological osmosis those of the Supreme Commander, until I became the first to say to hell with it, and excused myself—to bed."

Twenty years later Eisenhower toured the D-Day beaches of Normandy with Walter Cronkite and a television crew, and he remembered that he had thought of John. He said: "D-Day has a very special meaning for me, and I'm not referring merely to the anxieties of the day that were a natural part of an invasion where you know that hundreds of boys are going to die or be maimed forever.

"My mind goes back to the fact that my son was graduated from West Point on D-Day, and on the very day he was graduating men came here—American, British, our other Allies, and they stormed these beaches, not to gain anything for themselves, not to fulfill any ambitions that America had for conquest but just to preserve freedom, to establish systems of self-government in the world. Many thousands of men died for ideals such as these.

"Now, my own son has been very fortunate. He has had a very full life since then. But these young boys, many of them whose graves we have been looking at, contemplating their sacrifices—they were cut off in their prime. They had families who grieved for them. But they never had the great experience of going through life like my son."

Butcher was the first to get up that morning of June 6. "At H-hour, by coincidence, I was awake, that being 6:40, and was contemplating the underside of the drab tent roof, wondering how come such a quiet night in contrast with other D-nights, when this was supposed to be the biggest and most superduper of all." Just then a call came from Leigh-Mallory. He told Butcher that "only 21 of the 850 American C-47s were missing, and only four gliders had not been accounted for. The British had lost only eight C-47s out of 400. . . . I tiptoed down the cinder path to Ike's circus wagon to see if he was asleep and saw him silhouetted in bed reading a Western. Ike grinned as he lit a cigarette. I was almost the first with good news, but Admiral Ramsay was just on the phone, telling him things seemed to be going by plan and he had no bad news at all."

Mickey came to see him at 7:15, the usual hour. He said, "He [Eisenhower] was awake. There was a big ashtray piled with cigarette butts and it had been empty and clean when he went to bed. I thought, 'He hasn't had any sleep.' His face was drawn and he had only half a smile. I asked him how he felt, and he said, 'Not too bad, Mickey.' . . . He was waiting, the way we all were."

Eisenhower shaved; this time, unlike the morning he had sweated out TORCH inside the Rock of Gibraltar, there was hot water. A little later a soldier brought the supreme commander a copy of *Stars and Stripes* and morning newspapers from Portsmouth. Rome had fallen, and Mark Clark had issued a victory statement which some observers thought dealt too fully with Clark and not enough with the other Allied commanders and soldiers who had helped win the difficult victory. Vernon A. Walters, who was to become the translator for, among other presidents, Eisenhower, was Clark's senior aide at the time. He told the general about the landings in Normandy early on the morning of the 6th. Clark's reaction was not a happy one. He said, "The sons-a-bitches. They didn't even let us have the newspaper headlines for the fall of Rome for one day." Walters added, "The liberation of Rome, which otherwise would have been sensational headline news, was relegated, by the immensity of the Channel landings, to an inside page in the newspapers. These too are the vicissitudes of war."

At 8:00 on the morning of the 6th, Ike dictated a report to Marshall saying that while there were no reports on the actual landings, "All preliminary reports are satisfactory. Airborne formations apparently landed in good order. . . . Preliminary bombings by air went off as planned. Navy reports sweeping some mines, but so far as is known channels are clear and operations proceeding as planned. In early morning hours reaction from shore batteries was sufficiently light that some of the naval spotting planes have returned awaiting call."

He did not add that at Portsmouth the sun was shining.

The first news of the invasion reached the United States at 3:32 A.M. on the 6th. A radio broadcast from SHAEF headquarters said, "Under the command of General Eisenhower, Allied naval forces, supported by strong air forces, began landing Allied armies this morning on the coast of France." All over the country people called each other to pass on the good news. It was one of those rare nights that later everybody was to remember with precision. Nobody forgot where he had been that night or what he had done.

In Washington President Roosevelt appeared to take the news casually. He said at his morning press conference that the country was "thrilled by the news of the invasion" and that Eisenhower was "up to schedule." He warned, however, that "the war is by no means over yet." He said, "You don't just walk to Berlin; the sooner the country realizes that the better." He, like the supreme commander, realized that perhaps the greatest danger in the months, maybe years, ahead was that Americans would relax.

Eisenhower allowed the Germans to be the first to announce that the continent had been invaded; at 7:00 that morning the German radio said that Allied landings had been made from Le Havre to Cherbourg along the north coast of Normandy and on the south side of the bay of the Seine.

Ike's order of the day said:

Soldiers, Sailors, and Airmen of the Allied Expeditionary Forces: You are about to embark upon the Great Crusade, toward which we have striven these many months. The eyes of the world are upon you. The hopes and fears of liberty-loving people everywhere march with you. In company with our brave Allies and brothers-in-arms on other Fronts you will bring about the destruction of the German war machine, the elimination of Nazi tyranny over the oppressed peoples of Europe, and security for ourselves in a free world. . . .

Good Luck! And let us beseech the blessing of Almighty God upon this great and noble undertaking.

Like most Americans Mamie did not hear of the invasion until she got up that morning. She was at the Thayer Hotel at West Point for John's graduation later in the day. She was awakened at 7:30 by a woman reporter from the *New York Post*. What did she think of the invasion?

"The invasion?" said Mamie. "What invasion?" When she was told, she said—*Life* magazine had her saying it "wistfully"—"Why hasn't someone told me?"

Mamie later said John's graduation that day was to have been "one of the great personal moments [in Eisenhower's life]. . . . Writing [to him] about it would help, but . . . he would expect to *hear* me describe everything."

John said that he "woke up that morning worn out. June Week—five days preceding graduation—is hectic. . . . I had turned in my mattress the day before and had tossed fitfully through the previous night on an iron cot with two blotters as bedding. "As 1st Battalion cadet sergeant major, I took my place to march to breakfast for the last time. The battalion commander turned and regarded me quizzically. 'You heard, of course, that the Allies landed in Europe this morning.' That was the first I had heard. There was little time to ruminate over the news, however. . . . All of us went about our business, turning in our cadet chevrons, packing our footlockers, and preparing to depart."

John was not, he was to say, "part of the main drama of the day." Once again his father was that. "Mother and I found ourselves facing a bank of something like forty photographers, bulbs flashing unmercifully. I felt a swelling of resentment, caused not so much by the photographers' preemptory demands or even by the irritation of the flashbulbs; I hated being singled out conspicuously from those whose comradeship I valued—my classmates. Even after breaking ranks at the field house the chaos continued. The photographers insisted on a picture of Mother handing me a letter Dad had innocently written. He had intended it to be delivered on graduation day, not realizing the furor that circumstances would create."

Major General Francis B. Wilby, superintendent of the Academy, read the graduating class a message from John's father: "The American armies in Europe are delighted to join in welcoming into the commissioned ranks of the Army the West Point graduating class of 1944. . . . May the traditions of your alma mater sustain you, and good luck be with you all."

Eisenhower's friend Lieutenant General Bill Somervell made the main address to the graduates, and he made several changes in the speech because of the news from Normandy: "Today our forces began that grim, tough, and bloody march from the shores of the Atlantic to Berlin. Many of you will join in that march. . . ."

On June 9 Eisenhower sent a telegram to Mamie saying, "Due to previous plans it was impossible for me to be with you and John Monday [sic]. But I thought of you and hope you and he had a nice time with the family [the Douds]." West Point graduation was actually on Tuesday, June 6. According to John in Letters to Mamie, "Since D-Day was originally scheduled for June 5, General Eisenhower probably confused the dates." John said of his father's telegram that his "aversion to self-dramatization was sincere; it was also a valuable asset for an Allied commander. But at times he overdid it, seeming to relish expressing himself in an exasperatingly low-key manner, as in his June 9 telegram referring only to 'previous plans.' "

John, like his father, had not been an outstanding academic success at the Point; he ranked 138th in a class of 474. After the graduation ceremony, he was even more annoyed. "I was placed, despite my pleas and protests, in the superintendent's large black car with Mother and the superintendent. The three of us rode like royalty up the hill to barracks, my classmates observing and laughing sympathetically at my discomfiture."

The letter from his father must have given John some comfort, however; it had been written on May 24, and sent to Mamie to be handed to John immediately after graduation. It said, in part, "I hope you know how happy I am that both you and I are now officers of the great U.S. Army. I am especially proud of the fact that in all the years since your birth you have never once given your mother or me any cause for anxiety or worry and are now entering upon your chosen career splendidly equipped by character and training to meet its exacting demands."

There was another reason for John's feeling satisfaction that day. Two weeks earlier he had received secret orders to report that night to the New York port of embarkation where he would board the Queen Mary for a voyage to England; it had been General Marshall's idea that John being with his father during what was certain to be a tense time would be "beneficial" to the supreme allied commander. Since the mission was to be kept a secret from even John's closest friends, that morning John had "packed my uniforms as if I were proceeding to a vacation in the United States like the rest of my classmates."

At the Thayer, John replaced the suntans in his bag with the ODs (olive drab) that were being worn in Europe. "The process had to be camouflaged," said John. "Reporters came in a final time to take pictures of Mother and me listening to the radio." That night he boarded the *Queen* for the voyage to England.

In his broadcast to the people of Europe, Eisenhower had said:

People of Western Europe! A landing was made this morning on the coast of France by troops of the Allied Expeditionary Force. This landing is part of the concerted United Nations plan for the liberation of Europe, made in conjunction with our great Russian Allies. I have this message for all of you. Although the initial assault may not have been made in your own country, the hour of your liberation is approaching.

All patriots, men and women, young and old, have a part to play in the achievement of final victory. To members of resistance movements, whether led by national or outside leaders, I say: "Follow the instructions you have received." To patriots who are not members of organized resistance groups I say, "Continue your passive resistance, but do not needlessly endanger your lives until I give you the signal to rise and strike the enemy. The day will come when I shall need your united strength. Until that day, I call on you for the hard task of discipline and restraint."

Citizens of France! I am proud to have again under my command the gallant forces of France. Fighting beside their Allies, they will play a worthy part in the liberation of their homeland. . . .

Finally, at six o'clock that evening, de Gaulle spoke to his fellow countrymen. In his memoirs he said, "I spoke individually . . . a prey to intense emotions, declaring to my countrymen: 'The supreme battle has been joined. . . . It is, of course, the Battle of France, and the battle for France! For the sons of France, wherever they are, the simple and sacred duty is to fight the enemy by every means in their power. . . . The orders given by the French government and by the leaders which it has recognized must be followed precisely."

There was very little in what de Gaulle said to please Eisenhower, who was placing his major emphasis on the need for Allied unity. It was the French government and French leaders who "must be followed precisely." It was as if France alone was concerned with the battle, and its only leader was Charles de Gaulle. As might have been expected Roosevelt was not pleased either, and Anthony Eden told Churchill, "We must either break with de Gaulle—which means breaking with France—or conclude an agreement with him. There is no middle course. We must tell the President that de Gaulle must be supported."

Officially, the matter was out of Eisenhower's hands, but it was nevertheless very much his concern. He did not want to use Anglo-American troops to occupy

France; they were needed for the battle against Germany, and for that to happen, de Gaulle had to take over the civil administration of France as the supporters of the Vichy regime were removed from office. In addition, Ike desperately needed the military support that could be brought to the Allies by the mobilization of French forces. They took orders from General Pierre Joseph Koenig, de Gaulle's commander of the FFI (French Forces of the Interior).

Early on the morning of June 7 Eisenhower got aboard a British minelayer, *Apollo*, accompanied by Admiral Ramsay, several other British naval officers, Butcher, and Gault. The latter two brought along gas masks, helmets, and cameras. The *Apollo* dropped anchor near OMAHA Beach where the heaviest resistance had been met the day before. Bradley came aboard and was, as always, according to Eisenhower, "stout hearted and confident." Things had gone well— not quite as well as expected, but OVERLORD was clearly not another Dieppe.

It had been hoped that the beachheads would be six miles deep by the end of the first day in France, but in no place was the penetration more than five miles deep, and that was rare. And the casualties had been heavy. The Canadians had lost more than a thousand men, and the British had lost three times that many. Altogether the Allies had lost about 9,000 men. It was believed that a third of those had been killed. Still, more than 100,000 additional troops had been landed, and that day, while Eisenhower was still near the beachhead, the British attacked Bayeux, which on the 8th became the first French city to be liberated; Caen was only four miles away, but it would not be liberated that day or for some time to come.

General Sir Miles Dempsey, commander of the Second British Army, later said, "I never expected Third Division to get Caen on the first day and I always said that if we didn't get it on the first day it would take a month afterwards." But Monty when he came aboard the *Apollo* in the afternoon was enthusiastic about everything. His soldiers were "full of beans." They were in "tremendous form." They had "already taken the measure of the enemy."

Late in the afternoon, Eisenhower remembered, the *Apollo* was "going at a terrific speed, the equivalent of 40 miles per hour land speed; we hit a sand bank, and the boat just shook to pieces; all of us fell on our faces. . . . It was partly my fault because I'd insisted that we go as fast as we could so that we could get as close as possible." The party transferred to a destroyer, the H.M.S. *Undaunted*. They got back to Portsmouth at ten o'clock that night, and Eisenhower went immediately to his living quarters. Mickey said, "He looked tired and worn . . . I asked if we could get him something to eat. He shook his head . . . he said he was tired. . . . I think that night he slept. Anyway, he looked more rested the next day."

Only one correspondent—from Reuters—had gone on the trip, and he reported that during the four-and-a-half-hour voyage Eisenhower was at times only five miles away from the enemy. "It was almost unbelievable that this was D-Day-plus-one, so quiet and serene was the picture. It might have been a peacetime cruise along the coast of Hampshire. Only an occasional burst of fire from a nearby Allied warship broke the peace of the scene." The reporter missed the trip on the *Apollo,* but he said that the supreme commander had "got definitely more valuable information of the progress of the battle by personal meetings than by reliance on cross-channel signals. The cruise fully justified his hope."

On the morning of the 8th, Marty Snyder asked Ike how things were going on the beachhead. Ike said that things were "rough, but we're there to stay. The men are fighting magnificently."

Butcher thought Eisenhower seemed "tired and almost listless." The supreme commander agreed to an off-the-record press conference, during which he talked about the fact that the German 352d Division had "accidentally" been in on the 1st Infantry Division landing and had caused great and unexpected difficulties. He did not say that at one point Bradley had considered abandoning OMAHA Beach entirely. He did say that the whole operation was still "hazardous," although he did not want that word to be quoted because it did not quite represent what he felt about the operation. The weather, he said, had been unfortunate, and when he said that beginning the next day there might be good weather, he added, "You fellows pray for it, too."

Later in the day Beetle talked to the correspondents, and he was pessimistic in the extreme. It was better to do what Knute Rockne did with his football teams, emphasize your own weaknesses and the strengths of the other side. Besides, Caen had not been taken as predicted, and at that very moment the Germans were pushing back the Allied forces. The Associated Press report in the *New York Times* the next day was not quite so pessimistic. It said that Eisenhower had given a "confident appraisal of the first fifty-four hours of the Allied invasion." His faith in the sea, air, and ground units had been "completely justified." And Montgomery's ground forces were " 'performing magnificently.' "

Eisenhower wrote Mamie on the 9th:

As always when I go through these intense periods of strain and effort, I think of you, want you here, and try to write to you—but I'm afraid that even my short notes are rather incoherent.

Anyway, we've started. Only time will tell how great our success will be. But all that can be done by human effort, intense devotion to duty, and courageous execution, all by thousands and thousands of individuals, will be done by this force. The soldiers, sailors, and airmen are indescribable in their élan, courage, determination and fortitude. They inspire me.

How I look forward to seeing Johnny. It will be odd to see him as an *officer of the Army!* I'll burst with pride.

Eisenhower did not know it until later, but on June 9 GARBO, a German double agent, proved very useful to the Allies. He sent a message that went all the way to the German high command. It said, "The present operation [in Normandy], though a large-scale assault, is diversionary in character. Its object is to establish a strong bridgehead in order to draw the maximum of our reserves into the area of the assault and to retain them there so as to leave another area exposed where the enemy could attack with some prospect of success."

Hitler was so impressed with the message that he ordered two armored divisions that von Rundstedt had hoped to use in Normandy to the Pas-de-Calais area. They would be needed there when the principal Allied invasion landed. GARBO was also awarded an Iron Cross, Second Class, for his work.

On the 10th Eisenhower, according to Butcher, "had awakened in a snit." There was no news from Montgomery, none, and Monty had agreed on the 7th to furnish the Supreme Allied Commander a nightly bulletin. What's more, the weather was bad that day.

Kay drove him to WIDEWING, and Churchill hurried down, more insistent than ever that he be allowed to go to the beachhead. Eisenhower again said no, and again, they argued. Kay, who was there, reported that Eisenhower had been "cornered . . . in the office for a long chat." There was good news, however; Stalin had cabled Churchill that OVERLORD had been "conceived on a grandiose scale" and "has succeeded completely. . . . History will record this deed as an achievement of the highest order."

"Harmony was complete," said Churchill. In addition, Stalin had said that the Russians were starting a huge offensive, which got underway on the 22nd on four different fronts. On the first day, advances of up to eleven miles were said to have been made. The Russians had almost complete domination of the air, in part because a great many units of the Luftwaffe had been brought from the Eastern Front to the Western Front to fight against the British and American bomber offensive.

That day, too, Eisenhower met with three distinguished American visitors and friends, Marshall, Arnold, and King. He showed them and Churchill his headquarters, especially the war room. There Allied positions were shown on huge maps, and all four men were impressed. The three Americans had been planning this achievement for years. Churchill had been a late and reluctant convert, but now that it had happened, and the Channel was not choked with dead bodies, he congratulated Eisenhower on what he had accomplished. Their arguments for that summer were not over, however; indeed they had scarcely begun. As Eisenhower later said, Churchill "could bring in strong arguments in favor of his own pet plans and he could destroy your own in his own mind in ten minutes."

When Ike got back to Portsmouth that night, Butcher and Jim Gault, Ike's British aide, told him that they had seen Captain F. A. Grindle, skipper of the minelayer *Apollo*. He was in trouble because when his ship hit the sandbar it had been so badly damaged it would be laid up for two months, and Grindle was, Butcher said, "wallowing in despair."

It had been a busy day, a troublesome day; Eisenhower was tired, and he was cranky. The snit of the morning had not mellowed. Still, he said he would send a note on Grindle's behalf to his old friend Admiral Cunningham.

As another of Eisenhower's friends, Lucius Clay, once said, "Ike was a man who was always personally concerned with people, and he always demonstrated that concern. Even when he was president and I would visit him, he would always see me to the door. That may seem a small thing, but it was not. It was concern with others, genuine concern."

At 5:00 on the morning of the 11th Eisenhower was given a message from

Churchill. The prime minister had learned that the Germans had sent a message to their headquarters in France asking whether the Allied troops carried their gas masks with them or in baggage cars. The message had understandably upset Churchill. Eisenhower immediately ordered a quiet check to be sure that all the troops did have their gas masks. The Germans might use gas, he told Butcher, "to stave off final defeat." Butcher added, "We have lots [of poison gas] on hand for counterattack if they start the bad business."

On the 10th Eisenhower had told the prime minister that he "could not repeat not visit the bridgehead," but that same day a subordinate officer, inclined sometimes to forget that he was a subordinate, Montgomery, notified the prime minister that, in Churchill's words, "he was sufficiently established to receive a visitor." So Churchill forgot the gas threat. Given a choice between safety and an adventure that had in his mind too long been denied him, he chose the adventure, a visit to the beachhead. He was, after all, only seventy years old.

On the night of the 11th Marshall, Arnold, King, and the British Chiefs of Staff joined the prime minister on his private train for the overnight journey from London to Portsmouth. Forrest C. Pogue said, "There was an unmistakable air of an outing about the expedition to the battlefront. The irrepressible Prime Minister was exuberant."

Aboard the train—Smuts was another guest—they all had what Pogue describes as "a convivial meal around a long banquet table set up in one of the cars. Everyone seemed in a mood for celebration except King. Finally, after casting impish glances in the Admiral's direction, Churchill said, 'Don't look so glum. I am not trying to take anything away from the United States Navy just now.' "

Eisenhower met the party at Portsmouth. The British crossed the Channel to the British sector of the beachhead in a British destroyer; the Americans went in an American destroyer, *Thompson*. Eisenhower had not been in France since the summer of 1928, when he and Mamie arrived at Cherbourg.

Not unexpectedly, there was a good deal of confusion when, on June 12, the American visitors landed at OMAHA Beach. They were met by Bradley, however, and they soon found out that it was a good day to be there. Maxwell Taylor's Screaming Eagles had encircled the city of Carentan, and by six the paratroopers had driven into the city's streets to open the main road between the two American landing beaches, OMAHA and UTAH. The Allied forces on the seventh day in France were linked together on a front that was forty-two miles wide. Bradley was later to say, "We could now force our way across the Cotentin, then choke it off and capture the port of Cherbourg."

Chet Hansen had "parked two cars in the village square." Bradley said, "With General Marshall, King, Arnold, and Eisenhower . . . bunched together . . . an enemy sniper could have won immortality as a hero of the Reich." The Americans had lunch at Bradley's headquarters, C rations and biscuits, and late that afternoon, after several other stops, including a visit to Lightning Joe Collins' VII Corps headquarters at Utah Beach, they started back to Portsmouth, greatly cheered by what they had seen.

Two days later Marshall sent a report to Roosevelt:

> Conditions on the beachhead are favorable. . . . The Germans appear
> unable to muster a sizeable counterattack for some days to come. French
> Resistance good. Interruption of communications by air seems effective.

Bradley, he added, was calm and confident, and his corps commanders had an
"aggressive attitude."

Eisenhower got back to his headquarters at about 9:00 that night, and he,
Butcher, and George Allen, who was in England on a Red Cross assignment
concerning the exchange of prisoners of war, played bridge. Allen and Butcher
won; they played with a battered deck in which the joker substituted for the
six of clubs. According to Butcher, "George thought this extremely funny; the
Supreme Commander, whom George ardently and loudly proclaims the most
popular idol of the world at the moment, having to play bridge with a makeshift
deck."

Later that night Eisenhower told Allen and Butcher that Marshall had said
that after the war the young officers in the army would take charge, and Eisenhower, who was fifty-three, was one of those young men. " 'Why do you
think we've been pushing you?' Marshall had asked him. 'You will have ten
years of hard work in the Army after the war.'

"All Ike could say then was that he hoped to have a six months' rest."

★ ★ ★

STORMY WEATHER

John arrived in Scotland at dawn on June 13 and was met by "Tex"
Lee; they went to WIDEWING in what John described as "a luxurious
private train." Lee filled him in on what had happened since the
landings a week earlier. It seemed, he said, that the Allies were on the continent
to stay, although progress had not been as fast as planned. Caen had not yet
been taken by the British Second Army on the right; the American First Army
on the left was making progress—but slowly. Supplies were arriving on the
beachhead rapidly, and the bridgehead was deep enough to keep the beaches
free of artillery fire.

John reached his father's office early in the afternoon, and Eisenhower told
him about his trip to the beachhead the day before with Marshall, King and
Arnold, who had since left the theater. There were now, Eisenhower said, sixteen
American and British divisions in action.

The first visitor after John's arrival was Everett Hughes, "Uncle Everett,"
and he, having just been in France, did not agree with Tex Lee's earlier report
about supplies. He felt that they were not arriving fast enough. Ike immediately
picked up the phone and called J. C. H. Lee. "The call was blunt and to the
point," said John. "If Lee wanted to keep his job [commanding officer of

Services and Supply], Dad said, he had better get over there personally and see to it that things were stepped up. The telephone call of about half a minute duration over, Dad went on to other things."

John does not say that he was impressed with his first view of his father as supreme allied commander, but he surely was. Here was a man of decision, a man barking out orders and making threats to a lieutenant general who had graduated from West Point five years before he did and who for most of their army lives had outranked him.

John does say that his father was a "little fretful"; his job at the moment was coordinating land, sea, and air activity, waiting until large enough forces were ashore so that he could personally take command of things in the field. As a result Ike was feeling "housebound." Montgomery was making the on-the-spot decisions, John said. "This arrangement, though proper, seemed to make Dad a little fretful, like a football player sitting on the bench, anxious to get in the game. He covered his restlessness well, and only one close to him would be able to detect a trace of preoccupation in his manner. But the forced personal inactivity probably accounted for the unaccustomed curtness with which he had barked at General Lee that afternoon."

Later Ike and John drove to Telegraph Cottage, and as they were sitting outside that first evening John heard a buzzing sound and guns firing to the south. "Dad shrugged; he was aware that the cause was a new type of Nazi weapon, the V-1 [buzz bomb]." Hitler had for a long time been promising a secret weapon, and this was it.

Early that morning the buzzing sound had been heard over Bethnal Green in London. First a yellow and red flame moved swiftly through the sky, then the flame disappeared and the buzzing stopped. Thirty seconds later there was an explosion in the street. Six people were killed. The buzz bombs were at one time or another called "divers, pilotless aircraft, buzz bombs, doodle bugs, and robots." As Eisenhower later said, "It seems likely that, if the German had succeeded in perfecting and using these new weapons six months earlier than he did, our invasion of Europe would have proved exceedingly difficult, perhaps impossible. I feel sure that if he had succeeded in using these weapons over a six-months period, and particularly if he had made the Portsmouth-Southampton area one of his principal targets, OVERLORD might have been written off."

"To me, the buzz bomb was the most dreadful, impersonal, and nerve-wracking weapon of the war," Kay said. "Above all, it never stopped, day or night. Everyone in London became touchy-tempered from lack of sleep and the incessant strain. London office work was disrupted many times a day as the 'imminent danger' signal sounded, warning of at least one V-1 headed straight for that particular area. At WIDEWING that meant running out to blast shelters, clutching at Secret papers, listening with every pore and nerve, tight with the eternal waiting, waiting, waiting. Quite a few landed in the section around Bushy Park, indicating a German interest in our headquarters."

Eisenhower wrote Mamie on July 21, "This morning we had to go to our shelters nineteen times. Terrible bore, especially when one is trying, as I was, to write two long papers. Stenogs and I were in a flap.

"Have a headache today. Think my eyes are a bit strained."

Marty Snyder said, "General Eisenhower obeyed each air raid warning more to set an example than for his own protection. After each raid, he made quick inspections. Once, the WAC barracks was hit, killing three girls, and later the mess hall was so badly damaged that we were unable to use it for two days. Only after he was sure that everything was done for the injured did the General return to his desk."

Eisenhower later wrote, "The effect of the new German weapons was very noticeable upon morale. . . . When in June the Allies landed successfully on the Normandy coast the citizens unquestionably experienced a great sense of relief, not only at the prospect of victory but in the hope of gaining some insurance against future bombings. When the new weapons began to come over London in considerable numbers their hopes were dashed. Indeed, the depressing effect of the bombs was not confined to the civilian population, soldiers at the front began to worry about friends and loved ones at home, and many American soldiers asked me in worried tones whether I could give them any news about particular towns where they had been stationed in southern England."

At one point in early July the British Chiefs considered attacking the launching sites with poison gas. Eisenhower was outraged at the mere suggestion; he told Tedder, "Let's, for God's sake, keep our eye on the ball." The Chiefs agreed, and the idea was quickly rejected.

By mid-June the effect of the bombs was such that, as Butcher wrote, "most of the people I know are semi-dazed from loss of sleep and have the jitters, which they show when a door bangs, or the sounds of motors, from motorcycles to aircraft, are heard."

The British Chiefs of Staff asked Eisenhower to make the V-1 launching sites high-priority targets for allied bombers. The code name given to this offensive was CROSSBOW, and the sites in the Pas-de-Calais area were repeatedly bombed. According to Eisenhower, "It must be said, to the credit of the English leaders, that never once did one of them urge me to vary any detail of my planned operation merely for the purpose of eliminating this scourge."

There was one suggestion, however, that infuriated him. At a meeting on July 3 of the British Chiefs of Staff, retaliation by bombing the German civilian population was discussed. There was disagreement, but Eisenhower's old friend Admiral Cunningham, for one, thought that such retaliation might have some effect; he said, "We should not lightly discard anything which offered a chance of stopping the flying bomb attacks."

Eisenhower when he read the minutes of that meeting wrote to Tedder in longhand, "As I have before indicated, I am opposed to retaliation as a method of stopping this business—at least until every other thing has been tried and failed. Please continue to oppose." He was in a crusade to defeat the Nazis, but he had no intention of imitating them, despite the fact that in eleven weeks after the first bomb exploded 6,200 civilians were killed; 18,000 were injured; 750,000 houses were damaged, 23,000 of them completely destroyed. Hitler was determined, he said, to "convert the English to peace."

The defenses against the bomb became increasingly effective, and by the end of August only one out of seven bombs launched reached its target. On August

28 ninety out of ninety-four bombs launched failed to reach their target. On September 1, as Allied troops approached the launching sites, the attacks with V-1s stopped altogether. A week later, however, the first of the V-2s arrived. It was a thirteen-ton bomb with a ton of TNT in its nose, and during the next seven months more than 500 of them fell on London, killing 2,700 people and injuring seriously 6,500 more. As Kenneth S. Davis said in *Experience of War*, V-2 "casualty figures would have been much higher if the Germans had not been forced to launch from the farthest limit of the rocket's range, with consequent increase in its inaccuracy."

John remembered the time he spent with his father that summer with warmth but an awareness of the friction between them. He said, "On practically the first evening . . . as Dad and I were walking together at SHAEF, I asked him . . . : 'If we should meet an officer who ranks above me but below you, how do we handle this? Should I salute first and when they return my salute, do you return theirs?' The question was legitimate to my mind and has never been answered to my satisfaction; however, Dad's annoyed reaction was short: 'John, there isn't an officer in this theater who doesn't rank above you and below me.' "

Eisenhower was often sentimental, which was part of his great charm. John was a realist. He said, "We had a deep mutual affection, but there existed a certain military wall between us. I was not only his son; I was a young lieutenant who needed on occasion to be straightened out. Without a doubt, with my having grown up in a more relaxed Army than the one he had joined thirty years earlier, I think sometimes he considered me a sign that West Point had gone to hell."

Actually the father and son were much alike in their casual feelings about such matters as shining shoes and brass. Though John occasionally took the other side. In pictures of Eisenhower from North Africa he was often photographed, as John put it, "wearing his service cap . . . at a rakish angle." John wrote his father that by so doing he was "disillusioning the Corps of Cadets." On October 18, 1943, Ike responded:

I think I really deserved the hiding you gave me on my dress cap. The only point is, it is not a dress cap, it is a utilitarian thing that I use to shield my eyes from the sun and at the same time to allow me to ride comfortably in an automobile or in an airplane. When one wears the stiff wire ring inside the dress cap it has to be taken off if you try to get some rest while in any type of vehicle.

This is a rotten alibi and if any of my junior officers gave me the same one I would take his head off. However, you are some thousands of miles away and by the time you get this maybe I will put the wire back in the cap and try to conform to regular ideas of neatness in headdress.

In talking of his son to other people, Eisenhower was usually warmer, less formal, friendlier, more relaxed than he was with John himself. On the very day John arrived in England, Eisenhower wrote Mamie, "John will be in soon—

maybe in 1½ hours. I'm really as excited as a bride, but luckily I have so much to do I haven't time to get nervous." And later he wrote her, "I'm sure he's having a good time and what a Godsend he has been for me. I love to be with him."

On June 15th Eisenhower, John, and Tedder flew to the British sector of the beachhead. Kay drove them to the airfield; in *Strictly Personal*, written and published before his mother's death, John says that Kay was "an attractive Irish WAC, who was Dad's secretary and chauffeur." The plane landed on a small, temporary airfield about two miles from the front lines. According to John, "As we were clambering out of the plane, the co-pilot muttered that he wished those destroyers would quit shooting flak, as it made him nervous. Apparently we had flown in a little close for the Navy's comfort, and some-one had put up a couple of 20-mm shells to warn us away." The party's first stop was at Montgomery's headquarters; "Dad chuckled at a sign by the road which said, *Keep Left!* Everywhere else on the Continent vehicles drove on the right."

Monty was off seeing Bradley, which was part of his duty. He had, however, known Eisenhower was coming and to say that the fact had slipped his mind is not credible. John's charitable conclusion was that, "It is doubtful that he was being calculatingly impolite, but he lived in a world of his own and liked to go his own way. . . . Dad's lack of irritation can be explained only by as-suming that he was serious in refusing to interfere with his principal subordi-nate's activities." Nigel Hamilton said that Eisenhower's party "only left England around 9 A.M. and, accompanied by no less than thirteen P-47 Thunderbolts, their Flying Fortress arrived too late to catch Monty, who had gone to meet Bradley."

Later that morning the Eisenhower party visited Bayeux, stopping off on the way at the headquarters of the 15th Scottish Division, which Eisenhower had inspected back in England; many of the troops, who were on their way to the front, recognized him and yelled, "Hi, Ike." That pleased him, and he would smile and wave back. John observed that the supreme commander's visiting troops "was a fine thing for their morale. We noticed, however, that the soldiers riding in the trucks showed considerably more enthusiasm than those plodding on the road."

For the rest of the trip there were only three people in the car, Eisenhower, John, and Montgomery's aide, who drove. The driver told the supreme com-mander that General de Gaulle had visited Bayeux the day before and that on his first visit to France since he left in 1940 he had staged a parade. John realized that this was the first time his father had heard of the visit, and "I could see the old man's blood pressure rise." After all, no one was to visit the combat zone without his permission. Monty's aide also told Eisenhower that the French general had made a speech and was reported to have said, "The great virtue of the French was that they had never submitted to the Germans. Now, with the aid of the Allies they were reconquering their lost territory." John said, "I could see a certain humor in the situation; Dad could not. He sat in silence, the back of his neck red, for a couple of miles."

Later in the day Eisenhower returned to Monty's headquarters, and this time the British general was present. Hamilton said, "To Eisenhower, Montgomery outlined the administrative and supply problems hampering the Allied effort—and dutifully . . . Eisenhower made notes to take back to Supreme Headquarters with him." John said that on the afternoon of June 15th and later, his father treated Monty "with every courtesy, even deference . . . [though] as Supreme Commander, Dad was the ultimate boss. But he was obviously determined that any friction that might occur between the two would never be the result of any personal slight on his own part. Their differences would be based solely on military judgments in a common cause. Montgomery, on his part, never showed a noticeable sign of reciprocating."

They returned to London that evening, and John said, "As we drove back to Telegraph Cottage we were reminded of the lighthearted joshing we had received in Normandy over the fact that London was now under heavier fire than were the headquarters across the Channel. Indeed, if there was any single impression that remained with me from this first glimpse of a combat zone, it was the calm and peaceful atmosphere that prevailed only a few miles behind the lines, where men were dying every minute."

H. P. Willmott, a military historian on the staff of the Royal Military Academy, Sandhurst, has said, "The OVERLORD plan had been overwhelmingly concerned with two matters: the assault phase and creation of the beachhead, plus the provision of forces for the subsequent campaign in northwest Europe. Relatively little attention had been paid to the question of how operations were to be conducted once Allied forces were established ashore. This omission was natural but unfortunate."

For a time after the initial landings in Normandy, nothing seemed to go right, and as usual at such times Ike's health was poor. According to Kay, he "suffered several bad headaches, complained about his blood pressure, and, in a rare moment of fatigue, spent one morning in bed. . . . Several times . . . he drove off from the Southwick CP in a jeep, by himself, and took short flights in an L-5 observation plane to 'get away from it all . . . and you all.' "

Caen was not captured, as promised, by the 6th or 7th; it had not been captured—"liberated" was the operative word in France—by the 15th. On that night Butcher said in his diary, "Last night Ike was concerned that Monty couldn't attack until Saturday [June 17]. Ike was anxious that the Germans be kept off balance and that our drive never stop. But apparently Monty wants to tidy up his 'administrative tail' and get plenty of supplies on hand before he makes a general attack. . . . Ike also said that yesterday we had made no gains, which he didn't like."

The beachhead was still only seven miles deep, and almost 8,000 Americans were missing; nearly 13,000 had been wounded, and 3,283 were dead. By the 18th Montgomery had postponed his attack to the 19th, which would turn out to be an unfortunate choice of dates. On the 18th Eisenhower sent a letter to Monty:

> Recently I sent you a message by General de Guingand saying that I was going to forbid, for the time being, any further visits by V.I.P.s in the battle area. I won't have you bothered at this time by people who are not

in a position to help you directly in the battle effort and unless you personally desire to approve such visits I am quite certain that no further ones are necessary or desirable. . . .

The Chief of Staff tells me that the attack is to start tomorrow morning, after a forty-eight-hour delay. I can well understand that you have needed to accumulate reasonable amounts of artillery ammunition, but I am in high hopes that once the attack starts it will have a momentum that will carry it a long way. . . .

I thoroughly believe you are going to crack the enemy a good one.

Montgomery's crack at the enemy did not begin on the 19th. That morning what Stagg termed the worst storm of the previous twenty years struck the Channel. Fighter support for infantry activity was impossible; landing of supplies and of further troops was largely halted. One division, the 83d, was on board ship in the Channel when the storm struck, and five days later when Eisenhower visited the men of the division they had just reached shore, and, the supreme allied commander said, "I found a number of them still seasick and temporarily exhausted." John said of the beginning of the storm, "When Dad heard the news during the late afternoon at Telegraph Cottage, he paused for a few minutes, silent, and asked for a stiff Scotch and water . . . there was nothing he personally could do about the situation, and we spent the evening in a rather somber bridge game."

Mickey said, "Bad weather—the bad weather about which nobody was to say anything for publication—worried everybody; the General's satisfaction with the way things were going vanished . . . and his face was worried. At night he smoked instead of sleeping." "Most of that June the weather fought on the side of the Axis," said Beetle.

There was one comforting thought for the Supreme Commander. If he had postponed the invasion, the next date on which the moon and tides were favorable was June 19. In a note to Stagg, Eisenhower wrote, "thank the gods of war we went when we did."

During the storm John and his father went to visit Churchill at Whitehall. "The room was simple, with a fairly large-sized table and a huge map on the wall. The three of us sat in straight-backed chairs at one end. England's Prime Minister, slumped limply, was in a bad mood. He stared toward the floor at his side, almost motionless, speaking to Dad but really thinking out loud. 'This is the worst weather I have ever seen in my life,' he growled, emphasizing every word as he turned in his chair. Then, raising his voice, 'They have no right to give us weather like this.'

"In this respect, it seems that Churchill and General George Patton had an attitude in common. Dedicated to their respective missions, each seemed to feel that the Almighty had an obligation—a personal obligation—to render all necessary assistance to their accomplishments. The Old Man, on the other hand, seemed to view the situation more philosophically. Competitive to the extreme— and imbued with a hatred of Naziism and all it entailed—he appeared to approach his mission of defeating Hitler with the same attitude with which he attacked his opponents in bridge and poker—in both of which he was expert.

He appeared to view any situation with the cold, calculating attitude of a professional confident as he was throughout his life that the Almighty would provide him with a decent set of cards. He never wavered in his faith that he would win, but he appeared not to share the metaphysical feeling that God owed him anything specific, such as good weather on a given day. In short, the Old Man was far more hard-headed than either of his flamboyant friends Churchill or Patton."

Very few sons take the trouble to understand their fathers, and even fewer succeed. John took the trouble, and here at least he succeeded admirably.

On the 24th, after the storm, one of the worst of the century, had abated, Ike and John returned to France. Eisenhower said, "I flew from one end of the beach to the other and counted more than 300 wrecked vessels above small-boat size, some so badly damaged they could not be salvaged. . . .

"There was no sight of war that so impressed me with the industrial might of America as the wreckage on the landing beaches. To any other nation the disaster would have been almost decisive; but so great was America's productive capacity that the great storm occasioned little more than a ripple in the development of our build-up." That was one of the reasons, an important one, that Eisenhower for the rest of his life was impressed, at times, it seemed, awed by American industrialists and by how they had achieved the "industrial might" that turned a possible disaster into "no more than a ripple in the development of our build-up."

On the 24th Eisenhower did what he had planned to do before the storm broke, he visited Bradley's headquarters, again taking John with him. Bradley was glad to see him and understood how much the supreme commander had wanted to make the visit. He said, "For most of the 18 days we had been ashore, Eisenhower had paced impatiently inside the confines of that gaudy brass-bound prison known to the world as SHAEF. Now surfeited with high-level strategy, with statisticians, logisticians, and tacticians, Ike was eager to escape the rarefied air of SHAEF in England and find relief among the troops in the field. . . . Eisenhower found as I did that the wellsprings of humility lie in the field. For however arduous the task of a commander, he cannot face the men who shall live and die by his orders without sensing how much easier is his task than the one he has sent them to perform. . . . Throughout the war in Europe Eisenhower frequently escaped SHAEF to tramp in the field and talk with his men. There, like the others of us, he could see the war for what it was, a wretched debasement of all the thin pretensions of civilization."

In one exchange with a private in the 79th Division that day, Ike said, "Soldier, how many experts do you have in your rifle squad?"

"Three sir—I think."

"You think? Soldier, you had better know, damn it. Know exactly what you've got."

He spoke to another soldier, "And how many experts do you have?"

"Four. I'm one of them, sir."

"Good. That's fine. Where are you from?"

"Kentucky, sir."

"Got a good squad?"

"Best in the company, sir."

"Does the rest of the company think so?"

"Well, sir. . . ."

"Stupid bunch of people, aren't they!" According to Bradley, "Ike chuckled. The soldier grinned. We climbed back into the jeep."

Ike and John had lunch at Bradley's headquarters, and their old friend Gee Gerow joined them. His V Corps had run into very rough opposition at OMAHA Beach where it had run into a German division that had been in the area for maneuvers. After lunch Gee gave the two Eisenhowers some Camembert cheese he had no doubt liberated. According to John, "The atmosphere was calm and peaceful . . . here were officers who had been lifelong friends. . . . There was no cause for frenzy or excitement." They talked of trivial matters, and John said that those who criticized the military might have objected to that. But both Bradley and Gee had been in great personal physical danger at the time of the D-Day landings, and "Risks, gambles, and physical danger at times lay ahead for all three, including Dad. . . . this interlude was one in which all could enjoy, for a moment, a certain relative peace of mind." As Eisenhower and John left the Bradley headquarters Ike said, "Wish I didn't have to go back. I'll be mighty glad when we get moved over here with you."

They headed back to England, first aboard a DUKW, then on a PT boat, and finally on the destroyer that had brought them across the Channel in the morning. Both in the morning and the late afternoon they had passed long lines of LSTs. In the morning the landing craft had been returning from France, and while the Eisenhowers were returning to England, the LSTs were on their way to Normandy. The weather was clear, and the beachhead was secure. There was no longer any question about who would win the war. The question was when.

The next day Ike sent a message to Bradley:

> I most earnestly hope that you get Cherbourg tomorrow. As quickly as you have done so we must begin the preparations for the attack to the southward with all possible speed. The enemy is building up, and we must not allow him to seal us up in the northern half of the peninsula.

He also sent a message to Montgomery that would, he hoped, cause him to be more aggressive:

> I learn that your attack on the east flank started this morning. All the luck in the world to you and Dempsey.
>
> Please do not hesitate to make the maximum demands for any air assistance that can possibly be useful to you. Whenever there is any legitimate opportunity we must blast the enemy with everything we have.
>
> I am hopeful that Bradley can quickly clean up the Cherbourg mess and turn around to attack southward while you have got the enemy by the throat in the east. I am sure that Bradley understands the necessity of hitting hard and incessantly. Again good luck.

The next night Bradley cabled Ike that Cherbourg had been taken, though not before the port had been wrecked and heavily mined by the German defenders. The city had fallen to Collins' VII Corps. General Karl Wilhelm von Schlieben, the garrison commander, had surrendered without a struggle, and so had Admiral Walther Hennecke. Collins asked the general to surrender all his troops, but von Schlieben said that was impossible because he was out of touch with some of them. "I permitted him and the Admiral to wash up a bit," said Collins, "then started them back under an armed guard to First Army. After they left I had no compunction about instructing our psychological section to make maximum use of the charge that von Schlieben had saved his own skin while requiring his men to continue fighting." No wonder Allied troops, American GIs in particular, began saying and believing that the war would be over by Christmas or even Labor Day.

After their return to England, John and his father and very often Kay played bridge. They endured the buzz bombs, and commuted between Telegraph Cottage, Portsmouth, WIDEWING, and London. In *Crusade* Ike's memory of John's visit was somewhat different than that of his son. Eisenhower said that John "traveled with me everywhere, and his sole disappointment was my refusal to interfere in the normal routine for a young graduate and assign him to one of the infantry divisions then in Europe." John said, "Dad, never one to throw around posies, grumbled one day, 'Hell, if you weren't a regular officer with a career ahead of you, I'd just keep you here.' Such wishful thinking was counter to the facts. I was indeed a career officer, and my job was to go through Infantry School at Fort Benning and then join a division to fight. And I could never have borne the idea of spending the war as an aide—even to the Supreme Allied Commander. Dad knew this as well as I."

Later that month John got ready to return to the States. Eisenhower's own B-17 would be used to transport his son. Captain Mattie Pinette, Ike's personal secretary, was going along, and so were Sergeant Farr, his steward, and Tex Lee. Ike told Kay, "There's a spare place and I know you're anxious to meet Dick's mother. How would you like to go along?"

"I promptly forgot the war and entered into a little war of my own—an exit permit to leave England," said Kay. "My final attack on official lethargy was in the form of a telephone call from the Supreme Commander's office. The permit came through immediately."

Ike did not mention Kay's impending visit to Mamie until the day before the party left. That meant it was too late for Mamie to complain about Kay's visit or to forbid it. On June 29 he wrote:

> I suppose this is the first note I've ever written to you that is to be delivered by our son. He leaves tomorrow morning—and how I hate to see him go! He has been a great help to me, and I think he has enjoyed his visit.
>
> He was anxious to make the trip by air. Since I consider it the best way to go—particularly when conditions are favorable, I'm sending my own plane. To take advantage of the extra space in the ship, several people from my office are going on a short leave—and so John will have company. They

are Colonel Lee, my secretary, Mrs. Summersby, Capt. Pinette (WAC), and Sergeant Farr (my steward). They will probably play a bit of jack-leg bridge on the way, which will pass the time.

I guess Lee will go to see his mother at Indiana; Capt. Pinette will go to Maine. Mrs. Summersby is going to try to find Mrs. Arnold (mother of her late fiancé), and Sgt. Farr will go see his wife in Pa. So all are counting on having a big time for the week the plane will be in the U.S. The crew members are equally excited! The whole crowd of them have been very nice to Johnny.

Tomorrow I'll send you a teletype for our wedding anniversary. I've just sent a teletype to Stack asking him to send you roses on July 1. Hope it works OK. I will give Johnny the money to pay Stack. Wish I could come with them to deliver the flowers in person.

On July 1 he sent a telegram to be relayed to Mamie, knowing how she felt about flying and that she would be concerned about John's safety. He said that the route the plane would travel was the shortest, the pilot was excellent and Ike personally had "instructed him to take no chances if the weather is inclement." He hoped John would arrive "on the night of our anniversary." That was doubtful, however, "due to precautionary measures instilled in pilot."

That ought to ease Mamie's worries. She did not know, however, that, as Kay said, "Our send-off from the Germans was a buzz bomb. It landed several hundred yards away and rattled the car windows as we drove out to the airport. . . . All of us breathed a sigh of relief when London and the airport were far behind. In an airplane, the thought of being struck by a V-1 is particularly frightening."

All the passengers on the plane carried out their plans, and except by Kay, the trip was considered a success, particularly by Sergeant Farr. He spent a week with his wife in Pennsylvania, and exactly nine months later his wife had a baby.

Of the thirty-six-hour flight to Washington, Kay later said, "I got to know John Eisenhower a little better. . . . He seemed excessively honest, leaning almost too far backward in his anxiety to avoid unfair use of the Eisenhower name. He had an absolute horror of Brass. . . . John, incidentally, had the General's flair for writing and expression. And even an idiot could see he adored his father."

Mamie and Mrs. George Allen met the party at the airport, and, Kay said, "I found the general's wife an attractive, petite woman, her bangs the hint to a vivacious, friendly personality. We all chatted excitedly. Then Mrs. Eisenhower and Mrs. Allen went off to town, with John in tow, promising to call." Tex Lee had arranged for a room for Kay in a downtown Washington hotel, and though she was quickly to change her mind, her first impression of Washington was most favorable. "I could only bask in the peacetime atmosphere, the air of plenty," she said.

In *Eisenhower Was My Boss*, she said that the day after her arrival "I went up to the fashionable Wardman Park to visit Mrs. Eisenhower, who greeted me at the door with a welcome, tinkling, orange-filled Old Fashioned. Her cordiality helped me to meet the wives of various friends around headquarters, men I had known in North Africa and in England. In the beginning, I felt strange and foreign, much too British and much too militarized for this forgotten social side of femininity. But their natural friendliness soon thawed my embarrassment. Moreover, we had mutual interests, mutual friends: their husbands. I enjoyed meeting the wives of overseas friends, putting flesh on the name-skeletons rattled so continuously by lonely husbands abroad. . . . It was a lovely afternoon, and I enjoyed it thoroughly."

In *Past Forgetting* the account of the cocktail party is very different and possibly nearer to the truth; it is certainly less restrained. She said, "It was not much fun. I felt very stiff and foreign and military among these women in their fluttery light dresses. No other woman was in uniform. And certainly no other woman was being scrutinized as sharply as I was. As I sought out my hostess to say good-bye, John came up and told his mother that we were going to New York together and that he was going to take me to see *Oklahoma!*

"She made a face. 'Oh, I'm sure Miss Summersby doesn't want to go to New York in all this heat!'

" 'Yes, she does,' said John. 'We're going to New York and do the town.' . . . I have often wondered if perhaps Ike had asked John to do this."

Kay added, again in *Past Forgetting,* "It was in Washington that I became aware of the gossip about Ike and me. Of its virulence. No wonder the women at that cocktail party had been eyeing me so closely. Wherever I went, I began to feel as if I were on display. I became increasingly sensitive to the whispers. Ike must have been protecting me from a lot of this. Friends told me that there had been several gossip-column mentions of the General's glamorous driver and nastily pointed insinuations about our relationship."

Kay and John did a lot of sightseeing in Washington, "every building from the impressive Lincoln Memorial to the stately Capitol, from the White House to the Washington Monument." And in New York they did more sightseeing, but the city was less exciting than Washington and more familiar to Kay; she had seen it all in the movies, but *Oklahoma!* "was as lavish as any Hollywood musical; I was especially struck by the large number of males in the cast, which would have been impossible in wartime London."

When she returned to Washington, Kay said, "I spent most of the last hours stuffing piggishly, covering everything from milkshakes and orange juice to meat, salads, and fresh vegetables, all the delicacies I'd miss in London. . . . At the same time, I noticed a growing impatience with this selfish holiday. I wondered about the buzz-bombs, about Mother. I wondered about headquarters, about the official family, about Normandy. Tex, Mattie, and Sergeant Farr admitted to the same emotions.

"That old war-born sense of urgency surged through all of us as the B-17 took off, circled the lovely city of Washington for a final salute, and then headed 'home'—back to the war." Kay got back to Telegraph Cottage on Saturday, July 15. One buzz bomb had landed so close that the plaster had been knocked off an upstairs bedroom, and several windows had been broken. That night everybody slept in the shelter.

* * *

IRISH AND TRAGIC

For Ike Kay wasn't just a driver, a secretary, or a personal aide. She was his companion and confidante. Kay said he "made a practice of introducing me to all his friends and many of his British military associates. . . . 'I want you to know all these people, Kay. That way you can be even more helpful. I need someone to talk to and sort out my ideas with. Someone who knows the people and problems involved.' So just the fact of my knowing all these people and a little bit of how they would react to situations was useful." Anthea Saxe said, "He didn't know how to deal with the English aristocrats, and she helped. What you call a Lord and Lady, how to seat people at dinner parties, and this and that. She was a big help."

"Ike knew I was utterly discreet," Kay said, "and he had slowly got into the habit of talking things over with me in the car or over a drink when we arrived at Telegraph Cottage—after work—I never disagreed. I never made suggestions. I was just there. . . ." Kay told Anthea that "the general had said he couldn't trust his aides all that much. He said that Kay was the only person he could really trust. Kay was sort of his eyes and ears. She was very close-mouthed; never blabbered about anything . . . and I think he just trusted her as a terrific friend."

He permitted Kay to sit in on important meetings, including those of the senior staff officers at SHAEF at which secret matters were discussed. "We have no secrets from Kay," Ike would say. This surprised some of the staff, according to General James Gavin. "Chauffeurs do not normally join their generals for tea. . . . There was considerable gossip about Kay." George Patton was particularly upset by her presence and showed it. According to Larry Newman, "whenever Margaret Bourke-White or Clare Boothe Luce would come to the front, Patton would put on a typical Long Meadow Hunt country spread with all the wine and servants; and when Ike would bring Kay—sandwiches and coffee. He just did not put on the dog when Ike came with Kay." Nor would he talk to Ike in her presence. "I *do* have secrets from her," he would say.

Chet Hansen, General Bradley's aide during the war, said "there were people who did wonder. We thought it was kind of dumb once in a while to have a woman driver go into combat areas. It was just a dumb thing to do. If they were sleeping together it was their business. It was none of ours. He was the commander, he knew what he was doing."

Harrison Salisbury said that Eisenhower's relationship with Kay was general knowledge. "There was absolutely no secret about it, so far as—well, let's say anybody in the press corps or anybody in the Red Cross or anybody in headquarters. There are very few secrets in a headquarters of any kind. . . . Practically everybody had boyfriends or girlfriends, regardless of what their marital status was, when they were off during the war, and I think people rather liked this idea. It was a nice relationship and I think so far as the wartime period was concerned, nobody had any negative thoughts about it at all. It was good; it was fine. They enjoyed each other, and it gave them a little interlude in the war. You know, that's the sort of atmosphere that there was there."

One of the jokes circulating when I was a master sergeant concerned Ike and Kay. It seems one day Ike's car broke down. Kay gets out and lifts the hood and attempts to find out what's wrong. After working on the engine for a while Eisenhower picks up a tool in the car, goes out where Kay is working and asks, "Screw driver?" Kay looks out from under the hood and says, "We might as well, I can't get the damned thing fixed!"

Rumors circulated in Washington of the looseness of the WACs, the parties, the joy rides, and the "fallen" woman, Kay Summersby, who had been briefly married, divorced, made her money modeling and doing bit roles in movies— that is, before she became Ike's driver. When Kay visited Washington during the war, some of the army wives she met "left a bad taste in my memory." She was "hurt, then angered at the slander of WACs overseas. . . . How, I wondered, how could these Washington gossips . . . lump all overseas service women into one dirty group and then jab it with woman's cruelest weapon against woman; moral slander? I was even more upset at learning my own reputation was lost. I was a foreign woman—and I traveled with the High Brass. Therefore, I was a Bad Woman. . . . Nothing I could say or do would change this attitude. I was classified, labeled, and filed.

"A small, wicked voice inside cries out: 'Next war, My Girl, you may as well do all these things of which you're accused; they'll say you did anyhow!' "

Kay and Eisenhower shared many experiences at various headquarters throughout the war—in air raid shelters, on trips to the front, visiting troops. "She was particularly important to him," Anthea said, "because she allowed him to relax, by playing bridge with him." Kay said, "Our nightly bridge games did a lot to bring Ike and me together. We had an almost telepathic relationship. From the very beginning we played well together, and we soon became so attuned to each other's thinking that we were a very effective team." When time allowed they sometimes went sightseeing, and on more than one occasion slipped away for brief vacations. Unlike Mamie, Kay loved the outdoors. They went horseback riding—Kay was an excellent rider; they played golf, at which she was also good. In addition Kay was quite good looking. She was described in those days as "an extraordinarily attractive human being"; "Gay, witty, and charming." Anthea said she was "very glamorous. She really was. She really was a beauty. A lot of dash and verve. She just took his mind off things." John Eisenhower would one day describe her as "the Mary Tyler Moore of the headquarters. She was spunky, she was cute . . . I was very fond of her. . . . I wouldn't doubt that a bit but she was an asset. Whether she had designs on the Old Man, the extent to which he succumbed, I just don't know."

Anthea's husband, Ed, who became the executor for Kay's estate, said: "You have to think of each compartment separately. There may have been a time when Kay was more important to him than Mamie for reasons that were very specific at the time. This happens to all sorts of people and always will. But to take a day in the period of 1944 and make an assessment of his relationship with Mamie based on it isn't fair. You can make anything of this that you want to. I happen to think that the relationship was that which one would expect and I don't want to go any further. But I then say, 'So what?'

"She had it great during the war. . . . She was, after all, right up there at the pinnacle for so long, the whole world focusing on the war and her being there, this was the epitome of everything that mattered. And she had a close relationship with the man who was running it all."

When Ike first met Kay she was a private in the British Army and wound up a captain, an American citizen, and a WAC. Newman said, "Overnight she was in the U.S. Army, soon a second lieutenant, first lieutenant, and wound up a captain. I never asked her how she did it, and it still sort of baffles me, but I suppose during wartime you can do almost anything.

"She walked into it [the relationship] very slowly," Newman said, "but once she got into it, she was there. And she also knew from the beginning that it was a hopeless situation. She knew Ike's character better than anyone. She knew when the chips were down, that Mamie was going to have the ace. She had no chance. She served a purpose for Ike and she paid the price. She left the seat of power and he went on to do what he had to do."

Anthea said he never promised Kay marriage. "Judging from various bits and pieces that we saw, my own feeling was that the general probably was in love with her, but never, never to the point of leaving Mamie."

Shortly after Harry Butcher's death at the age of eighty-three in 1985, his widow, Mollie, who had been a British Red Cross worker in North Africa and had married Butcher after the war ended and he divorced his first wife, Ruth, announced in *Parade* magazine that "she [Kay] expected that Ike would eventually marry her and that they would spend at least one year in Tahiti. During the war, Ike must have mentioned Tahiti as a vacation paradise at least 100 times."

Mamie said of those rumors about her husband and his pretty driver, "I think all marriages are in jeopardy. That's where your good sense comes in. I wouldn't have stayed with him for five minutes if I hadn't had the biggest amount of respect in the world for him. People were afraid to tell me things to my face some times, but I knew most of the things that went on." As to the allegation that Eisenhower once thought of divorcing Mamie to marry Kay, John Eisenhower said it was "a spiteful falsehood."

When I wrote *Plain Speaking* in 1973, based on conversations I had with President Truman over a period of a year, I reported what Truman had told me, that "right after the war was over" Ike wrote Marshall, who was in Washington as army chief of staff, asking to be relieved of duty so that he could return to the United States to marry Kay. According to Truman, Marshall wrote back a letter "the like of which you never did see. He said that if he . . . if Eisenhower even came close to doing such a thing, he'd not only bust him out of the army, he'd see to it that never for the rest of his life would he be able to draw a peaceful breath. He said it wouldn't matter if he was in the army or wasn't. Or even what country he was in." Truman added that when he got wind of the correspondence he obtained the letters from the Pentagon and destroyed them.

Plain Speaking was not the first to suggest that Eisenhower was planning to divorce his wife to marry Kay. The fact that Ike wrote such a letter to Marshall was widely rumored when Eisenhower ran for the presidency in 1952. In fact it was said at the time that Eisenhower's telephones were tapped, so convinced were some Democrats that he still spoke to Kay on the phone.

There are two entries in Drew Pearson's diaries for 1952 pertaining to Kay Summersby. The first is dated February 21: "John Bennett stayed for dinner. He thinks Ike is afraid to come back for two reasons; one, he doesn't want to face Kay Summersby charges." The other reason, of course, was the "McCarthy blasts."

The second entry is on December 4: "John Bennett here for dinner, told about his talk with Eisenhower last Christmas when I sent Bennett to Paris with the Eisenhower Christmas cards. What Ike was chiefly concerned about was the General Patton letters and the fear that Mrs. Patton would release them. These are the letters in which Patton tells of Eisenhower's affair with Kay Summersby and his desire for divorce. Eisenhower wanted to know what the effect on the public would be if Mrs. Patton did release them. . . ."

Since I wrote *Plain Speaking*, Johns Hopkins University in Baltimore has found an exchange of postwar correspondence between Ike and Marshall bearing on the future of Ike, Mamie, and Kay. If this is the correspondence Truman described to me, the facts are completely at variance with his story and support John Eisenhower's contention "there is no evidence that divorce ever seriously crossed Dad's mind, even in the loneliest moments across the Atlantic."

According to these letters, nearly a month after V-E Day, on June 4, 1945, Eisenhower wrote Mashall requesting that he be permitted to bring Mamie to Europe to live with him.

Dear General:
Now that the time is approaching for my arrival in the United States I want to discuss with you one subject in which I must confess that my own conviction is somewhat colored by personal desire. It involves the possibility of enunciating some policy whereby certain personnel in the occupation forces could bring their wives to this country. . . . So far as my own personal case is concerned, I will admit that the last six weeks have been my hardest of the war . . . part of my trouble is that I just plain miss my family. . . . Moreover, the strain of the past three years has also been very considerable so far as my wife is concerned, and because of the fact that she has had trouble with her general nervous system for many years I would feel far more comfortable about her if she could be with me.

Marshall replied he would like to do anything he could for Eisenhower in his loneliness for his wife and son. There is no mention of "busting" Eisenhower out of the army as Truman said he had threatened. Moreover, Ike's wartime letters to Mamie, all handwritten, indicate much more explicitly that he planned to be with Mamie after the war, either in the States or in Europe.

He wrote to her from Algiers on April 12, 1943: ". . . my biggest ambition (aside from trying to help win this war) is to get home to you and never thereafter to leave your side."

And on June 11: "I could never be in love with anyone else—and . . . you fill my thoughts and hopes for the future always. . . . I'd rather be by your side than anywhere in the world."

And from Malta on July 9 of the same year: "It would be fun to have you and Johnny here with me . . . we could settle down to talk about family and what we're going to do when I come home again, and where we'll live and so on. . . ."

From Algiers on December 26: "I truly hope next year we'll be together; and I hope further that when we get this war won our long partings will be at an end."

From Bushy Park, London, on April 16, 1944: "I look forward to the day when we can travel and loaf together . . . I'd like to go to the corners of the earth—would you?"

From Versailles, January 3, 1945: "So far as you and I are concerned I hope you'll be ready to retire, so far into the country that it will take a visitor ten days by pack train to reach us."

From Reims April 4, 1945: "Just when this mess is to be over . . . I cannot even guess. But, thereafter, if I have to stay here indefinitely, you must come as soon as I can get a permanent abode."

A short time following the surrender he wrote: "Say nothing yet—but one thing is sure, I'm going to have a real visit with you!"

And on May 27: "I'm truly impatient to see you—I didn't realize how much so until the shouting stopped."

On the same day he wrote to Marshall, June 4, he wrote her: "What I'm most concerned in is the hope you can come back here very soon. I've written General Marshall. . . . I'd be willing to risk the cry of 'favoritism' to have you here. . . . I have a nice house that you'd love. While you might be lonely during the day, I could even occasionally get home for lunch and the nights I'd be away would be few."

Eisenhower left Frankfurt on Saturday, November 10, 1945, "to keep some engagements in Boston, Washington, and Chicago." Kay, in her first book, *Eisenhower Was My Boss*, indicates she thought he would be back, but according to Lieutenant Colonel Hortense Boutell who was on Eisenhower's staff in Germany after the war, "Kay wished he would, but I don't think there was much question at all that he would not be back. I don't think Kay realized the inevitability of what was going to happen. And she didn't want to think of it. Five of us, including Kay, lived in a house right within the compound of the General's house. Gradually we all teamed off and left. The last one there was Kay."

While in the States Eisenhower came down with a heavy cold and bronchitis and on November 22 entered Ashford General Hospital at White Sulphur Springs, West Virginia. In the interim the War Department conveniently changed his orders—he would not be returning to Europe—but would be stationed in Washington, D.C. Prior to leaving for the hospital, he dictated several letters, including the following to Beetle Smith:

Before you leave I think you should make arrangements to transfer Kay to General [Lucius] Clay, who wants her and has promised her a very good job with the promotion to which she is now entitled by reason of length of service in grade and the nature of her duties. It became completely impossible to continue her longer in my personal service due to the fact that she cannot become an American citizen until five years have passed, and an additional complication, just discovered, that since she, a foreigner, was commissioned for service in a specific theater, she would be automatically discharged upon arrival in the United States. . . . Since Kay has become far too widely publicized to hope to escape notice, there is nothing to do but to continue her in the European Theater until the day comes when all the WACs are disbanded and she will automatically come here because of the fact that her first paper business has been already initiated.

Along with the letter to Beetle was one to Clay.

Dear Lucius:
After looking over the situation here I find that it is entirely impossible to keep Kay Summersby in my personal office. I have explained the situation to Beedle [*sic*] and will attempt to do so in a letter to Kay herself. I hope you will find a really good job for her and I know that you will remember that she has not only served me with the utmost faithfulness and loyalty but has had more than her share of tragedy to bear in this war. Incidentally, she is about as close-mouthed a person about office business as I ever heard of.

In his letter to Kay he wrote:

I am terribly distressed, first because it has become impossible longer to keep you as a member of my personal official family, and secondly because I cannot come back to give you a detailed account of the reasons. . . .
In this letter I shall not attempt to express the depth of my appreciation for the unexcelled loyalty and faithfulness with which you have worked for the past three and a half years under my personal direction. . . .
I am sure you understand that I am personally much distressed that an association which has been so valuable to me has to be terminated in this particular fashion but it is by reasons over which I have no control. I shall watch your future with the greatest interest and I particularly request that at any time you believe I can be of any help you will let me know instantly,

either by a letter or by cable. After you come to this country I would be more than glad to do my best in helping you get a job in any place where anyone would have need for a person of your particular qualifications. . . . Finally, I hope that you will drop me a note from time to time— I will always be interested to know how you are getting along.

With lasting and warm regard, sincerely. . . .

That was the last really personal letter Eisenhower ever wrote to Kay; it was a kind of "Dear John" letter. Had Kay left it there, had she accepted it as a final good-bye she would have saved herself a lot of hurt and Eisenhower a lot of trouble.

Kay was transferred to Berlin, a place she found "depressing." She was assigned to General Clay's staff as a special officer in the Visitors Bureau. Her principal job was to handle VIPs, a job she found "uninteresting."

In reply to a letter from Beetle, Ike said he would try to write her a letter:

She is the only one of my personal official family who was left behind and yet she is the . . . one that, except for Lee, has been with me longest. I know that she feels very deserted and alone but I am certain that by following normal procedure she will obtain the best opportunity for a future job.

To a friend of Kay's, Margery Teulon Porter, a member of the Women's Royal Naval Service (WRNS), he wrote:

It became necessary to leave Kay behind. . . . I know she is badly disappointed because the group of us have been together so long that it has become second nature for her to work with that particular crowd and [she] will unquestionably feel lost in any other position.

Clay wrote to Eisenhower in March, the month Kay was promoted to captain, that Kay "had not enjoyed Berlin too much, as it involved making an entire new lot of friends." In another letter Clay said Kay "was anxious for her discharge at an early date." Ike, who planned to write his memoirs of the war, wanted a copy of Kay's diary and asked Clay if he would allow her to "make me a rough typewritten record. She is about the only one that could do it, for the reason that she probably made most of the entries in her own handwriting and abbreviations. I would be most appreciative—providing she has the time to do so—if you could have her undertake this job. I will enclose with this note a message to her because I want her to know that I will be personally appreciative of the work this would place upon her."

A note on the carbon indicates he did send Kay a handwritten message along with a letter of recommendation. The handwritten message is not with the Summersby file at the Eisenhower Library. The letter of recommendation he wrote is. In it he said:

TO WHOM IT MAY CONCERN

Subject: 1st Lieutenant Kay Summersby, WAC

Kay Summersby entered the employment of the American Forces in Europe in the summer of 1941 and has been continuously in the service of the War Department since that time. She was first employed as a civilian driver and later as a personal assistant in my office, and Secretary in charge of all mail.

Her outstanding characteristic is reliability, a trait that was particularly important during the war when her position made it impossible to keep from her knowledge operational secrets of the gravest type. She has an engaging personality and is particularly capable as receptionist and in managing appointments, which tasks she also carried out for me over a period of more than a year.

Any reader of this who may consider offering her a position, and wishing to communicate with me for more detailed exposition of her qualifications, need have no hesitation in doing so.

Lt. Summersby is definitely a superior type.

As far as Eisenhower was concerned, that was the end of Kay Summersby. But Kay was still in Berlin in September of 1946 when Ike arrived there on a trip with Mamie. Ike had no intention of seeing Kay, but he wanted to make sure she had made him a copy of her diary, and before leaving for Berlin had written General Clay:

Some time back Captain Summersby engaged to type out a diary kept by herself in my office during the European Campaign. It has become important that I learn timing of my movements during fall of 1944. Please ascertain if part of diary covering June 1944 through December 1944 has been typed. If so can a copy either be mailed here or handed to me when I arrive in Germany? Thanks.

In a note to Margaret Chick and Sue Sarafian (secretaries on Eisenhower's staff since 1943) on September 30, Kay said she had typed the material very quickly and hoped they would be "able to retype it for the Boss." The Boss did get her diary. Whether it was mailed or handed to him when he visited Germany is uncertain. One thing is certain, however: Kay did not hand it to him. A member of Clay's staff wrote to David Irving, author of *These Are the Generals*, on September 19, 1979:

As we were awaiting arrival of the plane I happened to look up and saw Kay S (with the dog Telek on leash) coming down the steps from the visitors' observation floor to the ground level where we were. I nudged Lucius [Clay] and pointed and he said, "Get rid of her." With considerable concern as to the outcome of the confrontation I met her at the foot of the steps. I said, "I'm sorry, Kay, but only the official greeting party is permitted down here." To which, to my great relief she replied, "Alright," and returned to the visitors' lounge. Mission accomplished. But I was somewhat nervous for the next few days.

Kay finally came to the United States in November of 1946, at which time she reported to Headquarters, Fourth Air Force, Hamilton Field, San Rafael, California. She was assigned to the PR Department while awaiting her discharge from the army. "She was still in the WACs," Anthea said, "and they had for some reason transferred her to California. By that time she saw the writing on the wall."

In the parking lot at Hamilton Field, Kay was attacked by someone who attempted to strangle her. Anthea said she escaped. "She screamed and screamed and somebody came and saved her." She recuperated from the experience at Butcher's home in California, and in a letter to him, Eisenhower said:

Kay went through a shocking experience but it was nice to know that every story and every reaction was on a sympathetic note. I can well imagine that she enjoyed the rest at your house after going through such an experience. . . .

Following the incident Kay became engaged to a man from San Francisco, and wrote to Eisenhower inviting him to the wedding. He replied saying he would be unable to attend as he was planning "to enter the hospital for his annual check-up and would be there for a few days."

Needless to say I wish for you and your husband every possible happiness. You served so long and so faithfully with the American forces and more particularly as one of my personal assistants, that I shall never lose the intense desire to see everything work out for the best for you and those close to you. . . .

But that, too, fell through. Kay found out that the man she was intending to marry thought she was enormously rich. Anthea said, "He was a real jerk and fortunately she found out just before the formal invitations went out. This was the story of Kay's life, though. One bad thing after another. So easily taken in, wasn't she? By men, anyway. She got out all right, and came to New York."

In his diary on December 2, 1947, Eisenhower recorded what under the circumstances cannot have been a surprise to him.

Heard today, through a mutual friend, that my wartime secretary (rather personal aide and receptionist) is in dire straits.

Then he proceeded to analyze what the trouble was with his "wartime secretary, rather personal aide and receptionist."

A clear case of a fine person going to pieces over the death of a loved one, in this instance the man she was all set to marry. Will do what I can to help, but it would seem hopeless. Too bad, she was loyal and efficient and the favorite of everyone in the organization. Makes one wonder whether any human ever dares become so wrapped up in another that all happiness and desire to live is determined by the actions, desires—or life—of the second. I trust she pulls herself together, but she is Irish and tragic.

Eisenhower's outstanding ability for self-justification was working full time that day. He knew perfectly well that Kay's being in "dire straits" had nothing to do with Dick Arnold's death. She had been deeply moved by that, but it had happened four years before. If Kay was "going to pieces" it was in response to her life since leaving Europe, the horror of the attack, the mistaken marriage she had almost made, and the fact that a man who had become central to her life had clearly abandoned her. He knew it, and he was ignoring it, even in the privacy of his diary.

By the time Kay got to New York she was undoubtedly a lost soul. Larry Newman knew Kay very well. "I took her out for a year, saw her regularly after the war, after California. I knew her after '47 all the way until she died. That guy was within a phone call of doing something. A lot of other people who were close to Ike, including Beetle Smith, all of them that I know of gave Kay a broad berth. When they were overseas it was 'Kay, whatever I can do for you.' "

It shocked Kay, at first, according to Anthea, that Eisenhower should cut the bonds of friendship. "I think even more of a shock was here in the States she didn't matter one bit. Couldn't get any sort of a decent job. She didn't do too well when she came back here. Having been, you know, really, having worked for someone like Eisenhower. You are sitting right outside his office, you get delusions of grandeur. . . . And Kay had a good opinion of herself, in a nice way. In her own funny way, she was a bit of a snob."

While living in New York Kay made a trip to Washington and went to see Ike at the Pentagon. He had told each member of his staff in Germany "to call on me when he or she comes through. . . . He had even issued orders that "whenever an old friend or acquaintance of the war days comes to my place he is to be assured that I will see him. . . . I will not have old friends turned away merely because I am busy. . . ." He said he was "delighted when women he knew from Europe who came to Washington stopped in to see him." According to Anthea, "Kay brought Telek and the general couldn't be nicer. He was very friendly and thrilled to see the dog."

After seeing Kay Ike wrote to a mutual friend:

I thought she looked very well, in spite of the many difficult things she has encountered in the past two or three months. I am sure there is going to come a time soon when she will get herself established and really settled in something she will like, and where she will be happy.

When Kay returned to her hotel room after visiting Ike, Anthea said "the general's office telephoned. I don't know how they put it, but the gist of it was 'don't come back to the general's office.' "

After that she received the same treatment in Washington as she had in New

York. Chet Hansen said, "No one would see her. No one would talk to her. No one would have anything to do with her. She had a hard time, a very hard time."

Eisenhower's book of war memoirs, *Crusade in Europe*, was published in 1948. In it Kay, who served "faithfully" by his side from 1942 to 1945, the "one that, except for Lee, has been with me longest," is mentioned one time. "Kay Summersby was corresponding secretary and doubled as a driver." And despite the fact she had given him a copy of her diary to use as a reference for the book, she is not mentioned in the acknowledgments. He says, "I am deeply indebted to a group of close friends for the assistance that allowed me quickly to concentrate and edit wartime notes, memoranda, and memories into a single narrative of my experiences in World War II. Among them the Hon. Joseph E. Davies . . . my wartime chief of staff, now Ambassador; Walter B. Smith; and Brigadier General Edwin Clark. . . ."

He was not without a spark of generosity, however. He mentions in his diary that he planned to give her $1,000 for her help with the book that was to make him a rich man.

According to Eisenhower's diary, "Long ago I determined that if ever I should publish a war memoir for which I should be paid, I would remember with substantial presents some of the people who served me so faithfully and unselfishly during the war, as members of my immediate personal staff." Kay Summersby was to be given $1,000.

Would Mamie have allowed it any other way? Would any jealous wife? Mamie certainly tried her best to keep Kay out of the TV series based on the book. According to Ken McCormick, who was working with Eisenhower on the memoirs, they had all gone down to the studio for a screening, and "When it came to the signing of the armistice, with all the generals crowding around, there, head bobbing behind for all to see, was Kay. Mamie saw that and privately blew her top and said, 'This will not do and she must not be in this.' "

So Ken McCormick asked Arthur Treudal, who was their contact with the TV studio, if it could be fixed. "He answered, 'Do you want me to tell you what you wish or do you want me to tell you what's got to be?' I said, 'Tell me what's got to be.' Treudal answered, 'We can't fix it.' The voice was just behind the picture and it was just enough sprockets off that if you took a scissor to it you'd clearly tampered with things and you ran out of sequence. So, you had to know she was there and watch for it. She wasn't on the screen two or three seconds, but just the fact she was there at all made Mamie angry. As far as I know it is still in the film strip."

After completing his memoirs, Ike came to New York to take on the presidency of Columbia University. Kay was also in New York working on her own account of the war, which would also be published that year. It was ghostwritten, but nevertheless, Hortense Boutell said, "Kay went through every bit of it. I know this for a fact because I was with her often as she stayed with me several times during that period. Nothing got in there if she didn't want it." Anthea said the first book was a "legitimate attempt on the part of Kay to write a truthful story. Forgetting the quality of the book. She felt she needed the money and she thought this was an opportunity to get some." John said of *Eisenhower Was My Boss*, "It was very accurate. I keep it as a reference."

On May 31 she wrote to Eisenhower telling him she was in New York working on a book and asked if she might stop in to see him. "I have had so much worry and trouble lately that it has been difficult to get down to letter writing." Her youngest sister had recently died, and her mother had become ill. Eisenhower replied on June 1:

Dear Kay:

It is distressing to learn of the tragedies in your family. I am deeply sympathetic in the grief I know you must feel because of the death of your sister. Your mother's breakdown must add immeasurably to your burdens.

I was somewhat astonished to learn that you were in New York working on a book. I thought that you had gone back to the WAC some months ago and assumed that you were somewhere on a military station. . . .

I can scarcely estimate when there might arise an opportunity for you to come past the office. The days are an unending series of conferences and work, and within a very few days I must take over direct responsibility for administration. My time is practically solidly booked through June and July, and in August I hope to take a trip to the west. It has been a fight to keep at least one afternoon a week free for golf, and I have discovered that without exercise I simply cannot go on. . . .

With kindest regards and very best wishes, Cordially . . .

Before publication of Kay's book, her literary agent, George Bye, visited Ike at which time he said he had no objections to the book's publication. What he did object to, as he told Myron Boardman, vice-president of Prentice-Hall, Kay's publisher, was the proposed title *Eisenhower's "Girl Friday."*

On July 16, Ike wrote Boardman:

So long as you have asked for my comment . . . I do have a reservation with respect to your proposed title which I deem to be inappropriate and inaccurate. Kay Summersby had an important position in my office and one which demanded complete reliability and loyalty on her part. However, there were a great number of individuals in that office, including a number of women. Therefore, I believe that to use the title you suggest is scarcely indicative of the situation.

I cannot myself suggest any title that I might deem suitable and which you might consider carried any particular sales appeal. But, if, as you say, you should like to be assured that I have no real objection to the book's publication, then I must tell you that I should like to see this particular point resolved.

Bye wrote a second appeal to Eisenhower to give his approval for the suggested title. On July 26 Ike replied:

I never heard of such an expression as "Eisenhower's Girl Friday." . . . It has struck me unfavorably, and I still believe that some other title would be more accurate and more descriptive. I do not understand, for example, why my name has to appear in the title, but again I realize that the publisher and yourself may have what you consider good reasons for this. . . . I do not see why some such title as "A WAC in SHAEF" or "A WAC in Eisenhower's Headquarters" would not be better:

On July 28 he wrote to Kay on the same matter:

Recently I have had letters from both your agent and from your publisher regarding the suggested title for your book. . . . The suggestion they made seemed to be a bit out of line and I informed them to this effect. You know, of course, I wish you the best of luck in this publishing venture, but since these people asked me for my honest opinion, I had to give it to them. . . .

Kay most certainly felt rejected when she read the end of the letter:

Ruth Briggs visited me recently just as I was leaving town. However, she and I had a few minutes to rush rapidly over old times. . . .

In other words, he found time in his "busy" schedule to see Ruth, but not her.

Kay's book, *Eisenhower Was My Boss,* was published in September of 1948. In portions of it published in four installments in *Life* magazine, Summersby was called "Eisenhower's 'Girl Friday.' " Ike wrote to Butcher:

the hue and cry was taken up by one or two columnists and, of course, the result was not pleasant for me. However, I have simply gone on in my own way and offered no word or criticism or defense to anyone.

Kay sent him a copy of the book, and on September 30 he acknowledged it, saying "I scarcely ever get to read but will seek an early opportunity to go through your account of the war." Four months later, in a letter to Butcher he said, "Actually, I never got to read Kay Summersby's book except for the first and last chapters."

But in 1952 when he was a candidate for the presidency there apparently were some people, particularly some Republicans running his campaign, who *had* read it and found it objectionable. The book suddenly became unavailable in Washington bookstores I am told, and the rumors were that the Republicans had bought up all the copies. And at the New York Public Library at Fifth Avenue and 42nd Street, all three copies which they owned suddenly and mysteriously disappeared.

Kay went on tour to promote the book, which kept her busy for a while, but then she returned to New York where she took a job as a salesclerk at Bergdorf Goodman's. She later met a stockbroker, Reginald Morgan, and on November 20, 1952, they were married. Kay sent Ike a wedding announcement and she received a note of congratulations in return.

As far as it is known there was no further communication or contact between Kay and Eisenhower after her marriage to Morgan and Ike's becoming president. Yet her name did come up from time to time in private conversation. Maude

Black recalled her husband bringing the subject up one evening in their apartment in New York. "Nothing to it," Ike told Douglas Black. "We were all too busy and tired out from the war."

William Bragg Ewald, who was a member of Eisenhower's White House staff and later worked with him on the two presidential memoirs, said that once after the presidency, when he and his wife and John were having dinner at the Gettysburg farm—Mamie was not present—"John brought up the name of Kay Summersby, Eisenhower's attractive British wartime secretary, whose association with him had for years inspired gossip and speculation. 'What was she doing now?' John asked. Ike handled it perfectly, I thought. A bit hurt, perhaps, he simply told John the little he knew. . . . No defense, no denial, no anger."

It is interesting that John should have mentioned so personal a subject to his father when other people were present rather than privately, little wonder that under the circumstances Eisenhower was possibly "a bit hurt." Eisenhower's response to the question was typical: He told what he knew without personal embellishment.

Other men might have tried to explain or apologize for a relationship that had become at least a prominent footnote to history. Eisenhower was not an explainer or an apologizer. Kay had been important to him, in whatever way, and important to the wartime effort at the time. This was no longer the time. The war was over.

What had become of Kay? Her marriage to Morgan did not work out at all and they were divorced in 1958. Larry Newman said "they fought like cats and dogs." Anthea said the same: "They fought all the time. He was attracted to her past, the glamor of it all. In fact, after Kay died, he came to see me to get some of his personal belongings and said, 'I know everyone is telling you how marvelous Kay was, but I'll tell you she was hell as a wife. Sometimes she would rip the phone out of the wall and throw it at me.' I said, 'Jack, I bet she had a good reason!' She wasn't happy with Morgan. She was very disappointed."

Kay returned to England for a year in the early seventies—she worked as a saleslady in an exclusive shop—but she wasn't happy living there and returned to New York. Her whole life was a terrible comedown after the war. She had to struggle, and the last years of her life, according to several sources, were "horrible."

Ed Saxe was able to secure her a position with CBS as a fashion coordinator—clothes for entertainers—but then in 1973 she became ill and doctors found she had terminal cancer. It was during this final illness that she signed a contract to write a second book, *Past Forgetting: My Love Affair with Dwight D. Eisenhower*. But on January 20, 1974, just a month after signing the contract, Kay died.

Past Forgetting was supposed to be the "true story of the passionate, moving secret love affair" between Kay and Eisenhower, but not according to her close friends.

Anthea Saxe said Kay was always very quiet about everything. "In fact, this last dreadful book was only written after her death. She never saw a word of it. That was absolutely not Kay. Just dreadful. She was dying and she had this friend who knew about it and this friend of hers, who was a writer, who in the end didn't write it but wanted to, said, 'Kay, why don't you tell the real story. I'll write it for you and you will make lots of money. You owe it to history.' Kay believed all this and took an advance of $10,000 or something—then she died. She never saw a single word of that dreadful book. A complete myth, the whole thing. A complete myth. It was made up. Absolutely. Absolutely. The book is so unlike Kay it was ridiculous."

Chet Hansen said he once asked Ed Saxe "why he didn't stop the damn thing. Saxe said, 'I couldn't; it was all bits and pieces. There was an agent who had a piece; there was a ghostwriter who had a piece; and there were a lot of others.' "

Hortense Boutell said she talked to Kay a couple of times before she died, "and I had a friend who knew the writer who worked on it and said that it was not Kay Summersby."

John Eisenhower said, "I personally think the second book [*Past Forgetting*] is pretty warped."

"For her to die as she did," Larry Newman said, "alone, and writing something for pure existence, the last book, in order to eat, to me it is one of the crying shames. She wrote it simply because she was desperate. She had such horrendous doctor bills and she had so few friends; she had some who helped and gave her money, but not nearly enough to see her through."

Still, Kay was never bitter, "not even at the end," Anthea said. Perhaps she believed what Eisenhower is said to have told her once, "that if there are two paths a man can take . . . then all things being equal, he should take the path along which he will do the most good, inflict the least hurt." With the general, duty would always come first.

★ ★ ★

OUT OF THE WOODS

Eisenhower had kept a diary, writing down everything that had happened while Kay was in the States. It had been a busy time. On July 1 Ike had returned to the beachhead. Mickey went with him, and he said, "We spent the next four days inspecting the front, looking at rocket and robot-bomb sites; getting the feeling of this new war." Bradley, who met the party at the air strip, said, "Although correspondents had begun to quip over Monty's recurrent failures at Caen, Eisenhower appeared neither disappointed in nor distressed by the course of our battle for the beachhead."

Eisenhower had dinner in Bradley's mess and spent the night at his CP. The next morning, Sunday, July 2, they went to Monty's new headquarters. Bradley said, "Whereas I preferred to live, work, and eat in the field with my staff, Monty sought the solitude of a lonely camp, removed and isolated from his main 21st Group CP." Gault, who was with the two Americans, said, "It was indeed a peaceful scene as General Montgomery's two puppies were playing in the grass and the only sign of war was a Panther and a Tiger tank which had arrived the day before." Eisenhower was furious when he found out from Bradley that the new 76-mm high-velocity guns, now the main armament of American Sherman tanks, could not penetrate the armor of the enemy tanks. "You mean our 76 won't knock these Panthers out?" he said. "I thought it was going to be the wonder gun of the war."

Bradley told the Supreme Commander that the 76 didn't have "the kick to carry her through the German armor. . . . Ike shook his head and swore. 'Why is it that I'm always the last to hear about this stuff? Ordnance told me this 76 would take care of anything the Germans had. Now I find you can't knock out a damn thing with it.' "

He didn't say so, but the Supreme Commander may have thought that he had had to deal with inadequate American tanks since shortly after the end of the First World War. And the United States was the greatest industrial nation on earth? True, the British had developed a weapon that could pierce the armor of the Panther, but Monty said they couldn't spare any for the Americans. "Obviously, if we were to deal with the Panthers we would have to improvise on our own," said Bradley.

By the beginning of July the Allies had landed 1,000,000 men in Normandy, thirteen American, eleven British, and one Canadian division. More than 566,000 tons of supplies had been brought ashore, as well as 171,532 vehicles. As Eisenhower later said, "It was all hard and exhausting work, but its accomplishment paid off in big dividends when finally we were ready to go full out against the enemy." During that same three-week period 41,000 prisoners had been taken; Allied casualties had reached 60,000. About 9,000 had been killed.

Eisenhower stayed on the beachhead until the morning of the 5th. During his stay, according to Mickey, "We went up to the lines and inspected men there; we went to hospitals and saw men. . . . We saw the [V-1] bomb sites from which the Germans had hoped to finish off the people on the other side of the Channel. We heard a lot of the noise of war . . . and a few times we were close enough to landing shells to have to jump. We got out of one corps headquarters only a couple of minutes before the German artillery opened up on it with all they had, which was plenty. We went across a bridge which was under shellfire, and we were always on roads the enemy would have liked to hit."

In a story of that visit to France the July 6 *New York Times* reported, "In a motor trip General Eisenhower . . . went past an enemy resistance pocket on the American side of the Normandy beachhead.

"General Eisenhower, intent on studying the entire front for himself, started on the British and Canadian sector in the east and worked over to the extreme west-coast positions of the Americans.

"He was in exposed positions most of the time, and twice German artillery barrages started just after he had left certain areas. Scorning a helmet, the general wore only a cloth hat."

After seeing Montgomery on the 2nd Eisenhower returned to Bradley's tent headquarters. According to his West Point classmate, "At dinner that evening over a captured bottle of good wine, Eisenhower relaxed in an evening of conversation. We pulled the blackout flaps on the mess tent and sat until long after dark."

Eisenhower said that several days before, he had asked a soldier his occupation, and the young man had said he was a wheat farmer from Kansas.

"How many acres have you got?" asked Eisenhower.

"Twelve thousand, sir," said the soldier.

"Twelve thousand?" said Eisenhower. "And how many do you have in wheat?"

"Nine thousand, sir."

"What's the yield?"

"Forty-one bushels to the acre."

"Mister," Eisenhower said, "just remember my name. When the war's over, I'll be around for a job."

In telling the story to Bradley, Eisenhower said, "When I was a kid, 250 acres of Kansas wheatland would have represented an honest ambition for any Abilene boy. Yessir, it would have looked mighty good to me—and I guess to you, too, Brad."

Bradley added, "In Moberly [Missouri] I would have settled for 160."

They left the mess tent to retire, and, according to Bradley, "As we walked through the wet grass toward my truck, a fire riveted the sky over Omaha five miles to the north. Ike stopped to look as the guns echoed over the beachhead.

" 'A bit noisier than London,' I said.

"He laughed. 'You haven't been back for the buzz bombs!' "

On the 3rd Eisenhower visited an unfinished site for the launching of buzz bombs. Then he went to Cherbourg. The Germans had mined and practically destroyed the port, and General von Schlieben was being difficult. He refused to eat the K rations he was given and complained that there was no shower in the farmhouse where he was kept. Only a month earlier, he pointed out, he had been guest of honor at a dinner in Cherbourg, and provided a menu to prove it. Lobster hollandaise had been served, pâté de foie gras, baked bluefish, roast leg of lamb, peaches and cream, château wines, vintage champagne, and Napoleon brandy. As Bradley's G-2 observed, after reading the menu, "Now he's going to England at the height of the brussels sprout season."

On the 4th of July Eisenhower made several other inspections, including a fighter airfield of the Ninth Air Force. Bradley, after celebrating the 4th by ordering that every nonconcealed gun in his army be fired at noon—it was the largest national salute the U.S. Army ever fired—returned to the CP to "find that Eisenhower had squeezed into the back seat" of a modified P-51 to be flown by Major General Elwood R. "Pete" Quesada, chief of the Ninth. The two men, said Bradley, "grinned like sheepish school boys caught in a watermelon patch. Quesada had been cautioned . . . to stick to the ground where he was worth more to us in a swivel chair than in the cockpit of a fighter. And Eisenhower was frightened for fear word of his flight might leak to the newsmen.

" 'General Marshall,' he admitted, 'would give me hell.'

"Then he added, 'All right, Brad, I'm not going to fly to Berlin.' "

When he got back, the field was crowded with fifty reporters and photographers, and on July 6 a headline in the New York Times said, EISENHOWER FLIES OVER NAZI LINES; a subhead added, FLIGHT FEATURES 5-DAY TOUR OF NORMANDY FRONT IN WHICH HE WAS OFTEN IN DANGER. There were pictures in newspapers everywhere in the United States and England, and, as Mickey observed, "The shots the photographers got of the General that day didn't show him with any too pleasant expression . . . as I've said, he hated anything that anybody might think was showing off. And he said there'd be hell to pay if the press interpreted that flight as a stunt. He was annoyed with himself for going on the flight."

In his report to Marshall after his return from France, Eisenhower said of his flight over the hedgerows of Normandy, "The nature of the country is playing such an important part that I took a quick flight over it yesterday, carefully escorted by a half-dozen fighters. I rode in a modified fighter myself and was up only about twenty or thirty minutes. Unfortunately, I hear that the newspapers, as usual, have gotten hold of the incident. . . . Actually, it was pure business (1) to see the country and (2) a gesture to our pursuit pilots who are doing yeoman work in attempting to find and plaster targets."

Marshall's reaction to the twenty- or thirty-minute unauthorized flight is not recorded, but on the 11th Eisenhower explained to Mamie, "Lately I saw a piece in the paper which intimated that on 4th July in France I was exceedingly reckless to 'show off.' Pay no attention to such tales. I'm most careful—and I'm not talking for effect. Ask Johnny how promptly I duck to the shelter when the 'buzzers' come around!"

There was one note of optimism in Eisenhower's July 5 message to Marshall; he said, "My latest reports on Cherbourg are more hopeful than they were at first. I personally visited the city, and while I do not know how long it will take us to get rid of the mine hazard, I must say that otherwise the place is not demolished anything like some of the other ports we have been forced to use in the past."

As for the infantry battles in France, he said, "The going is extremely tough, with three main causes responsible. The first of these is, as always, the fighting quality of the German soldier. The second is the nature of the country. Our whole attack has to fight its way out of very narrow bottlenecks flanked by marshes and against an enemy who has a double hedgerow and an intervening ditch almost every fifty yards as ready-made strong points. The third cause is the weather. Our air [force] has been unable to operate at maximum efficiency and on top of this, the rain and mud were so bad during my visit that I was reminded of Tunisian wintertime. . . . Even with clear weather it is extraordinarily difficult to point out a target that is an appropriate one for either air or artillery."

One of the American heroes in Normandy that summer was twenty-nine-year-old Curtis G. Culin, Jr., from New York City, a sergeant in an armored reconnaissance unit. In the meetings in London before OVERLORD, there was a great deal of discussion about the Germans, about the French underground, about the roads, the towns and the cities, and about the railways and the rivers. But there was almost no discussion of a problem that was to be almost as formidable an enemy in Normandy as the German soldiers, the hedgerows.

On the twentieth anniversary of D-Day, Eisenhower remembered in detail the hedgerows and the problem they presented. "The hedgerow isn't really a hedge," he said. "It's a bank of earth, sometimes four or five feet thick and four or five feet tall. The hedge itself grows right out of it, and the whole thing gets maybe ten feet or more tall. And the tanks simply couldn't get through it.

It is as hard as cement, and when the tanks tried to get through they were upended, their guns pointed straight to the sky.

"The hedgerows just put us out of action, and then a sergeant named Culin came up with a solution. He welded a steel snout to a tank so that it could cut right through the hedgerows, and, by the way, he used steel that had been left behind by the Germans.

"This idea got to General Bradley very quickly, and he was just ecstatic over it. Very soon two out of every three of our tanks were equipped with that snout; they were called Rhinos, for rhinoceros."

Actually the idea didn't originate with Culin. One day early that summer Captain James De Pew, commander of Culin's outfit, the 2d Armored's 102d Cavalry Reconnaissance, called his men together to talk over what could be done about the hedgerow problem. A man Max Hastings in his book *Overlord* identifies as "a Tennessee hillbilly named Roberts" said, "Why don't we get some saw teeth and put them on the tank and cut through these hedges?" Hastings wrote, "The crowd of men laughed, but Sergeant Culin, a notably shrewd soldier known in the outfit as a chess player and a man impatient with Army routines, said: 'Hang on a minute, he's got an idea there.' Culin it was who put Roberts' ill-articulated notion into effect and directed the first demonstration. The tankers—and shortly thereafter General Bradley—watched with awe as a hedgerow exploded before their eyes to make way for the Sherman bursting through. . . . It is difficult to overstate the importance of the 'Rhinos,' as they were called, for they restored battlefield maneuverability to Bradley's armour. Culin was later summoned to appear before an American press conference in Paris. An honest man, he tried hard to give some credit to Roberts. But the weight of the great propaganda and publicity machine was too much for him. He became a very American kind of national hero." Culin was given a Legion of Merit for his "invention." He later lost a leg in the Huertgen Forest. By the time of Bradley's breakthrough out of Normandy, which began on July 25, three out of every five American tanks had been equipped with the sergeant's steel tusks.

On July 10 Operation COBRA was born. As Ernie Pyle wrote at the time, "Surely history will give a name to the battle that sent us boiling out of Normandy, some name comparable with Saint-Mihiel or Meuse-Argonne of the last war. But to those of us there on the spot at the time it was known simply as the break-through. We correspondents could sense that a big drive was coming. . . . And then one evening Lieutenant General Omar Bradley, commanding all American troops in France, came to our camp and briefed us on the coming operation. It would start, he said, on the first day we had three hours of good flying time in the forenoon."

That day was July 25.

What Beetle often called "the Monty problem" continued, and as July went on it got worse. By the end of the month, Churchill was frequently expressing his dissatisfaction with Britain's most revered hero, and Tedder was saying openly that it might be necessary to sack the man. In his 1984 book about OVERLORD,

British writer Max Hastings said, "At the time and for some years after the war the extent of the breakdown of relations between Montgomery and Eisenhower was concealed. Today there is no doubt that by late July 1944, the American was wearied to death of his ground force commander." And on July 6 another troublesome general arrived on the continent, Patton.

In 1946 Eisenhower was sent the publisher's proof copy of a book called *Patton and His Third Army*. He apparently was asked to make corrections and comments, and he wrote in pencil in the front of the book, which he kept for his personal library, his frankest appraisal of the late Georgie:

> This book is about one of my oldest, dearest and most intimate friends covering a span of 26 years.
>
> I have hastily looked over some of the early pages of this book. It is a thrilling intimate account (generally very accurate) of a great operation. But it will be ruined if the author does not eliminate certain statements which seem to seek for George credit that can easily be proved to others, chiefly Bradley—who commanded the army group.
>
> George Patton was the most brilliant commander of an army in the open field that our or any other service produced. But his army was part of a whole organization and his operations part of a great campaign. Consequently, in those instances where Patton obeyed orders, the story only hurts itself by assuming that Patton conceived, planned and directed operations in which he was in fact—the brilliant executor.
>
> Within his own sphere Patton had exercised plenty of initiative but as far as shaping any boundaries and prescribing definite directions of attack were involved, Bradley had to do it—otherwise chaos.

Patton flew over from England late in the morning of July 6; he came in a flight of three C-47s with four P-47s as an escort; each of the C-47s carried a jeep. He went immediately to Bradley's headquarters and spent the night there. The next day he had lunch with Bradley, Monty, and de Guingand. He expressed his dissatisfaction with Montgomery in his diary that night:

> After lunch, Montgomery, Bradley and I went to the war tent. Here Montgomery went to great length explaining why the British had done nothing. Caen was their D-Day objective and they have not taken it yet.
>
> He tried to get Bradley to state that the Third Army would not become operational until the VIII Corps had taken Avranches. Bradley refused to bite because he is using me as a means of getting out from under 21 Army Group. I hope he succeeds.

Montgomery and Patton did not like each other, though Patton's distaste for Monty was more public and more colorfully expressed. But, as one of Patton's biographers, H. Essame, observed, "the two men had much in common. Both were athletic; both played to win; both were equally contemptuous of convention; both had highly developed histrionic tendencies. Both were ardent Episcopalians; both were communicants; both avidly read the Bible, including the blood-thirsty chapters of the Old Testament; both believed profoundly in the efficacy of prayer as an aid to victory." Eisenhower was "like an impresario with two stars in one play competing for popular acclaim."

In early July Patton was still on the sidelines, afraid the war would end without his help. Montgomery was very much in the center of things, but there was a strong feeling at Eisenhower's headquarters that the center was and would remain static. Perhaps Montgomery had outlived his usefulness. Drew Middleton once said, "After the war Eisenhower told me in Washington that we had to have Montgomery to get across the Channel, and a year later in Moscow Beetle said the same thing, that Montgomery was the only man who could have got us across the Channel. That was the kind of battle Monty fought best, the set piece battle. He wasn't all that good with an encounter battle and he wasn't all that great in pursuit, but if you said, 'We have to land there,' he would land you there and stay there."

Patton had brought with him his bull terrier, Willie, and one of the six volumes of E. A. Freeman's *History of the Norman Conquest*, the latter because he knew that while the Germans were in retreat—and he planned to have them retreating as soon as he could—they would have to use the same roads as those used by William the Conqueror, and if necessary Patton would pursue them down those roads, many of which were said still to exist.

Patton almost immediately decided that not only was Montgomery inadequate; so were his American colleagues. He said in his diary, "Neither Ike or Brad has the stuff. Ike is bound hand and foot by the British and does not know it. Poor fool. We actually have no Supreme Commander—no one who can take hold and say that this shall be done and that shall not be done. It is a very unfortunate situation to which I see no solution."

Hitler was also dissatisfied with his command structure. On July 1 Field Marshal Wilhelm Keitel, the fuehrer's commander in chief, had plaintively asked von Rundstedt, "What shall we do? What shall we do?"

Von Rundstedt said, "Make peace, you fools. What else can you do?" He was immediately replaced, but the man who succeeded him in Normandy, field Marshal Hans Günther von Kluge, soon reached the same conviction. He was not fired, but on his way to see Hitler a few weeks later he took a poison capsule and died. Rommel, who was also pessimistic about the outcome of the war, didn't have long to live either.

The Germans had lost the war, but Hitler didn't know that, and neither did tens of thousands of his troops.

By July 7 the time for confrontation with the Germans had definitely arrived. More and more Allied troops were pouring onto the beachhead, but there seemed to be no forward movement at all; there were those who said this war was becoming a repetition of the trench-warfare conditions of World War I, and somebody else said, "If we do not push inland shortly, we shall have to build skyscrapers to accommodate everyone." A great many people were afraid that Normandy might become another Anzio.

Beetle and Tedder urged Eisenhower to draft a letter which, as Tedder put it, "would tell Montgomery tactfully to get moving." Who dictated the letter is not known, possibly Morgan, now deputy chief of staff at SHAEF, or Beetle, but a draft was ready the next morning. Tedder felt it was *too* tactful. It said, in part:

> It appears to me that we must use all possible energy in a determined effort to prevent a stalemate or of facing the necessity of fighting a major defensive battle with the slight depth we have in the bridgehead. . . .
>
> I know that you are thinking every minute about these weighty questions. What I want you to know is that I will back you to the limit in any effort you may decide upon to prevent a deadlock and will do my best to phase forward any unit you might find necessary. For example, if you could use in an attack on your left flank an American armored division, I would be glad to make it available and get it to you as soon as possible. . . . Please be assured that I will produce everything that is humanly possible to assist you in any plan that promises to get us the elbow room we need. The air and everything else will be available.

The next day Tedder was asked what he thought of the British Second Army's plans and attacks. He replied, "Company exercises. That day [July 8] I phoned Portal." Portal "told me about his visit to Normandy on 7 July. He too was disturbed at the lack of progress by the Army. The problem was Montgomery, who could be 'neither removed nor moved' to action. Later that day, Generals Morgan and Gale, deputy chief of staff and senior administrative officer respectively, spoke to me of their apprehensions about the slow pace of our advance. . . . I gathered from Morgan that the Prime Minister was alive to the danger. To a member of my staff I remarked during the afternoon that in war all advantages are but questions of time. Unless we seized our opportunity at once, Germany would recover from the paralysis of industry, which bombing had helped to bring about. There were indications that her industry was being put rapidly underground."

Montgomery alone seemed unperturbed. He told the supreme commander that he did not need an armored division. He said, "I am, myself, quite happy about the situation. I have been working through on a very definite plan, and I now begin to see daylight. . . . We must," Monty continued, "be quite clear as to what is vital and what is not. If we get our sense of values wrong, we may go astray."

That last might be a remembered admonishment from Monty's tyrannical mother, Lady Maud, the wife of the Bishop of Tasmania. She was forever giving her son lectures in moral improvement and forever saying to the nearest listener, "Find out what Bernard is doing and tell him to stop." Ida Eisenhower spoke often of moral improvement, but she did it lovingly and with a smile. Maud never smiled, was never kind to her son, never loving. And he never forgave her, not even in death; he refused to attend her funeral.

Montgomery did begin operations against Caen on July 8, but that had been planned long before receipt of the tactful letter. Meanwhile, the American advance toward St.-Lô and farther south continued, slowly.

On the 9th Eisenhower stopped off at Chequers, and the prime minister, who was still in bed, gave him a lecture that in various forms he was to repeat until mid-August, saying that ANVIL, the plan for a landing in southern France, was a mistake. Eisenhower and Butcher then returned to their headquarters in Portsmouth, and late in the evening, in a visit to the war room, Butcher learned that "Caen had been practically taken. With this as a night cap, Ike went off to sleep."

Occasionally during those tense July days Ike went up in a Piper Cub with a co-pilot. According to Mickey that was "about the only opportunity he had to get away by himself. . . . He did that every chance he got in those last weeks in England, and I think it was the sport he liked best—more than pitching horseshoes, certainly, or playing badminton at Telegraph Cottage. Cub flying and horseback riding—those were the things the Boss really enjoyed most."

According to the original plans for OVERLORD, the city of St.-Lô was to have been liberated by June 11; that didn't actually happen until over a month later, and when the liberation was complete, there was not much left of the crucial city. An American private viewing the remains allegedly said, "We sure liberated the hell out of this place."

Bradley was already planning COBRA, and control of St.-Lô was essential to its success. The town was an important road center to the south of the beachhead. The Germans knew the importance of the city, and were determined to hold it. The bombing had continued without stopping since D-Day, but the firmly entrenched Germans fought on; in one case American riflemen called on a bulldozer to bury alive three German paratroopers who would not come out of a dugout.

The city was finally taken on July 18; its population had been 11,000, and in taking it, the Americans suffered almost half that number of casualties— 3,000 from the 29th Division, more than 2,000 from the 35th. There had been 40,000 American casualties *before* the breakout began, and, as the military historian, Russell F. Weigley, put it, "High as it is, the figure 40,000 does not adequately express the cost of the campaign. It does not include the especially heavy toll of psychologically wounded imposed by the *bocage* [hedgerow country], the victims of combat fatigue severe enough to cause at least temporary disablement, who numbered an additional 25 to 33 percent of 40,000."

Also on the 18th, at 5:30 in the morning, 6,000 one-ton bombs were dropped on German positions in three areas held by the Germans along the Orne River; an hour later almost 10,000 500-pound bombs were dropped on the same area. By the end of the day 4,500 Allied aircraft had been in action against the Germans there, and the air attacks were followed by massive artillery and naval gunfire.

The British ground attack, GOODWOOD, named after a British race track, began at 7:30 A.M. Three Allied armored divisions under the command of Lieutenant General Sir Miles Dempsey, were involved. According to Tedder, "Eisenhower thought that at last our whole front line would act aggressively against the enemy so that he would be the more vulnerable to a sharp thrust."

Much was expected of the operation, in large part because Montgomery had spoken of it as what one of his soldiers called "a big deal." Monty, a master at hyperbole, that day sent a message to Brooke, "Operation this morning a complete success. . . . The effect of the air bombing was decisive and the spectacle terrific . . . situation is very promising and it is difficult to see what the enemy can do just at present." In addition, Montgomery had one of his press conferences which resulted in elated reports in British newspapers, saying "a breakthrough"; "a wide corridor through German front"; "British Army in full cry." That was nowhere true.

The British force advanced three miles the first day, at the cost of 1,500 men and 270 tanks. On the 19th Montgomery made almost no gains at all but suffered losses of 1,100 men and an additional 131 tanks. Eisenhower was furious, particularly after reading Tedder's report. Tedder reported that "An overwhelming air bombardment opened the door, but there was no immediate deep penetration whilst the door remained open and we are now little beyond the immediate bomb craters. It is clear that there was no intention of making this operation the decisive one which you so clearly indicated [it should be]."

In his diary on the 20th Butcher said that Tedder called Ike from SHAEF Main on the evening of the 19th and "reflecting the disappointment of the air and the slowness on the ground, said that the British Chiefs of Staff would support any recommendation that Ike might care to make with respect to Monty for not succeeding in his big three-armored-division push."

What was not in the published diary is the fact that the supreme commander was ill. Butcher wrote, "Ike hasn't been feeling well these past few days. Driving down to camp on Monday evening [July 19 was Wednesday] I asked if he still had the ringing in his ears and he said yes. It has been bothering him for weeks. The treatment given by the doctor at SHAEF Main hadn't seemed to help, so I asked his permission to find another doctor. He grunted an assent. Yesterday I started the search, which came to the ears of M. G. Kenner [Major General Albert W. Kenner], the fine head of the SHAEF medical division, whose job is akin to that of an inspector general, to make sure the soldiers and all get proper medical treatment. He asked me to see him personally at his tent at the Forward Hdq. I soon discovered the reason for the privacy. He said ringing in the ears was a sign of high blood pressure and he was fearful that some ear man would not only suspect but likely gossip about the fact. This kind of news travels rapidly, he said, . . . It would get back to Washington and on his [Eisenhower's] record as well. . . . Kenner thought it would be wisest if he personally checked Ike and if he found the suspected pressure, give him some medicine to quiet him. . . . I felt very badly but suspected as much . . . the slowness of the battle, the desire to be more active in it himself, his inward but generally unspoken criticism of Monty for being so cautious, all these pump up his system. . . . He'll have to take care of himself, but his troubles are not from physical exertion, they are from the mental strain and worry. What a blow it would be to the world, not mentioning that to his personal followers if he should pull a Teddy Roosevelt! [TR died suddenly and unexpectedly of a blood clot in the heart.] At least he is in the care, more or less unwittingly, of a good and wise doctor."

The next day, again in an unpublished portion of the diary, Butcher said, "Yesterday Ike's blood pressure went down as a result of the slow-up medicine that Kenner gave him. . . . Kenner told me that while Ike's b.p. . . . was 176 over 110 (although he told Ike that it was only 166), today it had dropped to 156. . . . [From here on to end of paragraph the published diary is quoted.]

After Ike . . . had disposed of some picayunish problems, he retired to his caravan, where he dozed or slept much of the day, only getting up for dinner. Then he appeared quiet and rested, but blue as indigo over Monty's slowdown.

"The chief topic of conversation was who was to replace Montgomery—it being a foregone conclusion Monty was out." Monty was not out; he was not even close to being out, and he never would be. He was disliked and distrusted and found wanting by almost all the Americans and many of the British, excepting Brooke, but he had to survive. Much more than his own personal future was involved.

Max Hastings said, "It is impossible to imagine that Montgomery could have been sacked . . . without inflicting an intolerable blow to British national confidence. He whom propaganda has made mighty, no man may easily cast aside. . . . But it is difficult to guess what new pressures and directives might have been forced upon the Commander-in-Chief of the 21st Army Group had not the perspective of the Normandy campaign been entirely transformed by the American Operation COBRA."

On the 20th a fierce thunderstorm made furthering of GOODWOOD impossible even if Montgomery had been so inclined. Eisenhower was, Butcher said, "like a blind dog in a meat house—he can smell it, but he can't find it. How he will handle the situation remains the principal suspended interest of the diary, at the moment." The weather had grounded all planes, but Eisenhower ordered his B-25 into the air anyway. Bradley said it was the only plane in the air that day. He told Ike, "you're going to break your neck running around in a B-25 on a day like this. 'That's one of the privileges that goes with my job.' he said, 'no one over here can ground me.' "

Bradley and Ike discussed what was to become of Bradley's 12th Army Group, which would become operational on August 1. After that Eisenhower would take over direct control of the ground forces in Europe, and, as Chet Hansen, Bradley's aide, said in his diary, "Question of how graciously Monty looks on this." That afternoon before leaving for Monty's headquarters, Eisenhower looked at the threatening sky and told Hansen, "When I die, they ought to hold my body for a rainy day and then bury me in the middle of a storm. This damned weather is going to be the death of me yet." The weather had not improved when Eisenhower's plane returned him to Heston airfield later that day.

There is no record of what Ike and Monty said to each other, but one Montgomery biographer, Richard Lamb, said, "The openness and enthusiasm of Bradley . . . was in marked contrast to Montgomery's cold defensiveness and arrogance. When Eisenhower got back to London he complained bitterly to his chauffeur and confidante, Kay Summersby, who noted in her diary that he had said: 'Monty seems quite satisfied regarding his progress; says it is up to Bradley to go ahead.' . . . Eisenhower is not pleased at progress made." There had been 4,000 casualties in Monty's failed attempt, and 500 tanks had been lost. But as two British historians cheerfully reported in 1965, many of the tanks "were later recovered and repaired. . . . Although the Germans had completely foiled any British attempt at reaching Falaise, the GOODWOOD offensive had thoroughly alarmed them."

While Eisenhower was in Normandy, an attempt on Hitler's life was made by a group of anti-Nazis in Germany, some of them high-ranking officers and officials, who felt that the only way to save their country from certain disaster was to get rid of Hitler.

In the days that followed the failed assassination 5,000 people who had had nothing to do with it were murdered, and another 10,000, also innocent, were sent to concentration camps. Many of the actual conspirators were hanged. Rommel, who had been seriously injured when his car was strafed by an allied plane on the 17th, was named as one of the conspirators, and he was given the choice of being tried and found guilty of high treason, or commiting suicide, and he chose the latter, and was promised a state funeral and the safety of his wife and son.

Just what effect the assassination attempt had on the future of the Allied cause will never be known. What is known is that it had no effect at all on the German soldiers in the field or on most of their commanding officers; Hitler and Hitler alone was from that time on in total command of the army, and he was surrounded by worshipful puppets. Albert Speer said of the officers around the fuehrer: "As a result of their long cooperation, they not only developed an uncanny faith in him but also fell completely under his influence. They were in his spell, blindly subservient to him and with no will of their own."

Tedder said that when news of the attempted assassination reached SHAEF, "I saw the Supreme Commander at once, and told him that Montgomery's failure to take action earlier has lost us the opportunity offered by the attempt on Hitler's life. . . . I asked him to act at once . . . [to remove] Montgomery. Eisenhower agreed to do so, and said he would prepare a Paper. I intended, if the Supreme Commander would not act firmly, to put my views in writing to the Chiefs of Staff. I told Eisenhower that his own people would be thinking that he had sold them to the British if he continued to support Montgomery without protest. Later, I attended Bedell Smith's morning meeting, and thinking of the threat from 'V' weapons, remarked, 'Unless we get to the Pas-de-Calais quickly, southern England will have a bad time.' When Bedell Smith replied that we should not get there soon, I said, 'Then we must change our leaders for men who will get us there.' "

John Eisenhower later said, "The evening of July 20 was probably the lowest point in Allied fortunes since D-Day."

This time Eisenhower himself wrote the letter to Monty:

Dear Monty:

Since returning from your headquarters yesterday I have been going over the major considerations that, in my mind, must guide our future actions. This letter is to assure myself that we see eye to eye on the big problems.

You said:

1. We must get the Brittany peninsula. From an administrative point of view this is essential.

2. We do not want to get hemmed into a relatively small area. We must have space for maneuver, for administration and for airfields.

3. We want to engage the enemy in battle to write off his troops and generally to kill Germans. . . .

A few days ago, when Armored Divisions of Second Army, assisted by tremendous air attack, broke through the enemy's forward line, I was extremely hopeful and optimistic. I thought that at last we had him and were going to roll him up. That did not come about.

Now we are pinning our immediate hopes on Bradley's attack, which should get off either tomorrow or on the first good day. But the country is bad, and the enemy strong at the point of main assault, *and more than ever I think it is important that we are aggressive throughout the front* [Emphasis mine—M.M.]. . . . The enemy has no immediately available major reserves. We do not need to fear, at this moment, a great counter offensive. . . . Eventually the American ground strength will necessarily be much greater than the British. But while we have equality in size we must go forward shoulder to shoulder, with honors and sacrifices equally shared.

The letter seems direct and to the point, though somewhat condescending, and Tedder, reading it after it had been dispatched, found that it was "not strong enough. Montgomery can evade it. It contains no order." Tedder was right, as was clear from Montgomery's reply: "Have received your letter dated 21 July. There is not and never has been any intention of stopping offensive operations on the eastern flank." He added that he and the supreme commander saw "eye to eye on military problems. If not, do please let me know."

That reply in no way satisfied Eisenhower.

At 1:00 in the morning on July 25 Churchill called Eisenhower, saying not to awaken him if he was asleep. Butcher, in bedroom slippers and bathrobe, trudged down the cinder path to the caravan and, hearing no snoring, assumed Ike was awake. He wasn't, but he took the call in his office tent, and the first words Butcher heard him say were, "What do your people think of the slowness of the situation over there?" Butcher added in the unpublished portion of his diary, "This morning Ike said he had talked more than a half hour to the P.M. and that during the P.M.'s recent trip Monty obviously had sold Winston a 'bill of goods.' The P.M. was supremely happy with the situation. Then de Guingand phoned Ike to assure him that Monty had 'fattened up' the attack, and that one was on today in the British sector, as well as in the American. Ike said he had started to be alarmed at Monty's hesitance 10 days ago, had confided to Tedder his fears, and now Tedder is just reaching the phase of irritation in which Ike found himself several days ago."

Brooke was furious at what Eisenhower had said to the prime minister. He wrote in his diary, "I am tired to death with and by humanity and all its pettiness. Will we ever learn to 'love our Allies as ourselves???!!' I doubt it . . . it is equally clear that Ike knows nothing about strategy and is *quite* unsuited to the post of Supreme Commander as far as any of the strategy of the war is concerned."

Strategist or not, Ike remained dissatisfied with Monty's lack of progress. The supreme commander may never have said so, but Monty must have appeared to this baseball fan to be a bunter, and Eisenhower had said, "You can't hit a home run by bunting. You have to step up there and take your cut at the ball." If it can be said that Ike did not understand strategy—and it can't really—it can be said that Monty did not understand baseball.

The first step of what was to be a spectacular victory began not long after 5:00 A.M. on the morning of the 25th. More than 1,500 B-17s dropped 3,000 tons of bombs and medium and fighter-bombers dropped an additional 4,000 tons of bombs and napalm on a 7,000-yard front. The bombing continued throughout the morning, and the commander of a panzer division in the bombed area wrote:

By mid-day the entire area resembled a moon landscape, with bomb craters touching rim to rim, and there was no longer any hope of getting out any of our weapons. . . . The shock effect on the troops was indescribable. Several of the men went mad and rushed dementedly around in the open until they were cut down by splinters. Simultaneous with the storm from the air, innumerable guns of US artillery poured drumfire into our field positions. . . . Units holding the front were almost completely wiped out, despite, in many cases, the best possible equipment of tanks, anti-tank guns, and self-propelled guns.

In *Crusade* Eisenhower said, "Finally, on July 25, seven weeks after D-Day, the attack was launched, from the approximate line we had expected to hold on D-plus-5, stretching from Caen through Caumont to St.-Lô. A tremendous carpet, or area, bombing was placed along the St.-Lô sector of the American front and its stunning effect upon the enemy lasted throughout the day. Unfortunately a mistake on the part of the bombing forces caused a considerable number of casualties in one battalion of the 9th Division and in the 30th Division and killed General [Lesley] McNair, who had gone into an observation post to watch the beginning of the attack. His death cast a gloom over all who had known this most able and devoted officer." McNair, whose deafness had made him ineligible for active combat duty, had gone to the front despite warnings against it.

"Friendly" bombs that day killed 111 American soldiers and wounded 500 more.

Eisenhower's old friend, General Courtney Hughes, who was to become commander of the First Army, went to the command post of the 30th Division, and its commander told him, "We're good soldiers, Courtney, but there's absolutely no excuse, no excuse at all. I wish I could show some of those air boys, decorated with everything a man could be decorated with, some of our casualty clearing stations." A German general said of the American self-bombing, "It was hard to believe any living thing could be left alive in front of our positions. However, on moving to enemy-held territory, our men ran into some determined resistance."

Eisenhower spent part of the day with Bradley, watching the beginning of COBRA. It did not look like a blitzkrieg that day. Not only had there been the heartbreaking "short" drops; the bombs that had reached the enemy positions had not knocked them out. Bradley said, "When Eisenhower took off for England that evening, the fate of COBRA still hung in doubt. Several hundred U.S.

troops had been killed and wounded in the air bombing . . . and there was little reason to believe we stood at the brink of a breakthrough. Rather, the attack looked as though it might have failed."

On the way to the air strip, Eisenhower told a member of Bradley's staff that he would never again use heavy bombers against tactical targets. "I don't believe they can be used in support of ground forces," he said. "That's a job for artillery. I gave them a green light this time. But I promise you it's the last."

Later that evening back in England, however, reasonably good news arrived from Bradley. The attack had begun with the use of three infantry divisions. The 9th had gained 2,300 yards; the 4th, 1,200 yards, and the 30th, 1,300. Even so, Lightning Joe Collins' VII Corps had not reached its objectives and the question was whether the Germans had increased their strength, or was there to be relatively little opposition ahead? Collins, a remarkably optimistic man and one willing to take chances, decided to have his two armored divisions rolled ahead against relatively light resistance. His optimism paid off, as it was to do many times later that year. He later said, "I seldom complained in those days; the weather was so much better than it had been in Guadalcanal—I'd just come from Guadalcanal—that I didn't even mind the rain much. On the Canal it never stopped raining, and in the jungles we never saw the sky; it was always dark. In Europe even when it rained you could *see* the weather."

Eisenhower's mood improved, too. Kenneth Strong said of the supreme commander, "One of Eisenhower's greatest attributes was that he never lost his sense of proportion. But it was not until July 25 . . . that operations became sufficiently stabilized for the allies to launch a coordinated and successful attack and get into open country. As Eisenhower had forecast, the Allied commanders then made full use of their preponderance in armoured forces and the overwhelming air support they received. All the opportunities that offered themselves were seized with both hands."

By noon of the day after COBRA began, July 26, it was clear that what Bradley called "the initial crisis" had passed and that "the time had come for bold exploitation of the breakthrough."

On the 28th Bradley wrote Eisenhower, "To say that the personnel of the First Army headquarters is riding high tonight is putting it mildly. Things on our front really look good tonight." He told Chet Hansen, "We shall continue attacking, never giving him a chance to rest, never give him a chance to dig in."

Martin Blumenson in *Breakout and Pursuit* said, "After one week of action, U.S. troops held a line from Pontaubault eastward through Brécey and St-Pois to a point several miles north of the town of Vire. To be sure, the front line was held only by advance spearheads; the bulk of the First Army was still concentrated fifteen to twenty miles to the north. Nevertheless, the Allied forces had definitely seized the initiative, and there seemed to be no reason why they should relinquish it, particularly since the enemy disorganization was still unresolved. Brittany was at hand and the Seine had come within reach. The prospects for the future were unlimited."

On July 31 Field Marshal Günther von Kluge sent a message to his chief of staff: "It's a madhouse here [D'Este 407]. You can't imagine what it's like. . . . Unless I can get infantry and antitank weapons there, the [left] flank cannot hold. . . . Someone has to tell the Fuehrer that if the Americans get through at Avranches they will be out of the woods and they'll be able to do what they want. . . . It's a crazy situation."

On August 2 Eisenhower "was all smiles." He told Butcher, "If the intercepts are right, we are to hell and gone in Brittany, and slicing 'em up in Normandy." The intercepts were right. As Kluge wrote Hitler, "Whether the enemy can be stopped at this point is questionable. . . . Losses in men and equipment are extraordinary. The morale of our troops has suffered very heavily under constant murderous enemy fire. . . . In the rear areas of the front, terrorists, feeling the end approaching, grow steadily bolder. This fact, and the loss of numerous signal installations, makes an orderly command extremely difficult."

The "terrorists" von Kluge had mentioned were members of the heroic French Forces of the Interior, the FFI, who were to be increasingly helpful to Eisenhower and the troops under his command. But in the days ahead Eisenhower was to have to cope once again with that difficult, demanding, and uncontrollable French general, Charles de Gaulle. Moreover, neither the Monty nor the Patton problem had been solved, and with the addition of de Gaulle, the "impresario" would have three "stars" to contend with, and throughout most of August he was to have a fourth star on his hands as well, Churchill, with whom he would have "one of the longest-sustained arguments of the war."

★ ★ ★

CROSSING THE SEINE

It was always necessary to know what to do and how to do it successfully, but from time to time, something else was necessary, something Eisenhower seldom discussed but hoped he had, luck. He was fond of quoting Napoleon, who, when a staff member suggested that a certain colonel be appointed to the rank of general, said "What are his qualifications?" The staff officer started to list the courage and accomplishments in the field of the colonel, and Napoleon said, "I don't care if he is brilliant—is he lucky?" Of himself, Ike said, "There's a lot of changes or little bends in the way and finally you come to a particular spot. Regardless of character, dedication to the job, etc., there is still a lot of luck." Beetle described his boss as "not only a great commander but a lucky one."

By August 1 Ike was ready for a little good luck, and he had it. That day Bradley moved up from First Army to command the 12th Army Group. Brad believed in luck too. He said, "You have got to work hard, you have got to know your job, and there are certain characteristics of leadership you must always keep in mind. Then hope that you are lucky."

Bradley was content in leaving his beloved First Army in what he believed were good hands. Courtney Hodges was, he said, "an old crony from trap-shooting days at Benning. . . . Whereas Patton could seldom be bothered with details, Hodges studied his problems with infinite care and was thus better qualified to execute the more intricate operations. A steady, undramatic and dependable man with great tenacity and persistence, Hodges became the almost anonymous inside man who smashed the German Seventh Army while Patton skirted the end. In his way Hodges was as ideally suited for that mission as Patton was for his."

At noon that same day, Eisenhower officially activated Patton's Third Army, but no announcement was made. Ike had told Marshall, "In the interest of cover and deception there will be no repeat no announcement of this for some time. In due course an appropriate statement will be issued but I am particularly anxious that you do not permit any premature publicity from that end on the matter."

Actually, Eisenhower, who had been under heavy criticism for retaining Patton in command after the slapping incident, might have wished to take advantage of Patton's triumph by releasing his name at its height, thereby proving his (Ike's) judgment had been correct. And an earlier announcement would have pleased a great number of American officers at the time, particularly those of the Third Army, who feared SHAEF's silence was a plot to prevent Patton from getting credit for his offensive. Yet Eisenhower chose not to make an immediate announcement, and when urged by Butcher to do so said, "Why should I tell the enemy?"

Two days after Patton took command, his troops took Rennes, and in a little more than a week they had cleared most of Brittany. On the 2nd Eisenhower wrote Marshall:

It is my hope that once we have secured the Brittany peninsula we will find that our total capacity for receiving and maintaining additional divisions has been increased and that we can absorb all that can be brought in to us. . . . The next step would be aggressive action toward the northeast to destroy the bulk of the German mobile forces, all generally located along our present front and stretching up to include Pas-de-Calais. . . . regardless of the completeness of victory in the current battle, this command will continue to maintain the offensive to the absolute limit of his power. . . . Personally, I am very hopeful as to immediate results, and believe that within the next two or three days we will so manhandle the western flank of the enemy's forces that we will secure for ourselves freedom of action through destruction of a considerable portion of the forces facing us.

Also on that day, von Kluge was ordered to use eight of the nine panzer divisions in Normandy to cut off all U.S. forces in Brittany and south of Avranches. Then they would be without supply and could be driven back into the Channel. It was, the Hitler order said, "a unique, never recurring opportunity for a complete reversal of the situation." He added, however, "Von Kluge must believe in it." Von Kluge did not believe in it and said so, adding, "If, as I foresee, this plan does not succeed, catastrophe is inevitable."

The enemy counterattack came on the night of August 6, and the 2d Panzer Division penetrated a few miles southwest of Mortain but was stopped almost immediately by troops of the 35th Division. The Luftwaffe did not appear at all, and a German report said simply, "The air situation in the forenoon of 7 August stopped the whole counter-attack against Avranches—not even one of the announced 300 German fighters appeared."

Also on the 7th Montgomery started the First Canadian Army toward Falaise. By the evening of that crucial day, von Kluge was sure his counteroffensive was over, and news of the forthcoming Canadian attack did not cheer him. But a new order from Hitler faced none of these realities. It said, "I command the attack be prosecuted daringly and recklessly to the sea . . . regardless of the risk."

Eisenhower, however, was just as determined. He wrote Marshall, "My entire preoccupation these days is to secure the destruction of a substantial portion of the enemy forces facing us. Patton, on the marching wing of our forces, is closing in as rapidly as possible—his deployment through the bottleneck near Avranches was exceedingly difficult but we have now got the strength on that wing to proceed definitely about our business." As usual Ike was optimistic about the outcome: "If we can destroy a good portion of the enemy's army now in front of us we will have a greater freedom of movement in northern France, and I would expect things to move rapidly."

On the same day American troops had captured Avranches, Eisenhower's advance command post was moved from Portsmouth to an apple orchard near Tourniers in Normandy, code name SHELLBURST. There were tall hedgerows on three sides, on a fourth the hedgerows had been trimmed, and a landing field for liaison planes could be seen. The supreme commander's office was a good-sized tent with a board floor. Other tents were used for members of the staff and visitors, and as at Portsmouth, there would be many visitors.

It often seemed during the summer of 1944 that everybody in Washington wanted to visit the beachhead in France and to have his or her photograph taken with the supreme commander. By then Eisenhower was more than a mere celebrity; he had, as Kenneth S. Davis said, "achieved that intense fame and prestige which, possessing him as much as he possessed it, was destined to become one of the important facts of the postwar world. The fame, the prestige derived from great events in which millions of men played their part."

Whenever possible Eisenhower tried to prevent people from visiting him, among them Secretary of the Treasury Henry Morgenthau, Jr., a close friend and neighbor of the president at Hyde Park. But Morgenthau was persistent, and Eisenhower did see him, not in France, but in his mess tent at Portsmouth on August 7, just before he moved. Morgenthau brought with him an aide, Harry Dexter White, a seemingly shy, soft-spoken man with a Harvard Ph.D. Morgenthau was also accompanied by Fred Harris, a confidential advisor who after the war wrote a detailed account of the meeting at Portsmouth.

Eisenhower, as president, was to have a good deal of trouble remembering details of that meeting, and the so-called Morgenthau Plan calling for the harshest of treatment for Germany was either born at that meeting or it was not, and it was either Eisenhower's idea or it was not. In any case, as supreme commander,

Eisenhower had tried to prevent the meeting, and when it was over, even the reliable Butcher failed to record that it had taken place.

Small signs marked SHELLBURST guided the visitors to the new camp which, according to Butcher, "nestles in the general farm scene." The camp had a twenty-four-hour MP patrol as well as a number of slit trenches. It was only about twenty miles from the British front lines, and artillery fire was frequently heard. Kay, who lived in one of the tents close to Ike's, said, "It was so much calmer and more peaceful here just behind the front lines than it had been in England with the buzz bombs. . . . The weather was fine, and it was almost like a lovely country vacation, except that we had no time to enjoy it. . . . We were constantly on the go. One day I would drive Ike up to the front, where he would visit the commanders and talk with the men. The next day we would fly to Portsmouth, and I would drive him to London to confer with the P.M. or to SHAEF at Bushy Park." According to Mickey, "We were going places, and even if you didn't sense it all around you . . . you could tell it from the way the Boss looked and acted. He was in fine spirits those days."

As he had in England, Marty Snyder visited farmers around the camp and got fresh vegetables for the general's mess. The farmers, Marty said, willingly gave him vegetables, but when Beetle found out, he was furious. He told Marty, "General Eisenhower doesn't want us to take any food from the civilians." They need all they have. The men at the front are eating dehydrated food, and the general says so can we. After that, according to Snyder, "we ate dehydrated food." In an earlier letter to Mamie, Eisenhower had said, "I always feel guilty . . . when I eat anything special. These people, even including babies and the sick, have been so long without many items that we consider essential, that I feel almost like [I'm] cheating when someone sends me a bite of candy or an egg."

A few days later some French peasants gave a cow to Eisenhower so that he could have fresh milk. This gift could not be refused, and, according to Snyder, "The first morning we had it, Moaney, Hunt, and I gathered around the cow and tried to solve how to get milk out of it. Each of us tried, pulling, squeezing, massaging, but we couldn't get a drop. I heard, 'What's going on here?'

"It was General Eisenhower. 'We can't get this thing to work,' I said.

" 'Let me sit down,' he said. 'I'll show you how to do this.'

"I got up from the stool and the General sat down. Then, in steady, gentle strokes, he began to milk the cow. In a few minutes the bucket was full. Moaney, Hunt, and I watched, disgusted with ourselves. When he had finished, Eisenhower stood up and said, 'You city slickers have a lot to learn.' Then he laughed and went back to his trailer."

Some of the SHAEF personnel were in a hotel in nearby Granville, and Mickey supervised the cooking in the hotel kitchen. There was a clear indication of how the war was going for at least some German troops the second night the Americans were in the hotel. A small group of German soldiers from an offshore island sneaked into the village and attacked the hotel. According to Mickey, "We thought they were after General Eisenhower, and our retaliation was fierce.

But they were only after food. They rushed into the kitchen, grabbed boxes of canned stuff and ran away to the hills as fast as they could."

After establishing his advance headquarters in France, Eisenhower remained there only a little more than twenty-four hours. On the morning of the 8th, he visited his commanders. At Bradley's headquarters, according to Tedder, "Bradley was undecided whether to put a strong force into the Brittany Peninsula or whether to put our main strength into exploiting the breakthrough. . . . Eisenhower happened to be at his headquarters, and decided that the right policy was to make another and wider envelopment of the enemy forces toward the Seine and even the east of Paris.

On the 10th Eisenhower inspected the 82d and the 101st airborne divisions. James Gavin, who was soon to become commander of the 82d, was not always an admirer of Eisenhower, either as a general or as a human being. Of this occasion he said, "After the review General Eisenhower stopped at General Ridgeway's home . . . for tea. Some of the staff were surprised when his chauffeur, Kay Summersby, joined us. Chauffeurs do not normally join their generals for tea. She was an attractive woman, and she seemed to be a very nice person. I was struck once again, as I always was in my association with the British people, by how their women pitched in and supported the war effort as chauffeurs, clerks, staff officers; where they could contribute, they made an effort. There was considerable gossip about Kay Summersby. It must have been troublesome to General Eisenhower—if he was aware of it."

The following evening, the 11th, Eisenhower returned to SHELLBURST, and the next day he was in bed, the result of his old leg injury acting up. By the 14th, however, he was well enough to visit the 5th General Hospital near Carentan, and was depressed by what he saw and heard there. He found that 1,100 of the patients were suffering from self-inflicted wounds. Butcher said, "When he returned, he said he was depressed, and he looked it."

Also that day the supreme commander made public an order of the day.

To Troops of the Allied Expeditionary Force:
   Through your combined skill, valor, and fortitude you have created in France a fleeting but definite opportunity for a major Allied victory, one whose realization will make notable progress toward the final downfall of our enemy. . . .
   I request every airman to make it his direct responsibility that the enemy is blasted unceasingly by day and by night, and is denied safety either in fight or in flight.
   I request every sailor to make sure that no part of the hostile forces can either escape or be reinforced by sea, and that our comrades on the land want for nothing that guns and ships' companies can bring to them.
   I request every soldier to go forward to his assigned objective with the determination that the enemy can survive only through surrender; let no foot of ground once gained be relinquished nor a single German escape through a line once established.

The next day, at a press conference, Eisenhower officially announced the presence of the Third Army. He also revealed that Patton was its commander and that Lieutenant General Courtney H. Hodges had succeeded Bradley as commander of the First Army. Bradley had become commander of the 12th Army Group. Operation DRAGOON, code name for the landings in southern France, had begun earlier that day, and at the time he met with the press he was not sure the landings had been successful. DRAGOON was the operation that occasioned what Eisenhower called one of the "longest-sustained" arguments that he had with the prime minister during the war. He said, "This argument, beginning almost coincidentally with the breakthrough in late July, lasted through the first ten days in August. One session lasted several hours. The discussions involved the wisdom of going ahead with ANVIL, by then renamed DRAGOON, the code name for the operation that was to bring in General Devers' forces through the south of France."

Actually, the argument had begun long before the breakthrough. Late in June, Churchill had opposed the idea of bringing any troops from Italy for a landing in southern France. After the fall of Rome, Alexander was continuing his drive north, a drive that Churchill thought might eventually reach Vienna— before the Russians got there, of course. He cabled Roosevelt, "Let us resolve not to wreck one great campaign for the sake of another." Roosevelt's lengthy reply reminded Churchill that a landing in southern France had been agreed on at Teheran. "One of the early reasons for planning this attack," Eisenhower said, "was to achieve an additional port of entry through which the reinforcing divisions already prepared in America could pour rapidly into the European invasion."

Churchill was by no means finished arguing, however. The altercation continued throughout July, with the Americans, Eisenhower, Marshall, the U.S. Joint Chiefs, and Roosevelt for the landings and Churchill and the British Chiefs opposed. After the breakthrough, as Eisenhower said, the disagreement reached a new intensity. Churchill felt that the second landing in France should not be in the south but in one of the newly liberated ports in Brittany. He called it "the possibility of switching DRAGOON into the main and vital theater." The Russians were making rapid progress everywhere, particularly in southeastern Europe. They were also in Poland and Lithuania, and about to enter Czecho-slovakia and East Prussia. It seemed likely they would soon reach the Danube, Bulgaria and Yugoslavia and be on the borders of Greece and Turkey.

On August 4, when Lord Moran went into Churchill's bedroom, "he did not bother to hide his cares." In his diary, Moran wrote, "The fact is that he is no longer in good heart about the general situation. . . . I tried to comfort him, I said that victory was following victory—the Third Army had crossed the Seine— and that some of the Americans were talking already as if the war were over. He merely grunted, as if I did not understand. . . . He burst out: 'Good God, can't you see that the Russians are spreading across Europe like a tide; they have invaded Poland, and there is nothing to prevent them from marching into Turkey and Greece!'

"The American landings in the south of France are the last straw. He can see 'no earthly purpose' in them. 'Sheer folly,' he calls them. He had fought tooth and nail, he said, to prevent them. If only those ten divisions could have been landed in the Balkans . . . but the Americans would not listen to him; it was all settled, they said."

The next day, on August 5, Eisenhower had a six-hour meeting at Portsmouth with Churchill and his advisers. According to Butcher, the prime minister "had come for lunch and practically stayed for dinner." He pursued his argument for the Brittany landings at Brest, Lorient, and St.-Nazaire. According to Butcher, "Ike said no, continued saying no all afternoon, and ended saying no in every form of the English language at his command. . . . Ike argued so long and patiently that he was practically limp when the PM departed and observed that although he had said no in every language, the Prime Minister undoubtedly would return to the subject in two or three days." After the meeting, Eisenhower cabled Marshall, "I will not repeat not under any conditions agree at this moment to a cancellation of DRAGOON."

On the 8th Eisenhower received a message from the U.S. Joint Chiefs indicating that he was supported by Washington and that ANVIL "will go on as planned." Yet even after Eisenhower's emphatic opposition, and a message Roosevelt sent the prime minister on the 7th, saying he would not support any change in the ANVIL plan, Churchill persisted. Just as Eisenhower had predicted he would, Churchill, on the 9th, tried once more to call it off. On that day the supreme commander met again with the prime minister, this time at 10 Downing Street. The prime minister's refusal to admit defeat early in the war had made him, justifiably, a world hero; in early August 1944 the same kind of stubbornness was annoying, time-consuming, even absurd. The British historian John Ehrman said in *Grand Strategy* that Churchill's proposal for a landing in Brittany instead of the Riviera would have "abandoned a carefully planned operation on the eve of its execution, to alter the balance of the whole campaign in western Europe, and to abandon a strategy which they [the British] had worked out originally in concert with the Russians and only recently accepted with every appearance of finality." For one thing, the preparatory bombing of the proposed landing sites in southern France had already begun.

Nevertheless, at one heated point during the confrontation at 10 Downing Churchill said that he might find it necessary to go to the king and "lay down the mantle of my high office." Eisenhower knew Churchill well enough by then to realize that he was bluffing. The supreme commander was also aware that Churchill's arguments were for political reasons, not military, and in that case the prime minister should take the matter up with the president of the United States.

In *Crusade* Eisenhower said, "I did insist that as long as he argued the matter on military grounds alone I could not concede validity to his arguments. . . . I alone had to be the judge of my own responsibilities and decisions. . . . I am quite certain that no experienced soldier would question the wisdom, strictly from the military viewpoint, of adhering to the plan for attacking southern France." John Eisenhower said that when his father disagreed with a superior officer, as he had at least once with Marshall and several times with MacArthur, "He always seemed ready to lay his military career on the line; possibly it is more correct to say that when he believed he was right it never occurred to him to think of the consequences to his career. . . . This independence of spirit increased rather than diminished the mutual respect that Eisenhower enjoyed with relatively senior officers." Churchill was no exception. And Eisenhower seemed always to win in these confrontations; in any case he did win about ANVIL/DRAGOON, and when he wrote to Marshall about his meeting with Churchill, the supreme commander said:

I had a long conference with the Prime Minister and I must say his obvious reactions to latest decisions in the Mediterranean disturb me greatly. He seems to feel that United States is taking the attitude of a big, strong, and dominating partner rather than attempting to understand the viewpoint that he represents. . . . So far as I can determine he attaches so much importance to the matter that failure in achieving this objective would represent a practical failure of his whole administration. I am not quite able to figure out why . . . but one thing is certain—I have never seen him so obviously stirred, upset, and even despondent. . . . All this is for your confidential information only. I would feel guilty of eavesdropping and tale-bearing if it should go further.

He also wrote a letter to Churchill:

Sorry that you seem to feel we use our great actual or potential strength as a bludgeon in conference. The fact is that the British view has prevailed in many of our undertakings in which I have been engaged, and I do not see why we should be considered intemperate in our long and persistent support of ANVIL. . . . During all these months I have leaned on you often, and have always looked to you with complete confidence when I felt the need of additional support. This adds a sentimental to my very practical reasons for hoping most earnestly, that in spite of disappointment, we will adhere tenaciously to the concepts of control brought forth by the President and yourself two and one half years ago.

What he had said to Churchill was true. The British view did prevail in most meetings. The reason the U.S. won over ANVIL/DRAGOON, according to Tom Handy, was that "we just got as good as the British. In the beginning, we were always ahead of them on execution action, but on planning we were babes in the wood. Because they knew how to plan, and they could plan for both sides. They were awfully good at it. But we got organized and so we could kind of hold a candle to them."

On the night of August 14/15 paratroopers landed on the French Riviera near Le Muy. There was little opposition. The next morning half a million Allied troops began the planned landing; they had come in 450 ships accompanied by 230 warships and 1,500 aircraft. The fleet had sailed from Oran, Naples, Taranto, and Brindisi, and although it had taken five days to assemble, it had not been detected by the Germans.

A correspondent for *Yank*, the soldier's weekly, wrote:

On H-plus 20 we finally got orders to disembark. We walked through the open doors of our LST, across the narrow pontoon strips, and onto the short, sandy beach. The early morning air was damp and cold, and full of mist. Two hours later . . . the air became bright and warm, and, as we trudged up the road from the beach to the wooded slope that was to be our bivouac area, we felt the breeze coming from the hill.

As August 15 progressed, the German position deteriorated steadily. That afternoon, the Riviera beaches were teeming with Allied tanks, vehicles and crates of supplies, with more being landed in an endless stream. By evening, 2,000 prisoners and six towns had fallen to the Allied forces. Three more—Draguignan, Le Muy and Les Arces—were teetering on the edge of capture. All were to fall within thirty-six hours. In the words of a French observer, Henri Michel, "Everything went off as planned." By nightfall 86,000 men, 12,000 vehicles, and 46,000 tons of supplies had been landed.

It was the beginning of what the men called "the champagne campaign," according to one scarred veteran, "the only campaign of the war in Europe, perhaps the only one anywhere, in which a man could get himself a few drinks in a handsome bar, served by a beautiful French barmaid, pick up his rifle, walk a short distance, kill or frighten a few Germans, perhaps get shot at, although the Germans were retreating too quickly to do much shooting, and then return to the bar or maybe have a swim in the waters of the Mediterranean. Later the soldiers often got laid."

Churchill watched the landings from a British destroyer and he later said, "As far as I could see or hear not a shot was fired either at the approaching flotillas or on the beaches. The battleships had not stopped firing, as there seemed to be nobody there. . . . I had at least done the 'civil' to ANVIL! And indeed I thought it was a good thing I was near the scene to show the interest I took in it."

He telegraphed Eisenhower and said he admired "the perfect precision with which the landing was arranged and the intimate collaboration of British-American forces and organizations." When he wrote to Marshall about the message he had received "from the prime minister," Eisenhower said, "He seemed to be most enthusiastic about ANVIL. When I think of all the mental anguish I went through to preserve the operation, I don't know whether to sit down and laugh or cry. In any event, I sent him a wire and told him that since he had now apparently adopted the newborn child it would grow quickly and lustily."

In the north the Canadian II Corps, which began their attack against Kluge's forces on the 14th, had captured Falaise by the 16th. In his diary, Butcher said, "Ike's disposition . . . today is sunny, if not almost jubilant." By the 17th of August, after the fall of Falaise, Americans and Canadians were left with only a twelve-mile gap between them. The Allied air bombardment continued, and what remained was an awful shambles, the dead and the dying—men and animals—those trying to escape the pocket and those who tried but did not succeed. The British military historian John Keegan wrote that the dead, horses and men, "raised a stench against which the pilots of Allied light aircraft, surveying the devastation, wrinkled their noses at 1,500 feet."

In one of the most moving passages in *Crusade* Eisenhower said, "The battlefield of Falaise was unquestionably one of the greatest 'killing grounds' of any of the war areas. Roads, highways, and fields were so choked with destroyed equipment and with dead men and animals that passage through the area was extremely difficult. Forty-eight hours after the closing of the gap I was conducted through it on foot, to encounter scenes that could be described only by Dante. It was literally possible to walk for hundreds of yards at a time, stepping on nothing but dead and decaying flesh." Rommel summed it all up in one sentence. He said of the campaign, "It was one terrible blood-letting."

Kluge had been fired even before the end of the Falaise battle. A member of his staff said that he "took his dismissal quite calmly." That night he wrote a letter to Hitler imploring him to end the uneven battle in the West. Early on the 18th he said good-bye to his staff and set out in his car for Germany. At Metz he ordered his driver to stop. He took poison there, and was carried to a Metz hospital, a dying man. He was replaced by Field Marshal Walther Model, known for his ability to overcome crises, but what he faced in Normandy caused him to report to Hitler that the best that could be hoped for was to try to get as many of the soldiers trapped in the pocket out through the narrowing gap between Falaise and Argentan.

Despite Eisenhower's request in his order of the day not to let "a single German escape," many did escape what became known as the Argentan-Falaise Gap. Perhaps as many as 35,000, some of whom were later met by Allied forces in Germany. A German corporal caught up in the gap wrote his wife, "We had to retreat in a great hurry. I wonder what will become of us. The pocket nearly closed . . . I don't think I shall ever see my home again. However, we are fighting for Germany and our children, and what happens matters not." The fighting in the area ended on August 22.

Back on the Riviera, by the 24th Truscott's forces had pushed well up the Rhône River and were threatening Marseilles and Toulon. Four days later the last German forces in Marseilles surrendered to French units that were part of DRAGOON (ANVIL). That same day Toulon fell. About 37,000 prisoners fell into French hands at Marseilles and an additional 17,000 at Toulon. German casualties were uncountable, but they were certainly higher than the French losses of 2,700 killed and wounded at Toulon and 4,000 at Marseilles. When Marseilles fell, Operation DRAGOON was a whole month ahead of schedule.

Eisenhower got a large part of what he wanted from DRAGOON. Marseilles and Toulon, once cleared of the rubble of war, were able to handle vast quantities of reinforcements and supplies. Fourteen American divisions landed at Marseilles alone during the next weeks, and at one point 17,000 tons of supplies a day were coming in. DRAGOON also provided Eisenhower with ten more divisions for his autumn campaigns. It was no small matter, either, that on their way to join OVERLORD forces, these ten DRAGOON divisions captured 100,000 prisoners— so wiping out one-third of German forces in southern France. Their own losses stood at 3,000 American and 1,144 French killed and missing, and 4,500 American and 4,346 French wounded.

The intransigent Churchill, despite his "admiration" of the manner in which the campaign was conducted, still wrote in 1953 that though the victory had "brought important assistance to General Eisenhower by the arrival of another army on his right flank, and the opening of another line of communication . . . a heavy price was paid. The army in Italy was deprived of its opportunity to strike a most formidable blow at the Germans and very possibly to reach Vienna before the Russians, with all . . . that might have followed therefrom." That the Allied campaign in Italy was prolonged by the drain on men and matériel which DRAGOON imposed is evidenced by the fact that when the war came to an end, Allied forces had only just reached the north Italian border.

After the war Mark Clark, who had not been part of the operation, sourly observed that ANVIL/DRAGOON had been "one of the biggest political mistakes of the war." The general, who was inclined to doubt the wisdom or necessity of any undertaking of which he was not in charge, added that it was "the origin and the cause of Soviet expansion in Europe after the war."

Many historians who don't go as far as Clark's "origin" and "cause" theory have nevertheless concluded that considering what happened after the war, ANVIL/DRAGOON was indeed a political blunder. Brenda Ralph Lewis, in a 1976 assessment of the operation in *War Monthly,* said, "The political consequences of DRAGOON were just what Churchill said they would be. . . . Now, thirty years later, the Iron Curtain which afterwards came rattling down has not yet lifted, and the Cold War which ensued still had the power to kill."

To repeat Churchill's wise words on another occasion, "We know the results of what we have done. We cannot know what would have happened if we had done something different." Even he could not be sure that had DRAGOON not taken place, Allied forces would have reached Vienna first.

As for Eisenhower, he was in Europe to defeat the Germans as quickly and cheaply as possible. To do that he needed ports, and the ports that were opened by DRAGOON were used in the last months of 1944 to unload more tonnage than any others available to Allied forces. He said that it had been "the most decisive contribution to the complete defeat of Germany." That is what you might call Eisenhower hyperbole, but in 1944 the important point was that the American forces and the French who had landed on the Riviera and fought their way north with a minimum number of casualties met up with Patton's Third Army near Dijon on September 15, exactly one month after the operation began. And a little more than two weeks after Marseilles was captured with minimal damage, it was again open for business.

On August 19 Eisenhower wrote Montgomery:

> While you are carrying on your present operations, I would like for you to examine your needs, as C.-in C. of the Army group of the north in the advance to the Pas-de-Calais area. You can count on the full airborne command, including two U.S. Divisions already here and the one now coming if it can arrive in time. . . . The whole Airborne Command should be released as soon as practicable . . . so that it may prepare for further decisive operations. . . . you may or may not see a need for any U.S. ground units, after the crossings of the Seine have since been secured. This, I think, will depend upon the degree of destructive success we attain in the battling on this side of the river. Initial estimates of such additional forces

should be kept to the minimum, not only because of increased difficulties in maintenance if U.S. lines of communication are stretched too far, but because of the desirability of thrusting quickly eastward and severing almost all the hostile communications in the major portion of France. Moreover . . . you can always be reinforced quickly in case of need either from positions east or west of Paris.

On August 22, in a personal message to the Combined Chiefs, Eisenhower said:

The time is approaching when there will be put into effect the final system of command as planned from the beginning of this operation. . . . The target date is September 1, by which time the remaining elements of the enemy south of the Seine and west of Paris should have been destroyed and possible crossings secured over that river.

He then emphasized something he always considered essential to his command, that

. . . the Tactical Air Force, the United States Strategic Air Force and the Bomber Command each report independently to the Supreme Commander, who uses his deputy to assist in the coordination of the activities of these three forces. There will be no change in the general system except that the Commander of the Tactical Air Force together with representatives of the day and night bomber forces will be with the Supreme Commander in France.

That seemed simple enough and clear enough. He had said almost the same thing in April, before OVERLORD, but it had turned out to be neither simple nor clear then, nor was it to prove either now.

The August 22 message also said:

The Army Group of the Center, less portions necessarily employed otherwise . . . will advance, under General Bradley, to the east and northeast of Paris, from which area it can either strike northeastward . . . or, if the enemy strength in that region is not greater than I now believe, it can alternately strike directly eastward, passing south of the Ardennes. . . . Because of the additional supply commitments incurred in the occupation of Paris it would be desirable, from that viewpoint, to defer the capture of the city until the important matter of destroying the remaining enemy forces up to and including the Pas-de-Calais area. I do not believe this is possible. If the enemy tries to hold Paris with any real strength he would be a constant menace to our flank. If he largely evacuates the place, it falls into our hands whether we like it or not.

Liberating cities is always popular, but freeing Paris would be for political reasons, and Eisenhower considered that he had settled that matter once and for all during a great many lengthy, at times almost acrimonious meetings with Churchill over DRAGOON. There were many reasons for bypassing the city, in Eisenhower's mind all of them compelling. In liberating the city, he was convinced he would destroy it, "Every strategic and geographic reason" dictated that "the Germans would put up a strong fight for Paris." Besides, its people, three and a half million of them, were near starvation. They would soon be without gas, electricity, and coal. More than 4,000 tons of supplies would be needed every day to sustain the city.

Eisenhower said, "We wanted to avoid making Paris a battleground and consequently planned operations to cut off and surround the vicinity, thus forcing the surrender of the defending garrison. We could not know, of course, the exact condition and situation of the city's population. At the moment, we were anxious to save every ounce of fuel and ammunition for combat operations, in order to carry our lines forward the maximum distance, and I was hopeful of deferring actual capture of the city, unless I received evidence of starvation or distress among its citizens."

One thing Eisenhower wanted to make sure of was that there be no premature uprising within the French capital, and he had "firmly" instructed General Koenig to see to it "that no armed movements were to go off in Paris or anywhere else" until he, Eisenhower, personally had given the order. He told Koenig that it was essential that "nothing happens in Paris to change our plans."

On Sunday, August 20, Eisenhower had as visitors Anthony Eden and a party from the British foreign secretary's office, James Forrestal, Roosevelt's newly appointed secretary of the navy, and Charles de Gaulle.

De Gaulle stayed the longest and was the most trouble. The supreme commander gave him a detailed account of his plan to push Patton's Third Army around the south of Paris. Hodges' First Army would cross the Seine north of the city. Neither army was to enter the city itself. De Gaulle in his *Memoirs* said that he told Eisenhower, "Paris is a communications center which will later be essential and which it will be to your advantage to re-establish as soon as possible. If any place except the capital of France were in question, my advice would not commit you to any action for normally of course the conduct of operations is your responsibility."

Eisenhower had a different memory: "He [de Gaulle] made no bones about it; he said there was a serious menace from the Communists in the city, and that if we delayed moving in we would risk finding a disastrous political situation, one that might be disruptive to the Allied war effort."

On the 21st de Gaulle wrote that serious trouble should be expected in Paris because both the Germans and the police had left the city; he added that there was a shortage of food. He said, "I believe that it is really necessary to occupy PARIS as soon as possible with French and Allied forces, even if it should produce some fighting and some damage within the city. . . . If disorder now occurs in PARIS, it will later be difficult to take things in hand without serious incidents and that could, in my opinion, ultimately hinder future military operations." De Gaulle concluded that he was sending General Koenig, whom he had chosen to be the military governor of Paris, to confer with Eisenhower about the matter of occupying the city.

In a handwritten note to Beetle Smith on the 22nd, Eisenhower said, "I talked . . . to Koenig on this. It looks now as if we'd be compelled to go to Paris. Bradley and his G-2 think we can and *must* walk in."

The German commandant in Paris was General Dietrich von Choltitz, who had willingly destroyed Rotterdam and Sebastopol but who now wisely decided that the Germans had lost the war and that Hitler's orders to destroy Paris could be ignored. The fuehrer had ordered that the city be burned and that all of its bridges be blown up. Choltitz disobeyed, and in a message sent by the Swedish consul general in Paris to Stockholm for delivery to SHAEF headquarters in London, thence to Eisenhower, the German general made it clear that a hurried Allied entry into the city was not only possible but obligatory. That gave Eisenhower a military reason for entering the city, and on the afternoon of August 22 he gave the order to do so. He added that the degree of fighting must be "such as could be overcome by light forces." The entire operation was to be under the direct command of Major Gee Gerow of V Corps, but French forces would predominate.

The French 2d Armored Division was under the command of General Jacques Leclerc, a man who with some cause considered himself to be a modern d'Artagnan. He was brash and opinionated and very courageous. Eisenhower was a great admirer of the division. He said, "The veterans of this organization had started at Lake Chad three years before, made an almost impossible march across the Sahara Desert, and joined the Eighth Army to participate in the latter part of the French campaign." Thus, it seemed appropriate that it be chosen to receive the surrender of the city.

In a message to the Combined Chiefs of Staff on August 22, Eisenhower said, "When Paris is entered it is my intention to employ the French division for occupation. In entering the city it will be accompanied by token units of British and American forces. Some days thereafter General de Gaulle will be allowed to make his formal entry into the city. I will not personally go there until military considerations require."

That last turned out to be not quite accurate.

Leclerc began his drive toward Paris on August 23–24. There was scattered German resistance until his troops reached the city's outer defenses, when the German 88s opened up on the French columns. The guns along with the Tiger tanks, some concealed in haystacks, caused heavy losses, but von Choltitz had ordered most of his troops across the Seine; the bridges were intact and the city almost completely undamaged. Shortly after noon on August 25, one of Leclerc's young tankers burst into Choltitz's headquarters in the Hôtel Meurice in the Rue de Rivoli. "Do you speak French?" the young officer asked. "Probably better than you do," said Choltitz, who then allowed himself to be taken prisoner. The official surrender was signed later in the day. De Gaulle had arrived in France from Algiers on the morning of August 20, and five days later he was in Paris, about an hour after the signing.

On Saturday, August 26, Eisenhower, driven by Kay and accompanied by Gault, went to Bradley's headquarters in Chartres. Kay said that it was "a long, tiring trip." Eisenhower went a second time through the horror of the Falaise Gap. Kay writes, "I was glad when we emerged from the Falaise section, leaving the sickly odor and sight of death far behind. . . . Arriving at General Bradley's headquarters . . . we found the very air vibrating with one magic, romantic word, *Paris*."

There are various accounts of what followed. Eisenhower in *Crusade* said that at Chartres he "learned that General de Gaulle had already established his headquarters in one of the government buildings of Paris. I at once determined to push on into the city to make a formal call upon him." That makes the visit sound official, even necessary.

Kay said, "Everyone at headquarters agreed that the Supreme Commander himself should go into Paris for psychological reasons. The city needed a show of strength, of Allied unity; collaborationists still were active, unconvinced the occupation was over. . . . He acceded, asking General Bradley to accompany him and, always the SHAEF diplomat, messaging General Montgomery to ask if he wanted to come along to represent Britain. Monty declined the honor."

But, it would seem, not *everyone* at Bradley's headquarters thought Eisenhower did need to go to Paris "for psychological reasons." In an entry in his diary dated August 27, Chet Hansen said, "The decision to go to Paris was made yesterday when Ike came. Tho he would never admit it, I knew he was anxious to see the city. Kay certainly was; she seemed the most concerned about it. . . . Brad was not too keen on going. Told me he 'would never go if Ike hadn't come up and asked him.' Realized they would have to ask Monty and they drafted a wire to him. Jim [Gault] and Kay, neither of whom are Monty fanciers, bet he would not accept and hoped . . . that he would not 'steal the show.' Kay says he certainly would never want to share it with Ike."

Bradley's memory was different still: "The day after we had liberated Paris I returned from a hurried flight to Brest to find Eisenhower encamped on my doorstep. . . . Although he had come with more pressing issues in mind, Ike suggested we slip quietly into Paris for a glimpse of the city the following morning. 'It's Sunday,' he said. 'Everybody will be sleeping late. We can do it without any fuss.' "

Paris sleeping on a Sunday morning two days after its liberation? The appearance of the man largely responsible for the city's liberation would cause no fuss? Did Eisenhower really believe that? Perhaps. He certainly wanted to believe it. Kay wanted desperately to visit the city and what harm would be done?

The supreme commander's small convoy started for the City of Light a few minutes before 8:00 on Sunday morning, the 27th. Kay drove Bradley and Eisenhower, and Brigadier General Edwin Luther Sibert, G-2 for the 21st Army Group, led the way in a jeep, blowing his horn the whole time. Even before they reached the city itself the "fuss" started. The generals' car seemed to attract attention, possibly because it had four stars on its license plates as well as British, French, and American flags on the radiator cap.

According to Hansen, when the convoy reached the city people who had been asleep "came out in their pajamas to wave *bonjour* to us. Flags and shouting everywhere and the enthusiasm was infectious. I felt buoyant. . . . Now I understood why people grew sentimental about Paris." Kay said, "The sidewalks were packed with crowds who shouted and threw kisses at our convoy. Some held gifts of wine, fruit, or flowers."

Eisenhower had not been in Paris since 1928. He had not really got to know any Parisians during that sojourn; he had seldom ventured outside the American colony that surrounded him. His only memorable French adventure, the only one he mentioned anyway, was having onion soup on the Left Bank. As he told Kay later, in August 1944, "We lived on the Right Bank near the river, and I often used to walk up to the Arc de Triomphe with John, but nobody gave me a second look in those days."

Eisenhower's first stop on the 27th was to see de Gaulle. He said after the war, "I went to call on General de Gaulle promptly, and I did this very deliberately as a kind of de facto recognition of him as the provisional president of France. He was very grateful—he never forgot that. After all, I was commanding everything on the Continent, all the troops, all that de Gaulle could count on, everything supplied by America was under my orders. So he looked upon it as it was, and that was a very definite recognition of high political position and his place. That was of course what he wanted and what Roosevelt had never given him." John Eisenhower said, "In the many years of public service left to the two men, de Gaulle never failed to remember this gesture whenever they met."

De Gaulle asked for food and supplies, uniforms for the Free French forces so that they could be distinguished from the marauders and looters who were springing up everywhere. He also asked for equipment for the use of new divisions he was organizing. Most of this the supreme commander was able to give him.

De Gaulle also asked for the loan of two American divisions to help keep order in the city. This Eisenhower found "grimly amusing." He told the newspapermen who had come to the city in his convoy, "You fellows raised hell when I used existing authority to maintain order in North Africa. This time I'm following a hands-off policy. I'm playing along with the people the liberals support—and they now appeal to me to defend them against the excesses of their own group."

Still, Eisenhower said, he realized that de Gaulle was in "a tough spot." He could not "lend" two divisions, but he did provide the 28th Division, most of whose members were from Pennsylvania, to march down the Champs-Elysées on the 29th. The gesture was harmless enough, but much of the British press was outraged when photographs of the marchers were printed. There were indignant editorials saying that the Americans, as usual, were claiming full credit for something in which the British had played a major part. John later said, "Once again an innocent gesture had been misconstrued. But the pride of the British press and public sustained another, if minor, injury."

As for the 28th Division, it went on to the front later that same day; it fought throughout the rest of the war, including the battle of Huertgen Forest and in December in the Ardennes. One member of that division, although he did not join it until after the parade in Paris, was a Private Eddie Slovik, who in January 1945 was to become the only soldier since the Civil War to be executed for desertion. Eisenhower signed the order for Slovik's execution.

After Eisenhower left de Gaulle in Paris on the 27th, he made two other courtesy calls, and then, as he said in *Crusade*, "Word apparently got out that Bradley and I were in town, and when we went past the Arc de Triomphe on the Étoile we were surrounded by a crowd of enthusiastic citizens."

On the way to the Arc, Kay said, "People began to recognize him. The one word 'Eisenhower' roared up in growing symphony. By the time he and General Bradley got out of the car and paid their respects to the Unknown Soldier, the Étoile was a shoving, shouting mass of near-hysterical Parisians."

When Ike attempted to get back to his sedan, a group of MPs tried, without much success, to clear a path through the crowd; a large Frenchman kissed him on both cheeks, and, according to Bradley, "The crowd squealed in delight as Ike reddened and fought free." Brad was kissed on one cheek by a good-looking young woman. "Later as I rubbed a smear of her lipstick from my cheek, I joked Ike on my better fortune. 'I'll leave the accolades to you,' I told him, 'and take my chances with the crowd.' "

Eisenhower and Bradley returned to Bradley's headquarters at Chartres in time for late lunch. Eisenhower then drove back to his advance command post in Normandy.

On the 29th he sent the following message to his commanders—Ramsay, Montgomery, Bradley, Leigh-Mallory, Brereton, Spaatz, Harris, and Smith:

The German Army in the West has suffered a signal defeat in the campaign of the Seine and the Loire at the hands of the Combined Allied Forces. The enemy is being defeated in the East, in the South and in the North; he has experienced internal dissension and signs are not wanting that he is nearing collapse. His forces are scattered throughout Europe and he has given the Allied Nations the opportunity of dealing a decisive blow before he can concentrate them in the defense of his vital areas. We, in the West, must seize this opportunity by acting swiftly and relentlessly and by accepting risks in our determination to close with the German wherever met. . . . It is my intention to complete the destruction of the enemy forces in the West and then advance against the heart of the enemy homeland.

During this period there was a feeling back in the States and in SHAEF and at other army headquarters that the war might end in a very short time, probably with a total collapse of formal German resistance. A SHAEF communication said that the two and a half months of fighting since D-Day "have brought the end of the war within sight, almost within reach. The strength of the German armies in the West has been shattered. Paris belongs to the French again, and the Allied armies are streaming towards the frontiers of the Reich." And Churchill, who should have known better, had predicted a quick victory. At the beginning of August the prime minister had said that the war was "crashing onward toward its close." Even members of Eisenhower's staff were caught up in the euphoria. Major General Kenneth Strong, the usually reliable SHAEF G-2, said that the war would be over in three months. Beetle told the press early in September, "Militarily the war is won." Meanwhile army post exchange officers were planning to return Christmas presents for GIs that were already in the mail from the States. *Everybody* would be home by Christmas.

Eisenhower, however, was more cautious. He had told reporters in his August 15 conference that Hitler would either hang himself or be hanged, but before that he would fight to the bitter end, and most of his troops would fight with him. He said in a letter to Mamie, "Don't be misled by the papers. Every victory, even a partial one, is sweet—but the end of the war will come only with complete destruction of the Hun forces. So—always be optimistic and courageous, but not unduly expectant! (If that makes sense!)"

In another letter he said, "I wonder how people at home can be so complacent about finishing off the job we have here. There is still a lot of suffering to go through. God, I hate the Germans."

Later Eisenhower said, "With the capture of Paris, we were substantially on the line that had been predicted before D-Day as the one we would attain three or four months after our landing. Thus, in long-term estimate we were weeks ahead of our schedule, but in the important matter of supply capacity we were badly behind. Because almost the entire area had been captured in the swift movements subsequent to August 1, the roads, military lines, depots, repair shops, and basic installations required for the maintenance of continuous forward movement were still far to the rear of front lines." Now the heady days of August were over; a disappointing autumn and an alarming early winter were ahead.

★ ★ ★

A FRAGILE REED

In early September 1944 it looked as if nothing, certainly not the German army, could stop the Allies. They had landed more than 2,000,000 troops in northern France since D-day, as well as 3,000,000 tons of supplies. True, they had suffered almost a quarter of a million casualties, but the enemy had had nearly twice that many, including 200,000 men left behind in ports along the coast. About twenty-five panzer and regular infantry divisions had been destroyed and nineteen other panzer and infantry divisions had been seriously hurt. It looked to many people, including a good many newspapermen, as if nothing stood between the Allies and Germany but the Siegfried Line, which for many Allied soldiers was a joke. After all, "We're Gonna Hang Out the Washing on the Siegfried Line" had been a British music hall favorite since the days of the "phony war."

On September 1 Eisenhower took over from Monty operational command of the Allied ground forces on the continent. Those included the 21st Army Group under Montgomery and the 12th Army Group under Bradley. After the DRAGOON landings, the 6th Army Group was under Eisenhower's direction as well. That same day he officially took over his Continental headquarters in Granville, and Dieppe—the site of the disastrous 1942 Commando raid that was to teach the Allies so much about amphibious assaults—was liberated. And Monty was promoted to field marshal, giving him five stars to Ike's four.

In a postwar interview with Portal in London in 1947, the former marshal of the Royal Air Force told Forrest C. Pogue that he was convinced Eisenhower was reluctant to take over the ground command. Furthermore, said Portal, and he was certainly right about this, the job only caused Ike trouble. He did it because he didn't think he could name either Bradley or Montgomery. True, Portal pointed out, Monty had said that he would be willing to serve under Bradley; but he added, "It is easy to say you will do something publicly, when you know perfectly well that your superiors will never permit it. Neither Brooke nor Churchill would have agreed."

On August 23—by that time it was already known that Eisenhower would take over personal control of the ground forces—at a luncheon meeting at his headquarters, then in the apple orchard at Condé-sur-Noireau, Montgomery had lectured his supreme commander. That day he did not use a pointer as he had before, but he did insist that Bedell Smith, who had come with Ike, be excluded from the meeting, though Freddie de Guingand was at Monty's side. Eisenhower was furious at Beetle's exclusion from the meeting, and that didn't happen again.

Monty first explained his plan for Allied strategy; it was, to be sure, the only feasible plan. The most important part of the Montgomery strategy was for "the great mass of the Allied armies to advance northwards, clear the coast as far as Antwerp, establish a powerful air force in Belgium, and advance into the Ruhr. . . . The force must operate as one whole. . . . Singe control of the land operation is vital for success. This is a *whole time* job for one man."

Was it all clear so far? It was, but, as Eisenhower had told de Guingand earlier, he could not go along with it. The SHAEF planners had already decided that they wanted "a broad front both north and south of the Ardennes." Ike agreed with them fully on that, and he would be in charge.

Montgomery insisted that Eisenhower's and SHAEF's strategy was bound to fail. The immediate need was for a "firm and sound plan," which was the one he was proposing. The American plan would slow down the war and perhaps stop it altogether. At the very least "everyone" would be "fighting all the time." And as for Ike taking over direct command of the Allied toops, that was beneath him. "You must not," Monty said, "descend into the land battle and become a ground C-in-C. The Supreme Commander must sit in a lofty perch to be able to take a detached view of the whole intricate problem which involves land, sea, air, civil control and political problems, and someone else must run the battle for him."

A man more susceptible to flattery might have capitulated to Monty. Instead, Ike said that he would do just what he had planned to do, and when Monty rather desperately said that he would be willing to serve under Bradley because a unified command was so important, Eisenhower thanked him very much and said that on September 1 he would take over personally, and from that moment on Eisenhower had two enemies to fight, the Germans and Montgomery.

The disagreement between the British and the American general was more than a clash of wills. The two men honestly and totally disagreed about the relative merits of an overall advance, maintaining pressure over a broad Front on both sides of the Ardennes, versus a single deep thrust. Montgomery thought his forty divisions could and should make a rapid drive to Berlin. Eisenhower thought the first target should be the Rhine; then the subject of how to reach the heartland of Germany could be discussed.

On September 2, when Eisenhower had flown to Chartres to see Bradley, Patton, and, among others, Hodges, the supreme commander had already decided that Montgomery should push Sir Miles Dempsey's Second Army forward, with support from Hodges' First Army on his right. Patton said in his diary, "Ike was very pontifical and quoted Clausewitz to us, who have commanded larger forces than C ever heard of. He is all for cleaning up the Calais area. . . . We finally talked him into letting the V Corps of the First Army and the Third Army attack the Siegfried Line as soon as the Calais area stabilizes. Until this is done, we will not be able to get gas or ammunition for a further advance." Eisenhower did, however, agree that Patton could attack toward Frankfurt and Mannheim and gave permission to Bradley for the First Army to stay on Patton's left, south of the Ardennes.

When Montgomery found out that Patton was getting additional gasoline and that Hodges' First Army troops would advance on Patton's left flank, he was even angrier than before. Ike said that he was still giving Monty top priority, including supplies, but Monty said that that was not so and suggested—demanded is a more accurate word—that Eisenhower come back to his headquarters to discuss the matter. Such things were better talked over in person. In general what Monty said was true; Ike and Bradley and Ike and Hodges, for just two examples, could and did discuss anything. With Monty it was different. They never relaxed together; they were without humor when together, and Monty never even tried to learn how to get along with Eisenhower. Ike tried to get along with the field marshal, but he learned that fall and winter that Monty could never be persuaded to do something. He could only be ordered to do it.

Going to Montgomery's HQ again was a particularly unwelcome idea for Eisenhower at that moment. The meeting at Chartres had not been pleasant— both Patton and Bradley were in a rebellious mood over gasoline shortages and Ike's attempts to "appease" Monty—but the return to his headquarters in Granville was even less so. His C-47 had a broken muffler, and for the return from Chartres to Granville, he flew in an L-5 two-seater liaison plane, which due to unfavorable weather was forced to land on the beach not far from his villa. The tide was rising, and Eisenhower helped Captain Dick Underwood, the pilot, drag the plane to higher ground. While inching his way off the beach, which he feared might be mined, Eisenhower slipped, fell, and twisted his knee, his "good" knee, the right.

After that he and Underwood walked more than a mile and then flagged a jeep that was already somewhat overloaded with eight soldiers. Eisenhower said, "I asked them to take me to headquarters and so great was their concern that they practically lifted me into the front seat of the jeep. Then, careful to avoid crowding against my injured leg, they allowed no one except the driver to sit in front. I still do not understand how all the rest of them piled in and on the jeep and managed to get my pilot aboard, but they did." Eisenhower had to spend two days in bed and for a time wore a brace on his knee. The first press reports said that he was ill from overwork, after which, he said, "I had to publish the details of the affair, with the hope that my wife would not magnify the seriousness of the accident pending receipt of my letter of explanation."

The bad knee continued to bother Ike. On the 13th he wrote Mamie that:

the second I get back to headquarters, the doctors want me to lie down to rest my knee, otherwise, they say, I just keep on hurting it a bit more. It is exceedingly difficult for me to do anything when I'm lying down—even to read. I hate being cooped up. The docs have made a light cast which is strapped to my leg when I travel.

On the 19th he wrote:

Lately I've had to take treatment each day (baking and rubbing) of 1½ hours per day, and I have a hard time fitting in the date.

And on the 23rd:

My leg is improving, but not as rapidly as if I were 30 instead of almost 54. It is OK except for soreness, and I have to be so d—— careful. Annoying.

Whenever Ike was confined to bed he made full use of the time. Kay Summersby said he started keeping a journal of sorts, to justify the few short hours he "wasted" when confined to bed. "A note he made in my absence also indicated a new awareness of his spotlighted role in World War II: 'Dictated all p.m. Have started to put down some of the things that might be appropriate for me to say in a personal account of the war. Good way to occupy myself when flat on my back.' "

Despite the fact that he was in pain, Eisenhower continued to be optimistic in early September, and so did most of the troops under his command. Allied air offensives continued to be destructive. During the month, 112,400 tons of bombs were dropped by heavy bombers. Calais alone was the target for more than 6,000 tons.

By September 3 the Allies in Southern France had put ashore almost 200,000 men, 41,000 vehicles, and 220,000 tons of supplies. Lyon had been liberated on the 2nd; French units were brought forward so that they could enter the city first. In northern France, supply problems were beginning to worry the supreme commander. Douai, St.-Valery, and Lens were liberated by the Allies, and on the 3rd, units of the British Second Army entered Brussels. On the 4th, later to be called "the crucial day of the war in the west after D-day," troops of the British 11th Armored Division, aided by the Belgian "White Brigade," entered Antwerp, Europe's largest port and the one closest to the heart of the continent. The troops seized the twenty-mile-long harbor intact. The Germans had not yet had a chance to blow up the harbor area or the ten miles of docks, bridges, and sluice gates. There were celebrations in the city that night and in many Allied headquarters in Europe. Both Eisenhower and Montgomery were happy with what looked like a major accomplishment. Neither would have believed it if told that the port would not be usable until November 28. But September 4 was a crucial day in the war not so much for what was done as for what was not done. While Antwerp itself was taken, the Scheldt Estuary surrounding it was not. The latter was in the minds of many observers then and later a great strategic blunder, perhaps the Allies' greatest in Europe. Much more has been written and said about the Battle of the Bulge, but while the failure of the German counteroffensive somewhat hastened the end of the war in Europe, the fact that Antwerp was taken but not the surrounding estuary almost certainly prolonged that war.

On September 3 Ike's naval commander in chief, Admiral Sir Bertram Ramsay, had sent a telegram to Ike's HQ marked "For Action." That action was not taken for many weeks, and by the time it was, the Germans had made its aim costly, even for a time, impossible. Ramsay's telegram said:

It is essential that if Antwerp and Rotterdam are to be opened quickly—
  1. Enemy must be prevented from:
     (a) Carrying out demolitions and blocking the ports.
     (b) Mining and blocking Scheldt and the new waterway between Rotterdam and the Hook.
  2. Both Antwerp and Rotterdam are highly vulnerable to mining and blocking. If enemy succeeds in these operations the time it will take to open the ports cannot be estimated.
  3. It will be necessary for coastal batteries to be captured before approach channels to the river routes can be established.

A copy of Ramsay's memo was sent to Montgomery, and in one of his rare moments of humility Monty later wrote, "I must admit a bad mistake on my part—I underestimated the difficulties of opening up the approaches to Antwerp so that we could get the free use of the port. I reckoned the Canadian Army could do it while we were going for the Ruhr. I was wrong."

The two were not immediately related, but on the day Antwerp was taken by Montgomery's troops, Hitler told the Japanese ambassador to Berlin, Baron Hiroshi Oshima, that German forces were far from defeated. In fact, he said, "When the current replenishment of the air forces is completed . . . and the new army of more than a million men, which is now being organized, is ready, I intend to combine the new units with units to be withdrawn from all possible areas and to open a large-scaled offensive in the west."

"When might that be?" asked the baron.

"After the beginning of November," said Hitler.

The baron shortly thereafter sent the news to Tokyo, and since the Japanese code had long since been broken by the Americans, what Hitler had said about a November offensive was soon on the desks of officers in the Pentagon. No one paid the slightest attention, however, and when various indications of what the Germans were planning were discovered by Allied intelligence officers in Europe, they treated the matter with indifference.

At a press conference on September 7, after Third Army troops crossed the Moselle north of Metz, Patton, who could seldom be quoted, said, "I hope to go through the Siegfried Line like shit through a goose. That is not quotable. . . . Had we had the gas, which was a physical impossibility since we had gone much faster than we were supposed to, had we hit the Moselle four days earlier, it would have been like pissing in the wind."

On the 10th, when Eisenhower reluctantly and painfully flew to Monty's headquarters, now in Brussels, because of his knee he found it difficult to get on the plane and impossible to get off. Monty joined him on the plane, but the field marshall was not in a good mood as the conference began and his temper got worse as time went on. According to Tedder, who accompanied Eisenhower, "In our discussion Eisenhower explained again the precarious nature of our supply system and the need to gain the use of Antwerp promptly. He thought that without railway bridges across the Rhine, and without plentiful supplies, we would not maintain in Germany a force capable of penetrating to Berlin." Monty's manner, according to one biographer, was as if he were "addressing his Staff College pupils. As the tirade gathered fury Eisenhower stayed silent, but as soon as Montgomery stopped for breath, he leaned forward, put his hand on the other's knee, and said, 'Steady, Monty. You cannot talk to me like this. I am your boss!' Monty mumbled an apology, but relations between him and Eisenhower had reached new depths." Eisenhower later said, "Monty's suggestion is simple; give him everything, which is crazy."

Eisenhower was no happier with criticism than anybody else, but, unlike most people, he did not seem to brood over it. Fortunately during the difficult period in late 1944 and early '45 Marshall's backing of the supreme commander never wavered. Later Marshall remembered that, at the time, both Patton and Monty wanted more gas and that while the Third Army was getting most of the publicity because of "Patton's dash and showmanship," Hodges' First Army "was making very rapid moves in a very positive manner and getting very little credit for it in this country. . . . General Hodges was very quiet, and some very remarkable actions took place . . . for which General Hodges was entitled to the credit. . . . Montgomery wanted to go free and to go ahead on his part. Patton wanted to go free—with the great temptation of running right up to the Rhine— and there was almost no gasoline. . . . I think Eisenhower's control of the operations at that time was correct. And that all the others were yelling as they naturally would yell. There is nothing remarkable about that except that that one was commander of the British forces, which at that time were very small, and the other was a very high-powered, dashing commander who had the press at his beck and call—General Patton."

On the plane, Eisenhower and Monty did agree on what many people still believe was the bloodiest, most expensive, and most ill-advised operation of the European war, an airborne invasion of the Netherlands designed to seize seven vital bridges and hold open a corridor for tanks of the British Second Army to drive across the Rhine at Arnhem. Its code name was MARKET-GARDEN.

As will be seen, a great number of Allied leaders were neither particularly surprised nor much saddened at the failure of MARKET-GARDEN, which Bradley later called "the gallant defeat at Arnhem." The mild-mannered Bradley said of the first time he heard of the plan, "Had the pious, teetotaling Montgomery wobbled into SHAEF with a hangover, I could not have been more astonished than I was by the daring adventure he proposed. For in contrast to the conservative tactics Montgomery ordinaily chose, the Arnhem attack was to be made over a sixty-mile carpet of airborne troops. Although I never reconciled myself to the venture, I nevertheless freely concede that Monty's plan for Arnhem was one of the most imaginative of the war."

Other than the agreement on MARKET-GARDEN, the meeting between Eisenhower and Montgomery on the cramped plane in the Brussels airport on September 10 really accomplished nothing at all, though it did cause some additional discomfort for Ike's injured knee. The two men remained distrustful of each other; neither could agree to the other's plan for victory, and the British and American press continued to play up and exaggerate their differences. The British people were understandably in sympathy with a plan that Monty said would achieve a sure victory for the Allies before the end of the year. They had been in the war a very long time; they, both the civilians and the men and women in uniform, were weary, and everything they had, including patience, was in short supply. Another winter of fighting in Belgium, Holland, and Germany would be an almost unbearable additional strain. Churchill wanted to get the Allied armies as far east as possible, as quickly and with as little fuss as possible. The Russians never left his mind.

Brooke and the prime minister were on Monty's side in the argument, most of the time anyway, Brooke's support being somewhat sturdier and more dependable than the prime minister's. Churchill never entirely stopped feeling that he could and would win the war faster and at less cost by himself—if only his generals would leave him alone.

The Americans, on the other hand, the high command in particular, knew that the longer they fought, the stronger they would get. They saw no advantage at all in taking unnecessary risks. They were for slugging it out, and they didn't worry at all about their good friends in the USSR. Roosevelt, who was soon to meet with Stalin at Yalta, decided almost immediately that he understood old Joe and that he could handle the Russian Bear.

So Monty, though the strategy was largely his own, was doing what the British really wanted, planning to win the war in a hurry. Ike, though again the strategy was largely his own, was doing what the Americans wanted, fighting for a sure victory that might take a little longer. It is still not clear who was right. Eisenhower prevailed, and he was the supreme commander whose troops won the war. Perhaps Monty could have done it more quickly and at a lesser cost. But there was a fundamental difference between Eisenhower and Montgomery. Eisenhower seldom said he could do something until he was quite certain that he could do what he said, and then he did it. Monty was a man better at promise than at fulfillment.

One of Monty's less adoring biographers, Alan Chalfont, said, "The question of how far Montgomery's concept of the 'single thrust' was viable is clearer now than it seemed at the time. An analysis of the military events of September [1944] suggest that his skill as commander in mobile warfare was seriously limited; and that he was guilty of serious errors of judgment which cast doubt upon his whole understanding of the strategic problem.

"It seems clear beyond doubt that a great opportunity was missed during the first week of September, and that after that German defenses were far too strong to be defeated by a limited 'single thrust' type of operation."

What happened at Antwerp was a disaster, and Eisenhower and Montgomery could share the blame for that, though understandably neither seemed anxious to do so.

The day of the meeting between Ike and Monty in Brussels, Montgomery's steadfast supporter Brooke was on the *Queen Mary* on his way to the second conference with Churchill and Roosevelt in Québec. Brooke wrote in his diary of that day, "We had another meeting with Winston at 12 noon. He produced arguments to prove that operations could be speeded up so as to leave us an option till December before having to withdraw any forces from Europe. He knows no details, has only got half the picture in mind."

The conference meetings lasted from September 12 through the 16th, and most of the time Roosevelt and Churchill acted as if the war in Europe was over—well, nearly over, won anyway. The Russians were about to invade Hungary, which at the moment was highly applauded in Allied circles, though not by the prime minister. The Germans, it was said, would at any moment return to the Rhine, though that rampart did present problems. Both leaders agreed that China could be retaken, and the Philippines would be reconquered by the Americans. "Everything we have touched has turned to gold," said the prime minister, and at that moment there seemed no reason to doubt it, even at SHAEF.

Roosevelt seemed to have a new secretary of state, although old Cordell Hull still had the title officially. Roosevelt called Henry Morgenthau, his secretary of the treasury, the man who so recently had had a long and, from Morgenthau's point of view, satisfactory lunch with the supreme commander. The Morgenthau Plan for the treatment of Germany after the war was presented to the leaders at Québec by the treasury secretary himself. The Third Reich was to be made into an "agricultural and pastoral" country after the war. It must never again be allowed to rearm. The factories in the Saar and the Ruhr were either to be destroyed or removed as reparations.

None of these matters, which reached the press, especially the press in Germany, made things easier for the Allied armies. Many feared that the Germans would fight all the harder once they learned what the Allies had in mind for them. Actually, there is almost no evidence that either the Morgenthau Plan or the demand for unconditional surrender caused the Germans to fight any longer or any harder than they would have anyway. They simply fought on until Hitler was gone.

The conference did determine the partition of Germany after the war. There would be no Allied headquarters. According to Kay, Eisenhower "was told to plan for national boundaries, Russian, British, French, and American. His bosses also warned he might remain in Europe for a considerable length of time after the war. Aching for the end of the campaign and his job, homesick for leisure and his family, General Ike had to steel himself to the idea that he probably would command the occupation zone in Germany."

There seemed to be something to satisfy, if only temporarily, both Eisenhower and Montgomery in the decisions made at Québec. It was agreed that a northern approach into Germany had advantages over the southern approach. That one, Monty won, and the day after the conference in Québec ended, Monty's grandiose Operation MARKET-GARDEN began, and everybody had high, brief hopes for that. But, according to the editor of Brooke's diaries, Arthur Bryant, "The Combined Chiefs of Staff accepted Eisenhower's proposals for a broad advance instead of the single concentrated thrust on the Ruhr urged by Montgomery. The decision to leave overall operational control to the Supreme Commander had been agreed from the start, and it was impossible for the British Chiefs of Staff, at such a time of victory, to question the competence of the officer to whom both the Allied governments had entrusted their forces."

In a message to Marshall on the 18th Eisenhower said, "From what I can read in the paper, your Québec conference went off very nicely, but I suppose, as is usual, there was a lot under the surface that was not reported." The truth is, the second conference at Québec accomplished very little, and it was not until Yalta that, in the minds of millions, Roosevelt, old and tired and near death, "sold out" to Stalin. Many thought he had the backing of and perhaps the advice of Eisenhower. Meanwhile, it was clear by the time the Québec conference was over that the war in Europe was not, and the war in the Pacific was in a sense just beginning.

The war was not won. Eisenhower kept insisting on that. Mamie, perhaps Mamie most of all, had to be set straight on the matter, and on the 23rd in a letter to her Ike said:

So many people are certain that we've won the war that frequently I'm asked what I intend to do afterward. In the first place, the question usually makes me angry, because you can be certain this war is not "won" for the man that is shivering, suffering and dying up on the Siegfried Line. . . . My whole time and thought is tied up in winning this bloody mess—it will be fun, thereafter, putting in three months deciding whether I want to have my eggs boiled or scrambled for breakfast.

Despite the ailing knee and a great deal of trouble with, among others, Patton and Monty, Ike still found time during that disheartening fall and winter to make a great number of trips to the front to visit the troops under his command. On August 30 he had told Lieutenant General Brehon Somervell, an old friend who was head of the Services of Supply, about his need for a car. He told Somervell that it must have plenty of leg room in rear and with sufficient power and type of drive that will provide rapid pickup in passing convoys. . . . Due to difficulties in air travel I have to use automobiles a great deal in visiting headquarters, and unless the car is capable of rapid acceleration it is difficult to make any time. My present car is completely satisfactory except for this one item and it is possible that the one you have just shipped is identical. If this is the case will you try to locate a Buick of the type described. I will then turn over the Cadillac to General Lee or some other senior officer whose duties do not require so much road travel in rear of advancing armies. I am sorry to cause you all this trouble but I really need a vehicle of the kind described.

By the end of October, Ike had the car he needed, another Cadillac that he found "splendid." He wrote Somervell that it was "a satisfactory automobile. . . . It has room, power, and comfortable springs, all of which are necessary on longer winter trips. . . . The week before last I traveled more than 1000 miles by car, and the prospects are that all winter long I will have to depend upon the automobile to get about."

That fall Eisenhower went to the front to talk to several hundred members of the 29th Division. He spoke to them on a hillside that was both muddy and slippery, and when he turned to return to his jeep, he slipped and fell on his back. The soldiers laughed, and Eisenhower said, "From the shout of laughter that went up, I was quite sure no other meeting I had with soldiers during the war was a greater success than that one."

Eisenhower spent about a third of his time visiting troops. No parades or special inspections were held. He insisted that training continue without interruption, and most of the time there was no press coverage. He spent almost no time with high-ranking officers. He wanted to know from the soldiers themselves about their quarters and their food. He often talked to groups of soldiers on the loudspeaker attached to his jeep. He told them it was an honor to be their commanding officer and said, "You are the men who will win this war." He often said, "A commander meets to talk with his men to inspire them; with me it is the other way around. I get inspired by you."

At a time when his troops were getting ready to cross the Rhine, Eisenhower met a soldier on the bank of that river and asked, "How are you feeling, son?" "General," the soldier said, "I am awful nervous. I was wounded two months ago and just got back from the hospital yesterday. I don't feel so good."

Eisenhower said, "You and I are a good pair then, because I'm nervous, too. But we've planned this attack for a long time, and we've got all the planes, the guns, and airborne troops we can use to smash the Germans. Maybe if we just walk along together to the river we'll be good for each other."

It was impossible for him to come even close to visiting all the troops under his command, but he did draw closer to the men he met, and the stories were repeated and exaggerated until they reached thousands of men. In all the stories Ike emerged as warm and personal, and he was upset only when he read about his visits in the newspapers. He did not want anyone to think he made the trips for personal publicity purposes. Of course, a great many people inside and outside of the army did think that, and, although that wasn't his wish, there was a certain staginess in many of the visits. No one, division commander or private, was ever quite relaxed or quite natural in the presence of his supreme commander, but there was a certain comfort in just seeing him or just hearing from someone who had seen him that he was a real person. I did a great deal of traveling in the area in the fall and winter of 1944 and in early 1945, and I never heard anyone speak of Ike in any except the warmest terms.

Many people urged Eisenhower to cut down his visits, but he did not agree. "In the first place," he said, "I felt I gained accurate impressions of their [the soldiers'] state of mind. I talked to them about anything and everything . . . so long as I could get the soldiers to talk to me in return. This, I felt, would encourage men to talk to their superiors, and this habit, promotes efficiency. . . . There is among the mass of individuals who carry rifles in war, a great amount of ingenuity and initiative. If men can naturally and without restraint talk to their officers, the products of their resourcefulness become available to all. . . . Mutual confidence, a feeling of partnership, that is the essence of *esprit de corps*."

In an early November column in the *New York Times*, Anne O'Hare McCormick said, "General Eisenhower loves to talk about the Army. Nothing interests him more than an incident or observation that illustrated the spirit at the front. It is evident that all of the armies under his command are the Army in his mind. His popularity with all fighting units is due partly to their feeling that he is one of them and partly to his strong sense of the meaning of the title of Allied commander. He never refers to American, British, or French positions when discussing battlelines but always to this or that sector of the 'Allied front.' When he mentions 'our troops' he means not American but Allied troops."

In a message to his senior commanders on September 13, Eisenhower said that getting to the Rhine was still at the top of the priority list, that bridgeheads across the river must be secured, that the Ruhr must be seized, and then that—no, this was not what Monty wanted, though Ike didn't say so—the Allies "must concentrate [their] forces in preparation for a final drive into Germany." What followed was, however, for Monty's immediate attention. The supreme commander said:

> While this is going on we must secure bases as follows: Northern Group of Armies must promptly secure the approaches to Antwerp or Rotterdam so that one of these ports and the lines of communication radiating therefrom can give adequate maintenance to the Northern Group of Armies deep into the heart of Germany.

In his reply on the 15th, Monty did not mention Antwerp; he said that he hoped the Ruhr, the Saar, and the Frankfurt area would soon be in Allied hands. The Germans would really fight for the Ruhr and Frankfurt, but they would be defeated. He went on, "Clearly Berlin is the main prize, and the prize in defense of which the enemy is likely to concentrate the bulk of his forces. There is no doubt whatsoever, in my mind, that we should concentrate all our energies and resources on a rapid thrust to Berlin."

Whatever might or might not be said about Monty's letter, it was not an answer to Ike's letter. They might have been in two different armies fighting for two different goals, and in a sense, they were. Eisenhower could not fire Britain's greatest hero of the Second World War; no more could Monty, for all his finagling, get Roosevelt or Marshall to give Eisenhower's command to himself and Bradley.

John Eisenhower said that during this period "and for years afterward," whenever his father met with Montgomery, "he treated him with every courtesy, every deference. Monty often disappointed Dad—but in all positions except Supreme Commander, Montgomery held a status equal to his. Montgomery was not only commander of the 21st Army Group, he was also the senior British commander; he also had been senior British commander for the invasion. Dad wore the corresponding hat for the Americans. Naturally, as Supreme Commander, Dad was the ultimate boss. But he was obviously determined that any friction that might occur between the two would never be the result of any personal slight on his part. Their differences would be based solely on military judgment in a common cause."

On September 14th Ike told Marshall:

The fact is that we are stretched to the absolute limit in maintenance both as to intake and as to distribution after supplies are landed. . . . From the start we have always known that we would have to choose after breaking out of the original bridgehead, some line which would mark a relative slacking in offensive operations while we improved maintenance facilities and prepared for an offensive operation that could be sustained for another indefinite period. At first it seemed to me that the German would try to use some one of the lines available to him in France on which to make a rather determined stand, but due to the decisiveness of our victory below the Seine I determined to go all out in effort and in risk to continue the drive beyond the German border, up to and including the Rhine before we begin the process of regrouping and re-fitting.

While that was going on, Eisenhower said, Monty became "obsessed" with the idea that the 21st Army Group could rush into Berlin; all that was necessary was to give him "all the maintenance that was in the theater." The whole thing was based on "wishful thinking." He continued:

As opposed to this the only profitable plan is to hustle all our forces up against the Rhine, including Devers' forces, build up our maintenance facilities and our reserves as rapidly as possible and then put on one sustained and unremitting advance against the heart of the enemy country. Supporting this great attack will probably be subsidiary operations against the German ports on the left and against his southern industrial areas on the right.

What Eisenhower called "the great Airborne attack," MARKET-GARDEN, should be successful in carrying Montgomery up to and across the Rhine. Eisenhower then once again said of Montgomery that he must "quickly capture the approaches to Antwerp so that we may use that port." Once again Montgomery did not do it, and once again Ike was immobilized. In their unsatisfactory and uncomfortable meeting in Eisenhower's plane at Brussels, he had mentioned Antwerp. He had, according to Tedder, said that there was "The need to gain Antwerp promptly." But Monty did not remember that. In fact, he denied that the subject "was . . . ever mentioned at our conference on the 10th." In his office diary the next day, Ike wrote, "Monty seems unimpressed by necessity for taking Antwerp approaches."

Monty was indeed unimpressed with the tedious necessity of driving the Germans from their positions on both sides of the Scheldt Estuary; his mind and his imagination were concentrated on the challenge of Berlin. Tedder said of the SHAEF attitude at the time, "Eisenhower's view, with which I entirely agreed, was that it was fantastic to talk of marching to Berlin with an army which was still drawing on the great bulk of its supplies over the beaches of Bayeux." Meantime the Germans continued to mine the Scheldt and to pour men into the area to defend the estuary. Freeing it in November cost 13,000 men, half of them Canadians.

In the plane in Brussels on September 10, Eisenhower had agreed to Monty's most vivid, daring, and un-Monty-like plan, MARKET-GARDEN. It was an agreement the supreme commander may have regretted, but he never said so.

In *Crusade*, he said, "I instructed him [Monty] that what I did want in the north was Antwerp working, and I also wanted a line covering that port. Beyond this I believed it possible that we might with airborne assistance seize a bridgehead over the Rhine in the Arnhem region, flanking the defenses of the Siegfried Line. The operation to gain such a bridgehead—it was assigned the code name MARKET-GARDEN—would be merely an incident and extension of our eastward rush to the line we needed for temporary security."

Indeed, an operation like MARKET-GARDEN was something all of the airborne people wanted, and Marshall wanted a way to use the glider troops and paratroopers of the First Allied Airborne Army, commanded by Lieutenant General Lewis H. Brereton. It consisted of the British 1st and the U.S. 82d and 101st Airborne Divisions. The plan was for the 101st to secure the bridges at Zon and Veghel, near Eindhoven, the key bridges on the Waal and Maas rivers at Grave and Nijmegen. The British would land on the far side of the Rhine, near Arnhem, to the north. Then units of the British Second Army would come up from the south, meet with the airborne troops, and open the way into Germany.

It was the biggest airborne operation of all time, and it was a disaster. In his book *The War*, Louis L. Snyder said, "The airdrop did not go as well as expected, communications broke down, air support was lacking in the foggy weather, and worst of all, the complete Allied battle plan had been captured by the Germans after the first landings." The whole operation lasted nine days, and in the end what was left of the British 1st Airborne Division, known as the "Red Devils"—they wore bright red berets—were shooting their pistols at German tanks. Out of a division of 10,000 men, fewer than 2,200 made it back across the Rhine to be evacuated to the British Isles.

In 1966 Eisenhower defensively said of the failed operation, "I not only approved MARKET-GARDEN, I insisted upon it. What we needed was a *bridgehead* over the Rhine. If that could be accomplished I was quite willing to sit on all other operations. What this action proved was that the idea of 'one full-blooded thrust' to Berlin was silly." While he was at it, he might as well get in a little dig at Monty. Montgomery did not consider the operation a mistake. In his *Memoirs* he said, "I remain an unrepentant advocate of MARKET-GARDEN." But even Brooke deserted him on that one. On October 5 Brooks said in his diary, "I feel that Monty's strategy for once is at fault. Instead of carrying out the advance on Arnhem he ought to have made certain of Antwerp in the first place."

On September 20 Ike had moved his headquarters from Granville to Versailles. According to Marty Snyder, the supreme commander "did not want headquarters to be in a big city. Mickey said that he [Eisenhower] had been offered several sumptuous houses for his personal quarters, but he refused them all, including the Royal Palace at Versailles. He felt the palace was a monument which belonged to the people of France and should not be used as a residence by anyone. He finally decided on a modest house at St.-Germain [shared with Jimmy Gault]. Its previous occupant had been Rundstedt, the German general who had commanded occupied Paris. [Rundstedt was never commander of Paris but had occupied the house.] I wondered if Eisenhower's choice was meant to be symbolic of the liberation, but when I mentioned this to him he said that hadn't occurred to him.

" 'Symbolic gestures don't accomplish much," he said. 'We can't expect to liberate Europe just by taking over enemy generals' homes. Liberating cities isn't the reason for this war. We've got to liberate a lot of European minds from their distorted human values. That's the big job, and we won't start until after the fighting's over.' "

Eisenhower's office was in an annex to the hardly humble Trianon Hotel. His office was so huge that he ordered it broken up with a partition that did not reach the ceiling but was welcomed by Kay because it "gave me shameless opportunity to hear as much as a whisper in his sanctum. Thus, the official side of my job was made easier, for I could tell immediately when the General was available for interruption. I could write down the day's business in the diary without asking him what had transpired. And, as a normal female, I thoroughly enjoyed the luxury of eavesdropping on conversations in the Throne Room."

At Versailles, on the afternoon of September 22, Eisenhower held another meeting with all his commanders save one, Montgomery. Monty sent Freddie de Guingand, and Bradley was not surprised. Chet Hansen, his aide, had told him before the meeting that the SHAEF staff was making book that Monty would not attend. Although Eisenhower seemed not to care, Monty's absence was looked on by the other Allied leaders as a direct affront to the supreme commander.

It was perhaps just as well that Monty wasn't there, because early in the meeting Ike mentioned something that the field marshal would have found painful. Eisenhower asked for general agreement on the idea that "the possession of an additional major deep-water port on our north flank was an indispensable prerequisite for a final drive into Germany." He said that the main operations at the moment were those of the 21st Army Group, which would free the Antwerp approaches and attack the Ruhr from the north. Bradley would attack from the south. Brad was also to take over the British VIII Corps sector and as long as supplies were available continue the attack toward Cologne. Patton's Third Army would not do much of anything until the main Allied efforts had been fulfilled. When Patton got the news from Bradley the next day he said to an associate, "Well, how would you like to go to China?"

Monty's not being present at the meeting had its disadvantages for him, too. De Guingand wired him, "Ike supported your plan 100 per cent." That was not true. Montgomery had wanted complete control of the U.S. First Army. What he got was permission to communicate with that army's commander, Hodges, during emergencies. In his own rather vague report of the meeting to Monty, the supreme commander said that he was anxious "to get to the Ruhr quickly," which cannot have been news to the field marshal. And he might have found somewhat repetitious the last words of the message, "As I have told you, I am prepared to give you everything for the capture of the approaches to Antwerp, including all the air forces and anything else that you can support."

In his account of that meeting, Butcher added something that at the time seemed of minor importance. "Ike finds that Bradley's forces are getting fearfully stretched south of Aachen and that we may get a nasty little 'Kasserine' if the enemy chooses the right place to concentrate his strength."

Despite the fact that Eisenhower seemed always to be arguing with Montgomery and appeared most of the time to be demanding that Monty do what he didn't want to do, a great many American officers continued to think that Ike was agreeing to everything the field marshal and his British colleagues wanted. Thus, on September 24 Butcher, in Paris, had written in his diary, "I went out to Versailles today to bring Ike up to date on affairs at my level. I reported to him the comment from junior officers of the Third Army that 'Eisenhower is the best general the British have.' This disturbed him."

One of the supreme commander's minor worries that fall was whether or not he was putting on too much weight, possibly because he now had two cows providing milk and cream, and he was eating a good deal of candy. He insisted that Mickey have candy in his desk drawer at all times "in case he got hungry." There was a good deal of talk on the general's part about eating less and exercising more. The ever-loyal Mickey said, "I didn't think he was getting fat, but some of his clothes shrunk—the shirts particularly—and that may have made him think he was."

On September 29 in a report to the Combined Chiefs of Staff Ike said, "My general intention remains unaltered, that is, to press on with all speed to destroy the German Armed forces and to advance deep into Germany; and I have not deviated from my opinion that the best means of doing so is to strike at the Ruhr and the Saar, throwing the greater weight against the Saar."

It was clear by the end of September that Hitler's defeat, while certain, was not exactly imminent. The Fuehrer had not been idle while the Allies slowed down and sometimes stopped altogether. He had started building up his defenses as well as his depleted army allowed. True, many of the new recruits were boys, some of them as young as twelve and fourteen but imbued with Nazi fanaticism, and old men.

On the other hand, by the end of September the First Army alone had taken 185,000 prisoners of war, and several thousand others had been treated in Allied hospitals. More than 14,000 of the enemy had been killed and 50,000 wounded. The German garrisons at Brest, St.-Nazaire, and Bordeaux, indeed all the coastal fortresses, had been knocked out.

And despite the Allied letdown in morale and in activity at the end of September and throughout most of October, the campaign in France had been a great success. According to one American military historian, James L. Stokesbury, it "was one of the great campaigns of military history, certainly one of the great ones of the Second World War. . . . Under Eisenhower's direction, the campaign had gone smoothly and harmoniously. France and Belgium were liberated, ports were opened, supply problems mastered. All over Europe, the Germans were in disarray. . . . By day and by night the bombers still dropped their deadly loads on the Fatherland. It could only be a matter of time now. Within months, at most, the Master Race would be mastered."

The month of October began well—nothing spectacular, no heavy breakthroughs, no long lines of prisoners, nothing like North Africa in those last triumphant days or Normandy in midsummer. Still Hodges' First Army seemed to be doing well in its assault on the Siegfried Line near Aachen and in some areas had broken through the line, which had proved to be far less vulnerable than the song had predicted.

On October 6, at last, the Canadian II Corps began to eliminate some of the Germans holding the Scheldt Estuary. But the ground under foot was now wet and flooded; the troops made almost no progress. That morning the supreme commander, Bradley, and Beetle went to Orly to meet General Marshall and James F. Byrnes, head of the Office of War Mobilization, an office so important that Roosevelt called Byrnes the "Assistant President." It was his job to mobilize production for the whole Allied world and as Stalin correctly said, "Without American production the United Nations could never have won the war." By the end of the war the United States had produced almost 300,000 airplanes, 86,300 tanks as well as 8.5 million rifles. But Eisenhower's theater that fall and early winter never seemed to get enough supplies, and getting them to a port on the continent and then to the front-line troops at times seemed an impossible task.

Marshall, however, seemed unaware of the difficulties and setbacks the Allies had been experiencing. He flew to Bradley's headquarters on the 7th and, according to Brad, "It was apparent from the Chief of Staff's conversations that the chill which had caused us to revise our rosy September estimates on the end of the war had not yet filtered through to Washington and the War Department. While we were now resigned to a bitter-end campaign, he spoke with the cheery optimism we had discarded three weeks before. In approving our plans for a November offensive he predicted that our pressures would force the enemy to quit rather than endure another hard winter. This variation in outlook among distant echelons of command is usually present in any large-scale war where senior commands may be hundreds or thousands of miles from the front."

As a result, the chief of staff seemed to be concerned largely with things that were of more importance to a peacetime army than one engaged in a global war. He gave Butcher what the latter referred to as "an enormous job." He was asked to see to it that the army band be "identified with front-line troops." According to Butcher, Marshall had "almost despaired of bringing the Army band into the same prominence at home as that enjoyed by the Marine band." Butcher added that Marshall "had been after General Ike and Beetle since the early days in Africa to promote the Army Band, but correspondents naturally prefer to write news of actual battles, and stories of the Army Band are lost in the competition."

When Marshall spoke to Seventh Army troops, he tactlessly emphasized the war in the Pacific. It was, he said, so far ahead of schedule that the supply problem was difficult. He added that the work of establishing American army fronts throughout the world "had largely been completed." This was not exactly what the supreme commander in Europe, himself facing a crisis in a shortage of supplies and worried about where the replacements for his own decimated divisions were coming from, needed the chief of staff to say.

Before he left Europe, however, Marshall did concern himself with infantry replacements. He wanted to know how to bring elements of infantry regiments in the rear to relieve those on the front lines. On the 11th, in his first message to Marshall after the chief of staff returned to Washington, Eisenhower said that he had seen Bradley and "discussed the proposition of getting up Infantry for relief purposes."

On the 8th Marshall and Bradley flew to Montgomery's headquarters in Eindhoven. The journey to the Netherlands and what happened there must have pleased Eisenhower. Monty was in his usual bad temper, and the U.S. chief of staff recalled, that in private conversation in his office caravan, the field marshal said "there was a lack of grip, and operational direction and control was lacking. Our operation had, in fact, become ragged and disjointed, and we had now got ourselves into a real mess."

Marshall did not say much, but he did not hide the fact that he disagreed. In an interview with Forrest Pogue in 1956, he said that keeping quiet had been difficult. "I came pretty near to blowing out of turn," he said. "It was very hard for me to restrain myself because I didn't think there was any logic in what he said, but overwhelming egotism."

On October 10 Marshall visited Patton, and Georgie felt that the chief of staff was pleased with what he saw. "I have never known General Marshall to be so nice and human," he said in his diary. Marshall also found time to visit many front-line troops, and on the 10th, near Aachen, he stepped on German soil for the first time since 1919. When he returned to the United States, he got in touch with the families of dozens of officers and men to whom he had talked in Europe. He wrote Mamie:

I wanted to tell you that Eisenhower was looking very well and handling himself and his job beautifully. Of course he is under a very heavy strain but bears up under it wonderfully and has exhibited a store of patience to meet the various trying incidents of his position other than the direct conduct of the campaign.

Before returning to the States, Marshall spent the night of the 12th at Eisenhower's headquarters at Versailles. That day Eisenhower had held a press conference, warning the newsmen and, not incidentally, his own troops that the war in Europe was by no means over. According to the *New York Times*, he had "detected a public mood of impatience and concern at the comparative lack of Allied progress recently. . . . The present pause in the forward march into Germany, he explained, is inevitable to enable the Allies to re-establish lines of communications, after their rapid advancement."

Evidence of fraternization between Allied troops and Germans was already beginning to appear, and Ike said that "in Germany there will be no fraternization. We go in as conquerors. We shall treat them justly, in conformity with civilized standards as exemplified by our Governments."

Eisenhower spoke glowingly of MARKET-GARDEN, without, of course, referring to its code name or the fact that it had been a costly failure. He said that all of the airborne divisions, British and American, had done "beautiful work and I am proud of them all." He also said that the "British First Airborne Division . . . gave to all the Allied forces one of the most gallant examples of courage in all this war" and that "they enabled us to hold important bridges." He did not say that the operation had cost 172,000 casualties. True, there were bridgeheads across Maas and Waal rivers, and Monty had gained a sixty-five-mile corridor in the Netherlands, but the Rhine seemed as far away and as formidable as ever.

On the 14th King George VI was making a tour of the front, and that noon he, Eisenhower, Bradley, Patton, and the rest of the senior command had lunch at Hodges' First Army CP near Liège; the lunch was in what Bradley called a "barren dining room" in a run-down château, surrounded by mud. The dining room was cold, too, but Patton entertained the assembled generals and the king by telling the tale of his African campaign. Both the king and most of the others present had heard variations of the story. The last time the king had heard it was in Buckingham Palace in the summer of 1942, only then it involved Mexicans. According to Bradley, Patton "spoke of the thievery of Tunisian Arabs, sipped his coffee, and declared to the King, 'Why, I must have shot a dozen Arabs myself.'

"Ike looked up and with a wink toward me. 'How many, did you say, George?' he asked.

"Patton pulled on his cigar. 'Well, maybe it was only half a dozen—' he replied with a mischievous grin.

" 'How many?' Ike repeated the question.

"George hunched his shoulders, laughed, and turned to the King. 'Well, at any rate, sir, I did boot two of them squarely in the—ah, street at Gafsa.' "

After lunch Eisenhower and Bradley went to the new tactical headquarters of Brad's 12th Army Group in Luxembourg. Bradley said, "We motored down through the Ardennes, dank with the dampness of many rains, past the peat bogs of Belgium, and through the village of Bastogne. A mobile baking unit had rolled its ovens into a shed on the edge of town and a tantalizing odor of baking bread hung in the air."

The flag of the Grand Duchy of Luxembourg flew in the capital city, as well as several defiant banners proclaiming the national slogan, "We wish to remain what we are." It was a sad slogan, a reminder that the same sign might hang in almost every city in Europe. That was what the war was about; people, countries, and cities had wished to remain what they were.

A photograph of President Roosevelt hung in one of the shop windows; the merchant had made a slight mistake, however. The photograph was that of Teddy Roosevelt. Still the sentiment was right, and that evening was a most sentimental occasion for the supreme commander. Brad had remembererd, as nobody else had, that the 14th was Ike's fifty-fourth birthday, or "anniversary." A huge cake fom Paris was produced, decorated with four stars. Kay said there were also "champagne, cocktails . . . all the trimmings. It was a gay evening, despite nearness of the wars; General Eisenhower was deeply moved by Bradley's thoughtfulness and hospitality."

There was another celebration of the supreme commander's birthday back in Abilene; those present, Charlie Case, Jonah Callahan, Bill Sterl, Charlie Harger, and Gladys Harding Brooks had recorded a birthday greeting for Ike, and Case sent it on to him. In his thanks, written on December 8, the supreme commander said, "Yesterday the war completed its third year, so far as United States participation is concerned. . . . It seems a long time to me and I am so anxious to have it over and come home. When I think of how long England and some of the others have been in it, I feel a bit ashamed for voicing anything that sounds like a complaint. Nevertheless, I still wish it were over."

In October the supreme commander once more was afraid of "settling down," so on the 15th he moved his headquarters from Versailles to Gieux, "Goo" to most GIs. There he again lived in his favorite trailer, and Kay reported, "Whether he lived in Versailles or Gieux, Eisenhower's time, energy, and abilities were concentrated upon duties which fell into three distinct categories: (1) command problems, (2) trips, and (3) V-I-Ps. . . . General Eisenhower spent a good part of his waking hours trying to keep supplies en route to the advancing armies, trying to fulfill field commanders' every request."

At the end of September, Eisenhower had told the Combined Chiefs, "Except in the Low Countries, the enemy has now succeeded in establishng a relatively stable and cohesive front located approximately on the German frontier. He lost in France a million men and an enormous amount of equipment. While these losses cannot be made good, the enemy is taking every possible measure to mitigate his difficult position and there are no signs of collapse in morale or in the will to defend Germany."

Hitler, many of his people, and an enormous number of his soldiers still believed that a negotiated peace was possible. The population at large was constantly reminded of the zoning plan for postwar Germany, should the Allies win an unconditional surrender, and the Morgenthau Plan was still being advocated, German radio said with success, by powerful Jews in the United States. A handful of very high-ranking officers and Nazis knew about the planned counteroffensive in the Ardennes, but almost nobody except Hitler believed it would do anything more than shorten the war in favor of the Allies.

In mid-October there was not much cheer in the Allied camp, either. Eisenhower told Marshall, "We are having a sticky time in the North, but Montgomery has at least seen the light and is concentrating toward his west, left, flank in order to clear up the Antwerp situation." He added, "Today, the 15th, is probably the most miserable one we have had during this entire operation. It is raining proverbial cats and dogs. I am at my Forward Camp in the hope of flying down to see Devers tomorrow morning, but the prospects look dim, to say the least."

Earlier in the month, the U.S. First Army had begun breaking through some defenses in the Siegfried Line. The German soldiers there were like the German soldiers everywhere that autumn, deadly. And lest one forget what the "crusade" was all about, in October, the resistance of the Polish patriots in Warsaw came to a tragic end. More than 200,000 Poles had died in the fighting, as the Russians stood by—miles away. Much of the city had been destroyed, and Hitler ordered that the rest be razed.

Aachen, the first city in Germany to fall to the Allies, had no real strategic importance, but Hitler valued it for its symbolic and historical importance as Charlemagne's capital. The fight for the city lasted from September 11 until its commander surrendered it on October 21. The costly battle was not only from street to street; it was from house to house, room to room. Even the sewers were defended, and when the battle ended, not much was left of a city that had had a population of 160,000. The cathedral was, however, largely intact.

After the fall of the city, the Allied troops met with an experience that was to become quite common in the months that followed, both during and after the war. There were no Nazis in Aachen. In fact, everybody hated the Nazis. "Where have you been?" asked the natives. "We have been waiting for you," they said. As for Hitler, according to a young Czech war correspondent, everybody agreed that he was a "bloodhound, a bandit, a gangster. . . . We have been praying every day for you to come, said a woman with a pale, thin face." However, when I talked to some of the troops of the 1st Division who had done so much to take the city, none of them could remember seeing a single grateful German until well after the surrender.

At an October 18 meeting in Brussels with Montgomery and Bradley, Eisenhower announced—Bradley said it was "predicated . . . in part on a measure of hope"—that the Allies would continue to pound the enemy west of the Rhine, trying to split his forces, and then, in Bradley's words, "Perhaps . . . when we reached the river, the morale of the Reich would crack and bring the war to an end. Marshall had previously ventured this same thin hope. Eisenhower and I both clung to it, though we sensed it was a fragile reed."

Monty perforce attended this meeting which took place at his own headquarters. He and Bradley had an extended and familiar argument about the single versus the double thrust, or broad front. Eisenhower listened and decided in favor of Bradley. The battles ahead were to be the most dearly won of the war, and of those the fight for the Huertgen Forest was the most grueling, and perhaps the most unnecessary. It began in mid-September and did not end—if, in fact, it ever really *did* end—until December 16. General J. Lawton Collins in his postwar memoir sad that the Huertgen campaign and those for Aachen and Stolberg were "the most costly of the VII Cops [commanded by Collins] operations in Europe. . . . [But] it cost the Germans far more, and forced Rundstedt to employ divisions, tanks, and gasoline intended for the Ardennes counteroffensive, weakening that supreme German effort and subsequent defense of the Rhine."

Both in Europe and in the Pacific in the Second World War, GIs used to say of certain hard-won pieces of property, "Now that we've got it, what're they going to do with it?" That was the question asked when the Huertgen Forest was taken from the Germans—if, in fact, it *was* taken. "The Huertgen," the soldiers called it, always with contempt and fear. "The Huertgen" was fifty square acres of wooded land with rough, almost impassable foot trails instead of roads, and there were mines everywhere, mines and Germans and rain. It rained every day and every night, and there was trench foot. "Trench body," some soldiers said. Nobody was every dry, nobody was ever without fear, and soon after the end of October a renewed attack in the Huertgen was ordered by General Hodges to protect the right flank of the drive toward the Rhine. Hodges, as an enlisted man, had taken part in the First World War in the Meuse-Argonne offensive, for which he had received the Distinguished Service Cross. During the battle for "the Huertgen" in the Second World War, he used to have his jeep stop when he saw a truck carrying his First Army troops from the front, most of them wounded. He would get out of the jeep and stand by the side of the road until the truck passed. "I wish everybody could see them," he would say. Often he would cry.

Four infantry divisions—the 28th, the 8th, the 4th and the 9th—as well as a combat command of the 5th Armored Division were almost wiped out in "the Huertgen," a battle that has been called the Argonne of World War II. By December 13 more than 24,000 Americans were killed, missing, captured, or wounded, and another 9,000 suffered from battle fatigue or trench foot or debilitating illness caused by continued exposure on the front lines.

In his book *On to Berlin*, General James M. Gavin said that the Huertgen "was Hitler's last gamble. The bitter . . . fighting . . . was one of the most costly, most unproductive, and most ill-advised battles that our Army has ever fought. . . . I think it fair to say that little was learned from it. . . . No one, neither American nor German, had a clear idea of how intense and costly it would be. The Americans wanted to seize the eastern edge of the forest and in so doing protect the right flank of the U.S. Army, which was moving up to Cologne. But neither side could guess the other's objective, and both sides were surprised by the intensity and heavy cost of the fighting that followed."

The Germans were preparing for a surprise counteroffensive in the Ardennes. Their job was to protect the dams just behind the Siegfried Line, dams that controlled the flow of water into the Roer Valley. The Germans also wanted to hold the Americans back so that they would neither know about, delay or prevent the buildup for what would be called the "Battle of the Bulge."

Eisenhower mentions the Huertgen only twice in *Crusade;* he never dwelled on the failures or what at best might be called the dubious successes of the Allies in the war. He said, "The fall period [of 1944] was to become a memorable one because of bitterly contested battles, usually conducted under the most trying conditions of weather and terrain. Walcheren Island [in the Scheldt Estuary], Aachen, the Huertgen Forest, the Roer dams, the Saar Basin and the Vosges Mountains were all to give their names during the fall months of 1944 to battles that, in the sum of their results, greatly hastened the end of the war in Europe. In addition to the handicap of weather there was the difficulty of shortages in ammunition and supplies. The hardihood, courage, and resourcefulness of the Allied soldier were never tested more thoroughly and with more brilliant results than during this period."

Eisenhower also said, "Whenever veterans of the American 4th, 9th, and 28th Divisions referred to hard fighting they did so in terms of comparison with the Battle of Huertgen Forest, which they placed at the top of the list." By the end of October the 9th Division had gained only three thousand yards at the cost of one and a half casualties for each yard gained. Altogether the division lost 4,500 men. The words of its official report were even less sanguine than those of the supreme commander but still softer in judgment than those of most of the battle's veterans. The report said, "The real winner appeared to be the vast, undulating, blackish-green sea that virtually negated American superiority in air, artillery, and armor to reduce warfare to its lowest common denominator."

The opening of the port of Antwerp remained crucial to Allied success, and on the last day of October it was, as Butcher said, "still . . . the key to the logistics problem. Ike is prepared to wage a final all-out battle to cross the Rhine if we have the assurance of supply that Antwerp promises." Monty still seemed reluctant to do anything about the Scheldt approaches to the port. The Dutch islands of South Beveland and Walcheren, forming more than twenty miles of the northern shores of the Scheldt Estuary, were crowded with Germans who had been ordered to hold out as long as possible. The Germans as well as the Allies knew that the opening of the giant port of Antwerp was the key to getting across the Rhine. Monty's reluctance to undertake the task of getting rid of the German troops must always have puzzled Eisenhower. It was not a subject the field marshal was likely to discuss, and it was only some time after the end of the war that Brigadier Sir Edgar Williams—"Bill" Williams had been Monty's chief intelligence officer—revealed what he believed to be Montgomery's reasons. They did not add glory to Monty's reputation. Williams said, "Monty was reluctant to start the Battle of the Scheldt. Antwerp was fifty-five miles inland, and he knew that one day he must clear the banks of the estuary, which could so easily have been taken immediately after Antwerp fell. To him, it was not an interesting military operation . . . it lacked glamour from his point of view and so did not appeal to his vanity. He knew it would be a battle of attrition, with very heavy casualties (in the end nearly 13,000, mainly Canadians) and whatever the result, the Scheldt attack could not fit into the series of victories on which his reputation was based at that moment. His attitude was, 'If you finished the war, the Scheldt operation would be unnecessary since the Germans would soon capitulate without further casualties.' It wasn't just vanity—it was because of the feeling that the war was nearly over—and it would be a pity to get any more people killed in the doing of it; part of his 'economical' generalship psychology."

Bradley said, "Had Monty cleared the Scheldt as SHAEF suggested he do, Antwerp could have fitted into the scheme of supply much sooner and we might have been spared the famine that immobilized us in October. . . . Indeed of all the might-have-beens in the European campaign, none was more agonizing than this failure of Monty to open Antwerp. . . . We were forced to sit and wait until November for the long-line buildup from Cherbourg. By then the fall campaigning weather was gone; winter had set in. Meanwhile the German had not been idle. Between early September and mid-December he had tripled his forces on the Western front to 70 German divisions. And of his 15 panzer divisions, eight were refitted with Panther and Tiger tanks."

There is no such brief, bitter analysis of the situation created by Monty in *Crusade.* Eisenhower gently says of the Scheldt Estuary and Walcheren and South Beveland islands, "It was unfortunate that we had not been successful in seizing the area during our great norheastward march in the early days of September." And he added that the fault was partly his, saying, "The necessary forces for the attack could not be assembled until late October. If I had not attempted the Arnhem operation, possibly we could have begun the Walcheren attack some two or three weeks earlier."

The Canadian First Army advanced with difficulty along both sides of the estuary. Fighting was bitter. The Germans said their new V-2 rockets were destroying Antwerp, so why bother opening it at no matter what cost, but the Allied troops pressed onward. Walcheren Island surrendered on November 8, and 10,000 enemy troops were captured, one of them a division commander Eisenhower said, "For the entire series of operations in the area our own casualties, almost entirely Canadian and British, numbered 27,622. This compared to less than 25,000 in the capture of Sicily, where we defeated a garrison of 350,000."

Butcher said, "Ike . . . immediately expressed his grateful thanks to Monty personally." And there were no might-have-beens. There is no record of his ever saying to Monty or anyone else, "If you'd done so-and-so, then so-and-so wouldn't have happened."

Butcher said of the securing of the approaches to Antwerp, "I have seen Ike several times when he had received good news which normally he has discounted in advance, but on this occasion he could not hide his elation, for on the capture of Antwerp depended all of his future plans to end the war."

But now that Monty's troops had finished clearing the shores of the Scheldt, including the islands, the navy had to clear the estuary and port of mines and other obstacles; so it was not until November 28, twelve weeks after Antwerp was taken, that the first Allied ship entered the port unharmed.

In spite of Eisenhower's elation, his British G-2, Kenneth Strong, who was inclined particularly in his book *Intelligence at the Top: The Recollections of a British Intelligence Officer,* to look on the bright side of things, did not find much to be cheerful about in late October-early November. He said, "The Germans, except in the south, were back on their own frontiers. The next step was to close up to the Rhine, but the Germans conducted their operations skillfully and tenaciously, and the Allies were able to advance only slowly. It was a time of hard infantry fighting much resembling, I imagine, that of World War I. Freezing rain and blinding snow storms hampered all offensive movements. Antwerp not likely to be in full use until the end of November. . . . German morale . . . high."

The only good news for the Allies seemed to be coming from the Russians. The Red Army had isolated a German army group in Latvia, had advanced into East Prussia, reached the Vistula in Poland, crossed the Danube on a wide front isolating the Germans in Budapest, and captured Belgrade in Yugoslavia, aided by the partisans of Marshal Tito. But the Russians, too, had supply problems, and in November their army largely rested and regrouped.

Progress on the Western front continued to be slow. Still, Patton's troops did begin a limited offensive toward the Saar on the 8th. Of course it rained that morning. Eisenhower called Third Army headquarters. According to Patton, he said, " 'I expect a lot of you; carry the ball all the way.' I wonder if he ever made a decision to take risks when his best men advised caution. I doubt if he ever has," Patton added.

On November 11 Eisenhower told Marshall, "I am getting exceedingly tired of weather. Every day we have some report of weather that has broken records existing anywhere from twenty-five to fifty years. The latest case is that of the floods in Patton's area. His attack got off exactly as planned and with . . . extraordinarily fine . . . cooperation between the Eighth Air Force and the ground troops. Then the floods came down the river and not only washed out two fixed bridges, but destroyed his principal floating bridge and made others almost unuseable."

In a note to Patton the same day, he was more cheerful. He said that Georgie was not to be discouraged; the waters would go down, and Patton would get on with the job "as you always have." He wished him a happy birthday.

Patton's attacking troops, which were to drive through the Maginot Line defenses and fortresses in the area, hopefully reaching the West Wall (Siegfried Line), had received air support late in the morning of the 8th, when the attack began. The troops did eventually achieve their objective, one that Patton found too limited for comfort, and his Third Army troops reached Metz on November 18 and captured it on the 22nd.

In his November 11 message to Marshall, Eisenhower did have some good news to report: in "the last three days" he and Bradley had visited every division of the First and Ninth Armies. "Morale is surprisingly high and the men have succeeded in making themselves rather comfortable. There are no signs of exhaustion and the sick rate is not nearly as high as we would have a reasonable right to expect."

Eisenhower may have been suffering a lapse in his own usually high morale, though, for on November 12, in a letter John says "shows him at his testiest," he wrote to Mamie in the meanest and least sympathetic terms ever. The supreme commander was usually careful to keep his personal troubles to himself, but in between the lines his frustrations with the British, the weather, the slow progress of his own troops and the continued resistance of the Germans all somehow erupted (though they were not mentioned). Poor Mamie. The letter to him that provoked the outburst was probably no more self-pitying than most she wrote. It got to him, though, and he replied:

Yesterday, I arrived at my advanced camp after quite a tour along the front and found your letter, written just after Johnny had asked you to come down to see him. I fully understand your distress when contemplating his departure [for duty in the ETO]—I feel just as badly. But it always depresses me when you talk about "dirty tricks" I've played and what a beating you've taken, apparently because of me. You've always put your own interpretation on every act, look or word of mine, and when you've made yourself unhappy, that has, in turn, made me the same. . . .

It's true we've now been apart for 2½ years, and at a time that make separations painful and hard to bear. Because you don't have a specific war job that absorbs your time and thoughts I understand also that this distress is harder for you to bear. But you should not forget that I do miss you and do love you, and that the load of responsibility I carry would be intolerable unless I could have the belief that there is someone who wants me to come home—for good.

He mentioned that he received letters every day from members of the bereaved families of servicemen and from those who wanted soldiers sent home or at least kept out of danger. Then he said:

Now sweet, don't get me wrong in this letter. I'm not "fussing" at you. But please try to see me in something besides a despicable light and at least let me be *certain* of my welcome home. . . .

I truly love you and I do know that when you blow off steam you don't think of me as such a black-hearted creature as your language implies. I'd rather you didn't mention any of this again.

A family friend who asked not to be identified, whether dead or alive, said, "While Eisenhower learned to mask most of his emotions, Mamie never learned to keep any of her emotions secret. If she felt something, good or bad, she felt honor bound to share it."

On the 14th of November Brooke and Churchill had lunch wih Eisenhower at Rheims. The prime minister had just been in Paris paying tribute to de Gaulle, the French Resistance generals, and their supporters. In the published version of his diary, Brooke was only somewhat rude but not surprising in what he said. "We arrived at 11 A.M. and were met by Ike who drove us out to his camp situated on the golf links built by the big champagne merchants. He went over the dispositions on the front and seemed fairly vague as to what was really going on.

"We [including the prime minister] had lunch with him and then drove to the aerodrome where we took off for Northolt which we reached at 4:45 P.M. after a very comfortable flight."

The unpublished account was considerably more bitter. Brooke said that Eisenhower had made a most unfavorable impression on his guests because Kay Summersby had acted as hostess at the luncheon and that Churchill had sat on her right. He added, "This has done Ike no good with a lot of undesirable gossip. . . . Ike completely fails as Supreme Commander. He does nothing and lives in Paris out of touch. The war is drifting."

Arthur Bryant, in a footnote to *Triumph in the West*, said, "Accustomed to the more rigid hierarchy of the British Army, Brooke, during his visit, was surprised to find Mrs. Summersby presiding over the head of the luncheon table, with the Prime Minister on her right. Bryant also said, "Captain Butcher, and his [Eisenhower's] British lady driver and later personal secretary, Mrs. Kay Summersby . . . published books after the war describing this informal and very democratic arrangement [at the Rheims headquarters]."

If Churchill was shocked by Kay's presence as hostess at the luncheon, he does not say so in his account of it in *Triumph and Tragedy*. He says only, "De Gaulle returned to Paris and our half of the train carrying the men went on to Rheims arriving next morning, when I went to Ike's headquarters. In the afternoon I flew back to Northolt."

Actually, by that time Kay was no longer Eisenhower's driver; her last trip as a driver had been on October 10. On October 14 she had become a WAC second lieutenant, which was, she said, "a highlight of my wartime career, bringing reality to an old, old dream." Eisenhower, who had had a good deal to do with making it possible for Kay to become a WAC even though she was not a U.S. citizen, pinned the gold bars on her shoulders. As a WAC second lieutenant she could not, however, continue as Ike's chauffeur. Thereafter she spent her full time answering the letters, almost all admiring, written to him by people he didn't know personally. She said, "The days were so busy that I often had to remain in the office at night to catch up with correspondence. The only free hours were after the general left."

Eisenhower did not feel about Brooke the way he felt about Monty. Kenneth Strong said, "His first impression of Brooke was that he was adroit rather than deep, and shrewd rather than wise. He found his mannerisms and staccato speech disconcerting. Eisenhower . . . considered that Brooke did not have Marshall's ability to weigh calmly the conflicting factors of a problem and reach a rocklike decision. In spite of these reservations Eisenhower thought highly of Brooke. When they differed they did so forthrightly and honestly, and Eisenhower always listened carefully to Brooke's views. Brooke had been one of the leading opponents of the broad front strategy, but when he and Brooke stood together on the banks of the Rhine to watch the crossing by the Twenty-first Army Group and the American Ninth Army, Brooke turned to the Supreme Commander and said, 'Thank God, Ike, you stuck to your plan. . . . I am sorry if any fear of dispersed effort added to your burdens. The German is now licked. It is merely a question of when he chooses to quit. Thank God, you stuck by your guns.' "

Eisenhower's relations with the American press continued to be good. Early in November Anne O'Hare McCormick wrote that "General Eisenhower is a military dictator whose word is law on the ever-moving front that covers a large part of western Europe, but there is not much military pomp or punctilio about his simple headquarters. . . . His unlittered desk is drawn close to a wood fire— about the only form of heat in France these wintry days. In a plain soldier's blouse he looks younger, lighter and more compact than his pictures. His twinkling eyes, sandy hair, and shrewd grin are as American as Red Cross donuts, but the characteristic twinkle turns to steel when he speaks of the enemy, and changes into a flash of pride when he talks of the Army."

At a press conference on the 21st, Eisenhower said again that his troops were not getting enough supplies and that west of the Rhine the Germans would not risk retreat across a river over which the Allies had air supremacy. He said that, "The pressure must go up and continue to increase so that the highest point is on the day Germany surrenders. . . . I am an optimist, and I hope to prevent myself from becoming complacent."

He discussed the clearing of the Scheldt and said, "The Walcheren Island operation was one of the most gallant operations of the war. The number engaged was very small, but the losses were high proportionately. Unarmored craft with their small guns slammed right in the face of larger fixed guns and discharged their troops. The Navy deserves great kudos for this operation."

No one paid much attention to Ike's answer to one question that was to trouble a great many people later. A reporter mentioned that a few days earlier, in paying tribute to the Allied armies in the west, Stalin said that the Red Army would be in Berlin soon. Eisenhower replied, "Good for him. He will do a good job there, I think."

Churchill's reaction to the statement, if he read it, is not known, but we do know how the prime minister reacted later to what he considered Ike's cavalier attitude on that subject. Churchill, as we know, changed his mind about DRAGOON, but about Berlin and the Russians, never. Unlike some fringe Americans, Churchill never thought that what Eisenhower did was treasonous and possibly evidence that he was a member of the Communist Party. The prime minister thought only that the American general was hopelessly naive and should be protected from the folly he inflicted on the postwar world. Unfortunately, in this matter the prime minister could not count on the cooperation of his old friend Franklin Roosevelt, who was soon to demonstrate at Yalta that he knew how to handle the Russians—Stalin wanted nothing more urgently than to cooperate with the West once the troublesome war was over.

There must have been times when Churchill thought fondly of George III.

November 28 was a good day for the Allies. Antwerp was open, and while there would still be problems getting supplies from the port to the troops, the quays and the dock machinery were in fairly good order. German rockets had done very little damage to the port after all, and it seemed unlikely that shortages of supplies would limit and stop the Allied advance as they had so often in the past.

Montgomery had just returned from London where Brooke had convinced him, again, that he was a great general, a great strategist, and a man much put upon by those inferior to him in ability and intelligence, if not in rank. Eisenhower was first among those who in both Monty's mind and Brooke's was interfering with the triumphant end of the war. That was not a new idea for either of them, but when Eisenhower arrived at Monty's headquarters in Zonhoven on the 28th, Monty treated him with unmasked contempt. Eisenhower had decided before he arrived that what Monty said would not unsettle him, but had the field marshal had an eye for such matters, which he did not, he would have noticed that the more he talked the redder the supreme commander's face and neck got. Monty said several times, as if he were saying something new, "We must have a single Commander and concentrate our forces on a selected vital thrust instead of dissipating them all along the front."

It was clear in Monty's mind that that single commander would be himself. Eisenhower knew that that would never be, and he knew that Bradley would never serve under Monty and that under no circumstances would he reduce his command, giving any part of it to the field marshal. He knew, too, that nobody in Washington would go along with Monty and that, when the time came, Churchill probably wouldn't either. He did not say any of these things, however. He simply nodded a lot. Eisenhower's close friend Lauris Norstad once said, "There were times in my own experience when Ike would nod, and I would think that he was agreeing with what I was saying. Sometimes it did mean that—but not always. Sometimes it just meant that he had heard what I said."

Eisenhower spent the night, and after Monty had gone to bed at his usual time, the supreme commander indicated to at least one member of the field marshal's staff, Lieutenant Colonel C. P. Danay, that he did not agree with Monty. In fact, the next day when Montgomery said, after Ike left, "He agreed to everything I said," Danay said that he very much doubted it. Monty paid no attention to that blasphemy.

He almost immediately sent a message to Brooke boasting about his triumph. He said:

> Eisenhower visited me today and we had a very long talk. I put the following points to him:
> 1st. That the plan contained in his last Directive had failed and we had, in fact, suffered a strategic reverse. He agreed.

He said that the supreme commander had said that a new plan was necessary, one that would "concentrate our resources on a selected vital thrust." Of course Monty had said that, and Eisenhower had not agreed, not on November 28, never. Monty also said, and this was also inaccurate, "I proved to him that we had definitely failed and must make a new plan and next time we must quite definitely not (repeat not) fail. He admitted a grave mistake has been made and in my opinion is prepared to go almost any length to succeed next time. Hence his own suggestion I should be in full operational command north of the Ardennes. . . ."

Some men distorting the truth in such a way and believing that their distortions were the truth, might be advised to undergo psychiatric treatment. I do not know what was said privately in the higher echelons of command about the field marshal. I do know that among a few enlisted men of whom I was one and among various newspaper correspondents at the time it was said, "You've heard what happened to Montgomery?" "No, what happened to Montgomery?" "He started thinking he was Montgomery and had to be put away."

Monty had a second talk with Eisenhower on the morning of November 29, and of this he reported to Brooke, "He [Eisenhower] now definitely wants me to handle main business but wants Bradley to be in on it and, therefore, he will put him under me. In my opinion Ike will never agree to appointment of a Land Force Command for whole front as he wants to do this himself. If he reverts to the system we had in Normandy it means that I shall in reality be in operational charge and be able to influence whole land battle by direct approach to Ike himself."

Monty's summation of the way things went in Normandy is, to be kind, simplistic. After Normandy Montgomery was relieved of his position as commander of the ground forces in August; he was from then on commander of the 21st Army Group only. Ike by that time had realized, although it did not always seem clear from his actions, that Montgomery had to be ordered to do what was necessary. According to his biographer Chalfont, after Normandy Montgomery was "at last paying the price for his inability to communicate with his equals and most of his superiors."

On November 30 Monty, his sense of reality still absent, wrote Eisenhower a letter that the supreme commander never forgave nor forgot.

> *My dear Ike:*
> In order to clear my own mind I would like to confirm the main points that we agreed on during the conversations we had during your stay with me on Tuesday night.
> We have definitely failed to implement the plan contained in the SHAEF directive of October 28 . . . and we have no hope of doing so. We have therefore failed; and we have suffered a strategic reverse.
> We require a new plan. And this time *we must not fail.* . . . Bradley and I make a good team . . . things have not gone well since you separated us. . . . To be certain of success you want to bring us together and one of us should have full operational control north of the Ardennes. And if you decide that I should do that work—that is O.K. by me.

Monty suggested that they meet either on Wednesday, December 6, or Thursday, December 7. He added what Eisenhower and Beetle, who surely read the message first, must have considered the ultimate example of Monty's insensitivity. He said, "Will you let me know which day you select. I suggest that we want no one else at the meeting except Chiefs of Staff, who must not speak."

As for Beetle being silent, Ike said in his reply to Monty, written on December 1, "With respect to the Chiefs of Staff attending the conference, it makes no difference to me whether your Chief of Staff attends or whether Bradley's does. Mine will be there unless some unforeseen circumstance prevents. Bedell is my Chief of Staff because I trust him and respect his judgment. I will not by any means insult him by telling him that he should remain mute at any conference he and I both attend."

Eisenhower set the time of his next meeting with Monty at 11:00 A.M. on Thursday, December 7. He said that he did not understand what Monty meant by "strategic reverse. . . . I do not agree that things have gone badly since Normandy, merely because we have not gained all we had hoped to gain. . . . If we had advanced from the beginning *as we had hoped*, our maintenance services would have been in a position to supply us during the critical September days, when we actually reached the limit of our resources."

In other words, and surely Monty could not fail to understand, if you (Monty) had moved into Caen "as we had hoped," as you said you would, we would not have had a supply crisis in September. As for Patton and Hodges, Eisenhower had no intention of stopping their operations "as long as they are cleaning up your right flank and giving us the *capability of concentration*. On the other hand, I do not intend to push those attacks needlessly. It is going to be important to us later on to have two strings to our bow. Don't forget that you were very wise in making a provision for this at Mareth, and it paid off."

Then to the amenities: "We must look at this whole great affair stretching from Marsailles to the lower Rhine as one great theater. We must plan so when our next attacks start we will be able to obtain maximum results from all our forces, under the conditions now existing."

It was the toughest letter Monty had ever received from Eisenhower, and the field marshal responded immediately and abjectly. He had not meant to say that the Allied operation in Europe had failed; he had referred only to the SHAEF directive of October 28, which anybody would have to admit had not been carried out completely. That had been a far-reaching plan speaking of, among many other things, what should be done after the Rhine had been crossed. He was not criticizing overall policy; that had *not* resulted in failed strategy.

Ike replied immediately, and his reply, according to Richard Lamb showed the supreme commander had "displayed that quality of cat and mouse which was eventually to bring him to the Presidency of the United States." He said:

You have my prompt and abject apologies for misreading your letter of 30th November. In my haste to answer I obviously misread your paragraph 8 as a far more pessimistic statement than was justified. In any event, I am sorry if my letter gave offense; certainly I do not want to put words or meaning into your mouth, or ever do anything that upsets our close relationship. . . . Again I say that I am sorry that in my hurried reading of your letter I made an interpretation that you did not intend. I now see clearly exactly what you mean.

Eisenhower's humility—some people, including a number of his own American subordinates, would have found it too self-effacing—did not impress Monty, nor did it improve his conduct. He sent a message to Brooke on December 4 saying that he personally would take up the reorganization of the command in Washington. There was no indication that he had given up the idea of getting rid of Eisenhower. It would perhaps be more difficult than he had thought, but

"There is a sporting chance we may pull it off. But any outside interference at this juncture might be fatal."

Three days later, on December 7, when Monty met with Tedder, Bradley, and Eisenhower at Lieutenant General William Simpson's Ninth Army headquarters at Maastricht, the British field marshal was once again uncontrollable, rude, and felt that the other three men were ganging up on him. After all, he said, they had arrived together, and they left together.

If Monty's behavior that day was typical, so was Eisenhower's. He gave a modestly upbeat summary of what the Allies had done since September. The Germans were suffering very heavy losses which they could not long endure, particularly since a new Russian offensive would soon begin. As for crossing the Rhine, that, according to his staff, might not be possible, at least in a substantial way, until the following May.

Eisenhower then asked Monty for his comments, and the field marshal said that any future tactical plan against the enemy must cut off the Ruhr from Germany and must force the Germans into mobile war which would defeat them because they had neither enough fuel nor enough matériel. He said that such a mobile war could be fought only north of the Ruhr. Therefore, he said all resources must be put into a concentrated offensive across the Rhine north of the Ruhr.

Eisenhower had heard all this many times before; these were the arguments he had listened to in September and again in October and November. The difference was that now he knew Montgomery to be an untrustworthy man, and his patience with him was nearly exhausted. Ida used to talk a lot about Job. Eisenhower may have wondered what Job would have made of Monty. There was that verse, "Should a wise man utter vain knowledge, and fill his belly with the east wind?"

At the December 7 meeting, the supreme commander said that he believed that an area to the south, around Kassel and Frankfurt, was suitable for armor. And while he was still in favor of the northern advance, he also wanted to make not one but two thrusts, the better to make use of the fact that the German troops were relatively immobile. Montgomery wanted no part of that. He said that there was no chance that a thrust from the south would succeed and that as a result of such a failure his own drive north of the Ruhr would also fail.

Eisenhower disagreed. He said that the basic conception of what he proposed and what Monty proposed was the same, the principal drive would be north of the Ruhr, but it would be supported by a converging attack that would originate somewhere south of it. Montgomery once again brought up the question of command. He reiterated his position that all operations north of the Ardennes should be under one command and those south of the Ardennes should be under another. Eisenhower again disagreed.

Tedder said, "As for the future, we were all agreed that the pressure must be kept up throughout the winter, and if possible the enemy cleared back to the Rhine; that the main objective was to seal off the Ruhr from the rest of Germany, and thereby make the enemy fight; that the main attack should be north of the Ruhr, and that the starting point of the attack from the south could not yet be decided."

Monty was certain he had been surrounded by enemies at that meeting. He wrote to Brooke:

I played a lone hand against the three of them. . . . It is . . . clear that any points I made which caused Eisenhower to wobble would have been put right by Bradley and Tedder on the three-hour drive back to headquarters. . . . If you want the war to end within a reasonable period you have to get Eisenhower's hand off the tiller. I regret to say he just does not know what he is doing. And you will have to see Bradley's influence is curbed.

Eisenhower returned to Gieux the next morning; on the 10th he had lunch with members of the House Military Affairs Committee, including Mrs. Clare Boothe Luce, congresswoman from Connecticut. Among other things Mrs. Luce was to remember about that meeting was that the general was smoking heavily. At the time his consumption was up to five or six packs a day. Another congressman, chairman of the committee, Andrew May, brought a bottle of Kentucky bourbon. Butcher told Jim Gault, who was disturbed that the bourbon had been mentioned in a story and, thus, might cause trouble with the prohibitionists back in the States, to say that he, Butcher, had sent the whiskey to a field hospital. Eisenhower was very upset about the whole matter. He said that every member of the committee, including Mrs. Luce and May, would know that the story was not true and conclude that the supreme commander was a liar. Butcher said, "What did happen to the whiskey?"

"Why, damn it, the Congressmen drank it before lunch," the supreme commander said.

On the 12th, at Brooke's invitation, Eisenhower flew to London with Tedder. The three of them, Ike, Tedder, and the CIGS, had dinner with the prime minister at No. 10 Downing Street. According to Brooke they met at six in the Map Room. The prime minister and the entire British Chiefs of Staff were present, and Eisenhower explained again his plan for a double advance into Germany, close to Frankfurt and north of the Rhine. Brooke said, "I disagreed flatly with it, accused Ike of violating principles of concentration of forces, which had resulted in his present failures. . . . I stressed the importance of concentrating on one thrust. I drew attention to the fact that with his limited forces any thought of attack on both fronts could only lead to dispersal of effort."

The prime minister did not seem much interested. Brooke said, "Half the time his attention was concentrated on the possibility of floating mines down the Rhine. He must get down to detail."

At a second meeting, at dinner that night, also at No. 10, the prime minister, Ike, and Brooke were there, as well as Cunningham, Tedder, Portal, and Ismay. Brooke reported, "Conversation again on the same topic of the strategy, but I got no further in getting either Winston or Ike to see that their strategy is fundamentally wrong."

What Churchill told Brooke the next day did not improve the temper of the CIGS much. The prime minister said that he had gone along with Ike because he was the only American present. After all, Churchill said, Eisenhower was his guest. What Brooke had said did, however, make an impression on the prime minister, and he called a meeting of the war cabinet at 5:30 that afternoon. At the meeting Brooke once again "ran through the situation after the P.M. had given a general introduction." The prime minister did what politicians do at such times. He requested Brooke's staff and the Chiefs of Staff to prepare a report on the subject and give it to him.

Eisenhower returned to Versailles on the morning of the 13th, and on the morning of the 16th, before dawn, the Germans launched the offensive that many people feel was his real "baptism of fire." After it was over even those like Arthur Bryant felt that "Calamity acted on Eisenhower like a restorative and brought out all the greatness in his character. It was he who, as soon as news of defeat reached him, overruled Bradley, halted the offensive south of the Moselle and ordered Patton to march north against the Germans' flank; who threw in the two airborne divisions—his sole reserve—to hold the Bastogne and the Meuse crossings; who opened a conference of his senior commanders with the words, 'There will be only cheerful faces at this conference table,' and declared that the situation should be regarded as one not of disaster, but opportunity. His order of the day . . . continued the prophecy, 'By rushing out from his fixed defenses the enemy has given us the chance to turn his great gamble into his worst defeat.' "

* * *

A MERE INCIDENT

Replacements were needed everywhere in the Allied armies in Europe; there was, in fact, a shortage of everything, but the shortages were not as great as those facing the Germans, and in late December 1944 and on into the new year that factor was to be crucial.

The manpower shortage was especially worrisome to the American high command. Patton at the end of November said that 9,000 replacements were needed in the Third Army. "And none is in sight." On December 3rd he said, "I don't know what the young manhood of America is doing, but they certainly are not appearing over here. . . . People do not realize that 92% of all casualties occur in the infantry rifle companies, and that when the infantry division has lost 4,000 men, it has practically no riflemen left." By that time he said his Third Army needed 11,000 men. In December Bradley told Patton, "I would suppose that somebody in Washington had made a wrong guess as to the date on which this war will be over." And at the same time he told Eisenhower that without more replacements American infantry divisions would have no assault strength.

Still, as Beetle said, "Everywhere the front was kept in motion, though full power still waited on supply." In the long-planned offensive against the Saar, Patton's troops had crossed the Moselle and in several places was actually in Germany. Hodges' First Army and Simpson's Ninth Army were holding the high ground overlooking the Roer. The two armies had not recently had any twenty-five- to thirty-mile days. Instead they had advanced eight to nine miles in a month, and after the first snow fell in early November, the skies had been overcast, the air chilling. Only three miles to the south, German troops were still holding the key village of Schmidt and the Roer dams that were so essential to victory.

It was expected that when Allied forces crossed the Roer, the enemy would make "maximum use . . . of the flooding of the Roer in conjunction with his counterattack." Bradley added in *A Soldier's Story*, "The vigor with which von Rundstedt had met our attacks against those dams made it clear that he was thoroughly aware of the tactical ace he held."

It was at 0530 on the morning of December 16 that 2,000 German guns, the greatest artillery barrage heard since Normandy, roared out of the fog and darkness, sending shells hurtling into American positions along a broad front. At the same time, the Germans launched thirteen infantry and seven armored divisions toward the weakly held American positions. The positions were deliberately weak, and later a great many Americans said that Eisenhower, who had planned the strategy, had fallen on his face. Later in the day ten more German divisions, a thousand tanks, and a quarter of a million men moved into American-held territory.

On the 15th, the day before the German onslaught, Eisenhower wrote to Tom Handy, who was still in the Operations Division of the War Department. "To meet the manpower problem I have given the most stringent order to commanders for combing out people that could be replaced by limited service men or where actual reductions in the Table of Organization can be effected without detriment to the essential activities. Beyond this I have directed the greatest possible employment of civilian labor. . . . In every possible way we will try to find some means of distributing our shortages so as to prevent a complete breakdown in the machine due to the concentration of those shortages on the infantry element."

That same day Eisenhower received an upsetting and uncalled for note from Monty. The field marshal said that he would like to "hop over to England" so that he could spend Christmas with his son. Nothing wrong with that, but then he asked Ike to repay a personal debt, and he did it in a way that was calculatingly rude. He enclosed with the note a memorandum dated October 11, 1943. The memo said, "Amount: £5-. Eisenhower bets war with Germany will end before Xmas 1944—local time." Since Monty had been saying for weeks on every possible occasion that had he and not Eisenhower been in charge of the Allied land forces in Europe, the war would have been over in 1944, the note was hurtful, and, as one of Monty's biographers said, if it had been sent by anybody except Monty, it "might have seemed a macabre joke." Monty said in a handwritten note he attached to the October 1943 memo, "For payment, I think, at Christmas."

In his courteous reply Eisenhower said:

Dear Monty:

I am delighted that you can find opportunity to spend Christmas with your son. I envy you. . . .

The data contained in your memorandum respecting the bet is correct according to my own note. However, I still have nine days and while it seems almost certain that you will have an extra five pounds for Christmas, you will not get it until that day. At least you must admit we have gone a long way toward the defeat of Germany since we made our bet on the 11th of October 1943.

With best of Christmas wishes. . . .

That day the supreme commander also sent a holiday greeting to Churchill. "While there is scarcely anything that could add to your national and world stature, yet it is not too much to hope that more freedom-loving people everywhere will gain a clearer understanding of what we owe to you."

On the morning of the 16th, Montgomery wrote a report saying, "The enemy is a present fighting a defensive campaign on all fronts; his situation is such that he cannot stage major offensive operations." After finishing the report Montgomery flew to Eindhoven for a golf game, which was interrupted by an urgent message to return to headquarters.

Monty was not alone among the Allied brass in not knowing what the Germans were up to. The Allies simply did not believe that the enemy could build up enough forces for an attack of any strength, and it was known that he was short of gasoline. Because of the offensive operations then underway, Eisenhower said that the Allies had "a total of only three divisions on a front of some seventy-five miles between Trier and Monschau. . . . While my own staff kept in closest possible touch with this situation, I personally conferred with Bradley about it at various times. Our conclusion was that in the Ardennes region we were running a definite risk but we believed it a mistaken policy to suspend our attacks all along the front merely to make ourselves safe until all reinforcements arriving from the United States could bring us up to peak strength."

After the war a member of Hodges' G-2 staff told Forrest Pogue, author of *The Supreme Command*, that many people knew that the 6th Panzer Army was in the Ardennes region. He said, "The big question before the Ardennes was—Will the 6th SS Pz. be used to seal off a break in German line or will it be used for a counterattack. . . . Began to miss units in November and early December. Indications that they were pulllng out for something. Too many for rest only. PWs knew little; couldn't get many. . . . We knew 6th SS Pz. was around for something. Although we didn't have so much air recon at this period, a number of people passed the lines with some information."

The officer added that even if First Army intelligence had known the German offensive would be in the Ardennes, not a great deal could have been done about it "except have the men dig in more, set up some strongpoints, put in more mines." He added that throughout the fighting in the Huertgen Forest to the beginning of what would be called the Battle of the Bulge, the Ardennes was the most "thinly held area, and the troops were tired."

After the battle began, one of the critics of the failure in Allied intelligence was General Payton C. March, who had been Chief of Staff of the Army in the First World War. March, who was eighty, said that there had been 200,000 Germans involved in the attack, and there were just that many people in Richmond, Virginia. He said, "Imagine the population of Richmond being assembled across the Potomac and we not knowing it."

March added, "We have been lucky so far. In the occupied countries we had the advantage of the underground. They tipped us off as to the presence of the enemy. . . . But when we got to the border of Germany we faced a homogeneous population. We were up against a blank wall. Military intelligence cannot depend on aerial surveys."

It might have been some help if the Allies had known that General Josef "Sepp" Dietrich, commander of the 6th Panzer Army, later said of his assignment, "All I had to do was to cross the river, capture Brussels and then go on and take the port of Antwerp. And all this in December, January, and February, the worst three months of the year; through the Ardennes where snow was waist deep and there wasn't room to deploy four tanks abreast, let alone six armoured divisions; when it didn't get light until eight in the morning and was dark again at four in the afternoon and my tanks can't fight at night; with divisions that had just been re-formed and were composed chiefly of raw untrained recruits; and at Christmas time."

Still, the German troops did not know what lay ahead, and as von Rundstedt said, "The morale of troops taking part was astonishingly high at the start of the offensive. They really believed victory was possible—unlike the higher commanders who knew the facts."

Bradley came from Luxembourg to SHAEF headquarters on the 16th to discuss general strategy. The weather was bad, and he came by car to discuss, among other things, the problem of replacements. The general and members of his staff had lunch at the Ritz in Paris. His aide, Chet Hansen, said, "Paris looked deserted on a rainy Saturday afternoon; it was a depressing day and the city had lost much of its autumnal loveliness." After lunch Bradley went to Eisenhower's office at SHAEF. According to Hansen, "Ike was in generous spirits; he has just been given his fifth star and we congratulated him on it. 'God,' he answered, 'I just want to see the first time I sign my name as a General of the Army." That morning Eisenhower found out that Roosevelt had sent his nomination to become a General of the Army to the Senate. The rank had only recently been created, and he could go no further. He was now equal in rank to Marshall and MacArthur. And Monty. Ike, who had been a major for sixteen years, had been promoted from lieutenant colonel to five-star general in three years and six months.

It was a great honor, and Swede Hazlett wrote him a letter of congratulation. Nevertheless, as old friends will, Swede seemed to have some reservations in the matter. He said that he would have preferred for Ike to have been named a marshal but the fact that there was a George C. Marshall in the army had probably led to that idea being rejected. He also said, "I'm still prejudiced enough to think that the Navy usually does things better than the Army." General of the Army could not be shortened, he said, while Admiral of the Fleet could be, to Fleet Admiral. Swede was no longer teaching at Annapolis.

He was in charge of Naval ROTC at the University of North Carolina. He said with some bitterness that he had been eased out of the Naval Academy to make room for the "young, be-medaled heroes just back from the wars." He did give credit to the army for "digging deep in the hat and pulling you to the top when you were needed." Wryly he added, "I don't believe the Navy would ever have had the guts to shatter precedent to that extent." And maybe shattering precedent wasn't such a good idea. "As a matter of fact," he said, "it wasn't a very flattering commentary on the thousand odd files who outranked you, was it?"

Eisenhower in his reply on April 18 said that Swede's letter had taken almost three months to reach him. Then he got to what he considered the heart of the matter, those "thousand odd files" who had been bypassed when he got his awesome new title.

Nothing in your letter intrigued me more than your comparisons of the Army and Navy systems, as applied to their methods in selecting leaders in time of war. You seem to believe the Army was almost foolhardy in the matter but did believe that it took a certain amount of nerve to shatter precedent. Finally, it occurred to you that the Army system is not very flattering to the files that were jumped in the process. With this particular point I do not agree. As I see it, seniority, in itself, is of little moment in time of war. The head of the whole organization must make his best guesses as to the individuals he considers equipped for particular tasks, and then he perforce gives them the rank suitable to the task. . . . This process applies all the way down the line. Seniority normally means experience, and experience is always important. But experience and durability are not to be confused in their meaning, and experience alone will never meet the peculiar requirement of war leadership.

It was clear to Eisenhower and to the army that he had durability. Since Ike and Swede had not seen each other since they had been together for a few months in Washington, D.C., just before Ike went off to the Philippines, perhaps Swede needed to be reminded of the Eisenhower "durability." After all, at that time in Washington, Swede had felt that while Ike was becoming an army "comer" he was nevertheless "still a Major with no immediate prospects." In his reply of April 18 Eisenhower added:

Every day we are selecting men here for division or corps command, and our selections normally do not take seniority into account unless all other factors are so nearly equal that this one should govern. In the average case the ranks conferred are for the war only and everybody can go back to his old rank and seniority can again have its heyday.

Obviously General of the Army Eisenhower was not looking forward to that time.

Later on the morning of December 16 Eisenhower, Beetle, and most of the members of their staffs went to the chapel at the palace of Versailles for the wedding of Mickey and his WAC fiancée, Corporal Pearlie Hargrave. Eisenhower attended the ceremony and afterward gave a reception for the bride and groom at the house formerly occupied by von Rundstedt. According to Kay, there were "rivers of champagne, a beautiful French wedding cake, and a kiss for the bride from her boss." In her diary that night, Kay mentioned that Hodges' First Army was having a difficult time, "The German has advanced a little," she said.

Eisenhower gave the bride and groom a hundred-dollar war bond, but Mickey noticed that the general "was very busy that day. I didn't know then how busy he was or why; I just knew that he seemed more rushed than he had been for some time, and that, although he was smiling with us and seemed to be trying not to show it, he was worried."

Actually Eisenhower cannot have looked too worried about the Ardennes offensive during the day of December 16, for its extent was not yet known. Kenneth Strong, SHAEF's G-2 officer, wrote, "Saturday, 16 December 1944, the day of the German offensive, was bitterly cold in Versailles. It threatened later to become overcast in all areas near Paris; over much of the enemy-held area the ground was covered in snow and ice, and the fog and low cloud of the previous few days still persisted." Air reconnaisance of the enemy positions had, because of the weather, been impossible for several days. Strong continued, "Just before breakfast I received reports of an enemy attack during the night and early morning in the area of the Ardennes. Several enemy divisions had already been identified in action, perhaps rather more than one would normally expect on such an occasion."

Later in the day Strong found that at dawn two panzer armies, twenty-four divisions, had attacked three American divisions in the Ardennes, the 28th, which was tired and badly in need of reinforcements, the 99th, and the 106th, neither of which had been in combat before.

The members of Hitler's divisions, the 5th and 6th Panzer armies, were in part boys in their early teens and old men, but there were also battle-hardened veterans, an amazing number of them still eager to fight. The two panzer forces had been told they had enough fuel and ammunition for a lengthy battle. They were to plow through the weak American divisions and then continue on to the Meuse River. After that Belgium would be captured; Antwerp would be retaken, and the Allies, the British and Canadians on the one hand and the American troops on the other, would be split both geographically and politically. Hitler was convinced that the Allies would soon realize that they disliked each other and hated the Russians. A separate peace would be signed with the British and another with the Americans, possibly a third with the Russians.

Hitler was also much buoyed up by the idea that more than 2,000 German soldiers, speaking what they and many of their officers considered very good American English, would create chaos behind the lines in Allied-held areas. The German soldiers in this ill-planned operation had American pay books and wore American uniforms or parts of American uniforms that had been stolen from Red Cross prisoner-clothing stores.

At two o'clock in the afternoon of the 16th there was a meeting in the Map Room at Versailles. Strong was present, as well as Eisenhower, Bradley, Beetle, Tedder, Spaatz, SHAEF G-3 Major General Harold R. "Pinky" Bull, and British Major General J. F. M. "Jock" Whiteley, Ike's deputy chief of staff.

Of course Eisenhower wasn't worried then. Strong said he "for the moment dismissed . . . the Ardennes news, though the latest information was discussed very briefly." Much more important, or so it seemed, was the matter of replacements. And in the long run that may in fact have been the central crisis. In discussing the matter later, Drew Middleton of the *New York Times* said, "You had to find the men; you had to train them and bring them up. It's those problems that aren't associated with the battle front that really take up a great deal of a general's time and only a general with great organizational genius can handle them. Eisenhower had that."

Eisenhower proposed to keep on with the current offensives. Beetle asked Bradley what he felt about the chances of taking the dams over the Roer. At that moment, said Strong, "I was urgently called away. . . . My deputy, Brigadier General Betts, was at the door. Betts was normally a calm, phlegmatic man, but on this occasion he appeared to be rather shaken."

The news was still sketchy, but a major offensive seemed to be underway, particularly in the region in the Ardennes so thinly held by troops that were either untried or battle weary. Eisenhower said, "I immediately urged upon Bradley the movements of the 10th Armored Division from the south and the 7th Armored Division from the north, both toward the flanks of the attack. I urged him, also, to have Army Commanders on both flanks alert what divisions they had free, for instant movement toward that region if necessary." Bradley went to Eisenhower's office and called Patton, telling him to get the 10th Armored Division out of reserve and on its way to Luxembourg; its commanding general was to call Major General Troy Middleton, VIII Corp commander, for orders. Patton, as expected, protested. He said the Germans were just going through motions in a spoiling attack. Finally, however, Georgie decided, "He [Bradley] probably knows more of the situation than he can say over the telephone," and obeyed the order. Bradley also called his own headquarters and ordered the 7th Armored "to hit von Rundstedt on his flank."

Thus the decision for the basic strategy to end the German counteroffensive in the Ardennes was made, shortly after the attack began, by the supreme commander alone. His troops would drive von Rundstedt out by an attack on his flanks rather than frontally. Bradley discussed everything he did with Eisenhower and the two men went over what Eisenhower called "the list of reserves then available to us." The 82nd and the 101st Airborne divisions were the most battle tested but, because they had recently been involved in the fighting in Holland, "were not yet fully rehabilitated." They were, however, available. Montgomery to the north had a complete corps under his command and out of the line. The weather was once again on Hitler's side. Nothing could fly; thus, the Allies did not have the air cover advantage they had enjoyed in Normandy.

That night Bradley and Eisenhower had a leisurely dinner and stayed up late playing five rubbers of bridge and sharing a bottle of Highland Piper Scotch provided by Everett Hughes. The news that came in to SHAEF intelligence during the night made it official that seventeen divisions were involved in the counterattack. That was, Strong said, "more than we originally thought the Germans could make available." Bradley understandably decided to return to his own headquarters at Luxembourg.

Eisenhower, on receiving the latest intelligence, was not overly disturbed. In fact during the entire period when the Germans were being pushed away from the bulge they created in Allied lines, Ike did not seem to get excited or overly depressed, though Montgomery reported to Brooke a couple of days later that when the supreme commander spoke to him, he was "speaking very fast" and was "talking wildly." Monty added that he had had a bad connection. No one at SHAEF, however, noticed that Ike was doing or saying anything unusual; perhaps if he had been heeding the press reports, he might have been more pessimistic. Beetle said, "From newspapers I saw later, I gained the gloomy picture that the whole success of the Allied cause in Europe lay in the balance. General Eisenhower once said a little ruefully that he had never known we were in danger until he read about it in the papers. We were not unduly concerned over the final outcome, then or at any time. The German offensive moved far too slowly in its first days to gain important momentum. Enemy columns were advancing only five to seven miles a day, whereas in our great armored sweeps across France the tanks had often made advances of twenty-five to fifty miles in twenty-four hours."

Besides, the hoped-for raiding of American supply dumps had not been possible; when retreating American forces, as was rare, left such dumps behind, the supplies in them were carefully destroyed. From the beginning, German tanks abandoned because of lack of fuel seemed to be everywhere along the sides of the roads in the area of the counteroffensive.

But the press didn't know that. A temporary news blackout, instead of improving matters, made them worse; most correspondents wrote that American setbacks were more serious than they in fact were. A forty-eight-hour delay in announcing the news was tried for a time, but it didn't help much either. Finally, reporters reported the news as it happened, and the Allied successes became more evident every day.

On the 17th, in a message to Somervell, Eisenhower said, "Yesterday morning the enemy launched a rather ambitious counterattack east of the Luxembourg area where we have been holding very thinly. In order to concentrate on vital points we have had divisions holding thirty-mile fronts. However, we have some armor that is now out of the line and resting. It is closing in on the threat from each flank. If things go well, we should not only stop it [the counteroffensive] but should be able to profit from it." The supreme commander had already decided that no matter what else happened, the town of Bastogne, the important road center in Belgium, must be held. That day, when he mentioned to his staff—those outside of his immediate "family"—that he had been promoted, he remarked that his last promotion had been at the time of the German attack in the Kasserine Pass.

By the third day it was apparent that the German soldiers had not captured a single American gasoline dump. The key highway network south of Monschau had not been taken, and Nazi paratroopers were dropped at night near a vital road junction where they had thought their armor would link up with them. That did not happen, and after a wait of five days near the road junction, the paratroopers started back to German lines in disgust. In reporting the action, AP dispatch said tersely, "A few were captured early and the rest are now being eliminated."

The Germans did achieve some successes. The 106th "Golden Lion" Division had left the States only two months earlier. It was deployed in an area where, it was thought, its lack of experience would be unimportant, on a wooded ridge called the Schnee Eifel, near the town of St.-Vith. Its 15,000 men and officers were scattered along a twenty-seven-mile front on the foggy dawn of the 16th. German artillery plowed into the positions of the 106th, followed by tanks and infantry. The men fought as best they could but eventually were overrun. The 422nd and 423rd Regiments did not give up easily, however, fighting for almost two days in spite of dwindling supplies of food, water, and ammunition. In their last radio message, they said they were destroying their equipment.

The third regiment of the division, the 424th, was largely responsible for keeping the Germans out of the important communications center of St.-Vith. But altogether, the 106th division lost 8,633 men in the Bulge. Of these more than 7,000 were taken prisoner.

On the 18th a French delegation arrived at SHAEF headquarters to discuss the strategic situation with Beetle. As they were on their way to the War Room, Kenneth Strong noticed that the French officers were looking curiously into each office. One French general turned to Strong and said, "Why are you not packing? Aren't you making any preparations to leave?" At no point did the Americans plan to move.

One aspect of what Eisenhower called "Hitler's last bid" was designed to disrupt communications and create confusion in the Allied rear. It was called "Operation Greif," and was headed by dashing thirty-two-year-old Lieutenant Colonel Otto Skorzeny, who the year before, on Hitler's orders, had kidnapped Mussolini from a mountain hideaway in northern Italy. Skorzeny was thought by some Allied intelligence officers to be the most dangerous man in Europe. The German soldiers under his command wore captured American uniforms and carried false identification papers. They also presumably spoke English with an American accent, but when, after the first group of soldiers crossed American lines, a second group was asked to pronounce "Wreathe, writhe, or with," they failed, or as one of Bradley's G-2 officers put it, they "lisped themselves right into the jug."

Skorzeny and his men had gone to a great deal of trouble; spending time in prisoner-of-war cages with Americans, they had learned how to tear off the top of a cigarette package the way Americans supposedly did, and they were taught the basics of close-order drill, but when confronted it was found that none of them had dog tags and none knew his serial number. Of course, some Americans, myself included, got into trouble with American MPs who, soon after the first members of Skorzeny's team were discovered, began asking everybody in an American uniform about baseball. I, for one, did not know who had won the World Series in 1944 (Cardinals over Browns four games to two). But then Omar Bradley did not know who was married to Betty Grable (Harry James). Neither I nor the general got shot as a result of our ignorance of Americana, nor so far as I know did any other GI. Skorzeny's men were less fortunate. The German soldiers, most of them volunteers, had been informed that they could not be shot for appearing behind American lines in American uniforms if they wore their German uniforms underneath. This information was wrong, and eighteen of them were indeed shot.

On December 30 Patton wrote, "On this day four Germans in one of our jeeps, dressed in American uniforms, were killed, and another group of seventeen, also in American uniform, were reported by 35 Division as follows: 'One sentinel, reinforced, saw seventeen Germans in American uniforms. Fifteen were killed and two died suddenly.' "

The main objective of Operation Greif was to get to the Meuse. Ike met with failure, but Skorzeny's troops did cut a few lines of communication, and they delayed an American convoy for an hour by changing some road signs. A captured lieutenant said that one of the main purposes of the whole operation was to assassinate Eisenhower, Montgomery, Bradley, and other Allied generals. Before the assassinations, the Germans were to meet in Paris, at the famous Café de la Paix, and to help them out, several paratroopers were to be landed, disguised as nuns and priests. (As Kenneth Strong said, "Paratroopers *always* seem to disguise themselves as nuns and priests.") As a result, photographs of Skorzeny were circulated all over the city, and a number of men with the misfortune to resemble him were arrested and held for varying lengths of time.

The news of the assassination threat was brought to Eisenhower by a man he described as "a very agitated American colonel." The colonel was convinced that the supreme commander's life was in grave danger, and soon barbed wire was everywhere. According to Kay, "Several tanks moved in. The normal guard was doubled, tripled, quadrupled. The pass system became a strict matter of life and death, instead of the old formality. The sound of a car exhaust was enough to halt work in every office." Eisenhower said, "I discounted the murder theory but agreed to move my quarters closer to headquarters." Strong felt that "Eisenhower . . . did not believe that there was any personal danger to himself. I said I thought the whole thing was probably greatly exaggerated and doubted whether there was a Skorzeny man within a hundred miles of Paris. All the same I urged Eisenhower to remain in headquarters for a further couple of days 'just as a safety factor.' "

"Another night of uneasiness," Kay noted, "E. is just pinned to his office all day; at night he goes upstairs and sleeps in Tex's flat. I stay across the way from the office. Everyone's confined to the compound. What a life—." According to Kay, everyone, especially Ike, was depressed, but he "had to smother his own feelings and act as the eternal optimist, the confident bucker-upper. And he carried off the role with perfect aplomb."

The supreme commander was annoyed not only by personal inconveniences but also by the presence of so many troops standing guard in Paris who would be of far more use at the front.

For a time Lieutenant Colonel Baldwin B. Smith, who looked somewhat like Eisenhower, at least from a distance, moved into the von Rundstedt house and made a daily decoy trip to and from Ike's office. It was a game for which Eisenhower had little patience. He had for months, he said, "been driving everywhere around France with no more protection than that provided by an orderly and an aide who habitually rode in the car with me"; but he agreed to go through the motions for a time just "so you'll forget about this damned business and get back to the war." Butcher said, "I told him he now knows how it must feel to be President and guarded day and night by ever-watchful secret service men."

Mickey said of Colonel Smith that he was "supposed to look like the General. I never thought he did, particularly, except maybe from a long distance. . . . Every evening at about the time the Boss usually left the office and drove to St. Germain, Colonel Smith would come out wearing the general's overcoat and get in the car. Then Dry would run him out to the house in St. Germain, with the usual escort, and Colonel Smith would go in and take off the coat. Then, looking like a lieutenant colonel again, he would come back out quietly, and get in one of the jeeps and ride back to headquarters. That was supposed to fool the Germans, and maybe it did."

When Skorzeny was captured by the Seventh Army the following May, he "disclaimed any responsibility for espionage or sabotage behind American lines," according to the *New York Times*. But in fact Operation Greif set off a real spy mania in the American back areas.

On the morning of December 19 the supreme commander, Tedder, and Gault went to the rear headquarters of the 12th Army Group in Verdun. The supreme commander and his party traveled in a heavy bulletproof car accompanied by MPs in jeeps and staff cars. Bradley, Devers, and Patton, along with a few staff members each, were already there, as was Freddie de Guingand. Montgomery once again was not, and most of those present felt that the field marshal's absence was not only an insult to the supreme commander but to the other American commanders as well. The meeting was on the second floor of a ghostly French barracks heated only by a potbellied stove. Strong and G-3 "Pinky" Bull arrived late, and Eisenhower was annoyed. "Well," he said. "I knew my staff would get here; it was only a question of time."

After Eisenhower seated himself at the long table in the cold, damp room, he said, "The present situation is to be regarded as one of opportunity for us and not of disaster." He said that he was asking that the infantry regiments of divisions in the United States be shipped quickly. He also said that all offensive action was to be stopped and that, while some ground must be given to shorten Allied lines and free some reserves, no withdrawals at all were to go beyond the Meuse River. He discussed various other items of immediate business, then said that Patton's troops were to prepare to fight their way to Bastogne, and from there to push north in an attack with Hodges' First Army. "When can you start?" he asked Patton.

Georgie said, "As soon as you're through with me." Ike thought that Patton's answer was simply another example of his hyperbole and he asked him to be more specific. Patton was more specific; he said he could start on the morning of the 21st with three divisions.

Since that was about thirty-six hours away, Eisenhower at first thought that Patton still wasn't being serious. Martin Blumenson, editor of *The Patton Papers 1940–1945*, later said, "Patton's proposal was astonishing, technically difficult, and daring. It meant reorganizing his entire Army from an eastward direction to the north, a 90-degree turn that would pose logistical nightmares—getting divisions on new roads and making sure that supplies reached them from dumps established in quite a different context, for quite a different situation. Altogether, it was an operation that only a master could think of executing." Eisenhower gave his approval, and Patton wrote confidently to Bea, saying of the German counteroffensive, "Remember how a tarpon makes one big flop just before he dies."

After a tiring day, Eisenhower and his party started the tedious journey back to Versailles. It was late when Eisenhower got back to his office, but Jock Whiteley, generally considered to be one of the more alert and intelligent officers at headquarters—it was he who had first thought that a major Allied stand should be made at Bastogne—was still awake and pondering a telephone call from Montgomery. Monty, as usual, thought things outside his own command were totally confused and had said as much earlier in the day in a message to Brooke. There was, he had told the CIGS, "great confusion" everywhere, and, he added, "The command set-up has alway been very faulty and is now quite futile, with Bradley at Luxembourg [City] and the front cut in two." The latter was true; the front had been cut in two, but that fact did not worry Bradley. He had already decided not to move his headquarters from Luxembourg, and he said, "If we could omit von Rundstedt's penetration on the 35-mile gap between Malmédy and Bastogne while holding firm on the shoulders, we might force the enemy to funnel his strength due west into the Ardennes where the terrain would sponge it up. Between these two points only three mediocre roads meandered westward toward the Meuse."

Monty did not know what Bradley was thinking, and he wasn't particularly interested. He had called Whiteley to say that Eisenhower should put him in charge of all operations north of the penetration, and, if necessary, Winston Churchill should give Ike "a direct order . . . to do so." Whiteley was no partisan of Monty, but the more he thought the matter over, the more reasonable it seemed. If Bradley stayed in Luxembourg City, the northern part of the front might not get the attention it should. Further, all communications might be cut by the Germans. Hodges had moved his headquarters from Spa in Belgium to a city much loser to Liège, which seemed wise to Whiteley despite the difficulty of communications between First Army and SHAEF headquarters.

Whiteley shared Monty's suggestion and his own heretical thought that it might be a good idea with Strong, who agreed with him. Whiteley then called Beetle, who reacted strongly in the negative and said that Whiteley was "talking like a damned British staff officer."

Whiteley said that Smith could fire him if he wished, but he still thought that what Monty had suggested was right. Beetle listened, and, after hanging up, called Eisenhower. By that time the supreme commander was wearily familiar with Monty's attempts to get more power and larger command for himself and cannot have been overjoyed at the current proposal; besides, it was almost midnight, and he had had a bumpy and dangerous journey to and from Verdun that day. Still he went to the huge situation map on one wall of his office. Ed Folliard of the *Washington Post* visited Ike at SHAEF headquarters around this time, and he said that he was "very much impressed" by Ike. "His mind was like a great war map," Folliard said. "He knew where all the forces under his command were at that time. Talking about what the various forces were doing, he praised not only the Army forces but the Navy, the Air Force; he praised the British and the French, and I liked him for that very much."

On the night of December 19 Eisenhower, after studying the wall map, made the unwelcome decision that Montgomery was indeed right. The supreme commander realized that there would be understandable outrage and hurt at the decision; Bradley would be hurt, and Patton would be outraged. It would be to Georgie simply another example of Eisenhower's weakly selling out to the British. And some civilians would no doubt reach the same conclusion and decide that he had lost confidence in his own 12th Army Group commander. He had not, however, and the move was only for the duration of the crisis, so in the words of Charles B. MacDonald, *A Time for Trumpets: The Untold Story of the Bulge*, "With a grease pencil, he drew a line across the map from Gier on the Meuse River eastward through the Ardennes and across the German frontier to Prüm. All forces north of that line—the First and Ninth Armies, the First Canadian Army, and the Second British Corps—were to be temporarily under Montgomery; those south of the line—the VIII Corps and the Third Army—under Bradley."

When Beetle called Bradley with the news, he added, "It seems the logical thing to do." Bradley "asked if the changeover was to be a *temporary* one. Bedell agreed that it was and that it would last only as long as the Bulge." But Bradley was shaken. He was also angry. He felt that Ike had not indicated any unhappiness with him when they had met at Verdun. But here it was, and Brad had to admit, when Smith asked him, that "if Monty were an American commander, I would agree with you entirely. It would be the logical thing to do." Bradley could not say no to the proposal. The changeover was to take place on the 20th, and, Brad said, there might have been no trouble at all over the matter, but "Montomery unfortunately could not resist this chance to tweak our Yankee noses."

That morning, hoping to ease his classmate's feelings, Eisenhower called him and told him what he already knew, that the changeover would take place at noon. "I was to be left *temporarily* with only Patton's Third [Army]," said Bradley; Montgomery was to have, temporarily, the First and Ninth.

Bradley, later in his life, said that his agreeing to the changeover, no matter how temporary, was the greatest mistake he made in the war. He also said in *A Soldier's Story*, "Even . . . de Guingand, his chief of staff, was later to chide Monty for the manner in which he behaved. And while Eisenhower held his tongue only by clenching his teeth, he was to admit several years after the war that had he anticipated the trouble to be caused by it, he would never have suggested the change. Fortunately, the mischief was delayed until after our crisis in the Bulge had passed."

On the 21st Eisenhower proposed to Marshall that he promote Bradley and Spaatz "to four star rank." In Bradley's case, he said, "While there was undoubtedly a failure in the current operation to evaluate correctly the power that the enemy could thrust through the Ardennes, it must be remembered that . . . all of us were astonished at the ability of the *Volkssturm* division [made up of the young, the old and previous noncombatants] to act effectively. . . . Bradley has kept his head magnificently." Eisenhower added that this would "be a most opportune time" to give Bradley the promotion. Marshall agreed but pointed out that such a promotion was not possible at the moment because Congress was in recess. The promotion did not go through until the following March.

Churchill, in a telephone conversation with Eisenhower, said that the temporary change in command meant that "British troops will always deem it an honor to enter the same battle as their American friends." He later suggested that Bradley be given a consolation prize, a Bronze Star.

Chet Hansen said that, "Bradley said from the outset that if the change in command were not temporary, he would go home and fish. He would have, too, and it wouldn't have bothered him. He wouldn't have been bitter. He was totally his own man." Patton reacted exactly as his supreme commander had expected. He concluded that Ike was either "unwilling or unable to command Montgomery."

On the 21st the Belgian town of Bastogne was almost completely surrounded, but American forces on the northern flank, now under Montgomery's command, retook Stavelot, and the German LXVIII Corps had been halted. The change in command was considered coincidental, though Montgomery had already shown up in Simpson's Ninth Army and Hodges' First Army headquarters. A British officer with him said that he had entered Hodges' headquarters "like Christ come to cleanse the temple." Monty wrote Brooke that both commanders had "seemed delighted to have someone to give them orders."

That day Eisenhower wrote Mamie for the first time since the Bulge had begun. He made note that it was "the year's shortest day—how I pray that it may, by some miracle, mark the beginning of improving weather." He was busy, he said, "in fact that's gross understatement. There are so many things about this war that cannot be told now— possibly never—but they should make interesting talk between you and me when we're sitting in the sun, taking our elegant ease in our reclining days. But you'll probably be sick of hearing war— so maybe we'll just sit and fish or listen to the radio, or go visit John! With four grandchildren, I hope!" He had recently gone through Paris, he said, and seen their old apartment house from Pont Mirabeau. The house was "a bit dingy looking, otherwise unchanged. The river was overflowing its banks."

Mamie apparently was not aware that her husband had been promoted either. He said in his letter of the 21st, "I've been advanced in rank, with title of 'General of the Army.' Haven't yet received the regulations concerning insignia, etc. Five stars will be awkward unless I can get someone to embroider them on jackets." The five-star general was apparently successful in that, because Kay Summersby said, "So quietly that no one quite realized what had happened, he achieved the highest rung of all the military ladder. . . . The very tiny circle of five stars appeared on each Eisenhower shoulder almost by metamorphosis, refuting staff rumors that the new design would call for a straight, staggering line of five huge stars. . . . He wore collar insignia only when in combat jacket and he abandoned the overseas cap, which required rank, for the more sedate visored hat. If anything, the new five-star prominence was submerged as much as possible. Only the new red license plates on his car."

On December 22 Winston Churchill sent Ike a message that said, "I am putting this out tonight as mark of our confidence in you." The British government, he said, was making additional British soldiers available to Eisenhower, probably as many as a quarter of a million. They would be recruited with some difficulty and at some cost—transfers from the Navy and the RAF. Others would be called up from civilian life, and still others would be noncombatants from the British Army itself, retrained as combat men. When Beetle heard of Churchill's generous gesture he said that if the British could turn up 250,000 more men, the United States ought to be able to turn up 2,500,000 more men. Not only did that not happen, but an increasing number of U.S. soldiers were being sent to the Pacific.

In his thank-you note to the prime minister Ike said, "I realize that it [assigning the soldiers] was a most difficult decision to make and I can do no more than to express my appreciation and gratitude for this additional evidence of your unshaking resolution in prosecuting this war."

That same day Eisenhower sent identical telegrams to Simpson and Hodges, telling each that he and his army had "performed in your usual magnificent style"; he added that now that each man was under the field marshal "you will respond cheerfully and efficiently to every instruction he gives." Simpson had not been delighted to see Montgomery and take his orders as Monty had written to Brooke, but he was a man who kept his opinions, often sharp, to himself and shared them only with those officers in his command who kept their silence.

When Montgomery first saw Hodges, he thought that the American general was so exhausted that he might have to be relieved of duty, and Monty passed that conclusion along to Beetle. Smith told Monty that if Hodges had to go, Ike would do the firing. Eisenhower did not agree with Monty. In a message to the field marshal, he said, "Hodges is the quiet reticent type and does not appear as aggressive as he really is. Unless he becomes exhausted, he will always wage a good fight." So Hodges stayed, and Monty generously decided the quiet American "originally a bit shaken, very tired and in need of moral support is improving."

Brooke warned Monty to be cautious in his new assignment. He said, "Events and enemy action have forced on Eisenhower a more satisfactory system of command. It is most important that you should not even in the slightest rub this undoubted fact in to anyone at SHAEF or elsewhere. Any remarks that you make are bound to come to Eisenhower's ears sooner or later and that may make it more diffiult to ensure that this new set-up for command remains even after the present emergency has passed. I myself have felt that you were right all along."

On Christmas Day, when Bradley flew to the field marshal's headquarters at Zonhoven, Monty told his visitor that he would not join in a counterattack with the forces under the American's command. Bradley said, "I found him waiting expectantly for one last enemy blow. . . . Not until he was certain the enemy had exhausted himself would Montgomery plunge in for the kill."

Monty told Bradley that he had always said that the Allies should not attempt two thrusts at the same time; he had warned all along that neither would be strong enough. Now, he said triumphantly, "we are in a proper muddle." Bradley disagreed with everything Monty said, but since a number of his troops were under the Englishman's command at that moment, he made no rejoinder.

Monty wrote a colleague that the American general "looked thin and worn and ill at ease. . . . Poor chap, he is such a decent fellow and the whole thing is a rather bitter pill for him." Earlier in the day as Bradley passed through several villages on his way to Monty's headquarters he had noticed that a good many Hollanders were on the sidewalks in holiday dress, and he asked Chet Hansen the reason.

"It's Christmas, general," said Hansen.

While the supreme commander seemed to be able to do very little about American replacements, he did try to inspire those already under his command to "destroy the enemy on the ground, everywhere—destroy him." On the 22nd, in one of the few Orders of the Day he issued during the entire war, he not only asked the "troops of the A.E.F." to destroy the enemy, but added, "we cannot be content with his mere repulse. . . . By rushing out from his fixed defenses the enemy has given us the chance to turn his great gamble into his worst defeat. So I call upon every man, of all the Allies, to rise now to new heights of courage, of resolution, and of effort."

It was coincidental that the next day Eisenhower had to decide the fate of a man who would never do any of the things his supreme commander was asking. On November 11, 1944, Private Eddie—it seems unlikely that anyone ever called him Edward—D. Slovik had been tried for desertion to avoid hazardous duty, convicted, and sentenced to be shot because he could never quite bring himself to join the outfit to which he was assigned, the hard-luck 28th Division. The order to execute Slovick was signed by Eisenhower. The execution was intended to convince other soldiers not to desert, but like capital punishment in civilian life, it failed as a deterrent.

Looking back on the Bulge, Eisenhower said, "Not all soldiers were heroes. Seeking troops who could handle rifles or man guns along our extended lines, we offered men under certain court-martial sentences a pardon and a clean record if they would volunteer for the front. As I recall, all who had been sentenced to fifteen years or more of hard labor accepted the offer but very few of those with lighter sentences chose to abandon the stockade for the risk of combat. This refusal of duty by men wearing the American uniform was disheartening. But then, as now, I know that only a tiny majority create these doubts among their elders. Those who were in their seventies when I was in my teens . . . probably felt the same way about some of my generation's doings and vagaries.

"I believe that we can always rely, even as I had in the Battle of the Bulge and the concurrent winter fighting from the North Sea to the Italian Alps, on the willingness and readiness of Americans, including young ones, to endure greatly in their country's cause."

Kay said, "While plotting the battle itself, he devoted as much time as possible to the equipment and comfort of the fighting man. . . . Sometime he was faced by problems unknown to military regulations. . . . Replacements became a worrisome, then a pressing issue. General Eisenhower directed all rear-area commanders to use Allied civilians to the utmost, to shave down office forces to an absolute minimum. Even these and other measures were so inadequate that by the time Ardennes was past, more drastic measures had to be taken.

"Perhaps that was the reason for his impatience with Army criminals. He was especially impatient one day when, inspecting a Normandy hospital, he realized some of the men were there for self-inflicted wounds. And he was stern, as only a West Pointer and a dedicated war commander can be, with the hundreds of court-martial cases brought to his attention for final review every week."

At the time, everyone in and around SHAEF seemed to be talking about the American manpower shortage. Back in the States one young man out of eight was excused from military service for reasons that were not physical. There were 1,532,500 of them. Some were homosexuals; some had been classified as unstable or maladjusted, temperamentally unsuitable. Eddie Slovik almost certainly should have been one of those young men. Of the more than ten million men inducted into the armed services, only about two and a half million were trained for ground combat, and although nobody knew for sure exactly how many, perhaps a million of those avoided combat duty by means of bad-conduct discharge, self-inflicted wounds or what were diagnosed as psychological infirmities. About 40,000 men avoided combat by just taking off. Most were never apprehended. Slovik was one of the unlucky ones.

There is no mention of Private Eddie D. Slovik, 36896415, in *Crusade*; Eisenhower doesn't mention him in *At Ease*. Clearly the fate of the troublesome young man from Detroit was not something the former general and president discussed with his friends. Hundreds of letters to Eisenhower on the subject were never answered. Indeed the only time on record that Eisenhower mentioned Slovik at all was on the evening of February 11, 1963, in a television program with historian Bruce Catton entitled "Eisenhower on Lincoln as Commander-in-Chief." Eisenhower brought the matter up unexpectedly in the middle of the hour-long broadcast.

Catton had said that in the Civil War army discipline was lax and that many Union officers had complained that Lincoln as commander in Chief had "used the pardoning power too much. He was very reluctant to have a man shot for cowardice in battle. He used to say, well, a man has just got cowardly legs. You can't blame him for that. So he pardoned a great many people, and that was complained of rather bitterly. Do you think under the circumstances he did too much of that, or was that maybe a good thing for the morale?"

Eisenhower said he thought "it was probably a pretty good thing." Lincoln, he said, being president as well as commander in chief of the Union forces, had to keep in mind "the situation which was going to exist" in the country as a whole after the war. Ike also pointed out that the president of the United States no longer had to take part in these cases that involve the death sentence for crimes—military crimes in war. "And there's been only one man executed for a military offense since Mr. Lincoln's time." Catton, in the manner of people conducting television interviews, said, "Is that so."

Eisenhower replied, "As a matter of fact, I approved that one. It was for a repeated case of desertion. The man refused—he was one of those guard-house lawyers—he refused to believe that he'd ever be executed. And at the very last moment, I sent my Judge Advocate General to see him. He was on the gibbet.

And I said, 'If you will go back and serve in your company honorably until this war's over, you'll get an honorable discharge and not the death sentence.' And he said, 'Blarney,' or words to that effect. And so, he was executed. That's the only one."

It's a pity that in his only public mention of the execution of Eddie Slovik, the man who ordered it got almost everything wrong. It is surprising, too, because until the end of his life Eisenhower's memory was almost always accurate. Eddie D. Slovik was never on a gibbet, and there is no record of Edward C. Betts having visited him anywhere at all. The slow-witted Slovik could hardly have been, as Eisenhower said, a guard-house lawyer, and his desertions were not repeated. He did for a time believe that he would never be executed, but then nobody in the U.S. Army was executed for desertion, and he knew that. In the end he thought he was being executed for stealing bread when he was a boy. That wasn't true, of course, but the reason he was put to death wasn't quite clear. At the time nobody much knew about his execution except the men in the regiment that was supposed to be his, the 109th, and a few others in the division he never quite joined, the 28th. So if his death was intended to teach a lesson to other soldiers, that was a failure.

The case was certainly memorable. During the war in Europe, 454 GIs were sentenced to death. For one reason or another most of them were not executed. Seventy were, but with the exception of Slovik, they died for nonmilitary offenses like rape and murder.

U.S. Army discipline was often erratic in Europe. Many GIs seemed unable to tell the difference between Germans and other foreigners. They all spoke foreign languages, didn't they? Many of the French who had stayed behind in Normandy to welcome the liberating Americans were raped, murdered, had their possession vandalized and stolen. In Cherbourg, for instance, the first large city liberated by the Americans, the shooting of French civilians was all too common. A report from the Normandy base section noted, "Unfortunately, from the American angle, this created an unfavorable impression on the civilian population."

From first-hand experience with the 1st Division, from Normandy on until the end of the war, I can testify that the Big Red One almost never took prisoners, a practice which its commanding general, Clarence Huebner, encouraged. Nobody in authority in the theater seemed to mind. Eisenhower probably knew, but not officially, and, anyway, the 1st was not the only division to allow such a practice. But there were some disciplinary problems that could not be overlooked. The judge advocate general for the theater was Brigadier General Edward C. Betts, who seldom brought the supreme commander cheerful news. Usually he brought a number of dossiers describing GI criminals sentenced to death.

Eisenhower had a great many painful discussions with Betts. One day he made a note in the office diary:

Betts, 10:30. Reports that disciplinary conditions are becoming bad. Many cases of rape, murder and pillage are causing complaints by French, Dutch, etc. Am assigning special inspectors to the job at once. His reports substantiate those received from other sources.

Among the men involved in the troublemaking were those in two of Eisenhower's favorite divisions, the 101st and the 82nd Airborne. Kay said Ike emphasized to his staff, "Strong measures will be taken immediately, and he suggested strong medicine, a public hanging in case of rape." At one point there were 500 cases of rape a month, but no one was hanged in public.

Eddie Slovik was a hard-luck kid from the beginning, a product of the depression. He had been arrested for embezzling $59.60 when he was seventeen and working for a drugstore in Detroit. He had also taken candy, chewing gum, and cigarettes. He had been arrested for breaking and entering, petty theft, and disturbing the peace. After he got out of jail the first time, he was soon arrested again for "unlawfully driving away an automobile and violation of parole." He was sentenced to two and a half to seven years in prison. He got out of prison in April 1942 when he was twenty-two, and in November of that year he married an older women who was crippled and suffered from epilepsy.

Eisenhower knew none of these things when he looked over the charges against Slovik and the recommendation that he be put to death and receive no clemency. There is no reason to believe that if he had known them, his judgment would have been different. He was, as has been said, an Old Testament man, and in the Old Testament men were responsible for what they did.

Slovik's trial lasted a little over an hour and a half. The courtroom was in a public building in the small town of Rötgen, Germany, twenty miles south of Aachen. The bloodiest, most costly, most difficult battle of the war was going on only a few miles away, in the Huertgen Forest. He was found guilty and sentenced "To be dishonorably discharged [from] the service, to forfeit all pay and allowances due or to become due and to be shot to death with musketry."

When Eddie returned to the stockade after receiving the death sentence at his court-martial he felt, according to his sergeant, that he might be held in jail two or three months after the war was over. The sergeant said, "It never occurred to him or any other prisoner—even after he got the sentence—that he would actually be shot."

Presiding Officer Colonel Guy M. Williams, division finance officer, who presided at over a hundred courts-martial for the 28th Division, had this to say: "I think every member of the court thought that Slovik deserved to be shot: and we were convinced that, for the good of the division, he ought to be shot. But in honesty—and so that people who didn't have to go to war can understand this thing—this must be said. I don't think a single member of that court actually believed that Slovik would ever be shot. I know I didn't believe it . . . I had no reason to believe it . . . I knew what the practice had been. I thought that the sentence would be cut down, probably not by General Cota [commander of the 28th Division], but certainly by Theater Command. . . . And I thought that not long after the war ended—two or three years maybe—Slovik would be a free man."

On December 9 Slovik sent a five-page handwritten letter to Eisenhower, begging for clemency:

Dear General Eisenhower:
. . . [At] the time of my conviction or before my conviction I had no intentions of deserting the army whatsoever. For if I intended to I wouldn't

have given or surrendered myself as I did. I have nothing against the United States army whatsoever, I merely wanted a transfer from the line. I asked my CO when I came back if their [*sic*] was a possible chance of my being transferred cause I feared hazardous duty to myself, and because of my nerves, which no doubt in my mind we all have. I was refused this transfer.

I must tell you about my past criminal life in my younger stage of life. After being released from jail I was put on a two year parole after spending five years in jail. In them two years I was on parole I got myself a good job cause I was in class 4-F, the army didn't want anything to do with me at the time. So after five months out of jail I decided to get married which I did. I have a swell wife now and a good home. After being married almost a year and a half I learned to stay away from bad company.

I don't believe I ran away the first time as I stated in my first confession. I came over to France as a replacement, and when the enemy started to shelling us I got scared and nerves [nervous] that I couldn't move out of my fox hole. I guess I never did give myself the chance to get over my first fear of shelling. The next day their wasn't any American troops around so I turned myself over to the Canadian MPs. They in turn were trying to get in touch with my outfit about me. I guess it must have taken them six weeks to catch up with the American troops. Well sir, when I was turned over to my outfit I tried to explain to my CO just what took place, and what has happened to me. Then I asked for a transfer. Which was refused. Then I wrote my confession. I was then told that if I would go back to the line they would destroy my confession, however if I refused to go back on the line they would half [*sic*] to hold it against me which they did.

How can I tell you how humbley sorry I am for the sins I've committed. I didn't realize at the time what I was doing, or what the word desertion meant. What it is like to be condemned to die. I beg of you deeply and sincerely for the sake of my dear wife and mother back home to have mercy on me. To my knowledge I have a good record since my marriage and as a soldier. I'd like to continue to be a good soldier.

Anxiously awaiting your reply, which I earnestly pray is favorable, God bless you and in your Work for victory:

> I Remain Yours for Victory
> Pvt. Eddie D. Slovik

According to William Braford Huie in his book *The Execution of Private Slovik*, this letter was never read by Eisenhower. "He gets most of his information through the 'briefing process,' " Huie said. "The letter however, did go to the two reviewing organizations whose responsibility it was to 'brief' the general on such matters."

Whether Ike personally read the letter or was briefed about its contents, a reply signed by him was sent to Slovik on the 19th. It acknowledged receipt of Slovik's letter of the 9th requesting

that the Theater Commander exercise clemency and reduce the sentence for the offenses of which you were found guilty by general court-martial.

The evidence in every case tried by an Army court-martial is carefully and thoroughly reviewed before the sentence is carried out and the question of clemency is given due consideration in every case where the circumstances so warrant. . . . Final action has not been taken upon your case, but you may be sure that the evidence in the record of trial and the matters which you have presented in your letter will be carefully examined and that your plea for clemency will be given possible consideration before final action is taken.

Final action was taken on December 23, when Eisenhower approved and confirmed the sentence. Colonel Williams said, "When the news reached me . . . that Ike had ordered Slovik shot, I'll admit this, I probably was more surprised than Slovik was. That news hit me right between the eyes."

Lieutenant Colonel Henry J. Sommer, Judge Advocate, 28th Division, said, "Given the common practice up to that time, there was no reason for any of us to think that the Theater Commander would ever actually execute a deserter. But I thought that if ever they wanted a horrible example, this was one. From Slovik's record, the world wasn't going to lose much."

On January 13, Eisenhower sent the following message to the 28th Infantry Division:

Sentence of death imposed on Pvt. Eddie D. Slovik . . . has been confirmed. . . . The Provost Marshal, 28th Infantry will direct the execution under your supervision. Request designation of time and place of execution in order to permit publication of General Court-Martial.

In compliance with orders Private Slovik was shot to death by a firing squad on January 31, 1945, at Ste.-Marie-Aux-Mines, France. Major William Fellman, Provost Marshal, 28th Infantry Division, dispatched a report to Eisenhower that same day, through channels, notifying him of the execution and enclosing an in triplicate lengthy report of the proceedings, including a detailed description of the execution.

Two people who were present at the execution would later play an important part in Eisenhower's life, Lieutenant Colonel Henry Cabot Lodge, Jr., who was to be a member of President Eisenhower's cabinet, and Colonel Edward L. R. Elson, who was later to become head of the National Presbyterian Church, in Washington. Elson baptized Eisenhower after he became President. In January 1945 Elson was the ranking chaplain of XXI Corps, and many years later in an interview he recalled that he was "impressed with the majesty of the whole setting." He also recalled that a chaplain under his command who was carrying the black hood for Slovik, asked him when he was going to get more chaplains. He had, according to Elson, lost about a third of his chaplains in the Battle of the Bulge.

Father Cummings, the Catholic priest who was with Slovik that morning, recalled the prisoner saying: "I'm all right, Father. I want you to tell the fellows in the regiment that Eddie Slovik wasn't a coward—at least not today." And later he said, "Father, I'm getting a break that fellows up on the line don't get. . . . Here I get to sit with you and I know I'm going to get it. I know I'm going to die in a few minutes. But up there on the line you never know when it's coming, and it's that uncertainty that gets you. I guess that's what I couldn't take—that uncertainty."

Father Cummings added, "Slovik was the bravest man in the garden that morning." Eddie Slovik's regimental commander, Lieutenant Colonel James F. Rudder, said that Eddie and men like him had no right to live.

On December 23, 1944, the sky started clearing over the Ardennes, and the first wave of Allied planes resumed bombing. By the next day the Germans were being bombed on the roads on which they had hoped to escape. Traffic was unable to move either forward or backward. Most people, not including Eisenhower, said that the battle was over; later the supreme commander said that the enemy had been defeated by the third day of battle, the 19th, but the battle was far from over, even though imaginative news correspondents were thinking up bright things for the troops in Bastogne to say. For instance, the members of the 101st and other units were said to have said, "They've surrounded us, the poor bastards." They also never referred to themselves as "The Battered Bastards of Bastogne."

The enemy continued to attack, and Devers' 6th Army Group, which included the First French Army, was ordered by Eisenhower to pull out of an area that included the historic city of Strasbourg. De Gaulle was both frightened and furious when he found out. His feeling was understandable because if the Germans reoccupied the city, thousands of French citizens were certain to be killed. The Allies also lost St.-Vith. The 7th Armored, however, made a not-too-costly retreat and was soon able to return to battle and the withdrawal had delayed an entire German Corps and given Montgomery and Bradley time to organize a defense.

On the 23rd, too, with Eisenhower's morale very much in mind, Marshall sent a Christmas message to the supreme commander.

With sincere expressions of personal appreciation for the magnificent job you have done for the Allies and for the prestige and glory of America and the United States Army during the past year. . . . Good luck to you in the New Year. May the Lord watch over you. You have my complete confidence.

Eisenhower in his reply said that the letter was "the brightest spot in my existence since we reached the Siegfried Line. Short of a major defeat inflicted upon the enemy, I could not have had a better personal present."

Bastogne still held, but the men were short of supplies. In the frigid weather the Germans continued concentric attacks on the town. On the morning of the 22nd Brigadier General Anthony C. McAuliffe, West Point 1919, temporarily in command of the 101st Airborne, received a German demand for "the honorable surrender of the encircled town." McAuliffe in reply said "Nuts," and as a result made history. It was just the kind of reply the people of the United States, the people of the entire Allied world for that matter, needed at that moment. There were unsung but equally heroic stands in dozens of other towns and villages all over the Bulge area. Several of those towns have small memorials to the Allied soldiers who died there; in contrast, the entire town of Bastogne has been turned into what maybe the most vulgar tourist display in all of Europe.

On the 23rd supplies were dropped into Bastogne from the air, including a great deal of necessary artillery ammunition. Eisenhower also sent the 11th Armored Division, which had recently arrived in Europe, to Givet, just south of the deepest German penetrations, at Celles.

On Christmas Day the troops in Bastogne sent a message, "We're still holding out," and on the 26th McAuliffe greeted an officer in the first elements of the 4th Armored Division, commanded by Major General Hugh J. Gaffey. The tank men were somewhat bedraggled, but members of the 101st were clean shaven.

Captain William Dwight, the tank batallion G-3, saluted McAuliffe and said, "How are you, General?"

McAuliffe said, "Gee, I am mighty glad to see you."

On the 26th, Patton wrote Bea, "Ever since the 22, we have been trying to relieve Bastogne. Just now at 1845 Gaffey called to say we had made contact." On the 28th Berlin admitted on the radio that the Americans had broken open the "barrier positions" around the town. That same day a headline in the *New York Times* said, NAZIS ADMIT TURN IN TIDE OF BATTLE.

Christmas was not a happy day for the general. Kay said that he was "more depressed than at any time since I'd met him. He was low, really low." But the *Stars and Stripes* headline that day was cheerful. It said, YANKS STOP NAZI ATTACK, UNLEASH BIGGEST AIR BLOW. BULGE STABILIZED; COLUMNS HALTED 29 MILES FROM SEDAN—5500 PLANES ROCK ENEMY. True, due to the delay in the release of the news, those happenings had been thirty-six hours earlier. The next day Kay said, "Headquarters sensed a new air of confidence which started down at the lowest levels and surged right up to the Supreme Commander's office. Ike himself agreed, officially; the Germans were stopped."

When Patton told Beatrice, "The relief of Bastogne is the most brilliant operation we have thus far performed and is in my opinion the outstanding achievement of this war. Now the enemy must dance to our tune, not to his." Eisenhower's estimate of Bastogne and its meaning was less emotional than Patton's and considerably more accurate. He said, "The Bulge was a dangerous episode, but at Bastogne, the most publicized (but possibly not the most critical) stand in our furious defense, thousands of paratroopers, hemmed in, held out and wrecked the Nazis' time schedule. On a smaller scale, Bastogne was repeated in thousands of little places, hamlets and bridge crossings and road bends, where handfuls of men might for hours hold up a Nazi column."

It is interesting that in 1945 the supreme commander told Secretary of War Stimson that the Bulge was "a mere incident," but by 1967, in *At Ease*, it had become, in the mind of the retired supreme commander, "a dangerous episode." Ike was more nearly right in 1945; the Bulge was never really dangerous, and it had demonstrated one thing perfectly. The choice of Eisenhower for the job he held had been more than lucky; it had been right.

Eisenhower had been planning for some time to see Montgomery, but a number of things interfered, most often weather and/or security considerations. Ike intended to go to Brussels, but weather made it necessary to change the meeting to Hasselt, near Monty's TAC (tactical) headquarters. They met on the 28th, in Eisenhower's train—air and auto transport had seemed impossible—and, as usual, no one quite knew what to expect from the field marshal. The day before, when the supreme commander had been told that Monty might consider a counterattack, Eisenhower said, and with unaccustomed asperity, "Praise God from whom all blessings flow."

At the meeting, however, no mention of a counterattack was made. Eisenhower's information from Strong was that von Rundstedt's troops were all but knocked out physically and that the German commander was short of supplies. Ike wanted to attack as soon as possible and not give the German commander a chance to build up his position. Monty said that his information was that von Rundstedt would make a great attack against the First Army in the north. He would wait for that attack, stop it, and then launch a counterattack.

Eisenhower and Montgomery both repeated themselves, how often we do not know. It is certain that Eisenhower told the field marshal that if there was no German attack before the first of the year, Monty should strike on January 1.

At Hasselt Monty had emphasized that he and he alone must be commander of the counterattack that would include Bradley's Army Group, all of it, as well as his own. That was impossible, of course, and Monty knew it. Brad had made it clear from the beginning; he would go back to Missouri and fish before he would serve under Monty.

The next day Monty wrote the supreme commander reiterating most of his arguments; in writing they seemed even less palatable than they had orally. "My dear Ike," the letter began. "It was very pleasant to see you again yesterday and to have a talk on the battle situation. . . . I would like to refer to the matter of operational control of all forces engaged in the northern thrust towards the Ruhr, i.e. 12 and 21 Army Groups."

Monty said that when those two groups joined forces, "one commander must have powers to direct and control the operations; you cannot possibly do it yourself, and so you would have to nominate someone else." Subtlety was not one of Monty's strong points. Someone else indeed. Then Monty went on to tell Eisenhower exactly how to issue the desired order:

> I suggest your directive should finish with this sentence: "12 and 21 Army Groups will develop operations in accordance with the above instructions. From now onwards full operational direction, control, and coordination of these operations is vested in the C.-in-C. 21 Army Group, subject to such instructions as may be issued by the Supreme Commander from time to time.

The letter was signed with an affectionate flourish: "Yours always, and your very devoted friend, Monty."

Monty's letter understandably infuriated Eisenhower. He had not been pleased that English newspapers had for days been saying that Monty had saved the Americans from their dangerous errors by taking over part of their command, and that Monty could and should lead the Allied armies to victory. And that

Ike, who was a very nice guy, could sort of preside over things, do what he did best, be chairman of the board, while his deputy, Monty, triumphantly drove on to Berlin. As for Bradley, he had proved his incompetence in the early days of the Bulge. Why else did Monty have his job?

On the 30th Marshall sent Eisenhower a message saying what should have been clear to a bright lieutenant let alone a general about to wear five stars: that it was unacceptable to turn over to a British general any substantial portion of an American force as the London papers had been suggesting, in some cases demanding.

Eisenhower, of course, knew that; he said in his January 1 reply to Marshall. "You need have no fear as to my contemplating the establishment of a ground deputy." He added that he had divided Bradley's command earlier—though the matter had already been explained to Marshall—because the enemy "penetration was of such depth that Bradley could no longer command both flanks, while the only reserves that could be gathered on the north flank had to be largely British. Consequently single control had to be exercised on the north and on the south." Everything was working out fine, he said, and "we have at last succeeded in accumulating enough strength to start an attack of our own."

The receipt of Marshall's letter had not improved Eisenhower's temper, and on December 31 he wrote to Monty dispensing with diplomacy. He enclosed the "outline plan" that had been drawn up by Whiteley to be sent only to Monty, Bradley, Eisenhower, and SHAEF G-3, "covering operations as far as they can be foreseen." The covering letter said:

> The immediate thing is to give the enemy in the salient a good beating. . . .
> The plan gives to you and Bradley each a specific task. The plan also
> provides for great strength north of the Ruhr when the Rhine is crossed.
> In these principal features it repeats exactly my intentions as I gave them
> to you verbally on the train, on the 28th.

That meant that Monty's intention to delay an offensive was to be ignored, that, as Eisenhower had said, "The one thing that must now be prevented is the stabilization of the enemy salient with infantry, permitting him opportunity to use his Panzers at will on any part of the front. We must regain the initiative, and speed and energy are essential."

He added:

> You know how greatly I've appreciated and depended upon your frank
> and friendly counsel, but in your latest letter you disturb me by predictions
> of "failure" unless your exact opinions in the matter of giving you command
> are met in detail. I assure you that in this matter I can go no further.
>   For my part I would deplore the development of such an unbridgeable
> gulf of convictions between us that we would have to present our differences
> to the cc's [Combined Chiefs]. The confusion and debate that would follow
> would almost certainly damage the good will and devotion to a common
> cause that have made this Allied Force unique in history.

Montgomery was spectacularly insensitive to the feelings and opinions of others, but he had to know that if his disagreement with the supreme commander reached the Combined Chiefs of Staff, he had to lose. The disproposition between American and British troops grew daily. Too many in the United States would never agree to a Briton in command over American soldiers on a permanent basis; Roosevelt would have to side with his supreme commander, and Monty would be sent back to London, possibly to martyr to the British, but a martyr without a command. As for Eisenhower, even though he would almost certainly have survived the Allied fracture, he would have failed to do what he had primarily been assigned to do, create and maintain an Allied command.

Ike was fully aware of the possible consequences of his letter, and perhaps he only meant it as an unsent but shared threat. Whatever the plan, he cannot have counted on the superb help he got from Monty's chief of staff, Freddie de Guingand.

De Guingand had learned on a visit to Bradley's headquarters that Monty's reluctance to attack was considered deplorable by the Americans there, and that the field marshal's arrogance had made his continued presence intolerable. De Guingand immediately called his friend and admirer Bettle Smith, who confirmed Freddie's impression. The call had been made on December 30 while Monty's letter was still being read and reread by Ike's staff.

De Guingand sensed that the end might be near for his boss, and despite the fog and the snow and the fact that his pilot had been ordered not to leave the ground, Freddie flew to Paris. By the time he got to SHAEF headquarters, Ike had gone one step further. He was drafting a message to the Joint Chiefs saying that either he or Monty had to go. Whether Eisenhower expected that this letter would be sent is a question that can never be answered. It could still be made to serve its purpose with Monty, and that was what it was all about. In any case the letter, now, alas, nonexistent, was no doubt both powerful and persuasive. It may even be that if de Guingand hadn't voluntarily risked his life by flying to Paris Ike would have had Beetle call Freddie and ask him to come to Paris, saying something like, "By the way, Ike has written a letter that I don't really think should be sent"; but how much better to have Freddie appear on his own at SHAEF headquarters to explain to Beetle and Ike that Monty had no idea the fix he was in. Ike was angry, but it is doubtful that at that moment he was angry enough honestly to tell de Guingand that he was wasting his time, that Monty was finished. But that's what he said, though, again the exact words are lost to us, and, in a rare switch of roles, Smith was patient, understanding, and diplomatic. De Guingand persuaded Ike and Tedder, who had disliked Monty from the beginning, to wait and allow him, Freddie, to go to Monty and get him to back down.

Finally, Ike and Tedder agreed, and de Guingand—there ought to be a statue of this unsung war hero—sent a cable to Monty advising him to do nothing until he, Freddie, got back to the 21st Army Group headquarters. He returned the next day, again risking his life, and told Monty that he had to have a serious talk with him at once. According to Richard Lamb, "after tea they went to the latter's office. Years later in a BBC interview, de Guingand described their talk. At first Montgomery could not see the danger in which he had placed himself, but the other man brutally told him that if he did not climb down pretty fast he would be sacked and replaced by Alexander. De Guingand had already drafted a letter of apology, and he argued that it was essential that it should be sent immediately if the Field-Marshal was to keep his command."

Monty agreed, and the following message was immediately telegraphed to SHAEF headquarters:

31 December 1944

Dear Ike,

I have seen Freddie and understand you are greatly worried by many considerations in these very difficult days. I have given you my frank views because I have felt you like this. I am sure there are many factors which have a hearing quite beyond anything I realise. Whatever your decision may be you can rely on me one hundred per cent to make it work and I know Bradley will do the same. Very distressed that my letter may have upset you and I would ask you to tear it up.

Your very devoted subordinate,
Monty

That night de Guingand also found time to tell four British war correspondents that there was a crisis in the Allied high command and that a British ground commander in Europe would not be acceptable in the United States. He advised the correspondents, in effect, to take it easy, and they agreed to do so.

Before he went to bed that night, de Guingand called SHAEF headquarters and found that Monty's message had been received, that Eisenhower had been "most touched" by it. According to John Eisenhower, "The message to Washington was now in the wastebasket."

The long-delayed counterattack finally got underway on January 3, led by Lightning Joe Collins and his VII Corps. It was not the best morning for an attack of any kind. Collins said, "Snow and thick fog that swirled through the tree tops on the morning of the 3rd prevented air support and coated the narrow steep roads with ice, making them hazardous for tanks, even those with rubber treads. It was bitterly cold, freezing not only the ground but the hands and ears of advancing troops. For the next fornight snow piled up in drifts several feet deep, concealing mine fields and tank obstacles. Weather and rough terrain of the Ardennes offered more resistance initially than the lightly held enemy outposts, but as the weather worsened on January 7 and continued foul, the infantry accompanying and following the tanks had to bear more of the fighting."

Eisenhower had been rather busy the last few weeks, but Mamie was apparently not aware of it, and he said on the 7th, in a reply to what appears to have been a very critical letter from her:

It always distresses me when I get a message from you indicating anxiety or impatience because I have failed to write. Please, please understand that I go through periods when I simply cannot sit down and write a note. To hold a pen is sometimes sheer mental, almost physical agony. If ever I have to be in another war I'm going to take you along! I'll build you a shelter a hundred feet deep and then we'll not give a hoot for anything.

Both de Gaulle and Monty were giving Eisenhower trouble. It had from the beginning of the Bulge been necessary for the supreme commander to think of consolidating the long Allied front, which ran almost the full length of the Rhine, from Holland in the north to the Swiss frontier in the south. The French First Army was on the southern part of the line. Less than a month earlier it had liberated Strasbourg, which to many Frenchmen mattered as much as Paris. On December 26, the day after de Gaulle had visited the city to help celebrate its liberation, Eisenhower, to shorten the Allied line, had ordered that the French withdraw to defensive positions, with the Vosges Mountains at their back.

De Gaulle was infuriated, and he ordered the commander of the French First Army to "take matters into your own hands to guarantee the defense of Strasbourg." He also telegraphed both Churchill and Roosevelt, saying that Eisenhower's order would cause "extremely serious consequences . . . for France."

Roosevelt, as expected, ignored the matter—after all it was a military decision, but on January 3, Churchill got on a plane and flew to Paris, joining Brooke and others of the British at lunch. De Gaulle, who brought General Juin, chief of staff of the French National Defense, was also a guest, and he told Ike that for the Allies to withdraw from Strasbourg would be a national disaster for France. De Gaulle also said that if the Nazis reoccupied the city, they would kill thousands of innocent citizens in reprisal. Moreover, he said, if Eisenhower's order was carried out, the French people might forbid Ike's soldiers the use of indispensable French railways and communications facilities. He also threatened to withdraw French forces from SHAEF command.

Churchill agreed that Strasbourg should not be abandoned, however temporarily. He said he knew the importance of Alsace to the French people and added that "I support General de Gaulle that this fact must be taken into consideration." Eisenhower had at first thought de Gaulle's motives were purely selfish and that he was concerned only with his own political future. But the supreme commander became convinced that "my vast rear area might become badly involved through loss of service troops and through unrest." Eisenhower then told General de Gaulle that troops would be withdrawn "only from the salients in the northern end" of the line and that orders were "to hold Strasbourg firmly." De Gaulle was delighted, and Churchill told Eisenhower after the French general left, "I think you've done the wise and proper thing."

On his return to England, Churchill wrote Roosevelt, saying that he had spent two days with Eisenhower and Montgomery. Both felt the battle heavily, the prime minister said; both were sure of success. He added, "I hope you understand that, in case any troubles should arise, in the Press, His Majesty's Government have complete confidence in General Eisenhower. . . . He and Montgomery are very closely knit, and also Patton and it would be a disaster which broke up this combination which has in 1944 yielded us results beyond the dreams of military avarice. Montgomery said to me today that the breakthrough would have been most serious to the whole front but for the solidarity of the Anglo-American Army."

At noon on January 7 the U.S. First Army was returned to Bradley's command, and Monty wrote him in a most ingratiating letter, "What a great honour to command such fine troops. . . . How well they have all done." Unfortunatelv, Monty didn't leave it at that. No doubt encouraged by Churchill, the field marshal called a press conference in which he made it clear that without his timely intervention the Americans would have suffered a disaster. The field marshal was in an amiable mood throughout the day, and by the time of the press conference he was feeling so happy that, according to one British biographer, he was convinced "that he personally had won the Battle of the Bulge, and was as a result even more cocky than usual."

He gleefully told the press that early on in von Rundstedt's attack he, Monty, and he alone—at least that's what he seemed to be saying—had realized that the Germans were heading for the Meuse. He said, "As soon as I saw what was happening I took certain steps myself to ensure that if the Germans got to the Meuse they would certainly not get over the river. . . . I was thinking ahead." Then, in command of the northern flank, he had brought the British into the fight to save the Americans. "You have thus the picture of British troops fighting on both sides of American forces who have suffered a hard blow. This is a fine Allied picture, he said.

There was more, most of it designed to please not a single American. Monty said that the Bulge battle had been "most interesting . . . possibly one of the most interesting and tricky battles I have ever handled." He did say that one must not think that he had done all this alone. Eisenhower was "captain of our team." He and Monty were "the greatest friends." Moreover, he said, "I shall always feel that Rundstedt was really beaten by the good fighting qualities of the American soldier. . . ."—when given proper leadership.

The Germans made things worse by broadcasting, in English, a somewhat distorted version of the press conference; American soldiers thought the report was coming from the BBC. The final unbearable words of the German broadcast were, "his [Monty's] staff, which has been with him since Alamein, deserves high praise and credit. The Battle of the Ardennes can now be written off, thanks to Field Marshal Montgomery."

There was not much the supreme commander could do. Two days later he issued a Bronze Star to Bradley, and in the citation, he praised Brad for what he had done during the Bulge. Nobody seemed to care much, including Bradley, who after the war relegated his awards to the attic. He was not a man either impressed or assuaged by medals.

Churchill may later have best described what might be called Montgomery's unfortunate behavior. He said, "When Monty was given . . . the Army, after the Germans had broken through in the Ardennes, he made such a cock-a-doodle about it all the Americans said that their troops would never again be put under a British general." Patton's verdict was yet more succinct. He said, "Monty is a tired little fart. War requires taking risks, and he won't take them." Even Montgomery, when he got around to writing his memoirs in the 1950s, admitted that "I should have kept my mouth shut."

"By January 17, things had simmered down so much that even Monty and Patton were back into routine," said Kay. "The Field Marshal sent a message praising the First and Ninth U.S. Armies. General Patton telephoned, worried about nothing more than promotions." Patton had more on his mind, however. "I told the division and corps commanders that it will be necessary to continue the attack, and that I knew they are tired; therefore, they should try to arrange [to pull] one third of their forces out [of the line] to rest and warm up, because we are going to attack until the war is over."

On the 16th Monty had sent a friendly telegram to Eisenhower that began, "I have great pleasure in reporting to you that the task you gave me in the Ardennes is now concluded." The First Army had gone back to Bradley, and Monty graciously added that it had been "a great pleasure" to have it under his command.

In his reply Eisenhower said, "Thank you again for the way you pitched in to help out during the German thrust. I hope I can show my appreciation in a more lasting manner."

In that same message he looked beyond the Bulge and said:

We must substantially defeat the German forces west of the Rhine if we are to make a truly successful invasion with all forces available. . . . *We must make certain that he* [the enemy] *is not free, beyond a strong defensive line to organize powerful thrusts into our lines of communication.* As I see it, we simply cannot afford the large defensive forces that would be necessary if we allow the Germans to hold great bastions sticking into our lines at the same time that we try to invade his country. As an added thought, the more Germans we kill west of the Rhine, the fewer there will be to meet us east of the river.

On that day, the 16th, the U.S. First Army joined the U.S. Third Army across the river at Houffalize, Belgium, completing the pincer movement that cut off the Bulge at its waist. The bridge there had been badly damaged, but some few determined American soldiers had managed to use it. The Sixth Panzer Army, which a month earlier had appeared to some, not including its commander, Oberstgruppenführer Sepp Dietrich, to be invincible, had been decimated, and, Dietrich said, had lost "the will to fight." It was now pulled out of the Ardennes and sent to the Eastern front to engage in still another hopeless task, trying to stop the Russians. Although the 7th Armored Division did not recapture St.-Vith until January 23, "a mere incident" called the Battle of the Bulge was over.

On the 17th, Kay reported, "Ike asked General Spaatz and several of us over to his house that night for a home movie, insisting that Tooey bring his guitar. The two of them let off the past month's accumulated steam by booming out a medley of slightly off-key but boisterous West Point songs." She added, "The worst part of the war seemed over." Kay does not say so, but Ike and his guests undoubtedly had a few drinks and discussed what had yet to be done, and that was a lot. Two million men would soon be available for the final Allied round, and twice that many Russian soldiers were already engaged in what they considered a final assault.

On the first anniversary of the Bulge, in a report to Stimson, still secretary of war under Truman, Eisenhower said of the battle, "We smashed up his [the enemy's] last remaining reserves out in the open where we could get at them and rendered the subsequent conquest of the Siegfried [line] and of the Rhine much easier. I had pointed out at a press conference as early as August 15th [1944], that our major battle in the West was going to be on the frontiers of Germany and that I greatly hoped to fight this battle west of the Rhine, if possible *outside* the Siegfried. I think that any competent military critic would agree that it shortened the war very considerably."

Eisenhower also told Stimson in December 1945, "From my viewpoint the German winter offensive of December . . . 1944, was the outcome of a policy for which I was solely responsible . . . which, starting from the most meagre prospects in the minds of many doubters, ended in complete and unqualified victory. . . . I consider myself solely responsible for this portion of the campaign [the Bulge] just as I do for all other parts of the campaign that were waged under my direction."

It was said at the time of the battle, in many communiqués and by soldiers on the front lines, that while the cost of battle, and this definitely included the Ardennes in 1944, had been high for the Allies, it was twice as high for the Germans—two Germans killed, wounded, or missing for every Allied soldier. That was certainly not true in the Bulge. According to official statistics German casualties had been 81,834, of whom 12,652 were killed, 38,600 wounded, and 30,582 missing. The cost to the Americans had been 76,890 casualties, of whom 8,607 were killed, 47,139 wounded, and 21,144 missing. The Americans lost 733 tanks and tank destroyers as compared to German tank losses of between 350 and 400.

The Allied ground offensive had, Eisenhower said, been delayed six weeks, and the massive air attack on German industry had been delayed a month. On the other hand, before the Bulge an ever-increasing proportion of available supplies was being diverted to the Pacific; the Bulge reminded both the people of the United States as a whole, and those in Washington in particular, that the war in Europe was not yet over, and more supplies were sent across the Atlantic. In early 1945 Roosevelt was concentrating on the forthcoming conference at Yalta. Eisenhower was not to be at that conference to express his view but he ungently needed an uninterrupted Russian offensive in the east to support him in the west. Ike was very much afraid that the eighty-five divisions available to him for the spring offensive would not be enough to defeat the Germans. The German army in the Bulge had, however, suffered a debilitating defeat from which it never recovered. One soldier wrote home from the Ardennes, "If you actually saw me you would lift your hands in dismay. I am ragged and filthy. I have had the same underwear on for five weeks. If one doesn't get lice, it's a miracle. If only the war were over; it has lasted long enough already."

In early November Eisenhower had told Anne O'Hare McCormick of the *New York Times*, "This phase of the war is like climbing the last and hardest ascent of a high mountain in a thick fog. You can't see where the top is and you won't until you suddenly reach the turn and begin to go down the other side." The Allied forces had by now gone a considerable distance down the other side of the mountain.

★ ★ ★

THE LONG-DISTANCE RUNNER

In one way or another Eisenhower was to have a good deal to do with the Russians early in 1945, and he treated them as allies in the war not yet ended; a great many other people, Churchill in particular, were beginning to treat them with suspicion and even as prospective enemies.

Eisenhower sent Tedder to Moscow on December 31, a move that was approved by the Joint Chiefs of Staff, though it was unpopular in Western political circles. Tedder, accompanied by Brigadier General E. J. Betts and Major A. H. Birse, finally arrived, after a difficult journey, on January 14. Eisenhower said, "Tedder was authorized to give Russian military authorities full information concerning our plans for the late winter and spring, and was to obtain similar information concerning Russian projects." Tedder arrived in Moscow with a box of cigars for Stalin from Eisenhower. The Generalissimo took the pipe out of his mouth and said, "When do they go off?"

"They do not go off until I have gone," said Tedder.

The meetings went well. Stalin wanted to know if the Ardennes offensive had forced the Western Allies to hold back, and Tedder told him that was not the case. The Russian offensive had begun on January 12, hitting the Germans with more tanks than had ever been used in war, and with great superiority on the ground. In a few weeks the Red Army would be across the Oder, and Germany would be in grave trouble.

Stalin told Tedder and his party, "The Germans have more stubbornness than brains. In fact, they should never had undertaken the Ardennes offensive. That was very stupid of them." He also said that there was "no will inside Germany around which opposition to Hitler can coalesce."

At the end of the conference Stalin said, "We have no treaty, but we are comrades. It is proper, and also sound, selfish policy that we would help each other in time of difficulty. It would be foolish for me to stand aside and let the Germans annihilate you; they would only turn back on me when you are disposed of. Similarly it is in your interest to do everything possible to keep the Germans from annihilating me."

Shortly after the conference, Stalin wrote Eisenhower that the meeting had been "very useful." He said that the Soviet offensive was going along "in a satisfactory manner, in spite of unfavorable weather." It would, he said, cause the Germans "to renounce their offensive in the west. This will ease the positions of the Allied troops and . . . will accelerate preparation for your intended offensives."

Strong said at the time, "It would be difficult in the future to deny any claim by the Russians that the Allies in the West were unable to progress without Russian assistance."

By mid-February the Russians were threatening Berlin, Settin (Szczecin) and Dresden. It was all very impressive, and, as a result, Eisenhower said, "The Combined Chiefs of Staff authorized me to communicate directly with Moscow on matters that were exclusively military in character. Later in the campaign my interpretation of this authorization was sharply challenged by Mr. Churchill, the difficulty arising out of the old-age truth that politics and military activities are never completely separable."

Stalin had, however, lived up to his promises in the late winter of 1944–1945, including the promise that "the Russians would keep up a series of continuous operations that would, at the very least, prevent the Germans from reinforcing the Western front by withdrawing forces from the Russian sector."

The meeting of the Big Three at Yalta began on February 4 and lasted through the 9th. Eisenhower could not attend but sent Bedell. Just before the conference, however, Eisenhower went to Marseilles to see Marshall. He left Paris by train on January 26, had dinner, and spent the evening with his old friend Harry Hopkins and Jefferson Caffery, the American ambassador to France. Once again the subject of the appointment of a ground commander in chief was discussed, but Eisenhower had two powerful Americans to argue against it. Marshall said that if such a thing happened, he would resign as chief of staff. He also agreed with Eisenhower's general strategy to in effect do away with German resistance west of the Rhine. As for the supreme commander going to Yalta himself, both he and Marshall felt it would not be wise for him to leave the SHAEF command at that time, however briefly.

On the 29th, with Tedder and his party back from Moscow, Butcher said, "Ambassador Averell Harriman had been helpful and set word to General Ike that further information would be available from Stalin as to future plans of the Russians. "At last a direct contact has been made with Stalin so that the two great forces closing in on Hitler can act with proper intelligence." But later, in March, Eisenhower was to get into hot water for making "direct contact" with the Russian leader.

At the Yalta meeting, it was decided that Germany would be divided into three occupation zones, and later France was asked to occupy a zone. Berlin, two hundred miles east of the American zone, was to be a jointly controlled special zone within the Russian zone. An unconditional surrender still would be required from Germany, and Stalin agreed, as he had at Teheran, to enter the war in the Pacific.

Stalin, at a banquet on February 8, said that friendship between allies during a war was easy but "the difficult task comes after the war when diverse interests tended to divide the allies." He also said that "the present alliance would meet this test." Actually, it was already clear that "the present alliance" was in deep trouble. Some Americans were soon saying that Roosevelt had been sick and tired during the conference and had sold out to the Russians. Eisenhower himself, once the general turned politician, remembered, or so he said, that the president had told him not to worry about the Russians or Uncle Joe.

On February 12, shortly after the offensive in the West began, the supreme commander received a telegram from Roosevelt saying that he would be in Alexandria on his way home from Yalta. "If you have anything you particularly wish to see me about and the military situation permits, I will of course be glad to see you," the president said. At the time Eisenhower was still having trouble with his knee, and that day he had minor surgery on it. In his reply to the president the next day, the supreme commander said:

> Although I deeply regret my inability to meet you at the point suggested I am sure that my absence from here at this time would be most unfortunate. Floods have held up an important plan and some changes will probably have to be made that no one except myself can authorize. I truly appreciate the courtesy of your invitation.

Eisenhower must later have regretted that fact that he missed what would have been his last chance to see Roosevelt.

On February 6, John, who was on his way to join his combat unit with Bradley's 12th Army Group, stopped off to see his father for several days. John remembered that a physiotherapist was treating his dad and that from his sickbed one night, after he had had a rubdown—now submitted to daily—he called Monty. General Simpson's Ninth Army and the British Second as well as the Canadian First Army were to have attacked toward the Roer. Heavy rains and flooding of the river had held up Simpson, but the Canadians and British had gotten off as scheduled. Eisenhower wanted to make certain that the British understood why the Americans had been delayed. "The maintenance of good feeling between the forces of the two nationalities was a continuing consideration that Dad had to work on constantly," said John.

John said that, despite the knee injury, his father's "spirits were high." The Ninth's delay was only temporary, and the supreme commander's "confidence showed in sharp contrast to his somewhat frustrated state in Normandy when he had been in something of a quandary as to exactly what he was going to do." John mistakenly thought the Old Man was more serene than he really was. He was harassed by Churchill, annoyed by Monty, and frustrated by weather. But "he was, during this eleven months, exercising the professional skills and knowledge that he had been developing for thirty years. And he was doing so at the highest levels. Moreover, he was exercising his remarkable forte for maintaining morale, sustained by top-flight people."

Operation VERITABLE began on February 8; Lieutenant General Henry D. G. Crerar's Canadian First Army started south toward Nijmegen that day; the Ninth Army's Operation GRENADE had been scheduled two days later, but the retreating Germans had flooded the Roer Valley before the Americans arrived, and the weather was bad, preventing any immediate American action. As a result, the Ninth Army offensive across the Roer had to be delayed. It was February 23 before the first assault boats were launched, and March 2 before Ninth Army troops stood on the west bank of the Rhine.

Simpson and his staff saw no reason why his army should not cross the Rhine immediately upon reaching it, and had he been under American command he would have done so, but Montgomery said no. He gave a number of plausible reasons, but Simpson and most other Americans said that it was because Monty wanted nothing to interfere with his own crossing on March 23, when he allowed Simpson's army to be part of the larger panorama. The whole thing, Kay Summersby said, was "a typical Montgomery performance, with all the ingredients of incredible preparation, wheel-to-wheel barrage, mass assault, and victory."

By February 9 the British and Canadian forces captured Millingen, east of Nijmegen, and the U.S. Third Army was moving northward toward Prüm, while in the south the German resistance at Colmar ended. A German newspaper published for the Wehrmacht troops at the time said that if the enemy's news services speak in a disparaging way of the fact that 15-year-old German boys are fighting in the German lines, the Germans did not see in it anything derogatory or a sign of weakness but something to be proud of and a sign of their strength. One U.S. First Army officer said of the prisoners captured, "It was a pathetic sight—a bunch of toothless, rheumatic officers with a few schoolboys added. All of them belonged at home with their wives and mothers. After looking over this pitiful assemblage of the immature and the infirm, I ordered them back to the point of capture and released."

Not all the opposition was so weak, however; when on the 23rd there were heavy attacks on the Roer by the U.S. First and Ninth armies, the river was crossed in several places, but there was what one communiqué called "considerable" opposition from the Fifth Panzer Army and Fifteenth Army, which were part of Field Marshal Walther Model's Army Group B. A few weeks later, on April 17, Model, a true Nazi and disciple of Hitler, dismissed what remained of his army group, allowing its members to surrender, join another outfit, or go home. Then on April 21 he shot himself.

To the south the U.S. Seventh and Third armies were moving forward. On February 23, in Luxembourg, Patton entertained the press with some of his views on war and peace. He said, "A host of people who squat and piss say this will be the last war and that you only need clubs. . . . The only thing to do when a son-of-a-bitch looks cross-eyed at you is to beat hell out of him right then and there."

On the 24th Eisenhower was considerably more restrained at his meeting with reporters. Steve Early, Roosevelt's press secretary, who was visiting his friend Butcher after the Yalta conference, said that Eisenhower's was "the most magnificent performance of any man at a press conference that I have ever seen. He knows his facts, he speaks freely and frankly, and he has a sense of humor, he has poise, and he has command."

The February offensive involving First and Ninth armies by that time was well underway. Butcher said, "Ike talked for perhaps an hour, giving a general statement first, of developments since he had last talked to them, and then of the current offensive. . . . I marveled the way he turned possibilities for error into diplomatic but honest answers. One question had to do with Montgomery, which he covered by explaining the meaning of operational command. I think this satisified the correspondents."

That was my first Eisenhower press conference, and I recorded in my diary, "All future generals will have to know how to handle the press, probably more important than learning how to handle troops. . . . Ike is a master, though for my taste he smiles too much and says too little. Sometimes, when he chooses, he uses a great many words to say nothing at all, and much of it is—just words. He did that when he was asked about Montgomery; he took about five minutes to say absolutely nothing, but the boys and girls of the press acted as if they had heard Einstein explain relativity.

"The correspondents were struck by Ike's appearance of fitness. One asked his weight. Ike said he didn't know, as he hadn't weighed himself recently, he only judged by the tightness of his belt and lately had felt a tightening."

By March 3 Simpson's Ninth army had taken Krefeld, the largest city on the Cologne plain and only two miles from the Rhine. By the end of February the string of victories all along the Rhine had caused Brooke to make a major admission. For the first time he conceded that the Allied advance on a wide front was working. The "double attack," he said, "might soon become a pursuit and as such [was] fully justified."

Toward the end of the month Eisenhower and his staff moved from Versailles to Rheims—every soldier I knew pronounced it "Reams." Kay found the new headquarters less than satisfactory. "The space and the furnishings were a comedown from the Trianon in Versailles. Instead of a grand hotel in the shadow of a royal palace, we now worked in an old red schoolhouse. Later the site was to become historic . . . [but] in February . . . it was only an old red school-house, nothing more. The General's office was minute, an overgrown filing cabinet, not even as large as mine. Outside, trains and trucks, provided a factory-like atmosphere compounded mostly of dirt and noise."

Eisenhower's living quarters, however, were in the château of a champagne baron.

Kay, while not happy with the surroundings, was pleased that she had been promoted to first lieutenant and was "the first female five-star aide in American military annals. . . . My pay increased eighteen dollars per month and I put on a newly created insignia, a blue shield decorated with a circle of five white stars, topped by the aide's eagle."

On March 1 the supreme commander and Kay went to General Bradley's headquarters, which Eisenhower made his HQ for the next three days while he visited, among others, the Canadian First Army, the British Second, the U.S. First, Third, Ninth, and newly formed Fifteenth. Kay said that after he had seen a number of German cities, he told her, "I know you'll be glad, Kay, when I tell you this: they're all in ruins, just like Aachen. Maybe they'll make up for places like Coventry, London, Rotterdam, and St.-Lô."

There spoke the true Crusader, the vengeful Old Testament man.

When Eisenhower got back to Rheims on March 3, he learned that troops of the Canadian First and the U.S. Ninth armies had linked up near Geldern.

Third Army units had crossed over the Kyll, and in the sector of Lieutenant General Alexander M. Patch's Seventh Army, Forbach had been taken. It had been thought by the SHAEF planners that there would be a long, bloody battle for the city of Cologne, but on March 7 what was left of the city fell to Collins' VII Corps. The cathedral was intact, but the entire center of the city had been flattened. Collins said, "We had come well over 600 miles from Utah Beach, and the day before had captured our 140,000th prisoner." Eisenhower dropped by to congratulate Collins on his accomplishments, and on March 11 in the city stadium, where many Nazi celebrations had been held, Collins raised the American flag. He said, "I am . . . sure that the ceremony was not lost on the Germans passing by outside."

He added, "The day Cologne fell, March 7, the First Army's III Corps on our right scored an even greater coup." Ten years after that day, on March 7, 1955, President Eisenhower invited to the White House a number of men who had taken part in the crossing of the Rhine at Remagen. Eisenhower said, "Gentlemen, I have asked you to come here this morning because you know old soldiers' minds are bound to turn back once in a while to dramatic events of war—particularly of the kind that took place at the Remagen bridgehead.

"Now of course, this was not the biggest battle that ever was, but for me it always typified one thing: the dash, the ingenuity, the readiness at the first opportunity that characterizes the American soldier."

What happened on the bridge at Remagen that March day involved all of those qualities, though none of them belong exclusively to American soldiers. There were those who thought what happened at the bridge also involved a great deal of luck. But the decision to exploit the ingenuity, the dash, the readiness, and the luck was that of the supreme commander. Eisenhower, like Montgomery, preferred carefully prepared battle plans, but he could go beyond them when he thought it desirable, ignore them when he thought they were wrong, and, always, put them in perspective. Collins said of him, "He always knew where everybody was and what everybody was doing. Even when whoever it was had just moved."

Remagen became first celebrated for a hagiographical miracle. In 1164 the head of St. Apollinaris, a pupil of St. Paul, was being sent to Cologne, but the boat bearing it stopped, of its own will, at Remagen and refused to go the thirty miles further north. In March 1945 the reliquary containing the head was displayed with much pride to American GIs. When I paid a brief visit to Remagen several weeks later, small metal replicas of the silver reliquary were for sale at, as I recall, the equivalent of $10.

Many Allied soldiers thought of what happened at Remagen on March 7, 1945, as a sort of miracle. About one o'clock in the afternoon the lead infantry platoon of a tank-infantry command of the 9th Armored Division came out of a woods overlooking the Rhine to find the Ludendorff railroad and pedestrian bridge had not been destroyed by the retreating Germans. It was an impressive sight, more than a thousand feet long, with two planked-over railroad tracks and footpaths on either side, on which German soldiers were filing across to the east bank. Belated attempts by the Germans to demolish the bridge succeeded in damaging it and temporarily denying it to the tanks, but infantry was storming across the bridge, and not very much later someone put up a huge lettered sign, CROSS THE RHINE WITH DRY FEET—COURTESY OF THE 9TH ARMORED DIVISION. News traveled quickly to Hodges at First Army headquarters, and he called Bradley at 12th Army Group Headquarters. Brad was jubilant. "Hot dog, Courtney," he said. "This will bust 'em wide open. Shove everything you can across!" Bull was with Bradley, and he was less enthusiastic. What had happened, he said, did not fit into the plan; the plan called for the main Allied effort to be made north of the Ruhr. Persons in G-3 are often upset by diversions from plan; they have and probably need the minds of certified public accountants.

Bradley, a man not usually given to sarcasm, said, "What the hell do you want us to do, pull back and blow the bridge up?" Bradley then called Eisenhower, who was at dinner at Rheims. Ike said:

When he [Bradley] "reported that we had a permanent bridge across the Rhine I could scarcely believe my ears. He and I had frequently discussed such a development as a remote possibility but never as a well-founded hope. I fairly shouted into the telephone: "How much have you got in that vicinity that you can throw across the river?"

He said, "I have more than four divisions but I called you to make sure that pushing them over would not interfere with your plans."

I replied, "Well Brad, we expected to have that many divisions tied up around Cologne and now those are free. Go ahead and shove over at least five divisions instantly, and anything else that is necessary to make certain of our hold."

His answer came over the phone with a distinct tone of glee. "That's exactly what I wanted to do but the question has been raised here about conflict with your plans, and I wanted to check with you."

Bradley's "glee" no doubt stemmed not only from the fact that Bull, who had raised the question, was there to hear Eisenhower's answer, but from Brad's awareness that his rival, Montgomery, did not plan to cross the Rhine for at least two weeks.

The next day Eisenhower called Monty with the news of Remagen, which the field marshal took calmly. As he reported to Brooke, "I was consulted by Eisenhower by telephone this morning as to my opinion on the matter and said I considered it to be an excellent move, as it would be an unpleasant threat to the enemy and would undoubtedly draw enemy strength onto it and away from the business in the north."

Eisenhower may have expected something a little more enthusiastic from the field marshal, but, after all, the "business in the north" had been planned for many months. Monty's crossing of the Rhine, scheduled for March 23, would involve more than 250,000 men and would be the largest operation since OVERLORD.

Georgie Patton was also planning to cross the Rhine, before Monty if that was humanly possible. On the 9th he wrote in his diary:

All the Rhine bridges in my sector are out and it will take too much time to build one. I shall not wait for the Seventh Army [to cross the river].

Bradley was anxious for me to coordinate my plan with Patch, but since he cannot jump [the Rhine] until the 15th, I am going to attack as soon as possible, because at this stage of the war, time is more important than coordination.

Bradley told Patton to "take the Rhine on the run," and he did, making the second American crossing of the river before Monty—just—at 10:00 P.M. on March 22.

The Ludendorff Bridge turned out not to be as "permanent" as Eisenhower might have hoped. Immediately after American troops started pouring across the Rhine at Remagen, the Germans started shelling and bombing the bridge. German frogman loaded with explosives tried to demolish it from below, seriously weakening, but not destroying it. After ten days the central span of the bridge fell into the Rhine, drowning several engineers who were attempting to repair it. But by that time the bridgehead was eight miles deep and twenty miles wide. Beetle said, "It [the Ludendorff Bridge] did not last long, but while it did it was worth its weight in gold."

Undoubtedly, Bradley also benefited personally from his prompt exploitation of the bridge. As Strong said, "Eisenhower was now confirmed in the view he had so long that Bradley was a more enterprising commander than Montgomery when it came to offensive action, and that in the future he would be given wider scope and the greatest opportunities."

On the other hand, what happened at Remagen finally ended the career of von Rundstedt. He was succeeded by Field Marshal Albert Kesselring who said, "Never was there more bad luck at one place than at Remagen." When Kesselring took over command in the West in April, he referred to the rumors that had been circulating about a new "vengeance" weapon, successor to the V-1 and V-2, when he jokingly told his new staff, "Well, gentlemen, I am the new V-3."

On March 11 Eisenhower received an encouraging if premature report that Zhukov's troops had crossed the Oder River and were at Seelow, only twenty-eight miles from Berlin. (Actually the Russians did not get to Seelow for another month, but only the Russians knew that until after the war.)

The night of the 11th, Tooey Spaatz came to Ike's headquarters with his guitar. According to Butcher, they "banged out all the old ones and some new ones. . . . The singing was so good that everyone got into it. Ike led the basso profundos and really got into the whole swing of things again—the first evening I've seen him really enjoy since the Lord knows when. He is back in the office today, running the war with a new zip."

On the 13th Patton's XX Corps began attacks across the Moselle between Trier and Saarbrücken. Patton said in a letter to Bea that "the going is just terrible, just woods and mountains. Still they made about 4 miles. . . . We have taken 899,000 [prisoners] since Feb. 1 and got 9,000 plus yesterday, by far the biggest single bag we have had."

On the 16th Eisenhower and Beetle arrived at Georgie's headquarters in Luxembourg. He drove them from the airfield to his headquarters where he showed them his map room and exuberantly explained what he had done and what he planned to do. Eisenhower, Patton said, "was quite enthusiastic and complimentary, as was Smith." The next morning, Patton said, "Eisenhower spoke and paid me the first compliment he has ever vouchsafed. He stated that we of the Third Army were such veterans that we did not appreciate our own greatness and should be more cocky and boastful. . . . [Eisenhower was] extremely complimentary and stated that not only was I a good general but a lucky general and that Napoleon preferred luck to greatness."

The supreme commander then flew to Nancy in the Seventh Army sector and saw Patch before returning to Rheims for the night.

The news from the front continued good. On the 15th the Seventh Army had gone on the attack, this time in the area around Saarbrücken and Bitche. The Seventh Army joined the Third in what turned out to be a successful attempt to drive the Germans out of the Saar-Moselle sector. On the 17th the Remagen bridge collapsed, but by that time Army engineers had built several other bridges in the same area, and it seemed apparent that the advance over the Rhine was not about to be stopped. To the south the Third Army offensive over the Moselle took Koblenz and Boppard. Forward units of the Seventh Army had now crossed the German border.

None of these victories seemed to impress or cheer the supreme commander, however. He had had a cold earlier in the month, and he did not seem fully to recover. His injured leg also bothered him a good deal of the time. Kay said that she and Beetle decided that Eisenhower's "physical and emotional condition was worse than we had ever known it. The two of us were forever having talks about Ike's state of mind and state of health. Beetle was positive he was on the verge of a nervous breakdown."

Beetle told him, "Look at you. You've got bags under your eyes. Your blood pressure is higher than it's ever been, and you can hardly walk across the room." Fortunately, a wealthy American had said that he would be honored if the supreme commander would make use of his villa in Cannes, Sous le Vent. Ike finally agreed to rest there for a few days, insisting that Bradley join him. Tex, Kay, and three other WACs went along. Bradley and Chet Hansen arrived on March 20, the day after Eisenhower and his party got there. The WACs stayed in a villa about a mile and a half from Sous le Vent.

The flight to Cannes took three hours, and Kay said that the weather was perfect, and that it was "so wonderful to get away from Reims. . . . The villa where E. is staying . . . is a most delightful place. Never have I seen such wonderful bathrooms. We were told that the house cost over three million to build."

Eisenhower was unable to leave the grounds of the villa, but during the first two days that was unimportant because he slept, only waking up, Kay said, "long enough to eat. . . . He would eat lunch on the terrace and shuffle back to bed. After forty-eight hours of this, he began to look somewhat human, but he had had us all very seriously worried." Bradley said that he "cooperated in the therapy by avoiding any serious discussion of the war and filling in at the bridge table."

Mickey said, "The Boss was supposed just to relax and look at movies and enjoy himself. He did for about three days, although you could tell by the end of the third day it was wearing thin. The fourth day, when I went to his room in the morning he told me to pack up. He said: " 'Mickey, you and I are getting out of here and going on a trip. Pack enough stuff for about three days and let the other boys take the rest of the stuff back.' "

Bradley returned to his own headquarters at Namur, and Mickey and Eisenhower flew to the headquarters of the XVI Corps at Rheinberg, where Simpson's Ninth Army was to cross the Rhine in Operation PLUNDER, commanded by Montgomery. In anticipation of Monty's long-awaited Rhine crossing, Churchill had prepared a broadcast for the BBC, saying that the British under Monty's command had carried out the "first assault crossing of the Rhine in modern times." It was transmitted after PLUNDER began, and members of Hodges' and Patton's armies who of course were already across were greatly amused.

After his late night crossing at Oppenheim, south of Mainz, on the 22nd, Patton issued a statement to his men saying that from January 29 to that date they had "wrested 6,484 square miles from the enemy . . . captured 140,112 enemy soldiers and . . . killed or wounded an additional 99,000, thereby eliminating practically all of the German Seventh and First Armies. History records no greater achievement in so limited a time."

Meanwhile, Monty had lined up a quarter of a million men for his crossing; the main artillery barrage began at 1:00 A.M. on March 24. In addition to the artillery bombardment, Allied aircraft flew 7,500 sorties in support of the operation; 50,000 tons of bombs were dropped. The principal crossing, which included Simpson's Ninth Army, began at 2:00 A.M. Simpson and Eisenhower observed from a church belfry as more than 2,000 guns opened the attack. Eisenhower said, "Because the batteries were distributed in the flat plains on the western bank of the Rhine every flash could be seen. The din was incessant. Meanwhile infantry assault troops were marching to the water's edge to get into the boats. We joined some of them and found the troops remarkably eager to finish the job. There is no substitute for a succession of great victories in building morale."

Chalmers P. Wylie, who later became a congressman from Ohio, remembered after Eisenhower's death that while the 30th Division was moving into position for the attack at Wesel, "sporadic shell fire made us ill-at-ease and attested to the presence of the enemy and his intention to see that our mission failed. While we were marching gloomily in combat column, a staff car approached and stopped beside where I was walking.

"General Eisenhower stepped out. . . . I made a poor attempt to salute, which seemed the thing to do. The general extended his hand to shake mine, and said, I think, "Hi, soldier.' . . . The General walked up and down the column shaking hands and encouraging his troops. . . . I remember saying to a buddy, 'He shouldn't be here. Doesn't he know he is liable to be killed?' General Eisenhower was up with the troops risking his life but the inspiration his presence gave us cannot be imagined."

Some observers of PLUNDER were less impressed than Churchill. Monty's biographer Chalfont said, "Montgomery's crossing of the Rhine was a cumbersome, over-elaborate operation, with none of the speed and dash displayed by the Americans." The field marshal had even asked to have studies made of what one adviser called "sub-strata soil, depth of mud, etc." Patton never asked for such information. When Montgomery was asked why he had had his troops cross at one section of the river when on the other side they were confronted with cliffs 400 feet high, he said, "The impossible place is usually the least well-defended." Hodges was not that impractical.

The Americans and the British, however different their methods, had set the stage for taking the Ruhr, which Eisenhower had been planning since before OVERLORD. Before PLUNDER began, Monty had said, "Having crossed the Rhine, we will crawl about in the plains of northern Germany chasing the enemy from pillar to post." In his diary, Brooke said that on the morning of the 25th, Palm Sunday, he and Eisenhower had discussed what should be done when Kesselring and all the other German commanders surrendered. Brooke said, "Evidently the Boche is cracking and what we want now is to push him relentlessly, wherever we can, until he crumbles. In his present condition, we certainly have the necessary strength for a double envelopment strategy, which I did not consider applicable when he was still in a position to resist seriously."

Eisenhower agreed. Some weeks later he wrote Swede Hazlett, "I knew on March 24 that the enemy was absolutely whipped and was rapidly disintegrating. He had not the slightest chance and from then on it was merely a question of when we could get an orderly surrender to all the combined powers, or failing that completely occupy his country. During mid-April my mind was completely at ease so far as the actual fighting was concerned."

Bradley's role in the war had steadily grown since the January night when he lost command, however temporarily, of the First and Ninth armies. Now, Ike said to Butcher, "Bradley has never held back and . . . 'paused to regroup' when he saw an opportunity to advance." It was thus not surprising that Eisenhower sent new reserves to Bradley, rather than Montgomery. Bradley's troops would complete the encirclement of the Ruhr and after that, head east to link up with the Russians. On the 25th, First Army units under his 12th Army Group began to break out from the Remagen bridgehead, and additional Third Army units crossed the Rhine near Boppard.

One of the problems on Eisenhower's mind that spring was what to do about Berlin, and it seemed logical that he should consult Bradley. The basic directive Eisenhower had been given before leaving England was to "enter the continent of Europe, and, in conjunction with the other United Nations, undertake operations aimed at the heart of Germany and the destruction of her armed forces." There had been no mention of Berlin, as both men knew. The fact that Germany had now been divided into zones of occupation did not, as Eisenhower wrote, "influence our military plans for the final conquest of the country. Military plans, I believed, should be devised with the single aim of speeding victory; by later adjustment, troops of the several nations should be concentrated in their own national sectors."

Berlin had for a long time been considered "the main prize" of the offensive in Germany, but, as time went on, Eisenhower began to question its importance. Beetle said, "By the end of January 1945, the German government was evacuating the capital, fleeing to the temporary safety of the Thuringian Forest and south to Hitler's own retreat in mountainous Berchtesgaden. Deserted by its Nazi masters and ruined by our massive air bombardments, the city was becoming a shell—an empty symbol of the Nazis' brutal grandeur. It was losing all meaning as a military objective."

When Eisenhower made the decision about Berlin, he was aware of the distance between Montgomery's bridgehead and the Elbe. Marshal Zhukov already had more than a million men on or near the banks of the Oder, about thirty miles east of Berlin. When the Western Allies reached the Elbe, there would still be fifty miles of lowlands to be crossed before reaching the city.

Bradley said, "Here the western approach was studded with lakes, crisscrossed with streams, and interdicted with occasional canals. When Eisenhower asked me what I thought it might cost us to break through from the Elbe to Berlin, I estimated 100,000 casualties. 'A pretty stiff price to pay for a prestige objective,' I said, "especially when we've got to fall back and let the other fellow take over.'

"Had Eisenhower even contemplated sending Montgomery ahead to Berlin, he would have had to reinforce that British flank with not less than one American Army. I could see no political advantage accruing from the capture of Berlin that would offset the need for quick destruction of the German army on our front. As soldiers we looked naively on this British inclination to complicate the war with political foresight and nonmilitary objectives."

A few days after Montgomery's much-publicized crossing of the Rhine—American troops at the time said, "He didn't actually walk on the water, you know"—Eisenhower decided Bradley was right about the German capital—and indeed, according to the Russians, Bradley's estimate was very conservative. They later estimated that in the battle for the city they had suffered 304,000 casualties. But a great many critics felt and no doubt still feel that Eisenhower's strategy on Berlin was the greatest mistake of his military career.

Late in the afternoon of the 26th, after himself crossing the Rhine at Remagen, and visits to two corps headquarters, Eisenhower returned to Rheims far from jubilant. He was, according to Butcher, "feeling there will be guerrilla warfare after the German armies are beaten."

Despite the supreme commander's pessimism, the news was good. Units of the XV and VI Corps of Patch's Seventh Army had begun to cross the Rhine between Worms and Mannheim. In the north, too, the Allied armies were pushing forward.

Eisenhower had agreed to another press conference in Paris on March 27, and he opened it by saying that the Allies had "reached the end of one phase of this campaign and we are entering upon another. The Rhine has been symbolic not only in Germanic history and song, but it is a definite geographical and military plan which must be taken into consideration when you are trying to advance across it, either way."

He then, understandably and forgivably, spent a good deal of time reminding everybody that even back in England he had said that the Germans must be fought west of the Rhine. He reminded his listeners that there had been great opposition to that—he didn't identify the opponents—but he had followed through on his belief, and it had proved right. The German forces had been destroyed west of the Rhine. No, the war wasn't over. "No one knows what the German can do within his own country and it's certain that he's trying to do everything he possibly can. . . . [But] . . . he's not in the position today to do what he could have if the great victories this Allied force has achieved had not been so achieved."

A reporter asked, "Who do you think will be into Berlin first, the Russians or us?" Eisenhower said, "Well, I think mileage alone ought to make them do it. After all, they are thirty-three miles [away] and we are two hundred and fifty. I wouldn't want to make any prediction. They have a shorter race to run, although they are faced by the bulk of the German forces." Later he said, in *Crusade*, "When we stood on the Rhine in the last week of March we were three hundred miles from Berlin, with the obstacle of the Elbe still two hundred miles to our front. . . . It was desirable to thrust our spearheads rapidly across Germany to a junction with the Red forces, thus to divide the country and effectually prevent any possibility of German forces acting as a unit." It was also necessary to take the town of Lübeck so that all German troops in Denmark and Norway would be cut off, at the same time capturing Hamburg or Bremen or both. Control of the northern ports would shorten the Allied lines of supply.

Those were visible, understandable objectives for the Allies; a third, according to Eisenhower, "equally important" objective was not—to penetrate and destroy "the so-called 'National Redoubt.' . . . If the German was permitted to establish the Redoubt he might possibly force us to engage in a long-drawn-out guerrilla type of warfare, or a costly siege," Eisenhower said. "Thus he could keep alive his desperate hope that through disagreement among the Allies he might be able to secure terms more favorable than those of unconditional surrender. The evidence was clear that the Nazi intended to make the attempt and I decided to give him no opportunity to carry it out."

The Nazi had no such intention. The Redoubt, or *Die Alpenfestung*, as it was called in secret information gathered from various sources, was a combination of German hoax and American invention, and while it in no way affected the outcome of the war, it did influence Allied strategy in 1945.

As late as April 25 a correspondent of the *New York Times* who was with United States Third Army in Bavaria reported, "Adolf Hitler has chosen to make his last stand in the most formidable mountain region of Europe—a natural bastion 20 miles wide and 80 miles deep. The nucleus of the defending forces, it was learned, will be the elite Schutzstaffel, or SS troops, who came into being as Hitler's bodyguard and probably will end their days in the same capacity."

True, Hitler had planned to leave Berlin on April 20 for the Alpine retreat in Berchtesgaden; he had already sent his household staff there to get the villa, the Berghof, ready for him. Most of the ministerial offices had been evacuated to the south, but on April 25 Hitler was in a bunker in Berlin, a city that the Russians that day had encircled.

The *Times* correspondent in Bavaria believed that the Germans had in the so-called National Redoubt on April 25 enough supplies to last for six months. "Allied experience in Italy had already proved that fighting in mountain areas was costly, at times close to impossible," he wrote.

What was or was not in *Die Alpenfestung* (the Alpine fortress) had been a matter of concern to SHAEF ever since September 1944 when Eisenhower had assured Montgomery that the Allies "should concentrate all our energies and resources on a rapid thrust to Berlin." SHAEF's German sources had said that as many as a quarter of a million select German troops would be able to hold out in the area not for six months but for years. The British never paid much attention to those reports; the official history of the war said, "for Hitler the notion of a 'redoubt' was no more than a momentary idea that passed through his mind, only to vanish again immediately afterwards."

SHAEF, on the other hand, was fascinated by the reports, and in Strong's headquarters was a map of more than 20,000 mountainous acres of land south of Munich where the Redoubt was said to be. Strong said, "My own expressed view . . . was that it might not be there, but that we nevertheless had to take steps to prevent it being established. After the Ardennes, I was taking no more chances with the Germans. It was always possible that some such scheme might be regarded seriously by fanatical Nazis who could not bring themselves to accept the reality of the liquidation of the Third Reich. Eisenhower shared the skepticism, but he agreed that the stories could not be ignored and therefore took full account of the possibilities in his planning."

A report from SHAEF intelligence early in March had said that the mountain crags in the area were "practically impenetrable." It ominously added, "Here, defended by nature and by the most efficient secret weapons yet invented, the powers that have hitherto guided Germany will survive to reorganize her resurrection; here armaments will be manufactured in bombproof factories; food and equipment will be stored in vast underground caverns and a specially selected corps of young men will be trained in guerrilla warfare, so that a whole underground army can be fitted and directed to liberate Germany from the occupying forces."

Another frightening if unverifiable intelligence report at the time was that every week three to five "very long trains" went to *Die Alpenfestung*. On one such train was said to be "a new type of gun," and the report said that underground aircraft plants were being built in the area that could and would turn out Messerschmitts.

William L. Shirer later said of the Redoubt rumors: "It would seem as though the Allied Supreme Commander's intelligence staff had been infiltrated by British and American mystery writers." Bedell Smith was among the most credulous. He said in his postwar book, "After the Ruhr was taken, we were convinced there would be no surrender at all, so long as Hitler lived. Our feeling then was that we should be forced to destroy the remnants of the German army piece by piece, with the final possibility of a prolonged campaign in the rugged Alpine region of western Austria known as the National Redoubt. This we knew was the intent of mad Hitlerism. Even while the Ruhr fighting continued, photographs of the Redoubt area were building up evidence of new dugouts, extensive trenches, bunkers, and gun positions. Existing ditches and canals were being extended to form antitank obstacles. . . . There was every reason to believe that the Nazis intended to make their last stand among the crags."

When American troops arrived in the area south of Munich, they found no extensive entrenchment. True, there were, as the *Times* reporter had said on April 25, "outer defenses" that consisted "of road blocks, mines and scattered self-propelled guns." But the correspondent had also said that "the Germans have not had time to set up an adequate defense and are concentrating on the inner circle." There was no inner circle.

Even Bradley was taken in by the rumors. He said in *A Soldier's Story*, "G-2 had tipped us off to a fantastic enemy plot for the withdrawal of troops into the Austrian Alps where weapons, stores, and even aircraft plants were reported cached for a last-ditch holdout. There the enemy would presumably attempt to keep alive the Nazi myth until the Allies grew tired of occupying the Reich—or until they fell out among themselves. . . . It was this obsession with the Redoubt that accounted for my gloomy caution on the probable end of the war in Europe. As late as April 24 . . . I took a party of Congressmen who had been invited by Eisenhower to view the enemy's death camp [Buchenwald] . . . [I said] that 'we may be fighting one month from now and it may even be a year.' When a few of them looked alarmed, I told them of our apprehensions on a lingering campaign in the Redoubt."

On April 23, two days before Bradley told the visiting congressmen that the war in Europe might last another year, Lieutenant General Kurt Dittmar, the fifty-seven-year-old officer who every night broadast the latest communiqués from the front and was known as the "voice of the German high command," crossed the Elbe and surrendered to the U.S. 30th Infantry Division. Hitler was not in *Die Alpenfestung*, he said. When Dittmar was asked about the Redoubt, he said all that he knew was that he had read about it in a Swiss newspaper the previous winter. True, there were pockets of resistance in the north "including Norway and Denmark, and one in the south in the Italian Alps. . . . less by intention than by force of circumstance." But a great underground fortress in the Austrian Alps? That was nonsense. "That National Redoubt? It's a romantic dream. It's a myth," said Dittmar.

Bradley said, "Not until after the campaign ended were we to learn that the Redoubt consisted largely in the imaginations of a few fanatic Nazis. It grew into so exaggerated a scheme that I am astonished we could have believed it as innocently as we did."

Beetle was less forthright about having been taken in. He said in his 1956 book that at the beginning of May "our forces stormed into the National Redoubt, infantry leading armor through this difficult terrain. Whatever the Nazi plans had been for fanatical, last-ditch resistance in this area, they were frustrated by our swift advance."

The recollections of the supreme commander were no more candid. In *Crusade* he said, "The XXI and VI Corps of the Seventh Army crossed the Danube April 22 and advanced steadily toward the National Redoubt. On May 5 Innsbruck was taken, and the 103rd Division of the VI Corps pushed on into the Brenner Pass," where they met up with Mark Clark's Fifth Army troops advancing from Italy. Said Eisenhower, "My prediction of a year and a half before that I would meet the soldiers of the Mediterranean command 'in the heart of the enemy homeland' was fulfilled."

But whatever happened to those great factories in the Redoubt that could turn out Messerschmitts?

I sent a reporter to cover the battle of the National Redoubt for the Paris edition of *Yank* Magazine. He returned not long after the war ended, empty-handed. "There was nothing there but a lot of dark, deserted caves," he said. Since there had been dozens of stories in *Stars and Stripes* about the fearsome wonders said to be in those caves, I said, "*That's* the story."

Still, Bradley, a facer of facts, said, "However mistaken our estimate of the Redoubt might have been, this in itself was secondary in our rejection of Churchill's proposal to push on to the Baltic and Berlin."

When Eisenhower, driven by Kay, got back to Rheims on March 28, after the Paris press conference, he found a number of "For Eisenhower's Eyes Only" messages waiting for him. One was from Monty:

> Today I issued orders to Army commanders for the operations about to begin. . . . My intention is to drive hard for the Elbe using the [US] Ninth and [British] Second armies. The right of the Ninth Army will be directed on Magdeburg and the left on Hamburg. . . .
>
> I have ordered Ninth and Second armies to move their armoured and mobile divisions forwards at once to get through to the Elbe with all possible speed and drive.
>
> My Tac HQ moves to the northeast of Bonninghardt on Thursday, 29 March. Thereafter my HQ will move to Wesel, Münster, Wiedenbrück, Herford, Hanover—then by Autobahn to Berlin, I hope.

The field marshal had sent a copy of the message to Brooke, who found nothing in it to criticize. He said in his diary, "He [Monty] is planning a bold drive to the Elbe with most of his armour, and, judging by the general situation, he has every chance of bringing it off."

The fact that Eisenhower might be infuriated at the message seems not to have occurred to either Monty or Brooke. The field marshal was, after all, in a euphoric mood. His troops were advancing rapidly, with relatively light casualties, and to him Berlin was a "priority objective." Churchill had persuaded him that the city would play an important part in the peace—if the Allies got there before the Russians.

Eisenhower did not agree. Just when he decided he did not agree is not known; the subject is one about which he was afterward evasive and, if not untruthful, at least disingenuous. He said in *Crusade*, "A natural objective beyond the Ruhr was Berlin. It was politically and psychologically important as the symbol of remaining German power. I decided, however, that it was not the logical or the most desirable objective for the forces of the Western Allies. When we stood on the Rhine in the last week of March we were three hundred miles from Berlin. . . . The Russian forces were firmly established on the Oder with a bridgehead on its western bank only thirty miles from Berlin." In the first place, the Russians would "in all probability . . . be around the city long before we could reach there." In the second, a drive eastward by the Western Allies for the purpose of taking the city "would have meant the practical immobilization of units along the front. This I felt to be more than unwise; it was stupid. There were several other major purposes, beyond the encirclement of the Ruhr, to be accomplished quickly."

Monty's message wrongly assumed that he was to continue to have the U.S. Ninth Army under his control, and that he would be ordered by the supreme commander to lead the troops under his command to take Berlin. SHAEF Deputy G-3 Whiteley said, "Monty wanted to ride into Berlin on a white horse wearing two hats." Ike and Brad were not about to let that happen. General Sir Frederick Morgan, who had had so much to do with the early planning for OVERLORD and was now deputy to Beetle, said, "At that moment Monty was the last person Ike would have chosen for a drive on Berlin."

Eisenhower much later said of that period during the war, "Montgomery had become so personal in his efforts to make sure that the Americans—and me, in particular—got no credit, that, in fact, we hardly had anything to do with the war, that I finally stopped talking to him."

Monty was probably not uppermost in Eisenhower's mind the day he decided not to take Berlin, but neither can he have been absent. The Russians on the other hand were much on his mind that day. There was a message from Marshall as well as the one from Monty. The former, while not dealing with Berlin, did suggest a way of thinking about Allied strategy for the final weeks of the war. The chief of staff said:

From the current operations report, it looks like the German defense system in the west may break up. This would permit you to move a considerable number of divisions rapidly eastwards on a broad front. What are your views on . . . pushing U.S. forces rapidly on, say, the Nürnberg– or the Karlsruhe–Munich axis? The idea behind this is that . . . rapid action might prevent the formation of any organized resistance areas. The mountainous country in the south is considered a possibility for one of these.

The fact that organized resistance in "the mountainous country in the south" was considered seriously by Marshall and his suggesting the necessity for "rapid action" surely had something to do with Eisenhower's decision about Berlin. Marshall had gone on to say:

One of the problems which arises with disintegrating German resistance is that of meeting the Russians. What are your ideas on control and coordination to prevent unfortunate instances . . . ? One possibility is an agreed line of demarcation. The arrangements we now have . . . appear inadequate . . . steps should be initiated without delay to provide for communications and liaison.

Eisenhower took care of communications and liaison with the Russians immediately—though he had undoubtedly given the matter much prior throught. He acted on his own, without consulting any of the British, including his own deputy, Tedder, who was as surprised as everyone else. A great deal has been written about Eisenhower's message to Stalin on March 28, much of it making it seem that Eisenhower acted precipitously. On the contrary, it seems that almost everything that happened in early 1945 made the message, from Eisenhower's point of view, almost inevitable, certainly not too surprising. It was addressed to the Allied Military Mission in Moscow; the supreme commander asked its two members, John R. Deane and Ernest Archer, to "transmit a personal message from me to Marshal Stalin, and do anything you can to assist in getting a full reply."

In this first message to Stalin, Eisenhower said:

1. My immediate operations are designed to encircle and destroy the enemy forces depending the Ruhr, and to isolate that area from the rest of Germany. This will be accomplished by developing offensives around the north of the Ruhr and from Frankfurt through Kassel, until the ring is closed. The enemy enclosed in this ring will then be mopped up.

That operation, he added, would be over by the end of April "or even earlier." After that his job would be to "divide the enemy's remaining forces by joining hands with your forces."

For my forces the best axis on which to effect this junction would be Erfurt–Leipzig–Dresden; moreover, I believe, this is the area to which the main governmental departments are being moved. It is along this axis that I propose to place my main effort.

He then said that "before deciding firmly on my future plans" they should be coordinated with Stalin's. The liaison between the forces under his command and those under Stalin's must be perfected. "I am prepared to send officers to you for this purpose." Berlin was not mentioned.

Brooke immediately recognized the importance of the message, and it alarmed and angered him. The next day he said in his diary:

March 29th: A very long C.O.S. meeting with a series of annoying telegrams. The worst of all was one from Eisenhower direct to Stalin trying to coordinate his offensive with the Russians. To start with, he has no business to address Stalin direct, his communications should be through the Combined Chiefs of Staff; secondly, he produced a telegram which was unintelligible; and finally, what was implied in it appeared to be entirely adrift and a change from all that had been previously agreed on.

At 5:15 P.M. we were sent for by the P.M. to discuss Ike's telegram to Stalin, and our proposed action.

Meanwhile, Eisenhower had sent a second, "amplifying," cable to Moscow. Roosevelt that Easter weekend was going to Warm Springs, Georgia—he arrived on the 30th, Good Friday—and knew nothing about Eisenhower's cables to Stalin. Churchill was going to Chequers, but he read the cables before he left, and he was furious. Eisenhower, the agreeable American, the cooperative Allied commander, had done something without discussing the matter with him.

The prime minister knew that his old friend Roosevelt was not well and that he might have to handle this delicate matter without the president's help. He knew, too, that the U.S. Chiefs of Staff, dominated by Marshall, likely would be on the side of the supreme commander.

Later in the afternoon of the 28th Eisenhower had done something that upset the British even more. He had sent a reply to Monty, removing the Ninth Army from his command, thereby making impossible a 21st Army Group drive to Berlin. The next day very similar messages of confirmation were sent to Bradley and Devers.

The message to Monty said:

I agree in general with your plans up to the point of gaining contact with Bradley east of the Ruhr. However, thereafter my present plans are being coordinated with Stalin, as are outlined in following paragraphs.

As soon as you have joined hands with Bradley in this Kassel-Paderborn area, Ninth United States Army will revert to Bradley's command. Bradley will be responsible for mopping up and occupying the Ruhr and with the minimum delay will deliver his main thrust on the axis Erfurt-Leipzig-Dresden to join hands with the Russians.

The mission of your army group will be to protect Bradley's northern flank. . . . When your forces reach the Elbe, it may again be desirable for Ninth Army to revert to your operational control to facilitate the crossing of that obstacle. If so necessary orders will then be issued.

Devers will protect Bradley's right flank and be prepared later when the situation permits to advance to join hands with the Russians in the Danube Valley.

As you say, the situation looks good.

This situation did not look good to Monty at all or to Brooke or to the prime minister. In a message to General Ismay, his chief of staff, Churchill said:

It seems to me that the chief criticism of the new Eisenhower plan is that it shifts the axis of the main advance upon Berlin to the direction through Leipzig to Dresden, and thus raises the question of whether the Twenty-First Army Group will not be so stretched as to lose its offensive power, especially after it has been deprived of the Ninth United States Army. Thus we might be condemned to be an almost static role in the north and virtually prevented from crossing the Elbe until an altogether later stage in the operation has been reached. All prospect also of the British entering Berlin with the Americans is ruled out.

The 28th had been a very long day for Eisenhower; that morning he had come all the way from Paris to Rheims; he had had lunch with Bradley, and he had sent messages of some importance to the war and to the postwar world to Stalin and to Montgomery. Before retiring that night, he sent a cable to Marshall reporting that he had indeed communicated with the Russians and that a copy of the message to Stalin had been sent to the Combined Chiefs. As for coordinating Allied forces with those of the Russians, "I am still trying to do everything possible to perfect our liaison arrangements. . . . I do not think we can tie ourselves down to the suggestion that when our forces meet, either side will withdraw to its own occupational zone at the request of the opposite side."

Stalin, when he replied to Eisenhower's message, said, "Your plan to cut [off] the German forces by joining . . . [with] Soviet Forces entirely coincides with the plan of the Soviet High Command." The generalissimo then answered a question nobody had asked: "Berlin has lost its former strategic importance. . . . the Soviet High Command therefore plans to allot secondary forces in the direction of Berlin." That last was not quite true. The Russian forces that Stalin had assigned to take Berlin were under the command of Marshal Zhukov, three times proclaimed a Hero of the Soviet Union.

Kay remembered that the Allies had taken an average of ten thousand prisoners a day during March, "apart from heavy [German] losses in dead and wounded." She added, however, "I found the last day of March more noteworthy on the personal front because General Ike was already in the office, stern-faced and silently chastising, when we all showed up that morning."

That Easter Saturday, the 31st, Marshall told Eisenhower that the British Chiefs were apprehensive over his "implied change of plan" in transferring command of General William Simpson's Ninth Army from Montgomery to Bradley. They were most upset because it looked as if the Allied forces would make their most important move toward Leipzig, rather than north to Berlin. In his "immediate answer" Eisenhower said that there had been no change of plan. "Now that I can foresee the time my forces can be concentrated in the Kassel area I am still adhering to my old plan of launching from there one main attack calculated to accomplish, in conjunction with the Russians, the destruction of the enemy armed forces."

Later in the day, Kay made notes on a conversation between the supreme commander and the prime minister on the scrambler phone. Churchill, according to the notes, "does not agree with E. [on] future operation plans . . . he wants to keep a large force under Monty." The prime minister had said that, if Eisenhower was going to take forces from Montgomery, "I pray you not to do so until we reach Elbe, as such action would not help the great movement which is just beginning to develop."

Eisenhower in his reply said essentially what he had said to Stalin on the 28th, adding that if Montgomery in doing what he was assigned to do needed help "I propose to increase his forces." He added, "I trust this added information will make clear my present plans. Naturally, they are flexible and subject to changes to meet unexpected situations."

Eisenhower had now caused his most powerful friend in England to doubt his judgment, a situation that no doubt worried The Great Coordinator.

Churchill that day composed a message to the British Chiefs that was considerably less lofty in tone than the ones he was sending the Americans. He said he agreed with them in their disapproval of what Eisenhower had done but added, "we have only a quarter of the forces invading Germany and . . . the situation has . . . changed remarkably from the days of June 1944. . . . In short,

I see argumentative possibilities being opened to the United States Chiefs of Staff by our telegram, on which they will riposte heavily."

The U.S. Chiefs of Staff did exactly that, supporting Eisenhower. They said "the battle of Germany is now at the point where the Commander in the field is the best judge of the measures which offer the earliest prospect of depriving the German armies of their power to resist. . . . General Eisenhower should continue to be free to communicate with the Commander-in-Chief of the Soviet Army. . . . The single objective should be quick and complete victory." They added mildly that sending additional details of Allied plans to Moscow should be held up and that the supreme commander should give the Combined Chiefs more details on his plans for the future.

Eisenhower later said, "So earnestly did I believe in the military soundness of what we were doing that my inmates on the staff knew I was prepared to make an issue of it." Later in the day the supreme commander sent Montgomery a message "in further explanation of our recent exchange of telegrams reference future plans." He said, "My plan is simple and aims at dividing and destroying the German forces and joining hands with the Red Army."

He told Montgomery that "the bulk of my disposable strength" was to be used, first, to "attain our Leipzig objective." With that accomplished, those forces would move to the north "to seize the important naval, political, and shipping objectives across the Elbe or to the south to destroy any effective concentration of forces which the enemy may succeed in creating."

The south meant the Redoubt again. But, most important, lest the field marshal misunderstand, were the words: "I must adhere to my decision about Ninth Army passing to Bradley's command. . . . As I have already told you, it appears from this distance that an American command will again pass to you at a later stage for operations beyond the Elbe. You will note that in none of this do I mention Berlin. That place has become, as far as I am concerned, nothing but a geographical location, and I have never been interested in these. My purpose is to destroy the enemy's forces."

Holy Saturday was a big day for message-writing; Churchill, who was at Chequers, in addition to his message to the British Chiefs composed one to Eisenhower, in which he said that

the Ninth U.S. Army should march with the 21st Army Group to the Elbe and beyond to Berlin. . . . Why should we not cross the Elbe and advance as far eastward as possible? . . . I do not consider that Berlin has lost its military and certainly not its political significance. . . . The idea that the capture of Dresden and the juncture with the Russians there would be a superior gain does not commend itself to me. . . . Whilst Berlin remains under the German flag, it cannot in my opinion fail to be the most decisive point in Germany.

There were many other exchanges in the days that followed, largely repetitious, but Churchill appeared to end the discussion on April 6 by sending a message saying that he considered the whole matter closed. "To prove my sincerity," he said, "I will use one of my very few Latin quotations: *Amantium irae amoris integratio est.*" It meant, at least the War Department said it meant, "Lovers' quarrels are a renewal of love."

Brooke was less reconciled, but on April 1, Easter Sunday, he did say in his diary,

> Now that Ike has explained his plans it is quite clear that there is no very great change except for the fact that he directs his main axis of advance on Leipzig instead of Berlin. He also transfers the Ninth U.S. Army back to Bradley as soon as the Ruhr is surrounded and delays further advances whilst sweeping up this place. Most of the changes are due to national aspiration and to ensure that the U.S. effort will not be lost under British command. It is all a pity and straightforward strategy is being affected by the nationalistic outlook of allies. But, as Winston says, "there is only one thing worse than fighting with Allies, and that is fighting without them!"

On April 7, in what he called "my final radio on the subject to General Marshall," Eisenhower said that "it did not cross my mind to confer with the Combined Chiefs of Staff because I have assumed that I am held responsible for the effectiveness of military operations in this theater and it was a natural question to the head of the Russian forces to inquire as to the direction and timing of their next major thrust, and to outline my own intentions."

On April 4 the Ninth Army was returned to Bradley, and Simpson, who hadn't been told otherwise, decided that his troops would get to Berlin first. On April 9 some units of the Ninth went to Essen and reached the infamous Krupp armaments factories. The Ruhr pocket grew smaller every day.

On the 11th the First Army neared Leipzig, and the Ninth drove north of the Harz Mountains to the Elbe near Magdeburg. According to Bradley, five German divisions had withdrawn into the mountains for a siege. "At 8 P.M. on the evening of D plus 309," according to Bradley, a part of the 2nd Armoured Division had "closed to the banks of the Elbe. I had previously ordered Simpson to snatch a small bridgehead across the Elbe just as soon as he reached its bank. This was not in preparation for an advance on Berlin, as some observers immediately surmised, but only to establish a threat that might draw off German resistance from east of Berlin in front of the Russians."

It probably would have been possible to push on to Berlin, Bradley added, "had we been willing to take the casualties Berlin would have cost us." At that time the western forces were just about as close to Berlin as the Russians, but, Bradley said, "Zhukov's eastern approaches were infinitely more negotiable than the waterlogged path that confronted us in the west." In any case, Simpson was to be summoned by Bradley on the 15th and given a direct order from Eisenhower that the Ninth must stop where they were on the Elbe.

On the 12th Eisenhower flew to Wiesbaden where Bradley had his tactical headquarters, and the next day they flew to Hershfeld where Patton had his CIP. Looking down from the Cub as it flew low over the Autobahn, the two members of the West Point class of 1915 saw what must have been a satisfying sight. The two broad lanes of the highway were crowded with Allied soldiers, mostly Americans, and their vehicles on the way to the front. In the grassy divider between the two lanes of the highway were thousands of German refugees trudging to the rear. Patton met Ike and Bradley at an airport near Hershfeld and a little later took them to a salt mine containing a sizable part of the German gold reserve, much of it stolen from occupied countries.

Eisenhower had earlier told Marshall that a finance officer of the Third Army had seen what he estimated to be $250 million in gold bullion as well as over two thousand crates filled with "objects of fine art." He said, "Treasure is being moved to bank vaults in Frankfurt where it will be inventoried and held under my control and carefully guarded." When the supreme commander returned to Paris, he told Butcher about what Patton had shown him. Butcher wrote in his diary, "I reminded him that once at Gibraltar he and Wayne [Mark] Clark had talked of absconding with American expense money if TORCH proved unsuccessful. He said that there was plenty of expense money in the German cache, but the gold bars were too heavy to carry. He knew. He'd tried to lift one."

After inspecting the Nazi plunder, Eisenhower saw his first concentration camp, Ohrdruf, just outside the town of Gotha. "I have never been able to describe my emotional reactions when I came face to face with indisputable evidence of Nazi brutality and ruthless disregard of every shred of decency," said Eisenhower. "Up to that time I had known about it only generally or through secondary sources. I am certain, however, that I have never at any other time experienced an equal sense of shock. . . .

"I visited every nook and cranny of the camp because I felt it my duty to be in a position from then on to testify at first hand about these things in case there ever grew up at home the belief or assumption that 'the stories of Nazi brutality were just propaganda.' Some members of the visiting party were unable to go through the ordeal. I did so but as soon as I returned to Patton's headquarters that evening I sent communications to both Washington and London urging the two governments to send instantly to Germany a random group of newspaper editors and representative groups from the national legislatures. I felt that the evidence should be immediately placed before the American and British publics in a way that would leave no room for cynical doubt."

There can be no doubt that Eisenhower "visited every nook and cranny" of Ohrdruf. He was a man of insatiable curiosity, and he certainly would not have failed to find out, firsthand, everything he could about the camp that had given him the worst shock of his life. It is unusual, though, that he should have foreseen that an alarming number of Americans would say, in fact are still saying, that the concentration camps never existed, that they were "just propaganda."

Major General Hobart R. "Hap" Gay, who was with the party, said that as the members were waiting for transportation back to Third Army headquarters, an enlisted man bumped into one of the camp guards, and," said Gay, "from sheer nerves began to giggle.

"General Eisenhower fixed him with a cold eye and when he spoke, each word was like the drop of an icicle.

" 'Still having trouble hating them?' he said."

A few minutes later he told the others in the party, "I want every American unit not actually in the front line to see this place. We are told that the American soldier does not know wh at he is fighting for. Now, at least, he will know what he is fighting *against*."

In his report to Marshall, Eisenhower said that he had talked with three men "who had been inmates and through one ruse or another had made their escape." What they said combined with what he saw of "starvation, cruelty and bestiality were so overpowering as to leave me a bit sick," he said. "In one room . . . were piled about twenty or thirty naked men, killed by starvation. George Patton would not even enter. He said he would get sick if he did so."

Typically, Eisenhower embraced firsthand evidence of what the war was about. Patton never really understood it. To him wars were good things that a real man had to take part in—and enjoy. By fall of that year Patton was able to say, "The Nazi thing is just like a Democrat-Republican election fight." When some people protested, Georgie said that the uproar had been created by reporters who had nothing better to do than to "accuse me of being either pro-Fascist, pro-Republican, or pro-Communist, according to their desires."

In Warm Springs, on the morning of the 12th, Roosevelt read the *Atlanta Constitution*. Because of bad weather the papers from Washington had not yet arrived. The president saw that some of the troops were 115 miles from the Russians and 57 miles from Berlin. The war in Europe, which he had done so much to help win, was nearly over. At a little after 1:00 P.M. that day, Roosevelt complained of a "terrific headache"; at 3:35 he was pronounced dead.

That evening Eisenhower and Bradley returned to Patton's headquarters and had what Patton called a very pleasant evening. According to Gay, who was present, Eisenhower said that from a tactical point of view "it was highly inadvisable to take Berlin and he hoped political influence would not cause him to take the city. It had no tactical or strategic value, and would place upon American forces the burden for caring for thousands and thousands of Germans, displaced persons, Allied prisoners of war, etc." According to Gay, Patton said, "Ike, I don't see how you figure that one. We had better take Berlin and quick, and [then go eastward] on to the Oder [River]."

The three men went to bed around midnight. Patton, whose watch had stopped, turned on his radio to get the time. He said in his diary, "Just as I turned it on, the announcer reported the death of the President." He immediately told Eisenhower and Bradley. Patton said, "We had quite a discussion as to what might happen. It seems very unfortunate that in order to secure political preference, people are made Vice Presidents who were never intended, neither by Party nor by the Lord to be Presidents."

In remembering that night, Eisenhower said, "We pondered over the effect the President's death might have upon the future peace. We were certain that there would be no interference with the tempo of the war because we already knew some of the great measures afoot in the Pacific to accomplish the smashing of the Japanese. . . . None of us had known the president very well. I had, through various conferences, seen more of him than the others, but it seemed to me, from the international viewpoint, to be a most critical time to change national leaders. We went to bed depressed and sad."

The next morning when Mickey came to Eisenhower's room he saw that Roosevelt's death had come as a great shock to him. "There wasn't much to say about it," said Mickey. "He said the country had suffered a terrible loss." Harry Hopkins wrote Eisenhower that day, saying, "The President, as you must know, was devoted to you and had the utmost confidence that you could lead our armies to the sure victory. It must have been a great satisfaction to know the tyranny of Hitler was on the verge of defeat by your gallant armies."

That previous day Buchenwald, just outside Weimar, where the German Republic had been born, had been liberated by Allied forces. When he heard the news of the president's death, the American officer in charge announced that there would be a parade and memorial service for the dead Roosevelt. Of the 20,000 surviving prisoners 5,000 were able to lurch, stumble, and fall into some kind of order, and a lieutenant from Tennessee asked for the immediate surrender of all arms taken from the Nazis. He said that all thoughts of vengeance should be put aside. And he suggested that the prisoners shake hands with their guards and torturers, "rather," one prisoner said, "like an Olympic game. The winners would shake hands with the losers."

Eisenhower never thought that the war was a game, and when still another concentration camp was liberated on the last day of April he issued a brief and pointed communiqué. "Our forces liberated and mopped up the infamous concentration camp at Dachau. Approximately 32,000 prisoners were liberated; 300 S.S. guards were quickly neutralized."

Later on the 13th, Eisenhower went to First Army headquarters at Marburg where he met with Hodges and, to his great surprise, his son John. John had learned about Roosevelt's death at mess that morning. John was on duty at V Corps' command post at near Weissenfels. He said when he heard of Roosevelt's death, "I, like many others, experienced a sinking feeling, for although I had not been brought up to admire President Roosevelt, I felt the loss of a man who on any count had to be considered a great war leader."

Shortly afterwards John was summoned to First Army headquarters. His father was there and wanted to see him, he was told. "For all I knew Dad wanted me for something important. . . . I wondered if Truman was calling Dad back to be Chief of Staff of the Army, only to let someone else finish the job of conquering Germany," John said.

Eisenhower was not at Marburg when John got there, and a little later when the general arrived, he said to his son, "Well, what the hell are you doing here?"

"I was told to come here," John answered. "Someone gave me orders and sent me back by L-5 [liaison plane]."

The supreme commander, clearly not overjoyed, said that he had simply said that his son was probably somewhere in the vicinity. That had been interpreted as an order to get his son. John said, "Such mishaps, I later learned, are fairly frequent occurrences anywhere near the seat of power."

Eisenhower had just sent his condolences to Mrs. Roosevelt, and that night he, John, Bradley, and Hodges sat around talking for a while. "The thing most on his mind was the horror camp near Gotha," said John.

When discussing the Ohrdruf camp Eisenhower said, "The only spark of optimism I can see is that I really don't think the bulk of the Germans knew what was going on. When I saw that camp yesterday I ordered the mayor of Gotha to turn out the townspeople and make them clean up the mess. Last night he and his wife went home and hanged themselves. Maybe there's some hope after all."

Early the next morning John returned to his outfit.

On the night of April 12 units of the Ninth Army had crossed the Elbe near Magdeburg. On the 13th a bridgehead farther south was established. On the 14th the Germans drove the Americans back from the northern position, but the 83rd Division, which had crossed to the south, after repelling a counterattack, fought their way to the outskirts of Potsdam, about fifty miles from Berlin, before they were ordered to go no farther. That day, the 14th, the U.S. First and Ninth armies linked up in the Ruhr, splitting the pocket in two. Then, as Beetle put it, "on April 15, the defense simply fell apart."

The whole campaign had been planned back at Bushy Park in May 1944. Eisenhower and his staff had then decided that the Ruhr was the most important objective in Germany. The plan involved a double envelopment of the Ruhr, ending with the destruction of the German army within. The whole thing worked out just about as it had been envisioned, so much so that Beetle said, "I doubt that there had ever been a campaign in history where actual operations fitted so closely the initial plan of a commander, adopted so far in advance. Long before we set foot in Europe and tested the enemy's strength in battle, we had decided on the blueprint for his defeat."

Perhaps the fact that there was a new president in the White House encouraged Churchill, in mid-April, to have one last try at changing the strategy on Berlin. In any case, the British decided, despite the fact that the Ninth Army was now under American command, that Simpson, who very much wanted to do it, should be allowed to go to Berlin. Eisenhower did not agree. There was no guarantee that the Ninth Army could get to the German capital before the Russians, and he saw no reason for trying. The Redoubt still had to be conquered, and so did Lübeck. He told Marshall on the 15th, "I deem both of these to be vastly more important than the capture of Berlin—anyway, to plan for making an immediate effort against Berlin would be foolish in view of the relative situation of the Russians and ourselves at the moment. We'd get all coiled up for something that in all probability would never come off."

On the morning of the 17th Ike flew to London with Butcher, Gault, and Kay to discuss that and other matters with the prime minister. At dinner at No. 10 that night, he and the prime discussed arrangements that should be made with the Russians before each of the four powers (including the French) withdrew into their own occupation areas.

Kay and the general and Butcher spent the night at Telegraph Cottage. The supreme commander met with Churchill again the next morning, and, according to Butcher, "The Prime Minister walked with General Ike to the car. They were as homey as neighbors on adjoining Iowa farms. . . . Ike has grown very fond of Churchill and, although they occasionally differ on military questions, they are the best of friends."

Churchill finally cabled his last word in the matter to Foreign Secretary Anthony Eden in Washington:

> It would seem that the western Allies are not immediately in a position to force their way into Berlin. The Russians have two and a half million troops opposite that city. The Americans have only their spearheads . . . covering an immense front and at many points engaged with the Germans.

In fact the prime minister's estimate of the Russian strength—perhaps he got it from Eisenhower—gave Russia twice as many troops as she actually had "opposite" Berlin, but did that really matter?

Churchill could and did sway thousands of people, millions when he used the radio, as an orator; except on rare occasions, Eisenhower was not notable as a public speaker. But on a one-to-one basis and with small groups, he was, as his old friend Al Gruenther said, "irresistible." It had taken a long time, but the supreme commander had finally persuaded the prime minister to come round to his way of thinking.

Following Eisenhower's return from London, events moved rapidly. He later said, "The war was won before the Rhine was crossed. The enemy played into our hands by his insistence upon fighting the battle where he stood." As to why the Germans kept on fighting after that, Ike commented, "I have searched and searched to find their reason for prolonging the agony." He finally decided there were two reasons: Hitler, with his determination to stay on, and the "one hope" that the Allies would split apart. "They had that desperate hope, unquestionably. Otherwise there was no sense in taking the last month of pounding."

On April 25, the historic junction of the Russian and United States armies took place on the Elbe River, near the town of Torgau. Eisenhower had taken great care to see to it that there would be no mishap when the Russians and the Western Allied forces met. The Russians were, appropriately, to fire red rockets as the two armies came together. The Western Allies would identify themselves by firing green rockets. The U.S.-U.K. patrols, moreover, were not to go more than five miles beyond the Elbe and the Mulde rivers, an order that was widely, almost totally, ignored. It had also been agreed that when the two forces met, news of the event was to be announced simultaneously in London, Washington, and Moscow.

That day Eisenhower had met in Rheims with members of Congress who had flown in from Washington. On the 24th they had visited Buchenwald, along with a number of invited American journalists. The supreme commander told the group, "You saw only one camp yesterday. There are many others. Your responsibilities, I believe, extend into a great field, and informing the people at home of things like these atrocities is one of them. . . . Nothing is covered up. We have nothing to conceal. The barbarous treatment these people received in the German concentration camps is almost unbelievable. I want you to see for yourself and be the spokesmen for the United States."

Butcher noted in his diary, "Ike is showing signs of 'cabin fever, the close association with his staff makes him want to find some fresh faces and topics of conversation other than of the war. He's in swell health and, like the long-distance runner, he is now really hitting his stride in the final stretch run."

The next day, April 26, a patrol from the Third Army crossed the Austrian frontier, and early in May both the Third and the Seventh armies reached Berchtesgaden and the other Alpine crags where Eisenhower and so many others had thought there would be overwhelming German resistance.

Eisenhower was not much for second thoughts, and he never publicly discussed how he felt about the National Redoubt hoax. It surely occurred to him, however, that had he ordered his forces to go to Berlin, and especially to Prague, the postwar world would have been somewhat different. His perfect memory was distressingly imperfect when the subject of Berlin came up after the war. In *Waging Peace,* he wrote of Berlin in 1958, when Khrushchev announced that he was going to sign a "peace treaty" with East Berlin that would end all Allied rights in the city, "I had ample opportunity to think at length on Berlin. I had lived with this problem intermittently for the past thirteen years. Inevitably, despite intimate acquaintance with it, the question kept coming back to me: 'How, or rather why, did the Free World get into this mess? How did we ever accept a situation . . . [that] would likely mean the intitiation of World War III?' "

But on April 27, 1945, Russian, not American, troops controlled three-quarters of the German capital. On the 30th Hitler and his new bride, Eva Braun, died by suicide in the Berlin bunker, and Admiral Karl Dönitz, Hitler's successor, began the delicate job of negotiation, doing what he could to stall the final capitulation to allow as many German soldiers as possible to surrender to the Western Allies, rather than the Russians.

* * *

HIS GREATEST MOMENT

The first week of May saw the war in Europe racing to a climax. On May 2, in the palace of the Bourbon kings at Caserta, the unconditional surrender of the German forces in Italy took place. Ike wrote Mamie, "The front is crumbling rapidly—events march along. And how glad I'll be when it's all over." On the 3rd British forces took Hamburg. On the 4th, Ike issued the following statement:

The German forces on the Western Front have disintegrated. Today what is left of two German armies, surrendered to a single American division— the 102d, commanded by Major General Frank Keating.

In the north the remaining forces in Northwest Germany, Holland, Denmark and the Frisian Islands, including Heligoland, surrendered to Field Marshal Montgomery. In the South Allied troops from this command and from Italy have joined up. On the Czechoslovak border a Panzer division requested the privilege of giving up unconditionally.

Any further losses the Germans incur on this front are due to their failure instantly to quit. They know they are beaten and any hesitation is due to their own stupidity or that of the German Government. On land, sea, and air the Germans are thoroughly whipped. Their only recourse is to surrender.

That same day he wrote what turned out to be his last wartime letter to Mamie. In it he said:

These are trying times. . . . The enemy's armed forces are disintegrating, but in the tangled skein of European politics nothing can be done, except with the utmost care and caution, where the interests of more than one country are involved. . . . Last night I really expected some definite developments and went to bed early in anticipation of being waked up at 1, 2, 3 or 4 A.M. Nothing happened and as a result I was wide awake very early—with nothing decent to read. The Wild Wests I have just now are terrible—I could write better ones, left-handed.

When Montgomery spoke to Ike on the 4th he told him Admiral Dönitz was sending Admiral Hans-Georg von Friedeburg, the new head of the German Navy, to Rheims the following day to arrange for further surrenders. Eisenhower made it quite clear he had no intention of seeing any Germans until after the surrender was signed because of what his son John described as his "hatred of Nazism, inflamed by their useless prolongation of the war."

All day Saturday, the 5th, it rained. *Time*'s Charles Wertenbaker, described the day in Rheims, where Ike had his headquarters: "The gray-frayed clouds hung so low that they seemed to touch the chimneys . . . smoke from locomotives in the railroad yards sped slowly across the street and through the open windows of the École Technique, where Generals Eisenhower and Smith awaited the arrival of the Germans.

"Eisenhower was nervous but controlling his nervousness. He had just made recordings of his V-E Day proclamation, and when he walked back to his office his step was barely quicker than usual, his voice when he stopped to give an order only a little more incisive. . . . It was 3:30 in the afternoon. The Germans were expected at 4:30." A short time after 5:00 a car pulled up to the sidewalk in front of the red schoolhouse and German Admiral von Friedeburg stepped out. He appeared pale and tired. Beetle Smith and Kenneth Strong, whom Ike had delegated to negotiate with von Friedeburg, took him to a room just beyond the War Room. Beetle remembered, "Only the three of us were present. Friedeburg and I did most of the talking, with General Strong as interpreter. . . . Friedeburg's game was to play for time." He insisted he had no authority to sign a general surrender and asked for and was given permission to send a message to Dönitz. In his reply, Dönitz said he was sending Generaloberst Alfred Jodl, Chief of Staff of the German Army, to assist in the negotiations. Beetle brought Ike up to date on events and then, according to Butcher, "as there was nothing further to do, Ike left the building." That night, tired from the day's events, he decided to retire early, only to be awakened by a phone call from Churchill.

During the last three weeks of the war, Churchill called Ike at all hours of the day and night, most often at night. On the day of the actual surrender he telephoned Eisenhower eight times. As tired as Eisenhower was, he would always listen patiently. According to Wertenbaker, "Although Eisenhower's nerves were worn thin by the conflict between the need to enforce unconditional surrender and his eagerness to end the war and save lives, he lost his temper only once. That was with Himmler, not Churchill. When Churchill told him Himmler wanted to surrender to the Western Allies, he said, 'You wrap it up in diplomatic language and tell him to go to hell.' "

The next morning, Butcher said, Ike was "pretty well whipped down from the tension of waiting and interruptions to his sleep caused by the Prime Minister and others telephoning him." That afternoon Jodl arrived at Allied Advance Headquarters, and when he saw Beetle at 6:15 insisted on another forty-eight hours. Eisenhower, by now convinced the Germans were stalling for time, issued an ultimatum to the German delegation. He told Beetle, "You tell them that 48 hours from midnight tonight, I will close my lines on the western front so no more Germans can get through." This proved effective as the delegation agreed to come to the table without further delay. At 2:41 on the morning of the 7th, at a scarred oak table in the War Room, Jodl signed the surrender document before Bedell Smith and other Allied officers.

While waiting for word from the War Room, Ike paced up and down his office, "just as he did when dictating" Kay said. "The atmosphere was electric with his impatience . . . the silence was heavy with the contrast to the bustle in the War Room. It was nearing 3:00 A.M. when Beetle stomped in, half grinning, half grim. The surrender had been signed—officially.

"At the sound of heavy boots nearing the door, I rose from my desk in the same respectful attention I showed to any high-ranking officers. They [the Germans] marched straight by without as much as a glance, exact prototypes of filmland Nazis, sour-faced, glum, erect, and despicable. The whole thing seemed unreal.

"In the inner office, they came to a parade-ground halt, clicked their heels and saluted smartly, with no hint of the Nazi salute." In *Crusade in Europe*, Ike wrote of this scene, "I asked him [Jodl] through the interpreter if he thoroughly understood all provisions of the document he had signed. He answered, '*Ja.*' I said, 'You will, officially and personally, be held responsible if the terms of this surrender are violated, including its provisions for German commanders to appear in Berlin at the moment set by the Russian High Command to accomplish formal surrender to that government. That is all.' "

An Associated Press correspondent described the scene as follows: "General Eisenhower's famous smile was absent. There was a moment of heavy silence. Then General Eisenhower spoke. He was brief and terse as always. His voice was cold and stern. His steel-blue eyes were hard. In a few clipped sentences he made it plain that Germany was a defeated nation and that henceforth all orders to the German people would come from the Allies." Jodl nodded. "General Eisenhower stared silently in dismissal," Kay remembered. "The Germans half-bowed, saluted, did an about-face and marched back past my desk and out of the office. Afterward, General Ike's face stretched into the broadest grin of his career." Then he gathered the SHAEF officers around him, and some photographers took pictures. When all the newsmen had left, Smith said it was time to send a message to the Combined Chiefs. Everyone had a try at drafting an appropriate document. "I tried one myself," Smith later recalled, "and like all my associates, groped for resounding phrases as fitting accolades to the Great Crusade and indicative of our dedication to the great task just completed." Butcher said, "From time to time, we had joked as to the kind of heroic language that the Supreme Commander might use to tell the Combined Chiefs that the surrender had been achieved, 'We have met the enemy and they are ours,' or 'Don't give up the ship, we've just begun to fight.' "

Ike listened quietly to their proposals, he thanked everyone for their efforts, and then dictated the message himself. It read simply, "The mission of this Allied force was fulfilled at 0241, local time, May 7, 1945."

Later that year when Eisenhower was asked what he might term his "greatest moment," he replied:

Certainly my greatest moment should involve some incident in connection with the recent war, since, for millions of us, these years comprised the most dramatic of our experience.

I have tentatively thought of the hours just preceding the attack in North Africa; the critical risks that accompanied . . . the Salerno attack; the confidence and humility I felt in giving the order for the invasion of Europe; the breakthrough at St.-Lô; the complete defeat of the Nazi-counteroffensive; the crossing of the Rhine; the linking of the Russian and Allied forces; the surrender of the enemy forces in Northwest Europe to Field Marshal Montgomery . . . great moments all, but each merely a preliminary climax—to the Unconditional Surrender of all enemy forces . . . on all the Allied fronts in Europe. It was indeed a great moment for me when I dispatched on May 7, 1945, the message to my British and American superiors, in Washington and London, "The mission of this Allied force was fulfilled."

The occasion of the signing called for a bottle of champagne. Everyone "repaired" to Ike's house, Kay said, where "The next two hours or so bore more resemblance to a group sitting around discussing a just-ended bridge game than to people who had just seen the end of a war. There was no gaiety, no joking, no laughing. The Supreme Commander spent most of the time listing those to whom true credit belonged for successful conclusion of the war; there was no gloating; no personal pride, absolutely no buoyancy. Everyone simply seemed weary, indescribably weary."

Eisenhower, in describing how he felt that morning, said, "From Pearl Harbor Sunday until the German capitulation forty-one months later, I had been under all the pressures for which through my entire career I had been preparing myself. The size of the job, and the variety and uniqueness of the pressures, were unexpected, to say the least. No matter how jaunty my air at the conference table, some may have thought me cocksure—I wore a bit thin at times. Like so many other men and women who had been at war physically or emotionally, exhaustion rather than exultation was my first reaction to victory in Europe."

The group broke up as dawn came through the château windows, Kay said, Ike waiting up only long enough to get through on the phone to Bradley. "Brad, I've got good news. Get the word around," he said. Then he issued the final and climactic order of the war in Europe: "Make sure that all firing stops at midnight of the eighth."

Then, according to Butcher, when his nerves were still tense, Ike put himself to sleep reading *Cartridge Carnival*, a western by William Colt MacDonald.

At 11:30 P.M. on May 8, in Berlin, the final surrender document was signed by Field Marshal Keitch. Tedder represented the Western Allies, Marshal Zhukov, the Russians. The war in Europe was over.

For a brief time following the surrender Eisenhower enjoyed the freedom from decision making. It was during this period that he thought with nostalgia of West Point—June would make the thirtieth anniversary of his graduation—and he became excited by the idea of a purely sentimental venture—a short, one-day visit there to attend the graduation exercises. He began immediately to make preparations to gather all his classmates who were in Europe, to return with him for a private celebration. Ike developed such a high-pressure enthusiasm for the project he suggested "that each of my twenty classmates in Europe should send a secret message to his wife, asking her to meet him for a one-day reunion at West Point."

Marshall, however, "knocked the whole scheme into a cocked hat," Eisenhower said, when "he cabled to say that because our troops could not return home for victory parades—the divisions that we could spare from occupation duties in Europe were to be sent to the Pacific—he thought we should bring representative groups from all units—I do not remember how many groups were to go but each was to be made up from all grades, from the youngest recruit to the Commanding General."

Churchill, in the meantime, invited Ike to take part in a formal ceremony in London's ancient Guildhall, on June 12, where he was to be made a Freeman of the City of London. In responding to the invitation, Eisenhower said he sincerely hoped "that arrangements would be such as to avoid over-glorification of my own part in the victories." He said he had, for the past three years, "religiously kept from the public eye those affairs and decisions which necessarily had finally to be the responsibility of one man—myself." The honor he was to receive would require him to deliver a formal address, something he had never done before, although he had, for many years, written speeches for many of his senior officers, including MacArthur's Farewell Speech to the Army.

For over three weeks prior to the ceremony Ike worked on the speech. Butcher remembered there were "drafts and drafts." Ike knew what he wanted to say, but "wondered if he could say it well." Each evening, before he fell asleep, he sat propped up in his bed, yellow pad in hand, and went over the text. Soon he could quote it from memory, but, he said, to "fortify myself before I went to the ceremony . . . I wrote out on a small card the first words of each paragraph."

On the morning of June 12 Eisenhower rode to the Guildhall in an open landau drawn by two high-stepping bays. He was accompanied by Air Chief Marshall Tedder. Five policeman rode abreast on white horses in front and behind the carriage. He came through the old, battered streets, past thousands of Londonders who had been waiting for hours before the ceremonial ride began. He was met at the boundary of the City by the lord mayor and was escorted into London's ancient Guildhall, with its temporary roof and boarded windows, reminders of the Blitz, just as a string orchestra finished playing "My Old Kentucky Home." As he came through the door, past the Grenadier Guards, someone could be heard announcing "The Supreme Commander of the Allied Expeditionary Force!" The crowd rose to its feet, and Eisenhower came down the aisle behind slow-walking officials in fur-trimmed blue. He was bronzed and smiling, his tunic was decorated by six rows of ribbons. On the platform he sat beside the gold-and-scarlet-robed lord mayor, Sir Frank Alexander, and the prime minister.

Thirty years to the day after his graduation from West Point as a second lieutenant, Eisenhower became the fifth American to receive the freedom of the City. Presidents Ulysses S. Grant and Theodore Roosevelt, philanthropist George Peabody, and General John J. Pershing were the others.

Often during the ceremony, Eisenhower, who in Churchill's words "has shown the capacity for making great nations march together more truly united than they have ever been before," was moved and brought close to tears by the words of praise and the crowd's acclamation.

After the acting chamberlain had proffered the ceremonial "right hand of friendship" and reviewed Eisenhower's military career, Ike walked to the microphone and grinned. He appeared pale and nervous in the glare of the floodlights, and according to Kay, when he began to speak his voice could be heard only by those in front, "but then they fixed the microphone." Then he turned to the lord mayor and said something to the effect that if he didn't know he was among friends, he doubted if he could make his speech, and his voice almost failed. Butcher said it was his only departure from the text, "and sure enough, he got several 'heah-heahs. . . .' "

One person in the audience that day observed that for a few minutes Ike sounded like a high-school valedictorian who had committed his speech to memory. "But as he went on, he got better, and the crowd began to realize that Ike was doing all right."

The crowd gave him a big hand when he said:

Humility must always be the portion of any man who receives acclaim earned in blood of his followers and sacrifices of his friends. . . . I am not a native of this land. I come from the very heart of America. In the superficial aspects by which we ordinarily recognize family relationships, the town where I was born and the one where I was reared are far separated from this great city. . . . But I find myself today five thousand miles from that countryside, the honored guest of a city whose name stands for grandeur and size throughout the world. Hardly would it seem possible for the London Council to have gone farther afield to find a man to honor with its priceless gift of token citizenship. . . .

Much of his speech was devoted to eulogizing his British allies; and he spoke warmly of his staff

composed of chosen representatives of two proud and independent peoples . . . [whom] many feared . . . could never combine together in an efficient fashion to solve the complex problems presented by modern war.
I hope you believe we proved the doubters wrong. . . .

He referred to "the great team" he had led, saying:

No man alone could have brought about this result [the victory]. Had I possessed the military skill of a Marlborough, the wisdom of Solomon, the understanding of Lincoln, I still would have been helpless without the loyalty, vision, and generosity of thousands upon thousands of British and Americans. . . .

He received another big hand when he said:

A fact important for both of us to remember—neither London nor Abilene, sisters under the skin, will sell her birthright for physical safety, her liberty for mere existence.

Ike's words brought tears to the eyes of many, including Churchill, who later clapped the general on the back and said of the speech, "Well done, Ike, very well done." London's press agreed, and the next morning the *Daily Express* printed the Guildhall Address on the front page along with Lincoln's Gettysburg Address, "obviously intended favorably to compare the two," said Butcher.

The homage extended to Ike in London was to be repeated in many other places in the days, weeks, and months to follow. But on June 18, after three and a half years of war, when he stepped off the plane in Washington, Ike's first words were, "Oh, God, it's swell to be back!"

★ ★ ★

POSTSCRIPT

Merle Miller completed this book on the last Saturday of May 1986, and early the following Monday morning he entered Danbury Hospital. He never came out. On June 10 he died of complications resulting from what we all thought was a simple appendectomy.

On a warm, sunny day in June, at a spot less than 100 feet from the "glass house" in Brewster, N.Y., where he lived and worked, David W. Elliott, his friend of twenty-two years, and I buried his ashes, along with his typewriter, his thick-rimmed glasses, and a copy of the *New York Times*, three things he could never be without. This, then, is Merle Miller's last book. Not knowing it was his last, he considered it his best.

—Carol Hanley
June 1987

* * *

CHAPTER NOTES

* * *

WHERE IT ALL BEGAN

Most of the material describing Ike as a cadet is from an interview with Alexander M. "Babe" Weyand. Other sources are the recollections of classmates Hume Peabody, James A. Van Fleet, Charles C. Herrick, William H. Britton, and John E. Harris, which appeared in an article, "From Plebe to President" (*Collier's*, June 10, 1955); "Four Years at West Point, as of Fifty Years Ago," prepared by P.A.'s mother, Mrs. Roy C. Hodgson, based on letters P.A. wrote home during his stay at West Point; and "Recollections of Cadets Ike and Bradley," by Colonel W. H. Britton, prepared for the USMA Library at West Point.

Principal sources for the material describing Ike's feelings about West Point are Dwight D. Eisenhower's *At Ease: Stories I Tell to Friends* (Garden City, N.Y.: Doubleday, 1967); a September 13, 1966, CBS-TV broadcast, "Young Mr. Eisenhower" (filmed at Abilene, Kansas, and West Point); and correspondence between Eisenhower and General Maxwell D. Taylor.

The section on Ike's first roommate, John Henry Dykes, comes from an interview with Delmar Spencer Dykes, and correspondence between Ike and John Henry Dykes.

The paragraphs about Marty Maher come from his book, *Bringing Up the Brass* (New York: David McKay, 1951) and "The Legendary Sergeant," an article by Arthur Daly in the *New York Times* (January 20, 1961, Sports of the *Times*).

Grant's recollections of West Point are from his biography, *Grant*, by William S. McFeely (New York: W. W. Norton, 1981). Ike's feelings toward Grant come from his correspondence to William Elizabeth Brooks.

Other sources used in this chapter: Interviews with John Eisenhower and Mark Clark; Nancy Jansen McCarty's interview by the staff of the Eisenhower Library; Bela Kornitzer's *The Great American Heritage: The Story of the Five Eisenhower Brothers* (New York: Farrar, Straus and Cudahy, 1955); *At Ease;* Omar Bradley and Clay Blair's *A General's Life* (New York: Simon and Schuster, 1983); Robert Mancinelli's *The West Point Guidebook* (U.S. Military Academy, 1979); Eisenhower's Vertical File at the U.S. Military Academy Library.

* * *

WINNING AND LOSING

The material about Ike's football career and injury comes from an interview with Alexander M. "Babe" Weyand and "The Athletic Cadet Eisenhower," an article he wrote for the West Point alumni magazine, *Assembly* (vol. XXVII no. 1, Spring 1968); correspondence between Ike and Maxwell Taylor; "Four Years at West Point"; and the CBS-TV broadcast "Young Mr. Eisenhower."

The information about Jim Thorpe comes from correspondence between Ike and Bertram Jay Gumpert. The section about Ike's return to Abilene in the summer of 1913 comes from Earl J. Endacott's unpublished manuscript, "The Ike I Remember and Other Stories"; Kenneth S. Davis's *Soldier of Democracy* (Garden City, N.Y.: Doubleday, Doran, 1945); and an article by Earl Eisenhower, "I Grew Up with Ike," which appeared in the *American Weekly* magazine in 1954.

Other Sources: *At Ease;* "From Plebe to President."

★ ★ ★

A GOOD GAMBLE

Interviews with John Eisenhower and Mark Clark are the main sources for this chapter. The material about the end of Ike's football career comes from "The Athletic Cadet Eisenhower"; the CBS-TV broadcast "Young Mr. Eisenhower"; Edgar F. Puryear, Jr.'s interview with Ike on May 2, 1963, as related in Puryear's book *Nineteen Stars* (Washington, D.C.: Coiner Publications, Ltd., 1971); and correspondence between Eisenhower and Ruby Norman.

The section about smoking comes from Bernard Shanley's Diary; Clare Boothe Luce's interview by the staff of the Columbia History Project; the CBS-TV news special "Some Friends of General Eisenhower"; and John Gunther's *Eisenhower: The Man and the Symbol* (New York: Harper and Bros., 1952).

The account of the conversation between Ike and Colonel Shaw is from *At Ease*. The material pertaining to graduation day is from the Exercise Program for the Class of 1915.

Other sources: "From Plebe to President"; Harry C. Butcher's, *My Three Years with Eisenhower* (New York: Simon and Schuster, 1946); The March 29, 1969, CBS-TV broadcast, "Some Friends of General Eisenhower"; correspondence between Ike and George Ephraim Sokolsky, John Eisenhower, and Herman Beukema; and *The Howitzer* (1915), the West Point yearbook.

★ ★ ★

THE DOMINANT QUALITY

The principal source for this chapter is an interview with Nettie Stover Jackson. The material about Lane University comes from "Some Direct Quotations Concerning Lane University" by Clark Coan, instructor in social studies, Lawrence High School, Lawrence, Kansas; the section about Ida and David at the university comes from scrapbooks taken from the Abilene home. The account of the wedding is from newspaper clippings from the *Lecompton Monitor* and the *Hope Herald*.

Other sources: "Abilene's Ike," by C. M. Harger (*New York Times Magazine*, November 22, 1942); Kunigunde Duncan's *Earning the Right to Do Fanciwork* (Lawrence, Kans.: University of Kansas Press, 1957); Milton Eisenhower's *The President Is Calling* (New York: Doubleday, 1974); John Eisenhower's interview by the staff of the Eisenhower Library; an article by Mike Feinsilber "David: Ike Shy and Had Awful Temper"; (*City News*, September 20, 1978); *At Ease; The Great American Heritage: The Story of the Five Eisenhower Brothers;* correspondence between Eisenhower and Frances Curry; correspondence between Ike and Edgar Eisenhower; "I Grew Up with Eisenhower;" and an article by Lincoln Barnett in *Life* magazine, November 9, 1942.

★　★　★

A NICE LITTLE TOWN

An interview with Nettie Stover Jackson is the source for the information on Ida. Other sources: Correspondence between Ike and Ida's biographer, Kunigunde Duncan; a letter C. O. Musser wrote to Milton Eisenhower on July 10, 1945, attaching a list of errors he had found in the Alden Hatch book, *General Ike* (New York: Henry Holt, 1945), and eight pages of his recollections of David and Jacob Eisenhower; *The Great American Heritage: The Story of the Five Eisenhower Brothers;* and *At Ease.*

Most of the material describing Kansas is from Kenneth S. Davis's *Kansas: A Bicentennial History* (New York: W. W. Norton, 1976).

★　★　★

THE "RENEGADE TEXAN"

Most of the material describing Edgar is from *The Great American Heritage: The Story of the Five Eisenhower Brothers* and Edgar Eisenhower's *Six Roads to Abilene* (with John Dennis McCullum. Seattle: Wood & Reber, 1960).

The account of Ike's birth is from the "History of the Eisenhower Birthplace, Denison, Texas." Dr. D. H. Bailey, city health officer and doctor for the Katy is believed to have been the attending physician.

The material on Ike's visit to Denison in 1946 is from newspaper clippings and correspondence at the Sam Rayburn Library.

Other sources: Interview with Nettie Stover Jackson; *At Ease;* Ike's corrections of *Soldier of Democracy;* and *My Three Years with Eisenhower.*

★　★　★

AN ANGRY MAN

Much of the material used in this chapter on David Eisenhower comes from interviews with Nettie Stover Jackson, Aksel Nielsen, John Eisenhower and Earl J. Endacott. Eisenhower's quote concerning his father's death comes from Ike's Diary (Kevin McCann Papers, Eisenhower Library).

Other sources: CBS-TV broadcast "Some Friends of General Eisenhower"; *Six Roads to Abilene; Earning the Right to Do Fanciwork;* Henry Jamieson's, *They Still Call Him Ike* (New York: Vantage Press, 1972); *At Ease; The Great American Heritage: The Story of the Five Eisenhower Brothers;* John Eisenhower's *Strictly Personal* (Garden City, N.Y.: Doubleday, 1974); and John Eisenhower's interview by the staff of the Eisenhower Library.

* * *

THE STEPPING STONE

The material on the house on South East First Street comes from the official county records of Eisenhower properties. The information about the River Brethren comes from the *Kansas City Star* and the unpublished manuscript "The Religious Background of the Eisenhower Family," by Gladys Dodd.

The sources for the material on Abilene: "Eisenhower, as Seen Through the Pages of the *Abilene Reflector-Chronicle*," by Marcia Lee Lowther Longberg. (Master's thesis. Kansas State University, 1969); *The Heritage of Kansas*, edited by Everett Rich (Manhattan, Kansas: Flint Hills Book Co., 1960); Samuel Carter III's *Cowboy Capital of the World* (Garden City, N.Y.: Doubleday, 1973); and a folder, "Old Abilene Town," prepared and printed by The Abilene Town Co., Inc., Abilene, Kansas.

Other sources: Interviews with John Eisenhower, Henry Jamieson, Earl Endacott, and Tom Stephens; *The Great American Heritage: The Story of the Five Eisenhower Brothers; At Ease;* Mickey McKeogh's *Sergeant Mickey and General Ike* (with Richard Lockridge. New York: G. P. Putnam's Sons, 1946); *Overview*, the Eisenhower Foundation newsletter, vol. 9 no. 2, Fall 1983; *They Still Call Him Ike;* and Francis Trevelyan Miller's *Eisenhower: Man and Soldier* (Philadelphia: John C. Winston Co., 1944).

* * *

IN THE TRUTH

The account of Ida and the Jehovah's Witnesses comes from *The Watchtower*, October 15, 1980. The information about Eisenhower's presidency comes from "Religious Dimensions of Presidential Leadership: The Case of Dwight Eisenhower," by James David Fairbanks (*Presidential Studies Quarterly* vol. XII no. 2, Spring 1982); "Eisenhower's Fifties," by Robert Wright (*Antioch Review* vol. 38, Summer 1980); and Merlin Gustafson's "The Religion of a President," (*Christian Century*, April 30, 1969).

Other sources: Interviews with Nettie Stover Jackson and The Reverend Edward Elson; interviews of Robert Clark and John Bird by the staff of the Eisenhower Library; and the interview of Clare Boothe Luce by the staff of the Columbia Oral History Project; *The Great American Heritage: The Story of the Five Eisenhower Brothers; Eisenhower: Man and Soldier; Eisenhower: The Man and the Symbol;* William Lee Miller's *Piety Along the Potomac* (Boston: Houghton Mifflin, 1974); correspondence between Ike and Frances Curry; Ike's speech at the groundbreaking ceremony at the Eisenhower home in Abilene in 1952; and clippings from the *Denver Post* and the *New York Times*.

* * *

MARCHING THROUGH GEORGIA

The material in the chapter about Ike and Mark Twain comes from "Mark Twain and Dwight D. Eisenhower," by Cyril Clemens (*The Mark Twain Quarterly* vol. IX no. 3, Winter 1953).

David Eisenhower's comment on his grandfather's cooking comes from the *Sunday Patriot News*, Harrisburg, Pa. (July 5, 1981).

The paragraph on Ike's fishing and hunting quail with George Humphrey comes from the Eisenhower Foundation newsletter, *Overview* (vol. 10 no. 1, Spring 1984).

Other sources: Interviews with Nettie Stover Jackson, Bernard Shanley, Russell "Red" Reeder, and John Eisenhower; interviews of The Reverend Roy Witter, John Eisenhower, and James Stack by the staff of the Eisenhower Library; Delos Lovelace's *Ike Eisenhower: Statesman and Soldier of Peace* (New York: Thomas Y. Crowell, 1944); *Six Roads to Abilene; Eisenhower: American Hero,* by the editors of *American Heritage* magazine (New York: American Heritage Publishing Co., 1969); "The Ike I Remember and Other Stories"; *They Still Call Him Ike; At Ease; Soldier of Democracy; Eisenhower: The Man and the Symbol;* Vernon A. Walters' *Silent Missions* (Garden City, N.Y.: Doubleday, 1978); *Strictly Personal;* "Eisenhower's Toughest Fight," by Kenneth S. Davis (*Herald Tribune,* February 8, 1945); "Soldier and Civilian: Eisenhower Leads Crusades for Freedom in War and Peace"; (Undated, no source. Taken from the Eisenhower Library, shelf 2); "I Grew Up with Eisenhower"; "Mother Eisenhower Talks About Her Most Famous Son," by Elmer T. Peterson (*Better Homes and Gardens,* June 1943); "The President's Pet Peeves," by Jack Anderson and Fred Blumenthal (*Parade* magazine, March 20, 1955); the *Abilene Reflector-Chronicle* Memorial Issue (compiled from regular issues of the *Abilene Reflector-Chronicle* following the deaths of Ike and Mamie (March 28, 1969 and November 1, 1979, respectively); the *Dallas Morning News; Kansas City Star;* United Press; correspondence between Ike and Swede Hazlett; correspondence between Ike and Earl and Mrs. Ross Moffett, Provincetown, Mass.; and *The Mining Journal,* Marquette, Mich., January 28, 1960.

Miscellaneous sources used: Ike's comments on *Soldier of Democracy;* questionnaire Ike answered in 1954 for C. Wm. Chamberlain of Oceanside, Calif., who was writing a juvenile book on Ike's boyhood; CBS-TV broadcast "Young Mr. Eisenhower."

★ ★ ★

NOT AT THE TOP, BUT CLIMBING

The description of Ike is from an interview with Nettie Stover Jackson. The material about the class of 1909 comes from the Abilene High School yearbook, *The Helianthus,* and Abilene newspapers. Other sources used for the high school material: Interviews of Lelia Picking and John "Six" McDonnell by the staff of the Eisenhower Library.

Other sources: Merle Miller's *Plain Speaking: An Oral Biography of Harry S Truman* (New York: Berkley Books, 1973); *The Great American Heritage: The Story of the Five Eisenhower Brothers; At Ease; Eisenhower: Man and Soldier;* the *Tacoma News Tribune;* and correspondence between Ike and Minnie Stewart and Mame McInerney Riordan.

★ ★ ★

A MATTER OF AGE

The material pertaining to Ike's employment after high school comes from an interview with Earl J. Endacott; Ike's comment about this period comes from his corrections of *Soldier of Democracy.*

The account of Edgar's employment at the creamery comes from an interview of Orin Snider by the staff of the Eisenhower Library.

The information about the relationship between Swede and Ike comes from interviews with Mrs. Swede Hazlett and John Eisenhower. The account of the circumstances surrounding Ike's appointment to West Point comes from Swede's recollections prepared for the Eisenhower Library; *They Still Call Him Ike;* and correspondence between Swede and Ike in 1952.

The section on the age discrepancy comes from correspondence in the Senator Bristow Collection, Kansas State Historical Society, Topeka, Kansas; correspondence between Ike and Mrs. Nevie Bristow Remling; and U.S. Military Academy Library Archives records.

Other sources used in this chapter: *At Ease: The Great American Heritage: The Story of the Five Eisenhower Brothers;* Dwight D. Eisenhower's *Mandate for Change* (Garden City, N.Y.: Doubleday, 1963); *Soldier of Democracy; Eisenhower: Man and Soldier; Grant;* "Mother Eisenhower Talks About Her Most Famous Son"; CBS-TV broadcast, "Young Mr. Eisenhower."

★ ★ ★

THE SUMMER OF 1915

The most important sources for this chapter were interviews with Robert Brooks and Mary Jane Stineman; also letters Ike wrote to Gladys Harding and the diary she kept that summer.

Other sources: Interviews with Harry Anholt, Maude Black, and Henry Jamieson; *At Ease; The Great American Heritage: The Story of the Five Eisenhower Brothers; Soldier of Democracy;* "The Ike I Remember and Other Stories"; and William Shirer's *Twentieth Century Journey* (Boston: Little, Brown, 1984).

★ ★ ★

FORT SAM

Most of the material on Ike's recollections of Fort Sam comes from *At Ease.* Other sources: *Abilene Reflector-Chronicle* Memorial Issue; "Mamie and Ike Talk About 50 Years of Marriage," by Rosalind Massow (*Parade* magazine, June 26, 1966); *Eisenhower: Man and Soldier;* and correspondence between Eisenhower and Colonel George W. Helms and Ruby Norman.

★ ★ ★

MISS MAMIE

The account of Ike and Mamie's first meeting comes from an interview with her sister Mabel Frances "Mike" Doud Moore; "Mamie and Ike Talk About 50 Years of Marriage"; and Julie Nixon Eisenhower's *Special People* (New York: Simon and Schuster, 1977).

Most of the material on Elivera and John Doud also comes from an interview with Mike Moore; and from an interview with Aksel Nielsen.

Other sources: *Des Moines Register; Cedar Rapids Gazette; Rocky Mountain News* (Denver); *Twentieth Century Journey;* Alden Hatch's *Red Carpet for Mamie* (New York: Henry Holt, 1954); *Time* magazine; and *At Ease.*

★ ★ ★

THE NATURE OF THE DUTY

Interviews with Mabel Frances "Mike" Doud Moore, John Eisenhower, and Aksel Nielsen were used for this chapter. Other sources: Dorothy Brandon's *Mamie Doud Eisenhower: Portrait of a First Lady* (New York: Charles Scribner's Sons, 1954); *At Ease;* "The Ike I Remember and Other Stories"; Kirkpatrick Cobb's *Ike's Old Sarge* (Dallas, Texas: Royal Publishing Co., 1964); Lester and Irene David's *Ike and Mamie* (New York: G. P. Putnam's Sons, 1981); "Grandma's Going to the White House," by Mary Van Rensselair Thayer (*Denver Post,* January 11, 1953); "Mamie Eisenhower Talks About Fifty Years of Marriage," by Vivian Cadden (*McCall's,* September 1966); "I'll Always Be an Army Wife," by Vivian G. Milner (*Denver Post Magazine,* June 27, 1965); "Mamie and Ike Talk About 50 Years of Marriage"; several newspaper clippings from the *Denver Post* and the *Chicago Daily News;* and Barbara Walters' interview of Mamie at Gettysburg for an ABC-TV broadcast of *20/20* (November 23, 1979); correspondence between Ike and John, Ruby Norman, and Mamie.

★ ★ ★

THE ARMY WIFE

Lieutenant John B. Wogan's account of his first meeting with Mamie comes from the article "From Plebe to President." The paragraph on Mamie's return to Fort Sam forty-three years later comes from a memorial tribute in the House of Representatives by The Honorable Henry B. Gonzalez on March 31, 1969 (Dwight D. Eisenhower. Memorial Tributes Delivered in Congress. Washington, D.C., U.S. Gov. Printing Office, 1970).

Mamie's recollections of her early married life come from "Mamie and Ike Talk About 50 Years of Marriage"; *Special People;* "Mamie Eisenhower Talks About Fifty Years of Marriage"; and "Mamie and Ike: 49 Years," by Vivian G. Milner (the Sunday *Denver Post,* June 27, 1965).

The material on Ike's coaching comes from an article, "Former Players Remember Eisenhower as Great Leader," by Frank Klein, executive sports editor, (*San Antonio Sunday Express-News,* October 28, 1956); and clippings from the *San Antonio Express.*

The account of the march from Wilston to Austin, Texas, comes from *Ike's Old Sarge.* Other sources: Interviews with John Eisenhower and Aksel Nielsen; an interview of Merriman Smith by the staff of the Eisenhower Library; *At Ease;* and an interview of Mamie Eisenhower by Barbara Walters for *20/20* (ABC-TV November 23, 1979, at Gettysburg).

★ ★ ★

KEEPING THE COLONEL HAPPY

The most important source for the information on Camp Wilson and Leon Springs is *At Ease.* Other sources: An interview with John Eisenhower; Arthur Nevins's *Gettysburg's Five-Star Farmer* (New York: Carlton Press, 1977); *Mamie Doud Eisenhower: Portrait of a First Lady; Special People;* and *Soldier of Democracy.*

★ ★ ★

FULL CIRCLE

The material used in describing Mamie's feelings about Gettysburg comes from an interview of Mamie by the staff of the National Historic Site at Gettysburg, Pa.

The information on the flu epidemic comes for the most part from the *Gettysburg Times;* and the Historic Resource Study and Historical Base Map, Eisenhower National Historic Site, Gettysburg, Pa. (December 31, 1970).

Other sources: The unedited "Personal and Official Diary of General Dwight D. Eisenhower and Commander Harry C. Butcher, Naval Aide 1942–1945" (Eisenhower Library); William Manchester's *The Last Lion: Winston Spencer Churchill* (Boston: Little, Brown, 1983); Steve Neal's *The Eisenhowers: Reluctant Dynasty* (Garden City, N.Y.: Doubleday, 1978); "From Plebe to President"; *At Ease;* correspondence between Ike and George R. Goshaw, David Eisenhower, F. Summers, and Norman Randolph.

★ ★ ★·

GENUINE ADVENTURE

The material used in this chapter about the 1919 Transcontinental Motor Convoy comes from an article by Vaughn Smartt, "1919: The Interstate Expedition." (*Constructor* magazine, vol. LV no. 8, August 1973, published by the Associated General Contractors of America, Washington, D.C.); *Overview* (vol. 10 no. 3, Fall 1984); First Lieutenant E. R. Jackson's Ordnance Observer's Report; and *At Ease.*

Other sources: *Mamie Doud Eisenhower: Portrait of a First Lady; Mandate for Change;* and Eisenhower's official army 201 file.

★ ★ ★

THE TORTOISE AND THE HARE

The account of Ike's first meeting with Patton comes from *At Ease.* The portions of the article Eisenhower wrote on tanks, "A Tank Discussion" by Captain D. D. Eisenhower, Infantry (Tanks), come from the November 1920 issue of *Infantry Journal.*

Other sources: Interviews with John Eisenhower and Mark Clark; interview of Eisenhower by Puryear in *Nineteen Stars;* Martin Blumenson's *The Patton Papers: 1935–1940* (Boston: Houghton Mifflin, 1972); Ladislas Farago's *The Last Days of Patton* (New York: McGraw-Hill, 1981).

★ ★ ★

THE DARK SHADOW

The principal source for the account of Icky's death is *At Ease*. Mamie's discussion of Icky's death is from an interview at Augusta, Ga. by Barbara Walters for the *Today* show (NBC-TV March 26–27, 1970). The impact of Icky's death on Ike and Mamie comes from interviews with Mike Doud Moore and John Eisenhower.

The account of Icky's burial at the Eisenhower Center in 1966 comes from "The Ike I Remember and Other Stories."

Other sources: *Special People; Ike and Mamie; Strictly Personal;* Malcolm Moos's *Dwight D. Eisenhower* (New York: Random House, 1964); an article, "The Brave Journey of Helen Hayes," by Howard Teichmann for *Parade* magazine (November 24, 1985); correspondence between Eisenhower and Mamie, John Gunther, Louis Marx, and Helen Hayes.

★ ★ ★

A GRAVE OFFENSE

Most of the material used in this chapter comes from Eisenhower's official army 201 file. Other sources: *At Ease; Eisenhower: The Man and the Symbol;* and an interview of Merriman Smith by the staff of the Columbia Oral History Project.

★ ★ ★

THE INVISIBLE FIGURE

The most important sources for this chapter were interviews with Fox Conner, Jr., and Andrew Goodpaster; Bradford Chynoweth's interview by the staff of the U.S. Military History Institute, Carlisle Barracks, Pa.; and an interview of Eisenhower by the staff of the Hoover Library, West Branch, Iowa.

Other sources: *At Ease; Special People; Ike and Mamie;* Virginia Conner's *What Father Forbade* (Philadelphia: Dorrance & Co., 1951); correspondence between Col. Clarence Deems, Jr., and MacArthur; correspondence between Ike and Fox Conner; *Assembly,* Spring 1968; and a piece Lincoln Barnett wrote for the November 9, 1942, issue of *Life* magazine.

★ ★ ★

SLIGHTLY TO THE REAR

Most of the material used in this chapter comes from an interview with John Eisenhower; and interviews of Mamie, John, and David Eisenhower by the staff of the National Historic Site, Gettysburg, Pa.

The account of the relationship between Ike and Mamie after John's birth is from *What Father Forbade*. Hazlett's trip to Panama is from his recollections on file at the

Eisenhower Library in Abilene. The material on Eisenhower's appendectomy comes from his official army 201 file.

Other sources: Correspondence with Herb Mitgang; correspondence between Ike and Mamie; the transcript of Mamie's interview by Barbara Walters for the *Today* show (broadcast March 26–27, 1970); interview with William Ewald, Jr.; interview of John Bird by the staff of the Eisenhower Library; *Strictly Personal; The Great American Heritage: The Story of the Five Eisenhower Brothers; At Ease;* Peter Lyon's *Eisenhower: Portrait of the Hero* (Boston: Little, Brown, 1974); *Ike and Mamie; Eisenhower: The Man and the Symbol;* news clippings from the *New York Times;* and "Mamie and Ike: 49 Years."

★ ★ ★

THE WATERSHED

The material about the circumstances surrounding Ike's being chosen to go to the Command and General Staff School comes from correspondence between Ike and Fox Conner. The paragraphs on his preparing for the school come from an interview of Eisenhower by Puryear (in *Nineteen Stars*); and *At Ease.*

The sources for the information on the 1926 course at Leavenworth are letters written from Fort Leavenworth during the 1925/26 course by a student identified only as "A," which originally appeared in the *Military Engineer* and were reprinted by permission in *Cavalry Journal* (July 1926); and Ike's article "A Young Graduate" in the June 1927 issue of *Infantry Journal.*

Other sources: Interviews with Fox Conner, Jr.; the interview of Kevin McCann by the staff of the National Historic Site, Gettysburg, Pa.; interview of John W. Leonard by the staff of the Eisenhower Library; *The Patton Papers 1935–1940; At Ease; Mamie Doud Eisenhower: Portrait of a First Lady; Red Carpet for Mamie; Eisenhower: American Hero; Assembly* (vol. XXVII no. 1, Spring 1968); and *Strictly Personal.*

★ ★ ★

PRUDENS FUTURI

One of the most important sources for this chapter was a paper, "Dwight D. Eisenhower at the Army War College: 1927–28," prepared by Dr. Benjamin F. Cooling, and published in *Parameters*, the journal of the U.S. Army War College (vol. 5 no. 1, 1975). Mamie's comment on Ike at the War College is from "Mamie and Ike: 49 Years."

Other sources: Eisenhower's paper "An Enlisted Reserve for the Regular Army," prepared by Major D. D. Eisenhower, Infantry, March 28, 1928. Army War College, Washington, D.C., Command Course; *Strictly Personal; Eisenhower: Portrait of the Hero; The President Is Calling;* and *At Ease.*

★ ★ ★

SOME AMERICANS IN PARIS

The principal sources for this chapter are an interview with John Eisenhower, and an interview with George "Bo" Horkan, Jr., by the staff of the National Historic Site at Gettysburg, Pa.

The comments on Ike's inability to master other languages come from an interview with Vernon Walters, and his book *Silent Missions;* an interview with John Eisenhower; and *At Ease.*

The information about the seventeen-day tour Ike and Mamie took before returning to the States comes from the 1929 diary of William R. Gruber. Entries for August 28 to September 5, 1929, are in the handwriting of Eisenhower and are the material used in this chapter.

Other sources: *Strictly Personal; Red Carpet for Mamie;* Eisenhower's official army 201 file; correspondence between Eisenhower and George Horkan, Sr.; an interview with Aksel Nielsen; "Mamie and Ike Talk About 50 Years of Marriage"; and "Mamie and Ike: 49 Years."

★ ★ ★

THE ASSISTANT TO THE ASSISTANT

The information in this chapter about the years the Eisenhowers lived in Washington is from an interview with John, and from his book *Strictly Personal.* Most of the information on Eisenhower's work on industrial mobilization comes from his diary. The report of the inspection tour of the guayule rubber industry Ike made with Wilkes comes from a report submitted on June 6, 1930 (declassified on May 3, 1972).

Other sources: *Infantry Journal* (Nov./Dec. 1931); *The Industrial College of the Armed Forces: Thirty-First Anniversary. 1955* (Published by the American Ordnance Association, Washington, D.C.); *Strictly Personal;* Jordan A. Schwarz's *The Speculator: Bernard M. Baruch in Washington* (Chapel Hill, N.C.: University of North Carolina Press, 1981); *Eisenhower: Portrait of the Hero; Special People;* correspondence between Eisenhower and Bernard Baruch; and a letter from Eisenhower to Herbert Bayard Swope, dated September 19, 1946.

★ ★ ★

THE INSUBORDINATE GENERAL

The account of Ike's feelings about MacArthur and working in Washington during this period comes from an interview with Stan Swinton. The biographical material on MacArthur comes from William Manchester's *American Caesar: Douglas MacArthur 1880–1964* (Boston: Little, Brown, 1978).

The material on the Bonus Marches comes from an interview with Eisenhower by the staff of the Hoover Library in 1967; Eisenhower's Diary (Kevin McCann Papers, Eisenhower Library); Report from the Chief of Staff, U.S. Army, to the Secretary of War on the Employment of Federal Troops in Civil Disturbance in the District of Columbia; General George Van Horn Moseley's Papers in the Library of Congress; Roger Daniels'

The Bonus March: An Episode of the Great Depression (Contributions in American History, vol. 14. Westport, Conn.: Greenwood Publishing Co., 1971); "A Blunder Becomes Catastrophe: Hoover, the Legion, and the Bonus Army," by Donald J. Lisio (*Wisconsin Magazine of History,* Autumn 1967); and James F. and Jean H. Vivian's "The Bonus March of 1932: The Role of General George Van Horn Moseley" (*Wisconsin Magazine of History,* Autumn 1967).

Other sources: John P. Roche's article in the *New York Times Book Review* (June 28, 1981) on *The Eisenhower Diaries,* Robert H. Ferrell, editor (New York: W. W. Norton, 1981); *Eisenhower: Portrait of the Hero;* Samuel P. Huntington's *The Soldier and the State: The Theory and Politics of Civil-Military Relations,* Cambridge, Mass.: Harvard University Press, 1957; Gene Smith's *The Shattered Dream: Herbert Hoover and the Great Depression* (New York: McGraw-Hill, 1984); Richard Norton Smith's *An Uncommon Man: The Triumph of Herbert Hoover* (New York: Simon and Schuster, 1984); Arthur M. Schlesinger, Jr.'s *The Age of Roosevelt,* vol. 1, *The Crisis of the Old Order 1919–1933* (Boston: Houghton Mifflin, 1957); and T. Harry Williams's "The 'Macs' and the 'Ikes': America's Two Military Traditions" (*American Mercury,* vol. LXXV, October 1952).

★ ★ ★

GOOD MAN FRIDAY

The most important source for the year 1933 comes from Eisenhower's Diary (Kevin McCann Papers, Eisenhower Library). The paragraphs about Eisenhower and MacArthur come from Frazier Hunt's *The Untold Story of Douglas MacArthur* (New York: Devin-Adair Co., 1954).

The account of the reunion of Eisenhower and his brothers and Swede Hazlett comes from *Soldier of Democracy;* Stephen E. Ambrose's *Milton S. Eisenhower* (Baltimore: Johns Hopkins University Press, 1983); Ike's corrections of *Soldier of Democracy;* and Swede Hazlett's recorded recollections in the Eisenhower Library.

Other sources: Correspondence from the MacArthur Archives in Norfolk, Va.; and *At Ease.*

★ ★ ★

THE MISSION

The material on the defense of the Philippines comes from several reports Eisenhower prepared for MacArthur (on file at the MacArthur Archives, Norfolk, Va., under the heading Philippines, Defense Plan); Eisenhower's Philippine Diary (Kevin McCann Papers, Eisenhower Library); "Spearhead of Our Defense," by Jim Marshall (*Collier's,* September 5, 1936); "National Defense in the Philippines," by General Douglas MacArthur (1936, MacArthur Archives); a memorandum prepared by Brigadier General Charles Burnett, Chief of Bureau of Insular Affairs, on the Subject: Japanese Penetration of the Philippine Islands (MacArthur Archives. Confidential and undated); and *At Ease.*

The extracts from a letter written by a British manager of a sugar estate in Manaoag, Pangasinan Province, dated August 25, 1937, is from the MacArthur Archives (on file under the heading Philippines, Native Situation).

The material on flying comes from an interview of William L. Lee by the staff of the Eisenhower Library; and an article by Jesus A. Villamor, "He Knew How to Take It" (*The American Legion Magazine,* September 1960); an article by Jerry Lee, "Get

Going, Ike!" (Eisenhower Library. No source); and an interview with John Eisenhower.

The paragraphs on social life in the Philippines come from Johanna Ingersoll's *Golden Years in the Philippines* (Palo Alto, Calif.: Pacific Books, 1971); and "Can We Hold The Richest Land on Earth?" by W. B. Courtney (*Collier's,* July 1, 1939).

Most of the material on Mamie comes from *Red Carpet for Mamie* and *Mamie Doud Eisenhower: Portrait of a First Lady.*

The accounts of Ike's bridge playing come from columns by Alan Truscott in the *New York Times;* an interview with Mrs. Maude Black; correspondence between Ike and Al Gruenther; and the Hagerty Diaries.

Other sources: Clayton D. James's *The Years of MacArthur,* vol. 1, *1880–1941* (Boston: Houghton Mifflin, 1970); *The Untold Story of Douglas MacArthur; American Caesar; Gettysburg's Five-Star Farmer;* Kevin McCann's, *Man from Abilene* (Garden City: N.Y.: Doubleday, 1952); *Eisenhower: Portrait of the Hero; Strictly Personal;* and *At Ease.* Also, interviews with John Eisenhower and J. Lawton "Lightning Joe" Collins; an interview with Lucius Clay by the staff of the Military History Institute at Carlisle Barracks; Memorandum of the Terms of Agreement for Military Adviser to the President of the Philippine Commonwealth Government, Sept./Oct. 1935; Message of His Excellency Manuel L. Quezon to the National Assembly, November 25, 1935; Notes of an Interview with General MacArthur on Board the *President Coolidge* (1937); Speech Delivered by Field Marshal Douglas MacArthur at the Banquet given by His Excellency Manuel L. Quezon, August 24, 1936; "Information for Officers Ordered to the Philippine Islands," compiled in the office of Major T. K. Boles, A.C., of S.G-2, Philippine Department, principally by Captain H. C. Brenizer, F.A., and Captain R. T. Sothern, F.A. (*Infantry Journal,* vol. 33 no. 2, August 1928); correspondence between Eisenhower and T. J. Davis, James Ord, and MacArthur; and Eisenhower's official army 201 file.

* * *

THE ELECTRIC TRAIN

The information on Ike's three-month stay in the States in 1938 comes from an interview with John Eisenhower and his oral history file at the Eisenhower Library; "The Ike I Remember and Other Stories"; Ike's Philippine Diary; correspondence between Ike and MacArthur, T. J. Davis, and James Ord.

The material on Ike and Jews comes from correspondence between Ike and his brother Milton, and Maxwell Abbell; Ida Cowen's *Jews in Remote Corners of the World* (Englewood Cliffs, N.J.: Prentice-Hall, 1971); and *At Ease.*

With regard to the letter Eisenhower wrote his brother Milton on September 3, 1939: An attempt was made at the Eisenhower Library to see a copy of this letter, but a check of both the Milton Eisenhower Papers and Dwight D. Eisenhower's Pre-Presidential Papers revealed that neither collection contained a copy of the letter. It must therefore be assumed that Milton kept the letter in his own files.

Other sources: MacArthur Archives; *Strictly Personal; At Ease;* Martin Blumenson's *Mark Clark: Last of the Great World War II Commanders* (New York: Congdon & Weed, 1984); correspondence between Ike and Clark; Eisenhower's official army 201 file.

★ ★ ★

WAR GAMES

The account of the trip home is from Dwight D. Eisenhower's *Crusade in Europe* (Garden City, N.Y.: Doubleday, 1948); and *Eisenhower: Man and Soldier*.

The paragraphs on John and his decision to attend West Point come from an interview with John Eisenhower, his book *Strictly Personal*, and *At Ease*.

The principal sources for the material about Fort Lewis: Interviews with Mark Clark and Burton S. Barr; and Eisenhower's Diary (Kevin McCann Papers, Eisenhower Library).

Other sources: *Soldier of Democracy;* Maurine Clark's *Captain's Bride-General's Lady* (New York: McGraw-Hill, 1956).

★ ★ ★

A COLONEL NAMED EISENHOWER

The material on the Boettigers and Eisenhowers comes from an interview with John Eisenhower.

The account of John's first day at West Point is from *Strictly Personal*. The description of Tex Lee is from *Soldier of Democracy*. Mickey McKeogh's recollections of his arrival at Fort Sam are from *Sergeant Mickey and General Ike*.

The quote on ROUNDUP is from Robert E. Sherwood's *Roosevelt and Hopkins: An Intimate History* (New York: Harper and Bros., 1948).

Sources for the section about the Louisiana Maneuvers: "The Louisiana Maneuvers: Practice for War" by G. Patrick Murray (Doctoral candidate, Department of History, Kansas State University, Manhattan, Kansas; printed in *Louisiana History*, vol. 13, 1972); "The U.S. Army GHQ Maneuvers of 1941" by Christopher R. Gabel (Doctoral Thesis. Ohio State University, 1981); an interview with Robert Sherrod by the staff of the Columbia Oral History Project; Eric Sevareid's *Not So Wild a Dream* (New York: Alfred A. Knopf, 1969); Walter Krueger's *From Down Under to Nippon* (Washington, D.C.: Combat Forces Press, 1953); *At Ease;* correspondence between Eisenhower and General Kenyon Joyce; correspondence with Gee Gerow; and *Time* magazine.

The sources for the material on Ike's promotion are an interview with General Mark Clark and Ike's official army 201 file.

Other sources: *Strictly Personal;* correspondence—Ike to Everett Hughes, T. J. Davis; Mark Clark's *Calculated Risk* (New York: Harper and Bros., 1950); and an interview with James Stack by the staff of the Eisenhower Library.

★ ★ ★

THE FIRST ANSWER

The account of the attack on the American destroyer U.S.S. *Kearny*, and Roosevelt's speech on October 27, 1941, come from *Roosevelt and Hopkins*.

The material on December 7th comes from Forrest C. Pogue's biography, *George C. Marshall: Ordeal and Hope, 1939–1942* (New York: Viking Press, 1966); *Crusade in Europe:* and Katherine Tupper Marshall's *Together: Annals of an Army Wife* (New York: Tupper & Love, 1946).

The paragraph on the MacArthur-Marshall relationship is from *The Untold Story of Douglas MacArthur* and *George C. Marshall: Ordeal and Hope*.

The material on Ike's arrival in Washington and his meeting with Marshall comes from *Crusade in Europe; The President Is Calling; The Papers of Dwight David Eisenhower: The War Years*. vol. 1 (Alfred D. Chandler, Jr., ed. Baltimore: Johns Hopkins University Press, 1970).

Other sources: Correspondence between Ike and General Walter Krueger; Winston Churchill's *The Grand Alliance* (Boston: Houghton Mifflin, 1950); Eisenhower's Circular Diary (Kevin McCann Papers, Eisenhower Library); Kenneth S. Davis's *Experience of War* (Garden City, N.Y.: Doubleday, 1965).

★ ★ ★

A MAN OF RESPONSIBILITY

The biographical material on George C. Marshall comes from Leonard Mosely's *Marshall: Hero for Our Times* (New York: Hearst Books, 1982); *Together: Annals of an Army Wife;* and an interview with General Mark Clark.

Mrs. Marshall's account of the morning of June 6, 1944, is from an interview with Vernon Walters.

Ike's quotes on his feelings toward Marshall come from correspondence to Swede Hazlett and from *At Ease*.

The material on Ike and MacArthur used in this chapter comes from the Eisenhower Diaries for January and February 1944; messages between Ike and MacArthur; and *Reminiscenses*.

The paragraphs on the War Department come from an interview with John J. McCloy by the staff of the Columbia Oral History Project; Eisenhower's Diary; Helen Dunbar's Diary (Eisenhower Library); and Lucian K. Truscott, Jr.'s *Command Missions* (Salem, N.H.: Ayer Publishing Co., 1979, republication of a 1954 edition).

The material on the *Queen Mary* comes from Stephen E. Ambrose's *The Supreme Commander: The War Years of General Dwight D. Eisenhower* (Garden City, N.Y.: Doubleday, 1970) and *Crusade in Europe*.

The account of Ike's conversation with Marshall concerning promotions and his anger at promotions comes from *At Ease;* Eisenhower's Diary; and *Strictly Personal*.

Other sources: *Reminiscenses; Mamie Doud Eisenhower: Portrait of a First Lady; Sergeant Mickey and General Ike;* an interview of Merriman Smith by the staff of the Columbia Oral History Project; Ike's comments on *Soldier of Democracy;* Ike's army 201 file; correspondence between Eisenhower and Gee Gerow, Art Hurd, George Patton, Henry Maitland Wilson, George Marshall, and John and Edgar Eisenhower.

★ ★ ★

A KANSAN GOES TO LONDON

The material on the Marshall and Hopkins visit to London in April comes from Winston S. Churchill's *The Hinge of Fate* (Boston: Houghton Mifflin, 1950); and John Eisenhower's *Allies: Pearl Harbor to D-Day* (Garden City, N.Y.: Doubleday, 1982).

The paragraph on BOLERO is from Eisenhower's Diary.

The account of Eisenhower and Clark's trip to London in May is from *Calculated Risk;* Eisenhower's Diary; *Crusade in Europe;* and an interview with General Mark Clark by the staff of the U.S. Military History Institute, Carlisle Barracks.

Kay Summersby's description of her first meeting with Ike and his reaction to Montgomery is from *Eisenhower Was My Boss* (New York: Prentice-Hall, 1948) and *Past Forgetting* (New York: Simon and Schuster, 1976).

Other sources: *Command Missions; Milton S. Eisenhower;* Henry H. Arnold's *Global Mission* (New York: Harper and Bros., 1949); Sir Arthur Bryant's *The Turn of the Tide* (New York: Doubleday, 1957); memos and messages between Eisenhower, Marshall, and Roosevelt (Eisenhower Library).

★ ★ ★

A PRECIOUS FRIENDSHIP

The account of Eisenhower's appointment as commanding general, European Theater of Operations, comes from *Crusade in Europe* and his Diary.

The material on Churchill, Brooke, Ismay, and Lord Moran's trip to Washington to see Roosevelt in June comes from Lord Moran's *Churchill: Taken from the Diaries of Lord Moran* (Boston: Houghton Mifflin, 1966); *The Hinge of Fate; George C. Marshall: Ordeal and Hope;* and *Allies.*

The sources for John's visit to Washington the weekend before his father left for London are *Strictly Personal* and *Ike Eisenhower: Statesman and Soldier of Peace.*

The paragraph describing Ike's feeling toward Churchill comes from a eulogy he delivered at Churchill's funeral.

Other sources: Memoranda between Ike and Marshall; Eisenhower's Diary; an interview with General Thomas Handy by the staff of the Eisenhower Library; an interview with General Al Gruenther; *Turn of the Tide; Mamie Doud Eisenhower: Portrait of a First Lady;* and Alan Taylor's *War Lords* (New York: Atheneum, 1978).

★ ★ ★

20 GROSVENOR SQUARE

The material on Ike's return to London comes from an interview with Brigadier General Charles L. Bolte by the staff of the U.S. Military History Institute, Carlisle Barracks; and *Sergeant Mickey and General Ike.*

The account of how Ike dealt with his staff and the British comes from "He Is Our Eisenhower and This Is Our Hour" by Raymond Daniell (*Life* magazine, November 9, 1942); *Eisenhower Was My Boss;* and *Crusade in Europe.*

The source for the paragraphs on rations is Norman Longmate's *The G.I.s: The Americans in Britain, 1942–1945* (New York: Charles Scribner's Sons, 1975).

The source for the paragraph on censorship is *Crusade in Europe.*

The material on the Eisenhower-Churchill relationship comes from an interview with John Eisenhower and the CBS-TV broadcast "Some Friends of General Eisenhower."

Other sources: *Calculated Risk; The Turn of the Tide; My Three Years with Eisenhower; Eisenhower Was My Boss; Past Forgetting;* correspondence between Ike and Fox Conner; Lieutenant Colonel John Dawson Laurie; Charles Gailey, Jr.; and Mamie.

* * *

MAELSTROM

The material on Telegraph Cottage comes from *My Three Years with Eisenhower; Eisenhower Was My Boss;* and Ike's letters to Mamie.

The sources for the paragraphs on Robert Murphy are his biography, *Diplomat Among Warriors* (Garden City, N.Y.: Doubleday, 1964), and correspondence between Ike and Marshall. The paragraphs on de Gaulle are from Don Cook's biography, *Charles de Gaulle* (New York: G. P. Putnam's Sons, 1984).

The biographical information on Bedell Smith comes from interviews with Chet Hansen and Drew Middleton; an interview of Arthur Nevins by the staff of the National Historic Site at Gettysburg, Pa.; *George C. Marshall: Ordeal and Hope;* and *The Supreme Commander.*

The account of Clark's adventures on his way to meet with Mast comes from an interview with Mark Clark; *Calculated Risk;* and Martin Blumenson's biography of Clark.

The account of the six Flying Fortresses comes from *Allies.*

Other sources: *My Three Years with Eisenhower; Crusade in Europe; The Hinge of Fate; The Patton Papers; Past Forgetting; Eisenhower Was My Boss;* Harry C. Butcher's Unpublished Diary; John Eisenhower's editorial comments in *Letters to Mamie* (ed. John S. D. Eisenhower. Garden City, N.Y.: Doubleday, 1978); Thomas Handy's interview by the staff of the Eisenhower Library; and Peter Ziegler's biography, *Mountbatten* (New York: Alfred A. Knopf, 1984); and "Amateurs in Diplomacy: The American Vice Consuls in North Africa, 1941–1943," by Leon B. Blair (*Historian*, vol. 35 no. 4, 1973).

* * *

THE ROCK OF GIBRALTAR

The description of the offices inside the Rock comes from Colonel Benjamin A. Dickson's unpublished manuscript "From Algiers to the Elbe" and *Crusade in Europe.*

The material on the landings at Casablanca comes from *Allies* and "From Algiers to the Elbe." The story about the evening of the 6th and YBSOB is from an interview with Mark Clark.

The account of the meeting with Giraud comes from *Crusade in Europe; Calculated Risk* and an interview with Mark Clark.

Other sources: *Diplomat Among Warriors; Roosevelt and Hopkins;* Peter Tompkins's *The Murder of Admiral Darlan* (New York: Simon and Schuster, 1965); *Together: Annals of an Army Wife;* Harold Macmillan's *The Blast of War: 1939–1945* (New York: Harper & Row, 1967); correspondence between Ike and Cunningham, Beetle Smith, Mamie, Marshall, and the Combined Chiefs of Staff; and *My Three Years with Eisenhower.*

* * *

FRIDAY THE THIRTEENTH

The material on the meeting in Algiers between Admiral Darlan, Clark, and Giraud comes from an interview with Mark Clark and *Diplomat Among Warriors*. The background information on Admiral Darlan comes from *The Murder of Admiral Darlan*.

The sources for the paragraphs concerning Darlan's presence in Algiers are *Crusade in Europe;* correspondence between Eisenhower and the author Wallace Carroll and Eisenhower and Lauris Norstad; Memorandum for Record, September 14, 1946, and the draft in P & O 313.5, Case 60; Wallace Carroll's *Persuade or Perish* (Boston: Houghton Mifflin, 1948); and *My Three Years with Eisenhower*.

The account of Ike's trip back to Gibraltar from Algiers comes from the Associated Press dispatch, Allied Headquarters, North Africa, November 15.

Other sources: *Calculated Risk; Roosevelt and Hopkins; Eisenhower: Portrait of the Hero; Crusade in Europe; The Hinge of Fate; Allies; The President Is Calling; The Patton Papers;* Drew Middleton's *Our Share of Night* (New York: Viking Press, 1946); correspondence between Ike and Clark, Mamie, Beetle, and Marshall.

* * *

A BITTER DECISION

The account of Ike's arrival in Oran comes from an interview with General Lauris Norstad by the staff of the Eisenhower Library.

The material about the criticism of the "Darlan deal" and Darlan's assassination comes from the *New York Times;* the Associated Press; *Crusade in Europe; The Murder of Admiral Darlan; My Three Years with Eisenhower; Charles de Gaulle; The President Is Calling;* and an interview with Mark Clark.

Other sources: *The Taste of Courage: The War, 1939–1945* (Desmond Flower and James Reeves, eds. New York: Harper and Bros., 1960); *Sergeant Mickey and General Ike; Eisenhower Was My Boss; Soldier: The Memoirs of Matthew B. Ridgway* (as told to Harold H. Martin, New York: Harper and Bros., 1956); *The Patton Papers; Calculated Risk;* correspondence between Ike and Tom Handy, P. A. Hodgson, Mamie, John Eisenhower, Ismay, Beetle and the gang, Henry L. Stimson, Churchill, and Marshall.

* * *

POWER PLAYS

The account of the first meeting between Harold Macmillan and Ike comes from *The Blast of War*.

The sources for the material on Ike's plane trip to Casablanca are *At Ease* and *My Three Years with Eisenhower*.

The material on Casablanca comes from *Roosevelt and Hopkins; Crusade in Europe; My Three Years with Eisenhower; The Turn of the Tide; Experience of War; Charles de Gaulle;* and an interview with Thomas Handy by the staff of the Eisenhower Library.

The paragraphs on Marshall's visit to Algiers come from *Sergeant Mickey and General Ike* and *My Three Years with Eisenhower*. The paragraph on Churchill's visit comes from *The Hinge of Fate*.

Other sources: *George C. Marshall: Ordeal and Hope; Allies;* John Eisenhower's editorial comments in *Letters to Mamie;* Eisenhower's Diary; *Past Forgetting;* Margaret Bourke-White's article, "Women in Lifeboats, Torpedoed on an Africa-Bound Troopship, Photographer Finds Them as Brave in War as Men." (*Life*, February 22, 1943); *Diplomat Among Warriors; Eisenhower Was My Boss;* correspondence between Ike and Marshall, Handy, and Patton.

★   ★   ★

TURN OF THE TIDE

Most of the material used in this chapter on the Kasserine experience comes from Martin Blumenson's *Kasserine Pass* (Boston: Houghton Mifflin, 1967).

The paragraphs on Fredendall and his command post come from *Crusade in Europe;* correspondence between Ike and Gee Gerow, Marshall, and Fredendall; and *Command Missions*.

All Ernest N. Harmon quotes used in this chapter come from his book *Combat Commander* (with Milton and William Ross MacKaye. Englewood Cliffs, N.J.: Prentice-Hall, 1970).

Other sources: An interview with Thomas Handy by the staff of the Eisenhower Library; an interview with General Alfred Gruenther; *Sergeant Mickey and General Ike; Eisenhower Was My Boss;* John's comments in *Letters to Mamie; My Three Years with Eisenhower;* "From Algiers to the Elbe"; *The Patton Papers; Allies;* correspondence between Ike and Marshall, Mamie, Sir Alan Brooke, and Patton.

★   ★   ★

AN AUSPICIOUS OMEN

The material on the Bradley-Eisenhower relationship comes from Omar Bradley's *A Soldier's Story* (New York: Henry Holt, 1951); *A General's Life;* correspondence between Ike and P. A. Hodgson; and Dwight D. Eisenhower: Late a President of the United States. Memorial Tributes Delivered in Congress.

The paragraphs on Patton and II Corps come from *The Patton Papers;* Hubert Essame's *Patton: A Study in Command* (New York: Charles Scribner's Sons, 1974).

The account of Ike and Monty's second meeting comes from Nigel Hamilton's *Master of the Battlefield: Monty's War Years 1942–1944*. (New York: McGraw-Hill, 1984); and correspondence between Ike and Marshall.

The account of the dispute between Patton and Tedder comes from Lord Arthur Tedder's *With Prejudice* (Boston: Little, Brown, 1966); *The Patton Papers;* and correspondence between Ike and Patton.

The account of the meeting between troops of Monty's 8th Army and Patton's II Corps comes from Ralph G. Martin's *The G.I. War, 1941–1945* (Boston: Little, Brown, 1967).

The material on Hill 609 comes from *A Soldier's Story; Our Share of Night; My Three Years with Eisenhower;* and *Crusade in Europe*.

Other sources: John Gunther's *D-Day* (New York: Harper and Bros., 1944); *Master of the Battlefield;* Ladislas Farago's *Patton: Ordeal and Triumph* (New York: Ivan Obolensky, 1964); *The Blast of War;* correspondence between Ike and Patton, Bradley, Churchill, and Marshall.

★ ★ ★

THE FIRST STEP

The material on TRIDENT comes from *Roosevelt and Hopkins; Churchill: Taken from the Diaries of Lord Moran;* and *The Turn of the Tide.*

    The account of Churchill and Marshall's visit to Eisenhower (Algiers Conference) comes from *My Three Years with Eisenhower* and *The Hinge of Fate.*

The paragraphs on CORKSCREW come from *Crusade in Europe; Time* magazine; Memorandum for Personal Record written by Ike on July 1, 1943; and correspondence between Ike and Marshall.

The sources for the material on Dick Arnold's death and Kay's reaction to it are an interview with Anthea Saxe and urgent and personal messages between Truscott and Eisenhower.

Ewen Montagu's *The Man Who Never Was* (Philadelphia: J. B. Lippincott, 1954) tells how Operation MINCEMEAT was conceived and executed.

The description of Ike's office in Tunis and the account of the meeting between Ike and an officer of the 1st Canadian Division come from John Gunther's *D-Day.*

Other sources: An interview with Thomas Handy by the staff of the Eisenhower Library; correspondence between Ike and Marshall, Patton, Agnew, Mamie, and the Combined Chiefs.

★ ★ ★

HOLDING PATTON'S HORSE

The material on the Patton slapping incidents comes from *The Patton Papers;* correspondence between Ike and Patton, and Marshall; *Patton: Ordeal and Triumph;* the official army history report; *My Three Years with Eisenhower;* Arthur Krock's "In the Nation" (*New York Times,* November 24 and 25, 1943); and Oliver Pilat's *Drew Pearson: An Unauthorized Biography* (New York: Pocket Books, 1973).

    Other sources: Henri Michel's *The Second World War* (New York: Frederick A. Praeger, 1975); *The Blast of War; Experience of War;* Henry L. Stimson and McGeorge Bundy's *On Active Service in Peace and War* (New York: Harper and Bros., 1948); General Maxwell Taylor's *Swords and Plowshares* (New York: W. W. Norton, 1972); Winston Churchill's, *Closing the Ring* (Boston: Houghton Mifflin, 1951).

★ ★ ★

THE SOFT UNDERBELLY

De Gaulle's appraisal of Ike is from his *War Memoirs* (3 vols. New York: Simon and Schuster, 1958–1960).

    The source for the material on Messina is an interview with Eisenhower by H. H. Smith, Military History Institute, Carlisle Barracks, Pa., on June 12, 1948; the paragraph on GIANT II and the Italian surrender comes from Sir Kenneth Strong's *Intelligence at the Top* (Garden City, N.Y.: Doubleday, 1968); *Swords and Plowshares; Experience of War;* and *Crusade in Europe.*

The material on AVALANCHE comes from *The West Point Atlas of American Wars,* vol.

II, *1900–1953*. Map 95, World War II (chief editor: Colonel Vincent J. Esposito. New York: Frederick A. Praeger, 1959).

The account of Roosevelt's visit to Ike's villa comes from *Eisenhower Was My Boss* and *Roosevelt and Hopkins*.

The paragraphs on Roosevelt's decision that Ike command OVERLORD come from *Roosevelt and Hopkins;* Forrest C. Pogue's *George C. Marshall: Organizer of Victory, 1943–1945* (New York: Viking Press, 1973); and *Crusade in Europe.*

Other sources: *Calculated Risk; A Soldier's Story; The Blast of War;* Sir Francis de Guingand's *Operation Victory* (New York: Charles Scribner's Sons, 1947); Eisenhower's Diary; *Past Forgetting;* correspondence between Eisenhower and John, Mamie, Marshall, and Roosevelt.

★ ★ ★

THE SULTAN

The material concerning what Ike's title should be comes from *At Ease; Crusade in Europe;* and *Roosevelt and Hopkins.* The paragraph on Churchill's health comes from *Closing the Ring.*

The account of Ike's trip to Capri comes from *Eisenhower Was My Boss.* Churchill's quote on Anzio is from Louis L. Snyder's *The War: A Concise History* (New York: Julian Messner, 1960).

The pages on Ike's visit to Washington come from John Eisenhower's commentary in *Letters to Mamie; Crusade in Europe; Strictly Personal; George C. Marshall: Organizer of Victory; At Ease;* and *Soldier of Democracy.*

Other sources: *My Three Years with Eisenhower; The Turn of the Tide; The Blast of War; Master of the Battlefield; Churchill: Taken from the Diaries of Lord Moran;* the *New York Times;* Charles Christian Wertenbaker's "Eisenhower in Victory" in *Life* magazine, June 25, 1945; and correspondence between Ike and Beetle.

★ ★ ★

O.K., WE'LL GO

The material about the meeting at Norfolk House on January 21 comes from W. Bedell Smith's *Eisenhower's Six Great Decisions: Europe 1944–1945* (New York: Longmans, Green, 1956); James Gavin's *On to Berlin* (New York: Viking Press, 1978); *A Soldier's Story;* Montgomery's *The Memoirs of Field Marshal the Viscount Montgomery of Alamein, K. G.* (Cleveland and New York: World Publishing Co., 1958); and *Crusade in Europe.*

The paragraphs on SHINGLE come from *On to Berlin; Crusade in Europe;* and *My Three Years with Eisenhower.*

The pages on Patton come from *The Patton Papers; Patton: Ordeal and Triumph; Crusade in Europe;* and correspondence between Ike and Marshall.

The accounts of the meetings prior to the D-Day landings come from Carlo D'Este's *Decision in Normandy* (New York: E. P. Dutton, 1983); a June 5, 1964 CBS-TV broadcast "D-Day Plus 20 Years: Eisenhower Returns to Normandy," Walter Cronkite interview with Eisenhower; *Eisenhower's Six Great Decisions; Closing the Ring;* Alan Chalfont's *Montgomery of Alamein* (New York: Atheneum, 1976); Gordon A. Harrison's *Cross-Channel Attack* (Washington, D.C.: Office of the Chief of Military History, Department of the Army, 1951); *Intelligence at the Top;* and *Allies.*

Other sources: *Eisenhower Was My Boss; Past Forgetting;* Max Hastings' *Overlord:*

D-Day, June 6, 1944 (New York: Simon and Schuster, 1984); General J. Lawton Collins's *Lightning Joe* (Baton Rouge: Louisiana State University Press, 1979); Marty Snyder's *My Friend Ike* (with Glenn D. Kittler. New York: Frederick Fell, 1956); Mark Arnold Forster's *The World at War* (New York: Stein and Day, 1973); *The War: A Concise History;* interviews with Al Gruenther and Mark Clark; "From Algiers to the Elbe"; the *New York Times* and correspondence between Ike and Marshall, the Combined Chiefs, Mamie, and Henry Miller.

★ ★ ★

PIERCING THE HEART

The material on the messages broadcast over the radio prior to the D-Day landings comes from Warren Tute, John Costello, and Terry Hughes's *D-Day* (New York: Macmillan, 1974).

Most of Ike's quotes in this chapter come from the CBS-TV broadcast "D-Day Plus 20 Years."

The material on John's graduation day comes from *Strictly Personal* and the *New York Times;* John's editorial comments in *Letters to Mamie;* and correspondence between Ike and Mamie.

Other sources: *My Three Years with Eisenhower; Sergeant Mickey and General Ike;* John Keegan's *Silent Missions; Six Armies in Normandy* (New York: Viking Press, 1982); *Mamie Doud Eisenhower: Portrait of a First Lady; George C. Marshall: Organizer of Victory;* de Gaulle's *Memoirs;* David Irving's *The War Between the Generals: Inside the Allied High Command* (New York: Congdon & Lattes, 1981); the *New York Times* and the *Washington Post.*

★ ★ ★

STORMY WEATHER

The principal source for the section on John's visit is *Strictly Personal.*

The section about buzz bombs is compiled from *Eisenhower Was My Boss; Crusade in Europe;* and *Experience of War.*

The account of Ike and John's visit to Bradley comes from *A Soldier's Story* and *Strictly Personal.*

The information about Kay's trip to Washington comes from *Eisenhower Was My Boss* and *Past Forgetting.*

Other sources: *Sergeant Mickey and General Ike; My Three Years with Eisenhower; Lightning Joe; My Friend Ike; Master of the Battlefield; The Supreme Commander;* Ernie Pyle's *Brave Men* (New York: Henry Holt, 1944); correspondence between Ike and Mamie; and the *New York Times.*

★ ★ ★

IRISH AND TRAGIC

Principal sources for this chapter are interviews with Maude Black; Hortense Boutell; John Eisenhower; William Bragg Ewald; Chester "Chet" Hansen; Ken McCormick; Larry Newman; Anthea and Ed Saxe.

Other sources: *Eisenhower Was My Boss; Past Forgetting;* an interview with Harrison Salisbury by the staff of the Columbia Oral History Project; James M. Gavin's *On to*

Berlin; David Irving correspondence re. *The War Between the Generals;* and *The Eisenhower Papers.*

★ ★ ★

OUT OF THE WOODS

The section about the slowness of Montgomery's pace is compiled from *Overlord: D-Day, June 6, 1944;* an interview with Drew Middleton; correspondence between Ike and Montgomery; Richard Lamb's *Montgomery in Europe, 1943–45: Success or Failure?; With Prejudice;* and *My Three Years with Eisenhower.* (New York: Franklin Watts, 1984); Ike's comments on hedgerows is from the CBS-TV broadcast "D-Day Plus 20 Years."

Other sources: Russell F. Weigley's *Eisenhower's Lieutenants,* vol. I. (Bloomington, Ind.: Indiana University Press, 1981); Charles B. MacDonald's *The Mighty Endeavor* (New York: Oxford University Press, 1969); *Intelligence at the Top; A General's Life; A Soldier's Story; Sergeant Mickey and General Ike; The Patton Papers;* Martin Blumenson's *Breakout and Pursuit* (Washington, D.C.: Office of the Chief of Military History, Department of the Army, 1961); Butcher's Unpublished Diary for July 20; an interview with General J. Lawton Collins; the *New York Times;* and correspondence between Ike and Bradley.

★ ★ ★

CROSSING THE SEINE

Sources for the material on DRAGOON: Brenda Ralph Lewis's "Operation Dragoon." (*War Monthly* no. 27, June 1970); *Churchill: Taken from the Diaries of Lord Moran; Crusade in Europe;* interview with Thomas Handy by the staff of the Eisenhower Library; an interview with Mark Clark; Winston Churchill's *Triumph and Tragedy* (Boston: Houghton Mifflin, 1953); and messages between Ike and Marshall.

The account of Ike and Bradley's visit to Paris comes from *Eisenhower Was My Boss; Crusade in Europe;* Chet Hansen's Diary; *A Soldier's Story;* and *Past Forgetting.* The material on de Gaulle's return to Paris comes from his *Memoirs;* John Eisenhower's *The Bitter Woods* (New York: G. P. Putnam's Sons, 1969); *Charles de Gaulle;* and *Experience of War.*

Other sources: *Sergeant Mickey and General Ike; My Three Years with Eisenhower; The Second World War; With Prejudice; Six Armies in Normandy; Crusade in Europe; Breakout and Pursuit; Allies;* correspondence between Ike and Marshall, and Churchill; and letters to Mamie (published and unpublished).

★ ★ ★

A FRAGILE REED

The account of the August 23 meeting between Ike and Montgomery comes from *Montgomery in Europe 1943–1945: Success or Failure?* The material on their September 10 meeting is from *With Prejudice* and *Crusade in Europe.* The section on MARKET-GARDEN comes from *The War: A Concise History; Montgomery of Alamein;* Sir Arthur Bryant's *Triumph in the West* (Garden City, N.Y.: Doubleday, 1959). The paragraphs on the September 22 meeting at Versailles come from *A Soldier's*

Story; the W. B. Smith Collection (Eisenhower Library. Eyes Only Cables, September 22, 1944); and cables between Ike and Monty.

The source for the section on the Huertgen Forest is an article by James M. Gavin, "Bloody Huertgen: The Battle that Should Never Have Been Fought" (*American Heritage,* Dec. 1979). The account of Ike's meeting with Churchill on December 12 comes from *Triumph in the West.*

Other sources: A 1957 interview of George C. Marshall by Forrest C. Pogue (as reported in *George C. Marshall: Organizer of Victory*); *The Patton Papers; Eisenhower Was My Boss; With Prejudice; A Soldier's Story; The War: A Concise History; My Three Years with Eisenhower; Sergeant Mickey and General Ike;* James L. Stokesbury's *A Short History of World War II* (New York: William Morrow, 1980): *Lightning Joe;* an interview with Aksel Nielsen; the *New York Times;* and correspondence between Ike and Somervell.

★ ★ ★

A MERE INCIDENT

Sources for the material on the Battle of the Bulge: *Montgomery of Alamein; My Three Years with Eisenhower; Montgomery in Europe 1944–1945: Success or Failure?;* Forrest C. Pogue's notes at the Military History Institute, Carlisle Barracks, Pa.; B. H. Liddell Hart's *History of the Second World War* (New York: G. P. Putnam's Sons, 1970); *Intelligence at the Top;* Ike's Top Secret Memorandum dated December 23, 1944; *A Soldier's Story: Crusade in Europe; The Supreme Commander; Experience of War; The Taste of Courage; At Ease;* and the *New York Times.*

The information about Skorzeny and the rumored plot to assassinate Ike comes from *Crusade in Europe; Eisenhower Was My Boss; Sergeant Mickey and General Ike; My Three Years with Eisenhower; Intelligence at the Top;* and the *New York Times.*

The account of the December 19 meeting is from *The Mighty Endeavor;* the material about the December 20 changeover is from *A Soldier's Story* and Charles B. MacDonald's *A Time for Trumpets: The Untold Story of the Bulge* (New York: William Morrow, 1984).

Sources for the paragraphs on Ike's differences with de Gaulle: *Crusade in Europe* and *The Bitter Woods.*

Principal source for the section describing the execution of Eddie Slovik: Court-martial of Private Eddie Slovik. Record of the Trial (including the court-martial order; verbatim transcript; prosecution exhibits; staff judge advocate's review; board decision; and the report of execution) obtained from the Department of the Army, U.S. Army Judiciary, Falls Church, Va. Also helpful was William Bradford Huie's *The Execution of Private Slovik* (New York: Delacorte Press, 1954); and the February 11, 1963, NBC-TV special project "Eisenhower on Lincoln as Commander in Chief."

Other sources: *Eisenhower's Six Great Decisions; The Patton Papers;* an interview with Edward T. Folliard, a reporter for the *Washington Post,* by the staff of the Columbia Oral History Project; an interview with Chet Hansen; *On Active Service in Peace and War; Life* magazine; and the *New York Times.*

★   ★   ★

THE LONG-DISTANCE RUNNER

The account of Tedder's meeting in Russia with Stalin is from *With Prejudice* and *Crusade in Europe*. John's account of his February visit to see his father is from *Strictly Personal*.

The material on Operation VERITABLE is from *The Mighty Endeavor*. Sources for Remagen: *Crusade in Europe; Triumph in the West; The Patton Papers; The Supreme Commander; Operation Victory;* and *Life* magazine.

The section about Ike's trip to Cannes is from *Eisenhower Was My Boss; A General's Life;* and *Sergeant Mickey and General Ike.*

The information about the Redoubt comes from the *New York Times; Eisenhower's Six Great Decisions;* Ronald Lewin's *Ultra Goes to War* (New York: Pocket Books, 1981); William L. Shirer's *Rise and Fall of the Third Reich* (New York: Simon and Schuster, 1960); *A Soldier's Story;* and *Crusade in Europe.*

The material on Ike's visit to a concentration camp is from *Crusade in Europe* and his report to Marshall, dated April 15.

Sources for the material on Roosevelt's death and its aftermath: James MacGregor Burns's *Roosevelt: The Soldier of Freedom* (New York: Harcourt Brace Jovanovich, 1970); *The Patton Papers; Crusade in Europe; Sergeant Mickey and General Ike;* and *Strictly Personal.*

Other sources: An interview with General J. Lawton Collins; *Operation Victory; A General's Life; Past Forgetting; Montgomery of Alamein; Eisenhower's Six Great Decisions; The War Between the Generals;* Cornelius Ryan's *The Last Battle* (New York: Simon and Schuster, 1966); *Lightning Joe; My Three Years with Eisenhower;* the *New York Times;* and correspondence between Ike and Marshall, Churchill, and Eden.

★   ★   ★

HIS GREATEST MOMENT

Principal sources for this chapter are interviews with Sir James Gault and Sir Kenneth Strong; and two articles by Charles Christian Wertenbaker, "Eisenhower in Victory" and "Surrender at Reims," which appeared in *Life* magazine.

Other sources: *Eisenhower Was My Boss; My Three Years with Eisenhower; Letters to Mamie; Time* magazine; the *New York Times; Vital Speeches;* correspondence: Ike to Lieutenant Colonel R. M. G. Lloyd.

* * *

BIBLIOGRAPHY

* * *

INTERVIEWS BY THE AUTHOR:

Sherman Adams, Betty Allen, Harry Anholt, Robert Armstrong, Marvin Arrowsmith, Burton S. Barr, Maude Black (Mrs. Douglas Black), Robert Brooks, Herbert Brownell, Hortense Boutell, Dr. Arthur Burns, Gen. Edwin N. Clark, Gen. Mark W. Clark, Robert Clark, Gen. J. Lawton "Lightning Joe" Collins, Fox B. Conner, Jr., Miriam Dryhos, Delmar Spencer Dykes, John Eisenhower, The Rev. Edward L. R. Elson, George Etherington, William Bragg Ewald, Jr., Joel Fischer, Sir James Gault, Gen. Andrew Jackson Goodpaster, Gordon Gray, Robert Gray, Gen. Alfred E. Gruenther, Chester E. Hansen, Bryce Harlow, Gabriel Hauge, Ibby Hazlett (Mrs. Everett E. "Swede" Hazlett), William Hopkins, Nettie Stover Jackson, Wes Jackson, Henry Jamieson, Charles Kiley, Arthur Larson, Gen. Lyman J. Lemnitzer, The Hon. Henry Cabot Lodge, The Rev. Robert H. MacAskill, Ken McCormick, Leonard Marks, Drew Middleton, Arthur Minnich, Robert Montgomery, Mabel Frances "Mike" Doud Moore, Malcolm Moos, Larry Newman, Aksel Nielsen, Gen. Lauris Norstad, Jack Ramagna, Col. Russell P. "Red" Reeder, Jr., Charles Roberts, William P. Rogers, Anthea and Ed Saxe, Raymond Scherer, Bernard Shanley, Ellis D. Slater, Thomas Stephens, Mary Jane Stineman (Mrs. John Stineman), Sir Kenneth Strong, Stan Swinton, Sam Vaughan, Gen. Vernon Walters, Alexander M. "Babe" Weyand, Ann Whitman.

* * *

INTERVIEW BY JAMES PETERSEN, researcher, Kansas: Earl J. Endacott—June 26, 1982

* * *

ORAL HISTORY TRANSCRIPTS from the Dwight D. Eisenhower Library, Abilene, Kansas:

Levy Asper, Henry S. Aurand, John A. Bird, Gen. Charles L. Bolte, Charles R. Broshous, Herbert Brownell, Gen. Mark W. Clark, Robert Clark, Jacob L. Devers, John S. D. Eisenhower, Milton S. Eisenhower, Ivan Fitzwater, Abe Forney, Howard Funk, Gen. Thomas Handy, John Hightower, Nettie Stover Jackson, Helen S. King, William L. Lee, Gen. John W. Leonard, John H. Long, Mrs. Robert J. Long, John Krout, Nancy Jansen McCarty, John F. "Six" McDonnell, Arthur Nevins, Gen. Lauris Norstad, Lelia G. Picking, Irene Miller Sacco, J. Earl Schaefer, Inez G. Scott, Merriman Smith, Orin Snider, James Stack, Joseph Swing, Vernon A. Walters, The Rev. Roy I. Witter, Gen. Roscoe B. Woodruff.

★ ★ ★

ORAL HISTORY TRANSCRIPT—Herbert Hoover Presidential Library, West Branch, Iowa:

General Dwight D. Eisenhower—interviewed by Raymond Henle, director, on July 13, 1967, at Gettysburg, Pa.

★ ★ ★

ORAL HISTORY TRANSCRIPTS—The National Historic Site, Gettysburg, Pa.:

David Eisenhower, John Eisenhower, Mamie Eisenhower, George "Bo" Horkin, Jr., Kevin McCann, Arthur Nevins, Ethel Wetzel.

★ ★ ★

ORAL HISTORY TRANSCRIPTS—U.S. Army Military History Institute, Carlisle Barracks, Pa.:

Gen. Charles L. Bolte, The Bradford Chynoweth Papers, Gen. Omar N. Bradley, Gen. Mark W. Clark, Gen. Lucius D. Clay, Lt. Gen. Ira C. Eaker, Gen. Dwight D. Eisenhower, Gen. Andrew J. Goodpaster, Lt. Gen. James M. Gavin, Gen. Lyman L. Lemnitzer, Brig. Gen. S. L. A. Marshall, Gen. Elwood R. Quesada, Gen. Matthew B. Ridgway, Gen. Albert C. Wedemeyer.

★ ★ ★

ORAL HISTORY FROM COLUMBIA UNIVERSITY IN MICROFORM:

Elie Abel, Bertha Adkins, George David Aiken, George Venable Allen, Dillon Anderson, Evan Peter Aurand, Bill Becker, Charles Edward Bennett, Andrew H. Berding, Harold Boeschenstein, Robert Richardson Bowie, William Birrell Branke, Samuel Miller Brownell, Elmer La Mar Buckner, Carter L. Burgess, James Vincent Burke, Jr., Arthur Edward Burns, Earl Lauer Butz, Ralph Harlan Cake, Howard Alexander Cook, Charles Alexander Cook, William G. Cooper, Jr., Kenneth Gale Crawford, Thomas B. Curtis, Wesley Abner D'Ewart, Edward T. Dicker, George Douthit, William H. Draper, Jr., Roscoe Drummond, Milton Stover Eisenhower, Harold Engstrom, Luther Harris Evans, Leonard Kimball Firestone, Edward Thomas Folliard, Marion Bayard Folsom, Clarent Francis, Andrew Jackson Goodpaster, Arthur Gray, Jr., Robert Keith Gray, Nat R. Griswold, Richard L. Guylay, Najeeb E. Halaby, John Wesley Hanes, Jr., Wilson F. Harwood, Loy Wesley Henderson, John Baker Hollister, Albert Charles Jacobs, Neil H. Jacoby, Jacob Koppel Javits, Jesse Charles Johnson, Roger Warren Jones, Kenneth B. Keating, Henry Joseph Kellerman, William Fife Knowland, Robert Lowe Kunzig, Sigurd Stanton Larmon, Joseph Bracken Lee, Clare Boothe Luce, John Luter, Edward Aeneas McCabe, Kevin McCann, Carl Wesley McCardle, John Jay McCloy, James McClurg, Jr., Neil Hossier McElroy, Sidney Sanders McMath, Robert Edward Merriman, True Delbert Morse, Robert Daniel Murphy, Anchor Nielson, Herschel D. Newsom, Dennis O'Rourke, Don Paarlberg, John Sutton Patterson,

Charles Harting Percy, Richard M. Pittenger, Terrell E. Powell, Elwood R. Quesada, Maxwell M. Rabb, Ogden Rogers Reid, Ralph Waldo Emerson Reid, Edward E. Rice, Chalmers Roberts, Walter Spencer Robertson, Theodore McKeldin Roosevelt, Richard Halworth Rovere, Stanley Maddox Rumbough, Jr., Harrison Evans Salisbury, Irving Solomon, Leverett H. Saltonstall, Howland Sargeant, Raymond J. Saulnier, Leonard Andrew Scheele, Raymond Lewis Scherer, Dudley Crawford Sharp, Joseph S. Sheldon, William T. Shelton, James Robinson Shepley, Robert Lee Sherrod, Allan Shivers, David M. Shoup, Ellis Dwinnell Slater, Howard Kingsbury Smith, Merriman Smith, Mansfield Daniel Sprague, Elmer Boyd Staats, Theodore Streibert, Robert Helyer Thayer, Wayne Upton, James J. Wadsworth, Arthur V. Watkins, Anne W. Wheaton, Francis O. Wilcox, E. Grainger Williams, Henry Woods, Henry Merritt Wriston, Charles Richardson Yates.

★ ★ ★

BOOKS

Acheson, Dean. *Present at the Creation*. New York: W. W. Norton, 1969.

Adams, Henry H. *Harry Hopkins*. New York: G. P. Putnam's Sons, 1977.

———. *1942: The Year That Doomed the Axis*. New York: David McKay, 1967.

Adams, Sherman. *Firsthand Report: The Story of the Eisenhower Administration*. New York: Harper & Row, 1961.

Alexander, Charles C. *Holding the Line: The Eisenhower Era. 1952–1961*. Bloomington, Ind.: Indiana University Press, 1975.

———. *The Big Change: America Transforms Itself, 1900–1950*. New York: Harper and Bros., 1952.

Allen, Frederick Lewis. *Only Yesterday*. New York: Harper and Bros., 1931.

Allen, George E. *Presidents Who Have Known Me*. New York: Simon and Schuster, 1950.

Allen, Peter. *One More River: The Rhine Crossings of 1945*. New York: Charles Scribner's Sons, 1980.

Alsop, Joseph and Stewart. *The Reporter's Trade*. New York: Reynal and Co., 1958.

Alsop, Stewart. *The Center: People and Power in Political Washington*. New York: Harper & Row, 1968.

Ambrose, Stephen E. *Duty, Honor, Country: A History of West Point*. Baltimore: Johns Hopkins Press, 1966.

———. *Eisenhower and Berlin, 1945: The Decision to Halt at the Elbe*. New York: W. W. Norton, 1967.

———. *Ike: Abilene to Berlin*, New York: Harper & Row, 1973.

———. *Pegasus Bridge*. New York: Simon and Schuster, 1985.

———. *The Supreme Commander: The War Years of General Dwight D. Eisenhower*. Garden City, N.Y.: Doubleday, 1970.

Ambrose, Stephen E., and Richard H. Immerman. *Ike's Spies: Eisenhower and the Espionage Establishment*. Garden City, N.Y.: Doubleday, 1981.

———. *Milton S. Eisenhower*. Baltimore: Johns Hopkins University Press, 1983.

American Battle Monuments Commission. *Guide to the American Battlefields in Europe*. Washington, D.C.: U.S. Printing Office, 1927.

American Heritage Editors and United Press International. *Eisenhower: American Hero*. Introduction by Bruce Catton. New York: American Heritage Publishing Co., 1969.

Anderson, Clinton P., and Milton Viorst. *Outsider in the Senate*. New York: World Publishing Co., 1970.

Anderson, Jack, and James Boyd. *Confessions of a Muckraker*. New York: Random House, 1979.

Anderson, Jack, and Ronald W. May. *McCarthy: The Man, the Senator, the "Ism."* Boston: Beacon Press, 1952.

Anderson, J. W. *Eisenhower, Brownell and the Congress.* Tuscaloosa, Alabama: University of Alabama Press, 1964.

Army Times Editors. *The Challenge and the Triumph.* New York: G. P. Putnam's Sons, 1960.

Army Times Editors. *Warrior: The Story of General George S. Patton, Jr.* New York: G. P. Putnam's Sons, 1967.

Arnold, Henry H. *Global Mission.* New York: Harper and Bros., 1949.

Ayer, Frederick, Jr. *Before the Colors Fade: Portrait of a Soldier, George C. Patton.* Boston: Houghton Mifflin, 1964.

Bagni, Gwen, and Paul Dubov. *Backstairs at the White House.* Englewood Cliffs, N.J.: Prentice-Hall, 1978.

Bailey, Anthony. *America, Lost and Found.* New York: Random House, 1981.

Bailey, Ronald H., and eds. of Time-Life Books. *The Home Front: U.S.A.* Alexandria, Va.: Time-Life Books, 1977.

Baldwin, Hanson W. *World War I.* New York: Harper & Row, 1962.

Baruch, Bernard M. *Baruch: The Public Years.* New York: Holt, Rinehart & Winston, 1960.

Bayley, Edwin R. *Joe McCarthy and the Press.* Madison, Wisc.: University of Wisconsin Press, 1981.

Becker, Carl L. *Everyman His Own Historian.* New York: F. S. Crofts & Co., 1935.

Beesly, Patrick. *Very Special Intelligence.* New York: Doubleday, 1978.

Beitzell, Robert. *The Uneasy Alliance: America, Britain, and Russia, 1941–1943.* New York: Alfred A. Knopf, 1972.

Belfield, Eversley, and H. Essame. *The Battle for Normandy.* London: Batsford, 1965.

Bendiner, Robert. *Just Around the Corner.* New York: Harper & Row, 1967.

Bernstein, Irving. *Turbulent Years.* Boston: Houghton Mifflin, 1970.

Bidwell, Brigadier Shelford, Editorial Consultant. *Hitler's Generals and Their Battles.* Foreword by Brigadier General James L. Collins, Jr. New York: Chartwell Books. 1976.

Bishop, Jim. *FDR's Last Year.* New York: William Morrow, 1974.

Blake, I. George. *Paul V. McNutt: Portrait of a Hoosier Statesman.* Franklin, Indiana: Central Publishing Co., 1966.

Blumenson, Martin. *Breakout and Pursuit.* Washington, D.C.: Office of the Chief of Military History, Department of the Army, 1961.

———. *Kasserine Pass.* Boston: Houghton Mifflin, 1967.

———. *Mark Clark.* New York: Congdon & Weed, 1984.

———. *The Patton Papers, 1935–1940.* Boston: Houghton Mifflin, 1972.

———. *The Patton Papers, 1940–1945.* Boston: Houghton Mifflin, 1974.

Boldt, Gerhard. *Hitler: The Last Ten Days.* Translated by Sandra Bance. New York: Coward, McCann & Geoghegan, 1973.

Bosch, William J. *Judgment on Nuremberg: American Attitudes Toward the Major German War Crime Trial.* Chapel Hill, N.C.: University of North Carolina Press, 1970.

Bourke-White, Margaret. *"Dear Fatherland, Rest Quietly."* New York: Simon and Schuster, 1946.

Boussel, Patrice. *D-Day Beaches Revisited.* Garden City, N.Y.: Doubleday, 1964.

Bradley, Omar N. *A Soldier's Story.* New York: Henry Holt, 1951.

Bradley, Omar N., and Clay Blair. *A General's Life.* New York: Simon and Schuster, 1983.

Brandon, Dorothy. *Mamie Doud Eisenhower: Portrait of a First Lady.* New York: Charles Scribner's Sons, 1954.

Brett-Smith, Richard. *Hitler's Generals*. San Rafael, Calif.: Presidio Press, 1978.

Broad, Lewis. *Winston Churchill: The Years of Achievement*. New York: Hawthorn Books, 1963.

Brown, Anthony Cave. *Bodyguard of Lies*. New York: Harper & Row, 1975.

———. *The Last Hero: Wild Bill Donovan*. New York: Times Books, 1982.

Brown, Anthony Cave, and Charles B. MacDonald. *On a Field of Red: The Communist International and the Coming of World War II*. New York: G. P. Putnam's Sons, 1980.

Brown, Charles H. *The Correspondents' War*. New York: Charles Scribner's Sons, 1967.

Brown, John Mason. *Through These Men*. New York: Books for Libraries Press, 1956.

Bryant, Sir Arthur. *Triumph in the West: Based on the Diaries and Autobiographical Notes of Field Marshal the Viscount Alanbrooke*. New York: Doubleday, 1959.

———. *The Turn of the Tide*. New York: Doubleday, 1957.

Buchanan, A. Russell. *The United States and World War II;* vol. II. New York: Harper & Row, 1964.

Burlingame, Roger. *Don't Let Them Scare You: The Life and Times of Elmer Davis*. Philadelphia and New York: J. B. Lippincott, 1961.

Burner, David. *Herbert Hoover: The Public Life*. New York: Alfred A. Knopf, 1978.

Burns, James MacGregor. *Roosevelt: The Soldier of Freedom*. New York: Harcourt Brace Jovanovich, 1970.

Busch, Noel F. *Japan*. New York: American Heritage Publishing Co., 1972.

———. *TR: The Story of Theodore Roosevelt and His Influence on Our Times*. New York: Reynal & Co., 1963.

Butcher, Harry C. *My Three Years with Eisenhower*. New York: Simon and Schuster, 1946.

Calvocoressi, Peter. *Top-Secret Ultra*. New York: Pantheon Books, 1980.

Campion, Nardi Reeder, and Red Reeder (Russell Potter). *The West Point Story*. New York: Random House, 1956.

Carter, Paul A. *Another Part of the Twenties*. New York: Columbia University Press, 1977.

Catton, Bruce. *Gettysburg: The Final Fury*. Garden City, N.Y.: Doubleday, 1974.

Cavaioli, Frank J. *West Point and the Presidency*. New York: St. John's University Press, 1962.

Chalfont, Alun. *Montgomery of Alamein*. New York: Atheneum, 1976.

Childs, Marquis. *Eisenhower: Captive Hero*. New York: Harcourt, Brace, 1958.

Churchill, Allen. *The Year the World Went Mad*. New York: Thomas Y. Crowell, 1960.

Churchill, Winston S. *The Second World War:* vol. 1 *The Gathering Storm*. Boston: Houghton Mifflin, 1948.

———. vol. 2 *Their Finest Hour*. Boston: Houghton Mifflin, 1949.

———. vol. 3 *The Grand Alliance*. Boston: Houghton Mifflin, 1950.

———. vol. 4 *The Hinge of Fate*. Boston: Houghton Mifflin, 1950.

———. vol. 5 *Closing the Ring*. Boston: Houghton Mifflin, 1951.

———. vol. 6 *Triumph and Tragedy*. Boston: Houghton Mifflin, 1953.

The City of the Plains. Abilene. A Gem. Reprinted by Dickinson County Historical Society. Iowa: Burdette Co., 1887. (R & D Printers, 1976).

Clark, Mark W. *Calculated Risk*. New York: Harper and Bros., 1950.

———. *From the Danube to the Yalu*. New York: Harper and Bros., 1954.

Clark, Maurine. *Captain's Bride-General's Lady*. New York: McGraw-Hill, 1956.

Clay, Lucius D. *Decision in Germany*. Garden City, N.Y.: Doubleday, 1950.

Cobb, Kirkpatrick. *Ike's Old Sarge*. Dallas, Texas: Royal Publishing Co., 1964.

Cochran, Thomas C. *The Great Depression and World War II*. Glenview, Ill.: Scott, Foresman & Co., 1968.

Codman, Charles R. *Drive*. Boston: Atlantic Monthly Press, 1957.

Coit, Margaret L. *Mr. Baruch*. Boston: Houghton Mifflin Co., 1957.

Cole, Wayne S. *Charles A. Lindberg and the Battle Against American Intervention in World War II*. New York: Harcourt Brace Jovanovich, 1974.

Collins, General J. Lawton. *Lightning Joe*. Baton Rouge: Louisiana State University Press, 1979.

Colville, John. *The Fringes of Power*. New York: W. W. Norton, 1985.

———. *Winston Churchill and His Inner Circle*. New York: Wyndham Books, 1981.

Congdon, Don, ed. *Combat: European Theater. World War II*. Introduction by Merle Miller. New York: Dell Publishing Co., 1958.

Conner, Virginia. *What Father Forbade*. Philadelphia: Dorrance & Co., 1951.

Conroy, Pat. *The Lords of Discipline*. Boston: Houghton Mifflin, 1980.

Cook, Don. *Charles de Gaulle*. New York: G. P. Putnam's Sons, 1984.

———. *Ten Men and History*. Garden City, N.Y.: Doubleday, 1981.

Cooke, Alistair. *Six Men*. New York: Alfred A. Knopf, 1977.

Cortesi, Lawrence. *Last Bridge to Victory*. New York: Zebra Books, 1984.

Cowen, Ida. *Jews in Remote Corners of the World*. Englewood Cliffs, N.J.: Prentice-Hall, 1971.

Cozzens, James Gould. *Guard of Honor*. New York: Harcourt, Brace, 1948.

Craig, William. *Enemy at the Gates: The Battle for Stalingrad*. New York: E. P. Dutton, 1973.

Critchell, Laurence. *Four Stars of Hell*. New York: Declan X. McMullen Co., 1947.

Cruttwell, C. R. M. F. *A History of the Great War 1914–1918*. 2d ed. Oxford: Clarendon Press, 1936.

Cutler, Robert. *No Time for Rest*. Boston: Little, Brown, 1966.

Dallek, Robert. *Franklin D. Roosevelt and American Foreign Policy. 1932–1945*. New York: Oxford University Press, 1979.

Daniels, Jonathan. *The Man of Independence*. New York: J. B. Lippincott, 1950.

———. *The Time Between the Wars: Armistice to Pearl Harbor*. Edited by Lewis Gannett. Garden City, N.Y.: Doubleday, 1966.

Dastrup, Boyd L. *A Centennial History of the U.S. Army Command and General Staff College*. Manhattan, Kans.: Sunflower University Press, 1982.

David, Lester and Irene. *Ike and Mamie*. New York: G. P. Putnam's Sons, 1981.

Davis, Clyde Brion. *The Age of Indiscretion*. New York: J. B. Lippincott, 1950.

Davis, Kenneth S. *Experience of War: The United States in World War II*. Edited by Lewis Gannett. Garden City, N.Y.: Doubleday, 1965.

———. *Kansas: A Bicentennial History*. New York: W. W. Norton, 1976.

———. *A Prophet in His Own Country*. Garden City, N.Y.: Doubleday, 1957.

———. *Soldier of Democracy*. Garden City, N.Y.: Doubleday, Doran, 1945.

de Gaulle, Charles. *The War Memoirs of Charles de Gaulle: Salvation. 1944–46*. Translated by Richard Howard. New York: Simon and Schuster, 1960.

———. *The War Memoirs of Charles de Gaulle: Renewal and Endeavor*. New York: Simon and Schuster, 1970.

de Guingand, Maj. Gen. Sir Francis. *Operation Victory*. New York: Charles Scribner's Sons, 1947.

Deighton, Len. *Blitzkrieg: From the Rise of Hitler to the Fall of Dunkirk*. New York: Alfred A. Knopf, 1980.

———. *Fighter: The True Story of the Battle of Britain*. New York: Ballantine Books, 1982.

Delmer, Sefton. *The Counterfeit Spy*. New York: Harper & Row, 1971.

D'Este, Carlo. *Decision in Normandy*. New York: E. P. Dutton, 1983.

Deweerd, Harvey A. *President Wilson Fights His War*. New York: Macmillan, 1968.

Donovan, Robert J. *Conflict and Crisis: The Presidency of Harry S. Truman, 1945–1948*. New York: W. W. Norton, 1977.

Duncan, Kunigunde. *Earning the Right to Do Fanciwork: An Informal Biography of Mrs. Ida Eisenhower*. Lawrence, Kans.: University of Kansas Press, 1957.

Dupuy, R. Ernest, and Trevor N. *Brave Men and Great Captains*. New York: Harper & Bros., 1959.

Eisenhower, Dwight D. *At Ease: Stories I Tell to Friends*. Garden City, N.Y.: Doubleday, 1967.

———. *Crusade in Europe*. Garden City, N.Y.: Doubleday, 1948.

———. *The Eisenhower Diaries*. Robert H. Ferrell, ed. New York: W. W. Norton, 1981.

———. *Eisenhower's Own Story of the War*. New York: Arco Publishing Co., 1946.

———. *In Review: Pictures I've Kept*. Garden City, N.Y.: Doubleday, 1969.

———. *Letters to Mamie*. Edited by John S. D. Eisenhower. Garden City, N.Y.: Doubleday, 1978.

Eisenhower Foundation. *D-Day: The Normandy Invasion in Retrospect*. Foreword by Omar N. Bradley. Lawrence, Kans.: University of Kansas Press, 1972.

———. *Mandate for Change*. Garden City, N.Y.: Doubleday, 1963.

———. *The Papers of Dwight David Eisenhower: The War Years*, vols. 1–5. Edited by Alfred D. Chandler, Jr., and Stephen E. Ambrose. Baltimore: Johns Hopkins University Press, 1970.

———. *Waging Peace*. Garden City, N.Y.: Doubleday, 1965.

Eisenhower, John S. D. *Allies: Pearl Harbor to D-Day*. Garden City, N.Y.: Doubleday, 1982.

———. *The Bitter Woods*. New York: G. P. Putnam's Sons, 1969.

———. *Strictly Personal*. Garden City, N.Y.: Doubleday, 1974.

Eisenhower, Julie Nixon. *Special People*. New York: Simon and Schuster, 1977.

Eisenhower, Milton S. *The President Is Calling*. Garden City, N.Y.: Doubleday, 1974.

———. *The Wine Is Bitter*. Garden City, N.Y.: Doubleday, 1963.

Ellis, Joseph, and Robert Moore. *School for Soldiers: An Inquiry into West Point and the Profession of Arms*. New York: Oxford University Press, 1974.

Esposito, Col. Vincent J., et al., eds. *The West Point Atlas of American Wars*, 2 vols. New York: Frederick A. Praeger, 1959.

Eubank, Keith. *Summit at Teheran*. New York: William Morrow, 1985.

Ewald, William Bragg, Jr. *Eisenhower the President: Crucial Days 1951–1960*. Englewood Cliffs, N.J.: Prentice-Hall, 1981.

Eyewitness History of World War II, vol. I *Blitzkrieg;* vol. II *Siege;* vol. III *Counterattack;* vol. IV *Victory*. New York: Bantam Books, 1962.

Faber, Doris. *The Presidents' Mothers*. New York: St. Martin's Press, 1976.

Farago, Ladislas. *The Last Days of Patton*. New York: McGraw-Hill, 1981.

———. *Patton: Ordeal and Triumph*. New York: Ivan Obolensky, 1964.

Federal Writers' Project of the WPA for the state of Colorado. *Colorado: A Guide to the Highest State*. American Guide Series. Sponsored by the Colorado State Planning Commission. New York: Hastings House, 1945.

Federal Writers' Project of the WPA for the state of Iowa. *Iowa: A Guide to the Hawkeye State*. American Guide Series. New York: Hastings House, 1938.

Federal Writers' Project, Texas. *Denison Guide*. Published by the Denison Chamber of Commerce, Denison, Texas, 1939. Denison Kiwanis Club. Denison, Texas Centennial 1872–1972.

Feis, Herbert. *Between War and Peace: The Potsdam Conference*. Princeton, N.J.: Princeton University Press, 1960.

———. *1933: Characters in Crisis*. Boston: Little, Brown, 1966.

Ferrell, Robert H. *Off the Record: The Private Papers of Harry S Truman*. New York: Harper & Row, 1980.

Field, Rudolph. *Ike: Man of the Hour*. New York: Universal, 1952.

———. *Mister American*. New York: Rudolph Field Co., 1952.

Fischer, Louis. *The Road to Yalta*. New York: Harper & Row, 1972.

Fleming, Thomas. *The Officers' Wives*. New York: Warner Books, 1982.

———. *West Point: The Men and Times of the United States Military Academy*. New York: William Morrow, 1969.

Flower, Desmond, and James Reeves, eds. *The Taste of Courage: The War, 1939–1945*. New York: Harper and Bros., 1960.

Foner, Jack D. *Blacks and the Military in American History*. New York: Frederick A. Praeger, 1974.

Foot, M. R. D., and J. M. Langley. *MI 9: Escape and Evasion, 1939–1945*. Boston: Little, Brown, 1980.

Forman, Sidney. *West Point: A History of the United States Military Academy*. New York: Columbia University Press, 1950.

Forster, Mark Arnold. *The World at War*. New York: Stein and Day, 1973.

Fraser, David. *Alanbrooke*. New York: Atheneum, 1982.

Frye, William. *Marshall: Citizen Soldier*. Indianapolis, Ind.: Bobbs-Merrill, 1947.

Galloway, K. Bruce, and Robert B. Johnson, Jr. *West Point: America's Power Fraternity*. New York: Simon and Schuster, 1973.

Gammon, Roland. *All Believers Are Brothers*. Garden City, N.Y.: Doubleday, 1969.

Garlinski, Jozef. *The Enigma War*. New York: Charles Scribner's Sons, 1980.

Gavin, James M. *On to Berlin*. New York: Viking Press, 1978.

Goebbels, Joseph. *The Goebbels Diaries, 1942 to 1943*. Translated by Louis P. Lochner. Reprint of 1948 ed. Westport, Conn.: Greenwood Press, 1970.

Goldman, Eric. *The Crucial Decade and After: America, 1945–1960*. New York: Alfred A. Knopf, 1956.

Graff, Henry F., consulting editor. *The Life History of the United States* series, vols. 1–12. New York: Time, Inc., 1963.

Grey, Ian. *Stalin*. Garden City, N.Y.: Doubleday, 1979.

Grigg, John. *1943: The Victory That Never Was*. New York: Hill & Wang, 1980.

Gulley, Bill, and Mary Ellen Reese. *Breaking Cover*. New York: Simon and Schuster, 1980.

Gunther, John. *D-Day*. New York: Harper and Bros., 1943.

———. *Eisenhower: The Man and the Symbol*. New York: Harper & Bros., 1952.

———. *Inside Europe Today*. New York: Harper & Row, 1961.

———. *Roosevelt in Retrospect*. New York: Harper and Bros., 1950.

Hamby, Alonzo L. *Beyond the New Deal: Harry S Truman and American Liberalism*. New York: Columbia University Press, 1973.

Hamilton, Nigel. *Master of the Battlefield: Monty's War Years, 1942–1944*. New York: McGraw-Hill, 1984.

———. *Monty: The Making of a General, 1887–1942*. New York: McGraw-Hill, 1981.

Hansen, Harry, and Federal Writers' Project. *Louisiana: A State Guide*. Rev. ed. New York: Hastings House, 1971.

Harmon, Nicholas. *Dunkirk: The Patriotic Myth*. New York: Simon and Schuster, 1980.

Harriman, W. Averell, and Elie Abel. *Special Envoy to Churchill and Stalin, 1941–1946*. New York: Random House, 1975.

Harrison, Gordon A. *Cross-Channel Attack*. Washington, D.C.: Office of the Chief of Military History, Department of the Army, 1951.

Hart, Scott. *Washington at War: 1941–1945*. Englewood Cliffs, N.J.: Prentice-Hall, 1970.

Hastings, Max. *Overlord: D-Day, June 6, 1944*. New York: Simon and Schuster, 1984.

Haswell, Jock. *D-Day*. New York: Times Books, 1979.

———. *The Intelligence and Deception of the D-Day Landings*. London: Batsford, 1979.

Hatch, Alden. *Red Carpet for Mamie*. New York: Henry Holt, 1954.

Heckmann, Wolf. *Rommel's War in Africa*. New York: Doubleday, 1981.

Hess, Stephen. *The Washington Reporters*. Washington, D.C.: The Brookings Institution, 1981.

Higgins, Trumbull. *Winston Churchill and the Second Front, 1940–1943*. New York: Oxford University Press, 1957.

Higham, Robin, and Carol Brandt, eds. *The United States Army in Peacetime: Essays in Honor of the Bicentennial, 1775–1975*. Manhattan, Kans.: Military Affairs/Aerospace Historian Publishing, 1975.

Hoekema, Anthony A. *The Four Major Cults*. Grand Rapids, Mich.: William B. Eerdmans Publishing Co., 1963.

Horan, James D. *The Desperate Years*. New York: Bonanza Books, 1962.

Horne, Alistair. *The Price of Glory: Verdun 1916*. New York: St. Martin's Press, 1962.

Howarth, David. *Panama*. New York: McGraw-Hill, 1966.

Howe, Quincy. *Ashes of Victory: World War II and Its Aftermath*. New York: Simon and Schuster, 1972.

Hughes, David Ralph. *Ike at West Point*. Poughkeepsie, N.Y.: The Wayne Co., n.d.

Huie, William Bradford. *The Execution of Private Slovik*. New York: Delacorte Press, 1954.

Hunt, Corinne. *The Brown Palace Story*. Boulder, Colo.: A Rocky Mountain Writers Guild Publication, 1982.

Hunt, Frazier. *The Untold Story of Douglas MacArthur*. New York: Devin-Adair Co., 1954.

Hyde, H. Montgomery. *Stalin*. New York: Farrar, Straus and Giroux, 1971.

Ingersoll, Johanna. *Golden Years in the Philippines*. Palo Alto, Calif.: Pacific Books, 1971.

Ingersoll, Ralph. *Top Secret*. New York: Harcourt, Brace, 1946.

Irving, David. *The War Between the Generals: Inside the Allied High Command*. New York: Congdon & Lattes, 1981.

Ismay, Hastings. *The Memoirs of General Lord Ismay*. New York: Viking Press, 1960.

Jablonski, Edward. *A Pictorial History of the World War II Years*. New York: Doubleday, 1977.

Jackson, W. G. F. *The Battle for Rome*. New York: Bonanza Books, 1969.

Jamieson, Henry B. *They Still Call Him Ike*. New York: Vantage Press, 1972.

Janowitz, Morris. *The Professional Soldier: A Social and Political Portrait*. Glencoe, Ill.: The Free Press, 1960.

Johns, Glover S., Jr. *The Clay Pigeons of St.-Lo*. Harrisburg, Pa.: The Military Service Publishing Co., 1958.

Just, Ward. *Military Men*. New York: Alfred A. Knopf, 1970.

Kahn, E. J., Jr. *McNair: Educator of an Army*. Washington, D.C.: The Infantry Journal, 1945.

Kalb, Madeline G. *The Congo Cables: The Cold War in Africa from Eisenhower to Kennedy*. New York: Macmillan, 1981.

Keegan, John. *Six Armies in Normandy*. New York: Viking Press, 1982.

Kerr, Walter. *The Secret of Stalingrad*. New York: Jove Publications, 1979.

Kersuady, Francois. *Churchill and de Gaulle*. New York: Atheneum, 1982.

Killigrew, John W. *The Impact of the Great Depression on the Army*. Frank Freidel, ed. New York: Garland Publishing, 1979.

Kinch, Sam, and Stuart Long. *Allan Shivers: The Pied Piper of Texas Politics*. Austin, Texas: Shoal Creek Publishers, 1974.

Kinzer, Stephen, and Stephen Schlesinger. *Bitter Fruit: The Untold Story of the American Coup in Guatemala*. Garden City, N.Y.: Doubleday, 1982.

Kirkpatrick, Lyman B., Jr. *Captains Without Eyes: Intelligence Failures in World War II*. London: Collier-Macmillan, 1969.

Klein, Herbert G. *Making It Perfectly Clear*. New York: Doubleday, 1980.

Kluckhohn, Frank L., and Donald Ackerman. *The Real Eisenhower*. New York: Columbia Heights Press, 1969.

Knickerbocker, H. R., et al. *Danger Forward: The Story of the First Division in World War II*. Atlanta, Ga.: Albert Love Enterprises, 1947.

Koerner, James D. *Hoffer's America*. Peru, Ill.: Open Court Publishing Co., 1973.

Kornitzer, Bela. *The Great American Heritage: The Story of the Five Eisenhower Brothers*. New York: Farrar, Straus and Cudahy, 1955.

Kriepe, Werner, et al. *The Fatal Decision*. New York: William Sloane Assoc., 1956.

Krock, Arthur. *Memoirs: Sixty Years on the Firing Line*. New York: Funk & Wagnalls, 1968.

Langer, Paul F. *Japan: Yesterday and Today*. New York: Holt, Rinehart & Winston, 1966.

Lash, Joseph P. *Eleanor and Franklin*. New York: New American Library, 1973.

——. *Eleanor: The Years Alone*. New York: W. W. Norton, 1972.

Latham, Earl. *The Communist Controversy in Washington: From the New Deal to McCarthy*. Cambridge, Mass.: Harvard University Press, 1966.

Lee, R. Alton. *Dwight D. Eisenhower: Soldier and Statesman*. Chicago: Nelson-Hall, 1981.

Leuchtenburg, William E. *Franklin D. Roosevelt and the New Deal, 1932–1940*. New York: Harper & Row, 1963.

Lewin, Ronald. *The Chief: Field Marshal Lord Wavell*. New York: Farrar, Straus and Giroux, 1980.

——. *Montgomery*. New York: Stein and Day, 1971.

——. *Ultra Goes to War*. New York: Pocket Books, 1981.

Lewis, Lloyd. *Sherman, Fighting Prophet*. New York: Harcourt, Brace, 1932.

Liddell, Hart, B. H. *The German Generals Talk*. New York: William Morrow, 1948.

——. *History of the Second World War*. New York: G. P. Putnam's Sons, 1970.

Liebling, A. J. *Liebling Abroad*. New York: Playboy Press, 1981.

——. *Normandy Revisited*. New York: Simon and Schuster, 1958.

Lingeman, Richard R. *Don't You Know There's a War On? The American Home Front 1941–1945*. New York: G. P. Putnam's Sons, 1970.

Longmate, Norman. *The G.I.'s: The Americans In Britain, 1942–1945*. New York: Charles Scribner's Sons, 1976.

Longstreet, Stephen. *The General*. New York: G. P. Putnam's Sons, 1974.

Loewenheim, Francis L., Harold D. Langley, and Manfred Jonas, eds. *Roosevelt and Churchill: Their Secret Wartime Correspondence*. New York: E. P. Dutton, 1975.

Lyon, Peter. *Eisenhower: Portrait of the Hero*. Boston: Little, Brown, 1974.

MacArthur, Douglas. *Reminiscenses*. New York: McGraw-Hill, 1964.

McCann, Kevin. *Man From Abilene*. Garden City, N.Y.: Doubleday, 1952.

MacDonald, Charles B. *The Mighty Endeavor*. New York: Oxford University Press, 1969.

McFeeley, William S. *Grant*. New York: W. W. Norton, 1981.

McGivern, William P. *Soldiers of '44*. New York: Arbor House, 1979.

McKee, Alexander. *The Race for the Rhine Bridges*. New York: Stein and Day, 1971.

McKeogh, Michael J., and Richard Lockridge. *Sergeant Mickey and General Ike*. New York: G. P. Putnam's Sons, 1946.

Macmillan, Harold. *The Blast of War: 1939–1945*. New York: Harper & Row, 1967.

MacNeil, Neil. *Dirksen: Portrait of a Public Man*. New York: World Publishing Co., 1970.

Majdalany, Fred. *The Fall of Fortress Europe*. Garden City, N.Y.: Doubleday, 1968.

Manchester, William. *American Caesar: Douglas MacArthur 1880–1964*. Boston: Little, Brown, 1978.

Mann, Thomas. *The Magic Mountain*. Translated by H. T. Lowe-Porter. New York: Alfred A. Knopf, 1965.

Marshall, George C. *Memoirs of My Services in the World War 1917–1918*. Boston: Houghton Mifflin, 1976.

Marshall, Katherine Tupper. *Together: Annals of an Army Wife*. New York: Tupper and Love, 1946.

Marshall, S. L. A. *Bringing Up the Rear*. Edited by Kate Marshall. San Rafael, Calif.: Presidio Press, 1979.

———. *Night Drop: The American Airborne Invasion of Normandy*. Boston: Little, Brown, 1962.

Martin, Ralph G. *The G. I. War: 1941–1945*. Boston: Little, Brown, 1967.

Mason, David. *Who's Who in World War II*. Boston: Little, Brown, 1978.

Masson, Georgina. *Ancient Rome*. New York: Viking Press, 1974.

Masterman, J. C. *The Double-Cross System in the War of 1939 to 1945*. New Haven: Yale University Press, 1972.

Merriam, Robert L. *The Battle of the Bulge*. New York: Ballantine Books, 1957. (Copyright 1947 by Ziff-Davis Publishing Co. under the title *Dark December*).

Meyer, Karl E. *The New America*. New York: Basic Books, 1961.

Meyer, Robert, Jr., ed. *The Stars and Stripes Story of World War II*. New York: David McKay, 1960.

Michaels, Leonard, and Christopher Ricks, eds. *The State of the Language*. Berkeley, Calif.: University of California Press, 1980.

Michel, Henri. *The Second World War*. Translated by Douglas Parmee. New York: Frederick A. Praeger, 1975.

Middleton, Drew. *The Defense of Western Europe*. New York: Appleton-Century-Crofts, 1952.

———. *Our Share of Night*. New York: Viking Press, 1946.

———. *The Sky Suspended: The Story of the Battle of Britain*. New York: David McKay, 1960.

———. *The Struggle for Germany*. New York: Bobbs-Merrill, 1949.

Miller, Edward, and Betty Jean Mueller. *The Dwight D. Eisenhower Library*. New York: Meredith Press, 1966.

Miller, Francis Trevelyan. *Eisenhower: Man and Soldier*. Philadelphia: John C. Winston Co., 1944.

Miller, Lee G. *The Story of Ernie Pyle*. New York: Viking Press, 1950.

Miller, Merle. *Plain Speaking: An Oral Biography of Harry S Truman*. New York: Berkley Books, 1973.

Miller, Nathan. *F.D.R.: An Intimate History*. New York: Doubleday, 1983.

Miller, Walter L. *The Life and Accomplishments of Herbert Hoover*. Durham, N.C.: Moore Publishing Co., n.d.

Millis, Walter, ed. *The Forrestal Diaries*. New York: Viking Press, 1951.

———. *Arms and Men*. New York: G. P. Putnam's Sons, 1956.

Mollenhoff, Clark R. *The President Who Failed: Carter Out of Control*. New York: Macmillan, 1980.

Montagu, Ewen. *The Man Who Never Was*. Philadelphia: J. B. Lippincott, 1954.

Montgomery, B. L. *Memoirs of Field-Marshal the Viscount Montgomery of Alamein, K.G.* Cleveland and New York: World Publishing Co., 1958.

Montgomery, Brian. *A Field Marshal in the Family.* London: Constable, 1973.

Moorehead, Alan. *Eclipse.* New York: Harper and Bros., 1945.

———. *The March to Tunis.* New York: Harper and Bros., 1943.

———. *Montgomery.* New York: Coward-McCann, 1946.

Moos, Malcolm. *Dwight D. Eisenhower.* New York: Random House, 1964.

Moran, Lord (Sir Charles Wilson). *Churchill: Taken from the Diaries of Lord Moran.* Boston: Houghton Mifflin, 1966.

Morgan, Lt. Gen. Sir Frederick, K.C.B. *Overture to Overlord.* Garden City, N.Y.: Doubleday, 1950.

Morgan, Kay Summersby. *Past Forgetting: My Love Affair with Dwight Eisenhower.* New York: Simon and Schuster, 1976.

Morison, Samuel Eliot. *The Oxford History of the American People.* New York: Oxford University Press, 1965.

Mosely, Leonard. *Dulles: A Biography of Eleanor, Allen, and John Foster Dulles and Their Family Network.* New York: Dell Publishing Co., 1978.

———. *Hirohito: Emperor of Japan.* Englewood Cliffs, N.J.: Prentice-Hall, 1966.

———. *On Borrowed Time.* New York: Random House, 1969.

Mowat, Farley. *And No Birds Sang.* Boston: Little, Brown, 1980.

Muggeridge, Malcolm. *The Infernal Grove.* London: William Collins Sons, 1973.

Murphy, Robert. *Diplomat Among Warriors.* New York: Doubleday, 1964.

Nadich, Judah. *Eisenhower and the Jews.* New York: Twayne Publishers, 1953.

Navy Times Editors. *Operation Victory.* New York: G. P. Putnam's Sons, 1968.

Neal, Steve. *The Eisenhowers: Reluctant Dynasty.* Garden City, N.Y.: Doubleday, 1978.

Nelson, Raymond. *The Philippines.* New York: Walker & Co., 1968.

Nenninger, Timothy K. *The Leavenworth Schools and the Old Army.* Westport, Conn.: Greenwood Press, 1978.

Nevins, General Arthur S. *Gettysburg's Five-Star Farmer.* New York: Carlton Press, 1977.

New Yorker. *The* New Yorker *Book of War Pieces.* New York: Reynal & Hitchcock, 1947.

Nicolson, Harold. *The Diaries and Letters of Harold Nicolson: The War Years, 1939–1945.* Edited by Nigel Nicolson. New York: Atheneum, 1967.

Norman, Albert, Ph.D. *Operation Overlord, Design and Reality: The Allied Invasion of Western Europe.* Harrisburg, Pa.: The Military Service Publishing Co., 1952.

North, John, ed. *The Alexander Memoirs: Field Marshal Earl Alexander of Tunis.* New York: McGraw-Hill, 1961.

Novak, Michael. *Choosing Our King: Powerful Symbols in Presidential Politics.* New York: Macmillan, 1974.

O'Connor, Richard. *Black Jack Pershing.* New York: Doubleday, Co., 1961.

———. *Wild Bill Hickok.* New York: Doubleday, 1979.

O'Donnell, James P. *The Bunker: A History of the Reich Chancellory Group.* New York: Bantam Books, 1979.

Panter-Downes, Mollie. *London War Notes: 1939–1945.* Edited by William Shawn. New York: Farrar, Straus and Giroux, 1971.

Parmet, Herbert S. *Eisenhower and the American Crusades.* New York: Macmillan, 1972.

Parrish, Thomas, ed. *The Simon and Schuster Encyclopedia of World War II.* Chief consultant editor Brig. Gen. S. L. A. Marshall, New York: Simon and Schuster, 1978.

Patton, George S., Jr. *War As I Knew It.* Boston: Houghton Mifflin, 1947.

Perkins, Frances. *The Roosevelt I Knew.* New York: Harper and Bros., 1946.

Perrett, Geoffrey. *America in the Twenties.* New York: Simon and Schuster, 1982.

———. *Days of Sadness, Years of Triumph: The American People 1939–1945.* New York: Coward, McCann & Geoghegan, 1973.

——. *A Dream of Greatness*. New York: Coward, McCann & Geoghegan, 1979.

Persico, Joseph E. *Piercing the Reich*. New York: Ballantine Books, 1979.

Phillips, Cabell. *The 1940s: Decade of Triumph and Trouble*. New York: Macmillan, 1975.

——. *The Truman Presidency*. New York: Macmillan, 1966.

Pierce, Neal R. *The Great Plains States of America*. New York: W. W. Norton, 1973.

Pierpoint, Robert C. *At the White House: Assignments to Six Presidents*. New York: G. P. Putnam's Sons, 1981.

Pilat, Oliver. *Drew Pearson: An Unauthorized Biography*. New York: Pocket Books, 1973.

Pogue, Forrest C. *George C. Marshall: Education of a General*. New York: Viking Press, 1963.

——. *George C. Marshall: Ordeal and Hope, 1939–1942*. New York: Viking Press, 1966.

——. *George C. Marshall: Organizer of Victory, 1943–1945*. New York: Viking Press, 1973.

Powers, Thomas. *The Man Who Kept the Secrets: Richard Helms and the CIA*. New York: Alfred A. Knopf, 1979.

Pruessen, Ronald W. *John Foster Dulles: The Road to Power*. New York: The Free Press, 1982.

Pyle, Ernie, *Brave Men*. New York: Henry Holt & Co., 1944.

Reader's Digest Editors. *Illustrated Story of World War II*. Pleasantville, N.Y.: Reader's Digest, 1969.

Reeder, Colonel Red (Russell Potter). *Dwight David Eisenhower: Fighter for Peace*. Champaign, Ill.: Garrard Publishing Co., 1968.

Reilly, Michael. *Reilly of the White House*. As told to William J. Slocum. New York: Simon and Schuster, 1947.

Renaud, Alexandre. *Sainte-Mère Église*. France: Editions Odile Pathé, 1964.

Reston, James. *Sketches in the Sand*. New York: Alfred A. Knopf, 1967.

Reynolds, Quentin. *The Curtain Rises*. New York: Random House, 1944.

Ridgway, General Matthew B. *Soldier: The Memoirs of Matthew B. Ridgway*. As told to Harold H. Martin. New York: Harper and Bros., 1956.

Roberts, Chalmers M. *The* Washington Post: *The First Hundred Years*. Boston: Houghton Mifflin, 1977.

Rollins, Philip Ashton. *The Cowboy*. New York: Charles Scribner's Sons, 1926.

Romulo, General Carlos P. *I Walked with Heroes*. New York: Holt, Rinehart & Winston, 1961.

Rovere, Richard H. *The Eisenhower Years*. New York: Farrar, Straus, and Cudahy, 1956.

Ryan, Cornelius. *The Last Battle*. New York: Simon and Schuster, 1966.

——. *The Longest Day*. New York: Simon and Schuster, 1959.

Salisbury, Harrison. *Without Fear or Favor: An Uncompromising Look at* The New York Times. New York: Times Books, 1980.

Schell, Jonathan. *The Time of Illusion*. New York: Alfred A. Knopf, 1976.

Schlesinger, Arthur M., Jr. *The Age of Roosevelt*, vol. 2, *The Coming of the New Deal*. Boston: Houghton Mifflin, 1959.

——. *The Imperial Presidency*. Boston: Houghton Mifflin, 1973.

Schwarz, Jordan A. *The Speculator: Bernard M. Baruch in Washington*. Chapel Hill, N.C.: University of North Carolina Press, 1981.

Sevareid, Eric. *Not So Wild a Dream*. New York: Alfred A. Knopf, 1969.

Shavelson, Melville. *Ike*. New York: Warner Books, 1979.

Sheed, Wilfrid. *Clare Boothe Luce*. New York: E. P. Dutton, 1982.

Shenton, James P. *History of the United States from 1865 to the Present*. Garden City, N.Y.: Doubleday, 1964.

Sherwood, Robert E. *Roosevelt and Hopkins*. New York: Harper and Bros., 1948.

Shirer, William L. *The Rise and Fall of the Third Reich*. New York: Simon and Schuster, 1960.

———. *Twentieth-Century Journey*. New York: Simon and Schuster, 1976.

Sixsmith, E. K. G. *Eisenhower as Military Commander*. New York: Stein and Day, 1983.

Slater, Ellis D. *The Ike I Knew*. Privately printed. Copyright 1980 by the Ellis D. Slater Trust.

Smith, Bradley F., and Elena Agarossi. *Operation Sunrise*. New York: Basic Books, 1979.

Smith, Gene. *The Shattered Dream: Herbert Hoover and the Great Depression*. New York: McGraw-Hill, 1984.

Smith, Merriman. *Book of Presidents: A White House Memoir*. New York: W. W. Norton, 1972.

———. *Meet Mister Eisenhower*. New York: Harper and Bros., 1954.

Smith, R. Harris. *OSS: The Secret History of America's First Central Intelligence Agency*. Berkeley, Calif.: University of California Press, 1972.

Smith, Richard Norton. *An Uncommon Man: The Triumph of Herbert Hoover*. New York: Simon and Schuster, 1984.

Smith, W. Bedell. *Eisenhower's Six Great Decisions*. New York: Longmans, Green, 1956.

Smythe, Donald. *Guerrilla Warrior: The Early Life of John J. Pershing*. New York: Charles Scribner's Sons, 1973.

Snyder, Louis L., ed. *Masterpieces of War Reporting*. New York: Julian Messner, 1962.

———. *The War: A Concise History*. New York: Julian Messner, 1960.

Snyder, Marty, and Glenn D. Kittler. *My Friend Ike*. New York: Frederick Fell, 1956.

Speer, Albert. *Inside the Third Reich*. Translated by Richard and Clara Winston. New York: Macmillan, 1970.

———. *Spandau: The Secret Diaries*. Translated by Richard and Clara Winston. New York: Macmillan, 1976.

Sprague, Marshall. *Colorado*. New York: W. W. Norton, 1976.

Steinberg, Alfred. *Sam Rayburn: A Biography*. New York: Hawthorn Books, 1975.

Stern, Philip M. *The Oppenheimer Case: Security on Trial*. New York: Harper & Row, 1969.

Stevenson, William. *A Man Called Intrepid*. New York: Harcourt Brace Jovanovich, 1976.

Stillman, Edmund, and William Pfaff. *The New Politics: America and the End of the Postwar World*. New York: Coward-McCann, 1961.

Stokesbury, James L. *A Short History of World War II*. New York: William Morrow, 1980.

Stone, I. F. *In a Time of Torment*. New York: Random House, 1964.

Stratton, Joanna L. *Pioneer Women*. A Touchstone Book. New York: Simon and Schuster, 1982.

Strawson, John. *The Battle for North Africa*. New York: Bonanza Books, 1969.

Strong, Maj. Gen. Sir Kenneth. *Intelligence at the Top*. New York: Doubleday & Co., 1968.

———. *Men of Intelligence*. New York: St. Martin's Press, 1971.

Sullivan, Mark. *Our Times*. New York: Charles Scribner's Sons, 1927.

Sulzberger, C. L. *American Heritage Picture History of World War II*. New York: American Heritage Press, 1966.

Summersby, Kay. *Eisenhower Was My Boss*. Edited by Michael Kerns. New York: Prentice-Hall, 1948.

Swanberg, W. A. *Luce and His Empire*. New York: Charles Scribner's Sons, 1975.

Talese, Gay. *The Kingdom and the Power*. An NAL Book. New York: World Publishing Co., 1966.

Taylor, Alan, ed. and interpreter. *What Eisenhower Thinks*. New York: Thomas Y. Crowell, 1952.

Taylor, A. J. P., et al. *Churchill Revised: A Critical Assessment*. New York: Dial Press, 1969.

Taylor, Maxwell D. *Swords and Plowshares*. New York: W. W. Norton, 1972.

———. *The Uncertain Trumpet*. New York: Harper and Bros., 1960.

Taylor, Robert Lewis. *Winston Churchill: An Informal Study of Greatness*. Garden City, N.Y.: Doubleday, 1952.

Taylor, Telford. *Grand Inquest*. New York: Simon and Schuster, 1955.

Tedder, Lord Arthur. *With Prejudice*. Boston: Little, Brown, 1966.

Thompson, R. W. *Churchill and the Montgomery Myth*. New York: M. Evans, 1968.

———. *Montgomery the Field Marshal*. New York: Charles Scribner's Sons, 1969.

Time-Life Books Editors. *This Fabulous Century*, vol. I, 1900–1910. New York: Time-Life Books, 1969.

———. *This Fabulous Century*, vol. IV, 1930–1940. New York: Time-Life Books, 1969.

———. *The Old West: The Railroaders*. New York: Time-Life Books, 1973.

Toland, John. *Battle: The Story of the Bulge*. New York: Random House, 1959.

———. *Infamy: Pearl Harbor and Its Aftermath*. Garden City, N.Y.: Doubleday, 1982.

———. *The Last Hundred Days*. New York: Random House, 1966.

Tompkins, Peter. *The Murder of Admiral Darlan*. New York: Simon and Schuster, 1965.

Trevor-Roper, H. R. *The Last Days of Hitler*. New York: Macmillan, 1947.

Tucker, Glenn. *Lee and Longstreet at Gettysburg*. New York: Bobbs-Merrill, 1968.

Ubbelohde, Carl, et al. *A Colorado History*. Boulder, Colo.: Pruett Publishing Company, 1972.

Vandenberg, Philipp. *The Curse of the Pharaohs*. Translated by Thomas Weyr. New York: J. B. Lippincott, 1975.

Verckler, Stewart P. *Cowtown-Abilene: The Story of Abilene Kansas 1867–1875*. New York: Carlton Press, 1961.

Walters, Vernon A. *Silent Missions*. Garden City, N.Y.: Doubleday, 1978.

Warren, Earl. *The Memoirs of Chief Justice Earl Warren*. Garden City, N.Y.: Doubleday, 1977.

Watson, Mark S. *U.S. Army in World War II*. Washington, D.C.: The War Department Chief of Staff, Prewar Plans and Preparations, Historical Division, Department of the Army, 1950.

Weaver, John D. *Another Such Victory*. New York: Viking Press, 1948.

———. *Warren: The Man, the Court, the Era*. Boston: Little, Brown, 1967.

Weigley, Russell F. *Eisenhower's Lieutenants*. Bloomington, Ind.: Indiana University Press, 1981.

———. *History of the United States Army*. New York: Macmillan, 1967.

Welchman, Gordon. *The Hut Six Story: The Story of Breaking the Enigma Codes*. New York: McGraw-Hill, 1982.

Wertenbaker, Charles Christian. *Invasion*. New York: D. Appleton-Century Co., 1944.

West, John Anthony. *The Traveler's Key to Ancient Egypt*. New York: Alfred A. Knopf, 1985.

Wheeler, Richard. *We Knew William Tecumseh Sherman*. New York: Thomas Y. Crowell, 1977.

White, William Allen. *The Autobiography of William Allen White*. New York: Macmillan, 1946.

Willmott, H. P. *June 1944*. New York: Sterling Publishing Co., 1984.

Wilson, Theodore A., ed. *WW2: Readings on Critical Issues*. New York: Charles Scribner's Sons, 1972.

Winant, John Gilbert. *Letter from Grosvenor Square*. Boston: Houghton Mifflin, 1947.

Winterbotham, Frederick William. *The Ultra Secret*. New York: Harper & Row, 1974.

Woodward, Sir Lewellyn. *Great Britain and the War of 1914–1918*. London: Methuen & Co., 1967.

Yank Editors. *Yank: The Story of World War II as Written by the Soldiers*. New York: Crown Publishers, 1984.

Zhukov, Georgi K. *Marshal Zhukov's Greatest Battles*. Edited with an introduction and explanatory comments by Harrison E. Salisbury, translated by Theodore Shabad. New York: Harper & Row, 1969.

Zornow, William Frank. *Kansas: A History of the Jayhawk State*. Norman, Okla.: University of Oklahoma Press, 1957.

★ ★ ★

CORRESPONDENCE

Voluminous correspondence between members of the Eisenhower family, ranging from 1913 to 1967.

Correspondence from DDE 1913–67. The Eisenhower Library.

Letters from DDE to Gladys Harding Brooks 1914–1915.

Letters from DDE to Ruby Norman.

Correspondence between General Mark Clark and Eisenhower, 1939. The Citadel Archives. The Military College of South Carolina. Charleston, S.C. 29409.

Correspondence between Eisenhower and T. J. Davis. 1926 through 1943.

Correspondence between Eisenhower and Everett E. Hazlett.

Correspondence between Eisenhower and MacArthur, and Eisenhower and James Ord. MacArthur Archives. MacArthur Memorial. Norfolk, Va.

Correspondence between Eisenhower and Mamie. Published and unpublished, 1942–1945.

Correspondence between Eisenhower and General Maxwell D. Taylor.

★ ★ ★

DIARIES

Gladys Harding Brooks Diary—Summer of 1915.

Eisenhower and Harry C. Butcher's Personal and Official Diary—1942–1945.

Eisenhower's Diaries (Kevin McCann Papers, Eisenhower Library).

Eisenhower's Philippine Diary—December 1935–January 1940.

Eisenhower's Circular Diary—December 14, 1941–February 9, 1942.

Hagerty Diaries.

Chester Hansen Diary.

William R. Gruber's Diary of 1929.

Bernard Shanley Diaries—1952.

★ ★ ★

MANUSCRIPTS (UNPUBLISHED)

Dickson, Benjamin A. Colonel, AUS, Retired. "Algiers to the Elbe." No date.
Dodd, Gladys. "The Religious Background of the Eisenhower Family." No date.
Endacott, Earl J. "The Ike I Remember and Other Stories." Copyright notice; no date.

★ ★ ★

MISCELLANEOUS (PUBLISHED AND UNPUBLISHED)

Army War College—Eisenhower Paper—"An Enlisted Reserve for the Regular Army: Prepared by Major D. D. Eisenhower, Infantry, March 20, 1928." Army War College. Washington, D.C. Command Course.

Chronicle of the Belle Springs Creamery Co. of Dickinson County, Kansas, by Paul D. Hoffman. Kansas: Abilene Printing Co., Inc. 1975.

Corrections of the Kenneth S. Davis book *Soldier of Democracy* made by Dwight D. Eisenhower.

Corrections of the Alden Hatch book *Red Carpet for Mamie* made by C. O. Musser in a letter to Milton Eisenhower dated July 10, 1945.

Court-Martial of Private Eddie Slovik: Record of the trial, including court-martial order, verbatim transcript, prosecution exhibits, staff judge advocate's review board decision, and the report of execution. Department of the Army. United States Army Judiciary, Nassif Building, Falls Church, Virginia.

"Early Days in Abilene," by J. B. Edwards. Printed in the *Abilene Chronicle* in 1896 and reprinted in the *Abilene Daily Chronicle* in 1938 with added material from the papers of J. B. Edwards.

Eisenhower home inventory—compiled prior to June 22, 1947. Official county records of Eisenhower properties; additions and changes to home; floor plans; home furniture arrangement. Inventory of Books—titles; tourist description of the Eisenhower boyhood home.

Eisenhower's Vertical File at the U.S. Military Academy Library.

"Four Years at West Point as of Fifty Years Ago." Prepared by Mrs. Roy C. Hodgson on September 26, 1968, for the Thursday Afternoon Book Club of A.A.U.W., based on letters written home by P. A. Hodgson.

Hazlett Recollections. Eisenhower Library, Abilene.

Historic Resource Study and Historical Base Map. Eisenhower National Historic Site, Gettysburg, Pa., December 31, 1970.

"History of the Eisenhower Birthplace, Denison, Texas." Tourist guide available at birthplace.

The Howitzer—Class of 1915. (West Point yearbook.)

Records of the U.S. Military Adviser to the Philippine Commonwealth: correspondence; reports; news clippings from the MacArthur Archives, Norfolk, Va. (2 boxes).

Regulations for the Interior Police and Discipline of the United States Corps of Cadets, by the Commandant of Cadets. West Point: Press of the U.S. Military Academy, 1906.

Regulations for the United States Military Academy. Washington: Government Printing Office, 1911.

Sayler, H. S. Collection. Box 1. Vital Statistics—Class of 1915.

Scrapbook of Harry Anholt pertaining to Eisenhower.

Senator Bristow Collection. Kansas State Historical Society. Topeka, Kansas.

"Some Direct Quotations Concerning Lane University, Lecompton, Kansas, 1865–1903" by Clark Coan, Instructor in Social Studies; Lawrence High School, Lawrence, Kansas.

Statistical Study of the Class of 1915—U.S. Military Academy "The Class the Stars Fell On" "The Class That Reached the Stars" April 1975—Third Revision. Study compiled, published and distributed solely by H. Aurand, Class of 1915.

U.S. Army, Eisenhower's Official 201 File. 1911–death.

U.S. Military Academy Library Archives records.

U.S. Military Academy—West Point. An Official Directory and Guide published for West Point newcomers by Military Publishers, a private firm in no way connected with the Department of Army. San Diego, 1980.

U.S. Military Academy—1980 Cullum Memorial Edition Register of Graduates and Former Cadets. 1802–1980. Published by Association of Graduates, USMA. Revised and published annually. Chicago: R. R. Donnelly & Sons, 1980.

U.S. Military Academy. *The West Point Guidebook.* Copyright 1979. Robert A. Mancinelli.

U.S. Military Academy. The West Point 1979–80 Catalog.

★ ★ ★

PAPERS

Harry C. Butcher Papers. 1910–1959. Dwight D. Eisenhower Library, Abilene.

Bradford Chynoweth Papers, U.S. Army Military History Institute, Carlisle Barracks, Pa.

Chester B. Hansen Papers, U.S. Army Military History Institute, Carlisle Barracks, Pa. 17013.

Kevin McCann Papers. Dwight D. Eisenhower Library, Abilene, Kansas.

Thomas E. Stephens Personal Papers.

★ ★ ★

SYMPOSIUMS

Eisenhower Remembered Weekend. October 9–11, 1981. Eisenhower College, Seneca Falls, New York.

U.S. Military Academy Lecture Series and Symposium on the Theory and Practice of American National Security, 1945–1960. Presented in cooperation with the Association of Graduates, USMA, April 21–23, 1982. West Point, New York.

The American Dream. April 20–22, 1983. Dwight D. Eisenhower Library. Abilene, Kansas.

★ ★ ★

TV BROADCASTS

ABC. *20/20*. Barbara Walters' interview of Mamie Eisenhower at Gettysburg. Broadcast November 23, 1979.

CBS Reports—"D-Day Plus 20 Years: Eisenhower Returns to Normandy." Walter Cronkite interviews Eisenhower for segment of *CBS Reports*. Broadcast on June 5, 1964.

CBS news special—"Some Friends of General Eisenhower." Broadcast Saturday, March 29, 1969. Walter Cronkite.

CBS. "Young Mr. Eisenhower." Broadcast September 13, 1966.

NBC. The *Today* show. Barbara Walters with Mamie Eisenhower. Broadcast March 26–27, 1970.

NBC Television Special Projects—"Eisenhower on Lincoln, as Commander in Chief," broadcast on February 11, 1963.

★ ★ ★

THESES

"Eisenhower, as Seen Through the Pages of the *Abilene Reflector-Chronicle*." Marcia Lee Lowther Longberg. Master's thesis. Kansas State University, 1969.

"The U.S. Army GHQ Maneuvers of 1941." Christopher R. Gabel. Doctoral thesis. Ohio State University, 1981.

"The United States Military Academy in an Era of Educational Reform. 1900–1925." Roger H. Ny. Doctoral thesis. Columbia University, 1968.

* * *

PERMISSION ACKNOWLEDGMENTS

Permission is gratefully acknowledged from the following sources to reprint material in their control.

Abilene Reflector–Chronicle for material from the special commemorative edition of the *Abilene Reflector–Chronicle* following the deaths of Ike and Mamie.

American Bible Society Record for material from the July/August 1969 issue.

American Heritage for material from "My Roommate . . . is Dwight Eisenhower" by Edward M. Coffman, in the April 1973 issue, and "Bloody Huertgen: The Battle That Should Never Have Been Fought" by General James M. Gavin, in the December 1979 issue.

The American Legion Magazine for material by Jesus A. Villamor, copyright © 1960 by *The American Legion Magazine*.

The Association of Graduates United States Military Academy for material from "The Athletic Cadet Eisenhower" by Alexander M. Weyand, in the Spring 1968 issue of *Assembly*.

CBS News for excerpts from the following news broadcasts: "CBS Reports: D-Day Plus 20 Years" (6/5/64), copyright © 1964 by CBS Inc.; "CBS News Special: Some Friends of General Eisenhower" (3/29/69), copyright © 1969 by CBS Inc.; "CBS News Special: Young Mr. Eisenhower" (9/13/66), copyright © 1966 by CBS Inc.

Center for the Study of the Presidency for material from "Religious Dimensions of Presidential Leadership: The Case of Dwight Eisenhower" by James David Fairbanks, in *Presidential Studies Quarterly*, Vol. 2, Spring 1982.

The Columbia University Oral History Research Office for material from the oral histories of Robert B. Anderson, Clare Boothe Luce, Robert Clark, John Bird, Merriman Smith, Robert Sherrod, John J. McCloy and Arthur Nevins.

Doubleday and Company, Inc. for material from *Crusade in Europe* by Dwight D. Eisenhower, copyright © 1948 by Doubleday and Company, Inc.; *At Ease* by Dwight D. Eisenhower, copyright © 1967 by Dwight D. Eisenhower; *Strictly Personal* by John Eisenhower, copyright © 1974 by John S. D. Eisenhower; *Turn of the Tide* by Arthur Bryant, copyright © 1957 by Arthur Bryant; *Triumph in the West* by Arthur Bryant, copyright © 1959 by Arthur Bryant; *Diplomat Among Warriors* by Robert Murphy, copyright © 1964 by Robert Murphy; *Soldier of Democracy* by Kenneth S. Davis, copyright © 1945 by Kenneth S. Davis.

The Dwight D. Eisenhower Library for material from the Eisenhower Foundation newsletter.

Farrar, Straus & Giroux, Inc. for material from *The Great American Heritage* by Bela Kornitzer, copyright © 1955 by Farrar, Straus & Cudahy, Inc., copyright renewed © 1983 by Farrar, Straus & Giroux, Inc.

Harper and Row, Publishers, Inc. for material from *Roosevelt and Hopkins* by Robert E. Sherwood, copyright © 1948 by Robert E. Sherwood; *The Blast of War* by Harold Macmillan, copyright © 1967, 1968 by Thomson Newspapers Ltd.; *Calculated Risk* by Mark W. Clark, copyright © 1950 by Mark W. Clark.

Bill Heavey for material from "1919: The Interstate Expedition" by Vaughn Smartt, in the August 1973 issue of *Constructor.*

Houghton Mifflin Company for material from *The Hinge of Fate,* Volume IV of *The Second World War* by Winston S. Churchill, copyright © 1950 by Houghton Mifflin Company, copyright © renewed 1978 by Lady Spencer-Churchill, The Honorable Lady Sarah Audley and The Honorable Lady Soames; *The Patton Papers,* Volume 1, edited by Martin Blumenson, copyright 1972 by Martin Blumenson; *The Patton Papers,* Volume 2, edited by Martin Blumenson, copyright 1974 by Martin Blumenson.

Richard Lamb for material in "Operation Dragoon" by Brenda Ralph Lewis in the June 1970 issue of *War Monthly.*

McCalls for material from "Mamie Eisenhower Talks About Fifty Years of Marriage" by Vivian Cadden in the September 1966 issue.

The Meredith Corporation for material from "Mother Eisenhower Talks About Her Most Famous Son," reprinted from *Better Homes and Gardens,* June 1943, copyright © Meredith Corporation, 1943. All rights reserved.

The William Morris Agency for material from *A Soldier's Story* by General Omar Bradley.

NBC for material from a broadcast of Eisenhower on Lincoln as Commander in Chief, originally broadcast February 11, 1963, excerpt courtesy of National Broadcasting Company, Inc., copyright © 1987 National Broadcasting Company, Inc. All rights reserved.

The *New York Times* for material from "Eisenhower Redux" by John P. Roche (6/28/81 Book Review); Alan Truscott's column on bridge and Ike's expertise at the game; "In the Nation" by Arthur Krock (11/24/43 and 11/25/43); "General Eisenhower is a Military Dictator" by Anne O'Hare McCormick (11/4/44); "Abilene's Ike" by C. M. Harger (11/22/42 Magazine); "Eisenhower Plans Minutely, Then Strikes" by Drew Middleton (July 1943 Magazine).

Parade Publications, Inc. and Jack Anderson for material from "The President's Pet Peeves" by Jack Anderson and Fred Blumenthal, in the March 20, 1955 issue of *Parade;* Parade Publications, Inc. and Rosalind Massow for material from "Mamie and Ike Talk About 50 Years of Marriage" by Rosalind Massow, in the June 26, 1966 issue of *Parade;* and Parade Publications, Inc. and Howard Teichmann for material from "The Brave Journey of Helen Hayes" by Howard Teichmann, in the November 24, 1985 issue of *Parade.*

Parameters for material from "Dwight D. Eisenhower at the Army War College" in issue #1 of *Parameters,* 1975.

The Putnam Publishing Group for material from *Sgt. Mickey and General Ike* by Michael J. McKeogh and Richard Lockridge.

San Antonio Express and News for material from "Former Players Remember Eisenhower as Great Leader" by Frank Klein in the October 28, 1956 edition of the *San Antonio Express and News.*

Anthea Saxe for material from *Eisenhower Was My Boss* by Kay Summersby.

Charles Scribner's Sons for material from *Mamie Doud Eisenhower: A Portrait of a First Lady* by Dorothy Brandon.

Simon & Schuster, Inc. for material from *Special People* by Julie Nixon Eisenhower, copyright © 1977 by Julie Nixon Eisenhower; *Past Forgetting* by Kay Summersby Morgan, copyright © 1976 by The Estate of Kay Summersby Morgan; *My Three Years with Eisenhower* by Harry C. Butcher, copyright 1946, 1973 for Harry C. Butcher.

Thomas A. Tenney for material from "Mark Twain and Dwight D. Eisenhower" from the *Mark Twain Quarterly*, 9:3 (Winter 1953).

Barbara Walters for material from her interview with Mrs. Eisenhower, copyright © 1974 Meredith Corporation, with permission of Barbara Walters.

Watchtower Bible and Tract Society of Pennsylvania for material from "A Soldier Who Became a Preacher" in the October 15, 1980 issue of *The Watchtower*.

★ ★ ★

INDEX